THE TIMES

GUIDE TO
THE HOUSE OF
COMMONS

2010

THE TIMES

GUIDE TO
THE HOUSE OF
COMMONS

2010

Editor
Greg Hurst

Assistant Editor
Emily Gosden

Design Production Editor
Chris Davalle

Chief Sub-Editor
Matthew Lyons

TIMES BOOKS

First published in 2010 by Times Books

328.41005
Tm

HarperCollinsPublishers
77–85 Fulham Palace Road
Hammersmith
London W6 8JB

www.harpercollins.co.uk
www.thetimes.co.uk

© Times Newspapers Ltd 2010

The Times is a registered trademark of Times Newspapers Ltd

ISBN 978-0-00-735158-9

Special acknowledgements and thanks to:
Martin Barrow, Richard Dixon, Tim Hames, Robert Hands,
Lori Heiss, Jon Hill, Alex O'Connell, Peter Riddell, Paul Sanders

Production: Alison Gibson, Ed Pearson
Design & layout: Matt Ward

HarperCollins: Helena Nicholls, Ione Walder

Additional thanks to: Neil Bennett, Simon de Bruxelles,
Sam Coates, Lorraine Davidson, Laura Dixon, Francis Elliott,
Valerie Elliott, Alice Fishburn, Tim Glanfield, Fiona Hamilton,
Gary Hedgman, Zoe Holtermann, Jonathan Isaby, Suzy Jagger,
Russell Jenkins, Magnus Linklater, Samantha Lyster,
Angus Macleod, Andrew Norfolk, Matthew Parris, Alex Ralph,
David Sharrock, Ann Treneman, Philip Webster, Roland Watson,
Tom Whipple, Damian Whitworth, Nicola Woolcock,
Tony Garrett and *The Times's* graphics department, and the House
of Commons Information Office

Research on defeated candidates: Francesca Angelini,
Tom Brooks-Pollock, Marion Dakers, Rhiannon Edwards,
Kieran Fitzpatrick and Sean McCaffrey

Printed and bound in Great Britain by Butler, Tanner and Dennis

Contents

The new Parliament

The old era

The work of the House of Commons

General election 2010: results by constituency

Manifestos

Index to candidates

Photographs

Andy Rain/EPA; Stefan Rousseau/EPA pool; Fabio De Paola/Guardian; Dan Charity; Ben Gurr for The Times; Chris Radburn/PA; Chris Harris for The Times; Richard Pohle for The Times; Justin Kernoghan for The Times; Thomas Kellner/Getty Images; Chris Jackson/WPA Pool/Getty Images; Paul Barker/PA

THE ✤ TIMES

An aid to the navigation of uncharted political waters

Greg Hurst
Editor of the Guide

The general election of 2010 was a watershed: the first since February 1974 at which no single party won an overall majority. The inconclusive outcome was accompanied by a strong sense of paradox. The Conservative Party won the most seats, 305, with one additional seat expected, and duly delivered, in the election in Thirsk & Malton that was delayed by the death of a candidate. And yet, by falling short of an absolute Commons majority, David Cameron was widely held to have failed to seize fully, particularly in the final year, the opportunity presented to him as the outgoing Government, and Gordon Brown in particular, became steadily more unpopular.

The Liberal Democrats, clear winners of the campaign itself, were stunned actually to suffer a net loss of five seats, bringing their tally down to 57. They had expected significant gains after the television debates propelled Nick Clegg into the living rooms of voters unhappy with Mr Brown but with nagging doubts about Mr Cameron. The ten-point jump in support for the Liberal Democrats after the first leaders' debate was unprecedented in polling history. Even as the party's poll ratings began to glide downwards many Liberal Democrats hoped for, and expected, net gains of perhaps 20 or 30 seats.

The paradox was greatest within the Labour Party. Clear loser of the election, with a net loss of 90 seats, it endured its worst performance since 1931 during the Great Depression. Within Labour ranks, however, a grim sense of satisfaction was evident, even some pride, both at having clawed back from the prospect of being pushed into third place by the Liberal Democrats and at having denied Mr Cameron the majority that he wanted and, they may have calculated, he needed.

One refreshing aspect was that turnout, having reached a postwar low in 2001, rose again to 65.1 per cent, up by 3.7 per cent on 2005; if an election is interesting or the result uncertain, voters are more inclined to take part.

If the result appeared confusing to some, its immediate aftermath must have seemed doubly so. Gordon Brown, vanquished, returned to Downing Street. The Conservatives and Liberal Democrats, after weeks, months even, of fighting one another tooth and nail, dispatched teams to begin talks on a tentative arrangement for a minority administration or even a coalition. The outcome, Britain's first coalition since Churchill's cross-party administra-

tion during the Second World War, from 1940-45, and the first in peacetime since Ramsay MacDonald's National Government of 1929-35, and those that followed, ushered in a new era of British politics.

Coalition politics presents significant new challenges for the House of Commons. Ministers who are members of competing parties must find ways of working together that go beyond pragmatism and practical effectiveness and are based on trust, while maintaining their separate political entities and those of their parties. Backbench Members of both governing parties must find the language, tone and levers to criticise and influence individual aspects of policy or decisions of administration without tearing at the fabric of the coalition itself. There will be others unhappy about the very fact of coalition government, whose challenge is to advance their cause without being cast as wreckers. Such questions apply well beyond the exchanges on the floor of the Commons, to its select committees, public bill committees and its very culture as an institution.

For the Labour Party, in particular, the task of opposition carries heightened responsibilities. In the previous two Parliaments, the Liberal Democrats provided an increasingly significant alternative voice to that of the official Opposition, for example as the only British party to oppose the invasion of Iraq in 2003 and offering an alternative analysis during the financial crisis of 2008-09. Their entry into office gives the coalition Government an initial working majority in the Commons of 82 once the Speaker and Sinn Féin are excluded and leaves the main duty of opposition on Labour's shoulders alone. Furthermore, the coalition will have, between its peers, a large majority over Labour in the House of Lords, where cross-benchers do not vote as a block. This is the first time a Government has commanded majorities in both Houses of Parliament since John Major in 1997, and makes the opposition's work of scrutiny and challenge in the Commons doubly important.

Gordon Brown's resignation as Prime Minister and leader of the Labour Party heralded the opening of a new chapter for his party. Amid the uncertainty and fast-moving events of the post-election hiatus, this happened in two stages. First came an undertaking to step down at a future date if an alternative "progressive" coalition with the Liberal Democrats and minority parties could be negotiated. Then came his immediate departure as the coalition between Mr Cameron and Mr Clegg fell into place, although before its details were complete. Harriet Harman, Labour's deputy leader, took his place temporarily as Leader of the Opposition as the party agreed to a timetable of more than four months to elect a new leader for its annual conference in late September.

Two parties are represented in the new House of Commons for the first time: the Green Party, 11 years after it gained two seats in the European Parliament, thanks to its method of election by proportional representation, and the Alliance Party of Northern Ireland. The United Kingdom Independence Party and British National Party polled substantially more votes than the Greens, and both improved their share of the vote, without winning seats. The trend of independent Members of Parliament, re-established by Martin Bell in 1997, was reversed in mainland Britain with the defeat of Richard Taylor in Wyre Forest, where he served two terms, and Dai Davies in Blaenau Gwent. It was maintained only by the presence of Lady Sylvia Hermon, who broke with the Ulster Unionists to retain her seat with a large majority. Her victory reflects the very different politics of Northern Ireland.

The outcome of the general election, inconclusive as it was, nonetheless captured the mood of Britain in the late spring of 2010: dissatisfied with Labour (other than in Scotland, the only part of Britain where the party's vote went up, and Inner London); attracted in significant numbers by Mr Cameron, although with doubts harboured by some and antipathy among a minority; restless for change; and disenchanted with politics and the excesses of the previous Parliament.

The most important dynamic for the Commons itself is the scale of the turnover of its Members. More than one third, 227, are new to Parliament. This is fewer than the 242 new MPs returned in 1997, a postwar record, but is a massive transfusion for an institution that had lost touch with what the electorate expected from it. At the election 149 MPs stood down of their own volition (or their party's) rather than face the voters again, far more than the 115 who did so before the end-of-era election of 1997. Five former MPs also return after periods of broken service.

The Times Guide to the House of Commons 2010 has itself undergone change. Its commitment to accuracy and balance remain, but with even greater emphasis on analysis and comment. Writers from *The Times* explore the wider undercurrents that had an impact on the voters' view of politicians: the scandal of misuse of Commons allowances; the banking crisis and recession; and the handling of military campaigns in Iraq and Afghanistan. The *Guide* gives greater scope for the best of *The Times's* journalism beyond that of its writers, with the work of its photographers, illustrators, graphic artists and designers used to full effect.

Profiles of each Member of Parliament are livelier, intended to convey a sense of what each is like, what motivates them and how effectively they discharge their role, in addition to biographical details of what they have done. Information is included, too, on thousands of candidates who contested the election, were unsuccessful but attracted sufficient support to hold their deposit. Many among them, no doubt, will be the subject of fuller profiles in the next *Guide* as Members of Parliament.

Finally, and perhaps most importantly, there is a new chapter that explains and discusses the work of the House of Commons, its powers, recent reforms and their effect. Former Members of Parliament describe the reality of serving on the government and opposition benches, from the challenge of finding how to make their voice heard and the satisfaction of influencing events to the monotony of waiting, day after day, night after night, to vote.

The new Parliament is embarking on a journey of political change through waters familiar to much of continental Europe but, to date, largely uncharted by practitioners of politics, commentators, observers and electors in the United Kingdom. *The Times Guide to the Commons* seeks, as ever, to offer itself as their navigational aid.

State of the parties

Election May 2005

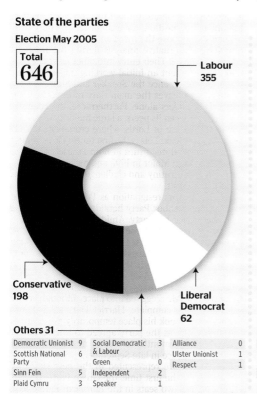

Total
646

Labour
355

Conservative
198

Liberal Democrat
62

Others 31

Democratic Unionist	9	Social Democratic & Labour	3	Alliance	0
Scottish National Party	6	Green	0	Ulster Unionist	1
Sinn Fein	5	Independent	2	Respect	1
Plaid Cymru	3	Speaker	1		

Election May 2010

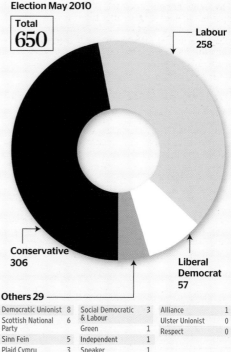

Total
650

Labour
258

Conservative
306

Liberal Democrat
57

Others 29

Democratic Unionist	8	Social Democratic & Labour	3	Alliance	1
Scottish National Party	6	Green	1	Ulster Unionist	0
Sinn Fein	5	Independent	1	Respect	0
Plaid Cymru	3	Speaker	1		

The House of Commons

The following were elected Members of the House of Commons in the 2010 general election

Alliance Alliance
C Conservative
DUP Democratic Unionist Party
Green Green
Ind Independent
Lab Labour

LD Liberal Democrat;
PC Plaid Cymru
SNP Scottish National Party
SF Sinn Féin
SDLP Social Democratic and Labour Party
Speaker Speaker

A

Abbott, Diane Hackney North & Stoke Newington	Lab
Adams, Gerry Belfast West	SF
Adams, Nigel Selby & Ainsty	C
Afriyie, Adam Windsor	C
Ainsworth, Bob Coventry North East	Lab
Aldous, Peter Waveney	C
Alexander, Danny Inverness, Nairn, Badenoch & Strathspey	LD
Alexander, Heidi Lewisham East	Lab
Alexander, Douglas Paisley & Renfrewshire South	Lab
Ali, Rushanara Bethnal Green & Bow	Lab
Allen, Graham Nottingham North	Lab
Amess, David Southend West	C
Anderson, Dave Blaydon	Lab
Andrew, Stuart Pudsey	C
Arbuthnot, James Hampshire North East	C
Austin, Ian Dudley North	Lab

B

Bacon, Richard Norfolk South	C
Bagshawe, Louise Corby	C
Bailey, Adrian West Bromwich West	Lab
Bain, Willie Glasgow North East	Lab
Baker, Norman Lewes	LD
Baker, Steven Wycombe	C
Baldry, Tony Banbury	C
Baldwin, Harriett Worcestershire West	C
Balls, Ed Morley & Outwood	Lab
Banks, Gordon Ochil & Perthshire South	Lab
Barclay, Stephen Cambridgeshire North East	C
Barker, Greg Bexhill & Battle	C
Baron, John Basildon & Billericay	C
Barron, Kevin Rother Valley	Lab
Barwell, Gavin Croydon Central	C
Bayley, Hugh York Central	Lab
Bebb, Guto Aberconwy	C
Beckett, Margaret Derby South	Lab
Begg, Anne Aberdeen South	Lab
Beith, Sir Alan Berwick-upon-Tweed	LD
Bell, Sir Stuart Middlesbrough	Lab
Bellingham, Henry Norfolk North West	C
Benn, Hilary Leeds Central	Lab
Benton, Joe Bootle	Lab
Benyon, Richard Newbury	C
Bercow, John Buckingham	Speaker
Beresford, Sir Paul Mole Valley	C
Berger, Luciana Liverpool Wavertree	Lab
Berry, Jake Rossendale & Darwen	C
Betts, Clive Sheffield South East	Lab
Bingham, Andrew High Peak	C
Binley, Brian Northampton South	C
Birtwistle, Gordon Burnley	LD
Blackman, Bob Harrow East	C
Blackman-Woods, Roberta Durham, City of	Lab
Blackwood, Nicola Oxford West & Abingdon	C
Blears, Hazel Salford & Eccles	Lab
Blenkinsop, Tom Middlesbrough South & Cleveland East	Lab
Blomfield, Paul Sheffield Central	Lab

Blunkett, David Sheffield Brightside & Hillsborough	Lab
Blunt, Crispin Reigate	C
Boles, Nicholas Grantham & Stamford	C
Bone, Peter Wellingborough	C
Bottomley, Peter Worthing West	C
Bradley, Karen Staffordshire Moorlands	C
Bradshaw, Ben Exeter	Lab
Brady, Graham Altrincham & Sale West	C
Brake, Tom Carshalton & Wallington	LD
Bray, Angie Ealing Central & Acton	C
Brazier, Julian Canterbury	C
Brennan, Kevin Cardiff West	Lab
Bridgen, Andrew Leicestershire North West	C
Brine, Steve Winchester	C
Brokenshire, James Old Bexley & Sidcup	C
Brooke, Annette Dorset Mid & Poole North	LD
Brown, Russell Dumfries & Galloway	Lab
Brown, Gordon Kirkcaldy & Cowdenbeath	Lab
Brown, Nicholas Newcastle upon Tyne East	Lab
Brown, Lyn West Ham	Lab
Browne, Jeremy Taunton Deane	LD
Bruce, Fiona Congleton	C
Bruce, Malcolm Gordon	LD
Bryant, Chris Rhondda	Lab
Buck, Karen Westminster North	Lab
Buckland, Robert Swindon South	C
Burden, Richard Birmingham Northfield	Lab
Burley, Aidan Cannock Chase	C
Burnham, Andy Leigh	Lab
Burns, Conor Bournemouth West	C
Burns, Simon Chelmsford	C
Burrowes, David Enfield Southgate	C
Burstow, Paul Sutton & Cheam	LD
Burt, Alistair Bedfordshire North East	C
Burt, Lorely Solihull	LD
Byles, Dan Warwickshire North	C
Byrne, Liam Birmingham Hodge Hill	Lab

C

Cable, Vince Twickenham	LD
Cairns, David Inverclyde	Lab
Cairns, Alun Vale of Glamorgan	C
Cameron, David Witney	C
Campbell, Ronnie Blyth Valley	Lab
Campbell, Sir Menzies Fife North East	LD
Campbell, Gregory Londonderry East	DUP
Campbell, Alan Tynemouth	Lab
Carmichael, Alistair Orkney & Shetland	LD
Carmichael, Neil Stroud	C
Carswell, Douglas Clacton	C
Cash, Bill Stone	C
Caton, Martin Gower	Lab
Chapman, Jenny Darlington	Lab
Chishti, Rehman Gillingham & Rainham	C
Chope, Christopher Christchurch	C
Clappison, James Hertsmere	C
Clark, Katy Ayrshire North & Arran	Lab
Clark, Greg Tunbridge Wells	C
Clarke, Tom Coatbridge, Chryston & Bellshill	Lab
Clarke, Kenneth Rushcliffe	C
Clegg, Nick Sheffield Hallam	LD

Clifton-Brown, Geoffrey Cotswolds, The	C
Clwyd, Ann Cynon Valley	Lab
Coaker, Vernon Gedling	Lab
Coffey, Ann Stockport	Lab
Coffey, Therese Suffolk Coastal	C
Collins, Damian Folkestone & Hythe	C
Colvile, Oliver Plymouth Sutton & Devonport	C
Connarty, Michael Linlithgow & Falkirk East	Lab
Cooper, Rosie Lancashire West	Lab
Cooper, Yvette Normanton, Pontefract & Castleford	Lab
Corbyn, Jeremy Islington North	Lab
Cox, Geoffrey Devon West & Torridge	C
Crabb, Stephen Preseli Pembrokeshire	C
Crausby, David Bolton North East	Lab
Creagh, Mary Wakefield	Lab
Creasy, Stella Walthamstow	Lab
Crockart, Michael Edinburgh West	LD
Crouch, Tracey Chatham & Aylesford	C
Cruddas, Jon Dagenham & Rainham	Lab
Cryer, John Leyton & Wanstead	Lab
Cunningham, Jim Coventry South	Lab
Cunningham, Alex Stockton North	Lab
Cunningham, Tony Workington	Lab
Curran, Margaret Glasgow East	Lab

D

Dakin, Nic Scunthorpe	Lab
Danczuk, Simon Rochdale	Lab
Darling, Alistair Edinburgh South West	Lab
Davey, Edward Kingston & Surbiton	LD
David, Wayne Caerphilly	Lab
Davidson, Ian Glasgow South West	Lab
Davies, David Monmouth	C
Davies, Glyn Montgomeryshire	C
Davies, Philip Shipley	C
Davies, Geraint Swansea West	Lab
Davis, David Haltemprice & Howden	C
de Bois, Nick Enfield North	C
de Piero, Gloria Ashfield	Lab
Denham, John Southampton Itchen	Lab
Dinenage, Caroline Gosport	C
Djanogly, Jonathan Huntingdon	C
Dobbin, Jim Heywood & Middleton	Lab
Dobson, Frank Holborn & St Pancras	Lab
Docherty, Thomas Dunfermline & Fife West	Lab
Dodds, Nigel Belfast North	DUP
Doherty, Pat Tyrone West	SF
Donaldson, Jeffrey Lagan Valley	DUP
Donohoe, Brian Ayrshire Central	Lab
Doran, Frank Aberdeen North	Lab
Dorrell, Stephen Charnwood	C
Dorries, Nadine Bedfordshire Mid	C
Dowd, Jim Lewisham West & Penge	Lab
Doyle, Gemma Dunbartonshire West	Lab
Doyle-Price, Jackie Thurrock	C
Drax, Richard Dorset South	C
Dromey, Jack Birmingham Erdington	Lab
Duddridge, James Rochford & Southend East	C
Dugher, Michael Barnsley East	Lab
Duncan, Alan Rutland & Melton	C
Duncan Smith, Iain Chingford & Woodford Green	C
Dunne, Philip Ludlow	C
Durkan, Mark Foyle	SDLP

E

Eagle, Maria Garston & Halewood	Lab
Eagle, Angela Wallasey	Lab
Edwards, Jonathan Carmarthen East & Dinefwr	PC
Efford, Clive Eltham	Lab
Elliott, Julie Sunderland Central	Lab
Ellis, Michael Northampton North	C
Ellison, Jane Battersea	C
Ellman, Louise Liverpool Riverside	Lab

Ellwood, Tobias Bournemouth East	C
Elphicke, Charlie Dover	C
Engel, Natascha Derbyshire North East	Lab
Esterson, Bill Sefton Central	Lab
Eustice, George Camborne & Redruth	C
Evans, Jonathan Cardiff North	C
Evans, Christopher Islwyn	Lab
Evans, Nigel Ribble Valley	C
Evans, Graham Weaver Vale	C
Evennett, David Bexleyheath & Crayford	C

F

Fabricant, Michael Lichfield	C
Fallon, Michael Sevenoaks	C
Farrelly, Paul Newcastle-under-Lyme	Lab
Farron, Tim Westmorland & Lonsdale	LD
Featherstone, Lynne Hornsey & Wood Green	LD
Field, Frank Birkenhead	Lab
Field, Mark Cities of London & Westminster	C
Fitzpatrick, Jim Poplar & Limehouse	Lab
Flello, Rob Stoke-on-Trent South	Lab
Flint, Caroline Don Valley	Lab
Flynn, Paul Newport West	Lab
Foster, Don Bath	LD
Fovargue, Yvonne Makerfield	Lab
Fox, Dr Liam Somerset North	C
Francis, Hywel Aberavon	Lab
Francois, Mark Rayleigh & Wickford	C
Freeman, George Norfolk Mid	C
Freer, Mike Finchley & Golders Green	C
Fullbrook, Lorraine South Ribble	C
Fuller, Richard Bedford	C

G

Gale, Roger Thanet North	C
Gapes, Mike Ilford South	Lab
Gardiner, Barry Brent North	Lab
Garnier, Edward Harborough	C
Garnier, Mark Wyre Forest	C
Gauke, David Hertfordshire South West	C
George, Andrew St Ives	LD
Gibb, Nick Bognor Regis & Littlehampton	C
Gilbert, Stephen St Austell & Newquay	LD
Gildernew, Michelle Fermanagh & South Tyrone	SF
Gillan, Cheryl Chesham & Amersham	C
Gilmore, Sheila Edinburgh East	Lab
Glass, Pat Durham North West	Lab
Glen, John Salisbury	C
Glindon, Mary Tyneside North	Lab
Godsiff, Roger Birmingham Hall Green	Lab
Goggins, Paul Wythenshawe & Sale East	Lab
Goldsmith, Zac Richmond Park	C
Goodman, Helen Bishop Auckland	Lab
Goodwill, Robert Scarborough & Whitby	C
Gove, Michael Surrey Heath	C
Graham, Richard Gloucester	C
Grant, Helen Maidstone & The Weald	C
Gray, James Wiltshire North	C
Grayling, Chris Epsom & Ewell	C
Greatrex, Tom Rutherglen & Hamilton West	Lab
Green, Damian Ashford	C
Green, Kate Stretford & Urmston	Lab
Greening, Justine Putney	C
Greenwood, Lilian Nottingham South	Lab
Grieve, Dominic Beaconsfield	C
Griffith, Nia Llanelli	Lab
Griffiths, Andrew Burton	C
Gummer, Ben Ipswich	C
Gwynne, Andrew Denton & Reddish	Lab
Gyimah, Sam Surrey East	C

H

Hague, William Richmond (Yorks)	C

Hain, Peter Neath	Lab
Halfon, Robert Harlow	C
Hames, Duncan Chippenham	LD
Hamilton, Fabian Leeds North East	Lab
Hamilton, David Midlothian	Lab
Hammond, Philip Runnymede & Weybridge	C
Hammond, Stephen Wimbledon	C
Hancock, Mike Portsmouth South	LD
Hancock, Matthew Suffolk West	C
Hands, Greg Chelsea & Fulham	C
Hanson, David Delyn	Lab
Harman, Harriet Camberwell & Peckham	Lab
Harper, Mark Forest of Dean	C
Harrington, Richard Watford	C
Harris, Rebecca Castle Point	C
Harris, Tom Glasgow South	Lab
Hart, Simon Carmarthen West & Pembrokeshire South	C
Harvey, Nick Devon North	LD
Haselhurst, Sir Alan Saffron Walden	C
Havard, Dai Merthyr Tydfil & Rhymney	Lab
Hayes, John South Holland & The Deepings	C
Heald, Oliver Hertfordshire North East	C
Healey, John Wentworth & Dearne	Lab
Heath, David Somerton & Frome	LD
Heaton-Harris, Chris Daventry	C
Hemming, John Birmingham Yardley	LD
Henderson, Gordon Sittingbourne & Sheppey	C
Hendrick, Mark Preston	Lab
Hendry, Charles Wealden	C
Hepburn, Stephen Jarrow	Lab
Herbert, Nick Arundel & South Downs	C
Hermon, Lady Sylvia Down North	Ind
Heyes, David Ashton-under-Lyne	Lab
Hillier, Meg Hackney South & Shoreditch	Lab
Hilling, Julie Bolton West	Lab
Hinds, Damian Hampshire East	C
Hoban, Mark Fareham	C
Hodge, Margaret Barking	Lab
Hodgson, Sharon Washington & Sunderland West	Lab
Hoey, Kate Vauxhall	Lab
Hollingbery, George Meon Valley	C
Hollobone, Philip Kettering	C
Holloway, Adam Gravesham	C
Hood, Jim Lanark & Hamilton East	Lab
Hopkins, Kris Keighley	C
Hopkins, Kelvin Luton North	Lab
Horwood, Martin Cheltenham	LD
Hosie, Stewart Dundee East	SNP
Howarth, Gerald Aldershot	C
Howarth, George Knowsley	Lab
Howell, John Henley	C
Hoyle, Lindsay Chorley	Lab
Hughes, Simon Bermondsey & Old Southwark	LD
Huhne, Chris Eastleigh	LD
Hunt, Tristram Stoke-on-Trent Central	Lab
Hunt, Jeremy Surrey South West	C
Hunter, Mark Cheadle	LD
Huppert, Julian Cambridge	LD
Hurd, Nick Ruislip, Northwood & Pinner	C

I

Illsley, Eric Barnsley Central	Lab
Irranca-Davies, Huw Ogmore	Lab

J

Jackson, Glenda Hampstead & Kilburn	Lab
Jackson, Stewart Peterborough	C
James, Margot Stourbridge	C
James, Siân Swansea East	Lab
Jamieson, Cathy Kilmarnock & Loudoun	Lab
Javid, Sajid Bromsgrove	C
Jenkin, Bernard Harwich & Essex North	C
Johnson, Gareth Dartford	C

Johnson, Diana Hull North	Lab
Johnson, Alan Hull West & Hessle	Lab
Johnson, Joseph Orpington	C
Jones, Susan Elan Clwyd South	Lab
Jones, David Clwyd West	C
Jones, Kevan Durham North	Lab
Jones, Andrew Harrogate & Knaresborough	C
Jones, Graham Hyndburn	Lab
Jones, Marcus Nuneaton	C
Jones, Helen Warrington North	Lab
Jowell, Tessa Dulwich & West Norwood	Lab
Joyce, Eric Falkirk	Lab

K

Kaufman, Gerald Manchester Gorton	Lab
Kawczynski, Daniel Shrewsbury & Atcham	C
Keeley, Barbara Worsley & Eccles South	Lab
Keen, Alan Feltham & Heston	Lab
Kelly, Chris Dudley South	C
Kendall, Elizabeth Leicester West	Lab
Kennedy, Charles Ross, Skye & Lochaber	LD
Khan, Sadiq Tooting	Lab
Kirby, Simon Brighton Kemptown	C
Knight, Greg Yorkshire East	C
Kwarteng, Kwasi Spelthorne	C

L

Laing, Eleanor Epping Forest	C
Lamb, Norman Norfolk North	LD
Lammy, David Tottenham	Lab
Lancaster, Mark Milton Keynes North	C
Lansley, Andrew Cambridgeshire South	C
Latham, Pauline Derbyshire Mid	C
Lavery, Ian Wansbeck	Lab
Laws, David Yeovil	LD
Lazarowicz, Mark Edinburgh North & Leith	Lab
Leadsom, Andrea Northamptonshire South	C
Lee, Dr Philip Bracknell	C
Lee, Jessica Erewash	C
Leech, John Manchester Withington	LD
Lefroy, Jeremy Stafford	C
Leigh, Edward Gainsborough	C
Leslie, Charlotte Bristol North West	C
Leslie, Christopher Nottingham East	Lab
Letwin, Oliver Dorset West	C
Lewis, Ivan Bury South	Lab
Lewis, Brandon Great Yarmouth	C
Lewis, Julian New Forest East	C
Liddell-Grainger, Ian Bridgwater & Somerset West	C
Lidington, David Aylesbury	C
Lilley, Peter Hitchin & Harpenden	C
Lloyd, Stephen Eastbourne	LD
Lloyd, Tony Manchester Central	Lab
Llwyd, Elfyn Dwyfor Meirionnydd	PC
Long, Naomi Belfast East	Alliance
Lopresti, Jack Filton & Bradley Stoke	C
Lord, Jonathan Woking	C
Loughton, Tim Worthing East & Shoreham	C
Love, Andy Edmonton	Lab
Lucas, Dr Caroline Brighton Pavilion	Green
Lucas, Ian Wrexham	Lab
Luff, Peter Worcestershire Mid	C
Lumley, Karen Redditch	C

M

Macleod, Mary Brentford & Isleworth	C
MacNeil, Angus Na h-Eileanan an Iar	SNP
MacShane, Denis Rotherham	Lab
Mactaggart, Fiona Slough	Lab
Mahmood, Shabana Birmingham Ladywood	Lab
Mahmood, Khalid Birmingham Perry Barr	Lab
Main, Anne St Albans	C
Mann, John Bassetlaw	Lab

Marsden, Gordon Blackpool South	Lab
Maude, Francis Horsham	C
May, Theresa Maidenhead	C
Maynard, Paul Blackpool North & Cleveleys	C
McCabe, Steve Birmingham Selly Oak	Lab
McCann, Michael East Kilbride, Strathaven & Lesmahagow	Lab
McCarthy, Kerry Bristol East	Lab
McCartney, Jason Colne Valley	C
McCartney, Karl Lincoln	C
McClymont, Gregg Cumbernauld, Kilsyth & Kirkintilloch East	Lab
McCrea, Rev William Antrim South	DUP
McDonagh, Siobhain Mitcham & Morden	Lab
McDonnell, Dr Alasdair Belfast South	SDLP
McDonnell, John Hayes & Harlington	Lab
McFadden, Pat Wolverhampton South East	Lab
McGovern, Jim Dundee West	Lab
McGovern, Alison Wirral South	Lab
McGuinness, Martin Ulster Mid	SF
McGuire, Anne Stirling	Lab
McIntosh, Anne Thirsk & Malton	C
McKechin, Ann Glasgow North	Lab
McKinnell, Catherine Newcastle upon Tyne North	Lab
McLoughlin, Patrick Derbyshire Dales	C
McPartland, Stephen Stevenage	C
McVey, Esther Wirral West	C
Meacher, Michael Oldham West & Royton	Lab
Meale, Joseph Mansfield	Lab
Mearns, Ian Gateshead	Lab
Menzies, Mark Fylde	C
Mercer, Patrick Newark	C
Metcalfe, Stephen Basildon South & Thurrock East	C
Michael, Alun Cardiff South & Penarth	Lab
Miliband, Ed Doncaster North	Lab
Miliband, David South Shields	Lab
Miller, Maria Basingstoke	C
Miller, Andrew Ellesmere Port & Neston	Lab
Mills, Nigel Amber Valley	C
Milton, Anne Guildford	C
Mitchell, Austin Great Grimsby	Lab
Mitchell, Andrew Sutton Coldfield	C
Moon, Madeleine Bridgend	Lab
Moore, Michael Berwickshire, Roxburgh & Selkirk	LD
Mordaunt, Penny Portsmouth North	C
Morden, Jessica Newport East	Lab
Morgan, Nicky Loughborough	C
Morrice, Graeme Livingston	Lab
Morris, Grahame Easington	Lab
Morris, James Halesowen & Rowley Regis	C
Morris, David Morecambe & Lunesdale	C
Morris, Anne-Marie Newton Abbot	C
Mosley, Stephen City of Chester	C
Mowat, David Warrington South	C
Mudie, George Leeds East	Lab
Mulholland, Greg Leeds North West	LD
Mundell, David Dumfriesshire, Clydesdale & Tweeddale	C
Munn, Meg Sheffield Heeley	Lab
Munt, Tessa Wells	LD
Murphy, Conor Newry & Armagh	SF
Murphy, Jim Renfrewshire East	Lab
Murphy, Paul Torfaen	Lab
Murray, Sheryll Cornwall South East	C
Murray, Ian Edinburgh South	Lab
Murrison, Andrew Wiltshire South West	C

N

Nandy, Lisa Wigan	Lab
Nash, Pamela Airdrie & Shotts	Lab
Neill, Bob Bromley & Chislehurst	C
Newmark, Brooks Braintree	C
Newton, Sarah Truro & Falmouth	C

Nokes, Caroline Romsey & Southampton North	C
Norman, Jesse Hereford & Herefordshire South	C
Nuttall, David Bury North	C

O

O'Brien, Stephen Eddisbury	C
O'Donnell, Fiona East Lothian	Lab
Offord, Matthew Hendon	C
Ollerenshaw, Eric Lancaster & Fleetwood	C
Onwurah, Chi Newcastle upon Tyne Central	Lab
Opperman, Guy Hexham	C
Osborne, Sandra Ayr, Carrick & Cumnock	Lab
Osborne, George Tatton	C
Ottaway, Richard Croydon South	C
Owen, Albert Ynys Mon	Lab

P

Paice, Jim Cambridgeshire South East	C
Paisley, Ian Junior Antrim North	DUP
Parish, Neil Tiverton & Honiton	C
Patel, Priti Witham	C
Paterson, Owen Shropshire North	C
Pawsey, Mark Rugby	C
Pearce, Teresa Erith & Thamesmead	Lab
Penning, Mike Hemel Hempstead	C
Penrose, John Weston-super-Mare	C
Percy, Andrew Brigg & Goole	C
Perkins, Toby Chesterfield	Lab
Perry, Claire Devizes	C
Phillips, Stephen Sleaford & North Hykeham	C
Phillipson, Bridget Houghton & Sunderland South	Lab
Pickles, Eric Brentwood & Ongar	C
Pincher, Christopher Tamworth	C
Poulter, Daniel Suffolk Central & Ipswich North	C
Pound, Stephen Ealing North	Lab
Primarolo, Dawn Bristol South	Lab
Prisk, Mark Hertford & Stortford	C
Pritchard, Mark Wrekin, The	C
Pugh, John Southport	LD

Q

Qureshi, Yasmin Bolton South East	Lab

R

Raab, Dominic Esher & Walton	C
Randall, John Uxbridge & Ruislip South	C
Raynsford, Nick Greenwich & Woolwich	Lab
Reckless, Mark Rochester & Strood	C
Redwood, John Wokingham	C
Reed, Jamie Copeland	Lab
Rees-Mogg, Jacob Somerset North East	C
Reevell, Simon Dewsbury	C
Reeves, Rachel Leeds West	Lab
Reid, Alan Argyll & Bute	LD
Reynolds, Jonathan Stalybridge & Hyde	Lab
Reynolds, Emma Wolverhampton North East	Lab
Rifkind, Sir Malcolm Kensington	C
Riordan, Linda Halifax	Lab
Ritchie, Margaret Down South	SDLP
Robathan, Andrew Leicestershire South	C
Robertson, Hugh Faversham & Kent Mid	C
Robertson, John Glasgow North West	Lab
Robertson, Angus Moray	SNP
Robertson, Laurence Tewkesbury	C
Robinson, Geoffrey Coventry North West	Lab
Rogerson, Dan Cornwall North	LD
Rosindell, Andrew Romford	C
Rotheram, Steve Liverpool Walton	Lab
Roy, Lindsay Glenrothes	Lab
Roy, Frank Motherwell & Wishaw	Lab
Ruane, Chris Vale of Clwyd	Lab
Rudd, Amber Hastings & Rye	C
Ruddock, Joan Lewisham Deptford	Lab

Ruffley, David Bury St Edmunds — C
Russell, Bob Colchester — LD
Rutley, David Macclesfield — C

S

Sanders, Adrian Torbay — LD
Sandys, Laura Thanet South — C
Sarwar, Anas Glasgow Central — Lab
Scott, Lee Ilford North — C
Seabeck, Alison Plymouth Moor View — Lab
Selous, Andrew Bedfordshire South West — C
Shannon, Jim Strangford — DUP
Shapps, Grant Welwyn Hatfield — C
Sharma, Virendra Ealing Southall — Lab
Sharma, Alok Reading West — C
Sheerman, Barry Huddersfield — Lab
Shelbrooke, Alec Elmet & Rothwell — C
Shepherd, Richard Aldridge-Brownhills — C
Sheridan, Jim Paisley & Renfrewshire North — Lab
Shuker, Gavin Luton South — Lab
Simmonds, Mark Boston & Skegness — C
Simpson, Keith Broadland — C
Simpson, Thomas David Upper Bann — DUP
Singh, Marsha Bradford West — Lab
Skidmore, Chris Kingswood — C
Skinner, Dennis Bolsover — Lab
Slaughter, Andy Hammersmith — Lab
Smith, Sir Robert Aberdeenshire West & Kincardine — LD
Smith, Nick Blaenau Gwent — Lab
Smith, Henry Crawley — C
Smith, Chloe Norwich North — C
Smith, Andrew Oxford East — Lab
Smith, Angela Penistone & Stocksbridge — Lab
Smith, Owen Pontypridd — Lab
Smith, Julian Skipton & Ripon — C
Soames, Nicholas Sussex Mid — C
Soubry, Anna Broxtowe — C
Soulsby, Sir Peter Leicester South — Lab
Spellar, John Warley — Lab
Spelman, Caroline Meriden — C
Spencer, Mark Sherwood — C
Stanley, Sir John Tonbridge & Malling — C
Stephenson, Andrew Pendle — C
Stevenson, John Carlisle — C
Stewart, Bob Beckenham — C
Stewart, Iain Milton Keynes South — C
Stewart, Rory Penrith & The Border — C
Straw, Jack Blackburn — Lab
Streeter, Gary Devon South West — C
Stride, Mel Devon Central — C
Stringer, Graham Blackley & Broughton — Lab
Stuart, Graham Beverley & Holderness — C
Stuart, Gisela Birmingham Edgbaston — Lab
Stunell, Andrew Hazel Grove — LD
Sturdy, Julian York Outer — C
Sutcliffe, Gerry Bradford South — Lab
Swales, Ian Redcar — LD
Swayne, Desmond New Forest West — C
Swinson, Jo Dunbartonshire East — LD
Swire, Hugo Devon East — C
Syms, Robert Poole — C

T

Tami, Mark Alyn & Deeside — Lab
Tapsell, Sir Peter Louth & Horncastle — C
Teather, Sarah Brent Central — LD
Thomas, Gareth Harrow West — Lab
Thornberry, Emily Islington South & Finsbury — Lab
Timms, Stephen East Ham — Lab
Timpson, Edward Crewe & Nantwich — C
Tomlinson, Justin Swindon North — C
Tredinnick, David Bosworth — C

Trickett, Jon Hemsworth — Lab
Truss, Elizabeth Norfolk South West — C
Turner, Karl Hull East — Lab
Turner, Andrew Isle of Wight — C
Twigg, Derek Halton — Lab
Twigg, Stephen Liverpool West Derby — Lab
Tyrie, Andrew Chichester — C

U

Umunna, Chuka Streatham — Lab
Uppal, Paul Wolverhampton South West — C

V

Vaizey, Ed Wantage — C
Vara, Shailesh Cambridgeshire North West — C
Vaz, Keith Leicester East — Lab
Vaz, Valerie Walsall South — Lab
Vickers, Martin Cleethorpes — C
Villiers, Theresa Chipping Barnet — C

W

Walker, Charles Broxbourne — C
Walker, Robin Worcester — C
Wallace, Ben Wyre & Preston North — C
Walley, Joan Stoke-on-Trent North — Lab
Walter, Bob Dorset North — C
Ward, David Bradford East — LD
Watkinson, Angela Hornchurch & Upminster — C
Watson, Tom West Bromwich East — Lab
Watts, Dave St Helens North — Lab
Weatherley, Mike Hove — C
Webb, Steve Thornbury & Yate — LD
Weir, Mike Angus — SNP
Wharton, James Stockton South — C
Wheeler, Heather Derbyshire South — C
White, Chris Warwick & Leamington — C
Whiteford, Eilidh Banff & Buchan — SNP
Whitehead, Alan Southampton Test — Lab
Whittaker, Craig Calder Valley — C
Whittingdale, John Maldon — C
Wicks, Malcolm Croydon North — Lab
Wiggin, Bill Herefordshire North — C
Willetts, David Havant — C
Williams, Hywel Arfon — PC
Williams, Roger Brecon & Radnorshire — LD
Williams, Stephen Bristol West — LD
Williams, Mark Ceredigion — LD
Williamson, Chris Derby North — Lab
Williamson, Gavin Staffordshire South — C
Willott, Jenny Cardiff Central — LD
Wilson, Sammy Antrim East — DUP
Wilson, Rob Reading East — C
Wilson, Phil Sedgefield — Lab
Winnick, David Walsall North — Lab
Winterton, Rosie Doncaster Central — Lab
Wishart, Pete Perth & Perthshire North — SNP
Wollaston, Dr Sarah Totnes — C
Wood, Mike Batley & Spen — Lab
Woodcock, John Barrow & Furness — Lab
Woodward, Shaun St Helens South & Whiston — Lab
Woolas, Phil Oldham East & Saddleworth — Lab
Wright, Iain Hartlepool — Lab
Wright, Jeremy Kenilworth & Southam — C
Wright, Simon Norwich South — LD
Wright, David Telford — Lab

Y

Yeo, Tim Suffolk South — C
Young, Sir George Hampshire North West — C

Z

Zahawi, Nadhim Stratford-on-Avon — C

The new Parliament

*"Come down, and we'll engage
in constructive negotiations
about power sharing"*

An ordinary beginning to an extraordinary campaign

Roland Watson
Political Editor

After asking the Queen to dissolve Parliament, Gordon Brown returned from Buckingham Palace to Downing Street and declared: "I come from an ordinary family in an ordinary town." As the opening line of the 2010 general election, it was designed to draw attention to the privileged background of his Eton-educated Conservative rival, David Cameron. It ill served as a guide for what followed, though, which was, by any standards of modern British political history, extraordinary.

None of the three leaders had led their parties into a general election and each faced a monumental task. Mr Brown was seeking an historic fourth term for Labour against the backdrop of the deepest recession for 60 years. He was also looking to overcome the memory of the election-that-never-was in October 2007 when, five months after inheriting the job from Tony Blair and revving up Labour's campaign machine, he ducked out of going to the country at the last moment.

Mr Cameron needed to achieve the biggest swing since the war to gain the 116 seats required for a Commons majority. His party had endured a jittery few months in which questions about its economic policy and a tightening in the polls fed off each other to spread deep unease through Tory ranks. He was beginning the campaign with a seven-point lead, well down from the double digits the Tories had enjoyed for most of the past year and not enough for an outright win.

Nick Clegg, the Liberal Democrat leader, needed to capitalise on the prospects of a hung Parliament. He also had the first televised debates between the leaders to look forward to. They would offer him a stage never before enjoyed by his predecessors: equal prime-time billing with his two rivals. Initially, though, the campaign conformed to type, focusing on the two established parties. Mr Cameron pre-empted Mr Brown's return from the Palace to stage a rally on the south bank of the Thames, across from Westminster. Waving his finger at the Houses of Parliament, he vowed to "make people feel proud again of that building over there". He was, he said, campaigning for "the Great Ignored", a group that encompassed black, white, rich, poor, town and country folk. It was a slogan he ignored for the rest of the campaign.

The styles of the Tory and Labour campaigns differed starkly from the start. As Mr Cameron tore round the country on a leased private plane, Mr Brown made political capital out of financial necessity, travelling by rail in standard class. Labour had raised less than half the Tories' £18 million war chest, and had spent much of it during the phoney war since the start of the year. Once at his campaigning destinations, Mr Brown rarely delivered speeches, preferring to meet small groups of voters in supermarket canteens or the living rooms of Labour supporters, fuelling questions about whether he was reaching swing voters. Mr Cameron, boasting a campaign team with a sharper eye for "optics", was pictured repeatedly, sleeves rolled up, in warehouses or stock rooms surrounded by workers and clearly visible logos of well-known brands.

The contrast carried through to their manifestos, in which Labour offered a "smarter" State, the Tories a smaller one. Mr Brown unveiled a traditional-looking pitch in a newly built and soon-to-be-opened wing of a Birmingham hospital. It promised to tailor public services to people's needs, giving them guarantees on rights of redress against schools, hospitals and police forces if services failed to reach certain standards.

The Tory manifesto was unusual and innovative, and not just for being presented in the semi ruins of Battersea power station. A hard-backed blue book on A5 paper titled *An Invitation to Join the Government of Britain*, it urged people to take more control over their workplaces, children's schools and how they are policed and ruled, offering a glimpse of life in what Mr Cameron billed the Big Society.

Mr Clegg chose the City of London as his launch pad, an attempt to show that the party often criticised for having uncosted policies was serious about its finances. The signature policy was to raise the starting threshold for income tax from £6,500 to £10,000, costing £17 billion. The document even included tax tables at the back to show that the sums added up, calculations immediately disputed by Labour and the Tories.

The choice between an empowered individual in a smaller Tory State and a smarter Labour State that provided service guarantees offered the central intellectual dividing line, although both sides fought surprisingly shy of their offering on the stump. Instead, the debate revolved around the economy, in particular whether the £6 billion of immediate savings the Tories were proposing to make in Whitehall, and subsequently used to ease Labour's proposed rise in national insurance contributions, would help or hinder the recovery.

So far, so normal. The campaign was turned on its head from the moment Mr Clegg stared into the cameras of the first TV debate, hosted by ITV in Manchester, and told the 10 million viewers that he was offering something other than business as usual. Presenting himself as a fresh alternative to the tired old parties he was fighting, he spoke crisply and directly about bringing fundamental change to politics. Mr Brown, sensing the early mastery of the medium shown by Mr Clegg and keen to isolate Mr Cameron, used the words "I agree with Nick" half a dozen times. (The following day, the phrase was appearing on Lib Dem badges, posters and banners.) But Mr Clegg would not be caught in a

Labour bear hug. Mr Cameron, expected to shine on a stage apparently made for the ease and informality of his communication skills, tried to look prime ministerial but instead appeared stiff and awkward.

Mr Clegg ran away with the verdict of viewers. In the course of 90 minutes he had wrested from Mr Cameron the mantle of change, in which the Tory leader had cloaked himself for the past four years. Within days, the Lib Dems shot up ten points in the polls. One found Mr Clegg to be the most popular political leader since Churchill. And so the game changed. Although campaigning continued, the oxygen sucked up by the first debate in effect suspended the state of the race while all sides waited for the second debate. Hosted by Sky in Bristol, it saw Mr Cameron recover some of his poise. Mr Clegg, despite his first success, refused to play safe, showed that his first offering was no fluke and cemented his place as a contender.

Shortly before the third debate, Mr Clegg, in an interview with The Times, said that the Lib Dems had replaced Labour as the progressive force in politics and that the election now boiled down to a two-horse race between him and Mr Cameron. Two weeks previously such an assertion would have been laughed out of court. With many polls showing the Lib Dems nudging ahead of Labour, it now carried weight.

Mr Clegg's success, or Cleggmania to give it its official media term, forced Labour and the Tories into tactical switches. They both turned their guns on Lib Dem policies, such as an amnesty on some illegal immigrants, softer sentencing and a refusal to guarantee the future of Britian's nuclear deterrent. The Tories did so with menaced warnings whereas Labour, with an eye on the possibilities of a Lib-Lab deal if voters returned a hung Parliament, were less harsh.

Mr Brown also re-wrote his personal campaign. Labour strategists, faced with selling a leader who was unpopular with voters, had kept the Prime Minister to a routine of small meetings largely behind closed doors. It had left Mr Brown frustrated. He would spend the final ten days meeting more "real people" and making more speeches. The new style made a calamitous start. In Rochdale, Mr Brown was accosted by a Labour-supporting grandmother, Gillian Duffy, who took him to task on issues ranging from student fees to immigration. She walked away happy to have had her say and quietly thrilled to have met the Prime Minister. He got into his official car and branded the mild confrontation a disaster, called her a bigoted woman and blamed an aide. The remarks were picked up by a radio microphone he had worn for his walkabout and had not yet taken off.

For the rest of the day Mrs Duffy became the centre of an extraordinary maelstrom. She was devastated to learn of Mr Brown's remarks, which were played repeatedly on news channels. They were doubly damaging: Mr Brown had appeared deaf to the concerns of millions of voters on immigration; and his apparent instinct to blame aides underlined a wider perception of character flaws. Over the next six hours, Mr Brown apologised six times. He tore up his schedule, abandoned preparation for the following day's final debate and returned to Rochdale where he spent 40 minutes in Mrs Duffy's living room trying to explain himself.

The third and final debate, hosted by the BBC in Birmingham, was Mr Brown's last chance to turn the campaign around. Labour aides had negotiated successfully for its theme to be the economy, Mr Brown's perceived strongest suit. Although he put in his best performance, he again trailed in third place, according to snap polls. In the final days, he was at his best, delivering his most passionate speech on social justice to an audience in London. Some wondered where this fiery campaigner had been for the previous three weeks, and why he had not been let loose. Others concluded that he was able to let himself go because he suspected he had lost.

On the eve of polling day Mr Cameron campaigned through the night, a self-consciously arduous bus trip from Scotland to Bristol via Grimsby where he met night workers in depots and sorting offices along the way. Such a gruelling final lap was hardly the best preparation for what was to follow.

Polling day itself was marred by near tragedy when Nigel Farage, an MEP and the former leader of the UK Independence Party, escaped with his life from a light plane crash after a campaign stunt went disastrously wrong. The aircraft carrying Mr Farage, who was standing against the Speaker, John Bercow, in Buckingham, was trailing a 15ft banner that read: "Vote for your country – Vote UKIP". The banner became entangled with the plane's tail about 10ft above the ground, causing it to nosedive. Mr Farage said that he and his pilot, Justin Adams, had had a miraculous escape.

On the stroke of 10pm, the exit poll commissioned by the BBC, ITN and Sky suggested that the Tories would win 307 seats, Labour 255 and the Liberal Democrats 59, pointing to the first hung Parliament for 36 years. Its forecasting was immediately doubted by psephologists, both amateur and professional, who believed that a survey of 18,000 voters at 130 polling stations would fail to catch the Lib Dem surge. In fact, it turned out to be remarkably prescient.

An eleventh-hour surge of voters, Lib Dem or otherwise, did, however, surprise election officials across the country. Queues of voters, some who had been waiting up to an hour, were turned away from polling stations in Sheffield, Leeds, Manchester, Chester, Lewisham and Hackney. There, officials applied the letter of the law and closed the door on anyone who had not been admitted and received a ballot paper. Their counterparts in Newcastle and Sutton Coldfield defied electoral law and stayed open past 10pm to let people vote. The scenes of chaos, to which the police were called in some cases, triggered a review by the Electoral Commission that could have far-reaching implications for the way Britain votes.

Britain woke on May 7 to a landscape unfamiliar to this generation of politicians. There was no clear winner and each party leader had reason to feel disappointed. Mr Cameron had failed to translate an economic crisis and weariness with 13 years of Labour into an overall Tory majority. Mr Brown had polled 29 per cent, only marginally above the party's disastrous showing in 1983, and had lost 91 seats. For all the enthusiasm that surrounded Mr Clegg during the campaign, he had lost five seats.

Voters had handed them not just the first hung Parliament for 36 years, but the most complicated Commons arithmetic since the 1920s. Mr Cameron, with 306 seats, was well short of the 326 that guaranteed a Commons majority. To soldier on alone as a minority government, he would at least need an assurance of broad Liberal Democrat support, known as a "confidence and supply" arrangement, under which the third party would not stand in the way of a Budget or Queen's Speech in return for some concessions.

On the other side, Labour, with 258 seats, and the Liberal Democrats, with 57, were also well short of being able to form a Lib-Lab pact that commanded a Commons majority. The only certainty was that the Queen would not be receiving any of the party leaders this post-election Friday. Instead, she, and the rest

Gordon Brown, announcing the election date in Downing Street, declared: "I come from an ordinary family"

of the country, witnessed an extraordinary three-act drama played out across Westminster as the three leaders began to play the hands dealt them by voters.

Mr Clegg moved first. Arriving at Liberal Democrat headquarters in Cowley Street after taking the dawn train from his constituency in Sheffield, he said that Mr Cameron had the right to try first to form a government. It was a momentous nod, but one that he had set himself up for by insisting during the campaign that he would respect the rights of the party that won the most seats and most votes.

Mr Brown was not for giving in. He pre-empted a Tory response with a brazen assertion of prime ministerial power, emerging from the front door of No 10 to remind the country that he remained in charge. He said his two leadership rivals should take as much time as they felt necessary to see if they could reach a deal. "For my part, I should make clear that I would be willing to see any of the party leaders."

Within the hour, Mr Cameron was making what he called "a big, open and comprehensive offer to the Liberal Democrats". Speaking at the St Stephen's Club in the shadow of a portrait of Churchill, himself at different times a Liberal and a Conservative, Mr Cameron sketched out a possible deal for "collaborative government" between the parties. He did not use the word coalition. After a night grappling with the possibilities, though, that was what he was pitching.

With theatrical timing, Saturday required the three leaders to attend the Cenotaph for the 65th anniversary of VE-Day. Normal service would have seen the Prime Minister approach to lay his wreath first, followed by the two other party leaders in turn. The occasion was choreographed, though, to reflect the election result: the three approached the Cenotaph together. The body language ranged from uncertain to icy.

The first public sign of the talks came on Sunday when the negotiating teams – William Hague, George Osborne, Oliver Letwin and Ed Llewellyn for the Tories; Danny Alexander, Chris Huhne, David Laws and Andrew Stunell for the Lib Dems – arrived at the Cabinet Office. The arrangement for the use of government property with civil servants on hand to answer questions about policies and costings was a first, codified in advance by Sir Gus O'Donnell, the Cabinet Secretary, in preparation for just such an electoral outcome.

To the background clatter of news helicopters overhead, a crowd of political tourists joined reporters outside the teal door of 70, Whitehall, to await news of who would govern and how. The parties left after nearly six hours without a deal. Meanwhile, ominously for the Tories, Mr Brown returned from Scotland and went almost immediately into a meeting with Mr Clegg at the Foreign Office. Cabinet ministers, including Lord Mandeslon, Lord Adonis, Alan Johnson, Ben Bradshaw and Peter Hain were offering increasingly vocal support for the idea of a "rainbow coalition" of Labour, the Liberal Democrats, the nationalist parties and independents. It was clear that Mr Clegg was making Mr Cameron sweat.

Tory perspiration turned to desperation on Monday when Mr Brown played his final card. After two further conversations with Mr Clegg, he stood in Downing Street to announce that the Liberal Democrats wanted to open formal talks with Labour and that he intended to step down. His announcement reversed the chronology of his discussions with Mr Clegg. The Liberal Democrat leader had made clear during the campaign that he could not prop up a defeated Mr Brown in Downing Street. The Prime Minister's departure, even if at a later date, was a pre-requisite for the start of Lib-Lab talks.

Nonetheless, Mr Brown's bombshell took the Tories by surprise. Labour, it turned out, had sent its own team of negotiators – Lord Mandelson, Lord Adonis, Ed Balls and Ed Miliband – to talk to the Liberal Democrats on Saturday. Throughout the weekend senior Liberal Democrats, including Lord Ashdown of Norton-sub-Hamdon, Charles Kennedy, Sir Menzies Campbell and Vince Cable, had been urging Mr Brown to budge and thus usher in the "progressive alliance" or realignment of the Left that they, in varying degrees, had devoted their political lives to achieving. The message received in Downing Street from the senior Lib Dems was clear: we do not want to go into coalition with the Tories.

Mr Cameron and those around him had woken on Monday believing that they were heading to Downing Street. Despite offering Mr Clegg a referendum on the alternative vote system and Cabinet seats, they went to bed fearing that they were out of the game. The proposed Lib-Lab deal hit immediate problems, however, on the Tuesday morning. First, senior Labour figures including David Blunkett and John Reid hit the airwaves to warn that the country would not wear what was being dubbed a "coalition of the losers". The maths were also against it: adding the three Welsh nationalists, four non-Unionist Ulster MPs, one independent Unionist and Britain's first Green MP to the Labour and Lib Dem ranks gave such a coalition only 324 MPs, hardly the basis for stable government.

Secondly, the two parties' negotiating teams fared badly. Labour subsequently accused the Liberal Democrats of making unrealistic spending demands; the Liberal Democrats accused Labour of posturing and failing to take them seriously. The upshot was that shortly after lunch, the Tory and Liberal Democrat negotiating teams were back in the Cabinet Office. There, they hammered out terms of a seven-page document that expressed where they agreed and where the Lib Dems would be allowed to opt out of government policy, such as on the future of Trident.

With every passing minute it became clearer that whatever emerged, Labour had lost the negotiations as well as the election. Mr Brown gathered his entourage in Downing Street for his farewell. With the sun beginning to set, and stung by accusations that in fulfilling his constitutional role to remain Prime Minister until an alternative emerged he had tried to cling to office, Mr Brown's dignity could wait no longer.

In a telephone conversation with Mr Clegg, witnessed by the photographer Martin Argles who was in No 10 to record Mr Brown's final hours for posterity, the Prime Minister said: "Nick, Nick, I can't hold on any longer. Nick, I've got to go to the Palace. The country expects me to do that. I have to go. The Queen expects me to go. I can't hold on any longer."

In Downing Street he ended 13 years of Labour rule that had begun with Tony Blair being cheered from Whitehall to the front door of No 10. In a moment of poignant self-awareness, he said that the job had taught him about the best in human nature and about its frailties "including my own".

He and his wife, Sarah, walked to the waiting car holding hands with their two sons, John and Fraser, a very rare sight of the family together after years in which the Browns had protected their sons' privacy.

Within the hour Mr Cameron travelled from a Buckingham Palace bathed in late evening sunshine to the gloom of Downing Street at dusk. He arrived as the youngest Prime Minister since 1812, the twelfth to serve under Elizabeth II and the first Tory for 31 years to depose a Labour prime minister.

How the polls really got it right

Andrew Cooper
Founder of Populus

The 2010 general election saw more opinion polls published than ever before – more than 90 polls during the course of the campaign: a rate of about three per day. Nearly half of these were from one organisation, YouGov, who produced a daily poll for *The Sun*, but during the campaign 11 different research companies produced voting polls.

The polling organisations between them used every conceivable mode of interviewing voters and deployed a wide range of ways to weight and adjust their data. These differing approaches, however, produced a fairly consistent picture as the election campaign kicked off, with the Conservatives 7 to 10 per cent ahead of Labour and the Liberal Democrats about a further 10 per cent behind. The polling story of the campaign was the subsequent abrupt surge in Liberal Democrat support, and its failure to materialise on election day.

Several polls picked up a growing frustration among many voters during the first week of the campaign. Even before the first TV debate the Populus poll for *The Times* published on April 14 found that more voters were hoping that the election would result in a hung Parliament than in a Conservative or Labour majority. The same poll found 75 per cent thinking that it was "time for a change from Labour", but only 34 per cent that it was also "time for a change to the Conservatives"; two fifths of the electorate wanting change, but unsure which party, if any, they trusted to deliver the kind of change they wanted. Furthermore, only 6 per cent of voters felt that the main parties were being completely honest about their plans for dealing with the deficit and only 4 per cent that they were being honest about their tax plans. These findings to a great extent defined the mood of the voters.

The first debate resulted in one of the most dramatic swings in party support ever seen, with the Liberal Democrats jumping by about 10 per cent more or less literally overnight, with the gain coming slightly more from the Conservatives than from Labour. There were nearly 40 polls published between the end of the first debate and the end of the third debate and the Lib Dems were in the lead in five of them and in second place, ahead of Labour, in all but four. When, on the stroke of 10pm on election night, the exit poll predicted that the Liberal Democrats would end up with fewer MPs than at the previous election it was met with widespread incredulity because it seemed irreconcilable with the consensus of pre-election polls. The exit poll turned out, of course, to be right.

Close analysis suggests that Lib Dem poll support was always frothy: it relied heavily on strong support from younger voters and people who had not voted at the previous election, groups that in past elections have been disproportionately likely to end up not voting at all. Most polls are weighted to take account of how likely respondents say they are to vote, but there is a tendency for people to overstate their own probability of voting and there is little or nothing pollsters can do systematically to compensate for those who insist that they are certain to vote and then do not.

Polls during the campaign also consistently suggested that Lib Dem support was softer: those saying that they were going to vote Lib Dem were also consistently more likely than Labour or Conservative voters to say that they had not definitely decided and may end up voting differently. The implication of these findings was that the election result was always likely to be worse for the Lib Dems than the mid-campaign polls implied. But voting polls are heavily modelled these days, applying adjustments intended to project what the result will look like, not just present a snapshot of responses. This means that by the end of the campaign the polls ought to have reflected the underlying softness in Lib Dem support in a lower vote share, and that did not happen. Furthermore all the opinion polls overstated support for the Lib Dems: if the polls overall were performing properly they should have scattered either side of the result, with some understating Lib Dem support, and that did not happen either.

There is some evidence that the swing away from the Lib Dems mainly occurred in the final 24 hours, too late to be properly reflected in the final pre-election polls. The *Times* poll published on election day, for example, put support for the Conservatives on 37 per cent (which is what they got), Labour on 28 per cent (they got 30 per cent) and Lib Dems on 27 per cent (they got 23.5 per cent). Fieldwork for this poll was done on the Tuesday and Wednesday before the election and the two halves of the sample produced revealingly different results. The 1,500 interviews conducted on Tuesday, May 4, would, if presented separately, have shown the Conservatives on 35 per cent, Labour on 26 per cent and Lib Dems on 29 per cent. But among the 1,000 people interviewed on Wednesday, May 5, the Conservatives were on 38 per cent, Labour on 30 per cent and the Lib Dems on 24 per cent. Conducting fieldwork over a longer timeframe – two or three days, rather than one – generally improves the chances of a poll sample being properly representative, capturing the views of busy and harder-to-reach voters. In this case it may have helped to obscure a very late swing away from the Lib Dems, principally to Labour.

It was not all bad news for the pollsters. All but one of the nine organisations that produced a poll on election-eve came within 2 per cent of the Conservative share, five were within 1 per cent and two got it exactly right. All but two of the final polls came within 2 per cent of the Labour share and two were within 1 per cent. Overall it was not as good a performance as 2005, when the polls as a whole were more accurate than ever before, but it was better than at many other elections.

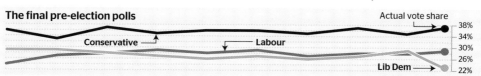

The final pre-election polls

Actual vote share

Conservative

Labour

Lib Dem

38%
34%
30%
26%
22%

A tremor that changed the political landscape

Peter Riddell
Chief Political
Commentator

The general election of May 6, 2010 was one of the most enthralling and exciting in living memory. Yet the dramas of the televised leaders' debates and of the negotiations leading to the creation of the Conservative-Liberal Democrat coalition Government have tended to obscure the big changes in voting patterns.

Although the Conservatives failed to secure an overall Commons majority, they still gained 100 seats and one of the largest swings of votes ever recorded. There were big variations in party performance in different parts of the country, and all three main parties both gained and lost seats. In detail, the election was notable for a big increase in turnout of 3.7 points up to 65.1 per cent. This was still well below the levels familiar before 2001 (a range of 71 to 79 per cent between 1955 and 1997) but it partly reversed the sharp decline in 2001, down to 59.4 per cent, with just a small recovery to 61.4 per cent in 2005. The Conservatives boosted their share of the vote by 3.7 points to 36 per cent. With the higher turnout, this gave them nearly 2 million more votes, up to 10.71 million. This was a clear 2 million ahead of Labour, which suffered a decline of nearly 1 million in its vote to 8.6 million. Its share of the vote fell by 6.2 points to 29 per cent, its lowest since 1983.

Many Labour MPs were relieved that the party had not done worse, partly because of fears towards the end of the campaign that it might come third in share of the votes and win only 200 to 220 MPs. Labour also did well in the borough elections in inner London and in district elections in some northern and big cities. But May 6 was still the party's second worst performance since 1918 and most of its gains achieved since the early 1990s in the Midlands and southern England outside the big cities were reversed.

More than a third of voters, 35 per cent, voted for parties other than the Tories and Labour, the highest proportion since 1918. Conversely, the creation of the coalition means that, together, the Conservatives and Liberal Democrats won, at 59 per cent, the highest percentage of the vote for any new government since 1945. The Liberal Democrats managed to raise their vote by nearly 850,000 to 6.83 million, an increase of 1 point to 23 per cent. The Democratic Unionists are now the second largest opposition party, although with just eight MPs after Peter Robinson, their leader and the First Minister, lost his seat to the Alliance party, which gained its first Westminster MP.

The Scottish Nationalists were unchanged on six seats (although they did lose a by-election gain) with Plaid Cymru on three seats. The UK Independence Party did, as usual in general elections, much less well than in the previous European Parliament elections, but boosted its vote by a third to 917,832, an increase of 0.9 points to 3.1 per cent. This partly reflected a rise of 62 in its number of candidates up to 558.

The British National Party, with 220 more candidates, at 339, nearly tripled its vote to 564,000, a rise of 1.2 points to 1.9 per cent. The Greens, who gained their first MP, maintained their vote in absolute terms at 286,000, but had a 0.1 point decline in share to 1 per cent.

The Conservatives always faced an uphill struggle to win an overall Commons majority. Their starting point of 198 MPs was less than Labour at its lowest point in 1983 of 209. Even after adjusting for the boundary changes that came into force in the May 2010 election and produced a notional gain for the Conservatives up to 209, the party still faced a huge mountain.

The swing of 4.9 per cent from Labour to the Tories was the third largest since 1945, exceeded only by the huge 10.2 per cent swing to Labour in the Blair landslide in 1997 and the 5.3 per cent swing to the Tories under Margaret Thatcher in 1979. The May 6 swing was exactly the same as the late Sir Edward Heath achieved when winning office in 1970, but it was still not enough to produce an overall Conservative majority, given the number of seats that had to be won.

The Tory share of votes cast, at 36 per cent, was the party's lowest lower for a century and a half, apart from the three Blair victories in 1997, 2001 and 2005. The most comparable performances were in the 1920s, another era of three-party politics. The Tories won 37 to 38 per cent of the total votes cast in three of the four general elections in the 1920s.

Nevertheless, the Conservatives gained a net 96 seats, rising to 306, only 20 short of an overall majority. This involved 100 gains and four loses (all but one to the Liberal Democrats). This is the largest number of seats gained by the Conservatives at a single general election since 1931 after the collapse of the Labour Government. It exceeds the 62 seats gained by Mrs Thatcher in 1979 and the 58 gained in 1983; and, in its turn, is exceeded only by Labour's 236 gains in 1945 and 147 in 1997.

Labour lost a net 90 MPs, with 94 losses and four gains (including from independents in Blaenau Gwent and Bethnal Green & Bow). This is by far the worst Labour performance since its debacle in 1931, when it was reduced to just 52 MPs. Since the 1945 election, the biggest Labour losses of seats have been 78 MPs in 1950, 76 in 1970, and 60 in 1983.

The Lib Dems suffered a net loss of 5 seats, down to 57. This involved a loss of 13 seats (all but one to the Tories) and a gain of 8 (5 from Labour and 3 from the Tories).

One of the most striking features of election night was how the Tories won seats very high up on their target list but failed to win ones lower down, the mirror image of the Labour performance. For instance, the Tories captured Cannock Chase on a 14 per cent swing, but failed to take Birmingham Edgbaston, which required a swing of only 2 per cent. Gisela Stuart, the victor in Egbaston, was one of the heroines in being an early winner in the Blair landslide of 1997 and, apart from a brief period as a minister, she has been an independent-minded backbencher, notably on Europe.

Of the 116 gains needed to win an overall majority, the Tories failed to capture 34, nearly half of which were successfully retained by the Lib Dems. The Lib Dems' net loss of seats was disappointing to them after the high expectations produced by Nick Clegg's success in the television debates. Yet the party did well in resisting the broader pro-Tory swing, notably in seats such as Cheltenham, Somerton & Frome, Eastleigh, Westmoreland & Lonsdale, Carshalton & Wallington and Taunton Deane (three held by future ministers in the coalition Government). The Tories also failed to win any of their target seats from the SNP.

The other Labour seats to hold out against the trend were Westminster North (held by Karen Buck against the controversial Tory barrister Joanne Cash), Eltham, Bradford West, Hammersmith, Halifax, Gedling, Poplar & Limehouse (where Jim Fitzpatrick easily saw off George Galloway, the former Respect MP), Elmet & Rothwell (where Ed Balls held on after a fierce campaign), Tynemouth, Bolton West and Bolton North East.

Labour did worse in England (down 7.4 points) and slightly worse in Wales (down 6.5 points) than it did nationwide (down 6.2 points), but managed to improve its relative share in Scotland by 3.1 points compared with 2005. In England, the best Labour performances were in London, where the swing to the Tories was just 2.5 per cent, half the UK average. This explains its success in holding on, against the trend, to the seats mentioned above, as well as in seeing off Lib Dem challenges in Islington South and the new Hampstead & Kilburn seat (where Glenda Jackson beat her Tory challenger by 42 votes in a tight three-way contest).

Labour's vote fell by 2.3 per cent in London, but 8.2 per cent elsewhere in England and, apart from Battersea, the Tory gains were concentrated in a band on the northwest of the capital, from Brentford & Isleworth, via Ealing Central & Acton, up to Harrow East and Hendon. Labour did well in seats with a large Muslim population, where the party suffered in 2005 because of the Iraq war, such as some in East London where Respect had done well in 2005 (East Ham, West Ham and Bethnal Green & Bow).

Outside London and the big industrial cities and towns of the North Labour did very badly along the motorway belts and in the East and West Midlands (together accounting for a third of their losses). Labour lost Middle England (but not Scotland and, partly, Wales) where Tony Blair's new Labour did so well in the 1990s. The map shows vividly how Labour was wiped out in the Medway towns, where it just held on in 2005 (Chatham & Aylesford, Dartford, Gillingham & Rainham); and on the other side of the Thames in Essex (Basildon South & Thurrock East, Thurrock, and Harlow); in its 1997 gains along the South Coast (Brighton Kemptown, Dover, Hastings & Rye, Hove, and Dorset South); in the southern East Midlands (both Milton Keynes and Northampton seats, Nuneaton and Rugby); in a belt of more than a dozen seats from Worcestershire up around Birmingham and into Staffordshire, Derbyshire and the northern East Midlands (such as Burton, Cannock Chase, Corby, Derbyshire South, Erewash, High Peak, Leicestershire North West, Lincoln, Stafford, Tamworth, Warwick & Leamington, Warwickshire North, Wolverhampton South West, Worcester and Redditch); in South York-

shire and Humberside (Brigg & Goole and Cleethorpes); and then in an unbroken group on either side of the Pennines (Colne Valley, Dewsbury, Keighley, Pendle, Pudsey, Rossendale & Darwen and South Ribble).

This analysis is reinforced by a social breakdown by Ipsos MORI, based on its campaign polls weighted to reflect the final result. This suggests that Labour lost the support of skilled manual workers, the C2s, by a huge 18 points on the 2005 election. The switch was even sharper among C2 women. This is classic aspirational Britain, highlighted by Lord Radice, the Labour peer and former MP who produced a detailed analysis for the Fabian Society after Labour lost in 1992. Entitled *Southern Discomfort*, this showed why the party was out of touch with the interests and hopes of this group: a problem that Mr Blair successfully addressed in 1997.

One of the perennial complaints of the Tories is that the electoral system is biased against them because of the way that boundary changes work. They point to the much larger number of votes required to elect a Tory MP compared with a Labour MP, and hence the much larger vote share required for a Tory majority.

This is only partly true. On average, seats won by the Conservatives had larger electorates than those won by Labour by a margin of 3,750: 72,350 to 68,600. But there is an uneven pattern: only four of the ten constituencies with the largest electorates are Tory held, six are Labour held. The main explanation is differential turnout where there is a much larger gap. For instance, the turnout in seats that the Tories won was 68.4 per cent, but it was only 61 per cent in those held by Labour. Hence the proposal by the Conservatives, reaffirmed by the coalition agreement, to equalise the size of constituencies will only partly address the imbalance in the system against the Tories because it will not and cannot address the issue of differential turnout.

The three safest seats in the country are held by Labour in Merseyside: Liverpool Walton, Liverpool West Derby and Knowsley. The safest Tory seat is Richmond, North Yorkshire, held by William Hague. (All three of the main leaders at the election had above-average personal results in their constituencies.) Five seats have majorities of under 100: Hampstead & Kilburn (Lab, 42); Warwickshire North (C, 54); Camborne & Redruth (C, 66); Bolton West (Lab, 92); Thurrock (C, 92); and the narrowest of all in Northern Ireland, where Sinn Féin held Fermanagh & South Tyrone by only 4 votes.

The election saw a further slight improvement in the gender and ethnic balance among candidates, even slighter among MPs. Just over a fifth of candidates were women: at 20.8 per cent, this represented a slight improvement on the figure of 20.3 per cent in 2005. About 30 per cent of Labour's candidates were women, against 24 per cent of Tories and 22 per cent of Lib Dems.

Just over a fifth (22 per cent) of the new MPs are women: at 142 the highest number and share ever. There are 48 Tory women MPs, 31 more than in 2005. The number of Labour women MPs is 17 less than in 2005 because of the party's overall losses but, at 81, is still well over half the total. The Lib Dems continue to perform poorly, with just seven women MPs.

A total of 26 MPs are from minority ethnic groups. The Tory total rose from two to eleven, while Labour numbers rose by two to fifteen. There are still no Lib Dem ethnic minority MPs.

The inconclusive result of the 2010 election leaves intriguing prospects for the next one. The Tories require a further two-point swing from Labour to gain an overall majority and Labour requires a swing from the Tories of 5 per cent to return to power with an absolute majority (exactly the same as the swing against it on May 6).

Who cares what the papers say?

Alexi Mostrous
Media Editor

In 2005, *The Sun* decided that the general election was so boring that it needed to employ a Page 3 girl to represent each of the three main parties. The paper followed up by announcing support for Mr Blair with a puff of red smoke from an office chimney. Five years on there were no such stunts. Political reporting was re-energised as Labour sought an historic fourth term. As doubts over David Cameron's prospects of victory increased, editors flooded pages with election copy. In the month before polling day on May 6, national newspapers printed 11,017 stories mentioning the election, compared with 9,263 during the same period in 2005.

After two elections in which the majority of the press supported Tony Blair and new Labour – overwhelmingly in 2001, begrudgingly in 2005 – Gordon Brown entered this campaign without the unequivocal support of a single national daily newspaper. *The Sun* abandoned Mr Brown in September 2009, defecting on the day of his speech to the annual Labour Party conference. After more than a decade of supporting Mr Blair, the News Corporation publication offered its 7½ million readers the front-page headline: "Labour's Lost It". The paper spent the next seven months gleefully capitalising on Mr Brown's unpopularity. A story in April revealed that even Peppa Pig, the children's television character, had apparently "turned her back" on Labour.

Less than a week before polling day, *The Times* came out for the Tories for the first time in 18 years. In a full-page editorial, the paper said that Mr Cameron had shown the "fortitude, judgment and character to lead this country". After supporting Labour in the past four general elections, the *Financial Times* also concluded that "on balance, the Conservative Party best fits the bill". Less surprisingly, *The Daily Telegraph's* 2 million readers were encouraged, for the 18th consecutive time since 1945, to vote Tory, as were the *Daily Mail's* 5 million.

In perhaps the most significant change, *The Guardian* decided to switch its support from Labour to the Liberal Democrats. "Invited to embrace five more years of a Labour government, and of Gordon Brown as prime minister, it is hard to feel enthusiasm," the paper told its million readers. Even the *Daily Mirror*, Labour's most loyal supporter since 1945, urged some of its 3.3 million readers to vote tactically for the Lib Dems.

At the same time, media cognoscenti were calling time on the very relevance of the press. Nick Clegg had supposedly broken the two-party mould with his barnstorming appearance in the first party leaders' debate on ITV. Like Susan Boyle before him, a virtuoso performance seemed to catapult Mr Clegg into the nation's consciousness. Unlike Susan Boyle, good first impressions did not translate into votes. The Lib Dem leader's approval ratings jumped by 11 percentage points but subsequently fell back, with the party winning fewer seats although more votes than in 2005.

Part of that disparity may be explained by the barrage of anti-Clegg stories unleashed by right-leaning newspapers after the first debate on April 15. On the morning of the second debate, the *Telegraph* used a massive front-page headline to reveal that some Liberal Democrat donors had been paying money directly into Mr Clegg's bank account. He produced bank statements showing that these were to fund part of a researcher's salary. The *Daily Mail* upped the ante with a front page accusing Mr Clegg of a "Nazi Slur". The story was based on remarks he made in 2002, when he wrote that Britain had a "more insidious . . . cross to bear" than Germany over Nazism. The scoop drew ire from Mr Clegg's supporters, who pointed out that the *Mail's* website at one point carried no fewer than eight anti-Clegg stories.

Private Eye provided some light relief. "Is Clegg A Poof?" ran a fake *Sun* headline in the satirical magazine. "Voting For Clegg Will Give You Cancer," a fake *Mail* page warned. "And Cause Collapse In House Prices."

Many journalists expressed excitement at Mr Clegg's elevation, however, not least because it added to the tantalisingly vague prospect of a hung Parliament. Nick Robinson, the BBC's political editor, told the Radio 4 *Today* programme that Cleggmania was "the reason people in our business are getting so excited". *The Sunday Times* ran a front-page story on a YouGov poll showing Mr Clegg to be more popular than Winston Churchill.

Whether the attacks on Mr Clegg had a significant effect is arguable. They may have slowed some of his momentum and left voters in doubt as to his party's ability to govern. Perhaps more likely is that voters showed themselves more influenced by sustained media exposure in the years before an election, which the Lib Dems have never enjoyed, than by a one-off television performance, however impressive. With Mr Clegg as Deputy Prime Minister, that disparity is likely to be corrected.

Mr Cameron and Mr Brown were convinced that newspapers move votes. Yet as Roy Greenslade, Professor of Journalism at City University, points out, the press has been mostly pro-Tory since 1945, but Labour has won more elections. According to an Ipsos MORI poll cited by Professor Greenslade, between 20 and 30 per cent of *Daily Mail* readers consistently voted Labour between 1997 and 2005, despite the paper's protestations. In 2010, however, the result may have been more similar to 1992, when only 14 per cent voted for Neil Kinnock.

Times readers appear to be even more independent: 64 per cent agreed with the paper when it advised them to vote Tory in 1992, according to Ipsos MORI, but in 2001, when the paper came out for Labour, 40 per cent of readers still said that they would support the Tories.

About 45 per cent of *Sun* readers pledged to vote Tory in 1992, when the paper put Neil Kinnock's head in a light bulb on polling day and ran the headline: "If Kinnock wins today will the last person to leave Britain turn out the lights." In contrast, only 29 per cent said that they would vote Conservative when the paper supported Mr Blair in 2001. A similar swing back to the Tories this year may have carried influence, especially in marginal seats.

Readers themselves do not consider newspapers to be influential at all. A survey by *Press Gazette* in March suggested that nine out of ten voters believed that their vote would be unaffected by any media organisation. Editors have to hope that Anthony Wells, a political commentator for YouGov, is right when he says: "The real impact is more subconscious, the long-term drip-drip of positive or negative coverage."

The great irony about reporting this election is found in the numerous editorials warning voters against a hung Parliament. In the event, the actual outcome of 2010 was one that no newspaper, save *The Independent*, endorsed.

And the winner is … television

Andrew Billen
Television Critic

The sky was dusty with volcanic ash and the airwaves thick with politics. Yet for a while the electorate refused to inhale. In a multichannel world, it is easy to avoid the news, easier still the election specials. ITV1's studio debates, *Campaign 2010 with Jonathan Dimbleby*, lost rather than gained audience as the election wore on. The regular political gabfests, BBC One's *Question Time* and *The Andrew Marr Show*, suffered dwindling not growing viewing figures. It was like soccer fans turning off *Match of the Day* during the World Cup.

If, like the grounded aeroplanes, the campaign was going to take off, it would take something new, and something different. It was supplied by three live, 90-minute election debates agreed between the politicians and networks after tortuous discussion. Their order having been decided by lottery, the first, ITV's on April 15, centred on domestic policy. Its MC, Alastair Stewart, proclaimed it historic. Its 9.5 million viewers – a figure that would not disgrace a Saturday night *Britain's Got Talent* – apparently agreed. But even Stewart could not have predicted that the commentariate and the focus-grouped would independently declare a clear winner in the Liberal Democrats' Nick Clegg or that his party's trend in the polls would go vertical. The debate was declared a "game changer".

As talent contests, the following debates on April 22 and April 29 were less decisive, mainly because, what by now could be seen as Clegg's challengers, Gordon Brown and, especially, David Cameron got better at them. Mr Cameron particularly mastered the "trick" of addressing the camera lens directly, a technique pioneered more than 50 years ago when hosts of *Sunday Night at the London Palladium* realised that faced with the choice of addressing the stalls or the nation's sitting rooms it was wise to talk to the many not the few.

The second debate, focusing on foreign policy and held by Sky News, was a success for a channel whose political editor, Adam Boulton, had campaigned hard for them to happen. Its 4.4 million viewers was a record audience for a Sky News production. Ofcom, the regulator, received many hundreds of complaints, however, mainly because Boulton, as chairman, broke protocol by asking a question of his own. Most confidently staged was the BBC's final "economic crisis debate", although it attracted fewer viewers than the first. Its experienced host, David Dimbleby, intervened more than either Stewart or Boulton, but only to repeat his audience's questions. In future such debates may have less constricted or more varied formats. It is, surely, impossible to imagine an election happening without them.

With even Jeremy Paxman's traditional roastings of the leaders producing few headlines, only once outside the set-pieces did television change the agenda, and then it was by accident. A Sky News radio mike was left on and attached to Mr Brown as he sped from an unsatisfactory encounter with a pensioner supporter. She was, he told an aide, a "bigoted woman". Within hours, his remarks were played back to him on Jeremy

The leaders' debates changed political broadcasting

Vine's Radio Two show. The camera showed him head in hands. After a self-immolating visit to Mrs Duffy's home in Rochdale, Mr Brown emerged before more cameras bashfully declaring himself a sinner but a penitent one. The mini-soap looked a disaster for Mr Brown, but, as it turned out, his ratings had nowhere further to fall.

The election night programmes for the first time featured an exit poll jointly paid for by the BBC, ITV and Sky. Its prediction of a hung Parliament, with Mr Cameron short of an overall majority by 19, was initially treated with scepticism by the studio pundits, mainly because it insisted that the Lib Dems' representation in Westminster would decline. It proved almost uncannily accurate. The result was so close that BBC One's election programme, which began at 9.55pm on the Thursday did not end until 8.45am on the Friday. David Dimbleby, showing stamina uncommon in a septuagenarian, resumed his anchorman's seat at 11am and carried on until 4pm. His efforts, showcased in a huge glass set built in Television Centre, earned the BBC more than 4 million viewers overnight. ITV1's show, hosted by Alastair Stewart, attracted only an average of 1.26 million and was beaten by a satirical commentary on the results from Channel 4. Sky News did worse than it had five years before, its 111,000 viewers probably depleted by its new-fangled HD transmission causing its sound to ride out of synch.

And so, like the old politics, the senior mass medium endured. Just as there was no decisive breakthrough for the third party, there was none for multichannel or the blogosphere. Had television turned the election into a beauty contest? By the end it appeared more likely that its debates had found a new way to scrutinise not only character but policy and that those of each contestant had been found wanting. The Friday after polling day, Sandy Toksvig, chairwoman of Radio Four's *The News Quiz*, made the Nick Clegg/*Britain's Got Talent* comparison explicit. We saw someone new, liked what we heard but, in the end, decided to vote for someone else. At least, however, by then we knew whom we were voting for. After a foggy start, it was a good election for television.

It will never be the same again

Daniel Finkelstein
Executive Editor

On Friday, May 7, 2010 David Cameron, the Leader of the Opposition, woke from a very short night's sleep and made an historic decision. It was one that would propel him into 10 Downing Street within five days and would change British politics for ever. He was, he determined, going to attempt to form the first coalition government since the Second World War.

Mr Cameron had long thought a hung Parliament rather likely. The number of seats that the Tories would have to win to have an overall majority was daunting. But his team had not, as Nick Clegg's Liberal Democrats had, spent a great deal of time agonising over what to do if it actually happened. Mr Cameron did not unveil a carefully developed plan. He acted on instinct.

But it was not just Mr Cameron's instinct that changed history. It was also the maths and Mr Clegg had always believed that the maths would be crucial. On May 7, the cold fact was that the Liberal Democrats and the Conservatives could together form a government with a majority of more than 80, but the Lib Dems and Labour would not have a majority even if they voted as a single block on everything.

So just before lunch on Friday, Mr Clegg arrived back at Lib Dem HQ and announced that he was sticking to the plan he had formulated before the election, one designed precisely for the sort of numerical position he was now in. He regarded the party with the largest support as having earned the right to seek to show that they were able to govern in the national interest. And that meant opening talks with the Conservatives.

What Mr Clegg had almost certainly not expected was Mr Cameron's response. The latter had quickly won support for coalition from his team, starting with his closest ally, George Osborne. Working with his adviser, Steve Hilton, he prepared a statement in which he said that while a mere pact with the Lib Dems was possible, he wanted to make a "big, open and comprehensive offer" to the third party. His aim: full coalition.

The negotiations began quickly, with the teams meeting that afternoon at the Cabinet Office for an initial session. Mr Osborne selected the venue. He wanted the Lib Dems to be able to see power out of the window. And so, looking over the Downing Street garden and in a sweltering room where the central heating had broken, the teams began to talk. Danny Alexander, David Laws, Chris Huhne and Andrew Stunnell for the Lib Dems quickly came to see that Mr Cameron was serious. They realised that his negotiating team – Mr Osborne, William Hague, Edward Llewellyn and Oliver Letwin – had come ready to make big concessions. Perhaps they did not quite realise why. From the word go, Mr Cameron realised that he needed a deal, but he also saw the whole thing as an opportunity.

First, the necessity. The Cameron team thought that a minority government was a very grim prospect indeed. Having introduced unpopular measures to deal with the deficit, the Government could be turfed out at the worst possible political moment.

There was raw political calculation in this, of course, but also consideration of the national interest. A minority government would not survive for long. It would need, or be forced, to fight an early election, making it impossible to begin the difficult work that the next administration needs to undertake. So the negotiators found themselves in an ironic position. The Lib Dems wanted policy concessions but were politically nervous of a full-scale coalition. The Tories, whom everyone assumed would play it tough, wanted to make policy concessions so that a proper long-term partnership could be formed.

One issue remained difficult: electoral reform. The Tories were offering a free vote in the Commons on a referendum on the Alternative Vote and that was not enough. That, plus the emotional pull of Lib Dems towards the Left, sent Mr Clegg's team talking to Labour. For a brief period a new Lib-Lab arrangement appeared a real possibility. But it was brief. Labour did not have the heart for it. Labour's negotiations – informally over the weekend and formally on the Monday after Gordon Brown announced his intention to resign – were half-hearted. They were not prepared to concede much, underestimated the progress the Lib Dems had made with the Tories, and thought that the numbers did not really stack up anyway.

It was also brief because the Tories made a big offer – a whipped vote to have a referendum on AV – and this offer, skilfully guided through the party in the hours after Mr Brown's departure had scared the Tories into imagining a Lib-Lab deal, brought Cameron not merely the premiership, but more besides: a great opportunity.

Finding it hard to gain even 40 per cent of the vote, the Conservative Party has, for years now, been threatened by the possible emergence of a unified progressive Left. Blair advisers such as Lord Mandelson and Lord Adonis have long seen this. They regard the split in the Left between Labour and the Liberals that took place at the beginning of the 20th century as having ushered in a Conservative century. They are probably correct. That split has been a very important reason for the election of Tory governments, particularly in the past 40 years.

If the Conservatives had won a small majority, it is not hard to imagine them being swept out in five years by an alliance, either explicit or implied, of Labour and Liberal Democrats. Something like that happened in 1997 and produced the Blair landslide. Now a combination of the new maths of the Commons and Cameron's boldness disrupted this and in doing so, changed politics for years. The Liberal Democrats have been picked up and put down in a different place, partly by Mr Clegg of course, but largely by a Cameron offer of partnership. The anti-Conservative majority is, in an extraordinary political coup, no longer an anti-Conservative majority. Things are more complicated now.

The second part of the opportunity relates to Mr Cameron's own party. Five years of work to rebrand the party did not change perceptions as much as his team had hoped. But now this. Mr Cameron has the potential to lift himself and the party above normal partisan politics.

And so, after some of the most dramatic days in modern politics, David Cameron found himself waving to the photographers outside No 10, flanked by Nick Clegg. But he has made a huge gamble. Could this move split his party? Might the Liberal Democrats prove not merely prickly partners, but impossible ones?

Unknown, unknowable. But this can be said with certainty. Politics has changed for ever.

Meet the Class of 2010, the new politics in person

Rachel Sylvester
Times columnist

There is a black-belt karate expert, a female football coach, a Mormon, a former television presenter and a bestselling author who has had the film rights to his life bought by Brad Pitt. A total of 232 new MPs were elected for the first time on May 6, 2010, including 147 Conservatives, 67 Labour members, 9 Liberal Democrats and the first representative of the Green Party, Caroline Lucas, who won in the Brighton Pavilion constituency.

They are the novices in the Virgin Parliament, the new boys and girls who were swept into Westminster on the wave of public revulsion that followed the expenses scandal in what was widely perceived to be a House of Whores. Some were elected purely as a result of the swing away from Labour to the Tories that came after 13 years of one party having been in power, but many replaced MPs who had either resigned or been voted out by an electorate angry about the duck houses, moats and mortgages. The turnover at the last election was unusually high. The result is that more than a third of those now sitting on the green benches in the House of Commons are innocent about the wiles of the whips, ignorant of parliamentary tricks and unequipped by the now-abolished John Lewis List. Half the Tory MPs have just been elected for the first time.

The Class of 2010 is the physical embodiment of "a new politics". They are younger on average than in 1997, the last time power changed hands: 34 per cent of the new MPs are aged in their thirties. There are more black and Asian faces on the green benches than ever before: 26 MPs from ethnic minorities and marginally more women. Three Muslim women were elected, including the bright and beautiful Rushanara Ali, who regained Bethnal Green for Labour from the Respect party's George Galloway.

Matthew Hancock, a former economist at the Bank of England who was an adviser to George Osborne before being elected Tory MP for West Suffolk at the election, says: "I'm 31 and I don't feel particularly young. There's a feeling of a huge generational shift."

Michael Dugher, a former aide to Gordon Brown who is now Labour MP for Barnsley East, agrees. "People are very keen to learn the lessons of the past," he says. "We are going to do things differently now. It is noticeable that the new MPs are hanging around with each other rather than the old hands. There is a togetherness about the new generation."

As the new arrivals gathered for training sessions on parliamentary procedure, security and the expenses regime at the start of the new session, it became clear that whatever their party allegiances they were united by a determination to represent a clean break with the dirty past. Nicholas Boles, the new Conservative MP for Grantham and Stamford, who until recently worked for Boris Johnson and is seen as one of the party's smartest policy brains, says: "Everybody is obsessed about not getting caught up in another expenses scandal. It is not that we are a bunch of self-righteous men and women in white suits but there is an overwhelming feeling that that was terrible, that we are at the beginning of our careers and the last thing we want to do is to have even the slightest hint of anything improper."

Among the new Tory and Liberal Democrat MPs there is a sense of excitement about the possibilities opened up by the coalition Government. One session of the induction course took place in the chamber and the two parties' members drifted to the Government side and sat among each other, intermingled. "We chatted very easily and got on in a way that would have been much more difficult for the old guard on either side," one Conservative member says.

The Class of 2010 is more professional than previous generations. About 20 per cent of the new MPs are defined as having come into the Commons from politics, having worked either as advisers or councillors, 15 per cent from business, 12 per cent consultancy, 12 per cent law and 10 per cent financial services. Only 6 per cent have come in from charities, 5 per cent from the education sector and 5 per cent from the media.

According to an analysis by the Sutton Trust, an educational charity, 35 per cent of MPs in the new Parliament went to independent schools. More than half of Conservative MPs were educated privately and 20 out of the 306 on the Tory benches went to one school – David Cameron's alma mater, Eton. On the Labour side, it is rather different. "There are a lot of regional accents, most of us are working class-made-good," says one new MP. Several union officials won seats, after a successful operation by Unite.

There does, though, also seem to be a hereditary principle at work in the House of Commons across the board. At least nine children of politicians were elected in 2010. They include Zac Goldsmith, the new Conservative MP for Richmond Park, who is the son of the late Referendum Party leader, Sir James Goldsmith; Ben Gummer, elected in Ipswich, the son of John Gummer, the former Tory Cabinet minister; and Anas Sarwar, who took over as Labour MP for Glasgow Central from his father, Mohammed Sarwar. Harriet Harman's husband, Jack Dromey, joins her in Parliament as MP for Birmingham Erdington and Valerie Vaz, Labour MP for Walsall South, is the sister of Keith Vaz, the longstanding Labour MP for Leicester East. Jacob Rees-Mogg, the son of the former Times Editor Lord Rees-Mogg, was elected in Somerset North East.

The new Conservative members are generally

Gloria De Piero, a former GMTV presenter, became MP for Ashfield, one of a total of 232 new faces

socially liberal and supportive of David Cameron's modernisation of their party. A few days after the election, the Tory leader held a meeting of all his new MPs and was rather astonished by the attitude he found. "The general mood of the group was that, if anything, we had not gone far enough on modernisation," one of those present says. "David said afterwards how remarkable it was, he was quite taken aback."

Like Mr Cameron, most of the new Conservative MPs, are also pretty Eurosceptic. According to George Eustace, the former campaign director of the anti-euro "no" campaign, who is now MP for Camborne and Redruth: "Most think we should be taking powers back from the EU, but the new intake is also very committed to the idea of social enterprises, charities and voluntary groups being involved in public services. The Iain Duncan Smith agenda is where traditional right-wing Conservatism can come together with the more liberal modernising wing of the party."

Other high-profile Tories include Rory Stewart, in Penrith and the Border, a former deputy governor of Iraq and bestselling author. He once walked across Afghanistan and also spent a summer as a tutor to Princes William and Harry. It is his life story that has been snapped up by Brad Pitt. Dan Byles, the new Tory MP for Warwickshire North, is almost as adventurous – he has rowed across the Atlantic and skied to the north pole with his mother.

Mr Goldsmith, the brother of Jemima Khan, will add a touch of glamour to the green benches, but could also clash with the leadership over green issues. Tracy Crouch, Tory MP for Chatham and Aylesford, is the qualified football coach. David Rutley, a former banker who represents Macclesfield, is the House of Commons's first Mormon. Helen Grant, in Maidstone and the Weald, is the first black woman Conservative MP. Dominic Raab, Tory MP for Esher and Walton, a lawyer by training, has represented Britain at karate.

On the Labour side there is a fighting spirit as well. Those to watch include Tristram Hunt, the television historian who has just been elected in Stoke-on-Trent Central, and Chuka Umunna, the new MP for Streatham, a former lawyer who has been described as a potential British Barack Obama. Rachel Reeves, in Leeds West, is a former Bank of England economist with a reforming zeal, and Gloria De Piero, who was until she became MP for Ashfield a GMTV presenter, is certain to attract plenty of attention. Two former ministers under Tony Blair who lost their seats in 2005 also returned to Parliament: Stephen Twigg in Liverpool West Derby and Chris Leslie in Nottingham East.

One new MP says: "It is nothing like 1997, when lots of people got in who never expected to. Everyone here now has got black under their fingernails from having scraped their way up. They are quite a brutal, hard-headed bunch. They don't look at the world through the prism of Blair-Brown or Left versus Right. They look at the world through the prism of Labour's defeat."

Whatever their party affiliation, those elected this year also look at the world through the prism of the MPs' expenses scandal. There is the possibility of a really quite dramatic change of culture, brought about by a younger, more independent-minded intake who are all too aware of voters' anger with politicians. Some of the Conservatives have been chosen in open primaries, which may make them less willing to toe the party line. Labour and Liberal Democrat MPs have used the election campaign to make clear their determination to alter the way in which politics is done. Across the board, the new intake is generally more receptive to constitutional reform, including changes to the voting system, than their parties' older grandees.

Just as the Blair Babes transformed how the House of Commons looked in 1997, bringing flashes of feminine colour to the rows of grey suits, so the Class of 2010 could alter for ever the way in which politics is conducted. One new Tory MP says: "We get the scale of the public's anger over the expenses scandal in a way that those who were in Parliament when it broke do not really get. We understand just how much change is needed."

Women failed to break through

Rosemary Bennett
Social Affairs Correspondent

The 2010 general election was, pretty much, a male affair. Senior women from the main parties were curiously absent from the campaign and silent during the rows that blew up over taxation and spending. Attention was resolutely focused on the three leaders as the TV debates dominated the campaign and, in the end, more column inches were devoted to their wives' outfits than equality.

At constituency level the story was not much better. In as many as 262 seats the three main parties all fielded male candidates, compared with just 11 seats where the main contenders were all women. The election was just too close to make gender an issue.

Not surprising, then, that there was no great breakthrough in the numbers of women entering Parliament. For all the talk of new dawns, it was old politics as usual when the 2010 intake took their seats for the first time. In terms of the numbers, there were 142 women MPs, compared with 126 in 2005, equivalent to 22 per cent of the total. That puts Britain on a par with the United Arab Emirates in terms of female representation.

The Conservatives made the most headway from their low base of just 18 MPs, 9 per cent of the parliamentary party, when the election was called. They emerged with 48 MPs, 16 per cent of the parliamentary party. Their success did not come easily. It was the result of considerable efforts, not in the approach to the election but throughout much of the previous Parliament, to make sure that a decent number of women candidates ended up in winnable seats.

For a while, they had the controversial "A" list comprising 50 per cent women from which the best seats were required to choose. In the end it was scrapped, such was its unpopularity, but it did help to boost the numbers. There was also a mentoring programme and, of course, plenty of encouragement from David Cameron.

In the end, though, it was not the sea change that the leadership had hoped for and privately senior party figures would admit that there was clearly farther to go.

Campaigners for equality worry that if this was the Conservatives' best chance to push the agenda then the results look particularly disappointing. "The Conservatives do deserve to be congratulated. They trebled the number of women MPs. But you cannot help being left with the feeling that they could have gone a lot further. They had a new leader, they were ahead in the polls. They might not have such a good opportunity in the future to push this agenda," Ceri Goddard, chief executive of the Fawcett Society, said.

Labour lost women MPs in terms of numbers, with 81 in the new Parliament compared with 94 in the last. In percentage terms the total rose slightly to 31 per cent from 27, largely owing to the party's use of all-women short lists in many winnable seats. That is unlikely to change in future elections.

The performance of the two main parties left the Lib Dems looking particularly feeble. They lost two of their already tiny pool of female MPs and now have only seven, equivalent to 12 per cent of the parliamentary party. Their poor record was underlined when the party had no woman MP senior enough to be in contention for the five Cabinet positions offered to the party under the deal.

Ms Goddard said that the Liberal Democrats were left looking very exposed, and had a fundamental problem if they were serious about increasing female representation. The party has an ideological opposition to positive action, a position backed powerfully by younger women in the party despite warnings from grandees such as Baroness Williams of Crosby that they will never get anywhere under existing procedures.

"To be fair to the party, they ran about half and half male and female candidates, but clearly the men were in the best seats. The party consistently refuses to adopt positive action to increase the number of women, which we think is an odd position given they are the party of electoral reform," Ms Goddard said.

So what do the new women MPs now amassed on the government benches want to do with their power?

Despite the derision of the Blair babes, Labour women used their numbers to push for more maternity leave and pay, and new rights for flexible work, very much bottom-up reforms. Conservative women say that they will push for even grater reform on flexible work so that as many men and women as possible can work part time and, perhaps surprisingly, equal pay. And they may make their presence felt most by opposing a key leadership policy, tax breaks for married couples, that many think is not the best use of money.

They may, however, have to expend their political capital in other ways too. There is already concern that the "new politics" of the coalition is perhaps not so much of an opportunity for women as a challenge. Women were absent from the coalition negotiations with both the Conservatives and Liberal Democrats fielding all-male sides. And in the scramble for a workable deal between the parties, the argument for fair representation at Cabinet level was somehow lost.

The first coalition Cabinet had just four women, and only one running a big department, with Theresa May at the Home Office. Analysts say it was not a great start. "Cameron and Clegg were acutely aware they have very few women on which they could credibly draw," said Colin Hay, Professor of political analysis at the University of Sheffield. "The politics of the past was gender discriminatory. The irony, in a way, is that the Cabinet remains a sort of last bastion of that old order."

Number of women MPs

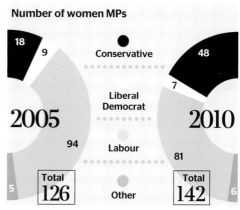

	2005	2010
Conservative	18 / 9	48
Liberal Democrat		7
Labour	94	81
Other	5	6
Total	**126**	**142**

Bad news for big spenders: money can't buy you votes

Sam Coates
Chief Political
Correspondent

For donors thinking of filling the coffers of Britain's political parties, there could be few worse advertisements than the previous Parliament. Three of its five years were stained by continuing police investigations; Scotland Yard interviewed a sitting Prime Minister for corruption offences; and more than half of its MPs had to hand back money after claiming for expenses they were not rightfully owed. Trust in politicians dropped to levels never seen before: only one in ten people thought MPs told the truth. Public antagonism was stoked by an often hostile media and insurgent blogosphere picking over the personal lives and motivations of public figures, especially donors who were often treated as if they had already been found guilty of paying for access to power.

Given the contempt with which so many politicians came to be held – one utterly blameless Lib Dem quit the Commons after his wife was spat on in the street – it is perhaps a surprise that just so many moneymen kept their faith and continued to write their cheques, mainly to the Conservatives. Over the course of the Parliament donors gave money to David Cameron at rates never seen before in British politics.

In his four years as Leader of the Opposition, from January 2006 to May 6, 2010, a record £122 million went through Tory coffers, by any international political yardstick an extraordinary amount. Barack Obama's presidential campaign committee in 2008 raised £450 million. That was to fund a campaign that won decisively in a country where campaigns hinge on TV advertising and with an electorate five times the size. In domestic terms this figure is also striking: Labour's income was £71 million over the same period, although £22 million of this came while Tony Blair was still in office. It also beats sums raised in previous Parliaments: the Tories' income was £49 million and Labour's £61 million between 2001 and 2005.

Perhaps more intriguing is the limited impact that this vast spending appeared to have. By Mr Cameron's own yardstick, set in a *Spectator* interview shortly before polling day, his own campaign was a failure. The Conservative vote increased by 3.8 percentage points on its 2005 vote: an increase of 2 million votes net, or, taking into account the higher number of votes received by rival parties, 1.1 million more than last time. In other words, every additional vote cost the Tories £111.

What is more, for the shrewd financial investor, the archetype of the modern Tory donor, the way the Conservative Party operated under the stewardship of Andy Coulson, Steve Hilton and ultimately George Osborne as general election co-ordinator, must have seemed horrific. At a national level, half a million pounds was gambled on cinema advertisements that were never shown, £400,000 on a January 2010 "cut the deficit not the NHS" poster campaign later disowned by some senior figures. About half a million was spent on a much-ridiculed "don't be a tosser" campaign on the national debt and the same sum again on a national newspaper campaign to recruit internet "friends of the Conservatives", which was never mentioned again by the leadership.

The previous Parliament brought the downsides of political giving into sharp relief. Of these, the loans-for-peerages saga, which overshadowed Mr Blair's final year in office, was perhaps the most seismic, involving the Prime Minister and senior staff, 136 people questioned by Scotland Yard's Special Crime Division, 6,300 documents handed to the Crown Prosecution Service and four people arrested, including a Downing Street aide at dawn. At its heart was an allegation, never tested in a court and strongly denied by all those involved, that Labour figures seduced wealthy donors with promises of peerages in return for vast secret loans to bankroll the party through the 2005 election campaign.

It came to light in 2006 after it emerged that four Labour supporters had been turned down for peerages by the House of Lords Appointments Commission. Chai Patel, the founder of the Priory healthcare group, publicly complained after his application was leaked to a newspaper, then rejected. It soon emerged that three other businessmen were put forward for peerages – Sir David Garrard, Sir Gulam Noon, and Barry Townsley – having all made huge loans to Labour before the election at the behest of Lord Levy, Mr Blair's gregarious fundraiser. Sir Gulam even revealed that he had been told by Lord Levy to remove references to his £250,000 loan to Labour from his peerage application form.

Despite an ignominious political tradition of peerages for donors, epitomised by Harold Wilson's Lavender List, opposition MPs started complaining that there had been a breach of the Honours (Prevention of Abuses) Act 1925, introduced after David Lloyd George sold honours for cash. An initial inquiry by the Public Administration Committee was halted after Scotland Yard agreed to investigate a complaint by Angus MacNeil, a Scottish Nationalist MP. The police investigation was initially treated lightly by Downing Street, until a number of arrests culminating with that of Lord Levy, who was brought in for questioning. Ruth Turner, an aide to Mr Blair, was arrested at dawn and questioned under suspicion of perverting the course of justice. The inquiry had reached the heart of No 10. In December 2006 Mr Blair became the first serving Prime Minister in history to face a police interrogation, seeing officers three times in Downing Street.

Mr Blair's staff had raised the stakes, warning Scotland Yard that the Prime Minister would resign if he was arrested while in office. In fact, Mr Blair left office before the investigation was complete. After 16 months, the inquiry was dropped without charges by the Crown Prosecution Service. The CPS said that it had never intended to go to court unless there was "unambiguous agreement" between two people that a gift would be made in exchange for an honour, adding: "There is no direct evidence of any such agreement."

Officers in the Speciality Crime Unit, which had pursued the case, were unhappy. They believed that they had two strong pieces of evidence: the diary of Sir Christopher Evans, who loaned money to Labour and was later arrested, which detailed conversations with Lord Levy. Detectives believed that this provided "spectacular" evidence of what they interpreted as an agreement for Sir Christopher to be ennobled in return for the loan. Detectives had also discovered that Downing Street officials initially drew up a plan to give peerages to eight of the twelve businessmen who secretly bankrolled Labour's 2005 general election campaign: four more than had been thought.

The reason for the CPS decision, apparently late on in the investigation, to demand "unambiguous" evidence as the basis of a criminal case and thus rule out the use of the two strongly circumstantial pieces of evidence in police hands remains a mystery. The investigation, which spanned the transition of power from Mr Blair to Gordon Brown, highlighted the culture clash between politicians and police, with the friction between both sides often played out in the media. It highlighted the levels of ignorance among many officials about the electoral reforms Labour had brought in during the first Parliament but now showed little sign of bothering with. It also came as the Labour Party was adjusting to life without large numbers of individual donors, forcing a return to a reliance on trade unions.

By the end of the Parliament, notions of abandoning the union link, once aired by Blairites such as Alan Milburn, seemed fanciful. At the lowest point in its popularity early in 2008, union funding accounted for 92 per cent of donations to Labour, amid claims that the party was solvent only because of a guarantee from Unite, the super-union, that it would never allow it to go bust. In November 2007, it emerged that Labour's third biggest donor, David Abrahams, had concealed his identity and given hundreds of thousands of pounds in the names of his secretary and a builder, illegal under electoral law. Mr Abrahams, a colourful Tyneside lawyer, said he had done so to avoid the limelight. Facing a police investigation, Mr Brown fired the Labour general secretary, Peter Watt, who carried the can for the arrangement set up by his predecessors. In May 2009 the CPS decided again that there was insufficient evidence for any prosecution.

The police also investigated the admission in December 2007 by Peter Hain that some donations to his own campaign to become Labour's deputy leader "were not registered as they should have been". The police inquiry, at the request of the Electoral Commission, cost him his post as Work and Pensions Secretary. He was cleared 11 months later, however, after prosecutors questioned the watchdog's interpretation of the law, suggesting that no one involved in Mr Hain's campaign could be prosecuted.

This was one of several uncomfortable moments for the Electoral Commission. In its first full term between 2001 and 2005 the watchdog, which oversees money in politics, was regarded as a largely benign if somewhat bureaucratic body. But its failure to see that political parties were taking out huge secret loans led to accusations that it was unfocused, too passive and failed to use its powers to investigate allegations of wrongdoing.

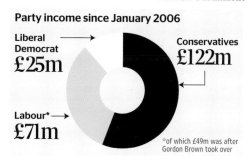

Party income since January 2006

Liberal Democrat **£25m**

Conservatives **£122m**

Labour* **£71m**

*of which £49m was after Gordon Brown took over

It defended itself vigorously, saying that it could only act using the laws passed by Parliament. Nevertheless, the commission strengthened its investigative capacity and started casting its spotlight elsewhere, bringing its own complications when it started picking over the donations by Lord Ashcroft to the Conservatives.

Lord Ashcroft, Tory vice-chairman, businessman and philanthropist, had long been a Labour hate figure whose funding they blamed for losing their party a number of seats in 2005. He revelled in his pariah status. After receiving his peerage in 2000 from William Hague, then Tory leader, he attempted unsuccessfully to become Lord Ashcroft of Belize, reflecting his dual citizenship. He stopped donating to the Conservatives under his own name in November 2001, fuelling suggestions, which he never denied, that he was no longer on the electoral register and giving instead through a small company, Bearwood Corporate Services.

In 2009 the Electoral Commission began examining suggestions that millions given to the Tories by Bearwood originated in Belize, possibly making the donations against electoral law. The money was reported to have been moved from Stargate Holdings based at Lord Ashcroft's bank in Belize City through two British holding companies and then to Bearwood Corporate Services. In a 15-month investigation, however, the watchdog was unable to discover what, if any, business the secretive Belize City-based Stargate conducted, and how it was financed. Lord Ashcroft was cleared.

He still ended up causing the party much embarrassment on the eve of the election, when it emerged that he had accepted his peerage on the understanding that he would pay full tax in Britain, only to remain secretly non-domiciled for tax purposes for a decade. This allowed him to save an estimated "tens of millions" of pounds of British tax on his overseas earnings while retaining his ermine.

Yet for all the fury directed at Lord Ashcroft, it is not clear that the marginal seats campaign he ran once he became the Conservatives' deputy chairman had the impact that many Conservatives had hoped for. His blueprint, outlined in a 2006 pamphlet Smell the Coffee, involved early candidate selection, relentless leafleting, repeated canvassing, candidate performance polling and targeted advertising as the key to winning marginal seats. Constituencies such as Hammersmith, Cheltenham and Bolton followed to the letter the Ashcroft plan yet all remained in Labour or Liberal Democrat hands. Indeed, research suggests that the spending advantage in the marginal seats helped the Tories to win at most an additional 14 seats above those that would have fallen anyway on the 5 per cent Labour to Tory swing.

Much analysis on the 2010 general election is yet to be done but the early indications suggest that it was one where, refreshingly, big money still failed to have a decisive impact on the result.

Little joy for the smaller parties

Jill Sherman
Whitehall Editor

The election of the Green Party's first MP as dawn broke on May 7, 2010 was one of the highlights of a long, unpredictable night. Caroline Lucas's breakthrough in Brighton Pavilion was some compensation for an otherwise disappointing result for the minority parties, who failed to exploit the disaffection with mainstream politics. Dr Lucas, leader of the Green Party since 2008, capitalised on her own popularity and activists' hard work for years in southern England to achieve, finally, a foothold at Westminster.

In the final stages of post-election negotiations between the parties after the inconclusive result, Dr Lucas, an MEP for the South East since 1999, briefly found herself being counted as part of a "progressive alliance" as the arithmetic meant that every additional seat was crucial. The plans fell apart but Dr Lucas turned her suitors down anyway, saying that she was interested in cooperation but not a formal coalition.

The Greens made their biggest push in a general election by fielding 335 candidates and spending £400,000 on their campaign. They had particularly high hopes in three target seats: Brighton Pavilion, Norwich South, and Lewisham Deptford. By early morning the day after the election, however, it became clear that Dr Lucas, a charismatic former CND-protester, was the only victor and the party's overall share of the vote fell slightly by 0.1 per cent from 2005.

The party argues that the decline was a result of a highly targeted election campaign in which it pooled most of its resources into those key seats, with busloads of Green activists brought in to campaign along the seafront each weekend. In the end, the tactic was vindicated, but it was a close race: despite being favourites to win the seat, after a nail-biting count the Greens eventually won with 1,252 votes.

While disappointing for Adrian Ramsay, the party's deputy leader, who lost in Norwich South, and Darren Johnson, who failed to make much headway in Lewisham Deptford, the most important thing for the party, was winning its first seat. As Dr Lucas said in an interview with The Times, she hopes she won't be there on her own for too long.

Most of the minority parties failed to recapture their success in the European elections the previous year. In 2010, squeezed out of the running by the three-horse race of the main parties, the smaller ones retained their 14 Westminster seats but took a smaller overall share of the vote, 11.9 per cent, than the previous year. It was, however, up 1.6 per cent from the general election in 2005, mainly because the parties fielded more candidates. The results were particularly disappointing because many of the smaller parties had looked likely to benefit more from the backlash against the main parties over MPs' expenses the previous year. The scandal may have stopped people voting for those individuals who had been at the centre of the expenses storm but in the end the minority parties failed to reap what should have been easy pickings.

The UK Independence Party, which had seen its popularity soar during the European elections, in which it took second place and 16.5 per cent of the vote, again failed to win a Commons seat. At one stage it looked as if Nigel Farage, the party's former leader, could be out of the race altogether when a light aircraft in which he was being flown crashed on the eve of the election. He was fortunate to escape without serious injury but was unable to oust John Bercow, the Commons Speaker, in Buckingham.

The British National Party also failed to make the breakthrough that many had feared after the party's shock success in 2009 when it won two European seats. It did, however, increase its share of the vote by a whisker, from 1.2 per cent in 2005 to 1.9 per cent. Nick Griffin, the party chairman and an MEP, raised his profile after appearing on Question Time on BBC One in autumn 2009, when he faced a barrage of criticism from other panellists. He was humiliated in the general election in Barking, where he stood against Margaret Hodge, the Labour incumbent, who increased her majority.

The BNP also targeted Stoke-on-Trent, where it had previously won a clutch of council seats, but Simon Darby the party's deputy chairman, was beaten into fourth place after Tristram Hunt, the Labour candidate parachuted into the constituency, won the seat.

George Galloway, the leader of the anti-war Respect party, also had his comeuppance. The colourful Mr Galloway, who made an embarrassing appearance on Celebrity Big Brother, failed to hang on in Poplar & Limehouse, East London, where he came third behind Labour and the Tories. He did not even turn up for his count. Respect's national share of the vote halved from 2005 to about 0.1 per cent mainly because the Iraq war was no longer a big central issue in the 2010 election.

The march of the independent MPs also came to a halt. In 2005 a record number stood and total votes cast for them reached 141,903. The betting money was on a further surge this year, with a predicted revolt against duck houses and flipped homes. But in the end it was the independents who were driven off the Commons green benches. Richard Taylor, the retired consultant who took Wyre Forest in 2001 on the back of a single-issue campaign to save his local hospital in Kidderminster, failed to retain his seat in 2010. Dr Taylor, who in his professional life wore a white coat, had taken the place of the white-suited Martin Bell, the former independent MP who seized Tatton on the back of the cash-for-favours scandal in 1997.

Dai Davies, who won a by-election at Blaenau Gwent in 2006 as an independent, was also unable to retain his seat. Even Esther Rantzen failed in her well-publicised bid to oust Labour in Luton South. The former That's Life presenter stood as an anti-sleaze candidate against Margaret Moran, the Labour MP who claimed £22,500 in Commons allowances to fix dry rot in a second home in Southampton. Ms Moran, however, decided to stand down before the election. Her replacement, Gavin Shuker, a 28-year-old church pastor, won 14,725 votes. Ms Rantzen came fourth with 1,872 votes and lost her deposit.

Only one MP was left holding the flag for the independents: Lady Sylvia Hermon, a former Ulster Unionist. Lady Hermon stood down from her party in March 2010 after the UUP formed an alliance with the Conservatives. Two months later she romped home to retain her North Down seat as an independent.

Don't emerge as sounding brass or tinkling cymbal

Matthew Parris
Times columnist

That no MP has yet suffered a heart attack in the minutes before making a maiden speech in the House of Commons, is some kind of miracle. The waiting is the worst. Sitting on those green leather benches, dreading the moment when the Speaker first calls your name, yet longing to get it over with as fast as possible, remains one of the most intense short periods of personal anxiety a man or woman can experience outside warfare.

I have parachuted freefall; aged 10 and dressed in a sailor-suit I have waited to launch into a song-and-dance routine of *I Whistle a Happy Tune* before a packed house in a repertory production of *The King and I*, as the orchestra struck up. Neither was as scary as awaiting my Commons maiden speech. But once you are on your feet, and you have your trembling hands and shaking notes under control, and you have started to talk, it is fine. You are away.

For me it went well. In light of what I shall tell you next I can tell you now that my maiden speech was considered one of the best of many maidens from the big and unusually talented parliamentary intake of 1979. That speech was a triumph. It was the rest of my parliamentary career that flopped. After my moment of glory I sank without trace in the Commons, never to resurface.

In all the seven years that followed at Westminster I did not say or do or achieve anything that came anywhere close to the success of that first Commons occasion, my maiden speech. My parliamentary career was undistinguished: for me a bitter if infinitely gentle disappointment. Cleverer new MPs than me, yes, but in time stupider ones too, overtook me one by one.

Why? My slow-burn failure baffled me. What had I overlooked? I wasn't lazy, crazy, or personally objectionable. Even after I had left I did not really understand. Only during the decades since, decades of thinking about politics as a journalist and commentator, has the truth dawned.

The truth is this: you will never get anywhere in the House of Commons speaking for yourself. You are the representative of people's interests, or you are nothing. There are, of course, ideals to be championed. There are arguments to be explained. There is policy logic to be pursued on its merits as well as its popular appeal. But, in the end, if what you say within that surprisingly small chamber carries no echo in the big country outside it then you are without point, and with discreet and subtle cruelty the very stones and carpets at Westminster will communicate to you that fact.

"Speaking for myself, Mr Deputy Speaker . . ." is a phrase that, sought in *Hansard's* electronic archive, would doubtless yield a generous harvest of instances. Do not be fooled. Whether they know it consciously or not, the most effective parliamentarians are never speaking mainly for themselves. They are inhabited by a kind of animal understanding of the beast that an MP is supposed to be: of what, in that remarkably large assembly of directly elected persons that with unintended accuracy we call the Lower House, an MP is for.

You, the MP, are there for the herd. You are there to speak for substantial groups of citizens with shared interests or desires. By no means are you there for the majority alone – or, necessarily, at all. You can usefully spend your whole career fighting for minorities. Groups for whom you speak may be beleaguered and outnumbered; but they must be groups. They must need and want a voice. You are their voice; they must respond to your voice, adding theirs; and your fellow parliamentarians must hear the noise. Your voice is your own, but if you are not somebody else's voice too, the place will not work for you.

You, the MP, are mainly there – not only, but mainly – as a messenger. You bring the message; you frame the message; you may have a talent for phrasing and targeting and marketing the message. You may even improve the message. You may have the skill so to express the message that it gathers force among those you represent. But you are seldom there to create the message, and unless and until it has gathered that force, you are the sounding brass or tinkling cymbal of St Paul's epistle. In the end the message comes not from inside your head but from outside the walls of Westminster, or it does not come at all. You, the MP, are there to carry it.

"Tribune" is an old-fashioned word whose meaning as we move into a new millennium is in danger of passing from the popular understanding. But if the word is out of date, what it signifies is not. Not for nothing have MPs been classically called the tribunes of the people. Their own beliefs and opinions carry most weight, and sometimes only carry weight at all, when they reflect the beliefs, opinions and *interests* of significant, numerous or powerful groups among the people who have sent them to Westminster.

Edmund Burke missed the point when he wrote: "Your Representative owes you, not his industry only, but his judgment; and he betrays, instead of serving you, if he sacrifices it to your opinion." Note the sly old propagandist's selection of the word "judgment" for the MP's view, and "opinion" for the elector's. But in rejecting Burke's advice I am not making a moral judgment. I am describing a dynamic. In our legislature, arguments born of the personal reflections of individual legislators do not prosper. Arguments carried into the chamber from the country outside do. Burke, in fact, knew that well enough, and in terms of his own personal career fared better articulating the external voice than advancing it within the chamber.

The Commons is not really about debate, it is about tug-o'-war; and your pull on the rope is a pull-by-proxy, for those not present.

How do I know this? I can only reply that it is not a matter of constitutional theory, but of experience. There was perhaps one moment during my seven years when I did, flickeringly, understand in heart as well as head what it meant to be an advocate – and I realised even at the time that it was on an arcane, minor and minority issue. I had become greatly exercised by the brutality and pointlessness of sending women convicted of prostitution to prison. In the event (with Robert Kilroy-Silk, then an MP) I managed to persuade my standing committee, and through them the Home Secretary, to change the law and remove imprisonment from the tariff.

Much of my argument was an argument in logic, but to bolster our case I invited the English Collective of Prostitutes to send down to the Commons a bus-load of their members (waiting for them in the Central Lobby I mistook a delegation on another issue from the Catholic Women's League for my own invitees, displeasing the League greatly) and led them to a committee room in Westminster Hall, where we addressed the other members of my standing committee, and took questions.

As I spoke, believing in the women's cause, and with many of them, real people, sitting around me, responding, I understood in the gut as well as the brain, what it means to be an MP.

Democracy as we British know it is not experienced in the intellect but in the stomach. What an MP is for is felt collectively at an unconscious level by a population few of whom could express it even if they cared to try. Popular sentiment is a current. It is a wind. It is a subterranean force. When you are with it – when it is with you – you just know. When you are not, you are that sounding brass or tinkling cymbal.

Time and again I rose to my feet in the chamber with what I thought, and still think, a brilliantly true idea to explain. How sure I was that we should adopt road-pricing in our country: that the economic theory of rationing a scarce commodity by price rather than by queue applied not just to turf or treacle tarts, but to tarmac too. Time and again I made speeches, asked questions, wrote newspaper articles, or argued in my Transport Select Committee, setting out a logical case that I knew, and still know, to be true and in the end inevitable.

Nobody listened. Nobody agreed. Nobody disagreed either. Nobody was interested. Nobody cared. Inevitable, yes: but not in 1986. Twentieth-century Britain was not ready for road pricing.

Or reform of the law on homosexuality. Time and again I argued the case for reducing the age of consent. Persistently I complained about police harassment of gay men. How cogently did I unpick the contradictions and expose the imperfections of the law relating to importuning in a public place. How assiduously did I collect evidence, interview defendants, correspond with the Commissioner of the Metropolitan Police and question ministers. How patiently I explained all this in the standing committee. How contemptuous I felt when a kindly Labour whip, the late Walter Harrison, took me aside to advise: "You will get nowhere in this place, lad, unless you leave all that alone." There is not (Walter went on to explain) the feeling for it in the country. How hotly I protested to myself, under my breath: "Well there ought to be."

Walter and I were both wrong. Public opinion on homosexuality was moving, changing. There existed the beginnings of an interest group among aggrieved gay men, the beginnings of the courage to stand up for themselves in public; and the beginnings of a supporting group of sympathisers among their millions of friends and relatives. HIV-Aids would in time bring all this to the surface. But 1982 was too early. Fifteen years later, Tony Blair, with his cannier instinct for the public mood, judged the moment right to propose change, as I had judged the moment wrong; and laws were duly amended. That was a time when young politicians and soon-to-be politicians such as David Cameron were changing their minds on social issues like these – or under the impression that they were changing their minds. What they were really doing was picking up, instinctively, a message from the people.

Time and again I spoke and wrote and asked Parliamentary Questions about the plight of the Sahrawi people in the Western Sahara, violently dispossessed by the Kingdom of Morocco. I visited them. I saw their plight. I heard their case. I studied their history. I was convinced. The case I made to the Foreign Secretary was unanswerable.

Indeed unanswered. He could not disagree and did not care to agree. Silence, that most eloquent of Commons responses, should have told me what no minister would put into words: the Sahrawi people have no constituency in the United Kingdom; and the United Kingdom has an interest in supporting Morocco. Silence said so; silence says so much at Westminster; but I was blocking my ears to the silence.

It is a funny feeling, speaking in the chamber when your argument carries no resonance outside it. Your fellow MPs do not howl you down. They just talk among themselves, or lope out for a drink or a cup of tea. You notice the Press Gallery above the Speaker's Chair clearing. Once you have gained a reputation for arguments that are disconnected from popular sentiment or headline news, your colleagues stop coming in when you are speaking. You argue into a void, like someone talking to the birds in a park. You wait for responses to your speech the next morning; but there is nothing, not even a report. And you reflect on that passage in Thornton Wilder's *The Bridge of San Luis Rey*, describing an early feminist: "The Abbess was one of those persons who have allowed their lives to be gnawed away because they have fallen in love with an idea several centuries before its appointed appearance in the history of civilisation. She hurled herself against the obstinacy of her time."

You hear it said, not of yourself but of others like you, that they are "frightfully clever" but "a bit of a loner". And if not remarkably thick-skinned (which, surprisingly, few MPs are) you become prey to feelings of injustice and self-pity.

They are misplaced. You are overlooking something rather obvious. The House of Commons is not a place where ideas are born and knows in its heart that it is not supposed to be. It is an echo-chamber in which interests and opinions are spoken for, and tested for resonance among more than six hundred other tribunes – and for their resonance, when reported, outside.

Resonance is not the same thing as rationality. During the last Parliament, Joanna Lumley, Nick Clegg and a small band of mostly backbench MPs understood how much more resonant was the case for special privileges for former Gurkhas than it was rational. Towards the end of the last century, Margaret Thatcher and much of her Cabinet failed to understand how much less resonant was the case for the Poll Tax, than it was reasonable. When the last Prime Minister, Gordon Brown, was Chancellor in 2000 he and his Cabinet colleagues were surprised (and threat-

Joanna Lumley and Nick Clegg understood the importance of the Gurkhas' case to the wider public

ened with a backbench rebellion) when they failed to anticipate that opposition to an entirely rational 75p per week increase in the state pension (in line with subdued inflation) would carry tremendous resonance outside the counting-houses of Whitehall. The same Cabinet entirely misjudged the (irrational) anger of motorists at (rational) increases in fuel duty, in line with rising prices.

Let us try to construct the profile of a fictional backbencher who made the right call on each of these judgments: the imaginary MP (let us call him Reg Smythe) who found himself on the right side of the argument on Poll Tax, Fuel Tax, pension increases, Gurkhas and Joanna Lumley. Three features, I would submit, stand out in Reg Smythe's profile. First, he is not unduly troubled by logic. Secondly, he has a keen sense of the importance to voters of their wallets. Thirdly, his ear is well-attuned to waves of popular sentiment.

But I would add this about Reg. He gets genuinely fired-up in the causes to which he attaches himself. His eyes prick with tears as he stands beside Dame Joanna and a cluster of ageing Ghurkhas, and the hard-heartedness of the Ministry of Defence infuri-

ates him. His rage at the 75p pension increase is not synthetic, and he knows many pensioners in his own constituency whose distress is real. He has entirely persuaded himself that fuel-tax increases are wrong not because motorists should not pay their share of environmental costs (Reg is passionate about the environment, too) but because transport is the lubricant of our whole economy, and these increases will hit entrepreneurs, road-hauliers and small business people.

And one further and most important remark. Not all these causes, and by no means all the arguments to which a dedicated tribune of the people may devote his energies, are majority causes. Some will be as unpopular among some voters as they are popular among others. Great parliamentary careers have rested, often enough, on the dogged association of an MP with a small but defined interest group, whose self-appointed guardian angel he becomes. He brings to the table that group, their concerns, and their potential support, and may not distract himself with larger causes. He is their man – or she their woman – and the MP the Chancellor takes aside for an anxious chat whenever the issue looks like trouble. An MP, in short, can fight for minorities all his life, while staying in tune with the type of democracy that energises a British parliamentary career.

In 1981 I was lucky to be among the seven backbenchers whose names were drawn from a hat, and who were invited to attend the Prince of Wales's wedding to Diana Spencer. Sitting among the huge congregation in St Paul's Cathedral I heard, over the loudspeakers, the questions – "Do you take this woman?" – and the responses. At each "I do" there came into the Cathedral, faintly but audibly, the distant-sounding roar of the crowds of tens of thousands, like the faint rumble of an ocean lapping at the steps of St Paul's.

That echo was for me the most moving thing of all. I wish I had followed its logic down Fleet Street, the Strand and Whitehall, to Westminster, and understood then what I understand now: that unless when you advance a case at Westminster you can hear in your imagination, and your fellow MPs can hear in theirs, that faint roar of approbation from the sea of public opinion, then prepare for the kindly obituaries many decades hence, after your knighthood and your sobriquet "veteran backbench MP" have long been earned. From the obituarist's phrase book will come those old favourites "brave thinker", "keen intellect", "gadfly", "never really a team player", "maverick", "radical theorist", "principled debater" . . . we can almost hear the chamber emptying as we read.

In less smart phraseology than the famous passage quoted above, Burke expressed the opposite view, but a truer one, when he wrote: "To follow, not to force the public inclination; to give a direction, a form, a technical dress, and a specific sanction, to the general sense of the community, is the true end of legislature."

Matthew Parris was Conservative MP for Derbyshire West from 1979 to 1986 and is a former parliamentary sketch writer for The Times.

The old era

"Let's just call it a damage limitation exercise"

The man who detoxified the Conservative brand

Francis Elliott
Deputy Political Editor

David Cameron best reveals his character and that of his political project at moments of defeat. He felt the blow of losing his first attempt at becoming an MP keenly in 1997, analysed correctly the reasons for the Tories' abject performance in 2001 but then misjudged why Michael Portillo's subsequent leadership bid fell short. The failure of Iain Duncan Smith's leadership forced him to reconsider his attitude to modernisation and his last doubts were extinguished by the third successive Conservative defeat under Michael Howard.

During his own period as Leader of the Opposition, Mr Cameron was at his best when he faced the greatest danger, tacking and trimming and finally out-manoeuvring Gordon Brown in the autumn of 2007 to scare the new Labour leader off an early election. When at last the poll was called in May 2010, Mr Cameron best showed his political gifts not during the campaign but in the days afterwards, converting an inconclusive result into a decisive outcome.

But if defeat best reveals the nature of the man and his project, it is in success that his closest friendships and alliances have been forged. The first of these is his relationship with Steve Hilton, whom he first met in the late 1980s when both worked for what was then Conservative Central Office. Their decades-long conversation about the Tories, their strengths and weaknesses, their prejudices and favourites, is the dialogue that most drives the project. At first sight the two men could hardly be more different. Mr Cameron's privileged background, social assurance and cultural Conservatism fitted him smoothly for the Conservative Research Department in the Tories' old HQ in Smith Square. Mr Hilton, the son of Hungarian immigrants and a scholarship boy who became a Conservative only at university, was less obviously a CRD Tory boy. Mr Cameron favoured red braces; Mr Hilton was known to wear a "voluminous poncho".

It is what they share, however, not what they do not, that most influences the modern Conservative Party. A passionate belief in the primacy of the individual over the collective – open in Mr Hilton's case, partly shielded from view in that of Mr Cameron – is their first shared value. Mr Hilton, whose family endured the Communist repression of Budapest in 1956, has a visceral dislike of the statist mindset.

Neither, however, is a straightforward economic liberal. The purpose of freeing individual action is so that people can better deliver social goods. And the State has a role in fostering and encouraging those other institutions, such as marriage, that help people to share responsibility for one another. The pair have tried a number of attempts to rebrand these strands of right-wing philosophy during their period at the helm of the Conservative Party. It has been known variously as "modern, compassionate Conservatism", the "post-bureaucratic age" and finally "the Big Society". For the second big thing that Mr Cameron shares with his closest ally is an abiding interest in and facility for political communication. Both schooled according to the exacting standards of a Margaret Thatcher-era CRD, they write crisply and without jargon or cant. In the run-up to the 1992 general election the pair were selected to manage the relationship with the Tories' advertising agency, Saatchi & Saatchi.

There is one final shared attribute: their age. They were part of a Smith Square "brat pack" in 1992 and were still young enough to weather the wilderness years so that they could emerge as part of the "next generation" just as new Labour was running out of steam.

In Stafford Leisure Centre in the early hours of May 2, 1997, however, those years outside power were just beginning. By then 31, the Conservative candidate, left hanging around as a loser at the count, knew that losing was no personal disgrace and certainly not a career-ending moment. Nonetheless, he felt it keenly when an elderly woman approached him in tears as the scale of the Tories' national defeat became clear. "I don't want to die under a Labour government," she said. The misery of that exchange still lingered when he wrote of it many years later.

Mr Cameron has suffered personal setbacks. The influence of the birth, life and death, aged 6, of his first son Ivan is well known. It is fair to say, however, that he has suffered less in the way of professional reverses than many other senior members of the Conservative leadership. After defeat in Stafford Mr Cameron went back to a well-paid City job as director of communications for the media company Carlton. It was a younger generation of Conservative staffers who tasted the most bitter fruits of opposition, and started to do the most original thinking about how to return to power.

Although they overlapped while the Tories were in government, Mr Cameron did not really know George Osborne until both were elected in 2001. He was not in Smith Square as Mr Osborne and a handful of other young staffers, including several defectors from the Social Democratic Party, began to think deeply about how to decontaminate the Conservative brand. Figures such as Andrew Cooper and Rick Nye, who went on to set up the polling firm Populus, began pointing out that voters tended to like Conservative policies, until they found out that they were Conservative policies. It was not the policies that were the problem.

Just as Europe divided the party during its previous years in power, so the question of "de-toxifying" the Tory brand fractured it in opposition. The modernisation of the Tories, started under William Hague, slowed as it became entangled in the Tories' *kultur* war over social issues such as gay adoption and marriage. Throughout it all Mr Hague's political secretary, Mr Osborne, had a ringside seat.

Mr Cameron, as he now privately admits, had a slower conversion to the modernisers' cause than some of his most senior allies. Less than a week after being elected in 2001 (having been selected for the safe seat of Witney) he was asked how the party should change. His answer is telling since it dwells on questions of presentation, not substance. "[The Conservative Party] needs to change its language, change its approach, start with a blank piece of paper and try to work out why our base of support is not broader. Anyone could have told the Labour Party in the 1980s how to become electable. It had to drop unilateral disarmament, punitive tax rises, wholesale nationalisation and unionisation. The question for the Conservative Party is far more difficult because there are no obvious areas of policy that need to be dropped." Almost as an afterthought, he then added: "We need a clear, positive, engaging agenda on public services."

Later, when he was leader, Mr Cameron was often asked when he would have a Clause Four moment, a reference to Tony Blair's totemic defeat of party critics. His answer was always a version of that first, raw, draft. The riposte might be caricatured as: "We're right, it's just that the voters don't realise it yet."

Although he backed Mr Portillo, the modernisers' candidate in the 2001 leadership election, the support was hesitant, even knowing. When Mr Portillo lost in an early round, the new Witney MP opted for Mr Duncan Smith over Kenneth Clarke. "What went wrong?" Mr Cameron mused in an online column. "Here was a leadership contender with buckets of charisma, a CV that included experience at the highest level of government and genuine cross-party appeal. Our man had offered leadership, radical change and ideas that challenged the party both in Parliament and the country. They simply weren't ready for it. In many ways it is view that I share."

Mr Cameron's early career as a backbencher is not littered with examples of him acting as a spokesman for the need for the party to broaden its appeal. He was, for example, a passionate defender of fox-hunting. (In fairness, he also took a brave and principled position on the decriminalisation of drugs.) Gradually, however, and partly as a result of a developing friendship with Mr Osborne, Mr Cameron started to think more deeply about what was needed, and in particular what a "clear, positive, engaging agenda on public services" might look like.

At the same time, Mr Cameron was receiving firsthand experience of the NHS as it cared for his son, who was born with Ohtahara syndrome, a serious neurological condition. If the Tories were really going to modernise, Mr Cameron came to realise, they had to embrace properly funded, high-quality, universally available public services. Michael Gove, then a journalist with *The Times*, Mr Hilton, Mr Osborne and others began to meet regularly in a Mayfair restaurant to plot a Conservative future.

There was still time to test to destruction the alternative model. Mr Howard, who replaced the ousted Mr Duncan Smith in 2003, flirted with a full-throated modernisation but came to view it as unauthentic, at least in his mouth, and opted like Mr Hague for a safety-first "core-vote" strategy in the 2005 election. Mr Cameron, who with Mr Gove helped to patch together the party's manifesto, saw at first hand the consequences of limiting Tory appeal to existing supporters.

Mr Cameron, then, emerged from another election disaster surrounded by two long-term friends, Mr Hilton and Mr Gove, and one newer ally, Mr Osborne. It was, however, someone he had known longer than any of them that pushed him hardest to run for the leadership. Andrew Feldman, a friend since Brasenose College, Oxford, set up the key meeting with Lord Harris of Peckham, a former Conservative treasurer, that helped to convince him to contest the leadership. Mr Feldman, who was later appointed chief executive of the party and then co-chairman, is an important, although non-political, member of the inner circle.

There were others who might have led the modernisers' charge against David Davis in 2005. Andrew Lansley, David Willetts, Francis Maude, even Oliver Letwin, had all, at various times, held the mantle. Mr Osborne, had he been a little older and a little more confident, might have challenged Mr Cameron's right to present the case. But he could see that Mr Cameron was exactly the reassuring figure that the party's grassroots would trust to carry out the sort of radical changes that were needed to restore the party's electoral fortunes. Together with Mr Hilton, the pair crafted a leadership campaign that balanced the modernising creed with a traditional message on the family. It was Mr Cameron's star performance in hustings at the Conservative Party conference in Blackpool, however, that landed him the job. He beat Mr Davis by a margin of two to one: 134,446 to 64,398.

Veterans of the early days of Mr Cameron's stint as Leader of the Opposition wonder, however, how they avoided disaster. It was not that the Tory leader lacked a solid backroom team: he had in Ed Llewellyn and Catherine Fall two long-term friends for his chief of staff and deputy chief of staff, and another former colleague reporting for duty was George Bridges. It was that the sheer, exuberant energy of the creative talents of Mr Hilton and Mr Letwin, coupled with Mr Cameron's own inexperience and a general lack of organisational clarity, led to some hair-raising scrapes.

A fascinated and largely supportive media did not seem to notice, at least at first, as it lapped up the youthful leader. The environment provided the theme and the backdrops for an initial repositioning. Carefully crafted photo-opportunities, the most famous involving dog-sledding in the Arctic Circle, challenged voters' preconceptions about what a Conservative leader looked like. Even the party's slogan in the 2006 council election – Vote Blue, Go Green – seemed designed to blur former associations.

The Conservative grassroots were a tougher audience, particularly on the sensitive issue of candidate selection. Local associations had seen off previous attempts to dilute their power to select representatives but the new leader knew that, if he was to make the party look more like modern Britain, this was a battle he had to win. His first attempt, the creation of a 100-strong "A-list" of preferred candidates, was a crass but ultimately effective opening gambit. In the new Parliament there are 48 women Conservative MPs and 11 who are black or from other ethnic minorities. In the previous Parliament there were just eight women and two non-white MPs on the Conservative benches.

But while candidate selection was a fight that Mr Cameron knew he had to have with his grassroots, the defining battle of this period was one that he did not mean to pick. Ill-judged briefing around the issue of grammar schools in May 2007 brought resentment over Mr Cameron's leadership to the surface among activists and MPs. That an Old Etonian was setting his face against state-funded selective education provided

David Cameron's star performance at the 2005 party conference in Blackpool landed him the job of leader

the first opportunity for critics to wheel out the issue of his class. Mr Cameron first tried to escalate the crisis making it a "key test" to establish whether it wanted just to be a "right-wing debating society". When the backlash grew fiercer, Mr Cameron made a tactical retreat. It was the start of an uncomfortable summer, the low point of his leadership in opposition. An increasingly restive party, Mr Brown's arrival in No 10 and the threat of an early election pushed the Tory leader to the right. Issues such as crime and immigration, deliberately ignored for two years, were foreshadowed.

Here Mr Cameron again showed his skills as a political communicator and the advantage of his youth. A thoughtful speech against multiculturalism won the distinction of an endorsement by Trevor Phillips, head of the new Equality and Human Rights Commission. Similarly, concerns about law and order were framed in the language of social justice. The emphasis was on the impact of crime, antisocial behaviour or welfare dependency on low-income households rather their better-off neighbours.

It took a straightforwardly old-fashioned Tory tax break, the offer to increase inheritance tax to a threshold of more than £1 million, to provide the Conservatives with the momentum at that year's conference to scare Mr Brown away from going to the country. As the Conservatives began to enjoy huge poll leads after that disastrous miscalculation by Labour, it seemed to Mr Cameron and his inner circle that he had at last resolved the party's brand problems. Mr Cameron could use the full palette of issues without being accused of lurching to the right. Even Nick Clegg's arrival as the new Lib Dem leader, another youthful leader offering change, failed to make a significant impact on poll ratings that seemed to pave a sure path to No 10.

The advent of the global economic crisis exposed such confidence as premature, although at first it seemed that it would deliver a landslide victory. Britain's galloping debt levels seemed to Mr Cameron and Mr Osborne to confirm, not challenge, the need for a smaller State. A tactical decision to match Labour's spending plans and deny Mr Brown his favoured "investment versus cuts" dividing line was abandoned in favour of a formula that "shared the proceeds of growth", code for cuts in spending. Expenditure would grow at a slower rate than GDP for all departments except in three ring-fenced areas, health, international development and education. This formulation was itself jettisoned as the recession took hold, however, and the Tories' economic credibility was tested.

Indeed the global nature of the crisis, and Mr Brown's relentless use of an international stage to illustrate the need for state action, undermined the Tory case. When framed as a choice between who could best cope with the economic storms, voters cooled on the Conservatives. Mr Cameron found his party's poll rating pegged back beneath 40 per cent, the share of the vote at which an overall majority was assured.

Throughout his leadership the party's private polling had consistently shown Mr Cameron to be more popular than his party. When the broadcasters' attention was on the Tory leader, the Conservative poll rating increased, when it was not they slipped back. The overall strategy of the campaign seemed simple enough: highlight Mr Cameron's personality while delivering a message of broad reassurance on public services and economic competence.

In fact, as the long campaign ground on through early spring it became clear that Mr Cameron had overestimated his own popularity with voters while underestimating the remaining suspicion voters harboured about the Conservative brand. In avoiding a Clause Four moment with his party, and then by using the economic crisis to seek a mandate for a smaller State directly, Mr Cameron left himself open to Labour claims that he represented the "same old Tories". It was Mr Clegg, however, who was best able to exploit the vulnerability. Voters wanting a change but not convinced about the Conservatives were offered a route out of their dilemma.

While the campaign exposed some of Mr Cameron's faults – a tendency to substitute personality for policy, an over-reliance on a small group of confidants – his pragmatism and speed of manoeuvre served him in excellent stead for its aftermath. The manner in which Mr Cameron fashioned his coalition and then drove it through a reluctant party impressed even his enemies.

His coalition with the Lib Dems offers the chance for the late and reluctant convert to complete the modernisation of the Tories.

Francis Elliott is co-author of David Cameron: The Rise of the New Conservatives *(2007)*

At long last it's OK to be a Tory

Alice Thomson
Times columnist

Who wants to be a Tory? In 2005 it was a lonely life. Even in the shires it was more embarrassing to say that you had voted blue than that you could not reverse a horse box. The Tories were in despair. They had liked the nice William Hague, the comprehensive-educated, northern lad with a pretty wife and lovely manners. It still rather hurt that the electorate had ridiculed his attempts to be more matey with his baseball caps and his 14 pints of beer.

This man seemed honourable and decent but Britain had rejected him. So they tried again. They chose an officer with four children, another charming, blonde wife and the shadow of a moustache. Iain Duncan Smith could put some backbone into the party, thought the loyalists. He would show the shallow Tony Blair how to be a gentleman.

But the quiet man soon went and Michael Howard, the former Home Secretary who promised cleaner hospitals and more school discipline, still could not make a dent in the polls.

The Tories were desperate. Who could save them from a life of slammed doors and dinner party jokes? The leadership contest of 2005 was a despondent affair. There was David Davis with his derring do and pick axe in his office and David Cameron, a Newbury boy with slicked-back hair.

As they met at the party conference in Blackpool, the mood was sombre. A few girls ran around wearing Mine's a DD, for David Davis, T shirts. The tone seemed set. The words running through the Blackpool rock were Tory Losers.

Then something miraculous happened. A young man bounded on to the stage, with no notes and began to talk. The grassroots, who had become pale and lifeless in the arid soil, suddenly felt as though they had been watered. Soon they were nudging each other, tapping their hearing aids, looking thoughtful and clapping ecstatically.

David Cameron brought the Conservative Party back to life. When he patted his wife's pregnant stomach at the end of his speech, the party knew that they had found their man. Here was an Old Etonian as at home in shorts as he was in plus fours, who gave them some credibility, no one sneered at him. Young women in wraparound dresses began to pour into Conservative Central Office, Oxbridge graduates were queuing for jobs as interns.

The leader wore things called Converse trainers that seemed to impress the press. He cycled to work (although there was that little hiccup when it was discovered that his chauffeur was following with his briefcase). His insistence on riding a sledge in Norway for a photoshoot was rather embarrassing but the country did not seem to mind so the grassroots were determined that they would not mind either. They turned a blind eye when Mr Cameron started hugging hoodies. The Heir to Blair, well that was a bit humiliating but never mind.

Onwards and upwards, the Tories were finally going places. Samantha Cameron was a working mother but she was not strident like Cherie Blair. And then there was Ivan. Mr Cameron was obviously a wonderful father to his disabled son.

It began to look rather promising. They soon started winning more council seats. The A list proved to be a blip. Then there was the question of grammar schools. Could they really accept a leader who didn't cherish these great institutions? But they did.

Then just as they thought they might finally be in with a chance, Gordon Brown became Prime Minister and extraordinarily the country decided they liked him.

Here was the first real wobble. Had they chosen the right man? Didn't he suddenly seem a bit young, a bit flash, a bit too toff? They should have stuck with Mr Hague. The party conference was a gloomy affair that year. Mr Major was wheeled in to provide extra support. Then young George Osborne did it. He promised to cut inheritance tax. The grassroots were relieved. They had not made a mistake, these boys knew on which side their crumpets were buttered. They would help the middle classes and wow Middle England. They had outbluffed Mr Brown, who could not now call a general election. The party was ecstatic. Mr Brown had become Mr Bean. The grassroots may have had a woman or ethnic minority candidate pressed on them but they proved to be decent chaps and chapesses. They would win.

Only, the polls changed again. By the beginning of 2010 it was clear that the Tories were not romping home. The recession had hit them hard. It was difficult to talk about GWB (General Well Being) when GDP was plummeting. People were not so polite any more. They thought the boys were a bit too aloof and distant. Their inner circle was too cliquey.

Mr Cameron sounded angry during the expenses scandal but he was not that clean either. Why should voters prune his wisteria? Who had let this happen? The grassroots felt let down by everyone now. The MPs whom they had served with scones and tea had done the dirty on them.

So they arrived at the election looking like an Eton mess, bits and pieces all jumbled together. Not really sure what they thought of their leader or their candidates or even their policies.

Then came Cleggmania, a slightly too clever Conservative manifesto (*Invitation to Join the Government of Britain*), the Big Society that none of them understood, and then days of uncertainty followed by a coalition, the kind of shabby deal that, a few days before, their leader had been writing off as disastrous.

Now they want to believe, they really do. They want to see the roses in the garden and the coalition and smile on it. They want to discover that they have two for the price of one, but they are nervous. Could they be the losers? The coalition manifesto drops many of their cherished plans and policies.

They worry that they have already had to give so much to the sandal-wearing yellows. It could all come at too high a price.

But they are emotionally shattered. They have given their all to this man in the past five years. They are staunch, they are loyal, they are tribal. And they are, after 13 long and lonely years, back in power where they believe that they belong. They will give him a chance.

Path to power: how the Lib Dems made history

Greg Hurst
Editor of the Guide

The Liberal Democrats scarcely looked like a party on the brink of power for much of the 2005-10 Parliament. Two leaders resigned after losing support and authority, twice pitching members into leadership elections that were bitterly fought and bruising, rather than cathartic, and left some participants damaged. Yet despite periods of intense turbulence, the party underwent a profound transition as the leadership passed to a new generation with a different outlook from the social liberalism that had been its dominant philosophy for decades. An influx of 20 new MPs, a third of the parliamentary party, many of whom were able, experienced and, above all, ambitious, was another important dynamic.

The general election of 2005 was a double-edged sword for the Lib Dems. A net gain of 11 seats took them to 62 MPs, the highest for a third party since 1922, with some huge swings from Labour. The Conservatives, who gained five seats but lost three to the Lib Dems, unnerved those MPs who survived with precarious majorities with a ferocious new style of locally targeted campaigning. Such were the expectations that many Lib Dems hoped for a bigger breakthrough and saw the election as an opportunity missed.

Charles Kennedy, exhausted two days after the birth of his son, had torpedoed his own manifesto launch during the campaign by floundering over the details of a flagship policy for a local income tax. He found himself under pressure from the outset of the new term. Disappointment with the election result, compounded by tensions between social and economic liberals and frustration among new MPs with the party's organisation in the Commons were compounded when Mr Kennedy drifted into one of his periodic bouts of introspection just as the party was crying out for leadership and strategic direction.

Although popular with many voters, Mr Kennedy was a source of increasing frustration with colleagues owing to an innate caution, chaotic organisation and reliance on a tight-knit inner circle of long-time friends. Although many suspected it, relatively few knew that he was an alcoholic who, when confronted by leading figures in the party in 2004, had agreed to undergo treatment but was subject to intermittent relapses. After months of tension, fresh drinking episodes in the autumn of 2005 proved to be the final straw for several of the younger generation of senior Lib Dem MPs, who began discussing plans for a multi-signature letter of no confidence in their leader.

A series of semi-public confrontations ensued during which Mr Kennedy, having previously appeared oddly detached, proved himself extraordinarily tenacious in seeking to cling on. Even when his alcoholism was disclosed, by a television journalist, he attempted a final throw of the dice by calling a leadership ballot of members in which he declared that he would be a candidate. His critics countered with a collective threat of resignation: 25 MPs declared that they would resign from their front-bench positions unless he fell on his sword. In a dignified statement the following day, Mr Kennedy duly stepped down.

The damage to the party did not stop there. Mark Oaten, a senior MP and, briefly, potential candidate for leader, was disgraced over liaisons with a male prostitute. Another candidate, Simon Hughes, Mr Kennedy's chief rival for much of his leadership, was forced to admit to past sexual relationships with men, despite telling journalists that he was not gay.

It was the nadir: in January 2006, a YouGov poll put Lib Dem support as low as 13 per cent. The party looked at though it might tear itself apart. The unlikely and unexpected victory in the Dunfermline & West Fife by-election the following month, for which Mr Kennedy himself returned to the spotlight to campaign, helped to steady the ship.

The front-runner to replace him was Sir Menzies Campbell, the deputy leader, who made his name articulating the party's opposition to the Iraq war. Any hopes of a coronation were dashed when Chris Huhne, a former MEP and one of the sharpest of the party's new MPs, entered the race despite previously pledging to support Sir Menzies. Mr Huhne's audacity enraged senior colleagues who had risked their reputations to topple Mr Kennedy but quickly won the admiration of many party activists, who mistrust anything that smacks of a stitch-up.

Sir Menzies won the election but Mr Huhne finished a strong second, after a vigorous campaign. Despite claims from supporters that Sir Menzies would bring a statesman's authority to the role, his opening appearances in the Commons proved to be disastrous, as he struggled to be heard in the bear pit of Prime Minister's Questions. In one early outing, as acting leader, he asked why one in five schools were without a permanent head. As his own party was itself without a leader, this provoked uproarious hilarity. Rapidly he was portrayed as too old, at 64, and out of touch. A determined man, he received coaching and his Commons performances improved but too late to rescue his reputation as an assured parliamentarian. Recriminations over his role in the traumatic resignation of Mr Kennedy also poisoned the well of the party's body politic.

This was the Lib Dems' awkward predicament as David Cameron, in his first year as Conservative leader, set about a re-branding exercise seeking to bite chunks out of their support. In a speech in Hereford, a precarious Lib-Con marginal constituency, Mr Cameron declared himself a "liberal Conservative" and ap-

Nick Clegg, the Lib Dem leader, with his predecessor Charles Kennedy on a campaign flight to Glasgow

pealed to Liberal Democrats to back him. His skilful championing of green issues threatened to wrest the mantle of environmental campaigning from the Lib Dems' complacent grasp: plans by Mr Cameron for a wind turbine on the roof of his house and travelling by husky sled to view melting glaciers in Norway were vivid pieces of political positioning, although his environmentalism proved short-lived.

Another Conservative overture, seeking to field the former BBC Director-General Greg Dyke as a joint Tory-Lib Dem candidate for London Mayor, was more deftly rejected by Sir Menzies. The Lib Dems' eventual candidate, Brian Paddick, proved to have questionable judgment and trailed in third place.

The following year, when Gordon Brown succeeded Tony Blair at No 10, the Lib Dems' defences were tested again. Mr Brown wanted to appoint two Lib Dems to his Cabinet: Lord Ashdown of Norton-sub-Hamdon and another peer who he hoped would defect to Labour, as he tried to construct a broad-based "government of all the talents". His plan leaked and was scuppered; oddly, Mr Brown assumed that Lib Dems would serve in a Labour administration, not a coalition with agreed policy concessions. The new Prime Minister settled on advisory posts for several Lib Dems: Lady Neuberger (on volunteering), Lord Lester of Herne Hill (on constitutional reform) and Baroness Williams of Crosby (on nuclear proliferation). Matthew Taylor, a former front-bencher, conducted an inquiry on rural housing.

The impact was deeply unsettling for the Lib Dems. It smacked of a crude attempt to divide the party's senior ranks, signalling to its left-of-centre supporters to return to Labour's embrace. Like many of Mr Brown's initiatives, the strategy soon unravelled but it again called into question the judgment of Sir Menzies and his closest adviser, Lord Kirkwood of Kirkhope, both of whom had presented his long-time friendship with Mr Brown as an asset.

Another unnerving factor for the Lib Dems was the unfolding narrative of the prosecution of their biggest donor, Michael Brown, whose donations of £2.4 million doubled their 2005 election budget. He was later convicted of money-laundering and theft and some wealthy investors who were his clients demanded that money be returned to them by the Lib Dems, who insisted that they had taken, and spent, the money in good faith. The episode severely damaged the Lib Dems' attempts to portray themselves as political reformers.

Under Sir Menzies' leadership, his party's poll ratings drifted slowly downwards, from 20 per cent in March 2006 to 15 per cent in the summer of 2007 and even 12 per cent that autumn, according to Populus, although they rose before and afterwards. When Mr Brown flirted with but abandoned a snap autumn election, Sir Menzies saw his chance and announced his resignation, knowing that his party had breathing space to elect his successor. His 18-month tenure, while difficult, saw important advances. Most notably he promoted to key spokesmanships and party positions a new generation eager to inject credibility on policy and greater professionalism into its organisation at Westminster: MPs such as David Laws, Ed Davey, Norman Lamb, Vince Cable and Nick Clegg. The forthcoming leadership election gave them a chance to complete their grip on the party's levers of power.

There was little doubt that this new generation would choose as its champion Nick Clegg, a former MEP who entered the Commons in 2005, took an erudite interest in policy, was articulate and effective on television but had a restless disrespect for convention and a keen appetite for reform. As Sir Menzies had, Mr Clegg began in the uncomfortable position of front-runner and, like him, faced a formidable challenge from Mr Huhne. Mr Clegg's campaign was cautious, holding back from his instinct to offer a bold, modernising agenda for fear of jeopardising his lead; Mr Huhne's was slightly populist and overtly aggressive, attacking his rival for "flip-flopping". His supporters at one point issued a rebuttal document entitled Calamity Clegg. The result was uncomfortably close, with Mr Clegg winning by about 500 votes.

Another by-product of the campaign was that the Lib Dems emerged with a new celebrity. Vince Cable, who was elected the party's deputy leader in place of Sir Menzies, found himself standing in at Prime Minister's Questions during the interregnum that followed his resignation. Dr Cable, who harboured leadership ambitions of his own before reluctantly ruling himself out because of his age, seized the moment.

His first attempt, when he cracked a joke, fell slightly flat: humour in the charged atmosphere on the floor of the House requires split-second timing and the ability to catch a mood. Undeterred, he tried again the following week. Mr Brown, having cancelled the autumn election, was embroiled in a scandal of hidden donations to Labour and the loss of child benefit records for 25 million families. "The House has noticed," Dr Cable began, "the Prime Minister's remarkable transformation in the last few weeks from Stalin to Mr Bean, creating chaos out of order, rather than order out of chaos." The Commons collapsed into laughter. Vince Cable became a household name almost overnight.

Mr Clegg, like all new Lib Dem leaders, struggled to make an impact with the electorate, often finding himself in the shadow of his energetic deputy leader, whose profile rose throughout the financial crisis that engulfed Britain's banks from autumn 2008. To frame the party's response to the economic crisis Mr Clegg convened a small group of experts and advisers; Vince Cable was a prominent member but Mr Clegg insisted on chairing it himself, asserting his authority rather than deferring to his more experienced deputy.

He took care to stay close to Mr Huhne, seeking his counsel often and holding him close rather than allowing any rift to open between them; Mr Huhne repaid him with loyalty. Meanwhile, Mr Clegg's allies were given key roles: David Laws played an increasingly key role in policy development, Ed Davey took charge of communications and Danny Alexander, who impressed Mr Clegg while working on his leadership campaign, became his chief of staff. Among backroom allies, he relied most on John Sharkey, a former advertising executive, for language in interviews and speeches; Polly MacKenzie to write his speeches; Jonny Oates for strategic media advice; Leana Pietsch on how issues would play in the press; and Alison Suttie to organise his office. This latter role was key: Mr Clegg, with three young children and impatient with the after-hours culture of the Commons, was ruthless in prioritising his diary and insisted on having time to take his boys to school or put them to bed, even if it meant returning to the Commons later. Much key party business was decided in conference telephone calls, with several advisers asked to ring a number with a PIN code at a given time for a focused discussion with the leader. It meant that the demands of managing a difficult and disparate party were contained and he could concentrate his energies elsewhere.

Mr Clegg's approach was to develop an irreverent, anti-Establishment edge to the Lib Dems, both as a strategy for being noticed and to differentiate himself from Labour and the Conservatives: when standing for leader he pledged to go to prison rather than comply with a national identity card register. This meant embracing some future hostages to fortune: opposing the replacement of the Trident nuclear deterrent, on which Mr Huhne had campaigned, and an "earned amnesty" for illegal immigrants, developed by Mr Clegg himself while home affairs spokesman. The lat-

ter, in particular, cost the Lib Dems many votes. Other key policy developments included dropping a symbolic commitment to a new 50p top rate of income tax, agreed under Sir Menzies' leadership and later implemented by Labour. Instead emphasis shifted towards taxing wealth, such as pensions contributions and capital gains, and exempting people earning beneath £10,000 a year from paying tax altogether, a policy revived from the 1997 manifesto. Mr Clegg made a further priority of improving education provision for children from poorer families.

An early test of his mettle was over Europe: Mr Clegg ordered his MPs to abstain on a Commons vote on whether the Lisbon treaty should be subject to a referendum, for which the Conservatives were campaigning. Several Lib Dems had pledged to constituents that they would back a referendum and could not comply, notably David Heath, Tim Farron and Alistair Carmichael in his Shadow Cabinet. Mr Clegg would not submit to a fudge by allowing them a free vote and accepted their resignations when they were among 15 Lib Dems to vote in favour.

If this episode was oblique, the issue that next introduced Mr Clegg to the voters was anything but. The Lib Dems inflicted on Gordon Brown his first significant Commons defeat, using one of their opposition days to table a motion to allow ex-Gurkha soldiers the right to live in Britain. The issue was simple for voters to understand and had the added appeal that the Gurkhas were backed by the television actress Joanna Lumley. Mr Cameron raced outside the Commons to join Mr Clegg celebrating with Ms Lumley for the television cameras. Mr Clegg again made waves by demanding the resignation of the Speaker, Michael Martin, over his inept handling of the MPs' expenses scandal, the first party leader in modern political history to do so. He appeared about to find his voice just at a moment when Conservative support was slipping while Mr Brown remained a deeply divisive Prime Minister. Yet his pre-election conference missed this opportunity, with several errors. Mr Clegg unwisely urged "savage" cuts in public spending, and appeared to ditch a commitment to scrap university tuition fees but was forced to back-track after a party backlash. Vince Cable provoked anger from MPs by unveiling, like a magician pulling a rabbit from a hat, a "mansion tax" on houses worth more than £1 million, later modified to £2 million.

Another of Sir Menzies' legacies was to have ordered preparations for an early election from 2007, meaning that target seat planning, candidate selection, fundraising and campaign staff recruitment were well advanced. The process was headed by Lord Rennard, the party's chief executive and architect of a string of by-election coups, but under Mr Clegg's leadership pressure developed for a new approach. Lord Rennard stood down in May 2009, coinciding with controversy over his Lords expenses claims, for which he was later cleared, meaning that none of Mr Clegg's core team had experience of running a general election.

Given Dr Cable's higher profile, they agreed long beforehand to make the campaign a double act. To avoid a repeat of the fraught "two Davids" SDP-Liberal Alliance duopoly of 1987, when reporters took delight in pouncing on differences between David Owen and David Steel, they campaigned together. The Clegg-Cable partnership worked well enough but was rapidly overtaken by events, as the television debates finally made Nick Clegg a national figure in his own right.

Greg Hurst is the author of Charles Kennedy: A Tragic Flaw *(2006)*

How Brown's rivalry with Blair proved to be Labour's undoing

Philip Webster
Election Editor

His voice breaking with emotion, Gordon Brown, wearing a borrowed red tie, said farewell to frontline politics outside the door of No 10 five days after the general election. His final attempt to keep his party in office with a last-ditch deal with the Liberal Democrats was doomed from the start. When it came unstuck he was impatient to go, setting off for the Palace to see the Queen when his successor, David Cameron, was barely ready to follow suit. It was the job for which he had yearned all his life, and particularly during the ten years it was held by Tony Blair.

When his dream to win an election in his own right was finally shattered, however, Mr Brown was in no mood to hang around. In just three years the two founding fathers of new Labour had gone and the Conservatives were back in government for the first time since 1997. It was a partnership that had made Labour electable again after 18 years in the wilderness, but when they looked back on the Blair-Brown years most Labour politicians reflected that it was the intensity of their relationship, and Brown's at times irrational desire to oust his old friend, that helped to destroy the project that they had worked so hard to create.

Mr Blair won the 2005 election having issued in advance an unprecedented promise that it would be his last, although he intended to serve for most of it. The move, taken at a time of weakness towards the end of the previous Parliament, was regretted by friends and other Blairites, who always harboured doubts about Mr Brown's ability to win an election.

In the year after his third victory the Brownites kept snapping at Mr Blair's heels and in the summer of 2006, The Times was dragged into the drama. Late in August we were invited to Chequers for an interview to mark Mr Blair's return from his summer holiday. Our expectation was that the intention was to allow Mr Blair to lay out a timetable for his departure. The opposite happened. Given at least eight opportunities to say that the autumn party conference would be his last, Mr Blair declined. Asked at lunch afterwards what we thought the story would be, we told Mr Blair that it would be: "Blair defies Labour over leaving." He did not demur.

Our splash the next day provoked an explosion throughout the Labour movement. Brown's allies were furious and some of them launched into a plot to remove him. A Wolverhampton curry house was the venue for a number of parliamentary aides and Tom Watson, a junior minister close to Brown, to plan a letter calling on Mr Blair to go. "Without an urgent change in the leadership of the party it becomes less likely that we will win the election," it said and its publication left the Prime Minister looking hugely vulnerable.

There was only one way to save his skin: to do what he had so deliberately avoided doing in his interview with The Times the previous week. He announced that the forthcoming conference would be his last as Labour leader, admitting that he would have preferred "to have done this in my own way". Mr Brown got his way, but as the years unfolded it began to look increasingly like a pyrrhic victory. Mr Blair's concession at least allowed the relationship between the two to return to something like the friendship they had once enjoyed.

Mr Brown was on course for the leadership and with no senior figures rising to challenge him he was crowned Labour king without a contest on June 24, 2007, promising to give the party not just policies but a soul. In his acceptance speech in Manchester, Mr Brown appointed a general election coordinator to show his party that it should be thinking of going to the country soon.

A far more dramatic announcement was, however, going to be part of Mr Brown's speech until only a short time before he delivered it. He and many of his closest aides were planning that Sunday morning to do what no other leader had done before and announce there and then that there would be a general election the following year. This was to be a new-style leadership, it was argued, so let's start doing things differently from the start. In the end it was removed; they concluded that it would be giving away far too much to the opposition parties, and there was even a fear that it might look disrespectful to the Queen, who is supposed to be told first of such matters. As later events were to show, however, it might have changed history.

It was left only for Mr Blair to take his bow the following week in the Commons, which he did with such customary élan that he had MPs from all sides rising in an unprecedented standing ovation at the end. He had managed ten years as Prime Minister, a remarkable feat. He had 28 minutes in the Palace saying goodbye to the Queen. Mr Brown went in later for a 57-minute audience and returned to No 10 as Prime Minister declaring: "Let the work of change begin."

Along with Peter Mandelson, Mr Brown and Mr Blair were the architects of the new Labour project. They were friends from their entry to the Commons together in 1983 but the tensions created when Mr Blair took the leadership never lifted until he finally left office. He gave his Chancellor unprecedented powers over domestic policy, ones that he exercised to an extraordinary degree. Decisions that might normally have been made in No 10 were taken at the Treasury; Mr Blair often learnt details of Brown Budgets at the last possible moment. His style was one of "Stalinist ruthlessness", according to a former Cabinet Secretary.

Mr Brown's most fervent supporters believe that the tragedy of their man was that he came to the post too late, when public enthusiasm for new Labour, eroded so much by the Iraq war, was already seriously on the wane. With three victories chalked up by Mr Blair, his successor was always going to find it hard to bring off a fourth. But within the wider Labour movement, the tragedy of Mr Brown was that both he and his allies overestimated his ability to do the hardest job in Britain. They never foresaw that the man who enjoyed strong levels of public support for most of his time as Chancellor could become so unpopular in the relatively short time he occupied No 10.

For all the tributes he received for the way he led the country, and to a lesser extent the world, during the financial crisis, the public took against him. David Cameron based his whole election campaign on a slogan warning of "five more years of Gordon Brown" because Conservative focus groups, like Labour's, told them that Mr Brown's personal position was irretrievable.

For those who know him well, the other tragedy of the outgoing Prime Minister is that the clunky, ill-at-ease, irascible man the public perceives is not the same person that Mr Brown, at his best, can be. That Mr Brown is a man utterly devoted to his family and friends, warm in his dealings with the public when the cameras are out of sight, funny when relaxing, as well-read as anyone could be, a sporting facts-and-figures nerd. His wife, Sarah, and sons, John and Fraser, quite obviously mean so much to Mr Brown, who married in his forties, and he has often told friends that the one consolation of being out of office would be being able to spend more time with them. Sadly, as even his closest friends admit, the public perception is not an accident and is justified by Mr Brown's behaviour over the years. His image as a bully is not accurate but he did get angry with himself, and with others, when things went wrong or they failed to meet his expectations.

It was, however, another personality trait that condemned Mr Brown to a political career that was to end without him winning a general election. During his long spell at the Treasury, and more crucially during those early weeks after he succeeded Mr Blair in 2007, Mr Brown acquired a reputation for dithering over big decisions. The habit was to cost him dear. As he almost announced on becoming leader, it had always been his intention on taking over to go to the country in 2008, but in the honeymoon period after he became Prime Minister, his popularity and that of Labour soared. The public liked the way he handled a run of national emergencies, including the floods and an outbreak of foot-and-mouth disease. So much so that Cabinet ministers were, by August, taking an autumn election for granted. Mr Brown, as a non-elected Prime Minister, could have rightfully asked for his mandate that September, ensuring that the party conferences were cancelled.

His inherent caution held sway. He needed more evidence that he was on a winner. He held the election threat over the Tory conference, believing that it would destabilise them. It was a disastrous miscalculation. He made the mistake of visiting British troops in Iraq on the day of the defence debate at the Conservative gathering, and a Tory charge of using the Forces as pawns got home. George Osborne's announcement that he was slashing liability to inheritance tax shook the Labour high command. Even so, as the conference season ended Mr Brown was still being urged by his closest allies to take the plunge and finish off Mr Cameron. But Mr Brown's pollsters, Deborah Mattinson and Stan Greenberg, who only weeks before had told him that he would win an election, began to back off. On the Thursday night figures such as Ed Balls went off to their constit-

The rivals: Tony Blair and Gordon Brown in 2001

uencies certain that an election would be announced within days.

The next day Mr Brown digested with his advisers the results of a poll of marginal constituencies taken after the conference. It suggested that the Tory conference had gone down well, particularly the inheritance tax cut. Mr Greenberg insisted that Mr Brown could still win, but he might not win well. For Mr Brown, whose only reason for going early was to increase his majority, that was devastating news and he went cold on the idea. Ministers who had been keen on a poll suddenly retreated. Having allowed his team to stoke speculation, a humiliated Mr Brown finally bottled it and called off the election the next day. His only real chance of winning in his own right had gone and his tight group of advisers, who had been with him throughout his Treasury days, were torn apart by the episode. Long friendships ended, never to be repaired, and loyal workers such as Spencer Livermore found themselves taking the blame.

In the years that followed it is the decision that

Mr Brown and his allies most regret. Most believe it is certain that he would have won then against the inexperienced Mr Cameron. It was only months into the Brown premiership but, viewed today, it was the beginning of the end. Britain was to have more than two further years of financial crisis and Mr Brown was to survive three serious attempts to oust him from office but something happened during that period that caused the country and some of his friends, however reluctantly, to doubt Mr Brown's capacity to win. For the band of Brownites who had stuck by the former Chancellor throughout his long period in office it was never to be the same.

Mr Brown was pitched into a series of financial earthquakes that brought out the best in him. History may judge his decision to nationalise Northern Rock early in 2008 to have been a success. His rescue of banks including Royal Bank of Scotland through taking a massive taxpayer stake in them may ultimately be seen to have saved the whole industry, with the taxpayer eventually making a profit. His handling of the G20 world summit over the banking crisis won plaudits from around the world. But at home Mr Brown was on a permanently downward spiral and it was a tribute to his prodigious resilience that he staggered on.

It was one of his last decisions as Chancellor, the abolition of the 10p rate of tax, that came back to haunt him. That part of his last Budget was largely ignored at the time because, with a typical Brown flourish, he had announced a cut in income tax, but the move hit millions of low-paid workers and, confronted by a mass backbench uprising, Brown had to ask his Treasury successor Alistair Darling to come forward with a mini-Budget to put it right.

In the summer of 2008, after dismal by-election defeats, Mr Brown faced his first serious coup attempt. MPs, many of them former Blair supporters, took to the airwaves to call for a leadership contest but no Cabinet ministers joined the rebellion and he survived. He was, though, was skating on thin ice and even his closest advisers realised that he badly needed to shore up his position. He did it in the most surprising way. For some months he had been talking to Peter Mandelson again. Mr Mandelson, in Brussels serving a stint as a commissioner, was worried about the survival of his new Labour project. The Prime Minister shocked him by asking him to come back to the Cabinet for the third time. He bit off Brown's hand and came back as a peer, Business Secretary and a host of other things. He was to be with Mr Brown to the end, finally running the election for him. The move was a masterstroke, virtually killing any chance that a Blairite would stand against Brown.

In June 2009, after terrible local elections, James Purnell, the Work and Pensions Secretary, resigned with an attack on the Prime Minister. Crucially David Miliband, as he had the previous year, failed to follow him over the top with Lord Mandelson warning him it would be disastrous. Again Mr Brown pulled through, but with more and more Labour MPs admitting privately that an election could not be won under him. Finally, in January 2010 Geoff Hoon and Patricia Hewitt, both former Cabinet ministers, mounted yet another unsuccessful putsch. No one who mattered followed them but the delay as ministers laboured to voice support spoke volumes. Somehow, Mr Brown made it through to the general election. He fought a strangely subdued campaign that he brought to life only with passionate speeches towards the end. The result was better than most in

Labour had expected but it was a defeat for which Mr Brown took responsibility.

Mr Brown's allies had always confided that if he felt at any time that his party would benefit from his departure he would go. His and their judgment was always that Labour would not be helped at all by the spectacle of a leader being forced out so close to an election. But on the night of the second television debate during the election campaign, Mr Brown told his closest political ally and friend, Ed Balls, that he would resign if Labour failed to get the highest number of seats and his continued presence was a block to a power-sharing deal.

As the results came in on Thursday night and Friday morning perhaps the biggest surprise was how well Labour had done. Topping 250 seats exceeded the expectations of most party strategists, the pollsters and the bookmakers. The better-than-expected showing followed a campaign in which Mr Brown was himself the reason massive numbers of voters gave to Labour candidates for not voting for their party. He was "cyanide on the doorstep", in the words of one unkind Labour minister. After the election, many Labour figures pondered whether if any other leader had been at the top of the party Labour would now be in its fourth term in a row.

Among Labour people it was a weekend of "if onlys". If only Mr Blair had taken on Mr Brown in a contest in 1994 after John Smith died and beaten him. Mr Blair would never then have had that sense of obligation to Mr Brown that in the end made him give way to him. If only Mr Blair had called Mr Brown's bluff and demoted him from the Treasury in the second term. If only Mr Blair had not announced before the 2005 election that it would be his last as leader. If only in 2006 Mr Blair had changed his mind, seen off the Brownite plot against him, and stood again in 2010.

On that dramatic Monday after the election Mr Brown announced plans to quit, as he had told friends he would. He called the cameras to Downing Street and said that he would stand down within months. He first told Nick Clegg. In so doing he removed the biggest obstacle to Mr Clegg doing a deal with Labour, if his attempts to wring further concessions from the Conservatives bore no fruit. As it happened, it was a final throw of the dice for Mr Brown and Labour and it did not work. Mr Clegg went with the Conservatives, even though he tried to keep open the prospect of a deal with Labour to the last. Mr Brown's Monday gambit was designed to give Labour its only chance of staying in power and it meant that when he finally resigned the next day he could go with dignity.

Exactly 1,048 days after he first kissed hands, Mr Brown was on his way back to the Palace to tender his resignation to the Queen, the eleventh prime minister to have done so. As he did so he could have been forgiven for wondering if his own and Labour's fortunes would have been better served if he had contained his ambitions. With Sarah by his side he left the stage saying that he had learnt about the very best in human nature and "a fair amount too about its frailties, including my own". The words spoke volumes. In those long years at the Treasury, getting Mr Brown to admit to mistakes, or even to human fallibility, was an impossible task. During his much shorter term as Prime Minister, Mr Brown seemed to learn much more about himself. He left the front line believing that Britain had become a better place during the Labour years. But no one is tougher on himself than Mr Brown. He will agree with the verdict that his years in No 10 did not live up to what had gone before.

Philip Webster was Political Editor of The Times *throughout the new Labour years*

Names of the dead were read to a silent Commons

Deborah Haynes
Defence Editor

British deaths on the front line were greater during the last Parliament than in any other since the Korean War. The toll, 369 service personnel, coupled with public anger over a lack of helicopters and armoured vehicles for troops in Afghanistan and Iraq, helped to draw the military into the political debate in a way not seen for a generation.

It did not happen straight away. Britain was a country at war on two fronts for most of the five years, but servicemen and women returning home would find themselves bemused at how little attention their efforts received. There was an underlying sense of disconnect between the politicians in Whitehall and the soldiers, sailors and airmen fighting and dying on their behalf in Helmand province and across southern Iraq. The sight of Tony Blair and after him Gordon Brown sporting flak jackets, helmets, sand-coloured boots and wide smiles on fleeting visits to fortified bases in both warzones did little to change this impression.

The political-military divide was further hindered by the rotation of four different defence secretaries in five years. Des Browne, who held the post from May 2006 until October 2008, was simultaneously made Secretary of State for Scotland when Mr Brown became Prime Minister, an appointment that many in the military saw as an insult, confirming their suspicion that the Government had failed to attach sufficient importance to its Armed Forces.

Mounting questions about the legality of the Iraq campaign, however, coupled with revelations in the media about the state of medical care for wounded troops, inadequate equipment on the front line and a litany of other shortfalls, began to create awkward political questions for ministers to answer. Driving home this sense of unhappiness, General Sir Richard Dannatt, then the head of the Army, broke with a tradition that frowns upon serving officers criticising the government and gave warning in September 2007 that the presence of British Forces in Iraq was worsening local militia attacks. He also spoke out on other emotive topics, such as inadequate accommodation for soldiers, unfair pay and the need for more boots on the ground in Afghanistan. Retired military chiefs added their voices to the chorus of complaints, with high-profile figures such as General Lord Guthrie of Craigiebank, a former chief of the defence staff, becoming a regular critic of Mr Brown, who was accused of cutting the defence budget during a time of war.

The mood of blame and betrayal differed sharply to the plaudits that Margaret Thatcher earned when she took Britain to war in 1982 to recover the Falkland Islands from Argentina. That successful campaign, despite the loss of 255 British lives, helped her to secure a landslide victory in a general election the following year. In contrast, the invasion of Iraq and its bloody aftermath, while defended by military commanders and politicians at the time, cast a shadow over the 2005-10 Parliament that did not disappear when Tony Blair stepped down. Instead, the Government's conduct in siding with the United States over Iraq began to be scrutinised in the Chilcot inquiry, set up to learn lessons from the Iraq campaign.

The previous Parliament also oversaw the deployment of British Forces into southern Afghanistan on a mission that was supposed to be about reconstruction but evolved into the bloodiest combat operation for the British military in decades. The punishing toll of casualties in Helmand over four summers belatedly captured people's attention back in Britain. Every week at Prime Minister's Questions the names of the dead were read out to a silent Commons, while television screens across the country tuned in to watch crowds line the street of a town called Wootton Bassett as convoys carrying the bodies of repatriated service members were escorted from a nearby military airbase. The reality of soldiers with missing limbs, horrific scars and the less obvious but equally debilitating problem of mental disorders also awoke a sense that Britain was at war and more needed to be done to help the Armed Forces. The Government came under increased scrutiny.

Public outrage at the continued use of Snatch Land Rovers, dubbed "mobile coffins" by the soldiers who used them because of their inability to protect against roadside bombs, was one of the emotive issues that changed the relationship between the military and the politicians. So, too, did anger at an inadequate pool of Chinook helicopters, which was forcing British troops to move by road, making them more vulnerable to improvised explosive devices, the biggest killer of British Forces in Afghanistan and Iraq.

The criticism added to a growing perception that the Government had tried to fight "Blair's wars" on a peacetime budget. Even coroners were calling into question how frontline soldiers were being kitted and trained. To their credit, ministers responded to urgent requests from commanders on the ground, with the Treasury signing off on new, improved armoured vehicles and helicopters in record time. The damage, however, had already been done and repeated assurances that no request had been turned down rang hollow amid the belief that the military had never been properly funded in the first place.

The issue became hugely sensitive, with the Conservatives and the Liberal Democrats keen to knock Labour's record, while the Government was anxious to demonstrate that it was doing everything possible to improve the situation. Highlighting the politicisa-

Processions of coffins through Wootton Bassett became a familiar sight, bringing home the reality of war

tion of what should be a military matter, a decision to replace the Snatch Land Rover with 200 new vehicles was revealed while Mr Brown was on a trip to Afghanistan. He embarked on the March visit immediately after giving evidence at the Chilcot inquiry in which he delivered a strong defence of his military spending record. He was, however, later forced to make an embarrassing correction to his evidence.

As well as requiring more of the Government, the growing political awareness and appreciation of defence also prompted the politicians to look more closely at how the Ministry of Defence conducted itself. The Defence Select Committee and the National Audit Office produced damning reports on its procurement record, with billions of pounds wasted on delayed projects.

Under Bob Ainsworth, Labour's final Defence Secretary, the MoD published a Green Paper that set the scene for a long-overdue Strategic Defence Review, although it was left to the Lib-Con coalition to implement. The failure to conduct a review sooner – the last one was in 1998, before the world-changing terrorist attack on September 11, 2001 and the wars in Iraq and Afghanistan – was regarded as another legacy of Labour's inability to understand the military and, arguably, a failure of commanders to push for it. As a result, many of the long-term programmes to which the MoD was committed, such as two new aircraft carriers, planes to fly off them, and scores of additional fast-jets, were seen as out-dated and no longer suited to equip Britain for the wars of the future with only limited resources available.

Separately, a realisation of cash shortages in MoD coffers to look after wounded personnel and veterans prompted the creation of a number of new military charities on top of the established organisations to raise extra money for serving and former members of the Armed Forces. They moved quickly to capitalise on the sudden, public appreciation of the military, with *The Sun* newspaper backing a charity called "Help for Heroes" that ran a hugely successful campaign selling blue and red wrist bands as well as a host of other money-raising events that further boosted the profile of the military.

Joanna Lumley added an unlikely dimension to the relationship between MPs and the military when she fronted a bid to secure Gurkha veterans with at least four years' service in the British Army the right to re-settle in Britain.

It was not just the Armed Forces that were in focus. *The Times* ran a campaign in 2007 to urge the Government to help hundreds of Iraqi interpreters who were facing death at the hands of militiamen in Iraq because of their association with the British military. In response, Mr Brown created a scheme to relocate the interpreters and their families in Britain or give them a cash payment.

Another unfortunate legacy was a growing pile of lawsuits against the Ministry of Defence ranging from allegations of torture and abuse by Iraqi detainees to claims of negligence by the families of soldiers who died in Snatch Land Rovers. This costly process will take a long time to resolve.

The increased awareness of the military among the public and politicians during the last Parliament failed to translate into a heightened interest in the general election. Military insiders had hoped that a debate would take place about what sort of country Britain aspires to be: does the nation want to maintain its costly but influential place on the top table as a nuclear power alongside the United States or is it happy to downgrade to a less-significant player?

This fundamental question was left to be answered in the Strategic Defence Review. Aligned to this will be the extent of expected cuts in the defence budget, which will affect the scope of future operations, from the size of the Armed Forces to the weapons at their disposal. Unlike the first half of the previous century, the number of MPs with military experience remained low, although the new Parliament has the highest tally in at least the past two decades – 19 Conservative MPs and one from Labour, according to Byron Criddle, of the University of Aberdeen. Despite a shortage of hands-on experience, MPs look set to retain their re-kindled appreciation of the military, at least for as long as British troops are deployed in Afghanistan.

Armed Forces Day, created by Mr Brown in June 2007, created an annual programme of events to celebrate all three services nationwide. The real test of Britain's relationship with its military, however, will occur in the decades ahead.

Hail and a fond farewell to the dearly departed

Ann Treneman
Sketch writer

So farewell, then, Manure Parliament. A solemn wave to those who are gone but not, as yet, forgotten. All in all, 147 MPs stood down before the election, some with honour and others not, exhausted, disillusioned, angry and shamed. On the night, many more joined them. Surely it is symbolic that, on a night when the overall swing to the Conservatives was 5 per cent, Mr Manure himself, David Heathcote-Amory, lost his seat in Wells, Somerset. Mr Manure, who had to pay back almost £30,000 in exes and submitted bills for dozens of sacks of manure for his garden, said: "Expenses damaged all incumbents and perhaps me particularly." I especially like that "perhaps".

His was not the only whiffy result. Many were surprised that Jacqui Smith, the first woman home secretary, stood for re-election in Redditch. Ms Smith, notorious for her claim for two porn videos for her husband, not to mention 88p for a bathplug, had fought a bizarre, almost guerrilla, campaign in which she did her best to avoid the press. Her best-known booster was Tony Blair, who popped in for tea one day. I am not sure if that helped or hindered: she lost with a 9.21 per cent swing to the Tories. She can now spend more time with her (second) home.

It was a bad night for former home secretaries. Charles Clarke lost his Norwich South seat by 310 votes to the Lib Dems. I shall miss Mr Clarke, a big beast of the Westminster village in every way, who fought a long and wonderfully personal campaign against Gordon Brown as Prime Minister. How sad for him that, in the end, he went before Gordo. Another Labour defeat was the minister Jim Knight, more talented than most, in the marginal Dorset South. I was not surprised to see that he was promptly made a peer.

I find it hard to imagine politics without Lembit Öpik, the celebrity-crazed Lib Dem just as well known for dating a Cheeky Girl whose big hit was called *The Cheeky Song (Touch My Bum)* and for believing that Earth could be destroyed by a meteorite. In the end, his career was wrecked by something much more mundane: a 13 per cent swing to the Tories. Hours after losing, Lembit popped up on the TV quiz show *Have I Got News for You* urging his fellow contestants to hurry up: "Can we get on with it? I've actually got an appointment at the JobCentre in about half an hour." Paul Merton responded: "They phoned earlier, they cancelled." Lembit loved this. He is a glutton for publicity.

Another shocker was Peter Robinson, Northern Ireland's First Minister and DUP leader, who lost his East Belfast seat. His defeat came after damaging revelations about himself and his wife, Iris, nicknamed the Swish Family Robinson after reports that they claimed more than £500,000 a year in salary and expenses. Iris, who always used to do a fine line in morality when she spoke in the Commons, had already stood down after it became known that she had obtained £50,000 for her teenage lover to fund his business. It is a sad tale but not without its moral.

In the pantheon of retiring MPs, I must make special mention of Sir Nicholas Winterton, Tory MP for Macclesfield since 1971. He and his wife, Ann, were known as Mr and Mrs Expenses. Sir Nicholas was wildly opinionated, red-faced and rambunctious (last year he slapped the bottom of the Labour MP Natasha Engel in the Commons tea room). But his retirement cannot pass without remembering his supremely ill-judged remarks about why he needed to travel first class: "If I was in standard class, I would not do work because people would be looking over your shoulder the entire time, there would be noise, there would be distraction. They are a totally different type of people: they have a different outlook on life. They may be reading a book but I doubt whether they are undertaking serious work or study."

So goodbye, Sir Nicholas, see you in economy. I will actually miss the rather gentle manner of Sir Peter Viggers, an MP for 36 years, who is now spending more time with his ducks, who never even liked their cute little house. Andrew MacKay, who with his wife, Julie Kirkbride, was another Mr and Mrs Expenses, was amazingly orange. His seat in the Commons, on the aisle, first bench back, will always have a tangerine hue for me. John Gummer, who seems to have been around for ever, is gone but not forgotten after his expenses got tangled up with his attempt to get rid of his moles. And then there is Mr Moat (aka Douglas Hogg), whose final act was to give an interview clarifying that he had not claimed for the moat per se and noting that, anyway, it wasn't a moat at all but a "broad dyke". Does that make it worse? After all, there is a certain majesty in a moat.

On Labour's side, in addition to the expenses villains, there are the lobbyists, not to mention the plotters. Stephen Byers, who once described himself as a cab for hire, is now out in the big bad world, his light on. I will never have to hear the patronising undulations of Patricia "Patsy" Hewitt's voice again. Geoff "Buff" Hoon, the man who specialised in never being there when it came to Iraq, now really won't be there. Despite it all I rather liked his plodding pedestrian ways. Other "hall of shame" retirees include Kitty Ussher, a once rising star, who wrote a two-page letter explaining why her London house needed major repairs: "Most of the ceilings have Artex coverings. Three-dimensional swirls. It could be a matter of taste, but this counts as 'dilapidations' in my book!" And Kitty, let us remember, was a member of the People's Party.

So where is the good in the good, the bad and the

ON THE BRIGHT SIDE, HORSE MANURE IS VERY GOOD FOR GREEN SHOOTS!

ST. STEPHEN'S ENTRANCE

ugly? Almost everybody else, actually. Of particular note is James Purnell, facial hair fashionista, whose sideburns will be missed by me. His shock resignation from the Cabinet almost brought down Gordon Brown. Mr Purnell was the brave one. It could have all been so different if he had succeeded.

For us sketch writers, John Prescott is simply irreplaceable: but he lives on, in the Twitter-sphere, boldly going where no one would have predicted he would. I will miss the bolshie proclamations of Labour's Andrew Mackinlay and the snide if somewhat forlorn comments of Chris Mullin, who proved to be a better diarist than politician. Others of note to go include Labour's Bob Marshall-Andrews, a man more or less permanently in opposition to his own side. In September 1997, commenting on an opinion poll that gave Tony Blair a 93 per cent approval rating, he said: "Seven per cent. We can build on that."

Others to be missed include

• Tony Wright, the much respected Labour MP who coined the phrase "Manure Parliament". He headed the eponymous committee on parliamentary reforms with tenacity and, dare I say it, wisdom.
• The Rev Ian Paisley, ancient Galapagos tortoise, who always spoke as if he was sermonising, possibly because he was.
• Michael Howard and Ann Widdecombe, linked forever by her "something of the night" comment about him. He was always worth watching, an astute and clever parliamentarian, and she was the only true reality TV star in the Commons: "I always imagined that when I was making my last speech, I would be sad. Instead I find that my uppermost sentiment is one of profound relief."
• David Howarth, a thoughtful Liberal Democrat, who returns to teach law at Cambridge. "People talk about

standing down. I am standing up!" he told me. He is gloomy about politics, saying that it is no longer a "high trust" profession. Like estate agents, MPs now must always be watched like hawks. Inevitably, he said, the result will be that it attracts less trustworthy people.
• Martin Salter, the Labour MP for Reading West, was larger than life and louder than it too. Before he left, I found him in his chaotic office brandishing a "stress banana", a gift. "I use my banana for pointing," he chortled. "People say, 'Don't Miliband me!'" His office was plastered with pictures of fish. "I am leaving politics to spend more time with my wife, my camper van and my fish, in that order."

Last but not least in any way is Sir Patrick Cormack, the Tory grandee who bowed out after 40 years. He was a bit of an old buffer but no one doubts that he loves Parliament (which he pronounced "Parl-i-ament", with a little wiggle). When I stopped by to see him in his magnificent office, which he was emptying out, there was palpable regret in his voice as he talked of his career ups and downs. He had wanted to be Speaker but, when he stood, received only 13 votes. "You take the rough with the rough!" he noted, his pug face crinkling. "Absolutely!"

So, at 71, he left to spend more time with his weekends. "It will be a terrible wrench. It has been my life for more than half my life. It is a very funny feeling at the moment: it is the last of this, the last of that. I am still behaving as normal but all the time I am sort of signing off." It is hard to imagine the chamber without Sir Patrick. For 40 years, whenever "Parl-i-ament" was sitting, he spent at least three hours a day seated in his place, the middle aisle seat towards the back. In his last speech, he ended with these words of Catullus: "Ave atque vale". Hail and farewell, indeed.
Ann Treneman is the author of Annus Horribilis: the Worst Year in British Politics *(2009)*

The tragedy of Gordon Brown

David Aaronovitch
Times columnist

It was the longest understudy, for one of the shortest performances. A decade of increasingly unquiet waiting for his moment to take over from Tony Blair was followed by just under three years in the long-coveted post. Departing No 10, Gordon Brown left behind a reputation for grumpiness, intellectual brilliance, ambition and, in the end, enduring personal tragedy.

The grey, jowly, plodding figure who left office was scarcely recognisable as the brilliant, Heathcliffian man who entered the Treasury in 1997. In opposition, Mr Brown had shredded his opponents with thunder and wit, which turned to lightning and cleverness early in new Labour's first term. In the first week of that term he announced the independence of the Bank of England, a reform that was to become accepted by his political rivals, but which was not even put to the Cabinet.

His most deployed political term in the first two years of the Labour Government was the legendary "prudence", who was invariably accompanied by "with a purpose". He knew exactly what he was doing; he was the great intellectual of modern politics. His supporters told anyone who would listen that he was the real brains behind new Labour. He was literally unassailable.

When writers use terms such as "paradox", "enigma" and "contradiction" it is often a sign that they simply do not understand the subject. Gordon Brown has had these words applied to him more often than any other modern British politician. It has been hard, throughout his career in government, to explain how his different characteristics coexisted within the same person.

Mr Brown was, famously, the "son of the manse" – a man built upon the bedrock of religious and social principles as bequeathed to him by his minister father. "Understand this about him," I was told more than once by Scots, "and you understand everything." And when he repeatedly used the word "values", like a mallet on a wooden tent-peg and pronounced with an almost unending first vowel, it sounded convincing and deeply meant.

In his international campaigns to reduce Third World debt and to increase aid to Africa, both hugely successful, it was easy to see high moral principle at work, although such goods are indeed oft interred with the politician's bones. These were real and important achievements, but ones unlikely to be appreciated by most journalists, let alone most voters.

It could also be that in 30 years the first historians of the 2000s will single out Gordon Brown's leadership during the banking crisis of 2008-09 as having been central to saving the world from a second full-scale Great Depression. For a year a formerly depressed Prime Minister was transformed into a man full of hectic energy and knowledgeable determination.

But then there was the thin-skinned, jealous, tricksy and occasionally even treacherous Brown, who seemed to stand at 90 degrees to the morals of the manse. This was the Chancellor who would cook the figures to make them more palatable and to suggest that he was being more generous than in fact he was; the colleague who allowed his closest advisers to run around Westminster bad-mouthing anyone who was considered to be an opponent; the Cabinet member who tried to keep his budgets secret from his own Prime Minister; the co-founder of new Labour who, for half a decade, connived secretly at the replacement of his one-time friend.

When, in the late Nineties, the first reports began to be written about rival camps forming around Tony Blair and Gordon Brown, some of us dismissed them as overblown – the product of junior aides shooting their mouths off and hacks anxious for a story. It seemed intrinsically unlikely that men who had been so disciplined and thoughtful in their pursuit of government should be so adolescent in their relationships with each other. I could not have been more wrong and gradually it became clear that this was not a matter of six of one and half a dozen of the other, but of a jealousy and resentment felt by Mr Brown towards Mr Blair.

So Gordon Brown became the man who opposed Tony Blair's attempts at public service reform when the latter was in office, and then embraced the same reforms once he had been pushed out.

And then, when in the post he had wanted so long, elected from a field of one, the politician who had moved decisively in 1997 on the question of the Bank of England, havered disastrously when, for a moment almost exactly ten years later, he might have won a general election in his own right.

In the televised debates in the 2010 campaign the former romantic lead came over as a rather querulous and awkward pensioner, barely restraining his innate grumpiness. Perhaps most ruinous to his long-term reputation, though, was the perception, widely shared and cleverly exploited by political opponents, that the economic crisis was somehow his fault, almost alone. The accusation was that Britain was particularly disadvantaged in responding to the crisis because of his earlier profligacy, saddling the nation with a mountain of public debt. When the Cameron-Clegg coalition began its governance of the country its main theme was blaming Mr Brown and his high-spending ways for any unpopular decision that it was about to make.

It might also be that Mr Brown is the last British leader in the modern era to be nothing like a television or film celebrity. His predecessor and his successor both possessed an easy public charm and a capacity to share their private existences in some way with the public and the media. Mr Brown palpably loathed this aspect of 21st-century politics, taking care to minimise the significant disability represented by his damaged eyesight, to play down the trauma of the loss of his first child in 2002, and to guard the privacy of his two young sons who, for one moment only, shared his last public appearance outside 10 Downing Street.

Gordon Brown was a substantial politician, a man of substantial achievement and significant faults, probably in the end too cautious, too thin-skinned and too cussedly human to be a great leader.

New Labour found its reforming stride too late

Phil Collins
Leader writer

The obituaries of the new Labour period in office are already being written, even though its time has only just passed. Politics always requires that you tell a clear story about what you are doing. In truth, in the maelstrom of internal conflict and external pressure, policy formation is often driven by scandal and panic as much as it is by principle and forethought. Much of the policy work the Labour Party did in opposition turned out to be inoperable. Policies enacted spawned unintended consequences. Then events occur that come to define the period in office that were never part of the original prospectus.

All that said, it still makes sense to divide the Labour period in office into three parts, broadly corresponding to changes in approach. The first period lasted from the golden glow of May 1997 until the winter crisis in the National Health Service in 2000. The failure of extra money alone to improve the service prompted the second, most fruitful, period of government between 2001 and the departure of Tony Blair from office in the summer of 2007. The premiership of Gordon Brown then marks a third phase in the Government, in which the pace of the second was slowed.

When the Blair Government was elected in May 1997 it came to office with a long history of policy development behind it. In office, though, it exhausted that preparatory work quite quickly. The granting of independence to the Bank of England was the most conspicuous policy, but really stood alone. There were three themes during this period in government. The governing idea of the administration was supplied by Mr Brown: the idea of work. The New Deal for the long-term unemployed, funded by a levy on the privatised utilities, and the introduction of tax credits to supplement the wages of those in work, heralded, it was said, a return to the idea that work was the best form of welfare.

The second notable theme of the first period was constitutional reform, although the half-hearted and incomplete programme indicated ambiguity on the part of senior personnel, not least the Prime Minister himself. Still, the devolved assemblies for Scotland and Wales are now a part of the political landscape accepted by all parties and the argument about the House of Lords is how to finish off Labour's near-abolition of the hereditary principle, rather than how to reverse it.

In the public services, the Government's strategy, which was essentially command and control from the central State, was well-equipped to deal with deep failure. There had been, for example, no progress on literacy for almost half a century. Placing a team in the department to force through curriculum change was an old-fashioned, and for a time very effective, use of state power. Hundreds of Public Service Agreements were set. The regimes of inspection and audit were toughened and the publication of information about services became commonplace.

The time ran out on this approach when the Chancellor of the Exchequer released the grip he had hitherto held on spending. The Government had come to office determined to shed Labour's historical association with profligacy. Mr Brown had, for that reason, submitted to the spending plans he had inherited from his Conservative predecessor. The paradox of releasing that restraint, though, was that it called forth the need for reform.

The standard Labour analysis, throughout the Thatcher and Major years, had been that there was not a great deal wrong with the public services that a lot of money could not put right. To some extent, that was true. Teachers, nurses, doctors and police officers had all fallen behind in the pay scales, relative to their professional counterparts in the private sector. Schools and hospitals were in a dilapidated state and the system was rationing provision in the only way it could – by queues. It was obvious that extra money was going to be part of the answer. That it was not the whole answer became clear when the money started to pour. The Prime Minister, late in 2000, realised that the analysis he had inherited from opposition was wrong. He realised too that the provision of extra money was a necessary accompaniment to the difficult reforms that, it was now clear, were needed.

The second phase of Labour government was dominated, in the coverage at the time and by the accounts of it since, by foreign policy. The terrorist atrocity on September 11, 2001 confirmed in the mind of the Prime Minister something that he had defined in a speech in Chicago in 1999: that terrorist threats could no longer be contained within national borders and that, therefore, the definition of what was in Britain's interest had to be hugely expanded. The attacks on Afghanistan and Iraq were the immediate consequences of the Chicago doctrine, applied to the terrorist attacks.

The last word will probably never be said on these decisions but it is not true that foreign policy meant that the Government's domestic momentum was lost. On the contrary, it started to speed up. Changes to the healthcare system began in earnest. The internal market bequeathed by the Conservatives, which Frank Dobson had torn up, was remade. A tariff was introduced to apply to procedures to change the incentives in the system. Private companies were encouraged to offer their services and patients were given a choice of which hospital to go to.

In education, the gradual demise of what Alastair Campbell famously called the "bog-standard" comprehensive began. City Academies, free from local authority control and aided by bequests from philanthropists, made the schools system more diverse. Again, the ideas inherited from the Major Government, which had been vanquished in the first term, were revived. Much to the chagrin of the Labour Party, which contains more than its fair share of defenders of municipal accountability, a new model school was established: independent and not wholly funded by the State. The dispute between the Labour leadership and the Labour Party reached a head over the 2005 Act, which sought to establish a new cadre of independent state schools. After a bruising battle, a very much diluted Act passed into statute, to no great effect.

Over time, a model of public service reform had developed that came to define the Government at its most radical. Pressure on the provider of the service came from three sources: from the users who could choose to go elsewhere; from the central State, which set targets for performance and ensured that services were audited and inspected; and from the threat that any failing institution would be subject to losing its franchise in competition with a private company.

The practice always fell some way short of the theory, not least because few Labour MPs could be assembled to agree with it. A more comfortable phase began when Mr Blair left office and was replaced by Mr Brown. Although, ostensibly, there was no serious change of direction, the Government slowed everything down. The reforms in health were slowed almost to a standstill. Education policy was almost entirely derailed by a crisis in child protection with the aftermath of the dreadful case of Baby P, a boy battered to death at the hands of his mother, her boyfriend and their lodger despite repeated visits by social workers. Only in welfare did the radicalism of the second phase continue as James Purnell tried to add greater conditions to the receipt of benefits and tried to widen the range of suppliers of welfare.

In a sense, the third phase of the Government brought it full circle. The emphasis during the Brown years on a multitude of small initiatives driven by central targets, now rebranded as guarantees, and the evident reluctance of the Government to open up the health and education markets were reminiscent of the Government's stuttering beginnings.

Of course, just as the Blair years will not be remembered for the travails of domestic policy, so the Brown years will be recalled as the moment that the banking system almost collapsed. The banking rescue, the small discretionary fiscal stimulus and the recession were events of great economic magnitude on which the Government chose, unsuccessfully as it turned out, to fight the general election.

By the time of that general election the ideas that had sustained the Labour Party through more than a decade of government were widely felt to have been emptied of content. And yet this was only a half truth. In the Conservative policy on free schools, for example, there were glimpses of where second-phase Labour was trying to get to. The social liberalism of the coalition Government owed something to Mr Cameron's desire to change his party, something to Nick Clegg and the Liberal Democrats, but rather more to the example of the Labour governments.

Phil Collins is a former speechwriter for Tony Blair

'This sucker's going down': diary of a financial crisis

Suzy Jagger
Politics & Business
Correspondent

For the man who told a reporter three years ago that he had no idea whether the US was heading into recession because he got a B in basic economics, President Bush showed astonishing prescience on the future of the world financial system. As Lehman Brothers collapsed in September 2008, almost dragging the global banking system down with it, the President declared: "This sucker's going down."

While Britain's "sucker" of a financial sector started to go down before its American rival, it was a US fiscal malaise that triggered the fall. Throughout the summer of 2007 banks who had lent extensively to borrowers on low incomes with bad credit histories began to warn publicly that in many cases they would not get their money back. HSBC, the owner of a US lender called Household International, startled the City and Wall Street in May of that year when it wrote off $5 billion of bad US debts. As the summer dragged on, more banks admitted that mortgage borrowers were defaulting on their repayments and that they would have to write the bad debts off. Banks started to become wary about lending to each other and by the end of the summer the wholesale lending market, where banks lend billions to each other for short periods, had dried up.

It was the crisis in this market that triggered the collapse of Northern Rock, sparking the first run on a British bank for more than a century. Its business model, devised by Adam Applegarth, its chief executive, had two main consequences. By choosing the wholesale lending market to fund Northern Rock's mortgage book, rather than backing it with savers' deposits, the former mutual was able to grow its business quickly and become Britain's fifth biggest provider of home loans. It also meant that when the wholesale lending market ground to a halt, Northern Rock was the most heavily exposed.

The public began to develop a new financial vocabulary. The word "liquidity" crept into headlines, television news alerts and ordinary conversations. It seemed, almost overnight, that everyone had become familiar with the term "sub-prime loan", even if they were not entirely sure what it meant. (It means a loan to a low-income borrower with a poor credit score.)

Central banks started to pump cheap money into the financial system to get capital markets moving again but it failed to stem the rot. If the British public had become nervous about the state of the banking sector, their anxieties took a turn for the worse on September 13, 2007. At about 10pm, the news ticker along the bottom of the BBC news screen reported that Northern Rock had gone to the Bank of England to beg for emergency funds. Once news of the approach leaked out, the bank was effectively dead. The next day, a Friday, the shares lost 32 per cent of their value. Savers, who formed long queues outside branches, withdrew £1 billion that day.

Bankers from other institutions rushed to reassure shareholders that they did not need Bank of England funds. It emerged rapidly that Northern Rock could not survive without being acquired by a rival but none volunteered, put off by a £2.7 billion refinancing bill, its shonky mortgage book and limited branch network.

The infection spread to other parts of the financial markets, such as bond insurers. Citigroup, then the biggest bank in the world, started to dump losses. Merrill Lynch admitted at the end of October to $7.9 billion of bad debts. Between December and March, central banks across the world started slashing interest rates in the hope that cheap money would cushion the strain. Brussels set up a $500 billion facility just to tide banks over the Christmas period.

In January 2008 major stock markets, including London, suffered their worst one-day fall since 9/11, prompting the US Federal Reserve to reduce the cost of borrowing in the biggest cut for 25 years. Alistair Darling, the Chancellor, announced the following month that Northern Rock was to be nationalised.

It took one month for the next major bank to break. Bear Stearns, the weakest of the five Wall Street banks, was acquired by its bigger rival JP Morgan Chase in a deal worth $240 million, having been valued at $18 billion the year before. The manner in which the acquisition was handled dictated the rescue terms of every other terminally fractured US bank over the next 18 months. Four men masterminded every subsequent US bank rescue deal: Henry Paulson, the former US Treasury Secretary; Ben Bernanke, the chairman of the Federal Reserve Board; Christopher Cox, the former head of the Securities and Exchange Commission; and Tim Geithner, then president of the New York Federal Reserve Bank, latterly President Obama's Treasury Secretary.

While hedge funds were allowed to snap like twigs under the financial strain, no US bank, large or small, was allowed to go bust on a weekday. The rescue talks often began in earnest on a Friday evening when world stock markets were shut. Mr Paulson was worried that if private rescue talks were leaked during the trading week, it could trigger wild swings in the stock market. The public statement declaring a troubled bank's new buyer or winding down arrangement would typically be made by early evening on a Sunday in the US, just before Tokyo opened for Monday morning business and 13 hours before New York. On the other side of the Atlantic, RBS, UBS, the Swiss bank, and Barclays begged existing investors to pay £27.2 billion of new money between them to repair their damaged balance sheets. A number of banks also sold stakes in themselves on the cheap to cash-rich foreign states such as Qatar. But existing small UK shareholders were reluctant to increase their holdings at all as they watched the value of their own homes fall for the first time in 12 years.

Two months later, in July 2008, HBOS, then Britain's biggest mortgage lender, tried to raise £4 billion from its own shareholders. It was a disaster. Only 8 per cent of investors agreed to buy more stock. Within days, the Chancellor warned Britain that it faced its worst economic crisis for 60 years and that the recession would last far longer than most had feared. Within a week, the world economy was plunged into the worst financial storm since the Wall Street crash of 1929.

The pace of the crisis accelerated to such an extent that almost each day delivered a new horror. On September 7, the mortgage lenders Fannie Mae and Freddie Mac, which accounted for almost half of all America's home loans, were bailed out by Washington in one of the biggest financial rescues in history. The US taxpayer was faced with guaranteeing $5 trillion of outstanding loans. Three days later, Lehman Brothers admitted that it had lost $3.9 billion in 12 weeks. Rumours spread across Wall Street and the City that Dick Fuld, the head of Lehman, had not been able to find a rescue buyer.

On September 12, 2008, office workers descending into Wall Street's subway on their way home may have noticed the stream of limousines pulling up around the corner. Like hearses, they delivered 30 of the world's most powerful financiers to the office of the Federal Reserve. Between them, the men controlled the world's banking system and they had been summoned by Mr Paulson to be told that Lehman was bust. He said that the US taxpayer was not going to bail it out and warned them that, if they failed to rescue Lehman or carve it up, they would all be caught up in the havoc. Those who attended included Lloyd Blankfein, chief executive of Goldman Sachs, and John Thain, his opposite number at Merrill Lynch. Mr Fuld was not invited.

By 3pm on Sunday, the rescue talks were off. Barclays had wanted to do a deal but was blocked by Britain, which demanded that the US Government should sweeten any deal with American money. With the collapse of Lehman now inevitable, employees of the bank in Canary Wharf and Manhattan were summoned back to their desks to calculate the bank's colossal exposure and prepare for bankruptcy.

Mr Thain realised that his bank would be the next casualty. As Lehman employees packed up their belongings, Mr Thain was secretly signing a deal to sell Merrill to Bank of America for $44 billion. He even made sure that $4 billion of bonus payments for himself and Merrill staff were accelerated before the agreement was signed.

Six weeks before US presidential elections, Mr Paulson was adamant that the American taxpayer would not be called upon to bail out Lehman. Just before midnight, Mr Fuld announced that the bank was bust. During the course of one day, half of Wall Street had either been taken over or been declared bankrupt.

A far bigger, immediate financial crisis loomed. AIG, the world's biggest insurer, was on the brink of collapse. Washington could not let AIG fail because it would have triggered a terrifying financial unravelling across the world. AIG, founded in Shanghai, owned substantial businesses. Most importantly, a huge financial markets business, with big operations selling products called credit default swaps, effectively writing insurance policies against other companies' bankruptcies. In September 2008, it controlled assets worth $1 trillion. By the end of Monday, Washington had bailed AIG out with $85 billion and taken control of a 79.9 per cent stake.

In London, Sir Victor Blank, venerable chairman of Lloyds TSB, was signing a deal to bail out HBOS. After a run on HBOS shares, the British Government agreed to waive all competition rules and allow Lloyds to buy the bank, grabbing a third of the UK mortgage and savings market in one go. The deal went through but the strain of assuming HBOS's bad debts on the healthier Lloyds became unsustainable. The transaction bought HBOS only a month before it needed to be bailed out.

The US Treasury Secretary became convinced that the whole banking system was vulnerable and came up with a plan three days later to rescue everybody. He proposed setting up a bailout fund into which $700 billion of taxpayer money would be pumped to buy lenders' bad debts so the banks would start trusting each other again and start lending. Despite all-night talks during which politicians were ordered to leave their BlackBerries outside and Mr Paulson went down on one knee to beg Nancy Pelosi, the leader of the House of Representatives, to be sympathetic, it failed. On September 29, Congress blocked the creation of the fund and the markets slumped.

Mr Paulson's counterparts on the other side of the Atlantic were also having a bad day. Having sought to secure HBOS days before, the Chancellor was forced to announce that Bradford & Bingley was to be nationalised and made the British taxpayer take control of £50 billion of its mortgages. To make matters worse, Iceland, whose own financial system was intertwined with the fate of British investors, started to collapse.

Desperate to create a fund that would help to restore some confidence in the US financial system, Mr Paulson endured new talks to persuade Washington to agree to the $700 billion rescue plan. On October 3 on the White House lawn, Mr Paulson announced his deal.

On the morning of October 7 in London a bloodbath broke out in the markets. A Treasury official phoned Mr Darling, who was in Europe at a meeting of finance ministers, to say that RBS stock was down 40 per cent, pulling the rest of the banking sector with it. A team led by the Prime Minister's trusted aide Baroness Vadera rapidly drew up a three-point plan to provide liquidity, guaranteed funding and capital injections. They agreed a new £50,000 threshold to guarantee retail deposits. They pulled together a rescue package of £50 billion for the banking system, supplemented by another £200 billion of support. By the end of the day, five central banks including the Bank of England had cut interest rates by half a percentage point.

Had observers been in any doubt about the purpose of releasing a wall of money on the British banking system, it would have become clear to them on the morning of October 13. The Government announced that it had pumped £37 billion into RBS, Lloyds and its new business, HBOS, to prevent the three lenders collapsing and part-nationalised them.

In the months that followed Wall Street and the City proved that they had emerged from the storm. The credit crisis began to spread to other industries, such as the automotive sector. But Westminster and Washington began the process of devising long-term assistance schemes and drawing up new regulatory regimes.

Within 18 months of the height of the banking crisis, Mr Paulson and Mr Darling had both been voted out of office. In neither case because they were seen to have personally failed to deal with the worst financial crisis for almost a century, but because politically both countries had moved on. Mr Paulson's battered mobile Motorola phone, which was used to negotiate every bail-out, is now an artefact in the Smithsonian Institute. Observers may hope that the banking crisis is contained, if not consigned, to history.

Suzy Jagger covered the American sub-prime crisis as US Business Correspondent until February 2009.

SNP pioneers of minority rule

Angus Macleod
Scottish Political Editor

Within the 2005 general election there lay a warning for Labour north of the Border that went largely unheeded. The party in Scotland, as everywhere else in Britain, had benefited for years from the Tony Blair "Big Tent" approach to building support across voter categories and divides. Yet, as opposition to the Iraq War lingered, that essential coalition of interests showed signs of breaking up in Scotland. Suddenly, middle-class Scottish voters who had supported the party since the mid-90s were increasingly exasperated and bitter. While its Scottish working-class heartlands stayed loyal, less committed Labour voters turned to the anti-war Liberal Democrats and SNP, to voice their dissent. Urban seats in Glasgow, Edinburgh, Aberdeen and throughout Scotland's central belt, while still returning Labour MPs, had become highly marginal.

If there was disillusion with Labour at UK level, the same was true at the Scottish Parliament. Devolution had recovered from early traumas over MSPs' expenses and controversy over the £400 million cost of the new Holyrood building, but it had not delivered the step change in public services that the Scots imagined it would. The Labour-led Scottish Executive had delivered groundbreaking policies, such as a ban on smoking in public places and free personal care for the elderly, but it was widely perceived to have governed looking over its shoulder for approval from London. For the Scots, devolution had not been Scottish enough.

The SNP, once more under the shrewd leadership of Alex Salmond, who returned to the post in 2004, was also recovering from a series of average election performances but Mr Salmond saw that the 2007 Scottish Parliament election would provide his party with its biggest chance yet to win power.

He saw that his party representing the Scottish interest and with no obligation to a wider party at UK level left him a golden opportunity. He set about professionalising the party machine, amassing an unprecedented £1 million election war chest from sympathetic business donors and presenting a set of policies that played into Scottish anxieties about escalating council tax bills, the NHS and education priorities.

Labour was flat-footed, perhaps believing that an SNP victory would never happen. In the months leading up to the 2007 election, it was obvious that only one party had momentum and it was not Labour. Anxieties about the SNP's core aim of independence were put to one side because voters knew that the break-up of Britain could not happen without a referendum. Labour's campaign was confused; the SNP's, with promises to abolish the council tax, cut class sizes and restore hospital A&E units, was exciting for many of those "soft" Labour voters who had deserted Labour in 2005 and were ready to do so again. To Labour's dismay and disbelief, the SNP emerged as the largest party. When their promise of an independence referendum proved an insuperable roadblock to forming a majority coalition with the Lib Dems, Mr Salmond opted for minority government, daring Labour and the other unionist parties to bring him down. His calculation proved prescient especially as his honeymoon in government turned out to be no nine-day wonder. He and his minority government set about delivering on manifesto promises that did not need legislation. Through delicate and skilful manoeuvring, he was able to attract enough support from at least one opposition party to get his annual budgets through Parliament.

Labour was dumbstruck. Unable to react, it became embroiled in an internal row over the leadership campaign expenses of Wendy Alexander, who succeeded Jack McConnell as Scottish leader. She resigned and was followed by Iain Gray, whose dogged but lifeless leadership meant that Mr Salmond, as First Minister, was able to retain his position as the major personality of devolved politics. As Labour's problems grew at Westminster under Gordon Brown, poll after poll showed that the SNP was, if anything, consolidating its position in Scotland.

The gloss was bound to come off the nationalists at some point. From mid-2009 it did. Their very status as a minority administration meant that a whole series of probably over-the-top manifesto priorities, such as cutting class sizes and abolishing student debt, had to be ditched. The SNP had delivered a council tax freeze, but the next step of abolishing the tax altogether and replacing it with a local income tax was also put on hold, simply because the nationalists did not have the parliamentary votes.

Labour, in the meantime, entered into an opposition coalition with the Lib Dems and the Conservatives over constitutional powers looked at by the Calman Commission, which recommended a tranche of new tax-raising and other powers for Holyrood. Calman was a direct riposte by the unionist parties to the SNP's independence agenda, although some unionists saw it as yet another concession to the nationalists. The SNP, for its part, was busy redefining what it meant by independence, talking loudly and often of a "social union" with the rest of the UK that would give Scotland full fiscal independence but with shared defence and diplomatic interests and retaining the Queen as head of state. It was dubbed independence-lite. It was also a recognition by the SNP that Scotland, for all the SNP spin about the "London" parties, remained firmly unionist while wanting their devolved Parliament to acquire more profile through greater autonomy from Westminster.

The 2010 election allowed Labour to present itself as more in tune than the SNP with Scots' wishes on the constitution while exploiting to the full Scots voters' fears about a Conservative government returning to the worst days of Thatcherism. Many found the latter tactic somewhat childish and disreputable, but there is no doubt that it worked. The key trend in the general election results of 2010 was that voters throughout Scotland voted for the party in their constituency most likely to keep the Tories out. Labour was the main beneficiary, returning 41 MPs, while the Lib Dems retained 11, the SNP repeated their 2005 performance with 6 MPs and the Tories returned a paltry 1, showing that whatever else, David Cameron was still regarded with suspicion north of the Border. But Labour, for the first time since devolution, found itself in opposition on both sides of the Border.

Northern Ireland comes back from the brink

David Sharrock
Ireland Correspondent

It was the parliamentary term in which the Northern Ireland peace process was finally completed, a time of extraordinary events that few could have imagined even five years earlier. The defining image must be that of the Rev Ian Paisley, the old warhorse of No Surrender Unionism, and Martin McGuinness, the former "Public Enemy No 1" in his role as Provisional IRA commander, laughing uproariously together in the company of Tony Blair, the Prime Minister, and his Irish counterpart, Bertie Ahern. And yet there should be no surprise that, this being Northern Ireland, the conclusion of the peace process does not mean the end of the Troubles nor the threat from violent Irish republicanism to the security of the State. A page was turned in the history of Britain's involvement with Ireland but the story was left far from over.

The backdrop was the usurpation of the Ulster Unionist Party, since the founding of the Northern Ireland state its "ruling party", by its rivals the Democratic Unionists in the 2005 general election. As disaffection with the outworking of the 1998 Good Friday Agreement and the dysfunctional power-sharing Executive led by David Trimble, the First Minister, reached new heights among Unionists, a sea change in voting patterns swept away the *ancien régime*, rewarding the DUP with nine Westminster seats and reducing the UUP to just one, North Down, held by Sylvia Hermon.

Mr Paisley's party promised an end to "pushover Unionism" and the experiment of sharing power with Sinn Féin, the political wing of the Provisional IRA. Yet even before the 2005 anointment of the DUP as the new voice of Northern Ireland's majority community, there were sufficient straws in the wind for Mr Blair's advisers to form the view that the real endgame in Ulster was to bring together the political extremes, abandoning the centre ground shared by the UUP and the SDLP, to create a new political status quo.

Indeed, Mr Blair's delayed departure from No 10 had much to do with the Prime Minister's determination to see his project reaching some definable goal, nearly a decade after the euphoria of the Good Friday Agreement. He courted Mr Paisley assiduously with a near-perfect reading of the psychology of Ulster's "Dr No". By now in his 80s and with a terrifying brush with mortality a recent memory, Mr Paisley was conscious that his political career was drawing to a close. He wanted, and was encouraged by Mr Blair in this with lengthy intimate chats about religion, to leave behind a legacy that subverted all the beliefs of his admirers and enemies.

At the same time Mr Blair's wingman in Ulster, the Northern Ireland Secretary Peter Hain, was given the job of playing Bad Cop to the PM's Good Cop. Mr Hain threatened the DUP with dire warnings that, if it failed to respond to the political progress that Sinn Féin was making, the British and Irish Governments would implement a Plan B – a far deeper green shade of Direct Rule for Northern Ireland bordering on joint sovereignty shared between London and Dublin.

Sinn Féin was suffering some game-changing setbacks. The manner in which Mr Blair had indulged Republican leaders for so long over the Provisional IRA's failure to decommission its vast arsenal of weaponry no longer impressed Washington, which began to threaten Gerry Adams's frequent trips to the United States with visa withdrawals. The Provisionals' murder of Robert McCartney, a working-class Roman Catholic from a strongly Republican Belfast district, in addition to the £26.5 million cash raid from the Northern Bank – at the time the largest robbery in UK criminal history – set an ominous new tone. Sinn Féin was in a corner and only the winding up of its military wing would extricate the party.

With time running out for Mr Blair, the scene was set for a final attempt at resolution with one more round of negotiations at a venue away from the pressures and distractions of Belfast. In October 2006 the parties and British and Irish leaders convened at St Andrews. Even the choice of a Scottish location played to Mr Paisley's Ulster-Scots roots. The DUP leader was said to be more enthusiastic than some of his party officers on signing a new international treaty between two sovereign governments that Mr Paisley would argue was an improvement on the 1998 Belfast Agreement.

The St Andrews Agreement contained more inducements for Mr Paisley than it did for Mr Adams and Sinn Féin, but the republicans also knew that they had fewer cards to play. Just as with Mr Blair, Sinn Féin's investment in years of developing a political strategy to achieve Irish unity without resort to violence now depended on the man who had made a career out of wrecking every attempt to reach an accommodation with nationalism. Sinn Féin agreed not only to recognise but to support the forces of law and order in the guise of the Police Service of Northern Ireland, a reformed Royal Ulster Constabulary shorn of its name and emblems, in return for the DUP's agreement to share power at Stormont. This was the moment when the sacred cow of the legitimacy of the Provisional IRA, a construct of the Irish liberation movement dating back to 1919, was finally dispatched. The following summer the Provos would quietly announce that they had formally ended their campaign to force Britain out of Ireland.

Symbolically this was a significant victory for Mr Paisley and the DUP, but it was still proving to be a hard sell to his grassroots, for so long weaned on the rhetoric of smashing Sinn Féin and republicanism. Mr Paisley demanded and got another Northern Ireland Assembly election, the tenth time that Northern Ireland had been called to the polls since 1998, to test his mandate for going into government with his former sworn enemies.

The March 2007 election rewarded the DUP with 36 seats in the 108-seat Assembly, reinforcing its primacy. The UUP managed only half that number and Sinn Féin also pulled away from the SDLP, taking 28 seats. On May 8, Mr Paisley was formally sworn in as First Minister. "If anyone had told me that I would be standing here today to take this office, I would have been totally unbelieving," he said. Mr Blair and the Provisional IRA's ruling Army Council, separated by just a few seats, watched from the Stormont gallery. Mr McGuinness took the oath as Deputy First Minister. Mr Blair left office with his peace project prize.

The "Chuckle Brothers" era was golden but brief, a honeymoon period in which the two former enemies laughed in public at one another's jokes even though Mr Paisley still refused to shake Mr McGuinness's hand. The former's fortunes soon waned. Having been schmoozed by the Establishment he had for so long spurned, even his wife Eileen was now a member of the House of Lords, he was rejected by the very Church he founded. Free Presbyterian elders forced him to stand down as Moderator over his decision to share power with "unreformed terrorists".

It was the tangled allegations of financial impropriety against his son Ian Jr that provided the excuse to get rid of him (the Stormont Ombudsman later cleared him). Mr Paisley tersely announced that he was retiring, to be replaced as DUP leader and First Minister by Peter Robinson. Mr McGuinness learnt of it from the radio news.

Mr Robinson promised a new era of "business-like" dealings with Sinn Féin: code for less grinning, which was going down badly with the grassroots. The DUP's foot-dragging over the transfer of policing and justice powers from Westminster to Stormont began to unnerve Sinn Féin, which withdrew its cooperation, effectively rendering the power-sharing Executive mute for many months. In local parlance, the Chuckle Brothers had become the Brothers Grim.

Northern Ireland slid in slow motion towards a new crisis. Sinn Féin privately briefed that its patience was not eternal and that if policing and justice were not devolved by Christmas 2009 they would bring down the institutions whose construction had taken so long to complete.

Then came the most unpredictable of crises for Northern Ireland's leaders. Gerry Adams was accused of covering up for decades the alleged sexual abuse by his brother Liam of Liam's daughter. Mr Robinson was revealed as a cuckold, his wife, Iris, MP for Strangford, having had an affair with a teenager. There was more. Iris had raised £50,000 from property developer friends to set her young lover up in business, pocketing a "commission" herself from the cash. Mr Robinson was accused in a BBC investigative documentary of having breached his office's code of conduct by not having made the authorities aware, a charge that he strongly denied.

The personal and political crises intertwined as Sinn Féin increased the pressure. Gordon Brown, whose interest in Northern Ireland had been minimal until now, was forced to fly with Brian Cowen, his Irish counterpart, to Belfast to hold emergency proximity talks. These failed and after three days the Prime Minister abandoned Hillsborough Castle, leaving Shaun Woodward, his Northern Ireland Secretary, to oversee two weeks of marathon negotiations, during which Mr Robinson temporarily stood down as First Minister.

Eventually the deal was done and sealed by the British and Irish leaders, who returned to unveil a firm date for the transfer of policing and justice powers, a hugely symbolic act for Sinn Fein since it could henceforth argue that the English were no longer running the show.

The extraordinary survival of Mr Robinson and Mr Adams as leaders of their respective parties was much commented upon, with most agreeing that neither could or would have remained in any other part of the United Kingdom or the Republic of Ireland. Yet there was one surprise in the general election of 2010. Mr Robinson's party saw off the challenge from a revived Ulster Unionist Party, now in alliance with the Conservatives, but also the Traditional Unionist Voice power-sharing rejectionists.

Establishing themselves beyond question as the voice of Unionism, talk began once more about a united Unionist party to challenge Sinn Fein's onward march towards becoming Northern Ireland's largest party. But Mr Robinson lost his East Belfast seat, which he had held for 31 years, to Naomi Long of the cross-community Alliance party, which designates itself neither Unionist nor nationalist. Across the city in West Belfast Mr Adams increased his share of the vote to 71 per cent.

As the parliamentary term drew to a close it seemed as if the self-denial about the threat of a fresh cycle of terrorism from a new generation of Irish Republican extremists was finally over. The Real IRA, a splinter of the Provisionals, bombed the Army's Palace Barracks outside Belfast where MI5 has its headquarters.

One phase of the Troubles had drawn to a close, but another was threatening to commence.

The Chuckle Brothers: McGuinness and Paisley

Welsh coalition complications

Greg Hurst
Editor of the Guide

Britain's first postwar coalition government involving the Conservatives and Liberal Democrats came within a whisker of being forged in Wales, three years before that agreed in Westminster. The two parties struck a deal to become junior partners in a coalition led by Plaid Cymru after the elections to the Welsh Assembly in 2007, only to see it unravel at the eleventh hour.

The collapse of Cardiff's "rainbow" coalition propelled Plaid into the arms of Labour, the dominant party of Wales, which remained in office to lead a red-green Government that was anathema to many supporters of both.

The biggest beneficiary was Rhodri Morgan, returning as First Minister to secure his place as the man who, more than anyone else, shaped the direction and tone of Welsh devolution. Donnish, quirky, consensual in approach but statist by instinct, Mr Morgan's achievement was to reach out well beyond Labour's strongholds in industrial South Wales to foster a sense of national purpose, often while his party did not. To do so, he had to lead, cajole and endure a Welsh Labour Party whose tribal instincts were directly contrary to the principles of pluralism on which Welsh devolution was built.

Unlike Donald Dewar, who led the parallel devolved Executive in Scotland from its creation to earn the mantle of father of the nation, Mr Morgan lost out in Labour's first election to lead the Welsh Assembly in 1999 after some heavy-handed intervention from Tony Blair in support of his chosen candidate, Alun Michael. Yet this opening battle was subsequently of enormous help to Mr Morgan because it illustrated his willingness to stand up to his party in London and do things his way. That became his approach as First Minister.

From the outset Labour's Assembly group refused to countenance coalition, despite being short of a majority, leading to the fall of Mr Michael and clearing the way for Mr Morgan to replace him, first in coalition with the Liberal Democrats from 2000-03 and subsequently, when Labour won 30 of the 60 Assembly seats in 2003, ruling alone.

Mr Morgan rejected new Labour's reforms to public services and sought to tackle inequality by extending the State: free bus passes for pensioners, free prescriptions for all, free breakfasts for primary school pupils.

The Assembly itself underwent a profound change in 2006 as the Government of Wales Act gave it law-making powers, known as "assembly measures", on areas of devolved policy, subject to the agreement of the Welsh Secretary and approval of both Houses of Parliament. It also separated the powers of the executive government from the Assembly.

Mr Morgan announced in 2005 that he would seek re-election to the Assembly in 2007 but, if successful, stand down some time in 2009, mid-way through the Assembly's term. The Assembly elections in 2007 coincided with a fall in Labour's popularity across Britain. Although the party in Wales tried to distance itself from Mr Blair, discouraging him from campaign visits, Labour lost four seats in the Assembly, leaving it well short of control.

In the ensuing vacuum, the opposition parties began an extraordinary attempt to oust Labour. Plaid, with a more professional campaign and fresh emblem of a yellow Welsh poppy in place of its traditional green, gained three seats to take its tally to 15. It also diluted its wish for Welsh independence to become a "long-term vision", making it a more palatable partner, opting instead for community campaigns against closing hospitals and sub-post offices and spending pledges such as a free laptop for every child at school.

Plaid's leader, Ieuan Wyn Jones, opened talks with the Welsh Conservatives, who had also nurtured a more distinctly Welsh identity, urging national status for the Welsh language and a bank holiday on St David's Day, and with the Liberal Democrats. The three had met regularly, and constuctively, to discuss oposition tactics; they now planned for government.

A week and a half later the three parties had hammered out a 20-page agreement, giving priority to education, renewable energy, a halt to hospital closures and a referendum on full law-making powers to the Assembly. Mr Wyn Jones was to become First Minister with the Conservative and Liberal Democrat leaders, Nick Bourne and Mike German, both as Deputy First Minister. It would have created the first Conservative ministers since 1997 and the first three-party coalition in Britain since Lloyd George was Prime Minister.

Incredibly, it was the party that stood to gain most, the Welsh Lib Dems, with just six Assembly seats, that pulled the plug. Their negotiating team backed the deal, as did their Assembly group, but a vote of their Welsh national executive committee split, nine in favour and nine against, with no provision in the rules for a casting vote. Furious, Plaid opened talks with Labour to agree a One Wales Agreement that confirmed a rethink on hospital closures and put emphasis on affordable housing and better transport links between North and South Wales. Mr Wyn Jones had to settle for the post of Deputy First Minister, with Mr Morgan back in charge.

The latter honoured his pledge to stand down, bowing out in December 2009 after almost a decade as the figurehead of Welsh devolution, declaring that he would spend more time digging his allotment and attending to his hobby of wood-carving. The election to succeed him was spirited but predictable with Carwyn Jones, the favourite of three candidates, emerging as the victor with 52 per cent of the vote. A barrister in criminal and family law, and Assembly Member for Bridgend since its creation, he had a relatively low profile other than during the foot-and-mouth outbreak in 2001, when he was Minister for Rural Affairs. His most recent post was that of Counsel General and Leader of the House.

The One Wales Agreement left little scope for him to make his mark in policy, other than by his choice of ministers and progress implementing the coalition programme, particularly the unfinished business of a referendum on full law-making powers for the Assembly. Labour's defeat in the general election of 2010 left Carwyn Jones one added responsibility, as the most senior Labour politician in power in Britain.

All change, the gravy train has hit the buffers

Ben Macintyre
Times columnist

There was the Rump Parliament (1649) and the Long Parliament (1640), the Mad Parliament (1258) and, quite simply, the Bad Parliament (1377). But what to call the 54th Parliament, which seemed so very long, so mad and, in many ways, so very bad? This will be, for ever, the Duck House Parliament. Little did Sir Peter Viggers imagine, when he ordered an obscure and expensive item of furniture for his pond, that he would be creating a grim leitmotif for an era of scandal that inflicted such damage on the institution he had served for 36 years. In a cruel twist, the wretched ducks did not even like their new house, which Sir Peter tried to include in his parliamentary expenses. They refused to live in it.

The Parliament ushered into being by the 2005 election and put out of its misery in April 2010, was one of astonishing turbulence, buffeted by scandal, economic meltdown and political acrimony. All the major parties changed leader: the Liberal Democrats twice. The Speaker was forced out of office for the first time since 1695. At the end of the Parliament, a remarkable 149 MPs stood down, including 100 Labour members and 35 Tories.

Far more important than the changing faces was the transformed relationship between the electors and the elected. Faith in politicians plummeted. After the expenses scandal of 2009, John Bercow, the new Speaker of the House of Commons, declared: "Let me be brutally honest about the scale of what has occurred. I cannot think of a single year in the recent history of Parliament when more damage has been done to it than this year, with the possible exception of when Nazi bombs fell on the chamber in 1941."

The bomb of the expenses scandal fell from a sky that was already overcast and stormy. The election of 2005 brought some notable newcomers to the House, including Nick Clegg and Ed Miliband. When Tony Blair won his third consecutive victory in 2005, with a reduced overall majority of 66, the Afghan war was already four years old and the war in Iraq had been under way for two years. The Parliament started in a truculent mood, which got steadily worse. Mr Blair was accused of misleading Parliament over the war and of ruling in presidential style. Mounting war casualties, the bitter grinding rivalry between Blair and Brown and the Prime Minister's growing unpopularity gave a sour, *fin de siècle* flavour of intrigue to the first two years of the Parliament, as it became ever clearer that Mr Blair would not fulfil a promise to serve a full third term.

David Cameron became leader of the Tories in October 2005 after a late surge of support. Sir Menzies Campbell took over leadership of the Liberal Democrats after Charles Kennedy resigned, citing a drink problem. Sir Menzies resigned after 19 months, paving the way for Mr Clegg to win the leadership by a wafer-thin margin. While the opposition parties forged new leaderships, the Blairites and Brownites traded blows and snide spin. The first attempted coup came in September 2006, when the Brownite parliamentary secretary at the Ministry of Defence, Tom Watson, signed a letter to Mr Blair asking that he resign to end the uncertainty over his succession. He was told to withdraw the letter or resign his ministerial position. He quit, with another broadside at Mr Blair: "I no longer believe that your remaining in office is in the interest of either the party or the country . . . the only way the party and the Government can renew itself in office is urgently to renew its leadership."

Mr Blair described Mr Watson's actions as "disloyal, discourteous and wrong". The plot thickened when it appeared that Mr Watson had visited Mr Brown's home in Scotland the day before the memo was sent. Mr Watson claimed that he had merely been dropping off a gift for the Browns' new baby son, Fraser.

The uncertainty, the rumours, the whiff of conspiracy and allegations of treachery set the tone for the rest of the Parliament: a poisonous legacy that Mr Blair would bequeath to Mr Brown, along with the premiership, in June 2007. Mr Brown's uncertainty over whether to call an election four months later, and his final decision to wait, compounded the impression, in some quarters, of a vacillating prime minister, untested at the polls and unwilling to throw the dice, holding on to office and motivated by expediency.

In April 2009, it emerged that Damian McBride, Mr Brown's special adviser and former head of communications at the Treasury, had discussed with the former Labour Party official Derek Draper the setting up of a website to post false and scurrilous rumours about the private lives of senior Tories and their spouses. Mr McBride resigned. Mr Brown was publicly apologetic and privately apoplectic. "Smeargate" left another stain.

This, then, was the unsettled backdrop for the great expenses explosion: creeping political disillusionment and war-weariness, a sense that after coming to power amid widespread euphoria Blair had done little to change parliamentary culture, a souring economy and the looming spectre of recession, and the peculiarly nasty aftertaste of Mr McBride's Smeargate. A series of smaller scandals paved the way, most notably when it emerged that the Conservative MP Derek Conway had employed his son, a full-time student at the time.

Under the old rules, MPs could claim expenses, including the cost of accommodation, "wholly, exclusively and necessarily incurred for the performance of a Member's parliamentary duties". A Freedom of Information Act request filed early in 2008, aimed at finding out exactly what MPs were claiming, was challenged by the House of Commons authorities as

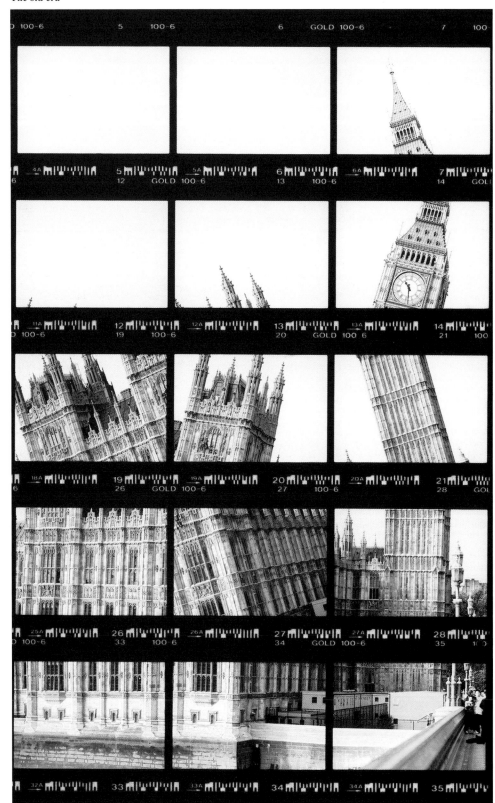

"unlawfully intrusive". When, after much legal wrangling, the House agreed to release the details, it did so with obvious reluctance, insisting that "sensitive" information be removed. Even before the touch-paper was lit, the House of Commons adhered firmly to the belief that how MPs chose to spend our money was their business, not ours.

On May 8, 2009 *The Daily Telegraph* obtained a full, uncensored copy of MPs' expenses claims dating back to 2004 and began publishing details: first those of the Labour Party, then the Tories, then the Liberal Democrats and finally the smaller parties. The scandal touched every corner of Westminster: ministers, Shadow Cabinet members, backbenchers, MPs and peers. It was, as *The Times* observed, "a full-blown political crisis". The ensuing outrage was focused on the abuse of parliamentary expenses relating to second homes: numerous MPs were accused of "flipping", the term for switching the designation of a second home between a constituency and London property, to ensure maximum expenses. Some MPs were renting out properties while simultaneously claiming for second homes. Home improvements in some cases went far beyond "making good dilapidations", suggesting that the expenses system was simply being milked as a way to increase property values, and turn a profit.

MPs were able to claim up to £400 a month for food, and many claimed every penny, every month, even when Parliament was not sitting. Items worth less than £250 could be claimed for without producing a receipt. A suspiciously large number of claims came in just under that mark.

The fallout was cataclysmic, and almost instantaneous. The headlines were devastating, revealing not only greed, but small-mindedness. Jacqui Smith, the Home Secretary, was found to have claimed for various domestic items, including pornographic films viewed by her husband; the Tory MP Douglas Hogg claimed for the expense of cleaning the moat at his country house; Frank Cook, a Labour backbencher, tried to claim back £5 he had donated at a Battle of Britain memorial service.

And then there was the duck house. The "Stockholm" model, which Sir Peter Viggers bought in 2006 for £1,645, was 5ft high and positioned on a floating island. This was only part of the £30,000 Sir Peter claimed towards gardening at his home, including £500 for manure. He was never actually reimbursed for the duck home, as a Commons official wrote "not allowable" beside the claim. "I paid for it myself and in fact it was never liked by the ducks," he said.

But it was the thought that counted.

Sir Peter made a statement: "I have made a ridiculous and grave error of judgment. I am ashamed and humiliated and I apologise." He also announced that he would not be standing at the next election.

The shockwaves crashed through Westminster. It was the detail that inflicted the lasting damage, as much as the sums involved. *The Daily Telegraph* reported that Hazel Blears, Secretary of State for Communities and Local Government, had been claiming the maximum allowable expenses for three properties, £4,874 on furniture, £899 on a new bed and £913 on a new TV, the second such television in under a year. She volunteered to pay the £13,332 capital gains tax she had avoided on the sale of her second home, and stood down in June.

All parties moved to try to limit the fallout: Mr Brown publicly apologised "on behalf of all politicians". Mr Cameron described some of the claims as "unethical and wrong" and announced that Shadow Cabinet

members would repay all questionable claims. A panel, under the former civil servant Sir Thomas Legg, was established to begin the detailed accounting. Eventually each MP involved would be informed whether they would have to repay any expenses. Three Labour MPs and one Conservative peer would finally face criminal prosecution for "false accounting".

Even more damaging than the accusations, in some cases, was the reaction of MPs to the charges. Some wriggled: Douglas Hogg insisted that the moat in question was more a "broad dyke". Some dug themselves in deeper: "I have done nothing criminal, that is the most awful thing," insisted the Tory MP Anthony Steen. "And do you know what it's about? Jealousy. I've got a very, very large house. Some people say it looks like Balmoral." Some seemed bizarrely sorry for themselves: Nadine Dorries, a Conservative MP, described the detailed media coverage of MPs' expenses as a sort of torture.

Never has the cultural chasm between voters and their representatives seemed so vast. While most of Britain reeled from rising unemployment and fretted over mortgage payments, here was a world of moated second homes and ride-on lawnmowers, where the ducks were pampered in special houses, and people bragged of living in their own Balmoral. The gulf between the MPs' sense of entitlement, and public outrage at the perceived pettiness and greed, could not have been wider. Publicly there was much handwringing, by those implicated and those in charge; privately, there was intense fury that the scandal had erupted, and then been left to swirl around unchecked. Many MPs felt hard done by, some with good reason, but there was no doubting the level of public anger over a system that was clearly seen, by far too many politicians, as an adjunct to their salaries, the trappings of an upper-middle-class lifestyle that they believed they deserved. Most seemed more angry than genuinely contrite.

At a time of deep financial uncertainty, the spectacle of MPs feathering their own nests, or duck houses, ignited a firestorm of public fury: two days after the scandal broke, the BBC programme *Question Time* attracted a viewership of nearly four million, the highest in its 30-year history.

The tale of sackings, de-selections, public apologies, repayment, retirement and, eventually, prosecutions, rumbling on for months, marked a low point in British political history. Some of the abuses were flagrant; some venial and some, frankly, irrelevant or unfair. Many decent, honourable and entirely honest MPs found themselves tarred by the overwhelming public perception that Westminster was rotten to the core. Some got their comeuppance; some watched, with horror, as the disillusionment that had marked the early stages of this Parliament turned to outright condemnation and calls for wholesale political reform.

The most high-profile casualty of all was the Speaker, Michael Martin. A Glasgow-born, hard-grained politician of the old-style Labour school, Mr Martin's election in 2000 was controversial from the start. Some suspected him of bias.

Mr Martin's own expenses had long been the subject of scrutiny: he used public money to employ a law firm to fight negative media stories, while his wife spent £4,000 on taxis. Refurbishing the Speaker's official residence within the Palace of Westminster cost the taxpayer an estimated £1.7 million over seven years.

There was more than a hint of tribalism in Mr Martin's resistance to the investigation of MPs expenses. His response to the exploding scandal appeared to be more concerned with the way the information had leaked out, than apologising, explaining or making amends.

To an increasing number, both inside and outside Parliament, Mr Martin was a symptom of the disease, a symbol of all that had gone wrong. Mr Clegg spoke for many when he declared that the Speaker had become an obstacle to reform. To his dwindling band of supporters, he was a scapegoat.

No Speaker had been forced out of office since Sir John Trevor was expelled for accepting bribes more than 300 years earlier. On May 19, 2009 the Conservative MP Douglas Carswell tabled a motion of no confidence, which was signed by 22 MPs. Later that day Mr Martin announced that he would resign from his position as Speaker of the House of Commons.

He took ermine in the Lords, becoming Lord Martin of Springburn. His throne in the House was occupied by John Bercow, elected on a promise to clean up Parliament. It subsequently emerged that the new Speaker had spent an additional £20,000 on refurbishing the grace-and-favour flat in the palace, again.

And so the Parliament – the "Rotten Parliament" as some were now calling it – wound down accompanied by a litany of recriminations, the familiar sound of plotting, and one last dollop of scandal.

In the autumn of 2008, Siobhain McDonagh, a junior government whip, who during her time in office had never voted against the Government, spoke of the need to discuss Mr Brown's position as party leader. She was swiftly sacked.

Then, in the month that Mr Martin stepped down, James Purnell, the Secretary of State for Work and Pensions, delivered another blow to Mr Brown's authority by announcing his resignation. This was not a statement of ambition but, far more threateningly, of principle. "I now believe your continued leadership makes a Conservative victory more, not less, likely . . . that would be disastrous for our country. I am therefore calling on you to stand aside to give our party a fighting chance of winning."

As speculation about Mr Brown's future swirled, his ministers backed him, with potential rivals such as Harriet Harman and David Miliband denying that they were preparing leadership bids. But with each plot, and each denial, his chances of clinging to power in the coming election seemed to recede. The final attempt to unseat him came in January 2010, when the former Health Secretary Patricia Hewitt and former Transport Secretary Geoff Hoon jointly called for a secret ballot on the future of Mr Brown's leadership. The plot fizzled. Mr Brown later called the abortive mini-coup "a form of silliness".

Perhaps the final symbolic motif for this grim Parliament came just before the election was announced, when Mr Hoon, Ms Hewitt and the former minister Stephen Byers were each caught out by undercover journalists posing as lobbyists. The former ministers appeared to be cashing in on their influence. Ms Hewitt explained that, for a fee of £3,000 a day, she could help "a client who needs a particular regulation removed, then we can often package that up". Mr Hoon was heard saying that he was "looking forward to . . . something that, frankly, makes money".

Above all, the crass remarks made by Mr Byers seemed to sum up the previous five years. "I am a bit like a sort of cab for hire," he explained to the fake lobbyist. "I still get a lot of confidential information because I am still linked to No 10." His trump card came close to self-parody: "We could have a word with Tony". Mr Blair was long gone from No 10, but his potential earning power lingered on.

At the start of the 54th Parliament, public confidence in politicians was already crumbling; by the end it was radically eroded. The perception that MPs lined their own pockets at taxpayer expense was widespread in 2005; by 2010 it was universal conventional wisdom. Unfairly, but understandably, Parliament had come to be seen as one large rank of cabs for hire. The tumult, sleaze and political skulduggery left the public jaundiced and angry, and many MPs traumatised and exhausted. Contemplating her own retirement, Ann Widdecombe spoke for many when she remarked: "I find that my uppermost sentiment is one of profound relief."

Like Oliver Cromwell, surveying the Rump Parliament, the public's patience had run out: "You have sat too long for any good you have been doing lately . . . Depart, I say; and let us have done with you. In the name of God, go!" And they went: in addition to the 149 MPs who stood down before the 2010 election, 76 were voted out of office in May of that year. In some ways, both the level of interest in the election, and a result giving no party an overall majority, were also an accurate reflection of the rancour and uncertainty of the five years that preceded it.

The unhappy 54th Parliament was, perhaps, a necessary trauma. Wholesale political reform became inevitable. Closer scrutiny of parliamentary expenses began. The gravy train hit the buffers, making a fantastic mess that will take many years to clear up.

Britain has a new Parliament, a new form of government and a large new crop of MPs. They will make their own mistakes and commit their own sins, but only this can be predicted with absolute certainty: no MP in the 55th Parliament will ever buy a duck house.

Ben Macintyre was parliamentary sketch writer for The Times *from 2002-04*

The work of the
House of Commons

*"Clearly you require a substantial
pay rise, Prime Minister"*

The growing powers of the humble backbencher

Peter Riddell
Chief Political
Commentator

One of the great paradoxes of the House of Commons is that just as its public standing has hardly ever been lower, MPs have seldom been more hard-working or potentially more effective. Procedural changes over the past dozen years have given backbench MPs more chance to play a creative role at Westminster.

The "declinist" view of Parliament has, of course, been reinforced by the expenses scandal (as discussed in an accompanying article). There is nothing new in such complaints. There never was a golden age. Every generation has had protests that the executive is too strong and the legislature too weak but, as the Hansard Society's Annual Audit of Political Engagement showed in March 2010, while the expenses row did not create a problem of trust, which has existed for many years, it did reinforce public scepticism. Less than two fifths of the public believe Parliament to be one of the two or three national institutions that have most influence on their everyday lives.

The counter view has been put most eloquently by Jack Straw, a former Leader of the Commons and closely involved in constitutional reform during his 13 years in the Cabinet. He argued, in a lecture to the Hansard Society in March 2010, that "the view that Parliament is irrelevant or powerless is complete nonsense". He acknowledged that the institution was far from perfect, and the balance remained tilted in the Government's favour, but changes in recent decades had strengthened the legislature. As Mr Straw pointed out, in the three decades from the mid-1940s until the mid-1970s, the executive was all powerful. Backbench MPs seldom rebelled: there were two whole sessions in the 1950s when not a single Conservative backbencher defied the whip and voted against the Government. There were few select committees. Those that did exist were mainly weak, apart from the Public Accounts Committee. Admittedly, many newspapers until the mid-to-late 1980s did carry full reports of what was said on the floor of the Commons, but radio broadcasting did not arrive on a regular and continuous basis until April 1978, and television cameras not until November 1989.

Select Committees

Since the 1970s, a number of far-reaching changes have been introduced, most significantly in 1979 with the creation of 12 broadly departmental select committees. Each big department is monitored by a select committee to examine its policymaking and performance. There have been variations in the number, titles and remit of committees to match changes in the machinery of government, but the principle has remained. This has created wideranging opportunities for MPs to question ministers, civil servants and interested bodies, and has unquestionably broadened the range of public debate. For instance, the opening up of decisions on setting interest rates, both in the mid-1990s and then with the creation of the Monetary Policy Committee in 1997, has meant that the Governor and senior directors of the Bank of England appear before the Treasury committee at least once a quarter.

There has been a similar opening up in other areas of policy. The banking crisis was examined frequently from autumn 2007 onwards by the Treasury Select Committee, when all the main players appeared at often uncomfortable hearings. The Defence Select Committee also pursued allegations that British troops in Iraq and Afghanistan were inadequately supplied and supported. The public gathering of evidence and the questioning of ministers has often been more important than the recommendations in the final reports.

There were three waves of reform during the Labour years: when Robin Cook was Leader of the Commons from June 2001 until March 2003; when Jack Straw was Leader from 2006 until 2007; and, finally, in the aftermath of the expenses scandal, when a special committee was set up under the respected Labour MP and political scientist Tony Wright to examine ways of strengthening the influence of the Commons and of backbenchers.

Among the changes have been a strengthening in the role of select committees in 2002 by giving them ten core tasks, including examining annual departmental reports and expenditure plans, aided by the creation of a central Scrutiny Unit to provide expert support in addition to the clerks and advisers to particular committees. But each committee has its own distinctive style, priorities and approach, notably reflecting the personality of the chairman. Additional pay for select committee chairmen was introduced from October 2003, while from 2007 the committees were given the additional role of holding pre-appointment hearings for those chairing a variety of public bodies. This is not, however, a veto power, as was shown when Ed Balls brushed aside the objections of the Childrens, Schools and Families Select Committee to an appointment in his area. In 2009, eight new regional committees were set up, despite the protests from the main opposition parties.

The Prime Minister was, for a long time, above this process, but, since July 2002, he has given evidence for about two and a half hours twice a year to the Liaison Committee, which consists of the chairmen of the main select committees. This enables a wide range of topics to be raised, but at times it can be too wide since neither Tony Blair nor Gordon Brown, in their very different ways, was ever discomfited during an appearance.

Wright committee

After the expenses scandal there was widespread agreement that the Commons not only needed to sort out this specific issue but also to address wider questions about the role of MPs. This led to the formation of the cross-party Select Committee on Reform of the House of Commons, generally known as the Wright committee. This was different from the Modernisation Committee, which had discussed most big changes since 1997 but had become dormant under Harriet Harman's leadership of the Commons. Whereas the Modernisation Committee had always been chaired by the Leader of the Commons, the Reform committee was chaired by a leading backbencher. Its remit was limited to what were seen as the most pressing problems: appointments to select committees, the arrangement of business in the House and the possibility of direct public initiation of issues in the chamber. The committee's report, Rebuilding the House, published in November 2009, concentrated on giving backbenchers more control and reducing the role of the party whips in determining the membership of select committees and the non-governmental business of the House.

The reform committee recommended that the chairmen of most select committees should be elected by the House as a whole and other members should be elected within each political party, with the basis of election being decided by each party. The party balance of committees and of the chairmen will continue to reflect the proportion of seats that each party holds in the House. The Speaker will determine what the balance should be between the parties and they will negotiate about which party will provide chairmen for which select committee. Nominations will be sought and candidates will submit manifestos. There may be hustings and elections will then take place.

The intention is that the chairmen and the members should be more independent than in the past, when there had been occasional rows on the floor of the House over attempts by the whips to prevent independent-minded MPs from being re-elected to chair committees. In addition, the size of departmental select committees was limited to 11, in the hope of ensuring greater attendance and higher commitment from MPs.

The most contentious proposal would involve ending the Government's exclusive hold on the agenda of the Commons. The reform committee proposed that a backbench business committee should be appointed to schedule backbench business and that, in time, a House business committee should be set up to schedule all business before the House. In March 2010, the Commons agreed with these proposals and with the establishment of a House business committee during the course of the following Parliament but the Labour Government and the party whips ensured that no time was available before the dissolution of the House and the election. Even the creation of a backbench business committee would represent a significant shift in the balance of power within Parliament, allowing backbenchers, rather than the party whips, to decide whether to have an increased number of short, topical debates and to give more time for discussion on select committee reports.

Legislation

The Commons scrutiny of legislation has commonly been regarded as one of the least satisfactory aspects of Parliament. The formal procedures are unchanging. A Bill is introduced without discussion, its first reading, then about ten days later it is debated in principle on the floor of the Commons in its second reading. Most Bills then go "upstairs" to be scrutinised line-by-line in what used to be called standing committees and are now known as public Bill committees. (Exceptions are constitutional Bills, the committee stages of which are always taken on the floor of the Commons, and the most controversial parts of the Finance Bill, which are again taken on the floor.)

This is the most criticised part of the process because government backbenchers are whipped to toe the line and constructive debate has been discouraged. Until a few years ago, the committee stages were allowed to run for a certain number of hours (often about 80) before the Ggovernment put down a guillotine motion limiting the time for further debate. This often left large parts of the Bill undebated before it got to the Lords. After a committee stage, a Bill returns to the floor of the Commons for a report stage, when further amendments can be made. This is often the stage at which controversial changes are debated. There is then a, usually short, third reading before the Bill goes to the Lords, where it follows similar procedures.

The main differences in the Lords are that there are seldom votes or divisions on the committee stages of Bills, which are increasingly taken in the Moses Room or a similar committee room. So the Lords allows votes on amendments on the third reading of Bills as well as at report stage. Each year some Bills are introduced in the Lords rather than the Commons to even out the workload between the two Houses. Money Bills, such as the Finance Bill, cannot be changed in the Lords and receive only a formal debate before being passed.

There have been a number of changes in these procedures. First, more Bills are being published in draft form, which allows time for examination either by a select committee or by a special committee (often a joint one of both Houses). These inquiries can lead to changes to Bills before they are formally introduced and it becomes a matter of the government's authority. The practice has been disappointing, however, with a marked decline over the past six years in the number of Bills published in draft form.

Secondly, the need for post-legislative scrutiny is now increasingly accepted, with Acts being examined five years after their passage. This is still in its early stages. Thirdly, Bills are now subject to formal timetables from their second reading onwards, with a programme motion stating when a committee stage has to be completed and how long there is for the report and third readings. This has led to complaints that opposition parties and backbenchers have been deprived of their rights to scrutinise, and occasionally, hold up Bills. Fourthly, standing committees were replaced in 2003 by public Bill committees, which permit brief scrutiny sessions when expert witnesses can give evidence immediately before the line-by-line examination of any measure. While, in theory, this offers scope for improving the scrutiny of Bills, the time allowed is often too short and the process needs to be reviewed.

Private Member's Bills

Most legislation is put forward by the Government, but in every session a few Bills sponsored by backbench MPs become law. Most of these emerge through a ballot held at the beginning of each session. A total of 13 Fridays in each session are allotted to Private Member's Bills, which go through the same stages as government Bills, but only seven Fridays are allotted to second readings: the other six are for later stages.

An MP who is lower than seventh will have to put their Bill down for a Friday on which it will not be the first to be debated. This involves astute tactics to judge which Bills will be controversial and therefore face op-

John Bercow, the Commons Speaker since June 2009, made his priority strengthening backbench MPs

The work of the House of Commons

position. Debates on important Bills often last most of the Friday sitting (from 9.30am to 2.30pm). Sponsors of Bills have to mobilise support among their fellow MPs since a closure motion to end the debate and have a second reading vote requires the support of 100 MPs, quite a high hurdle for a Friday when many MPs like to be back in their constituencies. Without a closure motion, a Bill can be blocked by a single MP shouting, "Object", in which case the debate is adjourned. The same happens to Bills that have not been debated. In practice, they then have virtually no chance of becoming law.

Bills introduced under this procedure vary enormously in importance, from highly controversial subjects such as hunting and abortion to minor adjustments of existing law. The Government sometimes offers backbenchers high in the ballot fully drafted Bills that have not found a place in the Queen's Speech programme. Pressure groups and constituents will also bombard MPs with ideas.

Another way for a backbencher to introduce legislation is under the ten-minute rule, which allows an MP the chance to make a brief speech in favour of introducing a Bill. Another MP can speak against and the proposal can then be voted upon. Even if successful, however, the Bill then has to take its chance for a second reading on a Friday. In practice, most ten-minute Bill debates, held in prime time twice a week after Question Time and any statements, offer a chance for an MP to get publicity for an issue. Bills can be introduced without debate by any backbench MP but they also have to compete for time on Fridays coming after the ballot bills. So they have very little chance of becoming law unless they are uncontroversial.

The chamber

It is a commonplace that the chamber of the Commons is not what it was. Debates are no longer reported in the press and most are poorly attended, but that is partly because there are now many other ways in which MPs can raise issues. The introduction of Westminster Hall as a secondary chamber has taken some of the pressure off the floor of the Commons. Westminster Hall holds debates from Tuesdays to Thursdays on constituency issues as well as national policy questions, with time regularly allocated for debates on select committee reports. In each case, a minister has to be present to give the government's response to either a narrow grievance or a broader policy issue.

Question Time, traditionally seen as the epitome of adversarial politics, has changed in a number of largely unappreciated ways. Each departmental Question Time now has a period for topical questions asked without any prior notice to the minister, while there is also a reduced notice period for tabling oral questions. MPs also table more written questions. Since 1997 Prime Minister's Questions has been a 30-minute session each Wednesday, later moving to noon, rather than two 15-minute sessions at 3.15pm on Tuesday and Thursday.

That has also reflected a series of changes in the timing of the parliamentary day. Monday and Tuesday sessions now begin at 2.30pm and last until between 10.30pm and 11pm, depending on the number of divisions at the end of the main business. The Wednesday session starts at 11.30am and ends at about 7.30pm; the Thursday session begins at 10.30am and ends at 6.30pm; and the much less frequent Friday sessions start at 9.30am and end by 3pm. This has had the effect of concentrating the parliamentary week from Monday evening until, usually, Wednesday early evening, and only occasionally Thursday.

John Bercow, elected as Speaker in June 2009, and re-elected in May 2010, has made a priority of strengthening the chamber and empowering the backbench MP. He has sought to speed up parliamentary business and ensure that more questions are asked of ministers. He has also allowed many more urgent questions, roughly one a sitting week compared with two in the 12 months before his election. Urgent questions allow any member to seek to compel a minister to come to the Commons to address an issue of importance. This has put pressure on the Government to volunteer statements of its own.

Opposition days

In each parliamentary session, the opposition parties are given the right to initiate debates on 20 sitting days. These days are allocated according to the strength of the parties in the Commons, to give the smaller groups such as the Scottish and Welsh nationalists and the Democratic Unionists a chance to have debates. The timing of such debate is in the hands of the Government but the subject for debate is entirely determined by the opposition party. The topics are normally urgent and controversial issues where the Opposition wishes to challenge or embarrass the Government.

These set-piece debates attract little media attention and often few MPs are in the chamber even for the opening or closing speeches. There have been suggestions in the past few years that the Opposition might exchange some of their time for shorter and more topical debates just after Question Time when a minister has to justify their policy and decisions. This possibility is likely to be explored in the current Parliament when a backbnech businss committee is set up to allocate time for non-government business.

Direct public involvement

The Commons has been slow to give voters a greater direct say. Proposals for direct e-petitions have been accepted in principle but nothing has been done to implement them, partly because of a lack of political will. The Wright committee made only vague suggestions for a new agenda initiative whereby a proposal attracting a certain amount of support would trigger a debate. There are two related, but separate, issues here: first, agenda-setting petitions that could trigger debates on a topic or even a Bill (although not binding MPs on how they should vote); secondly, more general e-petitions, as adopted in the Scottish Parliament, where members of the public can raise anything from individual cases of maladministration and local grievances to broader public policy problems requiring fresh legislation.

Conflicting roles

Any discussion of Parliament is complicated by the multiple loyalties of MPs: to their constituents, to their parties (locally and nationally) and to the House of Commons. That is partly because, unlike the United States, we do not have a separation of powers. So MPs have loyalties to either support or oppose the government of the day, which can conflict with or supersede their more parliamentary roles on, for example, select committees. This need not, and did not, prevent committees with a Labour majority in the last Parliament from publishing critical reports on the Brown Government's policies and performance. It is all a question of balance.

Peter Riddell is the author of six books on British politics, including two on Parliament. He has chaired the Hansard Society, a non-partisan charity for promoting understanding of Parliament, and is a Senior Fellow of the Institute for Government.

New intake foots bill for the old

Sam Coates
Chief Political Correspondent

It was designed as a punishment to fit the crime. Having hustled, exaggerated and bullied at least £1 million out of the expenses system to which they had no right, the eventual response of MPs in the last Parliament was to strip those in the next of the power to administer their own affairs. So MPs who returned to Parliament after the general election found themselves subtly but crucially disenfranchised. Theirs is the first generation of representatives with powers to make the laws of the United Kingdom, but banned from having input into the rules governing their own behaviour.

To its critics, Parliament and its centuries-old sovereignty was, at a stroke, subjugated beneath the control of an unaccountable quango. For those who witnessed repeated pitiful displays of self-interest by a Parliament unable to face up to the outrage caused by its own behaviour, however, there seemed to be no other route. Twice in the last Parliament, in 2008 and 2009, MPs debated changing the rules only to decide to cling on to as many of the perks, privileges and loopholes as they could. And twice they attempted to block or alter freedom of information laws to keep as much information about their claims secret as possible. Instead of agreeing to change, MPs would blame a hostile media and public misunderstanding for their predicament.

They were undoubtedly helped by a culture of compliance among those inside the Commons Department for Resources, affectionately known by its historic name, the Fees Office. These largely anonymous public servants waived through payments, some subsequently blaming bullying by MPs as the reason they signed off the payments. Yet on the rare occasions they were glimpsed in public, the senior figures appeared every bit the accessory in a relationship that had become too cosy. When Andrew Walker, then head of the Department of Resources, appeared publicly at a tribunal in 2008, he argued against greater transparency over MPs' expenses. His argument was that this would "distract them or lead to additional questions which they have to defend, even if they have (acted) perfectly sensibly, because there is a great desire to look at the private lives of public individuals".

Only when the full, unredacted publication of every receipt submitted for expenses was published in the summer of 2009 were MPs so cowed that they agreed to change the system for good. And so, at the end of 2009, the Independent Parliamentary Standards Authority (IPSA), arbiter of the conduct of the new generation of MPs, was born. Together with Sir Christopher Kelly, chairman of the Committee on Standards in Public Life, they have drawn up a new, far tougher regime.

Gone are the days when generous second-home allowances, coupled with rising property prices, combined to mean that a valuable property empire was a near inevitability for any MP beyond London. Also gone are the days when MPs in Zones 3-6 could classify themselves as living out of London, thereby helping themselves to a £20,000-plus second-home allowance. Farewell, too, to the so-called "food" payments, a monthly cheque of £400, no questions asked, no receipts required.

Today's MPs face a new austerity package of expenses that Sir Ian Kennedy, the chairman of IPSA, admits is a response to the expenses crisis. In effect, the new generation of MPs is paying for the crimes of the last. Many face the prospect of a lonely existence cut off from their families and living in one-bedroom flats in the cheaper districts of London, unless they supplement the cost from their £64,766 salary. Renting is now the only option. Only MPs who were re-elected and already have houses they own can continue claiming for mortgage payments, and then only until August 2012, forcing an earlier-than-expected sale of many homes.

London MPs will be defined as those who live within 20 miles of Westminster or can reach any part of their constituency within 60 minutes by public transport in peak hours, meaning that 128 MPs in this Parliament will be unable to claim for extra accommodation.

Beyond the housing allowance, the clampdown is equally severe. Only MPs with children under the age of 5 will be able to claim an extra travel allowance that takes into account their family circumstances. All MPs must travel in standard rather than first class, although ministers will still be allowed to travel first class under the government expenses scheme. One small concession by IPSA agreed to allow MPs to continue to employ one relative, continuing a long-established parliamentary tradition. This has still prompted howls of protest from some who pointed out that the first indication of the depth of the expenses scandal emerged when Derek Conway, then a Tory MP, was found to be paying his son but was unable to prove that he worked for him.

Yet in spite of the still-evident levels of public scorn at MPs' handling of their claims, several spent the early days of this new Parliament protesting about the new settlement. Some Members claimed that they were being forced to sack their researchers because of unexpected changes to pensions arrangements for staff. Others complained about over-zealous IPSA staff who would deal with personal queries only in writing by e-mail, then never reply, and require marriage and birth certificates before paying for family travel.

Meanwhile, some MPs were angry that IPSA hired three press officers, some paid more than backbenchers, while demanding that Members pay for expenses such as constituency offices out of their own pocket and claim the money back later. Some MPs reacted so badly to the new rules that they were warned to stop abusing staff or risk legal action. MPs now suffer the humiliation of being greeted with warning signs that read: "Abuse of staff will not be tolerated."

The new Parliament was unable to draw a clean line under the expenses affair. The first scalp of the session was David Laws, the Lib Dem MP for Yeovil, who was forced to quit as Chief Secretary to the Treasury less than three weeks into the job over £40,000 of rent claims that he paid to his partner, James Lundie. After 2006, payments to family members and partners were banned by the Commons, but Mr Laws demurred from declaring his relationship, kept secret even from his own family, to the parliamentary authorities. Mr Laws's insistence that privacy rather than profit was behind the move was not enough to justify an apparently straightforward breach of the rules nor prevent his resignation.

It was an early reminder of the toxic consequences of abnormal expenses arrangements, and how the general election had done little to dilute this.

A few words of friendly advice for aspiring MPs

Chris Mullin
Labour MP for Sunderland South 1987-2010.

A few days after I was selected, in June 1985, an editorial appeared in the *Daily Mail*. "Poor Sunderland," it began, "first its football team is relegated and now comes even worse news..." The Labour leader, Neil Kinnock, was not best pleased either. Not long afterwards, on a visit to the North East, he was overheard asking: "What has gone wrong in Sunderland?" He went on: "First they have an MP who is a boil on the arse of the Labour Party," a reference to my estimable colleague Bob Clay. "And now they have gone and selected a certifiable lunatic."

Despite this unpromising beginning, I was elected in 1987 with a swing to Labour more than double the national average. Being a friend of Tony Benn and having played a part in the uprising in the Labour Party in the early 1980s, I did not expect on arrival in Parliament to be carried shoulder high into the Tea Room and I was not disappointed.

At my first meeting of the parliamentary party there was a post-mortem examination on the outcome of the election – we had, after all, by now lost three in a row so it seemed a good idea to see what lessons could be learnt. I got up and made what I thought was a conciliatory little speech, the gist of which was that "we must turn our guns outwards and not shoot at each other".

Up got Roy Hattersley, then the deputy leader of the Labour Party. "What Chris ought to know," he said, "is that we aren't taking any prisoners."

And so it proved. For several years I put my name down for every vacancy on the Home Affairs Select Committee, without result. My fortunes began to change only when my campaign to free the various innocent people, 18 in all, convicted of just about all the main IRA bombings of the mid-1970s, bore fruit. A cause that had once seemed eccentric and extremist was now mainstream.

Suddenly I was respectable. I could no longer be denied a place on the Home Affairs Select Committee and scarcely an eyebrow was raised when, in due course, I became chairman and later a minister. Although I never scaled the Olympian heights, I like to think that I left the odd footprint in the sand during my 23 years in Parliament.

Here, for those who come afterwards, are a few tips that they may or may not find useful.

Take Parliament seriously
Given that we struggle so hard to get ourselves elected, it never ceases to amaze me that so many colleagues disappear as soon as the final bell rings each week. If we, the elected, don't take Parliament seriously, why should anyone else?

Never lose sight of the fact that our primary, albeit not the only, function, as Members of Parliament is to hold the executive to account for the considerable power that it wields. Something we do imperfectly. This need not consist of making brilliant speeches to an otherwise empty chamber. Well-targeted, prime-time interventions in ministerial speeches or statements are often much more effective.

Strike a balance between constituency and parliamentary work
So far as possible it is desirable for an elected representative to share the same sunshine and the same rainfall as his or her constituents. By all means live in your constituency and make sure that you are visible, hold surgeries, open an office, attend fairs, fêtes and concerts, but not to the exclusion of an active role in Parliament.

Some of my more modern colleagues, especially those in marginal seats, take the view, for which there is little hard evidence, that they will improve their chances of re-election if they rush around pretending to be fairy godmothers to their constituents ("Hello, I am your MP. Have you got a problem that needs solving?").

This, in my view, is a mistake. First, because it is beyond our powers to resolve the personal problems of many of our constituents and disappointment is the most likely outcome.

Secondly, because pavement politics (and I intend no disrespect) ought to be the preserve of local councillors. Thirdly, because excessive devotion to the small picture distracts from the primary function of an MP, which is to represent his or her constituents in Parliament. Please note, I am not saying neglect your constituents; only that there is a balance to be struck and that, in recent years, the pendulum has swung too far in favour of parochialism.

Put your name down for a place on a good select committee
Preferably one that deals with issues of interest to you and your constituents. You may not be successful at first, but do persist. Having been appointed, take it seriously.

The ground rules for a successful select committee member are as follows: (a) read the brief before the meeting; (b) turn up on time; (c) keep your backside on the seat throughout the proceedings (no nipping in and out to deal with supposedly urgent messages); (d) ask concise, relevant questions; and (e) do not indulge in petty politicking – conclusions should be reached on the basis of evidence, not prejudice. Active membership of a select committee can be one of the most fulfilling aspects of life in Parliament. The chairman of a good select committee has far more influence than most junior ministers, and these days they are also paid.

You are not an automaton

Do not waste time devising lollipop questions ("Could I trouble the Prime Minister to list his five greatest achievements?"). They do not impress anyone. By all means be constructive, support the programme on which your party was elected, but that does not mean that you have to sign up to every dot and comma, every piece of stupidity or foolishness devised by your political masters.

First, of course, make representations in private, but if all else fails and you want to be taken seriously there has to be a bottom line. On occasion, it may be necessary to vote against your party and in retrospect you may be vindicated, witness the Tory poll tax rebels or the 139 Labour MPs who voted against the Iraq adventure.

Do not be in too much hurry to become a parliamentary private secretary

By all means sign up with one of the big fish, prime minister, chancellor, home or foreign secretary, but not with one of the middle rankers. There are far too many PPSs and for the majority this will be the peak of their careers. Most do not have enough to do and while away their time hanging around the lobbies dishing out patsy questions. A sad fate for otherwise intelligent people.

Don't be afraid of cross-party alliances

One of the pleasant surprises of election to Parliament is the discovery that on many issues there are like-minded people in other parties and an alliance is often far more effective than ploughing a lone furrow. During the course of my miscarriages of justice campaign I teamed up with a ruddy-faced Tory backwoodsman, Sir John Farr, who, once engaged, was completely fearless. I inquired if our collaboration had caused him any trouble within his own ranks. "Only with the lawyers," he grunted, "and they're all arseholes."

Don't become a rent-a-quote

Try to stick to what you know about. Those who have opinions on everything are not taken seriously, even on their own side.

If at first you don't succeed, persist

In the land of the soundbite, he who can concentrate is king.

Never lose sight of the big picture

Most of us went into politics to make the world a better place and in the hope that we had something to contribute. Outcome, not process, is what matters.

If you get a call from a company inviting you to do a little lobbying, put the phone down.

Finally, a piece of advice that trumps all of the above.

Make time for your family

Politics is littered with broken marriages. Don't let yours be one of them. Quite apart from which, a little hinterland makes you a better politician.

Chris Mullin is the author of a volume of diaries, A View from the Foothills. *A further volume is due in 2010.*

A victorious Chris Mullin at the count in 1997, ten years after he was first elected as MP for Sunderland South

The pleasures of opposition

Paul Goodman
Conservative MP for Wycombe 2001-2010

I was first elected to Parliament in 2001. I departed nine years later after a further election, disagreeing with the consensus view that the Commons should be a chamber of professional politicians. In almost a decade, I never sat to the right of the Speaker's Chair, on the government benches. Although I served as a shadow minister for most of that period, standing down from David Cameron's front bench of my own accord in 2009, I did not get the chance to be a real one.

So, although I am unqualified to pronounce on life as a minister I am, if not exactly an expert on opposition, at least in a position to reflect on it. Is there a point to not proposing but opposing? If so, what is it? And is it best done from the front or back benches? Indeed, what is the role of a backbencher in any event?

The answer to all these questions is: it depends on what you believe an MP to be in the first place. If you think that having those two letters after a name is useless unless they are followed by a title (Minister for Holistic Governance and Horizon Scanning; Minister for Best-Practice Benchmarking and Blue-Sky Thinking) it follows that you will consider opposition a waste of time.

Some MPs who have been ministers enjoy opposition for a while, or semi-permanently as elder statesmen, able to pronounce on how much better life was when, well, they were ministers. This only goes to prove the point that most MPs want to be ministers in the first place. A few enter the Commons wanting to be backbenchers, and speak for their local area; fewer still come wanting to chair a select committee. But for many of their colleagues, the wish for red boxes is compulsive. Parliamentary life seems meaningless without being Under-Secretary of State for Community Engagement and Meaningful Dialogue (until, of course, one is an Under-Secretary of State, at which point parliamentary life seems meaningless without being a Minister of State, and so on).

It remains to be seen whether the growing tendency of voters to back local champions rather than future ministers, a shift given new impetus by the expenses scandal, alters the parliamentary balance in the medium term. In the short term, it will not: most members of the new Commons intake of 2010, like their predecessors, will want a desk in Whitehall and Westminster.

For those MPs who want to be ministers, then, being a shadow minister is merely a preparation for the real thing, although one tempered by the horrifying possibility that this happy transformation may never take place. After all, one may be sacked. Or one's party may lose the election. Or, worse still, one's party may win the election . . . and one may not be appointed. The ripe fruits of power may be snatched away by the whim or caprice of the prime minister of the day.

Nonetheless, those who enjoy opposing – tabling parliamentary written questions or, better still, freedom of information requests (since ministers do not answer written questions if they can get away with it); digging for stories damaging to the government; hauling into the light information that ministers want hidden; pouncing on their weaknesses, especially at times of crisis; utilising every procedural device (urgent questions, ministerial statements, opposition day debates) to gain advantage and, above all, using the media – will be as happy as pigs in dung.

This gross image is less disparaging than it sounds, because the low politics has a high point: the holding of government to account. Ministers must be answerable for their actions. And to whom should they be accountable, if not to our elected representatives? Furthermore, the odd shadow minister, when not scheming against ministers or schmoozing lobby groups, may be a creator of policy, picking good ideas from bad ones, like a man removing nuggets of gold from earth, thus preparing a future government to make Britain better. It follows that there is a case for taxpayer-funded shadow ministers, although not, in my view, a persuasive one. A political class of taxpayer-funded politicians, distinct and thereby distanced from those who elect them, is already in place. Its position should not be further entrenched.

The majority of MPs of any party will not, at any one time, sit on its front bench. They will soldier on as backbenchers, whether in government or opposition, willingly or unwillingly. And if to be a backbencher when one's party is in government is to be removed from the centre of events, being one in opposition is to be twice removed. The best chance of nudging one's way back towards them is to sit on a select committee. The quality of these committees varies greatly, but the better ones are well-chaired; have, therefore, a sense of purpose; cooperate across party lines; probe ministers and departments, performing an irreplaceable public service in so doing; and issue useful reports making strong recommendations.

Why, though, assume that the purpose of being an MP in opposition is to work towards the centre of events? Indeed, why think that this is the purpose of being an MP at all? I return to my first answer: it depends. If one believes that an MP's work is invalid if he does not sit on a front bench, one will look at such a person with scorn. But why take this view? Members of the local Conservative Association or Labour Party may bask in the reflected glory of being represented by a Cabinet minister. But, as previously noted, a growing number of constituents do not: they want a local champion, not a future minister, someone who will reply to their emails quickly and deal with their problems effectively (even if those problems are outside the scope or beyond the reach of the local MP). They are the masters now, in an age of soaring consumer expectations, not servants in an age of deference trooping meekly to the ballot box every five years and voting either Conservative or Labour on the basis of class. This is the "it" that "they just don't get".

A question follows. If being an MP is a job, how can MPs not only have outside interests, but work as ministers? After all, being a minister is also a job, one that has no intrinsic connection with representing Chuffnell Poges or Sin City South. In future years, the pressure to split the executive from the legislature may become irresistible. In such circumstances, opposition would be differently shaped and constituted, as would government. But until or unless this happens, the opposition backbencher, like his frontbench counterpart, must pack up his troubles in his old kit bag, pressing ministers on behalf of his constituents. After all, that is largely why he is there.

Life as a Member of Parliament

David Howarth
Liberal Democrat MP
for Cambridge 2005-2010

The central feature of parliamentary life is waiting: waiting for the division bell to go off; waiting to be called to speak; waiting for people to turn up for meetings or waiting for stories, good or bad, to appear in the media.

How one copes with waiting defines a parliamentary life. Some people manage to fill all those waiting hours with activity – signing piles of letters to constituents, replying to emails or (for London MPs) rushing to and from constituency engagements. Others, perhaps those whose constituents are not very demanding or who have organised their offices so efficiently that they have completed all their correspondence, engage in a parliamentary form of *dolce far niente*: hanging around the Tea Room (the best refuge in Parliament because the media are not allowed in), or, for the more distressed, the Strangers' Bar, or arranging some form of escape – in the past, before the scandals, a foreign trip with a select committee, or latterly an early return home on a Wednesday evening. Some even take an interest in legislation, and spend their time writing amendments to Bills, although that is very much a minority interest.

There is even an activity that manages to combine all three – giving the appearance of constituency activity and of taking an interest in parliamentary business but, in reality, doing nothing – namely signing early day motions. Members can be seen in every part of the building flicking through an important-looking blue document occasionally scribbling their signature on it. They are adding their names to EDMs. Technically, EDMs are motions the sponsors of which would like the House to debate some time soon, but on no specific day.

In reality, no one sponsoring an EDM expects, or even wants, the House to debate it. EDMs are merely a form of petition that only MPs can sign, a petition aimed at no one in particular that achieves precisely nothing. Even if every single MP signed an EDM, nothing would happen or change. They are, as someone once remarked, parliamentary graffiti.

Most EDMs are cobbled together by pressure groups with some simple-minded campaign message to promote, who have found some sympathetic, or fearful, MPs to act as proposers. The pressure groups' main purpose, however, is not to create pressure for change but to give their supporters something to do, or merely to build the group's database. Supporters are given pre-printed postcards to send to their MPs (or, increasingly, pre-prepared emails) urging the MP to 'sign EDM no XXX'. The pressure group always gives the impression that signing the EDM is a matter of vast importance, a deception many MPs are happy to go along with if it impresses constituents or a gullible local newspaper.

But the attraction of signing EDMs is that it takes far less energy than the other method of making sure that one's name appears in the local media, namely the intervention game. The intervention game consists of saying the name of one's constituency – or, better still, the name of one's local newspaper – on the record in the chamber or in Westminster Hall as many times as possible.

To achieve this end, MPs scan the agenda to look for opportunities to intervene in questions or debates and then rush from place to place so that they can pop up, utter the name of their constituency and disappear to the next opportunity as soon as is decent (or even sooner). The verb for this activity is 'to ketter', in honour of one of its greatest devotees in the 2005 Parliament, Philip Hollobone, the MP for Kettering, who managed to work the name of his constituency into almost every debate.

A determined ketterer will put down questions containing the name of his or her constituency to every department, including the Foreign Office and the House of Commons catering committee. If the question does not come out of the hat, the ketterer will turn up and 'bob' (stand up to try to catch the Speaker's eye) in the hope of being able to ask it anyway. The ketterer will also turn up at the start of every debate to intervene on the minister to ask a question of astounding irrelevance to the debate, but that, naturally, contains the name of the ketterer's constituency. Ketterers are, of course, a menace for those interested in parliamentary debate, but their party organisations love them, because, from the point of view of the party, the only point of an MP is to achieve re-election, and the only function of Parliament is to assist the MP in that task.

In days past, MPs would deal with all the waiting in another way, namely in other jobs. But second jobs have become very much frowned upon, to the extent that after the expenses crisis the House passed a motion that has been interpreted as meaning that MPs have to report how they spend not just in other paid work but even in volunteering.

This is the infamous 168-hour rule, the rule that MPs are MPs for every hour of the week, with no time off at all for anything else. Even writing a book or an article on politics, paid or not, is seen as a shameful activity to be reported to the authorities. One suspects that in the future those MPs who sleep more hours a night than Margaret Thatcher managed with will have to obtain permission from the Independent Parliamentary Standards Authority. But the effect of the 168-hour rule is that MPs will have to spend even more time just waiting.

One wonders what sort of people will want to be MPs in the future. The combination of minor celebrity status, with its constant observation by the media, enforced inactivity and being cooped up in the same place for weeks on end is reminiscent of only one thing. Welcome, then, to the Big Ben Brother House.

"Actually, I'm more of a voting floater"

MPs who stood down before the election

Conservative

Ainsworth, Peter Surrey East
Ancram, Michael Devizes
Atkinson, Peter Hexham
Boswell, Timothy Daventry
Browning, Angela Tiverton & Honiton
Butterfill, Sir John Bournemouth West
Cormack, Sir Patrick Staffordshire South
Curry, David Skipton & Ripon
Fraser, Christopher Norfolk South West
Goodman, Paul Wycombe
Greenway, John Ryedale
Gummer, John Suffolk Coastal
Hogg, Douglas Sleaford & North Hykeham
Horam, John Orpington
Howard, Michael Folkestone & Hythe
Jack, Michael Fylde
Key, Robert Salisbury
Kirkbride, Julie Bromsgrove
Lait, Jacqui Beckenham
Lord, Sir Michael Suffolk Central & Ipswich North
MacKay, Andrew Bracknell
Maclean, David Penrith & The Border
Malins, Humfrey Woking
Maples, John Stratford-on-Avon
Mates, Michael Hampshire East
Moss, Malcolm Cambridgeshire North East
Spicer, Sir Michael Worcestershire West
Spring, Richard Suffolk West
Steen, Anthony Totnes
Taylor, Ian Esher & Walton
Viggers, Sir Peter Gosport
Widdecombe, Ann Maidstone & The Weald
Wilshire, David Spelthorne
Winterton, Ann Congleton
Winterton, Sir Nicholas Macclesfield

Labour

Armstrong, Hilary Durham North West
Austin, John Erith & Thamesmead
Battle, John Leeds West
Blackman, Liz Erewash
Browne, Des Kilmarnock & Loudoun
Burgon, Colin Elmet
Byers, Stephen Tyneside North
Caborn, Richard Sheffield Central
Challen, Colin Morley & Rothwell
Chapman, Ben Wirral South
Chaytor, David Bury North
Clapham, Michael Barnsley West & Penistone
Clelland, David Tyne Bridge
Cohen, Harry Leyton & Wanstead
Cousins, Jim Newcastle upon Tyne Central
Cryer, Ann Keighley
Cummings, John Easington
Curtis-Thomas, Claire Crosby
Davies, Quentin Grantham & Stamford
Dean, Janet Burton
Devine, Jim Livingston
Ennis, Jeff Barnsley East & Mexborough
Etherington, Bill Sunderland North
Fisher, Mark Stoke-on-Trent Central
Follett, Barbara Stevenage
George, Bruce Walsall South
Gerrard, Neil Walthamstow

Griffiths, Nigel Edinburgh South
Grogan, John Selby
Hall, Mike Weaver Vale
Heal, Sylvia Halesowen & Rowley Regis
Henderson, Doug Newcastle upon Tyne North
Heppell, John Nottingham East
Hesford, Stephen Wirral West
Hewitt, Patricia Leicester West
Hill, Keith Streatham
Hoon, Geoff Ashfield
Howells, Dr Kim Pontypridd
Hughes, Beverley Stretford & Urmston
Humble, Joan Blackpool North & Fleetwood
Hutton, John Barrow & Furness
Iddon, Dr Brian Bolton South East
Ingram, Adam East Kilbride, Strathaven & Lesmahagow
Jones, Martyn Clwyd South
Jones, Lynne Birmingham Selly Oak
Kelly, Ruth Bolton West
Kemp, Fraser Houghton & Washington East
Kennedy, Jane Liverpool Wavertree
Kilfoyle, Peter Liverpool Walton
Laxton, Bob Derby North
Lepper, David Brighton Pavilion
Levitt, Tom High Peak
Mackinlay, Andrew Thurrock
Marshall-Andrews, Robert Medway
Martlew, Eric Carlisle
McAvoy, Thomas Rutherglen & Hamilton West
McCafferty, Christine Calder Valley
McCartney, Ian Makerfield
McFall, John West Dunbartonshire
McKenna, Rosemary Cumbernauld, Kilsyth & Kirkintilloch East
Milburn, Alan Darlington
Moffat, Anne East Lothian
Moffatt, Laura Crawley
Moran, Margaret Luton South
Morley, Elliot Scunthorpe
Mountford, Kali Colne Valley
Mullin, Chris Sunderland South
Murphy, Denis Wansbeck
Naysmith, Doug Bristol North West
O'Hara, Edward Knowsley South
Olner, Bill Nuneaton
Pearson, Ian Dudley South
Pope, Greg Hyndburn
Prentice, Bridget Lewisham East
Prescott, John Kingston upon Hull East
Purchase, Ken Wolverhampton North East
Purnell, James Stalybridge & Hyde
Reid, John Airdrie & Shotts
Salter, Martin Reading West
Sarwar, Mohammad Glasgow Central
Simon, Siôn Birmingham Erdington
Simpson, Alan Nottingham South
Smith, John Vale of Glamorgan
Southworth, Helen Warrington South
Stewart, Ian Eccles
Stoate, Dr Howard Dartford
Strang, Gavin Edinburgh East
Tipping, Paddy Sherwood
Todd, Mark Derbyshire South
Touhig, Don Islwyn
Truswell, Paul Pudsey
Turner, Des Brighton Kemptown
Turner, Neil Wigan

Ussher, **Kitty** Burnley
Vis, **Rudi** Finchley & Golders Green
Williams, **Alan** Swansea West
Williams, **Betty** Conwy
Wills, **Michael** Swindon North
Wright, **Tony** Cannock Chase
Wyatt, **Derek** Sittingbourne & Sheppey

Liberal Democrat

Barrett, **John** Edinburgh West
Breed, **Colin** Cornwall South East
Howarth, **David** Cambridge

Keetch, **Paul** Hereford
Oaten, **Mark** Winchester
Taylor, **Matthew** Truro & St Austell
Willis, **Phil** Harrogate & Knaresborough

Other

Conway, **Derek (Ind Con)** Old Bexley & Sidcup
McGrady, **Eddie (SDLP)** Down South
Paisley, **Ian (DUP)** Antrim North
Price, **Adam (PC)** Carmarthen East & Dinefwr
Salmond, **Alex (SNP)** Banff & Buchan
Short, **Clare (Ind Lab)** Birmingham Ladywood
Wareing, **Robert (Ind)** Liverpool West Derby

Defeated MPs

Conservative
Heathcoat-Amory, David Wells
Waterson, Nigel Eastbourne

Labour
Ainger, Nick Carmarthen West
 & Pembrokeshire South
Anderson, Janet Rossendale & Darwen
Atkins, Charlotte Staffordshire Moorlands
Baird, Vera Redcar
Barlow, Celia Hove
Berry, Roger Kingswood
Blizzard, Bob Waveney
Borrow, David S. South Ribble
Butler, Dawn Brent South
Cawsey, Ian Brigg & Goole
Clark, Paul Gillingham
Clarke, Charles Norwich South
Cook, Frank Stockton North
Dhanda, Parmjit Gloucester
Dismore, Andrew Hendon
Drew, David Stroud
Foster, Michael Worcester
Foster, Michael Jabez Hastings & Rye
Gilroy, Linda Plymouth, Sutton
Hall, Patrick Bedford
Hope, Phil Corby
Jenkins, Brian Tamworth
Keeble, Sally Northampton North
Keen, Ann Brentford & Isleworth
Kidney, David Stafford
Knight, Jim Dorset South
Ladyman, Stephen Thanet South
Linton, Martin Battersea
McCarthy-Fry, Sarah Portsmouth North
McIsaac, Shona Cleethorpes
McNulty, Tony Harrow East
Malik, Shahid Dewsbury
Mallaber, Judy Amber Valley
Marris, Rob Wolverhampton South West
Merron, Gillian Lincoln
Mole, Chris Ipswich
Morgan, Julie Cardiff North

Norris, Dan Wansdyke
O'Brien, Mike Warwickshire North
Palmer, Nick Broxtowe
Plaskitt, James Warwick & Leamington
Prentice, Gordon Pendle
Prosser, Gwyn Dover
Rammell, Bill Harlow
Reed, Andy Loughborough
Rooney, Terry Bradford North
Russell, Christine Chester, City of
Ryan, Joan Enfield North
Shaw, Jonathan Chatham & Aylesford
Smith, Angela E. Basildon South & Thurrock East
Smith, Geraldine Morecambe & Lunesdale
Smith, Jacqui Redditch
Snelgrove, Anne Swindon South
Starkey, Phyllis Milton Keynes South West
Taylor, Dari Stockton South
Waltho, Lynda Stourbridge
Ward, Claire Watford
Wright, Anthony Great Yarmouth

Liberal Democrat
Gidley, Sandra Romsey
Goldsworthy, Julia Falmouth & Camborne
Harris, Evan Oxford West & Abingdon
Holmes, Paul Chesterfield
Kramer, Susan Richmond Park
Öpik, Lembit Montgomeryshire
Rennie, Willie* Dunfermline & Fife West
Rowen, Paul Rochdale
Younger-Ross, Richard Teignbridge

Other
Davies, Dai (Ind) Blaenau Gwent
Galloway, George (Respect) Bethnal Green & Bow
Mason, John* (SNP) Glasgow East
Pelling, Andrew (Ind) Croydon Central
Robinson, Peter (DUP) Belfast East
Spink, Bob (Ind) Castle Point
Taylor, Richard (Ind) Wyre Forest

* Elected at by-election

The Cabinet table, June 2010

■ Conservatives

☐ Liberal Democrats

○ Civil Servant

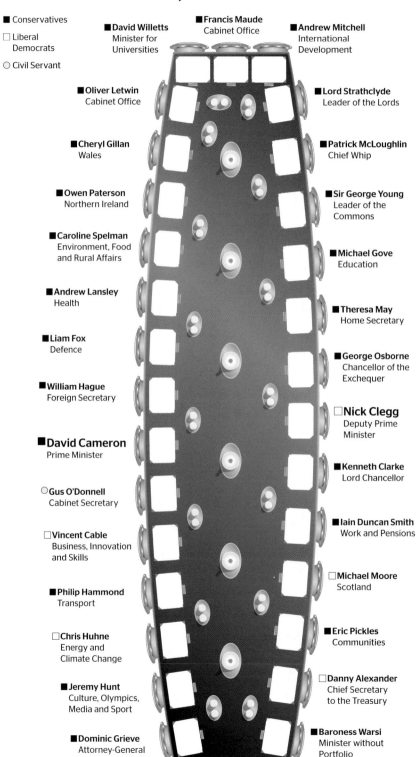

David Willetts
Minister for Universities

Francis Maude
Cabinet Office

Andrew Mitchell
International Development

Oliver Letwin
Cabinet Office

Lord Strathclyde
Leader of the Lords

Cheryl Gillan
Wales

Patrick McLoughlin
Chief Whip

Owen Paterson
Northern Ireland

Sir George Young
Leader of the Commons

Caroline Spelman
Environment, Food and Rural Affairs

Michael Gove
Education

Andrew Lansley
Health

Theresa May
Home Secretary

Liam Fox
Defence

George Osborne
Chancellor of the Exchequer

William Hague
Foreign Secretary

Nick Clegg
Deputy Prime Minister

David Cameron
Prime Minister

Kenneth Clarke
Lord Chancellor

○**Gus O'Donnell**
Cabinet Secretary

Iain Duncan Smith
Work and Pensions

☐**Vincent Cable**
Business, Innovation and Skills

☐**Michael Moore**
Scotland

Philip Hammond
Transport

☐**Chris Huhne**
Energy and Climate Change

Eric Pickles
Communities

Jeremy Hunt
Culture, Olympics, Media and Sport

☐**Danny Alexander**
Chief Secretary to the Treasury

Dominic Grieve
Attorney-General

Baroness Warsi
Minister without Portfolio

Her Majesty's Government

The Cabinet

Prime Minister, First Lord of the Treasury and Minister for the Civil Service	**David Cameron**
Deputy Prime Minister, Lord President of the Council (with special responsibility for political and constitutional reform)	**Nick Clegg**
First Secretary of State, Secretary of State for Foreign and Commonwealth Affairs	**William Hague**
Chancellor of the Exchequer	**George Osborne**
Lord Chancellor, Secretary of State for Justice	**Kenneth Clarke**
Secretary of State for the Home Department and Minister for Women and Equalities	**Theresa May**
Secretary of State for Defence	**Liam Fox**
Secretary of State for Business, Innovation and Skills	**Vincent Cable**
Secretary of State for Work and Pensions	**Iain Duncan Smith**
Secretary of State for Energy and Climate Change	**Chris Huhne**
Secretary of State for Health	**Andrew Lansley**
Secretary of State for Education	**Michael Gove**
Secretary of State for Communities and Local Government	**Eric Pickles**
Secretary of State for Transport	**Philip Hammond**
Secretary of State for Environment, Food and Rural Affairs	**Caroline Spelman**
Secretary of State for International Development	**Andrew Mitchell**
Secretary of State for Northern Ireland	**Owen Paterson**
Secretary of State for Scotland	**Michael Moore**
Secretary of State for Wales	**Cheryl Gillan**
Secretary of State for Culture, Olympics, Media and Sport	**Jeremy Hunt**
Chief Secretary to the Treasury	**Danny Alexander**
Leader of the House of Lords, Chancellor of the Duchy of Lancaster	**Lord Strathclyde**
Minister without Portfolio (Minister of State)	**Baroness Warsi**

Also attending Cabinet meetings

Minister for the Cabinet Office, Paymaster General	**Francis Maude**
Minister of State, Cabinet Office (providing policy advice to the Prime Minister in the Cabinet Office)	**Oliver Letwin**
Minister of State (Universities and Science), Department for Business, Innovation and Skills	**David Willetts**
Leader of the House of Commons, Lord Privy Seal	**Sir George Young**
Parliamentary Secretary to the Treasury and Chief Whip	**Patrick McLoughlin**

Also invited to attend Cabinet meetings when required

Attorney-General	**Dominic Grieve**

Departmental Ministers and Whips

Foreign and Commonwealth Office
First Secretary of State, Secretary of State for Foreign and
Commonwealth Affairs
William Hague (C)
Ministers of State
Jeremy Browne (LD), David Lidington (C),
Lord Howell of Guildford (C)
Parliamentary Under Secretaries of State
Henry Bellingham (C), Alistair Burt (C)

HM Treasury
Chancellor of the Exchequer
George Osborne (C)
Chief Secretary to the Treasury
Danny Alexander (LD)
Financial Secretary
Mark Hoban (C)
Exchequer Secretary
David Gauke (C)
Economic Secretary
Justine Greening (C)
Commercial Secretary
Sir James Sassoon (C)

Ministry of Justice
Lord Chancellor, Secretary of State for Justice
Kenneth Clarke QC (C)
Ministers of State
Lord McNally (LD) (and Deputy Leader of the House of
Lords), Nick Herbert (C) (jointly with the Home Office)
Parliamentary Under Secretaries of State
Crispin Blunt (C), Jonathan Djanogly (C)

Home Office
Secretary of State for the Home Department
and Minister for Women and Equalities
Theresa May (C)
Minister of State (Minister for Immigration)
Damian Green (C)
Minister of State (Minister for Police)
Nick Herbert (C) (jointly with the Ministry of Justice)
Minister of State (Minister for Security)
Baroness Neville-Jones (C)
Parliamentary Under Secretary of State
James Brokenshire (C)
Parliamentary Under Secretary of State
(Minister for Equalities)
Lynne Featherstone (LD)

Ministry of Defence
Secretary of State for Defence
Liam Fox (C)
Minister of State (Minister for the Armed Forces)
Nick Harvey (LD)
Parliamentary Under Secretaries of State
Gerald Howarth (C), Andrew Robathan (C)

Department for Business, Innovation and Skills
Secretary of State for Business, Innovation and Skills, and
President of the Board of Trade
Vincent Cable (LD)
Minister of State (Minister for Universities and Science)
David Willetts (C)
Ministers of State
John Hayes (C), Mark Prisk (C)

Parliamentary Under Secretaries of State
Edward Davey (LD), Ed Vaizey (C) (jointly with the
Department for Culture, Media and Sport),
Baroness Wilcox (C)

Department for Work and Pensions
Secretary of State for Work and Pensions
Iain Duncan Smith (C)
Ministers of State
Chris Grayling (C), Steve Webb (LD)
Parliamentary Under Secretary of State
Maria Miller (C)
Parliamentary Under Secretary of State
(Minister for Welfare Reform)
Lord Freud (C)

Department of Energy and Climate Change
Secretary of State for Energy and Climate Change
Chris Huhne (LD)
Ministers of State
Gregory Barker (C), Charles Hendry (C)
Parliamentary Under Secretary of State
Lord Marland (C)

Department of Health
Secretary of State for Health
Andrew Lansley (C)
Ministers of State
Paul Burstow (LD), Simon Burns (C)
Parliamentary Under Secretaries of State
Anne Milton (C), Earl Howe (C)

Department for Education
Secretary of State for Education
Michael Gove (C)
Ministers of State
Sarah Teather (LD), Nick Gibb (C)
Parliamentary Under Secretaries of State
Tim Loughton (C), Jonathan Hill (C)

Department for Communities and Local Government
Secretary of State for Communities
and Local Government
Eric Pickles (C)
Ministers of State
Greg Clark (C), Grant Shapps (C)
Parliamentary Under Secretaries of State
Andrew Stunell (LD), Bob Neill (C),
Baroness Hanham (C)

Department for Transport
Secretary of State for Transport
Philip Hammond (C)
Minister of State
Theresa Villiers (C)
Parliamentary Under Secretaries of State
Norman Baker (LD), Mike Penning (C)

Department for Environment, Food and Rural Affairs
Secretary of State for Environment, Food and Rural Affairs
Caroline Spelman (C)
Minister of State
James Paice (C)
Parliamentary Under Secretaries of State
Richard Benyon (C), Lord Henley (C)

Department for International Development
Secretary of State for International Development
Andrew Mitchell (C)
Minister of State
Alan Duncan (C)
Parliamentary Under Secretary of State
Stephen O'Brien (C)

Department for Culture, Media and Sport
Secretary of State for Culture, Olympics, Media and Sport
Jeremy Hunt (C)
Parliamentary Under Secretaries of State
John Penrose (C), Hugh Robertson (C), Ed Vaizey (C)
(jointly with the Department for Business, Innovation and Skills)

Northern Ireland Office
Secretary of State for Northern Ireland
Owen Paterson (C)
Minister of State
Hugo Swire (C)

Scotland Office
Secretary of State for Scotland (and providing ministerial support to the Deputy Prime Minister in the Cabinet Office)
Michael Moore (LD)
Parliamentary Under Secretary of State
David Mundell (C)

Wales Office
Secretary of State for Wales
Cheryl Gillan (C)
Parliamentary Under Secretary of State
David Jones (C)
Minister without Portfolio (Minister of State)
Baroness Warsi (C)

Office of the Leader of the House of Lords
Leader of the House of Lords,
Chancellor of the Duchy of Lancaster
Lord Strathclyde (C)

Office of the Leader of the Commons
Leader of the House of Commons, Lord Privy Seal
Sir George Young (C)
Parliamentary Secretary (Deputy Leader)
David Heath (LD)

Cabinet Office
Minister for the Cabinet Office, Paymaster General
Francis Maude (C)
Minister of State (providing policy advice to the Prime Minister in the Cabinet Office)
Oliver Letwin (C)
Parliamentary Secretaries
Mark Harper (C), Nick Hurd (C)

Law Officers
Attorney-General
Dominic Grieve QC (C)
Solicitor-General
Edward Garnier QC (C)
Advocate-General for Scotland
Lord Wallace of Tankerness QC (LD)

Whips – House of Commons
Chief Whip (Parliamentary Secretary to the Treasury)
Patrick McLoughlin (C)
Deputy Chief Whip (Treasurer of HM Household)
John Randall (C)
Deputy Chief Whip (Comptroller of HM Household)
Alistair Carmichael (LD)
Government Whip (Vice Chamberlain of HM Household)
Mark Francois (C)

Junior Lords of the Treasury
Government Whips (Lord Commissioners of HM Treasury)
Michael Fabricant (C)
Angela Watkinson (C)
Jeremy Wright (C)
Brooks Newmark (C)
James Duddridge (C)

Assistant Whips
Assistant Government Whips
Philip Dunne (C)
Stephen Crabb (C)
Robert Goodwill (C)
Shailesh Vara (C)
Bill Wiggin (C)
Chloe Smith (C)
Norman Lamb (LD) (and Chief Parliamentary and Political Adviser to the Deputy Prime Minister)
Mark Hunter (LD)

Whips – House of Lords
Lords Chief Whip (Captain of the Honourable Corps of Gentlemen at Arms)
Baroness Anelay of St Johns (C)
Deputy Chief Whip (Captain of The Queen's Bodyguard of the Yeomen of the Guard)
Lord Shutt of Greetland (LD)

Baronesses and Lords in Waiting
Baronesses in Waiting
Baroness Northover (LD), Baroness Rawlings (C)
Baroness Verma (C)
Lords in Waiting
Earl Attlee (C), Lord Astor of Hever (C)
Lord De Mauley (C),
Lord Taylor of Holbeach (C)
Lord Wallace of Saltaire (LD)

General Election 2010: results by constituency

*"How can you still be
making your minds up,
you bloody dimwits?"*

House of Commons, May 2010

Extensive boundary changes were made to the parliamentary constituencies in which the general election of 2010 was fought, larger in scale than the last such exercise before 1997. The net effect was to create four additional constituencies, taking the total to 650. The new boundaries complicate the presentation of results by constituency. To be meaningful, voting figures should be compared with those of the general election of 2005; yet so far-reaching were the boundary changes in many seats (outside Scotland, which underwent a similar process before the 2005 general election, and were unchanged this time) that such comparisons are often not possible.

In order to give a benchmark, notional voting figures for 2005 are used, based on projections by Professor Colin Rallings and Professor Michael Thrasher, of Plymouth University. Where a constituency has been redrawn extensively, or a new one created, the change from 2005 is based on these notional figures, signified by an asterisk above the column.

Each result is summarised as a 'hold' or 'gain' for the winning party. Again, in the majority of seats this description is a notional one, based on the Rallings-Thrasher calculation transferring the 2005 result into the new constituency boundaries. In a handful of seats, their calculation was that a constituency would have been won by a different party in 2005 had it been fought under the new boundaries: Thanet South in Kent, for instance, would have been gained by the Conservatives in 2005 rather than held by Labour. For consistency, the Guide therefore describes Thanet South, which the Tories gained in 2010, as a Conservative hold.

These results include the election in Thirsk & Malton, which was delayed by three weeks owing to the death during the general election campaign of the candidate for the United Kingdom Independence Party.

Constituencies are listed in alphabetical order. Those within cities, counties or towns are listed with the name of the city, county or town first: Manchester Central comes under 'M', above Manchester Gorton. Dorset West is under 'D', after Dorset South. City of York appears as York, City of.

The new boundaries confer added importance to the short profiles of each constituency in the results pages, a feature introduced in the Guide of 2001. Readers can refer to the colour maps featured elsewhere in the Guide to look up constituencies of interest to them. Short descriptions are provided of unsuccessful candidates who attracted more than 5 per cent of the vote in their constituency and thus held their deposit, where biographical details were supplied by candidates or were readily available. Not all were.

Profiles of each Member of Parliament retain their core purpose of a biographical summary of their background and political experience. To these have been added, where applicable, comments intended to answer the questions most readers may want to know: what is an individual MP like? What motivates them? How effective are they? Where do they fit within the jigsaw of politics? These are intended to be informative but are necessarily subjective; like the accompanying constituency descriptions, they represent the opinions of journalists and writers at *The Times*.
Greg Hurst

Party abbreviations

Parties with MPs
C Conservative; **Lab** Labour; **Lab Co-op** Labour and Co-operative; **LD** Liberal Democrat; **PC** Plaid Cymru; **SNP** Scottish National Party; **Green** Green; **DUP** Democratic Unionist Party; **SDLP** Social Democratic and Labour Party; **SF** Sinn Féin; **Alliance** Alliance

Minor parties
BB A Better Britain for All; **MP Expense** A Vote Against MP Expense Abuse; **South All** The South Party; **Green Soc** Alliance for Green Socialism; **Workers Lib** Alliance for Workers Liberty; **APP** Animal Protection Party; **Animals** Animals Count; **BCP** Basingstoke Common Man; **Blaenau Voice** Blaenau Gwent People's Voice; **Blue** Blue Environment Party; **BNP** British National Party; **BIC** Bromsgrove Independent Conservative; **BP Elvis** Bus-Pass Elvis Party; **BIB** Bushra Irfan of Blackburn; **CIP** Campaign for Independent Politicians; **Christian** Christian; **Ch M** Christian Movement for Great Britain; **Ch P** Christian Party; **CPA** Christian Peoples Alliance; **R and E** Citizens for Undead Rights and Equality; **City Ind** City Independent; **Clause 28** Clause 28, Children's Protection Christian Democrats; **CSP** Common Sense Party; **Comm Lge** Communist League; **Comm** Communist Party; **Comm Brit** Communist Party of Britain; **CNBPG** Community Need Before Private Greed; **Cornish D** Cornish Democrats; **Deficit** Cut the Deficit Party; **Dem Lab** Democratic Labour Party; **D Nat** Democratic Nationalist; **DDP** Direct Democracy Party; **Eng Dem** English Democrats; **Eng Ind** English Independence Party; **Parenting** Equal Parenting Alliance; **FDP** Fancy Dress Party; **Anti-War** Fight for an Anti-War Government; **F and R** For Freedom and Responsibility; **Snouts** Get Snouts Out The Trough; **YP** Go Mad and Vote For Yourself Party; **Humanity** Humanity; **Impact** Impact Party; **Ind** Independent; **Ind CHC** Independent Community and Health Concern; **Ind EACPS** Independent Ealing Action Communities Public Services; **Leave EU** Independent Leave-the-EU Alliance; **Ind People** Independent People Together; **Ind Rantzen** Independent Rantzen; **Green Belt** Independent Save Our Green Belt; **Ind Voice** Independent Voice for Halifax; **Ind Fed** Independents Federation UK; **UK Integrity** Independents Federation UK – Honest Integrity Democracy; **Save QM** Independents to Save Queen Mary's

Hospital; **Integrity** Integrity UK; **IZB** Islam Zinda Baad Platform; **J & AC** Justice & Anti-Corruption Party; **JP** Justice Party; **Land** Land is Power; **LTT** Lawfulness Trustworthiness and Transparency; **Lib** Liberal; **Libertarian** Libertarian Party; **Lincs Ind** Lincolnshire Independents; **LLPBPP** Local Liberals People Before Politics Party; **Magna Carta** Magna Carta Party; **Mansfield Ind** Mansfield Independent Forum; **Meb Ker** Mebyon Kernow; **Med Ind** Medway Independent; **Mid England** Middle England Party; **MRP** Money Reform Party; **Loony** Monster Raving Loony Party; **Nat Dem** National Democrat; **NF** National Front; **NFP** Nationwide Reform Party; **Ind CCF** New Independent Conservative Chelsea and Fulham; **Bean** New Millennium Bean; **No vote** No candidate deserves my vote; **ND** No description; **Nobody** Nobody Party; **NSPS** Northampton - Save Our Public Services; **PPN-V** Peace Party, non-violence, justice, environment; **PBP** People Before Profit; **PNDP** People's National Democratic Party; **PP Essex** Peoples Party Essex; **Pirate** Pirate Party UK; **Battersea** Putting the People of Battersea First; **RRG** Radical Reform Group; **Beer** Reduce Tax on Beer Party; **Reform** Reform 2000; **Respect** Respect the Unity Coalition; **George** Save King George Hospital; **SACL** Scotland Against Crooked Lawyers; **Jacobite** Scottish Jacobite Party; **SSP** Scottish Socialist Party; **SMA** Scrap Members Allowances; **Soc Dem** Social Democratic Party; **Soc Alt** Socialist Alternative Party; **SEP** Socialist Equality Party; **Soc Lab** Socialist Labour Party; **Soc** Socialist Party; **RA** Solihull and Meriden Residents' Association; **Staffs Ind** Staffordshire Independent Group; **TOC** Tamsin Omond to the Commons; **Tendring** Tendring First; **Best** The Best of a Bad Bunch; **Good** The Common Good; **Joy** The Joy of Talk; **Macc Ind** The Macclesfield Independent; **New Party** The New Party; **RP** The Restoration Party; **Science** The Science Party; **Speaker** The Speaker; **Poetry** The True English (Poetry) Party; **TUSC** Trade Unionist and Socialist Coalition; **TUV** Traditional Unionist Voice; **Trust** Trust; **UKIP** UK Independence Party; **Voice** United Voice; **UPS** Unity for Peace and Socialism; **Currency** Virtue Currency Cognitive Appraisal Party; **Reg Wessex** Regionalist Wessex; **UCUNF** Ulster Conservatives and Unionists - New Force; **WP** Workers' Party; **WRP** Workers' Revolutionary Party; **You** You Party; **YRDPL** Your Right to Democracy Party Limited; **Youth** Youth Party

Aberavon Labour hold

Hywel Francis
b. Jun 6, 1946
MP 2001-

Campaigner in the Welsh miners strikes and official historian of the miners' union. Son of Dai Francis, communist and NUM South Wales secretary. Chair, select committees: Welsh Affairs 2005-10 (member 2001-05). Member, Socialist Education Association, Co-op Party. Member European standing committee B. University professor, lecturer and tutor. Fellow, Royal Society of the Arts. Married, one daughter, two sons – one deceased. Ed: Whitchurch GS, Cardiff; Uni Coll of Wales, Swansea (BA history, PhD).

Keith Davies (LD) b. July 24, 1946. Retired petrochemical engineer. Contested Vale of Glamorgan 1992 and 1987. Ed: Neath Technical Coll, Neath.
Caroline Jones (C) Entrepreneur. Former teacher, local government officer and prison officer.
Paul Nicholls-Jones (PC) b. 1954. Renewable energy entrepreneur. Ed: Porth Grammar School.

Constituency
This South Wales seat encompasses a stretch of industrial coastline around Port Talbot. A controversial new power station lies by the mouth of the River Neath and Aberavon Sands, while the Corus steelworks is close to the Margam Sands. This is a working-class seat in which about a fifth of residents live in social housing and about 25 per cent work in manufacturing. Reaching inland, it includes Baglan, Cwmafan and Glyncorrwg. Once Ramsay MacDonald's seat, it has been solidly Labour for decades.

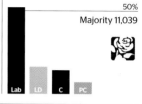

	Electorate	Turnout %	Change from '05 %
	50,789	61.0	
Francis, H Lab	16,073	51.9	-8.1
Davies, K LD	5,034	16.3	2.6
Jones, C C	4,411	14.3	4.2
Nicholls-Jones, P PC	2,198	7.1	-4.6
Edwards, K BNP	1,276	4.1	
Tutton, A Ind	919	3.0	
Beany, C Bean	558	1.8	
Callan, J UKIP	489	1.6	

50%
Majority 11,039

Lab | LD | C | PC

Aberconwy Conservative gain

Guto Bebb
b. Oct 9, 1968
MP 2010-

Former Plaid Cymru activist and Caernarfon party chair - the grandson of Ambrose Bebb, Plaid Cymru's co-founder. Defected to the Conservatives owing to Eurosceptic views (Member, Business for Sterling in Wales, Open Europe). Contested Conwy 2005, Ogmore 2002 by-election; Conwy 2003 Welsh Assembly election. Self-employed, Partneriaeth Egin Partnership (economic development consultancy). Business development director, Innovas Wales. Ran bookshop with wife. Married, two daughters, three sons. Ed: Ysgol Syr Hugh Owen; University of Wales, Aberystwyth (BA history); MIBA.

Ronald Hughes (Lab) b. Sep 14, 1948. Former maintenance fitter. Cllr, Conwy BC (former leader).
Mike Priestley (LD) b. 1966. Delivery office manager, Royal Mail; Cllr, Llandudno Junction. Ed: Ysgol Aberconwy.
Phil Edwards (PC) b. 1953. Cllr. Former Gen Sec of the North Wales Police Fed. Contested Clwyd West, Welsh Assembly elections 2007.

Constituency
This large North Wales seat reaches from Llandudno and Conwy on the coast to Llanrwst, Betws-y-Coed and beyond. Based on the old Conwy seat, it no longer includes Bangor, instead extending farther south. Much of the west of the seat lies within the Snowdonia National Park and tourism is a major employer. The old seat was safely Tory until Labour took it in 1997 and boundary changes reduced Labour's majority.

	Electorate	Turnout %	Change from '05 %
	44,593	67.2	☆
Bebb, G C	10,734	35.8	6.8
Hughes, R Lab	7,336	24.5	-8.5
Priestley, M LD	5,786	19.3	0.2
Edwards, P PC	5,341	17.8	3.8
Wieteska, M UKIP	632	2.1	1.0
Wynne-Jones, L Ch	137	0.5	

50%
Majority 3,398

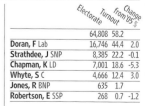

C | Lab | LD | PC

Aberdeen North Labour hold

Frank Doran
b. Apr 13, 1949
MP 1997-, 1987-92

Quietly spoken co-ordinator of trade union sponsored MPs. Member, select committees: CMS 2001-10. PPS to Ian McCartney 1999-2001; 1997-99. Opposition spokesman, Energy 1988-92. MP Aberdeen Central 1997-2005; Aberdeen South 1987-92. Solicitor. Chair Dundee mental health association. Divorced, two sons. Partner of Joan Ruddock MP. Ed: Ainslie Park School; Leith Academy; Dundee (LLB).

Joanna Strathdee (SNP) b. Dec 27, 1954. Cllr, Aberdeen (SNP group leader 2007-). Contested Gordon 2005.
Kristian Chapman (LD) b. April 12, 1988. Student. Ed: St. Bedes Catholic HS; Uni of Aberdeen.
Stewart Whyte (C) b. 1971. Secondary school teacher. Ed: Uni of Aberdeen. Contested Aberdeen South 2005 and Aberdeen Central 2001.

Constituency
Spanning south from the River Don to Aberdeen city centre, this seat includes the university and Aberdeen harbour, an important base for the North Sea oil industry. The large council estates of Seaton and Hilton typify the seat, although it also includes one rural ward to the west with villages such as Kingswells. This seat had major boundary changes in 1995 and 2005. It has returned Labour MPs since 1945 despite recent support for the Scottish National Party.

	Electorate	Turnout %	Change from '05 %
	64,808	58.2	
Doran, F Lab	16,746	44.4	2.0
Strathdee, J SNP	8,385	22.2	-0.1
Chapman, K LD	7,001	18.6	-5.3
Whyte, S C	4,666	12.4	3.0
Jones, R BNP	635	1.7	
Robertson, E SSP	268	0.7	-1.2

50%
Majority 8,361

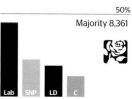

Lab | SNP | LD | C

Aberdeen South — Labour hold

Anne Begg
b. Dec 6, 1955
MP 1997-

Prominent disabled member. Ran Speakers' committee on representation. Elected Chair, cttee: Work & Pensions 2010-. Member cttees: Chairmen's Panel 2001-10; Work & Pensions 2001-10; Scottish Affairs 1997-2001. Member: Lab Party NEC 1998-99; PLP Lab Party policy forum; Educational Inst of Scotland; Gen Teaching Council for Scotland. Disabled Scot of the Year 1988. English teacher. Ed: Brechin HS; Aberdeen (MA history and politics); Aberdeen College of Education (Secondary teaching certificate).

John Sleigh (LD) b. May 17, 1985. Farmer and constituency assistant to Nicol Stephen MSP. Ed: Glasgow Uni.

Founded and chaired a farming collective in the area.
Amanda Harvie (C) b. Jan 5, 1965. MD of The Harvie Consultancy, previously chief exec of Scottish Financial Enterprise. Ed: London University.
Mark McDonald (SNP) b. 1980. Cllr, Aberdeen CC (Dep Leader SNP group). Ed: Dundee Uni; Aberdeen Uni.

Constituency
This seat covers the southern part of the city of Aberdeen, with the south harbour, the low-cost housing estates of the former fishing village of Torry, and Robert Gordon University. A mixed seat, it extends to the more affluent residential suburbs of Peterculter and Cults and rural areas to the west. In the 1980s and 1990s, the seat flipped between Labour and the Conservatives, most recently switching to Labour in 1997.

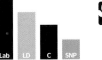

	Electorate	Turnout %	Change from '05 %
	64,031	67.2	
Begg, A Lab	15,722	36.5	-0.1
Sleigh, J LD	12,216	28.4	-5.0
Harvie, A C	8,914	20.7	3.6
McDonald, M SNP	5,102	11.9	2.0
Ross, S BNP	529	1.2	
Reekie, R Green	413	1.0	-0.9
Green, R SACL	138	0.3	

50%
Majority 3,506

Aberdeenshire West & Kincardine — Liberal Democrat hold

Sir Robert Smith
b. Apr 15, 1958
MP 1997-

Low-profile but effective performer. Baronet whose grandfather and cousin were Tory MPs in NE Scotland. LD: whip 2008-10; deputy shadow leader of House of Commons 2007-10; spokes Trade & Industry 2005-06; deputy chief whip 2001-06; whip 1999-2001; spokes Scotland 1999-2001. Cllr, Aberdeenshire 1995-97. JP 1997. Vice-convener Grampian Joint Police Board. Member, Electoral Reform Soc. Family estate manager. Married, three daughters. Ed: Merchant Taylor's School; Aberdeen (BSc).

Alex Johnstone (C) b. 1961. MSP 1999- (Rural affairs spokesman, former Scottish Conservative Chief Whip).

Contested Aberdeenshire West & Kincardine 2005.
Dennis Robertson (SNP) Client service manager for a sensory impairment charity. Ed: Royal Blind School, Edinburgh.
Greg Williams (Lab) b. Feb 5, 1984. Works for an oil industry company. Ed: Oxford Uni; York Uni (MA).

Constituency
This affluent rural seat includes a stretch of coastline south of Aberdeen, where historic towns such as Stonehaven are popular with commuters. Reaching inland, the main settlements of Banchory, Aboyne, Ballater and Braemar line the River Dee. Flanked by Cairngorm and Grampian Mountains and boasting attractions such as Highland Games and Balmoral Castle, this area is popular with tourists. Has been held by the Lib Dems since 1997.

	Electorate	Turnout %	Change from '05 %
	66,110	68.4	
Smith, R LD	17,362	38.4	-7.9
Johnstone, A C	13,678	30.3	2.0
Robertson, D SNP	7,086	15.7	4.5
Williams, G Lab	6,159	13.6	0.5
Raikes, G BNP	513	1.1	
Atkinson, A UKIP	397	0.9	

50%
Majority 3,684

Airdrie & Shotts — Labour hold

Pamela Nash
b. Jun 24, 1984
MP 2010-

The Baby of the House, one of the new "Facebook generation" intake of Scottish Labour MPs. Won all-female shortlist selection prompting resignation of local party chairman. Overcame personal tragedy of death of her mother and stepfather in 2002. Local candidate. Parliamentary researcher to John Reid. Worked for Boots chemists. Lasallion Developing World project. Young Fabians. Scottish Youth Parliament. Ed: St Margaret's Sch, Airdrie; Glasgow (Politics).

Sophia Coyle (SNP) Cllr, North Lanarkshire. Contested Scottish Parliament election, Airdrie & Shotts 2007.

Ruth Whitfield (C) b. 1978. Constituency PA for David McLetchie MSP. Trainee podiatrist. Ed: Edinburgh Uni.
John Love (LD) b. Aug 2, 1941. Retired accountant. Ed: Airdrie Academy, Airdrie. Former Conservative candidate for Airdrie and Shotts in the 1980s.

Constituency
The town of Airdrie lies east of Glasgow and in the northern half of this seat, which is bisected by the M8. To its south is Shotts, known for its high-security prison. Both towns were once dependent on traditional industries such as steel, and have not recovered from their decline. They are working-class and there is a large proportion of social housing. This seat and its predecessors have long been represented by Labour MPs, including John Smith, the late party leader.

	Electorate	Turnout %	Change from '05 %
	62,364	57.5	
Nash, P Lab	20,849	58.2	-0.8
Coyle, S SNP	8,441	23.6	7.1
Whitfield, R C	3,133	8.7	-1.1
Love, J LD	2,898	8.1	-3.3
McGeechan, J Ind	528	1.5	

50%
Majority 12,408

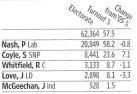

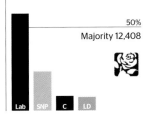

Gerald Howarth
b. Sep 12, 1947
MP 1997-; 1983-92

Diminutive, combative diehard Thatcherite, council member of The Freedom Association, founder member of No Turning Back Group. A champion of defence spending and outspoken on curbing immigration. Parly Under-Sec, Defence 2010-. Shadow Defence Minister 2002-10. PPS to Margaret Thatcher 1991-2. MP Cannock & Burntwood 1983-92. Qualified pilot, commissioned into RAFVR. International banker, Bank of America. Loan arranger, Standard Chartered Bank. Married, one daughter, two sons. Ed: Bloxham School, Banbury; Southampton (BA English).

Adrian Collett (LD) b. Mar 30, 1958. Cllr and Police Authority member. Contested Aldershot since 1992. Ed: Salesian Coll, Farnborough.
Jonathan Slater (Lab) b. May 6, 1977. Policy Officer in Children's Services. Ed: Essex Uni.

Constituency
In the northeastern corner of Hampshire, this is a densely populated seat. Aldershot itself lies in the south while to its north is Aldershot Military Town, known as "the home of the British Army", with up to 4,000 troops stationed here. Beyond this lie North Camp, Farnborough – astride the M3 and home to the airshow – and Blackwater. Boundary changes have removed Yateley. The seat is affluent, though less so than its neighbours, with patches of deprivation. It has a long tradition of Tory representation.

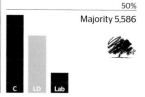

	Electorate	Turnout %	Change from '05 %
	71,469	63.5	☆
Howarth, G C	21,203	46.7	2.7
Collett, A LD	15,617	34.4	5.5
Slater, J Lab	5,489	12.1	-9.6
Snare, R UKIP	2,041	4.5	2.1
Crowd, G Eng	803	1.8	
Brimicombe, J Ch	231	0.5	

Majority 5,586

Richard Shepherd
b. Dec 6, 1942
MP 1979-

Passionate and emotional parliamentarian with contrarian instincts, strong defender of civil liberties and verged on tears in speeches on parliamentary sovereignty. A determined opponent of guillotining debates. Admired for his principles but not influential. An also-ran in 2009 election for Speaker. Maastricht rebel, lost whip 1994. Co-chair, Campaign for Freedom of Information. Former grocery business director; underwriter at Lloyds. Education: Isleworth Grammar School; LSE; Johns Hopkins School of Advanced International Studies. (MSc Economics).

Ashiq Hussain (Lab) b. Oct 15, 1955. Small business owner. Former Cllr, Derby and former Trade Union shop steward. Chaired a local Pakistani Community Centre. MBE.
Ian Jenkins (LD) b. Jan 10, 1951. Sales agent. Ed: Wolverhampton Polytechnic.

Constituency
Named after its two towns, this Walsall seat lies at the northeast of the West Midlands conurbation, on the border with Staffordshire. Aldridge, at the south, is very affluent and often referred to as a village. Brownhills, farther out, is a former mining community; manufacturing has had an important place in this seat and there are high numbers of working-class voters. The eastern Walsall suburbs of Pelsall and Rushall are also included. The seat has been Conservative since 1979.

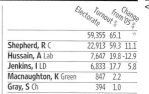

	Electorate	Turnout %	Change from '05 %
	59,355	65.1	☆
Shepherd, R C	22,913	59.3	11.1
Hussain, A Lab	7,647	19.8	-12.9
Jenkins, I LD	6,833	17.7	5.8
Macnaughton, K Green	847	2.2	
Gray, S Ch	394	1.0	

Majority 15,266

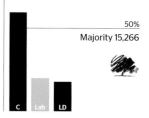

Graham Brady
b. May 20, 1967
MP 1997-

Genial right-winger, with a resemblance to Prince Andrew. Resigned from Cameron's front bench in row over grammar schools and has exploited martyrdom. Key figure in dealing with potential unrest among Tory MPs about coalition, as chairman of 1922 Committee 2010-. Shadow Minister: Europe 2004-07; Schools 2001-03. Parliamentary private secretary to Michael Howard 2003-04; Michael Ancram 1999-2000. Opposition whip 2000. PR career: Waterfront Partnership, Shandwick and Centre for Policy Studies. Married, one daughter, one son. Education: Altrincham Grammar School; Durham (BA Law).

Jane Brophy (LD) b. Aug 28, 1963. Sub-regional programme manager, NHS. Contested Eccles 2005. Education: Leeds Uni.
Tom Ross (Lab) b. Oct 7, 1981. Bank manager. Cllr, Trafford. Ed: Altrincham Grammar School; LSE.

Constituency
This city of Trafford seat is markedly different to most of the Greater Manchester conurbation to its northeast. The market town of Altrincham has recently undergone major development and, with Sale, has become a middle-class enclave. In the east of the seat the countryside is dotted with affluent villages. Conservative since the Second World War, in 2005 it was the last Tory seat in Manchester.

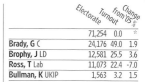

	Electorate	Turnout %	Change from '05 %
	71,254	0.0	☆
Brady, G C	24,176	49.0	1.9
Brophy, J LD	12,581	25.5	3.6
Ross, T Lab	11,073	22.4	-7.0
Bullman, K UKIP	1,563	3.2	1.5

Majority 11,595

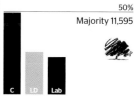

Alyn & Deeside — Labour hold

Mark Tami
b. Oct 31, 1962
MP 2001-

Amiable and well liked. Assistant government whip 2007-10. PPS to: John Healey 2005-06. Member, select committees: Joint committee Human Rights 2007; Joint committee Tax Law Rewrite Bills 2005-07; NI Affairs 2001-05. Member AEEU Amicus, TUC General Council. AEEU research & communications head; policy head. Norwich City fan. Married, two sons. Education: Enfield GS; Swansea (BA history).

Will Gallagher (C) b. 1981. Manages family garage business. Contested Welsh Assembly elections, Alyn and Deeside 2007. Education: Cambridge Uni.

Paul Brighton (LD) Tutor in local history, former Sixth Form head. Contested Alyn & Deeside 2005. Education: Exeter Uni.

Constituency

This seat borders Chester in England. Queensferry, Connah's Quay and Buckley dominate the north, with industrial works along the River Dee. The south, around Caergwrle, is more rural while Broughton at the east is home to a BAE Systems factory that builds wings for Airbus planes. The constituency's demographic is fairly evenly split across the middle and working classes, while manufacturing is a traditionally strong sector. This seat has been Labour since its inception in 1983.

	Electorate	Turnout %	Change from '05 %
	60,931	65.5	
Tami, M Lab	15,804	39.6	-9.2
Gallagher, W C	12,885	32.3	7.1
Brighton, P LD	7,308	18.3	1.0
Jones, M PC	1,549	3.9	0.2
Walker, J BNP	1,368	3.4	
Howson, J UKIP	1,009	2.5	-0.1

50%
Majority 2,919

Lab | C | LD

Amber Valley — Conservative gain

Nigel Mills
b. Oct 28, 1974
MP 2010-

Endured two recounts before winning seat. Cllr, Amber Valley BC 2004-; Heanor & Loscoe Town 2007-. Accountant: Deloitte; PriceWaterhouseCoopers (advising businesses on international tax issues). Institute of Chartered Accountants. Season ticket holder Notts County Cricket. Bereaved partner of Gillian Shaw, Tory PPC 2005, 2001 (died 2006). Education: Loughborough Grammar School, Newcastle-upon-Tyne (Classics).

Judy Mallaber (Lab) b. Jul 10, 1951. MP Amber Valley 1997-2010. Dir, Local Govt Info Unit; NUPE officer. Ed: Oxford Uni.

Tom Snowdon (LD) b. Jan 22, 1957. Chartered engineer. Contested NE Derbyshire 2005. Ed: Leic Uni (MBA), **Michael Clarke** (BNP) b. Nov 14, 1956. Self-employed upholstery designer. Ed: Swanwick Hall GS, Derbyshire.

Constituency

To the north of Derby city and to the west of the M1, this mixed seat is criss-crossed by A-roads, with the towns of Alfreton, Ripley and Heanor – where the BNP does well – and several villages around them. River Amber cuts through the northern corner. Manufacturing dominates economy and seat has high proportion of working-class residents. Pockets of deprivation, but much of area averagely well off. It was Conservative from 1983 until 1997. Under boundary changes it lost areas from the south and north west of the seat.

	Electorate	Turnout %	Change from '05 %
	70,171	65.5	☆
Mills, N C	17,746	38.6	4.7
Mallaber, J Lab	17,210	37.5	-9.0
Snowdon, T LD	6,636	14.4	2.1
Clarke, M BNP	3,195	7.0	
Ransome, S UKIP	906	2.0	0.3
Thing, S Loony	265	0.6	

50%
Majority 536

C | Lab | LD | BNP

Angus — Scottish National Party hold

Mike Weir
b. Mar 24, 1957
MP 2001-

Earnest, hard-working but lacking presence. SNP spokesman: environment 2007-10; trade & industry & energy 2005-10; work & pensions 2005-07; environment 2004; health 2004; trade & industry 2004. Cllr, Angus DC 1984-88. Solicitor. Law Soc of Scotland. Married, two daughters. Ed: Arbroath HS; Aberdeen (LLB).

Alberto Costa (C) Solicitor. Ed: Glasgow Uni.
Kevin Hutchens (Lab) b. Dec 18, 1957. Social Worker. Ed: Kent Uni.
Sanjay Samani (LD) b. April 12, 1973. IT project manager, small business owner. Ed: Loughborough Grammar School; Jesus Coll, Cambridge.

Constituency

This varied Scottish seat spans the coast north of Dundee, encompassing the port towns of Montrose and Arbroath. The latter is famous for the 1320 declaration of Scottish Independence and its smokies, the haddock delicacy. Reaching inland, the seat includes the market town of Forfar, amid the agricultural land of the Strathmore Valley, and farther inland to the Grampian Mountains, where hill farming dominates the economy of the Angus Glens. The seat and its predecessors have changed hands between the SNP and Tories historically and though the Nationalists have held it since 1987, their majorities have been thin.

	Electorate	Turnout %	Change from '05 %
	62,863	60.4	
Weir, M SNP	15,020	39.6	6.0
Costa, A C	11,738	30.9	1.5
Hutchens, K Lab	6,535	17.2	-0.7
Samani, S LD	4,090	10.8	-6.6
Gray, M UKIP	577	1.5	

50%
Majority 3,282

SNP | C | Lab | LD

Antrim East — Democratic Unionist Party hold

Sammy Wilson
b. Apr 4, 1953
MP 2005-

Bluff and good-humoured finance minister in the Northern Ireland Executive. A motorbike-loving sometime naturist (who sued a Sunday tabloid for publishing his naked holiday snaps), as environment minister he scoffed at global warming fears. DUP HoC spokes 2003-. MLA: East Antrim 2003-; Belfast East 1998-2003. Member, NI Policing Board. Cllr, East Belfast City 1981-, Lord Mayor 1986. DUP press officer. Schoolteacher (head of economics at grammar school). Ed: Methodist Coll; Queen's, Belfast (BA econ & pol); Stranmillis Coll (DipEd).

Rodney McCune (UCUNF) Criminal barrister. Ed: London.

Gerry Lynch (Alliance) b. Jul 28, 1977. Exec dir, Alliance Party of NI.
Oliver McMullan (SF) Publican. Cllr, Moyle DC 1993-. First Sinn Féin chair of local District Policing Partnership.
Justin McCamphill (SDLP) b. 1973. Teacher. Member of SDLP executive.
Sammy Morrison (TUV)

Constituency
The fourth most Protestant constituency in Northern Ireland, with the Catholic population concentrated at its southern and northern extremities. A coastal sliver, it begins as commuter belt for Belfast, runs through dormitory towns such as Carrickfergus, with its castle, and ends in the Glens of Antrim. Although there are pockets of deprivation, it is middle class and home to the Uni of Ulster campus at Jordanstown. The DUP took the seat in 2005, having lost out by a few votes to the UUP in 2001.

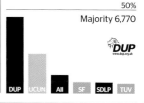

	Electorate	Turnout %	Change from '05 %
	60,204	50.7	
Wilson, S DUP	13,993	45.9	-1.0
McCune, R UCUNF	7,223	23.7	
Lynch, G Alliance	3,377	11.1	-3.6
McMullan, O SF	2,064	6.8	1.4
McCamphill, J SDLP	2,019	6.6	-0.8
Morrison, S TUV	1,826	6.0	

50%

Majority 6,770

| DUP | UCUN | All | SF | SDLP | TUV |

Antrim North — Democratic Unionist Party hold

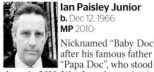

Ian Paisley Junior
b. Dec 12, 1966
MP 2010-

Nicknamed "Baby Doc" after his famous father "Papa Doc", who stood down in 2010. Was forced to resign in 2008 as a junior minister in the power-sharing Executive over his relationship with a property developer (though later cleared by the Stormont Ombudsman). MLA: North Antrim 2003-; North Antrim 1998-2003. Member, NI Policing Board. Elected member of NI Forum for political dialogue 1996-98. DUP Justice spokesman, press officer. Married, two daughters, two sons. Ed: Methodist Coll; Queen's, Belfast (MA Irish Politics, BA Modern History).

Jim Allister (TUV) b. Apr 2, 1953. Leader of TUV; resigned from DUP.

Criminal barrister, QC. Ed: Regent House GS; Queen's University, Belfast.
Daithi McKay (SF) b. Mar 2, 1982. SF environment spokes. Ed: St. Louis' GS.
Irwin Armstrong (UCUNF) Management consultant. Ed: Ballymena Academy; Ulster Uni.
Declan O'Loan (SDLP) b. Aug 5, 1951. Maths teacher. Ed: St MacNissi Coll, Garron Tower; Imperial Coll.

Constituency
Famous for the Giant's Causeway. The giant of Ulster politics, the Rev Ian Paisley, held the seat for the 40 years until this election. It is the Ulster Scots heartland, where resistance to Irish identity is strongest. The "capital" Ballymena is often referred to as the buckle in Ulster's Bible belt, a manufacturing centre reputed to be home to Northern Ireland's greatest number of millionaires.

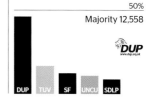

	Electorate	Turnout %	Change from '05 %
	73,338	57.8	*
Paisley Jr, I DUP	19,672	46.4	
Allister, J TUV	7,114	16.8	
McKay, D SF	5,265	12.4	-1.8
Armstrong, I UCUNF	4,634	10.9	
O'Loan, D SDLP	3,738	8.8	-2.2
Dunlop, J Alliance	1,368	3.2	0.2
Cubitt, L ND	606	1.4	

50%

Majority 12,558

| DUP | TUV | SF | UNCU | SDLP |

Antrim South — Democratic Unionist Party hold

Rev William McCrea
b. Aug 6, 1948
MP 2005-; 2000-01; 1983-87

"Singing Billy", a country and western recording artist who once shared a platform with a notorious loyalist terrorist. DUP spokes environment, food & rural affairs 2005-. MLA 1998-. Member, NI Assembly 1982-86. MP for Mid Ulster 1983-87. Cllr, Magherafelt DC 1973-. Civil servant, NI Dept of Health & Social Services Minister. Married, three daughters, two sons. Ed: Cookstown GS; Marietta Bible Coll, Ohio (Doctorate in divinity); Theological Coll of Free Presbyterian Church of Ulster.

Sir Reg Empey (UCUNF) b. Oct 26, 1967. Lord Mayor of Belfast 1993, 1989. UUP Leader 2005-10. Ed: Queen's Uni.

Mitchel McLaughlin (SF) b. Nov 29, 1945. Gen Sec SF 2003-07. MLA Foyle 1998-2007, Antrim South 2007-10.
Michelle Byrne (SDLP). Constituency aide to Conall McDevitt MLA. Ed: Queen's Uni, Belfast
Alan Lawther (Alliance). Commercial manager. Ed: Belfast Royal Academy; Cambridge.
Mel Lucas (TUV)

Constituency
A deceptively suburban constituency in spite of a rural landscape, its motorways and airport make South Antrim home to many Belfast commuters. It borders Lough Neagh, the largest freshwater lake in the British Isles. Antrim, its largest town, is blue-collar. Protestants account for two thirds of the population. The seat has been closely fought between the UUP and DUP, with supporters of other parties often voting tactically.

	Electorate	Turnout %	Change from '05 %
	63,054	53.9	*
McCrea, Rev W DUP	11,536	33.9	
Empey, R UCUNF	10,353	30.4	
McLaughlin, M SF	4,729	13.9	3.2
Byrne, M SDLP	2,955	8.7	-2.5
Lawther, A Alliance	2,607	7.7	-0.6
Lucas, M TUV	1,829	5.4	

50%

Majority 1,183

| DUP | UNCU | SF | SDLP | All | TUV |

Arfon

Hywel Williams
b. May 14, 1953
MP 2001-

Lyrical Welshman. PC spokes: defence, transport 2007-09; Treasury 2006-07; education & skills/CSF 2005-; culture, media & sport 2005-06; internet dev't 2004-; work & pensions, soc security, health 2001-; disability 2001-05. MP Caernarfon 2001-10. PC policy cabinet, policy developer for social security and older people. Social worker, project worker, social work and policy lecturer, consultant, author. Divorced, three daughters. Ed: Glan y Môr Sch; Wales Uni: Cardiff (BSc psychology); Bangor (CQSW social work).

Alan Pugh (Lab) b. Jun 9, 1955. Memb Welsh Assembly, Clwyd West 1999-2007. Dir, Snowdonia Society. Ed: Tonypandy GS; Glamorgan Uni.
Robin Millar (C) Local government managment consultant. Cllr, Forest Heath. Ed: Manchester Uni.
Sarah Green (LD) b. Apr 25, 1982. PR executive. Contested Ynys Môn 2005, Ed: Aberystwyth.

Constituency

This new Welsh seat is bounded by the Menai Strait, dividing it from Ynys Môn. The two main towns, Bangor and Caernarfon, both lie by the water, while Bethesda is slightly inland. The eastern half of the seat is more rural, much of it within the Snowdonia National Park. Hill farming is very important to the economy. The seat has one of the highest concentrations of Welsh-speakers. The old Caernarfon seat was held by Plaid Cymru since 1974 but the Bangor area from the old Conwy seat is seen as more Labour-leaning.

	Electorate	Turnout %	Change from '05 %
	41,198	63.3	☆
Williams, H PC	9,383	36.0	3.9
Pugh, A Lab	7,928	30.4	-3.5
Millar, R C	4,416	16.9	0.5
Green, S LD	3,666	14.1	-1.7
Williams, E UKIP	685	2.6	0.7

50%
Majority 1,455

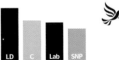

| PC | Lab | C | LD |

Argyll & Bute

Alan Reid
b. Aug 7, 1954
MP 2001-

Low profile. Lib Dem: whip 2009-10. LD shadow minister: Scotland 2007-10; Northern Ireland 2006-10; IT and Trade & Industry 2005-06. LD spokesman: Scotland 2004-05. LD whip 2002-10. Scottish Lib Dems vice-convener, member executive committee. Election agent to George Lyon, Scottish Parliament 1999. Cllr, Renfrew DC 1988-96. Computer project programmer. Teacher. Ed: Prestwick Academy; Ayr Academy; Strathclyde (BSc maths); Jordanhill College (teacher training); Bell Coll (computer data processing).

Gary Mulvaney (C) b. 1968. Chartered certified accountant, works for a local motor dealer. Cllr, Argyll & Bute DC.
David Graham (Lab) b. Feb 6, 1953. Community education worker.
Michael MacKenzie (SNP) Construction company owner. Ed: Allan Glens Sch; Glasgow Uni.

Constituency

This seat covers a vast, remote and beautiful swath of Scottish coastline and 26 inhabited islands including Mull, Jura and Bute. Inland, the seat reaches through Argyll moorland to the foot of the Grampians. The main towns are Oban, a ferry port, and Helensburgh, at the south of the seat and in commuter reach of Glasgow. Faslane, the base for the Trident nuclear submarine fleet, is also in the seat. It has been represented by the Tories, SNP and Liberal Democrats since the 1970s.

	Electorate	Turnout %	Change from '05 %
	67,165	67.3	☆
Reid, A LD	14,292	31.6	-4.9
Mulvaney, G C	10,861	24.0	0.6
Graham, D Lab	10,274	22.7	0.3
MacKenzie, M SNP	8,563	18.9	3.4
Morrison, E Green	789	1.8	
Doyle, G Ind	272	0.6	
Black, J Jacobite	156	0.4	

50%
Majority 3,431

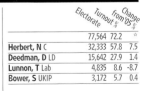

| LD | C | Lab | SNP |

Arundel & South Downs

Nick Herbert
b. Apr 7, 1963
MP 2005-

Diffident intellectual and former think-tank director, disinterested in personality politics. Inconsistent public performances have dented his reputation as a reliable front-line terrier and he is yet to make a big impact. A prominent homosexual; the first Tory MP openly gay at time of election. Missed out on secretarial brief in first coalition government. Min: Home/Justice (Police) 2010-. Shadow SoS: DEFRA 2009-10; Justice 2007-09. Co-founder, Reform 2002-05. Civil partnership. Ed: Haileybury Sch; Magdalene Coll, Cambridge (BA Law and land economy).

Derek Deedman (LD) b. Mar 25, 1947. Cllr, W Sussex CC. Contested Arundel & South Downs 2005, 2001. Local government career. Ed: Stourfield Sch.
Tim Lunnon (Lab) b. Dec 31, 1985. Engineer. Ed: Bath Uni.

Constituency

This vast rural constituency takes in the heart of West Sussex including, as the name suggests, the green hills of the Downs. Apart from Arundel, other small towns include Pulborough and Steyning. The area is generally relatively well off, with high numbers of professionals and a notable number of self-employed, especially in agriculture. Relatively minor boundary changes add the market town of Petworth and surrounding area. The seat has been Tory since its creation in 1997 but the party's dominance in the area stretches back far longer.

	Electorate	Turnout %	Change from '05 %
	77,564	72.2	☆
Herbert, N C	32,333	57.8	7.5
Deedman, D LD	15,642	27.9	1.4
Lunnon, T Lab	4,835	8.6	-8.7
Bower, S UKIP	3,172	5.7	0.4

50%
Majority 16,691

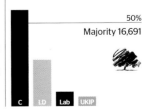

| C | LD | Lab | UKIP |

Ashfield

Gloria de Piero
b. Dec 21, 1972
MP 2010-

GMTV political cor-respondent, whose selection ten weeks before the general election led to allegations she had been parachuted into the seat. Glamorous appearance and youthful foray into topless modelling used by detractors to undermine her bright, working-class credentials. Raised by Italian-immigrant parents in Bradford without an inside toilet. Career: Chair, Labour students; BBC researcher. Education: Bradford & Ilkley College; Westminster Uni (BA Social Science); London (MSc Social & Political Theory).

Jason Zadrozny (LD) Actor, drama teacher and community centre worker.

Cllr: Notts CC; Ashfield DC. Ed: West Nottinghamshire Coll.
Garry Hickton (C) b. Jul 13, 1961. Manager, Co-op Group. Ed: Long Eaton GS; Co-operative Coll, Stanford Hall.

Constituency
Ashfield is on the border with Derbyshire. The M1 cuts through this seat, which is quite densely populated with the towns of Sutton-in-Ashfield, Kirkby-in-Ashfield and Eastwood and villages such as Annesley. The decline of coalmining and textile industries hit the area hard. Ashfield's last pit closed just after the millennium. D. H. Lawrence was born in Eastwood but the area's claim to literary fame is surpassed by its cricketing heritage. Five future England Test players worked at Annesley Colliery. The seat has a long Labour tradition, interrupted only by a Conservative by-election victory in 1977.

	Electorate	Turnout %	Change from '05 %
	77,379	62.3	☆
de Piero, G Lab	16,239	33.7	
Zadrozny, J LD	16,047	33.3	19.5
Hickton, G C	10,698	22.2	-2.2
Holmes, E BNP	2,781	5.8	
Ellis, T Eng	1,102	2.3	
Coleman, T UKIP	933	1.9	
Smith, E Ind	396	0.8	

50%
Majority 192

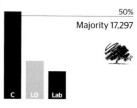

Ashford

Damian Green
b. Jan 17, 1956
MP 1997-

Nearly-man in talent and achievement; disappointed expectations he would lead modern pro-European faction. One-nation moderate, stood down from Howard's frontbench to argue for compassionate Conservatism. Backed David Davis for Tory leadership. Doggedly attacked Lab government; high-profile arrest over Home Office leaks and subsequent row may have revived his career. Min: Immigration 2010-. Shad Min: Immigration 2005-10. Shad SoS: Transport 2003-04; Education 2001-03. Defeated David Cameron in Ashford selection, 1997. Financial journalist: BBC, *The Times*. Special adviser, John Major's policy unity. Married, two daughters. Ed:

Reading Sch; Balliol Coll, Oxford (PPE; Pres, Oxford Union)

Chris Took (LD) b. May 13, 1980. Sales dir. Ed: Northwest HS, USA; Kent Uni.
Chris Clark (Lab) b. Apr 9, 1980. Employee comms exec, London Underground. Ed: Maidstone GS; KCL.

Constituency
In the heart of Kent, Ashford is a major town and has been designated a growth area, with £2.5 billion investment in homes and jobs over coming decades. A few pockets of mild urban deprivation are isolated in a generally affluent seat, with excellent travel connections as a Eurostar stop and with high-speed rail to London. Beyond Ashford the seat covers rural land including Romney Marsh, the North Downs and High Weald, stretching down to the East Sussex border. It has returned Tory MPs for decades.

	Electorate	Turnout %	Change from '05 %
	81,269	67.9	☆
Green, D C	29,878	54.1	2.7
Took, C LD	12,581	22.8	7.2
Clark, C Lab	9,204	16.7	-9.7
Elenor, J UKIP	2,508	4.5	1.4
Campkin, S Green	1,014	1.8	-1.6

50%
Majority 17,297

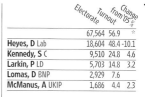

Ashton-under-Lyne

David Heyes
b. Apr 2, 1946
MP 2001-

Very low profile. Member, select committees: Public Administration 2001-. Cllr, Oldham Met BC 1992-2004. Manchester Citizens Advice Bureau (deputy district manager). Development worker. Computer graphics designer. Local government work. Advice service manager. Unison. Married, one daughter, one son. Education: Blackley Tech High School, Manchester; Open Uni (BA social sciences).

Seema Kennedy (C) Solicitor, family property company. Conservative constituency party chairman. Ed: Cambridge University.
Paul Larkin (LD) Cllr, Sefton Met BC. Defected from Labour to the Lib Dems

last year.
David Lomas (BNP)

Constituency
Failsworth, in Oldham borough, borders Manchester at the western end of this urban seat, the bulk of which is in Tameside borough. The relatively affluent and predominantly white small town of Droylsden is also at the west of the seat, while the much larger, predominantly working-class Ashton-under-Lyne is to the east. Ashton has large Indian and Pakistani communities and areas of deprivation ranked among the worst five per cent in the country. The seat has returned Labour MPs since 1935.

	Electorate	Turnout %	Change from '05 %
	67,564	56.9	☆
Heyes, D Lab	18,604	48.4	-10.1
Kennedy, S C	9,510	24.8	4.6
Larkin, P LD	5,703	14.8	3.2
Lomas, D BNP	2,929	7.6	
McManus, A UKIP	1,686	4.4	2.3

50%
Majority 9,094

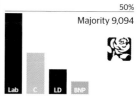

Aylesbury

David Lidington
b. Jun 30, 1956
MP 1992-

Intense, intellectual historian. Worthy and solid, he is an also-ran of politics – a born Minister of State. Twice victorious University Challenge captain. Min: FCO 2010-. Shadow Minister: Foreign Affairs 2007-10. Shadow Sec: NI 2003-07. Previously PPS to Howard as Home Sec. Worked for BP, Rio Tinto Zinc, then special adviser to Douglas Hurd. Married, four sons. Education: Haberdashers' Aske's School; Sidney Sussex College, Cambridge (MA history, PhD).

Steven Lambert (LD) b. Jun 11, 1970. Worked for Post Office. Cllr, Aylesbury Vale DC 2007-. Ed: Open Univ (BSc Social Sciences).

Kathryn White (Lab) Barrister in public, employment and education law. Ed: Balliol Coll, Oxford (BA History). **Chris Adams** (UKIP) b. Oct 9, 1963. UKIP political adviser, charity worker. Contested Aylesbury 2005.

Constituency
This Buckinghamshire constituency forms a geographically straggly arc, reaching from Aylesbury in the north, east to Wendover and the Chilterns, skirting the Risboroughs and turning southwest to the M40 at Stokenchurch. Between the villages lies a mixture of farms and woodland. Many big-name manufacturers such as Nestlé have deserted Aylesbury in the past decade and it is undergoing regeneration with extensive shopping development. The service and public sectors are significant employers but many people commute. The seat has been Tory for decades.

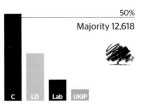

	Electorate	Turnout %	Change from '05 %
	77,934	68.2	☆
Lidington, D C	27,736	52.2	3.8
Lambert, S LD	15,118	28.4	-0.4
White, K Lab	6,695	12.6	-5.7
Adams, C UKIP	3,613	6.8	2.3

50%
Majority 12,618

C	LD	Lab	UKIP

Ayr, Carrick & Cumnock

Sandra Osborne
b. Feb 23, 1956
MP 1997-

Left wing, resigned from Government over Iraq war. Hard-working. PPS to: Helen Liddell 2002-03; George Foulkes 2001-02; Brian Wilson 1999-2001. Member, select cttees: Foreign Affairs 2005-10; European Scrutiny 2004-10; Scottish Affairs 1998-99; Information 1997-2000. MP Ayr 1997-2005. Cllr, Kyle & Carrick DC 1990-95, South Ayrshire Council 1994-97. Community worker. TGWU branch sec. Married, two daughters. Ed: Camphill Senior; Anniesland Coll; Jordanhill Coll; Strathclyde (dip community ed, dip/MSc equality & discrimination).

William Grant (C) Retired fireman. Left after 31 years service in 2005 and having reached the rank of deputy commander. Cllr, South Ayrshire. **Charles Brodie** (SNP) Business consultant. Contested Greenock & Inverclyde 2005, and 2001 as a Lib Dem. Ed: St Andrews Uni. **James Taylor** (LD) b. Jul 16, 1977. Music entrepreneur. Ed: Open Uni (MBA). Contested Scottish Parl elections, North Tayside 2007.

Constituency
This southwest Scottish seat fans out south and east from the main coastal town of Ayr. The Doon and Afton valleys and the prosperous rural area of Carrick lie to the south, while Girvan is the other main seaside town. At the east lies Cumnock, an industrial former mining town amid the old coalfields. This is more deprived, with many living in social housing and with problems of poor health. Traditionally a Labour area.

	Electorate	Turnout %	Change from '05 %
	73,320	62.6	
Osborne, S Lab	21,632	47.1	1.8
Grant, W C	11,721	25.5	2.4
Brodie, C SNP	8,276	18.0	4.9
Taylor, J LD	4,264	9.3	-4.7

50%
Majority 9,911

Lab	C	SNP	LD

Ayrshire Central

Brian Donohoe
b. Sep 10, 1948
MP 1992-

Lugubrious but publicity-hungry. PPS to Lord Adonis 2008-10. Member select cttees: Transport 2002-10; Transport, Local Gov't, Regions 2001-02; Environment, Transport & Regional Affairs 1997-2001. (MP Cunninghame South 1992-2005) Apprentice engineer Hunterston nuclear power station, ICI draughtsman. NALGO district officer. TGWU. Married, two sons. Ed: Irvine Royal Academy; Kilmarnock Tech Coll (nat cert engineering).

Maurice Golden (C) Environmental campaign manager. Ed: Dundee Uni. President of Conservative Futures Scotland. Contested Glenrothes by-election 2008; Scottish Parl elections 2007.
John Mullen (SNP) b. 1963. Businessman. Campaigns co-ordinator for the constituency in 2009 European elections. Ed: Marr Coll, Troon.
Andrew Chamberlain (LD) b. May 3, 1982. Cllr, Ayrshire North 2007-. Ed: Glasgow Univ (MA economics & philosophy).

Constituency
This southwest Scottish seat includes the prosperous seaside towns of Prestwick and Troon and some affluent rural towns. These contrast with the former mining communities that were the linchpins of the Ayrshire coalfield, and the large town of Irvine in the north. Once designated a New Town to relieve pressure on social housing in nearby Glasgow, it remains working-class. Labour enjoys a comfortable majority.

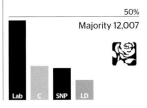

	Electorate	Turnout %	Change from '05 %
	68,352	64.3	
Donohoe, B Lab	20,950	47.7	1.3
Golden, M C	8,943	20.4	-1.7
Mullen, J SNP	8,364	19.1	7.6
Chamberlain, A LD	5,236	11.9	-4.1
McDaid, J Soc	422	1.0	-467

50%
Majority 12,007

Lab	C	SNP	LD

Ayrshire North & Arran

Labour hold

Katy Clark
b. Jul 3, 1967
MP 2005-

Left-winger and a serious rebel (voted against ID cards) but conscientiously attends the Chamber and speaks out often on constituency matters. Member, Socialist Campaign Group. Contested Galloway & Upper Nithsdale 2001. Head of membership legal services, Unison. Member TGWU, GMB, NUS. Solicitor. Ed: Kyle Academy; Aberdeen (LLB); Edinburgh (Dip Legal Practice).

Patricia Gibson (SNP) b. May 12, 1968. English teacher. Cllr, Glasgow CC 2007-. Ed: Glasgow Uni.
Philip Lardner (C) Teacher. Ed: Glasgow (law). Suspended by the party before the 2010 election after discov-

ered he had described gay people as "not normal" on his website.
Gillian Cole-Hamilton (LD) b. Sep 22, 1977. Primary school teacher. Contested Scottish Parl 2007. Ed: Aberdeen Uni.

Constituency

There is a distinct divide in this constituency. To the north, the commuting towns of Skelmorlie and Largs ensure a significant Conservative vote. This is eclipsed by the south, which is firmly Labour, thanks to the industrial areas around Kilbirnie and Dalry and the mining villages of the Garnock Valley. The seat also includes the islands of Arran and Cumbrae and a stretch of the Ayrshire coastline including Ardrossan, West Kilbride and the Hunterston nuclear power station. The seat and its predecessors have been Labour since 1987.

	Electorate	Turnout %	Change from 05 %
	74,953	61.5	
Clark, K Lab	21,860	47.4	3.5
Gibson, P SNP	11,965	26.0	8.1
Lardner, P C	7,212	15.6	-2.7
Cole-Hamilton, G LD	4,630	10.0	-6.4
McDaid, L Soc	449	1.0	-302

50%
Majority 9,895

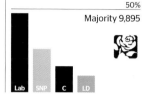

| Lab | SNP | C | LD |

Banbury

Conservative hold

Tony Baldry
b. Jul 10, 1950
MP 1983-

A survivor. Slightly pompous. A prominent Freemason. Euro-enthusiast and opposed Iraq war. Agriculture Minister (1995-97) during BSE crisis; nicknamed "Baldrick" by civil servants. Helped privatise electricity industry as Parly Under-Sec, Energy Department in 1990. Practising barrister, specialising in construction law. Extensive outside earnings from law and directorships. Served with TA, became honorary colonel. Divorced and re-married, one daughter and one son from first marriage. Education: Leighton Park; University of Sussex (BA social science, LLB, MA international development); Lincoln's Inn.

David Rundle (LD) History lecturer. Cllr, Oxford CC. Ed: King's Sch, Macclesfield; Christ Church, Oxford.
Les Sibley (Lab) b. Jan 29, 1949. MoD civil servant. Contested Banbury 2005, 2001. Cllr, Oxfordshire CC 2001-. Mayor of Bicester 1997-98.

Constituency

This northeastern strip of Oxfordshire borders Buckinghamshire, Nottinghamshire and Warwickshire and includes all but the southernmost reaches of the district of Cherwell, which were reassigned to the Henley constituency. Traditionally a farming economy, the population is concentrated in two burgeoning towns: Banbury, in the north, once home to an important livestock market; and Bicester, in the south, earmarked for development. It remains a safe Conservative seat.

	Electorate	Turnout %	Change from 05 %
	86,986	64.7	☆
Baldry, T C	29,703	52.8	5.9
Rundle, D LD	11,476	20.4	2.9
Sibley, L Lab	10,773	19.2	-8.9
Fairweather, D UKIP	2,806	5.0	2.8
White, A Green	959	1.7	-1.1
Edwards, R Ind	524	0.9	

50%
Majority 18,227

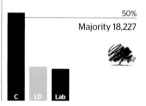

| C | LD | Lab |

Banff & Buchan

Scottish National Party hold

Eilidh Whiteford
b. Apr 24, 1969
MP 2010-

Long-term SNP activist, worked for Alex Salmond MP, Allan Macartney and Ian Hudghton MEPs and Irene McGugan MSP. Scottish campaigns manager, Make Poverty History. Co-ordinator, Scottish Carers' Alliance. Lecturer, Scottish Literature at Glasgow Univ and Newbattle Abbey Coll. Fed of Student Nats (Nat Organiser, President. Party spokesperson on Higher Education). Aberdeen-born, Macduff raised. Ed: Banff Academy; Glasgow (MA English & Scottish lit); Guelph, Ontario (MA English Lang & Lit); Glasgow (PhD Scottish Lit).

Jimmy Buchan (C) Fisherman. Chairman, the Scottish Fishermen's

Organisation. Convenor to the port of Peterhead.
Glen Reynolds (Lab) b. Apr 18, 1959. Journalist and lecturer. Contested Berwick-upon-Tweed 2005. Cllr, Darlington BC 2003-07.
Galen Milne (LD) b. Apr 2, 1951. Company dir of a UK-wide supplier to the life science research sector.

Constituency

This Aberdeenshire constituency is bounded by the North Sea on two sides and includes the major eastern fishing ports of Fraserburgh and Peterhead. Banff, Macduff and Portsoy line the north coast. In 2005, the largely farming area of Turriff was added. From 1987, this seat was the stronghold of Alex Salmond who made it the safest Scottish National Party seat in Scotland. He stood down in 2010 to concentrate on being First Minister.

	Electorate	Turnout %	Change from 05 %
	64,300	59.8	
Whiteford, E SNP	15,868	41.3	-9.9
Buchan, J C	11,841	30.8	11.5
Reynolds, G Lab	5,382	14.0	2.0
Milne, G LD	4,365	11.4	-2.0
Payne, R BNP	1,010	2.6	

50%
Majority 4,027

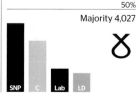

| SNP | C | Lab | LD |

Barking Labour hold

Margaret Hodge
b. Sep 8, 1944
MP 1994- (by-election)

Fought spirited campaign against BNP presence. Elected Chair, select cttee: Public Accounts 2010-. Minister: Culture, Media & Sport 2007-08; Trade & Industry 2006-07; Work & Pensions 2005-06; Education & Skills 2001-05. Parly Under-Sec Education & Employment 1998-2001. Chair select sub-cttee: Education & Employment 1997-98. Cllr, Islington 1973-94 (leader 1982-92). TGWU. Price Waterhouse consultant. Teacher. Market researcher. Divorced, one daughter, one son. Re-married, widowed. Two daughters. Ed: Oxford HS; LSE (BSc economics).

Simon Marcus (C) Businessman, worked at Brit Chamber of Commerce,

Brussels. Ed: King's Coll, London.
Nick Griffin (BNP) b. Apr 1, 1959. BNP leader 1999-. MEP for North West 2009-. Ed: Cambridge Uni.
Dominic Carman (LD) b. Aug 23, 1961. Journalist. Ed: Durham Uni.

Constituency
This East London seat is bounded by the Thames to the south and Barking Creek to the west, with a concentration of industry around the waterfront. The boundary was extended to include three densely populated wards in the north east. The ethnic minority population is not large by London standards, with about a fifth of residents. The BNP has increased tensions, especially over access to council housing, where about 40 per cent of residents live, and low-cost housing in new developments from the Thames Gateway project. The seat has been Labour since 1945.

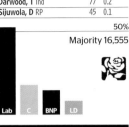

		Electorate	Turnout %	Change from '05 %
		73,864	61.4	☆
Hodge, M	Lab	24,628	54.3	4.7
Marcus, S	C	8,073	17.8	1.2
Griffin, N	BNP	6,620	14.6	-1.7
Carman, D	LD	3,719	8.2	-2.6
Maloney, F	UKIP	1,300	2.9	-0.6
Hargreaves, G	Ch	482	1.1	
Forbes, J	Green	317	0.7	-1.0
Chris, C	Dowling	82	0.2	
Darwood, T	Ind	77	0.2	
Sijuwola, D	RP	45	0.1	

50%
Majority 16,555

Lab | C | BNP | LD

Barnsley Central Labour hold

Eric Illsley
b. Apr 9, 1955
MP 1987-

Plain-speaking Yorkshireman overlooked as minister. Suspended from Labour whip May 19, 2009, following charges of false accounting over expenses claims. Opposition spokes: NI 1995-97; local government 1995; health 1994-95. Opposition whip 1991-94. Member, select committees: Yorks & Humber 2009-10; Chairmen's Panel 2000-10; Foreign Affairs 1997-2010; Procedure 1991-2010. Yorkshire area NUM official. Amicus. Married, two daughters. Education: Barnsley Holgate GS; Leeds (LLB).

Christopher Wiggin (LD) b. Sep 1, 1985. Self-employed online retailer. Education: York Uni.

Piers Tempest (C) b. Nov 10, 1973. Film producer. Education: Bristol University.
Ian Sutton (BNP), b July 12, 1963. Mechanical engineer. Education: Royston High School.

Constituency
Barnsley occupies a strategic position north of Sheffield, on the main commuter routes between the city and Leeds. Under boundary changes the seat has gained the relatively affluent village of Darton in the north west, alongside the M1. At the start of the Eighties, a fifth of Barnsley's workforce was in coalmining; pit closures hit the town hard. It has yet to recover fully but a £350 million redevelopment of the centre includes a transport interchange, digital media centre and indoor market. The seat has long been a Labour stronghold.

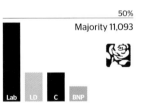

		Electorate	Turnout %	Change from '05 %
		65,543	56.5	☆
Illsley, E	Lab	17,487	47.3	-10.4
Wiggin, C	LD	6,394	17.3	-2.0
Tempest, P	C	6,388	17.3	2.5
Sutton, I	BNP	3,307	8.9	
Silver, D	UKIP	1,727	4.7	
Wood, D	Ind	732	2.0	
Devoy, T	Ind	610	1.7	
Robinson, T	Soc	356	1.0	

50%
Majority 11,093

Lab | LD | C | BNP

Barnsley East Labour hold

Michael Dugher
b. Apr 26, 1975
MP 2010-

Bluff, straight-talking, special adviser from TU background. Old-right Labour, grew up in working-class pit village of Edlington. Good friend, bad enemy. Rose to chief political spokesman for Gordon Brown after special adviser roles to Geoff Hoon and John Spellar. Contested Skipton & Ripon 2001. Unite, Unison, Fabian Society. Labour First, Labour Friends of Israel. UK Dir of Gov't Relations, EDS. Head of Policy, AEEU Engineering Union. Researcher and speechwriter to Frank Dobson. National Chair of Labour Students. Guitar player. Married, two daughters. Ed: St Mary's RC Sch, Edlington; McAuley RC Sch, Doncaster; Nottingham (BA Hons Politics).

John Brown (LD) b. June 27, 1947. Lecturer. Cllr, Congleton 1999-. Ed: Manchester Metropolitan Uni.
James Hockney (C) Businessman. Cllr, South Cambridgeshire DC 2004-. Ed: Cambridge Regional Coll.
Colin Porter (BNP) Joiner. Ed: Barnsley College, Barnsley.

Constituency
This constituency bears only a minimal resemblance to the old Barnsley East and Mexborough seat, having lost Mexborough and Dearne Valley and gained the communities of Worsbrough and Hoyland, south of Barnsley town. This scattering of urban areas includes some severe deprivation, with poor health and high unemployment typifying the former mining communities. Grimethorpe was the setting for the film *Brassed Off*. This has long been a staunch Labour area.

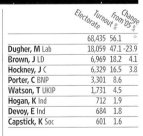

		Electorate	Turnout %	Change from '05 %
		68,435	56.1	☆
Dugher, M	Lab	18,059	47.1	-23.9
Brown, J	LD	6,969	18.2	4.1
Hockney, J	C	6,329	16.5	3.8
Porter, C	BNP	3,301	8.6	
Watson, T	UKIP	1,731	4.5	
Hogan, K	Ind	712	1.9	
Devoy, E	Ind	684	1.8	
Capstick, K	Soc	601	1.6	

50%
Majority 11,090

Lab | LD | C | BNP

Barrow & Furness
Labour Co-operative hold

John Woodcock
b. Oct 14, 1978
MP 2010-

Political spokesman to Gordon Brown as Prime Minister, though never very comfortable with the art of political spin. Worked as special adviser to John Hutton, from whom he inherits the seat. On the Progress wing of the party. Sheffield-born, former journalist at North West Evening Mail. Married (to former NUS president Mandy Telford), one daughter. Education: Tapton Comprehensive; Edinburgh.

John Gough (C) b. 1967. Contractor in the IT sector, former banker. Education: Ian Ramsey Comp Sch; Lancaster Uni.
Barry Rabone (LD) School sports co-ordinator. Former PE teacher.

Contested Barrow & Furness 2005, 2001. Education: Falmouth Grammar School; Cardiff College of Education.

Constituency
The working-class town of Barrow-in-Furness is located at the north side of Morecambe Bay, on Cumbria's southern peninsula. BAE Systems is the major employer, providing about 5,000 jobs and continuing Barrow's shipbuilding heritage and Labour-leaning tendencies. The seat juts up towards Broughton-in-Furness, taking in South Lakeland wards, including the town of Ulverston. These have more Conservative tendencies and the seat returned Tory MPs in the 1980s before switching back to Labour in 1992.

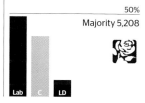

	Electorate	Turnout %	Change from 05 %
	68,758	64.2	☆
Woodcock, J Lab	21,226	48.1	2.9
Gough, J C	16,018	36.3	3.7
Rabone, B LD	4,424	10.0	-7.8
Smith, J UKIP	841	1.9	-0.1
Ashburner, M BNP	840	1.9	
Loynes, C Green	530	1.2	
Greaves, B Ind	245	0.6	

50%
Majority 5,208

Basildon & Billericay
Conservative hold

John Baron
b. Jun 21, 1959
MP 2001-

Unremarkable figure from mainstream Tory right, campaigned against large travellers site in his constituency. Opposition Whip 2007-10; Shadow Health Minister 2002-03, resigned as opposed Iraq war, reappointed 2003-07. Royal Regiment of Fusiliers (served in Berlin, Northern Ireland, Cyprus). Investment fund manager, director of Hendersons then Rothschild. Married, two daughters. Education: Several state and grammar schools, Queen's Coll, Taunton; Jesus Coll, Cambridge (BA history and economics); RMA Sandhurst.

Allan Davies (Lab) b. Jan 25, 1972. Communications manager. Ed: East

London Uni. Cllr, Basildon DC 2002-.
Mike Hibbs (LD) b. Nov 8, 1954. Architect. Ed: Birmingham Uni, London Metropolitan Uni. Contested Billericay 2005.

Constituency
This Essex seat takes the centre from the formerly separate Basildon and Billericay seats, including all of Billericay, at the north, and most of Basildon at the south. Basildon is the commercial centre of southern Essex and recipient of much Thames Gateway funding including the regeneration of the town centre and development of a new business park. There are areas of severe deprivation within the worst 10 per cent nationwide in Fryerns and Lee Chapel North. Basildon has been a bellwether in recent elections, but Billericay is more affluent and strongly Conservative.

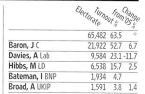

	Electorate	Turnout %	Change from 05 %
	65,482	63.5	☆
Baron, J C	21,922	52.7	6.7
Davies, A Lab	9,584	23.1	-11.7
Hibbs, M LD	6,538	15.7	2.5
Bateman, I BNP	1,934	4.7	
Broad, A UKIP	1,591	3.8	1.4

50%
Majority 12,338

Basildon South and Thurrock East
Conservative gain

Stephen Metcalfe
b. Jan 9, 1966
MP 2010-

Lifelong Essex man and longstanding Tory activist, contested Ilford South 2005. Selected by open primary. Cllr, Epping Forest DC 2002-07. Former Dep Chairman, Essex Area Conservative Party. Creative Director, Metloc Printers (family-owned printing business). Conservative Friends of Israel, Conservative Christian Fellowship. Amateur dramatics enthusiast. Active CofE. Married, one daughter, one son. Ed: Loughton School (head boy); Buckhurst Hill County High School Sixth form.

Angela Smith (Lab Co-op) b. Jan 7, 1959. MP 1997-2010. Min: Cabinet Office; Third Sector and for Social Exclu-

sion. Ed: Leicester Polytechnic.
Geoff Williams (LD) b. Jan 26, 1947. Non-exec dir and former FE lecturer. Cllr for 23 years. Ed: King's College.

Constituency
This new seat at the southwest of Essex comprises the eastern, greener half of the Thurrock borough and the southern part of the district of Basildon, including the hospital, the sought-after residential area of Kingswood and areas of deprivation in Langdon Hills and Nethermayne. Stanford-le-Hope is a key town in Thurrock and rural communities are established at East Tilbury and Orsett. London Gateway, a container port, is under construction, while the Petroplus refinery remains active. Two of the old seats had Labour MPs, the third a Tory.

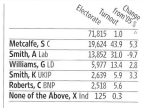

	Electorate	Turnout %	Change from 05 %
	71,815	1.0	☆
Metcalfe, S C	19,624	43.9	5.3
Smith, A Lab	13,852	31.0	-9.7
Williams, G LD	5,977	13.4	2.8
Smith, K UKIP	2,639	5.9	3.3
Roberts, C BNP	2,518	5.6	
None of the Above, X Ind	125	0.3	

50%
Majority 5,772

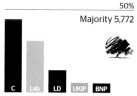

Basingstoke
Conservative hold

Maria Miller
b. Mar 26, 1964
MP 2005-

Quietly diligent, good on family policy. New breed Tory; hard-working mother who opposes all-women shortlists. Parly Under-Sec: Work & Pensions 2010-. Shadow Minister: Family 2007-10; Family Welfare 2006-07; Education 2005-06. Advertising, marketing and PR career; Texaco, Grey Advertising, Saatchi Rowland. Married, three children. Education: Brynteg Comprehensive, Bridgend; LSE (BSc economics).

John Shaw (LD) Chief executive of a carer charity. Contested Southampton Test 2001. Ed: Aberdeen Uni; Southampton Institute.
Funda Pepperell (Lab) Journalist and former international sprinter. Equal opportunities officer for Southampton Labour Party.

Constituency
This north Hampshire seat used to extend into extremely affluent rural land north and south of Basingstoke but boundary changes focus more tightly on the town, with only one rural ward. Basingstoke itself is fairly well off but includes some notably poorer areas than its neighbouring constituencies. About a fifth of residents live in social housing and there is a strong working class, although professional classes predominate. The M3 marks the town's southern boundary and there are large warehousing estates. Under previous boundaries it had a long Tory history but in 2001 the victory over Labour was by 880 votes.

	Electorate	Turnout %	Change from '05 %
	75,470	67.1	☆
Miller, M C	25,590	50.5	11.7
Shaw, J LD	12,414	24.5	2.6
Pepperell, F Lab	10,327	20.4	-12.2
Howell, S UKIP	2,076	4.1	1.9
Saul, S BCP	247	0.5	

50%
Majority 13,176

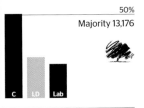

Bassetlaw
Labour hold

John Mann
b. Jan 10, 1960
MP 2001-

Plain-speaking, rarely misses passing bandwagon. PPS to: Tessa Jowell 2007-09; Richard Caborn 2005-07. Member, select committees: Treasury 2009-10, 2003-05; Unopposed Bills (Panel) 2004-10; Information 2001-05. Councillor, Lambeth BC 1986-90. National training officer TUC 1990-95. Head of research & education AEEU. Company director. Married, two daughters, one son. Education: Bradford Grammar School; Manchester University (BA economics); ITD diploma.

Keith Girling (C) Ex-soldier and entrepreneur. Education: Manvers Comprehensive School.

David Dobbie (LD) Key Skills tutor. Contested Bassetlaw 2005.

Constituency
This Nottinghamshire constituency is bordered by South Yorkshire to the north and is predominantly rural. It has been substantially redrawn since the last election in 2005 and has now increased by about 7,000 electors, gaining the town of Retford in the process, but losing Warsop on the outskirts of Sherwood Forest, which has large areas of severe deprivation. The coalfields seat was devastated by the decline of the mining industry. Premier Foods is a major employer, making Oxo in the industrial town of Worksop. The seat has a long history of loyalty to Labour.

	Electorate	Turnout %	Change from '05 %
	76,542	64.8	☆
Mann, J Lab	25,018	50.5	-2.5
Girling, K C	16,803	33.9	-1.2
Dobbie, D LD	5,570	11.2	-0.7
Hamilton, A UKIP	1,779	3.6	
Whithurst, G Ind	407	0.8	

50%
Majority 8,215

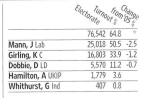

Bath
Liberal Democrat hold

Don Foster
b. Mar 31, 1947
MP 1992-

Veteran holder of myriad policy briefs. Prominent omission from first coalition government. Close to Paddy Ashdown's Lib-Lab project of the late 1990s. LD Shadow SoS: Culture, Media & Sport 2003-10; Olympics 2007-10; Transport 2002-03. LD spokes: Transport, Local Government, Regions 2001-02; Environment, Transport, Regions, Social Justice 1999-2001; Education, Employment 1992-97; Education 1992-95. Academic, consultant. Married, one daughter, one son. Ed: Keele Uni (BSc Physics & Psychology/CEd); Bath Uni (MEd).

Fabian Richter (C) Adviser to David Willetts MP. Education: Oxford Uni.

Hattie Ajderian (Lab) Youth worker and company secretary. Education: Oxford Uni.

Constituency
This seat has been redrawn to encompass just the city and exclude rural areas to the north and east. Famous for the only natural thermal waters in Britain, a 15th-century abbey and its Georgian stone crescents, Bath is a Unesco World Heritage Site. Tourism generates £195 million annually. Despite low unemployment, Bath is a city of contrasts. Much of it is in Britain's 20 per cent least deprived areas but some parts of Twerton and Abbey wards fall into the bottom 20 per cent. The Lib Dems took it from the Tories in 1992.

	Electorate	Turnout %	Change from '05 %
	65,603	71.8	☆
Foster, D LD	26,651	56.6	11.2
Richter, F C	14,768	31.4	-0.5
Ajderian, H Lab	3,251	6.9	-7.5
Lucas, E Green	1,120	2.4	-3.6
Warrender, E UKIP	890	1.9	0.2
Hewett, S Ch	250	0.5	
Anon Ind	69	0.1	0.0
Geddis, S Ind	56	0.1	
Craig, R South	31	0.1	

50%
Majority 11,883

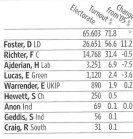

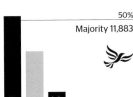

Batley & Spen
Labour hold

Mike Wood
b. Mar 3, 1946
MP 1997-

Unimpressive. Member, select committee: Broadcasting 1997-98. Probation officer. Social/community worker. GMB. Remarried. One daughter, one son from previous marriage. Two stepdaughters. Education: Nantwich & Acton GS; Salisbury/Wells Theological Coll (Cert theol); Leeds (CQSW); Leeds Met (BA History and Politics).

Janice Small (C) Media and marketing consultant, director of Conservative Action for Electoral Reform. Regional press officer working with Michael Howard in 2005. Ed: Blackheath and Bluecoat Grammar Sch.
Neil Bentley (LD) Solicitor. Contested

2005, 2001. Ed: Cambridge Uni, Leeds Metropolitan Uni.
David Exley (BNP) Self-employed electrician. Former cllr, Heckmondwike DC.

Constituency
Just south of Bradford, this seat has gained more than 10,000 constituents, mostly by the addition of the former mill town of Heckmondwike, which, like Batley, is predominantly working class and Labour leaning. Spen Valley at the west is more middle-class commuter territory. More than a quarter of residents work in manufacturing, many in traditional textile industries. About 15 per cent of the population is non-white, mainly of Indian Muslim heritage. The seat was Tory at its inception in 1983 but changed to Labour in 1997.

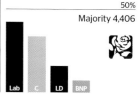

	Electorate	Turnout %	Change from 05 %
	76,732	66.6	☆
Wood, M Lab	21,565	42.2	-3.1
Small, J C	17,159	33.6	1.9
Bentley, N LD	8,095	15.8	0.4
Exley, D BNP	3,685	7.2	
Blakeley, M Green	605	1.2	-0.5

50%
Majority 4,406

Battersea
Conservative gain

Jane Ellison
b. Aug 15, 1964
MP 2010-

Europhile on the Tory left, whose selection by open primary caused consternation with local party. Friend of Matthew Offord MP from Barnet BC (Cllr, 2006-08, 1991-94). Contested Pendle 2005; Tottenham 2000; Barnsley 1997, 1996. John Lewis Partnership career: managed customer magazine, customer direct marketing. Bradford-born. Sings in choir, national trustee Sing for Pleasure. Spurs fan. Has partner. Ed: St Joseph's Coll, Bradford; St Hilda's Coll, Oxford (BA PPE).

Martin Linton (Lab) MP for Battersea 1997-2010. PPS to Harriet Harman, Peter Hain and Lord Falconer of Thoroton. Journalist.

Layla Moran (LD) Secondary school teacher. Ed: Imperial College, London.

Constituency
A long stretch of the Thames from the west side of Wandsworth Bridge almost to Vauxhall Bridge forms the northern boundary of this seat. At its heart are Clapham Junction railway station and the Northcote area, home to a large young professional population, with the proportion of those aged between 20 and 29 more than double the national average. Between the train tracks and the river are Battersea Park and power station. The seat extends south through Clapham Common to Balham. Labour took this seat from the Tories in 1997 but, by 2005, its majority was just 163 votes.

	Electorate	Turnout %	Change from 05 %
	74,300	65.7	☆
Ellison, J C	23,103	47.4	7.5
Linton, M Lab	17,126	35.1	-5.6
Moran, L LD	7,176	14.7	0.3
Evans, G Green	559	1.2	-3.1
MacDonald, C UKIP	505	1.0	0.2
Salmon, H Battersea	168	0.3	
Fox, T Ind	155	0.3	

50%
Majority 5,977

Beaconsfield
Conservative hold

Dominic Grieve
b. May 24, 1956
MP 1997-

Highly able barrister, tackled criminals more than once, one of few Tories to back Human Rights Act in maiden speech. Wiry, silkily spoken but rigorously intellectual. Incisive and an accomplished Commons performer on legal issues but can look posh and out of touch on other topics. Attorney General 2010-. Shadow Justice Sec of State 2009-10, Shadow Home Sec of State 2008-09, Shadow Attorney General 2003-2009, Shadow Minister: Criminal Justice; Scotland. Education: Westminster School, Magdalen College, Oxford (BA/MA modern history); London Polytechnic (Diploma in law). OUCA president. Son of Tory MP. Married with two children.

John Edwards (LD) Accountant. Former cllr, Slough BC.
Jeremy Miles (Lab) Lawyer. Education: Oxford Uni

Constituency
Beaconsfield, home to the famous Bekonscot model village, sits by Junction 2 on the M40 in the north of this Buckinghamshire constituency. Many residents of the market town, and of surrounding villages such as Gerrards Cross, make their daily commute to London or Heathrow, which lies just to the south of the seat. Despite its relative proximity to the busy international airport, it retains the rural charm of the Chiltern Hills and is an affluent area. In 1997 the Conservative vote share dipped below 50 per cent for the only time in living memory.

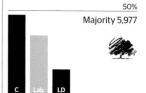

	Electorate	Turnout %	Change from 05 %
	74,982	70.0	☆
Grieve, D C	32,053	61.1	7.0
Edwards, J LD	10,271	19.6	-2.4
Miles, J Lab	6,135	11.7	-7.8
Gray-Fisk, D UKIP	2,597	5.0	0.5
Bailey, J Green	768	1.5	
Cowen, A MP	475	0.9	
Baron, Q Ind	191	0.4	

50%
Majority 21,782

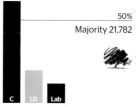

Beckenham | Conservative hold

Bob Stewart
b. Jul 7, 1949
MP 2010-

Decorated Army Colonel, nicknamed 'Bosnia Bob' (after high media profile as British Commander of UN Forces in Bosnia). Interested in Northern Ireland having served there. Freelance writer, broadcaster, lecturer. Political consultant. WorldSpace (MD); Hill & Knowlton (senior consultant). Friend of Martin Bell. Campaigned with Adam Holloway MP 2005. Illustrious military career, awarded DSO. Chief of Policy, Supreme HQ Allied Powers of Europe. Brought up in RAF family. Interested in care of disabled children - patron, ELIFAR charity. Divorced, re-married. Two children from first marriage, four children from second marriage. Ed:

Chigwell Sch; RMA Sandhurst; Uni of Wales (International Politics).

Steve Jenkins (LD) Departmental manager. Education: Uni of Surrey, Roehampton.
Damien Egan (Lab) Training consultant. Contested Weston-super-Mare 2005. Ed: St Mary's Roehampton.

Constituency
Sandwiched between Croydon and Bromley, this quiet and leafy suburban seat has been redrawn and lost Penge wards for the gain of the less populated and more affluent Bromley Common and Hayes and County Hall. Bromley town centre is a mix of mid 20th-century buildings and much older period ones. The population is overwhelmingly white and affluent. The seat has been held by the Tories for decades.

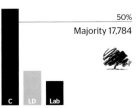

	Electorate	Turnout %	from '05 %	Change
	66,219	72.0		☆
Stewart, B C	27,597	57.9	-1.9	
Jenkins, S LD	9,813	20.6	4.5	
Egan, D Lab	6,893	14.5	-4.9	
Brolly, O UKIP	1,551	3.3	0.4	
Tonks, R BNP	1,001	2.1		
Garrett, A Green	608	1.3		
Eastgate, D Eng	223	0.5		

50%
Majority 17,784

C | LD | Lab

Bedford | Conservative hold

Richard Fuller
b. May 30, 1962
MP 2010-

Smooth, energetic local man and one-time student politician (Nat chair, Young Conservatives; chair, OUCA), who pursued international business career before returning to politics to contest Bedford 2005. Enthusiastic to bring business experience to improving Bedford town centre. Partner, Investcorp (venture capital) and Partner, LEK Consulting (management consultancy). Christian. Theatre enthusiast. Ed: Bedford Mod Sch; University Coll, Oxford (BA PPE); Harvard Business Sch (MBA).

Patrick Hall (Lab) MP for Bedford 1997-2010. PPS to Caroline Flint. Ed: Birmingham Uni.

Henry Vann (LD) Public affairs officer. Worked at the Department of Health. Ed: Cambridge Uni.

Constituency
This compact urban seat is dominated by Bedford on the Great Ouse, which cuts through the seat, but also includes Kempston to its southwest. Unilever and Argos are two of the biggest employers and there is a significant manufacturing sector in the economy. The central urban areas in Castle, Harpur and Cauldwell wards have some severe deprivation while the areas to the north and west such as Putnoe and Brickhill are some of the most affluent. There are notable Italian and Asian populations, mostly concentrated geographically: Queen's Park ward is more than 45 per cent non-white. The Tories had lost the seat to Labour in 1997.

	Electorate	Turnout %	from '05 %	Change
	68,491	65.9		☆
Fuller, R C	17,546	38.9	5.4	
Hall, P Lab	16,193	35.9	-5.7	
Vann, H LD	8,957	19.9	-2.0	
Adkin, M UKIP	1,136	2.5	0.1	
Dewick, W BNP	757	1.7		
Foley, B Green	393	0.9		
Bhandari, S Ind	120	0.3		

50%
Majority 1,353

C | Lab | LD

Bedfordshire Mid | Conservative hold

Nadine Dorries
b. May 21, 1957
MP 2005-

Feisty, unpredictable, publicity-hungry, populist blogger. Self-proclaimed "Bridget Jones of Westminster", seen as unreliable by colleagues. Social conservative, advocates reducing abortion limit. Some damage in expenses row, criticised for voicing fears of MP suicide. Member, cttees: Education 2005-06, Science 2007, IUS 2007-10, ECC 2009-10. Adviser to Oliver Letwin 2002-05. Contested Hazel Grove 2001. Businesswoman, sold healthcare firm to BUPA and served as a dir for them; nurse. Grew up on council estate. Divorced, three daughters. Ed: Halewood Grange; Warrington Dist Sch of Nursing.

Linda Jack (LD) Finance consultant. Contested Luton North 2005; five European elections. Cllr, Bedford BC 2002-07.
David Reeves (Lab) Accountant. Ed: Warwick University.

Constituency
The centre of Bedfordshire is a predominantly rural area, stretching from the outskirts of Milton Keynes at the west across to the border with Hertfordshire at the east. The hills of the Greensand Ridge run up the west of the seat and the constituency skirts up to the western side of Bedford. The main towns and villages are Ampthill and Flitwick in the centre and Shefford and Shillington to the east. The M1 cuts through the southwest corner of the seat and it is a popular area for affluent commuters. The seat has returned Tory MPs since the Second World War.

	Electorate	Turnout %	from '05 %	Change
	76,023	72.2		☆
Dorries, N C	28,815	52.5	5.9	
Jack, L LD	13,663	24.9	1.4	
Reeves, D Lab	8,108	14.8	-7.7	
Hall, B UKIP	2,826	5.2	2.4	
Bailey, M Green	773	1.4	-1.2	
Cooper, J Eng	712	1.3		

50%
Majority 15,152

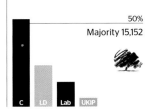
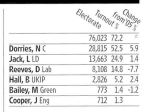

C | LD | Lab | UKIP

Bedfordshire North East — Conservative hold

Alistair Burt
b. May 25, 1955
MP 2001-; 1983-1997

Small, prim, mild-mannered Christian, on the Tory Left and with a slightly goody-goody reputation. Parly Under-Sec: FCO 2010-. Assistant Chief Whip and Dep Party Chair 2008-10, in charge of making new intake fit in. Plays for Con football team at conferences. Shadow Min: Local Government and Communities 2005-08. Unlikely choice as PPS for Iain Duncan Smith (2002-03) and kept on by Michael Howard (2003-05). Min: DSS 1995-97. Parly Under-Sec: DSS 1992-95. MP Bury North 1983-97. Cllr, Haringey. Solicitor, became headhunter (Whitehead Mann GKR) after 1997 defeat. Married, one daughter, one son. Education: Bury Grammar School; St John's College, Oxford (BA jurisprudence).

Mike Pitt (LD) Maths teacher. Cllr, Cambridge CC 2007-. Education: Cambridge University.
Edward Brown (Lab) Barrister. Education: Cambridge University.

Constituency
This is a big, rural seat that borders Northamptonshire at the north, arcs to the south east of Bedford, enclosing the city on three sides and extending south to the border of Hertfordshire. Sandy and Biggleswade are the two main towns, at the east. There is much arable farmland and the area is home to Jordans cereals, while another major employer, Saxon Valley Foods, shut with loss of hundreds of jobs in 2009. This seat has historically been safe for the Tories.

	Electorate	Turnout %	Change from '05 %
	78,060	71.2	☆
Burt, A C	30,989	55.8	5.9
Pitt, M LD	12,047	21.7	0.8
Brown, E Lab	8,957	16.1	-9.2
Capell, B UKIP	2,294	4.1	0.1
Seeby, I BNP	1,265	2.3	

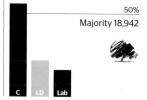

50%
Majority 18,942

Bedfordshire South West — Conservative hold

Andrew Selous
b. Apr 27, 1962
MP 2001-

Slightly moralistic do-gooder. Shadow Min: Work and Pensions 2006-10. Opposition whip 2004-06. PPS to Michael Ancram 2004. Member, select cttee: Work & Pensions 2001-06. Bow Group 1982-. Chair, Con Christian Fellowship 2001-. Director CNS Electronics 1988-94. Underwriter, Great Lakes Re (UK). TA officer, Hon Artillery Co, Royal Reg of Fusiliers 1981-94. Chartered insurer 1998. Married, three daughters. Ed: Eton; London School of Economics (BSc econ industry and trade).

Rod Cantrill (LD) Company director. Cllr, Cambridge CC 2002-. Ed: St Catharine's College, Cambridge.

Jennifer Bone (Lab) Building control surveyor. Ed: UCL (MA sustainable heritage).

Constituency
This seat comprises a small area of rural land with the population concentrated in two large urban areas either side. Leighton-Linslade is often referred to as Leighton Buzzard after the old market town with its shopping mews, but the area of Linslade, on the Grand Union Canal, is notable for its industries. Dunstable and Houghton Regis lie on the outskirts of Luton and have a strong concentration of manufacturing. Towards the Chilterns at the south is Whipsnade Zoo. B/E Aerospace is a notable employer in Leighton. This has long been a Tory stronghold.

	Electorate	Turnout %	Change from '05 %
	76,559	66.3	
Selous, A C	26,815	52.8	4.6
Cantrill, R LD	10,166	20.0	3.2
Bone, J Lab	9,948	19.6	-10.6
Newman, M UKIP	2,142	4.2	0.0
Tolman, M BNP	1,703	3.4	

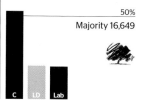

50%
Majority 16,649

Belfast East — Alliance gain

Naomi Long
b. Dec 13, 1971
MP 2010-

Her unseating of Peter Robinson provided the biggest story of the Northern Ireland count in 2010 with a 26.1 per cent swing and the Alliance party's first MP in its 40-year history. A senior guider in the Girl Guides and active Presbyterian. Lord Mayor, Belfast, 2009. Elected Alliance deputy leader 2006. MLA 2003-. Councillor Belfast 2001-. Consultant engineer. Married. Education: Bloomfield Collegiate School; Queen's, Belfast (MEng Civil Engineering).

Peter Robinson (DUP) First Minister in the Northern Ireland Assembly and leader of the Democratic Unionist Party. MP 1979-2010. Deputy leader of the Democratic Unionist Party 1980-2008. Member, cttee: Northern Ireland 1994-2007. Member of NI Assembly (1998-; 1982-1986). Ed: Annadale GS, Castlereagh College of FE.
Trevor Ringland (UCUNF), solicitor and ex-rugby player. Ed: Queen's, Belfast.

Constituency
Dominated by the huge Samson and Goliath cranes of the Harland and Wolff shipyard, this constituency is overwhelmingly Unionist and home to some of Belfast's poorest and wealthiest citizens. Stormont, the Northern Ireland Parliament, and the police headquarters are both here. The seat was held by Peter Robinson from 1979-2010 and in 2005 he took half of the votes cast.

	Electorate	Turnout %	Change from '05 %
	59,007	58.5	☆
Long, N Alliance	12,839	37.2	26.2
Robinson, P DUP	11,306	32.8	-19.6
Ringland, T UCUNF	7,305	21.2	
Vance, D TUV	1,856	5.4	
Donnelly, N SF	817	2.4	-0.1
Muldoon, M SDLP	365	1.1	-1.1

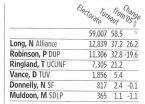

50%
Majority 1,533

Alliance

| All | DUP | UNCU | TUV |

Belfast North · DUP hold

Nigel Dodds
b. Aug 20, 1958
MP 2001-

Dour brains of the party who survived an IRA attack on himself and his wife while visiting their sick son in hospital. DUP Chief Whip HoC 2001-. DUP spokes: BERR, Justice 2007-; Business of HoC 2005-; treasury/work & pensions 2005-07. Sec Ulster DUP 1992-2008. Member, NI Assembly 1998- (Min: social devt 2001-02, 1999-2000). NI Forum for political dialogue 1996-98. Cllr, Belfast CC 1985- (Lord Mayor 1991-92, 1988-89). VP, Assoc of NI local authorities. Barrister. Eur Parl Secretariat. OBE. Married, one daughter, two sons. Ed: Portora Royal Sch; St John's Coll, Cambridge (BA law); Queen's Uni/Belfast Inst of Professional Legal Studies (Cert PLS).

Gerry Kelly (SF) Member, NI Assembly 1998-.
Alban Maginness (SDLP) Barrister. Member, NI Assembly 1998-.
Fred Cobain (UCUNF) Member, NI Assembly 1998-. Cllr Belfast CC 1985-2001.

Constituency
The patchwork of Protestant and Catholic working-class neighbourhoods made this constituency home to the highest levels of sectarian violence during the Troubles. As well as hosting what was known as "the Murder Triangle" there is also the grandeur of Cave Hill, from the peak of which Scotland can be seen. The DUP took the seat from the UUP in 2001, since when the Catholic population has risen and increasing numbers of Protestants have left.

	Electorate	Turnout %	Change from '05 %
	65,504	56.5	☆
Dodds, N DUP	14,812	40.0	-3.0
Kelly, G SF	12,588	34.0	7.1
Maginness, A SDLP	4,544	12.3	-4.5
Cobain, F UCUNF	2,837	7.7	
Webb, W Alliance	1,809	4.9	2.0
McAuley, M Ind	403	1.1	

50%
Majority 2,224

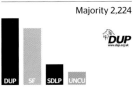

Belfast South · SDLP hold

Dr Alasdair McDonnell
b. Sep 1, 1949
MP 2005-

Big and sometimes abrasive, he bounced back from failing to win his party's leadership challenge. SDLP spokes, various, 2005-. Deputy leader SDLP 2004-. Member, NI Assembly for Belfast South 1998-. Councillor, Belfast City 1977-2001 (deputy Mayor 1995-96). Contested six GEs and one by-election between 1970-97. Hospital doctor/GP. Married, two daughters, two sons. Ed: St MacNissi's Coll; University Coll, Dublin (med school MC BCL BAO).

Jimmy Spratt (DUP) Member, NI Assembly 2007-. Contested Belfast South 2005.

Paula Bradshaw (UCUNF) Dir, community regeneration scheme. Ed: Ulster Uni.
Anna Lo (Alliance) Member, NI Assembly 2007-. Social worker. Ed: Ulster Uni.

Constituency
Home to Belfast's most exclusive residential districts, it is also Northern Ireland's most ethnically diverse constituency. In 2009 a group of Romanian Roma families sought refuge in a Protestant church after racist attacks. Lisburn Road is known locally as "Knightsbridge", with its boutiques and cafés. The Catholic population, now more than 40 per cent, is rising while Protestant numbers are falling. The seat was taken from the Ulster Unionists, who had held it for decades, in 2005 by the SDLP due to a split in the pro-Union vote.

	Electorate	Turnout %	Change from '05 %
	59,524	57.4	☆
McDonnell, A SDLP	14,026	41.0	10.9
Spratt, J DUP	8,100	23.7	-5.9
Bradshaw, P UCUNF	5,910	17.3	
Lo, A Alliance	5,114	15.0	7.7
McGibbon, A Green	1,036	3.0	

50%
Majority 5,926

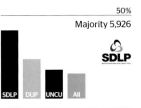

Belfast West · Sinn Féin hold

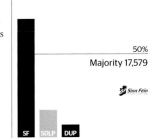

Gerry Adams
b. Oct 6, 1948
MP 1997-; 1983-92

A founding member of the Provisional IRA, leader from the mid-1970s and its most influential figure. Member, NI Assembly Belfast West 1998-. Member, NI Forum 1996, old Northern Ireland Assembly 1981. Sinn Féin: president 1983-; vice president 1978-83. Married, one son. Education: St Mary's Christian Brothers' School, Belfast.

Alex Attwood (SDLP) Solicitor. Member, NI Assembly 1998-. Cllr, Belfast CC, 1985-. Education: Queen's Uni, Belfast.
William Humphrey (DUP) Cllr, Belfast CC 2005-. Education: Boys' Model School.

Constituency
Northern Ireland's most Catholic and poorest constituency. More than two thirds of children were born to unmarried mothers in 2004, while 28 per cent of the population is under 16. The poorest ward is Shankill, a Protestant loyalist enclave with a towering "peace line" wall separating its population from the Falls Road. Bellicose political murals are painted on both sides. The seat is dominated by Sinn Féin, which was held by Mr Adams in 2005 with more than 70 per cent of the votes cast.

	Electorate	Turnout %	Change from '05 %
	59,522	54.0	☆
Adams, G SF	22,840	71.1	2.5
Attwood, A SDLP	5,261	16.4	0.4
Humphrey, W DUP	2,436	7.6	-3.3
Manwaring, B UCUNF	1,000	3.1	
Hendron, M Alliance	596	1.9	1.8

50%
Majority 17,579

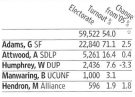

Bermondsey & Old Southwark

Simon Hughes
b. May 17, 1951
MP 1983-

One-time darling of Lib Dems' grassroots radicals and greens, his star waned after his bruising leadership campaign in 2006. LD Deputy Leader 2010-. LD Shad SoS: Energy & Climate Change 2009; Shad Leader of HoC 2007-09; Const affairs/justice 2006-07; LD Shad Attorney Gen 2005-07; ODPM 2005. LD dep whip 1988-99. Lib/Alliance/LD spokes various 1983-2004. Pres LD Party 2004-08. Contested LD leadership 2006, 1999. London mayoral candidate 2002/2004. Nat Young Liberals League. Member Liberal Lawyers Assocn. Barrister. Trainee EEC Brussels. Ed: Llandaff Cath Sch, Cardiff; Christ Coll, Brecon; Selwyn Coll, Cambridge (BA law/MA); Inns of Court Sch

of Law; Coll of Europe, Bruges (Cert in Higher Ed Studies).

Val Shawcross (Lab) GLA member 2000-. Ed: Liverpool.
Loanna Morrison (C) Journalist and businesswoman. Ed: Open University.

Constituency

This inner London seat spans the south bank of the Thames from Blackfriars Bridge to Greenland Docks. It includes Borough and Bankside, Bermondsey and Rotherhithe. Sought-after riverside areas exist but also large areas of deprivation. The Elephant & Castle area and Heygate estate are undergoing much-needed regeneration. There is a large student population and about a sixth of residents are black African. More than half live in social housing. Labour lost the seat to the Lib Dems in a 1982 by-election and never regained it since.

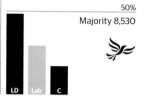

	Electorate	Turnout %	Change from '05 %
	77,623	57.5	☆
Hughes, S LD	21,590	48.4	0.7
Shawcross, V Lab	13,060	29.3	-2.4
Morrison, L C	7,638	17.1	4.2
Tyler, S BNP	1,370	3.1	
Chance, T Green	718	1.6	-1.4
Kirkby, A Ind	155	0.4	
Freeman, S ND	120	0.3	

50%
Majority 8,530

Berwick-upon-Tweed

Sir Alan Beith
b. Apr 20, 1943
MP 1973-

Seasoned parliamentarian. Candidate for Speaker in 2009, 2000. Stood against Paddy Ashdown for leadership of new Liberal Democrat party in 1988, pledging to protect "Liberal values". Chair, cttee: constitutional affairs / justice 2003- (re-elected unopposed 2010). Spokes, LD/SLD/Alliance/Lib spokes 1985-2002 (various, Cabinet/ Home/Treasury/Foreign). Lib chief whip 1976-87. Dep leader: Lib Dem 1992-2003; Lib Party 1985-88. Cllr, Tynedale DC 1974-75, Hexham RDC 1969-74. Lecturer. Widowed, remarried. One daughter, one son – deceased, from first marriage. Ed: King's Sch, Macclesfield; Nuffield Coll, Oxford (BA PPE); Balliol Coll, Oxford (BLitt/MA).

Anne-Marie Trevelyan (C) Accountant. Ed: Oxford Polytechnic.
Alan Strickland (Lab) Head of Policy, Volunteering England. Ed: Oxford University.

Constituency

The market town of Berwick-upon-Tweed lies just north of the river that forms the traditional border with Scotland; English for now, it has changed hands many times, often through battles. The huge Northumberland seat includes such attractions as the Holy Island of Lindisfarne, Alnwick Castle – used as Hogwarts in Harry Potter films – the beautiful Alnwick coast, Cheviot Hills and spectacular rolling moors of Northumberland National Park. The seat has high numbers of self-employed, middle classes and low-wage rural workers. A Lib Dem safe seat, it was previously Conservative.

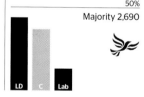

	Electorate	Turnout %	Change from '05 %
	57,403	67.0	☆
Beith, A LD	16,806	43.7	-8.9
Trevelyan, A C	14,116	36.7	7.7
Strickland, A Lab	5,061	13.2	-5.2
Weatheritt, M UKIP	1,243	3.2	
Mailer, P BNP	1,213	3.2	

50%
Majority 2,690

Berwickshire, Roxburgh & Selkirk

Michael Moore
b. Jun 3, 1965
MP 1997-

Serious-minded non-partisan figure close to Sir Menzies Campbell. Sec of State: Scotland 2010-. LD Shadow Sec of State: NI & Scotland 2008; International Devt 2007-10; Foreign Affairs 2006-07; Defence 2005-06. LD Shadow Minister: Foreign Affairs 2001-05. LD spokes (Scotland/Transport) 1997-2001. Member, cttee: Scottish Affairs 1997-99. Deputy Leader Scottish Liberal Democrats 2003-. MP Tweeddale, Ettrick & Lauderdale 1997-2005. Chartered accountant. MP research assistant. Married, one daughter. Education: Strathallan School; Jedburgh Grammar School; Edinburgh University (MA politics/ modern history).

John Lamont (C) MSP for Roxburgh & Berwickshire 2007-10 (Shadow Minister for Community Safety).
Ian Miller (Lab) Store manager.
Paul Wheelhouse (SNP) Economist.

Constituency

This large, rural Scottish seat reaches from the fishing town of Eyemouth, inland along the border with England and through the Cheviot Hills. It includes the major Borders towns of Hawick, Melrose, Galashiels, Duns, Jedburgh and Selkirk. The area is famous for its abbeys and rugby teams. Although prosperous in parts, there has been a decline in the traditional textile industry and it is reliant on agriculture. The seat has a strong Liberal Democrat tradition, but in 2007 its equivalent in the Scottish Parliament was taken by the Tories.

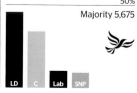

	Electorate	Turnout %	Change from '05 %
	73,826	66.4	☆
Moore, M LD	22,230	45.4	3.6
Lamont, J C	16,555	33.8	5.0
Miller, I Lab	5,003	10.2	-5.6
Wheelhouse, P SNP	4,497	9.2	0.6
Fowler, S UKIP	595	1.2	-0.1
Black, C Jacobite	134	0.3	

50%
Majority 5,675

Bethnal Green & Bow — Labour gain

Rushanara Ali
b. Mar 14, 1975
MP 2010-

Vivacious, elegant and eloquent, Bangladeshi-born high-flyer. One of the first intake of female Muslim MPs. A Bengali and British patriot. Spotted as a talent while still studying at university by Michael Young. Associate dir, Young Foundation. Worked for Oona King, her Labour predecessor. Career: Institute for Public Policy Research. FCO. Home Office. Co-founder, Tower Hamlets Summer University. Helped develop Language Line. Commissioner, London Child Poverty Commission. Speaks fluent Bengali. Moved to UK aged seven. Ed: Mulberry Sch; Tower Hamlets College; Oxford University (PPE).

Ajmal Masroor (LD) Media consultant. Ed: Birbeck College.
Abjol Miah (Respect) Drug prevention education officer. Ed: Goldsmiths.
Zakir Khan (C) Head of community Affairs, Canary Wharf Group plc.

Constituency
Brick Lane, famous for its art scene and curry houses, runs up the west of this inner London seat through Banglatown and Spitalfields where the majority of residents are Bangladeshi. The seat includes Bethnal Green, Stepney Green and Whitechapel and extends east to Mile End and Bow. It is generally deprived, with about 80 per cent social housing in some areas. The seat has been slightly reduced and no longer contains St Katharine's, Wapping or Shadwell. A traditional Labour stronghold, Respect capitalised on the antiwar vote for a dramatic win in 2005.

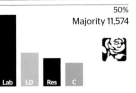

	Electorate	Turnout %	Change from '05 %
	81,243	62.4	☆
Ali, R Lab	21,784	42.9	8.5
Masroor, A LD	10,210	20.1	7.8
Miah, A Respect	8,532	16.8	-19.7
Khan, Z C	7,071	13.9	-7.0
Marshall, J BNP	1,405	2.8	
Bakht, F Green	856	1.7	-2.8
Brooks, P Ind	277	0.6	
van Terheyden, A Pirate	213	0.4	
Hikmat, H Voice	209	0.4	
Choudhury, H Ind	100	0.2	
Malik, A Ind	71	0.1	

50%
Majority 11,574

Beverley and Holderness — Conservative hold

Graham Stuart
b. Mar 12, 1962
MP 2005-

Genial, a regular in Commons Tea Rooms and lobbies. Elected Chair, select cttee: Education 2010-. Member, select cttees: Environmental Audit 2006-10; Education and Skills/Children Schools and Families 2007-10. Contested Cambridge 2001. Cllr, Cambridge CC 1998-2004. Sole proprietor, Go Enterprises; MD, CSL Publishing Ltd; Director, Marine Publishing Co Ltd. Married, two daughters. Ed: Glenalmond Coll; Selwyn Coll, Cambridge (BA law/phil).

Craig Dobson (LD) GP. Ed: Lord Lawson Comprehensive, Birtley; Glasgow Uni.

Ian Saunders (Lab) Manager in telecommunications.

Constituency
The market town of Beverley, which in 2008 topped a survey of towns where an affluent lifestyle could be achieved at the most affordable price, lies ten miles northwest of Hull. The constituency curves southeast around the city and along the Holderness coast, including the seaside towns of Hornsea and Withensea. It is prime commuter territory and relatively wealthy. The BP refinery at Saltend is in less prosperous territory. Tories traditionally dominated the area but won only narrow majorities after the seat's creation in 1997.

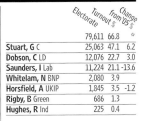

	Electorate	Turnout %	Change from '05 %
	79,611	66.8	☆
Stuart, G C	25,063	47.1	6.2
Dobson, C LD	12,076	22.7	3.0
Saunders, I Lab	11,224	21.1	-13.6
Whitelam, N BNP	2,080	3.9	
Horsfield, A UKIP	1,845	3.5	-1.2
Rigby, B Green	686	1.3	
Hughes, R Ind	225	0.4	

50%
Majority 12,987

Bexhill & Battle — Conservative hold

Greg Barker
b. Mar 8, 1966
MP 2001-

Wealthy, well-connected businessman. Smooth enough to remain a close confidante of David Cameron despite 2006 revelations of Mr Barker's homosexual affair and marriage breakdown. Environment and energy specialist. Min: Energy & Climate Change 2010-. Shadow Min: Climate Change 2005-10, having resigned as Opposition Whip (2003-05) to work on Cameron's leadership campaign. Career in corporate finance M&A, financial PR and two years with Russian oil company Sibneft, advising Roman Abramovich. Divorced, one daughter, two sons. Ed: Steyning GS; Lancing Coll; Royal Holloway Coll, London (BA history, economic history and politics).

Mary Varrall (LD) Garden designer. Contested Bexhill & Battle 2005. Ed: Prince Henry's Grammar Evesham.
James Royston (Lab) English teacher. Worked for Peter Skinner MEP.

Constituency
This large, rural East Sussex seat has been extended inland and includes the town of Heathfield, the Edwardian seaside resort of Bexhill, and Battle, which grew up around its abbey and is named after the Battle of Hastings in 1066. The dramatic moated Bodiam Castle lies just within the northern boundary. There are high numbers of self-employed and small business workers, partly due to a notable agricultural sector. Residents are generally well off, a few are extremely affluent and there are many retired people. The constituency has been Conservative since its inception in 1983.

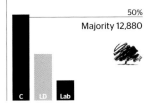

	Electorate	Turnout %	Change from '05 %
	79,208	68.9	☆
Barker, G C	28,147	51.6	-2.6
Varrall, M LD	15,267	28.0	5.3
Royston, J Lab	6,524	12.0	-5.9
Wheeler, S Trust	2,699	4.9	
Jackson, N BNP	1,950	3.6	

50%
Majority 12,880

Bexleyheath & Crayford

Conservative hold

David Evennett
b. Jun 3, 1949
MP 2005-; 1983-1997;

Unremarkable populist Essex Tory, won back seat in 2005 at second attempt. Shadow IUS/BIS Min 2009-10. Opposition Whip 2005-09. PPS to: Gillian Shepherd 1996-7; Baroness Blatch/David Maclean 1995-6; John Redwood 1993-5; Baroness Blatch 1992-3. MP Erith and Crayford 1983-97. Cllr, Redbridge BC. Teacher, insurance broker, City director, lecturer. Married, two sons. Education: Buckhurst Hill County High Sch for Boys, Ilford; LSE (BSc Econ, MSc Econ/politics).

Howard Dawber (Lab) Head of strategy for the Canary Wharf Group. Contested Cheadle 2001. Ed: KCL.

Karelia Scott (LD) Property entrepeneur. Ed: Ayr Grammar Sch; The Mount Sch, York; Uni of the West of England, Bristol.

Constituency
This seat is the easternmost London area south of the River Thames. Bexleyheath, at its west, is the main shopping hub. Crayford, farther east, is being regenerated having become rundown with vacant industrial sites. The seat curves up at the northeast to a small stretch of riverbank where Slade Green is one of the more deprived areas in what is otherwise a well-off seat. Relatively minor boundary changes do not significantly alter this seat, which was won by Labour on its creation in 1997, but taken by the Tories in 2005.

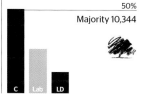

	Electorate	Turnout %	Change from 05 %
	64,985	66.5	☆
Evennett, D C	21,794	50.5	3.9
Dawber, H Lab	11,450	26.5	-7.7
Scott, K LD	5,502	12.7	-0.4
James, S BNP	2,042	4.7	
Dunford, J UKIP	1,557	3.6	0.4
Griffiths, J Eng	466	1.1	
Ross, A Green	371	0.9	

50%
Majority 10,344

C | Lab | LD

Birkenhead

Labour hold

Frank Field
b. Jul 16, 1942
MP 1979-

Agreed to chair independent review on poverty and life chances in coalition's first 'big tent' appointment. Maverick champion of welfare reform, had unhappy year as minister Welfare Reform 1997-98. Could not make progress as Speaker candidate 2009 because of lack of support on his own side. Long courted by Tories and popular with the press. Prominent Anglican, loves old churches. Chair, select committee: Social security 1990-97. Opposition spokesman: Education 1980-81. Director, Child Poverty Action Group, Low Pay Unit. Teacher. Education: St Clement Danes Grammar School; University of Hull (BSc Economics).

Andrew Gilbert (C) Law lecturer. Ed: University of East Anglia.
Stuart Kelly (LD) Councillor, electrician and tutor. Contested 2005 and 2001.

Constituency
Facing Liverpool across the Mersey, the Birkenhead constituency is bordered by docks to the north and the M53 to the west. Areas such as Tranmere, Rock Ferry and Bidston suffer from severe deprivation, with high crime and unemployment and poor-quality housing. The seat has been slightly extended in the southwest and includes the more affluent suburb of Prenton. This seat has long been a Labour stronghold.

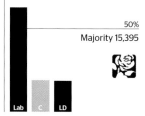

	Electorate	Turnout %	Change from 05 %
	62,773	56.3	☆
Field, F Lab	22,082	62.5	-2.3
Gilbert, A C	6,687	18.9	2.4
Kelly, S LD	6,554	18.6	-0.1

50%
Majority 15,395

Lab | C | LD

Birmingham Edgbaston

Labour hold

Gisela Stuart
b. Nov 26, 1955
MP 1997-

Independent-minded and articulate. Not afraid to take on her own party over Europe – a Eurosceptic after experience drafting EU constitution. Re-elected against the national swing with micro-community campaign. Parly Under-Sec: Health 1999-2001. PPS to Paul Boateng 1998-99. Member, select committees: Foreign Affairs 2001-10; Social Security 1997-98. Parly rep Convention on Future of Europe 2002-04. Amicus. Dep dir, London Book Fair. Lawyer. Lecturer, Worcester Coll of Tech & Birmingham Uni 1992-97. Divorced. Two sons. Education: Staatliche Realschule, Bavaria; Manchester Poly (business studies); London Uni (LLB).

Deirdre Alden (C) Freelance writer. Contested Edgbaston 2005.
Roger Harmer (LD) Charity manager and councillor. Ed: Oxford Uni.

Constituency
Just southwest of the city centre, Edgbaston contains a significant spill-over business district around Five Ways and Hagley Road, as well as Birmingham University. Stretching out to Bartley Green, on the border with rural Worcestershire, the rest of the seat is primarily residential. It encompasses Harborne, popular with young professionals. The seat becomes less affluent farther away from the centre. The economy is overwhelmingly service sector, and about a fifth of residents are members of an ethnic minority. The Conservatives held the seat from 1885 until Labour's victory in 1997.

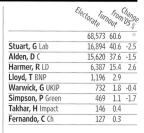

	Electorate	Turnout %	Change from 05 %
	68,573	60.6	☆
Stuart, G Lab	16,894	40.6	-2.5
Alden, D C	15,620	37.6	-1.5
Harmer, R LD	6,387	15.4	2.6
Lloyd, T BNP	1,196	2.9	
Warwick, G UKIP	732	1.8	-0.4
Simpson, P Green	469	1.1	-1.7
Takhar, H Impact	146	0.4	
Fernando, C Ch	127	0.3	

50%
Majority 1,274

Lab | C | LD

Birmingham Erdington | Labour hold

Jack Dromey
b. Sep 21, 1948
MP 2010-

Veteran union official who first emerged on public consciousness on Grunwick picket lines in 1970s. Husband of Harriet Harman MP. Elected deputy general secretary of Unite/TGWU in 2003 after losing to Tony Woodley for general secretary. Seen as acceptable face of Trade Unions by Blairites but missed out on a seat in 1997. Distanced himself from Blair in cash for honours, secret loans row in 2006, as Labour Party treasurer. Shoehorned into a seat once Brown took over. Former Secretary, Brent Trades Council. Machine minder, Alperton Carton Company. Married, one daughter, two sons. Ed: Cardinal Vaughan Grammar School, London.

Robert Alden (C) Cllr, Birmingham CC. Ed: Birmingham Uni.
Ann Holtom (LD) Cllr, Birmingham CC.

Constituency
This largely residential seat is bounded by the M6 to the southeast, dividing it from Birmingham city centre. It has significant areas of deprivation, especially in Kingstanding and Tyburn, although the Castle Vale estate in Tyburn improved with the replacement of tower blocks in the 1990s. Unemployment is high and the economy is more dependent on manufacturing than elsewhere. Tyburn is home to the Jaguar car assembly plant, where jobs have looked insecure, and the old Fort Dunlop complex, which has been turned into retail and office space. The seat has been Labour since its creation in 1974.

	Electorate	Turnout %	Change from '05 %
	66,405	53.5	
Dromey, J Lab	14,869	41.8	-11.1
Alden, R C	11,592	32.6	9.7
Holtom, A LD	5,742	16.2	0.3
McHugh, K BNP	1,815	5.1	
Foy, M UKIP	842	2.4	0.0
Tomkins, T Ind	240	0.7	
Williams, T NF	229	0.6	
Gray, T Ch	217	0.6	

50%
Majority 3,277

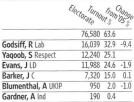

Birmingham Hall Green | Labour hold

Roger Godsiff
b. Jun 28, 1946
MP 1992-

Lumbering with a Cockney accent. Controversial, hard-edged ex-union official. Spoke out against immigration. GMB-sponsored. Former cricket special adviser to Richard Caborn 2002. (MP Birmingham Small Heath 1992-97) Cllr, Lewisham 1979-90: Lab chief whip 1974-77, mayor 1977. Member, Co-op party. Football fan, chair Charlton Athletic Community Trust. GMB senior research officer. Political officer APEX. Banker. Married, one daughter, one son. Education: Catford Comp Sch.

Salma Yaqoob (Respect) Leader of Respect. Psychotherapist. Contested

Birmingham Sparkbrook & Small Heath 2005.
Jerry Evans (LD) Archaelogical consultant.
Jo Barker (C) Runs a family business. Con Party Human Rights Commission.

Constituency
This southern seat has been substantially redrawn, changing its character, as well as boosting its size by about 16,000 electors. The affluent Hall Green, on the outskirts, remains but other outlying areas have been replaced by more deprived inner-city wards from the old Sparkbrook and Small Heath seat. Moseley is a mix of bohemian, artsy middle classes and traditional professionals. More than half the seat's residents are in ethnic minorities. Under the old boundaries, the seat was Conservative for 47 years before Labour's 1997 victory.

	Electorate	Turnout %	Change from '05 %
	76,580	63.6	
Godsiff, R Lab	16,039	32.9	-9.4
Yaqoob, S Respect	12,240	25.1	
Evans, J LD	11,988	24.6	-1.9
Barker, J C	7,320	15.0	0.1
Blumenthal, A UKIP	950	2.0	-1.0
Gardner, A Ind	190	0.4	

50%
Majority 3,799

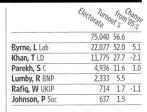

Birmingham Hodge Hill | Labour hold

Liam Byrne
b. Oct 2, 1970
MP 2004-

Clever but charmless, with a management consultant's manner, left infamous "there's no money left" handover note. Nicknamed Baldemort by civil servants. Chief Sec to Treasury 2009-10. Min: Cabinet Office 2008-09; Treasury 2008; West Midlands 2007-08; Home 2006-08. Parly Under-Sec, Health 2005-06. Adviser, 1997 election campaign. Director Business Liaison, Office of Leader of Lab Party. NVS nat exec. Co-founder EGS Gp Ltd. NM Rothschild. Anderson Consulting. Leader Manchester Uni Students Union. Married, one daughter, two sons. Ed: Burnt Mill Comp; University of Manchester (BA); Harvard (MBA).

Tariq Khan (LD), senior medical representative. Ed: University of Wolverhampton.
Shailesh Parekh (C), business owner.

Constituency
To the east of Birmingham city centre, this residential seat has increased by about 20,000 electors, gaining areas formerly in the old Sparkbrook and Small Heath seat. Hodge Hill is comfortably well off but otherwise this is a poor, densely populated seat, which, despite regeneration attempts, has high levels of deprivation, especially in Washwood Heath. The seat is predominantly an Asian area, but was once white and working-class. It is home to Birmingham City FC, whose fans painted the Sleeping Iron Giant sculpture to match their "bluenose" nickname. The seat has been Labour since 1950.

	Electorate	Turnout %	Change from '05 %
	75,040	56.6	
Byrne, L Lab	22,077	52.0	5.1
Khan, T LD	11,775	27.7	-2.1
Parekh, S C	4,936	11.6	1.0
Lumby, R BNP	2,333	5.5	
Rafiq, W UKIP	714	1.7	-1.1
Johnson, P Soc	637	1.5	

50%
Majority 10,302

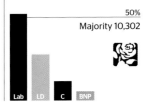

Birmingham Ladywood
Labour hold

Shabana Mahmood
b. Sep 17, 1980
MP 2010-

One of the first intake of female Muslim MPs. A passionate opponent of the Iraq war and 42-day detention, and an advocate of women's advancement and engagement in politics. Interested in jobs and housing. Daughter of Birmingham Lab Party chair – made for controversial selection. Brummie born and raised. Employed barrister, Berrymans Lace Mawer. Pupillage at 12 Kings Bench Walk. Teaches as volunteer. Member GMB. Speaks Mirpuri, Urdu and Punjabi. Daughter of Kashmiri/Pakistani immigrant parents. Enjoys creative writing. Ed: Small Heath Sch; King Edward VI Camp Hill Sch; Lincoln Coll, Oxford (law; JCR pres); Inns of Court Sch of Law (BVC).

Ayoub Khan (LD) b. May 5, 1973. IT consultant. Cllr. Ed: Birmingham Uni.
Nusrat Ghani (C) Charity worker. Ed: Uni of Central England; Leeds Uni.

Constituency
Birmingham city centre lies in this seat, with the main business district in Ladywood ward. The economy is overwhelmingly service sector and about a third of workforce is in financial or business sectors. Those living in sought-after residential properties in the centre are affluent but the seat is only averagely well off, with large areas of deprivation beyond the centre. About 44 per cent of residents are aged 24 and under, the most youthful demographic of all Birmingham seats. About two thirds are black or ethnic minorities, mainly Asian. This Labour-dominated seat had an independent MP after Clare Short had the whip withdrawn in 2006.

	Electorate	Turnout %	Change from '05 %
	73,646	48.7	
Mahmood, S Lab	19,950	55.7	3.0
Khan, A LD	9,845	27.5	-2.0
Ghani, N C	4,277	11.9	3.5
Booth, C UKIP	902	2.5	-3.0
Beck, P Green	859	2.4	2.1

50%
Majority 10,105

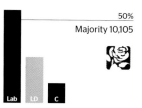

Lab LD C

Birmingham Northfield
Labour hold

Richard Burden
b. Sep 1, 1954
MP 1992-

Outspoken supporter of Palestinians (Chair, Britain-Palestine All Party Parliamentary Group). Motor sports adviser to Richard Caborn 2002-07. PPS to: Jeffrey Rooker 1997-2001. Member, cttee: Int Devt 2005-; Trade & Industry 2001-05. Former chair, Lab Campaign for electoral reform. Founded Joint Action for Water Services 1985 to oppose water privatisation. NALGO (branch officer, dist officer). Married, two stepdaughters, one stepson. Ed: Wallasey Tech GS; Bramhall Comp; St John's FE Coll, Manchester; York (BA pol); Warwick (MA industrial relations).

Keely Huxtable (C) b. 1981. Public sector worker. Ed: Cadbury College, Kings Norton.
Mike Dixon (LD) b. Aug 14, 1957. Lib Dems' organiser for Birmingham. Contested Birmingham Edgbaston 2005, Wolverhampton South West 2001.

Constituency
At the southwestern tip of Birmingham, this seat borders with the semi-rural Bromsgrove areas. Substantially increased by about 17,000 electors after gaining Kings Norton from the Selly Oak ward, it remains primarily residential and significantly less ethnically diverse than most of Birmingham. Although generally better off than many Birmingham seats, it was hit hard by the 2005 closure of the Longbridge Rover plant, which had dominated the economy. The seat changed hands several times between 1979 and 1992, when Labour won.

	Electorate	Turnout %	Change from '05 %
	71,338	58.6	
Burden, R Lab	16,841	40.3	-10.1
Huxtable, K C	14,059	33.6	3.2
Dixon, M LD	6,550	15.7	3.3
Orton, L BNP	2,290	5.5	
Borthwick, J UKIP	1,363	3.3	1.0
Pearce, S Green	406	1.0	
Rodgers, D Good	305	0.7	

50%
Majority 2,782

Lab C LD BNP

Birmingham Perry Barr
Labour hold

Khalid Mahmood
b. Jul 13, 1961
MP 2001-

Muslim who attracted controversy for putting his name to 'the five myths Muslims must deny' article supporting Afghanistan war, ghostwritten by Denis MacShane. PPS to Tony McNulty 2004-06. Member, select cttee: Broadcasting 2001-05. Cllr, Birmingham City 1990-93. Nat member Lab Finance & Industry group. Adviser, President of Olympic Council Asia. AEEU, former adviser Danish International Trade Union. Former engineer. Twice divorced, child from first marriage, daughter from second. Ed: University of Central England.

Karen Hamilton (LD) Accountant. Ed: University of Central England.

William Norton (C) Tax solicitor. Ed: University College London.

Constituency
This northwest Birmingham constituency is primarily residential and contains some relatively affluent, leafy suburbs. However, the Lozells and East Handsworth ward, nearest the city centre, is extremely deprived and has experienced racial tensions between black and Asian communities who together comprise more than 80 per cent of the ward's (and more than half of the seat's) residents. The manufacturing sector is stronger than in any other Birmingham seat, although many work in public services. Labour has held since 1974 with varying majorities.

	Electorate	Turnout %	Change from '05 %
	71,304	59.0	
Mahmood, K Lab	21,142	50.3	4.0
Hamilton, K LD	9,234	22.0	-4.1
Norton, W C	8,960	21.3	4.0
Ward, M UKIP	1,675	4.0	1.6
Tyrrell, J Soc	527	1.3	
Hey-Smith, D Ch	507	1.2	

50%
Majority 11,908

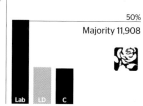

Lab LD C

Birmingham Selly Oak — Labour hold

Steve McCabe
b. Aug 4, 1955
MP 1997-

Machine politician, old-style Commons operator. Whip: government 2007-10; assistant 2006-07. PPS to Charles Clarke 2003-05. Member select committees: Joint Committee on House of Lords reform 2003-10; Home Affaird 2005-06; NI Affairs 1998-2003; Deregulation 1997-99. Cllr, Birmingham 1990-98. NALGO shop steward. Social worker/lecturer/researcher. MSF, Unite. Divorced, one daughter, one son. Education: Moray House Coll, Edinburgh (Cert Qual social work); Bradford (MA social work).

Nigel Dawkins (C) Runs own software consultancy company. Education: Imperial College Kensington.

David Radcliffe (LD) b. 1973. Doctor of Chemistry and university lecturer. Contested Corby 2005. Ed: Manchester Uni.

Constituency
This south Birmingham seat has been substantially redrawn, losing King's Norton and Moseley and King's Heath wards but gaining Billesley and Brandwood, on the outskirts of the city. These new areas are less affluent than Bournville – a model village built in 1893 by George Cadbury – and Selly Oak, which is home to large numbers of students. The seat is less ethnically diverse than much of the city. Under old boundaries it changed hands several times, won by Labour in 1992.

		Electorate	Turnout %	Change from '05 %
		74,805	62.3	☆
McCabe, S	Lab	17,950	38.6	-8.3
Dawkins, N	C	14,468	31.1	1.4
Radcliffe, D	LD	10,371	22.3	4.9
Orton, L	BNP	1,820	3.9	
Burgess, J	UKIP	1,131	2.4	-0.1
Burn, J	Green	664	1.4	-2.2
Leeds, S	Ch	159	0.3	

50%
Majority 3,482

Birmingham Yardley — Liberal Democrat hold

John Hemming
b. Mar 16, 1960
MP 2005-

Maverick. Contested Birmingham Yardley 2001, 1997 and 1992, Birmingham Small Heath 1987, Birmingham Hall Green 1983. Cllr, Birmingham City 1990- (group leader 1998-). Entrepreneur. Senior partner John Hemming & Co. Jazz pianist, heavy metal drummer. Married, two daughters and one son from marriage, one daughter from extra-marital affair with researcher. Education: King Edward's Sch, Birmingham; Magdalen Coll, Oxford (BA atomic, nuclear and theoretical physics, MA).

Lynnette Kelly (Lab) b. Nov 2, 1962. Former university lecturer. Education: Coventry Uni.

Meirion Jenkins (C) Director of a software company. International Trade Adviser for UK Trade and Investment. Education: Ashton Uni.

Constituency
In the southeast of the city the Yardley seat has been increased by about 21,000 electors. Manufacturing and construction are above the city average although the service sector still dominates. Attempts to develop areas of Stechford with new apartments failed to take off. All four wards have a mixture of deprived and fairly affluent areas. Traditionally a Conservative-Labour marginal seat, the Liberal Democrats took it in 2005.

		Electorate	Turnout %	Change from '05 %
		72,321	56.5	☆
Hemming, J	LD	16,162	39.6	-2.5
Kelly, L	Lab	13,160	32.2	-2.5
Jenkins, M	C	7,836	19.2	8.6
Lumby, T	BNP	2,153	5.3	
Duffen, G	UKIP	1,190	2.9	1.2
Morris, P	NF	349	0.9	

50%
Majority 3,002

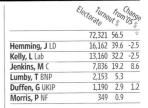

Bishop Auckland — Labour hold

Helen Goodman
b. Jan 2, 1958
MP 2005-

Popular, plain-speaking. Ally of Harriet Harman, earnest plotter. One-time Labour mole while civil servant in Treasury. Parly Under-Sec: Work & Pensions 2009-10. Asst Govt Whip 2008-2009. Deputy Leader of the House of Commons 2007-2008. PPS to: Harriet Harman 2007. Head of strategy, the Children's Society. Chief exec, Rails Safety and Standards Board. Dir, Commission on the Future of Multi Ethnic Britain. Chief exec National Association of Toy and Leisure Libraries. Married. Two children. Ed: Lady Manners Sch, Bakewell; Somerville Coll, Oxford (BA PPE).

Barbara Harrison (C) Self-employed management consultant. Former prison governor. Cllr, Durham CC. Ed: Bishop Barrington Comp.
Mark Wilkes (LD) b. Apr 30, 1975. Owns translation and interpretation business. Cllr. Ed: Sheffield University.

Constituency
Its southwestern expanse of Co Durham borders Cumbria in the west and is primarily rural Teesdale, with moors, commons and an Area of Outstanding Natural Beauty. The key town, in the middle, is Barnard Castle, on the banks of the Tees, home to a boarding school that produced several England rugby union internationals, including the Underwood brothers. While most of the area is well off, the urban concentration at the northeastern extremity – Bishop Auckland, Shildon and Spennymoor – have areas of deprivation. This seat has long been staunchly Labour.

		Electorate	Turnout %	Change from '05 %
		68,370	60.2	☆
Goodman, H	Lab	16,023	39.0	-11.1
Harrison, B	C	10,805	26.3	3.4
Wilkes, M	LD	9,189	22.3	-1.3
Walker, A	BNP	2,036	5.0	
Zair, S	LLPBPP	1,964	4.8	
Brothers, D	UKIP	1,119	2.7	-0.7

50%
Majority 5,218

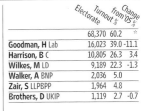

Jack Straw
b. Aug 03, 1946
MP 1979-

Survivor who was in Cabinet for the 13 years of Labour Government. Friendly, capable and fearless. Known for getting up on his soapbox in Blackburn and taking on anyone who wants to debate him. Lord Chancellor and SoS for Justice 2007-10. Leader of HoC 2006-07. SoS: Foreign 2001-06, Home 1997-2001. Shadow SoS: Home 1994-97; Environment 1992-94; Education 1987-92. Opp spokes: Environment 1983-87, Treasury/Econ 1980-83. Lab Party NEC 1994-95. Cllr, Islington BC 1971-78. Dep leader Inner London Education Authority 1973. Pres NUS 1969-71. GMB. Barrister. Visiting fellow, Nuffield Coll, Oxford. Divorced, re-married. One daughter from first marriage dec,

one daughter and one son from second marriage. Ed: Brentwood Sch; Leeds (LLB); Inns of Court Sch of Law.

Michael Law-Riding (C) Cllr. Worked for electronic security company.
Paul English (LD) b. Dec 24, 1968. Chief officer for Craven Vol Action.

Constituency
Once the weaving capital of the world, this seat has fought hard to combat the decline of its industries. Its plight is typified by rows of dilapidated terraced houses. A quarter of the population is of Indian or Pakistani origin. The town has avoided the extreme racial tension of neighbouring areas. The M65 extension, intended to boost the sluggish local economy, instead encouraged commuting elsewhere. Some suburban and rural fringes are more prosperous. There is a long Labour history.

	Electorate	Turnout %	Change from '05 %
	72,331	62.9	☆
Straw, J Lab	21,751	47.8	5.7
Law-Riding, M C	11,895	26.1	3.5
English, P LD	6,918	15.2	-5.4
Evans, R BNP	2,158	4.7	
Irfanullah, B BIB	1,424	3.1	
Anwar, B UKIP	942	2.1	-0.2
Astley, G Ind	238	0.5	
Sharp, J Ind	173	0.4	

50%
Majority 9,856

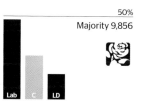

Lab | C | LD

Graham Stringer
b. Feb 17, 1950
MP 1997-

Successful, reforming council leader who became disaffected after three years in government. Experience was under-used by Blair and then Brown Governments. Govt whip 2001-02. Parly Sec Cab Office 1999-2001. Member, select cttees: IUS 2007-10; Science & Technology 2006-07; Modernisation of HoC 2006; Transport 2002; Environment, Transport & Regional Affairs 1997-99. Cllr Manchester CC 1979-98 (leader 1984-96). Amicus /Unite. Chair of Board Manchester Airport plc. Analytical chemist. Branch officer / shop steward, MSF. Avid Manchester United fan. Plays squash and real tennis. Married, one son, one stepdaughter, one stepson. Ed: Moston

Brook HS; Sheffield (BSc chemistry)

James Edsberg (C) Founder of economics research firm. Ed: Bristol Uni.
William Hobhouse (LD) b. Jan 17, 1963. Cllr, Rochdale. Dir, Composite Textiles. Ed: Cambridge Uni.
Derek Adams (BNP).

Constituency
The northernmost part of Manchester, formerly Blackley constituency, is joined by Broughton and Kersal, two deprived Salford wards divided from the rest of their borough by the River Irwell. Charlestown, on the edge of Manchester, is the city's least diverse ward while the population of Cheetham comprises 48.7 per cent ethnic minorities. It is also home to the prison formerly known as Strangeways. Harpurhey, with many housing estates, is very deprived. The seat has been Labour in recent decades.

	Electorate	Turnout %	Change from '05 %
	69,489	49.2	☆
Stringer, G Lab	18,563	54.3	-8.2
Edsberg, J C	6,260	18.3	5.3
Hobhouse, W LD	4,861	14.2	-4.9
Adams, D BNP	2,469	7.2	
Phillips, K Respect	996	2.9	
Willescroft, B UKIP	894	2.6	-2.7
Zaman, S Ch	161	0.5	

50%
Majority 12,303

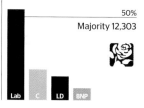

Lab | C | LD | BNP

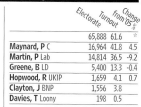

Paul Maynard
b. Dec 16, 1975
MP 1997-

Independent-minded, self-styled community champion. Proud Northerner. Long-standing special adviser to Liam Fox MP (1999-2007). Worked at Reform thinktank. Management consultant, Hodgart Temporal. Has mild cerebral palsy and epilepsy. Contested Twickenham 2005. Lay reader at local Catholic Church. Member, Twentieth Century Society. Northwich Victoria FC supporter. Ed: St Ambrose College; University College, Oxford (BA modern history).

Penny Martin (Lab) b. Dec 23, 1958. Co-ordinator for charity Lancashire Gulu Link. Education: University of Central Lancashire.

Bill Greene (LD) IT professional and risk manager.

Constituency
The Blackpool North seat used to extend up the coast to Fleetwood; after boundary changes its northern extremity reaches only Cleveleys, while it has gained the Park ward of Blackpool to the south. Park and Claremont wards are severely deprived and the seat is fairly poor with high unemployment — especially during the off-season. Blackpool had the lowest male life expectancy of all local authorities in England and Wales in 2007. The seat was Tory from the Second World War until Labour's landslide of 1997.

	Electorate	Turnout %	Change from '05 %
	65,888	61.6	☆
Maynard, P C	16,964	41.8	4.5
Martin, P Lab	14,814	36.5	-9.2
Greene, B LD	5,400	13.3	-0.4
Hopwood, R UKIP	1,659	4.1	0.7
Clayton, J BNP	1,556	3.8	
Davies, T Loony	198	0.5	

50%
Majority 2,150

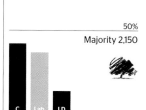

C | Lab | LD

Blackpool South | Labour hold

Gordon Marsden
b. Nov 28, 1953
MP 1997-

Earnest, constituency-focused loyalist. PPS to: Michael Wills 2007; Tessa Jowell 2003-05; Lord Irvine of Lairg 2001-03. Member, select cttees: Innovation, uni & skills 2007-10; Education & employment 1998-2001; Deregulation 1997-99. Pres, British Resorts Assoc. Historian/lecturer. English Heritage public affairs adviser. Ed: Stockport GS; New Coll, Oxford (MA history); London (PhD research combined historical studies); Harvard (Kennedy Scholarship).

Ron Bell (C) Retired management consultant. Education: Tyldesley secondary modern school.
Doreen Holt (LD) b. 1938. Retired.

Contested Blackpool South 2005, 2001, 1997. Ed: White Well Bottom Secondary Modern.

Constituency
The heart of Blackpool's traditional resort — with the iconic Pleasure Beach and Tower — is included in this seat, which has been cut in size in the northeast. The northwestern boundary is marked by the North Pier. The Blackpool Illuminations every autumn draw visitors but the town has struggled to adapt to changing markets. It had a casino-based regeneration bid rejected and much of the town is severely deprived, with Bloomfield ward the fifth worst in the UK. Labour took this seat from the Tories in 1997.

	Electorate	Turnout %	Change from '05 %
	63,025	55.8	☆
Marsden, G Lab	14,448	41.1	-7.5
Bell, R C	12,597	35.8	5.0
Holt, D LD	5,082	14.4	-0.7
Goodwin, R BNP	1,482	4.2	
Howitt, H UKIP	1,352	3.8	1.7
Thu, S Tun	230	0.7	

50%
Majority 1,851

Blaenau Gwent | Labour gain

Nick Smith
b. Jan 14, 1960
MP 2010-

Amiable local man from coal/steel industries family. Special interest in health issues. Cllr, Camden 1998-2006. Dir, Policy & Partnerships, Royal College of Speech and Language Therapists. Campaigns Manager, NSPCC. Nat Officer at Lab HQ. Sec Gen of European Parl Lab Party. Intl Democracy Adviser for US Democrats and Westminster Foundation for Democracy. Community, Unite and GMB. Campaigner, 'Salt our streets' and 'turn on the lights' (streetlights). Keen rambler. Fellow, Royal Geographical Society. Divorced, two daughters. Ed: Tredegar Comp; Coventry Poly; Birkbeck Coll (MSc Economic & Social Change).

Dai Davies (Blaenau Voice) b. Nov 26, 1959. MP Blaenau Gwent 2006 (by-election)-2010. Steel apprenticeship.
Matt Smith (LD) b. Mar 17, 1988. Pol student at University of Glamorgan.
Liz Stevenson (C) Corporate communications for the London Stock Exchange. Cllr, Herts DC 2004-08.

Constituency
A valleys seat including the former steel town of Ebbw Vale, and Tredegar, Beaufort, Brynmawr, and Abertillery. It is working class, with more than a quarter of residents living in social housing. Poor health is common. The area was dependent on coalmining and is steeped in Labour history, having been held by Aneurin Bevan and Michael Foot. Peter Law (ind) won here in 2005, having resigned from Labour in a row over all-women shortlists. He died in 2006 and his agent won the by-election.

	Electorate	Turnout %	Change from '05 %
	52,438	61.8	
Smith, N Lab	16,974	52.4	20.2
Davies, D Blaenau	6,458	19.9	
Smith, M LD	3,285	10.1	5.9
Stevenson, L C	2,265	7.0	4.7
Davies, R PC	1,333	4.1	1.7
King, A BNP	1,211	3.7	
Kocan, M UKIP	488	1.5	1.0
O'Connell, A Soc	381	1.2	

50%
Majority 10,516

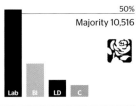

Blaydon | Labour hold

Dave Anderson
b. Dec 2, 1953
MP 2005-

Trade union activist who cut his teeth in the miners' strike 1984-85. Large man with strong Geordie accent. PPS to Bill Rammell 2006-. Member select cttees: North East 2009-10. Energy and Climate Change 2009-10, Procedure 2005-06, Northern Ireland Affairs 2005-10. Engineer National Coal Board mines. Elderly care worker Newcastle-upon-Tyne social services. Married. Educated: Maltby Grammar School. Doncaster Technical College; Durham Technical College (mining and mechanical engineering); Moscow Higher Trade Union School 1983; Durham University (DipSocSc).

Neil Bradbury (LD) b. Jul 21, 1976. Manager of a Citizens Advice Bureau. Newcastle University. Cllr, Northumberland CC, 2003-.
Glenn Hall (C) b. Oct 25, 1968. Commercial lawyer. Cllr, Tunbridge Wells BC 2007-. Ed: Durham University (history).

Constituency
From the town of Birtley and the iconic Angel of the North at the east, this seat encompasses the fringes of Gateshead, including part of the Team Valley industrial area. It extends west, taking in the huge Metrocentre shopping precinct and the towns of Whickham, Ryton and Blaydon; the 19th-century folk song Blaydon Races is Tyneside's unofficial anthem. The southern and western fringes of the seat are more rural. The seat has been Labour since 1935.

	Electorate	Turnout %	Change from '05 %
	67,808	66.2	☆
Anderson, D Lab	22,297	49.6	-2.0
Bradbury, N LD	13,180	29.4	-8.5
Hall, G C	7,159	15.9	7.9
McFarlane, K BNP	2,277	5.1	

50%
Majority 9,117

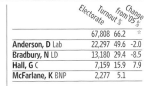

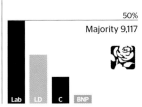

Blyth Valley — Labour hold

Ronnie Campbell
b. Aug 14, 1943
MP 1987-

Ruddy-cheeked, unre-constructed figure from Labour Left. Not so much old Labour as dinosaur Labour. Member select cttees: Catering 2001-10; Public Administration 1997-2001. Chair Lab MPs northern regional group 1999-. Cllr, Blyth Bor 1969-74, Blyth Valley 1974-88. NUM sponsored MP, former lodge sec Bates Colliery, Blyth. Miner for 28 years. Married, one daughter, five sons. Education: Ridley HS, Blyth.

Jeffrey Reid (LD) b. Sep 22, 1956. Salesman. Contested Blyth Valley 2005, 2001. Cllr, Northumberland CC (leader, Lib Dems). Education: Newcastle College.

Barry Flux (C) b. Oct 27, 1982. Office administrator. Education: Northumbria University.

Constituency

This densely populated urban seat lies on the coast just north of Newcastle upon Tyne. The two main population centres are Blyth, whose port handles 1.5 million tonnes of cargo each year and whose football team, Blyth Spartans, are famous for their giant-killing FA Cup exploits, and Cramlington, a former village that expanded rapidly after being designated a New Town in the 1960s. It has not fully recovered from the decline of the coalmining industry. The seat has a strong Labour tradition, though victories over the SDP in the 1980s were sometimes slim.

	Electorate	Turnout %	Change from '05 %
	64,263	60.0	
Campbell, R Lab	17,156	44.5	-10.4
Reid, J LD	10,488	27.2	-3.9
Flux, B C	6,412	16.6	2.7
Fairbairn, S BNP	1,699	4.4	
Condon, J UKIP	1,665	4.3	
Elliott, B Ind	819	2.1	
White, A Eng	327	0.9	

50%
Majority 6,668

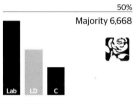

Bognor Regis & Littlehampton — Conservative hold

Nick Gibb
b. Sep 3, 1960
MP 1997-

Quiet and industrious. A big advocate of teaching phonics. Min: Schools 2010-. Shadow Min: Schools 2005-10. Opposition spokes: Trade and Industry 1999-2001; Treasury 1998-99. Chartered Accountant for KPMG. Educated: Maidstone Grammar School and Roundhay School, Leeds; Thornes House School, Wakefield; Durham Univ (BA law).

Simon McDougall (LD) b. Jan 5, 1967. Construction worker. Contested Bognor Regis 2005. Former Cllr, Bognor Regis TC. Ed: Bognor Regis Community College.
Michael Jones (Lab) b. Jan 22, 1976. Solicitor. Contested Bexhill and Battle

in 2005. Ed: Southampton University.
Douglas Denny (UKIP) b. March 31, 1948. Optometrist. Ed: Barrow Grammar School.

Constituency

A narrow strip of West Sussex coast stretches between the eponymous towns. Bognor Regis boasts the most hours of sunshine in Britain. A mixed seat socio-economically, both towns have some areas of relative deprivation typical of traditional seaside resorts where tourism has declined and employment is seasonal. They are home to many retired people. There are more affluent areas inland, which have been extended under relatively minor boundary changes to include Yapton. The seat has been Tory since its inception in 1997.

	Electorate	Turnout %	Change from '05 %
	70,812	66.2	☀
Gibb, N C	24,087	51.4	6.3
McDougall, S LD	11,024	23.5	1.7
Jones, M Lab	6,580	14.0	-11.0
Denny, D UKIP	3,036	6.5	-1.5
Moffat, A BNP	1,890	4.0	
Briggs, M Ind	235	0.5	

50%
Majority 13,063

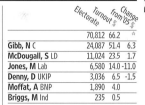

Bolsover — Labour hold

Dennis Skinner
b. Feb 11, 1932
MP 1970-

Assiduous, volatile left-wing Tory baiter, dubbed "Beast of Bolsover". Continues to fight the class war, sometimes by himself. Excels at one-line put-down of opponents, although sharpness has faded. Socialist Campaign Group. Chair Lab Party 1988-89 (Vice-Chair 1987-88). Lab Party NEC member 1999-; 1994-98; 1978-92. Cllr, Clay Cros UDC 1960-70; county cllr Derbyshire 1964-70. President Derbyshire Miners. Miner. Widowed. Two daughters, one son. Ed: Tupton Hall GS; Ruskin Coll, Oxford.

Lee Rowley (C) b. Sep 11, 1980. Banker at Santander. Councillor in Maida Vale since 2006. Ed: Oxford Uni (history)

Denise Hawksworth (LD) b. May 6, 1957. Officer manager for Paul Holmes MP. Contested Bolsover 2005; EU parliament 2009. Cllr, Chesterfield.
Martin Radford (BNP).

Constituency

Bolsover Castle overlooks the M1 in this seat, which lies to the east of Chesterfield and southeast of Sheffield. At the heart of the coalfields, this has always been working class but the closure of the pits left severe deprivation in many of the urban areas. Beyond the main towns of Bolsover and Shirebrook are several large villages. Regeneration projects are slowly improving the area but this is a seat that shares many of the challenges faced by post-industrial Yorkshire. It was made famous by Dennis Skinner and has been solidly Labour for decades.

	Electorate	Turnout %	Change from '05 %
	72,766	60.5	☀
Skinner, D Lab	21,994	50.0	-15.2
Rowley, L C	10,812	24.6	7.3
Hawksworth, D LD	6,821	15.5	-2.0
Radford, M BNP	2,640	6.0	
Calladine, R UKIP	1,721	3.9	

50%
Majority 11,182

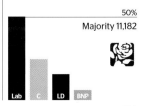

Bolton North East | Labour hold

David Crausby
b. Jun 17, 1946
MP 1997-

Sharper than first impressions may convey. Member, cttees: NW 2009-10; Quadripartite/Arms Export Controls 2006-10; Defence 2001-10; Social Security 1999-2001; Admin 1997-2001. Cllr, Bury 1979-92. Chair, Amicus group. Shop steward and works convenor AEEU; full-time works convenor. Engineer. Married, two sons. Ed: Derby GS, Bury; Bury Tech College.

Deborah Dunleavy (C) b. Jan 4, 1964. Company director. Contested Bolton South East 2005. Ed: Abraham Moss College.
Paul Ankers (LD) b. Aug 3, 1976. Full-time councillor (Chorlton 2007-). Ed: Humberside Uni.

Constituency
The northern constituency of this formerly industrial town includes most of central Bolton, with its shopping centres and old town hall — as featured by Peter Kay, its most famous export, in Live at the Bolton Albert Halls. The town has been the scene of significant regeneration in recent years. Beyond the centre are residential areas and the seat also includes some rural land at its northern extremities. It has generally returned an MP of the government of the day, with the exception of 1979-83.

	Electorate	Turnout %	Change from '05 %
	67,281	64.3	☆
Crausby, D Lab	19,870	45.9	-0.4
Dunleavy, D C	15,786	36.5	2.2
Ankers, P LD	5,624	13.0	-3.1
Johnson, N UKIP	1,815	4.2	2.4
Armston, N You	182	0.4	

50%

Majority 4,084

Bolton South East | Labour hold

Yasmin Qureshi
b. Jul 5, 1963
MP 2010-

One of first female Muslim MPs. Attentive, personable and hard-working. Opposed Iraq war, vocal about Muslim women's rights. Criminal law barrister and long-term Labour activist. Contested Brent East 2005. CPS prosecutor. Worked for UN Mission in Kosovo. Human rights adviser (voluntary role) to Ken Livingstone as Mayor of London. Citizens Advice Bureau voluntary work. British Institute of Human Rights. Special interest in poverty, mental health and child abuse issues. Usdaw/GMB. Pakistani-born, moved to Britain aged 9. Married to a prof cricketer. Ed: Westfield Comp, Watford; South Bank Uni (BA Hons Law); Council of Legal Ed; UCL (LLM).

Andy Morgan (C) Businessman. Cllr, Bolton 2002-.
Donal O'Hanlon (LD) Risk consultant at HSBC. Cllr, Bury. Ed: Hull Uni.

Constituency
The population of this seat is concentrated in south Bolton and Farnworth, which are sandwiched between the M61 and the railway that transports commuters the 11 miles to Manchester. Beyond this central avenue are woodland and open spaces with smaller communities. The traditionally industrial economy has diversified into service and public sectors but business parks remain and the area is less affluent, and has more council housing, than elsewhere in Bolton. About 12 per cent of residents are ethnic minorities. The seat has been Labour since its creation in 1983.

	Electorate	Turnout %	Change from '05 %
	69,928	56.6	☆
Qureshi, Y Lab	18,782	47.4	-8.3
Morgan, A C	10,148	25.6	2.9
O'Hanlon, D LD	6,289	15.9	-2.2
Spink, S BNP	2,012	5.1	
Sidaway, I UKIP	1,564	4.0	1.4
Johnson, A Green	614	1.6	
Syed, N CPA	195	0.5	

50%

Majority 8,634

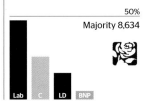

Bolton West | Labour hold

Julie Hilling
b. Apr 29, 1955
MP 2010-

Youth worker turned union official, who overcame public anger at expenses of Ruth Kelly, her predecessor, enduring a recount to hold off Tory challenge. Senior Regional Organiser, Transport Salaried Staffs' Association (union). NW Learning organiser, NASUWT. Community work, Wigan Council. Nat President, CYWU. Chair of Socialist Education Association. Long-term Atherton resident, lives on council estate. Member Amnesty, Cuba Solidarity, Howard League for Criminal Reform, Lab Friends of Palestine, Unite. Ed: Cedars Sch, Leighton Buzzard; Nottingham (BSc Chem); Manchester Poly (Dip youth & community work)

Susan Williams (C) b. May 1967. Cllr, Trafford 1998- (leader 20040). Contested Wythenshawe & Sale East 2001. Ed: Huddersfield Uni.
Jackie Pearcey (LD) b. Sep 23, 1963. IT trainer. Contested Gorton 1997, 2001; Davyhulme 1992. Cllr, Manchester CC 1991-. Ed: Bristol (BSc); Manchester (PhD).

Constituency
This seat sits predominantly to the west of Bolton and takes in only a slither of the town, instead containing large rural areas and the town of Atherton, in the Wigan ward. The town of Horwich, the new home of Bolton Wanderers FC, lies five miles northwest of Bolton amid the West Pennine Moors. Westhoughton, whose residents tend to be more affluent than in Bolton, is another popular small town in this seat. The seat was Tory until 1997 when it turned Labour.

	Electorate	Turnout %	Change from '05 %
	71,250	66.8	☆
Hilling, J Lab	18,327	38.5	-6.8
Williams, S C	18,235	38.3	4.9
Pearcey, J LD	8,177	17.2	-1.8
Lamb, H UKIP	1,901	4.0	2.6
Mann, R Green	545	1.2	
Jones, J Ind	254	0.5	
Bagnall, D You	137	0.3	

50%

Majority 92

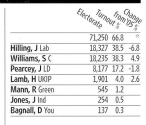

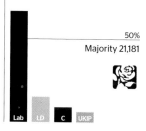

Joe Benton
b. Sep 28, 1933
MP 1990- (by-election)

Old-timer Liverpudlian. Opposition whip 1994-97. Member cttees: Chairmen's Panel 1998-2010; Parly Privilege 1997-2000; Education/Employment 1997-99. Cllr, Sefton Bor 1970-92 (leader Lab Group 1985-90). Member, RMT Parly Campaigning Group 2002-. Girobank. RAF national service. Married, four daughters. Ed: St Monica's Sch; Bootle Technical College.

James Murray (LD) Solicitor. Ed: Leeds (BSc) and Nottingham (LLM).
Sohail Qureshi (C) IT specialist.
Paul Nuttall (UKIP) b. 30 Nov, 1976. MEP, UKIP chairman. Ed: Savio HS, Netherton.

Constituency
Although it has retained the same name, the Bootle seat, just north of Liverpool, has been substantially extended to the north and encompasses the southern half of Crosby, which used to have its own seat. This deprived area is typified by high unemployment, low income, social problems and poor health. It is overwhelmingly white working class and regarded as the safest Labour seat in the country.

	Electorate	Turnout %	Change from '05 %
	71,426	57.8	*
Benton, J Lab	27,426	66.4	-4.6
Murray, J LD	6,245	15.1	-1.4
Qureshi, S C	3,678	8.9	1.6
Nuttall, P UKIP	2,514	6.1	2.8
Stewart, C BNP	942	2.3	
Glover, P TUSC	472	1.1	

50%

Majority 21,181

Mark Simmonds
b. Apr 12, 1964
MP 2001-

Campaigned for tighter regulation of gang masters who control agricultural labourers. Missed out on role in first coalition govt. Shad Min: Health 2007-10; Int Dev't 2005-07; Foreign Affairs 2004-05; Public Services/Health/Ed 2003-04; PPS to Michael Ancram 2002. Cllr, Wandsworth 1990-94. Chartered surveyor: partner, Savills, Strutt & Parker; dir, Hillier Parker. Married, two daughters, one son. Ed: Worksop College; Trent Poly (BSc urban estate surveying).

Paul Kenny (Lab) b. Mar 22, 1955. Community dev officer. Contested Boston 2005. Cllr, Lincolnshire CC 1993-2005. Ed: Uni of Birmingham.

Philip Smith (LD) b. Nov 16, 1963. Contested Doncaster South 2001; Mansfield 1997. Cllr, Mansfield 1999-.
Christopher Pain (UKIP) Contested Louth & Horncastle 2005.
David Owens (BNP)

Constituency
This seat spans from Skegness down to the River Welland. Much of Skegness and some parts of Boston, which lies inland, are severely deprived. In the 1630s, Boston lost a tenth of its population when 250 residents departed for a new life in Massachusetts. About 17,500 of the town's 75,000 residents are foreign citizens, mostly Eastern Europeans working in the agriculture and food processing industries that dominate local employment. The soaring population has put pressure on housing and services. Tory support has long been strong.

	Electorate	Turnout %	Change from '05 %
	70,529	61.2	*
Simmonds, M C	21,325	49.5	3.1
Kenny, P Lab	8,899	20.6	-10.9
Smith, P LD	6,371	14.8	5.4
Pain, C UKIP	4,081	9.5	0.0
Owens, D BNP	2,278	5.3	
Wilson, P Ind	171	0.4	

50%

Majority 12,426

David Tredinnick
b. Jan 19, 1950
MP 1987-

Maverick with consuming interest in alternative medicine. Suspended from Commons in first "cash for questions" scandal and forced to resign as PPS to Sir Wyn Roberts (1991-94) but survived on back benches. Career inc. manager, property co; marketing/comms; technology salesman; advertising account exec. Army – Guards officer. Divorced, one daughter, one son. Educated: Eton; Cape Town (MBA); St John's Coll, Oxford (MLitt).

Michael Mullaney (LD) b. Jun 5, 1980. Office manager. Ed: John Leas Sch; Northampton Uni.
Rory Palmer (Lab) b. Nov 19, 1981. Full-time councillor and cabinet member for adult and social care. Ed: Hartland Comprehensive School, Worksop and York University.

Constituency
This Leicestershire seat is named after the small town of Market Bosworth, in the centre of a large rural area, but its biggest population concentration is in Hinckley. The mining industry that once dominated the economy has long declined and the seat switched to Conservative in 1970. However, significant numbers of the working classes and manufacturing industry remain and the Tory margins of victory have not always been great.

	Electorate	Turnout %	Change from '05 %
	77,296	70.2	*
Tredinnick, D C	23,132	42.6	0.0
Mullaney, M LD	18,100	33.4	11.8
Palmer, R Lab	8,674	16.0	-15.9
Ryde, D BNP	2,458	4.5	
Veldhuizen, D UKIP	1,098	2.0	-1.9
Lampitt, J Eng	615	1.1	
Brooks, M Science	197	0.4	

50%

Majority 5,032

Bournemouth East
Conservative hold

Tobias Ellwood
b. Aug 12, 1966
MP 2005-

Popular and well-connected. Very gung-ho and eager, full of good ideas especially on specialist subjects such as Afghanistan. Overlooked in first coalition. Shadow Minister: CMS (2007-10). Opposition Whip (2005-07). Raised in the USA, Germany and Austria with UN-employed parents. Career: Army, including active service in Bosnia. Researcher to Tom King MP, business manager London Stock Exchange. Treasurer, Bow Group. Education: Vienna Int School; Loughborough University of Technology (design & tech); City (MBA).

Lisa Northover (LD) b. Jun 6, 1976.

Cllr, Bournemouth BC. Ed: St Peter's Catholic Comp, Bournemouth
David Stokes (Lab) Quantity surveyor. Ed: Beaufort Sch; Hatfield Polytechnic.
David Hughes (UKIP) Former electrical retailer. Ed: York University.

Constituency
This small urban seat includes most of the award-winning Bournemouth beach and large residential areas include above-average numbers of retired people. It is relatively affluent but Central Boscombe is in the top 1 per cent of deprived areas in Britain. Boscombe has constructed an artificial surf reef to increase tourism, already a large employer. Bournemouth is the biggest destination outside London for foreign students learning English. Finance and services are the other main sectors. Tory since the seat's creation but the margins of victory have not always been great.

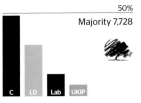

	Electorate	Turnout %	Change from '05 %
	71,125	61.9	☆
Ellwood, T C	21,320	48.4	3.1
Northover, L LD	13,592	30.9	-0.4
Stokes, D Lab	5,836	13.3	-5.3
Hughes, D UKIP	3,027	6.9	2.0
Humphrey, S Ind	249	0.6	

50%
Majority 7,728

C | LD | Lab | UKIP

Bournemouth West
Conservative hold

Conor Burns
b. Sep 24, 1972
MP 2010-

Right-wing Eurosceptic young fogey and ardent admirer of Margaret Thatcher. Belfast-born Catholic, pro-life. Member, Con Way Forward. Life-long Tory (chair Southampton Uni Conservative Assoc, member National Committee of Conservative Students). Cllr, Southampton CC 1999-2002. Contested Eastleigh 2005 (lost by 568 votes), 2001. Communications/finance career: Associate Dir, PLMR (lobbying); Head of Business Dev't, DeHavilland; Zurich Insurance. Board member, Spitfire Tribute Foundation. Lover of second hand books. Ed: St Columba's Coll, St Albans; Southampton (Mod Hist & Pol)

Alasdair Murray (LD) Director, Centreforum. Ed: King Edward VI Sch; Oxford University.
Sharon Carr-Brown (Lab) Proofreader. Ed: Bournemouth Sch; Durham Uni.
Philip Glover (UKIP) Writer. Ed: Bournemouth & Poole College; Southampton.

Constituency
A 2007 survey identified Bournemouth as the happiest place in Britain. The town centre is included in this seat, which has been redrawn to include wards from neighbouring Poole borough, Branksome East and Alderney, where there are large social housing estates. Kinson South is also relatively deprived but this seaside seat is generally fairly affluent, with residents working in finance, business and tourism. It has a staunchly Tory tradition.

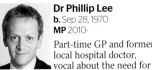

	Electorate	Turnout %	Change from '05 %
	71,753	58.1	☆
Burns, C C	18,808	45.2	5.6
Murray, A LD	13,225	31.8	-0.2
Carr-Brown, S Lab	6,171	14.8	-8.1
Glover, P UKIP	2,999	7.2	1.6
Taylor, H Ind	456	1.1	

50%
Majority 5,583

C | LD | Lab | UKIP

Bracknell
Conservative hold

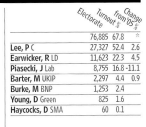

Dr Phillip Lee
b. Sep 28, 1970
MP 2010-

Part-time GP and former local hospital doctor, vocal about the need for more mathematicians and scientists in the Commons. Contested Blaenau Gwent 2005, placed on A-list and beat Rory Stewart to selection. Member, Conservative Way Forward. Special interest in energy security. Enjoys sports and travelling. Keen waterskiier and alpine skiier. C of E. Educated: Sir William Borlase's Grammar Sch, Marlow; King's College London / Keble College, Oxford (Human Biology and Biological Anthropology); St Mary's Hospital Med School at Imperial College (Medicine)

Ray Earwicker (LD) Retired civil servant. Contested Bracknell 2001. Ed: Oak Park County Sec Modern.
John Piasecki (Lab) Independent retailer. Ed: UMIST.

Constituency
Lying at Berkshire's border with Hampshire and Surrey, the constituency includes the eponymous town at its north, the smaller town of Crowthorne in the centre and the Royal Military Academy Sandhurst at its south. Much of it is covered in woodland. Easy commuting distances to Reading, Slough and London make it popular with professionals. Bracknell itself has a strong high-tech sector at the heart of the English "Silicon Valley". The seat has been Tory since its inception. Andrew MacKay, its long-serving MP, was one of the biggest casualties of the expenses scandal.

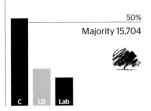

	Electorate	Turnout %	Change from '05 %
	76,885	67.8	☆
Lee, P C	27,327	52.4	2.6
Earwicker, R LD	11,623	22.3	4.5
Piasecki, J Lab	8,755	16.8	-11.1
Barter, M UKIP	2,297	4.4	0.9
Burke, M BNP	1,253	2.4	
Young, D Green	825	1.6	
Haycocks, D SMA	60	0.1	

50%
Majority 15,704

C | LD | Lab

Bradford East

Liberal Democrat gain

David Ward
b. Jun 24, 1953
MP 2010-

Long-serving community figure and councillor (Bradford 1984-2010; dep leader, LD group). Contested Bradford North 2005, 2001, 1992, 1990 by-elections. Business development manager, Leeds Met Uni, seconded to Bradford FC - community outreach/cohesion programmes. Director, Bantams Community Programme. Chair, Bradford East Sports Alliance. Accountant. NATFHE member. Amnesty International, Liberal Friends of Palestine. Married, two sons. Education: Boston Grammar School; North Kesteven GS; Trent Polytechnic (accountancy); University of Bradford (MBA, MPhil); University of Leicester (MSc).

Terry Rooney (Lab) MP Bradford North 1990-2010. Chair, cttee: Work & Pensions 2005-10. Welfare Worker. Ed: Horton Bank School; Buttershaw Comprehensive School; Bradford College. **Mohammed Riaz** (C) Managing director. Ed: London Uni; Bradford Uni.

Constituency
Essentially the old Bradford North, this new name more accurately reflects its position, reaching from the River Aire at the north down to the south east of the city centre. There is a large manufacturing sector but much unemployment, including high numbers of those who have never worked. About a quarter of residents are Asian, by far the biggest number of Pakistani origin. The constituency last changed hands in 1987, when Labour won.

	Electorate	Turnout %	Change from '05 %
	65,116	62.1	☆
Ward, D LD	13,637	33.7	3.9
Rooney, T Lab	13,272	32.8	-11.3
Riaz, M C	10,860	26.8	9.4
Poynton, N BNP	1,854	4.6	
Hussain, R Ind	375	0.9	
Shields, P Ind	237	0.6	
Robinson, G NF	222	0.6	

50%
Majority 365

Bradford South

Labour hold

Gerry Sutcliffe
b. May 13, 1953
MP 1994-

Genial Yorkshireman with passion for sport. Parly Under-Sec: Culture, Media & Sport; Minister: Sport 2007-10; Home Office/ Ministry of Justice 2006-07; Trade & Industry 2003-06. Whip: govt 2001-03; asst govt 1999-2001. Parliamentary private secretary to: Stephen Byers 1998-99; Harriet Harman 1997-98. Cllr, Bradford City 1982-84 (leader 1992-94). Sales/advertising/printing career. Sogat/GPMU dep branch sec. Married, three sons. Ed: Cardinal Hinsley GS, Bradford.

Matt Palmer (C) IT auditor. Ed: Ilkley Grammar; Bradford Grammar; Leeds Met. Bradford MBC councillor.

Alun Griffiths (LD) GP. Ed: Woodhouse Grove School; Welsh National School of Medicine. **Sharon Sutton** (BNP) Shop manager. Ed: Darton High School.

Constituency
From Queensbury, high in the Pennines at the west, this wide seat stretches over to Tong village in the east. It mostly skirts the south of Bradford centre and although jutting up north to include Lidget Green, scene of race riots in April 2001, it has by far the lowest ethnic minority population of the three Bradford seats. Areas of deprivation follow long-term decline of wool industries in a predominantly working-class seat with a long Labour tradition.

	Electorate	Turnout %	Change from '05 %
	63,580	59.8	☆
Sutcliffe, G Lab	15,682	41.3	-7.1
Palmer, M C	11,060	29.1	4.8
Griffiths, A LD	6,948	18.3	3.8
Sutton, S BNP	2,651	7.0	
Illingworth, J UKIP	1,339	3.5	2.0
Lewthwaite, J D	315	0.8	

50%
Majority 4,622

Bradford West

Labour hold

Marsha Singh
b. Oct 11, 1954
MP 1997-

Low-profile backbench loyalist. Parliamentary private secretary to Phil Woolas 2009-10. Member, select committee: Home 1997-. Former chair, Bradford West Lab Party/ dist Lab party. Bradford Community Health senior development manger. Unison. Widowed, remarried. One daughter, one son from first marriage, one stepdaughter, one stepson from second marriage. Education: Belle Vue Boys Upper School; Loughborough University (BA Languages, Politics & Economics of a Modern Europe).

Zahid Iqbal (C) Property investor. Ed: Priesthorpe Comprehensive; Leeds Metropolitan University.

David Hall-Matthews (LD) University lecturer. Ed: Christ's Hospital; Oxford University; SOAS.

Constituency
The eastern side of the constituency includes Bradford city centre, with its university, college and commercial hub. From there the seat stretches west to the suburbs of Clayton, home to many professionals. A mixed seat, there are still large areas of deprivation in what was once the wool capital of the world. It has one of Britain's largest ethnic minority populations and inner-city Manningham was the scene of race riots in July 2001. Though held by Labour from 1983, majorities were sometimes slim.

	Electorate	Turnout %	Change from '05 %
	62,519	64.9	☆
Singh, M Lab	18,401	45.4	5.7
Iqbal, Z C	12,638	31.2	-0.2
Hall-Matthews, D LD	4,732	11.7	-7.4
Sampson, J BNP	1,370	3.4	
Ali, A Respect	1,245	3.1	
Ford, D Green	940	2.3	-0.7
Smith, J UKIP	812	2.0	
Craig, N D	438	1.1	

50%
Majority 5,763

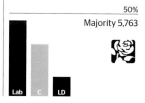

Braintree — Conservative hold

Brooks Newmark
b. May 8, 1958
MP 2005-

Very wealthy with a background in finance. Serious-minded and has published several papers through CPS. American-born. Government Whip 2010-. Opposition Whip, 2007-10. Co-Chair, Women2Win. Contested Braintree 2001, Newcastle Central 1997. Vice president, Lehman Bros 1984-87. Director, Newmark Bros. Principal Stellican Ltd. Partner, Apollo Management LP. Married, one daughter, four sons. Education: Bedford School; Harvard (BA history); Oxford University (politics postgrad research); Harvard (MBA).

Bill Edwards (Lab) Confectionery consultant. Education: Bradford.

Steve Jarvis (LD) Director of software company. Education: Francis Bacon School; St. Albans Hatfield Polytechnic.

Constituency
Effectively shifted north, this Essex seat has gained territory up to the border with Suffolk, formerly in the Saffron Walden seat, including the town of Halstead. From the south it cedes Witham, which gets its own seat. The southern boundary is now at Braintree, a market town with an ancient town hall. Regeneration projects are improving the two main towns and although the rest of the seat, which is mainly rural, suffers from poor access, the area is generally better off than much of Essex. The seat fell to Labour in 1997 but was regained by the Tories in 2005.

	Electorate	Turnout %	Change from '05 %
	71,162	69.1	☆
Newmark, B C	25,901	52.6	2.7
Edwards, B Lab	9,780	19.9	-10.8
Jarvis, S LD	9,247	18.8	5.2
Ford, M UKIP	2,477	5.0	2.6
Hooks, P BNP	1,080	2.2	
Blench, D Green	718	1.5	-1.5

50%

Majority 16,121

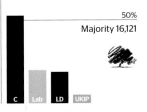

Brecon & Radnorshire — Liberal Democrat hold

Roger Williams
b. Jan 22, 1948
MP 2001-

Earnest party loyalist. LD shad SoS: Wales 2007-. LD Whip 2008-; 2004-07. LD Rural Affairs spokes 2002-. Member, cttee: EFRA 2005-; Welsh Affairs 2001-05. Cllr, Powys CC 1981-2002, Brecon Beacons National Park 1985- (chair 1991-95). Farmer. Former chair Brecon & Radnorshire NFU. Member, Rural Wales devt board. Chair mid Wales agri-food parternship. Lay sch insp. Married, one daughter, one son. Ed: Christ Coll, Brecon; Selwyn Coll, Cambridge (BA agriculture).

Suzy Davies (C) Contested Carmarthen East and Dinefwr 2005. Education: University of Exeter.

Christopher Lloyd (Lab) Researcher. Ed: Greenwich University.

Constituency
This rural South Powys seat reaches into the Black Mountains, around Crickhowell and Talgarth. Much of the south is within the Brecon Beacons National Park, by the town of Brecon. Llanwrtyd Wells, Llandrindod Wells, Builth Wells, Hay-on-Wye and Knighton are other settlements. The seat's demographic is most notable for large numbers of self-employed and small business owners, reflecting the dominance of agriculture, which employs about a tenth of the population. Before 1979 it was a safe Labour seat but since then has changed between Tory and Liberal parties, most recently being taken by the Liberal Democrats in 1997.

	Electorate	Turnout %	Change from '05 %
	53,589	72.5	
Williams, R LD	17,929	46.2	1.4
Davies, S C	14,182	36.5	1.9
Lloyd, C Lab	4,096	10.5	-4.5
Davies, J PC	989	2.6	
Easton, C UKIP	876	2.3	0.4
Robinson, D Green	341	0.9	
Green, J Ch	222	0.6	
Offa, L Loony	210	0.5	

50%

Majority 3,747

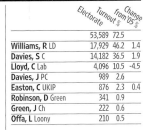

Brent Central — Liberal Democrat gain

Sarah Teather
b. Jun 1, 1974
MP Sep 2003-

Tenacious campaigner, early advocate of pupil premium which became coalition policy. Prominent role in resignation of Charles Kennedy in 2006. Min: Education 2010-. LD Shad Min: Housing 2008-10. LD Shad SoS: Business 2007-08; Education/Universities 2006-07; ODPM/CLG 2005-06. LD spokes: London 2004-05; Health 2003-2004. Chair, LD health policy working grp. Member, LD nat policy cttee. Cllr, Islington BC 2002-03. Macmillan Fund for Cancer Relief policy analyst. Ed: St John's Coll, Cambridge (BA pharmacology).

Dawn Butler (Lab) MP Brent South 2005-10. Asst govt whip 2008-10. First black woman to hold govt post. Ed: Waltham Forest Coll of FE (Dip).
Sachin Rajput (C) Barrister. Ed: Mill Hill County HS; Coll of Law, London.

Constituency
This new seat merges the remnant parts of the old Brent South and Brent East. Kensal Green lies at the southeast, neighbouring Stonebridge and Harlesden, which have a high concentration of black residents and severe deprivation. The southwest corner is dominated by the Park Royal industrial estate, the largest in Europe. To the west is Wembley Stadium, while the north reaches to Dollis Hill, through more areas of deprivation in Willesden Green and Neasden, which has Britain's largest Hindu temple. The Liberal Democrats took Brent East from Labour in a 2003 by-election and held on in 2005.

	Electorate	Turnout %	Change from '05 %
	74,076	61.2	☆
Teather, S LD	20,026	44.2	13.1
Butler, D Lab	18,681	41.2	-8.9
Rajput, S C	5,068	11.2	-1.9
Ali, S Green	668	1.5	-2.2
Williams, E Ch	488	1.1	
Duale, A Respect	230	0.5	
McCastree, D Ind	163	0.4	

50%

Majority 1,345

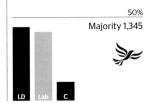

Brent North · Labour hold

Barry Gardiner
b. Mar 10, 1957
MP 1997-

Carefully spoken, well-groomed, self-important cheerleader for Tony Blair. Became unlikely critic of Gordon Brown, leading to his premature departure as PM's Special Envoy for Forestry (2007-08). Parliamentary private secretary to Lord Mandelson 2009-10. Parly Under-Sec: Environment, Food & Rural Affairs 2006-07; Trade & Industry 2005-06; Northern Ireland office 2004-05. Parliamentary private secretary to Beverley Hughes 2002-04. General Average Adjuster (arbitrator, maritime casualties). MSF, GMB. Education: Haileybury College; St Andrews (MA phil); Harvard (Kennedy scholarship); Cambridge (research).

Harshadbhai Patel (C) Qualified barrister. Ed: Fardar Patel Uni, Gurati State, India; Hon Soc of Inner Temple.
James Allie (LD) Lawyer. Contested Brent South in 2005. Ed: Leicester Uni.

Constituency

With leafy residential streets of between-the-wars semis in Northwick Park and Kenton and bordering Harrow to the west, this is the more affluent half of Brent. However, there are still areas of deprivation, especially in the south and centre. Brent has a majority non-white population and there is a large number of Asian residents concentrated in Queensbury and around Wembley. Boundary changes have extended it substantially at the south to include Alperton. The old seat was Tory from its creation in 1974 until it fell to Labour in 1997.

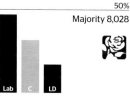

	Electorate	Turnout %	Change from '05 %
	83,896	62.3	
Gardiner, B Lab	24,514	46.9	-2.5
Patel, H C	16,486	31.5	2.2
Allie, J LD	8,879	17.0	-2.5
Malik, A Ind	734	1.4	
Francis, M Green	725	1.4	
Webb, S UKIP	380	0.7	
Vamadeva, J Ind	333	0.6	
Tailor, A Eng	247	0.5	

50%
Majority 8,028

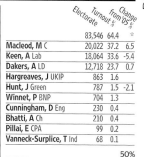

Brentford & Isleworth · Conservative gain

Mary Macleod
b. Jan 4, 1969
MP 2010-

Scottish-raised consultant who founded Westminster Women, forebear to Women2Win and the A-list. Contested Ross, Skye & Inverness West 1997. Management consultant, MD of own firm MCG; RBS; ABN AMRO; Andersen Consulting/Accenture. Policy adviser to HRH The Queen. Former Ambassador for Actionaid. Chartered Institute of Marketing, Chartered Institute of Personnel & Devt. Enjoys flying. Protestant. Ed: Dingwall Ac; Glasgow (literature & business).

Ann Keen (Lab) MP from 1997-2010. Parly Under-Sec: Health 2007-10. Ed: Surrey University.

Andrew Dakers (LD) Public affairs consultant. Contested seat 2005. Ed: Hampton Sch, Open University.

Constituency

Though the heart of this West London seat is Brentford and Isleworth, it also extends west to include most of Hounslow and east to Chiswick, with the northern boundary loosely following the M4. A seat of contrasts, Osterley Park and Chiswick Riverside have some affluent areas, but Brentford has pockets of deprivation that rank nationally among the worst 10 per cent. Central Hounslow is undergoing regeneration with the £220 million Blenheim Centre. Brentford is also home to GlaxoSmithKline. The Tories held this seat from its creation in 1974 until Labour took it in 1997.

	Electorate	Turnout %	Change from '05 %
	83,546	64.4	
Macleod, M C	20,022	37.2	6.5
Keen, A Lab	18,064	33.6	-5.4
Dakers, A LD	12,718	23.7	0.7
Hargreaves, J UKIP	863	1.6	
Hunt, J Green	787	1.5	-2.1
Winnet, P BNP	704	1.3	
Cunningham, D Eng	230	0.4	
Bhatti, A Ch	210	0.4	
Pillai, E CPA	99	0.2	
Vanneck-Surplice, T Ind	68	0.1	

50%
Majority 1,958

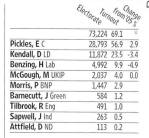

Brentwood & Ongar · Conservative hold

Eric Pickles
b. Apr 20, 1952
MP 1992-

The rotund face of municipal Conservatism, figurehead of 2010 election but largely as a cheerleader. Likes to be seen as a plain-speaking Yorkshireman but is political operator (Chairman, Con Party 2009-10). SoS: Communities & Local Gov't 2010-. Shadow SoS: CLG 2007-09. Dep Chair: Con Party, 2005-07. Shadow Min: Local Gov't/Regions 2002-03; Transport 2001-02. Opp spokesman: Social Security 1998-2001. Vice-Chair, Con Party 1993-97. Cllr, Bradford CC 1979-91 (leader). Industrial trainer. Ed: Greenhead GS; Leeds Poly.

David Kendall (LD) Owns cleaning business. Contested seat 2001. Cllr,

Brentwood 1991-. Ed: William Penn Sch; Havering Tech Coll.
Heidi Benzing (Lab) TU nat political officer. Ed: University of London.

Constituency

This Essex seat is primarily from Brentwood borough but also includes the rural area of Epping Forest district around the small town of Chipping Ongar, where much land is used for arable and animal farming and large areas of glasshouse horticulture. Brentwood is located within greenbelt land with villages dotted around. A well-connected town, predominantly home to affluent owner-occupiers. More than half the workforce commutes out while employment within the borough is mostly service sector. It gains just one ward, North Weald Bassett. The seat has been Tory for decades.

	Electorate	Turnout %	Change from '05 %
	73,224	69.1	
Pickles, E C	28,793	56.9	2.9
Kendall, D LD	11,872	23.5	-3.4
Benzing, H Lab	4,992	9.9	-4.9
McGough, M UKIP	2,037	4.0	0.0
Morris, P BNP	1,447	2.9	
Barnecutt, J Green	584	1.2	
Tilbrook, R Eng	491	1.0	
Sapwell, J Ind	263	0.5	
Attfield, D ND	113	0.2	

50%
Majority 16,921

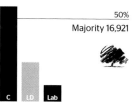

Bridgend

Madeleine Moon
b. Mar 27, 1950
MP 2005-

Unpredictable. PPS to: Lord Hunt of Kings Heath 2009-10; Jim Knight 2007-08. Cllr, Bridgend 1991-. Former mayor, Porthcawl. Residential care home inspector Care Standards Inspectorate. Social worker. Member: Fabian Society, Amnesty International. Married, one son. Education: Whinney Hill School; Durham Girls School; Madeley College, Staffordshire (CertEd); Keele University (BEd); Cardiff University (CQSW Dip SW).

Helen Baker (C) Former court clerk now works in husband's business. Contested seat in 2005. Ed: Cardiff University.

Wayne Morgan (LD) Cllr.

Constituency
This South Wales seat is dominated by Bridgend. Like Pyle, it is next to the M4, though the seat also reaches through rural land to the coast at Porthcawl. The Ford engine plant is a notable local employer. A series of teenage suicides has given unwanted attention to the area in recent years. Only minor boundary changes have been made to the seat, which has been held by Labour since 1987.

	Electorate	Turnout %	Change from '05 %
	58,700	65.3	☆
Moon, M Lab	13,931	36.3	-6.6
Baker, H C	11,668	30.4	5.4
Morgan, W LD	8,658	22.6	0.5
Thomas, N PC	2,269	5.9	-1.0
Urch, B BNP	1,020	2.7	
Fulton, D UKIP	801	2.1	0.7

50%
Majority 2,263

Lab C LD PC

Bridgwater & Somerset West

Ian Liddell-Grainger
b. Feb 23, 1959
MP 2001-

Unremarkable shire Tory. Cantankerous and and slightly bumptious. Member, select committees: Public Administration 2001-, Scottish Affairs 2002-05, Environment, Food & Rural Affairs 2003-05. Environmental Audit 2007-. President Tyne Bridge Conservative Association 1993-6. Cllr, Tynedale 1989-95. Former company managing director of own building and property company. Ran arable farm. Territorial Army, remains Major on Army reserve list. Married, two daughters, one son. Education: Millfield School, Somerset; South of Scotland Agricultural College, Edinburgh (National Certificate of Agriculture).

Theo Butt Philip (LD) Account executive in communications. Ed: Lancaster Uni.
Kathryn Pearce (Lab) Local government officer.

Constituency
The old Bridgwater constituency has been extended, reflected in the new name. It encompasses some of the best and worst of Somerset, from Exmoor and the Quantock and Brendon hills to the industrial town of Bridgwater, with its services on the M5. Other towns include Minehead and Watchet, along the lengthy stretch of coastline, and the area is reliant on tourism as well as agriculture. There are a large number of retired people and the seat has a long Tory tradition.

	Electorate	Turnout %	Change from '05 %
	76,560	71.2	☆
Liddell-Grainger, I C	24,675	45.3	-0.1
Butt, T Philip	15,426	28.3	
Pearce, K Lab	9,332	17.1	-8.5
Hollings, P UKIP	2,604	4.8	1.2
Treanor, D BNP	1,282	2.4	
Graham, C Green	859	1.6	-1.2
Cudlipp, B Ind	315	0.6	

50%
Majority 9,249

C LD Lab

Brigg & Goole

Andrew Percy
b. 1977
MP 2010-

Eurosceptic right-winger from humble background. State secondary school history teacher, advocates greater schools discipline. Researcher to David Davis MP. Councillor, Hull City Council 2000-10. Contested Normanton in 2005. Vice-Chair, Hull and Hoole Port Health Authority. Countryside Alliance, National Trust, Campaign Against Political Correctness. Member National Association of Schoolmasters Union of Women Teachers, VOICE. East Yorkshire-born and raised. Education: state comprehensive; York University (BA Hons); Leeds University (postgraduate diploma in Law); PGCE.

Ian Cawsey (Lab) b. Apr 14, 1960. MP for Brigg & Goole 1997-2010. Asst govt whip 2005-07. PPS to David Miliband 2002-05. Ed: Wintringham School.
Richard Nixon (LD) Supermarket store manager. Ed: Bispham College.

Constituency
Follow the Humber 28 miles inland from Hull and you will find Goole, a port town with a more prosperous past than now in construction and manufacturing. South of the river, in north Lincolnshire, villages and rural towns lie either side of Scunthorpe, which is not in the constituency. West lies Epworth, home of Methodism's founder, John Wesley, and to the east is Brigg. There is a strong agricultural sector and good transport links, due to the M180. Labour won the seat on its creation in 1997.

	Electorate	Turnout %	Change from '05 %
	67,345	65.2	☆
Percy, A C	19,680	44.9	6.9
Cawsey, I Lab	14,533	33.1	-12.7
Nixon, R LD	6,414	14.6	1.4
Wright, N UKIP	1,749	4.0	1.0
Ward, S BNP	1,498	3.4	

50%
Majority 5,147

C Lab LD

Brighton Kemptown

Conservative gain

Simon Kirby
b. Dec 22, 1964
MP 2010-

Attracted attention for decision to drop double-barrel of Radford-Kirby surname after selection. Grew up in council house. Local entrepreneur; co-founded Brighton radio station. Co-owner, C-Side pub & restaurant chain. Councillor: East Sussex County Council, 2005-09, 1992-93; Brighton Borough Council, 1995-97; Brighton and Hove City Council, 1996-99; Mid Sussex District Council, 1999-2001. Cites John Major as his political hero. Brighton & Hove Albion FC fan. Cof E. Married, two daughters, five sons - one deceased. Education: Hastings GS; Open Uni (BSc mathematical modelling); London School of Economics & Political Science.

Simon Burgess (Lab Co-op) Works in shipping and transport. Ed: University of Sussex.
Juliet Williams (LD) Barrister.

Constituency
The easternmost Brighton seat stretches from the pier, along the pebbled beach to the marina and beyond, encompassing Rottingdean, Saltdean and Peacehaven. Kemptown is known as the gay quarter and Brighton has the largest LGBT (lesbian, gay, bisexual and transgender) population in Britain. There are patches of relative deprivation in council housing in the west but the seat becomes more affluent as it moves farther east. It was part of Labour's seaside success story in 1997, overturning decades of Tory representation.

	Electorate	Turnout %	Change from 05 %
	66,017	64.7	☆
Kirby, S C	16,217	38.0	3.8
Burgess, S Lab	14,889	34.9	-4.1
Williams, J LD	7,691	18.0	1.1
Duncan, B Green	2,330	5.5	-1.1
Chamberlain-Webber, J UKIP	1,384	3.2	1.4
Hill, D TUSC	194	0.5	

50%

Majority 1,328

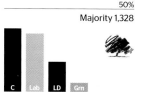

Brighton Pavilion

Green gain

Caroline Lucas
b. Dec 9, 1960
MP 2010-

Highly articulate and intelligent, the UK's first Green Party MP. Credited with making the Greens electable. Green Party leader 2008-, principal speaker 2003-08. Contested Oxford East 1992. MEP, South-East 1999-. Cllr, Oxon CC 1993-97. Twice arrested during protests. Member, Green Party Regional Council 1997-99. Co-chair Green Party Council 1989-90. Green Party nat press officer 1987-89. VP: RSPCA, Stop the War Coalition, Campaign Against Climate Change. CND national council. Oxfam adviser. Married, two sons. Ed: Malvern Girls' Coll; Exeter (BA English lit; PhD English & Women's studies); Kansas Uni, USA (scholarship).

Nancy Platts (Lab) Voluntary sector worker.
Charlotte Vere (C) Social entrepeneur. Ed: University College London.
Bernadette Millam (LD) Nurse. Ed: Chichester College.

Constituency
Named after the iconic Royal Pavilion, the constituency encompasses the heart of the city, with the alleyways of The Lanes and the bohemian North Laine shopping district. This seat combines the eccentric – Brighton had the most self-declared Jedi Knights in the 2001 Census – with the traditional grandeur of the small stretch of coastline, including The Grand Hotel. There is a large student population from the University of Sussex and some University of Brighton campuses and it is relatively affluent. In 1997, Labour overturned decades of Tory rule stretching back to its inception.

	Electorate	Turnout %	Change from 05 %
	74,004	70.0	
Lucas, C Green	16,238	31.3	9.4
Platts, N Lab	14,986	28.9	-7.5
Vere, C C	12,275	23.7	0.4
Millam, B LD	7,159	13.8	-2.2
Carter, N UKIP	948	1.8	0.6
Fyvie, I Soc	148	0.3	
Kara, S R&E	61.0	0.12	
Atreides, L ND	19	0.0	

50%

Majority 1,252

Green Party

Bristol East

Labour hold

Kerry McCarthy
b. Mar 26, 1965
MP 2005-

Seen as out-of-her-depth as Labour's 'Twitter tsar'. Assistant government whip 2009-10. PPS to: Douglas Alexander 2007-09; Rosie Winterton 2007. Councillor, Luton Borough Council 1995-2003. Director, London Luton Airport 1999-2003. Member, Labour National Policy Forum/ Economic Policy Commission 1998-2005. Unite. Solicitor. Head of public policy The Waterfront Partnership. Ed: Denbigh HS, Luton; Luton Sixth Form Coll; Liverpool (BA Russian, politics & linguistics); Law Society (CPE/final solicitors exams).

Adeela Shafi (C) University lecturer. Education: University of Bristol.

Mike Popham (LD) Company director Information Governance Ltd. Ed: Kingston Business School.

Constituency
This long, thin seat is bounded by the M32 at the north and stretches down the east of the city centre, reaching south beyond Brislington. It is predominantly residential, with only a few commercial parks, and is averagely well off; it has neither the deprivation of Bristol South nor the affluence of Bristol West. About 10 per cent of residents are ethnic minorities, concentrated in Eastville ward. The stronghold of Tony Benn from 1950 to 1983, it fell to the Tories until 1992, when Labour regained it.

	Electorate	Turnout %	Change from 05 %
	69,448	64.8	☆
McCarthy, K Lab	16,471	36.6	-8.9
Shafi, A C	12,749	28.3	0.2
Popham, M LD	10,993	24.4	4.7
Jenkins, B BNP	1,960	4.4	
Collins, P UKIP	1,510	3.4	0.7
Vowles, G Green	803	1.8	-0.9
Wright, S Eng	347	0.8	
Lynch, R TUSC	184	0.4	

50%

Majority 3,722

Bristol North West — Conservative gain

Charlotte Leslie
b. Aug 11, 1978
MP 2010-

Energetic and publicity-friendly – guest-blogger on several national newspapers. Local Bristol woman. Portland PR. Special adviser to David Willetts as Conservative Shadow Education Secretary. National Autistic Society. Education Associate, The Young Foundation. Author, More Good School Places (Policy Exchange). BBC/independent TV production (*The Weakest Link*). Bow Group. Former competitive swimmer, keen surfer. Education: Badminton Sch; Millfield Sch; Balliol College, Oxford (Classics).

Paul Harrod (LD) PR consultant.
Sam Townend (Lab) Barrister. Contested Reigate 2005. Ed: Cambridge.

Constituency

Docks at Avonmouth are the main focus of Bristol's maritime industries, divided from the rest of the constituency by the M5. Most of the seat is residential, though less densely populated than the rest of the city, with a smattering of green spaces. Boundary changes have removed the Stoke Gifford area and now include Stoke Bishop, nearer the city centre. Though this area and Canford are prosperous, elsewhere there is deprivation, especially on the Lawrence Weston council estate. The seat changed hands with the past two changes of government.

	Electorate	Turnout %	Change from '05 %
	73,469	68.5	*
Leslie, C C	19,115	38.0	5.5
Harrod, P LD	15,841	31.5	6.6
Townend, S Lab	13,059	25.9	-12.2
Upton, R UKIP	1,175	2.3	0.7
Carr, R Eng	635	1.3	
Dunn, A Green	511	1.0	

50%
Majority 3,274

Bristol South — Labour hold

Dawn Primarolo
b. May 2, 1954
MP 1987-

Left-winger once dubbed 'Red Dawn', close to Gordon Brown. Deputy Speaker 2010-. Minister: Children 2009-10; Public Health 2007-09. Treasury: Paymaster General 1999-2007; Financial Sec of State 1997-99. Opp spokeswoman: Treasury & economic affairs 1994-97; Health 1992-94. Cllr, Avon County 1985-87. Union member. Secretary/ voluntary worker/student. Patron, Terence Higgins Trust. Divorced, remarried. One son from first marriage. Education: Thomas Bennett Comprehensive; Bristol Polytechnic (BA social science).

Mark Wright (LD) Computer programmer. Cllr, Bristol CC 2005-. Ed: Bristol Uni (PhD)
Mark Lloyd Davies (C) Head of communications at Janssen-Cilag pharmaceuticals. Ed: Royal Holloway, University of London.

Constituency

The south of Bristol contains its most deprived areas: there are large social housing estates at Knowle West and Hartcliffe. This is a poor, white and working-class seat with a crime rate and unemployment that are both high, although the areas at the very north of the constituency, near the redeveloped Harbourside, boast more sought-after modern apartments. The seat has been Labour since the Second World War.

	Electorate	Turnout %	Change from '05 %
	78,579	61.6	*
Primarolo, D Lab	18,600	38.5	-10.1
Wright, M LD	13,866	28.7	4.9
Lloyd, M Davies C	11,086	22.9	
Chidsey, C BNP	1,739	3.6	
McNamee, C UKIP	1,264	2.6	-0.5
Bolton, C Green	1,216	2.5	-2.5
Clarke, C Eng	400	0.8	
Baldwin, T TUSC	206	0.4	

50%
Majority 4,734

Bristol West — Liberal Democrat hold

Stephen Williams
b. Oct 11, 1966
MP 2005-

Quiet, diligent, LD spokesman in opposition who missed out on a job in the first coalition Government. LD Shadow Sec of State: Innovation, Universities & Skills 2007-. LD Shadow Minister: Children, Schools & Families 2007; FE/HE 2006-07; Health 2005-06. Contested Bristol South 1997, Bristol West 2001. Cllr: Bristol CC 1995-99 (leader LD group/shadow council leader 1995-97); Avon 1993-96 (deputy leader/group chair LD group). Tax manager: Grant Thornton; Kraft Jacobs Suchard Ltd. Gay. Education: Mountain Ash Comp; University of Bristol (BA history).

Paul Smith (Lab) Local authority worker. Cllr, Bristol CC 1988–99. Ed: Newcastle University.
Nick Yarker (C) Works for DDB advertisers. Cllr, Westminster CC 2006-. Education: New College, Oxford (BA history).

Constituency

The heart of Bristol city lies in this seat, including the old industrial Floating Harbourside, now redeveloped with public squares and the financial centre – HBOS and Lloyds banks have bases hit by job cuts. Some of the city's most affluent areas are here, with multimillion-pound Victorian, Georgian and Regency houses. Lawrence Hill estate and Easton Road are in Britain's worst 1 per cent areas of deprivation. Once a Tory seat, it was taken by Labour in 1997 and Lib Dems in 2005.

	Electorate	Turnout %	Change from '05 %
	82,728	66.9	*
Williams, S LD	26,593	48.1	9.0
Smith, P Lab	15,227	27.5	-9.0
Yarker, N C	10,169	18.4	2.0
Knight, R Green	2,090	3.8	-1.9
Lees, C UKIP	655	1.2	-0.1
Kushlick, D Ind	343	0.6	
Baker, J Eng	270	0.5	

50%
Majority 11,366

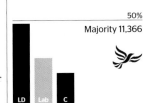

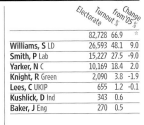

Keith Simpson
b. Mar 29, 1949
MP 1997-

Military historian with parade ground manner. Well-informed on foreign and defence issues while also a Commons man with whips' instincts. Shadow Minister: Foreign Affairs 2005-10; Defence 2002-05. Opposition Whip 1999-2001. Opp spokesman, Defence 1998-99, Environment, Food & Rural Affairs 2001-02. MP Mid Norfolk 1997-2010. Chair Conservative History Group. Member, Strategic Studies Internat Institute. Special adviser to Defence secretaries 1988-90. Military historian/defence consultant, Sandhurst lecturer. Con research department. Education: University of Hull (BA history); King's College London (PGCE).

Daniel Roper (LD) Probation officer. Cllr, 1995-. Ed: DeMontfort University; Lancaster University.
Allyson Barron (Lab) Sports therapist. Cllr, Suffolk CC 2005-09. Educated in Zimbabwe.

Constituency
This new seat is largely rural and extends from Fakenham – a base for manufacturing, especially of plastic and timber products – down through a large rural area reaching almost to Great Yarmouth. It includes the Taverham and Drayton suburbs from North Norwich as well as the market towns of Aylsham and Acle. Around the countryside are small villages with picturesque flint cottages. There is some agriculture but it is largely a residential seat for those commuting to nearby Norwich. There is a strong Tory history in the area.

	Electorate	Turnout %	Change from '05 %
	73,168	72.0	☆
Simpson, K C	24,338	46.2	2.8
Roper, D LD	17,046	32.4	2.9
Barron, A Lab	7,287	13.8	-9.8
Agnew, S UKIP	2,382	4.5	1.1
Crowther, E BNP	871	1.7	
Curran, S Green	752	1.4	

50%
Majority 7,292

Bob Neill
b. Jun 24, 1952
MP 2006-

Known as "Mr London Local Government". Short, bombastic, pompous but ever-smiling. Barrister, happiest in technical details of policy. Parly Under-Sec: CLG 2010-. Shadow Min: Local Gov't 2008-10 and Planning 2009-10; Shadow London Min 2007-08. GLA member 2000-08 (leader of Con group 2000-06), contested Dagenham in 1987, 1983 general elections. Served on former GLC and as Havering Cllr for 16 years. Barrister (criminal law). Married. Education: Abbs Cross GS; LSE (Law).

Sam Webber (LD) Media sales manager. Contested Bromley 2006. Ed: Dulwich Coll; East Anglia University.

Chris Kirby (Lab) Political researcher. Ed: University of Greenwich.

Constituency
Although now technically a London borough, Bromley bears much resemblance to Kent to which it once belonged. It is the largest borough town, with the Glades Shopping Centre and a pedestrianised high street. It is one of the least deprived areas in London. About 30 per cent of the borough's residents work in Bromley town, which has a mixed service sector economy. This seat has lost Bromley Common but gained the Cray Valley West ward, where there is some manufacturing. The seat has long been held by the Tories, but a 2006 by-election left them with a narrow majority.

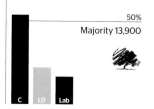

	Electorate	Turnout %	Change from '05 %
	65,427	67.3	☆
Neill, B C	23,569	53.5	8.5
Webber, S LD	9,669	22.0	-1.8
Kirby, C Lab	7,295	16.6	-7.9
Jenner, E UKIP	1,451	3.3	0.1
Savage, R BNP	1,070	2.4	
Robertson, R Green	607	1.4	-2.3
Cheeseman, J Eng	376	0.9	

50%
Majority 13,900

Sajid Javid
b. Dec 5, 1969
MP 2010-

Supremely confident, highly successful business career: youngest ever Vice President of Chase Manhattan Bank at age 24; later worked Deutsche Bank. Worked on investment in developing countries. Long-standing Tory activist and charity fundraiser. Pakistani-Muslim heritage - the son of an immigrant bus driver. Married, three daughters, one son. Education: Downend Sch, Bristol; Exeter Uni (Economics and Politics).

Sam Burden (Lab) Pensions consultant. Ed: East Anglia Uni.
Philip Ling (LD) Financial analyst. Ed: University of Bath (economics)

Constituency
Although not far from the main West Midlands conurbation, this northeast Worcestershire seat is separated by the Lickey Hills Country Park and is more rural; 90 per cent is greenbelt land. The main urban areas are around Bromsgrove and in the northeastern corner closest to Birmingham, with large villages such as Alvechurch and Wythall. Generally affluent, it is popular with commuters. The seat has traditionally been Conservative.

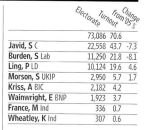

	Electorate	Turnout %	Change from '05 %
	73,086	70.6	
Javid, S C	22,558	43.7	-7.3
Burden, S Lab	11,250	21.8	-8.1
Ling, P LD	10,124	19.6	4.6
Morson, S UKIP	2,950	5.7	1.7
Kriss, A BIC	2,182	4.2	
Wainwright, E BNP	1,923	3.7	
France, M Ind	336	0.7	
Wheatley, K Ind	307	0.6	

50%
Majority 11,308

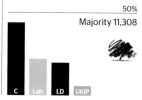

Broxbourne — Conservative hold

Charles Walker
b. Sep 11, 1967
MP 2005-

Pugnacious, chippy perpetual backbencher. Vice-chair, 1922 committee 2010-. Contested Ealing North 2001. Councillor, Wandsworth 2002-06. Director, Debtwise, LSM processing Ltd & Blue Arrow Ltd (recruitment); Comms Dir, CSQ Plc. Amicus member. Married, one daughter, two sons. Education: American School, London; Oregon (BSc pol/American hist).

Michael Watson (Lab) b. Dec 3, 1982. Political researcher for Bill Rammell MP. Cllr, Broxbourne BC 2008-. Ed: University of Essex.

Allan Witherick (LD), local government officer. Cllr, Hertfordshire CC 2005-. Ed: UCL.

Constituency
In the south of Hertfordshire, Broxbourne is focused on the conurbation that follows the River Lea, railway and A10 the length of the constituency, flanked by green belt land and the border with Essex. From Hoddesdon at the north, it merges into Broxbourne, Cheshunt and Waltham Cross in the south, by the junction with the M25. The economy has a strong manufacturing base and News International has a large printing works. There are small Italian and Turkish communities. The seat has been Tory since its creation in 1983.

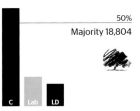

	Electorate	Turnout %	Change from 05 %
	71,391	64.0	
Walker, C C	26,844	58.8	5.0
Watson, M Lab	8,040	17.6	-7.9
Witherick, A LD	6,107	13.4	1.2
McCole, S BNP	2,159	4.7	0.0
Harvey, M UKIP	1,890	4.1	0.5
LeMay, D Eng	618	1.4	

50%
Majority 18,804

Broxtowe — Conservative gain

Anna Soubry
b. Dec 7, 1956
MP 2010-

Well-regarded, articulate lawyer and former television journalist. Contested Gedling 2005. Criminal barrister, KCH Chambers. Presenter/reporter, Central News TV/This Morning/Grampian North Tonight. Trainee reporter, Alloa. Former National Union of Journalists (NUJ) shop steward. Member, Tory Reform Group. Honorary president (Rector) of Stirling University. Student activist, first female Tory elected to NUS executive. Left Tories in 1980s, but later rejoined in 2002. Sport enthusiast. Divorced, two daughters. Education: Hartland Comprehensive School, Worksop; University of Birmingham (Law).

Nick Palmer (Lab) MP for Broxtowe 1997-2010. PPS to: Malcolm Wicks 2005-08; Margaret Beckett 2003-05; Ed: Copenhagen University; Birkbeck (PhD).
David Watts (LD) Academic. Cllr, Broxtowe 1999-. Ed: Huddersfield Poly.

Constituency
Broxtowe forms a corridor between Nottingham and the border with Derbyshire – with Derby not far to its west. The M1 is the spine of the seat, skirting the urban concentration of Stapleford and Beeston at the south and passing through a more rural area to smaller settlements such as Kimberley at the north. An affluent seat, it has large numbers of professionals and middle classes, with Boots a major employer. It was a notable victory for Labour in 1997.

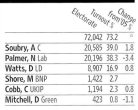

	Electorate	Turnout %	Change from 05 %
	72,042	73.2	
Soubry, A C	20,585	39.0	1.8
Palmer, N Lab	20,196	38.3	-3.4
Watts, D LD	8,907	16.9	0.8
Shore, M BNP	1,422	2.7	
Cobb, C UKIP	1,194	2.3	0.8
Mitchell, D Green	423	0.8	-1.1

50%
Majority 389

Buckingham — Speaker gain

John Bercow
b. Jan 19, 1963
MP 1997-

A florid orator, the surprise and controversial choice of Speaker (2009-) with backing of Labour MPs but few Tories. Sharp, but struggles to assert his authority. Made unlikely political journey from Thatcherite right-winger to social liberal. Shad SoS: Int Devt 2003-04. Quit as Shad Min for Work & Pensions (2002) to defy whip and support unmarried couples' adoption rights. Shad Chief Treasury Sec 2001-02. Spokes. Home 2000-01; Ed/Employment 1999-2000. Merchant banker, lobbyist (Saatchi & Saatchi), special adviser. Ran public speaking courses with Julian Lewis. Married to Sally, Lab Party member whose frank admissions of her past

and twitter usage attract attention. One daughter, two sons. Ed: Finchley Manorhill Sch; Essex (BA govt).

John Stevens (Ind)
Nigel Farage (UKIP) UKIP leader 2006-2009. MEP (South East) 1999-. Ed: Dulwich College.

Constituency
This large, rural constituency borders Milton Keynes in the north east; most of its employed residents commute to there or London, though local manufacturing and agriculture remain. Buckingham itself is a small market town on the Great Ouse, near the seat's northern boundary, and prides itself on green space typical of the constituency in general. Picturesque villages such as Wingrave are dotted amid the scenic countryside of the Vale of Aylesbury. This seat has been Tory since 1970.

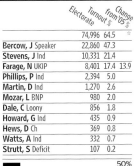

	Electorate	Turnout %	Change from 05 %
	74,996	64.5	
Bercow, J Speaker	22,860	47.3	
Stevens, J Ind	10,331	21.4	
Farage, N UKIP	8,401	17.4	13.9
Phillips, P Ind	2,394	5.0	
Martin, D Ind	1,270	2.6	
Mozar, L BNP	980	2.0	
Dale, C Loony	856	1.8	
Howard, G Ind	435	0.9	
Hews, D Ch	369	0.8	
Watts, A Ind	332	0.7	
Strutt, S Deficit	107	0.2	

50%
Majority 12,529

Spk Ind UKIP

Burnley — Liberal Democrat gain

Gordon Birtwistle
b. Sep 6, 1943
MP 2010-

Brusque, tough, local government stalwart. Will be Burnley's man in Westminster not the other way round. Capitalised on antipathy to Labour after Kitty Ussher's expenses claims and led high-profile campaigns against local hospital cutbacks. One-time Labour councillor who helped form the SDP. Contested Burnley 1997, 1992; for SDP 1982. LD Cllr, Burnley BC 1983-, Council Leader 2006-10. Mayor 2002-03. Labour Cllr, Great Harwood, 1974-76. Ran engineering/machine trading firm. Apprentice, Howard & Bullough. Married, two children. Ed: Accrington Coll; (HNC Production Engineering, HNC Mechanical Engineering).

Julie Cooper (Lab) Pharmacy director. Cllr, Burnley 2005-. Ed: Edge Hill Coll.
Richard Ali (C) Senior manager. Ed: Reading Uni.
Sharon Wilkinson (BNP) Cllr, Burnley. Ed: Gawthorpe Sch, Padiham.

Constituency
Violent clashes stoked by racial tensions in the summer of 2001 drew national attention to underlying problems in the East Lancashire town. The community has struggled with the decline of its textile and heavy industries and suffers from the chronic urban problems of ill health, high unemployment and a low-skilled workforce. Rows of derelict terraced houses typify the town, although the seat includes a rural area to the south. Burnley's population is about 7 per cent ethnic minority. The BNP has had success here but the seat has long returned Labour MPs.

	Electorate	Turnout %	Change from 05 %
	66,616	62.8	
Birtwistle, G LD	14,932	35.7	12.1
Cooper, J Lab	13,114	31.3	-7.1
Ali, R C	6,950	16.6	5.9
Wilkinson, S BNP	3,747	9.0	-1.3
Brown, A Ind	1,876	4.5	3.5
Wignall, J UKIP	929	2.2	1.3
Hennessey, A Ind	297	0.7	-0.3

50%
Majority 1,818

Burton — Conservative gain

Andrew Griffiths
b. Oct 19, 1970
MP 2010-

Eurosceptic, farming and rural affairs specialist. Contested Dudley North 2001. European Elections 2004 (West Midlands). Chief of Staff to: Eric Pickles MP; Hugo Swire MP; Theresa May MP. Special adviser to West Midlands MEP team in Brussels, helped set up European Inquiry into foot-and-mouth disease. Manager, commercial lending department of Leeds Permanent Building Society. Worked for family-run engineering business. Education: High Arcal Sch, Sedgley.

Ruth Smeeth (Lab) Charity campaigner. Education: University of Birmingham.

Michael Rodgers (LD) Furniture retailer. Cllr, East Staffordshire Borough Council since 2007.

Constituency
Forming a long, thin arc along the border with Derbyshire, this east Staffordshire seat is named after Burton-upon-Trent, at its southeastern corner, famed for its abbey and brewing. The town is primarily working-class and has areas of severe deprivation. As the seat stretches north through rural land to Uttoxeter and beyond, it becomes more rural and more affluent. Labour overturned 23 years of Tory rule when it took the seat in 1997.

	Electorate	Turnout %	Change from 05 %
	74,874	66.5	☆
Griffiths, A C	22,188	44.5	7.2
Smeeth, R Lab	15,884	31.9	-10.2
Rodgers, M LD	7,891	15.8	3.4
Hewitt, A BNP	2,409	4.8	
Lancaster, P UKIP	1,451	2.9	1.0

50%
Majority 6,304

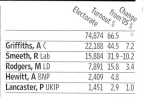

Bury North — Conservative gain

David Nuttall
b. Mar 25, 1962
MP 2010-

Anti-political correctness, anti-red tape Eurosceptic who capitalised on Labour's expenses trauma with outgoing MP David Chaytor. Councillor, Rotherham Metropolitan Borough Council 2004-06, 1992-96. Contested Bury North in 2005, Morecambe & Lunesdale in 2001 and Sheffield Hillsborough in 1997. Contested European elections representing Yorkshire & Humber in 1999. Self-employed Notary Public, Nuttalls Notaries. Member, Notaries Society. Solicitor, Sheffield. Bury Rotary Club. Active CofE (church warden). Married. Education: Aston Comprehensive School; London (LLB, by correspondence).

Maryam Khan (Lab) Solicitor and cllr, Manchester. Ed: Preston University.
Richard Baum (LD) NHS auditor and cllr, Bury. Ed: University of Birmingham.

Constituency
The constituency spans from Bury in the south to the market town of Ramsbottom, with its historic steam railway, in the north. Bury was once dominated by the textile industry but, on the northern bounds of Greater Manchester, it is now part of the middle-class commuter belt. It is famous for its black pudding. The seat was taken from the Tories by Labour in 1997 but its MP until 2010, David Chaytor, had the Labour whip withdrawn and was forced to stand down after being charged with false accounting of his expenses.

	Electorate	Turnout %	Change from 05 %
	66,759	67.4	☆
Nuttall, D C	18,070	40.2	3.4
Khan, M Lab	15,827	35.2	-6.7
Baum, R LD	7,645	17.0	1.9
Maude, J BNP	1,825	4.1	
Evans, S UKIP	1,282	2.9	1.8
Brison, B Ind	181	0.4	
Lambert, G Pirate	131	0.3	

50%
Majority 2,243

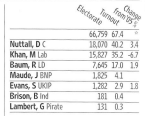

Bury South
Labour hold

Ivan Lewis
b. Mar 4, 1967
MP 1997-

Labour loyalist who was out of favour under Gordon Brown's leadership. Minister: Foreign and Commonwealth Office 2009-10. Parly Under-Sec: International Development 2008-09; Health 2006-08. Treasury: Econ Sec 2005-06. Parly Under-Sec: Education 2001-05. Parliamentary private secretary to: Stephen Byers 1999-2001. Councillor, Bury Borough Council 1990-98. Lab Friends of Israel (Vice-Chair 1997-2001). Unite. Charity Executive Chair, Bury MENCAP 1989-92. Trustee Holocaust Educational Trust. Man City fan. Jewish. Divorced, two sons. Education: William Julme Grammar School; Stand College; Bury FE College.

Michelle Wiseman (C) Chief executive of Manchester Jewish Community Care. Cllr. Education: Withington Girls School.
Vic D'Albert (LD) Accountant. Cllr, Bury BC. Contested seat 2005.

Constituency
Despite the name, this seat includes none of the official Bury wards. Instead, it encompasses Radcliffe, with its roots in coal and cotton, and settlements either side of the M60, which slices through the south of the constituency. Whitefield, north of the motorway, and Prestwich, to the south, are both sought-after commuter residential areas in this seat sandwiched between Manchester to the south east and Bolton to the north west. It switched to Labour in 1997.

	Electorate	Turnout %	Change from 05 %
	73,544	65.6	☆
Lewis, I Lab	19,508	40.4	-10.5
Wiseman, M C	16,216	33.6	5.5
D'Albert, V LD	8,796	18.2	1.1
Purdy, J BNP	1,743	3.6	
Chadwick, P UKIP	1,017	2.1	-0.5
Morris, V Eng	494	1.0	
Heron, G Green	493	1.0	

50%
Majority 3,292

Bury St Edmunds
Conservative hold

David Ruffley
b. Apr 18, 1962
MP 1997-

Sharp and clever, street-fighter henchman of David Davis. Economics and financial affairs specialist, made name on Treasury Select Committee (1998-2004). Overlooked in first coalition. Shadow Minister: Home 2007-; Work & Pensions 2005-07. Opposition Whip 2004-5. Special adviser to Ken Clarke 1991-96, Con Party strategic economic consultant 1996-97. Solicitor, Clifford Chance. Education: Bolton Boys' School; Queen's College, Cambridge (BA law).

David Chappell (LD) Contracts manager. Contested seat 2005. Cllr, Bury St. Edmunds. Ed: University of Edinburgh.

Kevin Hind (Lab) Editorial assistant, publishing. Education: University of Oxford.

Constituency
The historic town of Bury St Edmunds is at the west of the seat to which it gives its name, with the other major town of Stowmarket at the east. The economy had been stagnating but the new Arc shopping centre, which opened in 2009, has helped regeneration. Food manufacturing is a notable economic sector. Stowmarket is undergoing growth and redevelopment. The area is traditionally Tory but in 1997 the party held off Labour by just 368 votes.

	Electorate	Turnout %	Change from 05 %
	84,727	69.3	☆
Ruffley, D C	27,899	47.5	1.2
Chappell, D LD	15,519	26.4	6.7
Hind, K Lab	9,776	16.7	-10.7
Howlett, J UKIP	3,003	5.1	1.6
Ereira-Guyer, M Green	2,521	4.3	1.3

50%
Majority 12,380

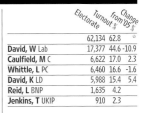

Caerphilly
Labour hold

Wayne David
b. Jul 1, 1957
MP 2001-

Unremarkable Labour loyalist and former MEP (1989-99). Organiser of Ed Miliband's campaign for Lab leadership 2010. Parly Under-Sec Wales 2008-10. Asst govt whip 2007-08. PPS to: Adam Ingram 2005-06. Team PPS MoD 2005. Member, cttees: European Scrutiny 2001-; Standards and Privileges 2004. Leader, European parly Lab Party 1994-98, ex-officio Lab Party NEC. Cllr, Cefn Cribwr 1985-91, chair 1986-87. VP Cardiff UN assosc. Pres Council for Wales of voluntary youth services. Teacher, tutor organiser, youth policy adviser. Divorced. Ed: Univ Coll, Cardiff (BA hist, Welsh hist; PGCE FE); Univ Coll, Swansea (econ hist research).

Maria Caulfield (C) Nurse. Ed: La Retraite School, London.
Lindsay Whittle (PC) Housing manager and Plaid Cymru group leader. Contested seat in 2005.
Kay David (LD) Retired teacher and part-time lecturer. Ed: Cardiff Uni.

Constituency
Lying just to the north of Cardiff, this seat's eponymous main town sits by the River Rhymney in the south, while Bargoed, Nelson and Ystrad Mynach form an urban triangle in the north. About a fifth of residents live in social housing in this formerly industrial area. There have been only minor boundary changes to this seat, which has returned Labour MPs for the best part of a century. Plaid Cymru has had strong support here, but this is more driven by anti-Labour sentiment than by demand for an independent Wales.

	Electorate	Turnout %	Change from 05 %
	62,134	62.8	☆
David, W Lab	17,377	44.6	-10.9
Caulfield, M C	6,622	17.0	2.3
Whittle, L PC	6,460	16.6	-1.6
David, K LD	5,988	15.4	5.4
Reid, L BNP	1,635	4.2	
Jenkins, T UKIP	910	2.3	

50%
Majority 10,755

Caithness, Sutherland & Easter Ross

Liberal Democrat hold

John Thurso
b. Sep 10, 1953
MP 2001-

Genial aristocrat. First hereditary peer to sit in Commons without disclaiming his title, Viscount Thurso. Grandson of Sir Archibald Sinclair, who was Liberal leader from 1935-45 and the last Liberal to serve in the Cabinet. LD Shadow Sec of State: Business (BERR/BIS) 2008-10; Scotland 2003-06; Transport 2003-05. LD whip 2001-02. Member, House of Lords 1995-99. LD Lords spokesman 2001-03. Member, Lib Dem federal policy committee 1999-2001. Hotelier, chairman/director. President/fellow Tourism Society. Married, one daughter, two sons. Education: Eton College; Westminster Tech Coll (HCIMA membership exam).

John Mackay (Lab) IT consultant. Ed: Strathclyde University.
Jean Urquhart (SNP) Cllr, Wester Ross, Lochalsh and Strathpeffer. SNP deputy leader. Contested Ross, Skye & Lochaber 2001.
Alastair Graham (C) Headmaster of secondary school. Cllr, Surrey.

Constituency
This constituency covers the northernmost tip of the British mainland. Much of the electorate is concentrated in Easter Ross, in the south, where there is a strong oil industry presence. Other industries to the north and west are fishing, farming and tourism – especially focused on John o' Groats. The seat is home to several distilleries. The seat's Labour MP, Robert Maclennan, defected to the SDP in 1981 and the seat has remained with the Lib Dems since.

	Electorate	Turnout %	Change from '05 %
	47,257	60.9	
Thurso, J LD	11,907	41.4	-9.0
Mackay, J Lab	7,081	24.6	3.7
Urquhart, J SNP	5,516	19.2	5.9
Graham, A C	3,744	13.0	2.8
Campbell, G Ind	520	1.8	-1.3

50%
Majority 4,826

Calder Valley

Conservative gain

Craig Whittaker
b. Aug 30, 1962
MP 2010-

Australian-raised, son of a left-wing union man. Self-assured, posits himself as a common-sense voice. Cllr, Calderdale MBC 2007-, 2003-04. Cabinet member for children's services at time of highly critical serious case review. Cllr, Heptonstall PC 1998-2003. Election agent to Elizabeth Truss, 2005. Retail general manager, PC World. Retail Manager, Wilkinson Home & Garden Stores. Member, Church of Latter Day Saints. Divorced, two daughters, one son. Education: Australian High School; Tighes Hill College.

Steph Booth (Lab) Teacher, journalist and academic. Step-mother of Cherie Booth. Education: Plymouth University.
Hilary Myers (LD) Development worker, Rochdale and District Mind. Education: Reading University.

Constituency
The western half of this Yorkshire seat is predominantly rural, with occasional settlements such as Todmorden and Hebden Bridge, a town with a bohemian reputation that is home to artists and writers. As the constituency curves round the southeast outskirts of Halifax it is more densely populated, with Elland and Brighouse, a centre of manufacturing, near the M62. An economically active seat, with above-average numbers of middle-class professionals and the working classes, it was held by the Tories from its 1983 creation until Labour's 1997 landslide.

	Electorate	Turnout %	Change from '05 %
	76,903	67.3	☆
Whittaker, C C	20,397	39.4	3.6
Booth, S Lab	13,966	27.0	-11.5
Myers, H LD	13,037	25.2	6.3
Gregory, J BNP	1,823	3.5	
Burrows, G UKIP	1,173	2.3	
Sweeny, K Green	858	1.7	-1.2
Cole, T Ind	194	0.4	
Greenwood, B Ind	175	0.3	
Rogan, P Eng	157	0.3	

50%
Majority 6,431

Camberwell & Peckham

Labour hold

Harriet Harman
b. Jul 30, 1950
MP 1982-

Tenacious women's libber, underestimated by critics. Masterminded Equality Bill. Dep ldr Lab Party 2007- (acting ldr 2010-). Ldr HoC 2007-10. Min: Women & Equality 2007-10. Constitutional Affairs 2005-. Chair, cttee Modernisation of HoC 2007-10. Solicitor Gen 2001-05. SoS: Social Security & Min: Women 1997-98. Shad SoS: Social Security 1996-97; Health 1996-96; Employment 1994-95. Shad Chief Treasury Sec 1992-94. Shad Min: Social Services 1984, 1985-87. Opp spokes: Health 1987-92. MP Peckham 1982-1997. Lab Party NEC 1993-98. QC 2001. Chair Childcare Commission. Legal officer, Nat Council for Civil Liberties. Solicitor. Married to Jack

Dromey MP. One daughter, two sons. Ed: St Paul's Girls' Sch; York (BA pol).

Columba Blango (LD) Teacher. Cllr. Ex-Mayor of Southwark.
Andy Stranack (C) Community devt worker. Stood for London mayor 2008.

Constituency
Previously the smallest electorate in England, this Southwark seat gains South Camberwell ward and parts of Livesey and Peckham Rye. The huge Aylesbury estate, in Walworth, struggles to shake off its reputation for urban decay but has recently received funding, which means the buildings will be replaced in the next 15 years. Camberwell Green and Peckham have pockets of severe deprivation. About 40 per cent of residents are black. About two thirds live in social housing. The seat has been Labour since 1945.

	Electorate	Turnout %	Change from '05 %
	78,618	59.4	☆
Harman, H Lab	27,619	59.2	-4.1
Blango, C LD	10,432	22.4	1.9
Stranack, A C	6,080	13.0	3.1
Jones, J Green	1,361	2.9	-1.7
Robby, Y Munilla Eng Dem	435	0.93	
Ogunleye, J WRP	211	0.5	
Sharkey, M Soc	184	0.4	
Francis, D Ind	93	0.2	
Robbins, S Ind	87	0.2	
Knox, P ND	82	0.2	
Mountford, J Workers	75	0.2	

50%
Majority 17,187

Cambourne & Redruth

George Eustice
b. Sep 28, 1971
MP 2010-

Self-effacing, straightforward, with quiet manner. Former aide to David Cameron who endured recount to take dramatic victory by narrow margin. Portland PR. Inspired to enter politics by James Goldsmith's Referendum Party of 1997, contested Euro 1999 election for UKIP. Press Secretary to David Cameron 2005-2007, squeezed out by arrival of Andy Coulson. Head of Press to Michael Howard, 2005 election. Campaign Dir, anti-Euro 'No Campaign'. Worked in family business, Trevaskis Fruit Farm. Keen runner. Has partner. Education: Truro Cathedral School; Truro School; Cornwall College.

Julia Goldsworthy (LD) MP Falmouth & Camborne 2005-10. LD Shad SoS: CLG 2007-10. LD Shad Chief Treasury Sec 2006-07. Ed: Cambridge Uni; Dai-ichi Uni of Economics; Birbeck Coll.
Jude Robinson (Lab) Charity fundraiser. Ed: University of Sussex.

Constituency
Camborne, Pool and Redruth form a five-mile urban corridor parallel to the west coast of Cornwall. Once prosperous from copper and tin mining, the area declined so much in 2000-06 that it qualified for funding as one of the poorest parts of the EU. Now a backwater in a county where tourism has supplanted industry – holidaymakers flock to the golden sands of St Ives Bay – the future may brighten from plans to resume tin mining. The seat has changed hands between all three main parties.

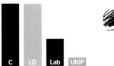

	Electorate	Turnout %	Change from '05 %
	63,968	66.4	☆
Eustice, G C	15,969	37.6	12.0
Goldsworthy, J LD	15,903	37.4	1.6
Robinson, J Lab	6,945	16.3	-12.4
Elliott, D UKIP	2,152	5.1	0.3
Jenkin, L Meb	775	1.8	
McPhee, E Green	581	1.4	
Hawkins, R Soc	168	0.4	

50%
Majority 66

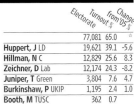

Cambridge

Julian Huppert
b. Jul 21, 1978
MP 2010-

Measured, thoughtful scientist wary of being pigeon-holed as a 'science MP'; keen interest in civil liberties. Member, Liberty national council. Research scientist at Cavendish Laboratory. Expert in DNA structures, has worked to develop anti-cancer drugs. Fellow of Clare College. Son of the scientist Herbert Huppert. Councillor, Cambridgeshire County Council, 2001-09 (leader Liberal Democrat group). Contested Huntingdon in 2005 general election. Humanist Jewish. Lives with partner. Keen cyclist. Education: The Perse School; Trinity College, Cambridge (BA Hons MSci in natural sciences and PhD in biological chemistry).

Nick Hillman (C) Ed: University of Cambridge.
Daniel Zeichner (Lab) Trade union and political officer. Contested Norfolk Mid 2005. Ed: Cambridge Uni.
Tony Juniper (Green) Environmental business adviser. Ed: Bristol Uni; UCL.

Constituency
The university dominates the city centre, with colleges, libraries and museums dotted around as well as the marketplace, river and lanes lined with small boutiques. It also influences the seat economically – with the "Silicon Fen" concentration of high-tech businesses – and politically, with a large student population that. It was Labour from 1992 to 2005. Minor boundary changes extend the seat to include the Trumpington ward, a leafy residential area to the south.

	Electorate	Turnout %	Change from '05 %
	77,081	65.0	☆
Huppert, J LD	19,621	39.1	-5.6
Hillman, N C	12,829	25.6	8.3
Zeichner, D Lab	12,174	24.3	-8.2
Juniper, T Green	3,804	7.6	4.7
Burkinshaw, P UKIP	1,195	2.4	1.0
Booth, M TUSC	362	0.7	
Old, H Ind	145	0.3	

50%
Majority 6,792

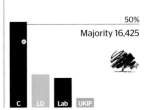

Cambridgeshire North East

Stephen Barclay
b. May 3, 1972
MP 2010-

Highly thought-of in the party but remains down-to-earth and approachable. Solicitor with career in financial crime prevention. Contested Lancaster & Wyre 2001 – lost by 481 votes; Manchester Blackley 1997. Adviser to Liam Fox as Conservative Party Chairman 2005. Chairman of Organising Committee of Carlton Political Dinner 2007-. Selected by open primary. Head of Anti-Money Laundering and Sanctions for Barclays Bank. FSA, Guardian Royal Exchange, Axa Insurance. Served briefly in army, sponsored through university. Rugby player and keen skydiver. Married. Ed: Peterhouse, Cambridge (history); College of Law, Chester.

Lorna Spenceley (LD) Training administrator, Lib Dems. Contested Harlow 2005. Ed: Uni of Cambridge and Open Uni.
Peter Roberts (Lab) Just completed Phd at Cambridge. Ed: University of Bath; LSE; University of Cambridge.

Constituency
The main settlements in this seat are Whittlesey, east of Peterborough; Wisbech, at the northeast of the seat; Chatteris, in the fork of the A141 and A142; and March, central in the seat. Between them lie the flat expanses of Fenland with long straight roads and dykes. Much land is given to arable farming, a notable economic sector. Manufacturing is also above average with high numbers of working and lower middle classes. The Tories have held this seat since 1987, when they took over from the Liberal MP Clement Freud.

	Electorate	Turnout %	Change from '05 %
	73,224	71.4	☆
Barclay, S C	26,862	51.4	4.5
Spenceley, L LD	10,437	20.0	2.9
Roberts, P Lab	9,274	17.7	-12.9
Talbot, R UKIP	2,991	5.7	0.4
Clapp, S BNP	1,747	3.3	
Jordan, D Ind	566	1.1	
Murphy, G Eng	387	0.7	

50%
Majority 16,425

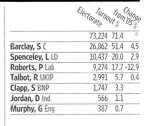

Cambridgeshire North West — Conservative hold

Shailesh Vara
b. Sep 4, 1960
MP 2005-

Serious, but quietly effective. Assistant government whip 2010-. Shadow: Deputy Leader of House 2006-10. Contested Northampton South 2001; Birmingham Ladywood 1997. Vice-Chair, Con Party 2001-05. Legal adviser/business consultant, London First. Solicitor, Richards Butler/CMS Cameron McKenna. Vice-President, Small Business Bureau. Married, two sons. Education: Aylesbury Grammar School; Brunel University (LLB).

Kevin Wilkins (LD) Political agent and manager of MP's office. Education: Cheltenham College; Queens College, Cambridge.

Chris York (Lab) Youth project worker with Cambridgeshire Constabulary, Peterborough City Council.
Robert Brown (UKIP)

Constituency

The south of the constituency forks either side of Huntingdon, taking in the rural expanses of Huntingdonshire with the market town of Ramsey and other affluent villages. To the north, it extends beyond Peterborough, including the parts of the city to the south of the River Nene. These are mostly modern residential developments, including some deprived areas. The countryside to the west is gently undulating limestone and clay hills. The seat has been Tory since its creation in 1997.

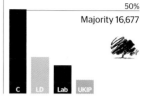

	Electorate	Turnout %	Change from 05 %
	88,857	65.6	*
Vara, S C	29,425	50.5	4.3
Wilkins, K LD	12,748	21.9	-1.0
York, C Lab	9,877	17.0	-8.7
Brown, R UKIP	4,826	8.3	3.0
Goldspink, S Eng	1,407	2.4	

Majority 16,677

Cambridgeshire South — Conservative hold

Andrew Lansley
b. Dec 11, 1956
MP 1997-

Erudite, never lost civil servants' manner. Tried to neutralise health as an issue for Tories. Not seen as team player in Shadow Cabinet. Has much confidence, less common sense, which has led to misjudgments. SoS: Health 2010-. Shadow SoS: Health 2003-10. Shadow Chancellor of Duchy of Lancaster 1999-2001, Min: Cabinet Office 1999-2001. Vice-Chair, Con Party 1998-99. Head of Private Office to Norman Tebbit 1985-87. British Chambers of Commerce. Dir, Con Research Department, public policy unit. CBE 1996. Divorced, remarried. Three daughters from first marriage, one daughter, one son from second marriage. Education: Exeter (BA politics).

Sebastian Kindersley (LD) Company director. Education: St Columbas College; Anglia Polytechnic University.
Tariq Sadiq (Lab) College fundraiser. Education: University of Durham; LSE.

Constituency

This seat contains outskirts of Cambridge such as Girton and a large spread of rural land to the west of the city, which is generally affluent. Most of the population live in villages, concentrated in the south where the M11 cuts through the seat. Boundary changes have removed Trumpington ward from the south of Cambridge and added the village of Cottenham to the north. The area has been Tory for decades.

	Electorate	Turnout %	Change from 05 %
	78,995	74.8	*
Lansley, A C	27,995	47.4	0.9
Kindersley, S LD	20,157	34.1	5.8
Sadiq, T Lab	6,024	10.2	-9.5
Page, R Ind	1,968	3.3	
Davies-Green, H UKIP	1,873	3.2	0.4
Saggers, S Green	1,039	1.8	-1.0

Majority 7,838

Cambridgeshire South East — Conservative hold

Jim Paice
b. Apr 24, 1949
MP 1987-

Long-serving MP whose slightly world-weary look belies a mischievous personality. A passionate issue-campaigner, marked as a farming specialist. Min: EFRA 2010-. Shadow Min: Rural Affairs 2006-10 and Agriculture 2005-10. Shadow SoS: Agriculture, Fisheries & Food 2004-05. Shadow Min: Police 2004; Home/Constitutional/Legal 2003-04. Parly Under-Sec: Education/Employment 1995-97; Employment 1994-95. PPS to: John Gummer 1990-94; Baroness Trumpington 1989-90. Farmer/farm manager and contractor. Training/management co. Dir. Cllr, Suffolk Coastal. Married, two sons. Ed: Writtle Agri Coll (nat agricultural dip).

Jonathan Chatfield (LD) Commercial manager, Network Rail. Ed: Weymouth Grammar School; Bradford University; Warwick Business School.
John Cowan (Lab) Company director. Ed: Cawston College; University of Suffolk.

Constituency

A rural block of Fenland to the east of Cambridge forms the bulk of this seat, with the small cathedral city of Ely in the north. The constituency has chunks missing from the west for Cottenham and east for Newmarket. The town's racecourse provides employment for many. Much of the seat is arable but constituents are mainly from middle and professional socioeconomic classes; many commute into Cambridge and work in high-tech industries. It has been Conservative since 1950.

	Electorate	Turnout %	Change from 05 %
	83,068	69.3	*
Paice, J C	27,629	48.0	0.8
Chatfield, J LD	21,683	37.6	6.2
Cowan, J Lab	4,380	7.6	-13.8
Monk, A UKIP	2,138	3.7	
Sedgwick-Jell, S Green	766	1.3	
Woollard, G Ind	517	0.9	
Bell, D CPA	489	0.9	

Majority 5,946

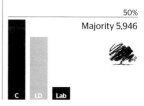

Cannock Chase
Conservative gain

Aidan Burley
b. Jan 22, 1979
MP 2010-

Highly driven and rather slick. Achieved one of the highest swings from Labour of the 2010 election. Worked for Nick Herbert on Cameron's Police Reform Taskforce. Cllr, Hammersmith & Fulham BC, 2006-10. Management consultant specialising in the public sector: Hedra (became Mouchel); Accenture. Political adviser/ speechwriter to Philip Hammond MP. Keen tennis player and rugby fan. Birmingham-raised. C of E. Ed: King Edwards VI School, Edgbaston; St John's Coll, Oxford (Theology)

Susan Woodward (Lab) Political adviser. Ed: Shire Oak GS; Leicester University; Birmingham University.

Jon Hunt (LD) Journalist.

Constituency
Just north of the West Midlands conurbation, the Staffordshire town of Cannock lies at the foot of this seat, with the urban area merging into nearby Hednesford. They are divided from Rugeley at the north by Cannock Chase, a large Area of Outstanding Natural Beauty with lowland heath and woodland and home to wild deer. Typically for the area, construction and manufacturing are strong sectors and, although this seat remains working-class, its economy is buoyant and it avoids extremes of deprivation. Under old boundaries it was taken by Labour in 1992.

	Electorate	Turnout %	Change from '05 %
	74,509	61.2	☆
Burley, A C	18,271	40.1	10.1
Woodward, S Lab	15,076	33.1	-17.9
Hunt, J LD	7,732	17.0	3.0
Majorowicz, T BNP	2,168	4.8	
McKenzie, M UKIP	1,580	3.5	-1.6
Turville, R Ind	380	0.8	
Jenkins, R Snouts	259	0.6	
Walters, M Ind	93	0.2	

50%
Majority 3,195

Canterbury
Conservative hold

Julian Brazier
b. Jul 24, 1953
MP 1987-

Exhibits excitable, slightly bombastic manner when debating favoured topics. Likeable but lightweight. 1922 executive committee, 2010-. A practising Roman Catholic and former pres, Con Family Campaign 1995-2001. Strong on defence issues; decorated TA officer (1972-82; 1989-92; TD 1993) from military family. Shadow Min: Trans 2005-10; Intl Affairs 2003-05; Home Affairs 2003, Work & Pensions 2002-03. Opp whip 2001-02. PPS to Gillian Shepherd 1990-1993. Chartered Consolidated Ltd and HB Maynard (management consultant). Married, three sons. Ed: Brasenose Coll, Oxford (BA maths & phil); London Bus Sch.

Guy Voizey (LD) Financial journalist. Contested Thanet South in 2001 and 2005. Ed: St Peter's Coll, Oxford.
Jean Samuel (Lab) Compliance director in Pharmaceuticals. Ed: Aylesbury HS; Pates GS; Hull.

Constituency
Centred on the affluent city of Canterbury, which has England's oldest cathedral, the seat includes East Kent countryside and stretches north to the coastal resort of Whitstable, famous for its oysters. Both working and middle classes are well represented in a demographic most notable for large numbers of students and professionals working in numerous education institutions, including the University of Kent. Minor boundary changes have removed Marshside ward. The seat has long been Tory, though majorities have not always been great in recent years.

	Electorate	Turnout %	Change from '05 %
	76,808	64.1	☆
Brazier, J C	22,050	44.8	0.3
Voizey, G LD	16,002	32.5	11.1
Samuel, J Lab	7,940	16.1	-12.0
Farmer, H UKIP	1,907	3.9	1.9
Meaden, G Green	1,137	2.3	-1.0
Belsey, A MRP	173	0.4	

50%
Majority 6,048

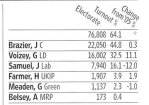

Cardiff Central
Liberal Democrat hold

Jenny Willott
b. May 29, 1974
MP 2005-

Gregarious and well-liked. Impressed during her time on the Public Administration select committee (2005-10). Became a councillor aged 23, MP at 29. LD shadow Sec: Chancellor of Duchy of Lancaster 2009-10; Work & Pensions 2008-09. LD shadow min: Justice 2008. LD dep chief whip 2006-08. LD Shadow Min: Youth Affairs 2006-07. Contested Cardiff Central 2001. Cllr, Merton BC 1998-2000. Area manager Victim Support Wales 2003. Head of advocacy Unicef UK. Married. Education: Wimbledon High School; Uppingham High School; St Mary's College, Durham (BA classics); LSE (MSc econ devt studies).

Jenny Rathbone (Lab) Estyn inspector. Ed: Essex University.
Karen Robson (C) Head of disability, UWIC. Ed: Durham Johnston School; Liverpool John Moores University.

Constituency
Bounded by the River Taff in the south west, this seat encompasses the heart of the Welsh capital, including the Millennium Stadium and Cardiff Castle. There are large numbers of professionals, in affluent areas such as Cyncoed. There is a huge student population, comprising more than 25 per cent of residents. Once a Tory seat, Labour held it from 1992 but the Liberal Democrats took it in 2005.

	Electorate	Turnout %	Change from '05 %
	61,162	59.1	
Willott, J LD	14,976	41.4	-8.3
Rathbone, J Lab	10,400	28.8	-12.10
Robson, K C	7,799	21.6	12.3
Williams, C PC	1,246	3.5	-0.1
Davies, S UKIP	765	2.1	1.1
Coates, S Green	575	1.6	
Saunders, R TUSC	162	0.5	
Beech, M Loony	142	0.4	
Mathias, A Ind	86	0.2	-0.2

50%
Majority 4,576

Cardiff North — Conservative gain

Jonathan Evans
b. Jun 2, 1950
MP 1992-1997; 2010-

Compassionate, conservative and outspoken proponent of electoral reform. Served in the Major government but lost seat in 1997. Spent intervening years as MEP (Wales, 1999-2009; leader, Conservative group 2001-04, Dir of Insurance for Eversheds and consultant on London insurance markets. MP Brecon & Radnor 1992-97. Parly Under-Sec, Wales 1996-97. Parly Sec, Lord Chancellor's Dept 1995-96. Min: Corporate and Consumer Affairs (DTI) 1994-95. PPS to Michael Mates 1992-94. Managing partner, Leo Abse & Cohen. FRSA. Avid football fan. Committed Christian. Ed: Howardian HS; Coll of Law, Guildford/London.

Julie Morgan (Lab) b. Nov 2, 1944. MP Cardiff North 1997-2010 (contested seat 1992). Campaigner for women and children. Social worker. Cllr, S Glamorgan. Ed: Howell's Sch Llandaff; KCL; Manchester Uni; Uni Coll, Cardiff.
John Dixon (LD) Creative services manager. Contested Welsh Assembly elections, Cardiff North 2003, 2001; European elections 1994. Ed: Isleworth GS, Hounslow; Uni Coll Cardiff.

Constituency
This seat follows the line of the M4 around the north of Cardiff, including areas such as Whitchurch and Heath, home to the hospital. Mostly smart residential suburbs with semi-detached homes lining leafy streets, these areas house high numbers of professionals. Held by Tories from its creation in 1982 until 1997, the seat switched to Labour, but by 2005 majorities were slim.

	Electorate	Turnout %	Change from 05 %
	65,553	72.7	
Evans, J C	17,860	37.5	1.0
Morgan, J Lab	17,666	37.1	-1.9
Dixon, J LD	8,724	18.3	-0.4
Rhys, L PC	1,588	3.3	-0.9
Gwynn, L UKIP	1,130	2.4	1.2
von Ruhland, C Green	362	0.8	
Thomson, D Ch	300	0.6	

50%
Majority 194

C | Lab | LD

Cardiff South & Penarth — Labour Co-op win

Alun Michael
b. Aug 22, 1943
MP 1987-

Blairite parachuted in to be First Secretary of Wales in 1999 but ousted a year later. Min: Trade & Industry 2005-06; Rural Affairs 2001-05. AM 1999-2000. SoS: Wales 1998-99. Min: Home 1997-98. Opp spokes: Voluntary Sector 1994-97; Home Affairs 1992-97; Welsh Affairs 1998-92. Cllr, Cardiff CC 1973-89. Co-op party nat exec. JP Cardiff. Journalist, youth/community worker. NUJ Branch sec. Married, three daughters, two sons. Ed: Colwyn Bay GS; Keele (BA lit/philosophy).

Simon Hoare (C) Planning & PR consultant. Contested Cardiff West in 1997. Ed: Bishop Hannon High School; Greyfriars College, Oxford.

Dominic Hannigan (LD) Researcher for the Welsh National Assembly. Contested Welsh Assembly elections, Cardiff South & Penarthin 2007. Ed: St Just; Penwith College, Cornwall; Cardiff University.

Constituency
Stretching along the Bristol Channel from the Barry Power Station and Sully, this seat reaches up through Penarth and along Cardiff's seafront to suburbs such as Rumney. It includes the docks and the National Assembly for Wales, which looks out over Cardiff Bay. The seat is a mixture of middle and working classes, but it and its previous incarnations have been Labour since 1945, with James Callaghan its MP until 1987.

	Electorate	Turnout %	Change from 05 %
	73,704	60.2	☆
Michael, A Lab	17,263	38.9	-7.7
Hoare, S C	12,553	28.3	4.4
Hannigan, D LD	9,875	22.3	2.5
Aslam, F PC	1,851	4.2	-1.1
Zeigler, S UKIP	1,145	2.6	1.2
Burke, G Ind	648	1.5	
Townsend, M Green	554	1.3	-0.6
Bate, C Ch	285	0.6	
Griffiths, R Comm	196	0.4	

50%
Majority 4,710

Lab | C | LD

Cardiff West — Labour hold

Kevin Brennan
b. Oct 16, 1959
MP 2001-

Plays guitar in cross-party MP rock band, MP4. Min: BIS/CSF 2009-10. Parly Sec: Cab office 2008-09. Parly Under-Sec: Children, Schools & Families 2007-08. Whip: govt 2006-07; assistant govt 2005-06. PPS to Alan Milburn 2004-05. Member, cttee: Public Administration 2001-05. Socialist Health Assocn. Lab campaign electoral reform. Cllr, Cardiff CC. Editor/organiser Cwmbran Community Press. Teacher. Research officer/special adviser to Rhodri Morgan as First Min of Wales. Married, one daughter. Ed: Pembroke Coll, Oxford (BA PPE); Univ Coll of Wales (PCGE hist); Glamorgan (MSc education management).

Angela Jones-Evans (C) Consultancy director. Ed: Aberystwyth; Sheffield.
Rachael Hitchinson (LD) Teacher. Ed: University of Liverpool; Cardiff.
Mohammed Sarul Islam (PC) Cllr. PC whip, Cardiff CC. Ed: Dhaka Uni.

Constituency
This seat covers the area of Cardiff to the west of the River Taff, including Llandaff with its cathedral and the smart village of St Fagans, by the River Ely. The M4 cuts through the middle of the seat and the northern half is rural, dotted with small settlements such as Pentyrch, separated by a ridge from Cardiff. The seat's mixed demographic includes professionals, but about a fifth of residents live in social housing. The seat has long been Labour, interrupted by one term of Tory rule from 1983-87. From 1976 until 1983 its MP George Thomas was Speaker.

	Electorate	Turnout %	Change from 05 %
	62,787	65.2	☆
Brennan, K Lab	16,893	41.3	-3.6
Jones-Evans, A C	12,143	29.7	7.0
Hitchinson, R LD	7,186	17.6	0.5
Sarul, M Islam PC	2,868	7.0	
Henessey, M UKIP	1,117	2.7	0.6
Griffiths, J Green	750	1.8	

50%
Majority 4,750

Lab | C | LD | PC

Carlisle
Conservative gain

John Stevenson
b. Jul 4, 1963
MP 2010-

Amiable, softly-spoken Scot. Independent-minded with measured, low-profile approach. Cllr, Carlisle CC 1999-. Solicitor: Bendles, Carlisle; Dickinson Dees, Newcastle. Cites Mandela and Gorbachev as political heroes. Well-travelled. Keen golfer and marathon runner. Church of Scotland. Has partner. Ed: Aberdeen Grammar School; Dundee (history & politics); College of Law, Chester.

Michael Boaden (Lab) Educational administrator. Contested Penrith & the Border 2001 & 2005. Ed: Thames Valley University.
Neil Hughes (LD) Bookstore assistant. Ed: Calday Grange GS, Merseyside.

Constituency
The remains of Hadrian's Wall run through Carlisle, the capital of Cumbria and the northernmost city in England. It is overwhelmingly working-class, with about one fifth living in council housing. The local economy is focused on distribution, retailing and health and social work and major employers include McVitie's, Pirelli and the local company Eddie Stobart. The area suffered during the 2001 foot-and-mouth outbreak and serious flooding in 2005. This seat has long been represented by Labour, although recent boundary changes have included some Tory areas beyond the city.

	Electorate	Turnout %	Change from '05 %
	65,263	64.7	☆
Stevenson, J C	16,589	39.3	5.9
Boaden, M Lab	15,736	37.3	-9.6
Hughes, N LD	6,567	15.6	-1.0
Stafford, P BNP	1,086	2.6	
Owen, M UKIP	969	2.3	0.0
Reardon, J Green	614	1.5	
Metcalfe, J TUSC	376	0.9	
Howe, P ND	263	0.6	

50%
Majority 853

C Lab LD

Carmarthen East & Dinefwr
Plaid Cymru hold

Jonathan Edwards
b. Apr 26, 1976
MP 2010-

Passionate but pragmatic nationalist. Down to earth and approachable, son of a working-class councillor and union man. Cllr, Carmarthen 2001-05, Sheriff of Carmarthen 2002. Public Affairs Officer, Citizens Advice Cymru. Chief of staff to Rhodri Glyn Thomas AM, Adam Price MP. Strategic adviser, PC Nat Campaigns Directorate. Christian. Keen cricketer and Swansea City FC fan. Education: Ysgol Gymraeg Rhydaman; Ysgol Gyfun Maes yr Yrfa; Uni of Wales, Aberystwyth (BSc hist & pol; MSc economic international history).

Christine Gwyther (Lab) Local govt officer. Member, Welsh Assembly

Carmarthen West & South Pembrokeshire 1999-2007.
Andrew Morgan (C) Works in pensions industry. Contested Welsh Assembly, Llanelli 2007.
Bill Powell (LD) Teacher. Cllr, Powys.

Constituency
This large, rural seat includes the towns of Llandeilo, Ammanford and Llandovery, which lie near the Black Mountains in the east. In the west, the boundaries take in the half of Carmarthen east of the River Towy. The northern boundary follows the line of the River Teifi, which splits Newcastle Emlyn in two, including the southern half. The seat's economy is heavily focused on agriculture. Plaid Cymru won its first Westminster berth here in 1966, with Gwynfor Evans. The seat has changed hands between the nationalists and Labour several times since.

	Electorate	Turnout %	Change from '05 %
	52,385	72.6	☆
Edwards, J PC	13,546	35.6	-10.2
Gwyther, C Lab	10,065	26.5	-1.8
Morgan, A C	8,506	22.4	8.7
Powell, B LD	4,609	12.1	2.4
Atkinson, J UKIP	1,285	3.4	1.7

50%
Majority 3,481

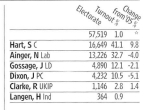

PC Lab C LD

Carmarthen West & Pembroke South
Conservative gain

Simon Hart
b. Aug 15, 1963
MP 2010-

Pugnacious, but mischievous and fun. Long-serving chief executive of Countryside Alliance prior to becoming MP - formerly their director of the Campaign for Hunting and press officer. Chartered surveyor in Carmarthen and Haverfordwest. Served with Territorial Army for five years. Keen cricketer. Married, one son, one daughter. Ed: Radley College; Royal Agricultural College, Cirencester (diploma rural estate management).

Nick Ainger (Lab) b. Oct 24, 1949. MP Carmarthen West and South Pembrokeshire 1992-2010. Government whip 2001-05; Parly Under-Sec: Wales 2005-07. Ed: Netherthorpe GS, Derbyshire.

John Gossage (LD) Economic consultant. Contested Welsh Assembly 2007. Ed: Christ's College, Cambridge; Birkbeck.
John Dixon (PC) Translator, adult education tutor. Plaid Cymru nat chair. Contested seat in 2005; Vale of Glamorgan in 1979, 1983, 1989 (by-election). Ed: Stanwell Comp, Penarth.

Constituency
This large, rural seat spans from the western half of Carmarthen to Carmarthen Bay where Tenby and Saundersfoot are among the main settlements. It carries on along the coast around the Angle Peninsula to Pembroke and its docks. Other towns inland include Narberth. Agriculture is important in this seat, which is relatively anglicised with few Welsh-speakers. It is popular with pensioners. Labour took the seat on its creation in 1997.

	Electorate	Turnout %	Change from '05 %
	57,519	1.0	☆
Hart, S C	16,649	41.1	9.8
Ainger, N Lab	13,226	32.7	-4.0
Gossage, J LD	4,890	12.1	-2.1
Dixon, J PC	4,232	10.5	-5.1
Clarke, R UKIP	1,146	2.8	1.4
Langen, H Ind	364	0.9	

50%
Majority 3,423

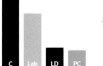

C Lab LD PC

Carshalton & Wallington
Liberal Democrat hold

Tom Brake
b. May 6, 1962
MP 1997-

Dislikes late-night Commons culture, commutes daily from Wallington. Liberal Democrat Shadow Minister: Home 2008-10; London & Olympics 2007-10; Communities & Local Government 2006-07. Liberal Democrat Shadow Sec of State: Transport 2005-06; International Development 2003-05. Liberal Democrat whip 2000-04. Liberal Democrat spokesman: Transport 2002-03; Environment/Transport/Regions/Social Justice 1997-2001. Councillor, Sutton 1994-98; Hackney 1988-90. IT manager. Married, one daughter, one son. Education: Lycee International, St Germain-en-Laye; Imperial College, London (BSc physics).

Dr Ken Andrew (C) Company director. Contested Carshalton 2005, 2001; Loughborough 1997; Ed: University of Wales, Cardiff.
Shafi Khan (Lab) Sixth form teacher. Cllr, Croydon 1994-. Ed: University of Dhaka.

Constituency
On the southern fringe of London, this seat is between South Croydon and Sutton. There are above-average numbers of workers in construction industries and pockets of deprivation around the St Helier estate and parts of South Beddington to the east. The south of the borough, around Carshalton Beeches, is more affluent, with large 1920s and 1930s detached houses and more rural expanses towards Clock House. The Lib Dems took the seat from the Tories in 1997.

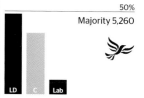

	Electorate	Turnout %	Change from '05 %
	66,520	69.0	☆
Brake, T LD	22,180	48.3	7.9
Andrew, K C	16,920	36.9	-0.6
Khan, S Lab	4,015	8.7	-8.6
Day, F UKIP	1,348	2.9	0.3
Lewis, C BNP	1,100	2.4	
Dow, G Green	355	0.8	-1.4

50%
Majority 5,260

Castle Point
Conservative gain

Rebecca Harris
b. Dec 22, 1967
MP 2010-

A strong advocate of localism. A-lister who was special adviser and researcher to Tim Yeo MP. Special interest in protecting the Green Belt and concerned with chemical storage close to population centres. Cllr, Chichester DC 1999-2003. Career at Phillimore & Co, publishers of British local history (marketing director). C of E. Married, one son. Education: The March School, Westhampnett; Bedales School; LSE (government).

Bob Spink (Green Belt) Conservative MP for Castle Point 1992-2008, sat as independent 2008-10. Education: PhD from Cranfield.

Julian Ware-Lane (Lab) IT consultant. Contested Raleigh 2005.
Brendan D'Cruz (LD) Ed: Plymouth University (PhD).

Constituency
The town of South Benfleet is on the Essex coast and shares this seat with Canvey Island, separated from the mainland by a series of creeks. Developed through the 20th century, it is predominantly urban although there are refinery industries at the west of the island. It has been undergoing regeneration and has below-average qualification levels. Traditionally Tory, it fell to Labour in 1997 and though regained in 2001, Bob Spink defected to UKIP in 2008.

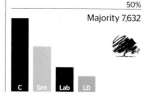

	Electorate	Turnout %	Change from '05 %
	67,284	66.9	
Harris, R C	19,806	44.0	-4.2
Spink, B Green	12,174	27.0	23.5
Ware-Lane, J Lab	6,609	14.7	-15.6
D'Cruz, B LD	4,232	9.4	-0.9
Howell, P BNP	2,205	4.9	

50%
Majority 7,632

Ceredigion
Liberal Democrat hold

Mark Williams
b. Mar 24, 1966
MP 2005-

Liberal Democrat Shadow Minister: Innovation, Universities & Skills 2007; Wales 2006-10; Education 2005-06. Contested Ceredigion 2001, 2000 by-election; Monmouth 1997. Former Pres, Ceredigion Liberal Democrats. Member, Welsh LD Exec 1991-92. Teacher. Member NASUWT. Const asst to Geraint Howells MP. Married, three daughters, one son. Education: Richard Hale School, Hertford; University College of Wales, Aberystwyth (BSc pol & econ); Plymouth (PGCE primary education).

Penri James (PC) Education: Bangor University.

Luke Evetts (C) Trainee solicitor. Ed: University of Wales, Aberystwyth.

Constituency
This rural seat stretches from Cardigan along the Welsh coast, taking in New Quay, Aberaeron, Aberystwyth and Borth, reaching to the estuary of the River Dovey. Inland, towns include the half of Newcastle Emlyn north of the River Teifi, and Lampeter. Agriculture dominates the economy and about 50 per cent of the population speak Welsh. Several Welsh Assembly departments have recently relocated to offices in Aberystwyth. The seat was won by Plaid Cymru in 1992, but fell to the Liberal Democrats. Voters here tend to choose personality over party.

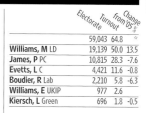

	Electorate	Turnout %	Change from '05 %
	59,043	64.8	☆
Williams, M LD	19,139	50.0	13.5
James, P PC	10,815	28.3	-7.6
Evetts, L C	4,421	11.6	-0.8
Boudier, R Lab	2,210	5.8	-6.3
Williams, E UKIP	977	2.6	
Kiersch, L Green	696	1.8	-0.5

50%
Majority 8,324

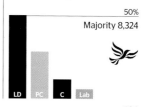

Charnwood
Conservative hold

Stephen Dorrell
b. Mar 25, 1952
MP 1979-

Wealthy, undistinguished. Once a leading light in pro-EU Tory left; rose to Health Sec of State (1995-97). Elected Chair, select cttee: Health 2010-. Brief stint as Shadow Sec of State: Education/Employment (1997-8) but returned to backbenches as increasingly involved in family clothing business, Wensum plc. It went through highly controversial pre-pack administration under his Chairmanship in 2009. Dir, new Wensum Group Ltd. SoS: National Heritage 1994-5. Financial Sec to Treasury 1992-4. Parly Under-Sec, Health 1990-2. MP Loughborough 1979-1997. Married, one daughter, three sons. Ed: Uppingham; Brasenose Coll, Oxford (BA law).

Robin Webber-Jones (LD) Manager.
Eric Goodyer (Lab) Engineer. Ed: De Montfort Uni.
Cathy Duffy (BNP) Cllr, Charnwood BC. Ed: All Hallows School, Manchester; Manchester University.

Constituency
Curving around the north of Leicester, this seat contains suburbs such as Birstall and Thurmaston at the east and Anstey and Glenfield at the west. The more rural areas farther from the city include part of Charnwood Forest. Although the demographic is skewed toward affluent middle-class professionals, skilled working classes who are comfortable are also in abundance. The seat has been Conservative since its creation in 1997.

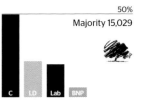

		Electorate	Turnout %	Change from 05 %
		74,473	71.9	☆
Dorrell, S	C	26,560	49.6	3.0
Webber-Jones, R	LD	11,531	21.5	3.2
Goodyer, E	Lab	10,536	19.7	-8.9
Duffy, C	BNP	3,116	5.8	
Storier, M	UKIP	1,799	3.4	0.4

50%
Majority 15,029

C   LD   Lab   BNP

Chatham & Aylesford
Conservative gain

Tracey Crouch
b. Jul 24, 1975
MP 2010-

Affable and well-connected with extensive Conservative party and lobbying experience. Epitome of new Tory, with east London accent. Head of public affairs, Aviva. Chief of Staff to: David Davis; Damian Green 2003. Political consultant: Westminster Strategy; Harcourt. Researcher for various MPs including Michael Howard 1996-98 Spurs fan. FA qualified coach. Lives with partner. Ed: Folkestone Sch for Girls; Hull (BA law and politics).

Jonathan Shaw (Lab) MP Chatham & Aylesford 1997-2010. Parly Under-Sec for fisheries 2007-08, Min for Disabled People 2008-10. Ed: West Kent Coll.

John McClintock (LD) EU civil servant. Education: Oxford (MSc).

Constituency
This straggly Kent-Medway constituency has two distinct urban areas. The large town of Chatham dominates the north. It is separated by the M2 and a rural area from the settlements of Snodland, Larkfield, Ditton and Aylesford, grouped round the M20 in the south. Chatham, on the Medway, is working-class with patches of severe deprivation, a legacy of the closure of the naval docks. It has been designated as the centre of Medway City, planned as part of Thames Gateway regeneration. Elsewhere, the seat is much more affluent. It was a surprise win for Labour at its creation in 1997.

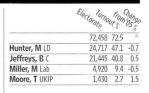

		Electorate	Turnout %	Change from 05 %
		71,122	61.6	☆
Crouch, T	C	20,230	46.2	9.4
Shaw, J	Lab	14,161	32.3	-12.7
McClintock, J	LD	5,832	13.3	-0.2
McCarthy-Stewart, C	BNP	1,365	3.1	
Newton, S	UKIP	1,314	3.0	0.0
Varnham, S	Eng	400	0.9	
Arthur, D	Green	396	0.9	
Smith, M	Ch	109	0.3	

50%
Majority 6,069

C   Lab   LD

Cheadle
Liberal Democrat hold

Mark Hunter
b. Jul 25, 1957
MP 2005-

Long-serving former councillor, from Lib Dems' centre-left. Assistant government whip 2010-. PPS to Nick Clegg 2007-10. LD Shadow Minister: Transport 2008-10; Foreign 2007; OPDM 2005-06. Contested Stockport 2001. Cllr: Stockport MBC 1996-2006 (leader 2002-05); Tameside MBC 1980-89. Marketing executive, Guardian Media Group. Married, one daughter, one son. Education: Audenshaw Grammar School, Manchester.

Ben Jeffreys (C) Teacher. Education: St Andrews University (MA in history).
Martin Miller (Lab) Education: Glasgow University.

Constituency
This atypical Greater Manchester seat is affluent and has the highest proportion of lower managerial and professional workers in the North. The market town of Cheadle sits by the M60, which runs along the top of the constituency heading northeast into neighbouring Stockport. The seat also takes in the leafy commuter towns of Cheadle Hulme and Bramhall. It has been marginal between the Lib Dems and Tories.

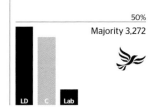

		Electorate	Turnout %	Change from 05 %
		72,458	72.5	☆
Hunter, M	LD	24,717	47.1	-0.7
Jeffreys, B	C	21,445	40.8	0.5
Miller, M	Lab	4,920	9.4	-0.5
Moore, T	UKIP	1,430	2.7	1.5

50%
Majority 3,272

LD   C   Lab

Chelmsford — Conservative hold

Simon Burns
b. Sep 6, 1952
MP 1987-

Urbane figure on the Tory left, popular with Opposition parties. Interested in US politics and, unusually for a Tory, backs the Democrats – and Hillary Clinton in 2008. Min: Health 2010-. Opposition Whip 2005-10. Shadow Min: Health 2004-05, Health and Education 2001-04. Parly Under-Sec: Health 1996-97. PPS to: Gillian Shepherd 1993-94; Timothy Eggar 1989-1993. Govt whip 1995-96; asst govt whip 1994-5. MP Chelmsford West 1997-2010. Political adviser, co dir and journalist. Institute of Directors policy exec. Divorced, one daughter, one son. Ed: Christ the King School, Ghana; Stamford School; Worcester Coll, Oxford (BA history).

Stephen Robinson (LD) Regional director, Royal Institute of British Architects. Contested Chelmsford West, 2001, 2005. Ed: University of Central Lancashire.
Peter Dixon (Lab) Works for freight company. Ed: London Guildhall Uni.

Constituency
In the centre of Essex, the county town of Chelmsford has its own seat after boundary changes. The modern town centre lies between the Rivers Can and Chelmer, while the suburbs are more affluent and attractive. There are patches of deprivation especially in Marconi ward. The majority work in the service sector, especially public sector, real estate and retail. Financial services and manufacturing have declined in recent years. Many residents commute. The seat has been Tory since 1950.

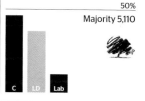

	Electorate	Turnout %	Change from 05 %
	77,529	70.4	*
Burns, S C	25,207	46.2	6.7
Robinson, S LD	20,097	36.8	6.6
Dixon, P Lab	5,980	11.0	-16.0
Wedon, K UKIP	1,527	2.8	-0.6
Bateman, M BNP	899	1.7	
Thomson, A Green	476	0.9	
Breed, C Eng	254	0.5	
Sherman, B Beer	153	0.3	

Majority 5,110

Chelsea & Fulham — Conservative hold

Greg Hands
b. Nov 14, 1965
MP 2005-

Clever, understands the City and will go far. Combative, media-friendly attack dog against Labour. Banker and local campaigner. Shadow Treasury Min 2009-10. MP Hammersmith & Fulham 2005-10. Cllr, Hammersmith & Fulham BC 1998-2006, leader of Con group 1999-2003. Born New York, has dual nationality, has campaigned for Republicans. Married, one daughter, one son. Ed: Dr Challoner's GS, Bucks; Robinson College, Cambridge (BA history).

Alexander Hilton (Lab) Internet consultant and writer. Cllr, Redbridge 2002-06. Contested Canterbury 2005. Ed: Redbridge Coll of FE.

Dirk Hazell (LD) Chief executive, Environmental Services Association. Conservatives regional chairman in London until 2008; Merton LBC councillor 1986-94. Ed: Trinity Hall, Cambridge.

Constituency
This new seat unites these two affluent areas on the north bank of the Thames. Fulham lies at the south west and Chelsea at the north east. Kings Road runs the length of the seat and is the retail and entertainment focus. House prices are high and the borough lives up to its wealthy reputation, although a small area of Fulham Broadway, traditionally a more working-class area, is in the worst 10 per cent for deprivation nationwide. The old Kensington & Chelsea seat was Tory, while Hammersmith & Fulham was held by Labour for two terms from 1997 to 2005.

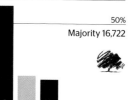

	Electorate	Turnout %	Change from 05 %
	66,295	60.1	*
Hands, G C	24,093	60.5	5.2
Hilton, A Lab	7,371	18.5	-6.9
Hazell, D LD	6,473	16.2	2.2
Stephenson, J Green	671	1.7	-2.5
Gittos, T UKIP	478	1.2	0.1
McDonald, B BNP	388	1.0	
Courtenay, R Ind	196	0.5	
Roseman, G Eng	169	0.4	
Spickernell, G Blue	17	0.0	

Majority 16,722

Cheltenham — Liberal Democrat hold

Martin Horwood
b. Oct 12, 1962
MP 2005-

Active in Chris Huhne's two leadership campaigns. Liberal Democrat Shadow Minister: Climate Change 2009-; Environment 2006-; Home 2005-06. Contested Cities of London & Westminster in 2001; Oxford East in 1992. Councillor, Vale of White Horse District Council 1991-95. Former President, Oxford Student Liberal Society. Chairman, Union of Liberal Students. Career as a marketing consultant. Member: Amnesty International, World Development Movement, Ashridge Management College Association. Married with one daughter and one son. Education: Cheltenham College, Gloucestershire; The Queen's College, Oxford.

Mark Coote (C) National fundraising director, Cancer Research. Contested Hastings & Rye in 2001 and 2005. Ed: Cheltenham Grammar School.

Constituency
Famous for its racecourse, Ladies' College and location on the edge of the Cotswold Hills, Cheltenham has a large tourism sector. GE Aviation is a big employer and GCHQ, the government communications centre, is here, so numbers of professionals are well above the national average. One of the West's most upmarket towns, the few less well-off spots are in the social housing area of Hesters Way. About 10 per cent of residents are students at the University of Gloucestershire. Liberal Democrats overturned decades of Tory representation in 1992.

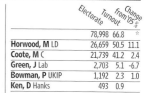

	Electorate	Turnout %	Change from 05 %
	78,998	66.8	*
Horwood, M LD	26,659	50.5	11.1
Coote, M C	21,739	41.2	2.4
Green, J Lab	2,703	5.1	-6.7
Bowman, P UKIP	1,192	2.3	1.0
Ken, D Hanks	493	0.9	

Majority 4,920

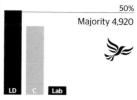

Chesham and Amersham — Conservative hold

Cheryl Gillan
b. Apr 21, 1952
MP 1992-

Hard-working but never got the headlines for the right reasons – rather for claiming dog food on expenses. SoS: Wales 2010-. Shadow Secretary: Wales 2005-10. Shadow Minister: Home, Constitutional and Legal Affairs 2003-05. Opposition whip 2001-03. Opposition Spokes. for Foreign & Commonwealth Affairs 1998-01; Trade & Industry 1997-98. Parly Under-Sec Education and Employment 1995-97; Parliamentary Private Secretary to Lord Privy Seal 1994-95. Senior marketing consultant, Ernst & Young 1986-91; marketing director, Kidsons Impey 1991-93. Married. Education: Cheltenham Ladies College; College of Law.

Tim Starkey (LD) Barrister. Education: Dr Chanoller's Grammar School; Amersham, Lincoln College, Oxford.

Constituency
Sharing the same boundaries as Chiltern District, the seat includes the pretty chalk hills that are designated an Area of Outstanding Natural Beauty. It has excellent transport links to London – the historic market towns of Amersham and Chesham are on the Metropolitan Underground line – making it a sought-after commuter area. A large professional population enjoys the high quality of life in this affluent constituency. It has long been a Tory safe seat.

	Electorate	Turnout %	Change from 05 %
	70,333	74.6	☆
Gillan, C C	31,658	60.4	6.8
Starkey, T LD	14,948	28.5	2.3
Gajadharsingh, A Lab	2,942	5.6	-8.0
Stevens, A UKIP	2,129	4.1	0.9
Wilkins, N Green	767	1.5	-2.0

50%
Majority 16,710

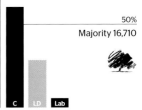

Chester, City of — Conservative gain

Stephen Mosley
b. Jun 22, 1972
MP 2010-

Energetic and very industrious. Not afraid to speak his mind. Cllr, Cheshire CC 2005-09; Chester CC 2000-09 (dep leader 2007-09). Member, Cheshire Fire & Rescue Authority. Dir, Severn Industrial Estates. Dir, Streamfolder. Dir, Weblong (IT consultancy). IBM (UK). C of E. Has family and business links to Malawi. Married, one daughter, one son. Ed: King Edward's Sch, Birmingham; Nottingham Uni (BSc (Hons) Chemistry).

Christine Russell (Lab) MP for Chester 1997-2010. Ed: Spalding HS, London Sch of Librarianship.
Elizabeth Jewkes (LD) b. May 28, 1957. Contested Vale of Clwyd 2005; Elles-

mere Port & Neston 1992. Wastewater operations for Dwr Cymru Welsh Water. Education: Newarke Girls Grammar School, Leicester, University of East London.

Constituency
With Roman heritage, historic city walls and a picturesque location on the River Dee, Chester is a popular tourist destination, as well as a sought-after location for affluent professionals. The largest private sector employer is Bank of America. There are small areas of deprivation such as in Blacon. The boundaries take in outlying areas to the north, south and east, while the western boundary is the border with Wales. Having been Conservative since the First World War, this seat was a surprise win for Labour in 1997.

	Electorate	Turnout %	Change from 05 %
	68,874	67.9	☆
Mosley, S C	18,995	40.6	3.8
Russell, C Lab	16,412	35.1	-3.9
Jewkes, E LD	8,930	19.1	-2.7
Weddell, A UKIP	1,225	2.6	0.9
Abrams, E Eng	594	1.3	
Barker, T Green	535	1.1	
Whittingham, J Ind	99	0.2	

50%
Majority 2,583

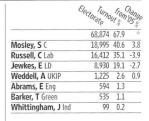

Chesterfield — Labour gain

Toby Perkins
b. Aug 12, 1970
MP 2010-

Great-grandson of Sir AP Herbert, the last MP for Oxford University. Cllr, Chesterfield BC 2003-. Founded rugby clothing company, Club Rugby. Recruitment industry, IT sales, CCS Media. Youth Training Scheme, Sheffield computer firm. Founder and chair, Chesterfield flood victims appeal. Unite. Qualified rugby coach, former Chesterfield & Derbyshire Rugby Union player. Married, one daughter, one son. Education: Trinity School, Leamington; Silverdale School, Sheffield.

Paul Holmes (LD) b. Jan 16, 1957. MP for Chesterfield 2001-10. LD Justice/Home spokes 2008-10. Cllr, Chesterfield. Ed: York Uni, Sheffield Uni.

Carolyn Abbott (C) b. Mar 28, 1969. Former stockbroker. Contested Barnsley East & Mexborough 2005; Sheffield Heeley 2001, Ed: Lancaster University (Philosophy, Politics and Economics)

Constituency
A historic market town with a famous crooked church spire, Chesterfield is on the boundary between rural and industrial Derbyshire. It lies to the south of Sheffield and at the heart of the old coalfield. Brimington and Inkersall, to the east, are also included in this seat. Regeneration projects have helped economic diversification and although patches of deprivation remain, the town is now averagely well off, with a large service sector. Once Tony Benn's parliamentary home, the Liberal Democrats overturned decades of Labour rule with victory in 2001.

	Electorate	Turnout %	Change from 05 %
	71,878	63.8	☆
Perkins, T Lab	17,891	39.0	-1.6
Holmes, P LD	17,342	37.8	-9.1
Abbott, C C	7,214	15.7	7.5
Phillips, D UKIP	1,432	3.1	0.9
Jerram, I Eng	1,213	2.7	
Kerr, D Green	600	1.3	
Daramy, J Ind	147	0.3	

50%
Majority 549

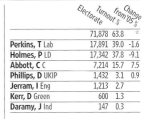

Chichester — Conservative hold

Andrew Tyrie
b. Jan 15, 1957
MP 1997-

Clever and very experienced from days as a special adviser (to John Major and Nigel Lawson). Elected Chair, select cttee: Treasury 2010-. Liberal Conservative interested in constitutional reform and human rights; big campaigner against rendition, voted against Iraq war. Also interested in economic and city issues. Shadow: Paymaster Gen 2004-05; Financial Secretary 2003-04. Previous career: senior economist, European Bank for Reconstruction & Development. BP. Fellow Nuffield College, Oxford. Education: Felstead School; Trinity College, Oxford (BA PPE); College of Europe, Bruges (econ dip); Wolfson Coll, Cambridge (MPhil internat relns).

Martin Lury (LD) Schoolmaster. Ed: Lancaster University.
Simon Holland (Lab) Printing. Ed: London School of Economics.
Andrew Moncrieff (UKIP) Owns irrigation business. Ed: Cambridge Uni, London Business School.

Constituency
This large, predominantly rural West Sussex seat runs from the border with Surrey through the South Downs to the coastal resorts of Selsey and the Witterings. The small cathedral city of Chichester and Georgian market town of Midhurst are the main population centres. There is a cluster of settlements near the border with Havant, in the west. There are a few poorer areas on the outskirts of Chichester. It has been Conservative since 1924 and in recent years has seen support for further-right parties such as UKIP.

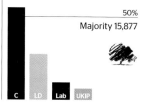

		Electorate	Turnout %	Change from '05 %
		81,462	69.7	☆
Tyrie, A	C	31,427	55.3	7.4
Lury, M	LD	15,550	27.4	-0.3
Holland, S	Lab	5,937	10.5	-8.1
Moncrieff, A	UKIP	3,873	6.8	1.0

50%
Majority 15,877

C　LD　Lab　UKIP

Chingford & Woodford Green — Conservative hold

Iain Duncan Smith
b. Apr 9, 1954
MP 1992-

The "quiet man" who reinvented himself as the voice of the Tory party's social conscience after a disastrous period as Leader of Opposition 2001-03. One of the few cases of a former leader having more influence when out of office than in; hugely influenced Party's thinking as Chairman of Centre for Social Justice 2005-10. Rewarded with Cabinet position (SoS Work & Pensions 2010-) also intended to placate Tory right. Prev: Shadow Sec: Defence 1999-2001; Soc Security 1997-99. Active service in Scots Guard then career at GEC-Marconi, property and printing. Married, two daughters, two sons. Education: Dunchurch College of Management; RMA Sandhurst;

Universita per Stranieri, Perugia; HMS Conway Cadet School.

Cath Arakelian (Lab) University lecturer. Education: Bristol University.
Geoffrey Seeff (LD) Chartered accountant. Contested Romford 2005. Education: Birmingham University.

Constituency
This northeast London seat covers borough boundaries. The Woodford Green area, from Redbridge in the east, includes the affluent, tree-lined streets of Monkhams. Chingford in the west is comfortably well off and forms the more prosperous northern half of Waltham Forest borough. Essentially white suburbia, Winston Churchill once held a seat here on old boundaries and, under Norman Tebbit and now Iain Duncan Smith, it remains a Tory stronghold.

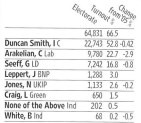

		Electorate	Turnout %	Change from '05 %
		64,831	66.5	
Duncan Smith, I	C	22,743	52.8	-0.42
Arakelian, C	Lab	9,780	22.7	-2.9
Seeff, G	LD	7,242	16.8	-0.8
Leppert, J	BNP	1,288	3.0	
Jones, N	UKIP	1,133	2.6	-0.2
Craig, L	Green	650	1.5	
None of the Above	Ind	202	0.5	
White, B	Ind	68	0.2	-0.5

50%
Majority 12,963

C　Lab　LD

Chippenham — Liberal Democrat hold

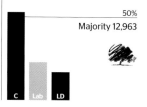

Duncan Hames
b. Jun 16, 1977
MP 2010-

Slight and quietly-spoken but diligent and determined. Special interest in marine renewable energy, schools and railways. Contested Westbury 2005, Watford 2001, Tottenham 2000. Cllr, West Wiltshire DC 2003-07. Owner and Director, Chippenham Consultants. Board member, SW England Regional Development Agency (chair, audit committee). Management consultant, Deloitte. VP, Lib Dem Youth & Students 2000-02. Keen runner. Education: Watford Boys Grammar School; New College, Oxford (BA PPE).

Wilfred Emmanuel-Jones (C) Television producer and farmer.

Greg Lovell (Lab) Online entrepreneur. Education: Dartford Grammar School, Sheffield University, BPP Law School.

Constituency
Poaching from the North Wiltshire, Devizes and old Westbury seats, boundary changes have given this large town its own seat, the most densely populated in Wiltshire. Blighted or blessed, depending on your view, by a prime location in the M4 corridor, this south Cotswolds area is popular with commuters working as far away as Reading in the east and Cardiff in the west. Bradford on Avon is an attractive town that has become a traffic bottleneck. The seats from which this one was made were Tory.

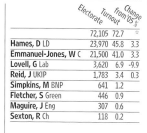

		Electorate	Turnout %	Change from '05 %
		72,105	72.7	☆
Hames, D	LD	23,970	45.8	3.3
Emmanuel-Jones, W	C	21,500	41.0	3.3
Lovell, G	Lab	3,620	6.9	-9.9
Reid, J	UKIP	1,783	3.4	0.3
Simpkins, M	BNP	641	1.2	
Fletcher, S	Green	446	0.9	
Maguire, J	Eng	307	0.6	
Sexton, R	Ch	118	0.2	

50%
Majority 2,470

LD　C　Lab

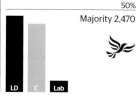

Chipping Barnet — Conservative hold

Theresa Villiers
b. Mar 5, 1968
MP 2005-

Earnest, yet to fulfil her potential. Over-promoted to shadow Cabinet after seven months in Commons and then denied Cabinet position in first coalition government. Min: Transport 2010-. Shadow Sec: Transport 2007-10. Shadow Chief Sec to Treasury 2005-07. Eurosceptic MEP, London 1999-2005. Barrister, Lincoln's Inn. Divorced. Education: Francis Holland Sch; Bristol (LLB); Jesus Coll, Oxford (BCL).

Damien Welfare (Lab) Barrister. Contested Norfolk North West 2005, Chipping Barnet 2001. Education: Cambridge Uni.
Stephen Barber (LD) Academic. Education: University of London.

Constituency
In the north of London, High Barnet is the last stop on the Northern Line. Surrounded by affluent residential streets of 1930s semi-detached houses, the seat has some deprived areas in the Underhill ward. The west and north of the seat give way to fields, with the village of Totteridge among them. Totteridge Lane, overlooking farmland, has some of the highest house prices in the capital. To the south the seat has been extended to include all of Coppetts ward, including Friern Village, a luxury development popular with celebrities. The seat has been Tory since 1950.

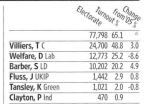

	Electorate	Turnout %	Change from '05 %
	77,798	65.1	☆
Villiers, T C	24,700	48.8	3.0
Welfare, D Lab	12,773	25.2	-8.6
Barber, S LD	10,202	20.2	4.9
Fluss, J UKIP	1,442	2.9	0.8
Tansley, K Green	1,021	2.0	-0.8
Clayton, P Ind	470	0.9	

50%
Majority 11,927

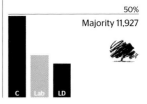

Chorley — Labour hold

Lindsay Hoyle
b. Jun 10, 1957
MP 1997-

Plain-speaking Lancastrian from party's traditional trade union Right, son of former Labour MP and peer Lord Hoyle. Deputy Speaker 2010-. Parliamentary assistant to Beverley Hughes 2008-10. Member, select committees: Quadripartite 2006-07; European Scrutiny 2005-10; Trade & Industry/Business 1998-10; Catering 1997-10. Cllr: Adlington TC 1980-98; Chorley BC 1980-98 (deputy leader 1994-97, Chorley Mayor 1997-98). Shop steward. Company director. Amicus member. Divorced, remarried, two daughters. Education: Lords College, Bolton; Horwich FE College; Bolton TIC (City & Guilds Construction).

Alan Cullens (C) Learning and development manager, aerospace industry. Cllr, Chorley BC 2004-. Past president, British Junior Chamber International.
Stephen Fenn (LD) Computer analyst. Cllr, Preston. Contested Chorley 2001. Ed: Bath Uni, Manchester Uni.

Constituency
The large market town of Chorley lies at the centre of this constituency in the south of Lancashire. The seat has been cut back, losing two of its most rural wards from the west. It is an area experiencing strong economic growth and becoming increasingly affluent. With three motorways passing through the seat and strong rail links nearby, the rural areas are sought-after commuter territory. The land to the east is part of the West Pennine Moors. This has tended to be a bellwether, but defied the trend in 2010.

	Electorate	Turnout %	Change from '05 %
	70,950	70.2	☆
Hoyle, L Lab	21,515	43.2	-7.6
Cullens, A C	18,922	38.0	3.6
Fenn, S LD	6,957	14.0	-0.8
Hogan, N UKIP	2,021	4.1	
Curtis, C Ind	359	0.7	

50%
Majority 2,593

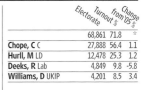

Christchurch — Conservative hold

Christopher Chope
b. May 19, 1947
MP 1983-1992; 1997-

Abrasive right-winger, a Thatcherite survivor and keeper of her flame; honorary VP and former chairman of Thatcherite Conservative Way Forward group. Outspoken critic of John Bercow as Speaker. Shadow Minister: Environment and Transport 2003-05; Transport 2002-03. Various Opposition spokes. roles. Parly Under-Sec: Transport 1990-2; Environment 1986-90. PPS to Peter Brooke 1986. MP Southampton Itchen 1983-92. Barrister. Long-serving Cllr, Wandsworth BC (leader 1979-83). Consultant (Ernst & Young). Married, one daughter, one son. Education: Marlborough College; St Andrews (LLB).

Martyn Hurll (LD) Investment marketing manager. Ed: Bournemouth Sch for Boys.
Robert Deeks (Lab) Chartered accountant. Ed: Bristol Uni.
David Williams (UKIP) Business owner. Contested Buckingham 2005.

Constituency
This coastal constituency lies on the eastern bank of the Stour, which divides Christchurch from the main Bournemouth and Poole conurbation. In Christchurch itself some 35 per cent of people are 60 or over and there is one of the highest proportions of retired people in Britain. The aerospace and tourist industries are significant employers. It has been solidly Conservative except for a dramatic 1993 by-election, when the Lib Dems won by 16,000 after the death of an MP whose majority was 23,000 the previous year.

	Electorate	Turnout %	Change from '05 %
	68,861	71.8	☆
Chope, C C	27,888	56.4	1.1
Hurll, M LD	12,478	25.3	1.2
Deeks, R Lab	4,849	9.8	-5.8
Williams, D UKIP	4,201	8.5	3.4

50%
Majority 15,410

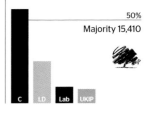

Cities of London & Westminster — Conservative hold

Mark Field
b. Oct 6, 1964
MP 2001-

Cheerful rebel. Served as Shadow Culture Minister (2005-06) but demoted in reshuffle after revelations of marriage-ending affair with Elizabeth Truss, now MP. Shadow Financial Secretary to the Treasury 2005; Shadow Minister for London 2003-05; Opposition Whip 2003-04. Parliamentary Panel on BBC Radio 4's weekly *Westminster Hour*. Solicitor, Freshfields Bruckhaus Deringer. CEO publishing and recruitment business. Divorced, remarried, one son. Education: Reading School; St Edmund Hall, Oxford, (BA Law); Chester College (Law Finals).

David Rowntree (Lab) Musician. Ed: University of London.
Naomi Smith (LD) Research and development manager at the Chartered Institute of Management Accountants. Ed: Leeds University.

Constituency

This seat stretches from Hyde Park in the west across to the banking and financial hub of the City in the east, and is bounded to the south by the Thames. It includes landmarks such as Buckingham Palace and the Houses of Parliament, retail centres such as Oxford Street and the entertainment districts of Soho, Covent Garden and the Strand. Only two small areas of deprivation exist, in the Churchill ward to the south, and around Chinatown, which is home to one of the largest Chinese populations in Britain. This is seen as a safe Tory seat.

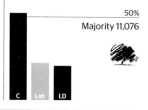

	Electorate	Turnout %	Change from '05 %
	66,489	1.0	☆
Field, M C	19,264	52.2	3.9
Rowntree, D Lab	8,188	22.2	-3.1
Smith, N LD	7,574	20.5	2.0
Chase, D Green	778	2.1	-2.2
Weston, P UKIP	664	1.8	0.7
Roseman, F Eng	191	0.5	
Delderfield, D Ind	98	0.3	
Nunn, J Pirate	90	0.2	
Cap'n, M Tom	84	0.2	

50%
Majority 11,076

C Lab LD

Clacton — Conservative hold

Douglas Carswell
b. Apr 3, 1971
MP 2005-

Fearless, anti-establishment maverick – happy to rock the boat and annoy the party whips. Waged ultimately successful campaign to bring down Michael Martin as Speaker, to displeasure of some colleagues. Blogger, author and media pundit. MP Harwich 2005-2010. Outspoken Better Off Out (anti-Europe) campaigner. Commercial television then fund management (Invesco). Married, one daughter. Grew up in Uganda and Kenya. Education: Charterhouse; University of East Anglia (BA history); King's College London (MA history).

Ivan Henderson (Lab) MP for Harwich 1997-2005. Education: Sir

Anthony Deane Comprehensive.
Michael Green (LD) Development banker. Education: Leeds University. Contested St Albans 2005.

Constituency

This seat is now named after Clacton-on-Sea. It is bounded by Brightlingsea Creek in the south east and Hamford Water in the north west. The once-popular resort of Clacton-on-Sea has dilapidated holiday homes with some of the lowest house prices in the country. Of more than 32,000 areas nationwide, Jayton is the third most deprived. About one in three residents is a pensioner and there are high levels of child poverty. As part of the Harwich seat, it was traditionally Tory, but had a Labour interlude in 1997-2005.

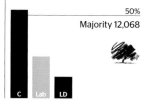

	Electorate	Turnout %	Change from '05 %
	67,194	64.2	☆
Carswell, D C	22,867	53.0	8.6
Henderson, I Lab	10,799	25.0	-10.9
Green, M LD	5,577	12.9	-0.6
Taylor, J BNP	1,975	4.6	
Allen, T Tendring	1,078	2.5	
Southall, C Green	535	1.2	
Humphrey, C Ind	292	0.7	

50%
Majority 12,068

C Lab LD

Cleethorpes — Conservative gain

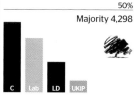

Martin Vickers
b. Sep 13, 1950
MP 2010-

Cleethorpes-born long-serving councillor. Contested Cleethorpes 2005. Cllr: NE Lincolnshire 1999- (cabinet member, environment); Great Grimsby 1980-94. Member regional transport boards Yorkshire/Hull & Humber. Constituency agent to Edward Leigh MP. Printing industry, retail trade. Anglican. Religion and railways buff. Lifelong Grimsby Town FC supporter. Went to university as mature part-time student, graduating in 2004. Churchwarden. Married, one daughter. Ed: Havelock Comp, Grimsby; Lincoln Uni (BA (Hons) politics).

Shona McIsaac (Lab) b. Apr 3, 1960. MP for Cleethorpes 1997-2010. PPS to:

Rt Hon Baroness Scotland of Asthal 2003-05; Adam Ingram 2001-05.
Malcolm Morland (LD) Lecturer, Cllr, NEt Lincs. Ed: North Lindsey Coll.
Stephen Harness (UKIP) Shift supervisor.

Constituency

From Barton-on-Humber, the southern entrance to the Humber Bridge, the seat stretches south to the downmarket holiday resort of Cleethorpes. It straddles the north and north east Lincolnshire boundaries but excludes Grimsby. Cleethorpes and Immingham, which with Grimsby is Britain's largest port by tonnage, have areas of severe deprivation. At North Killingholme, near Immingham, construction workers at the Lindsey oil refinery took strike action in 2009. Although the seat returned a Labour MP on its creation in 1997, the Tories had success in predecessor seats.

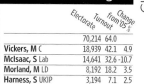

	Electorate	Turnout %	Change from '05 %
	70,214	64.0	
Vickers, M C	18,939	42.1	4.9
McIsaac, S Lab	14,641	32.6	-10.7
Morland, M LD	8,192	18.2	3.5
Harness, S UKIP	3,194	7.1	2.5

50%
Majority 4,298

C Lab LD UKIP

CLW

Clwyd South
Labour hold

Susan Elan Jones
b. Jun 1, 1968
MP 2010-

Seasoned charity fund-raiser. Cllr, Southwark 2006-2009 (resigned). Contested Surrey Heath 1997. Fundraiser, Housing Justice and medical research/church charities. Member of Institute of Fundraising (Cert). Labour Campaign for Electoral Reform. Christian Socialist. Unite. Speaks Welsh and Japanese; taught English in Japan for several years. Classical music enthusiast. Ed: Grango Comp; Ruabon Sch 6th form; Bristol (BA English, chair, Labour club); Cardiff (MA applied English lang studies).

John Bell (C) Teacher, lecturer. Contested Delyn 2005. Ed: Keele Uni.

Bruce Roberts (LD) Owns chartered accountancy business. Ed: Durham Uni; Lancaster.
Janet Ryder (PC) Former teacher. Member Welsh Assembly (North Wales) 1999-. Ed: Northern Counties Coll of Ed, Newcastle; Open Uni.

Constituency
The River Dee flows through this northeast Wales constituency, passing the main town of Llangollen in the centre. Ruabon is among other towns and the seat stretches to the border with Shropshire in the east. Both the agriculture and manufacturing sectors are bigger than average but the class demographic is unremarkable. About 25 per cent of residents live in social housing. The seat has been Labour since its creation in 1997, though recent boundary changes have removed some Labour-leaning wards.

	Electorate	Turnout %	Change from 05 %
	53,748	64.5	☆
Jones, S E Lab	13,311	38.4	
Bell, J C	10,477	30.2	4.8
Roberts, B LD	5,965	17.2	1.7
Ryder, J PC	3,009	8.7	-0.8
Hynes, S BNP	1,100	3.2	
Powell, N UKIP	819	2.4	0.4

50%
Majority 2,834

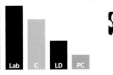

Lab | C | LD | PC

CLW

Clwyd West
Conservative hold

David Jones
b. Mar 22, 1952
MP 2005-

Affable and ambitious. Parly Under-Sec: Wales 2010-. Shadow Minister for Wales 2006-10. AM for North Wales 2002-03. Contested Chester 2001, Conwy 1997; Welsh Assembly elections 1999. Solicitor, Senior partner David Jones & Co, Llandudno. Married, two sons. Education: Ruabon Grammar; UCL (law); College of Law, Chester.

Donna Hutton (Lab) Regional organiser for Unison.
Llyr Huws Gruffydd (PC) Runs own PR company. Education: Cardiff University.
Michelle Jones (LD) Trustee, North Wales Mental Health Organisation,

Flintshire Disability Forum. Education: Cardiff University.

Constituency
This large North Wales seat forms an L-shape, with its northern boundary reaching from Colwyn Bay, through Abergele, to Kinmel Bay. The seaside is popular with pensioners. From here the seat reaches south to Clocaenog Forest, then east past Ruthin to the Clwydian mountain range. The agricultural sector is above average, but the health sector is notable. Labour won this seat from the Tories under new boundaries in 1997, only to lose it back to them in 2005.

	Electorate	Turnout %	Change from 05 %
	57,913	65.8	
Jones, D C	15,833	41.5	5.4
Hutton, D Lab	9,414	24.7	-11.3
Huws, L Gruffydd PC	5,864	15.4	
Jones, M LD	5,801	15.2	1.9
Nicholson, W UKIP	864	2.3	0.8
Blakesley, J Ind	96	0.3	
Griffiths, D Ch P	239	0.63	

50%
Majority 6,419

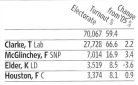

C | Lab | PC | LD

COA

Coatbridge, Chryston & Bellshill
Labour hold

Tom Clarke
b. Jan 10, 1941
MP 1982-

Undistinguished but dogged veteran backbencher who championed disabled rights, also interested in African poverty. Min: National heritage, CMS 1997-8. Shadow: Cab Min for Disabled People's Rights 1995-97; Sec: Int Dev't 1993-4; Scotland 1992-3. Min: Personal Social Services 1987-92. Opp Spokes 1993-4. MP Coatbridge & Chryston 1997-2005; Monklands West 1983-87; Coatbridge & Airdrie 1982-93. Cllr: Monklands DC 1974-82; Coatbridge TC 1964-74. JP 1972. Scottish Film Council. CBE. Ed: Columba High School; Scottish College of Commerce.

Frances McGlinchey (SNP) Charity manager. Contested Stirling 2005. Cllr,

North Lanarkshire. Ed: Queens College, Caledonian Uni.
Kenneth Elder (LD) Chartered management accountant. Cllr, Glasgow CC 2007-. Ed: Reading Uni.
Fiona Houston (C) Journalist.

Constituency
To the east of Glasgow, this seat has small rural areas to the north but is almost entirely urban, with more than its share of deprivation. It is dominated by the towns of Coatbridge and Bellshill. A solid Labour seat, in 2005 it gave Tom Clarke the largest numerical majority (19,519) of any MP.

	Electorate	Turnout %	Change from 05 %
	70,067	59.4	
Clarke, T Lab	27,728	66.6	2.2
McGlinchey, F SNP	7,014	16.9	3.4
Elder, K LD	3,519	8.5	-3.6
Houston, F C	3,374	8.1	0.9

50%
Majority 20,714

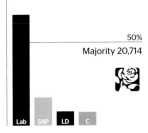

Lab | SNP | LD | C

Colchester Liberal Democrat hold

Bob Russell
b. Mar 31, 1946
MP 1997-

Low-profile backbencher who prides himself on his attendance record in Parliament. Lib Dem shadow minister: Defence 2005-10. LD whip 2003-10, 1999-2002, 1999-2002. LD spokesman: sport 1999-2005; home/legal affairs 1997-99. Member, select committees: Home Affairs 1998-10; Catering 2000-01. Cllr, Colchester BC 1971-2002 (leader 1987-91, mayor 1986-87). Journalist, publicity officer. Married, two daughters - one deceased, two sons. Education: St Helena Boys School, Colchester; NE Tech Coll (NCTJ Proficiency Cert).

Will Quince (C) Customer development manager. Ed: Aberystwyth University of Wales.
Jordan Newell (Lab) Voluntary sector worker.

Constituency
With its army garrison and prison, there is a strong military presence in Colchester. As Britain's oldest recorded town, it also has several historical attractions from the Norman keep of Colchester Castle to "Jumbo", the Victorian water tower. However, it is not dominated by tourism or any one industry. An affluent area, it has a mixed economy, with a strong financial and retail sectors and the University of Essex. The western boundary of this seat has been altered. Having traditionally been a Tory area, it was won by the Liberal Democrats on its creation in 1997.

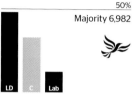

	Electorate	Turnout	Change from 05 %
	74,062	62.3	☆
Russell, B LD	22,151	48.0	0.3
Quince, W C	15,169	32.9	0.8
Newell, J Lab	5,680	12.3	-7.9
Pitts, J UKIP	1,350	2.9	
Chaney, S BNP	705	1.5	
Lynn, P Green	694	1.5	
Bone, E Eng	335	0.7	
Noble, G PP	35	0.1	
Shaw, P ND	20	0.0	

50%
Majority 6,982

| LD | C | Lab |

Colne Valley Conservative gain

Jason McCartney
b. Jan 29, 1968
MP 2010-

RAF officer turned TV journalist. Presenter, *Calendar News & Sport*, ITV Yorkshire. Reporter, BBC local radio. Leeds Metropolitan University. NUJ. Cites Mo Mowlam and Ronald Reagan among political heroes. RAF flight lieutenant, served Turkey, Las Vegas and Iraq. Governor, SportsAid. Huddersfield Town FC and Huddersfield Giants RLFC fan. CofE. Divorced, two daughters. Education: Lancaster Royal GS; RAF Coll, Cranwell; Leeds Trinity Coll (postgrad Diploma broadcast journalism).

Nicola Turner (LD) Managing director of manufacturing company. Education: Huddersfield New College.

Debbie Abrahams (Lab) Director of public health research unit. Education: Salford University.

Constituency
Large sweeps of rural land between Greater Manchester and Huddersfield make up the main area of this seat, but the population is concentrated in the north. This includes west Huddersfield, with its hospital, suburbs such as Golcar and the village of Honley. There are patches of deprivation here but the seat is economically active, with many middle-class professionals. The BBC comedy series *Last of the Summer Wine* is filmed at Holmfirth. The M62 loosely binds the constituency to the north. The seat has changed hands between the three main parties.

	Electorate	Turnout	Change from 05 %
	80,062	69.1	☆
McCartney, J C	20,440	37.0	4.1
Turner, N LD	15,603	28.2	3.7
Abrahams, D Lab	14,589	26.4	-9.0
Fowler, B BNP	1,893	3.4	
Roberts, M UKIP	1,163	2.1	
Ball, C Green	867	1.6	-1.2
Grunsell, J TUSC	741	1.3	

50%
Majority 4,837

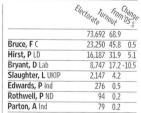

| C | LD | Lab |

Congleton Conservative hold

Fiona Bruce
b. Mar 26, 1957
MP 2010-

Long-term activist stalwart. Passionate about social mobility, proud of her northern mill-town upbringing. Interested in business and international aid work, ongoing work with school in Tanzania. Contested Warrington South 2005. Cllr War-rington BC 2004-10 (finance portfolio 2006-09). Award-winning businesswoman; founded successful law firm, Fiona Bruce & Co LLP and set up free legal advice service. Co-author, *There is Such as Thing as Society*. Kept a flock of sheep. Christian. Married, two sons. Education: Burnley High School; Howell's School, Llandaff; Manchester Uni (Law).

Peter Hirst (LD) Retired doctor. Contested Stroud 2005. Education: Manchester University.
David Bryant (Lab) Managing director of healthcare company. Education: Swansea University.

Constituency
The market town of Congleton, once famed for silk manufacture, lies at the east of this diamond-shaped seat. The other main towns are Alsager, in the south, Middlewich, in the west, and Sandbach, in between the two. The seat is very well off, with residents of its towns and villages enjoying the Cheshire countryside and excellent transport links on the M6. There are high numbers of professionals, and manufacturing, although in decline, remains significant. It has been safely Conservative since its inception in 1983.

	Electorate	Turnout	Change from 05 %
	73,692	68.9	☆
Bruce, F C	23,250	45.8	0.5
Hirst, P LD	16,187	31.9	5.1
Bryant, D Lab	8,747	17.2	-10.5
Slaughter, L UKIP	2,147	4.2	
Edwards, P Ind	276	0.5	
Rothwell, P ND	94	0.2	
Parton, A Ind	79	0.2	

50%
Majority 7,063

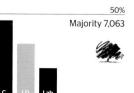

| C | LD | Lab |

139

Copeland — Labour hold

Jamie Reed
b. Mar 14, 1973
MP 2005-

Strong supporter of nuclear power industry. PPS to: Harriet Harman 2008-10; Tony McNulty 2006-08. Member, select committees: Environment, Food & Rural Affairs 2005-07; Regulatory Reform 2005-10. Media professional. Anti-racism campaigner. Member, GMB. Married, three sons. Education: Whitehaven School; Manchester Metropolitan (BA English); Leicester (MA mass communication).

Christopher Whiteside (C) Telecommunications manager. Contested Copeland 2005. Education: Bristol Uni. **Frank Hollowell** (LD) Nurse. Contested Copeland 2005. Education: Charles Feerers School of Nursing, Leicester.

Constituency
The coastline of this West Cumbria seat includes the working-class town of Whitehaven and the Sellafield nuclear power station, which has long defined the area economically. Tourism also plays a key economic role. The seat reaches into the centre of the Lake District National Park and includes England's deepest lake, Wastwater, and its highest mountain, Scafell Pike. Sheep farming is also notable, although it employs only about 3 per cent of the population. About a quarter of the population live in council housing and the seat has been Labour for decades.

	Electorate	Turnout %	Change from 05 %
	63,291	67.6	☆
Reed, J Lab	19,699	46.0	-0.7
Whiteside, C C	15,866	37.1	3.6
Hollowell, F LD	4,365	10.2	-3.7
Jefferson, C BNP	1,474	3.4	
Caley-Knowles, T UKIP	994	2.3	0.0
Perry, J Green	389	0.9	

50%
Majority 3,833

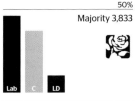

Corby — Conservative gain

Louise Bagshawe
b. Jun 28, 1971
MP 2010-

Feisty, ambitious and highly successful "chick-lit" novelist. Driven and very focused. Long-term Tory activist but had brief spell in Labour party. Brief music industry career: marketing executive, Sony Music; press officer, EMI records. Separated. Three children. Education: Sacred Heart School, Tunbridge Wells; Waldingham School; Christ Church, Oxford (BA English course two – Anglo-Saxon and Norse).

Phil Hope (Lab) MP 1997-2010. Minister for Care Services 2008-10. Parly Under-Sec: Voluntary sector 2007-08; skills 2005-07; ODPM 2003-05. Repaid £41,700 claimed in Commons expenses for London flat. Education: Exeter Uni.

Portia Wilson (LD) District nurse. Cllr, Northampton BC 2007-. Education: Northampton Uni.

Constituency
At the northeast end of Northamptonshire, this seat spans over the border with Cambridgeshire, taking in the smaller towns of Oundle, Raunds and Thrapston. Once a steel town, Corby has undergone significant regeneration, but there remains a large Labour-leaning working class, with about a fifth of residents in council accommodation, and serious deprivation. It is an economically active seat and also home to a significant middle class in the more affluent countryside. It was held by the Conservatives until 1997.

	Electorate	Turnout %	Change from 05 %
	78,305	69.3	☆
Bagshawe, L C	22,886	42.2	2.3
Hope, P Lab	20,991	38.7	-2052
Wilson, P LD	7,834	14.4	1.7
Davies, R BNP	2,525	4.7	

50%
Majority 1,895

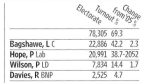

Cornwall North — Liberal Democrat hold

Dan Rogerson
b. Jul 23, 1975
MP 2005-

Constituency focused, from party's centre-left. Lib Dem shadow minister: Communities & Local Government 2007-10; Arts, Culture & Heritage 2007; OPDM/Communities & Local Government 2006-07; Environment, Food & Rural Affairs 2005-06. LD whip 2007-10. Contested Bedfordshire NE 2001. Cllr, Bedford BC 1999-2002. Campaigns officer Devon & Cornwall LDs 2002-04. Admin officer, De Montfort Uni. Research assistant, Bedford Bor Council. Unison. Married, one daughter, two sons. Education: St Mary's Sch, Bodmin; Bodmin Coll, Cornwall; Uni of Wales, Aberystwyth (BSc politics).

Sian Flynn (C) Company director. Cllr, Surrey CC 1991-99. Education: Exeter Uni.

Constituency
Dramatic boundary changes mean this seat loses Newquay – and about 20,000 electors. Bodmin, the largest town in North Cornwall, is "Gateway to the Moor", with its windswept, rugged landscape. Padstow is known as Padstein after the chef Rick Stein, whose culinary empire dominates the former fishing village. Bude lies to the north on a coastline whose beaches attract hordes of visitors. Tourism and dairy farming are important. Cornwall received EU funding for 2000-06 to boost its economy. The constituency changed hands numerous times before being won by Lib Dems in 1992.

	Electorate	Turnout %	Change from 05 %
	68,662	68.2	☆
Rogerson, D LD	22,512	48.1	5.8
Flynn, S C	19,531	41.7	6.3
O'Connor, M UKIP	2,300	4.9	-0.8
Hulme, J Lab	1,971	4.2	-8.3
Willett, J Meb	530	1.1	

50%
Majority 2,981

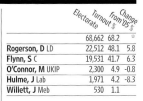
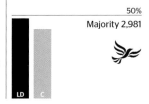

Cornwall South East Conservative gain

Sheryll Murray
b. Feb 4, 1956
MP 2010-

Passionate fishing industry campaigner; wife of a trawler skipper owner. Councillor: Caradon DC 2003-09 (leader Con group); Cornwall CC 2001-05. Member of the Objective One programme monitoring committee. Fishing industry representative: spokeswoman, Save Britain's Fish; director, the Fishermen's Association; Looe Fishermen's Protection Association; chairman of the South West Fish Producers' Organisation. Part-time doctor's receptionist for 20 years. Married, one daughter, one son. Education: Torpoint Comprehensive.

Karen Gillard (LD) Barrister. Cllr, Plymouth CC 2001-5 as LD and 2000

as Con. Contested Plymouth Sutton 2005. Education: Plymouth Uni.
Michael Sparling (Lab) Postgraduate student. Ed: University of Manchester.

Constituency
The main towns are Liskeard, in the centre, and Saltash and Torpoint, which sit across the Tamar Estuary from Devon and Plymouth, whose Devonport docks are a major employer. The Cornwall coastline draws tourists and retired people, while agriculture is also a notable economic sector. The most famous landmark is the Royal Albert Bridge created by the Victorian engineer Isambard Kingdom Brunel. Boundary changes have removed St Blaise and Stoke Climsland. The Lib Dems overturned 27 years of Tory representation with their victory in 1997.

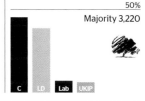

	Electorate	Turnout %	Change from '05 %
	72,237	68.7	*
Murray, S C	22,390	45.1	10.1
Gillard, K LD	19,170	38.6	-8.1
Sparling, M Lab	3,507	7.1	-3.4
McWilliam, S UKIP	3,083	6.2	1.1
Creagh-Osborne, R Green	826	1.7	
Holmes, R Meb	641	1.3	

50%
Majority 3,220

C · LD · Lab · UKIP

Cotswolds, The Conservative hold

Geoffrey Clifton-Brown
b. Mar 23, 1953
MP 1992-

Excitable, eccentric but well-meaning, bumbling shire Tory; a classic squire. Shadow Minister: various Trade/Foreign Affairs 2005-10; local government 2002-04. Assistant Chief Whip 2005; Opposition whip 2004-5; 1999-2001. PPS to: Douglas Hogg 1995-7. MP Cirencester and Tewkesbury 1992-7. Chartered surveyor and farmer. Divorced, one daughter, one son. Education: Eton; Royal Agricultural College, Cirencester.

Mike Collins (LD) Resources manager for Airbus UK. Chosen Hill School, Churchdown. Cllr, 1999-. Mayor of Bradley Stoke 2002-03.

Mark Dempsey (Lab) Environmental policy specialist. Contested Cotswold in 2005. Education: Gloucestershire University.

Constituency
This affluent seat covers a huge area of the beautiful Cotswold hills and quintessential English countryside dotted with picturesque villages. Cirencester, self-proclaimed Capital of the Cotswolds, lies near the south while the other main towns are Moreton-in-Marsh, Stow-on-the-Wold and Bourton-on-the-Water. Unsurprisingly, tourism is a large part of the economy and agriculture remains important. Boundary changes, adding Minchinhampton ward, are as minor as the change to the name, which used to be just Cotswold. The Conservatives have dominated this seat and its predecessors.

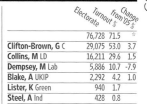

	Electorate	Turnout %	Change from '05 %
	76,728	71.5	*
Clifton-Brown, G C	29,075	53.0	3.7
Collins, M LD	16,211	29.6	1.5
Dempsey, M Lab	5,886	10.7	-7.9
Blake, A UKIP	2,292	4.2	1.0
Lister, K Green	940	1.7	
Steel, A Ind	428	0.8	

50%
Majority 12,864

C · LD · Lab

Coventry North East Labour hold

Bob Ainsworth
b. Jun 19, 1952
MP 1992-

Lugubrious manner masks tough political operator. Moustachioed. Liked and respected as an insider, but has little outside impact. Secretary of State: Defence 2009-10. Minister of State: Armed Forces 2007-09. Parly Under-Sec: Home 2001-03, Environment, Transport and Regions 2001. Whip: opposition 1995-97, govt 1997-2007: deputy chief 2003-07. Member select cttees: Accommodation and Works 2003-05, Selection 2003-05, Finance and Services 2003-05, Administration 2005-07. Councillor, Coventry CC 1984-93: dep leader 1988-91. MSF (formerly TGWU): shop steward, sr steward, sec jt shop stewards/ branch pres. Sheet metal worker, Jaguar Cars.

Married, two daughters. Education: Foxford Comprehensive School, Coventry.

Hazel Noonan (C) Care assistant. Cllr, Coventry CC 2008-.
Russell Field (LD) Computer programmer. Contested Coventry NE 2005. Cllr, Coventry 2003-. Education: De Montfort University (BSc).

Constituency
East of Coventry city centre, this working-class seat reaches to the M6. Traditionally focused on manufacturing, these industries have suffered job losses, gradually being replaced with service sector employment. Large areas of deprivation blight the seat. There are significant populations of residents of Indian and Pakistani origin in this traditionally Labour seat.

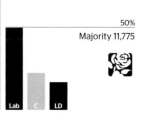

	Electorate	Turnout %	Change from '05 %
	73,035	59.4	*
Ainsworth, B Lab	21,384	49.3	-7.6
Noonan, H C	9,609	22.2	3.3
Field, R LD	7,210	16.6	0.1
Gower, T BNP	1,863	4.3	
Nellist, D Soc	1,592	3.7	
Forbes, C UKIP	1,291	3.0	0.2
Lebar, R Ch	434	1.0	

50%
Majority 11,775

Lab · C · LD

Coventry North West | Labour hold

Geoffrey Robinson
b. May 25, 1938
MP 1976-

Wealthy businessman at heart of 1990s New Labour project, close to Gordon Brown. Resigned from unsuccessful period in government (Paymaster General 1997-98) after loan to Mandelson revealed. Brought down by Blair-Brown feuding. Faced questions over collapse of engineering firm TransTec. Opp spokes: Trade & Industry, regional affairs 1983-87; science 1982-83. Chief exec TransTec plc. Dir, West Mids Enterprise Board. Triumph Motorcycles. Chief exec, Jaguar Cars Coventry. MD Leyland Innocenti. Lab party research asst. Married, one daughter, one son. Ed: Emmanuel Sch, London; Clare Coll, Cambridge; Yale Uni.

Gary Ridley (C) Commercial director. Cllr, Coventry 2002-. Education: Cardinal Newman RC Sch, Keresley, Coventry Uni.
Vincent McKee (LD) Company director and political writer. Contested Coventry S 2005, 2001; Coventry NE 1992. Education: Coventry Uni (BA), Birmingham City (MA), London Met (PhD).

Constituency
From severely deprived inner-city areas just beyond Coventry's commercial centre, this seat fans out to affluent semi-rural areas to the north west, home to relatively high numbers of professionals. However, Coventry's traditional working-class vote, built around the car manufacturing industry that dominated for decades, has tended to triumph, with Labour dominant since the Second World War.

	Electorate	Turnout %	Change from 05 %
	72,871	63.9	※
Robinson, G Lab	19,936	42.8	-5.2
Ridley, G C	13,648	29.3	2.7
McKee, V LD	8,344	17.9	-0.5
Sheppard, E BNP	1,666	3.6	
Nattrass, M UKIP	1,295	2.8	1.0
Clarke, J Ind	640	1.4	
Wood, J Green	497	1.1	
Downes, N Soc	370	0.8	
Sidhu, W Ch	164	0.4	

50%
Majority 6,288

Coventry South | Labour hold

Jim Cunningham
b. Feb 4, 1941
MP 1992-

Loyal footsoldier with taciturn manner. Engineering background makes him one of old generation with authentic links to shop floor. PPS to Mike O'Brien 2005-10. Member, select committees: Procedure 2005-06; ODPM 2005; Const affairs 2003-05; Chairmen's Panel 1998-2001; Trade & Industry 1997-2001; Home 1993-97. MP Coventry SE 1992-97. Cllr, Coventry 1972-92 (leader 1988-92). MSF shop steward. Engineer. Married, one daughter, one son, one stepdaughter, one stepson. Education: Columba HS, Coatbridge; Tillycoultry College; Ruskin courses (Labour Movement, Industrial Law).

Kevin Foster (C) Cllr, Coventry CC 2004-. Cabinet member for city services. Ed: Warwick Uni (Law).
Brian Patton (LD) Victim liaison officer. Cllr, Henley 1997–2008. Ed: Binley Park Comp, Coventry Uni.

Constituency
Coventry city centre lies at the north of this seat, with its cathedral, expanses of concrete offices and the university, which leads to a significant student vote in the seat. The residential tower blocks in St Michael's ward lie amid one of the most deprived areas in the country but south of the city centre it is more mixed, with the more middle-class areas of Earlsdon and Wainbody and large numbers of professionals. The seat was won by Labour on its creation in 1997.

	Electorate	Turnout %	Change from 05 %
	73,652	62.4	※
Cunningham, J Lab	19,197	41.8	-4.0
Foster, K C	15,352	33.4	2.8
Patton, B LD	8,278	18.0	0.4
Taylor, M UKIP	1,767	3.9	1.8
Griffiths, J Soc	691	1.5	
Gray, S Green	639	1.4	

50%
Majority 3,845

Crawley | Conservative gain

Henry Smith
b. May 14, 1969
MP 2010-

Very smooth and plausible, destined for ministerial office. Contested Crawley 2005, 2001. Own property investment company. Cllr, West Sussex CC 1997- (leader 2003-10); Crawley BC 2002-04. Co-author Direct Democracy, arguing for devolution of powers. Keen vexillologist and skiier. Married, one daughter, one son. Education: Frensham Heights, Farnham; UCL (BA philosophy).

Chris Oxlade (Lab) Presenter for Mercury FM. Ed: Hazlewick School.
John Vincent (LD) Head of safety analysis, EASA. Cllr, Surrey CC 1993-7. Contested Epson & Ewell in 2001, 1997. Contested European elections (South East), 2009, 2004. Ed: Coventry University.

Constituency
The borders are closely drawn round the large West Sussex town of Crawley, designated a New Town in 1947, and Gatwick, immediately to its north and by far the biggest source of employment. The affluent eastern half of the town contrasts with the relatively deprived south west, where densely packed terraced houses are home to much of the town's predominantly Asian ethnic minority population. Labour took the seat comfortably from the Tories in 1997 but margins of victory narrowed in subsequent elections, down to 80 votes in 2005.

	Electorate	Turnout %	Change from 07 %
	72,781	65.3	
Smith, H C	21,264	44.8	5.8
Oxlade, C Lab	15,336	32.3	-6.8
Vincent, J LD	6,844	14.4	-1.0
Trower, R BNP	1,672	3.5	0.5
French, C UKIP	1,382	2.9	0.7
Smith, P Green	598	1.3	
Khan, A JP	265	0.6	0.1
Hubner, A Ind	143	0.3	

50%
Majority 5,928

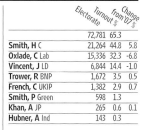

Crewe Nantwich · Conservative gain

Edward Timpson
b. Dec 26, 1973
MP May 2008-

Wealthy son of Timpson shoe repair / key cutting chain chief exec. Member, select committees: Children, Schools & Families 2008-10; Joint Cttee on Human Rights 2008-. Family law barrister. Married, two daughters, one son. Ed: Uppingham Sch, Rutland; Durham (BA politics); Law conversion; College of Law, London.

David Williams (Lab) Trade Union official for USDAW. Agent for Gwyneth Dunwoody MP. Ed: South Cheshire College.
Roy Wood (LD) Retired learning mentor. Contested Birkenhead, 1997, 2001. Ed: St Edwards Coll Liverpool, Liverpool Uni.

Constituency
This constituency in southern Cheshire has two distinct parts: the industrial, Labour-leaning railway town of Crewe with its tradition of car manufacture, and the more affluent, Conservative-voting Nantwich, famed for its cheesemaking, and the surrounding villages. Regeneration and housing renewal are gradually transforming Crewe. Labour held the seat from 1945 until the death of the Labour MP Gwyneth Dunwoody in 2008, when the Conservatives dramatically defeated her daughter, Tamsin, in a by-election.

	Electorate	Turnout %	Change from '05 %
	77,460	66.0	☆
Timpson, E C	23,420	45.9	12.9
Williams, D Lab	17,374	34.0	-14.4
Wood, R LD	7,656	15.0	-3.7
Clutton, J UKIP	1,414	2.8	
Williams, P BNP	1,043	2.0	
Parsons, M Ind	177	0.4	

50%
Majority 6,046

C | Lab | LD

Croydon Central · Conservative gain

Gavin Barwell
b. Jan 23, 1972
MP 2010-

Highly articulate political strategist, the ultimate party insider. A local Croydon man who served as Lord Ashcroft's right-hand-man at CCHQ high command (Director of Operations 2003-06). 1922 executive committee, 2010-. Consultant, own business. Cllr, Croydon 1998- (Cabinet Member for Community Safety & Cohesion). Advised John Gummer as Environment Sec. Married, three sons. Education: Trinity School, Croydon; Trinity College, Cambridge (BA theoretical physics & philosophy of science).

Gerry Ryan (Lab Co-op) BT technical officer. Contested Croydon South in 2001. Cllr, Croydon.

Peter Lambell (LD) Business analyst, Lloyds Banking. Cllr, Surrey CC 2009-.
Andrew Pelling (Ind) MP for Croydon Central 2005-10 (Conservative, then Ind). Member GLA 2000-2008.

Constituency
Reduced in size, this seat retains the retail centre of Croydon, which is based around the Whitgift shopping precinct. It extends southeast to the New Addington housing estate, which, along with the Ashburton area, is deprived. The rest of the centre is relatively affluent. Croydon has the highest levels of inequality of any London borough. Croydon's skyline has many high-rise buildings, including the tower housing Nestlé, a notable employer. Labour took this seat from the Tories in 1997 but lost it in 2005. Andrew Pelling lost the Tory whip in 2007 and then sat as an independent.

	Electorate	Turnout %	Change from '05 %
	78,880	63.1	☆
Barwell, G C	19,657	39.5	-0.9
Ryan, G Lab	16,688	33.5	-7.6
Lambell, P LD	6,553	13.2	0.4
Pelling, A Ind	3,239	6.5	
Le May, C BNP	1,448	2.9	
Atkinson, R UKIP	997	2.0	-0.2
Golberg, B Green	581	1.2	-1.0
Gitau, J Ch	264	0.5	
Cartwright, J Loony	192	0.4	
Castle, M Ind	138	0.3	

50%
Majority 2,969

C | Lab | LD | Ind

Croydon North · Labour hold

Malcolm Wicks
b. Jul 1, 1947
MP 1992-

Quietly deadly technocrat. Minister: Energy 2007-08; Trade & Industry 2005-07; Pensions 2003-05. Parly Under-Sec: Work & Pensions 2001-03; Education & Employment 1999-2001. Opposition spokesman: Social Security 1995-97. TGWU. Academic, research, analyst career. Married, two daughters, one son. Education: Elizabeth College, Guernsey; North West London Polytechnic; LSE (BSc sociology).

Jason Hadden (C) Solicitor. Education: Southampton University (BA Hons history).
Gerry Jerome (LD) Cllr, Sutton CC 2009-. Education: Kingsway College for FE, Sunderland Polytechnic, (BSc Hons pharmacology), Newcastle Polytechnic (BA applied computing).

Constituency
This residential seat to the north of Croydon town centre borders Lambeth and is more typical of London than the other Croydon seats. It is less affluent, with notable deprivation, especially in the Broad Green area. It is ethnically diverse, with white British a minority. More than a fifth of residents are black and about 15 per cent are Indian or Pakistani. Many of these are first-generation, with more than 30 per cent of residents born outside Britain. Labour took this seat from the Tories in 1992.

	Electorate	Turnout %	Change from '05 %
	85,212	60.7	☆
Wicks, M Lab	28,949	56.0	2.4
Hadden, J C	12,466	24.1	1.9
Jerome, G LD	7,226	14.0	-3.2
Khan, S Green	1,017	2.0	-0.9
Serter, J UKIP	891	1.7	0.0
Williams, N Ch	586	1.1	
Shaikh, M Respect	272	0.5	
Stevenson, B Comm	160	0.3	
Seyed, M Ind	111	0.2	

50%
Majority 16,483

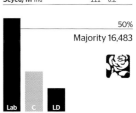

Lab | C | LD

143

Croydon South — Conservative hold

Richard Ottaway
b. May 24, 1945
MP 1992-; 1983-1987

Popular, but never really made it. Unsuccessful candidate for Chairman of 1922 committee, 2010. Elected Chair, select cttee: Foreign Affairs 2010-. Shadow Sec of State: Environment 2004. Opposition spokes. various 1997-2001. PPS to: FCO Mins 1985-87, Michael Heseltine 1992-95. Whip: gov't 1995-97, opposition 1997. MP Nottingham North 1983-87. London Mayoral nominee 2002. Solicitor – maritime and commercial law. Royal Navy officer 1961-70. Married. Education: Backwell School, Somerset; Bristol (LLB).

Simon Rix (LD) Book publisher. Education: Exmouth Community College;

University College London (BSc Hons in physics & astronomy)
Jane Avis (Lab) Cllr, South Norwood. Education: Reigate Priory School.

Constituency
Only the southern fringes of Croydon are in this seat and the Waddon area is one of the few areas of deprivation. Most of the seat is really Purley and Coulsdon with suburban areas reaching down to the Surrey border. There are above-average numbers of people in professional and managerial jobs, although Purley Way is known for warehousing and retail parks. It is the least ethnically diverse of the Croydon boroughs, at 80 per cent white British and with no other single ethnic group exceeding 4 per cent. This seat has been held by the Tories for decades.

		Electorate	Turnout %	Change from '05 %
		81,301	69.3	☆
Ottaway, R	C	28,684	50.9	-1.1
Rix, S	LD	12,866	22.8	2.4
Avis, J	Lab	11,287	20.0	-4.0
Bolter, J	UKIP	2,504	4.5	2.3
Ross, G	Green	981	1.7	

50%
Majority 15,818

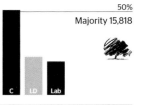

Cumbernauld, Kilsyth & Kirkintilloch East — Labour hold

Gregg McClymont
b. Jun 3, 1976
MP 2010-

Oxford academic, born and raised in Cumbernauld. Former speechwriter to Dr John Reid. Runs virtual think-tank Ideas Scotland. History Fellow, St Hugh's College, Oxford. Education: Cumbernauld High School; Glasgow (history); Pennsylvania (scholarship); Oxford (PhD history).

Julie Hepburn (SNP) Campaigner, education coordinator, human rights organisation. Ed: University of Edinburgh (politics), MA policy studies.
Rod Ackland (LD) Retired University IT support officer. Ed: Eastbourne College; Sussex University.
Stephanie Fraser (C) Head of development, Scottish Ballet.

Constituency
This Scottish seat has the longest constituency name in Britain. To the west it has rural areas around Lennoxtown, Twechar and Milton of Campsie, but it is largely urban and has a high concentration of social housing. The working-class voters of Cumbernauld, 15 miles northeast of Glasgow, Kilsyth, a former mining town, and in some wards of Kirkintilloch, make it safe for Labour.

		Electorate	Turnout %	Change from '05 %
		64,037	64.3	
McClymont, G	Lab	23,549	57.2	5.4
Hepburn, J	SNP	9,794	23.8	1.6
Ackland, R	LD	3,924	9.5	-5.3
Fraser, S	C	3,407	8.3	1.3
O'Neill, W	SSP	476	1.2	-1.8

50%
Majority 13,755

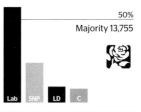

Cynon Valley — Labour hold

Ann Clwyd
b. Mar 21, 1937
MP 1984-

Left-winger tamed by Tony Blair with appointment as Special envoy to PM on Iraq human rights (2003). Now mainly single issue campaigner on Iraq and refugee issues. Chair PLP 2005-06. Assistant to John Prescott 1994-95. Opposition spokes various 1993-95. Shadow Sec: Nat Heritage 1992-3; Wales 1992; Int Dev't 1989-92. Shad Min: Education / Women's Rights 1987-88. Chair Tribune Group 1986-97. Lab Party NEC 1983-84. Journalist, broadcaster. MEP 1979-84. Married. Ed: Holywell GS; The Queen's Sch, Chester; Univ Coll of Wales, Bangor.

Dafydd Trystan Davies (PC) b. 1974. Development manager, Welsh-medium

higher education. Ed: Ysgol Gyfun Rhydfelen, Aberystwyth University (BA Hons international politics), PhD (Welsh economy and globalisation).
Lee Thacker (LD) Credit controller. Ed: King Alfred's School, Oxfordshire, Essex Uni.
Juliette Ash (C) Director, The Centre for Social Justice. Ed: University of Edinburgh, BSc (molecular biology).

Constituency
A chain of towns line the banks of the River Cynon, which runs the length of the seat. These include Abercynon, Mountain Ash and Aberdare. Only at the north does it give way to open expanses of rural land. This is a working-class seat, with an economy focused on manufacturing in the place of the old heavy industries. Health is poor in the area. This seat has a long history of returning Labour MPs.

		Electorate	Turnout %	Change from '05 %
		50,656	59.0	☆
Clwyd, A	Lab	15,681	52.5	-10.5
Trystan, D	Davies	6,064	20.3	
Thacker, L	LD	4,120	13.8	1.6
Ash, J	C	3,010	10.1	1.5
Hughes, F	UKIP	1,001	3.4	0.7

50%
Majority 9,617

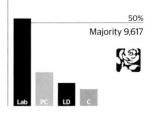

Dagenham & Rainham

Labour hold

Jon Cruddas
b. Apr 7, 1962
MP 2001-

Well-liked and widely respected left-winger who took on the BNP and won. Ran for deputy leadership. Member, cttee: Public Accounts 2003-10. Deputy Political Sec, PM's political office Downing St 1997-2001. Chief asst, General Sec Lab Party. Policy officer, Lab Party Policy Directorate 1989-94. TGWU, branch sec. Married, one son. Ed: Oaklands RC Comp, Portsmouth; Warwick (BSc economics, MA industrial relations, PhD industrial & business studies); Wisconsin.

Simon Jones (C) Consultant project and communications manager. Contested Pontefract & Castleford 2005, GLA top-up list 2004. Cllr, Waveney DC 2002-04. Ed: Anglia Ruskin University.
Michael Barnbrook (BNP) Retired police inspector. Contested Sidcup for UKIP in 2005. Ed: Plaistow GS.
Joseph Bourke (LD) Accountant. Ed: Thames Valley University.

Constituency
Dagenham's name is synonymous with the Ford Motor plant in the south of the seat, which now produces only car parts. The seat has been effectively shifted east under boundary changes, losing three working-class urban wards from the west but gaining three much larger, greener and more middle-class Tory wards from Havering borough in the south east. Patches of severe deprivation dotted through the seat, especially in the centre and the west, and the BNP has had most success in those areas. The old Dagenham seat was Labour.

	Electorate	Turnout %	Change from 05 %
	69,764	63.4	☆
Cruddas, J Lab	17,813	40.3	-8.9
Jones, S C	15,183	34.3	0.9
Barnbrook, M BNP	4,952	11.2	
Bourke, J LD	3,806	8.6	-0.5
Litwin, C UKIP	1,569	3.6	-0.4
Kennedy, G Ind	308	0.7	
Watson, P Ch	305	0.7	
Rosaman, D Green	296	0.7	

50%
Majority 2,630

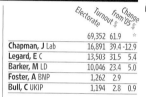

Darlington

Labour hold

Jenny Chapman
b. Sep 25, 1973
MP 2010-

Strong local campaigner and Darlington's first female MP. Cllr, Darlington 2007-. Researcher to Alan Milburn. Assistant prison psychologist, Durham/Dartmoor. Founder and chair, Newblood Live, youth music charity. Member, NE Strategic Partnership for Asylum & Refugee Support. Keen cyclist. Married, two sons. Education: Hummersknott Comprehensive, Darlington; Brunel (psychology); Durham Uni (medieval archaeology).

Edward Legard (C) Barrister, former soldier. Education: University of St Andrews.
Mike Barker (LD) Managing director, family business. Education: Forest GS,
Berkshire, University Coll Swansea (BA Hons political theory & govt).

Constituency
The large market town of Darlington, birthplace of the railways, lies at the south of County Durham, to the west of Middlesbrough. It has several large industrial parks and a larger-than-average construction sector. Main employers include the council, the hospital and Orange. The town centre has areas of deprivation. The seat is well connected: the A1(M) skirts its north west. It has changed hands a number of times postwar, most recently switching to Labour in 1992.

	Electorate	Turnout %	Change from 05 %
	69,352	61.9	☆
Chapman, J Lab	16,891	39.4	-12.9
Legard, E C	13,503	31.5	5.4
Barker, M LD	10,046	23.4	5.0
Foster, A BNP	1,262	2.9	
Bull, C UKIP	1,194	2.8	0.9

50%
Majority 3,388

Dartford

Conservative gain

Gareth Johnson
b. Oct 12, 1969
MP 2010-

Campaigned against tolls on Dartford crossing. Particularly interested in criminal justice, the Thames Gateway and IVF treatment. Contested Dartford 2005 (missed out by 706 votes), Lewisham West 2001. Cllr, Bexley 1998-2002. Defence solicitor in small firm, Thomas Boyd White. Keen cricketer. Married, one daughter, one son. CofE. Ed: Dartford GS; Coll of Law (LPC) Uni of the West of England (postgrad Diploma law)

John Adams (Lab) b. Feb 16, 1969. Financial journalist. Ed: University of Swansea.
James Willis (LD) b. 1977. Account manager.

Constituency
In the northwestern corner of Kent, Dartford borders Greater London and, with its position on the south bank of the Thames, is known for the Dartford river crossings north to Essex. It is a main growth centre as part of the Thames Gateway project and site of the huge Bluewater shopping centre. Its mixed socioeconomic make-up is not far from national averages, helping to explain why it has tended to change hands with the government of the day in recent decades.

	Electorate	Turnout %	Change from 05 %
	76,271	65.7	☆
Johnson, G C	24,428	48.8	7.6
Adams, J Lab	13,800	27.6	-15.5
Willis, J LD	7,361	14.7	4.6
Rogers, G Eng	2,178	4.4	
Palmer, R UKIP	1,842	3.7	0.7
Tindame, S Ind	264	0.5	
Crockford, J FDP	207	0.4	

50%
Majority 10,628

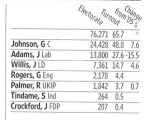

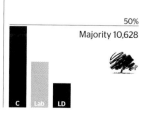

Daventry — Conservative hold

Chris Heaton-Harris
b. Nov 28, 1967
MP 2010-

Hardworking, combative, witty and fiercely Eurosceptic. Experienced: made name as MEP, East Midlands (1999-2009), wrote about EU budget process, contested Tory MEP leadership. Contested Leicester South 2004 by-election and 1997. Management and public affairs consultant. Prev: Eleven year, largely noctural, career for What 4 Ltd, family fruit & veg wholesale business in New Covent Garden Market. President of Earls Barton FC. Qualified and active football referee. Chairman, EU Sports Platform. Married, two daughters. Education: Tiffin Grammar School for Boys; Wolverhampton Polytechnic (didn't complete degree).

Christopher McGlynn (LD) b. Aug 25, 1958. Civil servant. Ed: Open University (environmental studies).
Paul Corazzo (Lab) b. Jul 9, 1975. Management, renewable energy firm. Former cllr, Kettering BC. Ed: Huddersfield University (history and politics).

Constituency
This Northamptonshire seat is barely recognisable from the old one of the same name, having effectively been shifted north under boundary reviews and cut by around 18,000 electors. It includes the Daventry district. Generally an affluent seat, with the exception of a few averagely prosperous areas in Daventry, the seat is home to high numbers of middle-class professionals and the Conservative tradition in the area goes back decades.

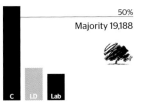

	Electorate	Turnout %	Change from '05 %
	71,451	72.5	
Heaton-Harris, C C	29,252	56.5	3.5
McGlynn, C LD	10,064	19.4	4.9
Corazzo, P Lab	8,168	15.8	-12.1
Broomfield, J UKIP	2,333	4.5	1.6
Bennett-Spencer, A Eng	1,187	2.3	
Whiffen, S Green	770	1.5	

50%
Majority 19,188

Delyn — Labour hold

David Hanson
b. Jul 5, 1957
MP 1992-

Highly forgettable, middle-of-the-road minister who was promoted after loyal stint as Tony Blair's PPS. Min: Home 2009-10; Justice 2007-09; NI Office 2005-07. PPS to Tony Blair 2001-05. Parly Under-Sec Wales 1999-2001, PPS to Alastair Darling 1997-98. Asst govt whip 1998-99. Member, cttee: Welsh Affairs 1992-95. Member, leadership campaign team 1994-97. Cllr, Vale Royal BC 1983-91 (leader), Northwich Town 1987-91. T&G, USDAW. Director, Re-Solv. Spastics Society. Manager, Plymouth Co-operative. Co-operative Union trainee. Married, two daughters, two sons. Education: Verdin Comp, Cheshire; Hull (BA drama, Cert Ed).

Antoinette Sandbach (C) Legal Aid barrister. Contested Welsh NA, 2007. Ed: Nottingham University (MA environmental law & international law).
Bill Brereton (LD) Management consultant. Ed: Cambridge University (BA Hons political theory and institutions).

Constituency
This Flintshire seat is across the Dee Estuary from the Wirral. Its main towns include Holywell and Mold and its economy has traditionally focused on manufacturing. The area has more in common with Merseyside and the industrial North West than it does with the traditional economy elsewhere in Wales. Once a Tory area, the seat was won by Labour in 1992.

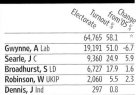

	Electorate	Turnout %	Change from '05 %
	53,470	69.2	
Hanson, D Lab	15,083	40.8	-4.9
Sandbach, A C	12,811	34.6	8.5
Brereton, B LD	5,747	15.5	-2.4
Ryder, P PC	1,844	5.0	-2.4
Matthys, J BNP	844	2.3	
Haigh, A UKIP	655	1.8	0.2

50%
Majority 2,272

Denton and Reddish — Labour hold

Andrew Gwynne
b. Jun 4, 1974
MP 2005-

Introduced successful Private Member's Bill to restrict activities of 'vulture funds' trading debts of developing countries. Chair, Lab Friends of Israel. PPS to: Ed Balls 2009-10; Jacqui Smith 2007-09; Baroness Scotland 2005-07. Cllr, Tameside MBC 1996-. European Co-ordinator Arlene McCarthy MEP. Researcher Andrew Bennet MP. National Computing Centre, Y2K team. ICL. Married, one daughter, two sons. Ed: Edgerton Park Community HS; Tameside Coll; NE Wales Inst (HND business & finance); Salford (BA politics & contemporary history).

Julie Searle (C) Consultant chemical engineer. Cllr, Adur DC 2000-. Educa-tion: Greenlands School, Blackpool, Bradford University.
Stephen Broadhurst (LD) Business consultant. Cllr, Macclesfield 2007-.
William Robinson (UKIP)

Constituency
Reddish, in Stockport borough, sits in the south west of this constituency, which extends through Tameside borough to Audenshaw and Dukinfield, by the River Tame, in the north. Denton, at the heart of this largely urban seat, is about six miles east of Manchester. The M60 and M67 pass through the middle of the constituency and it has benefited as part of the M60 investment corridor. The seat used to be industrial and retains above-average manual and skilled manual labourers. There is strong support for Labour.

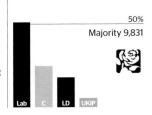

	Electorate	Turnout %	Change from '05 %
	64,765	58.1	*
Gwynne, A Lab	19,191	51.0	-6.7
Searle, J C	9,360	24.9	5.9
Broadhurst, S LD	6,727	17.9	1.6
Robinson, W UKIP	2,060	5.5	2.3
Dennis, J Ind	297	0.8	

50%
Majority 9,831

Derby North — Labour hold

Chris Williamson
b. Sep 16, 1956
MP 1910-

Extrovert, enthusiastic and not averse to confrontation. Tee-total vegan and outspoken against blood sports (trustee and former Chair, League Against Cruel Sports), past hunt sabateur (former Chairman of the Hunt Sabateurs Association). Life-long Derby resident: Cllr, Derby CC 1991- (Leader 2005-08, 2002-03). Vice-chair, Derbyshire Fire & Rescue authority. Chair, East Mids Empowerment Partnership. Non-exec Dir, Greater Derby NHS PCT. Varied career: welfare rights officer, social worker, market trader, bricklayer. Twice divorced, once widowed. One daughter, one son. Ed: Thomas More RC Sch; Castle Donnington Community Coll.

Stephen Mold (C) b. Jan 14, 1968. Marketing dir. Ed: Banbury School.
Lucy Care (LD) b. Jul 24, 1960. Chartered engineer. Cllr. Ed: Leamington Coll for Girls, Durham Uni.

Constituency
A residential seat, it excludes the centre of Derby, but includes a mixture of suburbs. Darley Abbey in the north is relatively affluent, while Chaddesden to the east and Mackworth to the west are less well off. Significant boundary changes have removed the affluent Conservative-leaning Allestree but brought in Mickleover and Littleover. The railway and aerospace industries are big private sector employers, but new investment has supported a shift from manufacturing to the service sector. Derby University provides a large student population. Labour won this seat from the Tories in 1997.

	Electorate	Turnout %	Change from '05 %
	71,484	63.1	☆
Williamson, C Lab	14,896	33.0	-9.0
Mold, S C	14,283	31.7	5.8
Care, L LD	12,638	28.0	0.5
Cheeseman, P BNP	2,000	4.4	
Ransome, E UKIP	829	1.8	-0.2
Gale, D Ind	264	0.6	
Geraghty, D Pirate	170	0.4	

50%
Majority 613

Derby South — Labour hold

Margaret Beckett
b. Jan 15, 1943
MP 1974-79; 1983-

Experienced party machine politician, used by Blair as a safe pair of hands. Cleverer than she appears but presided over major failings in EU farm payments scheme at DEFRA. Enthusiastic caravanner, devoted to older husband Leo, who is her PA. First female Foreign Sec 2006-07. Min: Housing (att. Cabinet) 2008-09. SoS: EFRA 2001-06. Leader of HoC 1998-2001. SoS: Trade & Industry 1997-98. Shad: Board of Trade Pres 1995-97. Shad SoS: Health 1994-95. Opp leader 1994. Dep leader Lab/Opp, 1992-94. Shad min 1984-94. Parly Under-Sec, Education/ Science 1976-79. Chair, HoC Modernisation 1998-2001. MP Lincoln 1974-79. Metallurgist. Married, two stepsons.

Ed: Notre Dame HS, Manchester Sci/ Tech Coll; John Dalton Poly.

Jack Perschke (C) b. Jun 6, 1978. Cllr, Runnymede BC 2006-2008. Management consultant. Infantry officer.
David Batey (LD) Cllr, Derby City.

Constituency
From Derby city centre, the seat fans out south to suburbs such as Normanton and Alvaston. Boundary changes have removed areas from the west and added Chellaston at the south. Manufacturing, although in decline, remains key to the economy and Rolls-Royce's factory in Sinfin is a major employer. A working-class seat with large numbers of long-term unemployed and those who have never worked. With 15 per cent of the population Asian, it is one of the most ethnically diverse seats in the East Midlands and has long been Labour.

	Electorate	Turnout %	Change from '05 %
	71,012	58.0	☆
Beckett, M Lab	17,851	43.3	-9.8
Perschke, J C	11,729	28.5	8.7
Batey, D LD	8,430	20.5	-3.7
Fowke, S UKIP	1,821	4.4	3.0
Graves, A Ind	1,375	3.3	

50%
Majority 6,122

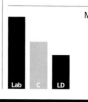

Derbyshire Dales — Conservative hold

Patrick McLoughlin
b. Nov 30, 1957
MP 1986 (by-election)

Plain-speaking working class Tory, an ex-coal miner. Skilled in Commons procedures and is a key figure in handling new MPs. Chief Whip 2010-. Opposition Whip: chief 2005-10; deputy chief 1998-2005; pairing 1997-98. Govt whip: 1996-97; assistant 1995-96. Parly Under-Sec: DTI 1993-94; Employment 1992-93; Transport 1989-92. PPS to: Lord Young of Graffham 1988-89, Angela Rumbold 1987-88. Cllr, Cannock Chase, Staffs. Agriculture then Littleton Colliery; NUM/NCB member. Married, one daughter, one son. Education: Cardinal Griffin Comprehensive; Staffs Agriculture College.

Joe Naitta (LD) b. Nov 18, 1963. Charity man. Cllr, Derby City 2008-. Education: Keele Uni.
Colin Swindell (Lab) b. Aug 25, 1982. Retail. Cllr, Derbyshire Dales 2009-.

Constituency
This rural seat, which was known as Derbyshire West, stretches from the west of Sheffield down to the northern fringes of Derby, the famous white peaks of limestone country. Most of the seat is in the Peak District National Park, including Bakewell. The towns of Ashbourne, Matlock and Wirksworth are just outside the park's boundaries. Several villages are dotted across the area. Tourism and farming are important in this largely affluent seat, which has been Conservative since 1950 and which is still influenced by the stately homes of Chatsworth and Haddon Hall.

	Electorate	Turnout %	Change from '05 %
	63,367	73.8	
McLoughlin, P C	24,378	52.1	5.6
Naitta, J LD	10,512	22.5	-1.9
Swindell, C Lab	9,061	19.4	-6.3
Guiver, I LD	1,779	3.8	1.3
Stockell, J Green	772	1.7	
Delves, N Loony	228	0.49	
Y'mech, A Humanity	50	0.1	

50%
Majority 13,866

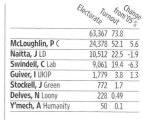

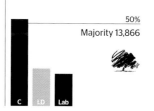

Derbyshire Mid — Conservative hold

Pauline Latham
b. Feb 4, 1948
MP 2010-

An experienced local government warhorse. Cut her political teeth fighting for grant maintained status for local secondary school, as a councillor on the (then) Labour-controlled Derbyshire County Council. As a grandmother, one of the oldest new Cameron cuties. Tends to know her onions. Cllr: Derby CC 1998-, 1992-96; Derbyshire CC 1987-93. Mayor of Derby 2007-08. Contested Broxtowe 2001; European elections 2004, 1999 (East Midlands). OBE. Dir, Michael St Development. Proprieter, Humble Plc. Led social action projects to Uganda. Enjoys horse-riding. Married, one daughter, two sons. Ed: Bramcote Hill Technical Grammar Sch.

Hardyal Dhindsa (Lab) Cllr, Derby CC 2004-, 1996-2002.
Sally McIntosh (LD) b. May 7, 1970. Learning resources manager. Education: Woodlands Community School, Hull Uni, Strathclyde Uni.

Constituency
This new constituency around the north of Derby has been created from parts of four different seats. Following the River Derwent north from the city, it includes the village of Duffield and busy market town of Belper. Reaching east, it includes the Derby suburb of Oakwood, a large council estate, and villages of Spondon and Borrowash amid semi-rural land. The sought-after modern suburb of Allestree, in the west of the city, is the site of the University of Derby, a notable employer. This seat is generally prosperous and home to affluent professionals.

	Electorate	Turnout %	Change from 05 %
	66,297	71.4	☆
Latham, P C	22,877	48.3	1.2
Dhindsa, H Lab	11,585	24.5	-10.2
McIntosh, S LD	9,711	20.5	4.5
Allsebrook, L BNP	1,698	3.6	
Kay, A UKIP	1,252	2.6	0.5
Seerius, R Loony	219	0.5	

50%
Majority 11,292

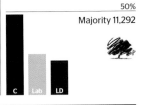

Derbyshire North East — Labour hold

Natascha Engel
b. Apr 9, 1967
MP 2005-

Sceptical about Commons reforms. PPS to: John Denham 2009-10; Liam Byrne 2008-09; Peter Hain 2007-08. Member, cttees: Reform of HoC 2009-; Work & Pensions 2005-07. Trade Union political fund ballot co-ordinator. Founder, Trade Union Co-ordinating Committee. Smith Institute. Subtitler for Teletext. Berlin-born and raised. Married, three sons. Education: King's School, Canterbury; King's College, London (BA German/Portuguese); Westminster Uni (MA technical/specialist translation).

Huw Merriman (C), b 1973, solicitor. Education: Durham College of Law. Cllr, Wealden DC.

Richard Bull (LD), GP. Education: Gosforth School, Henry Fanshawe School, University of Leeds, University of Sheffield.

Constituency
This C-shaped constituency surrounds Chesterfield on three sides. Once heavily dependent on mining, former coalfield towns such as Eckington and Killamarsh in the north and Clay Cross in the south are still less affluent than the rural area at the west, or the Sheffield suburb of Dronfield. These areas are home to many commuting professionals who enjoy the scenic location by the edge of the Peak District National Park. Though the seat has been Labour since 1935, margins of victory have sometimes been narrow.

	Electorate	Turnout %	Change from 05 %
	71,422	65.9	☆
Engel, N Lab	17,948	38.2	-10.1
Merriman, H C	15,503	33.0	7.0
Bull, R LD	10,947	23.3	1.8
Bush, J UKIP	2,636	5.6	1.2

50%
Majority 2,445

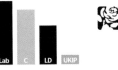

Derbyshire South — Conservative gain

Heather Wheeler
b. May 14, 1959
MP 2010-

Long-serving councillor experienced in urban regeneration. Selected by open primary. Cllr: South Derbyshire DC 1995- (leader 2007-10, leader con group 2002-10); Wandsworth BC 1982-86. Contested Coventry South 2005, 2001. City career: RICS Insurance; Stewart Wrightson Insurance Brokers; Stenhouse Insurance Brokers. Associate of the Chartered Insurance Institute. Enjoys renovating buildings and listening to The Archers. Married, one daughter. Ed: Grey Coat Hospital, Westminster; City of London Polytechnic (chartered insurance exams).

Michael Edwards (Lab), b Mar 13, 1961. IT project manager. Ed: Priory School, Shrewsbury, University of Birmingham. Cllr, Nottingham City 1993-.
Alexis Diouf (LD), b Feb 4, 1955. Deputy headteacher, NGO worker, social worker. St Gabriel College, Senegal, Sheffield City Polytechnic, Open Uni. Chesterfield borough cllr since 2003.

Constituency
Skirting around the south of Derby city, this seat stretches down through affluent semi-rural areas to Swadlincote, which was once the centre of the small South Derbyshire coalfield. This area remains less well off and more Labour-leaning but there is no real deprivation and the seat's residents are economically active. Two manufacturing giants, Toyota and JCB, have bases in the seat, but there is also a strong public sector. Much of the seat is within the National Forest. It has been a bellwether since 1970 and once sent Edwina Currie to Parliament.

	Electorate	Turnout %	Change from 05 %
	70,610	71.4	
Wheeler, H C	22,935	45.5	8.☆1
Edwards, M Lab	15,807	31.4	-11.5
Diouf, A LD	8,012	15.9	3.0
Jarvis, P BNP	2,193	4.4	
Swabey, C UKIP	1,206	2.4	
Liversuch, P Soc	266	0.5	

50%
Majority 7,128

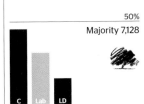

Claire Perry
b. Apr 3, 1964
MP 2010-

Relative newcomer to politics, only joined party in 2006 but quickly established within CCHQ as an adviser to George Osborne's team. Set to be a high-flyer. Won first selection attempt, Women2Win member. First person in family to go to uni. Career in City/US: Credit Suisse First Boston, McKinsey & Co, Bank of America. Homemaker 2000-07. Christian. Married, two daughters, one son. Education: Nailsea Comprehensive; Brasenose College, Oxford (geography); Harvard Business Sch (MBA).

Fiona Hornby (LD) Freelance mathematics tutor. Contested Devizes 2005. Cllr, Kennet DC 1995-1999. Education: Claverham School, Battle, Sussex University.
Jurab Ali (Lab) b. 1977. Electrician and restaurateur. Cllr, Swindon BC 2008-.

Constituency
The old constituency has been cut by more than 18,000 electors, removing Calne and Melksham. The new one is predominantly rural, with Devizes near the west and Marlborough by the downs to the north – this town has one of Britain's widest high streets. The Kennet and Avon Canal cuts through the centre of the seat. Tidworth, in the south, is a military town and boundary changes add further army bases in nearby villages. Large areas of Salisbury Plain are used for military training. The seat has been Tory since 1945.

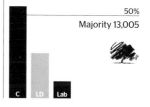

	Electorate	Turnout %	Change from '05 %
	67,374	68.8	☆
Perry, C C	25,519	55.1	4.0
Hornby, F LD	12,514	27.0	4.7
Ali, J Lab	4,711	10.2	-12.2
Bryant, P UKIP	2,076	4.5	0.2
Fletcher, M Green	813	1.8	
Houlden, M Ind	566	1.2	
Coombe, N Libertarian	141	0.3	

50%
Majority 13,005

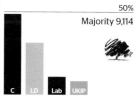

C LD Lab

Mel Stride
b. Sep 30, 1961
MP 2010-

Compassionate conservative with experience at Centre for Social Justice. Enthusiastic advocate of pavement politics, as modelled on Lib Dem grassroots activism. Campaigned against post office and hospital closures (Co-Chairman, Crediton Hospital Campaign Group). Launched "One Tonne Green Challenge". Founded Venture Marketing Group (runs National Franchise Exhibitions). Deutsche Morgan Grenfell. History and culture buff; qualified and award-winning tourist guide. Qualified pilot. Married, three daughters. Education: Portsmouth Grammar School; St Edmund Hall, Oxford (BA PPE, President Oxford Union, OUCA).

Philip Hutty (LD) b. 1965. Social worker. Education: Bristol Uni.
Moira Macdonald (Lab) b. Jun 3, 1950. Voluntary sector campaigner.
Bob Edwards (UKIP) b. Mar 4, 1946. Retired Royal Marines officer. Cllr for 15 years.

Constituency
The new, land-locked constituency takes roughly a third from each of the Mid Devon, Teighbridge and West Devon boroughs, plus the East Devon Exe Valley ward. There is substantial agriculture in a rural seat hit hard by the 2001 foot-and-mouth epidemic, when culling of uninfected herds caused almost as much misery as the disease. Tourism focuses on Dartmoor and thatched villages. The main town, Okehampton, is gateway to an army training camp. The area has a mixed history of Lib Dem and Tory support.

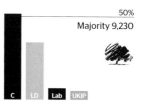

	Electorate	Turnout %	Change from '05 %
	71,204	75.7	☆
Stride, M C	27,737	51.5	7.7
Hutty, P LD	18,507	34.4	-4.4
Macdonald, M Lab	3,715	6.9	-4.7
Edwards, B UKIP	2,870	5.3	-0.6
Mathews, C Green	1,044	1.9	

50%
Majority 9,230

C LD Lab UKIP

Hugo Swire
b. Nov 30, 1959
MP 2001-

Close friend of David Cameron, had difficult time in last Parliament; sacked as Shad Culture Sec (2005-07) after advocating scrapping free entry to national museums. Min: NI Office 2010-. Prev. Shad Min: Arts 2004-5, Opp Whip 2003-04. PPS to Theresa May 2003. Member, select cttee: NI 2002-05. Non-Exec Chair, Photo-Me. Followed family footsteps in becoming Dir, Sotheby's. Prev. Nat Gallery head of development; financial consultant; MD; army. Once dated Jerry Hall. Keeps show pig. Married, two daughters. Ed: Eton; St Andrew's (Left after one year studying fine art, medieval history & Arabic culture); RMA, Sandhurst.

Paul Robathan (LD) b. May 11, 1948. Chair, South Somerset Strategic Partnership. Visiting Fellow, Imperial College. Cllr, South Somerset DC 2003-.
Gareth Manson (Lab) b. Apr 23, 1965. Teacher, Bristol Hospital Ed Service.
Mike Amor (UKIP)

Constituency
Redrawn almost beyond recognition, the seat retains its name despite losing the eastern tip of Devon. It gains outer Exeter and is geographically compact, the western boundary following the Exe down to Exmouth. East lie the resort of Sidmouth and historic Ottery St Mary. Residents are generally affluent, and ageing: about one in three is 65 or over. Scavengers from across Britain descended on Branscombe beach when a freighter ran aground in 2007, depositing car parts and BMW motorcycles. The old seat had been Tory since 1945.

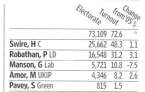

	Electorate	Turnout %	Change from '05 %
	73,109	72.6	☆
Swire, H C	25,662	48.3	1.1
Robathan, P LD	16,548	31.2	3.1
Manson, G Lab	5,721	10.8	-7.5
Amor, M UKIP	4,346	8.2	2.6
Pavey, S Green	815	1.5	

50%
Majority 9,114

C LD Lab UKIP

Devon North — Liberal Democrat hold

Nick Harvey
b. Aug 3, 1961
MP 1992-

Prominent in Paddy Ashdown's Lib-Lab project of 1990s. From Lib Dems' centre-right. Min: Defence (Armed Forces) 2010-. Spokesman for Commons Commission during expenses scandal. LD Shadow Secretary: Defence 2006-10. Member/spokes, HoC Commission 2005-. LD spokes: Culture, Media & Sport 2001-03; health 1999-2001; constitution 1997-99; trade & industry 1994-97; transport 1992-94. VP, Fed of Economic Devt Auths. Communications and marketing consultant and executive. Union of Liberal Students. Married, one daughter, one son. Education: Queen's College, Taunton; Middlesex Poly (BA business studies).

Philip Milton (C) b. Apr 29, 1962. Financial adviser, businessman.
Stephen Crowther (UKIP) b. Jan 19, 1957. Writer and communication consultant, assistant to MEPs.

Constituency
North Devon is a rural constituency with significant agriculture and villages dotted around rugged countryside. Main town and commercial centre is Barnstaple, which claims to be the oldest borough in Britain. Tourism is a big employer, benefiting from a long coastline with dramatic cliffs and sands that include award-winning Woolacombe beach. Two RAF search-and-rescue Sea King helicopters fly from the Royal Marine base at Chivenor. Seat has alternated between Tory and Liberal, most recently won by the Lib Dems in 1992.

	Electorate	Turnout %	from '05 %	Change
	74,508	68.9		☆
Harvey, N LD	24,305	47.4	0.9	
Milton, P C	18,484	36.0	0.3	
Crowther, S UKIP	3,720	7.3	2.0	
Cann, M Lab	2,671	5.2	-3.7	
Knight, L Green	697	1.4	-2.4	
Marshall, G BNP	614	1.2		
Cann, R Ind	588	1.2		
Vidler, N Eng	146	0.3		
Sables, G Comm	96	0.2		

50%
Majority 5,821

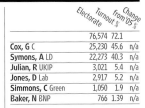

LD C UKIP Lab

Devon South West — Conservative hold

Gary Streeter
b. Oct 2, 1955
MP 1992-

Evangelical Christian, interested in human rights and overseas aid. Shadow Minister: International Affairs 2003-04. Shadow Sec of State: International Dev't 1998-2001. Parly under-Sec Lord Chancellor's Deptartment 1996-97. Parliamentary private secretary to: Sir Nicholas Lyell 1994-95; Sir Derek Spencer 1993-5. Opposition spokes 1997-98. Assistant government whip 1995-96. Vice-Chair Conservative Party 2001-02. Member of Parliament Plymouth Sutton 1992-7. Councillor Plymouth CC 1986-92. Solicitor, Foot & Bowden. Married, one daughter, one son. Education: Tiverton Grammar; KCL (LLB)

Anna Pascoe (LD) b. Dec 24, 1981. Hotel manager. Ed: Southampton Uni.
Luke Pollard (Lab) b. Apr 10, 1980. Head of public affairs for ABTA. Ed: Exeter Uni.
Hugh Williams (UKIP)

Constituency
From Dartmoor, at the north of the constituency, the River Erme tumbles down through the busy market town of Ivybridge, emerging on to a stretch of coastline that is less reliant on tourism than that in the neighbouring Totnes seat. Many commuters reside in the western end of South Hams and in the generally affluent red-brick settlements of Plympton and Plymstock, on the outskirts of Plymouth. The seat has returned Tory MPs with sizeable majorities in recent decades.

	Electorate	Turnout %	from '05 %	Change
	70,059	56.0		☆
Streeter, G C	27,908	56.0	11.6	
Pascoe, A LD	12,034	24.1	0.3	
Pollard, L Lab	6,193	12.4	-11.9	
Williams, H UKIP	3,084	6.2	-1.3	
Brean, V Green	641	1.3		

50%
Majority 15,874

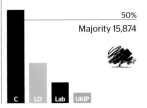

C LD Lab UKIP

Devon West & Torridge — Conservative hold

Geoffrey Cox
b. Apr 30, 1960
MP 2005-

Ruddy-cheeked, talented barrister from West Country family, son of a soldier. Member, NFU. Committee: Environment, Food & Rural Affairs (2006-10). Founded Thomas More Chambers, served as standing counsel to Mauritius. Appointed Queen's Counsel 2003. Married, one daughter, two sons. Education: King's College, Taunton; Downing College, Cambridge (English and law).

Adam Symons (LD) b. 1973. Cllr, Torridge DC. Education: Oxford University.
Robin Julian (UKIP) Farmer. Education: Wishmore Cross School, Camberley.

Darren Jones (Lab) b. Nov 13, 1986. Law student. Education: Plymouth University.

Constituency
Stretching north from the outskirts of Plymouth to Bideford Bay, this huge constituency contains much of Dartmoor and has a distinctly rural character, with significant agriculture and many self-employed residents. Visitors flock to the private 16th-century village of Clovelly, Lundy Island (resident population about 18) and Westward Ho!, the only place name in Britain with an exclamation mark. Once a safe Tory seat, voters embraced their MP's defection to the Lib Dems in 1995 and elected another Lib Dem at the next two elections, before the Tories won it back in 2005.

	Electorate	Turnout %	from '05 %	Change
	76,574	72.1		
Cox, G C	25,230	45.6	n/a	
Symons, A LD	22,273	40.3	n/a	
Julian, R UKIP	3,021	5.4	n/a	
Jones, D Lab	2,917	5.2	n/a	
Simmons, C Green	1,050	1.9	n/a	
Baker, N BNP	766	1.39	n/a	

50%
Majority 2,957

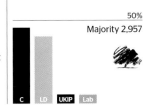

C LD UKIP Lab

Dewsbury — Conservative gain

Simon Reevell
b. Mar 2, 1966
MP 2010-

Criminal barrister specialising in defending service personnel at courts martial; re-trained in law after injury thwarted military career ambition (had army scholarship and cadetship). Born and brought up in West Yorkshire. Keen tennis player. Church warden. Married. Ed: Boston Spa Comp; Manchester Poly (BA Hons Economics); Poly of Central London (Dip Law); Inns of Court Sch of Law (BVC).

Shahid Malik (Lab) b. Nov 24, 1967. MP 2005-10. Britain's first Muslim Minister (Communities 2009-10). Parly Under-Sec: Justice 2008-09; Int Dev't 2007-08. Resigned while expenses were investigated, later cleared.
Andrew Hutchinson (LD) Manager of local business.
Khizar Iqbal (Ind) Owns dairy business. Cllr, Kirklees. Ex-Conservative.

Constituency
The hilly town of Dewsbury, roughly equidistant between Huddersfield to its west and Bradford and Leeds to the north, is at the northern extremity of the seat. Southern boundaries have been extended through the moorland to Denby Dale, increasing the electorate by 13,000. In 2005 Dewsbury had the highest BNP vote of any constituency, reflecting divisions between poor, white-dominated estates, such as Dewsbury Moor, home to the "kidnapped" schoolgirl Shannon Matthews, and enclaves such as Savile Town, where more than 90 per cent of people are Muslim. Labour had held since 1987.

	Electorate	Turnout %	Change from '05 %
	78,901	68.5	☆
Reevell, S C	18,898	35.0	3.3
Malik, S Lab	17,372	32.2	-8.4
Hutchinson, A LD	9,150	16.9	3.2
Iqbal, K Ind	3,813	7.1	
Roberts, R BNP	3,265	6.1	
Cruden, A Green	849	1.6	-0.5
Felse, M Eng	661	1.2	

50%
Majority 1,526

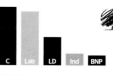

C | Lab | LD | Ind | BNP

Don Valley — Labour hold

Caroline Flint
b. Sep 20, 1961
MP 1997-

Glamorous Blairite with chequered career, never really made it as a minister. Quit as Europe Minister (2008-09) in a huff after being denied promotion, launched scathing attack on Brown's use of women as "window-dressing" but has had little impact since. Prev. Min: Housing (att. Cabinet) 2008. Min: Yorks & Humber 2007-08; Employment 2007-08; Public Health 2006-07. Parly-Under-Sec: Health 2005-07; Home 2003-05. PPS to: John Reid 2002-03; Peter Hain 2001-02. GMB researcher/pol officer. Shop steward. Divorced; re-married. One daughter, one son, one step-son. Education: Twickenham Girls School; Richmond Tertiary College; East Anglia (BA American history/literature, film studies).

Matthew Stephens (C) Business coach, keynote speaker.
Edward Simpson (LD) b. Nov 16, 1940. Councillor.

Constituency
Curving south and east of Doncaster, the South Yorks seat is mostly rural. At the west is Edlington, the former pit village where in 2009 two young brothers tortured two children. Rossington and Auckley are at the centre and Thorne, newly added in the north east, is a market town amid a flat, canalled landscape known as Little Holland. Severe deprivation has followed pit closures, but there has been regeneration. EU funding helped to build Robin Hood airport. The seat has a long Labour history.

	Electorate	Turnout %	Change from '05 %
	73,214	59.3	
Flint, C Lab	16,472	37.9	-18.6
Stephens, M C	12,877	29.7	2.7
Simpson, E LD	7,422	17.1	0.6
Toseland, E BNP	2,112	4.9	
Shaw, W UKIP	1,904	4.4	
Aston, B Eng	1,756	4.0	
Williams, M Ind	887	2.0	

50%
Majority 3,595

Lab | C | LD

Doncaster Central — Labour hold

Rosie Winterton
b. Aug 10, 1958
MP 1997-

Hardened veteran. Min: BIS/CLG 2009-10; Work & Pensions 2008-09; Yorkshire and the Humber 2008-; Transport 2007-08; Health 2003-07. Parly Sec, Lord Chancellor's Dept 2001-03. Parly officer. Head of John Prescott private office as Labour Party deputy leader 1994-97. MD Connect Public Affairs. TGWU branch officer. NUJ. Education: Doncaster GC; Hull (BA hist).

Gareth Davies (C) Works in asset management. Education: Nottingham University.
Patrick Wilson (LD) Careers adviser. Contested Doncaster Central 2005. Education: Huddersfield University.

Constituency
Set on the Don in the South Yorkshire coalfields, the town suffered from pit closures in the Eighties. Regeneration projects have injected £1 billion since the millennium but much of the borough remains severely deprived. Since the mid-Nineties, a series of scandals have made Doncaster a byword for local government corruption and incompetence, most recently with lamentable failings in its children's services. There is a small Pakistani community and the BNP and UKIP have had a presence in recent elections. Once held by the Tories, it has been Labour since 1964.

	Electorate	Turnout %	Change from '05 %
	75,207	55.5	
Winterton, R Lab	16,569	39.7	-11.3
Davies, G C	10,340	24.8	6.1
Wilson, P LD	8,795	21.1	-2.6
Parramore, L Eng	1,816	4.4	
Bettney, J BNP	1,762	4.2	
Andrews, M UKIP	1,421	3.4	0.0
Pickles, S Ind	970	2.3	
Williams, D R and E	72.0	0.17	

50%
Majority 6,229

Lab | C | LD

Doncaster North | Labour hold

Ed Miliband
b. Dec 24, 1969
MP 2005-

Brownite, seen as more personable than elder brother. Candidate for Labour leadership 2010. Sec of State: Energy & Climate Change 2008-10. Minister: Cabinet Office/Chancellor, Duchy of Lancaster, 2007-08. Parly Sec, Cabinet Office 2006-07. Special adviser to Gordon Brown as Chancellor 1997-2002. Chair, Council of Economic Advisers. Economics teacher, Harvard. TGWU/USDAW. Jewish, younger brother of David. Partner, one son. Education: Corpus Christi Coll, Oxford (BA PPE); London School of Economics (MSc Econ).

Sophie Brodie (C) Business journalist. Education: Oxford Uni.

Edward Sanderson (LD) b. Aug 23, 1986. Citizens Advice Bureau trainee adviser. Education: York University, Warwick University.
Pamela Chambers (BNP) b. Apr 20, 1959. Residential care officer. Education: Mexborough Secondary School.
Wayne Crawshaw (Eng Dem)

Constituency
Substantially larger than the old seat of the same name, the South Yorkshire constituency reaches to Mexborough in the west and covers largely rural areas north of Doncaster. Bentley lies on the northern banks of the Don and Adwick is farther north. The strongly working-class seat has yet to recover fully from the decline of the coal industry but large numbers work in construction and manufacturing. The seat routinely polls above 50 per cent for Labour.

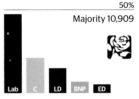

	Electorate	Turnout %	Change from '05 %
	72,381	57.3	☆
Miliband, E Lab	19,637	47.3	-3.8
Brodie, S C	8,728	21.0	1.8
Sanderson, E LD	6,174	14.9	-0.8
Chambers, P BNP	2,818	6.8	
Crawshaw, W Eng Dem	2,148	5.2	
Andrews, L UKIP	1,797	4.3	2.1
Rawcliffe, B TUSC	181	0.4	

Majority 10,909

Dorset Mid and Poole North | Liberal Democrat hold

Annette Brooke
b. Jun 7, 1947
MP 2001-

Local govt activist-turned-MP. LD Shad Min: Schools 2008-10; Young People 2007; Families 2006-10; Education 2005-06. LD spokes: children 2004-; home affairs 2001-04. LD whip 2001-03. Member, cttees: Children, Schools & Families 2007-; Public Accounts 2006-08; Procedure 2005-06; Public Admin 2001-05. Member, European Standing Cttee B 2001-02. Cllr, Poole BC 1986-2003 (mayor 1997-98; sheriff 1996-97). Head of Economics, Talbot Heath Sch Bournemouth. Business partner/owner. Counsellor / tutor, Open Uni. Married, two daughters. Education: Romford Tech Coll; LSE (BSc econ); Hughes Hall, Cambridge (CertEd).

Nick King (C) b. 1965. Entrepreneur and business owner. Education: North Devon College.

Constituency
A largely rural area north of Purbeck district, in the west, contrasts with more densely populated areas such as Corfe Mullen and Broadstone, on the outskirts of Poole in the east. Wimborne Minster lies at the seat's northeastern corner and is newly included after boundary changes. This is generally a fairly affluent constituency that is economically active, with sizeable working and middle classes. Only about one in ten residents lives in social housing. The seat was taken from the Tories by the Lib Dems in 2001.

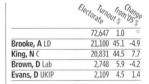

	Electorate	Turnout %	Change from '05 %
	72,647	1.0	☆
Brooke, A LD	21,100	45.1	-4.9
King, N C	20,831	44.5	7.7
Brown, D Lab	2,748	5.9	-4.2
Evans, D UKIP	2,109	4.5	1.4

Majority 269

Dorset North | Conservative hold

Bob Walter
b. May 30, 1948
MP 1997-

Avuncular pro-European old style one nation Tory. Out of sorts since party's Eurosceptic shift. Opposition spokes, Wales/constitutional affairs 1999-2001. Member, Western European Assembly 2001-. VP, Con Group for Europe 1997-2000. Contested Bedwelty 1979. Farmer; international banker, member London Stock Exchange; Dir, Aubrey G Lanston & Co. Keen sailor. Widowed, one daughter, two sons. Re-married, divorced. Education: Lord Weymouth School, Warminster; Aston University (BSc).

Emily Gasson (LD) b. Jun 23, 1970. Solicitor. Contested Dorset North 2005, 2001. Education: Durham Uni.

Constituency
This large rural seat has problems of remoteness and poor access for half the population, who live in villages. In the market towns of Blandford, Shaftesbury and Gillingham, population growth is high. The seat has one of the highest proportions of retired people but also higher numbers of young people than the rest of Dorset because of several boarding schools and an Armed Forces base. The seat has been held by the Tories since 1950 but margins of victory over Lib Dems in recent elections were sometimes narrow.

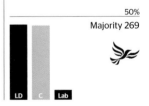

	Electorate	Turnout %	Change from '05 %
	73,698	73.5	☆
Walter, B C	27,640	51.1	4.6
Gasson, E LD	20,015	37.0	-0.9
Bunney, M Lab	2,910	5.4	-4.3
Nieboer, J UKIP	2,812	5.2	1.3
Hayball, A Green	546	1.0	-1.3
Monksummers, R Loony	218	0.4	

Majority 7,625

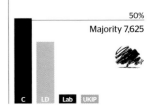

Dorset South · Conservative gain

Richard Drax
b. Jan 29, 1958
MP 2010-

Privileged former soldier and journalist, early critic of coalition deal. Lives in 7,000-acre Charborough House estate; runs as farming business. Chooses not to use full name, Richard Grosvenor Plunkett-Ernle-Erle-Drax. Worked in family agricultural firm. Journalist: BBC South Today, Radio Solent; Daily Telegraph; Daily Express; Tyne Tees TV; Yorkshire Evening Press. Soldier, Coldstream Guards. Divorced, re-married. Two daughters, two sons from first marriage. Education: Harrow School; RMA Sandhurst; Royal Agricultural Coll, Cirencester (Dip Membership, rural land management); Westminster press (Dip journalism).

Jim Knight (Lab) b. Mar 6, 1965. MP f 2001-10. Parly Under-Sec: Employment and Welfare Reform 2009-10; Schools 2005-9; Defra 2005-6. Publishing company manager.
Ros Kayes (LD) Secondary school teacher, lecturer; psychotherapist.

Constit uency
The densely populated coastal town of Weymouth and the Isle of Portland lie in the west of a constituency that arcs round Weymouth Bay to the rural Isle of Purbeck, with Swanage in the east. Weymouth is one of the least affluent towns in Dorset and the remote Isle of Purbeck has an ageing population. Second-home ownership leaves some villages all but deserted in winter and prices out young families. The Jurassic Coast and Corfe Castle are tourist attractions. Long a Tory seat, Labour took it in 2001.

	Electorate	Turnout %	Change from '05 %
	73,838	68.1	
Drax, R C	22,667	45.1	7.2
Knight, J Lab	15,224	30.3	-11.3
Kayes, R LD	9,557	19.0	3.3
Hobson, M UKIP	2,034	4.0	0.8
Heatley, B Green	595	1.2	
Kirkwood, A YP	233	0.5	

50%
Majority 7,443

C | Lab | LD

Dorset West · Conservative hold

Oliver Letwin
b. May 19, 1956
MP 1997-

Indefatigable intellectual with free-market instincts but acute social conscience. Clever and funny but unworldly; the Keith Joseph of his generation. Early Eurosceptic, prone to unguarded candour. Min: Cab Office (providing policy advice to PM in Cab office, attending Cabinet) 2010-. Chairman, Policy Review and CRD, 2005-. Shad SoS: EFRA 2005. Shadow Chancellor 2003-05. Shad Home Sec 2001-02. Shad: Chief Sec to the Treasury 2000-01 Fin Sec to the Treasury 1999-2000. Various opposition spokes. roles. Special adviser to Sir Keith Joseph. MD, NM Rothschild & Son. Married, one daughter, one son. Educated: Eton; Trinity College, Cambridge (BA hist, MA, PhD philosophy); London Business School.

Sue Farrant (LD) b. 1951. Director of a social research and consultation company. Contested Swindon South 2005.
Dr Steve Bick (Lab) b. Jul 26, 1961. GP.

Constituency
A long coastline reaches west to the fossil-encrusted cliffs of Lyme Regis. Other towns are Bridport – some of Britain's best fish and chips are sold from seafront huts – Sherborne and Dorchester. East lies Chesil Beach, an 18-mile shingle bank formed after the Ice Ages. Most of the countryside is designated an Area of Outstanding Beauty. In some coastal parishes, one in five houses is a second home. The population is ageing. Tories have held seat since 1945 but recent victories over the Lib Dems were narrow.

	Electorate	Turnout %	Change from '05 %
	76,869	74.6	
Letwin, O C	27,287	47.6	1.1
Farrant, S LD	23,364	40.8	-1.2
Bick, S Lab	3,815	6.7	-1.1
Chisholm, O UKIP	2,196	3.8	1.8
Greene, S Green	675	1.2	-0.6

50%
Majority 3,923

C | LD | Lab

Dover · Conservative gain

Charlie Elphicke
b. Mar 14, 1971
MP 2010-

Campaigned heavily against privatisation of port of Dover, at odds with Tories' 2005 stance, and secured pledge to review party position. Backed by the East Kent Hunt during election campaign. 1922 executive committee, 2010-. Cllr, Lambeth BC 1994-98. Research fellow, Centre for Policy Studies. Tax lawyer - partner, Hunton & Williams. Founded E-Print, recycled paper printing specialist business. Research scientist for ICI Pharmaceuticals. Contested St Albans 2001. Enjoys sailing and walking by the sea. Married, one daughter, one son. Ed: Felsted Sch, Essex; Nottingham (LLB); Inns of Court Sch of Law (Bar Finals)

Gwyn Prosser (Lab) b. Apr 27, 1943. MP for Dover 1997-2010 (contested seat 1992). Member, select cttee: Home Affairs 2001-10. Education: Swansea College of Technology.
John Brigden (LD) b. Apr 2, 1951. Director of public relations company. Cllr, Sevenoaks DC.

Constituency
Stretching from the Georgian town of Deal in the north, down the coast with its dramatic White Cliffs to just north of Folkestone, the seat focuses on the major port of Dover. This is the busiest passenger ferry port in the world, with shipping primarily crossing the Channel to Calais, and it dominates the economy and employment. The seat is averagely well off, with a large working class. Labour's victory here in 1997 followed 27 years of Tory representation.

	Electorate	Turnout %	Change from '05 %
	71,832	70.1	☆
Elphicke, C C	22,174	44.0	9.1
Prosser, G Lab	16,900	33.5	-11.8
Brigden, J LD	7,962	15.8	0.0
Matcham, V UKIP	1,747	3.5	0.8
Whiting, D BNP	1,104	2.2	
Walters, M Eng	216	0.4	
Clark, D CPA	200	0.4	
Lee-Delisle, G Ind	82	0.2	

50%
Majority 5,274

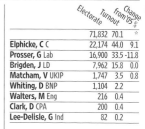

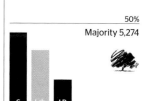

C | Lab | LD

Down North

Lady Sylvia Hermon
b. Aug 11, 1955
MP 2001-

Widow of former RUC chief constable Sir John Hermon, from mid-Ulster farming background First elected as UUP, but quit over party's links with the Conservatives. UUP spokes: Home, Trade & Industry, Youth & Women, Culture, Media & Sport 2001-05. Author, cttee member addressing Patten Report Criminal Justice Review 2000. Ulster Unionist Exec 1999. Law lecturer. Widowed. Two sons. Education: Aberystwyth (law); Chester College of Law (Part II Solicitors' Qualifying Examinations).

Ian Parsley (UCUNF) Runs a small PR company. Cllr, North Down BC.

Constituency
Home to the haves and the have-yachts, as the old joke goes, this is Northern Ireland's most affluent constituency with an air of detachment underscored by its preference for independent unionist MPs. The constituency is admired for its beautiful Belfast Lough coastline, golf courses and the old-fashioned pleasures of resort towns Bangor and Donaghadee.

	Electorate	Turnout %	Change from '05 %
	60,698	55.2	
Hermon, Lady S Ind	21,181	63.3	62.6
Parsley, I UCUNF	6,817	20.4	
Farry, S Alliance	1,876	5.6	-2.0
Kilpatrick, M TUV	1,634	4.9	
Agnew, S Green	1,043	3.1	
Logan, L SDLP	680	2.0	-1.1
Parker, V SF	250	0.8	0.1

50%
Majority 14,364

IND

Ind | UNCU | All

Down South

Margaret Ritchie
b. Mar 25, 1958
MP 2010-

An unfortunately wooden TV manner masks a steely ambition to revive the SDLP's fortunes. SDLP leader 2010-. Member, NI Assembly South Down 2003- (Social Dev't Minister 2007-). Councillor, Down District Council 1985-2009. Parly assistant to Eddie McGrady MP (her predecessor) 1987-2003. Education: Queen's University Belfast.

Caitriona Ruane (SF) b. 1962. Member, Northern Ireland Assembly (County Down). Minister of Education for Northern Ireland. Contested Down South 2005. Education: Convent of Mercy, Castlebar.

Jim Wells (DUP) b. Apr 27, 1947. Town planner. Cllr, Down DC 2001-. Contested Down South 2005, 2001. Education: Lurgan College, Queen's University Belfast.
John McCallister (UCUNF) b. Feb 20, 1972. Member, Northern Ireland Assembly (County Down). Education: Rathfriland High School, Greenmount Agricultural College.

Constituency
Held by Enoch Powell for 13 years, this rural constituency's capital is Downpatrick, the only town with a population in excess of 10,000. Mr Powell, on an Ulster Unionist ticket, remained despite a rising Catholic Nationalist population when he narrowly lost to Eddie McGrady of the SDLP in 1987.

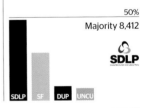

	Electorate	Turnout %	Change from '05 %
	70,784	60.2	☆
Ritchie, M SDLP	20,648	48.5	1.6
Ruane, C SF	12,236	28.7	1.7
Wells, J DUP	3,645	8.6	-7.6
McCallister, J UCUNF	3,093	7.3	
McConnell, I TUV	1,506	3.5	
Enright, C Green	901	2.1	
Griffin, D Alliance	560	1.3	0.0

50%
Majority 8,412

SDLP

SDLP | SF | DUP | UNCU

Dudley North

Ian Austin
b. Mar 6, 1965
MP 2005-

One-dimensional machine politician. One of trusted inner circle of Gordon Brown's henchmen. Parly Under-Sec, Communities & Local Gov't 2009-10. Asst gov't whip 2008-09. Minister for West Midlands 2008-10. PPS to Gordon Brown 2007-08. Special adviser to Gordon Brown 1999-2005. Dep dir, comms, Scottish Lab Party. Regional press officer, West Mids Labour. Married, one daughter, two sons. Education: Dudley School; Essex (BA govt).

Graeme Brown (C) b. 1979. Accountant for KPMG. Contested Ashton Under Lyme 2005. Ed: Newcastle Uni.
Mike Beckett (LD) Director, York and District Mind. Education: Goldsmiths, University of London.
Malcolm Davis (UKIP) Cllr, Dudley. Contested Dudley North 2005.

Constituency
To the west of Birmingham, Dudley is known as the capital of the Black Country and this seat includes the town centre, with its famous castle. Areas of severe deprivation exist, while farther out, towards the Staffordshire border, the small town of Segdley is more affluent. Suburban residential areas lie between the two town centres. Once reliant on collieries, the economy still has a manufacturing focus and the seat is strongly working-class, with more than a quarter living in council housing. Labour since 1994, the BNP has had some success.

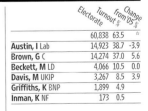

	Electorate	Turnout %	Change from '05 %
	60,838	63.5	☆
Austin, I Lab	14,923	38.7	-3.9
Brown, G C	14,274	37.0	5.6
Beckett, M LD	4,066	10.5	0.0
Davis, M UKIP	3,267	8.5	3.9
Griffiths, K BNP	1,899	4.9	
Inman, K NF	173	0.5	

50%
Majority 649

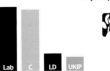

Lab | C | LD | UKIP

Dudley South

Conservative gain

Chris Kelly
b. Jun 3, 1978
MP 2010-

Youthful, softly spoken, uninspiring. Worked in Michael Howard's office. Conservative Way Forward. Euro-sceptic (Member, Business Council, Business for Sterling West Midlands). Company director, Keltruck. Oxford Uni Officers' Training Corps – Officer Cadet. Went on Project Umubano in Rwanda. Sport and fitness enthusiast. Ed: Wolverhampton GS; Oxford Brookes Uni (BA History & politics); Imperial Coll, London (MBA DIC).

Rachel Harris (Lab) b. Dec 4, 1957. Cllr, Dudley.
Jonathan Bramall (LD) b. Oct 10, 1982. Works in financial services. Contested Dudley South 2005. Education: King Edwards VI College; Essex University.
Philip Rowe (UKIP) b. Oct 16, 1952. Production Manager. Education: Sir Gilbert Claughton Grammar, Dudley Technical College.

Constituency
The southern half of this West Midlands town contains more industrial areas, especially in Brierley Hill near the canal in the east of the seat, and in the large Pensnett trading estate. White working classes traditionally employed in manufacturing are typical residents in these severely deprived areas, which contrast with the more affluent Kingswinford area in the west, dominated by residential suburbs. Labour won this seat in a 1994 by-election.

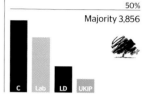

	Electorate	Turnout %	Change from 05 %
	60,572	63.0	☆
Kelly, C C	16,450	43.1	8.1
Harris, R Lab	12,594	33.0	-11.0
Bramall, J LD	5,989	15.7	3.0
Rowe, P UKIP	3,132	8.2	5.0

50%
Majority 3,856

Dulwich & West Norwood

Labour hold

Tessa Jowell
b. Sep 17, 1947
MP 1992-

Irrepressible Blairite, super-cheerful but with steely mettle. Min: London, Cabinet Office 2009-10. Paymaster Gen 2007-. Min: Olympics 2005-10. Attending Cabinet 2007-08. Sec: CMS 2001-07. Min: Women 2005-06, 1999-2001; Employment/Welfare 1999-2001; Health 1997-99. Opp spokes: Health 1996-97, 1994-95; Women 1995-96. Opp whip 1994-95. MP for Dulwich 1992-97. Councillor, Camden BC 1971-86. Care, social worker. Charities, academic career. Divorced, re-married (to David Mills). One son, one daughter, three stepchildren. Education: St Margaret's School, Aberdeen; Aberdeen (MA); Edinburgh; Goldsmiths, University of London.

Jonathan Mitchell (LD) Barrister. Contested Dulwich West & Norwood 2005. Education: Trinity College Dublin.
Kemi Adegoke (C) b. Jan 1, 1980. IT systems analyst. Education: Birkbeck, University of London.

Constituency
This South London seat, straddling the Lambeth-Southwark borough border, contains areas of contrasting affluence. Coldharbour, one of Brixton's most notorious areas and now included in this seat, is in the worst 10 per cent for deprivation nationwide, with estates such as Angell Town and Moorlands. But Thurlow Park and the leafy Dulwich area are at the opposite end. Dulwich is home to several prestigious independent schools. Labour took this seat from the Tories in 1992.

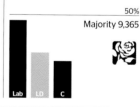

	Electorate	Turnout %	Change from 05 %
	72,817	66.2	☆
Jowell, T Lab	22,461	46.6	2.4
Mitchell, J LD	13,096	27.2	4.0
Adegoke, K C	10,684	22.2	-2.3
Collins, S Green	1,266	2.6	-3.7
Jones, E UKIP	707	1.5	0.8

50%
Majority 9,365

Dumfries & Galloway

Labour hold

Russell Brown
b. Sep 17, 1951
MP 1997-

Once again held off strong Tory challenge to retain his seat. PPS to: Gareth Thomas 2009-10; Jim Murphy 2008-10; Lord Drayson 2007; Douglas Alexander 2006-07; Alistair Darling 2005-06; Baroness Amos 2003-05, Lord Williams of Mostyn 2002-03. MP Dumfries 1997-2005. Cllr: Dumfries & Galloway Unitary 1995-97; Annandale & Eskdale DC 1988-96; Dumfries & Galloway Regional 1986-96. Chair, local community education project. ICI prod supervisor. TGWU branch sec/chair. Married, two daughters. Ed: Annan Academy.

Peter Duncan (C) b. Jul 10, 1965. MP for Galloway & Upper Nithsdale 2001-2005 during which he was the only Conservative MP in Scotland. Shadow Scot Sec 2003-05. Cllr.
Andrew Wood (SNP) b. 1956. Former director of a chemical and biocide company. Contested Dumfriesshire, Clydesdale & Tweeddale 2005.
Richard Brodie (LD) Teacher and cllr.

Constituency
This constituency stretches from Dumfries Burgh in the east to Stranraer and Cairnryan in the west and includes aspects of the Solway coastline. Labour edged it in 2005 from the Conservatives, mainly thanks to support in Dumfries, which was added to the seat. The rest of the electorate is in smaller towns such as Stranraer, Newton Stewart and Castle Douglas. The landscape around these towns makes the constituency one of the most agricultural in Britain.

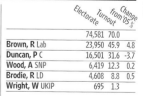

	Electorate	Turnout %	Change from 05 %
	74,581	70.0	☆
Brown, R Lab	23,950	45.9	4.8
Duncan, P C	16,501	31.6	-3.7
Wood, A SNP	6,419	12.3	0.2
Brodie, R LD	4,608	8.8	0.5
Wright, W UKIP	695	1.3	

50%
Majority 7,449

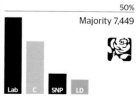

Dumfriesshire, Clydesdale & Tweedale — Conservative hold

David Mundell
b. May 27, 1962
MP 2005-

Underrated but conscientious. Immediately burdened with unlikely appointment as Shadow SoS for Scotland on entering the Commons as Scotland's only Tory MP, but missed out on Cabinet post due to Lib-Con coalition. Parly Under-Sec: Scotland 2010-. MSP, south of Scotland, 1999-2005; Transport/Telecoms/IT spokes. Corporate lawyer, Biggart, Baillie & Gifford. BT Scotland – head of national affairs. Cllr. Married; separated. One daughter, two sons. Ed: Lockerbie Academy; Edinburgh (Law); Strathclyde Uni Business Sch (MBA).

Claudia Beamish (Lab) Teacher. Ed: Queen Mary College.

Catriona Bhatia (LD) Cllr, Scottish Borders. Ed: George Watsons College; Westminster College.
Aileen Orr (SNP) Political lobbyist. Contested Roxburgh and Berwickshire & South of Scotland list in 2007; Berwickshire, Roxburgh and Selkirk 2005. Ed: Lockerbie Academy.

Constituency
Known as DCT, this large, rural constituency covers 2,000sq miles of the Southern Uplands and is the only Conservative seat in Scotland. To the south it is bounded by the Solway Firth. To the north and east, it stretches towards Edinburgh's commuter zone and in the west it includes Biggar. Labour is strong in Sanquhar and Douglas, while Conservative strength comes from Lockerbie and Moffat. The constituency contains the elopement town of Gretna.

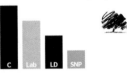

	Electorate	Turnout %	Change from '05 %
	66,627	68.9	
Mundell, D C	17,457	38.0	1.9
Beamish, C Lab	13,263	28.9	-3.3
Bhatia, C LD	9,080	19.8	-0.4
Orr, A SNP	4,945	10.8	1.7
McKeane, S UKIP	637	1.4	0.4
Ballance, A Green	510	1.1	

50%
Majority 4,194

Dunbartonshire East — Liberal Democrat hold

Jo Swinson
b. Feb 5, 1980
MP 2005-

Attracted attention when ousted sitting Labour MP to enter Commons aged 25. Was youngest MP for most of previous Parliament. Lib Dem Shadow Minister: Foreign 2008-10; Women & Equalities 2007. LD Shadow SoS: Scotland 2006-07. LD whip and CMS spokes, 2005-06. Contested Hull East 2001, Scottish Parliament Strathkelvin & Bearsden 2003. Cllr, Milngavie Community. Development officer, UK Public Health Association Scotland. Marketing manager, Spaceandpeople Ltd. Marketing exec, Viking FM. Education: Douglas Academy, Glasgow; LSE (BSc management).

Mary Galbraith (Lab) Consultant. Education: Glasgow University.
Mark Nolan (C) Cllr, Derby CC 2008-. Ed: University of Liverpool.
Iain White (SNP) Owner of small business. Contested Scottish elections, Ayr & South of Scotland list 2007. Ed: High School of Glasgow; University of Glasgow.

Constituency
This constituency is the embodiment of leafy, northeast Glasgow. The area is known for having the largest proportion of homeowners in the country, particularly in the suburbs of Milgavie and Bearsden. Despite its Labour traditions, this constituency fell to the Liberal Democrats in 2005.

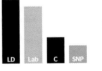

	Electorate	Turnout %	Change from '05 %
	63,795	75.2	
Swinson, J LD	18,551	38.7	-3.1
Galbraith, M Lab	16,367	34.1	1.0
Nolan, M C	7,431	15.5	-1.0
White, I SNP	5,054	10.5	4.7
Beeley, J UKIP	545	1.1	

50%
Majority 2,184

Dunbartonshire West — Labour hold

Gemma Doyle
b. 1981
MP 2010-

Part of self-proclaimed Facebook generation of new young Scottish intake. Contested European elections, Scotland 2004. Political officer, Parliamentary Labour Party. Conference development manager. Institute of Civil Engineers. Scottish Labour students, Chair Scottish Young Labour. Researcher to Cathie Craigie MSP. Part-time case worker. Member, Co-op, Unite. Enjoys crime and thriller novels. Catholic. Has long-term partner. Education: Our Lady and St Patrick's High School, Dumbarton; Glasgow (MA European Civilisation).

Graeme McCormick (SNP) Solicitor. Contested Strathkelvin & Bearsden in 1997 and Dumbarton local elections in 2007. Education: Paisley GS; Edinburgh Uni.
Helen Watt (LD) Charity volunteer. Vice convenor of Scottish Lib Dems 2006-. Contested Airdrie & Shotts 2005. Education: Glasgow Uni.
Martyn McIntyre (C) Policy officer. Contested Scottish parliament, Govan 2007. Education: Strathclyde Uni.

Constituency
The solid Labour seat contains three main population centres – the towns of Clydebank, Dumbarton and Alexandria. Shipbuilding used to be the mainstay industry in this area but much of the local employment is now in whisky production, which has an uncertain future. The constituency stretches up to the banks of Loch Lomond in the north west and Glasgow in the south east.

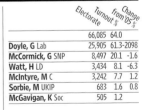

	Electorate	Turnout %	Change from '05 %
	66,085	64.0	
Doyle, G Lab	25,905	61.3	-2098
McCormick, G SNP	8,497	20.1	-1.6
Watt, H LD	3,434	8.1	-6.3
McIntyre, M C	3,242	7.7	1.2
Sorbie, M UKIP	683	1.6	0.8
McGavigan, K Soc	505	1.2	

50%
Majority 17,408

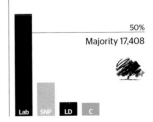

Dundee East

Stewart Hosie
b. Jan 3, 1963
MP 2005-

Regarded as competent and hard-working. SNP Chief Whip, Dep leader parly group 2007-; Treasury spokes 2005-. Contested Kirkcaldy 1997, 1992, Scottish Parl election 1999. SNP organisation convener/nat sec. IT career. Married, one daughter. Education: Carnoustie HS; Bell Street Tech (HND computer studies); Dundee Coll of Tech.

Katrina Murray (Lab) Manager for the NHS. President of Scottish TUC 2007. Education: Herriot Watt and Open University.
Chris Bustin (C) Manager. Contested Dundee East 2005; Scottish elections 2007. Education: Dundee University.

Clive Sneddon (LD) French teacher. Leader, NW Fife Council. Education: Oxford University (BA modern languages).

Constituency

This is a mostly urban seat, taking in the eastern, industrial side of Dundee. But it also contains more affluent, semi-rural areas from Angus outside the city, including the commuter-belt communities of Monifieth and Barnhill. The majority of the population is based in the city, particularly in the many large council estates. But, unlike much of Scotland, the Dundee estates are no longer solidly Labour. The Nationalists have made significant inroads and the SNP won the seat in 2005.

	Electorate	Turnout %	Change from '05 %
	65,471	62.0	
Hosie, S SNP	15,350	37.8	0.6
Murray, K Lab	13,529	33.4	-2.9
Bustin, C C	6,177	15.2	2.4
Sneddon, C LD	4,285	10.6	-0.7
Baird, S Green	542	1.3	
Arthur, M UKIP	431	1.1	0.3
Gorrie, A SSP	254	0.6	-0.7

50%
Majority 1,821

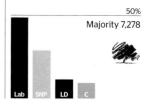

Dundee West

Jim McGovern
b. Nov 17, 1956
MP 2005-

Low-key footsoldier. Beat off Nationalist challenge to retain seat in 2010. PPS to Pat McFadden 2007-08. Member, select cttee: Scottish Affairs 2008-10, 2005-07. Tayside Regional Council 1994-96. GMB official. Glazier: Lynsey & Scott, Dundee DC. Married, one daughter, one son. Ed: Lawside RC Academy, Dundee; Telford Coll, Edinburgh (City and Guilds Glazing Craft).

Jim Barrie (SNP) Cllr, Dundee CC 2000-, convenor 2009-. Education: Harris Academy, Dundee.
John Barnett (LD) Postgraduate student at St Andrews. Education: Dundee University (LLB Law).

Colin Stewart (C) Education: Dundee High School, Dundee Uni.

Constituency

This always used to be a safe Labour seat. It has elected Labour MPs for the past 60 years but the Nationalists have worked hard in the area and this constituency is more of a Labour-SNP marginal than before. The modern Dundee West constituency has a larger rural hinterland than it used to, which has benefited the SNP. But it still retains its Labour-leaning urban base, some of which lies in the city's more deprived areas. Some of the housing is high-rise and there is a large proportion of rented social housing in this seat.

	Electorate	Turnout %	Change from '05 %
	63,013	58.9	
McGovern, J Lab	17,994	48.5	4.0
Barrie, J SNP	10,716	28.9	-1.1
Barnett, J LD	4,233	11.4	-3.0
Stewart, C C	3,461	9.3	1.0
McBride, A Ind	365	1.0	
McFarlane, J TUSC	357	1.0	

50%
Majority 7,278

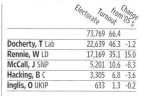

Dunfermline & Fife West

Thomas Docherty
b. Jan 28, 1975
MP 2010-

Cumbrian-born Account Director with Communications Consultancy. Contested Tayside North 2001. Communications Manager, Network Rail. Press & Public Affairs Officer, BNFL. Labour Party research assistant. Dunfermline Athletic FC fan. Married, one son. Ed: St Benedict's RC School, Whitehaven; studying at Open University (history).

Willie Rennie (LD) MP for Dunfermline & West Fife 2006-10 (won seat in by-election). LD Shadow Defence Minister 2008-10. Education: University of West Scotland.
Joe McCall (SNP) Teacher and fencing coach. Education: Aberdeen University.

Belinda Hacking (C) Clinical psychologist. Education: St Andrews University (PhD).

Constituency

The constituency is bordered by bridges, with the Kincardine across the Forth marking its westerly edge and the Forth Road Bridge marking its eastern fringe. The main population centre is the town of Dunfermline and the area used to be strongly Labour until it was won by the Liberal Democrats in a 2006 by-election. Industry is focused on the Rosyth Dockyard, which relies on work from the government.

	Electorate	Turnout %	Change from '05 %
	73,769	66.4	
Docherty, T Lab	22,639	46.3	-1.2
Rennie, W LD	17,169	35.1	15.0
McCall, J SNP	5,201	10.6	-8.3
Hacking, B C	3,305	6.8	-3.6
Inglis, O UKIP	633	1.3	-0.2

50%
Majority 5,470

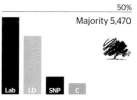

Durham, City of | Labour hold

Roberta Blackman-Woods
b. Aug 16, 1957
MP 2005-

Low profile. Interested in licensing houses in multiple occupation. Parliamentary private secretary to: David Lammy 2008-10; Des Browne 2007-08; Hilary Armstrong 2006-07. Parly assistant to Nick Brown as NE Minister 2008-. Member, select committee: IUS 2007-; Education/Skills 2005-06. GMB, UCU. Professor of social policy and associate dean, Northumbria Uni. Married, one daughter. Education: Methodist College, Belfast; Ulster (BSc and PhD social science).

Carol Woods (LD) Property investor. Cllr, Durham CC. Contested Durham East 2005, 2001. Education: Hull Uni (Zoology).
Nick Varley (C) Law student at Hull Uni.

Constituency
Built on a loop of the River Wear, the small city of Durham boasts cobbled streets, a prestigious university and a Unesco World Heritage Site enclosing the cathedral and castle. Rural areas surrounding it feature farms and woodland. Former mining settlements such as Sherburn to the east and Brandon to the west suffered with the decline of mining. Newton Hall, in the north, was once the largest housing estate in Europe. There are large student and elderly populations. Recently Lib Dems slashed the majorities in this once-certain Labour seat.

	Electorate	Turnout %	Change from '05 %
	68,832	67.2	
Blackman-Woods, R Lab	20,496	44.3	-2.8
Woods, C LD	17,429	37.7	-2.0
Varley, N C	6,146	13.3	3.9
Musgrave, R BNP	1,153	2.5	
Coghill-Marshall, N UKIP	856	1.9	
Collings, J Ind	172	0.4	

50%
Majority 3,067

Durham North | Labour hold

Kevan Jones
b. Apr 25, 1964
MP 2001-

Controversial figure, criticised for personal attacks on opponents and adversaries. Parly Under-Sec, Defence (Min Veterans) 2008-10. Member, select cttees: Defence 2001-09; Administration 2005-09. Cllr, Newcastle CC 1990-2001 (dep leader). GMB political officer/senior organiser. Parly assistant NH Brown MP. Golf enthusiast. Ed: Newcastle Poly (BA govt & public policy); Uni of Southern Maine, USA.

David Skelton (C) Management consultant. Ed: Hull Uni (politics).
Ian Lindley (LD) Risk assessor. Cllr, Northumberland CC 2008-. Ed: Sunderland Uni (PGCE).

Constituency
This relatively small seat between Durham and Sunderland is densely populated, with its chief towns of Chester-le-Street in the east and Stanley in the west. Both have areas of severe deprivation. The former's Riverside cricket stadium is the home of Durham CCC and recently hosted England one-day internationals and Test matches. Annfield Plain and smaller former pit villages are dotted through moorland and fells. The A1(M) and East Coast Main Line run through the seat, which is solidly Labour.

	Electorate	Turnout %	Change from '05 %
	67,548	60.7	*
Jones, K Lab	20,698	50.5	-13.6
Skelton, D C	8,622	21.1	4.3
Lindley, I LD	8,617	21.0	1.9
Molloy, P BNP	1,686	4.1	
Reid, B UKIP	1,344	3.3	

50%
Majority 12,076

Durham North West | Labour hold

Pat Glass
b. Feb 14, 1956
MP 2010-

Education specialist. Government adviser: National Strategies, Senior Regional Adviser (Special Educational Needs) Yorkshire & Humber Region. Acting Assistant Director of Education, City of Sunderland. Cites Nye Bevin and Barbara Castle as political heroes. Member: Fabian Soc, Amnesty Int, Co-operative Society. Medieval history/Wars of the Roses enthusiast. Roman Catholic. Unite union. Married, one son, one stepson. Ed: St. Leonard's Sch; Northumbria (MSc education and management); Sunderland (BEd).

Owen Temple (LD) Financial adviser. Cllr, Durham CC 2008-.
Michelle Tempest (C) Psychiatrist and lecturer. Education: Magdalen College, Cambridge.

Constituency
This large seat is mostly remote moorland, with occasional hamlets and arable farming. The main settlements are in the east and fairly deprived: the former steel-working town of Consett, in the north; the market town of Crook; and the former pit town of Willington, at the foot of the Pennines in the south, with Tow Law between. Other communities, such as the small town of Stanhope, are better off and line the banks of the Wear. This has long been a Labour seat.

	Electorate	Turnout %	Change from '05 %
	70,618	62.1	*
Glass, P Lab	18,539	42.3	-11.6
Temple, O LD	10,927	24.9	5.0
Tempest, M C	8,766	20.0	3.7
Stelling, W Ind	2,472	5.6	
Stewart, M BNP	1,852	4.2	
McDonald, A UKIP	1,259	2.9	

50%
Majority 7,612

Dwyfor Meirionnydd

Plaid Cymru hold

Elfyn Llwyd
b. Sep 26, 1951
MP 1992-

Earnest, slightly bumbling, but effective opponent of Iraq war in 2003. PC spokes 1997-, 1992-94. PC parly whip 1995-2001. Member, cttees: Welsh Affairs 1998-2001, 1992-97. Leader PC parly party 1999-. Member, PC policy cabinet. British-Irish parly body. Unicef parly panel. European Standing cttee B 2004-05. Barrister. Married, one daughter, one son. Ed: Dyffryn Conwy Sch; Llanrwst GS; Uni Coll of Wales, Aberystwyth (LLB); Chester Coll of Law.

Simon Baynes (C) Bookshop owner. Cllr, Powys CC 2008-. Contested Montgomeryshire 2005. Ed: Magdalen College, Cambridge (history).

Alwyn Humphreys (Lab) Manager for US co. Ed: Harper Adams Uni Coll.
Steve Churchman (LD) Shopkeeper/ sub-postmaster. Contested Welsh Assembly elections 2007, 2003; Barking 1992. Ed: Westminster Tech Coll.

Constituency
This new seat has been created from the old Meirionnydd Nant Conwy seat and parts of Caernarfon. It encompasses the Lleyn Peninsula, with a coastline stretching along Caernarfon Bay in the north, out to Bardsey Sound, and then around Cardigan Bay to the Dovey Estuary in the south. The main coastal towns are Pwllheli, Criccieth, Porthmadog, Barmouth and Tywyn. Inland are Dolgellau and Blaenau Ffestiniog. Hill farming is important to the area's economy and there are high numbers of Welsh speakers, helping to make this area safe for Plaid Cymru.

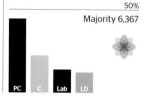

	Electorate	Turnout %	Change from 05 %
	45,354	63.7	☆
Llwyd, E PC	12,814	44.3	-6.4
Baynes, S C	6,447	22.3	8.1
Humphreys, A Lab	4,021	13.9	-7.8
Churchman, S LD	3,538	12.2	1.3
Hughes, L Ind	1,310	4.5	
Wykes, F UKIP	776	2.7	0.3

50%
Majority 6,367

| PC | C | Lab | LD |

Ealing Central & Acton

Conservative gain

Angie Bray
b. Oct 13, 1953
MP 2010-

Brash, outspoken, best known for leading campaign against London congestion charging. 1922 executive committee, 2010-. Contested East Ham 1997. London Assembly member (London West Central) 2000-08. Leader of London Assembly Con Group 2006-07. Media/public affairs consultant, Ian Greer Assocs, APCO. Press secretary to Chris Patten as Con Party Chair. Head of Broadcast Unit, CCHQ press office. Radio presenter/ journalist, LBC radio/ BFBS Gibraltar. VP, Conservative Arab Network, Con Friends of Poland. Keen tennis player and musician. Lives with partner. Ed: St Andrews (medieval hist); London Coll of Printing (radio journalism).

Bassam Mahfouz (Lab) Parliamentary researcher. Cllr, Ealing BC. Education: Gunnersbury Roman Catholic High School, Ealing; London Guildhall.
Jon Ball (LD) Company director. Cllr, Ealing BC. Ed: Hertfordshire Uni.

Constituency
Based on the old Ealing, Acton & Shepherd's Bush seat, which straddled borough borders, this new seat has lost the Shepherd's Bush area. It has been extended west to include the centre of Ealing, with the affluent area around Ealing Broadway Tube and common. Acton is in the east and is less prosperous. The north of the seat contains some of the Park Royal industrial estate. The old seat was won by Labour in 1997, but the Ealing area previously had a Tory MP.

	Electorate	Turnout %	Change from 05 %
	63,489	74.3	☆
Bray, A C	17,944	38.0	6.8
Mahfouz, B Lab	14,228	30.1	-3.2
Ball, J LD	13,041	27.6	-3.0
Carter, J UKIP	765	1.6	
Edwards, S Green	737	1.6	-3.3
Fernandes, S Ch	295	0.6	
Akaki, S Ind	190	0.4	

50%
Majority 3,716

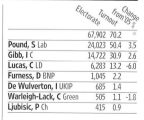

| C | Lab | LD |

Ealing North

Labour hold

Stephen Pound
b. Jul 3, 1948
MP 1997-

Wit and bon viveur. PPS to: Sadiq Khan 2009-10; Stephen Timms 2007-09; Hazel Blears 2005-07. Member, select committees: Standards & Privileges 2003-05; Northern Ireland Affairs 1999-; Broadcasting 1997-2001. Cllr, Ealing Borough Council 1982-98 (mayor 1995-96). T&GW branch officer. COHSE branch sec. Housing officer. Student. Hospital porter. Bus conductor. Seaman. Dir, Hanwell Community Centre. Married, one daughter, one son. Ed: LSE (BSc econ/ industrial relations dip; union pres).

Ian Gibb (C) Civil engineer. Cllr, Ealing BC 1992-. Contested North Warwickshire in 2005.

Chris Lucas (LD) Sales director. Education: Middlesex University.

Constituency
This seat includes Hanwell, with its 1930s semis, and the residential suburb of Perivale, which includes an industrial estate and the distinctive Art Deco Hoover Building (now Tesco). Both of these areas are affluent and the Greenford area is also comfortably well off. In Northolt, however, more than 30 per cent of residents have no skills and there are areas of severe deprivation. Ealing is home to the largest Polish community in London, with 21,000 in the borough given national insurance numbers between 2002 and April 2008. This has tended to be a bellwether seat.

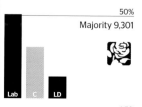

	Electorate	Turnout %	Change from 05 %
	67,902	70.2	☆
Pound, S Lab	24,023	50.4	3.5
Gibb, I C	14,722	30.9	2.6
Lucas, C LD	6,283	13.2	-6.0
Furness, D BNP	1,045	2.2	
De Wulverton, I UKIP	685	1.4	
Warleigh-Lack, C Green	505	1.1	-1.8
Ljubisic, P Ch	415	0.9	

50%
Majority 9,301

| Lab | C | LD |

Ealing Southall

Virendra Sharma
b. Apr 5, 1947
MP 2007-

Long-serving Ealing cllr (1982-), elected as MP in by-election in 2007 aged 70. Indian-born (moved to UK in 1968), fluent in Punjabi, Hindi and Urdu. PPS to Phil Woolas 2008-09. Member, cttees: International Development 2009-; Justice 2007-; Joint Committee on Human Rights 2007-. TGWU. Lab Party national ethnic minorities officer. Day services manager, learning disabilities. Bus conductor. Married, one daughter, one son. Ed: LSE (MA).

Gurcharan Singh (C) Cllr, Ealing BC 1982-, Mayor of Ealing 2003-4. Contested GLA elections 2000, 2004. Defected Lab to Con 2007. Ed: Meerut University, India.

Nigel Bakhai (LD) Operations support for Xerox. Contested Ealing Southall 2005, 2007 (by-election). Contested Euro elections 2004, 2009. Ed: Bradford Uni (BSc); Nottingham (MA)

Constituency

Reduced in size, the seat has lost more than 20,000 electors, with chunks towards central Ealing cut, but well-off residential areas such as Northfield and Elthorne gained. The seat's focus is Southall, to the west, known as "Little India", which has the biggest Indian population in London, as well as a notable Pakistani population. Its bustling streets are known for vibrant bazaars. Southall has a skills shortage with about 30 per cent of working-age residents having no qualifications and large areas among the 10 per cent most deprived. The seat has returned Labour MPs for decades.

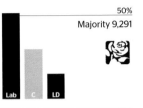

	Electorate	Turnout %	Change from '05 %
	60,379	70.8	☆
Sharma, V Lab	22,024	51.5	-5.8
Singh, G C	12,733	29.8	10.8
Bakhai, N LD	6,383	14.9	-3.3
Basu, S Green	705	1.7	-3.1
Anil, M Ch	503	1.2	
Chaggar, S Eng	408	1.0	

50%
Majority 9,291

Lab   C   LD

Easington

Grahame Morris
b. Mar 13, 1961
MP 2010-

Easington-born and locally raised constituency worker to outgoing MP John Cummings. Councillor, Easington District Council 1987-2002. NHS Medical Laboratory Scientific Officer. ASTMS Health Service Branch Secretary. Member national advisory committee for the NHS. Son of a colliery electrician and British Coal canteen worker/Labour councillor. First involved in politics through protesting with Anti-Nazi League. Sunderland FC fan. Roman Catholic. Married, two sons. Education: Peterlee Howletch Comprehensive; Newcastle Polytechnic (medical laboratory sciences BTec Higher National).

Tara Saville (LD) Teacher. Education: Cambridge University.
Richard Harrison (C) Dairy and arable farmer, food processing, property. Education: Royal Agricultural College, Cirencester.
Cheryl Dunn (BNP)

Constituency

From Seaham in the north, the seat stretches down the coast as far as Blackhall Colliery, with Peterlee, a New Town built in 1948, slightly inland. Lying between Tyne and Wear to the north and Tees Valley to the south, it enjoys their good rail and road links. Its economy and many communities were devastated by the closure of pits that employed more than half its men in the early 1980s. It has not yet recovered, with severe deprivation in much of the seat. Unsurprisingly, it is safely Labour.

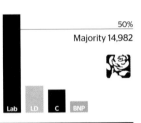

	Electorate	Turnout %	Change from '05 %
	63,873	54.7	☆
Morris, G Lab	20,579	58.9	-12.4
Saville, T LD	5,597	16.0	3.1
Harrison, R C	4,790	13.7	3.0
Dunn, C BNP	2,317	6.6	
Aiken, M UKIP	1,631	4.7	

50%
Majority 14,982

Lab   LD   C   BNP

East Ham

Stephen Timms
b. Jul 29, 1955
MP 1994-

Earnest technocrat. Survived stabbing at constituency event in May 2010. Parly Under-Sec, BIS 2009-10. Treasury: Financial Sec 2008-10, 2004-05, 1999-2001. Minister: Work & Pensions 2008; BERR 2007-08. Treasury: Chief Sec 2006-07. Minister: Work & Pensions 2005-06; Trade & Industry 2002-04; Education 2001-02; DSS 1999. Parly Under-Sec: DSS 1998-99. PPS to: Marjorie Mowlam (joint) 1998; Andrew Smith 1997-98. MP Newham North 1994-97. Cllr, Newham 1984-97 (leader 1990-94). Computer / telecoms career. Married. Ed: Farnborough Grammar School; Emmanuel College, Cambridge (MA maths, MPhil operational research).

Paul Shea (C) Founding partner of fund management business. Education: Oxford University.
Chris Brice (LD) Priest. Education: Cambridge University.

Constituency

This East London seat has been extended with the gain of the large, if sparsely populated, Royal Docks area along the Thames, which has been regenerated with conference venues such as ExCel. Its other main areas are Beckton, East Ham, Upton Park and Little Ilford, all with large areas of relative deprivation. Newham is the most ethnically diverse local authority in Britain. The Asian population is concentrated in the north of the seat, comprising about two thirds in Green Street and East Ham North, where the white population is 16 per cent. This seat has a solid Labour tradition.

	Electorate	Turnout %	Change from '05 %
	90,675	55.6	☆
Timms, S Lab	35,471	70.4	16.8
Shea, P C	7,645	15.2	1.4
Brice, C LD	5,849	11.6	0.9
O'Connor, B Eng	822	1.6	
Maciejowska, J Green	586	1.2	

50%
Majority 27,826

Lab   C   LD

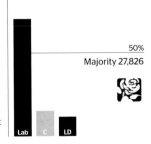

East Kilbride, Strathaven & Lesmahagow — Labour hold

Michael McCann
b. Jan 2, 1964
MP 2010-

Researcher and election agent to outgoing MP Adam Ingram. Councillor, S Lanarkshire 1999-, Deputy leader 2007-. Official, Civil & Public Services Association trade union. Civil servant, Department for International Development (then ODA). Married, one son, one daughter. Education: St Andrew's and St Bride's High School.

John McKenna (SNP) Firefighter.
Graham Simpson (C) Journalist. Contested East Kilbride in Scottish elections 2007. Education: St. Aiden's School, Carlisle.

John Loughton (LD) Scottish Policy and Communications Manager. Ex-reality show contestant. Education: University of Stirling.

Constituency
The heart of the constituency is East Kilbride, which was Scotland's first New Town. It also spreads south along the west side of the M74, taking in some rural villages. It includes the market town of Stathaven and the villages of Stonehouse and Blackwood. The seat has been held by Labour for several decades, but often with slim majorities.

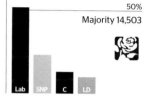

	Electorate	Turnout %	Change from '05 %
	76,534	66.6	
McCann, M Lab	26,241	51.5	2.8
McKenna, J SNP	11,738	23.0	5.2
Simpson, G C	6,613	13.0	3.0
Loughton, J LD	5,052	9.9	-6.6
Robb, K Green	1,003	2.0	-1.3
Houston, J Ind	299	0.6	-2.6

50%
Majority 14,503

East Lothian — Labour hold

Fiona O'Donnell
b. Jan 27, 1960
MP 2010-

Stepped in to fill the vacancy after sitting MP was deselected. Accomplished school debater - former debating partner of Charles Kennedy MP. Campaign specialist, Labour Party. Worked for Douglas Alexander MP, Hugh Henry, Trish Godman and Johann Lamont MSPs, and Catherine Stihler MEP. Voluntary sector work, mental health/child behaviour specialist: Capability Scotland, NCH Scotland, Stonham Housing Assoc. Member RSPB, GMB, Co-op. One daughter, three sons. Ed: Lochaber HS; Glasgow (English & history).

Michael Veitch (C) Head Scottish Con Research Unit in Scottish Parl.

Stuart Ritchie (LD) PR adviser for Engineering Employers Federation. Contested Ayrshire Central 2001.
Andrew Sharp (SNP) Owns media research business. Contested East Lothian in Scottish elections 2007.

Constituency
This coastal seat runs south and east of Edinburgh towards Dunbar. It is a commuter-belt town convenient for people working in the Scottish capital. The Cockenzie power station is within the constituency as are several picturesque villages including Aberlady. The constituency also takes in Prestonpans, a working-class area home to Tranent, a former mining town, and the market town of Haddington. The constituency is held in the Scottish Parliament by Iain Gray, the Scottish Labour leader.

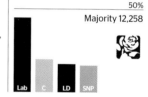

	Electorate	Turnout %	Change from '05 %
	73,438	66.9	
O'Donnell, F Lab	21,919	44.6	3.2
Veitch, M C	9,661	19.7	3.8
Ritchie, S LD	8,288	16.9	-7.9
Sharp, A SNP	7,883	16.0	2.9
Mackenzie, J Green	862	1.8	-0.7
Lloyd, J UKIP	548	1.1	0.4

50%
Majority 12,258

Eastbourne — Liberal Democrat gain

Stephen Lloyd
b. Jun 15, 1957
MP 2010-

Ousted sitting Tory MP in one of the Lib Dems' main election night triumphs. Contested Eastbourne 2005, Beaconsfield 2001. Trustee, LINK (deaf-support charity). Local campaigner against Post Office closures. Born and brought up in Mombasa, Kenya. Business development consultant: United Nations Environment Protection Finance Initiative, Federation of Small Businesses. Business development director, Grass Roots. Divorced, two step-children. Ed: St George's College, Weybridge.

Nigel Waterson (C) MP 1992-2010. Shadow Min: Pensions 2003-10. Opposition spokesman, Trade & Industry 2001-02. Shadow Min: DETR 1999-2001. Opposition Whip 1997-99. Solicitor. Ed: Queen's Coll, Oxford.

Constituency
The East Sussex town of Eastbourne, at the foot of the South Downs, is a popular resort, boasting an impressive coast that stretches from sandy beaches to the dramatic white cliffs that have made Beachy Head a popular beauty spot – and infamous suicide location. The seat is predominantly affluent and notable for its many retired people. Conservative dominance since the First World War was interrupted in 1990, when Lib Dems took the constituency in a by-election after the murder of its MP, Ian Gow, by the IRA. The Tories regained it in 1992 but margins of victory were slim in recent elections and the Lib Dems regained it in 2010.

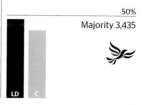

	Electorate	Turnout %	Change from '05 %
	77,840	67.0	☆
Lloyd, S LD	24,658	47.3	5.7
Waterson, N C	21,223	40.7	-2.3
Brinson, D Lab	2,497	4.8	-6.0
Shing, S Ind	1,327	2.6	
Needham, R UKIP	1,305	2.5	0.0
Poulter, C BNP	939	1.8	
Baldry, M Ind	101	0.2	
Gell, K Ind	74	0.1	

50%
Majority 3,435

Eastleigh
Liberal Democrat hold

Chris Huhne
b. Jul 2, 1954
MP 2005-

Emerged as figurehead for party's left/green grassroots, despite liberal economic outlook. Ruthless streak. Sec of State: Energy & Climate Change 2010-. Contested LD leadership 2006, 2007. LD Shad Sec: Home 2007-10, Justice/Lord Chancellor 2008-09; EFRA 2006-07; Chief Sec to Treasury 2005-06. MEP for SE 1999-2005 (dep leader LD group, EP LD spokes on economics). Contested Oxford W & Abingdon 1987, Reading E 1983. MD and founder, Sovereign Risk Ratings IBCA Ltd. Journalist/editor. Trainee journalist. NUJ. Married, one daughter, two sons, two stepdaughters. Ed: Westminster Sch; Sorbonne; Magdalen Coll, Oxford (PPE).

Maria Hutchings (C) Campaigner for special needs services. Ed: Goldsmiths University.
Leo Barraclough (Lab) Journalist. Ed: Manchester University.

Constituency
From the marinas and yacht clubs of Hamble, on the Hampshire coast, the seat curves round Southampton and north to Eastleigh itself, a former railway town undergoing regeneration. The seat's many commuters generally enjoy higher salaries in Southampton than those available in the constituency. Retail is the chief economic sector and there is a sizeable working class. Lib Dems overturned decades of Tory dominance in a 1994 by-election after the infamous death of the MP, Stephen Milligan. They held on in subsequent terms but the 2001 majority was 568.

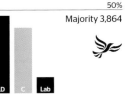

	Electorate	Turnout %	Change from '05 %
	77,435	69.3	
Huhne, C LD	24,966	46.5	8.2
Hutchings, M C	21,102	39.3	2.1
Barraclough, L Lab	5,153	9.6	-11.5
Finch, R UKIP	1,933	3.6	0.2
Pewsey, T Eng Dem	249	0.46	
Stone, D Ind	154	0.3	
Low, K Nat	93	0.2	

50%
Majority 3,864

Eddisbury
Conservative hold

Stephen O'Brien
b. Apr 1, 1957
MP 1999-

Genial, competent, from party's mainstream. Parly Under-Sec: Int Devt 2010-. Shadow Minister for: Health 2005-10; Skills 2005. Shadow Sec: Industry 2003-05. Shadow Minister: Treasury 2002-03. Opposition whip 2001-02. PPS to Francis Maude 2000. Businessman, manufacturing industrialist, solicitor. Married, one daughter, two sons. Ed: various Kenya/UK; Emmanuel College, Cambridge (MA law); College of Law.

Robert Thompson (LD) Retired. Local Councillor. Ed: Nottingham Uni.
Pat Merrick (Lab) Youth worker. Cllr, Cheshire West & Chester (dep Lab group leader). Ed: Chester Uni.

Constituency
This seat comprises a large expanse of rural Cheshire, between Chester and Crewe, and one significant town, Winsford, at the northeastern corner. A notable agricultural sector, predominantly dairy farming, employs about 5 per cent of the population. Within easy reach of Manchester and Liverpool to the north, the rural area is also home to many affluent, Conservative-voting professionals. Winsford, built around the salt mining industry, is less affluent and tends to be Labour-leaning, meaning that Conservative margins of victory here have been slim.

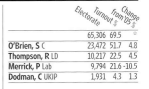

	Electorate	Turnout %	Change from '05 %
	65,306	69.5	☆
O'Brien, S C	23,472	51.7	4.8
Thompson, R LD	10,217	22.5	4.5
Merrick, P Lab	9,794	21.6	-10.5
Dodman, C UKIP	1,931	4.3	1.3

50%
Majority 13,255

Edinburgh East
Labour hold

Sheila Gilmore
b. Oct 1, 1949
MP 2010-

Aberdeen-born but Edinburgh-raised, long-serving councillor (Moredun, 1991-2007; convenor for housing 1999-2007). Contested Edinburgh Pentlands, Holyrood election 2007. Election agent to Nigel Griffiths MP. Solicitor, specialising in women's rights and on legal aid cases. Helped found Edinburgh Women's Rape Crisis Centre. Teacher. Keen cyclist. Married, three daughters, one son. Ed: George Watson's College, Edin; Kent (History & Politics); Law

George Kerevan (SNP) Associate editor and columnist at *The Scotsman*. Education: Glasgow University.

Beverley Hope (LD) Constituency organiser for West Edinburgh Liberal Democrats. Education: Cardiff University; St Andrews University.
Martin Donald (C) Politics researcher. Education: Aberdeen Uni.

Constituency
The constituency is home to some of the capital's most notable tourist attractions including Arthur's Seat, the main peak of the group of hills that form most of Holyrood Park and tower over the Royal Palace of Holyroodhouse, St Giles Castle and Princes Street Gardens. Towards the south and east it also comprises some of Edinburgh's more deprived areas such as the Craigmiller housing estate. It is traditionally a safe Labour seat.

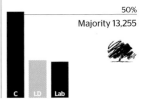

	Electorate	Turnout %	Change from '05 %
	60,941	65.4	
Gilmore, S Lab	17,314	43.4	3.4
Kerevan, G SNP	8,133	20.4	3.4
Hope, B LD	7,751	19.4	-5.0
Donald, M C	4,358	10.9	0.6
Harper, R Green	2,035	5.1	-0.6
Clark, G TUSC	274	0.7	

50%
Majority 9,181

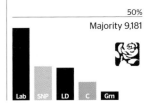

Edinburgh North & Leith

Mark Lazarowicz
b. Aug 8, 1953
MP 2001-

Reputation as cerebral but with a strong local profile. PM's special representative on carbon trading 2008-10. PPS to: David Cairns 2007-08. Member, SERA, Co-operative party, Scottish Labour party (Chair 1989-90). TGWU. Advocate. Gen Sec, British Youth Council Scotland. Organiser Scottish Ed and Action for Devt. Married, one daughter, three sons. Education: St Benedicts School, London; St Andrews University (MA moral philosophy & medieval history); Edinburgh University (LLB).

Kevin Lang (LD) Public affairs consultant. Education: Edinburgh University.

Iain McGill (C) Director of employment agency. Contested Midlothian 2005, Airdrie & Shotts in Scottish parliament elections.
Calum Cashley (SNP) SNP policy adviser and blogger. Stood for Dundee West in Scottish parliament election 1999. Ed: Napier Uni.

Constituency

This seat takes in Edinburgh's famous shopping area Princes Street as well as some of the Neo-Classical streets of New Town. It also runs to the port of Leith, which has been transformed from a heavy engineering and shipbuilding area to a thriving and trendy community with many bars and restaurants. It also has redeveloped flats that have attracted young professionals. The less prosperous parts of the constituency such as Pilton ensure that Labour has high levels of support.

	Electorate	Turnout %	Change from '05 %
	69,204	68.4	
Lazarowicz, M Lab	17,740	37.5	3.23
Lang, K LD	16,016	33.8	4.7
McGill, I C	7,079	15.0	-3.7
Cashley, C SNP	4,568	9.7	-0.4
Joester, K Green	1,062	2.2	-3.6
Hein, J Lib	389	0.8	
Black, W TUSC	233	0.5	
Jacobsen, D Soc	141	0.3	
MacIntyre, C Ind	128	0.3	

Majority 1,724

Edinburgh South

Ian Murray
b. Aug 10 1976
MP 2010-

Edinburgh-born and raised local businessman, came through recount to hold off Lib Dem challenge and admitted he didn't expect to win. Cllr, Edinburgh CC 2003- (Finance and Social Inclusion spokes). Partner, Aspen Bar & Grill. Campaign manager, Edinburgh Pentlands 2001, 1997. Member, US-DAW. Supporter, Care for the Wild. Has partner. Education: Wester Hailes Ed Centre; Edinburgh (social policy & law).

Fred Mackintosh (LD) Advocate. Contested Livingstone 1992; Midlothian 2005. Education: Edinburgh Uni.

Neil Hudson (C) Lecturer in vetinary surgery.
Sandy Howat (SNP) Financial adviser. Ed: Edinburgh Uni.

Constituency

This is a prosperous constituency that begins to the south of Edinburgh city centre. It takes in affluent residential areas such as Marchmont, Merchiston and Morningside as well as the more suburban Fairmilehead at the foot of the Braid Hills. It extends to the city bypass and takes in several council estates including Gilmerton, Kaimes and Moredun. The seat has been held by Labour since 1987 but the Liberal Democrats took its Scottish Parliament equivalent in 2003.

	Electorate	Turnout %	Change from '05 %
	59,354	73.8	
Murray, I Lab	15,215	34.7	1.5
Mackintosh, F LD	14,899	34.0	1.8
Hudson, N C	9,452	21.6	-2.5
Howat, S SNP	3,354	7.7	1.5
Burgess, S Green	881	2.0	-1.2

Majority 316

Edinburgh South West

Alistair Darling
b. Nov 28, 1953
MP 1987-

The great survivor who lasted the entire 13 years in the Labour Cabinet. Popular, low-key, skilled technocrat with famous eyebrows. Admired for asserting political independence and being possibly the only one who successfully stood up to Gordon Brown. Chancellor of the Exchequer 2007-10. SoS: Trade & Industry 2006-07; Scotland 2003-06; Transport 2002-06; Soc Security/Work & Pensions 1998-2002. Chief Sec to Treasury 1997-98. Opposition spokes: Treasury/econ affairs/City 1992-97; Home 1998-92. Lab Party econ commission 1994-97. MP Edinburgh Central 1987-2005. Cllr, Lothian Regional Council 1982-87. Solicitor,

advocate. Married, one daughter, one son. Ed: Loretto Sch; Aberdeen (LLB).

Jason Rust (C) Solicitor. Cllr, Edinburgh CC 2004-.
Tim McKay (LD) Retired uni lecturer and chartered accountant. Cllr, Edinburgh CC 2007-. Contested Hamilton 1987; East Lothian 1992.
Kaukab Stewart (SNP) Primary school teacher.

Constituency

The seat takes in old tenement areas such as Dalry and Fountainbridge as well as the more affluent suburbs of Colinton and Craiglockart. It also contains the villages of Balerno and Currie, which have been Tory strongholds. Labour took this seat's predecessor from the Tories in 1997 and the boundary changes before the 2005 election boosted Labour's core vote.

	Electorate	Turnout %	Change from '05 %
	66,359	68.5	
Darling, A Lab	19,473	42.8	3.1
Rust, J C	11,026	24.3	0.9
McKay, T LD	8,194	18.0	-3.0
Stewart, K SNP	5,530	12.2	1.6
Cooney, C Green	872	1.9	-1.5
Fox, C SSP	319	0.7	-0.6
Bellamy, C Comm	48	0.1	

Majority 8,447

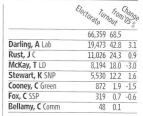

Edinburgh West — Liberal Democrat hold

Michael Crockart
b. Mar 19, 1966
MP 2010-

Former police officer with Lothian & Borders Police. Long-standing Lib Dem activist. Contested Edinburgh North & Leith 2005, Scottish Parliament elections 2007. Systems developer and IT project manager, Standard Life. Born and brought up in Perth. Enjoys photography and listening to classical music. Married, two sons. Education: Perth High School; Edinburgh University (BSc Social Sciences).

Cameron Day (Lab) Youth participation co-ordinator.
Stewart Geddes (C) Accountant.
Sheena Cleland (SNP) Assistant to Roseanna Cunningham MEP,

translator. Contested Edinburgh West in 2005; Scottish election 2007.

Constituency
The constituency, safe in recent times for the Liberal Democrats, lies to the west and north west of Edinburgh city centre. It takes in working-class areas such as Stenhouse as well as the affluent Murrayfield area. It also broadens out to take in the leafy suburbs of Costorphine, Gyle and Cramond, and reaches along the Firth of Forth to South Queensferry and Edinburgh airport.

	Electorate	Turnout %	Change from '05 %
	65,161	71.3	
Crockart, M LD	16,684	35.9	-13.6
Day, C Lab	12,881	27.7	9.1
Geddes, S C	10,767	23.2	3.8
Cleland, S SNP	6,115	13.2	4.1

50%
Majority 3,803

Edmonton — Labour Co-op hold

Andy Love
b. Mar 21, 1949
MP 1997-

Affable mainstream plodder. PPS to: John Healey 2008-09; Jacqui Smith 2001-05. Member, cttees: Treasury 2005-; Regulatory Reform 1999-05; Public Accounts 1997-2001. TGWU/Unite, NACO. Co-op party. Chartered Secretary. Married. Ed: Greenock HS; Strathclyde (BSc physics).

Andrew Charalambous (C) Property dealer, social landlord, barrister. Ed: William Foster School, Tottenham; Southgate Technical Coll, London.
Iarla Kilbane-Dawe (LD) Atmospheric scientist. Contested Edmonton in 2005. Ed: St Ignatius' Coll, Galway; Trinity Coll Dublin; Cambridge Uni.

Constituency
The distinctive social housing blocks of Edmonton Green rise up above its shopping centre, looking out over North London. The area bordering Tottenham to the south shares its deprived characteristic, as does the newly included Ponders End ward to the north. The seat is bounded by reservoirs, manufacturing and warehouses to the east, but the western end around Bush Hill Park is much more affluent, with leafy residential streets. The seat is ethnically diverse, with a notable Cypriot community. From 1983 to 1997 the Tories interrupted Labour's dominance of this seat.

	Electorate	Turnout %	Change from '05 %
	63,902	63.2	
Love, A Lab	21,665	53.7	-2.3
Charalambous, A C	12,052	29.9	2.3
Kilbane-Dawe, I LD	4,252	10.5	-1.5
Freshwater, R UKIP	1,036	2.6	0.3
Johnson, J Green	516	1.3	-1.0
Basarik, E Reform	379	0.9	
Morrison, C Ch	350	0.9	
Mclean, D Ind	127	0.3	

50%
Majority 9,613

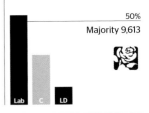

Ellesmere Port & Neston — Labour hold

Andrew Miller
b. Mar 23, 1949
MP 1992-

Known as 'windy Miller', earnest and dull. Concerned with Vauxhall plant. Elected Chair, select cttee: Science & Tech 2010-. Chair, cttee: Regulatory Reform 2005-10. PPS to: T & I mins 2001-05. Member, select cttees: Sci/Tech 1992-97; Information 1992-2001; Joint Cttee on Human Rights 2001. Pres computing for Labour. Chair, Leadership Campaign Team 1997-98. Member, First steps team. Technician/geology analyst. MSF regional official. Keen cricketer. Married, one daughter, two sons. Ed: Hayling Island Sch; Highbury Tech Coll; LSE (ind relations dip).

Stuart Penketh (C) Geological

consultant. Ed: Manchester University.
Denise Aspinall (LD) Senior lecturer in nursing, Liverpool John Moores University; mental health nurse. Ed: Liverpool Uni; Liverpool John Moores University.

Constituency
The seat spans the base of the Wirral peninsula, with Ellesmere Port on the Mersey and Neston on the Dee. Ellesmere Port is heavily industrialised and famous for the Vauxhall plant, which remains the largest employer. To the east is Stanlow refinery and there are patches of severe deprivation along the Mersey waterfront. Other parts are more affluent: Neston was originally a market town, while the flat expanse of land in between is mostly rural with villages that have good transport links to Liverpool. The seat switched from Conservative to Labour in 1992.

	Electorate	Turnout %	Change from '07 %
	63,097	70.1	☆
Miller, A Lab	19,750	44.7	-4.1
Penketh, S C	15,419	34.9	2.1
Aspinall, D LD	6,663	15.1	-0.7
Crocker, H UKIP	1,619	3.7	0.8
Starkey, J Ind	782	1.8	

50%
Majority 4,331

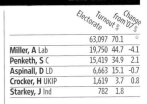

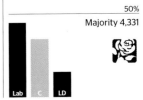

Elmet & Rothwell
Conservative gain

Alec Shelbrooke
b. Jan 10, 1976
MP 2010-

Independent-minded. Interested in Middle Eastern politics. Contested Wakefield 2005. Cllr, Leeds CC 2004-10. Campaign manager Elmet 2001. Project manager for Nanofactory at Leeds University; became researcher/assistant to pro vice-chancellor. Mechanical engineer, Lucas Heavy Duty Engineering. Ed: St George's CofE School, Gravesend; Brunel (Hons mechanical engineering).

James Lewis (Lab) Cllr, Leeds CC 2003-. Ed: Boston Spa Comp School, Leeds.
Stewart Golton (LD) Cllr, Leeds CC (leader LD group). Ed: Leeds GS; Park Lane College, Leeds; Newcastle Uni.

Constituency
Elmet is the old name for the sweep of West Yorkshire countryside that comprises the bulk of this seat, to the eastern side of Leeds, including the affluent commuter town of Wetherby. Further south are former mining communities which, though relatively prosperous, remain Labour-leaning. The boundaries have been extended to include the populous and less well-off Rothwell, at the southwestern extremity. The constituency was Conservative from its inception in 1983 until 1997.

	Electorate	Turnout %	Change from '05 %
	77,724	71.8	☆
Shelbrooke, A C	23,778	42.6	8.1
Lewis, J Lab	19,257	34.5	-11.4
Golton, S LD	9,109	16.3	-1.0
Clayton, S BNP	1,802	3.2	
Oddy, D UKIP	1,593	2.9	
Nolan, C Ind	250	0.5	

50%
Majority 4,521

Eltham
Labour hold

Clive Efford
b. Jul 10, 1958
MP 1997-

Cockney ex-cabbie, an energetic and effective constituency campaigner. Brownite. PPS to: John Healey 2009-10; Margaret Beckett 2008-09. Member, select cttees: Transport 2002-09; Standing Orders 1999-2000; Procedure 1997-2001. Vice-Chair, London Group of Lab MPs. Member, Lab Friends of India. Cllr, Greenwich Bor 1986-98. TGWU. Partner, family-owned jewellery/watch repair business. Passionate Millwall FC supporter. Married, three daughters. Ed: Walworth Comp; Southwark FE Coll.

David Gold (C) Director of marketing, Brighton College. Contested Brighton Pavilion 2001. Ed: Brighton College; Royal Holloway; University of London.
Steven Toole (LD) Geographer. Contested Erith and Thamesmead 2005. Ed: Newcastle Uni; Swansea Uni (PhD in geography).

Constituency
Just south of Greenwich & Woolwich, this South London seat is generally more affluent than its riverside neighbours, from which it gains a couple of wards after boundary changes. In the west of the seat, however, there are areas in the 10 per cent most deprived nationally. About 30 per cent of residents live in social housing. Eltham Palace and the town centre have distinctive historical architecture. The south and east of the seat border Bexley borough and share more of its suburban characteristics. Labour took this from the Tories in the 1997 landslide.

	Electorate	Turnout %	Change from '05 %
	62,590	67.1	☆
Efford, C Lab	17,416	41.5	-0.7
Gold, D C	15,753	37.5	2.9
Toole, S LD	5,299	12.6	-4.7
Woods, R BNP	1,745	4.2	
Adams, R UKIP	1,011	2.4	-0.4
Hayles, A Green	419	1.0	
Tibby, M Eng	217	0.5	
Graham, A Ind	104	0.3	

50%
Majority 1,663

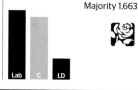

Enfield North
Conservative hold

Nick de Bois
b. Feb 21, 1959
MP 2010-

Ran 'Backing Local Business' campaign and highlit business credentials as MD, Rapiergroup marketing agency. Contested same seat in 2005 and 2001, Stalybridge & Hyde in 1997. PR assistant, Advertising Standards Authority. Ran Backing Local Business campaign. From services family. Rugby fan. Speaks French & German. Divorced, remarried. Three daughters and one son, from first marriage. Education: Culford Sch; Cambridge Coll of Arts & Tech (HND Business studies).

Joan Ryan (Lab) MP for Enfield North 1997-2010. PM special rep for Cyprus 2007-08. Parly Under-Sec: Home 2006-07. Whip: govt 2003-06; asst govt 2002-03. PPS to Andrew Smith 1997-2002. Former Teacher. Cllr, Barnet 1990-1997. Ed: St Joseph's Sch; City of Liverpool Coll; South Bank Polytechnic, London.
Paul Smith (LD) Computer programmer. Education: Oxford University.

Constituency
This is the northernmost constituency in London, its outer boundary following the M25, which separates it from Hertfordshire. A large area of greenbelt open park and farmland covers the north and west of the seat, while the southern boundary cuts through Enfield town centre. The east, around Enfield Lock, has more industrial heritage and more deprived areas. Labour took this seat from the Tories in 1997.

	Electorate	Turnout %	Change from '05 %
	66,258	67.1	☆
de Bois, N C	18,804	42.3	
Ryan, J Lab	17,112	38.5	-2.3
Smith, P LD	5,403	12.2	0.7
Avery, T BNP	1,228	2.8	
Jones, M UKIP	938	2.1	0.3
Linton, B Green	489	1.1	
Williams, A Ch	161	0.4	
Weald, R Eng	131	0.3	
Athow, A WRP	96	0.2	
Daniels, G Ind	91	0.2	

50%
Majority 1,692

Enfield Southgate Conservative hold

David Burrowes
b. Jun 12, 1969
MP 2005-

Social conservative. Shadow Minister: Justice 2007-. Member Public Administration Select Committee 2005-10. Cllr, Enfield BC 1994-2004. Co-founder and trustee, Conservative Christian Fellowship. Solicitor specialising in criminal law, Shepherd Harris and Co, Enfield. Married, two daughters, four sons. Education: Highgate School; Exeter (LLB Law).

Bambos Charalambous (Lab) Solicitor. Cllr, Enfield 1994-. Contested Epping Forest 2005. Education: Chace Boys Comp Sch, Tottenham; Liverpool Polytechnic; University of London.
Johar Khan (LD) Business development manager. Cllr, Waltham Forest

BC 2006-2010. Ed: Norlington School, Leyton; East London Uni.

Constituency
The western end of Enfield borough, bordering Barnet, is the most affluent, particularly in the large areas of green space around Cockfosters. It is typified by wide leafy residential streets with semi-detached houses. The few small patches of deprivation lie to the south, on the border with Haringey. This seat was the scene of the most memorable defeat of the 1997 election, when Michael Portillo was ousted from what had been a safe Tory seat for decades. His replacement, Stephen Twigg, was then a major scalp for the Tories in 2005.

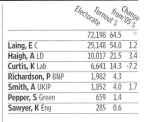

	Electorate	Turnout %	Change from '05 %
	64,138	69.2	☆
Burrowes, D C	21,928	49.4	5.7
Charalambous, B Lab	14,302	32.3	-8.8
Khan, J LD	6,124	13.8	2.7
Krakowiak, P Green	632	1.4	-1.4
Brock, B UKIP	505	1.1	-0.1
Mukhopadhyay, A Ind	391	0.9	
Billoo, S Respect	174	0.4	
Weald, B Eng	173	0.4	
Malakounides, M ND	88	0.2	
Sturgess, J BB	35	0.1	

50%
Majority 7,626

Epping Forest Conservative hold

Eleanor Laing
b. Feb 1, 1958
MP 1997-

Hard-working and excitable, but can be shrill and has never made a great impact. Shadow Minister: Justice 2007-10; Women and Equality 2005-07. Shadow Sec of State: Scotland 2005. Shadow Min: Women 2004-05; Children 2003. Opposition whip 1999-2000. Spokes, various. Special adviser to John MacGregor 1989-94. Solicitor. Divorced, one son. Education: St Columba's Sch; Edinburgh (BA/LLB; first female President, Edinburgh Univ Union).

Ann Haigh (LD) Children's guardian, social work consultant. Contested East Ham 2005. Ed: Gowan Lea School; North East London Polytechnic.

Katie Curtis (Lab) Trade unionist. Candidate in European elections, Eastern region 2009.

Constituency
This Essex seat is divided from the capital by Epping Forest. At the end of the Central Line, it is prime commuter territory. It includes the market town of Epping and suburban areas of Loughton, Waltham Abbey, Buckhurst Hill and Chigwell. It has been marginally redrawn with the loss of one ward – North Weald Bassett. There are large industrial estates and recent development in Loughton and Waltham Abbey but it is an affluent area. Winston Churchill was MP for what was the Epping seat in 1924-45 and it has remained Conservative in recent decades.

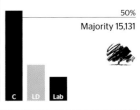

	Electorate	Turnout %	Change from '05 %
	72,198	64.5	☆
Laing, E C	25,148	54.0	1.2
Haigh, A LD	10,017	21.5	3.4
Curtis, K Lab	6,641	14.3	-7.2
Richardson, P BNP	1,982	4.3	
Smith, A UKIP	1,852	4.0	1.7
Pepper, S Green	659	1.4	
Sawyer, K Eng	285	0.6	

50%
Majority 15,131

Epsom & Ewell Conservative hold

Chris Grayling
b. Apr 1, 1962
MP 2001-

Imposing, 'attack-dog', sometimes effective but questions arise over his judgment. Heavy-handed in terms of questioning. Predictable but humiliating demotion to Min: Work & Pensions 2010- after stint as Shadow Home Sec 2009-0. Shadow SoS: Work and Pensions 2007-09; Transport 2005-07. Shadow Leader of the House of Commons 2005. Shadow Min: Health 2005; Higher Ed 2004-05; Public Services, Health & Education 2003-04. Opposition whip 2002. Cllr, Merton. Media career. Change consultant and European marketing dir Burson Marsteller. Married, one daughter, one son. Ed: Sidney Sussex Coll, Cambridge (BA history).

Jonathan Lees (LD) Charity worker. Cllr, Epsom BC 2003-. Contested Epsom & Ewell in 2005.
Craig Montgomery (Lab) Solicitor. Ed: Rawlins Community Coll, Leicestershire; Glasgow Uni (LLB); St Edmund Hall, Oxford (BCL)

Constituency
More densely populated than most of Surrey, the constituency is dominated by a chain of affluent commuter settlements running from Ashtead in the south and through Epsom, Ewell and Stoneleigh to Worcester Park in the north. These are flanked on either side by parkland and the Epsom Downs, whose racecourse is best known as the home of the Derby. The constituency has returned a Conservative MP since 1885.

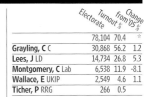

	Electorate	Turnout %	Change from '05 %
	78,104	70.4	☆
Grayling, C C	30,868	56.2	1.2
Lees, J LD	14,734	26.8	5.3
Montgomery, C Lab	6,538	11.9	-8.1
Wallace, E UKIP	2,549	4.6	1.1
Ticher, P RRG	266	0.5	

50%
Majority 16,134

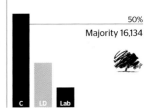

Erewash — Conservative gain

Jessica Lee
b. Apr 7, 1976
MP 2010-

Brisk, straightforward family law barrister who worked on "Breakdown Britain" report for Centre for Social Justice. Particularly interested in child protection, adoption and education. Also worked on Commission into Social Work review. Tory activist since age 15. Contested Camberwell & Peckham 2005. Ed: Loughborough HS; Royal Holloway, Uni of London (hist & pol); law.

Cheryl Pidgeon (Lab) b. Apr 8, 1958. Secretary for Midlands TUC. Cllr, Nottingham 1995-. Ed: Long Eaton GS; Nottingham Trent Uni.
Martin Garnett (LD) b. May 10, 1956. University lecturer. Contested Erewash 2005, 2001 and 1997. Education: Bentley Grammar School, Calne, University College Swansea, University College, London.

Constituency

Erewash lies between Derby and Nottingham, bounded by the Trent and Derwent rivers in the south and the River Erewash in the east. Ilkeston is in the north while Sandiacre and Long Eaton flank the M1, which passes through the south of the seat. Manufacturing is the linchpin of the economy and though predominantly working-class, there are patches of great affluence, especially in the semi-rural south west. This area has, however, been significantly cut back to accommodate the new Derbyshire Mid seat. It has been Tory since its creation in 1970 until Labour's victory in 1997.

	Electorate	Turnout %	Change from '05 %
	69,654	68.4	☆
Lee, J C	18,805	39.5	10.4
Pidgeon, C Lab	16,304	34.2	-10.5
Garnett, M LD	8,343	17.5	4.0
Bailey, M BNP	2,337	4.9	
Sutton, J UKIP	855	1.8	-0.1
Fletcher, L Green	534	1.1	
Wilkins, L Ind	464	1.0	

Majority 2,501

Erith & Thamesmead — Labour hold

Teresa Pearce
b. Feb 1, 1955
MP 2010-

Left-winger and long-term constituency activist, backed in selection as candidate by predecessor MP John Austin in face of national party support for Georgia Gould, the daughter of Blair's pollster Lord (Philip) Gould. Cllr, Erith 1998-2002. Campaigned against incinerator in constituency. Lancashire-born but London-raised, became single mother aged 18, two daughters, relied on council housing. Senior manager, Pricewaterhouse-Coopers tax investigations team. Inland Revenue. Education: St Thomas More School.

Colin Bloom (C) b. 6 Sep, 1970. Company director. Contested Halton 2005.
Alexander Cunliffe (LD) Lawyer. Education: King's School, Worcester, University of Wales.

Constituency

This riverside seat straddles two London boroughs: the former New Town of Thamesmead in the west of the seat is from Greenwich, while Erith and surroundings in the east of the seat from Bexley. About 30 per cent of residents live in social housing and areas in Thamesmead are in the most deprived 10 per cent nationwide. These give way to warehouses in Belvedere, the second-largest manufacturing area in the capital. The Thames Gateway project aims to regenerate the area. About 25 per cent of residents are ethnic minorities. Labour took this seat on its creation in 1997.

	Electorate	Turnout %	Change from '05 %
	69,918	60.8	☆
Pearce, T Lab	19,068	44.9	-7.7
Bloom, C C	13,365	31.5	5.0
Cunliffe, A LD	5,116	12.0	-0.8
Saunders, K BNP	2,184	5.1	
Perrin, P UKIP	1,139	2.7	-1.1
Williams, L Eng	465	1.1	
Akinoshun, A ND	438	1.0	
Cordle, S CPA	379	0.9	
Powley, M Green	322	0.8	

Majority 5,703

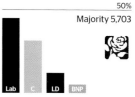

Esher & Walton — Conservative hold

Dominic Raab
b. Feb 25, 1974
MP 2010-

Likeable, clever ex-FCO adviser and lawyer. Civil libertarian-in-chief of the new MPs; author, *The Assault on Liberty* (2009). Selected by open primary. Chief of staff to David Davis as Shadow Home Sec then Dominic Grieve as Shadow Justice Sec. FCO posting to The Hague. Linklaters career, secondment to Liberty. Cites "stubborn optimists" Ronald Reagan and Mother Teresa as political heroes. Black belt, third dan karate – former member, British squad. Boxer. Son of Czech refugee. Widely travelled. Married. Education: Dr Challoners Grammar Sch, Amersham; Lady Margaret Hall, Oxford (Law); Jesus College, Cambridge (International law LLM).

Lionel Blackman (LD) b. Oct 7, 1960. Solicitor. Education: Sutton Grammar, Leicester University.
Francis Eldergill (Lab) b. Sep 20, 1963. Computing manager. Education: Goldsmiths University of London.

Constituency

Named for its two principal towns – Walton-on-Thames and Esher – the constituency includes a number of affluent villages such as Cobham and Stoke D'Abernon, and Hampton Court Palace in the northern end. Property prices are sky high as the middle-class professionals who dominate the area, utilising the excellent travel connections to London, have vociferously opposed new developments. The seat has returned Tory MPs for decades.

	Electorate	Turnout %	Change from '05 %
	75,338	72.4	☆
Raab, D C	32,134	58.9	13.2
Blackman, L LD	13,541	24.8	-4.7
Eldergill, F Lab	5,829	10.7	-8.7
Collignon, B UKIP	1,783	3.3	0.0
Popham, T Ind	378	0.7	
Chinnery, C Loony	341	0.6	-0.6
Kearsley, M Eng	307	0.6	
Lear, A Best	230	0.4	

Majority 18,593

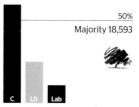

Exeter — Labour hold

Ben Bradshaw
b. Aug 30, 1960
MP 1997-

Deft lightweight. Supporter of electoral reform. Sec of State: Culture, Media & Sport 2009-10. Min: South West 2007-09; Health 2007-09; DEFRA 2006-07. Parly Under-Sec: DEFRA 2003-06; Privy Council Office 2002-03; FCO 2001-02. PPS to John Denham 2000-01. Member, cttee: European Scrutiny select cttee. Member, Lab Campaign for Electoral Reform, Lab Movement for Europe. BBC Radio 4 reporter (Sony News Reporter Award 1993) Journalist (BBC correspondent during fall of Berlin Wall). Has civil partner. Education: Thorpe St Andrew Sch, Norwich; Sussex (BA German); Freiburg Uni, Germany.

Hannah Foster (C) Human resources director. Ed: University of Sunderland. **Graham Oakes** (LD) b. Nov 29, 1959. Charity executive. Contested South Dorset 2005, Wells 2001, Exeter 1992. Ed: Westfield Comprehensive, Somerset School of Nursing.

Constituency
All but two Exeter city wards are in the constituency, bisected by the Exe. The commercial centre climbs up the hill to the historic cathedral, which stands out in a city mostly rebuilt after wartime bombing. Regeneration brought the £230 million Princesshay shopping and leisure complex, opened in 2007. Parliament Street is officially the narrowest in Britain. The Met Office is the biggest employer in a largely service sector economy and university students form about a tenth of residents. The seat has been Labour only since 1997.

	Electorate	Turnout %	Change from '05 %
	77,157	67.7	☆
Bradshaw, B Lab	19,942	38.2	-4.0
Foster, H C	17,221	33.0	8.1
Oakes, G LD	10,581	20.3	-0.7
Crawford, K UKIP	1,930	3.7	0.3
Gale, C Lib	1,108	2.1	
Black, P Green	792	1.5	-2.3
Farmer, R BNP	673	1.3	

50%
Majority 2,721

Falkirk — Labour hold

Eric Joyce
b. Oct 13, 1960
MP 2000-

Soldier who entered politics after criticising Army class system. Ultra-loyalist, but became disaffected over policy on Afghanistan. Parliamentary private secretary to: Bob Ainsworth 2009-10; John Hutton 2006-09; Margaret Hodge 2005-06; Mike O'Brien 2003-05. Member, select committees: Scottish Affairs 2001-03; Procedure 2001-05. MP for Falkirk West 2000-05. Executive member, Fabian Society. Unison. Former Army Major. Private, Black Watch regiment. Married, two daughters. Education: Perth Academy; Stirling (BA religious studies); RMA Sandhurst; Bath (MA education); Keele (MBA).

John McNally (SNP) b. Feb 1, 1951. Councillor, hairdresser. Education: St Modan's High School. **Katie Mackie** (C) Public affairs adviser to the Scottish Grocers' Federation, Education: Manchester Met University. **Kieran Leach** (LD) b. July 12, 1967. PhD student. Education: Broughton High School, Newcastle University.

Constituency
Set in Scotland's old industrial heartland, the seat combines the town of Falkirk with several smaller towns and villages. The electorate is concentrated in Falkirk where there is a strong Labour base. The Falkirk Wheel has boosted tourism in the area and helped it to recover from its industrial past. The constituency also incorporates some affluent rural areas in the south east towards Edinburgh.

	Electorate	Turnout %	Change from '05 %
	81,869	62.0	
Joyce, E Lab	23,207	45.7	-5.1
McNally, J SNP	15,364	30.3	8.9
Mackie, K C	5,698	11.2	1.3
Leach, K LD	5,225	10.3	-5.7
Goldie, B UKIP	1,283	2.5	

50%
Majority 7,843

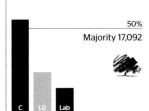

Fareham — Conservative hold

Mark Hoban
b. Mar 31, 1964
MP 2001-

Clever. Financial Sec to Treasury 2010-. Shadow Minister: Treasury 2005-10; Education 2004-05; Public Services, Health and Education 2003-04. Opposition whip 2002-03. General election campaign manager 1992, 1987. Chartered Accountant, PricewaterhouseCoopers. Married. Education: St Leonard's Comprehensive School, Durham; LSE (BSc economics).

Alex Bentley (LD) b. Apr 18, 1952. Company director of tailoring business. Lord Mayor City Portsmouth 1993. Contested Havant 2005, NW Hampshire 2001, Portsmouth north 1992. Education: Warblington Sec Sch.

James Carr (Lab) b. Jul 22, 1947. Teacher. Contested Fareham 2005, 2001. Education: Newcastle University.

Constituency
Fareham lies on the Hampshire coast, in the northwestern tip of Portsmouth Harbour. The seat encompasses the neighbouring suburban areas of Locks Heath and Warsash and is bounded by the River Hamble, a popular sailing area, in the west. Though traditionally linked to maritime industries in the nearby harbours, it is predominantly home to middle classes. The M27 runs along the top of the seat, taking commuters to Portsmouth or Southampton. Generally an affluent constituency, it has returned Tory MPs with large majorities since its inception in 1974.

	Electorate	Turnout %	Change from '05 %
	75,878	71.6	
Hoban, M C	30,037	55.3	5.6
Bentley, A LD	12,945	23.8	2.1
Carr, J Lab	7,719	14.2	-11.4
Richards, S UKIP	2,235	4.1	1.2
Doggett, P Green	791	1.5	
Jenkins, J Eng	618	1.1	

50%
Majority 17,092

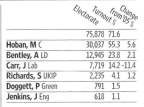

Faversham & Kent Mid

Conservative hold

Hugh Robertson
b. Oct 9, 1962
MP 2001-

A likeable, low-key sports enthusiast. Parly Under-Sec: CMS 2010-. Shadow Minister: Sport 2005-10. Opposition spokes. sport 2004-05. Opposition Whip 2002-04. Special adviser to Shadow NI Sec 1998-2001. Army Officer (The Life Guards). Assistant director, Schroder Investment Management. Married, one son. Education: King's School, Canterbury; Reading (BSc land management); RMA Sandhurst.

David Naghi (LD) b. May 13, 1957. Builder. Contested same seat 2005. Cllr, Maidstone BC 2002-. Ed: Vinters Boys' School, Maidstone.
Ash Rehal (Lab) b. Dec 13, 1952.

Consultant psychologist. Education: University of London.

Constituency
Stretching from the coast at the Swale estuary to Headcorn at its southern extremity, the seat encompasses a large rural area of the North Downs and High Weald. The medieval town of Faversham, in the north, lies amid a fruit farming area. The western border reaches the outskirts of Maidstone, where the urban cluster of Bearstead and Shepway lies by the M20, which cuts through the seat. This area is less affluent than the countryside that surrounds it. The seat has been Tory since its inception in 1997.

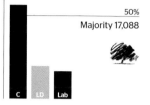

		Electorate	Turnout %	Change from '05 %
		68,858	67.8	*
Robertson, H	C	26,250	56.2	6.1
Naghi, D	LD	9,162	19.6	2.9
Rehal, A	Lab	7,748	16.6	-12.5
Larkins, S	UKIP	1,722	3.7	1.1
Valentine, T	Green	890	1.9	
Kemp, G	NF	542	1.2	
Knorm, H	Davidson	398	0.9	

50%
Majority 17,088

C LD Lab

Feltham & Heston

Labour Co-operative hold

Alan Keen
b. Nov 25, 1937
MP 1992-

One half of "Mr & Mrs Expenses" with wife Ann, who lost her seat in 2010. Member, committees: CMS 1997-10; Deregulation 1995-96; Education 1995-96. Sec, Lab FPTP group. Cllr, Hounslow Bor. Part-time tactical scout, Middlesbrough FC. Private industry and commerce (fire protection industry). Married, one daughter, two sons. Education: St William Turner's Sch, Cleveland.

Mark Bowen (C) Information manager for BA. University of Greenwich. Cllr, Hounslow BC 2002-.
Munira Wilson (LD) Works in communications. Cllr, Richmond upon Thames BC. Ed: Cambridge

Constituency
The name of the seat reflects two relatively distinct areas flanking Heathrow, which has a massive influence on the local economy. Heston and Cranford lie to its east, under the main flight path and bisected by the M4, and Feltham, Bedfont and Hanworth, to the airport's south. Hanworth has some particularly deprived areas such as the Butts Farm estate, while Bedfont Lakes is a commercial base for companies such as IBM. Labour retook this seat from the Conservatives in 1992.

		Electorate	Turnout %	Change from '05 %
		81,058	59.9	*
Keen, A	Lab	21,174	43.6	-4.5
Bowen, M	C	16,516	34.0	5.2
Wilson, M	LD	6,669	13.7	-3.0
Donnelly, J	BNP	1,714	3.5	
Shadbolt, J	UKIP	992	2.0	0.5
Anstis, E	Green	530	1.1	-1.2
Tripathi, D	Ind	505	1.0	
Khaira, A	Ind	180	0.4	
Williams, R	Ind	168	0.4	
Linley, M	WRP	78	0.2	

50%
Majority 4,658

Lab C LD

Fermanagh & South Tyrone

Sinn Féin hold

Michelle Gildernew
b. Mar 28, 1970
MP 2001-

Her popularity crosses the sectarian divide in one of NI's most polarised constituencies – holding her seat by just four votes from a unity Unionists challenge. SF social devt spokes. NI Assembly 1998-2001: Employment & learning cttee, dep chair Social Devt cttee, Centre cttee. SF Internat Dept/ Inter-Party talks team member, former women's issues spokes, press officer 1997. London office head. Married, two sons. Education: St Joseph's PS, Caledon; St Catherine's College, Armagh; Ulster University.

Rodney Connor (Ind) Former chief executive, Fermanagh District Council. Unity unionist candidate – DUP and

Ulster Unionists stood aside to allow him clear run.
Fearghal McKinney (SDLP) Journalist, formerly with Ulster Television. Recent recruit to party.

Constituency
A naturally Catholic nationalist constituency. The main town is Enniskillen, between the Upper and Lower Loughs Erne. The Irish border is a defining feature, explaining the strong presence of Republican irredentism. The 1981 election victory of the IRA hunger striker Bobby Sands is accepted as the starting point of the peace process and the rise of Sinn Féin, which holds the seat.

		Electorate	Turnout %	Change from '05 %
		67,908	68.9	
Gildernew, M	SF	21,304	45.5	7.3
Connor, R	Ind	21,300	45.5	
McKinney, F	SDLP	3,574	7.6	-7.2
Kamble, V	Alliance	437	0.9	
Stevenson, J	Ind	188	0.4	

50%
Majority 4

 Sinn Féin

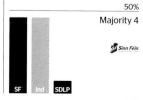

SF Ind SDLP

169

Fife North East — Liberal Democrat hold

Sir Menzies Campbell
b. May 22, 1941
MP 1987

Left-leaning elder states-man, made his mark articulating his party's opposition to Iraq war. Not a success as leader. No role in first coalition government. LD Leader 2006-07. LD Shadow Sec: Foreign Affairs 1997-2006. Lib Dem/SLD/Lib Dem spokes 1987-2001. Advocate. Competed 1964 Olympics, 1966 Commonwealth Games. UK athletics team capt. UK 100m record holder 1967-74. CBE. Married. Ed: Hillhead HS; Glasgow (MA arts, LLB law); Stanford, USA (postgrad law studies).

Miles Briggs (C) Political adviser. Member, Scottish Countryside Alliance. Ed: Perth Grammar School, Aberdeen Business School, Robert Gordon University.
Mark Hood (Lab) Self-employed project manager in financial services sector. Cllr, Fife.
Rod Campbell (SNP) b. 1953, Advocate. Contested Roxburgh and Berwickshire 2001, 2003 Scottish elections, North East Fife 2005 and 2007 Scottish elections. Solicitor. Ed: Reading School, Exeter University.

Constituency
A largely coastal constituency, stretching from Leven in the Firth of Forth to Earlsferry, Elie, Pittenweem, Anstruther and St Andrews to the Firth of Tay. The area has a thriving tourist business thanks to its spectacular golf courses and picturesque villages. Sir Menzies Campbell has turned this into a safe seat for the Liberal Democrats.

	Electorate	Turnout %	Change from 05 %
	62,969	63.6	
Campbell, M LD	17,763	44.3	-7.8
Briggs, M C	8,715	21.8	2.3
Hood, M Lab	6,869	17.2	4.5
Campbell, R SNP	5,685	14.2	3.8
Scott-Hayward, M UKIP	1,032	2.6	1.2

50%
Majority 9,048

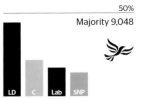

Filton & Bradley Stoke — Conservative hold

Jack Lopresti
b. Aug 23, 1969
MP 2010-

Strong voice for the TA; served five month tour in Afghanistan as Gunner, Gloucester Volunteer Artillery. Passionate about social mobility having left school at 15. Cllr, Bristol CC 1999-2007. Contested Bristol East 2001; European Parliament 2004 (South West). Member Freedom Association, Conservative Way Forward. Consultant/manager in financial services and residential property sectors. Worked in family ice cream & catering business. Interested in military and political history (member, International Churchill Society, General George Patton Historical Society – cites George Patton as hero). Married, one daughter, two sons. Ed: Brislington Comp Sch.

Ian Boulton (Lab) b. May 17, 1968. Company director. Cllr.
Peter Tyzack (LD) b. Dec 7, 1946. Contested Bristol SW 2001, Bristol E 1997. Cllr, S Gloucestershire 1995-.

Constituency
This new South Gloucestershire seat has a rural area northwest of the M5. The inner area is urban, centred on the Filton suburb of Bristol, a large employment centre. Pioneers built aircraft there before the First World War, a tradition represented by BAE Systems, Rolls-Royce and Airbus. From other constituencies have come the modern town of Bradley Stoke, social housing estates in Patchway and, southeast around the M32-M4 junction, the affluent village of Winterbourne and Victorian terraced suburb of Staple Hill. This has been a bellwether seat since 1950.

	Electorate	Turnout %	Change from 05 %
	69,003	70.0	
Lopresti, J C	19,686	40.8	5.3
Boulton, I Lab	12,772	26.4	-7.5
Tyzack, P LD	12,197	25.3	-3.1
Knight, J UKIP	1,506	3.1	0.0
Scott, D BNP	1,328	2.8	
Lucas, J Green	441	0.9	
Johnson, R Ch	199	0.4	
Zero, V None the Above	172	0.36	

50%
Majority 6,914

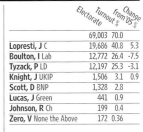

Finchley & Golders Green — Conservative hold

Mike Freer
b. Jun 29, 1960
MP 2010-

Energetic Thatcherite. Pioneer of new "easy-Council" local government model as Cllr, Barnet 2001-2010 (leader 2006-2009); 1990-94. Faced criticism over council's deposits in Icelandic banks. Contested Harrow West 2005. Self-employed consultant on regeneration and local gov't and marketing advisor. Banking career: Barclays Bank; Bradford & Bingley; National & Provincial building soc. Management consultant, Deloitte Touche Tohmatsu. Prev retail catering career: KFC, Pizza Hut. Keen cyclist. Gay, in Civil Partnership. Ed: Chadderton GS; Manchester & St Aidan's Sch Carlisle; Stirling (accountancy & business law – did not take finals); BT Vital Vision exec MBA (Harvard, Stamford, Berkley).

Alison Moore (Lab) b. Nov 8, 1958. Science researcher and lecturer. Ed: Leeds University.
Laura Edge (LD) April 6, 1978. Solicitor. Cllr, Haringey 2006-.

Constituency
Golders Green, at the south of this seat, is renowned for its Jewish community, which makes up about a fifth of the population with especially high numbers of Orthodox Jews. Hampstead Garden Suburb, founded by Dame Henrietta Barnett in 1907, is the most affluent ward in Barnet, with its sought-after architecture. Farther northeast, however, there are concentrations of council housing in East Finchley. Margaret Thatcher's seat from 1959 to 1992, it notably turned Labour in 1997.

	Electorate	Turnout %	Change from 05 %
	77,198	61.1	☆
Freer, M C	21,688	46.0	6.2
Moore, A Lab	15,879	33.7	-5.4
Edge, L LD	8,036	17.0	-0.1
Cummins, S UKIP	817	1.7	0.6
Lyven, D Green	737	1.6	-1.0

50%
Majority 5,809

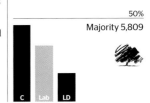

Damian Collins
b. Feb 4, 1974
MP 2010-

Highly focused and very smooth. Former chief of staff to Michael Howard, whose seat he inherits. Contested Northampton North, 2005. Political Officer, The Bow Group. PR/advertising career: Lexington Communications; Influence Communications; M&C Saatchi. Conservative Research Department and Press Office. Founding Director of the Conservative Arts and Creative Industries Network. Catholic. Manchester Utd / cricket fan. Married, one daughter, one son. Educated: St Mary's High School / Belmont Abbey School, Herefordshire; St Benet's Hall, Oxford (Modern History; OUCA president).

Lynne Beaumont (LD) b. Jan 8, 1958. Carer. Cllr, Shepway 2003-. Education: West London Institute of Higher Education.
Donald Worsley (Lab) b. Mar 23, 1951. Solicitor. Ed: Nottingham Trent Uni.

Constituency
From the eponymous towns at the foot of the North Downs, the seat stretches down the coast at St Mary's Bay to Dungeness at its southern tip. The Channel Tunnel car terminal is at Folkestone and the M20 runs down to the town. Although there are areas of deprivation in the town, the immediate surroundings are affluent. Farther south, villages line the coast while inland Romney Marsh and Walland Marsh define the landscape. The personal profile of Michael Howard, MP for 1983-2010, helped to bolster the Tory vote in what had been a marginal seat.

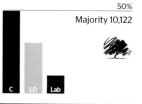

	Electorate	Turnout %	Change from '05 %
	78,003	67.7	☆
Collins, D C	26,109	49.5	-4.5
Beaumont, L LD	15,987	30.3	0.7
Worsley, D Lab	5,719	10.8	-1.8
McKenna, F UKIP	2,439	4.6	3.3
Williams, H BNP	1,662	3.2	
Kemp, P Green	637	1.2	-0.3
Plumstead, D Ind	247	0.5	

50%

Majority 10,122

C   LD   Lab

Mark Harper
b. Jun 26, 1970
MP 2005-

Solid. Parly Sec: Cabinet Office 2010-. Shadow Minister: Disabled People 2007-10; Defence 2005-07. Auditor, KPMG. Analyst and manager, Intel. Own chartered accountancy practice. Enjoys travelling and cinema. Married. Education: Headlands School, Swindon; Brasenose College, Oxford (BA PPE).

Bruce Hogan (Lab) b. Jul 5, 1949. Retired teacher. Cllr 1987-2009. Education: Beaminster Comprehensive; Cardiff University.
Chris Coleman (LD) b. Nov 11, 1978. Solicitor advocate. Contested Forest of Dean 2005, Stoke on Trent 2001. Cllr, 2002-08. Education: St Edwards

School, Cheltenham and University College Northampton.

Constituency
From the border with Wales in the south west, the constituency stretches up to Worcestershire in the north. Bounded by the Severn to the east, the Forest of Dean is overwhelmingly rural. Main towns include Lydney, Coleford and Newent. The forest has a reputation for strange goings-on – one priest warned parishioners not to dabble in the occult. Once driven by mining, the economy is dominated by small businesses and low-wage, seasonal employment in tourism. A quarter of residents commute to work elsewhere. Tories held the seat from 1979 to 1997 and regained it from Labour in 2005.

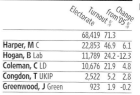

	Electorate	Turnout %	Change from '05 %
	68,419	71.3	
Harper, M C	22,853	46.9	6.1
Hogan, B Lab	11,789	24.2	-12.3
Coleman, C LD	10,676	21.9	4.8
Congdon, T UKIP	2,522	5.2	2.8
Greenwood, J Green	923	1.9	-0.2

50%

Majority 11,064

C   Lab   LD   UKIP

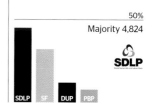

Mark Durkan
b. Jun 26, 1960
MP 2005-

A dry wit. SDLP leader 2001-10, Chair 1990-95. Member, Northern Ireland Assembly Foyle 1998- (Dep first minister 2001-02, Minister of Finance & personnel 1999-2001). Cllr, Derry City 1993-2000. Member SDLP talks team 1996-98, 1991-92. Assistant to John Hume MP. Deputy President, Union of Students in Ireland. Married, one daughter. Education: St Columb's College, Derry; Queen's University, Belfast.

Martina Anderson (SF) Member, Northern Ireland Assembly 2007-.
Maurice Devenney (DUP) Farmer. Deputy Mayor, Derry CC 2008-.

Eammon McCann (PBP) b. 1943. Journalist. St Columb's College.

Constituency
Encompasses the city of Londonderry, or Derry (sometimes called the Maiden City to avoid having to make a choice between the two names). After West Belfast it is Northern Ireland's most Catholic constituency. Protestants have retreated from the Cityside or West Bank, under the assault of the IRA's campaign, and decamped to the Waterside across the River Foyle.

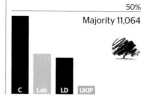

	Electorate	Turnout %	Change from '05 %
	65,843	57.5	
Durkan, M SDLP	16,922	44.7	-1.7
Anderson, M SF	12,098	31.9	-1.4
Devenney, M DUP	4,489	11.9	-2.2
McCann, E PBP	2,936	7.8	
Harding, D UCUNF	1,221	3.2	
McGrellis, K Alliance	223	0.6	

50%

Majority 4,824

SDLP

SDLP   SF   DUP   PBP

Fylde — Conservative hold

Mark Menzies
b. May 18, 1971
MP 2010-

Interested in energy security and the planning system. Contested Selby 2005, Glasgow Govan 2001. Brought up in Ayrshire by widowed mother. Marketing career: ASDA, Morrisons. Won IGD/Unilever Social Innovation Marketing award 2007. Marks & Spencer graduate trainee. Educated: Keil School (assisted place); Glasgow (Economic and social history)

Bill Winlow (LD) b. Feb 17, 1945. Contested Fylde 2005, Leeds North East 1997. Cllr, Leeds 1986-99. Medical writer. Education: Newcastle University, St Andrews university.
Liam Robinson (Lab) b. Jul 19, 1982. Railway station manager. Cllr, Liverpool. Education: University of Manchester.

Constituency
This seat on the north bank of the River Ribble is one of the most affluent areas in Lancashire. The rural areas are popular with commuters, with the M55 bisecting the seat and connecting to the M6. The BAE Systems base at Warton dominates the economy. St Anne's remains a popular seaside town and, like many coastal areas, has high numbers of retired people, as does neighbouring Lytham. The other main town is Kirkham. Blackpool airport is within the seat, which has returned Tory MPs since 1945.

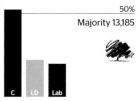

	Electorate	Turnout %	Change from '05 %
	65,917	66.3	*
Menzies, M C	22,826	52.3	-2.1
Winlow, B LD	9,641	22.1	6.2
Robinson, L Lab	8,624	19.7	-5.9
Bleeker, M UKIP	1,945	4.5	
Mitchell, P Green	654	1.5	

50%
Majority 13,185

C | LD | Lab

Gainsborough — Conservative hold

Edward Leigh
b. Jul 20, 1950
MP 1983-

Outspoken and over-excitable. Catholic, family-values right-winger with ruddy complexion. Enjoyed limelight as coruscating chairman of Public Accounts Committee (2001-10). Parly Under-Sec, DTI, 1990-3. PPS to John Patten 1990. Councillor, Richmond/GLC, Member Con Research Dept, private secretary to Margaret Thatcher. Barrister, arbitrator. Married, three daughters, three sons. Education: Oratory School; French Lycée, London; Durham (BA history).

Pat O'Connor (LD) b. Oct 21, 1959. Administrative officer for Lincolnshire Police. Cllr, Lincolnshire 1999-. Education: St Philip's Sch, Birmingham.

Jamie McMahon (Lab) b. Jan 30, 1989. Political organiser. Education: Nottingham University.

Constituency
This vast rural seat north of Lincoln is named after the small market town of Gainsborough at its western boundary. Market Rasen, best known for its racecourse, is the largest town to the east. Regeneration projects are attempting to reduce patches of severe deprivation in Gainsborough, but most of the seat is affluent, albeit isolated. There is an ageing population and though arable farming shapes the landscape, agriculture is in decline and the service sector dominates. The seat was last represented by a non-Conservative MP in 1924.

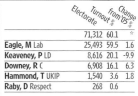

	Electorate	Turnout %	Change from '05 %
	72,144	68.3	*
Leigh, E C	24,266	49.3	5.4
O'Connor, P LD	13,707	27.8	1.8
McMahon, J Lab	7,701	15.6	-10.5
Pearson, S UKIP	2,065	4.2	0.1
Porter, M BNP	1,512	3.1	

50%
Majority 10,559

C | LD | Lab

Garston & Halewood — Labour hold

Maria Eagle
b. Feb 17, 1961
MP 1997-

Committed tribalist. Min: Justice/Government Equalities Office 2009-10. Parly Under-Sec: Justice 2007-09; GEO 2008-09; Northern Ireland Office 2006-07; Education 2005-06; DWP (disabled people) 2001-05. PPS to John Hutton 1999-2001. Member, cttee: Public Accounts 1997-99. Press officer/political education officer, Labour Party. Campaigns officer. Solicitor. Voluntary sector. Education: Formby High School; Pembroke College, Oxford (BA PPE); London College of Law.

Paula Keaveney (LD) b. Dec 29, 1959. University lecturer. Cllr, Liverpool CC. Education: Edinburgh University.

Richard Downey (C) b. May 10, 1983. Businessman. Education: Liverpool College, Durham University.

Constituency
The majority of the old Liverpool Garston constituency remains in this seat, but the new name reflects the addition of the suburb of Halewood, formerly in Knowsley South. The area in the south of the seat, around John Lennon airport and Garston Docks, is extremely deprived, as is the Belle Vale district in the north. The suburb of Woolton, however, is one of the most affluent in Liverpool and salaries compare favourably with the national average. The predecessor seats were both Labour.

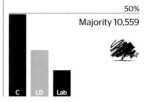

	Electorate	Turnout %	Change from '05 %
	71,312	60.1	*
Eagle, M Lab	25,493	59.5	1.6
Keaveney, P LD	8,616	20.1	-9.9
Downey, R C	6,908	16.1	6.3
Hammond, T UKIP	1,540	3.6	1.8
Raby, D Respect	268	0.6	

50%
Majority 16,877

Lab | LD | C

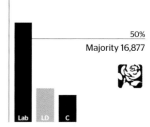

Gateshead Labour hold

Ian Mearns
b. Apr 21, 1957
MP 2010-

Owlish, plain-speaking with heavily authentic Tyneside accent. Very experienced in local government. Interested in regional development, energy and the environment. Cllr, Gateshead 1983-10 (dep leader 2002-10). Led campaign for North East Assembly prior to 2004 referendum. Chaired Council of Local Education Authorities. LGA representative, held several board roles. Member, Association of North East Councils. North East Regional Assembly. Member, Unison and Unite. Has partner. Two children from previous marriage. Education: St Mary's Technical School, Newcastle.

Frank Hindle (LD) b. 1952. Uni lecturer. Cllr, Gateshead 1991-. Contested Gateshead E & Washington W 2005. Ed: Heathfield Sch; Sheffield Uni.
Hazel Anderson (C) Full-time mother, former teacher. Ed: Cambridge Uni.

Constituency
This new dense urban seat reaches from Dunston in the west to Felling in the east, with Gateshead in the middle. Residents live in a mix of terraced housing, densely packed maisonettes and tower blocks. Though there are large areas of deprivation, regeneration on the south bank of the Tyne has created a cultural quarter that includes the Baltic Centre for Contemporary Art and the Sage Gateshead music complex, designed by Lord Foster of Thames Bank. The area has a long Labour heritage.

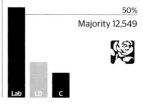

	Electorate	Turnout %	Change from '05 %
	66,492	57.5	☆
Mearns, I Lab	20,712	54.1	-7.3
Hindle, F LD	8,163	21.3	0.6
Anderson, H C	5,716	14.9	4.8
Scott, K BNP	1,787	4.7	
Tennant, J UKIP	1,103	2.9	-0.4
Redfern, A Green	379	1.0	
Brunskill, E TUSC	266	0.7	
Walton, D Ch	131	0.3	

50%
Majority 12,549

Gedling Labour hold

Vernon Coaker
b. Jun 17, 1953
MP 1997-

Solid, hard-working, reliable and respected. Unspectacular, but his discretion and loyalty means his views carry weight. Manager for Ed Balls' leadership campaign. Min: Children, Schools & Families 2009-10; Home 2008-09. Parly Under-Sec: Home 2006-08. Whip: govt 2005-06; Asst govt 2003-05. PPS to: Tessa Jowell 2003-03; Estelle Morris 2002; Stephen Timms 1999-2002. Member, cttee: Social Sec 1998-99. Cllr, Rushcliffe Bor 1983-97. Member: European Standing Cttee B 1998. Friends of the Earth, League Against Cruel Sports. Hon fellow, Unicef. Teacher, member of NUT. Married, one daughter, one son. Ed: Drayton Manor GS; Warwick (PGCE,

Trent Poly).
Bruce Laughton (C) b. 1957. Farmer and businessman. Cllr: Newark & Sherwood DC; Notts CC 2001-. Contested Sherwood 2005. Ed: Nottingham University.
Julia Bateman (LD) b. Mar 13, 1976. Non-practising barrister. Ed: University College London.

Constituency
This densely packed urban seat lies to the east of central Nottingham, with the communities of Arnold, Carlton and Gedling merging to form a large suburban sprawl. The large village of Burton Joyce is to the east. Generally well off, it is a very economically active seat with both middle and working classes well represented. After decades of Conservative dominance it was a notable victory for Labour in 1997.

	Electorate	Turnout %	Change from '05 %
	70,590	68.3	☆
Coaker, V Lab	19,821	41.1	-5.5
Laughton, B C	17,962	37.3	0.3
Bateman, J LD	7,350	15.3	1.5
Adcock, S BNP	1,598	3.3	
Marshall, D UKIP	1,459	3.0	1.3

50%
Majority 1,859

Gillingham & Rainham Conservative gain

Rehman Chishti
b. Oct 4, 1978
MP 2010-

Controversial former adviser to Benazir Bhutto. Contested Horsham 2005 for Labour against Francis Maude; defected and became special adviser to Maude as Chairman of Conservative Party. Now seen as an "on-message" Tory party loyalist. Tory Cllr, Medway 2006-. Labour Cllr, Medway 2003-2006. Pakistani-born. Barrister, Lincolns Inn. Keen cricketer and runner. Education: Fort Luton HS; Sixth Form Rainham Mark Grammar School, Chatham GS; University of Wales, Aberystwyth (Law).

Paul Clark (Lab) b. Apr 29, 1957. MP Gillingham 1997-2010. Parly Under-Sec Transport 2008-10. PPS to John

Prescott as Deputy PM 2005-08. Assistant government whip 2003-05. PPS to: Lord Falconer 2001-03; Lord Irvine 1999-2001. Cllr, Gillingham BC 1982-90.
Andrew Stamp (LD) Environment officer. Cllr, Medway 2007-.

Constituency
At south of the Medway, in the north of Kent, this is a densely populated urban seat. The two towns are contrasting: Rainham is affluent and contrasts with pockets of severe deprivation in Gillingham, a legacy of the closure of the naval dockyards. Though renamed, the seat has been only marginally redrawn; the old Gillingham constituency already included Rainham. However, the loss of a less affluent area by the river is not favourable to Labour, whose win here in 1997 was dramatic after decades of Tory representation.

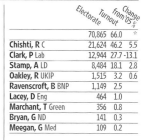

	Electorate	Turnout %	Change from '05 %
	70,865	66.0	☆
Chishti, R C	21,624	46.2	5.5
Clark, P Lab	12,944	27.7	-13.1
Stamp, A LD	8,484	18.1	2.8
Oakley, R UKIP	1,515	3.2	0.6
Ravenscroft, B BNP	1,149	2.5	
Lacey, D Eng	464	1.0	
Marchant, T Green	356	0.8	
Bryan, G ND	141	0.3	
Meegan, G Med	109	0.2	

50%
Majority 8,680

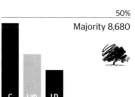

Glasgow Central Labour hold

Anas Sarwar
b. Mar 14, 1983
MP 2010-

Smooth, confident and charming. Glasgow born and bred, Pollokshields man – son of predecessor and first UK Muslim MP, the controversial Mohammed Sarwar. Contested Scottish Parliament 2007 (top of regional list). Unite. Founder, Y-Vote youth political engagement programme and Scottish Muslim Network. NHS Dentist, member Gen Dental Council. Campaigned to save Govan shipyard. Muslim. Married, one son. Education: Hutchesons' Grammar School; Glasgow (dentistry).

Osama Saeed (SNP) Chief executive, Scottish-Islamic Foundation.
Chris Young (LD) b. May 11, 1974. Actor and writer. Contested Scottish Parliament 2007. Education: Forest School, near Snaresbrook; University of St Andrews; University of Glasgow; Glasgow Sch of Law.
John Bradley (C) b. May 2, 1983. International relations PhD student. Education: Bristol Grammar & Rugby; Universities of Oxford, London and Edinburgh.

Constituency
This has been dubbed the most well-educated constituency in Scotland as it contains two of Glasgow's universities. It also has the city centre, the main rail stations and visitor attractions such as Kelvingrove Art Gallery and Glasgow Cathedral. As well as the stylish Merchant City area, it has the largest ethnic minority population of any Scottish seat. It has been Labour since 1950.

		Electorate	Turnout %	Change from 05 %
		60,062	50.9	
Sarwar, A	Lab	15,908	52.0	3.8
Saeed, O	SNP	5,357	17.5	2.8
Young, C	LD	5,010	16.4	-1.3
Bradley, J	C	2,158	7.1	0.8
Whitelaw, A	Green	800	2.6	-2.3
Holt, I	BNP	616	2.0	-0.4
Nesbitt, J	SSP	357	1.2	-2.8
Urquhart, R	UKIP	246	0.8	
Archibald, F	Pirate	128	0.4	

50%
Majority 10,551

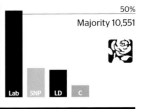

Glasgow East Labour gain

Margaret Curran
b. Nov 24, 1958
MP 2010-

Feisty and tough. Will be "dual mandate" MP and MSP until she stands down from Holyrood at Scottish elections in 2011. Contested Glasgow East by-election 2008. MSP for Glasgow Baillieston 1999 – (Communities minister in Scottish Executive 2003 -2007). Lecturer. Member, TGWU. Married, two sons. Education: Our Lady & St Francis, Glasgow; Glasgow (MA history & economic history); Dundee Coll (postgrad cert, community education).

John Mason (SNP) b. May 15, 1957. MP Glasgow East 2008-10. Spokesman, Work and Pensions, 2008-10. Cllr, Glasgow CC, 1998-2008. Chartered accountant. Education: Hutchisons' Grammar School, Glasgow; Glasgow (accountancy).
Kevin Ward (LD) b. 1984. University administrator. Ed: University of Strathclyde.

Constituency
This had the most dramatic by-election result of recent times when the SNP won it from Labour in 2008. It takes in the former Glasgow Baillieston seat and about 40 per cent of the old Glasgow Shettleston constituency. Its most famous landmark is Parkhead, the home of Celtic FC. It also contains the deprived Easterhouse estate and stretches from Gallowgate near the city centre to the outskirts of Coatbridge in North Lanarkshire.

		Electorate	Turnout %	Change from 05 %
		61,516	52.3	
Curran, M	Lab	19,797	61.6	0.9
Mason, J	SNP	7,957	24.7	7.7
Ward, K	LD	1,617	5.0	-6.8
Khan, H	C	1,453	4.5	-2.4
Finnie, J	BNP	677	2.1	
Curran, F	SSP	454	1.4	-2.1
Thackeray, A	UKIP	209	0.7	

50%
Majority 11,840

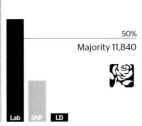

Glasgow North Labour hold

Ann McKechin
b. Apr 22, 1961
MP 2001-

Popular and loyal. Parly Under-Sec, Scotland 2008-10. PPS to: Jacqui Smith 2005. Member, select committees: International Development 2005-09; Standing Orders 2001-10; Scottish Affairs 2001-05. MP for Glasgow Maryhill 2001-05. Solicitor. Council member, world development movement. TGWU, Unite. Education: Sacred Heart High School, Paisley; Paisley Grammar School; Strathclyde (LLB Scots law).

Katy Gordon (LD) b. Jan 23, 1966. Project manager, Glasgow careers service. Contested Glasgow South West 2005. Ed: Aberdeen University, Napier University.
Patrick Grady (SNP) Policy officer, Scottish Parliament. Education: University of Strathclyde.
Erin Boyle (C) b. Jul 21, 1983. Former political researcher in Scottish Parliament. Education: Holyrood Secondary Sch; Glasgow Uni.

Constituency
This constituency contains more of a rich and poor mix than any other in the city, with large parts of the very affluent West End as well as the working-class areas of Maryhill, Summerston and Ruchill that, in the past, have given Labour its majority.

		Electorate	Turnout %	Change from 05 %
		51,416	57.6	
McKechin, A	Lab	13,181	44.5	5.1
Gordon, K	LD	9,283	31.4	4.0
Grady, P	SNP	3,530	11.9	-1.0
Boyle, E	C	2,089	7.1	-1.7
Bartos, M	Green	947	3.2	-4.5
Main, T	BNP	296	1.0	
McCormick, A	TUSC	287	1.0	

50%
Majority 3,898

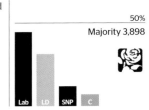

Glasgow North East

Willie Bain
b. Nov 29, 1972
MP 2009- (by-election)

Good local organiser who fought off tough challenge from SNP to take 2009 by-election. Parliamentary private secretary to Sadiq Khan 2010-. Member, select committee: Joint committee on Tax Law Rewrite bills. Election agent to Michael Martin. Lecturer, researcher: University of Strathclyde Law School; London Southbank University. Unite, Progress, Fabian Society, Amnesty International. Education: St Roch's School; Strathclyde (LLB).

Billy McAllister (SNP) Cllr, Glasgow CC.
Eileen Baxendale (LD) b. Apr 16, 1945. Social worker. Cllr, South Lanarkshire. Education: Queen Victoria High School, Stockton-on-Tees; University of London; Columbia University; University of Manchester.
Ruth Davidson (C) b. Nov 10, 1978. Journalist. Education: Buckhaven High School and University of Edinburgh.

Constituency
One of the poorest seats in Britain, this part of Glasgow is affected by gangs, deprivation and drugs. While areas such as Dennistoun have moved upmarket, the rest of the constituency is severely deprived. This is the old seat of the former Commons Speaker Michael Martin and had the final by-election of the last parliament in November 2009 when Labour held off the SNP.

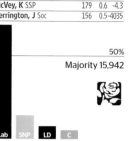

	Electorate	Turnout %	Change from 05 %
	59,859	49.1	
Bain, W Lab	20,100	68.4	9.1
McAllister, B SNP	4,158	14.1	-3.5
Baxendale, E LD	2,262	7.7	5.4
Davidson, R C	1,569	5.3	0.1
Hamilton, W BNP	798	2.7	-0.5
Campbell, G TUSC	187	0.6	
McVey, K SSP	179	0.6	-4.3
Berrington, J Soc	156	0.5	-4035

50%
Majority 15,942

Lab SNP LD C

Glasgow North West

John Robertson
b. Apr 17, 1952
MP 2000-

Affable and popular. Parliamentary Private Secretary to Yvette Cooper 2009-10; Kim Howells 2005-08. Member select committees: European Scrutiny 2003-10; Scottish Affairs 2001-10. MP for Glasgow Anniesland 2000-05. Amicus. CWU/NCU political, education officer. GPO, Post Office, BT. Election agent for Donald Dewar MP/MSP. Married, three daughters. Education: Shawlands Academy; Langside College (ONC electrical engineering); Stow College (HNC electrical engineering).

Natalie McKee (LD) b. Mar 2, 1980. Optometrist. Glasgow City Council candidate 2009. Education: Notre Dame High School, Glasgow; Glasgow Caledonian University.
Mags Park (SNP) Management trainer. Contested Rutherglen and Hamilton West 2005.
Richard Sullivan (C) Management consultant. Education: Stirling University.

Constituency
This safe Labour seat lies on the north bank of the River Clyde and includes upwardly mobile areas such as Scotstoun and Jordanhill with more deprived areas such as the Drumchapel housing estate. Under previous boundaries as Glasgow Garscadden, the core of this seat was represented by Donald Dewar and Labour held the seat after his death.

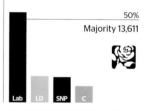

	Electorate	Turnout %	Change from 05 %
	60,968	58.4	
Robertson, J Lab	19,233	54.1	5.0
McKee, N LD	5,622	15.8	-3.7
Park, M SNP	5,430	15.3	1.6
Sullivan, R C	3,537	9.9	0.4
Crawford, M Green	882	2.5	-1.4
Mclean, S BNP	699	2.0	
Livingstone, M Comm	179	0.5	

50%
Majority 13,611

Lab LD SNP C

Glasgow South

Tom Harris
b. Feb 20, 1964
MP 2001-

Runs respected political blog. Not afraid to take tough line on issues such as asylum-seekers. Parly Under-Sec: Transport 2006-08. Parliamentary private secretary to: Patricia Hewitt 2005-06; John Spellar 2003-05. Member, committee: Science & Technology 2001-04. MP Glasgow Cathcart 2001-05. Lab Friends of Israel. Reporter. Press officer, PR career: Strathclyde Passenger Transport Exec; E Ayrshire Council; Glasgow CC; Strathclyde RC; Scottish Lab Party. NUJ, Amicus, Unison. Divorced, remarried. Three sons (one from first marriage). Education: Garnock Academy, Ayrshire; Napier College (HND journalism).

Malcolm Fleming (SNP) Charity campaigner. Contested Galloway and Upper Nithsdale 2001. Education: Biggar High School, Glasgow, University of Aberdeen.
Shabnum Mustapha (LD) Charity manager. Scottish Parliament candidate 2007. Education: Shawlands Academy, University of Glasgow.
Davena Rankin (C) Commercial manager, Glasgow Caledonian University. Education: Knightswood Secondary School, Glasgow; University of Sussex.

Constituency
While this constituency includes one of the few Conservative-voting council wards in the city in Maxwell Park, other parts such as Langside and Shawlands are Labour. Deprived social housing estates typify the seat and there is a large Pakistani community. About a third of residents are Catholic.

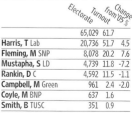

	Electorate	Turnout %	Change from 05 %
	65,029	61.7	
Harris, T Lab	20,736	51.7	4.5
Fleming, M SNP	8,078	20.2	7.6
Mustapha, S LD	4,739	11.8	-7.2
Rankin, D C	4,592	11.5	-1.1
Campbell, M Green	961	2.4	-2.0
Coyle, M BNP	637	1.6	
Smith, B TUSC	351	0.9	

50%
Majority 12,658

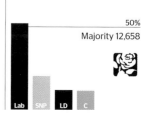

Lab SNP LD C

Glasgow South West — Labour Co-op hold

Ian Davidson
b. Sep 8, 1950
MP 1992-

Troublesome left-winger with flair for publicity. Passionately Eurosceptic and anti-Euro. Elected unopposed as Chair, select committee: Scottish Affairs 2010-. Member, select committees: Public Accounts 1997-10; Scottish Affairs 2005-10. MP Glasgow Govan 1992-97, Glasgow Pollok 1997-2005. Member, Co-operative Party. Founder, Labour against the Euro. Councillor, Strathclyde Regional Council 1978-92. Member, new Europe advisory council. Secretary, Labour MPs trade union group. Project manager, MEP researcher, chairman/president student associations. Married with one daughter and one son. Education: Jedburgh GS; Galashiels Academy; University of Edinburgh (MA); Jordanhill College.

Chris Stephens (SNP) Trade unionist. Son of a shipyard welder. Works for Glasgow CC.
Isabel Nelson (LD) IT consultant. Langside College, Glasgow; University of Glasgow. Contested Glasgow Central in 2005.
Maya Henderson Forrest (C) b. Aug 13, 1991. Student. Ed: Glasgow Uni.

Constituency
This seat is blighted by poverty, deprivation, high crime and poor health. It includes Ibrox Park, the home of Glasgow Rangers FC as well as one of the last remaining Clyde shipyards at Govan. Made up of parts of the former Glasgow Pollok and Glasgow Govan constituencies, this area has long been safe Glasgow territory for Labour.

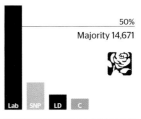

	Electorate	Turnout %	Change from 05 %
	58,182	54.6	
Davidson, I Lab	19,863	62.5	-1802
Stephens, C SNP	5,192	16.3	1.0
Nelson, I LD	2,870	9.0	-2.6
Henderson Forrest, M C	2,084	6.6	
Sheridan, T TUSC	931	2.9	
Orr, D BNP	841	2.7	

50%
Majority 14,671

Lab | SNP | LD | C

Glenrothes — Labour hold

Lindsay Roy
b. Jan 19, 1949
MP 2008-

Cerebral headmaster who won crucial by-election in 2008. Relative political newcomer but personal friend of Gordon Brown. Member, select committee: Scottish Affairs 2009-. Executive Member, International Confederation of Principals. President, Headteachers Association of Scotland. Chairman, Curriculum & Student Affairs Committee, Carnegie College. Associate assessor, HM Inspectorate of Education. Rector at Kirkcaldy High School and Inverkeithing High School. Teacher. Fellow, Royal Society for the Arts. Married with one daughter and two sons. Education: Perth Academy; Edinburgh (BSc geography).

David Alexander (SNP) b. May 26, 1954. Cllr, Falkirk (leader 2001-07).
Harry Wills (LD) Business consultant. Contested Glenrothes by-election 2008. Ed: Strathclyde Business Sch.
Sheila Low (C) Business development manager, Baker Tilly. Ed: University of Aberdeen.

Constituency
This central Fife constituency is named after the Glenrothes New Town but also encompasses small industrial areas such as Methil and Buckhaven on the north edge of the Firth of Forth. The area has long been seen as a Labour heartland, although the constituency was the scene of a keenly fought by-election in 2008 when Labour held off a strong SNP challenge.

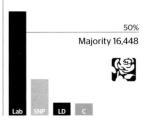

	Electorate	Turnout %	Change from 05 %
	67,893	59.7	
Roy, L Lab	25,247	62.3	10.4
Alexander, D SNP	8,799	21.7	-1.6
Wills, H LD	3,108	7.7	-4.9
Low, S C	2,922	7.2	0.1
Seunarine, K UKIP	425	1.1	-0.1

50%
Majority 16,448

Lab | SNP | LD | C

Gloucester — Conservative gain

Richard Graham
b. Apr 4, 1958
MP 2010-

Suave former investment banker, diplomat and airline manager. Cllr, Cotswold DC 2003-07. Contested European parl 2004 (SW England). Adviser to David Willetts as Shadow SoS for Pensions. Director/Head of Int Business, Baring Asset Management. Founder Chair, British Chamber of Commerce Shanghai. FCO diplomacy: First Sec of British High Commission in Kenya/Peking. British Trade Commissioner China. General manager, John Swire & Sons; Cathay Pacific. Vice-chair, Board of Airline Representatives, Philippines. Dir, Care for Children Ltd. RAFVR. Keen cricketer. Married, one daughter, two sons. Ed: Christ Church, Oxford (history).

Parmjit Dhanda (Lab) b. Sep 17, 1971. MP 2001-10. Candidate for Speaker 2009. Parly Under-Sec: Communities 2007-8; Education 2006-07. Asst govt whip 2005-6. Ed: Mellow Lane Comp Sch, Hayes; Nottingham Uni.
Jeremy Hilton (LD) Cllr, Gloucester.

Constituency
With its Victorian dock and a cathedral featured in the Harry Potter films, tourism is big business in the city of Gloucester. Traditional manufacturing dependence has diversified and the financial sector is strong. Yet this is the most deprived district in Gloucestershire, with particular deprivation in Barton and Westage. Under boundary changes the seat has been slightly cut, with the loss of the more affluent Longlevens ward. The ethnic minority population of 7.5 per cent is high for the area. The seat was Conservative from 1970 to 1997.

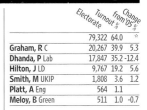

	Electorate	Turnout %	Change from 05 %
	79,322	64.0	
Graham, R C	20,267	39.9	5.3
Dhanda, P Lab	17,847	35.2	-12.4
Hilton, J LD	9,767	19.2	5.6
Smith, M UKIP	1,808	3.6	1.2
Platt, A Eng	564	1.1	
Meloy, B Green	511	1.0	-0.7

50%
Majority 2,420

C | Lab | LD

Gordon
Liberal Democrat hold

Malcolm Bruce
b. Nov 17, 1944
MP 1983-

Veteran of Liberal-SDP Alliance era, has never quite made it to top of Scottish party. Candidate for LD leader in 1999, deputy leader in 2003. Chair, select cttee: International Devt 2005- (re-elected unopposed 2010). LD Shad SoS: Trade & Industry 2003-05; EFRA 2001-02. Spokes, various 1985-99. Leader Scottish: Lib Dems 1989-92, Social & Lib Dems 1988-89. Barrister. Trainee journalist, buyer, research/info oddicer, dir, editor/publisher. Divorced, remarried. One daughter, one son from first marriage; two daughters, one son from second. Ed: Wrekin Coll; St Andrews (MA econ & pol science); Strathclyde (MSc marketing); CPE & Inns of Court Sch of Law.

Richard Thomson (SNP) b. Jun 16, 1976. Contested Tweeddale, Ettrick and Lauderdale 2001. Former Head of Research SNP. Journalist/MBA student. Ed: Tynecastle High School, Edinburgh; University of Stirling; Edinburgh Business School.
Barney Crockett (Lab) b. Apr 28, 1953. Ed: Aberdeen University.
Ross Thomson (C) b. 1987. Accounts manager. Contested Scottish parl, Coatbridge & Chryston 2007.

Constituency
The area is dominated by farming and forestry and there are several whisky distilleries around its picturesque hills and rivers. Traditionally a Liberal Democrat constituency, it includes the market towns of Huntly, Keith and Inverurie but the seat stretches far enough into the commuter belt around Aberdeen to include the airport.

	Electorate	Turnout %	Change from 05 %
	73,420	66.4	
Bruce, M LD	17,575	36.0	-9.0
Thomson, R SNP	10,827	22.2	6.3
Crockett, B Lab	9,811	20.1	-0.1
Thomson, R C	9,111	18.7	1.1
Edwards, S Green	752	1.5	
Jones, E BNP	699	1.4	

50%
Majority 6,748

Gosport
Conservative hold

Caroline Dinenage
b. Oct 28, 1971
MP 2010-

Selected by open primary, the daughter of TV presenter Fred Dinenage. Attracted attention for an airbrushed campaign poster. Contested Portsmouth South 2005. Director - Recognition Express (manufacturer of corporate identity products). Christian. Sporty. Special interest in military personnel and their families; is married to a Naval Officer. Two children. Education: Oaklands Roman Catholic Comp, Waterlooville; University of Wales, Swansea.

Rob Hylands (LD) b. Dec 9, 1957. Cllr, Gosport BC. Licensee. Ed: Brune Park Secondary School.

Graham Giles (Lab) b. Mar 21, 1957. Charity execuitve. Former consultant to World Bank. Ed: Spurgeons College, London.

Constituency
The town of Gosport lies on the western side of Portsmouth Harbour, connected to the city by regular ferry services. The seat has a long naval history and, although Haslar Royal Naval Hospital closed amid protests in 2009, the MoD still owns about a fifth of the land here. Many residents work at Portsmouth naval base. The generally well-off seat includes Lee-on-the-Solent, which is popular with retired people, and extends west along the coast as far as Stubbington. Held by the Tory MP Peter Viggers since 1974, he was forced to stand down after his duck house became the most notorious symbol of the expenses scandal.

	Electorate	Turnout %	Change from 05 %
	72,720	64.6	
Dinenage, C C	24,300	51.8	7.1
Hylands, R LD	9,887	21.1	4.5
Giles, G Lab	7,944	16.9	-14.5
Rice, A UKIP	1,496	3.2	-1.1
Bennett, B BNP	1,004	2.1	
Shaw, B Eng	622	1.3	
Smith, A Green	573	1.2	-1.7
Smith, D Ind	493	1.1	
Read, C Ind	331	0.7	
Hart, B Ind	289	0.6	

50%
Majority 14,413

Gower
Labour hold

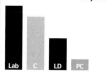

Martin Caton
b. Jun 15, 1951
MP 1997-

Cheerful left-winger with a fondness for bow ties. Member, cttees: Environmental Audit 2005-; Chairmen's Panel 2003-; Joint cttee on Consolidation of Bills 2001-; Welsh Affairs 1997-2005. Member, Socialist Health Assoc, SERA. Chair, Welsh regional group of Lab MPs 2002-. Cllr: Swansea CC 1988-97; Mumbles Community 1986-90. Agriculture/political (MEP) research. IPCS section treasurer/membership sec. Married, two stepdaughters. Ed: Newport GS; Norfolk Agriculture Sch; Aberystwyth FE Coll (Nat Agriculture Cert, Higher Nat Cert applied biology).

Byron Davies (C) b. Sep 4, 1952. Contested Welsh elections, Gower 2007.

Mike Day (LD) b. Jul 23, 1953. Cllr. Management consultant.
Darren Price (PC) b. 1980. Cllr, Swansea CC

Constituency
The Gower Peninsula lies between the Bristol Channel and the River Loughor's estuary, and is designated an Area of Outstanding Natural Beauty. The affluent Mumbles and Port-Eynon are the main towns on its southern coast. Apart from the peninsula the seat encompasses an area of the Lliw Valley inland to the north east, including Gorseinon, Clydach and Pontarddulais. A comfortably well-off seat, it is home to celebrities such as Catherine Zeta-Jones and Bonnie Tyler. The service sector is the main source of employment, but industry was traditionally the linchpin of the economy, helping to explain Labour's dominance historically.

	Electorate	Turnout %	Change from 05 %
	61,696	67.5	☆
Caton, M Lab	16,016	38.4	-4.0
Davies, B C	13,333	32.0	6.5
Day, M LD	7,947	19.1	0.6
Price, D PC	2,760	6.6	-1.2
Jones, A BNP	963	2.3	
Triggs, G UKIP	652	1.6	-1.6

50%
Majority 2,683

Grantham & Stamford — Conservative hold

Nicholas Boles
b. Nov 2, 1965
MP 2010-

Trusted Cameron member of the Notting Hill Tory set - one of the original Tory modernisers. A former flatmate of Michael Gove. CCHQ staffer responsible for planning policy implementation. Contested Hove 2005 and London Mayoral primary 2007. Forced to withdraw after Hodgkins Lymphoma diagnosis. A-lister, won seat candidature in open primary later same year then became Chief of Staff to Boris Johnson 2008. Cllr, Westminster (1998-2002). Founded Policy Exchange think tank. Ran own paint/decorating supply co. Overseas work. Gay. Ed: Winchester; Magdalen College, Oxford (PPE); Harvard (Kennedy Scholarship).

Harrish Bisnauthsing (LD) Mayor of Stamford in 2002-03. Consultant.
Mark Bartlett (Lab) b. Oct 1, 1960. Recruitment agent.

Constituency
This southwest Lincolnshire seat is predominantly rural and the towns, both close to the A1, are at its northern and southern extremities. Bourne is the other main town. Grantham, hometown of Margaret Thatcher, has some patches of severe deprivation and is significantly less affluent than the rest of the seat. Manufacturing was traditionally important, while much of the rural land is given over to agriculture, despite employing relatively few. Traditionally a Conservative voting area, it had a Labour MP from 2007 after the defection of Quentin Davies.

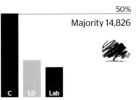

	Electorate	Turnout %	from '05 % Change
	78,000	67.7	☆
Boles, N C	26,552	50.3	3.4
Bisnauthsing, H LD	11,726	22.2	5.7
Bartlett, M Lab	9,503	18.0	-13.2
Robinson, C BNP	2,485	4.7	
Wells, T UKIP	1,604	3.0	-0.2
Horn, M Lincs	929	1.8	

50%
Majority 14,826

Gravesham — Conservative hold

Adam Holloway
b. Jul 29, 1965
MP 2005-

An action man who knows a lot about defence. Member, Defence Select Committee 2006-10; Arms Export Controls 2009-10. Commissioned Grenadier Guards. Media career; Presented World In Action, Granada TV, reported for ITN. Education: Cranleigh School, Surrey; Magdalene College, Cambridge (MA theology and social and political science); Imperial College, London (MBA); RMA Sandhurst.

Kathryn Smith (Lab Co-op) Consultant. Cllr, Bexley 1994-2006.
Anna Arrowsmith (LD) b. Jan 15, 1952. Pornographic film director.

Constituency
From Gravesend and Northfleet on the south bank of the Thames, this Kent seat stretches towards the North Downs. The north of the constituency is predominantly urban, has patches of deprivation and forms part of the Thameside regeneration project. The rest, south of the A2, is rural, much of it green belt land, and generally affluent. The seat has the biggest black and minority ethnic population in Kent, the largest proportion of Indian origin. It has changed hands many times; Labour took it in 1997 but the Tories won it back in 2005.

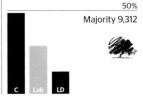

	Electorate	Turnout %	from '05 % Change
	70,195	67.4	
Holloway, A C	22,956	48.5	4.9
Smith, K Lab	13,644	28.8	-13.4
Arrowsmith, A LD	6,293	13.3	2.6
Clark, G UKIP	2,265	4.8	2.9
Uncles, S Eng	1,005	2.1	-651
Crawford, R Green	675	1.4	
Dartnell, A Ind	465	1.0	

50%
Majority 9,312

Great Grimsby — Labour hold

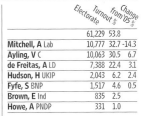

Austin Mitchell
b. Sep 19, 1934
MP 1977-

Eccentric veteran left-winger (Socialist Campaign Group). Self-publicist who once changed name to Haddock to promote local fish industry. Appeared cantankerous and out of touch on reality show. Opp spokes: Trade & Industry 1988-89. Opp whip 1979-85. PPS to John Fraser 1977-79. MP for Grimsby 1977-83. Member, select cttees: Public accounts 2005-; EFRA 2001-05; Agriculture 1997-2001. Lab econ policy group. Vice-Chair, Hansard Soc. Uni lecturer/fellow. Long-serving anchor for Yorkshire TV's evening magazine programme. Divorced, remarried. Two daughters from first marriage; one daughter, one son from second marriage to journalist

Linda McDougall. Ed: Woodbottom Council Sch; Bingley GS; Manchester (BA history/MA); Nuffield Coll, Oxford (MA, DPhil).

Victoria Ayling (C) Cllr.
Andrew de Freitas (LD) Cllr, NE Linc.
Henry Hudson (UKIP) Deputy Chair Grimsby Conservatives until 2009.

Constituency
The port of Grimsby lies on the south bank of the Humber, near the estuary mouth. Although the fishing industry that traditionally dominated the constituency has declined, Grimsby's biggest private employer remains Young's Seafood. Chemical and petrol companies have a strong presence. Overwhelmingly white and strongly working-class, the seat suffers from high unemployment. It has been Labour since the Second World War.

	Electorate	Turnout %	from '05 % Change
	61,229	53.8	
Mitchell, A Lab	10,777	32.7	-14.3
Ayling, V C	10,063	30.5	6.7
de Freitas, A LD	7,388	22.4	3.1
Hudson, H UKIP	2,043	6.2	2.4
Fyfe, S BNP	1,517	4.6	0.5
Brown, E Ind	835	2.5	
Howe, A PNDP	331	1.0	

50%
Majority 714

Great Yarmouth

Brandon Lewis
b. Jun 20, 1971
MP 2010-

Ambitious businessman, who runs independent primary schools as Director, Woodland Schools Ltd. Ally of Eric Pickles MP; worked as his campaign manager in 2005. Contested Sherwood 2001. Cllr: Brentwood 1998-2009 (Leader 2004–2009). Barrister. Runs communications company. C of E. Marathon runner. Married, one daughter, one son. Education: Forest School; Buckingham (LLS Hons Law); Kings College, London (LLM commercial law); Buckingham (BSc economics).

Tony Wright (Lab) b. Aug 12, 1954. MP 1997-2010. Member, cttee: Business & Enterprise 2005-10; Public Admin 2000-02. Ed: Hospital Secondary Modern; Great Yarmouth Coll of FE.
Simon Partridge (LD) Councillor. Hotelier.

Constituency
With 15 miles of beaches, Great Yarmouth – the easternmost seat in Norfolk – is a major seaside resort, but its popularity with tourists has declined in recent decades. The seat is small and mainly urban, including Gorleston to the south. Fishing and manufacturing industries have declined and there is high unemployment, while pockets of severe deprivation exist. There is a large working class and the seat is a base for servicing and supplying the southern North Sea gasfields. The population is overwhelmingly white and relatively ageing. Once a Tory safe seat, this was one of Labour's great seaside wins in 1997.

	Electorate	Turnout %	Change from '05 %
	70,315	61.2	
Lewis, B C	18,571	43.1	5.0
Wright, T Lab	14,295	33.2	-12.3
Partridge, S LD	6,188	14.4	3.4
Baugh, A UKIP	2,066	4.8	0.6
Tann, B BNP	1,421	3.3	
Biggart, L Green	416	1.0	
McMahon-Morris, M LTT	100	0.2	

50%
Majority 4,276

C | Lab | LD

Greenwich & Woolwich

Nick Raynsford
b. Jan 28, 1945
MP 1986-87; 1992-

Stolid. More comfortable with policy detail than politics. Briefly considered standing against Ken Livingstone as Labour candidate for Mayor of London. Min: ODPM 2002-05; Local Gov't & Regions 2001-02; Housing & Planning 1999-2001. Parly Under-Sec, Environment, Transport & Regions. Opp spokes: Housing/Construction/London 1994-97; Transport & London 1993-94. PPS to Roy Hattersley 1986-87. MP Greenwich 1992-97, Fulham 1986-87. Cllr, Hammersmith & Fulham 1971-75. GMB. Housing consultant. Married but separated. Three daughters. Ed: Repton Sch; Sidney Sussex Coll, Cambs (BA hist); Chelsea Sch of Art (art & design).

Spencer Drury (C) Cllr, 2002-. Teacher. Ed: Colfe's School.
Joseph Lee (LD) Director of estate agency.

Constituency
All but one of the wards in this marginally redrawn seat have areas in 10 per cent of the most deprived in the country. These are concentrated around Woolwich at the east, which has not recovered from the closure of the old Royal Arsenal. At the other end of the seat, Greenwich Village has relatively affluent areas along with the Cutty Sark and Royal Observatory. Thames Gateway regeneration is needed and the peninsula is scene of one of the biggest housing projects with the Millennium Village. The seat has been a Labour stronghold for years.

	Electorate	Turnout %	Change from '05 %
	65,489	62.9	
Raynsford, N Lab	20,262	49.2	-3.3
Drury, S C	10,109	24.5	7.0
Lee, J LD	7,498	18.2	-1.5
Rustem, L BNP	1,151	2.8	
Hewett, A Green	1,054	2.6	-1.9
Adeleye, E Ch	443	1.1	
Wresniwiro, T Eng	339	0.8	
Kasab, O TUSC	267	0.7	
Alingham, T Ind	65	0.2	

50%
Majority 10,153

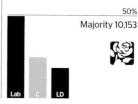

Lab | C | LD

Guildford

Anne Milton
b. Nov 3, 1955
MP 2005-

Petite former nurse with slightly intense manner. Worked in the NHS for 25 years. Parly Under-Sec: Health 2010-. Shadow Minister: Health 2007-10; Tourism 2006-07. Vice-Chair, Conservative Medical Society. Cllr, Reigate Borough Council 1999-2004. RCN union steward. National Childbirth Trust. Married, one daughter, three sons. Education: Haywards Heath Grammar, West Sussex; St Bartholomew's Hospital (RGN); South Bank Polytechnic (Dip District Nursing).

Sue Doughty (LD) MP Guildford 2001-05. Consultant. Education: Mill Mount GS; Northumberland College.

Constituency
The eponymous town is in the north of this hourglass-shaped constituency and Cranleigh, which claims to be the largest village in England, is to the south. The western part of Guildford includes the University of Surrey, hospital and modern cathedral, which overlooks the River Wey to the historic central shopping area rising up the hill. The firm Tory hold since 1906 was broken in 2001 after an anti-incinerator campaign by the Lib Dems, but the Tories won it back in 2005.

	Electorate	Turnout %	Change from '05 %
	77,082	72.1	
Milton, A C	29,618	53.3	9.8
Doughty, S LD	21,836	39.3	-4.0
Shand, T Lab	2,812	5.1	-4.8
Manzoor, M UKIP	1,021	1.8	0.6
Morris, J PPN-V	280	0.5	

50%
Majority 7,782

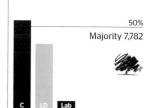

C | LD | Lab

Hackney North & Stoke Newington — Labour hold

Diane Abbott
b. Sep 27, 1953
MP 1987-

Surprise candidate for Labour leadership, 2010, with last-minute nominations. Left-wing firebrand (member of Socialist Campaign Group) turned serene television pundit; now a veteran MP, but wielded little influence to date. Was Britain's first black female MP. Member select cttees: Foreign Affairs 1997-2001; Treasury and Civil Service 1989-97. Member Lab Party NEC 1994-97. Cllr, Westminster CC 1982-86. Member, GLA advisory cabinet for women and equality 2000-, RMT parly campaigning group 2002-. Equality officer/admin trainee, ACTT. Admin trainee Home Office, race relations officer NCCL. Researcher Thames TV, reporter *TV-am*, press and PR officer GLC; Lambeth Council. Divorced, one son. Ed: Harrow County Girls' GS; Newnham Coll, Cambridge (history).

Keith Angus (LD) b. 1977. Investment manager. Ed: Open University.
Darren Caplan (C) b. 1973. Public affairs consultant. Ed: Birmingham.

Constituency
This inner London seat includes large areas of severe deprivation as well as the up-and-coming Stoke Newington, popular with young professionals. It is diverse, with less than half the residents white British: about a fifth are black, concentrated in the south of the seat, and there is a significant Indian population in the east. There is religious diversity, too, with a large Muslim population and a notable Turkish community. The seat has been Labour for decades.

	Electorate	Turnout %	Change from '05 %
	73,874	1.0	☆
Abbott, D Lab	25,553	55.0	6.0
Angus, K LD	11,092	23.9	0.8
Caplan, D C	6,759	14.5	-0.1
Sellwood, M Green	2,133	4.6	-5.1
Hargreaves, M Ch	299	0.6	
Moore, S ND	285	0.6	
Knapp, K Loony	182	0.4	
Shaer, P Ind	96	0.2	
Williams, A Ind	61	0.1	
Pope-De-Locksley, J Magna	28	0.1	

Majority 14,461

Hackney South & Shoreditch — Labour hold

Meg Hillier
b. Feb 14, 1969
MP 2005-

Quiet but exudes confidence. Parly Under-Sec, Home Office 2007-10. Parliamentary private secretary to Ruth Kelly 2006-07. Member, select cttee: NI Affairs 2005-06. Cllr, Islington Borough Council. Mayor of Islington 1998/99. GLA member for NE London 2000-04. Journalist; *Housing Today* features ed. Merchant Navy service. Member, TGWU, Fabian Society. Married, one daughter, one son. Ed: Portsmouth HS; St Hilda's Coll, Oxford (BA PPE); City (dip newspaper journalism).

Dave Raval (LD) Public affairs consultant. Ed: Cambridge. Uni.

Simon Nayyar (C) Consultant. Ed: York Uni.

Constituency
Shoreditch and Hoxton are the innermost London parts of the seat, known for their popularity with artists. With the exception of this area and small pockets on the southern and western borders, this seat is within the most deprived 20 per cent nationwide. More than 25 per cent of residents are black. Although many tower blocks have been demolished, more than half live in social housing. Further regeneration is coming with the Olympic Village, a third of which lies inside the seat's eastern boundary. The seat has returned Labour MPs for decades.

	Electorate	Turnout %	Change from '05 %
	72,816	58.9	
Hillier, M Lab	23,888	55.7	3.0
Raval, D LD	9,600	22.4	1.1
Nayyar, S C	5,800	13.5	-0.3
Lane, P Green	1,493	3.5	-2.1
King, M UKIP	651	1.5	
Rae, B Lib	539	1.3	
Williams, J Ch	434	1.0	
Sen, N DDP	202	0.5	
Davies, P Comm	110	0.3	
De La Haye, D Ind	95	0.22	
Tuckett, J Ind	26	0.1	
Spinks, M Ind	20	0.1	

Majority 14,288

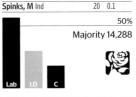

Halesowen & Rowley Regis — Conservative gain

James Morris
b. Feb 4, 1967
MP 2010-

Passionate advocate of localism agenda; Chief Executive, Localis (local government/localist think tank). Director, London Policy Institute. Small businessman specialising in computer software. Founder, Mind the Gap - campaign to promote civic engagement. Cricketer. Married, one daughter, one son. Ed: Nottingham HS; Birmingham (English Lit); Oxford University (Postgrad research); Cranfield Management school (MBA).

Sue Hayman (Lab) Contested Bexleyheath & Crayford 2005.
Philip Tibbets (LD) BAE Systems. Ed: King Edward VI College, Stourbridge; University of St Andrews.

Derek Baddeley (UKIP).

Constituency
This West Midlands seat, to the south of Dudley, is bordered by the M5 to the east. There is a significant number of affluent middle classes around Halesowen and residential housing typifies the south of the seat, while at the very south is an area of farmland on the border with rural Worcestershire. Farther north, Blackheath and Rowley Regis are more industrial and working-class areas, which helped Labour to win in 1997. Turner's Hill looks out over the north of the seat.

	Electorate	Turnout %	Change from '05 %
	63,693	69.1	☆
Morris, J C	18,115	41.2	4.6
Hayman, S Lab	16,092	36.6	-9.7
Tibbets, P LD	6,515	14.8	2.3
Baddeley, D UKIP	2,824	6.4	1.8
Thompson, D Ind	433	1.0	

Majority 2,023

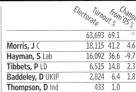

Halifax — Labour hold

Linda Riordan
b. May 31, 1953
MP 2005-

Whips' nightmare; replaced left-wing rebel Alice Mahon in 2005 but proved just as rebellious from the outset. Member, select committees: Justice 2008-10; Procedure 2006-10; Crossrail Bill 2006-07; Environmental Audit 2005-10. Cllr, Calderdale MBC. Chair, Ovenden Initiative. Non-executive Director, Calderdale & Huddersfield NHS Trust. Board member, Pennine Housing. Worked as secretary for Alice Mahon MP. Widowed. Education: K H Whitley Secondary Modern, Yorkshire; Bradford University (BA politics and history).

Philip Allott (C) b. 1959. Owns PR company. Contested Bolton West 2005, Brent North 2001. Ed: King James' Sch, Knaresborough; Leeds Met.
Elisabeth Wilson (LD) Uni lecturer. Contested Colne Valley 2005.
Tom Bates (BNP) b. Oct 31, 1969. Forklift truck driver. Cllr, Calderdale MBC. Ed: Heath GS, Halifax.

Constituency
Halifax gave its name to the bank whose current incarnation, the troubled HBOS, is the biggest private employer in this West Yorkshire seat. Once a wool town, it retains a large working-class and manufacturing presence, returning a Labour MP for most of its recent history. The seat briefly turned blue during the Thatcher years. About 10 per cent of the population is of Asian origin and the BNP has had some success. Labour has held the seat since 1987 but margins of victory have often been narrow.

	Electorate	Turnout %	Change from '05 %
	70,380	61.9	☆
Riordan, L Lab	16,278	37.4	-4.5
Allott, P C	14,806	34.0	0.9
Wilson, E LD	8,335	19.1	1.2
Bates, T BNP	2,760	6.3	
Park, D Ind	722	1.7	
Sangha, J UKIP	654	1.5	

50%
Majority 1,472

| Lab | C | LD | BNP |

Haltemprice & Howden — Conservative hold

David Davis
b. Dec 23, 1948
MP 1987-

Swaggering right-winger from humble background, raised by single mother on council estate. Resigned as Shadow Home SoS (2003-08) to fight bizarre, almost uncontested, by-election over terrorism powers. Twice contested Tory leadership. Effective champion of civil liberties and campaigner against torture. Shadow Dep PM 2002-03. Chair, PAC 1997-2001. Minister of State FCO 1994-97. MP Boothferry 1987-97. Career, Tate & Lyle. Weekend soldier, Territorial SAS. Married, two daughters, one son. Ed: Warwick (BSc molecular/computing science); London Business School (MSc business studies); Harvard Business School (AMP).

Jon Neal (LD) b. Nov 12, 1975. Media manager for research organisation. Contested seat 2005, 2001. Ed: Hull.
Danny Marten (Lab) b. Oct 19, 1986. Researcher for Diana Johnson MP.

Constituency
The constituency, dominated by farmland, stretches along the M62, from commuter villages, including Cottingham, west of Hull that contain 70 per cent of the electorate to Howden, a few miles north of Goole. The Press Association is a main employer in Howden and BAE Systems is the big name at Brough. The economy is dominated by professionals in service sectors. Although traditionally Tory, the Lib Dems have been a strong second in some recent elections. In 2008 David Davis, MP since 1987, forced an unopposed by-election to highlight civil liberties.

	Electorate	Turnout %	Change from '05 %
	70,403	69.2	☆
Davis, D C	24,486	50.2	3.2
Neal, J LD	12,884	26.4	-10.0
Marten, D Lab	7,630	15.7	2.2
Cornell, J BNP	1,583	3.3	
Robinson, J Eng	1,485	3.1	
Oakes, S Green	669	1.4	

50%
Majority 11,602

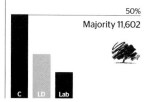

| C | LD | Lab |

Halton — Labour hold

Derek Twigg
b. Jul 9, 1959
MP 1997-

Unremarkable survivor, little impact as minister. Parly Under-Sec: Defence 2006-08; Transport 2005-06; Education & Skills 2004-05. Whip: govt 2003-04; asst govt 2002-03. PPS to: Stephen Byers 2001-02; Helen Liddell 1999-2001. Cllr, Halton Borough Council 1983-97, Cheshire County Council 1981-85. GMB. Political consultant. Civil servant, Dept for Education & Employment. Branch sec/chair. Married, one daughter, one son. Education: Bankfield High School, Widnes; Halton College of Further Education.

Ben Jones (C) b. 1978. Management consultant. Ed: University of Liverpool.

Frank Harasiwka (LD) b. Apr 4, 1959. Company director. Contested Bolton South East 2005, 2001, 1997, 1987; European elections, Greater Manchester West 1994.

Constituency
Although technically part of Chester, this constituency lies on either side of the Mersey, where it narrows at the Runcorn Gap. The postwar New Town of Runcorn lies to the south and long-established Widnes to the north. Both have large areas of severe deprivation. Overwhelmingly white, working-class and traditionally reliant on the chemical industry, this seat has been Labour since its inception in 1983.

	Electorate	Turnout %	Change from '05 %
	68,884	60.0	☆
Twigg, D Lab	23,843	57.7	-5.4
Jones, B C	8,339	20.2	0.3
Harasiwka, F LD	5,718	13.8	-3.2
Taylor, A BNP	1,563	3.8	
Moore, J UKIP	1,228	3.0	
Craig, J Green	647	1.6	

50%
Majority 15,504

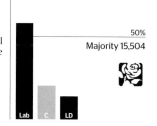

| Lab | C | LD |

Hammersmith — Labour hold

Andy Slaughter
b. Sep 29, 1960
MP 2005-

Ponderous former local councillor, manner reminiscent of an allotments committee chairman, but effective local campaigner. PPS to: Lord Malloch-Brown 2007-09; Lord Jones 2007-08; Stephen Ladyman 2005-07. Member, cttees: Court of Referees 2007-10; CSF 2007-; Regulatory Reform 2005-07. MP, Ealing Acton & Shepherds Bush 2005-10. Contested Uxbridge 1997. Cllr, Hammersmith & Fulham 1986- (leader 1996-, dep leader 1991-96). Barrister, specialising in criminal, housing and personal injury law. Member: Co-op party. GMB, Unite. Education: Latymer Upper School; Exeter University (BA English).

Shaun Bailey (C) b. 1971. A-lister. CEO of a charity. Ed: South Bank Uni.
Merlene Emerson (LD) Solicitor and commercial mediator. Ed: Kings College London; Cambridge Uni.

Constituency
This new inner London seat extends from Fulham Reach in the south to Wormwood Scrubs prison and Imperial College in the north. Hammersmith is the base for several multinationals, while the BBC is in White City. The area changed dramatically with the opening of the Westfield Shopping Centre in 2008. The seat includes some deprived areas, with 45 per cent of residents in College Park and Old Oak renting from housing associations. The old Hammersmith & Fulham seat was taken by the Tories in 2005, while the Shepherds Bush area was previously in a Labour seat.

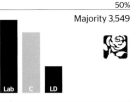

	Electorate	Turnout %	Change from '05 %
	72,348	65.6	☆
Slaughter, A Lab	20,810	43.9	1.5
Bailey, S C	17,261	36.4	2.4
Emerson, M LD	7,567	16.0	-3.0
Miles, R Green	696	1.5	-2.6
Crichton, V UKIP	551	1.2	0.6
Searle, L BNP	432	0.9	
Brennan, S Ind	135	0.3	

50%
Majority 3,549

| Lab | C | LD |

Hampshire East — Conservative hold

Damian Hinds
b. Nov 27, 1969
MP 2010-

Career in pubs, brewing and hotel industries as strategist / marketer. Contested Stretford & Urmston in 2005. Chairman of Bow Group 2001-02. Freelance consultant. Strategy director, Greene King plc. InterContinental Hotels plc/Holiday Inn Worldwide. Management consultant, Mercer Management. Lists Margaret Thatcher and Ronald Reagan among political heroes. Catholic. Married, one daughter. Education: St Ambrose Grammar School, Altrincham; Trinity College, Oxford (PPE; president, Oxford Union).

Adam Carew (LD) b. Mar 20, 1963. Ecologist & part-time lecturer.

Contested Hampshire North East 2005.
Jane Edbrooke (Lab) b. Mar 10, 1981. Communications manager for NHS London. Ed: LSE

Constituency
In dramatic boundary changes, the seat has lost a large area towards Havant in the south and gained an area on the Surrey border in the north east, a net reduction of 10,000 electors. Main settlements are the historic market towns of Alton and Petersfield and the newly included former military town of Whitehill and Bordon, with a budding eco-town project. The urban areas are comfortably off, albeit not as affluent as surrounding countryside, much of which is within the South Downs National Park and home to many commuting professionals. Under old boundaries the constituency had a long Tory tradition.

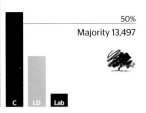

	Electorate	Turnout %	Change from '05 %
	72,250	71.0	☆
Hinds, D C	29,137	56.8	9.8
Carew, A LD	15,640	30.5	-3.5
Edbrooke, J Lab	4,043	7.9	-8.6
McGuinness, H UKIP	1,477	2.9	0.3
Williams, M Eng	710	1.4	
Jerrard, D JAC	310.0	0.6	

50%
Majority 13,497

| C | LD | Lab |

Hampshire North East — Conservative hold

James Arbuthnot
b. Aug 4, 1952
MP 1987-

Urbane, able but ponderous barrister. Eeyore-like, gloomy manner. Low public profile but behind-the-scenes operator: close to William Hague, ran successful 1997 leadership campaign and later served as Opp Chief Whip (1997-2001). Relinquished Shadow SoS, Trade (2003-05) to become Chair, Defence Sel Cttee (2005-, re-elected 2010-). Took role in inquiring into mistakes of Iraq and Afghanistan mil campaigns. Chair, Con Friends of Israel. Min: Defence Procurement 1995-7. MP Wanstead & Woodford 1987-97. Married, three daughters, one son. Keeps Alpaca. Ed: Eton; Trinity Coll, Cambridge (law).

Denzil Coulson (LD) b. Sep 2, 1972. Primary school teacher. Ed: Settler's School, Cape Town: University of Cape town; University of South Africa.
Barry Jones (Lab) b. Aug 16, 1947. Retired systems engineer. Contested Hampshire North East 2001. Ed: Imperial College London.

Constituency
The seat has been substantially redrawn; though most of Hart district remains, it no longer includes any of east Hampshire. Instead, it extends west, flanking Basingstoke to the north and south. The M3 cuts through the centre of the seat and the main town of Fleet lies just to its south, running into Church Crookham. Other settlements include Bramley and Hook, and the Lib Dem-leaning town of Yateley. The seat remains affluent and under previous boundaries had a long Tory history.

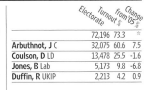

	Electorate	Turnout %	Change from '05 %
	72,196	73.3	☆
Arbuthnot, J C	32,075	60.6	7.5
Coulson, D LD	13,478	25.5	-1.6
Jones, B Lab	5,173	9.8	-6.8
Duffin, R UKIP	2,213	4.2	0.9

50%
Majority 18,597

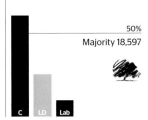

| C | LD | Lab |

Hampshire North West — Conservative hold

Sir George Young
b. Jul 16, 1941
MP 1974-

Popular, bicycling Baronet. Shrewd Tory wet. Leader of HoC, Lord Privy Seal (attending Cabinet) 2010-. Influential in toughening Commons discipline as Chair, Cttee Standards & Privileges (2001-09) after failing to become Speaker in 2000. Contested again 2009. Shadow Leader HoC 2009-10. Shadow: Leader of HoC/Constitutional Affairs 1999-2000; Leader of HoC/Chancellor of Duchy of Lanc 1998-99. Shadow SoS: Defence 1997-98. SoS: Transport 1995-97. Financial Sec Treasury 1994-5. Min: Environ 1990-94. Gov't whip 1990. Parly under-sec 1979-86. Opp whip 1976-79. MP Ealing Acton 1974-97. Cllr 1968-73. Economist, Nat Econ Devt Office. Econ adviser, Post Office Corp. Married, two daughters, two sons. Ed: Eton; Christ Church, Oxford (PPE); Surrey (MPhil econ).

Thomas McCann (LD) Contested Slough 2005.
Sarah Evans (Lab) b. Feb 21, 1971. Works in communications.

Constituency
This large, rural constituency spans an area from the western outskirts of Basingstoke across to the border with Wiltshire. The main towns are Tadley, bordering Berkshire in the northeastern extremity, and Andover, in the south west of the seat. Other settlements include Whitchurch and Quidhampton. This is an affluent seat with a large middle class. Manufacturing and agriculture are traditionally important. It has been a safe Tory seat for decades.

	Electorate	Turnout %	Change from '05 %
	76,040	70.1	☆
Young, G C	31,072	58.3	7.8
McCann, T LD	12,489	23.4	-1.5
Evans, S Lab	6,980	13.1	-7.8
Oram, S UKIP	2,751	5.2	1.4

50%
Majority 18,583

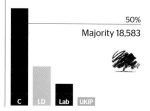

Hampstead & Kilburn — Labour hold

Glenda Jackson
b. May 9, 1936
MP 1992-

Star of big screen (Oscar-winning actress in 1971, 1974) who has struggled to play the part of politician. Grumpy. Had difficult period as a junior minister, later a vocal critic of Blairism. Survived fierce three-way battle to hold seat by a whisker. Parly Under-Sec, Environment Transport & Regions 1997-99 – resigned. Opp Transport spokes 1996-97. MP Hampstead & Highgate 1992-2010. GLA advisory cabinet for homelessness. Campaigner: Oxfam/Shelter/Friends of the Earth. President, the National Toy Libraries Assoc. CBE. Divorced, one son. Education: West Kirby County Grammar School for Girls; RADA.

Chris Philp (C) b. Jul 6, 1976. Businessman. Cllr, Camden BC 2006-10. Education: Oxford.
Edward Fordham (LD) b. Mar 13, 1971. Senior officer, LGA. Contested Hampstead & Highgate 2005. Education: Nottingham.

Constituency
After significant boundary changes, leafy Hampstead with its Victorian terraces is no longer paired with Highgate to its north east. Instead, it gains a chunk of neighbouring Brent borough to the south west, encompassing Brondesbury, with its large detached houses, Queen's Park and Kilburn, which includes an area of deprivation in an otherwise affluent seat. Traditionally home to many Irish residents, there are a mix of ethnicities. The other centres are Swiss Cottage and Belsize. Labour won the old Hampstead & Highgate seat in 1992.

	Electorate	Turnout %	Change from '05 %
	79,713	66.3	☆
Jackson, G Lab	17,332	32.8	-3.5
Philp, C C	17,290	32.7	9.8
Fordham, E LD	16,491	31.2	-4.0
Campbell, B Green	759	1.4	-3.2
Nielsen, M UKIP	408	0.8	0.1
Moore, V BNP	328	0.6	
Omond, T TOC	123	0.2	
Alcantara, G Ind	91	0.2	

50%
Majority 42

Harborough — Conservative hold

Edward Garnier
b. Oct 26, 1952
MP 1992-

Solid if undramatic; certain to be a big influence on legal policy. Urbane and posh, excellent barrister-like questioning but can sound out of touch. Solicitor General 2010-. Shadow Attorney General 2009-10; Shadow Minister: Justice 2007-10; Home Affairs 2005-07. Shadow Attorney General 1999-01; Shadow Minister Lord Chancellor's Department 1997-99. Parliamentary private secretary to: Roger Freeman 1996-97; Sir Nicholas Lyell/Sir Derek Spencer 1995-97; Alastair Goodlad/David Davis 1994-95. Barrister. Married, one daughter, two sons. Ed: Wellington Coll; Jesus College, Oxford (BA mod hist); College of Law.

Zuffar Haq (LD) b. Jun 15, 1966. Businessman. Contested Leicester West 2005. Ed: De Montfort Uni.
Kevin McKeever (Lab) b. Oct 8, 1980. Works in PR. Ed: Durham University.

Constituency
This Leicestershire seat reaches from Market Harborough on the border with Northamptonshire up through rural land to the densely populated neighbouring towns of Oadby and Wigston, which lie just south of Leicester city. This is an economically active seat, with large numbers of professionals and middle-class commuters living in affluent country villages. There is also a sizeable working class, especially in the more deprived Wigston. About 7 per cent of residents are of Indian origin. The seat has been Tory for decades but the Liberal Democrats narrowed the majorities in some recent elections.

	Electorate	Turnout %	Change from '05 %
	77,917	70.5	☆
Garnier, E C	26,894	49.0	6.0
Haq, Z LD	17,097	31.1	-3.5
McKeever, K Lab	6,981	12.7	-6.6
Dickens, G BNP	1,715	3.1	
King, M UKIP	1,462	2.7	-0.5
Ball, D Eng	568	1.0	
Stephenson, J Ind	228	0.4	

50%
Majority 9,797

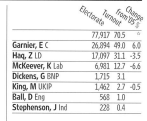

Harlow — Conservative gain

Robert Halfon
b. Mar 22, 1969
MP 2010-

Organised petition to make St George's Day a public holiday. Contested Harlow 2005, 2001. 1922 executive committee, 2010-. Member, Conservative Way Forward. Political consultant, including to Conservative Friends of Israel. Former Chief of Staff to Oliver Letwin. Board member, Centre for Social Justice. Cites Solzhenitsyn and Natan Sharansky as political heroes. Took part in Project Umubano. Has walking disability. Season ticket holder, Chelsea FC. Collects watches. Lives with partner. Jewish. Ed: Highgate school; Exeter Uni (BA politics; MA Russian & East European politics).

Bill Rammell (Lab) b. Oct 10, 1959. MP 1997-2010. Min: Armed Forces 2009-10; FCO 2008-09; Ed/Uni 2005-08.
David White (LD) b. Sep 29, 1983. Business analyst.

Constituency
Harlow town, in the west of Essex, was built around the original village to house displaced London residents after the Second World War. Although home to one of the UK's first tower blocks, The Lawn, it is generally green. It has a relatively youthful population and unusually high reliance on large employers. Workplace earnings are significantly higher than residents', meaning some of the best jobs are taken by those commuting from London. It has a higher number of ethnic minorities than most of Essex at about 8 per cent. It was working-class Tory territory, but Labour took it in 1997.

	Electorate	Turnout %	Change from '05 %
	67,439	65.1	☆
Halfon, R C	19,691	44.9	4.1
Rammell, B Lab	14,766	33.7	-7.7
White, D LD	5,990	13.7	0.7
Butler, E BNP	1,739	4.0	
Croft, J UKIP	1,591	3.6	1.1
Adeeko, O Ch	101	0.2	

50%
Majority 4,925

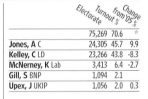

C Lab LD

Harrogate & Knaresborough — Conservative gain

Andrew Jones
b. Nov 28, 1963
MP 2010-

Proud Yorkshireman. Approachable and quick-witted. Cllr, Harrogate BC 2003-. Former chairman, Bow Group. Interested in renewable energy and recycling. Sales and marketing, Bettys & Taylors of Harrogate. Career: M&C Saatchi; Going Places; Kingfisher (Superdrug, B&Q). Contested Harrogate & Knaresborough 2001. Enjoys cricket, squash. Ed: Bradford Grammar School; Leeds (BA English).

Claire Kelley (LD) b. Sep 17, 1956. Caseworker for Phil Willis. Ed: Maidenhead HS; University of Sussex.
Kevin McNerney (Lab) b. Dec 5, 1964. Barrister. Ed: Northumbria University.

Constituency
Sixteen miles north of Leeds, these neighbouring towns form the core of a small seat extended to include a rural area to the north east, formerly in the Skipton & Ripon seat. Parts of Harrogate are within the least deprived 1 per cent of Britain and it has six of Yorkshire's ten most expensive streets. Its spa and the English tea time treats produced by Bettys and Taylors of Harrogate make it important for tourism. Before turning Lib Dem in 1997 it was staunchly Conservative.

	Electorate	Turnout %	Change from '05 %
	75,269	70.6	☆
Jones, A C	24,305	45.7	9.9
Kelley, C LD	23,266	43.8	-8.3
McNerney, K Lab	3,413	6.4	-2.7
Gill, S BNP	1,094	2.1	
Upex, J UKIP	1,056	2.0	0.3

50%
Majority 1,039

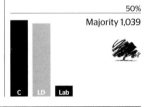

C LD Lab

Harrow East — Conservative gain

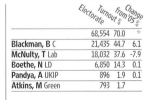

Bob Blackman
b. Apr 26, 1956
MP 2010-

A highly divisive but successful political operator, eventually making it into parliament despite the wishes of some in his own party. From the mainstream Tory right. Cllr, Brent 1986- (leader Conservative group 1990; council leader 1991-96). Contested Brent North 2005; Bedford & Kempston 1997; Brent South 1992. Greater London Assembly member 2004-2008 (defeated). Career at BT (rose to Regulatory Compliance Manager). Previously worked in sales for Unisys. Devoted Spurs fan. Enjoys bridge and chess. Married. Christian (United Reform). Ed: Preston Manor High School; Liverpool University (Union president).

Tony McNulty (Lab) b. Nov 3, 1958. MP Harrow East 1997-2010. Cllr, Harrow DC 1986-97. Contested Harrow East 1992-2010. Lecturer.
Nahid Boethe (LD) b. Apr 28, 1948. Charity fundraiser; President of Rotary Club of Harrow. Contested Hendon 2005; Hayes & Harlington 2001.

Constituency
In the north west of London, this seat is divided demographically between the outermost areas around Harrow Weald and Stanmore Park, which are more than 75 per cent white, and the more densely populated Kenton, Queensbury and Edgware areas where a substantial majority of residents are black or ethnic minorities. The area is fairly affluent commuter territory and deprivation is low. This seat has swung between the two main parties and held by Labour from 1997 to 2010.

	Electorate	Turnout %	Change from '05 %
	68,554	70.0	☆
Blackman, B C	21,435	44.7	6.1
McNulty, T Lab	18,032	37.6	-7.9
Boethe, N LD	6,850	14.3	0.1
Pandya, A UKIP	896	1.9	0.1
Atkins, M Green	793	1.7	

50%
Majority 3,403

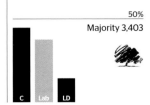

C Lab LD

Harrow West
Labour Co-op hold

Gareth Thomas
b. Jul 15, 1967
MP 1997-

Very busy and quite forgettable. Minister: International Development 2008-10; BERR 2008-09. Parly Under-Sec: Trade 2007-08; DfID 2003-08. PPS to Charles Clarke 1999-2003. Member, select cttee: Environmental Audit 1997-99. Chair Co-op party 2000-. Cllr, Harrow 1990-97. Vice-Chair, Assocn of Local Govt Soc Services Cttee. Amicus. Teacher. Ed: Hatch End HS; Lowlands Coll; Uni Coll of Wales (BSc econ/politics); Uni Coll of Wales, Aberystwyth; King's Coll, London (MA imperial & commonwealth studies); Greenwich (PGCE).

Dr Rachel Joyce (C) NHS doctor.

Ed: Uni of Wales Med Sch; Uni Coll, Cardiff; London Uni.
Christopher Noyce (LD) b. Oct 14, 1957. Solicitor. Contested Harrow West 2005, 2001. Cllr, Harrow DC. Ed: Harrow County Grammar School for Boys; Pembroke College, Oxford; College of Law Guildford.

Constituency
After boundary changes this northwest London seat loses the large Pinner area, and gains more of Harrow in the east. With several Tube stops in the seat, most residents commute to work elsewhere and it is generally affluent. The Rayners Lane estate in Roxbourne is one of the main areas of social housing and the most densely populated. There are high numbers of ethnic minorities. This was held by the Tories for decades until falling to Labour's landslide in 1997.

	Electorate	Turnout %	Change from '05 %
	71,510	64.5	☆
Thomas, G Lab	20,111	43.6	-5.0
Joyce, R C	16,968	36.8	6.4
Noyce, C LD	7,458	16.2	-2.5
Crossman, H UKIP	954	2.1	0.8
Langley, R Green	625	1.4	

50%
Majority 3,143

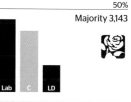

Hartlepool
Labour hold

Iain Wright
b. May 9, 1972
MP 2004-

Boyish Teesider made good, elected as successor to Peter Mandelson after he became European Commissioner in 2004. Parly Under-Sec: Children 2009-10; CLG 2007-09. PPS to Rosie Winterton 2005-06. Member, cttees: Public Accounts 2007; Modernisation of HoC 2006-08; Public Administration 2005-06. Cllr, Hartlepool BC 2002-05. GMB. Chair Lab Friends of Israel 2005-06. Chartered accountant. Married, one daughter, three sons. Ed: Manor Comp, Hartlepool; Hartlepool Sixth Form Coll; UCL (BA hist, MA).

Alan Wright (C) b. 1947. Current affairs presenter/producer, BBC.

Reg Clark (LD) b. Mar 15, 1958. Consultant/investor. Contested Hartlepool 1997.
Stephen Allison (UKIP) b. Apr 28, 1960. Contested Hartlepool 2004.

Constituency
The northeastern coastal town of Hartlepool, developed around the port and distinctive headland, was traditionally known for shipbuilding and steel. Though a shadow of their old selves, significant manufacturing and construction centres remain. Warehousing and industries dominate much of the coast along Hartlepool Bay and there is a nuclear power station. Most of this working-class town remains severely deprived. Hartlepool FC's mascot, H'Angus the Monkey, was famously elected mayor in 2002. The seat, Labour since 1964, was represented by Peter Mandelson for 12 years.

	Electorate	Turnout %	Change from '05 %
	68,923	55.5	
Wright, I Lab	16,267	42.5	-9.0
Wright, A C	10,758	28.1	16.7
Clark, R LD	6,533	17.1	-13.3
Allison, S UKIP	2,682	7.0	3.5
Bage, R BNP	2,002	5.2	

50%
Majority 5,509

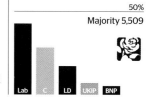

Harwich & Essex North
Conservative hold

Bernard Jenkin
b. Apr 9, 1959
MP 1992-

Good-looking, veteran, Eurosceptic right-winger who never quite made it. Close to Iain Duncan Smith as leader. Tasked with boosting diversity through A-list as Dep Chair Con Party 2005-06. Elected Chair, select cttee: Public Admin 2010-. Wife, Anne, is a maverick who ran Women2Win. 1922 executive cttee, 2010-. Shad Min: Trade & Industry 2005. Shad SoS: Regions 2003-05; Defence 2001-03. Shad Min: Transport 1998-2001. PPS to Michael Forsyth 1995-7. MP N Essex 1997-2010; N Colchester 1992-97. Var opp spokes roles. Pol adviser to Leon Brittan 1986-88. Venture capital manager. Married, two sons. Ed: William Ellis; Corpus Christi, Cambridge (BA Eng lit).

James Raven (LD) Professor of History. Contested Essex North in 2005. Ed: Cambridge Uni; Oxford Uni.
Darren Barrenger (Lab) b. Jul 2, 1967. IT project director for BT.

Constituency
Only the northern tip of the old Harwich seat remains. The Mayflower was built here and the area retains a strong maritime connection with one of the largest container ports in Britain. The port is joined with the old, predominantly rural, North Essex seat, which has lost its southwest extremity to the new Witham seat. There are large numbers of pensioners and high levels of deprivation and child poverty. The villages and towns through the countryside inland are more affluent. The old Harwich seat fell to Labour in 1997, but the North Essex seat remained Tory.

	Electorate	Turnout %	Change from '05 %
	70,743	69.3	☆
Jenkin, B C	23,001	46.9	4.3
Raven, J LD	11,554	23.6	4.3
Barrenger, D Lab	9,774	20.0	-10.9
Anselmi, S UKIP	2,527	5.2	1.5
Robey, S BNP	1,065	2.2	
Fox, C Green	909	1.9	-1.8
Thompson, P Bates	170	0.4	

50%
Majority 11,447

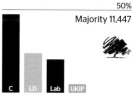

Hastings & Rye — Conservative gain

Amber Rudd
b. Aug 1, 1963
MP 2010-

Extremely well-connected and highly focused former banker. Rather earnest. Was 'aristocracy adviser' to *Four Weddings and a Funeral*. Contested Liverpool Garston 2005. Interested in education, entrepreneurship and rail travel. Recruitment consultant. Financial journalist for Corporate Finance. Chairman, Travel Intelligence. Venture capital, Lawnstone Ltd. Banker, JP Morgan. Chair, Hastings Local Traders Group. Cites Barbara Castle, Rab Butler, Margaret Thatcher and Oliver Cromwell as political heroes. Divorced (from journalist A A Gill), one daughter, one son. Ed: Edinburgh (MA history); Pennsylvania Uni (history).

Michael Foster (Lab) b. Feb 26, 1946. MP Hastings & Rye 1997-2010. Solicitor. Ed: Hastings GS; Leicester University.
Nicholas Perry (LD) Mental health social worker. Ed: University of London. Ed: Cambridge University.

Constituency
The East Sussex coastal town of Hastings, with its beach-launched fishing fleet, is the main population hub. The constituency extends east up the coast, round Rye Bay and inland to Rye itself, with its charming cobbled streets. Hastings has several areas within the 10 per cent most deprived in England. There is a relatively large working class and many self-employed; few parts of this seat are truly affluent. Its was the scene of one of Labour's most impressive seaside victories in 1997, overturning 95 years of Conservative representation.

	Electorate	Turnout %	Change from 05 %
	78,000	63.9	☆
Rudd, A C	20,468	41.1	3.0
Foster, M Lab	18,475	37.1	-3.5
Perry, N LD	7,825	15.7	-0.1
Smith, A UKIP	1,397	2.8	0.1
Prince, N BNP	1,310	2.6	
Bridger, R Eng	339	0.7	

50%
Majority 1,993

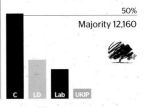

C | Lab | LD

Havant — Conservative hold

David Willetts
b. Mar 9, 1956
MP 1992-

Likeable intellectual with Tiggerish manner, nicknamed "two brains". Fell out of favour under David Cameron after backing David Davis in 2005 and attacking grammar schools in 2007. Min: BIS (Universities and Science; att. Cabinet) 2010-. Shadow Min: Uni & Skills 2009-. Shadow SoS: IUS 2007-09; Ed & Skills 2005-07; Trade & Ind 2005; Welfare Reform 2004-05; Work & Pensions 2001-05; Soc Security 1999-2001, Ed/Employment 1998-99. Opp spokes 1997-98. Paymaster Gen 1996, Parly Sec 1995-96. Gov't whip 1995, ass't 1994-5. PPS to Sir Norman Fowler 1993-94. Head of Policy Co-ord, Con Party 2003-04. Political/policy/co dir. Married, one

daughter, one son. Ed: Christ Church, Oxford (BA PPE).

Alex Payton (LD) b. Feb 6, 1974. Barrister. Ed: Oxford Uni.
Robert Smith (Lab) b. Aug 30, 1982. Teacher. Ed: Hull Uni.

Constituency
Just east of Portsmouth, this unusually shaped constituency encompasses Hayling Island, with its beaches and holiday resorts, and Havant, Emsworth and Purbrook on the mainland. A seat of contrasts, there are affluent areas along the coast but areas of severe deprivation, especially in the huge Leigh Park council housing estate. Hayling Island is particularly popular with retired people and the constituency has a large working class, with manufacturing and construction traditionally strong. There is a long Tory tradition.

	Electorate	Turnout %	Change from 05 %
	69,712	63.0	☆
Willetts, D C	22,433	51.1	6.8
Payton, A LD	10,273	23.4	3.2
Smith, R Lab	7,777	17.7	-11.0
Kerrin, G UKIP	2,611	6.0	3.5
Addams, F Eng	809	1.8	

50%
Majority 12,160

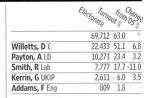

C | LD | Lab | UKIP

Hayes & Harlington — Labour hold

John McDonnell
b. Sep 8, 1951
MP 1997-

Left-wing rebel, enjoyed attention of bid for Labour leadership in 2007 (received marginal support); candidate again in 2010, withdrew to allow Diane Abbott through. Consistent but little-noticed champion of socialism. Member, cttees: Unopposed Bills 1999-2004; Deregulation & Regulatory Reform 1999-2002. Cllr, GLC 1981-86. Chair, Britain & Ireland Human Rights Centre. Shop steward, Unison. NUM/TUC researcher/ Camden council policy unit head. Chief exec, Assocn of London Authorities/Govt. Editor Lab Herald. Divorced, remarried. Two daughters from first marriage, one son from second. Ed: Brunel (BSc govt & pol); Birkbeck Coll (MSc pol & soc).

Scott Seaman-Digby (C) b. 1972. Director of commercial management consultants. Cllr, Hillingdon. Ed: University of London (BA); Liverpool.
Satnam Kaur Khalsa (LD) b. Jul 15, 1955. Accountant. Contested Feltham and Heston in 2005.

Constituency
The M4 bisects this seat. To the south are Harlington and Heathrow, while to the north are Hayes and West Drayton. Once described by George Orwell as "one of the most godforsaken places I have ever struck", Hayes is predominantly a residential suburb with industrial sites and has little in the way of cultural assets. A number of Hayes areas are within the most deprived 20 per cent nationwide. This seat historically returned Labour MPs, but was held by the Tories from 1983 to 1997 before Labour recaptured it.

	Electorate	Turnout %	Change from 05 %
	70,233	60.7	☆
McDonnell, J Lab	23,377	54.8	-1.6
Seaman-Digby, S C	12,553	29.4	1.7
Kaur, S Khalsa LD	3,726	8.7	
Forster, C BNP	1,520	3.6	
Cripps, A NF	566	1.3	
Dixon, C Eng	464	1.1	
Lee, J Green	348	0.8	-0.6
Shahzad, A Ch	83	0.2	

50%
Majority 10,824

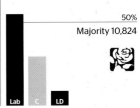

Lab | C | LD

Hazel Grove — Liberal Democrat hold

Andrew Stunell
b. Nov 19, 1942
MP 1997-

Member of Lib Dem coalition negotiating team. Chief Whip during crisis in Charles Kennedy's leadership in 2005. Former Baptist lay preacher. Parly Under-Sec: Communities & Local Government 2010-. LD shad sec: ODPM/CLG 2006-07. LD whip: chief 2001-06; dep chief 1997-2001. LD spokes: energy 1997-2005. Chair, LD local election campaign 2007. Member, LD federal/conference cttees. Cllr: Stockport MBC 1994-2002; Cheshire CC 1981-91; Chester CC 1979-90. Pres, NW Constitutional Convention. VP, Local Govt Assoc. Vice-Chair Assoc of County Councils. Architectural assistant/political sec. OBE. Married, two daughters, three sons. Education: Surbiton GS; Manchester (architecture RIBA pt II exemption); Liverpool Polytechnic.

Annesley Abercorn (C) Adviser to Oliver Letwin MP. Ed: Highgate, University of London.
Richard Scorer (Lab) Solicitor. Ed: Edinburgh Uni; UPenn.

Constituency
Just east of Stockport, this seat stretches to the foot of the Pennines. Hazel Grove, in the south of the seat, was traditionally focused on silk mills and coalmining but is now an affluent commuter hub. Marple, which lies in a picturesque setting in the Goyt Valley along the Peak Forest Canal, and Romiley, are also sought-after locations in this middle-class seat. The Lib Dems ousted the Tories in 1997.

	Electorate	Turnout %	Change from '05 %
	63,074	66.6	☆
Stunell, A LD	20,485	48.8	-1.5
Abercorn, A C	14,114	33.6	3.3
Scorer, R Lab	5,234	12.5	-3.6
Whittaker, J UKIP	2,148	5.1	1.9

Majority 6,371

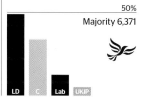

Hemel Hempstead — Conservative hold

Mike Penning
b. Sep 29, 1957
MP 2005-

A burly ex-fireman with an estuary accent. Dull, but surprisingly effective working class patriot, has no pretensions to be an intellectual; a populist right-winger. Was Deputy Head of Media for Iain Duncan Smith. Parly Under-Sec: Transport 2010-. Shadow Minister: Health 2007-10. Member, Health Select Committee 2005-07. Contested Thurrock 2001. Adviser to William Hague's Shadow Cabinet. Political journalist. Served in Army with Grenadier Guards, then became fireman. Married, two daughters. Educated: Appleton Comp, King Edmund Comp, Essex.

Dr Richard Grayson (LD) b. Apr 18, 1969. Former LD Director of Policy. Head of Politics, Goldsmiths. Contested Hemel Hempstead 2005.
Ayfer Orhan (Lab) b. Dec 25, 1959. Contested Cambridgeshire NW 2005.

Constituency
In the west of Hertfordshire, the town of Hemel Hempstead is the main focus, although it also includes affluent rural areas to the north, reaching up to the border with Buckinghamshire. The retail town centre focuses on the Marlowes area. The wider economy is mixed, with a strong real estate sector and technology cluster; Dixons has its headquarters here and Kodak is a major employer. More than 25 per cent live in social rented housing but Hemel Hempstead is generally affluent. The seat was taken by Labour on its creation in 1997 but fell to the Tories in 2005.

	Electorate	Turnout %	Change from '05 %
	72,754	68.0	☆
Penning, M C	24,721	50.0	9.9
Grayson, R LD	11,315	22.9	6.0
Orhan, A Lab	10,295	20.8	-18.9
Price, J BNP	1,615	3.3	
Alexander, D UKIP	1,254	2.5	-0.7
Young, M Ind	271	0.6	

Majority 13,406

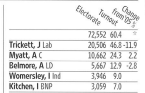

Hemsworth — Labour hold

Jon Trickett
b. Jul 2, 1950
MP 1996-

Leading figure in grass-roots left organisation Compass. Among the first to call for Blair's resignation. PPS to: Gordon Brown 2008-10; Peter Mandelson 1997-98. Member, select cttees: Public Accounts 2001-06; Education & Employment 2001; Unopposed Bills (Panel) 1997-. Cllr, Leeds City 1984-86 (leader 1989-96). GMB. Plumber, builder. Married, two daughters, one son. Ed: Roundhay Sch, Leeds; Hull (BA politics); Leeds (MA political sociology).

Ann Myatt (C) Education: University of Leeds.
Alan Belmore (LD) b. 1990. Accountant.

Ian Womersley (Ind) b. Sep 3, 1958. Keyworker. Cllr, Hemsworth 2008-. Ed: Hemsworth Communirt Coll.
Ian Kitchen (BNP)

Constituency
Lying southeast of Wakefield, much of this West Yorkshire constituency is green belt land, untouched by motorways. The population is concentrated in Hemsworth and South Kirkby, towns at the seat's southern boundary that have severe deprivation. An economy dependent on coalmining was devastated by pit closures. Associated problems of poor health persist and large numbers of people work in routine occupations. This was traditionally seen as one of Labour's safest seats.

	Electorate	Turnout %	Change from '05 %
	72,552	60.4	☆
Trickett, J Lab	20,506	46.8	-11.9
Myatt, A C	10,662	24.3	2.2
Belmore, A LD	5,667	12.9	-2.8
Womersley, I Ind	3,946	9.0	
Kitchen, I BNP	3,059	7.0	

Majority 9,844

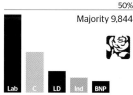

187

Hendon — Conservative gain

Matthew Offord
b. Sep 3, 1969
MP 2010-

Athletic. Friend of Jane Ellison MP from Barnet Council days (Cllr, Barnet 2002-; deputy leader to Mike Freer MP as council leader). Contested Barnsley East & Mexborough 2001. Political advisor: Local Government Association; Conservative Central Office. Media analyst: BBC; MediaLink. Keen scuba diver, sailer and wild swimmer. Member, Surfers against Sewage. Elected Fellow of Royal Geographical Society. Former trustee Hendon & Mill Hill Alms Houses. Christian. Married. Ed: Amery Hill School, Alton; Nottingham Trent (BA Photography); King's College London (PhD)

Andrew Dismore (Lab) b. Sep 2, 1954. MP Hendon 1997-2010. Chair, Joint Human Rights Cttee 2005-10. Ed: Bridlington GS; Warwick Uni; LSE.
Matthew Harris (LD) b. Feb 24, 1971. Works in PR. Ed: Christ's Coll, Finchley; Brasenose Coll, Oxford (Eng).

Constituency
The M1 runs the length of this northwest London seat, from the green spaces by the border with Hertfordshire, finishing at Brent Cross at the southern boundary. Burnt Oak and Colindale, on the western border, are the poorest areas, and along with West Hendon have large council housing concentrations. Edgware, towards the north of the seat, has a large Jewish community comprising nearly a fifth of the seat's residents. Labour took this seat in 1997 but, under different boundaries, it had been held by the Tories for 47 years.

	Electorate	Turnout %	Change from '05 %
	78,923	58.8	☆
Offord, M C	19,635	42.3	5.3
Dismore, A Lab	19,529	42.1	-3.0
Harris, M LD	5,734	12.4	-1.8
Lambert, R UKIP	958	2.1	0.6
Newby, A Green	518	1.1	-0.7

50%
Majority 106

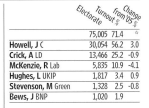

Henley — Conservative hold

John Howell
b. Jul 27, 1955
MP 2008-

Won by-election following Boris Johnson's election to Mayor of London; lives in the shadow of his predecessor. Member, select committee on Work and Pensions 2008-10. Business career: partner, Ernst&Young; led British business delegations to G7 meetings; Board member, Know How Fund. Business journalist, BBC World Service. Amateur dramatist. Married, two daughters, one son. Education: Battersea Grammar School; Edinburgh (MA archaeology); St John's Coll, Oxford (DPhil prehistoric archaeology).

Andrew Crick (LD) b. Feb 7, 1969. Assistant consultant. Ed: Staffordshire University, Sheffield Uni.

Richard McKenzie (Lab) b. Feb 23, 1966. Businessman, lollipop man. Ed: St George's College, Weybridge, Reading Uni.

Constituency
Picturesque Henley-on-Thames, famed for its royal regatta, is near the south of this physically huge constituency, which takes in expanses of sparsely populated Chiltern Hills and Oxfordshire countryside. Other towns, such as Goring and Wheatley, are popular with commuters in one of the most affluent seats in the country. It has been extended to include the Cherwell borough wards of Kirtlington and Otmoor. The seat has been Tory for decades.

	Electorate	Turnout %	Change from '05 %
	75,005	71.4	☆
Howell, J C	30,054	56.2	3.0
Crick, A LD	13,466	25.2	-0.9
McKenzie, R Lab	5,835	10.9	-4.1
Hughes, L UKIP	1,817	3.4	0.9
Stevenson, M Green	1,328	2.5	-0.8
Bews, J BNP	1,020	1.9	

50%
Majority 16,588

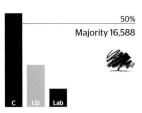

Hereford & Herefordshire South — Conservative gain

Jesse Norman
b. 1962
MP 2010-

Thoughtful, friend and Eton contemporary of Boris Johnson. Wrote key 'Cameroon' text Compassionate Conservatism but departed the leadership policy with Churchill's Legacy: The Conservative case for the Human Rights Act. Policy adviser to Boris Johnson during mayoral campaign and George Osborne as Shadow Chancellor Philosophy researcher/teacher, UCL. Worked at Barclays. Worked for and ran educational project giving away textbooks in Eastern Europe. Married, three children. Ed: Eton Coll; Oxford University; UCL (MPhil, PhD).

Sarah Carr (LD) b. Mar 3, 1974. Political adviser. Ed: Telford Coll; Wulfrun

Coll; Portsmouth Uni.
Philippa Roberts (Lab) b. Feb 16, 1975. Environmental consultant. Ed: Manchester University.

Constituency
From the county town of Hereford, the seat fans out to Ross-on-Wye in the south east and the border with Wales in the west. Agriculture accounts for an important economic sector, with a weekly livestock market in Hereford, as does tourism, with a Norman cathedral and pretty countryside. After decades of Tory dominance it was won by the Liberal Democrats in 1997.

	Electorate	Turnout %	Change from '05 %
	71,435	67.7	☆
Norman, J C	22,366	46.2	5.2
Carr, S LD	19,885	41.1	-2.3
Roberts, P Lab	3,506	7.3	-3.0
Smith, V UKIP	1,638	3.4	1.2
Oliver, J BNP	986	2.0	

50%
Majority 2,481

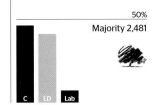

Herefordshire North
Conservative hold

Bill Wiggin
b. Jun 4, 1966
MP 2001-

Former school-mate of David Cameron. Assistant Government whip 2010-. Opp Whip 2009-10. Shad Min: Agriculture/Fisheries 2005-09; Environment 2005. Shad Sec: Wales 2003-05. Shad Min: EFRA 2005, 2003. MP Leominster 2001-2010. Contested Burnley 1997. Banker. Manager structured products Commerzbank. City of London Freeman. Owns smallholding with Hereford cattle, Ryeland sheep. Countryside Alliance. Shooting/fishing hobbies. TA Officer. Married, one daughter, two sons. Ed: Eton Coll; University College of North Wales (BA economics)

Lucy Hurds (LD) Book-keeper.

Neil Sabharwal (Lab) b. Dec 14, 1980. Solicitor. Cllr, Lambeth BC. Ed: Dulwich College; Cambridge University.

Constituency
This seat has lost territory from Worcestershire and gained Old Gore in the south. Its renaming reflects the huge rural area surrounding Leominster town, including other market towns of Kington, Bromyard and Ledbury. Cattle and sheep farming remains important in this seat, which has one of the highest proportions of residents employed in the agricultural sector in the country. It has been Conservative since 1906.

	Electorate	Turnout %	Change from 05 %
	66,525	71.5	☆
Wiggin, B C	24,631	51.8	-0.7
Hurds, L LD	14,744	31.0	7.0
Sabharwal, N Lab	3,373	7.1	-8.4
Oakton, J UKIP	2,701	5.7	2.4
Norman, F Green	1,533	3.2	-1.5
King, J Ind	586	1.2	

50%
Majority 9,887

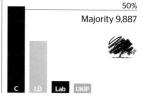

C · LD · Lab · UKIP

Hertford & Stortford
Conservative hold

Mark Prisk
b. Jun 12, 1962
MP 2001-

Small business background. Min: BIS 2010-. Shadow Minister: Business 2005-10. Opposition Whip 2004-05. Shadow: Paymaster General 2003-04; Financial Sec 2002-03. Founder East Hertfordshire Business Forum. Member Prince's Trust. Founding Chair, Youth for Peace through NATO. 1983-86. Chartered Surveyor, then formed marketing consultancy. Married. Education: Truro School; Reading (BSc land management).

Andrew Lewin (LD) b. Jan 1, 1987. Junior PR consultant. Ed: Bishop's Stortford HS, York Uni (politics).
Steve Terry (Lab) b. Oct 16, 1962. Trade Union official.

Constituency
The market town of Bishop's Stortford is on Hertfordshire's border with Essex, and its leafy avenues are home to many affluent commuters to London. The Havers Estate is a rare pocket of deprivation. The town is just the other side of the motorway from Stansted airport, which provides employment for many residents and has attracted a large European immigrant population. Farther south is Sawbridgeworth, while the town of Hertford and neighbouring Ware lie to the west. The economy is predominantly service sector, unemployment is low and the area is mostly prosperous. It has returned Tory MPs since its creation in 1983.

	Electorate	Turnout %	Change from 05 %
	78,459	70.6	☆
Prisk, M C	29,810	53.8	3.6
Lewin, A LD	14,373	26.0	7.5
Terry, S Lab	7,620	13.8	-10.5
Sodey, D UKIP	1,716	3.1	1.0
Harris, R BNP	1,297	2.3	
Xenophontos, L Ind	325	0.6	
Adams, M Ind	236	0.4	

50%
Majority 15,437

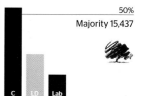

C · LD · Lab

Hertfordshire North East
Conservative hold

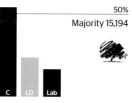

Oliver Heald
b. Dec 15, 1954
MP 1992-

Genial figure uncomfortable with rough-and-tumble of frontline politics; solid but unspectacular. If not a minister he could be a leading backbencher or chairman of a select committee. Shadow Sec of State: Constitutional Affairs 2004-7 (Shadow Chancellor of the Duchy of Lancaster 2005-07). Shadow Leader of the House 2003-. Shadow Minister: Work and Pensions; 2002-03. Opposition spokes. roles 2000-02, whip 1997-2000. Parly Under-Sec, DSS,1995-7. PPS to William Waldegrave 1994-5, Sir Peter Lloyd 1994. Barrister. Married, two daughters, one son. Educated: Reading School; Pembroke College, Cambridge (MA law).

Hugh Annand (LD) Translator.
David Kirkman (Lab) b. Aug 10, 1964. IT professional, secretary. Essex Labour Party.

Constituency
This large seat reaches from Letchworth and Baldock on the border with Bedfordshire, clockwise to Royston on the Cambridgeshire border. It goes through the area between Stevenage and Essex where Buntingford is one of the few towns, and down to the western side of Hertford. Baldock's Georgian and Victorian buildings contrast with Letchworth – the first garden city founded in 1903, with further large modern housing estates added through the century. Much of the land in this seat is given to agriculture, primarily arable. A safe Tory seat, it narrowly withstood Labour's 1997 onslaught.

	Electorate	Turnout %	Change from 05 %
	72,200	69.8	☆
Heald, O C	26,995	53.5	5.5
Annand, H LD	11,801	23.4	3.1
Kirkman, D Lab	8,291	16.4	-11.9
Smyth, A UKIP	2,075	4.1	0.8
Bland, R Green	875	1.7	
Campbell, R Ind	209	0.4	
Ralph, D YRDPL	143	0.3	
Reichardt, P Ind	36	0.1	

50%
Majority 15,194

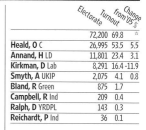

C · LD · Lab

Hertfordshire South West Conservative hold

David Gauke
b. Oct 8, 1971
MP 2005-

Thoughtful Eurosceptic from Tory right. Knowledgable on economics. Exchequer Secretary, Treasury 2010-. Shadow Minister: Treasury 2007-10. Centre for Policy Studies member. Con Friends of Israel. Solicitor, Macfarlanes. Married, three sons. Education: Northgate High School, Ipswich; St Edmund Hall, Oxford (Law LLB); Chester College of Law.

Christopher Townsend (LD) Senior risk manager. Cllr, Dacorum BC 2007-. Education: UCL, Imperial College.
Harry Mann (Lab) Lecturer, LSE. Contested North Yorkshire 2005. Education: King's College, London.

Constituency
Running along the boundary of Hertfordshire, the northern half is from the Dacorum district and the southern half the Three Rivers district. Rickmansworth and nearby Chorleywood are served by the M25 and the Tube network. It has some affluent areas such as Moor Park. There are light industrial areas with companies such as Renault-Nissan and high-tech and media industries with the Leavesden film studios. Asian-Indian communities make up around 21 per cent of the population in Moor Park and Eastbury. The seat has long been Conservative.

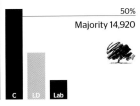

	Electorate	Turnout %	Change from '05 %
	78,248	72.5	☆
Gauke, D C	30,773	54.2	7.2
Townsend, C LD	15,853	27.9	-2.1
Mann, H Lab	6,526	11.5	-9.3
Benson, M UKIP	1,450	2.6	0.3
Gates, D BNP	1,302	2.3	
Hannaway, J Ind	846	1.5	

50%
Majority 14,920

Hertsmere Conservative hold

James Clappison
b. Sep 14, 1956
MP 1992-

A worthy dull. Shadow Minister: Work & Pensions 2007; Treasury 2002; Work 2001-02. Parly Under-Sec: Education 1995-7. PPS to Baroness Blatch 1994-5. Barrister. Owns 27 acre family-inherited farm. Property portfolio of 24 rental houses. Married, three daughters, one son. Education: St Peter's School, York; The Queen's College, Oxford (BA PPE).

Sam Russell (Lab) b. Jan 18, 1984. Railway manager. Education: University of Kent.
Anthony Rowlands (LD) b. Aug 11, 1952. Director, Centre Forum think-tank. Contested Isle of Wight 2005; St Albans 1997. Cllr, St Albans DC

1984-2003; Hertfordshire CC 1993-7. Education: Oxford (BA Modern History), Cambridge (PGCE) and London (MA Educational Administration) universities.

Constituency
Two motorways run through this seat, with the M1 fencing off the town of Bushey in the west, the M25 separating Potters Bar at the east, and Radlett and Borehamwood between them. Surrounded by 80 per cent green belt land the towns are popular with commuters and more than 60 per cent work outside the seat. Radlett and Aldenham are affluent but there are areas of deprivation in Borehamwood. Elstree Studios is a major employer. The ethnic minority population is about 12 per cent and there is a large Jewish community at more than a tenth of the population. This is a safe Tory seat.

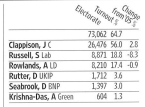

	Electorate	Turnout %	Change from '05 %
	73,062	64.7	
Clappison, J C	26,476	56.0	2.8
Russell, S Lab	8,871	18.8	-8.3
Rowlands, A LD	8,210	17.4	-0.9
Rutter, D UKIP	1,712	3.6	
Seabrook, D BNP	1,397	3.0	
Krishna-Das, A Green	604	1.3	

50%
Majority 17,605

Hexham Conservative hold

Guy Opperman
b. May 18, 1965
MP 2010-

Barrister who won 2007 Bar Pro Bono Award for Free Representation Unit work, and judicial review challenge and campaign against local hospital closures. Contested Caernarfon 2005; North Swindon 1997. Adviser to Michael Ancram as Shadow Foreign Sec. Cllr, Wiltshire 1995-99. Amateur steeplechase jockey, survived serious accident 2006. Marathon-runner. Member, Countryside Alliance. Has long-term partner. Ed: Harrow; Buckingham (law); Lille, France (Diploma).

Andrew Duffield (LD) b. Jan 12, 1963. Accommodation agent. Contested Hexham 2005, Sedgefield 2001. Ed: Plymouth College, Durham Uni.

Antoine Tinnion (Lab) b. Apr 5, 1970. Barrister. Ed: Cambridge (LLB), Oxford (MA pol/econ), Harvard (MA Law).

Constituency
Atypically for Northumberland, there are relatively high numbers of professionals and well-off middle classes in this large constituency. Hexham is surrounded by open countryside with villages dotted through, especially north towards the Cheviot Hills and Kielder, Britain's largest man-made lake. To the south is Hadrian's Wall and the North Pennines, with settlements at Haltwhistle, Prudhoe – a former mining town – and the affluent commuter hub of Ponteland, near Newcastle. Conservatives have held the seat since 1924, despite a significant coalmining Labour vote, but in 1997 they won by only 222 votes.

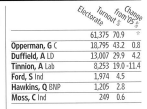

	Electorate	Turnout %	Change from '05 %
	61,375	70.9	
Opperman, G C	18,795	43.2	0.8
Duffield, A LD	13,007	29.9	4.2
Tinnion, A Lab	8,253	19.0	-11.4
Ford, S Ind	1,974	4.5	
Hawkins, Q BNP	1,205	2.8	
Moss, C Ind	249	0.6	

50%
Majority 5,788

Heywood & Middleton — Labour hold

Jim Dobbin
b. May 26, 1941
MP 1997-

Organiser of Catholic Labour MPs on conscience issues. Member, select committees: Communities & Local Gov't 2007-09; European Scrutiny 1998-10, joint cttee on consolidation of bills 2001-10. Cllr, Rochdale BC 1994-97 (leader 1996-97), 1983-92. Member European Standing Cttee C 2002-. NHS microbiologist. Married, two daughters, two sons. Education: St Columba's RC HS, Cowdenbeath; St Andrew's RC HS, Kirkcaldy; Napier Coll, Edinburgh (BSc bacteriology/virology).

Michael Holly (C) b. 1949. Chartered accountant. Cllr, Rochdale BC 2006-. Education: Jesus Coll, Oxford (BSc Chemistry).

Wera Hobhouse (LD) b. 1960. Cllr, Rochdale BC 2004-. Ed: Muenster Uni (History).
Peter Greenwood (BNP)

Constituency
This seat lies between Bury to the west and Oldham to the south. It takes in a southwestern part of Rochdale town but, unlike the neighbouring seat, it is 96 per cent white. It is solidly working-class and, although it has a significant hotel and catering sector, it suffered from the decline of the textiles industry. It has been hit by the recession, with Woolworths one of the big names closing. This has long been a safe Labour seat.

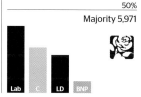

	Electorate	Turnout %	Change from '05 %
	80,171	57.5	☆
Dobbin, J Lab	18,499	40.1	-8.2
Holly, M C	12,528	27.2	5.4
Hobhouse, W LD	10,474	22.7	2.5
Greenwood, P BNP	3,239	7.0	
Cecil, V UKIP	1,215	2.6	0.7
Lee, C Ind	170	0.4	

50%
Majority 5,971

High Peak — Conservative gain

Andrew Bingham
b. Jun 23, 1962
MP 2010-

Proud of his credentials as a life-long constituency resident, keen to develop the High Peak tourism trade. Strong local campaigner on pensions system for employees for Federal Mogul. Contested High Peak 2005. Cllr, High Peak BC 1999-. Dir, family firm distributing engineering equipment. Enthusiastic cook. Buxton FC supporter. Married. Ed: Long Lane Comp Sch, Chapel-en-Frith; High Peak FE College (catering).

Caitlin Bisknell (Lab) Journalist. Cllr, Buxton 1999-.
Alistair Stevens (LD) b. 1958. Estate agent. Cllr, New Mills TC 2007-. Education: Burnage High School,
Manchester Metropolitan (BA history and politics).

Constituency
The Pennines run down the length of the seat, which spans the space between Greater Manchester and Sheffield. Most of it is within the Peak District National Park, with the exception of the settlements in the west, which run between Glossop and Buxton, once famed for its spring waters and now for its opera house. These towns both have significant industry and are Labour-leaning. Overall the seat is very affluent and home to many commuters to the nearby cities. The seat was Tory for 27 years until 1997.

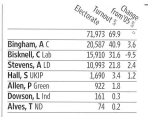

	Electorate	Turnout %	Change from '05 %
	71,973	69.9	☆
Bingham, A C	20,587	40.9	3.6
Bisknell, C Lab	15,910	31.6	-9.5
Stevens, A LD	10,993	21.8	2.4
Hall, S UKIP	1,690	3.4	1.2
Allen, P Green	922	1.8	
Dowson, L Ind	161	0.3	
Alves, T ND	74	0.2	

50%
Majority 4,677

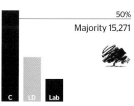

Hitchen & Harpenden — Conservative hold

Peter Lilley
b. Aug 23, 1943
MP 1983-

Issue-oriented survivor from Tory Cabinets of Thatcher and Major eras. Stood for leader in 1997, helping to split Tory right. Shadow Chancellor 1997-8. Dep Opposition leader 1998-99. Sec: Soc Security 1992-7; Trade and Industry 1990-2. Treasury: Financial Sec 1989-90; Economic Sec 1987-89. PPS to: Nigel Lawson 1984-87; Lord Bellwin/William Waldegrave 1984. MP St Albans 1983-97. Economic consultant, financial analyst specialising oil and energy. Chair, Bow Group 1973-75. Married. Ed: Dulwich College; Clare College, Cambridge (BA nat/econ science).

Nigel Quinton (LD) b. Jun 1, 1961.
Company director. Cllr, Welwyn Hatfield BC 2006-. Ed: Cambridge Uni
Oliver de Botton (Lab) b. Jan 7, 1981. Works for CfBT Ed Trust. Cllr, Hackney BC 2010-. Ed: Cambridge.

Constituency
The medieval market town of Hitchin is in the north, while Harpenden is to the south, the only major town in the mostly rural northern half of St Albans city authority. Both towns have excellent transport connections, making them popular for commercial and industrial hubs and affluent residents, particularly professional and managerial. Rothamsted Experimental Station in Harpenden is one of the largest agriculture research stations. There are several industrial estates with the rest of the seat rural with pretty villages and hamlets. The seat has returned Tory MPs since its creation.

	Electorate	Turnout %	Change from '05 %
	73,851	74.1	☆
Lilley, P C	29,869	54.6	5.2
Quinton, N LD	14,598	26.7	0.2
de Botton, O Lab	7,413	13.6	
Wilkinson, G UKIP	1,663	3.0	1.3
Wise, R Green	807	1.5	
Henderson, M Ind	109	0.2	
Byron, S R&E	108	0.2	
Hannah, E YRDPL	90	0.2	
Rigby, P Ind	50	0.1	

50%
Majority 15,271

191

Holborn & St Pancras — Labour hold

Frank Dobson
b. Mar 15, 1940
MP 1979-

Bearded veteran. Traditional Labour figure, smarter and not as nice as he looks. Has a stock of rude jokes. Cabinet career ended when persuaded by Blair to contest inaugural London mayoral election (lost to Ken Livingstone). SoS: Health 1997-99. Shadow SoS: Environment 1994-97. Shadow Min: London 1993-97. Shadow SoS: Transport 1993-94; Employment 1992-93; Energy 1989-92. Shadow Leader HoC and Campaigns Co-ordinator 1987-89. Shad Min: Health 1983-87. Opp spokes 1981-83, 1989-97. Cllr Camden BC; leader 1973-75. Asst Sec Office of Local Ombudsman. Electricity Council. CEGB HQ. Married, one daughter, two sons. Education:

Archbishop Holgate's Grammar School; London School of Economics (BSc econ).

Jo Shaw (LD) Barrister. Ed: Leeds Uni.
George Lee (C) Management consultant. Ed: Cambridge Uni.

Constituency
This Camden borough seat includes Holborn and Covent Garden in the heart of Central London, and the King's Cross-St Pancras transport hub. Retaining its old name, this redrawn seat extends farther north to include Gospel Oak and the affluent Highgate. Other prosperous areas are Primrose Hill and near Regent's Park, but overall this is the less affluent half of Camden, with large council estates around Kentish Town and deprivation around the railway station. The seat has been Labour since its creation in 1983.

	Electorate	Turnout %	Change from '05 %
	86,863	62.9	*
Dobson, F Lab	25,198	46.1	1.0
Shaw, J LD	15,256	27.9	1.8
Lee, G C	11,134	20.4	-0.5
Bennett, N Green	1,480	2.7	-4.8
Carlyle, R BNP	779	1.4	
Spencer, M UKIP	587	1.1	
Chapman, J Ind	96	0.2	
Susperregi, M Eng	75	0.1	
Meek, I Ind	44	0.1	

50%
Majority 9,942

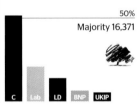

Hornchurch & Upminster — Conservative hold

Angela Watkinson
b. Nov 18, 1941
MP 2001-

Right-wing populist. Govt whip 2010-. Opp Whip 2005-10. Shadow Min: Local Gov't Affairs/Communities 2005; Education 2004-05; Health/Education 2004. Opp whip 2002-04. Member, Con Way Forward. Cllr, Essex CC 1997-2001, Havering 1994-98. Local gov't officer. Committee manager Basildon DC. Worked in special sch. Early career, banking. Divorced, two daughters, one son. Education: Wanstead County HS; Anglia (HND public admin).

Kath McGuirk (Lab) b. Feb 27, 1964. Parly assistant. Cllr, Barnet BC.
Karen Chilvers (LD) b. Apr 3, 1971. Marketing consultant. Cllr, Brentwood BC. Education: Gaynes School, Upminster; Chartered Institute of Marketing (Diploma in Marketing).
William Whelpley (BNP)

Constituency
The two old seats that give their name to this new one have not fared equally, with almost all the old Upminster territory included, but only two wards from Hornchurch. These include the town centre of Hornchurch itself, which, like Cranham and Upminster, is prosperous. There are some patches of deprivation in the north of the seat. The easternmost point in London, and the end of the District Line, this seat feels more like Essex, with which it borders. Both the predecessor seats here switched to Labour in 1997, with Upminster going back to the Tories in 2001 and Hornchurch in 2005.

	Electorate	Turnout %	Change from '05 %
	78,487	68.0	*
Watkinson, A C	27,469	51.5	4.0
McGuirk, K Lab	11,098	20.8	-10.3
Chilvers, K LD	7,426	13.9	5.4
Whelpley, W BNP	3,421	6.4	
Webb, L UKIP	2,848	5.3	3.2
Collins, M Green	542	1.0	-0.1
Durant, D Ind	305	0.6	
Olukotun, J Ch	281	0.5	

50%
Majority 16,371

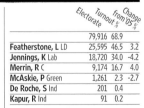

Hornsey & Wood Green — Liberal Democrat hold

Lynne Featherstone
b. Dec 20, 1951
MP 2005-

Feisty campaigner, early enthusiast for political blogging. Active in Chris Huhne's leadership campaigns of 2006 and 2007. Parly Under-Sec (Min for Equalities): 2010-. LD shadow Min: Youth & Equalities 2008-10. LD shadow Sec of State: Int Devt 2006-07. LD spokes: London 2006-07; Home 2005-06. Member, committee: Environmental Audit 2005-06. Member GLA 2000-05. Chair (Chair, Assembly Committee on Transport 2003-05). Councillor, Haringey (leader of opposition) 1998-2003. Strategic design consultant. Divorced, two daughters. Education: S Hampstead High School; Oxford Poly.

Karen Jennings (Lab) b. Feb 11, 1953. Head of health, Unison.
Richard Merrin (C) b. Jul 4, 1966. Managing director. Education: Collingwood Comprehensive, Surrey; Manchester University (BA politics and modern history).

Constituency
This is the much better-off, western half of the North London borough of Haringey. From leafy Highgate and Stroud Green in the south, it stretches through the mainly affluent Muswell Hill to the poorer Wood Green in the north. The seat includes concentrated patches of social housing. Hornsey, one of the more diverse wards, is the focus of significant Turkish, Greek, Cypriot and black communities. Having been held by Labour, the seat fell to the Lib Dems on a 14 per cent swing in 2005.

	Electorate	Turnout %	Change from '05 %
	79,916	68.9	
Featherstone, L LD	25,595	46.5	3.2
Jennings, K Lab	18,720	34.0	-4.2
Merrin, R C	9,174	16.7	4.0
McAskie, P Green	1,261	2.3	-2.7
De Roche, S Ind	201	0.4	
Kapur, R Ind	91	0.2	

50%
Majority 6,875

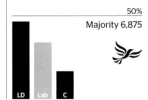

We can't go on like this. WITH SUSPICIOUS MINDS

YEAR FOR CHANGE

Read our plan for change at conservatives.com

Don't let him take Britain back to the 1980s.

Labour

www.labour.org.uk

Fire up the Quattro. It's time for change.

(Idea kindly donated by the Labour Party)

Vote for change. Vote Conservative

Billboard wars: Conservative campaign posters were defaced, Labour's attempt to attack David Cameron backfired

Campaign trail: (l-r, from top) David Cameron toured warehouses in shirtsleeves; and pledged to restore pride to Parliament; Nick Clegg and Vince Cable toured as a doubleact; Clegg was backed by actor Colin Firth; Gordon Brown, confronted in Rochdale by Gillian Duffy; Brown at a supporters' garden party

William Hague and the Tory team (above) leave coalition talks with Liberal Democrats, led by Danny Alexander

The end: Gordon Brown leaves Downing Street with his wife Sarah and, unusually in public, sons John (left) and Fraser

There at last: David Cameron arrives at Downing Street with Samantha, his wife

David Cameron and Nick Clegg's first joint press conference in Downing Street's rose garden, dubbed the "love-in"

The House of Commons

2010

650 seats

Conservative	306
Labour	258
Liberal Democrat	57
Other	29

2005
646 seats

Labour	355
Conservative	198
Liberal Democrat	62
Other	31

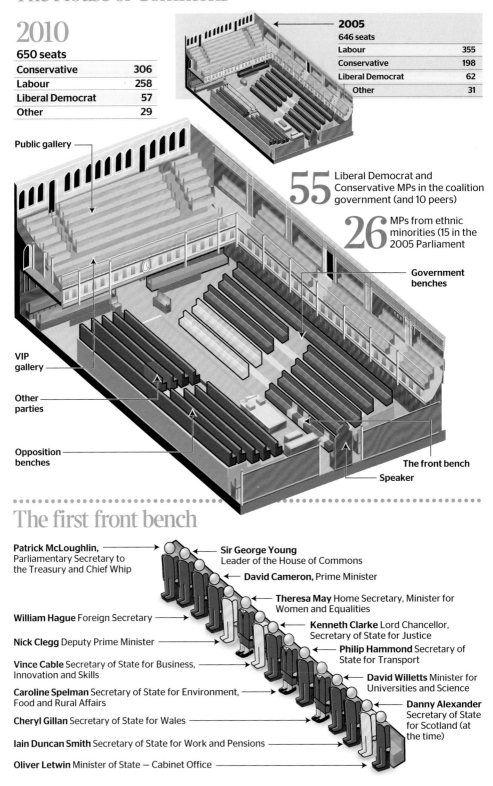

Public gallery

55 Liberal Democrat and Conservative MPs in the coalition government (and 10 peers)

26 MPs from ethnic minorities (15 in the 2005 Parliament

Government benches

VIP gallery

Other parties

Opposition benches

The front bench

Speaker

The first front bench

Patrick McLoughlin, Parliamentary Secretary to the Treasury and Chief Whip

Sir George Young Leader of the House of Commons

David Cameron, Prime Minister

Theresa May Home Secretary, Minister for Women and Equalities

William Hague Foreign Secretary

Kenneth Clarke Lord Chancellor, Secretary of State for Justice

Nick Clegg Deputy Prime Minister

Philip Hammond Secretary of State for Transport

Vince Cable Secretary of State for Business, Innovation and Skills

David Willetts Minister for Universities and Science

Caroline Spelman Secretary of State for Environment, Food and Rural Affairs

Danny Alexander Secretary of State for Scotland (at the time)

Cheryl Gillan Secretary of State for Wales

Iain Duncan Smith Secretary of State for Work and Pensions

Oliver Letwin Minister of State – Cabinet Office

2010 election results

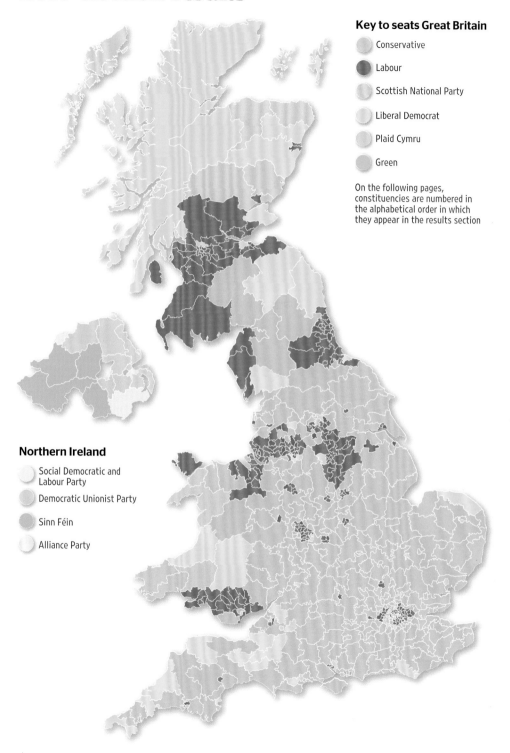

Key to seats Great Britain

- Conservative
- Labour
- Scottish National Party
- Liberal Democrat
- Plaid Cymru
- Green

On the following pages, constituencies are numbered in the alphabetical order in which they appear in the results section

Northern Ireland

- Social Democratic and Labour Party
- Democratic Unionist Party
- Sinn Féin
- Alliance Party

South East

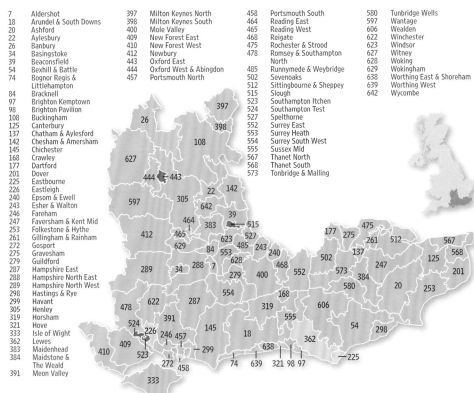

Greater London

East

South West

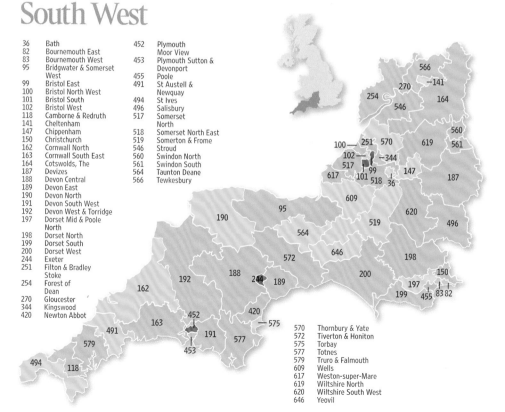

East Midlands

North East

Tyne & Wear

Tyne & Wear

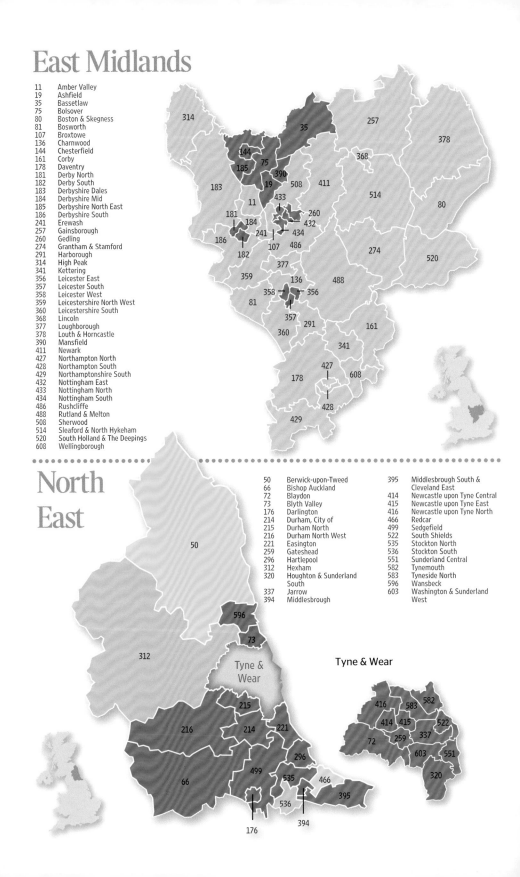

West Midlands

Birmingham

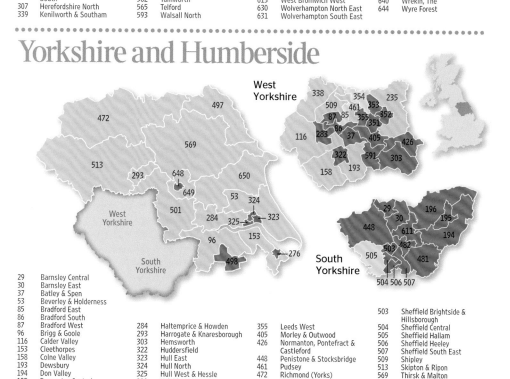

Birmingham

8	Aldridge-Brownhills	367	Lichfield	594	Walsall South
57	Birmingham Edgbaston	379	Ludlow	598	Warley
58	Birmingham Erdington	392	Meriden	601	Warwick & Leamington
59	Birmingham Hall Green	413	Newcastle-under-Lyme	602	Warwickshire North
60	Birmingham Hodge Hill	435	Nuneaton	612	West Bromwich East
61	Birmingham Ladywood	467	Redditch	613	West Bromwich West
62	Birmingham Northfield	483	Rugby	630	Wolverhampton North East
63	Birmingham Perry Barr	510	Shrewsbury & Atcham	631	Wolverhampton South East
64	Birmingham Selly Oak	511	Shropshire North	632	Wolverhampton South
65	Birmingham Yardley	516	Solihull		West
105	Bromsgrove	528	Stafford	633	Worcester
110	Burton	529	Staffordshire Moorlands	634	Worcestershire Mid
124	Cannock Chase	530	Staffordshire South	635	Worcestershire West
165	Coventry North East	537	Stoke-on-Trent Central	640	Wrekin, The
166	Coventry North West	538	Stoke-on-Trent North	644	Wyre Forest
167	Coventry South	539	Stoke-on-Trent South		
204	Dudley North	540	Stone		
205	Dudley South	541	Stourbridge		
282	Halesowen & Rowley Regis	543	Stratford-on-Avon		
306	Hereford & Herefordshire	557	Sutton Coldfield		
	South	562	Tamworth		
307	Herefordshire North	565	Telford		
339	Kenilworth & Southam	593	Walsall North		

Yorkshire and Humberside

West Yorkshire

South Yorkshire

West Yorkshire

South Yorkshire

29	Barnsley Central				
30	Barnsley East				
37	Batley & Spen				
53	Beverley & Holderness				
85	Bradford East				
86	Bradford South			503	Sheffield Brightside &
87	Bradford West	284	Haltemprice & Howden	355	Leeds West		Hillsborough
96	Brigg & Goole	293	Harrogate & Knaresborough	405	Morley & Outwood	504	Sheffield Central
116	Calder Valley	303	Hemsworth	426	Normanton, Pontefract &	505	Sheffield Hallam
153	Cleethorpes	322	Huddersfield		Castleford	506	Sheffield Heeley
158	Colne Valley	323	Hull East	448	Penistone & Stocksbridge	507	Sheffield South East
193	Dewsbury	324	Hull North	461	Pudsey	509	Shipley
194	Don Valley	325	Hull West & Hessle	472	Richmond (Yorks)	513	Skipton & Ripon
195	Doncaster Central	338	Keighley	481	Rother Valley	569	Thirsk & Malton
196	Doncaster North	351	Leeds Central	482	Rotherham	591	Wakefield
235	Elmet & Rothwell	352	Leeds East	497	Scarborough & Whitby	611	Wentworth & Dearne
276	Great Grimsby	353	Leeds North East	498	Scunthorpe	648	York Central
283	Halifax	354	Leeds North West	501	Selby & Ainsty	649	York Outer
						650	Yorkshire East

North West

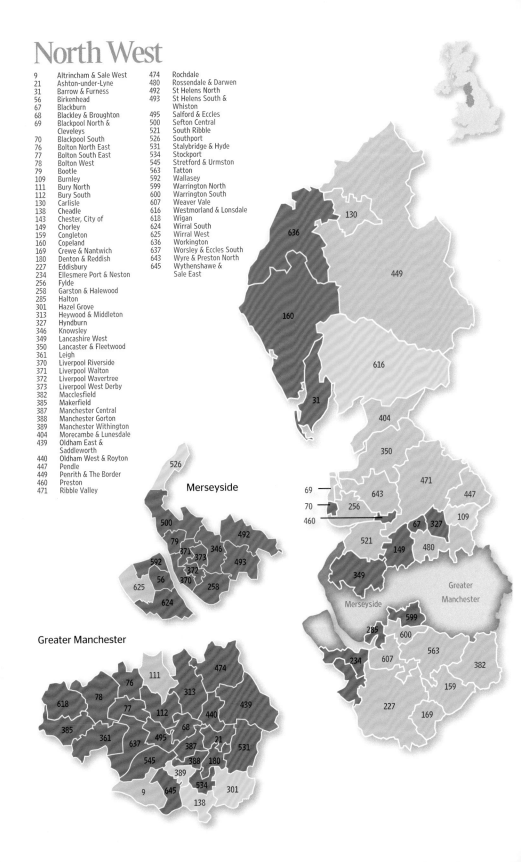

Merseyside

Greater Manchester

Wales

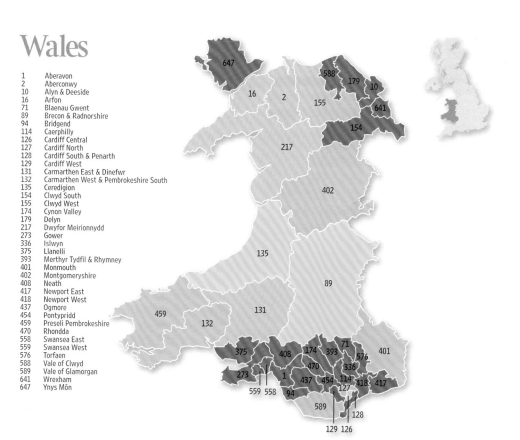

Northern Ireland

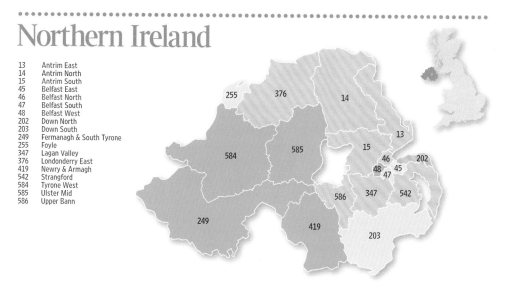

Scotland

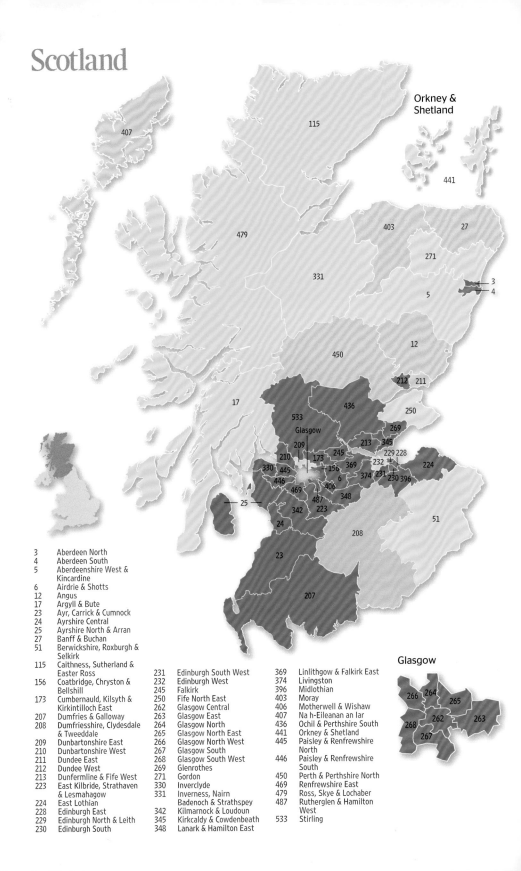

Orkney & Shetland

Glasgow

Horsham
Conservative hold

Francis Maude
b. Jul 4, 1953
MP 1997-; 1983-92

Arch Conservative moderniser, who missed out on the Major years. The architect of Cameron's A-list of candidates and had a key role in planning for a Tory government by heading the implementation team. Son of Tory minister Angus Maude. SoS: Cab Office, Paymaster General (att. Cabinet) 2010-. Shadow Min: Cab Office 2007-10. Shadow Chancellor of Duchy of Lancaster. Con Party Chair, 2005-07. Shadow SoS: Foreign 2000-01. Shadow Chancellor 1998-2000. Shadow SoS: CMS 1997-98. Financial Treasury Sec 1990-92. Min: FCO 1989-90. Parly Under-Sec DTI 1987-89. Gov't whip 1985-87. PPS to Peter Morrison 1984. MP North Warwicks 1983-92. Co-founded

Policy Exchange think-tank 2002. Westminster cllr, banker, barrister. Married, three daughters, two sons. Ed: Abingdon; Corpus Christi, Cambridge (MA history); College of Law.

Godfrey Newman (LD) Retired teacher. Former Cllr, Horsham DC.
Andrew Skudder (Lab) IT worker.

Constituency
Centred on the eponymous West Sussex town, the seat includes a substantial rural area, reaching down beyond the town of Billingshurst in the south west and surrounding Crawley on three sides in the north east, bordering Surrey. There are high numbers of professionals in this affluent constituency and the nearby Gatwick is a notable employer. In 2005, the Tories' still enviable 50 per cent vote share was their lowest since 1945, albeit under varying boundaries.

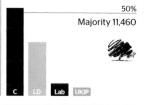

	Electorate	Turnout %	Change from '05 %
	76,835	72.7	☆
Maude, F C	29,447	52.7	3.4
Newman, G LD	17,987	32.2	4.5
Skudder, A Lab	4,189	7.5	-9.2
Aldridge, H UKIP	2,839	5.1	0.4
Fitter, N Green	570	1.0	
Lyon, S Ch	469	0.8	
Duggan, J PPN-V	253	0.5	
Kissach, D Ind	87	0.2	

50%
Majority 11,460

C LD Lab UKIP

Houghton & Sunderland South
Labour hold

Bridget Phillipson
b. Dec 19, 1983
MP 2010-

The first MP elected to the new Parliament. Has composed manner. Interested in housing, transport, family and Armed Forces. Member Labour Party national policy forum. Women's refuge manager, Wearside Women in Need. Worked on regeneration projects for Sunderland City Council. Member, GMB, Co-operative party. Cites Aung San Suu Kyi as political hero. Roman Catholic. Married. Ed: St Robert of Newminster Sch, Washington; Hertford Coll, Oxford (modern history; chair, OULC).

Robert Oliver (C) b. 1972. History and politics teacher. Cllr, Sunderland CC 2004-. Contested Sunderland S 2005.

Chris Boyle (LD) Human rights lawyer. Cllr, Newcastle CC 2003-.
Colin Wakefield (Ind) Retired BAE technical specialist. Cllr, Sunderland CC.

Constituency
At the extreme south of Tyne and Wear, this coalfields constituency centres on the town of Houghton-le-Spring. Boundary changes remove Washington from the north and add the Doxton area from the southwestern fringe of Sunderland, where South Rainton Bridge business park is a new centre of employment – npower moved in from Newcastle. In the north is the Penshaw Monument, Sunderland's most prominent landmark. Modelled on the Theseum in Athens, it was built in 1844 by public subscription. A white, working-class area, predecessor seats were strongly Labour-voting.

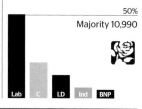

	Electorate	Turnout %	Change from '05 %
	68,729	55.3	☆
Phillipson, B Lab	19,137	50.3	-11.7
Oliver, R C	8,147	21.4	5.2
Boyle, C LD	5,292	13.9	-0.6
Wakefield, C Ind	2,462	6.5	
Allen, K BNP	1,961	5.2	
Elvin, R UKIP	1,022	2.7	

50%
Majority 10,990

Lab C LD Ind BNP

Hove
Conservative gain

Mike Weatherley
b. Jul 2, 1957
MP 2010-

Rock and heavy metal music fan who once presented *House of Rock* community radio show. Cllr, Crawley BC 2006-07. Contested Brighton Pavilion 2005, Barking 2001. Vice-president (finance & admin), Motion Picture Licensing Company. Finance Dir, Custommatic. Financial Controller, Pete Waterman Group. Finance Dir/part-owner, Cash Bases. Chartered management accountant. Enjoys skiing and football. Married, one daughter, two sons. Education: Kent Coll, Canterbury; South Bank Poly (BA business studies).

Celia Barlow (Lab) b. Sep 28, 1955. MP for Hove 2005-2010. PPS to Ian Pearson 2006-09. Contested Chichester 2001. TV producer. Ed: Cambridge; Uni Coll, Cardiff; Central St Martin's.
Paul Elgood (LD) b. Nov 10, 1971. Cllr, Brighton & Hove. Contested Hove & Portslade 2005.

Constituency
Immediately west of Brighton, Hove's stretch of seafront is defined by its multicoloured beach huts and has long been a popular resort. It is also a popular residential area, with impressive Regency architecture, and home to many professionals. Stretching inland through suburbs such as Aldrington and Mile Oak, it reaches to the foothills of the South Downs. It is generally well off. Demographic change in recent years, with increasing student numbers, has been seen as a factor that helped Labour to overturn decades of Tory rule with its 1997 victory.

	Electorate	Turnout %	Change from '05 %
	71,708	69.5	☆
Weatherley, M C	18,294	36.7	0.3
Barlow, C Lab	16,426	33.0	-4.5
Elgood, P LD	11,240	22.6	4.6
Davey, I Green	2,568	5.2	-0.6
Perrin, P UKIP	1,206	2.4	1.1
Ralfe, B Ind	85	0.2	

50%
Majority 1,868

C Lab LD Grn

Huddersfield Labour hold

Barry Sheerman
b. Aug 17, 1940
MP 1979-

Blairite, unlikely leader of attempts to overthrow Gordon Brown in 2009. Knowledgeable on education policy, well-connected charity entrepreneur. Chair, select committees: Children Schools & Families 2007-10, Education & Skills 2001-07. Opp spokes: Disabled People's Rights 1992-94; Home Affairs 1988-92; Employment & Education 1983-88. MP Huddersfield East 1979-83. Uni lecturer. AUT, Amicus. Married, three daughters, one son. Education: Hampton Grammar School; Kingston Tech College (econ & politics); London School of Economics (BSc econ); London (MSc pol sociology).

Karen Tweed (C) NHS worker. Education: Brooksbank School, Elland.
James Blanchard (LD) b. Mar 23, 1977. Charity worker. Contested Hackney North & Stoke Newington 2005. Education: Shipshed High School, Hind Leys, Leicestershire, Leeds University.

Constituency
About ten miles south of Bradford, the town of Huddersfield was built around the wool industry and retains its working-class roots. Areas of deprivation blight the centre and there is a high proportion of social housing and much unemployment. But there is a strong education sector and because of the town's university one in ten electors is a student. About one in five residents is of ethnic minority origin, the largest community being Pakistani. Labour has held the seat since its creation in 1950.

	Electorate	Turnout %	Change from '05 %
	66,316	61.1	*
Sheerman, B Lab	15,725	38.8	-7.6
Tweed, K C	11,253	27.8	6.7
Blanchard, J LD	10,023	24.7	0.6
Cooper, A Green	1,641	4.1	-0.6
Firth, R BNP	1,563	3.9	
Cooney, P TUSC	319	0.8	

50%
Majority 4,472

Hull East Labour hold

Karl Turner
b. Apr 15, 1971
MP 2010-

Local man inheriting the seat from John Prescott – a close friend of his councillor father – and beating Prescott's own son in the selection process. Involved with John Prescott "East Hull pride" campaign. Barrister (Wilberforce Chambers; Max Gold Solicitors). Took A levels and degree as mature student having been self-employed antiques seller on leaving school. Rugby player. Education: Bransholme High School; Hull College; Hull (law).

Jeremy Wilcock (LD) Retired manufacturing worker. Education: King's Coll, Taunton. Queen Mary Coll, Buckinghamshire Coll.
Christine Mackay (C) Health scientist.

Education: Hull University, Humberside University (MA).
Mike Hookem (UKIP)

Constituency
On the Humber Estuary, Kingston-upon-Hull is better known just as Hull. The seat covers people living east of the River Hull, which flows through the city from north to south. It includes industrial docks on the Humber waterfront and is strongly working-class and overwhelmingly white. The BP refinery is a big employer. Regeneration has focused on housing. A third of the population lives in council or social housing. John Prescott, the former Deputy Prime Minister, announced his retirement after colourfully representing the constituency for 40 years.

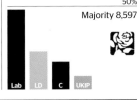

	Electorate	Turnout %	Change from '05 %
	67,530	50.6	*
Turner, K Lab	16,387	47.9	-8.1
Wilcock, J LD	7,790	22.8	2.6
Mackay, C C	5,667	16.6	3.6
Hookem, M UKIP	2,745	8.0	
Uttley, J NF	880	2.6	
Burton, M Eng	715	2.1	

50%
Majority 8,597

Hull North Labour hold

Diana Johnson
b. Jul 25, 1966
MP 2005-

Made little impact as minister. Parly Under-Sec: Children, Schools & Families 2009-10. Assistant government whip 2007-09. PPS to: Stephen Timms 2005-07. Cllr Tower Hamlets 1994-2002. Employment/immigration/education barrister. Legal member Mental Health Act Commission. Family lawyer McCormacks. Volunteer/locum lawyer, Tower Hamlets Law Centre. Law clerk, Hamilton, Ontario. Paralegal, Herbert Smith. Law clerk, Philadelphia. TGWU, Unison. Education: Northwich County Grammar School; Sir John Deans Sixth Form College, Cheshire; Brunel (Modern history); Queen Mary College, London (Law).

Denis Healy (LD) Local campaigner. Contested Hull North 2005.
Victoria Aitken (C) Entrepreneur.

Constituency
Set back from the Humber Estuary, this northern half of Hull is a seat of contrasts. There is a large student population – about 13 per cent of residents – attending the University of Hull, but also traditional, and deprived, working-class residential areas. One of them is Bransholme, an isolated urban wasteland five miles northeast of the city centre. One of Europe's largest council estates, it is viewed by many as a monument to the errors of 1960s town planners. The seat has returned Labour MPs since 1966.

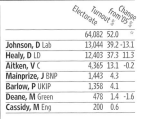

	Electorate	Turnout %	Change from '05 %
	64,082	52.0	*
Johnson, D Lab	13,044	39.2	-13.1
Healy, D LD	12,403	37.3	11.3
Aitken, V C	4,365	13.1	-0.2
Mainprize, J BNP	1,443	4.3	
Barlow, P UKIP	1,358	4.1	
Deane, M Green	478	1.4	-1.6
Cassidy, M Eng	200	0.6	

50%
Majority 641

Hull West & Hessle — Labour hold

Alan Johnson
b. May 17, 1950
MP 1997-

Genial ex-postman and orphan made good. Failed to make impact at highest level. Secretary of State: Home 2009-10; Health 2007-09; Education & Skills 2006-07; Trade & Industry 2005-06; Work & Pensions 2004-05. Min: Education & Skills 2003-04; Trade & Industry 2001-03. Parly Under-Sec: Trade & Industry 1999-2001. Parliamentary private secretary to: Dawn Primarolo 1997-99. Labour Party NEC member 1995-97. Postman. TUC General Council member. General sec: Union of Communication Workers, CWU. Divorced, two daughters, one son. Remarried, one son. Education: Sloane Grammar School, Chelsea.

Mike Ross (LD) Cllr, Hull 2002-.
Gary Shores (C) b. Dec 22, 1971. Teacher. Cllr, East Riding 2007-. Education: Hull Further Education College, Hull University.

Constituency
The retail heart of Hull city is included in this seat, along with a stretch of estuary including Humber Quays which, after extensive regeneration, has become a base for Royal Bank of Scotland, PricewaterhouseCoopers, Barclays and other financial service companies. Most of the waterfront remains warehousing and the south of the constituency is generally deprived. In the west of the seat, Hessle is a more affluent commuter suburb. The seat has been Labour since its creation in 1955.

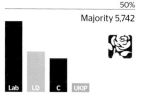

	Electorate	Turnout %	Change from '05 %
	69,017	45.7	☆
Johnson, A Lab	13,378	42.5	-12.6
Ross, M LD	7,636	24.2	3.2
Shores, G C	6,361	20.2	-0.5
Hordon, K UKIP	1,688	5.4	
Scott, E BNP	1,416	4.5	
Mawer, P Eng	876	2.8	
Gibson, K TUSC	150	0.5	

50%
Majority 5,742

Huntingdon — Conservative hold

Jonathan Djanogly
b. Jun 3, 1965
MP 2001-

Wealthy, son of multimillionaire textile magnate and philanthropist, Sir Harry. Some damage in expenses scandal. Parly Under-Sec: Justice 2010-. Shadow Business Minister, Solicitor General 2005-10. Shadow Minister: Home Affairs 2004-05. Cllr, Westminster CC 1994-2001. Solicitor (partner SJ Berwin LLP). Ran mail order retail business with wife. Married, one daughter, one son. Education: University College school; Oxford Poly (BA law and politics); Guildford Coll of Law.

Martin Land (LD) Lib Dem campaign manager.
Anthea Cox (Lab) Disability rights campaigner. Contested Cambridgeshire

North West 2001. Education: Allerton High School, Birmingham University.
Ian Curtis (UKIP)

Constituency
Huntingdon is in the north of this seat, roughly halfway between Peterborough and Cambridge. St Ives and St Neots are the other main towns. They are between A-roads that criss-cross the constituency and more than 35 per cent commute out to work. A major employer is Huntingdon Life Sciences. Huntingdon North has some deprived areas but this is an overwhelmingly white, affluent seat with a good quality of life and strong Conservative vote; more than 60 per cent for most of the years that John Major was MP.

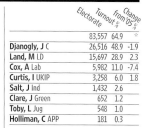

	Electorate	Turnout %	Change from '05 %
	83,557	64.9	☆
Djanogly, J C	26,516	48.9	-1.9
Land, M LD	15,697	28.9	2.3
Cox, A Lab	5,982	11.0	-7.4
Curtis, I UKIP	3,258	6.0	1.8
Salt, J Ind	1,432	2.6	
Clare, J Green	652	1.2	
Toby, L Jug	548	1.0	
Holliman, C APP	181	0.3	

50%
Majority 10,819

Hyndburn — Labour hold

Graham Jones
b. Mar 3, 1966
MP 2010-

Campaigned on local, everyman ticket as life-long constituency resident working in printing company. Keen blogger. Refers to himself as MP for Haslingden & Hyndburn. Friend of Jon Cruddas. Endured recount despite relatively wide margin of victory. Cllr: Hyndburn BC 2002-10 (Lab leader 2006-10); Lancashire CC 2009-. Graphic designer, specialising in pre-press. Has a golf handicap of 9. Has partner. One son, one daughter. Education: St Christopher's CofE School, Accrington; UCLAN (BA (Hons) Applied social studies).

Karen Buckley (C) b. 1968. Solicitor. Education: Queen Mary Girls School,

Lytham St Anne's, Uni of Central Lancs.
Andrew Rankine (LD) b. Feb 26, 1952. Self-employed. Cllr, Skipton TC (deputy leader). Education: Ryebank School, Liverpool, Bradford University, Bolton Institute (MSc).

Constituency
Bisected by the M65, this seat lies towards the east of Lancashire, between Blackburn and Burnley. The main settlements of Oswaldtwistle, Great Harwood and Accrington are situated near the motorway, while Haslingden, in the south, is on the A56. There is a strong manufacturing sector but the economy is generally sluggish and deprivation and unemployment are relatively high. The Tories narrowly held this seat from its creation in 1983 until 1992, when Labour gained it.

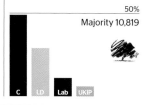

	Electorate	Turnout %	Change from '05 %
	67,221	63.5	☆
Jones, G Lab	17,531	41.1	-4.6
Buckley, K C	14,441	33.8	1.9
Rankine, A LD	5,033	11.8	-2.6
Shapcott, D BNP	2,137	5.0	
Barker, G UKIP	1,481	3.5	1.6
Logan, K CPA	795.0	1.9	
Gormley, K Green	463	1.1	
Reid, C Eng	413	1.0	
Hall, C Ind	378	0.9	

50%
Majority 3,090

Ilford North
Conservative hold

Lee Scott
b. Apr 6, 1956
MP 2005-

Working class Tory and proud of it. Member, Select Committees: Health 2007-10; Transport 2005-08. Cllr, Redbridge Borough 1998-. Director, Scott & Fishell. Sales Executive for companies including Toshiba. Campaign director/provincial director United Jewish Israel Appeal 1988-98. Married, three daughters, two sons. Education: Clarke's College, Ilford, Essex; College of Distributive Trades.

Sonia Klein (Lab) Management consultant.
Alex Berhanu (LD) Teacher and lecturer. Education: British School, Addis Ababa. Reading University, Wolverhampton University.

Constituency
This outer London seat borders Essex to the north. It includes part of Woodford in the west, separated by the M11 from the rest of the seat, encompassing Clayhall, Fairlop and Hainault in the east. This is leafy, suburban territory with greenbelt land, forest and parks and overwhelmingly white residents. It included a Labour MP from 1997 to 2005, in a seat traditionally considered Conservative.

	Electorate	Turnout %	Change from 05 %
	71,995	65.3	☆
Scott, L C	21,506	45.7	2.0
Klein, S Lab	16,102	34.3	-5.4
Berhanu, A LD	5,966	12.7	-1.1
Warville, D BNP	1,545	3.3	
van der Stighelen, H UKIP	871		
Allen, C Green	572	1.2	
Hampson, R CPA	456.0		

50%
Majority 5,404

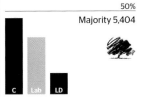

Ilford South
Labour Co-operative hold

Mike Gapes
b. Sep 4, 1952
MP 1992-

Worthy, dull hard-worker with modest impact but respected in the chamber. Chair, select committee: Foreign Affairs 2005-10. PPS to: Lord Rooker 2001-02; Paul Murphy 1997-99. Lab party nat policy forum member 1996-2005. Chair, Co-op party parly group 2000-01. NATO parly assembly. Teacher/union official. TGWU member. West Ham fan. Divorced. One daughter, two stepdaughters. Education: Buckhurst County HS; Fitzwilliam Coll, Cambridge (MA econ); Middlesex Poly, Enfield (dip industrial relations).

Toby Boutle (C) b. 1980. Barrister. Former speech-writer for William Hague. Education: Magdalen Coll, Oxford (PPE).
Anood Al-Samerai (LD) b. Dec 10, 1980. Constituency office manager for Simon Hughes MP. Cllr, Southwark 2007- (leader, LD group). Education: Prendergast School, Lewisham, Keble College, Oxford.

Constituency
This East London seat is ethnically diverse: a minority is white British, with large Indian and Pakistani communities as well as sizeable numbers of black residents in the Clementswood area in the centre of the seat. There are patches of deprivation, but few residents live in social housing and most of the seat is averagely well off. Under varying electoral boundaries it has changed hands from Labour to Conservative frequently.

	Electorate	Turnout %	Change from 05 %
	75,246	68.0	
Gapes, M Lab	25,301	49.4	-2035
Boutle, T C	14,014	27.4	0.2
Al-Samerai, A LD	8,679	17.0	-3.6
Chowdhry, W Green	1,319	2.6	
Murray, T UKIP	1,132	2.2	0.6
Jestico, J King	746	1.5	

50%
Majority 11,287

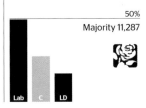

Inverclyde
Labour hold

David Cairns
b. Aug 7, 1966
MP 2001-

A former Catholic priest who required a change of law to allow him to stand for Parliament in 2001. Resigned from government job in Scotland Office (Min: Scotland 2007-08) having called for Gordon Brown to step down in summer 2008. Parly Under-Sec: NI 2006-07; Scotland 2005-07. PPS to: Malcolm Wicks 2003-05. MP Greenock & Inverclyde 2001-05. Dir, Christian Socialist Movement. Cllr, Merton 1998-2002. Research assistant to Siobhain McDonagh. Ed: Notre Dame HS; Gregorian Univ, Rome; Franciscan Study Centre, Canterbury.

Innes Nelson (SNP) Cllr, Inverclyde.
Simon Hutton (LD) b. Feb 22, 1985. Physics teacher. Contested Scottish parliament election West Renfrewshire West of Scotland Region 2007. Ed: Greenock Academy; Glasgow University.
David Wilson (C) Cllr. Education: Bellahouston Academy, Glasgow; Glasgow University.

Constituency
The Inverclyde area used to be home to some of the Clyde's busiest dockyards but is now a mixed constituency, with the grand houses of former shipyard owners along the redeveloped banks of the river. It is similar throughout the rest of this West Coast seat, which includes the leafy Kilmacolm suburb of Glasgow and some of the poorest parts of Greenock and Port Glasgow.

	Electorate	Turnout %	Change from 05 %
	59,209	63.3	
Cairns, D Lab	20,993	56.0	5.3
Nelson, I SNP	6,567	17.5	-2.0
Hutton, S LD	5,007	13.4	-3.6
Wilson, D C	4,502	12.0	1.8
Campbell, P UKIP	433	1.2	

50%
Majority 14,426

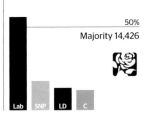

Inverness, Nairn, Badenoch & Strathspey — Liberal Democrat hold

Danny Alexander
b. May 15, 1972
MP 2005-

Diffident manner belies sharp political skills; key Lib Dem strategist. Chief Secretary to the Treasury 2010-. Chief of Staff to Nick Clegg, 2007-10. LD Shadow SoS: Work & Pensions 2007-08. LD Shadow Chancellor of Duchy of Lancaster 2007. LD whip 2006-07. LD spokes Work & Pensions 2005-07. Head of Comms: Cairngorms Nat Park; Britain in Europe. Dep dir/ head of comms/press officer, European Movement. Election aide to Jim Wallace MP 1997. Press officer, Scottish Lib Dems. Researcher, Campaign for Freedom of Information. Married, one daughter. Ed: Lochaber HS, Fort William; St Anne's Coll, Oxford (BA PPE).

Mike Robb (Lab) b. Aug 21, 1956. Company director. Education: Edinburgh University (BSc Physics).
John Finnie (SNP) b. Dec 13, 1956. Retired police officer. Cllr, Highland 2007-. Education: Lochaber High and Oban High.
Jim Ferguson (C) Company director.

Constituency
The booming city of Inverness is by far the biggest population centre in this rural constituency that stretches from the Moray Firth in the north to Speyside and Grantown-on-Spey farther inland. The retirement and golfing centre of Nairn, with its long sandy beach, is the other notable population centre in this constituency, which relies on whisky and forestry as its two key industries. It is held by the Liberal Democrats.

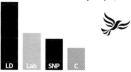

	Electorate	Turnout %	Change from 05 %
	72,528	64.9	
Alexander, D LD	19,172	40.7	0.5
Robb, M Lab	10,407	22.1	-8.8
Finnie, J SNP	8,803	18.7	5.2
Ferguson, J C	6,278	13.3	3.0
Boyd, D Ch	835	1.8	
MacLeod, D Green	789	1.7	-0.7
Durance, R UKIP	574	1.2	
MacDonald, G TUSC	135	0.3	
Fraser, K Joy	93	0.2	

50%
Majority 8,765

| LD | Lab | SNP | C |

Ipswich — Conservative gain

Ben Gummer
b. Feb 19, 1978
MP 2010-

Entered parliament as his father, John Gummer, the former Cabinet minister, left. Campaigned on services at Ipswich hospital and wrote contract to voters, pledging to be positive. Worked for Sancroft, his father's corporate responsibility consultancy. Ran small engineering firm. Author of *The Scourging Angel*, a history book about the black death. Education: Peterhouse College, Cambridge (BA history, MA. Starred double first).

Chris Mole (Lab) b. Mar 16, 1958. MP for Ipswich 2001-10. Parly Under-Sec, Transport 2009-10. TU organiser. Ed: Dulwich Coll, Kent Uni (Electronics).

Mark Dyson (LD) b. Apr 1, 1957. Journalist and company dir. Ed: Magdalen Coll Sch, Oxford; Pembroke Coll, Oxford (BA/MA Experimental Psychology).

Constituency
Ipswich is polarised between the deprived west and south of the town, with some areas in the worst 10 per cent nationwide, and the north east and east, some of the most affluent in the country. The seat includes the medieval city centre and the Waterfront, where old mills and warehouses have been replaced with restaurants, bars and yachts. Major employers include AXA. This seat has had brief spells of Tory representation, most recently in 1987-92, but has generally voted Labour.

	Electorate	Turnout %	Change from 05 %
	78,371	59.9	☆
Gummer, B C	18,371	39.1	8.0
Mole, C Lab	16,292	34.7	-8.2
Dyson, M LD	8,556	18.2	-2.9
Streatfield, C UKIP	1,365	2.9	0.2
Boater, D BNP	1,270	2.7	
Glover, T Green	775	1.7	
Christofi, K Ch	149	0.3	
Turtill, P Ind	93	0.2	
Wainman, S Ind	70	0.2	

50%
Majority 2,079

| C | Lab | LD |

Isle of Wight — Conservative hold

Andrew Turner
b. Oct 24, 1953
MP 2001-

Apt to put his foot in it. Right-winger, recovered from serious stroke in 2006. 1922 executive cttee, 2010-. Member, select cttees: Justice 2008-10; Education & Skills 2001-05. Vice-Chair (campaigning) Con Party 2003-. Cllr, Oxford CC 1979-96. Sheriff of Oxford 1994-95. Ed consultant; Dir, Grant-Maintained Schs Foundation; Special Adviser to SoS for Social Services; Con researcher; teacher. Has long-term partner. Ed: Rugby; Keble Coll, Oxford (BA geog/MA); Birmingham (PGCE); Henley Management Coll.

Jill Wareham (LD) b. 1951. Cllr, Isle of Wight CC 1993-2005. Clerk to governors.

Mark Chiverton (Lab) b. Sep 3, 1954. Trade union organiser. Contested Isle of Wight 2005.

Constituency
Famously having the biggest electorate of any UK parliamentary seat, it covers the entire Isle of Wight. Its white cliffs, beaches and the yachting mecca of Cowes make it a prime holiday destination and its economy is focused on tourism. Its regular ferry links to the mainland are vital. It is a popular retirement location, reflected in the ageing population. Small patches of deprivation exist in the east of Newport, the main town in the centre of the island, and in Ryde in the north east, but it is generally comfortably off. The seat has frequently changed hands between the Tories and Liberals, most recently being won back by the Tories in 2001 after a term of Lib Dem representation.

	Electorate	Turnout	Change from 05 %
	109,966	63.9	
Turner, A C	32,810	46.7	-2.2
Wareham, J LD	22,283	31.7	2.2
Chiverton, M Lab	8,169	11.6	-5.5
Tarrant, M UKIP	2,435	3.5	0.0
Clynch, G BNP	1,457	2.1	
Dunsire, I Eng	1,233	1.8	
Keats, B Green	931	1.3	
Martin, P Mid	616	0.9	
Harris, P Ind	175	0.3	-0.6
Randle-Jolliffe, P Ind	89	0.1	-0.7
Corby, E Ind	66	0.1	-0.7

50%
Majority 10,527

| C | LD | Lab |

197

Islington North
Labour hold

Jeremy Corbyn
b. May 26, 1949
MP 1983-

Totally unchanged, archetypal bearded 1980s left-wing rebel, admirably unwavering in convictions, more likeable than he looks. Refusal to send son to grammar school instead of local comprehensive contributed to marriage breakdown. Socialist Campaign group member. Member, select cttee: Social Security 1991-97. Cllr Haringey Bor 1974-84. Former NUPE full-time organiser. Tailor and Garment workers and AUEW. Married; separated. Three sons. Education: Adams Grammar School, Shropshire.

Rhodri Jamieson-Ball (LD) Transport planner. Cllr, Islington BC 2005-. Education: SOAS (BSc development economics); UCL (MSc transport).
Adrian Berrill-Cox (C) Barrister for the FSA. Education: Reading University (LLB Law).

Constituency
From Holloway prison, Tufnell Park and Upper Holloway in the west, the seat spans through Finsbury Park in the centre to Highbury in the east, including Arsenal's Emirates Stadium. There are extremes of wealth and poverty with some leafy residential streets but also large areas of social housing, concentrated in the north. A diverse seat where about half of residents are white British. There is no dominant ethnic group, but African or Caribbean totals about 12 per cent. The seat has been held by Labour's Jeremy Corbyn since its inception in 1983.

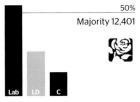

	Electorate	Turnout %	Change from '05 %
	68,120	65.4	
Corbyn, J Lab	24,276	54.5	3.4
Jamieson-Ball, R LD	11,875	26.7	-3.2
Berrill-Cox, A C	6,339	14.2	2.4
Dixon, E Green	1,348	3.0	-4.1
Lennon, D UKIP	716	1.6	

50%
Majority 12,401

Lab | LD | C

Islington South & Finsbury
Labour hold

Emily Thornberry
b. Jul 27, 1960
MP 2005-

Bustling loyalist with a wonderful throaty voice and a good sense of humour. PPS to Joan Ruddock 2009-10. Member, cttees: Environmental Audit 2005-07; Communities & Local Govt 2006-09. Barrister, Mike Mansfield's Chambers: Tooks Court. Unite. Married, one daughter, two sons. Ed: CofE Secondary Modern, Guildford; Burlington Danes, Shepherd's Bush; Kent (BA Law).

Bridget Fox (LD) Contested Islington South 2005. Cllr, Islington BC 1998–2006. Education: Balliol College, Oxford (BA history & French); Polytechnic of North London (MA library sciences).

Antonia Cox (C) Journalist. Education: University of Cambridge.

Constituency
This seat stretches from Farringdon north to Holloway and is centred on the shopping streets around the Angel Tube. The seat includes Old Street's "Silicon Roundabout", a high-tech business cluster. But Islington is polarised in terms of wealth and, beyond the Georgian townhouses, the majority of residents live in social housing, in some of the most deprived areas in the country. This is a densely populated seat, typically with above-average unemployment, and has returned Labour MPs for decades.

	Electorate	Turnout %	Change from '05 %
	67,649	64.4	
Thornberry, E Lab	18,407	42.3	2.5
Fox, B LD	14,838	34.1	-4.2
Cox, A C	8,449	19.4	4.6
Humphreys, J Green	710	1.6	-3.1
McDonald, R UKIP	701	1.6	0.1
Dodds, J Eng	301	0.7	
Deboo, R Animals	149	0.3	

50%
Majority 3,569

Lab | LD | C

Islwyn
Labour Co-operative hold

Christopher Evans
b. Jul 7, 1976
MP 2010-

Speaks with lilting Rhondda valley accent. Constituency researcher to the previous MP Don Touhig, won controversial selection. Contested Cheltenham 2005. Member: Unite, the Fabians, Co-operative party. Official, Union of Finance Staff. Marketing executive, University of Glamorgan. Personal account manager, Lloyds TSB. Bookmaker. Education: Porth County Comprehensive; Pontypridd College; Trinity College, Carmarthen (history).

Daniel Thomas (C) Building society employee. Education: Blackpool Comprehensive; Exeter Uni (BA politics). **Steffan Lewis** (PC) b. 1984. Plaid Cymru press officer. Contested Blaenau Gwent 2006 (by-election). **Asghar Ali** (LD) Cllr, Cardiff CC 2004-. Contested Welsh assembly elections 2007, South Wales Central.

Constituency
Islwyn is in southeast Wales, with towns built around three Gwent valleys. Between the Rhymney and Sirhowy rivers in the west lie Pontllanfraith and Blackwood. Risca, Crosskeys, Abercarn and Newbridge line the River Ebbw and Monmouthshire and Brecon Canal in the east. The area has received money from the EU to diversify the economy in what was once the heartland of industrial mining. It remains working-class and about a fifth of residents live in social housing. Unsurprisingly it has a long Labour history, including being represented by Neil Kinnock.

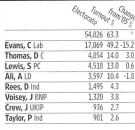

	Electorate	Turnout %	Change from '05 %
	54,826	63.3	✳
Evans, C Lab	17,069	49.2	-15.2
Thomas, D C	4,854	14.0	3.0
Lewis, S PC	4,518	13.0	0.6
Ali, A LD	3,597	10.4	-1.8
Rees, D Ind	1,495	4.3	
Voisey, J BNP	1,320	3.8	
Crew, J UKIP	936	2.7	
Taylor, P Ind	901	2.6	

50%
Majority 12,215

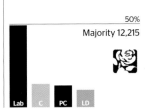

Lab | C | PC | LD

Jarrow
Labour hold

Stephen Hepburn
b. Dec 6, 1959
MP 1997-

Football-loving Geordie, a loyal Labour footsoldier. Member, select committees: Administration 2009-10; Northern Ireland Affairs 2004-10; Accommodation and Works 2003-05; Defence 1999-2001; Administration 1997-2001. Cllr, South Tyneside 1985- (dep leader 1990-97). Labourer, South Tyneside MBC. Member, UCATT. Research asst to Don Dixon MP. Education: Springfield Comprehensive, Jarrow; Newcastle (BA).

Jeffrey Milburn (C) b. 1959. Company director. Cllr, South Tyneside 2006-. Education: Whitburn Comprehensive.
Tom Appleby (LD) Law student. Cllr, Tynedale DC 2006-. Education:

Prudhoe Community High School; Northumbria University (BA politics)
Andy Swaddle (BNP)

Constituency
Associated for ever with the march of 1936, the town of Jarrow sits to the south of the River Tyne, just east of Newcastle. It still suffers severe deprivation caused by the decline of traditional industries, most notably shipbuilding. To its west is Hebburn while to the south and east it extends to the villages of Boldon and the more affluent Cleadon. After boundary changes, it no longer reaches the coast. This has long been a safe Labour seat.

	Electorate	Turnout %	Change from '05 %
	64,350	60.3	☆
Hepburn, S Lab	20,910	53.9	-4.9
Milburn, J C	8,002	20.6	7.8
Appleby, T LD	7,163	18.5	-4.0
Swaddle, A BNP	2,709	7.0	

50%
Majority 12,908

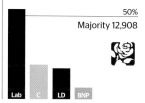

| Lab | C | LD | BNP |

Keighley
Conservative gain

Kris Hopkins
b. Jun 8, 1963
MP 2010-

Former soldier. Cllr, Bradford 1998- (leader 2006-10, dep leader 2004-06). Chair: Bradford Local Strategic Partnership; Yorkshire & Humber Housing and Regeneration Board. Contested Halifax 2005, Leeds West 2001. Tory Reform Group. Cites Douglas Hurd and William Hague among political heroes. Lecturer in media theory, comms and digital media. Former Army private, Duke of Wellington's Regiment; served Kenya, Northern Ireland and Germany. Keen runner, walker and photographer. Married, one daughter. Education: Oakbank School, Keighley; Leeds (Communications and cultural study).

Jane Thomas (Lab) b. Mar 29, 1956. Public affairs consultant. Education: Swansea Uni (BA politics).
Nader Fekri (LD) History lecturer. Contested Keighley 2005. Cllr, Hebden Royd TC.

Constituency
This West Yorkshire seat has dramatic contrasts in wealth. It is centred on the poor, working-class town of Keighley, northwest of Bradford, where manufacturing is strong. Surrounding rural communities, including Haworth, once home to the Brontë sisters, are far more affluent. Commuter-belt Ilkley, in the north, has one of Britain's highest proportions of millionaires. About one in ten residents is ethnic minority and Nick Griffin garnered 9 per cent of votes for the BNP in 2005. Labour overturned 14 years of Tory representation in 1997.

	Electorate	Turnout %	Change from '05 %
	65,893	72.4	
Hopkins, K C	20,003	41.9	7.7
Thomas, J Lab	17,063	35.8	-8.9
Fekri, N LD	7,059	14.8	3.0
Brons, A BNP	1,962	4.1	-5.1
Latham, P UKIP	1,470	3.1	
Smith, S NF	135	0.3	

50%
Majority 2,940

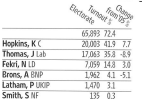

| C | Lab | LD |

Kenilworth & Southam
Conservatiive hold

Jeremy Wright
b. Oct 24, 1972
MP 2005-

Tory supporter of John Bercow. Government whip 2010-. Opposition whip 2007-10. Member, select cttee: Constitutional Affairs 2005-07. MP Rugby & Kenilworth 2005-10. Criminal law barrister. Married, one daughter. Ed: Taunton School; Trinity School New York; Exeter (law); Inns of Court Sch (BVC).

Nigel Rock (LD) Cllr, Stratford DC. Consultant.
Nicholas Milton (Lab) b. Dec 25, 1966. Employed by Commission for Rural Communities. Contested Congleton 2005. Ed: Herts Uni.

Constituency
This new seat consists of a large rural area centred on Southam in the east, and a branch out to the west between Coventry and Warwick, including the main historic town of Kenilworth with its ruined castle. The M40 runs through the seat, assisting affluent commuting. The area has traditionally been Conservative but, under previous boundaries, Kenilworth was twinned with Rugby and had a Labour MP between 1997 and 2005.

	Electorate	Turnout %	Change from '05 %
	59,630	81.2	
Wright, J C	25,945	53.6	3.2
Rock, N LD	13,393	27.7	5.6
Milton, N Lab	6,949	14.4	-11.2
Moore, N UKIP	1,214	2.5	0.5
Harrison, J Green	568	1.2	
Rukin, J Ind	362	0.8	

50%
Majority 12,552

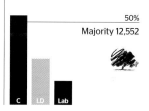

| C | LD | Lab |

Kensington Conservative hold

Sir Malcolm Rifkind
b. Jun 21, 1946
MP 2005-; 1974-97

Very experienced elder statesman whose come-back in 2005 after eight years disappointed, with a short-lived and failed leadership bid. Chose not to serve on frontbench under Cameron, instead making wise backbench speeches on foreign and defence issues. Shadow Sec of State: Work & Pensions 2005-. Sec of State: Foreign 1995-7; Defence 1992-5; Transport 1990-2; Scotland 1986-90. Minister: Foreign 1983-86. Parly-Under-Sec: Foreign 1982-83. Minister: Scotland 1979-82. MP Edinburgh Pentlands 1974-97. Lecturer Uni College of Rhodesia. Barrister, QC (Scotland). Education: George Watson's College; Edinburgh (LLB MSc Law).

Sam Gurney (Lab) b. Dec 19, 1973. TUC policy officer. Ed: Holland Park Comprehensive; Sussex Uni. **Robin Meltzer** (LD) b. Sep 26, 1977. TV producer. Ed: Cambridge Uni.

Constituency
This new inner London seat includes the cluster of national museums in South Kensington, skirts around Hyde Park and stretches north to the council estates of Golborne. Dotted with cosmopolitan areas such as Portobello Road, with its famous market, the north has deprived areas, as has the western boundary around Earl's Court. The centre, south and east are affluent. Notting Hill has been gentrified but retains its diversity, celebrated in the annual carnival. The old Kensington & Chelsea seat was Tory, but the old Regent's Park & North Kensington had been held by Labour since 1997.

	Electorate	Turnout %	Change from '05 %
	65,961	53.3	☆
Rifkind, M C	17,595	50.1	6.3
Gurney, S Lab	8,979	25.5	-4.1
Meltzer, R LD	6,872	19.6	-0.6
Caroline, L Pearson	754	2.2	
Ebrahimi-Fardouee, Z Green	753	2.1	-2.4
Adams, E Green	197	0.6	-4.0

50%
Majority 8,616

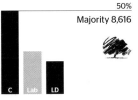

Kettering Conservative hold

Philip Hollobone
b. Nov 7, 1964
MP 2005-

One of new breed of unremarkable yet hyper-active Tory MPs elected in 2005 who covet high rankings in theyworkforyou.com, based on number of speeches and questions. Proud of how little he claims in parliamentary expenses. Member, Transport Select Committee, 2006-10. Cllr, Kettering 2003-; Bromley 1990-94. Investment bank analyst. Served in TA. Married, one daughter, one son. Education: Dulwich College, London; LMH, Oxford (BA modern history & economics).

Phil Sawford (Lab) b. Jun 26, 1950. MP for Kettering 1997-2005. Training manager. Education: Kettering Grammar; University of Leicester.

Chris Nelson (LD) b. Mar 1, 1986. Campaigns assistant, Northampton Liberal Democrats & Bill Newton Dunn MEP. Education: LSE Community College, Kettering; LLB (hons), Oxford Brookes Uni.

Constituency
Dramatically cut down, the Northamptonshire seat of Kettering has lost a large area of Daventry countryside from its south west and is more tightly focused around Kettering and the nearby smaller towns of Burton Latimer, Rothwell and Desborough. There are areas of severe deprivation in Kettering. Labour won with a tiny majority of 189 in 1997 and held it for two terms before the Tories took it back in 2005.

	Electorate	Turnout %	Change from '05 %
	68,837	68.8	☆
Hollobone, P C	23,247	49.1	6.2
Sawford, P Lab	14,153	29.9	-12.7
Nelson, C LD	7,498	15.8	3.6
Skinner, C BNP	1,366	2.9	
Hilling, D Eng	952	2.0	
Bishop, D BP	112	0.2	

50%
Majority 9,094

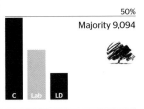

Kilmarnock & Loudoun Labour Co-operative hold

Cathy Jamieson
b. Nov 3, 1956
MP 2010-

Reputation as hard-working and ultra-loyal MSP at Holyrood 1999- (Min for Justice / Education & Young People, Dep Leader of Labour in Scots Parly), will be dual mandate until 2011. Stood unsuccessfully for post of Scottish leader of Labour in 2008. Social worker. Principal Officer, Who Cares? Scotland (advocacy organisation for young people in residential care). Robert Burns and local history enthusiast, fanatical Kilmarnock FC supporter. Married, one son. Ed: James Hamilton Academy; Glasgow School of Art (BA Hons); Goldsmiths Coll (art therapy); Glasgow (dip Social Work); Glasgow Caledonian (Cert Management).

George Leslie (SNP) b. 1938. Veterinary surgeon. Former Deputy Leader of SNP.
Janette McAlpine (C) Knowledge transfer manager, Glasgow Caledonian Uni. Contested Scot Parl elections 2007, Kilmarnock and Loudoun.
Sebastian Tombs (LD) b. Oct 10, 1949. Architect. Contested Edinburgh North & Leith 2001, and Scot Parl 1999, 2003.

Constituency
This traditional Labour seat takes in the top half of North Ayrshire. The large town of Kilmarnock is the hub for this constituency, which also encompasses the Irvine Valley. The smaller towns of Darvel, Newmilns and Galston increased the SNP share of the vote but Labour's strength in Kilmarnock and other working-class towns such as Auchinleck and Catrine have ensured that this remains a solid Labour seat.

	Electorate	Turnout %	Change from '05 %
	74,131	62.8	☆
Jamieson, C Lab	24,460	52.5	5.3
Leslie, G SNP	12,082	26.0	-1.7
McAlpine, J C	6,592	14.2	2.9
Tombs, S LD	3,419	7.3	-3.8

50%
Majority 12,378

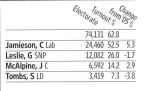
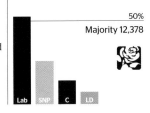

Kingston & Surbiton — Liberal Democrat hold

Edward Davey
b. Dec 25, 1965
MP 1997-

Leading figure of a new generation at the helm of the Liberal Democrats. Chairman of the party's 2010 election campaign. Parly Under-Sec: BIS 2010-. LD shadow SoS: Foreign & Commonwealth 2007-10. Chief of Staff to Sir Menzies Campbell 2006-07. LD shadow SoS: Trade & Industry 2006; Education & Skills 2005-06; Chief Sec to Treasury 2001-02. LD Whip 1997-2000. LD spokes: ODPM 2002-05; London 2000-03; economy 1999-2001; Treasury 1997-99. Member, Federal Policy cttee. LD Clls Assoc. Economic adviser to senior Lib Dem Mps. Management consultant. Royal Humane Soc hon testimonial. Married, one son. Ed: Nottingham HS; Jesus Coll, Oxford (BA PPE); Birkbeck Coll, London (MSc econ).

Helen Whately (C) Management consultant, Healthcare. Ed: Westminster Sch, Oxford Uni.
Max Freedman (Lab) b. Apr 24, 1979. Parliamentary Asst. Ed: Warwick Uni.

Constituency
The main retail centre of Kingston upon Thames, with the large Bentalls Centre and old market square, is at the northern boundary of this seat. Farther east is New Malden, which has the largest Korean population in Europe. In the centre of the seat lies Surbiton, while at the south is Chessington, known for its theme park. The area is generally well off, with only one small area of Norbiton in the 20 per cent most deprived nationally. The Lib Dems took this traditionally Tory seat in 1997.

	Electorate	Turnout %	Change from 05 %
	81,116	70.4	*
Davey, E LD	28,428	49.8	-1.3
Whately, H C	20,868	36.5	3.6
Freedman, M Lab	5,337	9.3	-3.8
Greensted, J UKIP	1,450	2.5	1.2
Iker, C Green	555	1.0	
Drummer, M Loony	247	0.4	
May, A CPA	226	0.4	

Majority 7,560

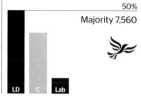

Kingswood — Conservative gain

Chris Skidmore
b. May 17, 1981
MP 2010-

Achieved one of the highest swings of the 2010 election. Tory party education adviser; director, Public Services Improvement group. Chaired Bow Group. Historian - wrote biography of Edward VI and taught part-time at Bristol University. Journalist, People Magazine. Plays guitar. Education: Bristol Grammar School; Christ Church, Oxford (history).

Roger Berry (Lab) b. Jul 4 1948. MP for Kingswood 1997-2010. Member, select cttees: Deregulation 1994-95; Trade & Industry 1995-2010. Cllr, Avon CC (Deputy Leader 1985-86). Lecturer. Ed: Huddersfield New Coll; Bristol Uni; Sussex Uni.

Sally Fitzharris (LD) Researcher for Baroness Northover. Ed: King's College London (MA medieval studies); Magdalen Coll, Oxford (MA Lit Hum); PG dip. Journalism; PGCE.

Constituency
Though retaining its name, the constituency has been redrawn, losing the Bristol wards of Frome Vale and Hillfields but still covering the city's fringes. Kingswood is an old industrial town with a coalmining heritage. It is a mix of Victorian terraces and newer estates, with social and private housing. The eastern edge of the seat just reaches into rural land with the relatively affluent villages of Upton Cheney and Siston. A large science park is planned for Emersons Green. The seat switched to Labour in 1992 but was won back by the Conservatives in 2010.

	Electorate	Turnout %	Change from 05 %
	66,361	72.2	*
Skidmore, C C	19,362	40.4	8.3
Berry, R Lab	16,917	35.3	-10.6
Fitzharris, S LD	8,072	16.9	-1.2
Dowdney, N UKIP	1,528	3.2	0.8
Carey, M BNP	1,311	2.7	
Foster, N Green	383	0.8	
Blundell, M Eng	333	0.7	

Majority 2,445

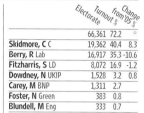

Kirkcaldy & Cowdenbeath — Labour hold

Gordon Brown
b. Feb 20, 1951
MP 1983-

Bombastic "clunking fist" who all but forced Tony Blair out but then, as Prime Minister himself, floundered. The economic brains of New Labour. Prime Minister and Labour Party leader 2007-10. Chancellor of Exchequer 1997-2007. Shadow: Chancellor of Exchequer 1992-97; spokes Trade & Industry 1989-92, 1985-87; Chief Sec to Treasury 1987-88. MP Dunfermline East 1983-2005. Former member Lab Party NEC. Chair Scotland Lab Party 1983-84. Joint hon sec Commonwealth parly assocn. University rector, lecturer, journalist, editor. Married, one daughter deceased, two sons. Education: Kirkcaldy High School; Edinburgh (MA, PhD).

Douglas Chapman (SNP) Cllr, Fife.
John Mainland (LD) Local government officer. Contested Dunfermline East 2001. Education: Kirkcaldy High School; University of Dundee MA politics, social policy & management; Heriot-Watt University postgraduate diploma in housing.
Lindsay Paterson (C)

Constituency
This is one of the safest Labour seats in the country. Guarded by the Firth of Forth to its south, this constituency contains many of southern Fife's former coalfield communities, including Lochgelly and Cowdenbeath, which used to be known as Little Moscows because of socialist ties. The area is struggling with its post-industrial role, but voters have remained with Labour.

	Electorate	Turnout %	Change from 05 %
	73,665	62.2	*
Brown, G Lab	29,559	64.5	6.5
Chapman, D SNP	6,550	14.3	-0.2
Mainland, J LD	4,269	9.3	-3.7
Paterson, L C	4,258	9.3	-1.0
Adams, P UKIP	760	1.7	0.4
Archibald, S Ind	184	0.4	-46.6
MacLaren of MacLaren, D Ind	165	0.36	
Jackson, D Land	57	0.1	

Majority 23,009

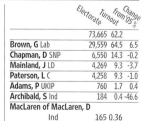

Knowsley — Labour hold

George Howarth
b. Jun 29, 1949
MP 1986-

Thoughtful, from Lab right, close to Jack Straw. Parly Under-Sec: NI 1999-2001; Home 1997-99. Opp spokes: home 1994-97; environment 1989-94. Member, select cttee: Modernisation of HoC 2005-10; Public Accounts 2002-03. Cllr: Huyton Urban C 1971-75; Knowsley BC 1975-86 (dep leader 1982-83). Prev. MP Knowsley North/&Sefton East. Teacher. Engineer. Chief exec Wales TUC sponsored co op centre, Cardiff 1984-86. Married, one daughter, two sons. Education: Liverpool Poly (BA soc sciences).

Flo Clucas (LD) b. May 9, 1947. Retired teacher. Cllr, Liverpool CC. Contested Knowsley North and Sefton East 2005; Liverpool Garston 1997; Crosby 1992. Education: Bellerive Grammar School, Liverpool University.
David Dunne (C) Barrister. Education: St Edward's College, West Derby, King's College London.

Constituency
This new seat to the east of Liverpool unites the bulk of Knowsley borough, formerly divided between two seats, excluding only the Halewood and Whiston areas in the south. The population is concentrated in two very deprived areas: Huyton in the south and Kirkby in the north. The M57 runs the length of the seat, passing through some more affluent areas near Knowsley Park in the centre, while the M62 cuts through the southwestern corner near the prosperous Roby. Both the predecessor seats here were Labour.

	Electorate	Turnout %	Change from 05 %
	79,561	56.1	☆
Howarth, G Lab	31,650	70.9	-0.9
Clucas, F LD	5,964	13.4	-0.4
Dunne, D C	4,004	9.0	-2.3
Greenhalgh, S BNP	1,895	4.2	
Rundle, A UKIP	1,145	2.6	

50%
Majority 25,686

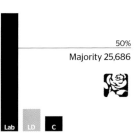

Lagan Valley — DUP hold

Jeffrey Donaldson
b. Dec 7, 1962
MP 1997-

Defected to the DUP, causing a re-alignment of unionist politics, and won it again for his new party in 2005. DUP spokes: Home / Defence 2007-; Transport, Int Devt 2005-07; Education, Defence 2004-05. UUP spokes 1997-2003. Member, NI Assembly 2003-, 1985-86. VP Ulster Unionist Council 2000-03. NI Forum 1996-98. Partner, financial services / estate agency business. MPs agent / personal asst. Ulster Defence Regiment. Married, two daughters. Education: Kilkeel High School; Castlereagh College.

Daphne Trimble (UCUNF) b. Jul 25, 1953. Solicitor. Education: Queen's University Belfast.
Trevor Lunn (Alliance) b. Jun 29, 1946. Cllr, Lisburn CC. Education: Belfast Royal Academy.
Keith Harbinson (TUV) Solicitor. Education: Queen's University Belfast.

Constituency
One of the five seats that form the suburban ring around Belfast, it contains Lisburn, which was recently granted city status despite its proximity to Belfast and not having a hotel. The constituency includes parts of strongly republican West Belfast but it is mainly middle-class and Protestant. Hillsborough and its rural hinterland have not had a significant Catholic population since before the Plantation. It was held for decades by James Molyneaux, the former Ulster Unionist leader, succeeded in 1997 by Jeffrey Donaldson, who defected to the DUP and won it again for his new party in 2005.

	Electorate	Turnout %	Change from 05 %
	65,257	56.0	☆
Donaldson, J DUP	18,199	49.8	-8.5
Trimble, D UCUNF	7,713	21.1	
Lunn, T Alliance	4,174	11.4	0.5
Harbinson, K TUV	3,154	8.6	
Heading, B SDLP	1,835	5.0	1.5
Butler, P SF	1,465	4.0	-0.3

50%
Majority 10,486

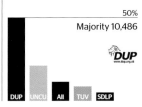

Lanark & Hamilton East — Labour hold

Jim Hood
b. May 16, 1948
MP 1987-

Undemonstrative "Old Labour" type. Chair, select committee: European Scrutiny 1998-2006. MP Clydesdale 1987-2005. Member, Co-op party. Councillor, Newark & Sherwood Dist 1979-97. NUM official. Leader Notts striking miners in 1984-85 national miners' strike. Mining engineer. Married, one daughter, one son. Education: Lesmahagow Higher Grade School; Coatbridge College; Nottingham Uni (economics, industrial relations, communications).

Clare Adamson (SNP) Cllr, North Lanarkshire. Education: Glasgow Caledonian University.
Colin McGavigan (C) Business consultant. Education: Queen's College Belfast.
Douglas Herbison (LD) Trade Association chief executive. Contested Banff and Buchan 2001, Inverclyde 2005. Education: Caledonian University.

Constituency
Tucked in between the cities of Edinburgh and Glasgow, this seat has a semi-urban, semi-rural make-up. The towns are not prosperous, but are generally working-class, with Hamilton, Uddingston and Carluke some of the most populous examples. The SNP has a presence in this area.

	Electorate	Turnout %	Change from 05 %
	74,773	62.3	
Hood, J Lab	23,258	50.0	4.0
Adamson, C SNP	9,780	21.0	3.3
McGavigan, C C	6,981	15.0	2.3
Herbison, D LD	5,249	11.3	-7.3
McFarlane, D Ind	670	1.4	0.5
Sale, R UKIP	616	1.3	0.3

50%
Majority 13,478

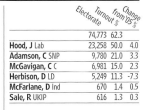

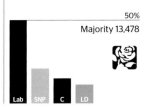

Lancashire West — Labour hold

Rosie Cooper
b. Sep 5, 1950
MP 2005-

Former Lib Dem. PPS to: Ben Bradshaw 2009-10; Lord Rooker 2006-07. Contested NW region 2004 European Parliament electiond for Labour. For Lib Dems: contested Liverpool Broadgreen 1992, Knowsley N 1986/1987, Cllr, Liverpool City 1973-2000. Lord Mayor of Liverpool 1992-93. PR and communications professional. USDAW. Director, Merseyside Centre for Deaf People. Education: Bellerive Convent Grammar School; Liverpool University.

Adrian Owens (C) b. 1965. Business consultant. Contested Ribble South 2001. Education: Trinity College, Cambridge.

John Gibson (LD) Cllr, Sefton Metropolitan BC. Education: Durham University, Cambridge University.

Constituency
At the southwestern tip of Lancashire, this is a seat of contrasts. Small towns and villages are popular with commuters to Manchester and Liverpool, while the market town of Ormskirk thrives with Edge Hill University. Skelmersdale, however, built in the 1960s as a New Town for manufacturing workers from Liverpool, suffers from deprivation from the decline of industries and outdated town planning. Regeneration is under way and Matalan has its headquarters here. With the exception of a Tory interlude from 1983 to 1992, this has generally been a Labour seat.

	Electorate	Turnout %	Change from '05 %
	75,975	63.8	
Cooper, R Lab	21,883	45.1	-2.9
Owens, A C	17,540	36.2	2.3
Gibson, J LD	6,573	13.6	-0.4
Noone, D UKIP	1,775	3.7	1.6
Cranie, P Green	485	1.0	
Braid, D Clause 28	217	0.45	

50%
Majority 4,343

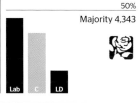

Lancaster & Fleetwood — Conservative gain

Eric Ollerenshaw
b. Mar 23, 1950
MP 2010-

Tough, straight-talking former teacher who had prominent role as leader of the Conservative group on the Greater London Assembly (2002-04; member, 2000-04). Cllr, Hackney BC 1990-2007. London Development Agency board. Contested Heywood & Middleton 1992. Chief of Staff to Baroness Warsi as Shadow Minister for Community Cohesion & Voluntary Action. Long-serving teacher at state comprehensives. Cites Metternich, Churchill and Thatcher as political heroes. OBE. Roman Catholic. Education: Hyde County Grammar School, Cheshire; London School of Economics (BSc Economics).

Clive Grunshaw (Lab) b. Oct 7, 1961. Councillor, Preston. Education: Lancaster University.
Stuart Langhorn (LD) Teacher. Contested Lancaster & Wyre 2005. Education: Lancaster University.

Constituency
The M6 and West Coast Main Line railway form the spine of this new seat, passing through Lancaster, with its historic castle and two universities, at the northern boundary. To the east lies rural land, while, to the west, the seat extends to Fleetwood, divided from the rest of the seat by the River Wyre. Fleetwood has pockets of deprivation in an otherwise prosperous seat. Traditional fishing industries have declined but there are still fish processing businesses. Fleetwood was previously in a Labour seat, while Lancaster was Tory.

	Electorate	Turnout %	Change from '05 %
	69,908	61.1	☆
Ollerenshaw, E C	15,404	36.1	2.5
Grunshaw, C Lab	15,071	35.3	-7.1
Langhorn, S LD	8,167	19.1	3.5
Dowding, G Green	1,888	4.4	-1.4
McGlade, F UKIP	1,020	2.4	-0.1
Kent, D BNP	938	2.2	
Riley, K Ind	213	0.5	

50%
Majority 333

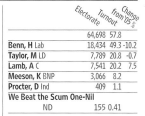

Leeds Central — Labour hold

Hilary Benn
b. Nov 26, 1953
MP 1999- (by-election)

Likeable intellectual with communitarian instincts, lacks ruthlessness; never known to take a controversial stand or offend anyone. Son of Tony Benn. Sec: Environment, Food & Rural Affairs 2007-; Int Dev't 2003-07. Min: DFID 2003. PPS: Home 2002-03; DFID 2001-02. David Blunkett special adviser 1997-99. Cllr, Ealing Bor; dep leader 1986-90. Contested Ealing North 1987, 1983. Chair London Authorities Education Cttee Assocn. MSF research officer, head of policy and communications. Unite. Widowed, remarried. One daughter, three sons. Education: Holland Park Comprehensive; University of Sussex (BA Russian/East European studies).

Michael Taylor (LD) b. Apr 7, 1950. Senior lecturer. Contested Halifax 2005. Cllr, various for 22 years. Ed: Ulster (BSc Economics); Manchester (PG Dip Economic Development and PhD); Leeds (PGCE) universities.
Alan Lamb (C) Pub and restaurant manager. Cllr, Leeds CC 2007-.
Kevin Meeson (BNP)

Constituency
Leeds business and retail centre is at the heart of the constituency. Despite this relatively prosperous hub, the seat is severely deprived residentially, typified by row upon row of terraced houses, home to Labour-inclined working classes. There is high unemployment. The two universities produce a significant student population. Boundaries to the south have been expanded substantially to include the suburbs of Middleton and Belle Isle.

	Electorate	Turnout %	Change from '05 %
	64,698	57.8	
Benn, H Lab	18,434	49.3	-10.2
Taylor, M LD	7,789	20.8	-0.7
Lamb, A C	7,541	20.2	7.5
Meeson, K BNP	3,066	8.2	
Procter, D Ind	409	1.1	
We Beat the Scum One-Nil			
ND	155	0.41	

50%
Majority 10,645

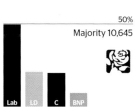

Leeds East — Labour hold

George Mudie
b. Feb 6, 1945
MP 1992-

Key supporter of Gordon Brown. Asst govt whip 2009-10. Parly Under-Sec, Education 1998-99. Whip; govt dep chief 1997-98; pairing and accommodation 1995-97; opp 1994-97. Member, select cttees: Treasury 2001-09; Selection 1995-99; Finance & Services 1997-99; Public Accounts 1994-95; Accommodation & Works 1992-98. Cllr, Leeds City 1971-92 (leader 1980-90). NUPE engineer/union official. Leeds Utd fan. Married, two children. Ed: Waid Academy; Newbattle Abbey (social sciences).

Barry Anderson (C) Cllr, Leeds CC 1999-. Contested Leeds East 2001. Ed: Edinburgh Napier Uni.

Andrew Tear (LD) Former soldier.
Trevor Brown (BNP) b. Jan 16, 1952. Retired railwayman. Education: Ashfield Secondary Modern Sch, York; Margaret McMillan Coll of Education.

Constituency

This predominantly residential seat has large areas of severe deprivation, particularly in areas such as Gipton and Harehills, where tower blocks look out over rundown council housing and boarded-up properties. Over a third live in social housing in this staunchly Labour seat. There are patches of greater affluence in the south east, with the disparity said to fuel crime rates. Employment is low but health sector employment is well above average, with Seacroft Hospital in the constituency.

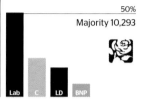

	Electorate	Turnout %	Change from '05 %
	65,067	58.1	*
Mudie, G Lab	19,056	50.4	-9.4
Anderson, B C	8,763	23.2	1.6
Tear, A LD	6,618	17.5	0.3
Brown, T BNP	2,947	7.8	
Davies, M Green	429	1.1	

50%
Majority 10,293

Leeds North East — Labour hold

Fabian Hamilton
b. Apr 12, 1955
MP 1997-

Survivor from left. Took party to court to halt all-women shortlists before 1997 election. Member, select committees: Foreign Affairs 2001-10; Quadripartite 2006-10; Administration 1997-2001. Vice-Chair Lab Friends of Israel. Member, Co-operative Party, Fabian Soc. Cllr, Leeds City 1987-98. Unite. Apple Mac consultant/dealer. Graphic designer. Taxi driver. Married, two daughters, one son. Ed: Brentwood Sch; York (BA soc sciences).

Matthew Lobley (C) b. 1975. Company chairman. Cllr, Leeds CC 2003-. Contested Leeds NE 2005. Education: Sheffield University (BSc maths).

Aqila Choudhry (LD), b Mar 15, 1962. Charity manager. Ed: Open University.

Constituency

A seat with extremes of wealth, Leeds North East has lost a chunk of the sparsely populated, affluent and semi-rural area from its north and gained further densely populated inner-city areas in the south. These are a mixture of prosperous professional parts and pockets of severe deprivation where many live in social housing. Chapeltown's back-to-back Victorian terraces house a large ethnic minority population that forms a tenth of the electorate. Under previous boundaries the seat was long held by the Tories before Labour took over in 1997.

	Electorate	Turnout %	Change from '05 %
	67,899	70.0	*
Hamilton, F Lab	20,287	42.7	-3.0
Lobley, M C	15,742	33.1	2.9
Choudhry, A LD	9,310	19.6	-2.1
Hendon, W UKIP	842	1.8	
Redmond, T BNP	758	1.6	
Foote, C Green	596	1.3	

50%
Majority 4,545

Leeds North West — Liberal Democrat hold

Greg Mulholland
b. Aug 31, 1970
MP 192005-

Able, slightly self-regarding. LD shad min: Health 2007-10; Schools 2006-07; Int Devt 2005-06. Member, cttee: Work & Pensions 2005-. Cllr, Leeds City 2003- (lead member, corporate services 2004-). Acc dir: CPM; Field Marketing; The Marketing Store; Biggart Donald. Member, Institute of Sales Promotion 1999. Member CAMRA. Co-founder Campaign for an English National Anthem. Campaigner, CAFOD. Married, one daughter. Ed: St Ambrose Coll, Altrincham; York (BA politics, MA public admin & public policy).

Julia Mulligan (C) b. 1967. Director of a marketing company. Cllr, Craven DC.

Judith Blake (Lab) b. Jul 23, 1953. Cllr, Leeds CC. Contested Leeds NW 2005. Ed: Kent Uni.

Constituency

This triangular seat stretches north and west from Headingley, home to cricket and rugby league stadiums and a large Leeds Metropolitan University campus. It takes in the suburban villages of Adel, Yeadon and Bramhope, the market town of Otley and Leeds Bradford International Airport. This affluent constituency is home to many professionals and notable for a student population comprising above a quarter of the electorate. Once regarded as a safe Conservative seat, it switched to Labour in 1997 before being taken by the Lib Dems in 2005.

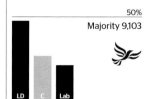

	Electorate	Turnout %	Change from '05 %
	65,399	66.5	*
Mulholland, G LD	20,653	47.5	10.6
Mulligan, J C	11,550	26.6	-0.3
Blake, J Lab	9,132	21.0	-10.9
Bulmer, G BNP	766	1.8	
Thackray, M UKIP	600	1.4	
Hemingway, M Green	508	1.2	-1.5
Procter, A Eng	153	0.4	
Bavage, T Green	121	0.3	-2.4

50%
Majority 9,103

Leeds West — Labour hold

Rachel Reeves
b. Feb 13, 1979
MP 2010-

Very highly thought of within the party, very bright. Columnist for Blairite Progress. Author, *Why Vote Labour?*. Contested Bromley & Chislehurst 2005 (with slogan 'from Bromley, for Bromley') and 2006 by-election (pushed to fourth place after low-key campaign). Economist: HBOS; Bank of England (inc stint at Brit Embassy in Washington). Amicus. Member: Fawcett Society, Amnesty, Fabian Society, Co-operative Party. Sister, Ellie, is member NEC. In a relationship. Ed: Cator Park Sch; New College, Oxford (PPE); LSE (MSc Economics) Likes walking, reading, swimming. Political heroes include Aneurin Bevan and Clement Attlee.

Ruth Coleman (LD) LD group support manager, Kirklees Council.
Joe Marjoram (C) Former Royal Navy officer. Cllr, Leeds CC 2008-.
Joanna Beverley (BNP) b. Jun 22, 1983. Housewife.

Constituency
The deprived working-class area north of this seat, around Bramley, is dominated by council housing, It contrasts with the averagely well-off south; the middle classes are well represented in the greener streets of Wortley and Farnley. Leeds Metropolitan University lies on the other side of the northeastern boundary but makes Kirkstall, home to a ruined abbey, increasingly popular with students, who comprise about one in ten electors. Labour has represented the seat since the Second World War except for a Liberal interlude between 1983 and 1987.

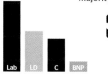

	Electorate	Turnout %	Change from '05 %
	67,453	57.5	☆
Reeves, R Lab	16,389	42.3	-13.9
Coleman, R LD	9,373	24.2	6.8
Marjoram, J C	7,641	19.7	5.6
Beverley, J BNP	2,377	6.1	
Blackburn, D Green	1,832	4.7	-2.5
Miles, J UKIP	1,140	2.9	1.1

50%
Majority 7,016

Leicester East — Labour hold

Keith Vaz
b. Nov 24, 1956
MP 1987-

Irrepressible but controversial figure, survived inquiries into financial affairs. Suspended for one month for several breaches of MP code of conduct. Prominent figure and socialite in British-Indian community. Chair, select cttee: Home Affairs 2003- (re-elected 2010-; member 1987-92). Min: FCO 1999-2001. Parly Sec, Lord Chancellor's Dept 1999. PPS to: Ross Cranston 1998-99; Lord Falconer 1997-98; John Morris 1997-99. Opp spokes: Environment 1992-97. Unison. Lab Party regional exec 1994-96. British Council board member. Barrister. Married, one daughter, one son. Ed: Cambridge (BA law/MA/ MCFI); London Coll of Law.

Jane Hunt (C) Project manager. Cllr, Charnwood BC.
Ali Asghar (LD) b. Aug 12, 1951. Welfare officer. Cllr, Nottingham CC. Ed: Trent Bridge Sec Sch; Nottingham Trent Uni (BA English language).

Constituency
An East Midlands city built around manufacturing, Leicester's textiles and clothes industries remain important and this seat is overwhelmingly working-class. It is also notable as a seat in which white British are a minority, while two fifths are of Indian origin. The seat covers the Evington, Humberstone, Nether Hall and Rushey Mead areas of the city, including some industrial estates. It has long been seen as a safe Labour seat, although in 1981 its MP defected to the Social Democratic Party and the subsequent split allowed the Tories to win for one term.

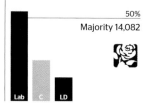

	Electorate	Turnout %	Change from '05 %
	72,986	65.8	☆
Vaz, K Lab	25,804	53.8	-5.0
Hunt, J C	11,722	24.4	4.6
Asghar, A LD	6,817	14.2	-2.3
Gilmore, C BNP	1,700	3.5	
Taylor, M Green	733	1.5	
Ransome, F UKIP	725	1.5	
Sadiq, A UPS	494	1.0	

50%
Majority 14,082

Leicester South — Labour hold

Sir Peter Soulsby
b. Dec 27, 1948
MP 2005-

From mainstream left, a critic of the Iraq war. Member, select committees: East Mids 2009-10; Transport 2009-10; Procedure 2009-10; Modernisation of HoC 2007-10; Environment Food & Rural Affairs 2005-10. Contested Harborough 1979, Leicester South 2004. Cllr, Leicester City 1973-2003, Council leader 1995-99, 1981-94. Election agent to Jim Marshall. Special educational needs teacher. Married, three daughters. Ed: Minchenden Sch, Southgate; City of Leicester Coll (BEd).

Parmjit Singh Gill (LD) b. Dec 20, 1966. Management consultant. MP for Leicester South 2004–5; contested Leicester South 2001, 2005.

Ross Grant (C) b. 1970. Cllr, Leicester CC 2004-. Ed: Lancaster Boys' Comp; Aston Uni.

Constituency
From the city centre with its cathedral and covered market, this seat encompasses Leicester and De Montfort universities, with students nearly a fifth of the residents. Farther out are the suburbs of Aylestone, Knighton and Stoneygate. The seat is also notable for a large ethnic minority population at about 40 per cent. About 25 per cent live in social housing. Once seen as a safe Labour seat, it was Conservative in 1983-87 and even more briefly Liberal Democrat, from a 2004 by-election, until 2005.

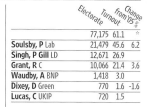

	Electorate	Turnout %	Change from '05 %
	77,175	61.1	☆
Soulsby, P Lab	21,479	45.6	6.2
Singh, P Gill LD	12,671	26.9	
Grant, R C	10,066	21.4	3.6
Waudby, A BNP	1,418	3.0	
Dixey, D Green	770	1.6	-1.6
Lucas, C UKIP	720	1.5	

50%
Majority 8,808

Leicester West — Labour hold

Elizabeth Kendall
b. Jun 11, 1971
MP 2010-

Bright, capable and highly ambitious former special adviser who inherited the seat of her former boss, Patricia Hewitt. Also worked for Harriet Harman. Health specialist. Dir, Ambulance Services Network. Dir, Maternity Alliance. Lead researcher, health & social care, IPPR. Health think-tank the King's Fund. Ed: Watford Girls; Queens College, Cambridge (history).

Celia Harvey (C) b. 1962. Businesswoman. Colonel in TA.
Peter Coley (LD) BT project manager. Cllr, Leicester CC 1992-. Ed: Gateway Grammar; City and Guilds (HNC Business and Finance).

Gary Reynolds (BNP)

Constituency

Extending primarily northwest of Leicester centre, this is the most working-class of the three seats, with a strong manufacturing sector. It includes areas such as New Parks and Beaumont Leys, with residential estates interspersed with industrial parks, recreational sites and a hospital. It is less ethnically diverse than the other two, although still with a sizeable ethnic minority population at around a fifth. The seat has been Labour since the 1920s.

	Electorate	Turnout %	Change from 05 %
	64,900	55.2	☆
Kendall, E Lab	13,745	38.4	-12.4
Harvey, C C	9,728	27.2	2.8
Coley, P LD	8,107	22.6	4.4
Reynolds, G BNP	2,158	6.0	
Ingall, S UKIP	883	2.5	
Forse, G Green	639	1.8	-3.1
Huggins, S Ind	181	0.5	
Score, S TUSC	157	0.4	
Dyer, S Pirate	113	0.3	
Bowley, D Ind	108	0.3	

50%
Majority 4,017

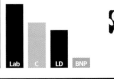

Leicestershire North West — Conservative gain

Andrew Bridgen
b. Oct 28, 1964
MP 2010-

Eurosceptic (member, Business for Sterling, The NO campaign). The Institute of Directors (former East Midlands chair). Formed AB Produce Ltd. Trained with Royal Marines. Christian. Enjoys skiing, fishing and country pursuits. Military history buff. Married, two sons. Ed: The Pingle Comp, Swadlincote; Nottingham (Biological Science).

Ross Willmott (Lab) b. Nov 4, 1957. Research fellow at De Montfort Uni. Leader, Leicester CC 1993– 2003, 2007-. Ed: London Uni; Warwick Uni.
Paul Reynolds (LD) Political and economic adviser. Pol adviser to Coalition forces (SAO) in Iraq in 2003.

Ian Meller (BNP) b. May 25, 1965. Bricklayer. Cllr, NW Leicestershire 2007-. Ed: St Martin's School, Stoke Golding; Desford College.

Constituency

Bordering with Derbyshire, this semi-rural seat contains a large area of the National Forest at its south. The main towns are Ashby-de-la-Zouch and Coalville, while the M1 runs up the east of the seat, passing by East Midlands Airport and Castle Donington in the north. This former coalfields seat retains a strong Labour-leaning working class and there are some patches of deprivation, but generally it is well off and also home to sizeable middle classes. It last changed hands in 1997.

	Electorate	Turnout %	Change from 05 %
	71,219	73.0	
Bridgen, A C	23,147	44.6	
Willmott, R Lab	15,636	30.1	-2113
Reynolds, P LD	8,639	16.6	4.6
Meller, I BNP	3,396	6.5	3.4
Green, M UKIP	1,134	2.2	-1.1

50%
Majority 7,511

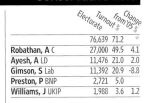

Leicestershire South — Conservative hold

Andrew Robathan
b. Jul 17, 1951
MP 1992-

Rather ra ra and military - a former SAS man with belligerent tribal instincts. Opposition Deputy Chief Whip 2005-10. Shadow Minister: Defence 2004-05; Internat Devt 2003; Trade & Industry 2002-03. PPS to Ian Sproat 1995-7. MP Blaby 1992-2010. Cllr, Hammersmith & Fulham 1990-92. City of London freeman. 15-year Coldstream Guards/SAS career, then worked for BP. Married, one daughter, one son. Education: Merchant Taylor's Sch; Oriel College, Oxford (BA modern history); RMA Sandhurst; Army Staff College.

Aladdin Ayesh (LD) Senior lecturer at De Montfort University.

Sally Gimson (Lab) b. Aug 27, 1964. Public relations. Ed: Cambridge Uni.
Paul Preston (BNP).

Constituency

The seat formerly known as Blaby has been renamed, reflecting the inclusion of much of the neighbouring Harborough district. The south of the seat contains the main town of Lutterworth but is generally more rural, while settlements such as Narborough, Blaby and Whetstone are clustered nearer Leicester toward the north. The M1 and M69 run through the seat, converging near the city and the good transport links make it popular with commuters. Once Nigel Lawson's seat, it has long been Conservative.

	Electorate	Turnout %	Change from 05 %
	76,639	71.2	☆
Robathan, A C	27,000	49.5	4.1
Ayesh, A LD	11,476	21.0	2.0
Gimson, S Lab	11,392	20.9	-8.8
Preston, P BNP	2,721	5.0	
Williams, J UKIP	1,988	3.6	1.2

50%
Majority 15,524

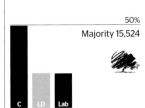

Andy Burnham
b. Jan 7, 1970
MP 2001-

Trying unsuccessfully to shed lightweight image. Candidate for Labour Party leadership 2010. Passionate football fan (Everton). Secretary of State: Health 2009-10; CMS 2008-09. Chief Sec to Treasury 2007-08. Min: Health 2006-07. Parly Under-Sec, Home 2005-06. PPS to: Ruth Kelly 2004-05; David Blunkett 2003-04. Co-op party. TGWU/Unison. Chair, Supporters Direct. Special adviser to Chris Smith. Football Task Force administrator. Parliamentary officer, NHS confederation. Married, two daughters, one son. Education: St Aelred's Roman Catholic High School, Merseyside; Fitzwilliam College, Cambridge.

Shazia Awan (C) CEO of an underwear company. Ed: Cardiff Uni (MA International Relations). Set up Wales Conservative newsletter.
Chris Blackburn (LD) b Jun 9, 1982. Business development manager. Ed: Runshaw College; Manchester Uni.
Gary Chadwick (BNP)

Constituency
Substantially redrawn, the seat has effectively shifted east, losing Hindley to Wigan and gaining Tyldesley and the rural area around Astley Green. The bird reserve lake of Pennington Flash was formed from mining subsidence and lies just outside the town of Leigh, which, like most settlements in the seat, was historically dependent on cotton and coal industries. It has been Labour since 1922, usually with at least 50 per cent of the vote.

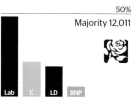

	Electorate	Turnout %	Change from 05 %
	76,350	58.1	☆
Burnham, A Lab	21,295	48.0	-9.8
Awan, S C	9,284	20.9	4.5
Blackburn, C LD	8,049	18.2	-0.9
Chadwick, G BNP	2,724	6.1	
Lavelle, M UKIP	1,535	3.5	
Bradbury, N Ind	988	2.2	
Dainty, T Ind	320	0.7	
Hessell, R Ch	137	0.3	

50%
Majority 12,011

Lab | C | LD | BNP

Norman Baker
b. Jul 26, 1957
MP 1997-

Vigorous campaigner with maverick streak and reputation for prolixity. Parly Under-Sec: Transport 2010-. LD Shadow Secretary of State: Transport 2007-10; Min Cab Office & Chancellor of Duchy of Lancaster 2007; Environment/EFRA 2002-06. Environment & Transport spokesman 1997-. Member, select cttees: Joint Cttee on Human Rights 2001-03; Broadcasting 2000-01; Environmental Audit 1997-2000. LD HoC environment campaigner. Cllr: Lewes DC 1987-99 (leader 1991-97), East Sussex CC 1989-97. Teacher/lecturer/company dir. Education: Royal Liberty School, Gidea Park; Royal Holloway College (BA German).

Jason Sugarman (C) b. 1969. Barrister, specialises in criminal law and complex fraud. Ed: Brighton Coll; Durham Uni (history); Westminster (law dipoma).

Constituency
Centred on the eponymous town, this East Sussex constituency encompasses the surrounding rural area, at the end of the South Downs, which is generally affluent and includes such famous place names as Glyndebourne. It stretches down to the coast at Seaford and Newhaven, the latter being less well off. About 10 per cent of residents are in social housing. There is an ageing demographic and although the middle and self-employed classes are numerous, there is a sizeable working class. Health and education are large employment sectors. A Liberal Democrat victory in 1997 overturned more than a century of Tory dominance.

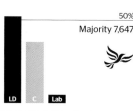

	Electorate	Turnout %	Change from 05 %
	68,708	72.9	☆
Baker, N LD	26,048	52.0	0.5
Sugarman, J C	18,401	36.7	2.1
Koundarjian, H Lab	2,508	5.0	-4.3
Charlton, P UKIP	1,728	3.5	1.2
Murray, S Green	729	1.5	-0.8
Lloyd, D BNP	594	1.2	
Soucek, O Ind	80	0.2	

50%
Majority 7,647

LD | C | Lab

Joan Ruddock
b. Dec 28, 1943
MP 1987-

Left winger who gained prominence as Chair of CND in 1980s. Strong on women's issues. Min: DECC 2009-10. Parly Under-Sec: DECC 2008-09; DEFRA 2007-08; Women 1997-98. Opp spokes: Environmental Protection 1994-97; Home 1992-94; Transport 1989-92. Unite. ARCS. Member IPU. Dir: research/publications Shelter, Nat Homeless Campaign, Oxford Housing Aid Centre. Council officer/CAB manager. Separated and later widowed from first husband. Partner of Frank Doran MP. Ed: Imperial Coll, London (BSc botany).

Tam Langley (LD) b. Jan 21, 1976. Public affairs director and campaigner.

Gemma Townsend (C) Works with GLA on policing and crime.
Darren Johnson (Green) b. 1966. Chair of the London Assembly and leader of the six-strong Green Group on Lewisham Council.

Constituency
This is the most deprived of the seats in the southeast London borough of Lewisham, partly because of the legacy of the dock closures at Deptford. Efforts to regenerate it as part of the Thames Gateway area are under way along with new transport links. The seat is primarily residential, with many commuting out to work, and about 40 per cent living in social housing. There are more affluent areas around Crofton Park and Hilly Fields. About a third of residents are black. The seat has long returned Labour MPs.

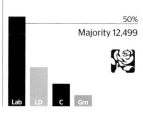

	Electorate	Turnout %	Change from 05 %
	67,058	61.5	☆
Ruddock, J Lab	22,132	53.7	-1.7
Langley, T LD	9,633	23.4	5.4
Townsend, G C	5,551	13.5	0.8
Johnson, D Green	2,772	6.7	-3.4
Page, I Soc	645	1.6	
Martin, M CPA	487	1.2	

50%
Majority 12,499

Lab | LD | C | Grn

Lewisham East — Labour hold

Heidi Alexander
b. Apr 17, 1975
MP 2010-

Pragmatic and highly capable former councillor (Lewisham 2004-10; Deputy Mayor and Cabinet Member for Regeneration 2006-10). Has formidably direct manner. First in family to go to university. Unite member. Chair, Greater London Enterprise. Dir, Lewisham's Local Education Partnership. Campaign manager, Clothes Aid. Researcher to Joan Ruddock MP. Lives with long-term partner. Education: Churchfields Comp, Swindon; Durham (BA geography; MA, urban & regional change).

Pete Pattisson (LD) Teacher and campaigner. Cllr, Lewisham BC 2007-10. Chair of the ENOUGH! campaign.

Jonathan Clamp (C) b. Feb 1971. Senior manager, BT. Cllr, Kensington & Chelsea BC 2002-06.

Constituency
This southeast London seat focuses on Catford and stretches north to Blackheath. Pockets of deprivation are significantly concentrated in Whitefoot, Downham and Rushey Green, which, along with Catford South, is included after boundary changes. About 30 per cent of the seat's residents live in social housing. The seat had been Tory from 1983 until 1992, when Labour took it.

	Electorate	Turnout %	Change from '05 %
	65,926	63.3	☆
Alexander, H Lab	17,966	43.1	-4.6
Pattisson, P LD	11,750	28.2	8.3
Clamp, J C	9,850	23.6	-0.7
Reed, R UKIP	771	1.9	-0.4
Cotterell, P Green	624	1.5	-2.7
Rose, J Eng	426	1.0	
Hallam, G CNBPG	332	0.8	

50%
Majority 6,216

Lewisham West & Penge — Labour hold

Jim Dowd
b. Mar 5, 1951
MP 1992-

Interested in animal welfare, member of League Against Cruel Sports, WWF, IFAW, RSPB. Member, select committee: Health 2001-10. Whip: government 1997-2001; opposition 1993-95. Member: Co-op party; Labour Friends of Palestine and the Middle East; Unite; GMB. Cllr, Lewisham BC 1974-94: mayor 1992. Member, Lewisham and North Southwark District Health Authority. Electronics engineer, Plessey Co. Education: Sedgehill Comp; London Nautical Sch.

Alex Feakes (LD) b. Mar 31, 1975. Owns a film & video production company, finance director of an art gallery. Cllr, Lewisham BC. Contested Lewi-

sham West 2005; Lewisham Mayoral 2002. Ed: Imperial Coll, London (BSc physics); Birkbeck Coll, London (MSc bioinformatics).
Chris Phillips (C) b. 1957. Architect. Cllr, Bromley BC. Ed: Royal College of Art.

Constituency
The new name for this seat reflects significant boundary changes, which effectively shift it southwest, gaining Penge, Crystal Palace and Clock House. The latter two and the Lewisham ward of Bellingham have areas of severe deprivation. Across the seat about 30 per cent live in social housing. This is mainly a residential seat with some manufacturing in Sydenham. Labour took this from the Tories in 1992.

	Electorate	Turnout %	Change from '05 %
	69,022	65.2	☆
Dowd, J Lab	18,501	41.1	-5.2
Feakes, A LD	12,673	28.1	1.0
Phillips, C C	11,489	25.5	3.9
Staveley, P UKIP	1,117	2.5	-0.1
Phoenix, R Green	931	2.1	-0.4
Hammond, S CPA	317	0.7	

50%
Majority 5,828

Leyton & Wanstead — Labour hold

John Cryer
b. Apr 11, 1964
MP 1997-2005; 2010-

Tough, hard-left union official, former rebel MP defeated in 2005. Returned to his old place in the Commons - on the rebels' front bench, below the gangway next to Dennis Skinner. Son of left-wing MPs Ann Cryer and the late Bob Cryer. Member, cttee: Deregulation & Reform 1997-2002. Eurosceptic. Member of Bennite Socialist Campaign Group. Political officer, Unite, Aslef. Journalist: Tribune; Morning Star; Labour briefing; The Guardian; GMPU Journal; Lloyd's of London Publications. Member, Amnesty International. Married, two sons, one daughter. Ed: Oakbank Sch, Keighley; Hatfield Poly; London Coll of Printing.

Farooq Qureshi (LD) b. Jul 7, 1942. Restaurateur. Ed: Pakistan.
Ed Northover (C) Solicitor, specialist in mergers and acquisitions and private equity. Ed: Merton College, Oxford (modern history).

Constituency
Straddling borough boundaries, this East London seat combines deprived areas around Leyton, from Waltham Forest in the west, with the better-off Wanstead area, from Redbridge in the east. It is ethnically diverse with the biggest minority groups Pakistani and black Caribbean. It is also economically varied with both numbers of professionals and of those who have never worked above the London average. The seat has been Labour since its creation in 1997.

	Electorate	Turnout %	Change from '05 %
	63,541	63.2	☆
Cryer, J Lab	17,511	43.6	-2.2
Qureshi, F LD	11,095	27.6	2.9
Northover, E C	8,928	22.2	-0.6
Wood, G UKIP	1,080	2.7	0.9
Gunstock, A Green	562	1.4	-3.0
Clift, J BNP	561	1.4	
Bhatti, S Ch	342	0.9	
Levin, M Ind	80	0.2	

50%
Majority 6,416

Lichfield Conservative hold

Michael Fabricant
b. Jun 12, 1950
MP 1992-

Ebullient. Endures speculation over authenticity of resplendent blond hair. Govt whip 2010-. Opposition Whip 2005-10. Shadow Minister: Economic Affairs 2003-05; Trade & Industry 2003. PPS to: Michael Jack 1996-97. MP Mid-Staffs 1992-97. Senior Director and Co-founder of an international broadcast manufacturing/management group. Lawyer. Chartered electronics engineer. Ed: Brighton, Hove and Sussex Grammar School; Loughborough (BSc economics and law); Sussex (MSc systems and econometrics); Oxford/London/ South California (PhD econometrics and economic forecasting).

Ian Jackson (LD) b. Jul 2, 1949. Accountant. Former chair of a local action group fighting green belt development.
Steve Hyden (Lab) b. Jun 14, 1958. Case maker. School governor, parish councillor.

Constituency
The population of this West Midlands seat is concentrated in its south, in the cathedral city of Lichfield and large town of Burntwood. It becomes more rural as it stretches farther north away from the Birmingham conurbation, into areas in the National Forest. Typical of the area, manufacturing is an important sector and this is an economically active seat, with high numbers of professionals. The seat has been Conservative in recent years, but the margin of victory in 1997 was just 238 votes after a recount.

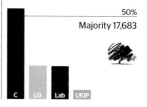

	Electorate	Turnout %	Change from '05 %
	72,586	71.0	*
Fabricant, M C	28,048	54.4	5.7
Jackson, I LD	10,365	20.1	4.2
Hyden, S Lab	10,230	19.8	-12.4
Maunder, K UKIP	2,920	5.7	2.4

50%
Majority 17,683

C LD Lab UKIP

Lincoln Conservative hold

Karl McCartney
b. Oct 25, 1968
MP 2010-

Mainstream, traditionalist interested in the Commonwealth, education and transport. Cllr, Wrothan PC 1997-2003. Contested Lincoln 2005. Magistrate. Self-employed corporate strategy and communications consultant, clients including TFL and the Strategic Rail Authority. Conservative party researcher/agent for MPs including Dame Angela Rumbold. Dir, IT consultancy company founded by his brother. PR manager for Norton Rose. Keen rugby and football fan. Married, two sons. Ed: Birkenhead Sch for Boys; Neston HS; Willink Sch, Burghfield; St David's University Coll (BA geography, SU president); Kingston Uni (MBA).

Gillian Merron (Lab) MP Lincoln 1997-2010. Min: Health 2009-10. Parly Under-Sec, Foreign Office 2008-09, Int Devt 2008-09. Parly Sec, Cabinet Office 2007-08. PPS to John Reid, MP 2001-02. Asst govt whip 2002-04.
Reg Shore (LD) Performing arts specialist and teacher. Cllr, West Lindsey DC. LD Group Leader.

Constituency
Lincoln's imposing Gothic cathedral towers over the city, with its university and castle. There is a strong working class, although traditional industries have declined and been replaced by retail and public sector. The seat also takes in the huge housing estate of Birchwood. Deprivation here and in the north and east of the city contrasts with the more affluent centre and west. Labour's 1997 victory overturned 18 years of Tory representation in this seat.

	Electorate	Turnout %	Change from '05 %
	73,540	62.2	
McCartney, K C	17,163	37.5	3.3
Merron, G Lab	16,105	35.2	-8.5
Shore, R LD	9,256	20.2	1.9
West, R BNP	1,367	3.0	
Smith, N UKIP	1,004	2.2	-1.5
Coleman, E Eng	604	1.3	
Walker, G Ind	222	0.5	

50%
Majority 1,058

C Lab LD

Linlithgow & Falkirk East Labour hold

Michael Connarty
b. Sep 3, 1947
MP 1992-

Left-wing but thoughtful champion of mining communities. Taciturn but acute, chair European Scrutiny 2006-10 (member 1998-) and not afraid to take on his own side. PPS to: Tom Clarke 1997-98. Member, select cttees: Info 1997-2001; European Scrutiny 1998-. MP Falkirk East 1997-98. Cllr, Stirling DC: leader 1980-90. JP 1977-90. Teacher. Chair, Stirling Econ Devt Co. Pres student assocn. Married, one daughter, one son. Ed: St Patrick's High School; Stirling University (BA economics); Glasgow; Jordanhill Coll of Ed (DCE).

Tam Smith (SNP) b. Feb 12, 1942. Businessman.

Stephen Glenn (LD) b. Sep 1969. Data analyst. Contested Linlithgow and East Falkirk in 2005.
Andrea Stephenson (C) b. 1980. Political operations co-ordinator.

Constituency
This seat combines traditional Scottish central belt with industry and Edinburgh's commuter fringe. It was created from two contrasting seats: the working-class Falkirk and the Edinburgh commuter town of Linlithgow - once home to Scottish monarchs. The mixed feel of this seat is completed by the industrial area around Bathgate and Bo'ness, which has the Grangemouth oil refinery. It has long had Labour MPs.

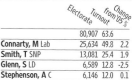

	Electorate	Turnout %	Change from '05 %
	80,907	63.6	
Connarty, M Lab	25,634	49.8	2.2
Smith, T SNP	13,081	25.4	1.9
Glenn, S LD	6,589	12.8	-2.5
Stephenson, A C	6,146	12.0	0.1

50%
Majority 12,553

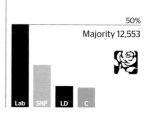

Lab SNP LD C

209

Liverpool Riverside — Labour hold

Louise Ellman
b. Nov 14, 1945
MP 1997-

Fiercely pro-Israel (Vice-Chair APPG: Israel 2002-; council against anti-Semitism 2003-. Vice-Chair Lab Friends of Israel). Chair, Transport select committee 2008- (re-elected unopposed 2010; member, Transport cttee in its various incarnations 1997-). Cllr: Lancs CC 1970-97 (leader 1981-97); W Lancs DC 1974-87. Founder chair NW Regional Assocn. Open Uni tutor/ FE lecturer. Member, Co-Op party, TGWU. Married, one daughter, one son. Ed: Manchester HS for Girls; Hull (BA sociology); York (MPhil soc admin).

Richard Marbrow (LD) Campaigns officer for Chris Davies MEP. Cllr, Liverpool, CC 1998-2007.
Kegang Wu (C) b. 1961. Scientist, lecturer and businessman. Chief China adviser for the British Chambers of Commerce.

Constituency

Liverpool city centre, with its cathedrals, museums and the iconic Albert Dock, has undergone major regeneration in recent years and its designation as European Capital of Culture 2008 confirmed its new image. Liverpool borough, however, remains the most deprived in England and this seat, extending either side of the centre along the banks of the Mersey, generally remains extremely poor, especially around the dilapidated terraced houses of Princes Park ward, which has an ethnic minority population of almost 40 per cent. The seat has long been a Labour stronghold.

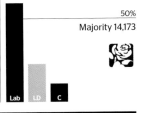

	Electorate	Turnout %	Change from '05 %
	74,539	52.1	*
Ellman, L Lab	22,998	59.3	0.0
Marbrow, R LD	8,825	22.7	-0.6
Wu, K C	4,243	10.9	1.9
Crone, T Green	1,355	3.5	-1.7
Stafford, P BNP	706	1.8	
Gaskell, P UKIP	674	1.7	0.1

Majority 14,173

Liverpool Walton — Labour hold

Steve Rotheram
b. Nov 4, 1961
MP 2010-

Runaway victor over union/party insiders in controversially shortlisted selection. Cllr, Liverpool 2002-10. Mayor of Liverpool 2008. Dep Lord Mayor 2007-08. Senior business manager, Learning Skills Council. Returned to education as mature student. Bricklayer who founded construction company and worked in construction training/teaching. Married, three children. Ed: Ruffwood Comp; John Moores (MA contemporary urban renaissance).

Patrick Moloney (LD) b. Apr 6, 1960. Software engineer. Former cllr, Liverpool CC.
Adam Marsden (C) Works in finance.

Constituency

This seat contains some of the most deprived wards in England, notably the terraced streets of Everton around the football club. Liverpool FC's Anfield base is also in this seat. In the north of the city, the seat is primarily residential. It is overwhelmingly white and working-class with high unemployment - a legacy of the decline of the docks. It has been Labour since 1964.

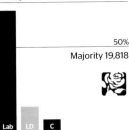

	Electorate	Turnout %	Change from '05 %
	62,612	54.8	*
Rotheram, S Lab	24,709	72.0	0.2
Moloney, P LD	4,891	14.2	-2.7
Marsden, A C	2,241	6.5	0.1
Stafford, P BNP	1,104	3.2	
Nugent, J UKIP	898	2.6	-0.7
Manwell, J CPA	297	0.9	
Ireland, D TUSC	195	0.6	

Majority 19,818

Liverpool Wavertree — Labour Co-op hold

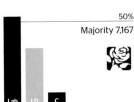

Luciana Berger
b. May 13, 1981
MP 2010-

Faced criticism for lack of local knowledge. Partner of Siôn Simon, former Birmingham Erdington MP. Shot to prominence in 2005 due to friendship with Euan Blair and resignation from NEC of the NUS in anti-Semitism dispute. Labour Friends of Israel. Government Strategy Unit, Accenture; Government and Parliamentary Manager, NHS Confederation Dir; Lab Friends of Israel. Member of Unite, the Cooperative Party, the Fabian Society and Progress. Jewish. Likes Bollywood films, running and weight training. Ed: Haberdashers' Aske's Sch; Birmingham (BCom commerce & Spanish); Birkbeck Coll (MSc gov, pol & policy).

Colin Eldridge (LD) Director of Wash and Press Centre Ltd. Ed: University of the West of England, Bristol. Former cllr, Liverpool CC.
Andrew Garnett (C) Compliance officer advising on financial regulation. Ed: Manchester University.

Constituency

The boundaries have been changed but the seat remains, essentially, a residential area to the east of the city centre. There is a geographical divide in terms of affluence, with semi-detached houses lining leafy streets in the middle-class suburbs of Church and Childwall to the south, and dilapidated terraced and council houses in Kensington and Fairfield to the north. Although an old seat of the same name was strongly Conservative until it was abolished in 1983, this seat was won by Labour in 1997.

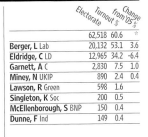

	Electorate	Turnout %	Change from '05 %
	62,518	60.6	*
Berger, L Lab	20,132	53.1	3.6
Eldridge, C LD	12,965	34.2	-6.4
Garnett, A C	2,830	7.5	1.0
Miney, N UKIP	890	2.4	0.4
Lawson, R Green	598	1.6	
Singleton, K Soc	200	0.5	
McEllenborough, S BNP	150	0.4	
Dunne, F Ind	149	0.4	

Majority 7,167

Liverpool West Derby

Labour Co-op hold

Stephen Twigg
b. Dec 25, 1966
MP 1997-2005; 2010-

The face of the 1997 election landslide when unseated Michael Portillo, returning to parliament in new safe seat after defeat in Enfield Southgate in 2005. Giggly, doesn't take self too seriously. Once seen as über-Blairite but has repositioned self with spell at think-tanks (Chair, Progress and Dir, Foreign Policy Centre) following electoral defeat. Min: Schools 2004-05. Parly Under-Sec: Education 2002-04. Dep Leader of HoC 2001-02. Cllr, Islington 1992-97; part of 'Islington mafia' with James Purnell. Amicus, Co-op. Pol consultant, Rowland Sallingbury Casey. Gen Sec, Fabian Soc. Research asst to Margaret Hodge. Parly officer, Amnesty Int.

Pres, NUS. Gay. Ed: Oxford Uni (PPE/ politics & econ).

Paul Twigger (LD) b. Feb 20, 1981. Field officer for Age Concern.
Stephen Radford (Lib) Part-time manager. Cllr, Liverpool CC.
Pamela Hall (C)

Constituency
West Derby, in the north east of Liverpool, is one of the more affluent areas and lies at the centre of this seat, with middle classes also concentrated around Croxteth Hall and Country Park in the north east. This band of relative prosperity is flanked by areas of severe deprivation in the estates of Norris Green in the north west and the Dovecot and Yew Tree areas to the south east. Bob Wareing took this seat for Labour in 1983 but was deselected in 2007 and then sat as an independent.

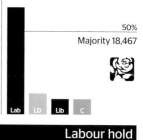

	Electorate	Turnout %	Change from '05 %
	63,082	56.7	☆
Twigg, S Lab	22,953	64.1	3.6
Twigger, P LD	4,486	12.5	-2.7
Radford, S Lib	3,327	9.3	
Hall, P C	3,311	9.3	1.0
Jones, H UKIP	1,093	3.1	1.1
Andersen, K Soc	614	1.7	

50%
Majority 18,467

| Lab | LD | Lib | C |

Livingston

Labour hold

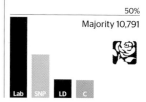

Graeme Morrice
b. Feb 23, 1959
MP 2010-

Long-serving local councillor (West Lothian DC 1987-) and council leader (1995-2007). Wholesale and retail career. Member, West Lothian Healthcare NHS Trust, NHS Lothian Board. Former Chair, W Lothian Community Health & Care Partnership. Scottish Enterprise & Lothian Ltd. Member, Unite. Music enthusiast. Lives with partner. Education: Broxburn Academy, West Lothian; Napier, Edinburgh (business studies).

Lis Bardell (SNP) Former lecturer. Education: Edinburgh University (law); Bristol University (social policy & social work). Previously managed a children's development project.

Charles Dundas (LD) b. Jul 19, 1978. Campaigner. Contested Glasgow Baillieston 2001; Holyrood elections Glasgow Springburn 2003. Agent to Sir Menzies Campbell MP in North East Fife 2005. Ed: Glasgow Uni (MA Hons history).
Alison Adamson-Ross (C)

Constituency
Livingston is the only New Town in the Lothians. Ruled by a confusing battalion of roundabouts, this was once a thriving mining community. This largely concrete conurbation now depends on the electronics sector for much of its employment. Bordering the southwestern fringes of Edinburgh, Livingston has been a Labour seat with a strong SNP presence.

	Electorate	Turnout %	Change from '05 %
	75,924	63.1	
Morrice, G Lab	23,215	48.5	-2.6
Bardell, L SNP	12,424	25.9	4.4
Dundas, C LD	5,316	11.1	-4.3
Adamson-Ross, A C	5,158	10.8	0.7
Orr, D BNP	960	2.0	
Forrest, A UKIP	443	0.9	0.6
Hendry, A SSP	242	0.5	-1.3
Slavin, J Ind	149	0.3	0.1

50%
Majority 10,791

| Lab | SNP | LD | C |

Llanelli

Labour hold

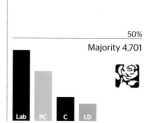

Nia Griffith
b. Dec 4, 1956
MP 2005-

Left-winger from South Wales valleys. PPS to: Harriet Harman 2008-10; Hilary Benn 2007-2008. Deputy Mayor of Carmarthen 1998-1999; Sheriff of Carmarthen 1997-1998; Cllr, Carmarthen Town 1987. School teacher/faculty head. Adviser for LEA/schools inspector. Divorced. Ed: Somerville Coll, Oxford (BA modern languages); Uni Coll of N Wales Bangor (PGCE).

Myfanwy Davies (PC) b. Dec 1975. Academic. Campaigned with Jill Evans MEP. Patron, Breakthro' Llanelli. Secretary of Llanelli Fairtrade Coalition. Associate member, Llwynhendy WI.

Christopher Salmon (C) b. 1978. Former army officer, investment adviser, developing markets.
Myrddin Edwards (LD)

Constituency
This South Wales seat reaches from Kidwelly and Pembrey Forest, around to the north side of the Loughor Estuary, taking in Burry Port and Llanelli. Once focused on coal and steel industries, Llanelli now has a more diverse manufacturing base but remains working-class, with a large population living in social housing and severe deprivation around the seafront. The coast is home to many pensioners. The seat has a long Labour tradition, although the identical seat for the Welsh Assembly has returned Plaid Cymru politicians - including in 2007 - reflecting a sizeable Welsh-speaking population.

	Electorate	Turnout %	Change from '05 %
	55,637	67.3	
Griffith, N Lab	15,916	42.5	-4.4
Davies, M PC	11,215	29.9	3.5
Salmon, C C	5,381	14.4	0.7
Edwards, M LD	3,902	10.4	-2.4
Marshall, A UKIP	1,047	2.8	

50%
Majority 4,701

| Lab | PC | C | LD |

Londonderry East — DUP hold

Gregory Campbell
b. Feb 15, 1953
MP 2001-

Sharp-tongued hardliner who starred with his nemesis Martin McGuinness in banned BBC documentary 'At the Edge of the Union'. DUP spokes: Work & Pensions 2007-; CMS 2005-; Defence 2005-07. Member, Northern Ireland Assembly 1998- (Minister for Culture, Arts, Leisure 2008-9, Min for Regional Devt 2000-03, Whip 1998). NI pol dialogue forum 1996-98. Old NI Assembly 1982-86. Cllr, Londonderry CC 1981-. Civil servant. Self-employed businessman. Married, three daughters, one son. Education: Londonderry Technical College; Magee College (extra-mural political studies certificate).

Cathal Ó hOisín (SF) Cllr, Limavady BC 2005-10, currently Mayor. Party leader on Limavady District Policing Partnership.
Lesley Macaulay (UCUNF), runs training/consultancy business. Youth worker, Church of Ireland. Fundraising manager, NSPCC; Chest, Heart & Stroke NI.
Thomas Conway (SDLP) Cllr, Derry CC.
William Ross (TUV) b. 1936. Party president. Former MP for East Londonderry 1974-2001.

Constituency
A strong Unionist seat centred on the North Coast with its golf courses and rich farmland. It includes pockets of high prosperity and poor estates dominated by loyalist paramilitaries. The DUP took it from the UUP's Willie Ross, a hardliner, in 2001.

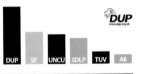

	Electorate	Turnout %	Change from '05 %
	63,220	55.3	☆
Campbell, G DUP	12,097	34.6	-6.4
Ó hOisín, C SF	6,742	19.3	
Macaulay, L UCUNF	6,218	17.8	
Conway, T SDLP	5,399	15.5	-3.9
Ross, W TUV	2,572	7.4	
Fitzpatrick, B Alliance	1,922	5.5	3.1

50%

Majority 5,355

Loughborough — Conservative gain

Nicky Morgan
b. Oct 10, 1972
MP 2010-

Interested in financial markets regulation and higher education. Contested Loughborough 2005, Islington South & Finsbury 2001. Solicitor - corporate lawyer specialising in M&A: Travers Smith; Allen & Overy; Theodore Goddard. Christian. Sings with a choir. Married, one son. Ed: Surbiton HS; St Hugh's Coll, Oxford (BA law, MA); College of Law, Guildford (LPC)

Andy Reed (Lab Co-op) b. Sep 17, 1964. MP Loughborough 1997-2010. PPS to: Kate Hoey MP 2000-01; Margaret Beckett MP 2001-03. Education: Longslade Community Coll, Birstall; De Montfort University.

Mike Willis (LD) b. Oct 1945. Logistics manager, College Radio Station. Lecturer in media and multimedia at New College, Nottingham.

Constituency
Midway between Leicester and Nottingham, this seat includes the large town of Loughborough, on the River Soar and Grand Union Canal, and Shepshed, near the M1. To the east it encompasses an area of countryside, with farms and hamlets. The university provides a large student population, at around a fifth. The seat's demographic is a representative mixture across the social classes, while the economy has an important high-tech sector. Boundary changes in 1997 helped Labour to win from the Tories, but minor alterations this time were in favour of the Conservatives.

	Electorate	Turnout %	Change from '05 %
	77,502	68.2	☆
Morgan, N C	21,971	41.6	4.3
Reed, A Lab	18,227	34.5	-6.7
Willis, M LD	9,675	18.3	0.4
Stafford, K BNP	2,040	3.9	
Foden, J UKIP	925	1.8	-0.6

50%

Majority 3,744

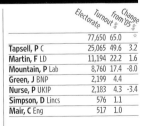

Louth & Horncastle — Conservative hold

Sir Peter Tapsell
b. Feb 1, 1930
MP 1959-1964; 1966-

Archetypal pin-striped, plummy-voiced Edwardian Tory. Octogenarian, future Father of the House. Opposition spokes: Treasury 1977-78; Foreign & Commonwealth Office 1976-77. MP Lindsay East 1983-97; Horncastle 1966-83; Nottingham West 1959-64. Member, UN Business Advisory Council. PA to Anthony Eden as PM. Adviser to central banks/international companies. Council Member, Institute for Fiscal Studies. London Stock Exchange member 1957-90. Divorced, one son deceased. Remarried. Education: Tonbridge School; Merton College, Oxford (BA modern history; Dip economics).

Fiona Martin (LD) Cllr, Horncastle TC 1979-2010. Former mayor of Horncastle. Cllr East Lindsey DC, former chair.
Patrick Mountain (Lab) b. 1959. Lecturer in countryside management & agriculture.

Constituency
This large stretch of Lincolnshire coastline includes the seaside resorts of Mablethorpe and Sutton-on-Sea, where severe deprivation is evident after the decline of the tourism industry. The seat's eponymous towns lie inland amid a rural area of the Lincolnshire Wolds where farming is an important sector. It is more averagely well off, but with a few patches of affluence. The Conservatives have been dominant for decades, but some of the poorest areas supported Labour in 1997.

	Electorate	Turnout %	Change from '05 %
	77,650	65.0	☆
Tapsell, P C	25,065	49.6	3.2
Martin, F LD	11,194	22.2	1.6
Mountain, P Lab	8,760	17.4	-8.0
Green, J BNP	2,199	4.4	
Nurse, P UKIP	2,183	4.3	-3.4
Simpson, D Lincs	576	1.1	
Mair, C Eng	517	1.0	

50%

Majority 13,871

Philip Dunne
b. Aug 14, 1958
MP 2005-

Sharp, clever and could do well in office. Successful businessman who co-founded Ottaker's plc, the now sold-off bookstores. Very financially able, proved his knowledge during the banking crisis. Assistant government whip 2010-. Opposition Whip 2008-10, Deputy Chairman Conservative Party 2008-10. South Shropshire District councillor, 2001-04. Former merchant/investment banker/adviser in New York, Hong Kong and London. NFU member; responsible for family farm. Former director, Juvenile Diabetes Research Foundation. Married, two daughters, two sons. Education: Eton College; Keble College, Oxford (BA PPE).

Heather Kidd (LD) b. Jan 31, 1954. Science teacher. Cllr, South Shropshire DC 1996-2010.
Anthony Hunt (Lab) b. Jan 31, 1980. Political aide to Paul Murphy MP.

Constituency
This vast rural constituency spans southern Shropshire, from the border with Wales in the west to Staffordshire in the east. This is one of the most agricultural in England and earnings are below national and county averages, with many living in isolated rural areas. More affluent areas lie near the amenities of the towns of Bridgnorth, Church Stretton and Ludlow - a renowned foodie destination with an annual festival and two Michelin-starred restaurants. The Liberal Democrats broke more than a century of Tory dominance in 2001 but the seat was won back by the Conservatives in 2005.

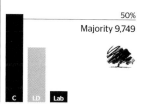

	Electorate	Turnout %	Change from '05 %
	66,631	73.1	
Dunne, P C	25,720	52.8	7.8
Kidd, H LD	15,971	32.8	-7.9
Hunt, A Lab	3,272	6.7	-3.9
Gill, C UKIP	2,127	4.4	2.7
Evans, C BNP	1,016	2.1	
Morrish, J Green	447	0.9	-0.9
Powell, A Loony	179	0.4	

50%
Majority 9,749

C | LD | Lab

Kelvin Hopkins
b. Aug 22, 1941
MP 1997-

Diminuitive left-winger with gnome-like demeanor. Active member of Socialist Campaign Group. Adviser on yachting to Richard Caborn 2002-07. Member, cttees: Public Admin 2002-; Broadcasting 1999-2001. Vice-Chair central region Lab Party. Cllr, Luton Bor 1972-76. Delegate, Luton TUC. NALGO/Unison policy/research officer. TUC Econ Dept. Married, one daughter, one son. Ed: Queen Elizabeth's GS, High Barnet; Nottingham (BA pol/econ, maths with stats).

Jeremy Brier (C) Barrister. Ed: Christ's College, Cambridge (BA Hons law); City University, London (dip law).

Rabi Martins (LD) b. Jul 5, 1945. Business management consultant and executive director. Cllr, Watford BC 2004-. Ed: Dodoma Secondary School, Tanzania.

Constituency
This compact urban seat is beyond the centre and primarily residential. The Barnfeld area is particularly middle-class, but the numbers of managerial and professional workers are still below national average. There are large communities from Pakistani, Indian and black Caribbean heritage. The M1 passes through and the large Willowgate Trading Estate is nearby. Labour ousted the Tories in 1997.

	Electorate	Turnout %	Change from '05 %
	65,062	66.1	☆
Hopkins, K Lab	21,192	49.3	0.7
Brier, J C	13,672	31.8	-0.4
Martins, R LD	4,784	11.1	-4.5
Brown, C UKIP	1,564	3.6	0.4
Rose, S BNP	1,316	3.1	
Hall, S Green	490	1.1	

50%
Majority 7,520

Lab | C | LD

Gavin Shuker
b. Oct 10, 1981
MP 2010-

Very fresh-faced and squeaky-clean pastor of the City Life Church, Luton, determined to improve the town's reputation. Kept the swing to the Tories below the national average, despite the high-profile expenses/lobbying record of outgoing Margaret Moran. Received strong support from the Christian Socialist Movement. Formerly associate pastor, City Life Church Cambridge. Worked for Fusion UK charity. Worked for Endis, web development company. Member, Unite. Married. Ed: Icknield HS; Luton Sixth Form Coll; Girton Coll, Cambridge (BA social & political science).

Nigel Huddleston (C) b. 1970. Director,

management consultancy. Ed: UCLA (MA business administration).
Qurban Hussain (LD) Employment adviser. Cllr, Luton BC 2003-2007, deputy leader 2005-07.

Constituency
This seat covers the central parts of the town and extends south, including Caddington and London Luton airport, neighbouring on the old Vauxhall site at Napier Park. The M1 runs down the west of Luton while the town centre dominates the town. There are also industrial areas with plant workers concentrated in Dallow ward. There is a high proportion of people who have never worked and about 20 per cent of residents were born outside Britain. The two largest ethnic groups are Pakistani, at more than 10 per cent, and Bangladeshi at nearly 6 per cent. Labour took this from the Tories in 1997.

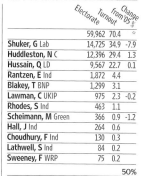

	Electorate	Turnout %	Change from '05 %
	59,962	70.4	☆
Shuker, G Lab	14,725	34.9	-7.9
Huddleston, N C	12,396	29.4	1.3
Hussain, Q LD	9,567	22.7	0.1
Rantzen, E Ind	1,872	4.4	
Blakey, T BNP	1,299	3.1	
Lawman, C UKIP	975	2.3	-0.2
Rhodes, S Ind	463	1.1	
Scheimann, M Green	366	0.9	-1.2
Hall, J Ind	264	0.6	
Choudhury, F Ind	130	0.3	
Lathwell, S Ind	84	0.2	
Sweeney, F WRP	75	0.2	

50%
Majority 2,329

Lab | C | LD

Macclesfield — Conservative hold

David Rutley
b. Mar 7, 1961
MP 2010-

Special adviser from the Major government years, experienced in big business. Won open primary. Contested St Albans, 1997. Member, Bow Group. Special adviser to Cabinet Office / MAFF / HM Treasury 1994-96. Barclays Bank (marketing dir); Halifax General Insurance; ASDA Stores (dir, e-commerce / financial services); Safeway Stores; PepsiCo Int. Mountaineer, rock climber, ornithologist. Practising Mormon. Married, two daughters, two sons. Education: Priory School, Lewes; LSE (BSc Econ); Harvard (MBA).

Roger Barlow (LD) b. Oct 13, 1970. Director Deloitte. Ed: Robert Pattison School; Christ's Church, Oxford.
Adrian Heald (Lab) b. Mar 7, 1961. Consultant Physician.

Constituency
Macclesfield, with its cobbled streets and former textile mills, lies at the centre of the seat, surrounded by Cheshire countryside, the eastern half of which lies within the Peak District National Park. Poynton, on the outskirts of Stockport, and Bollington are the other main settlements. This well-off seat is home to well-educated and well-paid professionals, many of whom commute north to Manchester. The seat has been Conservative since 1918.

	Electorate	Turnout %	Change from 05 %
	73,417	68.2	☆
Rutley, D C	23,503	47.0	-2.7
Barlow, R LD	11,544	23.1	3.5
Heald, A Lab	10,164	20.3	-8.7
Murphy, B Macc	2,590	5.2	
Smith, J UKIP	1,418	2.8	
Knight, J Green	840	1.7	

Majority 11,959

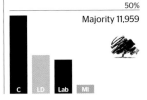

Maidenhead — Conservative hold

Theresa May
b. Oct 1, 1956
MP 1997-

Clergyman's daughter, moderniser with penchant for fashionable shoes, struggled with some policy spokesperson roles; has long endured 'token woman' tag. Shock appointment as Home Sec 2010-. Likeable but had previously made little impact on big issues. Coined 'nasty party' term as Chair Con Party 2003-03. Shadow SoS: Work & Pensions 2009-10. Shadow Min: Women 2007-. Shadow Leader of the HoC 2005-09. Shadow SoS: CMS 2005; Family 2004-05; Environment/ Transport 2003-04; Transport 2002; Local govt/Transport/regions 2001-02; Education/Employment 1999-2001. Merton cllr, payment clearing services career, Internat affairs adviser. Married. Education: Wheatley Park Comp; St Hugh's Coll, Oxford (BA geog, MA).

Tony Hill (LD) b. Aug 14, 1944. Retired school headmaster. Ed: Christ's College, Cambridge.
Pat McDonald (Lab) b. Dec 2, 1983. Barrister. Ed: Durham University.

Constituency
This seat spans the eponymous town, near Slough in the east, and Twyford and the suburban outskirts of Reading in the west. With the M4 running through the south and Heathrow near by, it is well connected. The Thames forms the northern boundary and, with attractive villages, helps to make it a popular area for affluent, commuting professionals. Main employers in Maidenhead itself include Hitachi. The area has a strong Tory tradition but local issues helped the Lib Dems to reduce majorities.

	Electorate	Turnout %	Change from 05 %
	72,844	73.8	☆
May, T C	31,937	59.5	7.6
Hill, T LD	15,168	28.2	-8.0
McDonald, P Lab	3,795	7.1	-2.1
Wight, K UKIP	1,243	2.3	0.9
Rait, T BNP	825	1.5	
Forbes, P Green	482	0.9	
Prior, P F&R	270		

Majority 16,769

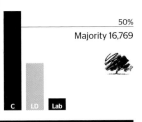

Maidstone & The Weald — Conservative hold

Helen Grant
b. Sep 28, 1961
MP 2010-

Polished A-lister from a tough background; raised by single mother on Carlisle council estate. The Conservative's first female black MP. Solicitor, founded own firm. Specialist on family law and sat on reform commission for Centre for Social Justice. Con Social Mobility Task Force; Con Social Justice Policy Group. Joined Tories 2006; Labour member 2004-05. Non-exec dir, Croydon PCT. Christian. Married, two sons. Education: St Aidans Comp/Trinity Comp, Carlisle; Hull (Law); College of Law, Guildford.

Peter Carroll (LD) Entrepreneur. Ed: University of Manchester.

Rav Seeruthun (Lab) b. Jun 6, 1973.

Constituency
From Maidstone at its northern extremity, this seat snakes down through the affluent mid-Kent countryside of the Weald. Boundary changes have removed Hawkhurst and Sandhurst from the south and it now finishes near Benenden, home of the famous school. Other settlements include the medieval market town of Cranbook, Staplehurst and Marden. Maidstone itself is relatively affluent with only small patches of deprivation, helping to explain decades of Conservative representation.

	Electorate	Turnout %	Change from 05 %
	71,041	68.9	☆
Grant, H C	23,491	48.0	-3.8
Carroll, P LD	17,602	36.0	13.2
Seeruthun, R Lab	4,769	9.8	-12.6
Kendall, G UKIP	1,637	3.4	0.3
Jeffery, S Green	655	1.3	
Butler, G NF	643	1.3	
Simmonds, H Ch	131	0.3	

Majority 5,889

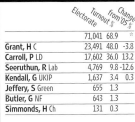
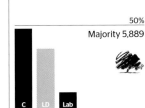

Yvonne Fovargue
b. Nov 29, 1956
MP 2010-

Inherits the seat from Ian McCartney, for whom her husband, Paul Kenny, was a press officer; he was the first declared candidate before the imposition of an all-women shortlist. Cllr, Warrington BC 2004-. Chief Exec, St Helens Citizens Advice Bureau. Housing Officer, Moss Side Estate. Estate Manager, Manchester City Council Member: Co-op party, Unite. Married, one daughter. Education: Sale Girls Grammar School; Leeds University (English).

Itrat Ali (C) b. Oct 16, 1973. Key account manager. Ed: Hecmondwike GS; Loughborough University.

David Crowther (LD) Cllr, St Helens 2006-; 1988-1996. Ed: Newton GS.
Bob Brierley (Ind)
Ken Haslam (BNP) b. May 19, 1940. Retired haulage contractor. Ed: Ashfield Secondary Modern (now Cansfield High), Wigan.

Constituency
This Greater Manchester constituency has lost a couple of wards to Wigan but gained Hindley and Hindley Green from neighbouring Leigh. With them comes Bickershaw Colliery, which in 1992 became the last pit to close in the borough. Ashton-in-Makerfield is the third-largest town in Wigan borough and, along with the other former mining communities in this seat, is white, working-class and solidly Labour.

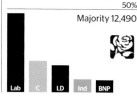

	Electorate	Turnout %	Change from '05 %
	73,641	59.4	☆
Fovargue, Y Lab	20,700	47.3	-14.8
Ali, I C	8,210	18.8	5.2
Crowther, D LD	7,082	16.2	4.8
Brierley, B Ind	3,424	7.8	
Haslam, K BNP	3,229	7.4	
Mather, J Ind	1,126	2.6	

50%

Majority 12,490

Lab | C | LD | Ind | BNP

John Whittingdale
b. Oct 16, 1959
MP 1992-

A key figure in the Tory right. Very close to Baroness Thatcher since serving as her political secretary (1988-92). Vice-chair, 1922 committee 2010-. Skillful select committee chair (CMS 2005-; re-elected unopposed 2010). Shadow SoS: CMS 2004-05; Agriculture/Fisheries/Food 2003-04; CMS 2002-03; Trade & Industry 2001-02. PPS to William Hague 1999-2001. Opp Treasury spokes 1998-99. Opp whip 1997-98. PPS to Eric Forth 1994-96. Pol adviser/researcher. Manager, NM Rothschild & Sons. OBE 1990. Divorced, one daughter, one son. Ed: Winchester; UCL (BSc economics).

Elfreda Tealby-Watson (LD) b. Mar 6, 1965. Consultant.
Swatantra Nandanwar (Lab) b. Apr 17, 1944. Cllr. Teacher. Contested Saffron Walden 2005.

Constituency
This redrawn seat spans the southern parts of Maldon district and Chelmsford borough, skirting the southern fringe of the county town. The eastern part covers the "Dengie Peninsula", the area between the Blackwater and Crouch estuaries. The traditional seaside town of Maldon is at the head of the Blackwater Estuary, from which sea salt was traditionally harvested. Burnham-on-Crouch is in the south. The western half of the seat is also rural, with the town of South Woodham Ferrers also on the Crouch. The area has long been Conservative.

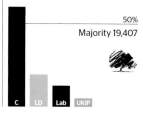

	Electorate	Turnout %	Change from '05 %
	68,861	69.6	☆
Whittingdale, J C	28,661	59.8	3.5
Tealby-Watson, E LD	9,254	19.3	4.3
Nandanwar, S Lab	6,070	12.7	-11.5
Pryke, J UKIP	2,446	5.1	0.6
Blaine, L BNP	1,464	3.1	

50%

Majority 19,407

C | LD | Lab | UKIP

Tony Lloyd
b. Feb 25, 1950
MP 1983-

Low public profile but respected chair, Parly Lab Party (2006-), close union links. Min: FCO 1997-99. Opp spokes: FCO 1995-97; Environment/ London 1994-95; Education 1992-94; Employment 1993-94; 1988-92; Transport 1988-89. MP Stretford 1983-97. Cllr, Trafford DC 1979-84. Uni lecturer. GMB. Married, three daughters, one son. Ed: Stretford GS; Nottingham (BSc maths); Manchester Business Sch (dip business admin).

Marc Ramsbottom (LD) b. Nov 27, 1963. Contested Manchester Central 2005, cllr 2000-. Employment Tribunal Advocate. Ed: Manchester Poly; University of Leicester.

Suhail Rahuja (C) Financial analyst. Cllr. Ed: Oxford University.

Constituency
Manchester city centre, substantially rebuilt after the devastation of the 1996 IRA bombing, is the heart of this seat and home to the banking and service sectors. Its Northern Quarter, once a wasteland, has been redeveloped into a vibrant cultural area, while the distinctive Urbis building is being converted to house the National Football Museum. The varied constituency also includes the deprived estates of Moss Side, the City of Manchester Stadium and old warehouses along the Manchester Ship Canal. The seat has been Labour since its creation in 1974.

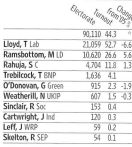

	Electorate	Turnout %	Change from '05 %
	90,110	44.3	☆
Lloyd, T Lab	21,059	52.7	-6.6
Ramsbottom, M LD	10,620	26.6	5.6
Rahuja, S C	4,704	11.8	1.3
Trebilcock, T BNP	1,636	4.1	
O'Donovan, G Green	915	2.3	-1.9
Weatherill, N UKIP	607	1.5	-0.3
Sinclair, R Soc	153	0.4	
Cartwright, J Ind	120	0.3	
Leff, J WRP	59	0.2	
Skelton, R SEP	54	0.1	

50%

Majority 10,439

Lab | LD | C

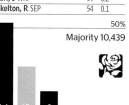

215

Manchester Gorton — Labour hold

Gerald Kaufman
b. Jun 21, 1930
MP 1970-

Ex-journalist's gift for eye-catching turn of phrase but well past his peak. Shadow Sec of State: Foreign 1987-92; Home 1983-87; Environment 1980-83. Minister: Industry 1975. Parly Under-Sec: Industry 1975; Environment 1974-75. Opp spokes 1979-80. Chair, select committee: Culture, Media & Sport 1997-2006. Member, select committee: Liaison 1992-2005. MP Ardwick 1970-83. Lab Party parly pres liaison officer. Journalist. Education: Leeds GS; The Queen's College, Oxford (MA PPE).

Qassim Afzal (LD) b. Feb 8, 1960. Contested Birmingham Sparkbrook 2001, Manchester Gorton 2005. CEO ABI Media Marketing Company. Ed: University of Central Lancashire.
Caroline Healy (C)

Constituency
Gorton, a traditionally white suburb now undergoing regeneration, lies in the east of this Manchester seat, just south of the city centre. The constituency also encompasses Manchester's Curry Mile, the residential suburb of Levenshulme, an antiques and market hub, and Fallowfield, with its student halls of residence and a youthful demographic. The westernmost ward, Whalley Range, has a diverse community and boasts parks and woodland. The seat has been Labour for most of the past century.

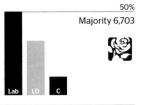

	Electorate	Turnout %	Change from '05 %
	75,933	50.5	☆
Kaufman, G Lab	19,211	50.1	-3.0
Afzal, Q LD	12,508	32.6	-0.9
Healy, C C	4,224	11.0	1.2
Hall, J Green	1,048	2.7	
Reissman, K TUSC	507	1.3	
Zulfikar, M Respect	337	0.9	
Harrison, P Ch	254	0.7	
Dobson, T Pirate	236	0.6	

50%
Majority 6,703

Manchester Withington — Liberal Democrat hold

John Leech
b. Apr 11, 1971
MP 2005-

Surprise winner of seat in 2005 after controversial campaign to 'save' Christie hospital, Manchester. LD shad min: Transport 2006-10. Member, cttee: Transport 2005-10. Cllr, Manchester CC (dep leader of opposition) 1998-. Dep leader, Manchester Lib Dems Group. Customer relations, RAC Ltd. Assistant restaurant manager, McDonald's Restaurant Ltd. Ed: Manchester Grammar School; Loretto College, Edinburgh; Brunel University (history & politics).

Lucy Powell (Lab) b. Oct 10, 1974. Social investment, NESTA. Ed: Kings College, London.

Christopher Green (C) b. 1973. Engineer.

Constituency
The popular residential areas comprising this Manchester constituency are home to a very high proportion of yuppies and students - around 35 per cent of the population of Withington ward are aged 20-24. The seat, which lies about three miles south of the city centre, is relatively affluent and sought-after because of large old houses, mostly now split up for rental. It has a varied political history, having switched from Tory to Labour under Margaret Thatcher before a surprise win for the Lib Dems in 2005.

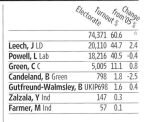

	Electorate	Turnout %	Change from '05 %
	74,371	60.6	☆
Leech, J LD	20,110	44.7	2.4
Powell, L Lab	18,216	40.5	-0.4
Green, C C	5,005	11.1	0.8
Candeland, B Green	798	1.8	-2.5
Gutfreund-Walmsley, B UKIP	698	1.6	0.4
Zalzala, Y Ind	147	0.3	
Farmer, M Ind	57	0.1	

50%
Majority 1,894

Mansfield — Labour hold

(Joseph) Alan Meale
b. Jul 31, 1949
MP 1987-

Unimpressive backbencher close to John Prescott. Adviser to Richard Caborn 2002-05. Parly Under-Sec: Environment; Transport & Regions 1998-99. Parliamentary private secretary to John Prescott 1994-98. Opposition whip 1992-94. Member, Co-op party. Author/editor/MP researcher. Aslef gen sec asst. Nacro officer. Michael Meacher parly/political adviser. Married, one daughter, one son. Ed: St Joseph's RC School, Co Durham; Durham; Ruskin Coll, Oxford; Sheffield Hallam.

Tracy Critchlow (C) Bookkeeping and secretarial business. Cllr, Derbyshire Dales 2000-.

Michael Wyatt (LD) Regional administration assistant. Cllr, Leicestershire DC 2003-.
Andre Camilleri (Mansfield Ind).
David Hamilton (UKIP).

Constituency
This Nottinghamshire seat is on the border with Derbyshire. With the exception of the Meden Valley it is predominantly urban and, after boundary changes, includes Warsop to the north, as well as Mansfield and Mansfield Woodhouse. The area suffered with the decline of the coalmines and other manufacturing industries and much of it is severely deprived, with typically high unemployment, low incomes and poor health. It has a long Labour tradition.

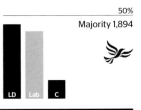

	Electorate	Turnout %	Change from '05 %
	80,069	60.4	☆
Meale, J Lab	18,753	38.8	-11.4
Critchlow, T C	12,741	26.3	7.6
Wyatt, M LD	7,469	15.4	1.4
Camilleri, A Mansfield	4,339	9.0	
Hamilton, D UKIP	2,985	6.2	
Hill, R BNP	2,108	4.4	

50%
Majority 6,012

Meon Valley
Conservative hold

George Hollingbery
b. Oct 12, 1963
MP 2010-

Interested in housing, development and elder care. Contested Winchester 2005, campaign manager for Andrew Hayes 2001. Cllr, Winchester CC 1999-2010; Alresford TC 1999-2003. Business career: Thompson Sowerbutts (property investment); chairman, Companion Care Ltd (national chain of vets); chair & founder, Pet Depot Ltd. Venture capitalist. Stockbroker, Robert Fleming & Co. Keen fly fisherman and garden designer. Ed: Radley Coll; LMH, Oxford (Human Sciences); Wharton Sch, Philadelphia Uni (MBA).

Liz Leffman (LD) b. Mar 23, 1949. Consultant, company director.

Howard Linsley (Lab) b. Aug 5, 1944. Cllr and Chair, Liss PC; Vice Chair, East Hants Assoc of Parish and Town Councils.

Constituency
This new seat has been created by taking large chunks from the Winchester, North East and East Hampshire constituencies. Much of it falls within the South Downs National Park and, as the name indicates, the River Meon flows through the middle of the seat. The population is concentrated in Horndean and Waterlooville, near Havant in the south east of the seat, while West Meon, Bishop's Waltham and Wickham are dotted through the countryside. Although an affluent seat, popular with commuters, its predecessors were not uniformly Tory and the Lib Dems had success in Winchester.

	Electorate	Turnout %	Change from '05 %
	70,488	72.7	☆
Hollingbery, G C	28,818	56.2	10.4
Leffman, L LD	16,693	32.6	-8.4
Linsley, H Lab	3,266	6.4	-4.2
Harris, S UKIP	1,490	2.9	0.4
Harris, P Eng	582	1.1	
Coats, S APP	255	0.5	
Quar, G Ind	134	0.3	

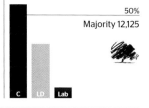

50%

Majority 12,125

Meriden
Conservative hold

Caroline Spelman
b. May 4, 1958
MP 1997-

Earnest and articulate, but dull; failed to make impact in several high-profile jobs. Goody-two-shoes image tarnished lengthy inquiry into nanny-gate affair, forced to repay money and apologise for inadvertent breach of rules. Resulted in demotion from Con Party Chair (2007-2009) to Shadow SoS: DCLG (2009-10). SoS: EFRA 2010-. Shadow SoS: DCLG/ODPM 2005-07; Local Govt 2004-05; Environment 2003-04. Int Devt 2001-03. Shadow Min: Women 2001-04. Var opp spokes roles 1999-2001, whip 1998-99. Sec/research fellow/business consultant. Married, one daughter, two sons. Ed: Queen Mary College (BA European studies).

Ed Williams (Lab)
Simon Slater (LD) b. Sep 26, 1981. Teacher. Cllr, Solihull BC 2006-.

Constituency
The bulk of this oddly shaped seat is rural, occupying the area between Solihull and Coventry and scattered with affluent commuter towns such as Dorridge, Balsall Common and Meriden, the geographical centre of the country. A branch snakes up to the east of Birmingham, including the international airport and the National Exhibition Centre. Beyond these lies a residential concentration, with deprived areas such as Kingshurst and Chelmsley Wood where there is tension between white working classes and Asians. The area has been earmarked for regeneration funds. The seat was a Labour-Tory marginal before the Conservative victory of 1979.

	Electorate	Turnout %	Change from '05 %
	83,826	62.2	☆
Spelman, C C	26,956	51.7	4.1
Williams, E Lab	10,703	20.5	-11.8
Slater, S LD	9,278	17.8	1.1
O'Brien, F BNP	2,511	4.8	
Allcock, B UKIP	1,378	2.6	-0.7
Stanton, E Green	678	1.3	
Sinclaire, N RA	658	1.3	

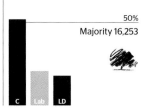

50%

Majority 16,253

Merthyr Tydfil & Rhymney
Labour hold

Dai Havard
b. Feb 7, 1950
MP 2001-

Earthy, chatty Welshman with a twinkle in his eye and no time for metropolitan niceties; once attacked Tory "toffocracy" and "policy wonks" who wanted to withdraw from EU Social Chapter. Hard-left, interested in the military. Member, select committees: Defence 2003-; Regulatory Reform 2001-05. Member European standing committee C. MSF union officer: studies tutor/researcher/education/ official. Amicus. Married but separated. Ed: Various secondary modern/grammar technical/comprehensive schools; St Peter's College, Birmingham (Cert Ed); Warwick University (MA industrial relations).

Amy Kitcher (LD) Domestic abuse charity worker. Ed: Aston; Sussex.
Maria Hill (C) Solicitor. Ed: UWE Law School.

Constituency
This southeast Wales seat has four rivers, with the population concentrated in the two biggest valleys: the River Rhymney and its eponymous town are at the east, while the River Taff in the west includes Merthyr Tydfil. In the valley lies Aberfan, where coal waste slid down the hillside and engulfed the village in 1966, killing 144, mostly children. The seat has an overwhelmingly working-class demographic with about 25 per cent living in social housing and some of the worst health problems in Britain. The area has been Labour since the time of Keir Hardie.

	Electorate	Turnout %	Change from '05 %
	54,715	58.6	
Havard, D Lab	14,007	43.7	-16.7
Kitcher, A LD	9,951	31.0	17.1
Hill, M C	2,412	7.5	-1.4
Tovey, C Ind	1,845	5.8	
Cennydd, G Jones PC	1,621	5.1	
Barnes, R BNP	1,173	3.7	
Brown, A UKIP	872	2.7	0.4
Cowdell, A Soc	195	0.6	-0.3

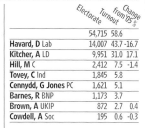

50%

Majority 4,056

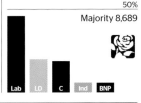

Middlesbrough Labour hold

Sir Stuart Bell
b. May 16, 1938
MP 1983-

Old school parliamentarian from Labour right. Part of the Speaker's commission establishment, tried to defend belated attempts at reform, having opposed it previously. Chair, cttee: Finance & Services 2009-10; 2000-05. Opp spokes: T & I 1992-97; NI 1984-87. PPS to Roy Hattersley 1983-84. Second Church Estates commissioner 1997-. Vice-Chair Interparly union. HoC commission member 2000-. Cllr, Newcastle CC 1980-83. Fabian Soc, Soc of Lab Lawyers. Barrister/clerk/reporter/novelist. Knighted 2004. Ed: Gray's Inn Legal Educational Council.

Chris Foote-Wood (LD) b. Dec 15,
1940. Author and publisher.
John Walsh (C)
Joan McTigue (Ind)
Michael Ferguson (BNP)

Constituency
At the heart of Teesside, Middlesbrough was dubbed the Hercules of Britain because of its industry. It has yet to recover from their decline, with Corus closures in 2009 compounding the misery. Deprivation and unemployment are severe. Middlehaven, the old dockland, is earmarked for a £500m regeneration and a merger with neighbouring Stockton is planned for the next 20 years. Ray Mallon, its mayor, was dubbed Robocop when he ran Middlesbrough CID until a corruption scandal. Predominantly working-class and white, the seat had returned a Labour MP with more than 50 per cent in every election since 1935.

	Electorate	Turnout %	Change from '05 %
	65,148	51.4	☆
Bell, S Lab	15,351	45.9	-11.7
Foote-Wood, C LD	6,662	19.9	1.2
Walsh, J C	6,283	18.8	2.3
McTigue, J Ind	1,969	5.9	
Ferguson, M BNP	1,954	5.8	
Parker, R UKIP	1,236	3.7	1.3

50%

Majority 8,689

| Lab | LD | C | Ind | BNP |

Middlesbrough South & Cleveland East Labour hold

Tom Blenkinsop
b. Aug 14, 1980
MP 2010-

Officer for Community (steel union) and con-stituency researcher to former MP Dr Ashok Kumar, who died March 2010. Strong supporter of AV voting system, having been selected by local Labour party using this method. Married. Education: Newlands School FCJ, Saltersgill; St Mary's Sixth Form College, Saltersgill; Teeside (BSc PPE); Warwick (MA continental philosophy); TUC Organising Academy

Paul Bristow (C) b. 1979. Public affairs officer.
Nick Emmerson (LD) b. 1970. Corporate lawyer. Ed: Newcastle University; York College of Law.

Constituency
Only the very southern fringes of Middlesbrough are included in this seat, which stretches out to the coast. Straddling borough boundaries, it encompasses the pretty market town of Guisborough in the centre and Saltburn-by-the-Sea, Brotton and Loftus in the east. Prosperity varies from pockets of severe deprivation in Stainton to affluent areas near Roseberry Topping, the oddly shaped hill. On the whole it is better off and less staunchly Labour than the main town constituency, having changed political hands several times.

	Electorate	Turnout %	Change from '05 %
	72,664	1.0	☆
Blenkinsop, T Lab	18,138	39.3	-11.1
Bristow, P C	16,461	35.6	3.8
Emmerson, N LD	7,340	15.9	2.1
Lightwing, S UKIP	1,881	4.1	2.6
Gatley, S BNP	1,576	3.4	
Allen, M Ind	818	1.8	

50%

Majority 1,677

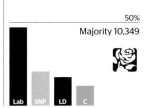

| Lab | C | LD |

Midlothian Labour hold

David Hamilton
b. Oct 24, 1950
MP 2001-

Friendly, left-of-centre, ex-miner. Spent two months in prison before acquittal during the strikes of the 1980s. PPS to Ed Miliband 2008-10. Member, select cttees: Procedures 2001-, Broadcasting 2001-, Scottish Affairs 2001-, Work and Pensions 2003-. Vice-chair all-party occupational safety and health group 2004-. Cllr, Midlothian Council 1995-2001. Joint NUM chair 1981-87. Member: European standing cttee A 2003, RMT parly campaigning group 2002-. Miner, employment training scheme supervisor, placement/training officer, chief exec Craigmillar Opportunities Trust. Married, two daughters. Ed: Dalkeith High School.

Colin Beattie (SNP) b. Oct 17, 1951. Former banker. Cllr, Midlothian 2007-. Contested Midlothian 2005, Scottish parl 2007.
Ross Laird (LD) Company director. Ed: Auchmuty High; Glasgow Uni.
James Callander (C)

Constituency
The Midlothian area to the south of Edinburgh used to house the industry that fuelled the Scottish capital, particularly mining. The Labour traditions of those days are still in this seat, even though the mining has gone. Several large towns dominate this constituency, most notably Dalkeith, Penicuik, Bonnyrigg, Gorebridge and Loanhead. There is hope locally that the area will become revitalised by the reintroduction of the Waverley Line train service from Edinburgh to the Borders.

	Electorate	Turnout %	Change from '05 %
	61,387	63.9	
Hamilton, D Lab	18,449	47.0	1.6
Beattie, C SNP	8,100	20.6	3.7
Laird, R LD	6,711	17.1	-9.1
Callander, J C	4,661	11.9	2.5
Baxter, I Green	595	1.5	
Norrie, G UKIP	364	0.9	
McCleery, G Ind	196	0.5	
Duncan, W TUSC	166	0.4	

50%

Majority 10,349

Milton Keynes North — Conservative gain

Mark Lancaster
b. May 12, 1970
MP 2005-

One of a few soldiers in the House of Commons; Army officer then major with TA, undertook active service in Afghanistan in 2006 parliament summer recess. Shadow Minister: International Development. Opposition Whip 2006-07. Councillor, Huntingdon District Council, 1990-99. Director, Kimbolton Fireworks. Married but separated. Education: Kimbolton School, Huntingdon; Royal Military Academy Sandhurst; University of Buckingham (BSc business studies); University of Exeter (MBA).

Andrew Pakes (Lab)

Jill Hope (LD) Former banker, NHS worker. Ed: Headlands Grammar School; Southampton (English), City of London School of Management.

Constituency
A slightly redrawn constituency loses wards in the east of the town and with them the "North East" name. It now includes the entire Campbell Park ward, home to The Centre, the enormous shopping and leisure complex, and some newer estates. Original areas such as Newport Pagnell remain and the constituency extends north of the M1 to include rural parts and the town of Olney. Labour narrowly took the seat from the Tories in 1997, only for it to be won back in 2005.

		Electorate	Turnout %	Change from '05 %
		85,841	62.8	☆
Lancaster, M	C	23,419	43.5	7.3
Pakes, A	Lab	14,458	26.8	-11.1
Hope, J	LD	11,894	22.1	1.5
Phillips, M	UKIP	1,772	3.3	0.5
Hamilton, R	BNP	1,154	2.1	
Francis, A	Green	733	1.4	-0.8
John, R	Lennon	206	0.4	
Bananamatt, M	Fensome	157	0.3	
Vyas, A	Ind	95	0.2	

50%
Majority 8,961

Milton Keynes South — Conservative gain

Iain Stewart
b. Sep 18, 1972
MP 2010-

Scottish-raised headhunter who worked for Virginia Bottomley at Odgers, Ray & Berndston. Contested Milton Keynes South West 2005, 2001; Glasgow Rutherglen Scottish Parliament 1999. Ran independent Westminster political research unit, advised the Tories. Accountant, Coopers & Lybrand. Enjoys opera, good wine and whisky, and running marathons. Education: Hutchesons' Grammar School, Glasgow; Exeter (BA politics); Chartered Management Institute (dip management)

Phyllis Starkey (Lab) b. Jan 4, 1947. MP 1997-2010. Chair, CLG select cttee 2005-10. PPS to: Denis Macshane

2002-05; (team) FCO 2001-02. Cllr, Oxford CC 1983-97; leader 1990-93. Research scientist/univ lecturer/ science policy administrator/party fellow 1974-78. Ed: Lady Margaret Hall, Oxford (Biochemistry); Clare Hall, Cambridge (PhD).
Peter Jones (LD) Sales director. Ed: Malvern College, UEA.

Constituency
Slightly more densely populated than its northern neighbour, this seat contains many modern estates and the Second World War code-breaking centre of Bletchley. It has gained a couple of eastern wards, so bringing in the Open University, Milton Keynes's biggest single employer. As with Milton Keynes in general, the seat has a notably young population. Labour took it from the Tories in 1997 but lost it back in 2010.

		Electorate	Turnout %	Change from '05 %
		90,487	61.2	☆
Stewart, I	C	23,034	41.6	3.9
Starkey, P	Lab	17,833	32.2	-8.6
Jones, P	LD	9,787	17.7	2.5
Pinto, P	UKIP	2,074	3.8	0.2
Tait, M	BNP	1,502	2.7	
Deacon, K	Green	774	1.4	-1.3
Nti, S	CPA	245	0.4	
Worth, J	NFP	84	0.2	

50%
Majority 5,201

Mitcham and Morden — Labour hold

Siobhain McDonagh
b. Feb 20, 1960
MP 1997-

Blairite, unlikely public face of attempted coup against Gordon Brown in autumn 2008. Asst govt whip 2007-08. PPS to John Reid 2005-07. Member, cttees: Unopposed Bills 2004-; Health 2000-05; Social Security 1997-98. Cllr, Merton BC 1982-97. GMB. Battersea church housing trust devt co-ordinator; housing adviser; Wandsworth homeless persons unit; housing benefits asst; clerical officer DHSS. Ed: Holy Cross Convent, New Malden; Essex (BA govt).

Melanie Hampton (C).
Diana Coman (LD) Local government consultant.

Constituency
The Underground passes through Collier's Wood in the north of the seat and terminates in Morden, but the Tube station and town centre are just over the boundary in the neighbouring Wimbledon seat. It includes a small portion of the 1930s St Helier housing estate and is less affluent than its western neighbour. It has pockets of deprivation in Figges Marsh. It is also more diverse, with black and ethnic minority populations at 50 per cent in some wards and Sri Lankan, South African and Polish communities. The seat reaches southwest as far as Lower Morden and east to Mitcham Common, both more prosperous areas. Labour unseated the Tories here in 1997.

		Electorate	Turnout %	Change from '05 %
		65,939	66.4	☆
McDonagh, S	Lab	24,722	56.5	-0.3
Hampton, M	C	11,056	25.2	0.6
Coman, D	LD	5,202	11.9	-2.1
Martin, T	BNP	1,386	3.2	
Mills, A	UKIP	857	2.0	
Roy, S	Green	381	0.9	-2.6
Alagaratnam, R	Ind	155	0.4	
Redgrave, E	Ind	38	0.1	

50%
Majority 13,666

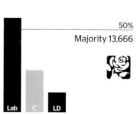

Mole Valley — Conservative hold

Sir Paul Beresford
b. Apr 6, 1946
MP 1992-

Practising dentist, New Zealand born and bred. Has a low profile but is shrewd and can be aggressive. Junior Minister: Environment 1994-97. MP Croydon Central 1992-97. Knighted in 1990 for work on inner-city rehabilitation; long-serving Wandsworth Cllr (1978-94) and leader (1983-92). Married, one daughter, three sons. Education: Waimea College, New Zealand; Otago (NZ).

Alice Humphreys (LD) Solicitor. Education: Nottingham University.
James Dove (Lab) b. Dec 2, 1983. Barrister. Education: Durham University.

Constituency
At the heart of Surrey, and geographically its largest constituency, Mole Valley centres on the charming antiques haven of Dorking, at the foot of the North Downs. Its other town is Leatherhead, to the north, home to light industry and a high street once voted one of the worst in Britain. Affluent commuter villages such as Bookham, Brockham and Shere are scattered across picturesque countryside in what is still regarded as a safe Tory constituency.

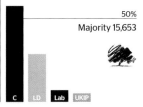

	Electorate	Turnout %	Change from '05 %
	72,612	74.8	
Beresford, P C	31,263	57.6	2.8
Humphreys, A LD	15,610	28.7	-1.7
Dove, J Lab	3,804	7.0	-3.7
Jones, L UKIP	2,752	5.1	2.1
Sedgwick, R Green	895	1.7	

50%
Majority 15,653

C | LD | Lab | UKIP

Monmouth — Conservative hold

David Davies
b. Jul 27, 1970
MP 2005-

Unpredictable, populist, often over-the-top headline-seeker. Happy to be quoted. Distinguished from near-namesake by "T.C." middle initials. Deeply right-wing, Welsh-speaker. Ran campaign against devolution, Member, Welsh Assembly 1999-2007, arguing against extension of its powers. Elected unopposed as Chair, cttee: Welsh Affairs 2010-. Obsessive about the police, Special Constable for Brit Transport Police. Cttee member: Home 2007-10. Brief stint at British Steel and in TA, years spent travelling and working odd jobs abroad. Lorry driver, took over family haulage/tea-importing business. Married, two daughters, one son. Ed: Bassaleg Comp, Newport.

Hamish Sandison (Lab) b. Mar 21, 1952. Solicitor. Ed: Uni of Cambridge.
Martin Blakebrough (LD) b. 1962. CEO drug and alcohol charity. Ed: Richard Challoner Sch; Thames Poly; Cardiff and Kingston Universities.

Constituency
This large South Wales seat lies on the border with England. From Chepstow, the seat follows the River Wye north to Monmouth. Usk and Abergavenny are other towns on the River Usk popular with game fishermen. Picturesque and rural, this is also one of the more anglicised areas, with relatively few Welsh-speakers. With large numbers of middle-class residents, this was once a safe Tory area. Taken by Labour in a 1991 by-election, it reverted to the Tories before Labour won again in 1997 and the Tories regained it in 2005.

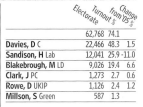

	Electorate	Turnout %	Change from '05 %
	62,768	74.1	
Davies, D C	22,466	48.3	1.5
Sandison, H Lab	12,041	25.9	-11.0
Blakebrough, M LD	9,026	19.4	6.6
Clark, J PC	1,273	2.7	0.6
Rowe, D UKIP	1,126	2.4	1.2
Millson, S Green	587	1.3	

50%
Majority 10,425

C | Lab | LD

Montgomeryshire — Conservative gain

Glyn Davies
b. Feb 16, 1944
MP 2010-

Achieved one of the highest profile scalps of election night 2010 in ousting Lembit Öpik. Very interested in health issues after overcoming serious illness. Member, Welsh National Assembly 1999-2007. Councillor, Montgomeryshire DC 1979-89 (Chair 1985-89). Contested Montgomeryshire 1997. Former farmer. Chair, Development Board for Rural Wales. Member: Wales Tourism Board, Welsh Development Agency. President, Campaign for Protection of Rural Wales. Recently learnt Welsh to fluency. Keen golfer. Married, four children. Education: Caeveinon High School; University of Aberystwyth (international politics).

Lembit Öpik (LD) b. March 2, 1965. MP for Montgomeryshire 1997-2010. LD spokesman Wales, NI 1997-2007, Business 2007, Housing 2007-08.
Heledd Fychan (PC) b. Sep 20, 1980. Plaid Cymru press officer.
Nick Colbourne (Lab) b. Sep 14, 1957. Magistrate. Former Cllr, Wrexham. Retired police officer.

Constituency
Named after the small town of Montgomery, by the Offa's Dyke path on the border with England, this rural seat also includes Newtown, Welshpool, Llanidloes and Machynlleth, the starting point for the Laura Ashley empire. The west is home to more Welsh-speakers than the east of the seat. Agriculture is important, employing about a tenth of the population. There is a strong Liberal tradition, which was interrupted only by one term with a Tory MP from 1979.

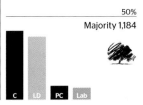

	Electorate	Turnout %	Change from '05 %
	48,730	69.4	*
Davies, G C	13,976	41.3	13.8
Öpik, L LD	12,792	37.8	-12.5
Fychan, H PC	2,802	8.3	1.3
Colbourne, N Lab	2,407	7.1	-5.2
Rowlands, D UKIP	1,128	3.3	0.4
Ellis, M NF	384	1.1	
Lawson, B Ind	324	1.0	

50%
Majority 1,184

C | LD | PC | Lab

Moray

SNP hold

MOR

Angus Robertson
b. Sep 28, 1969
MP 2001-

Affable with tendency towards pomposity. Leader, SNP Westminster group 2007-. Dep Leader 2005-07. SNP spokes: Europe, ODPM 2005-07; foreign affairs/defence 2001-. Member, cttee: European Scrutiny 2001-. Nat organiser Student Nationalists Federation. Member: nat exec young Scottish nationalists, SNP internat bureau. European policy adviser, SNP group Scottish Parl. Communication consultant. Journalist. NUJ. Ed: Broughton HS, Edinburgh; Aberdeen (MA pol/international relations).

Douglas Ross (C) Dairy farmer. Cllr, Moray. Ed: Alves Primary and Forres Academy, Scottish Agricultural Coll.

Kieron Green (Lab) Science technician at Lossiemouth HS. Former member of Stuart MacLennan's campaign. Ed: Edinburgh Uni (astrophysics)
James Paterson (LD) Parliamentary assistant to Jamie Stone MSP and John Farquhar Munro MSP since 1999. Ed: Gordonstoun School.

Constituency
Moray is one of the SNP's safest seats in the country. It is a large constituency, taking in the Moray council area. It is predominantly rural, with many small towns and villages, ranging from the fishing communities around the mouth of the Findhorn to the distilleries of Speyside inland. The RAF bases at Kinloss and Lossiemouth are among the biggest employers in the area with whisky production and agriculture also strong.

	Electorate	Turnout %	From '05 % Change
	65,925	62.2	
Robertson, A SNP	16,273	39.7	3.2
Ross, D C	10,683	26.1	4.2
Green, K Lab	7,007	17.1	-3.3
Paterson, J LD	5,956	14.5	-4.7
Gatt, D UKIP	1,085	2.7	

50%
Majority 5,590

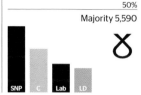

Morecambe & Lunesdale

Conservative gain

MOR

David Morris
b. Jan 3, 1966
MP 2010-

Hairdresser who ran his own salon. Interested in tourism and business. Son of a lifeboat inspector, from a nautical family. Contested Carmarthen West & South Pembrokeshire 2005; Blackpool South 2001. Member, Institute of Directors. Adviser to Greenwich University on study into effects of minimum wage. Former musician and songwriter. Divorced, two sons. Education: Kowloon School, Hong Kong; St Andrews Nassau, Bahamas; Lowton School, Lancashire.

Geraldine Smith (Lab) b. Aug 29, 1961. MP for Morecambe and Lunesdale 1997-2010. Member, select committee: Science and Technology 2001-05.

Education: Lancaster and Morecambe College
Leslie Jones (LD) Lecturer. Education: BA (Hons) economics and education.

Constituency
From the border with Cumbria, the northernmost seat in Lancashire stretches down Morecambe Bay to the River Lune. The major settlements are Carnforth, Morecambe, the old seaside resort, and Heysham, a busy port. Efforts are under way to regenerate Morecambe as a tourist destination but it has declined greatly and there are areas of severe deprivation. British Energy is a major employer, with two nuclear power ports at Heysham, while the White Lund industrial estate is nearby. Labour took this seat from the Tories in 1997.

	Electorate	Turnout %	From '05 % Change
	69,965	62.3	☆
Morris, D C	18,035	41.4	4.0
Smith, G Lab	17,169	39.4	-9.7
Jones, L LD	5,971	13.7	0.1
Knight, M UKIP	1,843	4.2	
Coates, C Green	598	1.4	

50%
Majority 866

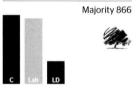

Morley & Outwood

Labour Co-operative hold

MOR

Ed Balls
b. Feb 25, 1967
MP 2005-

A divisive figure. Close to Gordon Brown and disliked by many other ministers; seen as arrogant and aggressive. Has vast capacity to absorb information. Candidate for Lab leadership 2010. SoS: Children, Schools and Families 2007-10. Econ SoS, Treasury 2006-07. MP Normanton 2005-10. Chair, Fabian Soc 2007-08. Chief Econ adviser to HM Treasury 1999-2004, Econ adviser to Gordon Brown 1994-99. Econ leader writer and columnist, *Financial Times*. Teaching fellow Dep of Econ Harvard. Mem, TGWU/Unison. Married (to Yvette Cooper MP), two daughters, one son. Ed: Nottingham HS; Keble Coll, Oxford (BA PPE); JFK Sch of Govt, Harvard (MPA).

Antony Calvert (C) Partner, Curtin & Co. Cllr, Wakefield CC 2004-07.
James Monaghan (LD) b. Feb 10, 1976. Cllr, Leeds CC. Small business owner.
Chris Beverley (BNP) b. May 2, 1980. Parly assistant to Andrew Brons MEP.

Constituency
Morley is an old market town to the south west of Leeds that has fought resolutely to maintain independence from the city on its doorstep. Boundary changes have removed nearby Rothwell but added the more prosperous Outwood, forming a constituency criss-crossed by the M1, M62 and M621. Strong road links are helping to turn these former mining and textile communities into commuter territory. There remains a strong working-class presence and about a sixth of the population lives in social or council housing. Predecessor seats were Labour.

	Electorate	Turnout %	From '05 % Change
	74,200	65.8	☆
Balls, E Lab	18,365	37.6	-8.4
Calvert, A C	17,264	35.3	10.3
Monaghan, J LD	8,186	16.8	6.7
Beverley, C BNP	3,535	7.2	
Daniel, D UKIP	1,506	3.1	

50%
Majority 1,101

Motherwell & Wishaw — Labour hold

Frank Roy
b. Aug 29, 1958
MP 1997-

Life-long Motherwell and Labour man, held key organising role in recent Scottish by-election campaigns. Whip: govt 2006-10; asst govt 2005-06. PPS to: Helen Liddell 2001, 1998-99; John Reid 1999-2001. Member, select cttees: Selection 2008-; Defence 2001-05; Social Security 1997-98. GMB. Shop steward, ISTC. PA to Helen Liddell. Steelworker, Ravenscraig works. Married, one daughter, one son. Ed: St Joseph's HS, Our Lady HS, Motherwell; Motherwell Coll (HNC marketing); Glasgow Caledonian (BA consumer and management studies).

Marion Fellows (SNP) Business studies lecturer, West Lothian Coll. Contested Scottish Parliament, Motherwell & Wishaw. Education: Belmont High, Ayr and Carrick Academy, Heriot-Watt University (BSc accountancy and finance).
Stuart Douglas (LD) Student. Education: University of Glasgow (LLB Hons. Law 2006-).
Patsy Gilroy (C)

Constituency
This Clyde Valley constituency embodies the post-industrial character of much of central-belt Scotland. The area once thrived on heavy industry, based around Ravenscraig, but it has struggled to find a new identity since the closure of the steelworks in 1992. The constituency includes Strathclyde Country Park but the towns of Motherwell and Wishaw still dominate this North Lanarkshire seat that has been solidly Labour since the Second World War.

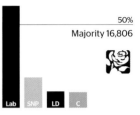

	Electorate	Turnout %	Change from 05 %
	66,918	58.5	
Roy, F Lab	23,910	61.1	3.7
Fellows, M SNP	7,104	18.2	1.8
Douglas, S LD	3,840	9.8	-2.2
Gilroy, P C	3,660	9.4	0.1
Gunnion, R TUSC	609	1.6	

50%
Majority 16,806

Na h-Eileanan an Iar — SNP hold

Angus MacNeil
b. Jul 21, 1970
MP 2005-

Gained overnight fame as MP who brought "cash for honours" claims of peerages linked to secret loans to Labour to attention of Scotland Yard. SNP spokes: Scotland 2008-; Work & Pensions 2007-08; transport 2005-; environment 2005-07; food & rural affairs, fishing & tourism 2005-. Contested Inverness East, Nairn & Lochaber 2001. Convener, Lochaber branch SNP. Education lecturer part-time, Inverness College. Teacher. Married, three daughters. Education: Castlebay School, Isle of Barra; Nicolson Inst, Stornoway; Strathclyde (BEng civil engineering); Jordanhill College (PGCE primary teaching and bilingualism).

Donald John MacSween (Lab) b. May 9, 1949. Dir, housing charity, Former cllr, Stornoway.
Murdo Murray (Ind) b. Dec 4, 1954. Dir, M A Murray Consulting Ltd.
Jean Davis (LD) b. May 26, 1954. Occupational physician. Contested Na h-Eileanan an Iar 2005.

Constituency
Formerly known as the Western Isles, the seat changed to its Gaelic name in 2005 to reflect the importance of the language in the Outer Hebrides. It has the smallest electorate in the country in what is one of the largest geographic spreads. The seat stretches 130 miles from the Butt of Lewis in the north to Barra Head in the south. Crofting and fishing are the two main industries in an area where local issues dominate election campaigns. The SNP took this from Labour in 2005.

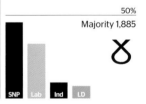

	Electorate	Turnout %	Change from 05 %
	22,266	66.1	
MacNeil, A SNP	6,723	45.7	0.8
John, D MacSween Lab	4,838	32.9	
Murray, M Ind	1,412	9.6	
Davis, J LD	1,097	7.5	-0.5
Norquay, S C	647	4.4	0.0

50%
Majority 1,885

Neath — Labour hold

Peter Hain
b. Feb 16, 1950
MP 1991-

Former liberal skilled at wooing Labour grassroots. Populist instincts irritate colleagues. Damaged by controversy surrounding undeclared donations to his dep leadership campaign; forced to resign from Cabinet in 2008 during police investigation; no charges, but had to apologise to House. SoS: Wales 2009-10; DWP 2007-2008; Wales 2002-2008; Northern Ireland 2005-2007. Leader of HoC/Lord Privy Seal 2003-05. Min: Europe, FCO 1999-2001. Parly Under-Sec Welsh Office 1997-99. Opp: spokes 1996-97, whip 1995-96. Chairman, select cttee: Modernisation of HoC 2003-2005. Member Co-op. Leader Young Libs. Head of research, CWU. Divorced, two sons. Remarried. Ed: Queen Mary Coll, London (BSc pol sci); Sussex (MPhil).

Alun Llewelyn (PC) b. 1961. Cllr, Neath Port Talbot C (Dep Leader of Opp).
Frank Little (LD) IT consultant.
Emmeline Owens (C) Worked for Abbey, HBOS, Brit Chambers of Comm.

Constituency
The town of Neath lies at the south of this seat, with small villages dotted along the Vale of Neath. Farther north, the Swansea Valley has another cluster of settlements, including Ystalyfera, while at the northern tip lies Graun-Cae-Gurwen. Once industrial, the seat remains working-class with a focus on manufacturing, although EU funding and regeneration projects have helped to diversify the economy and the health sector is also notably strong. The seat has been held by Labour for decades.

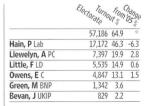

	Electorate	Turnout %	Change from 05 %
	57,186	64.9	*
Hain, P Lab	17,172	46.3	-6.3
Llewelyn, A PC	7,397	19.9	2.8
Little, F LD	5,535	14.9	0.6
Owens, E C	4,847	13.1	1.5
Green, M BNP	1,342	3.6	
Bevan, J UKIP	829	2.2	

50%
Majority 9,775

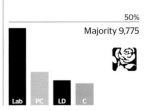

New Forest East
Conservative hold

Julian Lewis
b. Sep 26, 1951
MP 1997-

A passionate champion of nuclear defence, who sees European integration as a threat to Britain's independent nuclear deterrent. Very pro-Israel. Combative style not to all colleagues' tastes. He once ran speaking courses with John Bercow and is his leading supporter on the Tory benches. Shadow Minister: Defence 2005-10 and 2002-5; Cabinet Office 2004-05. Opposition Whip 2001-02. Joint organiser of campaign against Lab Party militant infiltration. Royal Naval Reserve. Defence consultant/political researcher (dep dir. CRD). Ed: Dynevor Grammar, Swansea; Balliol College, Oxford (MA philosophy/politics); St Antony's College, Oxford (DPhil strategic studies).

Terry Scriven (LD) Former colonel in the Royal Military Police, member of the South East Regional LSC Board. Ed: Portsmouth Uni (diploma in management studies); Leicester Uni. **Peter Sopowski** (Lab) b. Jun 10, 1949. Teacher. Ed: University of East Anglia.

Constituency
The physical bulk of the seat contains much of the New Forest National Park and towns such as Brockenhurst and Lyndhurst are focal points for tourism. The most densely populated areas are those concentrated along the western bank of Southampton Water: Holbury (by the huge Fawley oil refinery, an important employer), Hythe, Marchwood and Totton. Socioeconomically diverse, the seat has nevertheless been resolutely Tory for decades.

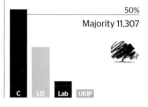

	Electorate	Turnout %	Change from 05 %
	72,858	68.7	☆
Lewis, J C	26,443	52.9	3.4
Scriven, T LD	15,136	30.3	-3.0
Sopowski, P Lab	4,915	9.8	-2.4
Day, P UKIP	2,518	5.0	-0.1
Golden, B Green	1,024	2.1	

50%
Majority 11,307

C LD Lab UKIP

New Forest West
Conservative hold

Desmond Swayne
b. Aug 20, 1956
MP 1997-

Eager enthusiast, mainly known for closeness to Cameron with whom he runs. Right-winger who opposed Britain's EEC membership in 1975 referendum. TA officer, called up and served in Iraq July-Dec 2003. Swims daily in the Serpentine. PPS to David Cameron 2005-; Michael Howard 2004-05. Shadow Minister: NI 2004; Int. Affairs 2003-04. Opposition whip 2002-03. Opposition spokes: Defence 2001-02; Health 2001. Systems analyst and teacher. Manager, Risk Management Systems, Royal Bank of Scotland. Married, two daughters, one son. Education: Bedford School; St Mary's College, University of St Andrew's (MA theology).

Mike Plummer (LD) b. Jun 12, 1955. College lecturer. Former cllr, Poole. **Janice Hurne** (Lab) b. Feb 7, 1950. Retired lecturer. School governor. Education: University of Cardiff.

Constituency
This large, rural seat along Hampshire's border with Dorset is affluent. The population is concentrated in sought-after towns by the coast such as Lymington, New Milton and Barton-on-Sea, while inland – just on the boundary of the New Forest National Park – lie Fordingbridge and Ringwood. The forest and tourism are important economic sectors and there are many small business owners. Middle-class professionals enjoy the location, in easy commuting reach of Bournemouth and Southampton. The constituency has been safely Conservative for decades.

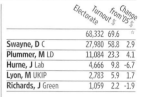

	Electorate	Turnout %	Change from 05 %
	68,332	69.6	☆
Swayne, D C	27,980	58.8	2.9
Plummer, M LD	11,084	23.3	4.1
Hurne, J Lab	4,666	9.8	-6.7
Lyon, M UKIP	2,783	5.9	1.7
Richards, J Green	1,059	2.2	-1.9

50%
Majority 16,896

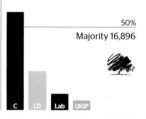

C LD Lab UKIP

Newark
Conservative hold

Patrick Mercer
b. Jun 26, 1956
MP 2001-

Highly decorated Army man. Sacked from front-bench (Shadow Minister: Homeland Security 2003-07) over comments about ethnic minorities in the Armed Forces. Later agreed to advise Gordon Brown's Government on defence but resigned role soon after. Member, Home Affairs committee: 2007-10. Chair, sub-committee: Counter-terrorism 2008-10. Member, Defence committee 2001-03. BBC journalist. Married, one son. Education: King's School, Chester; Exeter College, Oxford (MA modern history) RMA Sandhurst; Staff College.

Dr Ian Campbell (Lab) b. Jun 6, 1960. GP. Sch gov. Ed: Uni of Glasgow.

Pauline Jenkins (LD) Sec sch teacher. Cllr, Southwell and Trent TC 1998-2003, 2006. Ed: Manchester Uni.

Constituency
A vast rural seat with much of the eastern half of Nottinghamshire, Newark has been slightly redrawn, effectively shifting it to the south, losing Retford to the north but gaining an affluent collection of commuter villages near the small town of Bingham. Newark-on-Trent is near the border with Lincolnshire and has patches of deprivation. A few miles to its west is the more prosperous Southwell, which has a cathedral. Under its former boundaries it was Labour before 1979, then Conservative until 1997. After one troubled term as Labour MP, Fiona Jones was defeated by the Tories in 2001.

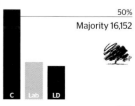

	Electorate	Turnout %	Change from 05 %
	71,785	71.4	☆
Mercer, P C	27,590	53.9	3.4
Campbell, I Lab	11,438	22.3	-6.0
Jenkins, P LD	10,246	20.0	1.6
Irvine, T UKIP	1,954	3.8	1.0

50%
Majority 16,152

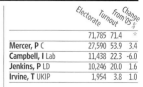

C Lab LD

223

Newbury — Conservative hold

Richard Benyon
b. Sep 4, 1960
MP 2005-

Genial. Archetypal rural, ex-military man, enjoys shooting and fishing. Son of former MP Bill Benyon and great-great-grandson of former Prime Minister Lord Salisbury. Close family links with Cameron. Parly Under-Sec: EFRA 2010-. Shadow Min: EFRA 2009-10, previously Opposition Whip 2007-09. Newbury District Cllr 1991-95, led Con group, contested Newbury 1997 and 2001. Served in the army before qualifying as chartered surveyor, ran business as land agent then took over family farm. Education: Bradfield Coll, Reading; Royal Agricultural Coll (dip real estate management, land economy). Divorced and remarried, five sons (three from first marriage).

David Rendel (LD) b. Apr 15, 1949. MP for Newbury 1993-2005. LD spokes Higher Ed 2001-05; Welfare 1997-99; Local Govt 1993-97. Ed: Eton; Oxford.

Constituency
In west Berkshire, this large rural seat borders Oxfordshire, Wiltshire and Hampshire. The noisy M4 cuts it in two, with the main town of Newbury, neighbouring Thatcham and Hungerford in the southern half, along the Kennet and Avon Canal. Excellent transport links and pretty countryside make it popular with middle-class commuters. Vodafone headquarters is an important employer. The area is famous for horse racing and an environmental battle in 1996 over the Newbury bypass. A seat long held by Tories, a 1993 by-election gave the Lib Dems a shock victory. They held on in two general elections before the Tories won it back in 2005.

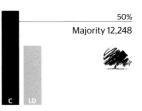

	Electorate	Turnout %	Change from '05 %
	83,411	70.2	☆
Benyon, R C	33,057	56.4	7.4
Rendel, D LD	20,809	35.5	-7.1
Cooper, H Lab	2,505	4.3	-1.7
Black, D UKIP	1,475	2.5	1.0
Hollister, A Green	490	0.8	
Burgess, B Ind	158	0.3	
Yates, D AD	95	0.2	

50%
Majority 12,248

Newcastle-under-Lyme — Labour hold

Paul Farrelly
b. Mar 2, 1962
MP 2001-

Left-of-centre, playing leading role in opposing higher university tuition fees as new MP in 2005. Abstained after heavy pressure. Member, cttees: CMS 2005-10; Unopposed Bills (Panel) 2004-10; Sci/Tech 2003-05; Joint cttee on consolidation of bills 2001-10. Member, Socialist Education Assoc. Journalist: The Observer, Independent on Sunday, Reuters. Manager, corporate finance division, Barclays De Zoete Wedd. Education: Wolstanton County GS; Marshlands Comp; St Edmund Hall, Oxford (BA PPE).

Robert Jenrick (C) b. 1982. Solicitor. Member of the 2005 David James Review of Government Efficiency.

Education: Wolverhampton Grammar School; St John's College, Cambridge. **Nigel Jones** (LD) Cllr. Former teacher. **David Nixon** (UKIP) Cllr, Staffordshire CC and Newcastle-under-Lyme BC.

Constituency
The Staffordshire town of Newcastle-under-Lyme lies at the bottom of this seat, with its suburbs sprawling north and barely separated by A-roads and a brook from neighbouring Stoke-on-Trent. Towards the northern border with Cheshire lies the town of Audley amid semi-rural land. The M6 runs through this seat, with Keele University nearby. With potteries and coalmining history this is traditionally working class and Labour-leaning, although better off than Stoke.

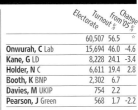

	Electorate	Turnout %	Change from '05 %
	69,433	62.2	
Farrelly, P Lab	16,393	38.0	-7.3
Jenrick, R C	14,841	34.4	9.5
Jones, N LD	8,466	19.6	0.7
Nixon, D UKIP	3,491	8.1	4.5

50%
Majority 1,552

Newcastle upon Tyne Central — Labour hold

Chi Onwurah
b. Apr 12, 1965
MP 2010-

Highly experienced chartered engineer, worked on bringing wireless comms to Africa. Head international tech strategy, Ofcom. Partner, Hammatan Ventures tech consultancy. Dir, Market Devt, Telegent. Dir, Product Strategy, Global Telesystems. Cable & Wireless, Nortel. Anti Apartheid, Fabians, Co-operative Society. Institute of Engineering and Technology. Advisory Board, OU Business Sch. Wallsendborn to working class Geordie mother and Nigerian father, moved to Nigeria as infant but forced back by Biafran Civil War (father fought) and grew up in Newcastle. Ed: Kenton Comp; Imperial Coll (BEng Elec Eng); Manchester Bus. Sch (MBA).

Gareth Kane (LD) Manager, environmental research centre. Cllr, Newcastle CC. Ed: Methodist Coll Belfast, Christ's Coll, Cambridge; Newcastle University **Nick Holder** (C) Senior manager for a consultancy business.
Ken Booth (BNP)

Constituency
Boundaries have been slightly redrawn to include a greater stretch of riverside at the south and the historic city centre around Grainger town. It loses some areas, predominantly from the east. There are high numbers of professionals but also areas of severe deprivation. The seat is ethnically diverse by northeastern standards and includes Chinatown. St James' Park, home of Newcastle United FC, looks down on the city from its elevated location. The seat is traditionally Labour but Lib Dems have made advances in recent years.

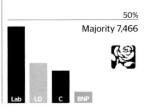

	Electorate	Turnout %	Change from '05 %
	60,507	56.5	☆
Onwurah, C Lab	15,694	46.0	-4.6
Kane, G LD	8,228	24.1	-3.4
Holder, N C	6,611	19.4	2.8
Booth, K BNP	2,302	6.7	
Davies, M UKIP	754	2.2	
Pearson, J Green	568	1.7	-2.2

50%
Majority 7,466

Newcastle upon Tyne East — Labour hold

Nicholas Brown
b. Jun 13, 1950
MP 1983-

Tough political enforcer devoted to Gordon Brown. Very conspiratorial and hates Blairites. Opera-loving. Govt whip: Chief 2008-; Deputy 2007-08; Chief 1997-98. Min: DWP 2001-02; MAFF 1998-2001. Opp whip: Deputy 1995-97. Various opp spokes 1994-95, 1985-94. Dep to Margaret Beckett 1992-94. MP Newcastle upon Tyne E & Wallsend 1997-2010. Cllr, Newcastle upon Tyne CC 1980-83. Legal adviser GMBATU. Proctor & Gamble advertising dept. Gay. Ed: Tunbridge Wells Tech HS; Manchester (BA).

Wendy Taylor (LD) b. Jul, 1955. Doctor. Cllr, Newcastle CC. Ed: Newcastle University.

Dominic Llewellyn (C) b. 1984. Works for The Shaftesbury Partnership. Governor of Excelsior, and a Director of OWN IT, an educational charity. Ed: Newcastle University.

Constituency
Socioeconomically, the constituency has contrasting halves. Two universities dominate the north, providing many students and young professionals in Jesmond and Heaton. The south has large council estates and severely deprived areas, including Byker Wall estate, notorious as home of the child burglar "Ratboy" in the 1990s but famous as the setting for the children's TV show Byker Grove, which launched the careers of Ant McPartlin and Declan Donnelly. The seat has lost Wallsend and almost reaches the city centre to include the distinctive Millennium Bridge. The seat is traditionally Labour.

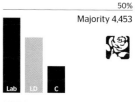

	Electorate	Turnout %	Change from '05 %
	64,487	58.7	☆
Brown, N Lab	17,043	45.0	-7.8
Taylor, W LD	12,590	33.3	1.5
Llewellyn, D C	6,068	16.0	3.0
Spence, A BNP	1,342	3.6	
Gray, A Green	620	1.6	
Levy, M Comm	177	0.5	

50%
Majority 4,453

Lab | LD | C

Newcastle upon Tyne North — Labour hold

Catherine McKinnell
b. Jun 8, 1976
MP 2010-

Newcastle born and raised, one of eight children. Solicitor (employment specialist), Dickinson Dees. Assists husband in café/events business. Finance Officer, Edinburgh Uni Students Association. Married, two children . Ed: Sacred Heart Comp; Edinburgh (politics & history); Northumbria (CPE; LPC).

Ronald Beadle (LD) b. Jan 28, 1966. Academic at Northumbria University. Contested Newcastle North 2005. Ed: Westminster Sch; LSE (BSc government & history, MSc)
Stephen Parkinson (C) b. 1982. Director of the Centre for Policy Studies. Helped produce electoral literature for the Crewe & Nantwich, Henley, and Norwich by-elections. Education: Cambridge University, BA (Hons) hist.

Constituency
This seat covers the northwestern fringes of Newcastle, including Westerhope and the eastern part of the middle-class commuter suburb Gosforth, which the new boundary cuts in half down the High Street. The seat extends into the countryside, with towns and villages such as Throckley and Newburn in the south and Dinnington in the north. Newcastle international airport lies at the western edge. Residents are comfortably well off but although the area is increasingly middle-class, it is shaped politically by the legacy of old Tyneside industries and has a long Labour history.

	Electorate	Turnout %	Change from '05 %
	67,110	65.5	☆
McKinnell, C Lab	17,950	40.9	-9.0
Beadle, R LD	14,536	33.1	0.1
Parkinson, S C	7,966	18.1	3.4
Gibson, T BNP	1,890	4.3	
Proud, I UKIP	1,285	2.9	
Heyman, A Green	319	0.7	

50%
Majority 3,414

Lab | LD | C

Newport East — Labour hold

Jessica Morden
b. May 29, 1968
MP 2005-

Instinctive party loyalist, brought in to run the Labour party's operations Wales, where politics has traditionally been noticeably male dominated due to coal and steel industries. PPS to Peter Hain 2009-10, 2007-08; Paul Murphy 2008-09. Member, select cttees: Welsh Affairs 2005-07; Modernisation of HoC 2005-06; Constitutional Affairs/Justice 2005-10. Gen sec, Welsh Lab Party. Worked for GMB, and Llew Smith and Huw Edwards MPs. Has partner, one daughter, one son. Education: Croefceiliog Comprehensive; Birmingham Uni (BA history).

Ed Townsend (LD) Public relations consultant. Cllr, Newport CC (Dep Leader). Education: Wallasey Gramm; Horace Mann School, New York, University of Leicester, BA (Politics), Cardiff Business School, (MBA).
Dawn Parry (C) Local businesswoman. Cllr, North Somerset.

Constituency
At the southeast corner of Wales, this seat spans along the River Severn, from Caldicot, by the second Severn crossing, to the River Usk, which divides Newport in two. The eastern half of the town included in this seat is home to many of Newport's prefab houses, which are being replaced. The M4 runs near the north of the seat. The Llanwern steelworks was a major employer but has been closed down. The seat remains working-class and has historically been represented by Labour.

	Electorate	Turnout %	Change from '05 %
	54,437	63.3	
Morden, J Lab	12,744	37.0	-8.2
Townsend, E LD	11,094	32.2	8.5
Parry, D C	7,918	23.0	-0.4
Jones, K BNP	1,168	3.4	
Cross, F PC	724	2.1	-1.7
Rowlands, D UKIP	677	2.0	-1.0
Screen, L Soc	123	0.4	-259

50%
Majority 1,650

Lab | LD | C

Newport West

Paul Flynn
b. Feb 9, 1935
MP 1997-

Veteran left-winger and outspoken anti-war. Conscientious attender in Commons. Opp spokes: social security 1989-90; health & social security 1988-89. Member, select cttees: Environmental Audit 2003-05; Welsh Affairs 1997-98. Sec, Welsh group of Lab MPs. Cllr: Gwent 1974-83; Newport 1972-81. Member, UK delegation to Council of Europe and Western European Union. POST board member. Chemist. Radio broadcaster. Labour MEP research officer. Re-married. One stepson, one stepdaughter, one son, one daughter (deceased) from first marriage. Education: St Illtyd's College; University College of Wales, Cardiff.

Matthew Williams (C) b. 1973. Political adviser to David Tredinnick MP.
Veronica German (LD) Teacher. Cllr, Newport CC 2003. Contested National Assembly, Rhondda 1999.

Constituency
On the northern banks of the Severn and the western banks of the River Usk, this seat includes much of the town centre. A museum part-focused on the uprising of the Newport Chartists in 1839 is here. It also includes suburbs such as Rogerstone, beyond the M4. It curves round the town and crosses the Usk to include the Celtic Manor Resort, the 2010 host of the Ryder Cup golf. This seat is more middle-class than its eastern neighbour and the service sector is important. It returned a Tory on its creation in 1983 but Labour MPs thereafter.

	Electorate	Turnout %	Change from '05 %
	62,111	64.0	
Flynn, P Lab	16,389	41.3	-3.5
Williams, M C	12,845	32.3	2.8
German, V LD	6,587	16.6	-1.3
Windsor, T BNP	1,183	3.0	
Moelwyn, H Hughes	1,144	2.9	-845
Rees, J PC	1,122	2.8	-0.8
Bartolotti, P Green	450	1.1	-0.4

50%
Majority 3,544

Newry & Armagh

Conor Murphy
b. Jul 10, 1963
MP 2005-

Former Provisional IRA prisoner, jailed in 1985 for possession of explosives. Member, NI Assembly (Newry & Armagh) 1998- (Min for Regional Dev 2007-). SF group leader, NI Assembly. Contsted Newry & Armagh 2001 gen election. Cllr, Newry & Mourne Dist 1989-97. Married, one daughter, one son. Education: St Colman's Coll, Newry; Queen's, Belfast.

Dominic Bradley (SDLP) b. Nov 18, 1954. Teacher and educational adviser. Member, NI Assembly 2003-. Education: St Paul's High School Besbrook, Abbey Grammar School, Newry (BA English language and English literature).

Danny Kennedy (UCUNF) b. Jul 6, 1959. UUP Member, NI Assembly, Newry & Armagh 1998-. Cllr, Newry & Mourne, 1985-. Education: Newry High School.
William Irwin (DUP) b. Dec 12, 1956. DUP Member, NI Assembly 2007-. Cllr, Armagh 2005-. Education: Clounagh Junior High School.

Constituency
The only constituency in Northern Ireland that can claim two cities. Co Armagh's apple orchards deserve greater fame but lose out to the "bandit country" of its southern fringe, where the writ of the Provisional IRA has run for decades and contributed to a local form of "ethnic cleansing". Towns such as Crossmaglen are 99 per cent Catholic. A safe Sinn Féin seat.

	Electorate	Turnout %	Change from '05 %
	74,308	60.4	
Murphy, C SF	18,857	42.0	0.7
Bradley, D SDLP	10,526	23.4	-1.7
Kennedy, D UCUNF	8,558	19.1	
Irwin, W DUP	5,764	12.8	-5.5
Frazer, W Ind	656	1.5	0.2
Muir, A Alliance	545	1.2	

50%
Majority 8,331

Sinn Féin

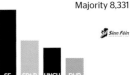

Newton Abbot

Anne-Marie Morris
b. Jul 5, 1957
MP 2010-

Has family from Brixham stretching back to William of Orange. Senior Council for Devon. Cllr, West Sussex CC 2005-07. MD, Manteion (marketing/executive coaching). Solicitor. Federation of Small Businesses. Keen rower, horse rider. Singing and amateur dramatics enthusiast. Has partner, step-children. Ed: Bryanston Sch; Hertford Coll, Oxford (law); Coll of Law, London; Open Uni (MBA); Harvard (leadership programme); Strathclyde Uni school of coaching (dip executive coaching).

Richard Younger-Ross (LD) b. Jan 29, 1953. MP for Teignbridge 2001-2010. LD spokes, Culture, Media and Sport 2007-10. Education: Ewell Technical College, Oxford Brookes
Patrick Canavan (Lab)
Jackie Hooper (UKIP)

Constituency
The old Teignbridge constituency is replaced by a much smaller seat – 20,000 fewer electors – that takes in coast between Exmouth and Torbay. The market town of Newton Abbot, on the Teign Estuary, is the main retail centre and site of a racecourse. The 22 miles of coast are the focus of a growing tourism industry and much of the area remains rolling Devon countryside. High numbers of retired people produce an ageing demographic. The old seat was safely Tory until taken by the Lib Dems in 2001, who held it until 2010.

	Electorate	Turnout %	Change from '05 %
	69,343	69.6	
Morris, A C	20,774	43.0	8.0
Younger-Ross, R LD	20,251	41.9	-3.6
Canavan, P Lab	3,387	7.0	-4.4
Hooper, J UKIP	3,088	6.4	-0.1
Lindsey, C Green	701	1.5	
Sharp, K Ind	82	0.2	

50%
Majority 523

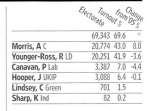

George Freeman
b. Jul 12, 1967
MP 2010-

A former NFU parliamentary officer, who grew up on a farm and enjoys country pursuits. Involved with Small Business Policy Task Force. Contested Stevenage 2005 with "Positive Politics" campaign. Launched "Mind the Gap" civic action campaign 2003, "Positive Politics" 2005. Founded 4D-Biomedical consultancy business. Adviser, Norwich Research Park, Non-Exec Dir, Elsoms Seeds. Venture capitalist. Spitfire fan. Married, one son, one daughter. Education: Radley Coll; Girton Coll, Cambridge (geography).

David Newman (LD) b. Jun 10, 1969. Vice President at Citibank in the United Arab Emirates since 2006.

Contested Surrey Heath 1997. Education: Guildford County Sch, Chartered Insurance Institute.
Elizabeth Hughes (Lab) b. Mar 30, 1964. Technical manager in manufacturing. Education: Manchester Met Uni.
Toby Coke (UKIP)

Constituency
This rural seat has been redrawn and effectively shifted south and east to make way for the new Broadland seat. It is mostly from Breckland district, of which the council is a major employer in the large and economically growing town of Dereham. Other towns are Attleborough, which is home to business parks, and Watton, which has suffered from decline of agriculture. The seat has also gained Wymondham and Hingham. Under old boundaries the seat was historically Conservative, but in 1997 the margin of victory was narrow.

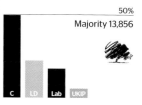

	Electorate	Turnout %	Change from '05 %
	74,260	68.4	☆
Freeman, G C	25,123	49.5	3.0
Newman, D LD	11,267	22.2	3.0
Hughes, E Lab	8,857	17.5	-12.8
Coke, T UKIP	2,800	5.5	1.5
Birt, T Green	1,457	2.9	
Kelly, C BNP	1,261	2.5	

50%
Majority 13,856

C LD Lab UKIP

Norman Lamb
b. Sep 16, 1957
MP 2001-

Influential figure in Lib Dems' Orange Book movement, architect of plan for part-privatisation of Royal Mail, adopted as coalition government policy. Asst Govt whip 2010- (and Chief Parliamentary and Political Adviser to the Dep PM). LD Shadow Sec: Health 2006-10. Chief of Staff to Sir Menzies Campbell 2006. LD Shadow Sec: Trade & Industry 2005-06. PPS to Charles Kennedy 2003-05. LD spokes: Treasury 2002-05; Int Devt 2001-02. Member, cttee: Treasury 2003-. Cllr, Norwich CC 1987-91. Member, European Standing Cttee A. Solicitor/consultant. Married, two sons. Ed: George Abbott Sch, Guildford; Wymondham Coll, Norfolk; Leicester (LLB).

Trevor Ivory (C) b. 1978. Solicitor. Ed: University of East Anglia (LL.B Law).
Phil Harris (Lab) Contested seat 2005.
Michael Baker (UKIP)

Constituency
This seat spans 45 miles of coastline, with the resorts of Wells, Sheringham and Cromer. They attract tourists, many with second homes in the area, and the retired, who comprise more than 25 per cent of residents. Holt and North Walsham, the main manufacturing base, is slightly inland, as are Stalham and Hoveton. About 50 per cent of the population live in rural villages and the majority work in small businesses in the towns, which have received funding to compete with Norwich. The seat lost almost 13,000 electors to the new Broadland seat. The Tories held from 1970 until the Lib Dems' victory in 2001.

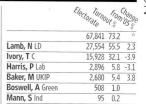

	Electorate	Turnout %	Change from '05 %
	67,841	73.2	☆
Lamb, N LD	27,554	55.5	2.3
Ivory, T C	15,928	32.1	-3.9
Harris, P Lab	2,896	5.8	-3.1
Baker, M UKIP	2,680	5.4	3.8
Boswell, A Green	508	1.0	
Mann, S Ind	95	0.2	

50%
Majority 11,626

LD C Lab UKIP

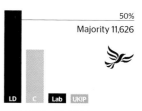

Henry Bellingham
b. Mar 29, 1955
MP 2001-; 1983-97

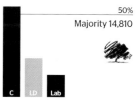

Has the manner of an unreconstructed Norfolk squire, looks like a throwback to the 19th century. Enjoys country sports, passionate on rural issues. Enthusiastic member of Lords and Commons cricket team. Parly Under-Sec: FCO 2010-. Shadow Constitutional Affairs/Justice Minister 2006-10, Opposition Whip 2005-06, Shadow Small Business Minister 2002-05. Ran consultancy firm 1997-2001 after election defeat. Previous roles include parliamentary private secretary to Malcolm Rifkind 1991-97. Barrister. Married, one son. Education: Eton; Magdalene College, Cambridge (BA Law).

William Summers (LD) Works for non-profit housing organisation. Volunteer for re-election campaign of Norman Lamb MP, 2005.
Manish Sood (Lab) b. Jul 11, 1971. Cllr, Leicester.

Constituency
King's Lynn is the main town, located on the River Great Ouse that runs down to the coast at The Wash. A significant number of residents take advantage of good train links to Cambridge or London to commute, but arable agriculture and manufacturing dominate the economy. There is a low-skilled workforce with below-average numbers of professionals. King's Lynn is undergoing regeneration and has pockets of severe deprivation within the worst 10 per cent nationwide. After one term of Labour, the Tories won it back in 2001.

	Electorate	Turnout %	Change from '05 %
	73,207	65.3	☆
Bellingham, H C	25,916	54.2	4.3
Summers, W LD	11,106	23.2	8.5
Sood, M Lab	6,353	13.3	-18.3
Gray, J UKIP	1,841	3.9	0.2
Fleming, D BNP	1,839	3.9	
de Whalley, M Green	745	1.6	

50%
Majority 14,810

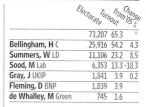

C LD Lab

227

Norfolk South — Conservative hold

Richard Bacon
b. Dec 3, 1962
MP 2001-

Enthusiastic and very likeable. Works forensically on the Public Accounts Committee (2001-) but may be regarded as a single issue campaigner. His arcane interests make him a loner. Makes terrible jokes involving pigs. Uncovered foreign prisoners scandal that helped bring down Charles Clarke as Home Secretary; earned Backbencher of the Year 2006. Financial journalist, investment banker (Barclays), PR career at Brunswick and own business, English Word Factory. Married, one son. Choral singer and bongo player. Education: King's School, Worcester; LSE (BSc (Econ) politics and economics).

Jacky Howe (LD) b. Jul 31, 1976. Self-employed management and fund-raising consultant. Cllr, Norfolk CC. Ed: Open University (MBA).
Mick Castle (Lab) b. Dec 20, 1949. Community development worker. Member of Great Yarmouth Strategic Partnership. Cllr, Great Yarmouth (leader Labour group).

Constituency
Diss, Loddon and Harleston are the main towns, while villages are dotted amid the fields and meadows, with the Norfolk Broads waterways running through them. The seat has been slightly redrawn, losing Wymondham and Hingham from the west. Agriculture and associated manufacturers such as BOCM Pauls are important to the economy. This is one of the most affluent seats in Norfolk and has been safely Tory since 1950.

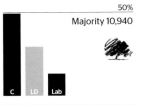

	Electorate	Turnout %	Change from 05 %
	76,165	72.2	☆
Bacon, R C	27,133	49.3	5.2
Howe, J LD	16,193	29.5	-1.3
Castle, M Lab	7,252	13.2	-9.0
Heasley, E UKIP	2,329	4.2	1.4
Mitchell, H BNP	1,086	2.0	
Willcott, J Green	1,000	1.8	

50%
Majority 10,940

C   LD   Lab

Norfolk South West — Conservative hold

Elizabeth Truss
b. Jul 26, 1975
MP 2010-

Self-confident. Proved her mettle in ugly showdown with local party over extra-marital affair. Deputy director, Reform think-tank 2008-09. Cllr, Greenwich BC 2006-2010. Contested Calder Valley 2005; Hemsworth 2001. Energy/telecoms career: The Communication Group; Cable & Wireless; Shell Int. Member, Chartered Institute of Management Accountants. Christian. Married, two daughters Education: Roundhay School, Leeds; Merton College, Oxford (PPE).

Stephen Gordon (LD) b. Sep 13, 1949. Healthcare practitioner. Chairman, SW and Mid Norfolk LD Constituency Party.

Peter Smith (Lab) b. Dec 14, 1987. Teacher. Ed: Durham University; York University.
Kay Hipsey (UKIP)

Constituency
This large, rural constituency is based around the towns of Thetford, Swaffham and Downham Market. It includes Thetford Forest and open arable land where a number of the population are employed in agriculture. Associated manufacturing is a major employment sector, especially in Thetford, where it pays about 50 per cent of the workforce. The decline of agriculture has left Thetford with patches of severe deprivation and it received funding from the EU. The seat has been cut by about 16,000 electors, with the loss of the Breckland area around Watton. It has been Conservative since 1964.

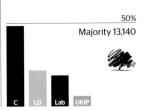

	Electorate	Turnout %	Change from 05 %
	74,298	66.2	☆
Truss, E C	23,753	48.3	3.4
Gordon, S LD	10,613	21.6	2.4
Smith, P Lab	9,119	18.6	-11.4
Hipsey, K UKIP	3,061	6.2	1.5
Pearce, D BNP	1,774	3.6	
Allen, L Green	830	1.7	

50%
Majority 13,140

C   LD   Lab   UKIP

Normanton, Pontefract & Castleford — Labour hold

Yvette Cooper
b. Mar 20, 1969
MP 1997-

Elfin looks mask fierce intellect and steely determination. Very ambitious. Not popular with civil servants. SoS: Work & Pensions 2009-10. Chief Sec to the Treasury 2008-09. Min: Housing (att. Cabinet) 2007-08; Housing/Planning 2005-07. Parly Under-Sec: ODPM 2003-05; Lord Chancellor's Dept 2002-03; Health 1999-2002. Leader writer, *The Independent*. Economist. Policy adviser to Lab treasury teams 1992-94. Domestic policy specialist, Bill Clinton 1992 pres campaign. Econ researcher to John Smith 1990-92. TGWU,GMB. Married (to Ed Balls MP), two daughters, one son. Ed: Oxford; Harvard (Kennedy Scholar); LSE.

Nick Pickles (C) Works for a small IT company. Former president of Durham Students' Union.
Chris Rush (LD) b. Jun 8, 1985. Ed: Wakefield Coll (Travel and Tourism).
Graham Thewlis-Hardy (BNP)

Constituency
Normanton, previously at the eastern extremity of its own seat, is now added to the western extremity of the Pontefract & Castleford constituency. These three towns and Knottingley are clustered around the motorways that criss-cross the seat. This area, southeast of Leeds, is comprised of overwhelmingly white, working-class, former mining communities, with patches of severe deprivation. Regeneration is helping to improve the towns' economic prospects. The constituency has long been staunchly Labour.

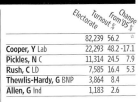

	Electorate	Turnout %	Change from 05 %
	82,239	56.2	☆
Cooper, Y Lab	22,293	48.2	-17.1
Pickles, N C	11,314	24.5	7.9
Rush, C LD	7,585	16.4	5.3
Thewlis-Hardy, G BNP	3,864	8.4	
Allen, G Ind	1,183	2.6	

50%
Majority 10,979

Lab   C   LD   BNP

Northampton North

Michael Ellis
b. Oct 13, 1967
MP 2010-

Constitutional history and monarchy buff, broadcast contributor. Lifelong Northampton man, selected by open primary. Criminal Barrister, works on many legal aid cases. Former cllr, Northampton CC. Worked with the Youth Offending Team. Society of Conservative Lawyers. Jewish. Enjoys gym and theatre. Education: Wellingborough School; Buckingham University (Law); Inns of Court School of Law (BVC).

Sally Keeble (Lab) b. Oct 13, 1951. MP for Northampton North 1997-2010. Parly Under-Sec: Transport, Local Government and Regions 2001-2002; International Development 2002-03.

Education: Cheltenham Ladies College; St Hugh's College, Oxford.
Andrew Simpson (LD) Cllr, Northampton BC 2007-. Education: Leicester University (Combined Studies).

Constituency

North of the city centre, this seat is primarily residential but also includes the University of Northampton and several warehousing estates. After boundary changes it lost wards to its southern neighbour. There are areas of deprivation at the east and centre, but this is the more affluent of the two city seats and an above-average working class is balanced by a more prosperous middle class, with the outskirts in the north especially well off. Labour took this traditionally Tory seat in 1997.

	Electorate	Turnout %	from '05 %	Change
	64,230	62.7	☆	
Ellis, M C	13,735	34.1	4.4	
Keeble, S Lab	11,799	29.3	-9.4	
Simpson, A LD	11,250	27.9	1.0	
Beasley, R BNP	1,316	3.3		
Macarthur, J UKIP	1,238	3.1	0.6	
Lochmuller, T Green	443	1.1		
Fitzpatrick, E Ind	334	0.8		
Webb, T Ch	98	0.2		
Mildren, M Ind	58	0.1		

50%
Majority 1,936

C Lab LD

Northampton South

Brian Binley
b. May 1, 1942
MP 2005-

Maverick, successful businessman and Freemason, with manner of doorstep insurance salesman; populist, common-man style. Treasurer, 1922 committee, 2010-. Treasurer, Cornerstone Group. Ordered to apologise to house and repay money over expenses claim. Chair, Conservative Parliamentary Enterprise Group (2006-). Founder, chairman, BCC Marketing. Co-founded Beechwood House publishing. Northampton Town FC devotee. Married, two sons (one from previous relationship). Education: Finedon Mulso C of E Sec Modern.

Clyde Loakes (Lab) b. Mar 6, 1970. Former civil servant and cllr. Chair of

the North London Waste Authority 2009-.
Paul Varnsverry (LD) Cllr, Northampton BC 2007-.

Constituency

The newly created seat has removed a substantially affluent, rural area to the south as well as the prosperous outskirts of the city. In return it has gained a small industrial area in the west of the city, with the net effect of losing about 20,000 electors. With the exception of Duston and Weston, most of this seat is relatively deprived. It encompasses the city centre, Delapre Park, industrial estates and residential suburbs. Under different boundaries, it turned Labour in 1997 but was won back by the Tories in 2005.

	Electorate	Turnout %	from '05 %	Change
	66,923	58.2	☆	
Binley, B C	15,917	40.8	3.1	
Loakes, C Lab	9,913	25.4	-16.1	
Varnsverry, P LD	7,579	19.4	5.9	
Clarke, T Ind	2,242	5.8		
Clark, D UKIP	1,897	4.9	2.8	
Sills, K Eng	618	1.6		
Hawkins, J Green	363	0.9		
Green, D NSPS	325	0.8		
Willsher, K Ind	65	0.2		
Costello, L SMA	59	0.2		

50%
Majority 6,004

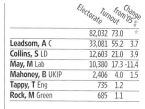

C Lab LD Ind

Northamptonshire South

Andrea Leadsom
b. May 13, 1963
MP 2010-

Interested in early years mental health and early intervention, and in banking reform and regulation. Advocate of localism. Contested Knowsley South 2005. Cllr, S Oxon DC 2003-07. Head of Corporate Governance, Invesco Perpetual. MD, start-up hedge fund. Financial institutions director, Barclays Bank. Cites Aung San Suu Kyi as political hero. Married, three children. Education: Tonbridge Girls' Grammar; Warwick (political science).

Scott Collins (LD) Cllr, Northampton BC 2007-. Chair of the Diverse Communities Forum.

Matthew May (Lab) b. Nov 23, 1971. Teacher. Education: University of London (history).

Constituency

This new seat spans most of the district of the same name, formerly in the Daventry seat, as well as areas up to the south of Northampton. The market towns of Towcester and Brackley are situated amid an expanse of countryside, which reaches almost to Milton Keynes. Silverstone racetrack is also in the seat. This is an affluent area with the number of middle-class professionals above national averages. The working class is also well represented, with few economically inactive. The area has a Conservative tradition stretching back decades.

	Electorate	Turnout %	from '05 %	Change
	82,032	73.0	☆	
Leadsom, A C	33,081	55.2	3.7	
Collins, S LD	12,603	21.0	3.9	
May, M Lab	10,380	17.3	-11.4	
Mahoney, B UKIP	2,406	4.0	1.5	
Tappy, T Eng	735	1.2		
Rock, M Green	685	1.1		

50%
Majority 20,478

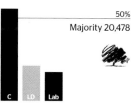

C LD Lab

Norwich North Conservative gain

Chloe Smith
b. May 17, 1982
MP 2009-

Surprise choice as government whip, ruffled feathers among more experienced Conservative MPs. Coy about her job and links to Tory preparation team during by-election. Assistant government whip 2010-. Member, select committee: Work & Pensions 2009-10. Deloitte career, seconded to Conservatives' implementation unit (assistant to James Clappison as shad work & pensions minister). Education: Methwold High School, Norfolk; Swaffham Sixth Form College; York (BA English literature).

John Cook (Lab) b. Jul 9, 1964. Former Party Organiser.

John Stephen (LD).

Constituency
North of the River Wensum, this seat excludes Norwich city centre and instead covers the suburbs of Catton Grove, Crome and Mile Cross, with pockets of severe deprivation in the latter two. Outlying areas such as Hellesdon, Sprowston and Thorpe St Andrew form part of the same conurbation. Most residents work in the centre where financial services are a major employer. Boundary changes have removed Taverham and Drayton. Under old boundaries a by-election was forced in 2009 by the resignation of the Labour MP Ian Gibson over his expenses and the seat fell to the Conservatives.

	Electorate	Turnout %	Change from '05 %
	65,258	65.2	☆
Smith, C C	17,280	40.6	10.1
Cook, J Lab	13,379	31.4	-15.7
Stephen, J LD	7,783	18.3	2.2
Tingle, G UKIP	1,878	4.4	2.1
Goldfinch, J Green	1,245	2.9	-0.3
Richardson, T BNP	747	1.8	
Holden, B Ind	143	0.3	
Holland, A Ch	118	0.3	

50%
Majority 3,901

Norwich South Liberal Democrat gain

Simon Wright
b. Sep 15, 1979
MP 2010-

Diminutive former maths teacher who ousted the Labour big beast to achieve one of the major scalps of the 2010 election. Eager and earnest. Cllr, North Norfolk DC 2003-07. Constituency agent to Norman Lamb MP. Secondary school teacher. Musician. Norwich City FC fan. Christian. Married. Ed: Dereham Neatherd HS, Norfolk; Imperial Coll, London (BSc Hons mathematics); Kings Coll London (PGCE).

Charles Clarke (Lab) b. Sep 21, 1950. MP for Norwich South 1997-2010. Home Sec 2004-06. Secretary of State for Education and Skills 2002-04

Antony Little (C) Cllr, Norwich CC (leader of Conservatives).
Adrian Ramsay (Green) b. 1981. Green Party deputy leader. Cllr, Norwich CC 2003-10. Contested Norwich S in 2005.

Constituency
Central Norwich, with its Norman cathedral, castle and medieval alleyways, lies in this seat. It is a tourist attraction as well as a base for those visiting the Broads and coastline. Finance is the main economic sector, employing about a third of the workforce, with Aviva among the big companies. Affluence varies from some severe deprivation in Wensum to wealthy areas of Eaton and the "Golden Triangle", which runs from the city centre to the University of East Anglia. Victorian terraced houses are popular with students and young professionals in the area. The seat was won by Labour in 1987.

	Electorate	Turnout %	Change from '05 %
	73,649	64.6	☆
Wright, S LD	13,960	29.4	-0.6
Clarke, C Lab	13,650	28.7	-8.7
Little, A C	10,902	22.9	1.1
Ramsay, A Green	7,095	14.9	7.5
Emmens, S UKIP	1,145	2.4	1.0
Heather, L BNP	697	1.5	
Polley, G WRP	102	0.2	

50%
Majority 310

Nottingham East Labour Co-op hold

Chris Leslie
b. Jun 28, 1972
MP 2010-; 1997-2005

The "baby of the house" of the 1997 intake when he took the rock-solid Tory seat of Shipley, from unlikely background working as an office administrator and photocopying for Gordon Brown. Set up think-tank, New Local Government Network, after losing seat in 2005. Ran Gordon Brown's leadership campaign and became embroiled in Labour donations row. Personable and an important Brownite, his long search for a seat was frustated by Labour rules on all-women shortlists, until late selection Nottingham East. Parly Under-Sec: Const Affairs 2003-05 (stint as junior min marred by postal voting problems.); ODPM 2002-03. Parly Sec: Cabinet Office 2001-02.

PPS to Lord Falconer 1998-2001. Ed: Bingley GS; Leeds (BA politics & parly studies, MA ind and lab studies).

Sam Boote (LD) Cllr, Rushcliffe BC.
Ewan Lamont (C) Senior producer and programme manager.

Constituency
Encompassing the part of Nottingham city centre north of Parliament Street, including the Victoria Shopping Centre, theatres and a campus of Nottingham Trent University, this seat is predominantly suburban. Steinton, towards the racecourse and country park in the east, has areas of severe deprivation, as does St Ann's, just north of the city centre. Farther north, Sherwood and Mapperley Park are leafier and better off. Labour took this seat from the Tories in 1992.

	Electorate	Turnout %	Change from '05 %
	58,707	56.4	☆
Leslie, C Lab	15,022	45.4	-1.3
Boote, S LD	8,053	24.3	2.5
Lamont, E C	7,846	23.7	1.2
Wolfe, P UKIP	1,138	3.4	0.9
Hoare, B Green	928	2.8	-2.4
Sardar, P Ch	125	0.4	

50%
Majority 6,969

Nottingham North
Labour hold

Graham Allen
b. Jan 11, 1953
MP 1987-

Tall, hard-working and nerdish. Obsessive about constitutional reform, interest in pre-school intervention for poor children. Elected Chair, select ctee: Political & Constitutional Reform 2010-. Govt whip 1997-2001. Shad Min: Environment 1996-97; Transport 1995-96; Media & Broadcasting 1994-95; Constitutional Affairs 1992-94; Soc Security 1991-92. Warehouseman Nottingham. Officer: Lab Party research 1978-83, Local Govt GLC 1983-84. Political Fund ballots nat co-ordinator 1984-86. GMBATU research/education officer 1986-87. Married, one daughter. Ed: Forest Fields GS, Nottingham; City of London Poly (BA pol & econ); Leeds Uni (MA political sociology).

Martin Curtis (C) b. 1964. Cllr, Cambridge CC. Former Army technician and civil servant at MoD. **Tim Ball** (LD) b. Sep 16, 1959. Computer programmer. Ed: Ilkeston School; Birmingham University.

Constituency
This is the most deprived seat in the city. It is mainly working-class, two fifths live in social housing, typified by the concentric rings of red-brick homes in Aspley ward, where one area ranked the 26th most deprived out of more than 32,000 nationally in 2007. There tends to be high unemployment and large numbers of residents have never worked. Major economic sectors include manufacturing and health, with a hospital in the seat. With the exception of a narrow Tory victory in 1983, this seat has been Labour since its inception in 1955.

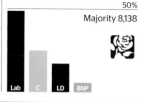

	Electorate	Turnout %	Change from 05 %
	63,240	54.2	☆
Allen, G Lab	16,646	48.6	-10.6
Curtis, M C	8,508	24.8	6.7
Ball, T LD	5,849	17.1	-0.3
Brindley, B BNP	1,944	5.7	
Marriott, I UKIP	1,338	3.9	-1.5

50%
Majority 8,138

Nottingham South
Labour hold

Lilian Greenwood
b. Mar 26, 1966
MP 2010-

Union official (Unison regional organiser/manager/officer). Research officer, Civil & Public Services Association, Local Authority conditions of service advisory board. Member Co-operative party, Compass, the Fabian Society, Fawcett Society. Keen runner and hill-walker. Married, three daughters. Ed: Canon Slade Sch, Bolton; St Catherine's Coll, Cambridge (BA economics and social & political sciences); Southbank Polytechnic (MSc sociology and social policy).

Rowena Holland (C) b. Nov 15, 1968. Has worked in Pharmaceuticals for 3M Healthcare in Loughborough and Merck Sharp Dohme.

Tony Sutton (LD) b. Jan 13, 1948. Cllr, Nottingham CC (deputy leader, LD group). Semi-retired consultant food technologist.

Constituency
This seat encompasses most of the pedestrianised areas of the city, Notts County FC, Nottingham University, the Queen's Medical Centre and affluent residential areas such as Wollaton and Radford to the west of the city centre. Farther south are big industrial parks and Clifton, which has a large council estate and the main university campus. Central and some southern parts of the seat have areas of severe deprivation but this is the wealthiest of the three Nottingham constituencies and is home to a large student population, comprising more than 25 per cent of residents. Labour took it from the Tories in 1992.

	Electorate	Turnout %	Change from 05 %
	67,441	60.5	☆
Greenwood, L Lab	15,209	37.3	-8.6
Holland, R C	13,437	32.9	6.2
Sutton, T LD	9,406	23.1	-0.4
Woodward, T BNP	1,140	2.8	
Browne, K UKIP	967	2.4	-1.5
Butcher, M Green	630	1.5	

50%
Majority 1,772

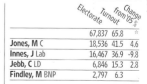

Nuneaton
Conservative gain

Marcus Jones
b. Apr 5, 1974
MP 2010-

Forthright mainstream Tory. Interested in local government and the housing market. Cllr, Nuneaton & Bedworth BC 2005- (leader 2008-09; leader Con group 2006-09). Conveyancing manager for Tustain Jones & Company Solicitors. Keen angler. Married, one son. CofE. Ed: St Thomas More RC School, Nuneaton; King Edward IV Sixth Form College.

Jayne Innes (Lab) b. Aug 19, 1970. Consultant, working mainly with charities. Former aide to Geoffrey Robinson MP. Contested Birmingham Yardley 2005. Ed: University of Wolverhampton. **Christina Jebb** (LD) Cllr, Staffordshire Moorlands DC. Hypnotherapist and holistic therapist. Ed: Doncaster College; Open University. **Martyn Findley** (BNP) Cllr, Nuneaton & Bedworth BC 2008-2010.

Constituency
In Warwickshire, just north of Coventry, Nuneaton is within easy reach of the West Midlands conurbation and is increasingly popular with commuting professionals. However, it grew around industries and there remains a strong working class and areas of deprivation. This substantially redrawn seat has gained a small semi-rural area west of Hartshill at the north, for the loss of a much larger and more affluent expanse from its south. Under old boundaries the Tories held it from 1983 to 1992 before Labour won it back.

	Electorate	Turnout %	Change from 05 %
	67,837	65.8	☆
Jones, M C	18,536	41.5	4.6
Innes, J Lab	16,467	36.9	-9.8
Jebb, C LD	6,846	15.3	2.8
Findley, M BNP	2,797	6.3	

50%
Majority 2,069

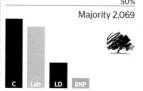

Ochil & Perthshire South | Labour hold

Gordon Banks
b. Jun 14, 1955
MP 2005-

Reputation as highly intelligent and good election campaign organiser. PPS to James Purnell 2006-09. Member, select cttees: Regulatory Reform 2005-; Unopposed Bills (Panel) 2005-; Scottish Affairs 2005-06; NI Affairs 2005-06. Contested Mid Scotland & Fife regional list 2003 Scottish Parl. Unite. Dir, Cartmore Building Supply. Chief buyer, Barratt Developments. Married, one daughter, one son. Ed: Glasgow Coll of Building (City & Guilds construction tech & concrete practice); Stirling (hist/pol).

Annabelle Ewing (SNP) b. Aug 20, 1960. MP for Perth 2001-05. Contested Falkirk East 2007.

Gerald Michaluk (C) Marketing consultant. Member of the Market Research Society and Fellow of the Chartered Institute of Marketing.
Graeme Littlejohn (LD) b. Feb 5, 1984. Media and campaigns officer for George Lyon MEP.

Constituency
This constituency in the heart of rural Scotland takes in parts of the old local authority areas of both Clackmannanshire and Kinross. It edges alongside both Perth and Stirling, containing most of the towns and villages between these two big population hubs. The seat has something of a dual personality, with the traditional Tory strongholds of Auchterarder and Crieff alongside the more working class, Labour/SNP towns of Alloa and Alva. Boundary changes helped to reduce Labour's majority over the SNP in 2005.

	Electorate	Turnout %	Change from '05 %
	75,115	67.2	
Banks, G Lab	19,131	37.9	6.6
Ewing, A SNP	13,944	27.6	-2.2
Michaluk, G C	10,342	20.5	-0.9
Littlejohn, G LD	5,754	11.4	-1.9
Bushby, D UKIP	689	1.4	0.8
Charles, H Green	609	1.2	-0.9

50%
Majority 5,187

Lab | SNP | C | LD

Ogmore | Labour hold

Huw Irranca-Davies
b. Jan 22, 1963
MP 2002-

Mildly rebellious instincts curbed by appointment to government. Parly Under-Sec: Environment, Food & Rural Affairs 2008-10; Wales 2007-08. Assistant government whip 2006-07. PPS to: Tessa Jowell 2005-06; Jane Kennedy 2003-05. Member, select committees: Joint Cttee on Statutory Instruments 2002-04; Procedure 2002-. Leisure facility management. Swansea Institute of Higher Ed senior lecturer and course director. Married, three sons. Education: Gowerton Comp; Crewe and Alsager College (BA combined studies); Swansea Inst of Higher Ed (MSc European leisure resort management).

Emma Moore (C) b. 1981. Works in banking. Contested European elections, North East 2009.
Jackie Radford (LD) Researcher, National Assembly for Wales.
Danny Clark (PC) Electrical contracts manager. Chairs the community council.

Constituency
The towns of Pencoed and Pontyclun lie near the seat's southern border, which roughly follows the route of the M4. Farther north, Maesteg is the main town. The seat takes its name from Ogmore Forest. Former mining communities such as Blaengarw have suffered deprivation and the area was in the media spotlight after several youth suicides in recent years. This is an overwhelmingly working-class seat in which manufacturing still dominates. It has been Labour since 1918.

	Electorate	Turnout %	Change from '05 %
	55,527	62.4	☆
Irranca-Davies, H Lab	18,644	53.8	-7.2
Moore, E C	5,398	15.6	1.4
Radford, J LD	5,260	15.2	0.5
Clark, D PC	3,326	9.6	-0.6
Thomas, K BNP	1,242	3.6	
Passey, C UKIP	780	2.3	

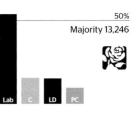

50%
Majority 13,246

Lab | C | LD | PC

Old Bexley & Sidcup | Conservative hold

James Brokenshire
b. Jan 8, 1968
MP 2005-

Diligent but dry. Parly Under-Sec, Home 2010-. Shadow Minister: Home Affairs 2006-10. Member, select cttee: Constitutional Affairs 2005-2006. MP Hornchurch 2005-10 (seat abolished). Corporate lawyer; partner at Jones Day Gouldens. Former national vice-chairman Young Conservatives. Interested in community radio and cricket. Married, two daughters, one son. Education: Davenant Foundation GS; Cambridge Centre for Sixth Form Studies; Exeter (LLB Law).

Rick Everitt (Lab) b. Jan 7, 1963. Head of Club Development at Charlton FC. Cllr, Bexley BC 2002-06. Education: Reading University.

Duncan Borrowman (LD) Campaigns manager. Cllr, Bromley BC. Education: BETHS Grammar Sch; Open University.

Constituency
This suburban southeast London seat reaches almost to Dartford and is dominated by rows of 1930s semi-detached houses, the vast majority of which are owner-occupied. The Coca-Cola plant in Sidcup is a notable employer and the majority of working people are employed within the borough. St Mary's is the most affluent part of a well-off seat. It was held by Ted Heath for 14 terms and remained Tory. It has been represented by an independent since 2008 after Derek Conway had the whip removed over his expenses.

	Electorate	Turnout %	Change from '05 %
	65,665	69.3	☆
Brokenshire, J C	24,625	54.1	4.1
Everitt, R Lab	8,768	19.3	-8.7
Borrowman, D LD	6,996	15.4	1.5
Brooks, J BNP	2,132	4.7	
Coburn, D UKIP	1,532	3.4	-1.2
Cheeseman, E Eng	520	1.1	
Hemming-Clark, J Save	393	0.9	
Rooks, J Green	371	0.8	
Dynamite, N Loony	155	0.3	

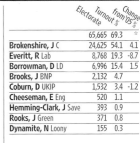

50%
Majority 15,857

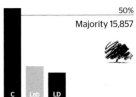

C | Lab | LD

Oldham East & Saddleworth — Labour hold

Phil Woolas
b. Dec 11, 1959
MP 1997-

Combative but sociable. Ran Peter Hain's campaign for deputy leader 2007. Minister: NW 2009-10; Borders & Immigration (Home/Treasury) 2008-; Environment, Food & Rural Affairs 2007-08; ODPM/CLG 2005-07. Deputy Leader of House of Commons 2003-05. Whip: govt 2002-03; assistant government 2001-02. PPS to Lord Macdonald 1999-2001. Dep leader leadership campaign team 1997-99. Head of comms, GMB. Chair, Tribune newspaper. Award-winning TV producer. NUS president. Married, two sons. Education: Nelson Grammar School; Walton Lane High School; Nelson & Colne College; Manchester University (BA philosophy).

Elwyn Watkins (LD) Cllr, Rochdale BC 2004-; chair, Rochdale Township. **Kashif Ali** (C) Barrister. Previous co-ordinator of Conservative campaigning activities across Oldham East & Saddleworth. Former Deputy Chairman of the Manchester Conservative Federation.

Constituency
This seat previously included some Rochdale wards but is now drawn from Oldham borough and stretches over to the Pennines, which rise up above the affluent villages of Saddleworth Moor. The eastern parts of Oldham town centre include large Pakistani populations concentrated in St Mary's and Alexandra wards, the scene of infamous race riots in 2001. The seat is marginal. Conservative until 1995, it was won by the Lib Dems in a dramatic by-election and has been Labour since 1997.

	Electorate	Turnout %	Change from '05 %
	72,765	61.2	☆
Woolas, P Lab	14,186	31.9	-10.7
Watkins, E LD	14,083	31.6	-0.5
Ali, K C	11,773	26.4	8.7
Stott, A BNP	2,546	5.7	
Bentley, D UKIP	1,720	3.9	1.8
Nazir, G Ch	212	0.5	

50%
Majority 103

Oldham West & Royton — Labour hold

Michael Meacher
b. Nov 4, 1939
MP 1970-

Left-winger with greenish tinge. Tried to stand for leader 2007, little support. Min: Environment 1997-2003. Shadow Cabinet 1983-97, Principal Opp spokes for: Environmental Protection; Education & Employment; Transport; Citizen's Charter & Science; Overseas Devt & Co-operation; Social Security; Employment; Health & Social Security. Parly Under-Sec: Trade 1976-79; Health/Social Security 1975-76; Industry 1974-75. Lab NEC 1983-89. Uni lecturer. Divorced, remarried. Two daughters, two sons, all from first marriage. Ed: Berkhamstead Sch; New Coll, Oxford (BA Greats); LSE (dip social administration).

Kamran Ghafoor (C) Self-employed. Ed: Salford Uni.
Mark Alcock (LD) Cllr, Oldham MBC 2007-. Former ALDC political officer. **David Joines** (BNP) b. Jul 11, 1955. Retired pipeline manager. Contested South Derbyshire 2005.

Constituency
Oldham lies around seven miles northeast of Manchester and the seat includes the towns of Royton to the north and Chadderton to the west. Oldham once produced a third of the world's spun cotton but the industry declined and the town is better known for the race riots of 2001. The west of Oldham town centre includes a large Bangladeshi population in Coldhurst ward and a Pakistani community in Werneth. The BNP polled more than 16 per cent in 2001 but the seat has been Labour since its creation in 1950.

	Electorate	Turnout %	Change from '05 %
	72,651	59.1	☆
Meacher, M Lab	19,503	45.5	-2.9
Ghafoor, K C	10,151	23.7	2.6
Alcock, M LD	8,193	19.1	-2.2
Joines, D BNP	3,049	7.1	
Roberts, H UKIP	1,387	3.2	0.7
Miah, S Respect	627	1.5	

50%
Majority 9,352

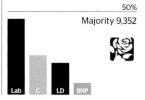

Orkney & Shetland — Liberal Democrat hold

Alistair Carmichael
b. Jul 15, 1965
MP 2001-

Combative, media-friendly figure from the Lib Dems' centre-left. Quit LD front bench to vote for EU referendum in 2008. Deputy Chief Whip (Comptroller of HM Household) 2010-. LD Shadow Sec of State: NI/Scotland, 2008-, 2007-08; Transport 2006-07. LD deputy spokesman: Home 2004-05; NI 2002-05. Scottish LD spokes, energy review 2001-02. Member, select committees: Scottish Affairs 2001-; Internat Devt 2001-02. Member, LD federal policy cttee 2004-. Solicitor. Procurator fiscal depute Procurator Fiscal Service. Hotel manager. Married, two sons. Ed: Islay HS; Aberdeen (Scots law LLB, Dip LP).

Mark Cooper (Lab) b. 1984. Youth and student officer, Edinburgh South CLP. **John Mowat** (SNP) SNP convenor, election agent, organiser. **Frank Nairn** (C) Farmer. Contested Orkney & Shetland 2005. **Robert Smith** (UKIP)

Constituency
This is Britain's most northerly constituency and also has the most disparate population. The Orkney and Shetland Islands share many of the same concerns. Shetland's economy is based around the oil terminal at Sullom Voe. Orkney also has significant oil interests at Flotta, but relies on a significant beef sector, too. Tourism is important for both island groups but transport links are also key, particularly ferry links with the mainland. The seat has a strong Liberal Democrat tradition.

	Electorate	Turnout %	Change from '05 %
	33,085	58.5	
Carmichael, A LD	11,989	62.0	10.5
Cooper, M Lab	2,061	10.7	-3.5
Mowat, J SNP	2,042	10.6	0.3
Nairn, F C	2,032	10.5	-2.7
Smith, R UKIP	1,222	6.3	3.9

50%
Majority 9,928

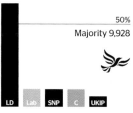

Orpington

Joseph Johnson
b. Dec 23, 1971
MP 2010-

Respected financial journalist, nicer and saner than his elder brother Boris – with whom he struggles to avoid endless comparisons. Head of Lex Column & Associate Editor of the *Financial Times*, previously South Asia bureau chief. Corporate financier, investment banking division of Deutsche Bank. Married, two children. Education: Balliol College, Oxford (modern history); Institut d'Etudes Europeennes, Universite Libre de Bruxelles; INSEAD (MBA).

David McBride (LD) b. Dec 20, 1973. Teacher. Cllr, Bromley BC (Leader of the Liberal Democrats).

Stephen Morgan (Lab) b. Jun 1, 1977. Cllr, Lambeth BC 2006-.

Constituency
This seat has been reduced and Orpington lies towards the north of the seat. The boundaries stretch south through rural areas to Biggin Hill, home of the air show, stopping short of the M25. Technically in the London borough of Bromley, it is often thought of as Kent. It is well off and more than 90 per cent white British. The seat has been Tory since 1970.

	Electorate	Turnout %	Change from '05 %
	67,732	72.2	☆
Johnson, J C	29,200	59.7	8.5
McBride, D LD	12,000	24.5	-15.9
Morgan, S Lab	4,400	9.0	3.0
Greenhough, M UKIP	1,360	2.8	0.4
Culnane, T BNP	1,241	2.5	
Galloway, T Green	511	1.0	
Snape, C Eng	199	0.4	

50%
Majority 17,200

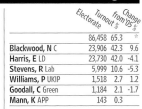

C | LD | Lab

Oxford East

Andrew Smith
b. Feb 1, 1951
MP 1987-

Loyal, competent ally of Gordon Brown, stepped down from Cabinet to concentrate on successful battle to hold seat against Lib Dem challenge. Teased for lacking personality. In opposition, attacked Tory plans to privatise NATS declaring "our air is not for sale", before implementing the sell-off when in government. SoS: Work & Pensions 2002-04. Chief Sec to Treasury 1999-2002. Min: Education/Employment 1997-99. Shadow Sec: Transport 1996-97; Chief Sec Treasury 1994-96. Opp spokes: Education 1988-92; Treasury & econ affairs 1992-96. Oxford/Swindon Co-op Soc relations officer. PC. Married, one son. Ed: St John's College, Oxford.

Steve Goddard (LD) French lecturer, University of Oxford. Cllr, Oxford CC 1996-2002. Contested Oxford East 2001, 2005.
Edward Argar (C) b. 1977. Works for consulting and business services firm. Cllr, Westminster CC.

Constituency
A constituency once defined by Cowley car plant and Blackbird Leys housing estate, and accordingly Labour-leaning, its character has been dramatically changed by the inclusion of Carfax and Holywell wards, which contain the bulk of Oxford's historic centre. The industrial fringe now shares constituency with dreaming spires, punts on the Isis and the students who comprise a fifth of residents and who helped the Lib Dems when in the Oxford West and Abingdon seat.

	Electorate	Turnout %	Change from '05 %
	81,886	63.1	☆
Smith, A Lab	21,938	42.5	6.6
Goddard, S LD	17,357	33.6	-1.6
Argar, E C	9,727	18.8	1.5
Dhall, S Green	1,238	2.4	-2.1
Gasper, J UKIP	1,202	2.3	0.6
O'Sullivan, D SEP	116	0.2	
Crawford, R Parenting	73	0.1	

50%
Majority 4,581

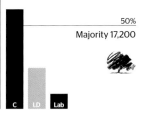

Lab | LD | C

Oxford West & Abingdon

Nicola Blackwood
b. Oct, 1979
MP 2010-

Civil libertarian, classically trained musician. CCHQ volunteer 2005 election. Researcher to Andrew Mitchell MP. Works with Conservative party Human Rights Group. Co-founder, Conservative Party Social Action Project. Adviser to Conservative International Development team. Seasoned volunteer on overseas aid projects. Ed: home-schooled; Trinity Coll of Music (classical singing from age 14); St Anne's Coll, Oxford (Music); Emmanuel Coll, Cambridge (MPhil Musicology); studying for DPhil.

Evan Harris (LD) b. Oct 21, 1965. MP Oxford West and Abingdon 1997-2010.

Richard Stevens (Lab) b. May 3, 1979. Cllr, Oxford West & Abingdon. Solicitor.

Constituency
The seat has lost all but a handful of Oxford colleges, although it retains the smart intellectual areas of Jericho and Summertown. The constituency extends to the large, modern village of Kidlington in the north and to the historic market town of Abingdon in the south. In between lie countryside, farmland and a scattering of affluent villages, such as North and South Hinksey. It was Conservative until 1997 but tactical voting helped the Lib Dems to retain it until 2010.

	Electorate	Turnout %	Change from '05 %
	86,458	65.3	☆
Blackwood, N C	23,906	42.3	9.6
Harris, E LD	23,730	42.0	-4.1
Stevens, R Lab	5,999	10.6	-5.3
Williams, P UKIP	1,518	2.7	1.2
Goodall, C Green	1,184	2.1	-1.7
Mann, K APP	143	0.3	

50%
Majority 176

C | LD | Lab

Paisley & Renfrewshire North

Jim Sheridan
b. Nov 24, 1952
MP 2001-

Adaptable but with left-wing roots. PPS: MoD team 2005-06; resigned over Lebanon conflict. Member, select cttees: Chairmen's Panel 2009-; Internat Devt 2007-09; Public Accounts 2003-05; Broadcasting 2003-05; Information 2001-04. MP for West Renfrewshire 2001-05. Cllr, Renfrewshire 1999-. TGWU convener/stand down official. Print room asst, painter, M/C operator, material handler. Married, one daughter, one son. Ed: St Pius Sec Sch.

Mags MacLaren (SNP) b. 1966. Operations manager, housing charity. Ed: University of Paisley (BA business administraion and IT).

Alistair Campbell (C) Businessman.
Ruaraidh Dobson (LD) b. Apr 18, 1990. Student of microbiology, University of Glasgow. Helped in Katy Gordon's campaign for Glasgow North and Jo Swinson MP's work in East Dunbartonshire. Co-founded Liberal Youth Scotland in 2008.

Constituency
This seat on the north west of Glasgow is based around the town of Paisley, but also takes in a large part of West Renfrewshire. It is a mixed constituency, ranging from Glasgow airport through former industrial areas to the more leafy and affluent edges of Glasgow. Despite the more desirable, suburban fringes, the working-class centre of Paisley still provides the bulk of the electorate, giving Labour its base of support.

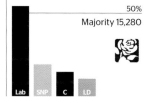

	Electorate	Turnout %	Change from '05 %
	63,704	68.6	
Sheridan, J Lab	23,613	54.0	8.3
MacLaren, M SNP	8,333	19.1	0.3
Campbell, A C	6,381	14.6	1.0
Dobson, R LD	4,597	10.5	-7.7
Pearson, G Ind	550	1.3	
Rollo, C SSP	233	0.5	-1.1

50%
Majority 15,280

Lab SNP C LD

Paisley & Renfrewshire South

Douglas Alexander
b. Oct 26, 1967
MP 1997-

"Wee" Dougie, the baby-faced acolyte of Gordon Brown, blamed for aborted plan for autumn 2007 election. Struggling to escape Brown's embrace and establish his independence. His sister is Wendy Alexander (MSP, Scottish Lab leader 2007-08). SoS: Internat Devt 2007-; Transport and Scotland 2006-07. Min: Europe 2005-06; FCO & DTI 2004-05; Cabinet Office and Duchy of Lancaster 2003-04; Cabinet Office 2002-03; DTI 2001-02. GE campaign co-ordinator 2007-, 1999-2001. Speechwriter/researcher for Gordon Brown MP, 1990. Solicitor, Brodies WS/Digby Brown. Married, one daughter, one son. Ed: Edinburgh; Pennsylvania, USA.

Andy Doig (SNP) Cllr. Previously worked in rehabilitation. Also a licensed Eucharistic assistant within the Scottish Episcopal Church.
Gordon McCaskill (C) Retired police officer. Cllr, East Renfrewshire 2007-2010.
Ashay Ghai (LD) Policy & equality officer in the third sector. Cllr, East Dunbartonshire. Contested Holyrood election, Clydebank & Milngavie 2007.

Constituency
This constituency was modelled on the old Paisley South seat. It is based around the southern part of Paisley, including Paisley University and most of the town centre, but spreads west to Elderslie then out to the rural towns and villages around Kilbarchan and Lochwinnoch. It has a mixed electorate but the Labour vote from the urban areas dominates.

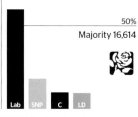

	Electorate	Turnout %	Change from '05 %
	61,197	65.4	
Alexander, D Lab	23,842	59.6	7.1
Doig, A SNP	7,228	18.1	0.6
McCaskill, G C	3,979	10.0	1.5
Ghai, A LD	3,812	9.5	-8.1
Mack, P Ind	513	1.3	0.8
Kerr, J SSP	375	0.9	-1.1
Hendry, W Ind	249	0.6	0.2

50%
Majority 16,614

Lab SNP C LD

Pendle

Andrew Stephenson
b. Feb 17, 1981
MP 2010-

One of the youngest Conservative MPs, selected back in 2006. Campaigned against hospital and healthcare cuts. Cllr, Macclesfield BC 2003-07. Self-employed insurance broker, Stephenson & Threader. Member, Selrap (railway campaign group). National deputy chair, Conservative Future 2001-02. Methodist. Education: Poynton County High School; Royal Holloway (BSc business management).

Gordon Prentice (Lab) b. 1951. MP for Pendle 1992-2010. Member of the Public Administration Select Committee. Ed: University of Glasgow (MA politics and economics).

Afzal Anwar (LD) Barrister. Community representative to the Whitefield Regeneration Partnership. Governor, Ghausia Girls HS.
James Jackman (BNP)

Constituency
Pendle lies in the east of Lancashire, bordering Yorkshire. The main settlements — Brierfield, Nelson and Colne — are grouped around the end of the M65 in the south of the seat. Barnoldswick, in the north, is the home of the Rolls-Royce factory, a major employer. About 30 per cent of the population work in manufacturing. There are pockets of severe deprivation and much of the urban terraced housing stock is unfit to live in, although rural areas toward the Ribble Valley are more affluent. Labour took this seat from the Tories in 1992.

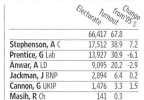

	Electorate	Turnout	Change from '05 %
	66,417	67.8	
Stephenson, A C	17,512	38.9	7.2
Prentice, G Lab	13,927	30.9	-6.1
Anwar, A LD	9,095	20.2	-2.9
Jackman, J BNP	2,894	6.4	0.2
Cannon, G UKIP	1,476	3.3	1.5
Masih, R Ch	141	0.3	

50%
Majority 3,585

C Lab LD BNP

Penistone & Stocksbridge — Labour hold

Angela Smith
b. Aug 16, 1961
MP 2005-

Famously came to brink of resignation over abolition of 10p tax row but persuaded not to. PPS to Yvette Cooper 2005-08. Member, select cttees: Transport 2009-; Court of Referees 2007-; Regulatory Reform 2005-07. MP Sheffield Hillsborough 2005-2010. Cllr, Sheffield City (cabinet member for education). Unison. Sheffield First for Learning & Work. Married, one stepdaughter, one stepson. Ed: Toll Bar Sch; Nottingham (BA English studies); Newnham Coll, Cambridge (PhD).

Spencer Pitfield (C) Teacher at Birkdale School, Sheffield. A local magistrate for seven years sitting on the Sheffield Bench. Ed: Sheffield University (PhD in British clarinet and piano music).
Ian Cuthbertson (LD) Consultant and company director. Ed: Bradford Grammar School; University of Bradford (computing).

Constituency
Straddling the border between the borough of Barnsley in the north and Sheffield district in the south, this new seat is named after two small towns amid large areas of the rural Pennines to the west. While livestock farms cover much of the land, many residents are affluent commuters. The seat is bounded by the M1 at the east and Ecclesfield lies at the southeastern corner, on the outskirts of Sheffield. The predecessor seats in this area were both Labour.

	Electorate	Turnout %	Change from 05 %
	68,501	67.9	☆
Smith, A Lab	17,565	37.8	-7.4
Pitfield, S C	14,516	31.2	7.5
Cuthbertson, I LD	9,800	21.1	-3.7
James, P BNP	2,207	4.7	
French, G UKIP	1,936	4.2	2.5
McEnhill, P Eng	492	1.1	

50%
Majority 3,049

Penrith & The Border — Conservative hold

Rory Stewart
b. Jan 3, 1973
MP 2010-

Eccentric but brilliant former soldier, diplomat, award-winning author and Harvard professor. Charismatic, polite and engaging. Unideological. Whips' nightmare. Former Labour supporter. Officer, Black Watch. Diplomat, Indonesia/Montenegro. Coalition Deputy Governor of two Iraqi provinces. Walked 6,000 miles including through Afghanistan. Founded Turquoise Mountain (NGO in Afghanistan). Professor & Director of Carr Center for Human Rights, Harvard University. Episcopalian. Privately tutored Princes William and Harry. OBE. Education: Eton; Balliol College, Oxford (history & PPE).

Peter Thornton (LD) b. 1951. Photographer and caterer. Cllr.
Barbara Cannon (Lab) b. Oct 25, 1954. Cllr, Cumbria CC. Former chair of Northumbria Health Authority Trust.

Constituency
This huge Cumbrian seat stretches from the edge of the Yorkshire Dales to the border with Scotland, skirting around Carlisle. In the west lies Wigton and some of the Lake District National Park. In the centre is the Eden Valley, with the main market town of Penrith sitting astride the M6. In the east are the Pennines, including Alston, England's highest market town. Tourism is a key industry but agriculture — especially sheep and dairy farming — dominates the economy, employing about 10 per cent of residents. It is a solidly Conservative seat.

	Electorate	Turnout %	Change from 05 %
	64,548	69.9	☆
Stewart, R C	24,071	53.4	2.0
Thornton, P LD	12,830	28.5	2.7
Cannon, B Lab	5,834	12.9	-6.1
Stanyer, J UKIP	1,259	2.8	0.3
Davidson, C BNP	1,093	2.4	

50%
Majority 11,241

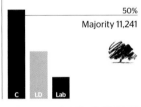

Perth and Perthshire North — SNP hold

Pete Wishart
b. Mar 9, 1962
MP 2001-

Attention-seeking but hard-working. Plays keyboard in MP's rock band, MP4. SNP Chief Whip 2001-07. SNP spokesman: CMS 2001-; Constitution 2005-07; Overseas aid 2005-07; Home, Justice, International Development 2007-; Transport, Rural Affairs 2001-05. MP North Tayside 2001-05. Member, national council/ NEC. Executive vice-convener fundraising SNP. Musician (Big Country, Runrig). Musicians Union. Community worker. Scotland against drugs campaign cttee. Married but separated, one son. Education: Queen Anne High School, Dunfermline; Moray House College of Education (Dip CommEd).

Peter Lyburn (C) Worked for a recycling and environmental consultancy business. Contested Dunfermline West 2007.
Jamie Glackin (Lab) b. Sep 18, 1972. Company director of renewable energy consultants.
Peter Barrett (LD) Cllr, Perth 2007-.

Constituency
This is a huge rural constituency in the centre of the map of Scotland. It is bordered by the Grampian mountains in the north west, the Tay Estuary and the edges of Dundee in the east and Perth in the south. In rural Perthshire, it contains some of the most beautiful "lochs and glens" countryside in Scotland. The Tories and the SNP vie for control in these areas, while Labour and the Liberal Democrats have strong pockets of support in Perth.

	Electorate	Turnout %	Change from 05 %
	72,141	66.9	☆
Wishart, P SNP	19,118	39.6	6.0
Lyburn, P C	14,739	30.5	0.2
Glackin, J Lab	7,923	16.4	-2.3
Barrett, P LD	5,954	12.3	-3.8
Taylor, D Trust	534	1.1	

50%
Majority 4,379

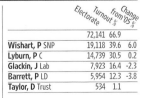

Peterborough Conservative hold

Stewart Jackson
b. Mar 13, 1965
MP 2005-

Unremarkable. Overlooked in first coalition government. Shadow Minister, Communities and Local Government 2008-10. Opposition whip 2007-08. Bank manager, Lloyds TSB, and various business roles inc. Aztec Training and Enterprise Council, Business Link for London. Married, one daughter. Education: London Nautical School; Chatham House Grammar School; Royal Holloway College (BA economics); Thames Valley University (MA human resources management).

Ed Murphy (Lab) b. Mar 13, 1961. Director of local charity, former housing adviser. Ed: Essex University.
Nick Sandford (LD) Cllr, Peterborough CC 1996- (leader of LD group). Works for the Woodland Trust in Grantham. Education: MA (Hons) natural sciences, Oxford University.
Frances Fox (UKIP)

Constituency
This constituency includes the parts of the city north of the River Nene, with the cathedral at its centre. It has also been extended to include two rural wards to the north east. Rows of Victorian terraced houses in Central ward are home to a significant Pakistani community, while Bretton in the west is dominated by council estates. The city is low-waged, low-skilled and has patches of severe deprivation. A £1 billion regeneration programme, Opportunity Peterborough, began in 2005. The seat was redrawn before the 1997 election, pushing Labour to victory, but the Tories won it back in 2005.

	Electorate	Turnout %	Change from '05 %
	70,316	63.9	☆
Jackson, S C	18,133	40.4	-2.9
Murphy, E Lab	13,272	29.5	-4.8
Sandford, N LD	8,816	19.6	2.9
Fox, F UKIP	3,007	6.7	3.5
King, R Eng	770	1.7	
Radic, F Green	523	1.2	
Swallow, J Ind	406	0.9	

50%
Majority 4,861

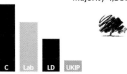

Plymouth Moor View Labour hold

Alison Seabeck
b. Feb 20, 1954
MP 2005-

Very low profile, interested in local government. PPS to Geoff Hoon 2008-09, 2006-07. Assistant government whip 2007-08. Member/official Amicus-MSF. Fawcett Society. Labour Women's Network. Parliamentary adviser to Nick Raynsford. MP 1992-2005. Parly assistant to Lord Hattersley as Shad Home Sec. Unite. Divorced. Two daughters. Education: Harold Hill GS; NE London Poly (gen studies).

Matthew Groves (C) Lawyer. Cllr, Tanbridge. Education: St. Bedes Secondary School.
Stuart Bonar (LD) Public affairs officer. Education: Devonport High School for Boys; Royal Holloway, University of London, (BA modern history, economic history & politics); Birkbeck College, University of London (MSc American politics).
Bill Wakeham (UKIP)

Constituency
The seat retains the bulk of the old Plymouth Devonport constituency but has been renamed after the eastern Moor View ward since the loss of Devonport, with its naval base. Large housing estates and maritime-related industries define the constituency, whose traditional fisheries and military economies have been in long-term decline. Unemployment levels are some of the highest in the region and the constituency has been Labour since 1992, when the former Social Democrat leader David Owen, who had held the seat for 18 years, stood down.

	Electorate	Turnout %	Change from '05 %
	67,261	61.7	☆
Seabeck, A Lab	15,433	37.2	-7.2
Groves, M C	13,845	33.3	8.3
Bonar, S LD	7,016	16.9	-2.1
Wakeham, B UKIP	3,188	7.7	0.0
Cook, R BNP	1,438	3.5	
Miller, W Green	398	1.0	
Marchesi, D Soc	208	0.5	

50%
Majority 1,588

Plymouth Sutton & Devonport Conservative gain

Oliver Colvile
b. Aug 26, 1959
MP 2010-

Affable, straightforward communications consultant from a naval family. Made it third time lucky to take the seat (contested Plymouth Sutton 2005, 2001). Dir, Polity Communications. Proprietor, Oliver Colvile & Associates. Account Dir of a division, Saatchi & Saatchi. Company director. Conservative Party agent. Member, Federation Vice-Pres, Plymouth Cricket Club; Plymouth Albion Rugby Club. Ed: Stowe Sch, Buckingham.

Linda Gilroy (Lab Co-op) b. Jul 19, 1949. MP for Plymouth Sutton from 1997-2010. PPS to Min for Local Govt and Regions 2001-05 and Min for Science 2008-09. Assnt to Regional Minister for South West 2009-10.
Judy Evans (LD) Doctor.
Andrew Leigh (UKIP) b. Jan 1, 1964. Chartered financial planner.

Constituency
The seat takes in Plymouth's modern centre and touristy waterfront, from whose Mayflower Steps the Pilgrim Fathers sailed for America. Redrawn, it includes Devonport dockyard, home to Europe's largest naval base and responsible for 10 per cent of the city's income. The Labour Government repeatedly insisted that the dockyard, which directly or indirectly supports 24,000 jobs, was secure, despite persistent closure rumours. Residential wards vary from the more affluent Stoke and Compton to the housing estates of Efford. Under varying boundaries, the seat was Tory before Labour took it in 1997.

	Electorate	Turnout %	Change from '05 %
	71,035	61.8	☆
Colvile, O C	15,050	34.3	4.7
Gilroy, L Lab	13,901	31.7	-9.0
Evans, J LD	10,829	24.7	2.1
Leigh, A UKIP	2,854	6.5	-0.1
Brown, N Green	904	2.1	
Gerrish, B Ind	233	0.5	
Hawkins, R Soc	123	0.3	

50%
Majority 1,149

237

Pontypridd — Labour hold

Owen Smith
b. May 2, 1970
MP 2010-

Interested in urban regeneration and welfare reform. Contested Blaenau Gwent by-election 2006. BBC producer with Radio 4 *Today* programme. Special adviser to Paul Murphy as Sec of State for Wales and Northern Ireland. Director, Amgen (world's largest biotech company). Son of Prof Dai Smith, Welsh Arts Council chair and close friend of outgoing MP Kim Howells. Member, Unite. Cites Jean Jaures among political heroes. Local man, Pontypridd RFC fan. Enjoys fishing. Married, two sons, one daughter. Education: Coed-y-Lan Comp, Pontypridd; Sussex Uni (history and French).

Michael Powell (LD) Self-employed heating and plumbing engineer. Cllr. **Lee Gonzalez** (C) b. Aug 21, 1981. Research fellow, Cardiff University 2010-. **Ioan Bellin** (PC) Press and communications officer for Assembly members.

Constituency
To the north west of Cardiff, this seat has numerous small towns lining the A-roads that criss-cross it. These include Llantrisant, Pontyclun and Beddau in the south, and Church Village and Ponrypridd in Taff Vale in the north east. These areas were once mining towns and the seat retains a manufacturing presence. It is home to a large middle-class population, a strong service sector and a popular university, which attracts adult learners. The seat has been reduced under boundary changes but the remaining area has a strong Labour tradition.

	Electorate	Turnout %	Change from '05 %
	58,219	63.0	*
Smith, O Lab	14,226	38.8	-15.4
Powell, M LD	11,435	31.2	11.2
Gonzalez, L C	5,932	16.2	4.6
Bellin, I PC	2,673	7.3	-3.7
Bevan, D UKIP	1,229	3.4	0.8
Parsons, S Soc	456	1.2	
Watson, D Ch	365	1.0	
Matthews, J Green	361	1.0	

50%
Majority 2,791

| Lab | LD | C | PC |

Poole — Conservative hold

Robert Syms
b. Aug 15, 1956
MP 1997-

Uncharismatic member of Tory Right, active constituency MP. Shad Min: Local Govt Affairs/Communities 2005-07; Local/Devolved Gov't Affairs 2003-05. Opp Whip 2003. Vice-Chair Con Party 2001-03. Opp. spokes 1999-2001. PPS to Michael Ancram 1999-2000. Cllr, N Wilts Dist 1983-87, Wilts County 1985-87. Ran family haulage and plant hire business. Fellow, Chartered Institute of Building. Divorced, remarried but separated. One daughter, one son. Education: Colston's School, Bristol.

Philip Eades (LD) Licensee. Cllr, Poole 2003-. Education: BA(Hons) business studies.

Jason Sanderson (Lab) b. Nov 27, 1955. Retired lecturer. Former cllr, Poole. Education: Cardiff University.

Constituency
Poole town centre runs from the quay, where old merchant houses adjoin modern buildings, to the Dolphin shopping centre. Alongside commerce and the marine industry – Poole is home to the Special Boat Service – are large residential areas of varied character. Sandbanks, at the entrance to the world's second-largest natural harbour, was recently valued as the world's fourth most expensive property area. The constituency has lost Branksome East ward but gains Creekmoor. Regeneration is due, with planned construction of the Twin Sails Bridge. The seat has been Tory since 1950.

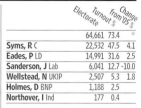

	Electorate	Turnout %	Change from '05 %
	64,661	73.4	*
Syms, R C	22,532	47.5	4.1
Eades, P LD	14,991	31.6	2.5
Sanderson, J Lab	6,041	12.7	-10.0
Wellstead, N UKIP	2,507	5.3	4.4
Holmes, D BNP	1,188	2.5	
Northover, I Ind	177	0.4	

50%
Majority 7,541

| C | LD | Lab | UKIP |

Poplar & Limehouse — Labour hold

Jim Fitzpatrick
b. Apr 4, 1952
MP 1997-

Genial Scotsman. Notorious for walking out of a Muslim wedding because of segregation from wife. Min: DEFRA 2009-10. Parly Under-Sec: Transport 2007-09; T&I 2006-07; ODPM 2005-06. Parliamentary private secretary to Alan Milburn 1999-2001. Whip: govt 2002-05; asst govt 2001-02. Mem, committee: Selection 2003. London Lab Exec/Chair Greater London Lab Party 1991-2000. Hon Treas London Lab MPs reg group. Firefighter, driver, trainee; fire brigade long service and good conduct medal. Fire Brigades Union NEC. GPMU. Divorced, remarried. One daughter, one son from first marriage. Education: Holyrood Senior School.

Tim Archer (C) b. 1974. Associate of the Institute of Financial Services. Former Cllr, Tower Hamlets. **George Galloway** (Respect) b. Aug 16, 1954. MP Bethnal Green/Bow 2005-10. **Jonathan Fryer** (LD) b. Jun 5, 1950. Writer, lecturer and broadcaster.

Constituency
Poplar used to be twinned with Canning Town, to the east, but has been cut back, gaining a much smaller area to the west, extending as far as St Katharine Docks and the News International base at Wapping. The south of the seat follows the Thames through Shadwell to Limehouse, which includes the most deprived area in London. Just a short way southeast is Canary Wharf. To the south the seat includes the Isle of Dogs and north it reaches to Bromley-by-Bow, which has high levels of social housing. Labour has historically been strong here.

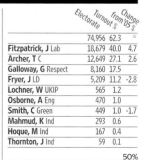

	Electorate	Turnout %	Change from '05 %
	74,956	62.3	*
Fitzpatrick, J Lab	18,679	40.0	4.7
Archer, T C	12,649	27.1	2.6
Galloway, G Respect	8,160	17.5	
Fryer, J LD	5,209	11.2	-2.8
Lochner, W UKIP	565	1.2	
Osborne, A Eng	470	1.0	
Smith, C Green	449	1.0	-1.7
Mahmud, K Ind	293	0.6	
Hoque, M Ind	167	0.4	
Thornton, J Ind	59	0.1	

50%
Majority 6,030

| Lab | C | Res | LD |

Portsmouth North
Conservative gain

Penny Mordaunt
b. Mar 4, 1973
MP 2010-

One-time magician's assistant turned corporate comms director and healthcare specialist. Contested Portsmouth North 2005. Con Party Head of Youth (under Major), Head of Broadcasting (under Hague). Chief of Staff to David Willets 2005. Head of foreign press to George Bush in 2000 presidential election. Healthcare consultant. Centre for Social Justice commission for older people. Dir, Diabetes UK. Associate, Hanover Comms. Media Intelligence Partners. Created Veterans Reunited. Comms dir: National Lottery; Freight Transport Assn; Kensington & Chelsea BC. Royal Navy reservist. Fellow, RSA. Mem, British Astronomical Assn. Asst to former

Magic Circle pres Will Ayling. Ed: Oaklands RC Comp; Reading Uni.

Sarah McCarthy-Fry (Lab Co-op) b. 1955. MP for Portsmouth North 2005-10. Exchequer Sec to Treasury 2009-10. **Darren Sanders** (LD) Account manager. Former cllr.

Constituency
Covers the northern part of Portsea Island; rows upon rows of terraced houses in North End, and warehouses and council estates in Hilsea. Also a stretch of mainland with sharp contrast between severely deprived working-class areas in Paulsgrove and Wymering and parts of Cosham in the west, and far more affluent Drayton and Farlington in the east. Taken by Labour in 1997 after 18 years of Tory representation, the seat has undergone slight boundary changes, adding further Tory-leaning areas.

	Electorate	Turnout %	Change from '05 %
	70,329	62.7	☆
Mordaunt, P C	19,533	44.3	6.5
McCarthy-Fry, S Lab	12,244	27.8	-10.8
Sanders, D LD	8,874	20.1	-0.2
Fitzgerald, M UKIP	1,812	4.1	0.7
Knight, D Eng	1,040	2.4	
Maclennan, I Green	461	1.0	
Tosh, M TUSC	154	0.4	

50%
Majority 7,289

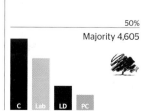

Portsmouth South
Liberal Democrat hold

Mike Hancock
b. Apr 9, 1946
MP 1997-; 1984-87

Populist survivor from SDP era. LD spokes Planning 2000-10; Defence 1997-99. Member, select cttees: Chairmen's Panel 2000-10; Defence 1999-10; Public Admin 1997-99. MP SDP 1984-87. Member: Soc Dem Party 1981-87; Lab Party 1968-81. Council of Europe, Western European Union, NATO. Cllr, Hants CC 1973-97 (leader 1993-97); Portsmouth CC 1971. Dir, BBC daytime. Mencap district officer. Vice-Chair, Portsmouth Docks. CBE. Married, one daughter, one son. Ed: Copnor & Portsea Sch.

Flick Drummond (C) b. 1962. Former insurance broker, OFSTED inspector and cllr, Winchester cllr. Contested

Southampton Itchen 2005.
John Ferrett (Lab) b. Aug 21, 1965. TU official, chief immigration officer.

Constituency
The southern half of Portsea Island includes Portsmouth city centre, undergoing a £350 million redevelopment, and the historic dockyard, home to the Royal Navy – a huge employer – and the Mary Rose. The most densely populated city beyond inner London, the largely residential south east of the seat is almost entirely comprised of terraced housing. The western half near Portsmouth Harbour and docks is significantly more deprived than the east, which enjoys a seafront and beach at the mouth of Langstone Harbour. Mike Hancock held this as SDP MP for 1984-87, after a by-election, and regained it from the Tories as a Liberal Democrat in 1997.

	Electorate	Turnout %	Change from '05 %
	70,242	58.8	☆
Hancock, M LD	18,921	45.9	4.2
Drummond, F C	13,721	33.3	-0.4
Ferrett, J Lab	5,640	13.7	-8.7
Martin, C UKIP	876	2.1	-0.2
Crompton, G BNP	873	2.1	
Dawes, T Green	716	1.7	
DuCane, I Eng	400	1.0	
Cummings, L J&AC	117.0	0.28	

50%
Majority 5,200

Preseli Pembrokeshire
Conservative hold

Stephen Crabb
b. Jan 20, 1973
MP 2005-

Quiet, solid, local man, contested the same seat in 2001. Asst Govt whip 2010-. Opposition whip (2009-10) and could rise in the Whips Office. Interested energy policy, human rights; Election Observer OSCE Bosnia-Herzegovina 1998. Chair: North Southwark and Bermondsey Conservative Assn (1998-2000). Policy and Campaigns manager, London Chamber of Commerce. Marketing consultant. Marathon runner. Married, one daughter, one son. Ed: Tasker Milward Vice-Chair Sch, Haverfordwest; Bristol (pol); London Business Sch (MBA).

Mari Rees (Lab) b. Aug 29, 1959. Ed: St David's Ursuline Convent.

Nick Tregoning (LD) b. Feb 2, 1952. Cllr, Swansea,
Henry Jones-Davies (PC) b. 1949. Publisher of *Cambria – The National Magazine of Wales.*

Constituency
This large rural seat boasts a stunning coastline, encompassing the Pembrokeshire Coast National Park around St Brides Bay and into Cardigan Bay. The western half of the seat is particularly anglicised and the influx of people with second homes from South Wales and England to towns such as St David's, Goodwick and Fishguard has led to this area being dubbed the "New North Cornwall". Milford Haven is the site of large oil refineries. Inland, the main town is Haverfordwest. The seat returned Labour MPs for two terms after its creation in 1997, but it was narrowly won by the Tories in 2005.

	Electorate	Turnout %	Change from '05 %
	57,419	69.0	☆
Crabb, S C	16,944	42.8	6.4
Rees, M Lab	12,339	31.2	-3.7
Tregoning, N LD	5,759	14.5	1.5
Jones-Davies, H PC	3,654	9.2	-3.3
Lawson, R UKIP	906	2.3	1.0

50%
Majority 4,605

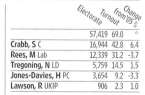

Preston — Labour Co-operative hold

Mark Hendrick
b. Nov 2, 1958
MP 2000-

Parliamentary private secretary to: Ivan Lewis 2009-; Jack Straw 2007-08; Margaret Beckett 2003-07. Member, committees: International Dev't 2009-; European Scrutiny 2001-04. MEP Lancs Central 1994-99. Cllr, Salford CC 1987-95. Member, Co-operative party. Member, GMB. Engineer/lecturer. Married. Education: Salford GS; Liverpool Poly (BSc electrical & electronic engineering); Manchester (MSc computer science, Cert Ed); Volkshochschule, Hanau (Germany).

Mark Jewell (LD) b. Aug 5, 1964. Project manager. Cllr, Preston CC. Education: Thames Polytechnic BSc (Hons) mechanical engineering; postgraduate diploma engineering management (DipEM).
Nerissa Warner-O'Neill (C) b. 1977. Councillor, Waverley. Former lawyer. Education: Durham University (LL.B Law).

Constituency
Preston is at the heart of Lancashire and this seat contains all but its northern residential suburbs. The University of Central Lancashire is based here with 32,000 students and 3,000 staff skewing the seat's demographic and contributing to a science sector of the economy. The city has significant areas of deprivation, with St Matthew's and Deepdale wards among the worst 10 per cent nationwide. Booths supermarkets has its headquarters in Ribbleton, in the north east of the seat. It has been Labour since its creation in 1983.

		Electorate	Turnout %	from '05 %	Change
		62,460	52.0	☆	
Hendrick, M	Lab	15,668	48.2	-0.4	
Jewell, M	LD	7,935	24.4	4.6	
Warner-O'Neill, N	C	7,060	21.7	0.7	
Muirhead, R	UKIP	1,462	4.5	1.7	
Ambroze, G	Ch	272	0.8		
Tayya, K	Ind	108	0.3		

50%
Majority 7,733

Pudsey — Conservative gain

Stuart Andrew
b. Nov 25, 1971
MP 2010-

Experienced charity fundraiser. Cllr, Leeds CC 2003-. Contested Wrexham 1997. Spent early years in Llanfairpwllgwyngyllgogerychwyrndrobwllllantysiliogogogoch. Fundraising manager, Martin House Children's Hospice. Member, Institute of Fundraisers. Previously: East Lancashire Hospice; Hope House Children's Hospice; British Heart Foundation. Has long-term partner. Ed: Ysgol David Hughes, Menai Bridge Anglesey.

Jamie Hanley (Lab) b. Nov 14, 1973. Lawyer. Ed: Hull University
Jamie Matthews (LD) b. May 11, 1984. Cllr, Leeds 2008-. Ed: Cardiff University (European politics).

Constituency
Pudsey town lies in the south of this seat, which is popular with commuters and is sandwiched between Leeds and Bradford. In the north are Calverley, Horsforth, a Domesday Book settlement that became Britain's largest village in the late 19th century, and the town of Guiseley, home to the original Harry Ramsden's fish and chip shop. Affluence varies from prosperous, semi-rural areas to aspirational urban communities. The constituency was Conservative from 1922 until a dramatic win by Labour in 1997.

		Electorate	Turnout %	from '05 %	Change
		69,257	70.9	☆	
Andrew, S	C	18,874	38.5	4.8	
Hanley, J	Lab	17,215	35.1	-10.3	
Matthews, J	LD	10,224	20.8	2.7	
Gibson, I	BNP	1,549	3.2		
Dews, D	UKIP	1,221	2.5	-0.3	

50%
Majority 1,659

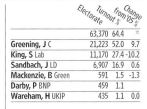

Putney — Conservative hold

Justine Greening
b. Apr 30, 1969
MP 2005-

Smiling face of the modest Conservative gains on 2005 election night. Has worked hard to develop her skills on the front bench as a combative performer. Very serious. A rising star whose ordinary manner may be a political asset. Economic Secretary to the Treasury 2010-. Shadow Minister: Communities & Local Government 2009-10; Treasury 2007-09. Bow Group member, former officer. Sales/business/finance manager, Centrica, GSK, SmithKline Beecham. Auditor, PWC. Education: Oakwood Comprehensive, Rotherham; Southampton (business economics & accounting); London Business School (MBA).

Stuart King (Lab) b. Dec 27, 1970. Events organiser. Education: Nottingham University.
James Sandbach (LD) Policy officer, Citizens Advice. Contested Castle Point 2005. Ed: University of St Andrews, University of London, University of Westminster, BPP Law School, City University, Inns of Court.

Constituency
The sought-after Putney area lies along a small stretch of river in the west of Wandsworth and is home to many professionals. Roehampton, farther west, has its own university. The A3 cuts through the seat; at its south is Putney Heath and Southfields, reaching down to the top of Wimbledon Park. This seat is less ethnically diverse than the London average, at 84 per cent white. It was won by Labour in 1997, but retaken by the Tories in 2005.

		Electorate	Turnout %	from '05 %	Change
		63,370	64.4	☆	
Greening, J	C	21,223	52.0	9.7	
King, S	Lab	11,170	27.4	-10.2	
Sandbach, J	LD	6,907	16.9	0.6	
Mackenzie, B	Green	591	1.5	-1.3	
Darby, P	BNP	459	1.1		
Wareham, H	UKIP	435	1.1	0.0	

50%
Majority 10,053

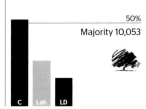

Mark Francois
b. Aug 14, 1965
MP 2001-

Quiet and unassuming. Staunchly Eurosceptic, lost out on preferred brief in coalition deal. Govt whip (Vice-Chamberlain of HM Household) 2010-. Shadow Minister for Europe 2007-10 (Shadow Cabinet 2009-10); Shadow: Paymaster General 2005-07, Economic Secretary to the Treasury 2004-05; Opposition whip 2002-04. Infantry officer in TA. Public affairs consultant. Divorced. Education: St. Nicholas Comprehensive School, Basildon; Bristol (BA history); King's College, London (MA war studies).

Susan Gaszczak (LD) Cllr. Founder member of the Richmond Youth and Students branch.

Michael Le-Surf (Lab) b. Mar 14, 1964. Works in healthcare with people with learning disabilities.

Constituency
The Crouch and Roach rivers frame the east of this seat, from which the old Rayleigh seat extended to the southern boundaries of Chelmsford. It has lost that area and instead extends due west to Wickford, from the old Billericay seat. Wickford is undergoing regeneration through the Thames Gateway project. Most of this seat is fairly affluent and drawn from the Rochford district, including the market town of Rayleigh and villages such as Hawkwell and Hockley amid pretty countryside. Predecessor seats were Tory.

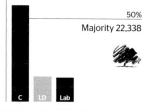

	Electorate	Turnout %	Change from 05 %
	75,905	69.0	☆
Francois, M C	30,257	57.8	3.9
Gaszczak, S LD	7,919	15.1	-0.3
Le-Surf, M Lab	7,577	14.5	-12.0
Hayter, J Eng	2,219	4.2	
Callaghan, T UKIP	2,211	4.2	0.1
Evennett, A BNP	2,160	4.1	

50%
Majority 22,338

C   LD   Lab

Rob Wilson
b. Jan 2, 1965
MP 2005-

The first MP selected by an open primary, keen advocate of consultative politics that reaches beyond his party. Opp whip 2009-10. Shadow Min: Higher Ed 2007-09. Cllr, Reading Bor 2003-06; 1992-96. Contested Carmarthen West & Pembrokeshire South 2001 and Bolton NE 1997. Conservative Campaign manager Reading East 1992. Entrepreneur health/comms. Adviser to David Davis MP. Married, four children. Education: Wallingford Sch; Reading (BA history).

Gareth Epps (LD) Community relations manager. Education: Magdalen College School, Oxford; University of Manchester (BA (Hons) modern

languages, MA European politics & Policy).
Anneliese Dodds (Lab) b. Mar 16, 1978. Lecturer and researcher. Education: Oxford University.

Constituency
From Reading town centre, dominated by the huge Oracle shopping and leisure complex, the seat stretches out in three arms: north to Caversham; south to part of the less affluent Whitley; and east to Woodley. Part of the increasingly popular University of Reading lies in this constituency and much of the student population lives here. Otherwise, demographics are skewed toward professionals and the non-white population, which is above national average, in particular those of Pakistani origin. Labour overturned decades of Tory representation in 1997 but lost in 2005.

	Electorate	Turnout %	Change from 05 %
	74,922	66.7	☆
Wilson, R C	21,269	42.6	6.9
Epps, G LD	13,664	27.3	3.0
Dodds, A Lab	12,729	25.5	-8.5
Pitfield, A UKIP	1,086	2.2	0.2
White, R Green	1,069	2.1	-1.4
Lloyd, J Ind	111	0.2	
Turberville, M Ind	57	0.1	

50%
Majority 7,605

C   LD   Lab

Alok Sharma
b. Sep 7, 1967
MP 2010-

Selected for the first seat he applied for. Worked as chartered accountant, company auditor, consultant and tutor. Ran own business. Reticent to disclose further details of career history. Former chair, Bow Group's economic affairs committee. Fellow, Royal Society for the encouragement of Arts, Manufacturing and Commerce. Enjoys cycling and walking. Married, two daughters. Ed: Reading Blue Coat Sch; Salford (Bsc Hons applied physics with electronics).

Naz Sarkar (Lab) b. Dec 12, 1975. Teacher. Education: Bristol University.
Daisy Benson (LD) Cllr, Reading BC 2006-. Education: Edinburgh

University, (MA English Literature and Politics).

Constituency
From just beyond the town centre, this Berkshire seat stretches out west through suburbs such as Southcote and Calcot before reaching the increasingly rural Tilehurst and Purley-on-Thames. Beyond the conurbation the seat includes the affluent countryside around picturesque Pangbourne, by the Thames, which forms the northern boundary. To the south is an industrial area including sewage works and rugby and football stadiums. Reading has areas of some deprivation and relatively high numbers of working classes but the middle classes predominate. The seat was a surprise win for Labour in 1997 after years of Tory representation.

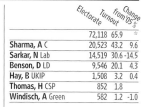
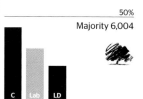

	Electorate	Turnout %	Change from 05 %
	72,118	65.9	☆
Sharma, A C	20,523	43.2	9.6
Sarkar, N Lab	14,519	30.6	-14.5
Benson, D LD	9,546	20.1	4.3
Hay, B UKIP	1,508	3.2	0.4
Thomas, H CSP	852	1.8	
Windisch, A Green	582	1.2	-1.0

50%
Majority 6,004

C   Lab   LD

Redcar — Liberal Democrat gain

Ian Swales
b. Apr 5, 1953
MP 2010-

Long-term Redcar resident and party member since SDP days. Contested Redcar 2005. Founded own training/consultancy business. ICI career – financial and business management roles, rising to global head of leadership development. Previously Yorkshire Electricity. Married, One daughter, two sons. Education: Ashville Coll, Harrogate; UMIST (BSc chemical engineering).

Vera Baird (Lab) b. Feb 13, 1951. MP for Redcar 2001-10. Solicitor General, 2007-10. Parly Under-Sec, Constitutional Affairs 2006-07. QC. Education: Chadderton Grammar School; Northumbria University (law).

Steve Mastin (C) Teacher. NUT local executive branch member. Education: St Andrew's University; Cambridge University.

Constituency

From Redcar and Marske-by-the-Sea, the constituency reaches inland to the fringes of Middlesbrough. Bordered by the Tees to the north, an expanse of land by the river is dominated by heavy industrial works sites, much of it vacant after extensive redundancies from Corus steel in 2009. This devastated the economy and compounded deprivation that was already severe in pockets of the town and the area around South Bank and Skippers Lane industrial estate. The seat has been Labour since its inception in 1974.

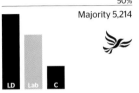

	Electorate	Turnout %	Change from '05 %
	67,125	62.5	
Swales, I LD	18,955	45.2	25.0
Baird, V Lab	13,741	32.8	-18.6
Mastin, S C	5,790	13.8	-4.0
Bulmer, M UKIP	1,875	4.5	3.0
Broughton, K BNP	1,475	3.5	1.0
Walter, H TUSC	127	0.3	

50%

Majority 5,214

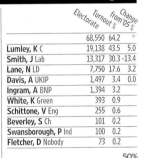

Redditch — Conservative gain

Karen Lumley
b. Mar 28, 1964
MP 2010-

A TV regular from the outset of Jacqui Smith's expenses trauma. Interested in education. Cllr: Redditch BC 2001-03; Clwyd CC 1993-96; Wrexham BC 1991-96. Contested Redditch 2005, 2001; Delyn 1997. Deputy Chair, Welsh Conservative Party. Company secretary, RKL Geological Services. Assistant act John Bull Group. Trainee accountant, Ford Motor Company. Trainer, Westminster Foundation for Democracy. Enjoys knitting. CofE. Married, one daughter, one son. Education: Rugby High School for Girls.

Jacqui Smith (Lab) b. Nov 3, 1962. MP for Redditch, 1997-2010. Home Sec 2007-09. Chief Whip 2006-07, Min for

Mental Health/Industry/Schools 2001-06. Ed: Hertford Coll, Oxford (PPE).
Nicholas Lane (LD) b. Jul 10, 1983. Barrister. Researcher to Norman Baker MP. Ed: Bristol Uni; KCL; Coll of Law.

Constituency

This Worcestershire seat lies 15 miles south of the West Midlands conurbation. The population is concentrated in Redditch, in the north east of the seat, which was designated a New Town in 1964 to accommodate overspill from Birmingham. There are areas of deprivation around the town centre, but the boundaries encompass a more affluent rural area in the south. The large Inkberrow ward has been slightly extended under boundary changes. The seat was won on its creation in 1997 by Jacqui Smith, whose expenses and troubled stint as Home Secretary led to a predictable defeat.

	Electorate	Turnout %	Change from '05 %
	68,550	64.2	☆
Lumley, K C	19,138	43.5	5.0
Smith, J Lab	13,317	30.3	-13.4
Lane, N LD	7,750	17.6	3.2
Davis, A UKIP	1,497	3.4	0.0
Ingram, A BNP	1,394	3.2	
White, K Green	393	0.9	
Schittone, V Eng	255	0.6	
Beverley, S Ch	101	0.2	
Swansborough, P Ind	100	0.2	
Fletcher, D Nobody	73	0.2	

50%

Majority 5,821

Reigate — Conservative hold

Crispin Blunt
b. Jul 15, 1960
MP 1997-

One Nation Tory from a military background, knowledgeable on defence issues (served 1979-1990, rising to Captain). Miscalculated by quitting as Shadow Trade and Industry Minister (2002-03) in first, unsuccessful, attempt to topple Iain Duncan Smith, returned to frontbench under Howard. Parly Under-Sec: Justice 2010-. Shadow Minister: National Security 2009-10. Opposition Whip 2004-09. Forum of Private Business representative, political consultant, special adviser to Malcolm Rifkind 1993-97. Married, one daughter, one son. Ed: Wellington Coll; RMA Sandhurst; University Coll, Durham (BA politics); Cranfield Institute of Technology (MBA).

Jane Kulka (LD) Finance manager, RNIB Redhill College. Former Reigate councillor. Ed: De-Burgh Secondary School, Tadworth and NESCOT, Ewell.
Robert Hull (Lab) b. Jan 25, 1956. Works in PC Support (IT.) Education: Thomas Bennett Community College.

Constituency

Bisected by a designated Area of Outstanding Natural Beauty and the M25, the constituency includes the neighbouring towns of Reigate and Redhill to the south and Banstead village to the north. About 70 per cent is green belt which, combined with population growth well above the national average, makes demand for housing a key issue. This is commuter-belt territory and is a junior member of the financial services satellite towns. It has returned a Tory MP in every election since 1945.

	Electorate	Turnout %	Change from '05 %
	71,604	69.8	☆
Blunt, C C	26,688	53.4	4.8
Kulka, J LD	13,097	26.2	3.1
Hull, R Lab	5,672	11.4	-10.2
Fox, J UKIP	2,089	4.2	-0.3
Brown, K BNP	1,345	2.7	
Essex, J Green	1,087	2.2	

50%

Majority 13,591

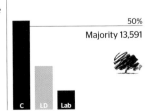

Jim Murphy
b. Aug 23, 1967
MP 1997-

Easygoing manner but good political touch with proven ministerial record. Received credit for Labour performance in Scotland in 2010 general election. Sec of State: Scotland 2008. Minister: FCO 2007-08; DWP 2006-07. Parly Sec, Cabinet Office 2005-06. Whip: govt 2003-05, asst govt 2002-03. Parliamentary private secretary to: Helen Liddell 2001-02. MP Eastwood 1997-2005. Co-op party. Former Chair Labour Friends of Israel. Scots Labour Party project manager. Director, Endsleigh Insurance. Pres NUS. Married, one daughter, two sons. Education: Bellarmine Secondary School; Milnerton High School, Cape Town; Strathclyde.

Richard Cook (C) b. 1967. Commercial manager for Biffa Waste Services.
Gordon Macdonald (LD) Scottish Parliamentary Officer for Christian public affairs charity CARE, policy officer for the anti-euthanasia coalition "Care Not Killing".
Gordon Archer (SNP) Convenor of the Cathcart branch. Former senior adviser and spokesperson for John Swinney MSP. Former cllr, Glasgow.

Constituency
This prosperous seat on the southern edge of the city has been called Glasgow's "stockbroker belt" and was once the safest Conservative seat in Scotland. Jim Murphy took it for Labour in 1997. Apart from Barrhead, the seat is mainly semi-rural and includes Eaglesham, the first conservation village in Scotland.

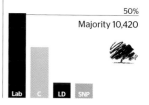

	Electorate	Turnout %	Change from '05 %
	66,249	77.3	
Murphy, J Lab	25,987	50.8	6.9
Cook, R C	15,567	30.4	0.6
Macdonald, G LD	4,720	9.2	-9.0
Archer, G SNP	4,535	8.9	2.0
MacKay, D UKIP	372	0.7	

50%
Majority 10,420

| Lab | C | LD | SNP |

Chris Bryant
b. Jan 11, 1962
MP 2001-

Fervent pro-EU, led summer 2006 revolt against Tony Blair. Likeable, excitable and funny – but not taken seriously since underpants episode. Former clergyman, first MP to hold civil partnership at Commons. Parly Under-Sec, FCO 2009-10. Dep Leader HoC 2008-09. PPS to: Harriet Harman 2007-08; Lord Falconer 2005-06. Const Affairs team 2005-. Cllr, Hackney 1993-98. BBC European Affairs head. Lab party local govt devt officer/agent. Chair, Lab Movement for Europe, Christian Socialist Movement. Ordained priest. Freelance author. Ed: Cheltenham Coll; Mansfield Coll, Oxford (BA Eng, MA); Ripon Coll, Cuddesdon (MA Cert Theol).

Geraint Davies (PC) b. 1948. Pharmacist. Cllr, Rhondda Cynon Taffr. Member, Welsh Assembly (Rhondda) 1999-2003.
Paul Wasley (LD) b. 1950. Runs own engineering company.
Philip Howe (Ind)
Juliet Henderson (C)

Constituency
The Rhondda Valley in South Wales encompasses two river valleys. Towns such as Tonypandy, Treorchy and Treherbert line Rhondda Fawr ("large") in the west, while smaller settlements such as Tylorstown and Ferndale follow Rhondda Fach ("small") at the east. Porth lies where the two converge in the south. A working-class seat with strong manufacturing sector, many of the old mining communities suffer from poor health. The seat has been held by Labour since 1910.

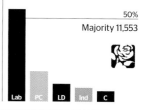

	Electorate	Turnout %	Change from '05 %
	51,554	60.3	
Bryant, C Lab	17,183	55.3	-12.7
Davies, G PC	5,630	18.1	2.2
Wasley, P LD	3,309	10.7	0.3
Howe, P Ind	2,599	8.4	
Henderson, J C	1,993	6.4	0.9
John, T UKIP	358	1.2	

50%
Majority 11,553

| Lab | PC | LD | Ind | C |

Nigel Evans
b. Nov 10, 1957
MP 1992-

Voluble, excitable, combative Thatcherite who speaks out frequently. Popular, but never quite made it. Owns longstanding family-run Swansea newsagents. Deputy Speaker 2010-. Shadow Sec of State: Wales 2001-03. Con Vice-Chair 1999. Parliamentary private secretary to: William Hague 1996-97, Tony Baldry 1995-96, David Hunt 1993-95. Education: Dynevor School; University College (BA politics).

Paul Foster (Lab) b. Nov 11, 1970. Project manager for renewable energy company.
Allan Knox (LD) b. Sep 22, 1964. Works in IT for Lancashire CC and in-ternet service provider. Clitheroe Town Mayor 2005-07 Ed: Barrhead High Sch, Aberdeen Uni (BSc chemistry).
Stephen Rush (UKIP) Works in family machinery manufacturing business. Former chairman of Clitheroe Football Club. Education: St Mary's College, Blackburn.

Constituency
One of the most affluent areas in Lancashire, the Ribble Valley is a predominantly rural seat centred on the large market town of Clitheroe. BAE Systems has a base at Samlesbury and traditional dairy farms have diversified to cater for tourism in the attractive Forest of Bowland. The seat has traditionally been Tory but the Lib Dems held it for one year in 1991 after winning a by-election triggered by the resignation of the former Home Secretary David Waddington.

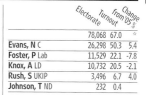

	Electorate	Turnout %	Change from '05 %
	78,068	67.0	
Evans, N C	26,298	50.3	5.4
Foster, P Lab	11,529	22.1	-7.8
Knox, A LD	10,732	20.5	-2.1
Rush, S UKIP	3,496	6.7	4.0
Johnson, T ND	232	0.4	

50%
Majority 14,769

| C | Lab | LD | UKIP |

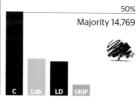

Richmond (Yorkshire) Conservative hold

William Hague
b. Mar 26, 1961
MP 1989- (by-election)

Funny, accomplished orator, hugely popular with Tory grassroots as voice of provincial party. Foreign Sec of State 2010-. Shadow Sec of State: Foreign 2005-10. Conservative Party leader: 1997-2001. Sec of State: Wales 1995-97. Minister: Social Security and Disabled People 1994-95. Parly Under-Sec DSS 1993-94. PPS to Norman Lamont 1990-93. Political adviser to Sir Geoffrey Howe, Leon Brittan. ShellUK/McKinsey/JCB pol and econ adviser. Married. Education: Magdalen College, Oxford (PPE); INSEAD Business School, France.

Lawrence Meredith (LD) Official with European Commission, previously civil servant. Education: Queen's College, Oxford (BA (Hons) modern languages, Russian and French).
Eileen Driver (Lab) b. Jul 28, 1948. Retired teacher.

Constituency
Bordering Cumbria to the west, this large rural seat stretches east from the Pennines to the Vale of York and has been enlarged to the south. The two main towns are Richmond and Northallerton but much of the population lives in villages, many within the Yorkshire Dales National Park, the linchpin of the tourism sector. There is a large agricultural sector, especially sheep farming. Catterick Garrison, Britain's largest army base, has 7,500 regular soldiers and thousands of recruits and civilian staff. This is one of the safest Tory seats.

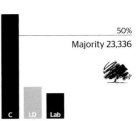

	Electorate	Turnout %	Change from '05 %
	79,478	67.2	☆
Hague, W C	33,541	62.8	3.5
Meredith, L LD	10,205	19.1	2.2
Driver, E Lab	8,150	15.3	-5.3
Rowe, L Green	1,516	2.8	-0.3

50%
Majority 23,336

C | LD | Lab

Richmond Park Conservative gain

Zac Goldsmith
b. Jan 20, 1975
MP 2010-

Multi-millionaire environmentalist and former green adviser to David Cameron. Known for prettyboy looks and charming manner. Principled green campaigner who vowed not to be lobby fodder. Faced scrutiny over tax status. Dep chair, Tory Quality of Life policy group. Son of Sir James Goldsmith. Edited *The Ecologist*. Smokes roll-up cigarettes. Separated, two daughters, one son. Education: Eton Coll (expelled).

Susan Kramer (LD) b. Jul 21, 1950. MP for Richmond Park 2005-10. LD spokesman Families and Cabinet Office 2007-10; Trade and Industry 2006-07. LD candidate for London Mayor 2000. Education: St Paul's Girls School; St Hilda's College, Oxford (BA Hons. politics, philosophy and economics); University of Illinois (MBA).

Constituency
The vast expanse of the park dominates the centre of seat with the urban areas concentrated either side. At the north are the affluent centres of Richmond, Barnes and Kew, with the Royal Botanical Gardens, all by the Thames. At the south is Coombe and the residential northern half of Kingston upon Thames. The private Coombe Estate has multimillion-pound homes but the rest of Coombe is more affordable and diverse. The Lib Dems took this from the Tories in 1997 but lost it back in 2010.

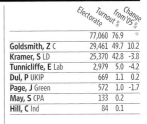

	Electorate	Turnout %	Change from '05 %
	77,060	76.9	
Goldsmith, Z C	29,461	49.7	10.2
Kramer, S LD	25,370	42.8	-3.8
Tunnicliffe, E Lab	2,979	5.0	-4.2
Dul, P UKIP	669	1.1	0.2
Page, J Green	572	1.0	-1.7
May, S CPA	133	0.2	
Hill, C Ind	84	0.1	

50%
Majority 4,091

C | LD | Lab

Rochdale Labour hold

Simon Danczuk
b. Oct 24, 1966
MP 2010-

Triumphed despite misfortune of "bigot-gate", the biggest gaffe of the election 2010, taking place while Gordon Brown was canvassing with him in Rochdale. Cllr, Blackburn with Darwen BC 1993-2001. Co-founder and director, Vision 21 social research agency. Researcher: The Big Issue; Opinion Research Corporation; Bolton TEC. Founder member, Labour Friends of Palestine, AEU, GMB. Raised in Burnley. Started work in factory aged 16, retrained and went to university as mature student. Married, one daughter, one son. Education: Gawthorpe Comprehensive; Lancaster University (economics & sociology).

Paul Rowen (LD) MP for Rochdale 2005-10. LD spokes: Transport 2005-07, Work & Pensions 2007-10.
Mudasir Dean (C) Runs a community cohesion project. Ed: Bolton University.

Constituency
In the north of Greater Manchester, this seat extends from Rochdale across the South Pennine Moors. It has not yet recovered from the decline of the textile industry. There are high levels of unskilled manual workers and those who have never worked. The large ethnic minority population includes about 15 per cent Pakistanis and community cohesion is an important issue. As the home of the co-operative movement, it is an atypical working-class seat with strong Liberal tendencies. Labour lost it to the Lib Dems in 2005, but won it back in 2010 – aided by boundary changes which gave them a notional majority.

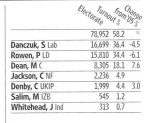

	Electorate	Turnout %	Change from '05 %
	78,952	58.2	
Danczuk, S Lab	16,699	36.4	-4.5
Rowen, P LD	15,810	34.4	-6.1
Dean, M C	8,305	18.1	7.6
Jackson, C NF	2,236	4.9	
Denby, C UKIP	1,999	4.4	3.0
Salim, M IZB	545	1.2	
Whitehead, J Ind	313	0.7	

50%
Majority 889

Lab | LD | C

Rochester & Strood
Conservative hold

Mark Reckless
b. Dec 6, 1970
MP 2010-

Radical libertarian Eurosceptic who was best man to Daniel Hannan. Happy to defy whips; endorsed by UKIP. Cllr, Medway 2007-. Contested Medway 2005, 2001. Solicitor, Herbert Smith. UK economist, Warburgs investment bank. Barings. Conservative Party Policy Unit. Ed: Marlborough Coll; Christ's Church, Oxford (PPE); Columbia (MBA); College of Law (LLB).

Teresa Murray (Lab) b. May 29, 1959. Further education college manager. Cllr, Medway.
Geoffrey Juby (LD) b. Feb 7, 1954. Works in catering. Contested Medway 2005, 2001. Ed: East Dereham Sch.

Constituency
This new seat is essentially the old Medway one but now includes all of Rochester, on the eastern bank of the Medway across from Strood. The two towns, containing most of the seat's residents, are a target of Thames Gateway regeneration. The physical bulk of the constituency is sparsely populated, however, covering marshland and nature reserves as it stretches north to the Blythe Sands on the Thames Estuary. A mixed constituency demographically of middle and working classes, it has tended to change hands with the party of government.

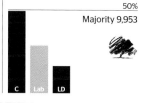

	Electorate	Turnout %	Change from '05 %
	73,882	64.9	☆
Reckless, M C	23,604	49.2	6.6
Murray, T Lab	13,651	28.5	-13.1
Juby, G LD	7,800	16.3	3.9
Sands, R Eng	2,182	4.6	
Marchant, S Green	734	1.5	

50%
Majority 9,953

Rochford & Southend
Conservative hold

James Duddridge
b. Aug 26, 1971
MP 2005-

Has a slightly intense manner but a mischevious sense of humour. Opposition Whip 2008-10. Banker, Barclays, ran operations in Botswana. Founder member, YouGov. Previous Tory involvement inc. research assistant to Bernard Jenkin, campaign manager Stephen Shakespeare, Exec Committee Conservative Way Forward. Contested Rother Valley 2001. Married, two sons. Ed: Huddersfield New College; Wells Blue School; Essex (BA government).

Kevin Bonavia (Lab) b. Aug 9, 1977. Solicitor (commercial fraud). Former chair, Young Fabians. Ed: Birmingham University (BA Hons history).

Graham Longley (LD) b. Aug 1, 1948. Cllr, Southend BC 1983- (leader 1994-2000, Mayor 2000). Contested Rochford & Southend East 2005. Education: Fairfax High School.

Constituency
The boundary of this coastal Essex seat, at the mouth of the Thames Estuary, has remained largely unchanged, losing only a couple of partial wards. Including the old market town of Rochford, it contains little else from the district and is drawn from the Southend-on-Sea borough. It includes the heart of the seaside resort. It has struggled to maintain its old tourism industry and has above-average unemployment. It also has an active nightclub scene that is more lively than other resorts. The seat has historically been a Tory stronghold and was represented by Sir Teddy Taylor.

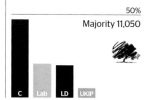

	Electorate	Turnout %	Change from '05 %
	71,080	58.6	☆
Duddridge, J C	19,509	46.9	1.5
Bonavia, K Lab	8,459	20.3	-11.3
Longley, G LD	8,084	19.4	4.7
Moyies, J UKIP	2,405	5.8	0.9
Strobridge, G BNP	1,856	4.5	
Vaughan, A Green	707	1.7	-1.8
Chytry, A Ind	611	1.5	

50%
Majority 11,050

Romford
Conservative hold

Andrew Rosindell
b. Mar 17, 1966
MP 2001-

Epitome of Essex Tory with robust right-wing outlook and attack-dog instincts. The opposite of a metropolitan sophisticate. Local populist who campaigned with Spike, his Staffordshire Bull Terrier adorned in a Union Jack flag. Was forced to quit Monday Club with Iain Duncan Smith. Vice-Chair Conservative Party 2004-. Member, National Union Executive Committee Conservative Party 1986-88, 1992-94. Councillor, Havering 1990-2002. Central Press Features, freelance journalist. Parliamentary researcher to Vivian Bendall MP. Director, European Foundation. Education: Marshalls Park Comprehensive, Romford.

Rachel Voller (Lab) b. Jun 29, 1976. Midwife, formerly a nurse.
Helen Duffett (LD) Former caseworker for Lynne Featherstone MP. Active blogger.
Robert Bailey (BNP)

Constituency
Romford is technically at the northeastern fringe of London, but thought of as Essex. It is overwhelmingly white and largely well off, with above-average numbers of owner-occupiers and self-employed. Under boundary changes it lost part of Emerson Park but took the populated Hylands from the western edge of Hornchurch. The northern end of the seat includes Collier Row and Havering Country Park. Labour overturned 23 years of Tory representation to take this in 1997, but the Tories won it back in 2001.

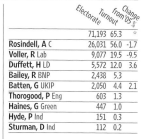

	Electorate	Turnout %	Change from '05 %
	71,193	65.3	☆
Rosindell, A C	26,031	56.0	-1.7
Voller, R Lab	9,077	19.5	-9.5
Duffett, H LD	5,572	12.0	3.6
Bailey, R BNP	2,438	5.3	
Batten, G UKIP	2,050	4.4	2.1
Thorogood, P Eng	603	1.3	
Haines, G Green	447	1.0	
Hyde, P Ind	151	0.3	
Sturman, D Ind	112	0.2	

50%
Majority 16,954

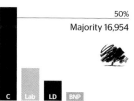

Romsey & Southampton North Conservative gain

Caroline Nokes
b. Jun 26, 1972
MP 2010-

The daughter of Roy Perry, a pro-European former Tory MEP. Interested in farming and food issues. Contested Romsey 2005, Southampton Itchen 2001. Cllr, Test Valley BC 1999-. Chief exec, National Pony Society. Christian. Married, one daughter. Education: La Sagesse Convent, Romsey; Peter Symonds College, Winchester; Sussex University (BA government & politics).

Sandra Gidley (LD) b. 1957. MP for Romsey from 2000-2010. Liberal Democrat spokeswoman on Women, 2001-06; Health 2006-10. Education: Eggars Grammar School, Alton; Bath University.

Aktar Beg (Lab) b. Feb 19, 1945. Office manager/chartered surveyor. Former cllr, Waltham Forest. Ed: Royal Institute of Chartered Surveyors.

Constituency
This large Hampshire seat is predominantly rural and largely affluent, bordering Wiltshire in the west and spreading from near Andover in the north, down the Test Valley to the outskirts of Southampton in the south. Though including most of the old Romsey seat, home to many commuting professionals, it has lost Chandler's Ford and Hiltingbury. The new name reflects an increased area of Swaythling added from Southampton city, including the Ford Transit van factory. The Lib Dems won the old Romsey constituency in a 2000 by-election and then kept it for two full terms, but in 2005 by just 125 votes - and lost to the Tories in 2010.

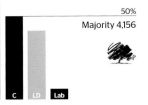

	Electorate	Turnout %	Change from '05 %
	66,901	73.2	☆
Nokes, C C	24,345	49.8	6.6
Gidley, S LD	20,189	41.3	-2.4
Beg, A Lab	3,116	6.4	-4.6
Meropoulos, J UKIP	1,289	2.6	0.3

50%
Majority 4,156

Ross, Skye & Lochaber Liberal Democrat hold

Charles Kennedy
b. Nov 25, 1959
MP 1983-

Enigmatic figure. Opposed coalition, abstained when MPs voted on the agreement. Lib Dem leader 1999-2006, resigned after admitting to a drink problem. Genial, still popular with the public. Vice-Pres, Liberal International 2006-. President, European Movement 2008-. Alliance/ SDP/LD spokes, various roles, 1987-99. LD party pres 1990-94. Member LD federal exec cttee, policy cttee. Journalist, broadcaster. Married, one son. Ed: Lochaber HS, Fort William; Glasgow (MA politics/philosophy/English); Indiana Uni.

John McKendrick (Lab) b. Aug 31, 1976. Lawyer. Ed: LSE; Oxford Uni.

Alasdair Stephen (SNP) Architect and partner in Dualchas Building Design. Director of Hebridean Contemporary Homes. Member, Saltire Housing Panel. Ed: Strathclyde University, Sabhal Mor Ostaig, Skye (Gaelic).
Donald Cameron (C) b. 1976. Legal advocate. Stood as the Scottish Conservative candidate in Linlithgow for the Scottish Parliamentary elections in May 2007. Ed: Oxford University (BA Hons modern history).

Constituency
The biggest constituency in Britain physically is also the fortress of the Liberal Democrat Charles Kennedy. It forms a triangle to take in some of the most scenic parts of northwest Scotland, from the Black Isle in the east to the Isle of Skye in the west. It also takes in Fort William to the south.

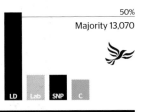

	Electorate	Turnout %	Change from '05 %
	51,836	52.6	
Kennedy, C LD	18,335	52.6	-6.1
McKendrick, J Lab	5,265	15.1	0.2
Stephen, A SNP	5,263	15.1	5.5
Cameron, D C	4,260	12.2	2.2
Scott, E Green	777	2.2	-1.1
Anderson, P UKIP	659	1.9	0.4
Campbell, R Ind	279	0.8	0.2

50%
Majority 13,070

Rossendale & Darwen Conservative gain

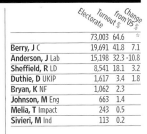

Jake Berry
b. Dec 29, 1978
MP 2010-

Smart, unpretentious and approachable Liverpudlian lawyer. Interested in social housing and supporting manufacturing. Agent to Amber Rudd 2005. Solicitor (commerical property specialist): City Law Partnership, DWF, Halliwells. Shareholder, Tung Sing Housing Association. Enjoys walking and water-skiing. Married. Ed: Liverpool Coll; Sheffield (law); College of Law, Chester.

Janet Anderson (Lab) b. Dec 6, 1949. MP for Rossendale & Darwen 1992-2010. Government whip 1997-98, Opposition whip 1994-96, Shadow Min: Women 1996-1997.

Ed: Trowbridge Girls High; Central London Poly.
Robert Sheffield (LD) b. Apr 6, 1947. Semi-retired. Carport manufacturer, marine surveyor.

Constituency
At the southeastern corner of Lancashire and just north of the Bolton-Rochdale conurbation, this seat straddles borough boundaries. Darwen, with its imposing tower, lies near Blackburn in the west, and is divided by Pennine moors from Rossendale in the east, where Rawtenstall is the main settlement. There is a strong manufacturing presence. Scout Moor is home to 26 wind turbines, the largest onshore site in England. There are pockets of deprivation in the urban centres, having suffered major redundancies from Airtours. Labour won this seat from the Tories in 1992.

	Electorate	Turnout %	Change from '05 %
	73,003	64.6	☆
Berry, J C	19,691	41.8	7.1
Anderson, J Lab	15,198	32.3	-10.8
Sheffield, R LD	8,541	18.1	3.2
Duthie, D UKIP	1,617	3.4	1.8
Bryan, K NF	1,062	2.3	
Johnson, M Eng	663	1.4	
Melia, T Impact	243	0.5	
Sivieri, M Ind	113	0.2	

50%
Majority 4,493

Rother Valley — Labour hold

Kevin Barron
b. Oct 26, 1946
MP 1983-

Solid reputation as a hard-working backbencher; quietly influential. Chair, select committee: Health 2005-10. Member, select committee: Standards & Privileges 2005-10; Liaison 2005-10. Opp spokes: Health 1995-97; Employment 1993-5; Energy 1988-92. PPS to Neil Kinnock 1985-88. National Coal Board. Amicus. Widowed, two daughters, one son. Ed: Maltby Hall; Sheffield (day release, social sciences); Ruskin Coll, Oxford (dip Labour studies).

Lynda Donaldson (C) b. 1961. Works in Financial Services. Cllr, Rotherham.
Wesley Paxton (LD) Ed: Warwick University (BA economics and industrial studies); Hull University (Cert Ed).
Will Blair (BNP) b. Nov 16, 1942. General store owner. Cllr, Rother DiC 2008-. Ed: Doagh Secondary School, County Antrim.
Tina Dowdall (UKIP)

Constituency
At the very south of Yorkshire, this seat has large rural expanses dotted with suburban areas such as Broom, Whiston and Swallownest. Well-connected by the M1, they are popular with commuters to Rotherham (to the north) and Sheffield (to the west). Farther east there are less affluent former mining settlements such as Maltby – where deprivation is evident in both the old housing and new council estates – and the former pit village of Thurcroft. This constituency has long been staunchly Labour.

	Electorate	Turnout %	Change from '05 %
	72,841	64.2	
Barron, K Lab	19,147	41.0	-10.6
Donaldson, L C	13,281	28.4	5.3
Paxton, W LD	8,111	17.4	1.2
Blair, W BNP	3,606	7.7	
Dowdall, T UKIP	2,613	5.6	1.3

50%
Majority 5,866

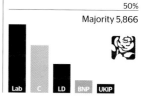

Lab | C | LD | BNP | UKIP

Rotherham — Labour hold

Denis MacShane
b. May 21, 1948
MP 1994-

Multi-lingual EU enthusiast, detailed knowledge of European politics. Combative with clownish streak. Min: FCO 2002-05. Parly Under-Sec: FCO 2001-02. PPS: joint to FCO 1999-2001 and 1997-99; to Geoff Hoon 1999. Chair, Fabian Society 2001-02. Journalist: BBC producer, Pres NUJ. Internat Metal Workers Federation policy dir. Dir European Policy Institute. Divorced. One son, four daughters – one deceased, from previous relationship. Ed: Merton Coll, Oxford (MA mod hist); Birkbeck Coll, London (PhD international econ).

Jackie Whiteley (C) Careers adviser. Ed: Leeds Met Uni.
Rebecca Taylor (LD) Senior researcher, International Longevity Centre. Contested Euro elections 1999.
Marlene Guest (BNP)
Peter Thirlwall (Ind)

Constituency
Across the M1 to the north east of Sheffield, Rotherham is a former steel and coal town that has suffered from the industries' decline. South Yorkshire received EU funding for regeneration in the past decade but further recent job cuts have hit hard. From the terraces of Masbrough, in the centre, to council estates farther out, much of the town remains severely deprived. Rotherham's ethnic minority community is concentrated in the north, with some tensions reflected in BNP success locally. The seat has been Labour since 1933.

	Electorate	Turnout %	Change from '05 %
	63,565	59.0	
MacShane, D Lab	16,741	44.6	-13.1
Whiteley, J C	6,279	16.7	3.4
Taylor, R LD	5,994	16.0	-0.4
Guest, M BNP	3,906	10.4	
Thirlwall, P Ind	2,366	6.3	
Vines, C UKIP	2,220	5.9	2.0

50%
Majority 10,462

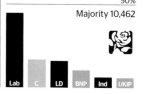

Lab | C | LD | BNP | Ind | UKIP

Rugby — Conservative gain

Mark Pawsey
b. Jan 16, 1957
MP 2010-

Interested in land use and planning issues. Contested Nuneaton 2005. Cllr, Rugby BC 2002-07. Son of James Pawsey (MP Rugby 1979-97). Successful businessman - founded catering trade supply firm with brother; firm acquired by FTSE100 company. Enjoys rugby and wine appreciation. Married, two daughters, two sons. Ed: Lawrence Sheriff Sch, Rugby; Reading (estate management).

Andy King (Lab) b. Sep 14, 1948. MP for Rugby and Kenilworth 1997-2005. Ed: Missionary Institute; Hatfield Polytechnic.
Jerry Roodhouse (LD) b. Jun 26, 1953. Self-employed businessman. Ed: Harris CE High School, Rugby.

Constituency
After substantial boundary changes, Rugby was split from the Kenilworth area and given its own seat, stretching north from the town through Fosse, Wolvey and Bulkington, to the edge of Nuneaton. This affluent rural area and southern Rugby, which tend to be Conservative-voting, contrast with the less affluent and more Labour-leaning industrial north of the town, where there are patches of deprivation. The seat is home to Rugby School where the game of rugby football was invented in 1823.

	Electorate	Turnout %	Change from '05 %
	68,914	68.9	
Pawsey, M C	20,901	44.0	5.7
King, A Lab	14,901	31.4	-12.1
Roodhouse, J LD	9,434	19.9	4.9
Badrick, M BNP	1,375	2.9	
Sandison, R Green	451	1.0	
Milford, B UKIP	406	0.9	-1.1

50%
Majority 6,000

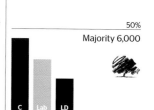

C | Lab | LD

Ruislip, Northwood & Pinner | Conservative hold

Nick Hurd
b. May 13, 1962
MP 2005-

Urbane son of former Foreign Secretary Lord Hurd, making him the fourth successive generation in his family to become an MP. Quietly impressive and well-liked. Parly Under-Sec: Cabinet Office 2010-. Shadow Minister for Charities 2008-10. Opposition Whip 2007-08. Kensington & Chelsea Borough Champion for Steve Norris 2003. Member, Vote No to the EU Constitution Campaign. Business consultant, banker, represented British bank in Brazil. Chief of staff to Tim Yeo MP. Married, two daughters, two sons. Education: Eton; Exeter Coll, Oxford (BA classics).

Anita McDonald (Lab) b. Dec 18, 1968. Teacher. Cllr, Hillingdon 2006-.
Thomas Papworth (LD) b. 1972. Cllr, Bromley BC. Ed: Royal Holloway University (history); University of Kent (Masters in international relations).

Constituency
On the northwestern fringe of London, bordering with Buckinghamshire to the west and Hertfordshire to the north. This seat has been substantially redrawn to take in Pinner in the north east, from Harrow borough, and Ickenham in the south west from the old Uxbridge seat. It lost Manor, South Ruislip and Cavendish from the southeast. Its affluent residential areas have good transport links with several Underground and overground stations. This has been safely Tory for decades.

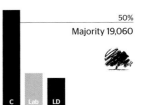

	Electorate	Turnout %	Change from '05 %
	70,873	70.8	☆
Hurd, N C	28,866	57.5	2.8
McDonald, A Lab	9,806	19.5	-4.5
Papworth, T LD	8,345	16.6	0.3
Pontey, J UKIP	1,351	2.7	1.2
Edward, I NF	899	1.8	
Lee, G Green	740	1.5	0.0
Akhtar, R Ch	198	0.4	

50%
Majority 19,060

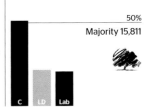

C | Lab | LD

Runnymede & Weybridge | Conservative hold

Philip Hammond
b. Dec 4, 1955
MP 1997-

Mild-mannered millionaire, with the air of a provincial bank manager. An archetypal old-fashioned Tory. Respected as a solid performer in previous role as Tories' public spending supremo. Had to make-do with SoS: Transport 2010-, having missed out on preferred Treasury brief in first coalition deal. Shadow Chief Sec to the Treasury 2007-10; 2005. Shadow Sec: Work and Pensions 2005-07. Shadow Min: Local Govt 2002-05; T & I/Small Business 2001-02; Health 1998-2001. Business career, director roles inc property, oil & gas. Malawi govt consultant. Married, two daughters, one son. Ed: Shenfield Sch, Brentwood; University College, Oxford (MA PPE).

Andrew Falconer (LD) Careers adviser, Royal Holloway University. Former asst to Sir Robert Smith MP.
Paul Greenwood (Lab) b. May 4, 1953. Employee of fire service. Member, Agricultural Association.
Toby Micklethwait (UKIP) Retired businessman. Contested Runnymede and Weybridge in 2005.

Constituency
The constituency spreads from the town of Weybridge in the southeast to Runnymede meadows in the north of the borough that is named after them. Here King John signed Magna Carta in 1215. Affluent commuter settlements that crowd round the M25-M3 interchange include Egham, Chertsey, Virginia Water and Thorpe, site of an industrial estate and eponymous theme park. Prettier rural areas are to be found in the south west of this safe Conservative seat.

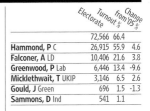

	Electorate	Turnout %	Change from '05 %
	72,566	66.4	
Hammond, P C	26,915	55.9	4.6
Falconer, A LD	10,406	21.6	3.8
Greenwood, P Lab	6,446	13.4	-9.6
Micklethwait, T UKIP	3,146	6.5	2.6
Gould, J Green	696	1.5	-1.3
Sammons, D Ind	541	1.1	

50%
Majority 16,509

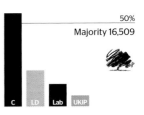

C | LD | Lab | UKIP

Rushcliffe | Conservative hold

Kenneth Clarke
b. Jul 2, 1940
MP 1970-

Pugnacious, red-faced populist veteran with unrivalled ministerial experience including successful tenure as Chancellor (1993-97). Knowledge-able but better at broad brush than detail and can be dangerously off-message. A traditionalist about parlia-ment. Europhile views thrice thwarted party leadership bids: came second in 1997 and 2001; eliminated first round 2005. Returned to frontline politics in 2009. Lord Chancellor, SoS for Justice 2010-. Shadow SoS: Business 2009-10. Prev SoS: Home 1992-3; Ed/Sci 1990-2; Health 1988-90. Barrister. Cigar-smoking former non-exec dir of BAT. Married, one daughter, one son. Ed: Gonville & Caius Coll, Camb (BA LLB).

Karrar Khan (LD) Pharmaceutical devt consultant. Cllr, Rushcliffe BC.
Andrew Clayworth (Lab) b. Jul 18, 1958. Biomedical scientist for the NHS.

Constituency
The southern tip of Nottinghamshire lies in this seat, which was formerly one of the biggest constituencies in terms of population. It has lost a substantial area from its north east including Bingham. Its population is concentrated in the West Bridgford area, on the southern outskirts of Nottingham, while other settlements include Ruddington, Keyworth and East Leake. Both Trent Bridge cricket ground and the City Ground, home to Nottingham Forest FC, are just inside the northern boundary. This is generally an affluent seat, whose Conservative vote has been cemented by the appeal of Kenneth Clarke, MP since 1970.

	Electorate	Turnout %	Change from '05 %
	72,955	73.6	☆
Clarke, K C	27,470	51.2	3.2
Khan, K LD	11,659	21.7	4.4
Clayworth, A Lab	11,128	20.7	-6.7
Faithfull, M UKIP	2,179	4.1	1.6
Mallender, R Green	1,251	2.3	-1.2

50%
Majority 15,811

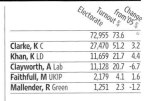

C | LD | Lab

Rutherglen & Hamilton West
Labour Co-op hold

Tom Greatrex
b. Sep 30, 1974
MP 2010-

Special adviser to Secretary of State for Scotland (Jim Murphy, Des Browne, Douglas Alexander) 2007-10. Member Cooperative Party, GMB. Dir, Corporate Affairs, NHS 24. Head of Policy & Public Affairs, East Dunbartonshire Council. Industrial organiser, GMB. Special adviser to Nick Brown 1997-99. Researcher, Lab Party whips office. Avid Fulham FC fan. Married, twin daughters. Ed: The Judd School, Tonbridge; LSE (BSc economics, government & law).

Graeme Horne (SNP) b. Sep 22, 1969. Deputy Leader, South Lanarkshire Council SNP Group. Ed: Coatbridge College; Stow College, Glasgow.

Ian Robertson (LD) Maths teacher. Contested Glasgow East 2005 and by-election 2008.
Malcolm Macaskill (C) Contested Rutherglen & Hamilton West 2001.

Constituency
This is a compact, suburban constituency on the southeastern edge of Glasgow. Much of it used to be in Glasgow Rutherglen but these were combined with parts of Hamilton South to form a new seat before 2005. It is bordered by the M74 on its eastern edge and the constituency is based around the communities of Rutherglen and Cambuslang. This area still carries echoes of heavy industry and is dominated by high-density housing. It remains Labour.

		Electorate	Turnout %	Change from '05 %
		76,408	61.5	
Greatrex, T	Lab	28,566	60.8	-2344
Horne, G	SNP	7,564	16.1	2.2
Robertson, I	LD	5,636	12.0	-6.3
Macaskill, M	C	4,540	9.7	1.3
Murdoch, J	UKIP	675	1.4	0.4

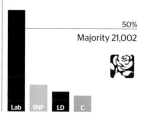

50%
Majority 21,002

Lab | SNP | LD | C

Rutland & Melton
Conservative hold

Alan Duncan
b. Mar 31, 1957
MP 1992-

Flirtatious, dapper Thatcherite-turned-moderniser, nicknamed "Hunky Dunky"; the best-dressed man in the Commons. Very quotable. Demoted from shadow cabinet for comments over MPs expenses 'rations' and will probably not make the top now. Min: Int Dev 2010-. Shadow Min: Prisons 2009-10. Shadow Leader of House 2009. Shadow Sec: Trade & Industry/Business (2005-09); Trans 2005; Int Dev 2004-05; Constitutional Affairs 2003-04. Con Party Vice-Chair 1997-98. Opp spokes roles and PPS to: William Hague 1997-98; Dr Brian Mawhinney 1993-94. Civil partner. Ed: St John's Coll, Oxford (BA PPE; pres, Oxford Union); Harvard.

Grahame Hudson (LD) Senior lecturer in the Faculty of Art and Design at De Montfort University.
John Morgan (Lab) b. Mar 5, 1968. Prison officer at HMP Stocken.

Constituency
This huge rural seat in the East Midlands encompasses the borough of Melton, which has Melton Mowbray at its centre, and the district of Rutland, with the main towns of Oakham and Uppingham. It also covers four rural wards of Harborough District. Rutland was the second least deprived local authority in the country in 2007 and Melton is also relatively affluent. It has been Conservative since 1945.

		Electorate	Turnout %	Change from '05 %
		77,185	71.5	
Duncan, A	C	28,228	51.1	-0.1
Hudson, G	LD	14,224	25.8	7.2
Morgan, J	Lab	7,893	14.3	-10.7
Baker, P	UKIP	2,526	4.6	1.4
Addison, K	BNP	1,757	3.2	
Higgins, L	Ind	588	1.1	

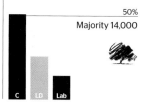

50%
Majority 14,000

C | LD | Lab

Saffron Walden
Conservative hold

Sir Alan Haselhurst
b. Jun 23, 1937
MP 1970-74; 1977-

Courteous old-style Tory; was prominent as a pro-European Tory Wet but since 1997 has been a mainstay of the Commons establishment. Popular and very competent in the chair as deputy speaker. Stood unsuccessfully for Speaker, 2009. Chairman, Ways and Means, and Deputy Speaker 1997-. PPS to Mark Carlisle 1979-81. MP Middleton and Prestwich 1970-74. Chemicals/plastics exec. Public affairs consultant. Knighted 1995. Married, one daughter, two sons. Ed: Cheltenham; Oriel College, Oxford.

Peter Wilcock (LD) b. Mar 20, 1953. Social researcher. Cllr, Uttlesford DC 1995-. Ed: Magdalen Coll Sch, Oxford.

Barbara Light (Lab) b. Dec 9, 1951. University lecturer in London.

Constituency
This seat still covers a large rural area at the northwest corner of Essex despite having lost a chunk from the east under boundary changes. The market town of Saffron Walden lies at the north. It acts as a hub for myriad villages dotted around it and nearby Audley End is the main point for London commuters. Stansted airport is a feature of the seat as a major employer and a source of contention over its expansion. This affluent seat has been safely Tory for decades.

		Electorate	Turnout %	Change from '05 %
		76,035	71.5	
Haselhurst, A	C	30,155	55.5	4.6
Wilcock, P	LD	14,913	27.4	-2.2
Light, B	Lab	5,288	9.7	-4.5
Lord, R	UKIP	2,228	4.1	1.4
Mitchell, C	BNP	1,050	1.9	
Hossain, R	Green	735	1.4	

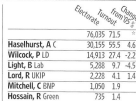

50%
Majority 15,242

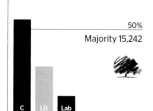

C | LD | Lab

St Albans
Conservative hold

Anne Main
b. May 17, 1957
MP 2005-

Dogged if slightly plodding Commons performer. Bruised by expenses controversy. Member, select committee DCLG 2005-. Cllr, Beaconsfield PC 1999-2002, South Bucky District 2001-. Teaching and family 1979-80; Home-maker 1980-90; Carer for terminally ill husband 1990-91; Single parent and supply teacher 1991-95. Widowed, remarried. Two daughters, one son from first marriage, one son from second. Ed: Bishop of Llandaff Sch; Swansea (BA English); Sheffield (PGCE).

Sandy Walkington (LD) b. Dec 5, 1953. Comms consultant. Contested St Albans for Lib/SDP Alliance 1983, 1987.

Roma Mills (Lab) b. Aug 20, 1951. Cllr, St Albans DC 1988-. Ed: Bristol University (English, philosophy and politics); Hertfordshire University.

Constituency
The cathedral city is at the north of this seat and the M25 passes through to the south. Banking and finance account for more than 25 per cent of jobs and the public sector a similar proportion, both replacing the manufacturing industries that declined in the Nineties. However, more than 50 per cent of residents commute out – mostly to highly paid managerial or professional jobs in London – and about 40 per cent of jobs are taken by people commuting in. Labour secured a shock win in 1997, but it returned to the Tories in 2005.

	Electorate	Turnout %	from '05 %	Change
	70,058	75.4		☆
Main, A C	21,533	40.8	3.5	
Walkington, S LD	19,228	36.4	11.0	
Mills, R Lab	9,288	17.6	-16.8	
Stocker, J UKIP	2,028	3.8	2.3	
Easton, J Green	758	1.4		

50%
Majority 2,305

St Austell & Newquay
Liberal Democrat hold

Stephen Gilbert
b. Nov 6, 1976
MP 2010-

Mainstream Lib Dem, interested in affordable housing and community cohesion. Cllr: Haringey BC 2002-05; Restormel BC 1998-2002. Business consultant in Cornwall. Public Affairs Manager, Fidelity International (fund management house). Adviser to Investment Management Association. Researcher to Lembit Öpik MP and Robin Teverson MEP. Keen gym and cinema-goer. Gay. Ed: Fowey Community Sch; St Austell Coll; Aberystwyth (BScEcon international politics); LSE (MScEcon international relations).

Caroline Righton (C) b. Feb 26, 1958. Journalist, television presenter, producer.

Lee Jameson (Lab) b. Sep 19, 1974. Local government officer. Education: Hull University.

Constituency
St Austell, just inland on the southern coast of Cornwall, was previously grouped with Truro. The redrawn constituency extends northwest to the busy tourist resort and surfing centre of Newquay. St Austell has undergone multimillion-pound regeneration in the Aylmer Square area and is a tourist hub because of the nearby Eden Project. The seat includes the well-preserved Georgian harbour at Charlestown, which frequently appears on film and television. More than 20 per cent of residents are pensioners. The previous seat returned Liberal MPs since 1974.

	Electorate	Turnout %	from '05 %	Change
	76,346	61.9		☆
Gilbert, S LD	20,189	42.7	-4.5	
Righton, C C	18,877	40.0	5.1	
Jameson, L Lab	3,386	7.2	-6.6	
Cole, D Meb	2,007	4.3		
Medway, C UKIP	1,757	3.7	-0.4	
Fitton, J BNP	1,022	2.2		

50%
Majority 1,312

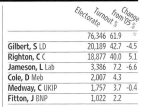

St Helens North
Labour hold

Dave Watts
b. Aug 26, 1951
MP 1997-

Liverpudlian, former council leader - a more authentic local representative than constituency neighbour Shaun Woodward. Govt whip 2005-10. PPS to: John Prescott 2003-05; John Spellar 1999-2002. Member, cttees: Finance & Services 2005-06; 1997-2001. Cllr, St Helens MBC 1979-97 (leader 1993-97). Vice-Chair assocn of metropolitan authorities. UK pres Euro group of industrial regions. MP research asst. Shop steward Utd Biscuits AEU. Married, two sons. Ed: Seel Rd Sec Modern.

Paul Greenall (C) Cllr, West Lancs BC, 2001. Ed: Brookfield Comprehensive.

John Beirne (LD) Self-employed, hairdresser. Cllr, St Helens 2004-.

Constituency
From the northern half of St Helens, the seat fans out through rural land, with Rainford at the affluent western end, Billinge in the centre and Haydock and Newton-le-Willows in the east. The coal and glass industries have declined from their heyday, leaving areas of deprivation, but manufacturing remains above average and the public service sector is also strongly represented. The seat's core is white, working-class and Labour-voting.

	Electorate	Turnout %	from '05 %	Change
	74,985	59.4		☆
Watts, D Lab	23,041	51.7	-5.6	
Greenall, P C	9,940	22.3	3.5	
Beirne, J LD	8,992	20.2	-0.7	
Robinson, G UKIP	2,100	4.7	1.8	
Whatham, S Soc	483	1.1		

50%
Majority 13,101

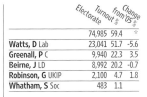
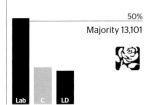

St Helens South Labour hold

Shaun Woodward
b. Oct 26, 1958
MP 1997-

Turncoat, ex-Tory MP and Conservative official who defected to Labour. In 1999 unlikely member of Gordon Brown's team. Very wealthy wife. SoS: NI 2007-. Parly Under-Sec: CMS 2006-07; NI 2005-06. Conservative Opp spokes, Environment, Transport & Regions 1999. Member, select cttees: Joint cttee on Human Rights 2001-05; Broadcasting 2000-01; Foreign Affairs 1999; European Scrutiny 1998-99; Broadcasting 1997-99. MP St Helens South 2001-10, Witney, 1997-2001. Dir Con Party comms 1991-92. BBC TV news/current affairs. Dir, English Nat Opera. Married, three daughters, one son. Ed: Bristol GS; Jesus Coll, Cambs (MS Eng Lit).

Brian Spencer (LD) Cllr, St Helens (leader 2006-).
Val Allen (C) Self-employed, engineering business. Ed: Bishop Rawstorne Secondary Modern School; Wigan Technical College.

Constituency
St Helens town centre lies at the north of this seat, which also includes Prescot in the west. St Helens has a strong industrial heritage, notably in glassmaking, and its decline has left deprivation and high unemployment. Regeneration efforts include a planned transformation of the derelict United Glass site into a new stadium for the St Helens rugby league club. The M62 runs through the south, linking to Liverpool and Manchester on either side. The old St Helens South seat, which was held by Labour, has been substantially increased in size with the addition of Whiston.

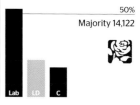

	Electorate	Turnout %	Change from '05 %
	77,975	1.0	☆
Woodward, S Lab	24,364	52.9	-2.7
Spencer, B LD	10,242	22.2	-6.6
Allen, V C	8,209	17.8	5.7
Winstanley, J BNP	2,040	4.4	
Sumner, J UKIP	1,226	2.7	0.8

50%
Majority 14,122

St Ives Liberal Democrat hold

Andrew George
b. Dec 2, 1958
MP 1997-

Professional Cornishman. Liberal Democrat Shadow Secretary: International Development 2005-06. LD Shad Min: Food & Rural affairs 2002-05. PPS to Charles Kennedy 2001-02. LD Shad Min: Disabilities 1999-2001; Fisheries 1997-99. Member, cttee: Agriculture 1997-2000. Rural community devt council 1994-97. Married, one daughter, one son. Ed: Helston GS; Helston Sch; Sussex (BA cultural/community studies); Univ Coll, Oxford (MSc agricultural economics).

Derek Thomas (C) b. 1972. Community development manager. Cllr, Penwith DC.

Philippa Latimer (Lab) b. Apr 7, 1983. Public afffairs manager, BCSE. Ed: Sussex University.
Mick Faulker (UKIP)

Constituency
The seat curves round Mounts Bay on Cornwall's south coast, stretching from Land's End, the most westerly point in England, to Lizard Point, the most southerly. Penzance and numerous fishing villages nestle in the bay while, on the northern coast, St Ives sits on its eponymous bay. It still attracts artists with its luminous light and turquoise seas but is overrun with tourists. The constituency includes the Isles of Scilly. Nearly 50 per cent of constituents are aged 45 or over. The Lib Dems took this former Tory stronghold in 1997.

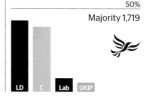

	Electorate	Turnout %	Change from '05 %
	66,930	68.6	☆
George, A LD	19,619	42.7	-9.1
Thomas, D C	17,900	39.0	11.7
Latimer, P Lab	3,751	8.2	-4.4
Faulkner, M UKIP	2,560	5.6	1.3
Andrewes, T Green	1,308	2.9	-1.1
Rogers, J Cornish	396	0.9	
Reed, S Meb	387	0.8	

50%
Majority 1,719

Salford and Eccles Labour hold

Hazel Blears
b. May 14, 1956
MP 1997-

Pint-sized Blairite redhead, relentless enthusiasm diminished by expenses controversy. Made messy resignation from Cabinet which destabilised Brown then disappeared from public view to dedicate herself to surviving in Salford. SoS: CLG 2007-09. Min: Without Portfolio 2006-07; Home 2003-06. Parly Under-sec: Public Heath 2003-03; Health 2001-02. PPS to Alan Milburn 1998-99. Member, Nat Policy Reform/ leadership campaign team 1997. Cllr, Salford 1984-92. Solicitor. Chair, Salford Community Health Council. Branch sec, Unison. Unite, USDAW. Keen motorcyclist. Married. Ed: Trent Poly (BA Law); Chester Coll of Law.

Norman Owen (LD) Cllr, Salford CC. Contested Salford 2005.
Matthew Sephton (C) Primary school teacher, Stockport.
Tina Wingfield (BNP) PA to Nick Griffin MEP.

Constituency
This Greater Manchester seat combines most of the old Salford seat with the northern part of Eccles, once known for the number of Coronation Street stars among its residents. The seat is bordered by the River Irwell to the east and Manchester Ship Canal to the south. The Salford Quays have undergone regeneration in recent years and several BBC departments are due to move here in 2011. Much of the rest of the seat remains deprived and about 25 per cent of residents say that they have a limiting, long-term illness. The seat has been Labour for decades.

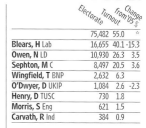

	Electorate	Turnout %	Change from '05 %
	75,482	55.0	☆
Blears, H Lab	16,655	40.1	-15.3
Owen, N LD	10,930	26.3	3.5
Sephton, M C	8,497	20.5	3.6
Wingfield, T BNP	2,632	6.3	
O'Dwyer, D UKIP	1,084	2.6	-2.3
Henry, D TUSC	730	1.8	
Morris, S Eng	621	1.5	
Carvath, R Ind	384	0.9	

50%
Majority 5,725

Salisbury — Conservative hold

John Glen
b. Apr 1, 1974
MP 2010-

Wiltshire-born and bred, committed Christian. Magistrate. Contested Plymouth Devenport 2001, won Salisbury candidature through open primary. Management consultancy career at Accenture interspersed with stints at Conservative Research Department; seconded to Head of Political Section during William Hague's leadership, returned as Deputy Director/Director 2004-06. Prev parliamentary researcher. Board, Centre for Policy Studies, 2009-. Married, one step-daughter, one step-son. Ed: King Edward's Sch, Bath; Mansfield Coll, Oxford (MA modern history; JCR President); Judge Institute, Cambridge Uni (MBA).

Nick Radford (LD) Self-employed, renewable energy business. Ed: Oxford Uni (BA Hons Biological Sciences).
Tom Gann (Lab) b. Jun 9, 1982. Ed: Bishop Wordsworth's School; University of Warwick.

Constituency
The city of Salisbury is a big tourist destination for its cathedral, medieval centre and proximity to Stonehenge. It is the commercial centre of an otherwise largely rural seat. A military base at Wilton is due for closure this year but military training will continue on Salisbury Plain. Chalk downs dipping down to dense woodland are a feature of the south east. The seat has returned Tories since 1945. Sir Edward Heath, the former Conservative Prime Minister, was a long-time resident of one of the grandest homes in Cathedral Close.

	Electorate	Turnout %	Change from 05 %
	67,429	71.9	☆
Glen, J C	23,859	49.2	2.8
Radford, N LD	17,893	36.9	10.0
Gann, T Lab	3,690	7.6	-11.0
Howard, F UKIP	1,392	2.9	-1.3
Witheridge, S BNP	765	1.6	
Startin, N Green	506	1.0	-2.4
Arthur, K Ind	257	0.5	
Holme, J Ind	119	0.3	

50%
Majority 5,966

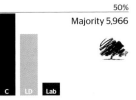

Scarborough & Whitby — Conservative hold

Robert Goodwill
b. Dec 31, 1956
MP 2005-

Staunch Eurosceptic. Asst govt whip 2010-. Shadow Minister: Transport 2007-10. Opposition Whip 2006-07. MEP for Yorkshire and the Humber, 1999-2004 (spokesman for environment 2001-04), having contested two general elections (Redcar 1992; NW Leicestershire 1997) and two European parliament elections. NFU member, has 250-acre family farm. Steam traction engine fan. Married, one daughter, two sons. Education: Bootham School, York; Newcastle (BSc Agriculture).

Annajoy David (Lab) b. Oct 5, 1963. Businesswoman/company director. Former Vice-Chair, CND.

Tania Exley-Moore (LD) b. May 30, 1959. Teacher, sixth form college. Contested Scarborough & Whitby, 2005. Ed: Teesside University (BA Hons humanities), Nottingham University (MA Victorian literature).

Constituency
The two towns are the main population centres of a seat covering a vast stretch of North Yorkshire coastline, extending inland to the North York Moors National Park. Scarborough, home of the playwright Sir Alan Ayckbourn and a cricket festival, is the larger, more traditional seaside resort. Whitby, with its ruined Gothic abbey and narrow cobbled streets surrounding a working port, has a more upmarket reputation. Fishing and tourism have declined from their heydays, giving rise to pockets of deprivation. Voters surprisingly elected a Labour MP in 1997-2005.

	Electorate	Turnout %	Change from 05 %
	75,443	65.3	☆
Goodwill, R C	21,108	42.8	1.8
David, A Lab	12,978	26.3	-12.0
Exley-Moore, T LD	11,093	22.5	6.6
James, M UKIP	1,484	3.0	1.0
Scott, T BNP	1,445	2.9	
Cluer, D Green	734	1.5	-1.1
Popple, P Ind	329	0.7	
Boddington, J Green	111	0.2	-2.4

50%
Majority 8,130

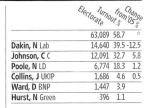

Scunthorpe — Labour hold

Nic Dakin
b. Jul 10, 1955
MP 2010-

Former council leader with expertise in education from teaching career. Cllr, N Lincs 1996-2007 (Leader 1997-2003). Principal of the John Leggott Sixth Form College in Scunthorpe. English teacher, apart from brief spell as a trainee accountant. Christian. Member: NUT, Friends of the Earth, Child Poverty Action Group, Lincolnshire Wildlife Trust, RSPB. Keen squash player and avid Scunthorpe Utd fan. Married, two daughters, one son. Education: Longslade Upper School, Birstall, Leicestershire; Hull (history).

Caroline Johnson (C) Doctor. Ed: Newcastle University (Medicine).

Neil Poole (LD) b. Dec 9, 1952. Family business. Cllr, North Lincolnshire. Ed: North Lincolnshire Tech Coll; Bishop Burton Coll of Agriculture.

Constituency
Scunthorpe lies at the north with a rural area, separated by the M180, to the south. Known as the "industrial garden town", it was built round the steel industry and has suffered with its decline. Corus remains the chief employer but has made redundancies. Once grouped with other areas, Scunthorpe has been represented by a variety of parties, but since gaining its own seat in 1997 has been seen as safely Labour. Its outgoing MP, Elliot Morley, stood down after he was accused of false accounting of his expenses.

	Electorate	Turnout %	Change from 05 %
	63,089	58.7	☆
Dakin, N Lab	14,640	39.5	-12.5
Johnson, C C	12,091	32.7	5.8
Poole, N LD	6,774	18.3	1.2
Collins, J UKIP	1,686	4.6	0.5
Ward, D BNP	1,447	3.9	
Hurst, N Green	396	1.1	

50%
Majority 2,549

Sedgefield

Labour hold

Phil Wilson
b. May 31, 1959
MP 2007-

Friend and former aide to Tony Blair, whom he helped to win the selection as Labour's candidate for Sedgefield in 1983. Local miner's son with a world-weary manner. PPS to: Andy Burnham 2009-10; Vernon Coaker 2008-09. Member, select cttees: Public Accounts 2007-; Regulatory Reform 2007-; NE 2009-. Usdaw, CSPA, TGWU, GMB. Adviser, Gala Coral. Has partner, two children, three stepchildren. Ed: Trimdon Secondary Modern; Sedgefield Comprehensive.

Neil Mahapatra (C) Private equity. Ed: Oxford University (BSc Biological Sciences); Harvard (MBA).

Alan Thompson (LD) Engineer and businessman. Cllr, Northumberland CC 2007-. Ed: Higher National Certificate (Chartered Engineering). **Mark Walker** (BNP)

Constituency
This large seat almost encircles Darlington in the south and stretches northeast nearly to the coast. Former colliery villages here include Trimdon, the constituency home of Tony Blair in 1983-2007. Many remain severely deprived since the Eighties pit closures. So are many of the densely populated council estates of Newton Aycliffe, which in 1947 was the North's first New Town. Sedgefield itself has large housing developments around the historic village. President Bush and Tony Blair shared a lunch of fish, chips and mushy peas at its Dun Cow pub in 2003. This has long been a safe Labour seat.

		Electorate	Turnout %	Change from 05 %
		64,727	62.1	☆
Wilson, P	Lab	18,141	45.1	-13.9
Mahapatra, N	C	9,445	23.5	9.3
Thompson, A	LD	8,033	20.0	8.2
Walker, M	BNP	2,075	5.2	
Gregory, B	UKIP	1,479	3.7	2.1
Gittins, P	Ind	1,049	2.6	

50%

Majority 8,696

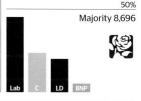

Sefton Central

Labour hold

Bill Esterson
b. Oct 27, 1966
MP 2010-

Tall, with diffident manner. Long-serving Medway councillor (1995-2010), passionate about education and children's services. Cites Dennis Skinner as his political hero for his constituency dedication and party loyalty. Director, Leaps & Bounds training consultancy. Worked with Coopers & Lybrand accountancy firm. Manages a hockey team. Married, one daughter, one son. Education: Rochester Mathematical School; Leeds University (maths & philosophy).

Debi Jones (C) Cllr, Sefton Met BC 2006-. Contested Crosby 2005. **Richard Clein** (LD) Journalist and associate director, PR company.

Constituency
From Formby in the north, this seat stretches down the coast towards Liverpool, encompassing the northern half of Crosby town and extending inland to Maghull. It is generally well off, with commuters enjoying good transport links to the nearby cities, although the area immediately between the M57 and M58 is more deprived. The Crosby and Knowsley North and Sefton East constituencies from which this new seat was formed were both Labour.

		Electorate	Turnout %	Change from 05 %
		67,512	71.8	☆
Esterson, B	Lab	20,307	41.9	-3.7
Jones, D	C	16,445	33.9	0.4
Clein, R	LD	9,656	19.9	0.7
Harper, P	UKIP	2,055	4.2	3.5

50%

Majority 3,862

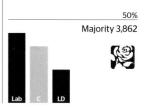

Selby & Ainsty

Conservative hold

Nigel Adams
b. Nov 20, 1966
MP 2010-

Professional Yorkshire-man. Successful businessman from humble, local background; son of a school cleaner and caretaker. Rejected from A-list but his constituency party snubbed A-listers including Anne McIntosh MP to select him. Champion of businesses, devised Selby Means Business cheque book. Interested in energy policy. Contested Rossendale & Darwen 2005. Dir, NGC Networks. Founded/Dir, Advanced Digital Tel-ecom, having left school at 17. Early career selling advertising for newspapers/Yellow Pages. C of E. Keen cricketer. Married, one son, three daughters. Ed: Selby High Sch.

Jan Marshall (Lab) b. Jul 11, 1952. Cllr, North Yorkshire CC, 2001-2005. Auditor and librarian; former branch sec SCPS and IPCS Trade Unions. **Tom Holvey** (LD) Cllr, York CC 2004-. Econ Policy Manager at Leeds CC.

Constituency
Selby, a market town on the Ouse, remains at the heart but the seat has lost an area on the outskirts of York. It curves northwest, skirting Leeds and extending almost to Harrogate. The seat is mostly rural with commuter villages dotted through the flat, fertile Vale of York. Coalmines have closed but the Drax coal power station remains and there is a strong manufacturing sector. A small monument by a field near Tockwith marks the Civil War Battle of Marston Moor in 1644. Traditionally a Tory area, the seat switched to Labour in 1997.

		Electorate	Turnout %	Change from 05 %
		72,789	71.1	☆
Adams, N	C	25,562	49.4	2.3
Marshall, J	Lab	13,297	25.7	-17.1
Holvey, T	LD	9,180	17.8	7.8
Haley, D	UKIP	1,635	3.2	
Lorriman, D	BNP	1,377	2.7	
Michael, G	Eng	677	1.3	

50%

Majority 12,265

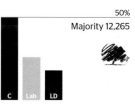

Sevenoaks Conservative hold

Michael Fallon
b. May 14, 1952
MP 1983-92; 1997-

Thatcherite with good inquisitor instincts on financial matters. Chair Treasury Sub-Committee 2001-. Parly Under-Sec: Schools 1990-1992; Government whip 1988-1990; PPS to Cecil Parkinson 1987-88. MP Darlington 1983-92. Former company director of Quality Care Homes plc (nursing homes) and Just Learning Ltd (nurseries). Married, two sons. Education: Epsom College, Surrey; St Andrews (MA classic and ancient history).

Alan Bullion (LD) Agricultural editor; university lecturer. Nat exec member, European Movement. Contested Hammersmith & Fulham 2005.

Gareth Siddorn (Lab) Charity work, UNICEF; National Executive of Labour Environmental Campaign.

Constituency
This Kent seat borders East London and is criss-crossed by the M25, M20 and M26. The main town of Sevenoaks lies near the south of the seat and, like the settlements in the rural North Downs surrounding it, is generally extremely affluent. Swanley, in the northwestern tip, is the other main town, slightly less well-off. The constituency is typified by middle-class professionals living in detached houses, commuting to work in London. It has been represented by the Tories since 1924.

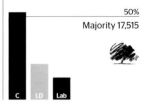

	Electorate	Turnout %	Change from 05 %
	69,591	71.0	☆
Fallon, M C	28,076	56.8	5.5
Bullion, A LD	10,561	21.4	-0.8
Siddorn, G Lab	6,541	13.2	-8.0
Heath, C UKIP	1,782	3.6	0.6
Golding, P BNP	1,384	2.8	
Uncles, L Eng	806	1.6	
Ellis, M Ind	258	0.5	

50%
Majority 17,515

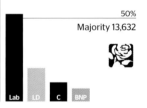

C | LD | Lab

Sheffield Brightside & Hillsborough Labour hold

David Blunkett
b. Jun 6, 1947
MP 1987-

Tribal loyalist, helped sink remote prospect of Lib-Lab coalition 2010. Chaired Labour's election development board. Diminished figure after controversy over fast-tracking of visa for his lover's nanny. Cleared by inquiry but largely sidelined since second resignation; makes worthy speeches with little impact. SoS: Work & Pensions 2005; Home 2001-04; Education/Employment 1997-2001. First blind Cabinet minister. Shadow Sec: Educat/Employment 1995-97; Ed 1994-95; Health 1992-94. Opp spokes 1988-92. Lab Party: member NEC 1983-98; chair 1993-94. Unison. Indust relats/politics tutor. Shop steward GMB EMGB. Divorced, remarried.

Three sons from first marriage; one son from other relationship; three stepdaughters from second marriage. Ed: Sheffield (BA pol theory/inst); Huddersfield Coll of Ed (PGCE).

Jonathan Harston (LD) Cllr, Sheffield CC 1999-. Teacher.
John Sharp (C) Cllr, Wakefield DC.

Constituency
From the edge of the city centre, the constituency rises up the hillsides to the north and latches Hillsborough, home to Sheffield Wednesday FC, to the old Brightside seat. It encompasses areas such as Burngreave, Parsons Cross, Shirebank and Wincobank, as well as the Northern General Hospital, a significant employer. A very working-class seat, with almost half its residents living in social housing, this is the poorest Sheffield seat and safely Labour.

	Electorate	Turnout %	Change from 05 %
	68,186	57.1	☆
Blunkett, D Lab	21,400	55.0	-14.6
Harston, J LD	7,768	20.0	6.9
Sharp, J C	4,468	11.5	1.7
Sheldon, J BNP	3,026	7.8	
Sullivan, P UKIP	1,596	4.1	1.1
Bowler, M TUSC	656	1.7	

50%
Majority 13,632

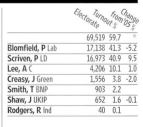

Lab | LD | C | BNP

Sheffield Central Labour hold

Paul Blomfield
b. Aug 25, 1953
MP 2010-

Advocate of electoral and constitutional reform, who narrowly held off Lib Dem challenge. Long-term Sheffield resident and district party chairman. General manager, Sheffield University Student Union. Former gov, Sheffield City Polytechnic. Chair, Sheffield City Trust (1997-2008). Anti-Apartheid Movement campaigner; founded Sheffield branch in youth. Unison and Amicus member. Married (to MEP Linda McAvan), one son. Education: Abbeydale Boys GS; Tadcaster GS; St John's Coll, York (Theology).

Paul Scriven (LD) b. 1966. Cllr, Sheffield CC, 2000-. Leader 2008-.

Andrew Lee (C) Cllr, North Yorkshire CC. School governor.

Constituency
The city centre contains the cathedral, city hall and shopping centre. Development has transformed it, with highlights including the enclosed Winter Garden, Millennium Galleries and new-look railway station. The seat reaches east to the deprived Manor council estate and to the west branches out in a triangle, with Walkley and Nether Edge at the extremities. The University of Sheffield and Sheffield Hallam University mean that a quarter of residents are students. Another quarter are from an ethnic minority background. Labour has long represented the seat.

	Electorate	Turnout %	Change from 05 %
	69,519	59.7	☆
Blomfield, P Lab	17,138	41.3	-5.2
Scriven, P LD	16,973	40.9	9.5
Lee, A C	4,206	10.1	1.0
Creasy, J Green	1,556	3.8	-2.0
Smith, T BNP	903	2.2	
Shaw, J UKIP	652	1.6	-0.1
Rodgers, R Ind	40	0.1	

50%
Majority 165

Lab | LD | C

Sheffield Hallam

Liberal Democrat hold

Nick Clegg
b. Jan 7, 1967
MP 2005-

Engaging face of new political era. Interested in policy, restlessness with Commons convention lies in part behind wish for political reform. Deputy Prime Minister 2010-. Leader, Lib Dems 2007-. LD Shad SoS: Home 2006-07. LD spokes Foreign 2005-06. MEP East Midlands 1999-2004 (member, Maghreb & Arab Maghreb Union Delegation 2002-04). European Commission official – led negotiations with Russia, China. Lobbyist, GPlus. Married (to Spanish national), three sons. Ed: Westminster Sch; Cambridge (MA social anthropology), Minnesota Fellowship Award; Coll of Europe, Bruges (dip European affairs).

Nicola Bates (C) Communications professional, charity volunteer with 'Crisis'. Ed: University of York.
Jack Scott (Lab) Charity worker, Youth Action Network, Foundation for Social Inclusion. Ed: Northampton Grammar School; University of Sheffield.

Constituency
In a city divided between haves and have-nots, with a 14-year difference in life expectancy, this second wealthiest seat beyond London and the South East is resolutely for the haves. It encompasses western fringes of Sheffield and the countryside beyond. More than a third of residents are professionals; the number of "higher professionals" is double the national average and triple that for Yorkshire and the Humber. A fifth of residents are students. The Lib Dems took the constituency with a dramatic swing in 1997.

	Electorate	Turnout %	Change from 05 %
	69,378	73.7	☆
Clegg, N LD	27,324	53.4	7.1
Bates, N C	12,040	23.6	-6.6
Scott, J Lab	8,228	16.1	-1.7
James, N UKIP	1,195	2.3	1.0
Barnard, S Green	919	1.8	-0.8
Wildgoose, D Eng	586	1.2	
Fitzpatrick, M Ind	429	0.8	
Green, R Ch	250	0.5	
Adshead, M Loony	164	0.3	

50%
Majority 15,284

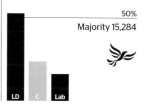

Sheffield Heeley

Labour hold

Meg Munn
b. Aug 24, 1959
MP 2001-

Personable Blairite. Likeable but undynamic, very upset when sacked by Gordon Brown. Unlikely member of revolt against Gordon Brown's leadership in 2009. Parly Under-Sec: Foreign & Commonwealth Office 2007-08; Women & Equality 2006-07; Trade & Industry 2005-06. PPS to: Margaret Hodge 2002-05; Education team 2003-04. Cllr, Nottingham CC 1987-91. Co-op party. Soc worker. Assistant director, City of York council. Nalgo shop steward. Unison, GMB, USDAW. Married. Ed: Rowlinson Comp Sch; York (BA langs); Nottingham (MA soc work); Soc Work Qual Cert; Management Studies Cert/ Dip.

Simon Clement-Jones (LD) Cllr, Sheffield CC, 2004-.
Anne Crampton (C) GP, Crowthorne, Berkshire. Cllr, Eversley PC.

Constituency
To the south of Sheffield city centre, the seat stretches down to the border with Derbyshire. It is mixed: a third of people live in council or social housing and there are patches of deprivation in the north and south but some lower-middle class groups are well represented, as are skilled manual workers. There are fewer students or top professionals than in the centre and the population is predominantly white. The area has had a diverse political history under varied boundaries but since 1983 has been represented by Labour.

	Electorate	Turnout %	Change from 05 %
	65,869	62.1	☆
Munn, M Lab	17,409	42.6	-11.5
Clement-Jones, S LD	11,602	28.4	7.0
Crampton, A C	7,081	17.3	3.0
Beatson, J BNP	2,260	5.5	
Arnott, C UKIP	1,530	3.7	1.4
Roberts, G Green	989	2.4	-1.2

50%
Majority 5,807

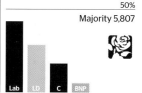

Sheffield South East

Labour hold

Clive Betts
b. Jan 13, 1950
MP 1992-

Led backbench revolt to force through higher MPs' housing allowance in 2001. Suspended for seven days in 2003 for giving Commons pass to gay lover, a former male escort. Elected Chair, select cttee: CLG 2010-. Whip: govt 1998-2001; asst govt 1997-98; opp 1996-7. Member Lab leader campaign team 1995-96, Lab housing group. Cllr, Sheffield CC 1976-92; leader 1987-82. Economist: TUC, Derbyshire CC, S Yorks CC, Rotherham BC. Chair S Yorks Pension Authority. Sheffield Weds fan. Ed: Pembroke Coll, Cambridge (BA econ/pol).

Gail Smith (LD) Foot-Health practitioner. Cllr, Sheffield CC 1992-.

Ed: Foot Health Practitioner Diploma.
Nigel Bonson (C) Former police officer, adviser on neighbourhood regeneration and managememnt of offenders.
Chris Hartigan (BNP)

Constituency
This seat could more accurately be called Sheffield East, based as it is on the old Sheffield Attercliffe seat. It has been extended slightly towards the city centre but remains less cosmopolitan than its neighbour. It is home to a greater proportion of white residents and more working and lower-middle classes. Many steelworks were once here and there are still large industrial parks in the north, joined by the huge Meadowhall shopping centre and Sheffield City airport. The constituency has traditionally returned huge Labour majorities.

	Electorate	Turnout %	Change from 05 %
	67,284	61.5	☆
Betts, C Lab	20,169	48.7	-11.6
Smith, G LD	9,664	23.3	6.4
Bonson, N C	7,202	17.4	3.0
Hartigan, C BNP	2,345	5.7	
Arnott, J UKIP	1,889	4.6	0.2
Andrew, S Comm	139	0.3	

50%
Majority 10,505

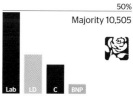

Sherwood — Conservative gain

Mark Spencer
b. Jan 20, 1970
MP 2010-

Farmer and business-man, endured recount to take the seat. On the liberal wing of the Conservative party, advocates localism. Cllr, Gedling BC 2003-; Notts CC 2005-. Member, East Midlands regional assembly 2009-10. Runs Spring Lane Farm Shop, selling produce from family farm, and Floralands Garden Village, Lambley. Married, two children. Education: Colonel Frank Seeley Sch, Calverton; Shuttleworth Agricultural College.

Emilie Oldknow (Lab) NHS worker. Education: Colonel Frank Seely School; Newcastle University.

Kevin Moore (LD) Provides learning support for adults. Worked in financial services. Cllr, Ashfield DC.

Constituency
Forever associated with Robin Hood, Sherwood is a large rural area to the north of Nottingham, dominated by the forest. The main towns lie at opposing ends with Hucknall by the River Leam and Ollerton and Boughton, a former pit town, by the River Maun. Most of this old coalfields seat is not well off and has generally voted Labour, although the smaller settlements such as Ravenshead, Calverton and Woodborough are more affluent. The Conservatives held this for one term from 1983.

	Electorate	Turnout %	Change from 05 %
	71,043	68.9	☆
Spencer, M C	19,211	39.2	5.8
Oldknow, E Lab	18,997	38.8	-10.6
Moore, K LD	7,283	14.9	1.4
North, J BNP	1,754	3.6	
Parker, M UKIP	1,490	3.0	-0.7
Swan, R Ind	219	0.5	

50%
Majority 214

C | Lab | LD

Shipley — Conservative hold

Philip Davies
b. Jan 5, 1972
MP 2005-

Wildly outspoken torchbearer for the old-fashioned anti-EU Tory right. Opposes sex education in schools. 1922 executive committee, 2010-. Member: Better Off Out; Campaign Against Political Correctness. Member ctees: CMS 2006-; Modernisation of the House 2007-. Became Executive at Asda, having worked his way up from cashier through management trainee scheme. Married, two sons. Ed: Old Swinford Hospital Sch; Huddersfield (BA historical and political studies).

Susan Hinchcliffe (Lab) b. 1968. Marketing manager, Daily and Sunday Telegraph. Girlguiding ambassador.

John Harris (LD) Former secondary school teacher.

Constituency
This West Yorkshire seat's three main settlements of Shipley, Baildon and Bingley are clustered at the centre, a few miles north of Bradford. With semi-rural land on either side, this is primarily a residential seat, home to large numbers of middle-class professionals, and is predominantly white. Saltaire village, a Unesco World Heritage Site, lies between Shipley and Bingley. Only small patches of deprivation exist, concentrated in central Shipley, but Labour nevertheless held here from 1997 to 2005.

	Electorate	Turnout %	Change from 05 %
	67,689	73.0	☆
Davies, P C	24,002	48.6	9.7
Hinchcliffe, S Lab	14,058	28.4	-9.4
Harris, J LD	9,890	20.0	4.9
Warnes, K Green	1,477	3.0	-0.4

50%
Majority 9,944

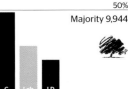

C | Lab | LD

Shrewsbury & Atcham — Conservative hold

Daniel Kawczynski
b. Jan 24, 1972
MP 2005-

Excitable shire Tory, distinctive as one of the tallest MPs. Not very effective. Strong right-winger and strong Polish connections. Member Committees: Int Devt 2008-; Justice 2007-09; Environment Food & Rural Affairs 2005-07. Life-long Tory activist, contested Ealing Southall 2001, Chairman Sterling Uni Con Assoc. Career, telecoms account manager. Married, one daughter. Ed: St George's College; Stirling University (BA business studies with French/Spanish).

Charles West (LD) GP. Former cllr, Shropshire CC. Ed: Priory Boys School; Birmingham (Mb. ChB. MHSM).

Jon Tandy (Lab) Employed by Royal Mail, CWU representative and deputy assistant area health and safety officer. Cllr, Shrewsbury.

Constituency
The town of Shrewsbury, with its historic English and Welsh bridges, lies at the centre of this seat, surrounded by Shropshire countryside. There are affluent areas to the west of the town centre and in the rural areas within easy commuting distance. However, more deprived areas, home to disaffected youth, are found to the east and in the isolated outlying countryside. The service sector dominates the economy. Once a safe Tory seat, it was taken by Labour in 1997 only for Paul Marsden to defect to the Lib Dems after the 2001 election. The Conservatives regained it in 2005.

	Electorate	Turnout %	Change from 05 %
	75,438	70.3	☆
Kawczynski, D C	23,313	44.0	6.3
West, C LD	15,369	29.0	6.2
Tandy, J Lab	10,915	20.6	-13.5
Lewis, P UKIP	1,627	3.1	0.4
Whittall, J BNP	1,168	2.2	
Whittaker, A Green	565	1.1	-1.2
Gollings, J Impact	88	0.2	

50%
Majority 7,944

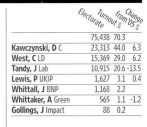

C | LD | Lab

Shropshire North
Conservative hold

Owen Paterson
b. Jun 24, 1956
MP 1997-

Journeyman of the right, close to Iain Duncan Smith. Lacks political skills. SoS: NI 2010-. Shadow Sec: NI 2007-10. Shadow Minister: Transport 2005-7; EFRA 2005; PPS to: Iain Duncan Smith 2001-03. Opposition whip 2000-01. Member, 92 and No Turning Back groups, Con Way Forward. Tanner, president COTANCE. British Leather Co Ltd. Married, one daughter, two sons. Ed: Radley College; Corpus Christi College, Cambridge (MA history).

Ian Croll (LD) Qualified accountant; teacher; board member of local Chamber of Commerce; treasurer elect of local Drugs forum.

Ian McLaughlan (Lab) Business development manager, North Staffordshire Chamber of Commerce. Cllr, Stoke-on-Trent CC 2004-2008. Ed: Brasenose College, Oxford (modern languages).

Constituency
This seat's biggest town, Oswestry, lies near the border with Wales, while Market Drayton is the self-proclaimed home of gingerbread and the base for Müller yoghurt production. The other main towns are Whitchurch, Wem and Ellesmere, site of Ellesmere College. Agriculture is a defining feature of politics and the economy here, with earnings below county and national averages and farmers defensive of their interests. The idyllic landscape also attracts tourists. The Tories have represented this seat for decades, usually with safe majorities.

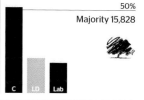

	Electorate	Turnout %	Change from '05 %
	78,926	65.7	
Paterson, O C	26,692	51.5	2.0
Croll, I LD	10,864	21.0	1.3
McLaughlan, I Lab	9,406	18.1	-7.7
List, S UKIP	2,432	4.7	-0.1
Reddall, P BNP	1,667	3.2	
Boulding, S Green	808	1.6	

50%
Majority 15,828

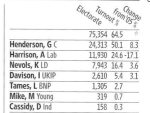

Sittingbourne & Sheppey
Conservative hold

Gordon Henderson
b. Jan 27, 1948
MP 2010-

Proud Kent man and staunch Eurosceptic (Member, Better Off Out group) who narrowly missed out on same seat after recount in 2005. Also contested Luton South 2001. Cllr, Swale BC 1986-95 (dep leader), Kent CC 1989-93. Conservative party agent, former constituency agent to Roger Gale MP. Grew up on council estate, long-standing Isle of Sheppey resident. Self-employed management consultant. Operations Manager, Beams UK. Dir, Unwins Wine Group. Senior contracts officer, GEC Marconi. Worked his way up from stockroom assistant to senior store manager, Woolworths. Unpublished novelist. Instructor, Army Cadet Force. Dir,

Swale Community Action Project. Christian. Married, two daughters, one son. Ed: Fort Luton Sch.

Angela Harrison (Lab) Cllr, Swale BC; Kent CC.
Keith Nevols (LD) Local party secretary.

Constituency
This North Kent seat combines the Isle of Sheppey with the mainland area round Sittingbourne, from which it is divided by the Swale. Relative deprivation is evident in much of Sheppey and in small patches of Sittingbourne, but the mainland is generally better off. The seat has been slightly increased and now includes all of Teynham and Lynsted. Labour won in this formerly Tory area at the seat's inception in 1997 but by 2005 its majority had fallen to 75.

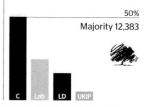

	Electorate	Turnout %	Change from '05 %
	75,354	64.5	※
Henderson, G C	24,313	50.1	8.3
Harrison, A Lab	11,930	24.6	-17.1
Nevols, K LD	7,943	16.4	3.6
Davison, I UKIP	2,610	5.4	3.1
Tames, L BNP	1,305	2.7	
Mike, M Young	319	0.7	
Cassidy, D Ind	158	0.3	

50%
Majority 12,383

Skipton & Ripon
Conservative hold

Julian Smith
b. Aug 30, 1971
MP 2010-

Responsible for bringing Carol Vorderman into Tory role. Co-authored Arculus Report on regulation and red tape with Ken Clarke. Founder and managing director, Arq International, executive recruitment business. Involved with training schemes/charities - Training for Life, Hoxton Apprentice. Junior international squash player. Plays violin and piano to Grade 8. Brought up in remote farming village. Married. Ed: Balfron High; Millfield Sch (sixth form bursary); Birmingham (English & history).

Helen Flynn (LD) Commissioning editor at a publisher; businesswoman, community work; manages play group.

Claire Hazelgrove (Lab) b. Jul 16, 1988. Executive Committee, South Northamptonshire CLP. Youth officer, women's officer.

Constituency
The name reflects the two biggest market towns in a rural North Yorkshire seat that encompasses sweeps of moorland and hills – much of the west is in the Yorkshire Dales National Park. Slightly redrawn, it loses some villages on the outskirts of Harrogate but reaches farther east, beyond Ripon. Traditional trades of quarrying and agriculture remain, though in decline, and tourism and financial services are big employers. The seat is comfortably off but has few truly affluent areas. It has been Tory since its inception in 1983.

	Electorate	Turnout %	Change from '05 %
	77,381	70.7	※
Smith, J C	27,685	50.6	0.6
Flynn, H LD	17,735	32.4	5.8
Hazelgrove, C Lab	5,498	10.1	-8.2
Mills, R UKIP	1,909	3.5	-1.1
Allen, B BNP	1,403	2.6	
Bell, R Ind	315	0.6	
Gilligan, D Youth	95	0.2	
Leakey, R Currency	84	0.2	

50%
Majority 9,950

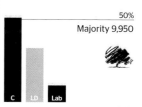

Sleaford & North Hykeham

Stephen Phillips
b. Mar 9, 1970
MP 2010-

Barrister and unpaid adviser to Michael Gove on special educational needs; chair of governors at only sign-bilingual school in the UK. Selected by open primary having missed out on selection in Woking, where he spent his early years. Made one of the youngest Queen's Counsel in the country in 2009, Crown Court Recorder. Specialises in insurance law. Served in the Army with Welsh Guards. Went by the name Stephen Trafalgar-Phillips while at university. Married, two daughters, one son. Education: Sydenham School, Bridgewater; Hardye's School, Dorchester; Canford School, Wimborne; Oriel Coll, Oxford (Law).

David Harding-Price (LD) b. 1956. Mental health professional.
James Normington (Lab) b. Oct 5, 1980. Barrister.
Marianne Overton (Lincs) b. May 22, 1959. Cllr, Lincs CC; North Kesteven DC. Non-exec dir, NHS.

Constituency
This seat in western Lincolnshire is rural, made up of arable farmland and open space with small settlements. Lincoln is just over the northern border, making it easily accessible for affluent commuters. Much of the population lives in North Hykeham and other settlements to the south. The other main town is Sleaford, in the south. Former RAF bases north of Sleaford gave Lincolnshire the nickname "Bomber County" during the Second World War. The seat and its predecessors have a long Tory tradition.

	Electorate	Turnout %	Change from '05 %
	85,550	69.6	*
Phillips, S C	30,719	51.6	1.0
Harding-Price, D LD	10,814	18.2	0.1
Normington, J Lab	10,051	16.9	-9.5
Overton, M Lincs	3,806	6.4	
Doughty, R UKIP	2,163	3.6	-1.3
Clayton, M BNP	1,977	3.3	

50%
Majority 19,905

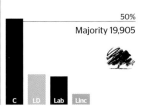

Slough

Fiona Mactaggart
b. Sep 12, 1953
MP 1997-

Opera-loving heiress, surprising but effective match for this working-class constituency. From Labour's centre-left. Owlish looks belie fearless, outspoken manner. Successfully treated for ovarian cancer in 2003. Parly Under-Sec: Home 2003-06. PPS to Chris Smith 1997-2001. Member, cttee: Public Administation 1997-98. Cllr, Wandsworth 1986-90. VP, national sec NUS. Press/PR officer NCVO. Chair, Liberty. Teacher/PR officer/lecturer. Gen sec joint council for immigrants welfare. Ed: Cheltenham Ladies Coll; King's Coll, London (BA Eng); Goldsmith's Coll, London (postgrad teaching cert); Inst of Education (MA).

Diana Coad (C) Timber-broker after haute-couture modelling career. Cllr, Slough BC 2006-.
Chris Tucker (LD) Maths teacher.

Constituency
"Come, friendly bombs, and fall on Slough," implored John Betjeman in 1937. The industry he despised has diversified but the Berkshire town is typified by grey housing estates and concrete office blocks. It struggles to shake off the soulless image of *The Office*, despite regeneration attempts. The Mars bar was invented here; other big employers in a productive town with good links to London and Heathrow include O2 and Ferrari. The non-white population is 40 per cent; the largest communities are Indian and Pakistani and there are the highest number of Sikhs in Britain. Labour overturned three terms of Tory representation in 1997.

	Electorate	Turnout %	Change from '05 %
	77,068	62.0	*
Mactaggart, F Lab	21,884	45.8	-0.3
Coad, D C	16,361	34.3	7.9
Tucker, C LD	6,943	14.5	-2.2
Mason-Apps, P UKIP	1,517	3.2	-0.5
Kennet, M Green	542	1.1	-0.9
Chaudhary, S Ch	495	1.0	

50%
Majority 5,523

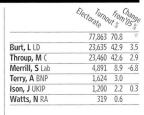

Solihull

Lorely Burt
b. Sep 10, 1954
MP 2005-

Surprise victor in 2005 after stealth campaign caught Conservatives napping. First woman to chair Lib Dems' parliamentary party. LD shad min: BIS 2009-10; BERR 2007-09; Small Business, Women & Equality 2006-07; NI 2005-06. LD whip 2005-06. Member, cttee: Regulatory Reform 2006-10; Treasury 2005-06. Contested Dudley South 2001. Personnel management. Prison Service. Dir, marketing consultancy company. Founder, Licensed retail company. Married, one daughter, one stepson. Ed: High Arcal Grammar School, Dudley; University College of Wales, Swansea (BSc econ); Open University (MBA).

Maggie Throup (C) Former medical laboratory scientist, runs marketing and PR Consultancy. Ed: Bradford Girls' Grammar School; Manchester (Biology).
Sarah-Jayne Merrill (Lab) Ed: University of York.

Constituency
In the south east of Birmingham, this is generally a very affluent seat with residential concentrations around Solihull and Shirley. The National Exhibition Centre and Birmingham International airport lie just beyond the seat's northwestern boundary and bring business tourism to the area, but the decline of traditional manufacturing has been seen, particularly with job losses from the seat's Land Rover plant. Traditionally staunchly Conservative, it was a surprise win for the Lib Dems in 2005.

	Electorate	Turnout %	Change from '05 %
	77,863	70.8	*
Burt, L LD	23,635	42.9	3.5
Throup, M C	23,460	42.6	2.9
Merrill, S Lab	4,891	8.9	-6.8
Terry, A BNP	1,624	3.0	
Ison, J UKIP	1,200	2.2	0.3
Watts, N RA	319	0.6	

50%
Majority 175

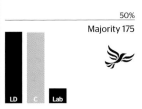

Somerset North — Conservative hold

Dr Liam Fox
b. Sep 22, 1961
MP 1992-

Indefatigable, the big beast of the right: aggressive, dogged, with neo-conservative instincts. Coined 'broken society' phrase during 2005 leadership contest. Committed and knowledgeable on Defence brief: SoS 2010-, Shadow Sec 2005-10. Prev Shadow Sec: Foreign 2005; Health 1999-2003. Ran Michael Howard's 2003 leadership campaign. Rewarded with co-chairman, Con Party 2003-05. Spokes Const. affairs 1997-99. Parly Under-Sec, FCO, 1996-7. Government whip 1995-96; Assistant government whip 1994-95. PPS to Michael Howard 1993-94. Chair Conservative Health/ Social Services Policy Committee 2001. GP. Married, one daughter, one son.

Ed: St. Bride's High School; Glasgow (MB Medicine, MRCGP) .

Brian Mathew (LD) Career in African sanitation and health programmes. **Steven Parry-Hearn** (Lab) Charity worker, Shaw Trust.

Constituency
Though a tiny boundary change adds an extra 181 electors (as of the last census), this is essentially the old Woodspring seat with a new name. A coastal strip between the Severn Estuary and the M5 includes the towns of Clevedon and Portishead, while inland from the motorway is Nailsea and a predominantly rural area dotted with villages. This is a fairly affluent constituency with about a third of the population commuting to work, mostly in Bristol and Bath. The old seat returned Tory MPs.

	Electorate	Turnout %	Change from '05 %
	77,304	75.0	☆
Fox, L C	28,549	49.3	7.5
Mathew, B LD	20,687	35.7	5.5
Parry-Hearn, S Lab	6,448	11.1	-10.7
Taylor, S UKIP	2,257	3.9	1.4

50%

Majority 7,862

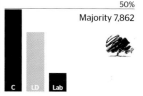

Somerset North East — Conservative hold

Jacob Rees-Mogg
b. May 24, 1969
MP 2010-

Resolutely genteel young fogey. Son of former *Times* Editor Lord Rees-Mogg. Outspoken and gaffe-prone, once implied those not privately/Oxbridge educated were "potted plants". Eurosceptic. Contested The Wrekin 2001, Central Fife 1997 (infamously campaigned with his nanny). Investment banker (pension fund manager). Founded, Somerset Capital Management. Dir, Lloyd George Management, including spell in Hong Kong. J Rothschild Investment Management. Centre for Policy Studies. Keen cricketer. Married, one son, one daughter. Ed: Eton; Trinity Coll, Oxford (history, president OUCA).

Dan Norris (Lab) b. Jan 28, 1960. MP for Wansdyke 1997-2010. Asst govt whip 2001-03, PPS to Peter Hain 2006-07, David Miliband 2007-10. **Gail Coleshill** (LD) Science teacher. Cllr, S Somerset DC; Bath CC.

Constituency
Largely the old Wansdyke seat, it no longer contains any south Gloucestershire wards and instead encircles the Bath city seat. Only a third of the population lives in urban areas: Midsomer Norton, a traditional market town on the River Somer, neighbouring Radstock, a former coalmining town, and Keynsham, on the outskirts of Bristol. The rest of the constituency is rural, with the gentle hills of the Chew Valley a particularly affluent area. The economy is strong. Once seen as safely Tory, the seat was won by Labour in 1997.

	Electorate	Turnout %	Change from '05 %
	67,412	76.0	☆
Rees-Mogg, J C	21,130	41.3	2.2
Norris, D Lab	16,216	31.7	-7.0
Coleshill, G LD	11,433	22.3	2.7
Sandell, P UKIP	1,754	3.4	1.3
Jay, M Green	670	1.3	

50%

Majority 4,914

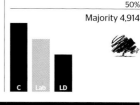

Somerton & Frome — Liberal Democrat hold

David Heath
b. Mar 16, 1954
MP 1997-

Classic bearded Liberal. Keen parliamentarian, effective orator. Quit Liberal Democrat front bench to vote for EU referendum in 2008. Deputy Leader of House of Commons 2010-. LD Shadow: Leader of HoC 2009-10. LD Shadow Sec: Justice/Lord Chancellor 2007-08. LD spokes, various 1997-2007. Member: LD Federal Exec 1993-95, 1990-92; Liberal Party Nat Exec 1988-89. Audit Commission. Cllr, Somerset 1985-97 (leader 1985-89). Chair Avon/Somerset Police Authority. Optician. CBE. Married, one daughter, one son. Ed: Millfield School; St John's College, Oxford (MA physiological sciences); City (ophthalmic optics).

Annunziata Rees-Mogg (C) Journalist, *The Daily Telegraph*; deputy editor of *MoneyWeek* and editor *European Journal*. Contested Aberavon 2005.

Constituency
From Wincanton at the centre of the seat, one arm extends north to Frome – pronounced "Froom" – which boasts more than 500 listed buildings, more than Bath has. Another branch extends west to Somerton and beyond. Tweaks to the boundaries include gaining Baltonsborough and Butleigh and losing Ivelchester. The seat is largely rural, with agricultural land, especially around Blackmoor Vale, that gives rise to food and dairy businesses. The constituency has returned Lib Dems with narrow victories since they first won by 130 votes in 1997.

	Electorate	Turnout %	Change from '05 %
	81,548	74.3	☆
Heath, D LD	28,793	47.5	3.8
Rees-Mogg, A C	26,976	44.5	1.9
Oakensen, D Lab	2,675	4.4	-6.4
Harding, B UKIP	1,932	3.2	1.3
Warry, N Leave	236	0.4	

50%

Majority 1,817

259

South Holland & The Deepings | Conservative hold

John Hayes
b. Jun 23, 1958
MP 1997-

A smart right-winger with a bulldog appearance, he is a leading figure of the "faith, flag and family" Tory right. Min: BIS 2010-. Shadow Minister: BIS 2009-10; Higher Ed 2009; Vocational Ed 2005-09; Transport 2005; Local Govt 2003-05; Agriculture 2002-03. Opposition whip 2001-02. Member, 1922 group. Cllr Notts CC 1985-88. IT company director, The Data Base. Married, two sons. Education: Colfe's Grammar School; Nottingham (BA politics, PGCE history/English).

Jennifer Conroy (LD) Cllr, Northampton DC. Community activist involved in local residents' association. Educa-

tion: Northampton (BA history).
Gareth Gould (Lab) b. Aug 29, 1978. Education: University of Lancaster.
Richard Fairman (UKIP)

Constituency
This seat encompasses the southernmost stretch of Lincolnshire coastline, reaching up to the River Welland, which flows out from the main town of Spalding. A Georgian market town, it has historic trade links with the Netherlands, and is central to the British flower industry, celebrating with an annual tulip parade. The other main settlements are the affluent Deepings, in the south west, and Holbeach. There is a significant agricultural sector, particularly in flower and vegetable growing. Typical of farming areas it is averagely affluent, but has long been Conservative.

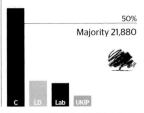

	Electorate	Turnout %	Change from '05 %
	76,243	1.0	☆
Hayes, J C	29,639	59.1	2.1
Conroy, J LD	7,759	15.5	2.6
Gould, G Lab	7,024	14.0	-10.5
Fairman, R UKIP	3,246	6.5	2.5
Harban, R BNP	1,796	3.6	
Baxter, A Green	724	1.4	

50%
Majority 21,880

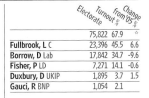

South Ribble | Conservative gain

Lorraine Fullbrook
b. Jul 28, 1959
MP 2010-

Lively and approachable. Credited by George Osborne with influencing the Conservatives' inheritance tax policy pledge. Contested South Ribble 2005. Cllr, Hart DC 2000-04 (council leader 2003-04). Dir, Women2Win but opponent of all-women shortlists. Self-employed PR consultant. Trade sector controller at senior management level, Bryant & May. Media & PR adviser to James Arbuthnot MP. Married. Ed: Kilmarnock Academy; Caledonian Uni (dropped out in third year).

David Borrow (Lab) b. Aug 2, 1952. MP South Ribble 1997-2010. PPS: to Tport Min 2003-10, to Higher Education Min 2004-05. Cllr, Preston BC (leader 1992-

94 and 1995-97). Education: Coventry Uni (BA economics).
Peter Fisher (LD) NHS non-executive director; JP administrator, national charity.

Constituency
South Ribble, which includes about two thirds of the borough of the same name, also encompasses wards from Chorley and West Lancashire. The northern boundary follows the River Ribble out to the coast, while the main settlements are concentrated to the east of the seat near the M6, which runs past longitudinally. These include Penwortham, a suburb of Preston, Leyland, home to the truck manufacturers, and Eccleston. Comfortably affluent and held by the Tories until Labour's landslide of 1997.

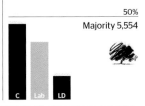

	Electorate	Turnout %	Change from '05 %
	75,822	67.9	☆
Fullbrook, L C	23,396	45.5	6.6
Borrow, D Lab	17,842	34.7	-9.6
Fisher, P LD	7,271	14.1	-0.6
Duxbury, D UKIP	1,895	3.7	1.5
Gauci, R BNP	1,054	2.1	

50%
Majority 5,554

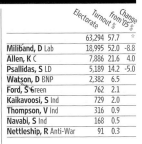

South Shields | Labour hold

David Miliband
b. Jul 15, 1965
MP 2001-

Regarded by Blairites as the true keeper of new Labour flame. Erudite on policy, but questions exist over his people skills and political courage, twice holding back from challenging Gordon Brown. Candidate for Lab leader 2010. SoS: Foreign 2007-10; EFRA 2006-07. Min: CLG/ODPM 2005-06; Cab Off 2004-05; Ed & Skills 2002-04. Founder, Centre for Eur Reform. Head: PM's policy unit 1997-2001; Leader of Opp's policy office 1994-97. SoS, Comm on Social Justice. Research fellow, Inst for Public Policy Research. NCVO, parly officer. TGWU. Jewish, older brother of Ed. Married, two adopted sons. Ed: Haverstock Comp; Corpus Christi Coll, Oxford (BA PPE); MIT (MSc pol sci).

Karen Allen (C) Financial sector. Member, Conservative Way Forward (CWF), Conservative Future Executive.
Stephen Psallidas (LD) Project manager, sustainable development. Cllr.
Donna Watson (BNP)

Constituency
On the south bank of the Tyne, this is a working-class and overwhelmingly white constituency. A big manufacturing presence includes Barbour's Simonside plant, which produces the wax jackets. Rekendyke and Horsley Hill are especially deprived. The boundary now includes a strip of coastline south of the town, to the village of Whitburn. For a passionate argument about football, South Shields is the place: half the town supports Sunderland, the other half their sworn enemies, Newcastle United. Politically the seat has been Labour for decades.

	Electorate	Turnout %	Change from '05 %
	63,294	57.7	☆
Miliband, D Lab	18,995	52.0	-8.8
Allen, K C	7,886	21.6	4.0
Psallidas, S LD	5,189	14.2	-5.0
Watson, D BNP	2,382	6.5	
Ford, S Green	762	2.1	
Kaikavoosi, S Ind	729	2.0	
Thompson, V Ind	316	0.9	
Navabi, S Ind	168	0.5	
Nettleship, R Anti-War	91	0.3	

50%
Majority 11,109

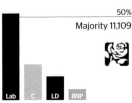

Southampton Itchen — Labour hold

John Denham
b. Jul 15, 1953
MP 1992-

Won respect as most senior minister to resign over Iraq war. Less effective on return to Brown's cabinet, leading short-lived Dept for Innovation, Univs & Skills. Leading Lab adv of elec reform. SoS: DCLG 2009-10; IUS 2007-09. Chair, cttee: Home 2003-07. Min: Home 2001-03; Health 1999-2001; Soc Sec 1997-98. Parly Under-Sec: Soc Sec 1997-98. Opp spokes: soc sec 1995-97. Cllr: Southampton CC 1989-92; Hants CC 1981-89. Advice worker, transport campaigner, head of youth affairs, consultant to vol orgs. War on Want. PC. Divorced, has partner. One daughter, one son from first marriage, one son with partner. Ed: Woodroffe Comp; Southampton (BSc chemistry).

Royston Smith (C) RAF ground engineer. Cllr, Southampton CC.
David Goodall (LD) Senior project leader, Roke Manor Research. Cllr, Eastleigh BC 2002-.

Constituency
Spanning the mouth of the River Itchen, the constituency contains the city centre on the western bank, including Eastern Docks, the retail and commercial hub and two university campuses. Stretching farther up the eastern bank of the Itchen, it covers a larger residential area, including suburbs such as Woolston, Sholing and Bitterne. This is predominantly a working-class area with some deprivation but the city has undergone extensive regeneration. The seat last changed hands when Labour regained it by a narrow majority in 1992 after two Tory terms.

		Electorate	Turnout %	Change from 05 %
		74,532	59.6	*
Denham, J	Lab	16,326	36.8	-11.5
Smith, R	C	16,134	36.3	9.1
Goodall, D	LD	9,256	20.8	0.1
Kebbell, A	UKIP	1,928	4.3	0.6
Spottiswoode, J	Green	600	1.4	
Cutter, T	TUSC	168	0.4	

50%
Majority 192

Southampton Test — Labour hold

Alan Whitehead
b. Sep 15, 1950
MP 1997-

Expert on local government, policy thinker largely overlooked in Government. Brief ministerial career caught up in John Prescott's muddled Whitehall empire. Parly Under-Sec: Transport 2001-02. PPS to: Baroness Blackstone 1999-2001; David Blunkett 1999-2000. Member, cttees: Energy & Climate Change 2009-10; Standards & privileges 2005-10; Constitutional Affairs 2003-10; Environment, Transport & Regional Affairs 1997-99. Lab Party Nat Policy Forum. Cllr, Southampton CC 1980-92 (leader 1984-92). Prof of public policy. Dir: Outset/BIIT/Southampton Environment Centre. Married, one daughter, one son. Ed: Southampton (BA pol/phil, PhD pol sci).

Jeremy Moulton (C) b. 1976. Pensions manager, Winterthur Life (AXA) Cllr, Cab Min for Resources and Finance.
David Callaghan (LD) Journalist; The Guardian; freelance. Cllr, Sutton TC 2006-. Deputy Mayor, 2008-09.

Constituency
The western half of Southampton is in this seat, which runs along the River Test in the south. The waterfront is used predominantly by the Western Docks; Southampton is the cruise departure capital of Britain and a leading deep-water container port, especially for vehicle import and export (Ford Transit vans are produced just beyond the northern boundary). Inland, the seat encompasses suburbs such as Shirley and takes in Southampton Common and the main University of Southampton campus – there is a large student population. The constituency was Tory in 1979-97.

		Electorate	Turnout %	Change from 05 %
		71,931	61.4	*
Whitehead, A	Lab	17,001	38.5	-5.7
Moulton, J	C	14,588	33.0	8.0
Callaghan, D	LD	9,865	22.3	-1.8
Hingston, P	UKIP	1,726	3.9	0.9
Bluemel, C	Green	881	2.0	-1.7
Sanderson, C	Ind	126	0.3	

50%
Majority 2,413

Southend West — Conservative hold

David Amess
b. Mar 26, 1952
MP 1997-; Basildon 1983-97

A classic local populist who was the grinning face of John Major's unlikely 1992 election victory, when filmed holding swing seat of Basildon for Tories. Committed Roman Catholic, active in conservative social policy areas. 1922 executive committee, 2010-. PPS to: Michael Portillo 1988-97; Lord Skelmersdale 1988; Edwina Currie 1987-88. Junior school teacher, underwriter, consultant to agencies supplying accountants. Married, four daughters, one son. Ed: St Bonaventure's GS; Bournemouth Coll of Technology (BSc economics).

Peter Welch (LD) Public sector auditor at NAO. Ed: Exeter Uni (politics).

Thomas Flynn (Lab) Party organiser, previously worked for School of Nursing. Ed: Southampton Uni (economics; MA in interactive production).

Constituency
This small, densely populated urban seat includes some of the seaside town's coastline around Leigh and Chalkwell Ooze. West of the town centre and pier, it is mainly a residential area and has better escaped the decline of the tourism industry than the neighbouring seat. It remains popular with relatively affluent commuters to London. The seat has returned Tory MPs for decades, though their margin of victory fell significantly in 1997.

		Electorate	Turnout %	Change from 05 %
		66,527	65.6	
Amess, D	C	20,086	46.1	-0.1
Welch, P	LD	12,816	29.4	5.4
Flynn, T	Lab	5,850	13.4	-9.2
Cockrill, G	UKIP	1,714	3.9	0.5
Gladwin, T	BNP	1,333	3.1	
Bolton, B	Green	644	1.5	
Vel, D	Ind	617	1.4	
Phillips, T	Eng	546	1.3	

50%
Majority 7,270

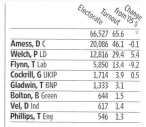

Southport | Liberal Democrat hold

John Pugh
b. Jun 28, 1948
MP 2001-

Co-founder of Beveridge Group to protect Lib Dems' social liberal heritage. LD Shadow Min: Health 2009-10; Treasury 2008-10; Health 2006-07; Transport 2005-06. LD spokes: education 2002-05. Former member Merseyside Police Authority. North West Arts Board, Merseyside Partnership. Teacher, philosophy head, Merchant Taylors Boys Sch, Crosby. Married, three daughters, one son. Ed: Prescott GS; Maidstone GS; Durham (BA phil); Liverpool (MA logic, MEd); Nottingham (MPhil theology); Manchester (PhD logic).

Brenda Porter (C) b. 1954. Manager, charitable and religious organisations.

Cllr, Sefton BC, 2000-.
Jim Conalty (Lab) b. Jun, 1963. Senior research & information officer, Sefton Children's Services; Director/Trustee M.Path European Mental Health Trust. Ed: Ainsdale High; Hugh Baird College.

Constituency
Encompassing a stretch of coastline roughly halfway between the Ribble and Mersey estuaries, Southport seat contains the eponymous town, as well as Birkdale and Ainsdale to the south. Southport is a relatively upmarket seaside resort with a large number of professionals commuting to nearby cities but it does have a few pockets of deprivation along the seafront. It is also home to a high number of retired people. It has been marginal between Conservatives and Lib Dems since the 1980s.

	Electorate	Turnout %	Change from '05 %
	67,202	65.1	
Pugh, J LD	21,707	49.6	3.3
Porter, B C	15,683	35.8	-1.2
Conalty, J Lab	4,116	9.4	-3.4
Durrance, T UKIP	2,251	5.1	3.3

50%
Majority 6,024

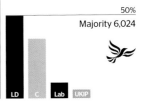

| LD | C | Lab | UKIP |

Spelthorne | Conservative hold

Kwasi Kwarteng
b. May 26, 1975
MP 2010-

Highly intelligent and articulate with calm, confident demeanour. Contested Brent East 2005; London Assembly List 2008. Chairman of the Bow Group 2005-06. Financial analyst: WestLB, JP Morgan Cazenove and Odey Asset Management. Journalist and author, *Ghosts of Empire*. Born in UK to Ghanaian parents. Education: Eton (King's Scholar; Newcastle Scholar); Trinity College, Cambridge (BA classics & history, MA; PhD history; was on winning *University Challenge* team); Harvard (Kennedy Scholar).

Mark Chapman (LD) Technical and sales office manager for a distribution company. Cllr, Bedfordshire DC, 2004-

07. Contested Mid-Beds 2005.
Adam Tyler-Moore (Lab) Practising solicitor. Ed: University of Bristol.
Christopher Browne (UKIP) Contested Runnymede and Weybridge 2001; 2005.

Constituency
In the northern tip of Surrey, this densely populated urban constituency is atypical of the county, although it shares the commuter-driven high house prices. The settlements of Ashford, Shepperton, Staines, Stanwell and Sunbury sprawl across most of Spelthorne and about 30 per cent is flood plain or reservoir. Just south of Heathrow, the airport and associated sectors employ about a quarter of the working population. The seat has been Tory for decades, although majorities dipped in 1997.

	Electorate	Turnout %	Change from '05 %
	70,479	67.1	
Kwarteng, K C	22,261	47.1	-3.3
Chapman, M LD	12,242	25.9	8.9
Tyler-Moore, A Lab	7,789	16.5	-10.7
Browne, C UKIP	4,009	8.5	3.9
Swinglehurst, I Ind	314	0.7	
Littlewood, R Best	244	0.5	
Couchman, P TUSC	176	0.4	
Gore, J CIP	167	0.4	
Leon-Smith, G Ind	102	0.2	

50%
Majority 10,019

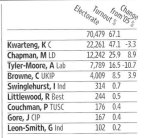

| C | LD | Lab | UKIP |

Stafford | Conservative gain

Jeremy Lefroy
b. May 30, 1959
MP 2010-

Coffee and cocoa trader with extensive business and charitable experience in Tanzania. Contested Newcastle-under-Lyme 2005; European parliament (West Mids) 2004. Cllr, Newcastle-under-Lyme BC 2003-07. MD, African Speciality Products. Worked in Tanzania for 11 years with Schluter Group. Co-founder, Equity for Africa charity. Chartered accountant, Arthur Andersen. Grad trainee, Ford Motor Co. Member Amnesty, Countryside Alliance. Keen musician and sportsman. Christian. Married, two children. Education: Highgate School; King's College, Cambridge (classics).

David Kidney (Lab) b. 21 Mar, 1955. MP for Stafford 1997-2010. Parly Under-Sec, Energy & Climate Change 2009-10.
Barry Stamp (LD) Cllr Stafford BC 1991. Ed: West Midlands Coll; St. Peter's Coll, Birmingham; Open Uni.

Constituency
The M6 forms the spine of this seat, at the centre of Staffordshire. The main town of Stafford and the smaller Penkridge to the south run alongside the motorway, while the seat also includes substantial rural land reaching to the border with Shropshire. This is an economically active seat, in which there are high numbers of professionals, as well as working classes from the traditional manufacturing sector. Labour overturned decades of Tory dominance – and defeated a young David Cameron – when they won in 1997.

	Electorate	Turnout %	Change from '05 %
	70,587	71.2	☆
Lefroy, J C	22,047	43.9	4.7
Kidney, D Lab	16,587	33.0	-10.2
Stamp, B LD	8,211	16.3	2.0
Goode, R UKIP	1,727	3.4	0.1
Hynd, R BNP	1,103	2.2	
Shone, M Green	564	1.1	

50%
Majority 5,460

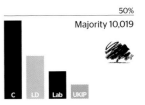

| C | Lab | LD |

Staffordshire Moorlands
Conservative hold

Karen Bradley
b. Mar 12, 1970
MP 2010-

Chartered accountant who came to politics when seconded to Michael Howard's shadow treasury team by KPMG. Sure-footed. Contested Manchester Withington 2005, Richmond BC 2006. Accounting career: KPMG. Conservative Policy Unit. Policy Exchange. Deloitte. Associate Member, Institute of Chartered Accounts in England and Wales (ACA) and Chartered Institute of Taxation (CTA). Special interest in beer and pub issues having grown up in family running The Queen's Head, Buxton. Detective fiction enthusiast. Married, two sons. Church of England. Ed: Buxton Girls Sch; Imperial College, London (BSc Hons mathematics).

Charlotte Atkins (Lab),MP for Staffordshire Moorlands 1997-2010. Parly-Under-Sec, Dept for Tport 2004-05, PPS to Baroness Symons of Vernham Dean 2001-02. Ed: LSE, London.
Henry Jebb (LD) Runs small printing business. Cllr. Staffordshire Moorlands DC. Ed: Keele (BA).
Steve Povey (UKIP)

Constituency
Spanning from the former mining town of Biddulph in the west to part of the Peak District National Park in the east, this seat centres on the town of Leek. Substantial boundary changes resulting in a net loss of electors brought the loss of the mining town Kidsgrove but the gain of the Brown Edge and Endon areas in the east of Stoke-on-Trent, and Alton, home to the Alton Towers theme park. Labour overturned 27 years of Tory dominance when it won in 1997.

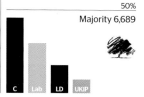

	Electorate	Turnout %	Change from '05 %
	62,071	70.6	☆
Bradley, K C	19,793	45.2	5.4
Atkins, C Lab	13,104	29.9	-6.0
Jebb, H LD	7,338	16.8	-0.8
Povey, S UKIP	3,580	8.2	1.4

50%
Majority 6,689

Staffordshire South
Conservative hold

Gavin Williamson
b. Jun 25, 1976
MP 2010-

Interested in manufacturing, involved in Staffordshire pottery industry: helped turn around one company; brought another out of administration. Contested Blackpool North & Fleetwood, 2005. Cllr, North Yorks 2001-05. Managing Director, architectural design practice. Christian. Well travelled. Married, two daughters. Education: Raincliffe School, Scarborough; Uni of Bradford (social science).

Kevin McElduff (Lab) Director of public services, TMS Insight Group.
Sarah Fellows (LD) Sales manager.
Mike Nattrass (UKIP) MEP West Midlands.

Constituency
Forming a long arc around the north west of Wolverhampton, this semi-rural area is made up of suburban villages, the four largest being Codsall, Great Wyrley, Perton and Wombourne. Typically for the West Midlands, manufacturing is a strong sector but this is overwhelmingly a white, middle-class area, home to many prosperous professionals. Accordingly, it has been Conservative since its creation.

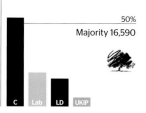

	Electorate	Turnout %	Change from '05 %
	73,390	68.7	☆
Williamson, G C	26,834	53.2	2.6
McElduff, K Lab	10,244	20.3	0.3
Fellows, S LD	8,427	16.7	3.3
Nattrass, M UKIP	2,753	5.5	-4.7
Bradnock, D BNP	1,928	3.8	
Morris, A Ind	254	0.5	

50%
Majority 16,590

Stalybridge & Hyde
Labour hold

Jonathan Reynolds
b. Aug 28, 1980
MP 2010-

Aide to outgoing MP James Purnell, selected amid huge row with Peter Mandelson's involvement after failing to make initial shortlist. Cllr, Tameside 2007-. Dep Chair, Longdendale & Hattersley Dist Assembly. Trainee solicitor, Addleshaw Goddard. Lab Party NEC 2003-05. Member, Co-operative Party, Unite. Married, one son. Ed: Houghton Kepier Comp; Sunderland City Coll; Manchester (BA politics & modern history); BPP Law School, Manchester.

Rob Adlard (C), professional musician. Local Conservative branch chairman. Ed: High Tunstall Comprehensive; University of Manchester.

John Potter (LD), chair of Preston Lib Dems 2008-. Ed: media and journalism.
Anthony Jones (BNP)

Constituency
At the eastern extremity of Greater Manchester, this seat extends through a vast stretch of moorland at the foot of the Pennines. The main settlements form an urban band up the west side of the seat. Hyde, by the M67 in the south, includes Werneth ward, with more than half of the borough's total Bangladeshi population. Stalybridge, in the centre, and Mossley, to the north, are more predominantly white. The seat was traditionally working-class owing to old mill industries and, in recent years, Labour has polled around 50 per cent.

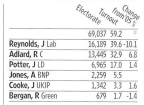

	Electorate	Turnout %	Change from '05 %
	69,037	59.2	☆
Reynolds, J Lab	16,189	39.6	-10.1
Adlard, R C	13,445	32.9	6.8
Potter, J LD	6,965	17.0	1.4
Jones, A BNP	2,259	5.5	
Cooke, J UKIP	1,342	3.3	1.6
Bergan, R Green	679	1.7	-1.4

50%
Majority 2,744

Stevenage | Conservative gain

Stephen McPartland
b. Aug 9, 1976
MP 2010-

Formerly Tory party local agent (NE Herts), called on the party to create a dedicated urban campaigning unit. Membership director, British American Business. Trustee, The Living Room charity. Avid reader. Stevenage FC fan. Married. Education: Liverpool Coll; Liverpool (BA (Hons) history); Liverpool John Moores (MSc technology management).

Sharon Taylor (Lab Co-op) Worked for British Aerospace and Hertfordshire Constabulary. Cllr, Stevenage BC 1997-; Cllr, Hertfordshire CC 2007-. Education: Stevenage Girls Grammar. **Julia Davies** (LD) Secondary school teacher. Education: Merchant Taylors School; University of London. Contested Stevenage 2005.

Constituency
Stevenage was the first New Town after the Second World War. It is averagely affluent, with the highest proportion of residents in social housing in eastern England. To the other side of the A1(M) is Knebworth, which has grown to become a small town. Main employers include GlaxoSmithKline, Fujitsu and the John Lewis Partnership. Labour took this seat from the Tories in 1997.

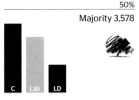

	Electorate	Turnout %	Change from '05 %
	68,937	64.8	☆
McPartland, S C	18,491	41.4	6.4
Taylor, S Lab	14,913	33.4	-9.7
Davies, J LD	7,432	16.6	-1.7
Mason, M UKIP	2,004	4.5	1.4
Green, A BNP	1,007	2.3	
Vickers, C Eng	366	0.8	
Phillips, S No	327	0.7	
Cox, D Ind	80	0.2	
Ralph, A YRDPL	31	0.1	

50%

Majority 3,578

Stirling | Labour hold

Anne McGuire
b. May 26, 1949
MP 1997-

Feisty performer who pulls no punches. Parly Under-Sec: Work & Pensions 2005-08; Scotland 2002-05. Whip: govt 2001-02; asst govt 1998-2001. PPS to Donald Dewar 1997-98. Labour party Scottish exec 1984-97. Chair Labour Party Scotland 1992-93. Cllr, Strathclyde RC 1980-82. Teacher, voluntary sector development worker/ senior manager. Deputy director Scottish Council for Voluntary Organisations. GMB national executive 1987-91. Married, one daughter, one son. Education: Our Lady of St Francis School, Glasgow; Glasgow (MA politics with history); Notre Dame College of Education (Diploma secondary education).

Bob Dalrymple (C) b. 1975. Marketing executive, whisky industry. Contested Stirling, Scottish Parliament elections 2007. Education: Edinburgh (law). **Alison Lindsay** (SNP) Cllr. Worked in National Health and Education Services. Ed: Edinburgh nursing and midwifery; Sterling (BA). **Graham Reed** (LD) b. 1947. Cllr, self-employed consultant. Cllr, Stirling CC 2007-. Ed: Stirling Uni (BA politics).

Constituency
This is a big rural constituency with the town of Stirling at the centre. It has strong Conservative support in the countryside and Labour votes in the town. At the last election, the Labour vote won out, as it has done since 1997. Agriculture is a big employer in the countryside with tourism, particularly round Bannockburn, a major employer in the more urban parts.

	Electorate	Turnout %	Change from '05 %
	66,080	70.8	
McGuire, A Lab	19,558	41.8	5.8
Dalrymple, B C	11,204	23.9	-1.1
Lindsay, A SNP	8,091	17.3	4.7
Reed, G LD	6,797	14.5	-6.2
Ruskell, M Green	746	1.6	-1.4
Henke, P UKIP	395	0.8	0.4

50%

Majority 8,354

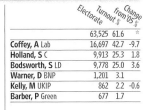

Stockport | Labour hold

Ann Coffey
b. Aug 31, 1946
MP 1992-

Unremarkable, low-key establishment figure. Known for penchant for dangling earrings. Joint parliamentary private secretary to: Alistair Darling 1998-; Tony Blair as PM 1997-98. Opposition health spokesperson 1996-97. Opposition whip 1995-96. Cllr, Stockport MBC 1984-92. Social worker, fostering team leader. USDAW. Divorced, one daughter. Remarried. Education: Bodmin & Bushey Grammar School; South Bank Poly (BSc sociology); Walsall College of Education (Postgrad Education Certificate); Manchester (MSc psychiatric social work).

Stephen Holland (C) b. 1975. Cllr. Stockport DC 2006-. Chartered tax adviser. Education: Oxford (modern languages).
Stuart Bodsworth (LD) Junior diplomat, foreign office; adviser to Bedford Council Lib Dems; business owner.

Constituency
Situated to the south east of Manchester, Stockport sits astride the M60. The sandstone market town was traditionally industrial, with a specialist millinery heritage, but is now a busy urban centre. It has fairly average socioeconomic class distribution but the highest percentage of economically active residents in Greater Manchester, further bolstered by recent regeneration work. It switched from Tory to Labour in 1992.

	Electorate	Turnout %	Change from '05 %
	63,525	61.6	☆
Coffey, A Lab	16,697	42.7	-9.7
Holland, S C	9,913	25.3	1.8
Bodsworth, S LD	9,778	25.0	3.6
Warner, D BNP	1,201	3.1	
Kelly, M UKIP	862	2.2	-0.6
Barber, P Green	677	1.7	

50%

Majority 6,784

Stockton North — Labour hold

Alex Cunningham
b. May 1, 1955
MP 2010-

Humble community figure. Cllr: Stockton on Tees BC 1999-; Cleveland CC 1984-97. Runs own PR/ web design consultancy having worked in PR for the gas industry (head of comms, Transco). Trained journalist, previously worked in newspapers and radio. Christian. Member, Socialist Education Association. Cites Michael Foot and Tony Benn among political heroes. Married, two sons. Education: Branksome Comp; Queen Elizabeth Sixth Form Coll; Coll of Technology, Darlington.

Ian Galletley (C) Headteacher and education inspector, writer. Cllr, Darlington BC 2006-.

Philip Latham (LD) Teacher. Cllr, Tynedale DC 1995-. Contested Hexham 2001.

Constituency
The northeastern half of Stockton-on-Tees encompasses not only the commercial and retail town centre but the sprawling expanses of industrial works along the north banks of the river, which stretch east to Billingham and have long defined the area's economy. The entire riverside is severely deprived and the town was dubbed Britain's capital of childhood obesity in 2009. The seat includes rural areas and Wolviston at the north is well off. Regeneration is under way, with a 20-year plan to merge Stockton and Middlesbrough into one "green" city. This has been a Labour stronghold since 1945.

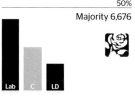

	Electorate	Turnout %	Change from 05 %
	67,363	58.6	☆
Cunningham, A Lab	16,923	42.9	-12.0
Galletley, I C	10,247	25.9	4.7
Latham, P LD	6,342	16.1	-2.6
Macpherson, J BNP	1,724	4.4	
Cook, F Ind	1,577	4.0	
Parkin, G UKIP	1,556	3.9	1.2
Saul, I Eng	1,129	2.9	

50%
Majority 6,676

Stockton South — Conservative gain

James Wharton
b. Feb 16, 1984
MP 2010-

Fresh-faced centrist, local Stockton on Tees man. The second youngest MP in the Commons. Wants to encourage investment in carbon capture and new green technologies in his area. Chairman of Stockton Conservative Assocation 2002-07. Company Law solicitor at BHP Law, Darlington. Member of Officers Training Corps at university. Christian. Education: Yarm School; Durham (Law)

Dari Taylor (Lab) b. 1944. MP Stockton S 1997-2010; PPS to: Lewis Moonie and Lord Bach 2001-03, Hazel Blears, MP 2003-05. Cllr, Sunderland 1986-97. Lecturer, Basford College of FE then Westbridgeford College of FE.

Education: Burnley Municipal College; Nottingham (BA); Durham (MA).
Jacquie Bell (LD) Hospital social worker. Education: Bangor (BA social theory and institutions); Edinburgh (diploma in social work); CQSW, certificate in practice teaching.

Constituency
The southwestern part of Stockton includes the Bowesgate and Preston Farm industrial estates but the seat on the whole is more residential. Though Thornaby, the main town, is fairly deprived, the rest of the area is reasonably prosperous, especially by the region's standards. It includes the Fairfield suburb of Stockton and the communities of Egglescliffe, Ingleby Barwick and Yarm, which flank the Tees to the south. The Tories held the seat from its 1983 creation until Labour won in 1997.

	Electorate	Turnout %	Change from 05 %
	74,552	67.5	☆
Wharton, J C	19,577	38.9	4.7
Taylor, D Lab	19,245	38.3	-9.4
Bell, J LD	7,600	15.1	-1.0
Sinclair, N BNP	1,553	3.1	
Braney, P UKIP	1,471	2.9	0.9
Hossack, Y Ind	536	1.1	
Strike, T Ch	302	0.6	

50%
Majority 332

Stoke-on-Trent Central — Labour hold

Tristram Hunt
b. May 31, 1974
MP 2010-

Urbane, smooth Blairite TV historian and friend of Peter Mandelson, controversially seen to have helped him into the seat, prompting locals to stand against him. Son of Labour peer. Volunteered Millbank 1997, 2001. BBC / Channel 4 documentaries. Lecturer in British history at Queen Mary Uni of London. Critically-acclaimed author on English Civil War and Victorian Cities. Fellow, Royal Historical Society. Trustee, Heritage Lottery Fund. Associate Fellow, Centre for History & Economics, King's Coll Cambridge. Research Fellow, IPPE. Ed: University Coll Sch; Trinity Coll, Cambridge (history); Chicago (postgrad fellowship); King's Coll, Cambridge (PhD history).

John Redfern (LD) Worked for Improvement and Development Agency. Cllr, Staffordshire Moorland DC. Contested Stoke Central 2005.
Norsheen Bhatti (C) b. 1977. Financial services. Parliamentary researcher.
Simon Darby (BNP) b. 1964. Computer consultant. Deputy leader of BNP.

Constituency
Stoke-on-Trent is comprised of six original Staffordshire pottery towns, with two included in this seat: Hanley, the city centre, and Stoke itself, home to the celebrated Portmeirion, in the west. This overwhelmingly working-class seat with areas of severe deprivation is also home to a large number of students at the University of Staffordshire. There is a small Pakistani population and the BNP has had success locally. For most of the last century this seat has been strongly Labour.

	Electorate	Turnout %	Change from 05 %
	60,995	53.2	☆
Hunt, T Lab	12,605	38.8	-13.6
Redfern, J LD	7,039	21.7	3.1
Bhatti, N C	6,833	21.0	3.7
Darby, S BNP	2,502	7.7	
Lovatt, C UKIP	1,402	4.3	1.1
Breeze, P Ind	959	3.0	
Elsby, G Ind	399	1.2	
Ward, B City	303	0.9	
Walker, A Ind	295	0.9	
Wright, M TUSC	133	0.4	

50%
Majority 5,566

Stoke-on-Trent North

Joan Walley
b. Jan 23, 1949
MP 1987-

Wearingly earnest manner, interested in environmental policy. Opp spokes: Transport 1990-95; Environmental Protection & Devt 1988-90. Elected Chair, select cttee: Environmental Audit 2010-. Member, select cttees: West Mids 2009-10; Chairmen's Panel 2008-10; Environ Audit 1997-; Trade & Industry 1995-98. Cllr, Lambeth 1981-85. Nacro devt officer. Local govt officer. Alcoholics recovery project. Unison, Unity. SERA, SEA. Married, two sons. Ed: Biddulph GS, Staffs; Hull (BA social admin); Uni Coll of Wales (Dip community work devt).

Andy Large (C) Company director. Ed: Alsager School; Durham Uni.

John Fisher (LD) Retired teacher. Cllr, Staffs Moorlands DC 1995-; Leek TC. Contested Staffs Moorlands 2005.
Melanie Baddeley (BNP)
Geoffrey Locke (UKIP)

Constituency
Burslem, the birthplace of Josiah Wedgwood, is known as the mother town of the Staffordshire potteries and the closure of Royal Doulton's factory here in 2004 was symbolic of the industry's decline. Hopes are set on the regeneration of the former site. Tunstall has similarly suffered from the closure of ceramics firms. Boundary changes have removed territory from the east of the seat, but it has gained the former mining town of Kidsgrove in the north. With large areas of severe deprivation, this working-class seat returned large Labour majorities throughout the second half of the last century.

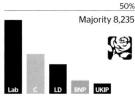

	Electorate	Turnout %	Change from '05 %
	72,052	55.8	*
Walley, J Lab	17,815	44.3	-11.5
Large, A C	9,580	23.8	6.0
Fisher, J LD	7,120	17.7	4.2
Baddeley, M BNP	3,196	8.0	
Locke, G UKIP	2,485	6.2	2.1

50%

Majority 8,235

Stoke-on-Trent South

Rob Flello
b. Jan 14, 1966
MP 2005-

Parliamentary private secretary to: Hazel Blears 2007-09; Lord Falconer 2006-07. Member, committee: Science/Technology 2005-07. Cllr, Birmingham City 2002-04. Regional Organiser Labour Party. CEO Malachi Community Trust. Unite, Unity, USDAW. Ancient history enthusiast. Divorced, one daughter, one stepson. Education: Kings Norton Boys' School; University of Wales, Bangor (BSc chemistry).

James Rushton (C) Accountant and business adviser. Ed: Stoke-on-Trent Sixth Form Coll; London University.
Zulfiqar Ali (LD) Doctor. Cllr, Stoke-on-Trent CC 2008-. Education:

medicine; Royal College of Physicians of Ireland (Postgrad).
Michael Coleman (BNP)

Constituency
Longton and Fenton are two of the six original Staffordshire pottery towns, although Fenton was famously forgotten in Arnold Bennett's novels. Unemployment from the decline of the ceramics industries has been high in recent years and there are large areas of deprivation in this working-class seat, with many in non-skilled occupations. About a fifth live in council housing, although there are some more affluent areas in the south west. Its Labour record stretches back to before 1945.

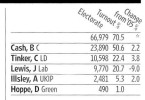

	Electorate	Turnout %	Change from '05 %
	68,031	58.6	*
Flello, R Lab	15,446	38.8	-8.1
Rushton, J C	11,316	28.4	4.2
Ali, Z LD	6,323	15.9	0.8
Coleman, M BNP	3,762	9.4	
Barlow, M UKIP	1,363	3.4	0.7
Follows, T Staffs	1,208	3.0	
Breeze, M Ind	434	1.1	

50%

Majority 4,130

Stone

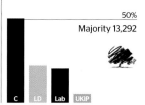

Bill Cash
b. May 10, 1940
MP 1984-

Tall, bespectacled, favour's lawyers pin-striped suits. Extremely obsessive opponent of European Union (led Maastricht rebels); knowledgeable, but can be a bore. Shadow Attorney General (2001-03). Committee Member, European Scrutiny 1998-. MP Stafford 1984-97. Solicitor with own practice. Married, one daughter, two sons. Stoneyhurst College; Lincoln College, Oxford (MA history).

Christine Tinker (LD) Worked in banking, Armed Forces and fitness industry, executive director of British Tennis Coaches' Association. Education: Warwick University (BA politics).

Jo Lewis (Lab) b. 1969. Teacher, previously constit. secretary for local MPs. Education: Staffordshire (BSc); Keele (PGCE).
Andrew Illsley (UKIP)

Constituency
This predominantly rural mid-Staffordshire seat is a straggly shape, curving up either side of the Stoke-on-Trent and Newcastle-under-Lyme seats in the north, as well as either side of the Stafford seat in the south. The town of Stone lies in the centre, with the other main population concentration in Cheadle in the north east. The M6 runs through the seat and its good connections make it popular with affluent professionals. It has been held by the Tories since its creation in 1997.

	Electorate	Turnout %	Change from '05 %
	66,979	70.5	*
Cash, B C	23,890	50.6	2.2
Tinker, C LD	10,598	22.4	3.8
Lewis, J Lab	9,770	20.7	-9.0
Illsley, A UKIP	2,481	5.3	2.0
Hoppe, D Green	490	1.0	

50%

Majority 13,292

Stourbridge — Conservative gain

Margot James
b. Aug 28, 1957
MP 2010-

Independent-minded Thatcherite Tory whose business acumen has generated much respect among peers. Contested Holborn & Pancras 2005. Cllr, Kensington & Chelsea BC 2006-08. Vice-Chair Conservative party (for women's issues). Head of European Healthcare, Ogilvy & Mather advertising agency. Founder / CEO, Shire Health Group (PR/medical education). Worked for Maurice James Industries, father's business. Lesbian, has partner. Education: Millfield Sch; LSE (BSc Economics).

Lynda Waltho (Lab) b. May 22, 1960. MP for Stourbridge 2005-10. Member, Modernisation Committee 2005-07.

Schoolteacher/political adviser. Ed: Keele Uni (economics and geography). **Christopher Bramall** (LD) b. Apr 2, 1942. Retired. Former cllr, Stourbridge. Education: Latymer Upper Sch, Christ's Coll, Cambridge (MA, economics and politics)

Constituency
In the southwestern corner of the West Midlands conurbation, this seat borders Staffordshire and Worcestershire and includes some very affluent semi-rural areas at its outskirts. The commercial centre of Stourbridge and Lye, a deprived industrial town, lies to the south of the River Stour, while Quarry Bank is a residential area to its north. It is a mixed seat, with both middle-class professionals and working classes well represented. It has changed hands many times, with Labour winning in 1997.

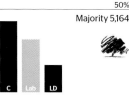

		Electorate	Turnout %	Change from '05 %
		69,637	67.8	*
James, M	C	20,153	42.7	3.4
Waltho, L	Lab	14,989	31.7	-10.4
Bramall, C	LD	7,733	16.4	0.4
Westrop, M	UKIP	2,103	4.5	1.8
Weale, R	BNP	1,696	3.6	
Duckworth, W	Green	394	0.8	
Nicholas, A	Ind	166	0.4	

Majority 5,164

Strangford — DUP hold

Jim Shannon
b. Mar 25, 1955
MP 2010-

Countryside pursuits enthusiast who describes himself as a self-employed pork retailer. Served in Ulster Defence Regiment 1974-77, Royal Artillery 1977-88. Member, NI Assembly 1998-, Forum for Political Dialogue 1996-98, Cllr, Ards, 1985-. Married, three sons. Ed: Coleraine Academical Inst.

Mike Nesbitt (UCUNF) b. 1957. Former commissioner of "Victims and Survivors" committee, NIA. Former UTV Presenter. Education: Campbell College, Belfast, Jesus College, Cambridge (MA, English literature), Queen's University, Belfast (diploma in business administration).

Deborah Girvan (Alliance) b. Nov 28, 1950. Part-time marketing director. **Claire Hanna** (SDLP) International development agency worker. Active trade unionist.
Terry Williams (TUV)

Constituency
This overwhelmingly Unionist constituency is one of five forming a ring around Belfast, mixing the suburban with some of the finest rural landscape in the British Isles, curling around Strangford Lough. Its MP Iris Robinson took the Chiltern Hundreds after her sexual and financial affairs with a teenage lover were revealed by a BBC documentary. The DUP took the seat from the Ulster Unionists in 2001.

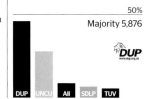

		Electorate	Turnout %	Change from '05 %
		60,539	53.7	*
Shannon, J	DUP	14,926	45.9	-8.9
Nesbitt, M	UCUNF	9,050	27.8	
Girvan, D	Alliance	2,828	8.7	0.5
Hanna, C	SDLP	2,164	6.7	-1.8
Williams, T	TUV	1,814	5.6	
Coogan, M	SF	1,161	3.6	-0.1
Haig, B	Green	562	1.7	

Majority 5,876

Stratford-on-Avon — Conservative hold

Nadhim Zahawi
b. Jun 2, 1967
MP 2010-

Well-spoken co-founder and CEO of YouGov. Interested in immigration and business. Contested Erith & Thamesmead 1997. Cllr, Wandsworth BC 1994-2006. Sits on board of a FTSE 250 business. European marketing dir, Smith & Brooks (children's merchandise firm). Enjoys horseriding and show jumping. CofE. Married, two sons. Ed: King's Sch, Wimbledon; UCL (BSc chemical engineering).

Martin Turner (LD) b. 1966. Warwickshire NHS director of communications. Contested Halesowen & Rowley Regis 2005, Sutton Coldfield 2001; European parl elections 2004. Ed: King Edward's Sch, Birmingham; Oxford Uni.

Robert Johnston (Lab) b. Sep 20, 1982. Trade Union official. Education: Liverpool University.

Constituency
An historic market town synonymous with Shakespeare, Stratford-upon-Avon sits in the middle of this seat, with rural land extending to its north west and south east. The seat has, however, been cut back, losing a vast area that used to extend up to Southam in its north east. Tourism is a major sector and the seat is home to large numbers of well-off professionals, many commuting north to Birmingham. Traditionally Conservative, it had a Labour MP for two years when Alan Howarth defected to Labour in 1995.

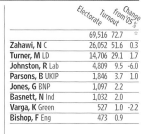

		Electorate	Turnout %	Change from '05 %
		69,516	72.7	*
Zahawi, N	C	26,052	51.6	0.3
Turner, M	LD	14,706	29.1	1.7
Johnston, R	Lab	4,809	9.5	-6.0
Parsons, B	UKIP	1,846	3.7	1.0
Jones, G	BNP	1,097	2.2	
Basnett, N	Ind	1,032	2.0	
Varga, K	Green	527	1.0	-2.2
Bishop, F	Eng	473	0.9	

Majority 11,346

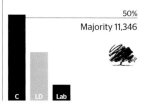

Streatham — Labour hold

Chuka Umunna
b. Oct 17, 1978
MP 2010-
Very smooth, very plausible. Charismatic, articulate and ambitious. Darling of the soft/pragmatic Left; mentored by Jon Cruddas. Friend of David Lammy. Management cttee, Compass pressure group. Inevitably hailed as the British Obama. Shrewd campaign won plaudits. Strong on youth engagement issues. Trustee, Anthony Bourne Foundation. Specialist employment law solicitor: Rochman Landau; Herbert Smith. Board member, Generation Next. Member, GMB, Unite. Nigerian/Irish/English descent, Streatham-raised. Compass pressure group. Ed: St Dunstan's Coll, Catford; Manchester (English & French law); Burgundy Uni; Nottingham Law Sch.

Chris Nicholson (LD) b. Apr 18, 1958. Economist. Specialist adviser to parliamentary select cttees. Ed: Manchester GS, Cambridge Uni (Econ).
Rahoul Bhansali (C) Financial consultant.

Constituency
From the eastern half of Clapham Common this seat stretches down to Streatham in the south, taking in large African and Caribbean communities in a seat where 30 per cent were born outside Britain. Less affluent than the other Lambeth constituencies, there are sought-after residential areas around the Abbeville Road area and along the edges of Tooting Bec Common. Like much of South London, it also has pockets of severe deprivation, especially in Brixton Hill and Knight's Hill. About 30 per cent live in social housing. Labour took this seat from the Tories in 1992.

	Electorate	Turnout %	Change from '05 %
	74,531	62.8	☆
Umunna, C Lab	20,037	42.8	-4.2
Nicholson, C LD	16,778	35.8	6.3
Bhansali, R C	8,578	18.3	2.0
Findlay, R Green	861	1.8	-3.7
Macharia, G Ch	237	0.5	
Polenceus, J Eng	229	0.5	
Lepper, P WRP	117	0.3	

50%
Majority 3,259

Stretford & Urmston — Labour hold

Kate Green
b. May 2, 1960
MP 2010-
Well-regarded, Scottish-born poverty and families campaigner (chief exec, Child Poverty Action Group; Dir, National Council for One Parent Families) unafraid to criticise Labour. Contested Cities of London & Westminster 1997. GLA candidate West London 2000. Member: Fawcett Society, Fabians. AMICUS. Chair London Child Poverty Commission, member Nat Employment Panel. Trustee, IFS. Whitehall & Industry Group secondee to Home Office. Magistrate. Former career, Barclays Bank. OBE. Divorced. Ed: Currie HS; Edinburgh (LLB).

Alex Williams (C) b. 1975. Accountant. Cllr, Trafford. Education: King Edward VI School, Southampton and Nottingham University (mathematics).
Steve Cooke (LD) University lecturer. Cllr, Salford CC.

Constituency
This mostly residential area of Trafford is separated from Salford to the north by the Manchester Ship Canal. The M60 cuts through the seat, dividing the towns of Urmston and Stretford. The Old Trafford area reaches almost to central Manchester, bordering on Moss Side and sharing its deprived characteristics. It is home to Manchester United FC, the cricket ground, the Trafford shopping centre and a large business park. The seat was won by Labour on its creation in 1997, but one of its predecessor seats had been Conservative.

	Electorate	Turnout %	Change from '05 %
	70,091	64.1	☆
Green, K Lab	21,821	48.6	-2.8
Williams, A C	12,886	28.7	-1.4
Cooke, S LD	7,601	16.9	3.0
Owen, D UKIP	1,508	3.4	1.2
Westbrook, M Green	916	2.0	
Jacob, S Ch	178	0.4	

50%
Majority 8,935

Stroud — Conservative gain

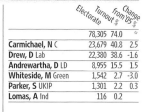

Neil Carmichael
b. Apr 15, 1961
MP 2010-
Former cow and sheep farmer turned PR consultant. Very fluent. Contested Stroud 2001, Leeds East 1992. Chief exec, Strategic Impact (public affairs / business advisors - investment in Eastern Europe). Consultant, JBP (Bristol). Non-exec dir, Artloan. Proprietor, TLB Carmichael - environment scheme and woodland developer. Member NFU. Chair of Northumbria Daybreak charity. Visiting lecturer in British political history and rural economics at Sunderland and De Montford universities. Renovating a Massey Ferguson 135 tractor. Interested in English Civil War history. Married, two daughters, one son. Ed: St Peter's Sch, York; Nottingham (politics).

David Drew (Lab Co-op) b. Apr 13, 1952. MP for Stroud 1997-2010. Ed: Uni of Nottingham, Uni of Birmingham, Uni of the West of England.
Dennis Andrewartha (LD) b. Jan 11, 1947. Cllr, Lib Dem leader, Stroud DC.

Constituency
The constituency reaches well beyond Stroud town to the River Severn in the west and Cotswold hills in the east, and is bisected by the M5. The population is concentrated in Stroud, Cam, Dursley and Wotton-under-Edge, former wool mill areas. Stroud town has a bohemian reputation, boasts Britain's first fully organic café and has had local Green Party success. Laurie Lee's Cider with Rosie was set in the Slad Valley. The economy is based on small businesses, including dairy farming. It was Conservative for 40 years until the Labour landslide of 1997.

	Electorate	Turnout %	Change from '05 %
	78,305	74.0	☆
Carmichael, N C	23,679	40.8	2.5
Drew, D Lab	22,380	38.6	-1.6
Andrewartha, D LD	8,955	15.5	1.5
Whiteside, M Green	1,542	2.7	-3.0
Parker, S UKIP	1,301	2.2	0.3
Lomas, A Ind	116	0.2	

50%
Majority 1,299

Suffolk Central & Ipswich North — Conservative hold

Dr Daniel Poulter
b. Oct 30, 1978
MP 2010-

Healthcare specialist, worked as NHS hospital doctor (obs/gynae). Won open primary. Ran medical and lifestyle advice clinics for the homeless and people with alcohol or substance misuse problems. Worked on Preston Home Energy and Water Conservation Project as Cllr, Reigate & Banstead (Deputy Leader 2008-10). Cllr, Hastings BC 2006-07. Names Benjamin Disraeli as political hero. Engaged to be married. Keen cricketer and rugby player. Education: Battle Abbey School; Guys, Kings and St Thomas' School of Medicine (Medicine); Bristol University (Law).

Andrew Aalders-Dunthorne (LD) b. Nov 3, 1969. Cllr, Norwich CC. Education: Bowthorpe HS, City Coll Norwich, Uni of East Anglia.
Bhavna Joshi (Lab) b. Sep 22, 1977. Works in pharmaceuticals. Education: King's College London.

Constituency

This is a largely rural seat, encompassing a small corner of northwest Ipswich, around Castle Hill, and the small suburban town of Kesgrave to the east. From here, the seat extends north to the border with Norfolk, taking in the town of Framlingham with its 12th-century castle. Much of the surrounding area is agricultural land and the seat is generally well off, although it has declined in recent years. There are some pockets of deprivation in the urban fringes of Ipswich. The Tories have held this seat since 1951.

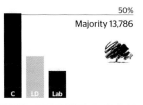

	Electorate	Turnout %	Change from 05 %
	75,848	1.0	☆
Poulter, D C	27,125	50.8	6.3
Aalders-Dunthorne, A LD	13,339	25.0	4.7
Joshi, B Lab	8,636	16.2	-12.3
Philpot, R UKIP	2,361	4.4	1.0
Stringer, A Green	1,452	2.7	-0.6
Trevitt, M Ind	389	0.7	
Vass, R New	118	0.2	

50%
Majority 13,786

Suffolk Coastal — Conservative hold

Therese Coffey
b. Nov 18, 1971
MP 2010-

Forthright. Scientist and businesswoman. Contested Wrexham 2005; European South-East 2009, 2004. Roman Catholic. BBC property department following career at Mars; rose to finance director, Mars Drinks UK. Qualified chartered management accountant. Football and live music fan, CAMRA member. Ed: St Mary's College, Rhos on Sea; St Mary's College, Crosby; St Edward's College Liverpool; UCL (PhD chemistry).

Daisy Cooper (LD) b. Oct 29, 1981. Senior strategic planner, Commonwealth Secretariat. Ed: Leeds Uni (LL.B Hons law), Nottingham Uni (LL.M in public international law).

Adam Leeder (Lab) b. Jul 2, 1986. Researcher for Labour MP. Ed: University of Sheffield.
Stephen Bush (UKIP) Professor.

Constituency

From Felixstowe, the seaside town and largest container port in Britain, this seat extends north up the coast. It includes Woodbridge, a town near Ipswich with pockets of great affluence, especially in the Martlesham. Major employers are BT and the Sizewell power station, which is on the coast near Aldeburgh. Farther north, the seat includes the towns of Leiston, Saxmundham, Southwold and Halesworth. Most of the seat is averagely well off, with poorer areas at Wrentham and the southern reaches of Felixstowe. Traditionally a Tory seat, Labour came a close in 1997.

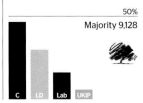

	Electorate	Turnout %	Change from 05 %
	76,687	71.6	☆
Coffey, T C	25,475	46.4	1.8
Cooper, D LD	16,347	29.8	7.7
Leeder, A Lab	8,812	16.1	-10.1
Bush, S UKIP	3,156	5.8	
Fulcher, R Green	1,103	2.0	-1.3

50%
Majority 9,128

Suffolk South — Conservative hold

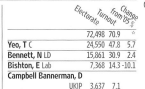

Tim Yeo
b. Mar 29, 1945
MP 1983-

Seasoned centrist figure with an interest in renewable energy. Elected Chair, Energy & Climate Change 2010-. Chair, Environ Audit Cttee 2005-10. Shad SoS: Environ/Transport 2004-05; Public Services, Health, Ed 2003-04; Trade & Industry 2002-03; CMS 2001-02. Shad Min: MAFF 1998-2001. Opposition spokes 1997-98. Joint Parly Under-sec: Environ 1993-94; Health 1992-93; Environ 1990-92. PPS to Douglas Hurd 1988-90. Vice-Chair Con Party 1998. Investment banker, company director. Chief executive, Scope. Cambridge Uni Air Squadron. Married, one daughter, one son. Education: Charterhouse; Emmanuel College, Cambridge (MA history).

Nigel Bennett (LD) b. Jul 21, 1966. Cllr.
Emma Bishton (Lab) b. Apr 4, 1967. Senior public health specialist, NHS.
David Campbell Bannerman (UKIP) b. May 28, 1960. MEP (Eastern) 2009-.

Constituency

This wide rural seat stretches from the market and antiques town of Clare, in the far west, along the River Stour, which forms the county border with Essex, as far as Shotley Gate, where the Stour and Orwell estuaries meet. It is predominantly drawn from Babergh district and includes the towns of Sudbury and Hadleigh as well as the Pinebrook area on the fringes of Ipswich. An attractive, prosperous and relatively well-connected seat, its economy varies from traditional shops in market towns to industrial fringes, as well as some tourism. It has been Tory for decades.

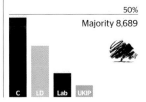

	Electorate	Turnout %	Change from 05 %
	72,498	70.9	☆
Yeo, T C	24,550	47.8	5.7
Bennett, N LD	15,861	30.9	2.4
Bishton, E Lab	7,368	14.3	-10.1
Campbell Bannerman, D UKIP	3,637	7.1	

50%
Majority 8,689

Suffolk West — Conservative hold

Matthew Hancock
b. Oct 2, 1978
MP 2010-

Economic adviser (Chief of Staff to George Osborne 2005-10) who sacrificed career in No 11 to forge his own path. Clever but socially awkward. Cheshire born and raised, worked on family computer software firm then at Bank of England before joining Tory high command. Longstanding activist. Married, one daughter, one son. Education: King's School Chester; Exeter Coll, Oxford (BA PPE); Christ's Coll, Cambridge (Masters, econ).

Belinda Brooks-Gordon (LD) b. Jun 6, 1962. Reader, psychology and social policy. Education: Middlesex University (psychology), Cambridge University (MPhil criminology, PhD).

Ohid Ahmed (Lab) b. Jan 26, 1965. Cllr, Tower Hamlets. Education: University of East London (MBA).
Ian Smith (UKIP) b. Nov 15, 1966. Cllr, Lakenheath PC. Education: The Billericay School.

Constituency
The main towns in this seat are the industrial Brandon, on the border with Norfolk in the north, Mildenhall on the River Lark, and the affluent horse-racing centre of Newmarket. The seat also arcs around the north of the Bury St Edmunds seat, reaching as far as the manufacturing hub of Haverhill. The demographic is skewed by two of the largest US Air Force bases in the country, at Mildenhall and Lakenheath; 21 per cent of residents were born outside the EU. This seat has been Tory for decades.

	Electorate	Turnout %	Change from 05 %
	74,413	64.6	☆
Hancock, M C	24,312	50.6	1.7
Brooks-Gordon, B LD	11,262	23.4	6.2
Ahmed, O Lab	7,089	14.7	-14.2
Smith, I UKIP	3,085	6.4	1.5
Johns, R BNP	1,428	3.0	
Appleby, A Ind	540	1.1	
Young, C CPA	373	0.8	

50%
Majority 13,050

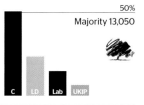

Sunderland Central — Labour hold

Julie Elliott
b. Jul 29, 1963
MP 2010-

Sunderland born and raised, from a working-class family. Political/Policy/Media/Research officer, GMB. Regional organiser, National Asthma Campaign. Regional organiser, Labour Party (agent Tynemouth 1997). Four children. Education: Seaham Northlea Comprehensive; Newcastle Poly (Government & Public Policy).

Lee Martin (C) Cllr, Sunderland CC, 2004-. Education: University of Sunderland.
Paul Dixon (LD) b. Nov 10, 1965. Property manager. Cllr, Sunderland CC 2008. Education: Bede Comprehensive School.

Constituency
Boundary changes unite into one constituency all but the very western fringes of Sunderland, built on the mouth of the Wear. The southern coastline is dominated by industry and warehousing but north there are beaches at Roker and Seaburn. The Stadium of Light is north of the river, just off Keir Hardie Way – a reminder of the seat's Labour tradition. The decline of old industries has left severe deprivation – most of the city centre is in the worst 5 per cent nationally – and high unemployment. The University of Sunderland provides a large student presence.

	Electorate	Turnout %	Change from 05 %
	74,485	57.0	☆
Elliott, J Lab	19,495	45.9	-4.1
Martin, L C	12,770	30.1	5.6
Dixon, P LD	7,191	16.9	0.1
McCaffrey, J BNP	1,913	4.5	
Featonby-Warren, P UKIP	1,094	2.6	

50%
Majority 6,725

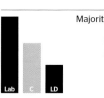

Surrey East — Conservative hold

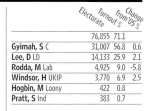

Sam Gyimah
b. Aug 10, 1976
MP 2010-

British-born but spent childhood in Ghana. Chairman Bow Group, 2005. Lauded as successful businessman but faced questions over liquidation of business ClearStone, which he founded. Dir, Workology (underwent restructuring). Former chairman CareerAbility. Former investment banker, Goldman Sachs (M&A). Arsenal fan. Divorced. Ed: Achimota Secondary School, Ghana; Freman Coll, Herts; Somerville College, Oxford (PPE; President, Oxford Union).

David Lee (LD) b. May 1, 1974. Customer services trainer. Ed: Oakwood Sch Horley; Reigate 6th Form Coll; Uni of Portsmouth (German studies).

Mathew Rodda (Lab) b. Dec 28, 1966. Charity project manager. Survived Paddington rail crash, 1999.
Helena Windsor (UKIP) b. 1956. Microbiologist, director of local business. Ed: Langley Park school; North East London Polytechnic.

Constituency
In the eastern extremity of Surrey, bordering Kent, the constituency comprises the town of Horley and district of Tandridge, which has about 90 per cent green-belt land. The towns of Caterham and Oxted and villages such as Godstone lie amid agricultural land, woodland and open countryside. Half the working population commutes out, including many to Crawley and Gatwick airport, the biggest single employer. A Tory stronghold since 1918, even in 1997 the party took more than 50 per cent of the vote.

	Electorate	Turnout %	Change from 05 %
	76,855	71.1	☆
Gyimah, S C	31,007	56.8	0.6
Lee, D LD	14,133	25.9	2.1
Rodda, M Lab	4,925	9.0	-5.8
Windsor, H UKIP	3,770	6.9	2.5
Hogbin, M Loony	422	0.8	
Pratt, S Ind	383	0.7	

50%
Majority 16,874

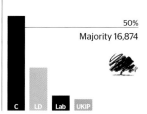

Surrey Heath | Conservative hold

Michael Gove
b. Aug 26, 1967
MP 2005-

Arch moderniser, skilled debater, with resemblance to a meerkat. Excitable and loves a media fight – an adept broadcast performer. Very pro-Israel. Author, *Celsius 7/7*. Sec of State: Education 2010-. Shadow Sec of State: Children, Schools and Families 2007-10. Shadow Minister: Housing (2005-07). Journalist: *The Times*, BBC News, Scottish Television, Aberdeen Press and Journal. Married, one daughter, one son. Education: Robert Gordon's College, Aberdeen; LMH, Oxford (BA English).

Alan Hilliar (LD) Business consultant. Cllr Guildford BC 1985-95.

Matthew Willey (Lab) b. Sep 12 1977. Communications consultant. Ed: Worthing HS; Southampton (MSc internat relations and security studies).
Mark Stroud (UKIP) b. 1960. Social and private housing worker. Contested European elections (south east) 2009. Ed: Thames Valley University.

Constituency
In the west of the county, bordering Hampshire and Berkshire, the constituency is named after its extensive rural areas but is home to the sizeable towns of Camberley and Frimley, and Chobham, Bagshot and Ash. There is a strong military presence because of Royal Military Academy Sandhurst, just beyond the northern boundary, and Deepcut Barracks, due for closure in about 2013. Frimley Green hosts the World Darts Championships. This is a safe Tory seat.

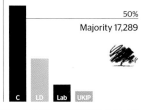

	Electorate	Turnout %	Change from '05 %
	77,690	70.0	
Gove, M C	31,326	57.6	6.2
Hilliar, A LD	14,037	25.8	-3.0
Willey, M Lab	5,552	10.2	-6.4
Stroud, M UKIP	3,432	6.3	3.3

50%
Majority 17,289

C LD Lab UKIP

Surrey South West | Conservative hold

Jeremy Hunt
b. Nov 1, 1966
MP 2005-

Amiable yet ambitious, from the soft Tory left. Plucked from the relatively obscure culture brief to be one of the five "faces" of the Tory campaign. His telegenic appeal and ability to deliver speeches without notes has won him fans. Smooth and likeable, a future leader-but-one or two. Sec of State: Culture, Olympics, Media & Sport 2010-. Shadow Sec of State, Culture, Media and Sport 2007-10. Shadow Minister, Disabled People, 2005-07. Management consultant Outram Cullinan & Co. Taught English in Japan. Founder and managing director, Hotcourses. Education: Charterhouse, Surrey; Magdalen College, Oxford (MA PPE).

Mike Simpson (LD) Charity chief executive, YMCA. Contested North West Hampshire 1992. Ed: The King's Grammar School, Ottery St Mary, Devon (BA economics). Founded YMCA partnership project in Bethlehem.
Richard Mollet (Labour)

Constituency
Much of Waverley borough is included in a constituency that borders Sussex and Hampshire and features the Devil's Punchbowl, a dramatic heathland hollow. The historic market towns of Farnham, Godalming and Haslemere, affluent commuter hubs, lie at the periphery. The centre remains rural, with a third covered by woodland. Once regarded as safe for the Tories, in 2001 they had less than a 2 per cent margin over the Lib Dems, who retained a reasonable presence in 2005 but have since lost popularity over local disputes.

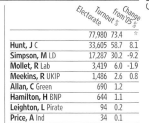

	Electorate	Turnout %	Change from '05 %
	77,980	73.4	*
Hunt, J C	33,605	58.7	8.1
Simpson, M LD	17,287	30.2	-9.2
Mollet, R Lab	3,419	6.0	-1.9
Meekins, R UKIP	1,486	2.6	0.8
Allan, C Green	690	1.2	
Hamilton, H BNP	644	1.1	
Leighton, L Pirate	94	0.2	
Price, A Ind	34	0.1	

50%
Majority 16,318

C LD Lab

Sussex Mid | Conservative hold

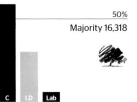

Nicholas Soames
b. Feb 12, 1948
MP 1983-

Bombastic, anachronistic with exceptionally courtly manners. Brightens the chamber. Grandson of Sir Winston Churchill and son of Lord Soames. One Nation Tory with close interest in the military. Linked with Labour's Frank Field in a campaign to limit immigration. 1922 executive committee, 2010-. Shadow SoS: Defence 2003-05. Minister: Armed Forces 1994-97. Joint Parly Sec MAFF 1992-94. PPS to: Nicholas Ridley 1987-89, John Gummer 1984-86. MP Crawley 1983-97. Commissioned into 11th Hussars. Equerry to Prince of Wales. Stockbroker then PA to Sir James Goldsmith. Asst dir Sedgwick Group. Married, one daughter, two sons. Ed: Eton Coll.

Serena Tierney (LD) Solicitor and international mediator. Member, LD Federal Policy cttee 2001-03, chair of Commerce Policy Working Group.
David Boot (Lab) Journalist.

Constituency
Though this seat is in West Sussex, the name reflects its border with East Sussex. The three main towns, dotted amid the countryside, are Haywards Heath, Burgess Hill and East Grinstead, which lies at the border with Surrey in the north. The constituency has been slightly extended west to take in Bolney and surrounding area. This is classic commuter-belt territory for London and Brighton. Generally affluent, it is home to many professionals and middle classes, mostly owner-occupiers, and a service sector dominates the economy. It has long been represented by Conservatives.

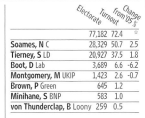

	Electorate	Turnout %	Change from '05 %
	77,182	72.4	
Soames, N C	28,329	50.7	2.5
Tierney, S LD	20,927	37.5	1.8
Boot, D Lab	3,689	6.6	-6.2
Montgomery, M UKIP	1,423	2.6	-0.7
Brown, P Green	645	1.2	
Minihane, S BNP	583	1.0	
von Thunderclap, B Loony	259	0.5	

50%
Majority 7,402

C LD Lab

Sutton & Cheam — Liberal Democrat hold

Paul Burstow
b. May 13, 1962
MP 1997-

Low-key manner but effective political organiser, ran Sir Menzies Campbell's leadership campaign in 2006. Min: Health 2010-. LD Chief Whip 2006-10. LD spokes: London 2005-06. LD Shadow Sec of State: Health 2003-05. LD spokes: older people 1999-2003; local govt 1997-99; disabled people 1997-98. Former member SDP/Liberal Alliance, London regional LD exec, federal policy cttee. Political sec, LD Cllrs Assoc 1996-97. Cllr, Sutton 1986- (deputy leader 1994-99). Organising sec, buyer. Married, two daughters, one son. Education: Glastonbury High School; Carshalton FE College; South Bank Poly (BA business studies).

Philippa Stroud (C) b. 1965. Co-founder and exec dir, Centre for Social Justice. Worked on homelessness projects.
Kathy Allen (Lab) b. Nov 22, 1947. Local government officer.

Constituency
Technically part of London, this seat has more in common with Surrey, which it borders. Predominantly white, with no major ethnic groups, this is a generally affluent seat with only small numbers of residents in social housing and above-average numbers in managerial or professional occupations. Cheam and Belmont are often referred to as villages, with affluent residential streets, while Sutton has a pedestrianised retail centre. In the north of the seat, Kempton is a more industrial area and around Rosehill is less affluent. The Lib Dems took this from the Tories in 1997.

	Electorate	Turnout %	Change from 05 %
	66,658	72.8	☆
Burstow, P LD	22,156	45.7	-1.2
Stroud, P C	20,548	42.4	1.7
Allen, K Lab	3,376	7.0	-4.9
Clarke, J BNP	1,014	2.1	
Pickles, D UKIP	950	2.0	
Hickson, P Green	246	0.5	
Dodds, J Eng	106	0.2	
Connolly, M CPA	52	0.1	
Cullip, M Libertarian	41	0.1	
Hammond, B UK	19	0.0	

50%
Majority 1,608

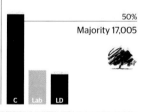

Sutton Coldfield — Conservative hold

Andrew Mitchell
b. Mar 23, 1956
MP 2001-; 1987-97

Very smooth. A close ally of David Davis and Lord Ashcroft. Lost his original Gedling seat in 1997. Committed to international development, especially in Africa. Son of a Tory MP, wealthy descendant of El Vino wine merchant founders, in which he held a stake. SoS: Int Dev't 2010-. Shadow Sec: Int' Dev't 2005-10, organises Tories' Project Umubano in Rwanda. Shadow Minister: Home 2004-05; Econ 2003-04. Parly Under-Sec DSS 1995-97. Whip: ass't gov't 1992-3, gov't 1993-5. PPS to: John Wakeham 1990-92, William Waldegrave 1998-90. Banker with Lazards. Served in Army, UN Cyprus. Married, two daughters. Ed: Jesus Coll, Cambridge (MA history).

Robert Pocock (Lab) b. Aug 22, 1952. Chief executive of a research and consultancy company. Ed: Royal Holloway College. Contested Sutton Coldfield 2001 GE.
Richard Brighton (LD) Doctor. Former member of the North Birmingham Primary Care Trust. Contested Birmingham Selly Oak in 2005 GE.

Constituency
Physically the largest of the Birmingham seats, Sutton Coldfield lies in the north of the city and is a town in its own right, distinct in character and prosperity. It includes rural areas on the outskirts as well as Sutton Park. The town centre, in Trinity ward, has a concentration of businesses but it is otherwise largely residential. This is a very affluent seat, home to overwhelmingly white middle classes. It has been Conservative since its creation in 1945.

	Electorate	Turnout %	Change from 05 %
	74,489	67.9	☆
Mitchell, A C	27,303	54.0	1.4
Pocock, R Lab	10,298	20.4	-5.5
Brighton, R LD	9,117	18.0	1.4
Grierson, R BNP	1,749	3.5	
Siddall-Jones, E UKIP	1,587	3.1	-1.8
Rooney, J Green	535	1.1	

50%
Majority 17,005

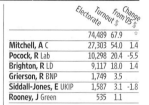

Swansea East — Labour hold

Siân James
b. Jun 24, 1959
MP 2005-

PPS to: Gareth Thomas 2008-09. Member, select cttees: Constitutional Affairs/Justice 2006-; Procedure 2005-. Dir, Welsh Women's Aid. Lobbyist. National Trust. Save The Children. Nat Fed Young Farmers' Clubs. Enthusiast of antiques, model railways and dolls houses. Married, one daughter, one son. Ed: Cefn Saeson Comp; Uni of Wales, Swansea (Welsh).

Robert Speht (LD) b. 1972. Wind energy manager. Contested Swansea East 2005, 2001. Former cllr, Swansea. Ed: Swansea (mechanical engineering with German), Loughborough (MSc in Renewable Energy Systems).

Christian Holliday (C) b. 1980. Planning consultant. Member of Lord Heseltine's Cities Taskforce, 2006. Ed: Swansea Coll; Swansea Uni; Cardiff Uni; UWE
Dic Jones (PC) BT senior engineer.
Clive Bennett (BNP)

Constituency
This seat includes the Swansea Docks on the River Severn and crosses the River Tawe to stretch northwest as far as Port Mead and Penderry. There are areas of severe deprivation here and in the south. The seat encompasses the Swansea Enterprise Park, which has offices and out-of-town retailers that create the mainstay of the formerly industrial economy. More than a fifth of residents live in social housing and there is a large working class. The M4 passes through the north of the seat. Labour has represented here since 1922.

	Electorate	Turnout %	Change from 05 %
	59,823	54.6	☆
James, S Lab	16,819	51.5	-5.1
Speht, R LD	5,981	18.3	-1.8
Holliday, C C	4,823	14.8	4.8
Jones, D PC	2,181	6.7	-0.2
Bennett, C BNP	1,715	5.3	2.8
Rogers, D UKIP	839	2.6	0.4
Young, T Green	318	1.0	-0.6

50%
Majority 10,838

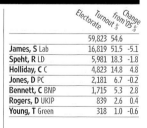

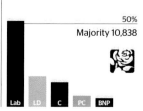

Swansea West ·   Labour hold

Geraint Davies
b. May 3, 1960
MP 2010-; 1997-2005

Returning to the Commons to represent his native Wales having served eight years as a loyal backbencher as MP Croydon Central (1997-2005). PPS: Justice Team 2003-05. Member, select committee: Public Accounts 1997-2003. Cllr, Croydon 1986-97. GMB, Co-op. After 2005 defeat worked for Environment Agency Wales. Chair, Lab Finance & Industry Group Wales. Company director. Parly ambassador, NSPCC. School governor. Marketing manager, Colgate Palmolive. Group product manager, Unilever. Member, MSF. Married, three daughters. Education: Llanishen Comprehensive, Cardiff; Jesus College, Oxford (BA PPE).

Peter May (LD) Cllr, Swansea CC. Cabinet Member for Housing and Older People.
Rene Kinzett (C) b. 1975. Public relations and government affairs consultant. Cllr, Swansea CC (leader of Conservative group).

Constituency
This seat includes the centre of Swansea, its university and marina, as well as industrial estates, works and a chocolate factory. There is deprivation in the east, especially in the wards of Townhill and Castle; the west is more affluent. There are large numbers of students and also high numbers of the middle classes, with the health and education sectors dominating the economy. More than a fifth of residents live in social housing. The seat was briefly held by the Tories before Alan Williams won it for Labour in 1964.

	Electorate	Turnout %	Change from '05 %
	61,334	58.0	
Davies, G Lab	12,335	34.7	-7.1
May, P LD	11,831	33.2	4.3
Kinzett, R C	7,407	20.8	4.9
Roberts, H PC	1,437	4.0	-2.5
Bateman, A BNP	910	2.6	
Jenkins, T UKIP	716	2.0	0.2
Ross, K Green	404	1.1	-1.1
McCloy, I Ind	374	1.1	
Williams, R TUSC	179	0.5	

50%
Majority 504

Lab   LD   C

Swindon North   Conservative gain

Justin Tomlinson
b. Nov 5, 1976
MP 2010-

Runs TB Marketing, a major print supplier of for local Conservative parties. Cllr, Swindon 2000-10. Contested North Swindon 2005. Marketing executive, Point to Point. Sales & Marketing Manager, First Leisure. Student politician, became national chair, Conservative Future. Separated. Education: Harry Cheshire High School, Kidderminster; Oxford Brookes (BA business & marketing)

Victor Agarwal (Lab) b. 11 Dec, 1973. Airline employee. Cllr, Surrey CC. Education: University of Surrey.
Jane Lock (LD) b. 19 Jul, 1955. Businesswomen. Clr, Somerset CC.

Constituency
At the northern extremity of Wiltshire, this seat has been redrawn slightly, losing Cricklade. It includes a small rural area round Highworth but is mostly north of Swindon. Honda and BMW have factories, hard hit by the recession, and there are many more industrial and trading estates. Penhill has a large social housing estate and the constituency is relatively working-class. Swindon is due to become Britain's first "wireless city", supplying free broadband to every home. The seat was won by Labour at its creation in 1997.

	Electorate	Turnout %	Change from '05 %
	78,391	64.2	
Tomlinson, J C	22,408	44.6	5.7
Agarwal, V Lab	15,348	30.5	-14.6
Lock, J LD	8,668	17.2	4.4
Halden, S UKIP	1,842	3.7	1.4
Bates, R BNP	1,542	3.1	
Hughes, B Green	487	1.0	

50%
Majority 7,060

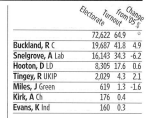

C   Lab   LD

Swindon South   Conservative gain

Robert Buckland
b. Sep 22, 1968
MP 2010-

Barrister interested in the detail of criminal justice policy, and in local planning and development issues. Member, Conservative Group for Europe, Tory Reform Group. Contested South Swindon 2005, Preseli Pembrokeshire 1997, Islwyn 1995. Cllr, Dyfed CC 1993-96. Crown Court Recorder. Society of Conservative Lawyers. Co-ordinator, Swindon Special Educational Needs Network. Anglican. Married, two children. Ed: St Michael's School, Bryn; Hatfield Coll, Durham (BA Hons Law)

Anne Snelgrove (Lab) b. 7 Aug, 1957. MP Swindon South 2005-10. PPS to Gordon Brown. Teacher. Education:

Ranelegh School, City University London.
Damon Hooton (LD) b. 29 Jan, 1959. Conveyancing executive. Mayor of Frome. Councillor, Mendip DC 2003-, Frome TC, 2007-. Military.

Constituency
In this seat is Swindon's town centre, developed with the arrival of the Great Western Railway in 1840 and now undergoing regeneration. The Old Town is a sought-after residential area. The Parks and Walcott areas have large social housing estates. A mixed economy includes heavy manufacturing, light engineering and commercial and financial sectors. The M4 cuts through the seat, dividing Swindon from a more rural area to the south. The constituency had a long Labour tradition and the party regained it in 1997 after a 14-year Tory interlude.

	Electorate	Turnout %	Change from '05 %
	72,622	64.9	
Buckland, R C	19,687	41.8	4.9
Snelgrove, A Lab	16,143	34.3	-6.2
Hooton, D LD	8,305	17.6	0.6
Tingey, R UKIP	2,029	4.3	2.1
Miles, J Green	619	1.3	-1.6
Kirk, A Ch	176	0.4	
Evans, K Ind	160	0.3	

50%
Majority 3,544

C   Lab   LD

Tamworth — Conservative gain

Christopher Pincher
b. Sep 24, 1969
MP 2010-

IT consultant and history buff; cites Duff Cooper and William Pitt among political heroes. Midlander, born in Walsall and raised in Wombourne. Contested Tamworth 2005; Warley 1997. Conservative Way Forward. Consultancy career at Accenture. Grand prix and horse racing enthusiast. Education: Ounsdale School, Wolverhampton; LSE (government & history).

Brian Jenkins (Lab) b. 19 Sep, 1942. MP for Tamworth 1997-2010, SE Staffordshire 1996-97 (by-election). Education: Coleg Harlech, London School of Economics.

Jenny Pinkett (LD) b. 23 Ap, 1945. Retired teacher. Education: Wrexham College of Education, Open University.

Constituency
This Staffordshire seat lies just north of the Birmingham conurbation. The population is heavily concentrated in Tamworth, although the seat includes semi-rural areas to its north and west. Manufacturing and distribution are important sectors, with the M6 Toll road running through the west of the seat. A very active seat economically, professionals are well represented, as well as traditional working classes. Under old boundaries, Labour took the seat from the Conservatives in a 1996 by-election.

	Electorate	Turnout %	Change from '05 %
	72,693	63.8	
Pincher, C C	21,238	45.8	8.7
Jenkins, B Lab	15,148	32.7	-10.3
Pinkett, J LD	7,516	16.2	2.1
Smith, P UKIP	2,253	4.9	2.1
Detheridge, C Ch	235	0.5	

50%
Majority 6,090

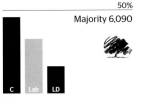

C Lab LD

Tatton — Conservative hold

George Osborne
b. May 23, 1971
MP 2001-

Shrewd political operator, feared rather than loved within his own party and beyond. Inextricably linked to Cameron. Masterminded 2010 election campaign. Thin-skinned but clever. Politically courageous but seen as arrogant by many Tory MPs. Was caught up in "yacht-gate". Chancellor of the Exchequer 2010-. Shad Chancellor 2005-10; Shad Chief Sec to Treasury 2004-05; Shad Min: Econ Affairs 2003-04. Opp whip 2003. Head of CRD political section 1994-5. 10 Downing St pol office 1997, Shad Cab sec / William Hague political sec 1997-2001. Freelance journalist. Married, one daughter, one son. Ed: St Paul's Sch; Magdalen Coll, Oxford (BA hist).

David Lomax (LD) b. Jan 10, 1956. Special needs teacher. Cllr, High Peak BC, 1991-.
Richard Jackson (Lab) b. May 29, 1972. Vet. Education: Bristol University.

Constituency
Centred on the market town of Knutsford, the Tatton constituency covers an extremely affluent area of north Cheshire, popular with professionals who commute north to Manchester. The biggest town is Wilmslow by Manchester airport at the northern boundary. The village of Alderley Edge is known for astronomically high house prices. AstraZeneca is a key employer. Some rural areas to the south are less well off. The seat has been solidly Conservative with the notable exception of the Independent anti-sleaze MP Martin Bell's defeat of Neil Hamilton in 1997.

	Electorate	Turnout %	Change from '05 %
	65,689	68.9	☆
Osborne, G C	24,687	54.6	3.1
Lomax, D LD	10,200	22.6	0.8
Jackson, R Lab	7,803	17.3	-6.5
Flannery, S Ind	2,243	5.0	
Gibson, M Poetry	298	0.7	

50%
Majority 14,487

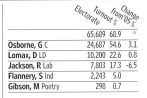

C LD Lab

Taunton Deane — Liberal Democrat hold

Jeremy Browne
b. May 17, 1970
MP 2005-

Pro-market reformer from Lib Dems' centre-right. Well spoken and serious minded. Min: FCO 2010-. LD Shad Chief SoS to Treasury 2007-10. LD Shad Min Home 2007. LD whip 2006-07. LD Shad Min: Foreign 2005-07. Member, cttee: Home 2005-08. Contested Enfield Southgate 1997. Public affairs consultant: Reputation Inc, Edelman Worldwide. LD dir of press & broadcasting. Dewe Rogerson. Divorced. Education: Bedales; Nottingham (BA politics).

Mark Formosa (C) b. 1977. Cllr, Newquay TC, Restormel BC, 2003-. Contested North Cornwall 2005. Ed: Newquay Treviglas School.

Martin Jevon (Lab)

Constituency
Having lost a large rural area from West Somerset, the old Taunton seat has been renamed to match the borough with which it now shares a boundary. Project Taunton is a £1 billion regeneration scheme to build 18,000 homes, much needed as prices outstrip incomes. Wellington is the other main town. The rest of the constituency is rural, with the Blackdown, Brendon and Quantock hills and a small farming sector. Once solidly Conservative, the seat was won by the Lib Dems in 1997, Tories in 2001 and Lib Dems again in 2005.

	Electorate	Turnout %	Change from '05 %
	82,537	70.5	
Browne, J LD	28,531	49.1	4.7
Formosa, M C	24,538	42.2	1.1
Jevon, M Lab	2,967	5.1	-7.0
McIntyre, T UKIP	2,114	3.6	1.3

50%
Majority 3,993

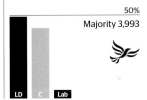

LD C Lab

David Wright
b. Dec 22, 1966
MP 2001-

Known as "demolition Dave" for his record in levelling tower blocks. Asst govt whip 2009-10. PPS to: Jane Kennedy 2007-08; John Hutton 2006; David Miliband 2005-6; Rosie Winterton 2004-05. Member, cttees: Procedure 2001-; Environmental Audit 2001-; Administration 2001-02. Cllr: Oakengates Town 1989-2000; Wrekin DC 1989-97. Local govt officer. Housing strategy manager Sandwell MBC. Married. Ed: Wrockwardine Wood Comp, Shropshire; New Coll, Telford; Wolverhampton Poly (BA humanities).

Tom Biggins (C) Cllr, Shropshire CC, 1997-. Works for family cheese business. Ed: Oxford University.

Phil Bennion (LD) Cllr, Lichfield DC, 2002-. Farmer. Agricultural adviser to Lib Dem MPs and MEPs.
Denis Allen (UKIP)

Constituency
About 30 miles west of Birmingham, the roundabouts and charmless but convenient modern centre of Telford testify to its status as a postwar New Town, although the original towns in its urban sprawl retain a sense of identity. It grew dramatically, only to suffer from economic decline and high unemployment in the early 1990s. A large number of people are employed in manufacturing, especially in the electronics and polymers sectors, but there is also a growing service sector and EDS is a major employer. The seat was won by Labour when it was created in 1997.

	Electorate	Turnout %	Change from '05 %
	65,061	63.5	☆
Wright, D Lab	15,974	38.7	-9.5
Biggins, T C	14,996	36.3	3.2
Bennion, P LD	6,399	15.5	1.4
Allen, D UKIP	2,428	5.9	1.2
Spencer, P BNP	1,513	3.7	

50%
Majority 978

| Lab | C | LD | UKIP |

Laurence Robertson
b. Mar 29, 1958
MP 1997-

The Nicholas Winterton of his day. Right-winger whose comments on immigration have caused controversy. Elected unopposed as Chair, select cttee: Northern Ireland 2010-. Shadow Minister: NI 2005-10; Economic Affairs 2003-05; Trade and Industry 2003. Opposition Whip 2001-03. Consultant in industrial management, charity fundraising and PR. Factory owner. Marathon runner. Married but separated, two stepdaughters. Education: St James' CoE Secondary School; Farnworth Grammar; Bolton Higher Ed Inst (Management Service Dip)

Alistair Cameron (LD) b. Apr 8, 1960. Human resources officer. Cllr,

Cheltenham BC, Gloucestershire CC. Contested Tewkesbury 2005. Education: Bristol Uni (BA History).
Stuart Emmerson (Lab) b. Feb 4, 1978. Political officer in local government. Education: York Uni.

Constituency
The M5 runs through this semi-rural constituency, from the suburban sprawl between Cheltenham and Gloucester in the south to the historic riverside town of Tewkesbury in the north. An affluent seat, it is home to many highly qualified commuters working for such companies as Group 4 Securities and enjoys beautiful countryside and good transport links. Flooding devastated large areas of the seat in 2007. The constituency has been Conservative since the Second World War.

	Electorate	Turnout %	Change from '05 %
	76,655	70.4	☆
Robertson, L C	25,472	47.2	-1.0
Cameron, A LD	19,162	35.5	7.1
Emmerson, S Lab	6,253	11.6	-8.7
Jones, B UKIP	2,230	4.1	
Sidford, M Green	525	1.0	-2.2
Ridgeon, G Loony	319	0.6	

50%
Majority 6,310

| C | LD | Lab |

Roger Gale
b. Aug 20, 1943
MP 1983-

Belligerent backbencher – aggressive, dislikes the media but keen on animals. Vice-Chairman Conservative Party 2001-03. PPS to: Jeremy Hanley 1993-94; Archibald Hamilton 1992-93. Television producer, director and broadcaster; rose to BBC director of children's television. Belonged to NUJ and acting unions. Divorced twice, remarried. One daughter from second marriage, two sons from third marriage. Education: Hardye's School; Guildhall School of Music and Drama.

Michael Britton (Lab) b. Apr 16, 1946. Printing industry worker and trade unionist. Trade Union chair for Amnesty International.

Laura Murphy (LD) b. Feb 2, 1956. Business director. Education: University of Brighton (MBA).
Rosamund Parker (UKIP) b. Sep 23, 1941. Therapist. Education: Roedean School, University of Kent.

Constituency
From the resort of Margate, the seat stretches along the North Kent coast as far as Herne Bay, with its brightly coloured beach huts, encompassing the northwestern half of Thanet district and wards within Canterbury authority. Other settlements include Westgate, Birchington, Beltinge and Minster. Kent International airport is in the seat. Boundary changes have removed Cliftonville from the east. Health and social work is an important sector and the seat is notable for a high number of retired people. There is a long Tory tradition.

	Electorate	Turnout %	Change from '05 %
	69,432	62.4	☆
Gale, R C	22,826	52.7	4.7
Britton, M Lab	9,298	21.5	-11.2
Murphy, L LD	8,400	19.4	3.8
Parker, R UKIP	2,819	6.5	2.6

50%
Majority 13,528

 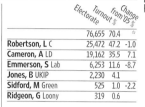

| C | Lab | LD | UKIP |

Thanet South — Conservative hold

Laura Sandys
b. Jun 5, 1964
MP 2010-

Extremely well connected and personable political consultant. Daughter of the colourful wartime MP Lord Duncan Sandys, she sacrificed chance at university to care for him following his stroke. Later specialised in Iraq as mature student, led to role as senior research associate, Centre for Defence Studies, King's College. Member, Cameron's Democracy Task Force. Journalist, policy strategist. Opposed the war. Work in Caucasus. Founded and ran own PR/marketing firm. Trustee, Open Uni. Dep Chair, Civic Trust. Founder, Cons Women's Muslim group. Married. Ed: several secondary schs; Wolfson Coll, Cambridge (Masters, Intl Relations).

Dr Stephen Ladyman (Lab) b. Nov 6, 1952. MP South Thanet 1997-2010. Parly-Under Sec for Health 2003-05, Min of State for Transport 2005-07.
Peter Bucklitsch (LD) Cllr.
Trevor Shonk (UKIP)

Constituency
Could more accurately be called Thanet East, stretching as it does along the easternmost coastal fringe of Kent, encompassing Ramsgate, Broadstairs and, since boundary changes, Cliftonville from Thanet district. It includes a rural area from Dover district, to the south beyond the River Stour, around the well-preserved medieval town of Sandwich. The huge Pfizer pharmaceutical company is a leading employer. The seat was once seen as safely Tory but Labour ousted the disgraced Jonathan Aitken in 1997 and held on with narrowing majorities in the subsequent two terms.

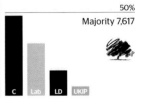

	Electorate	Turnout %	from '05 % Change
	71,596	64.2	*
Sandys, L C	22,043	48.0	6.8
Ladyman, S Lab	14,426	31.4	-8.1
Bucklitsch, P LD	6,935	15.1	2.9
Shonk, T UKIP	2,529	5.5	0.7

50%
Majority 7,617

| C | Lab | LD | UKIP |

Thirsk & Malton — Conservative hold

Anne McIntosh
b. Sep 20, 1954
MP 1997-

Slight but combative barrister, strongly pro-European. Absolutely dogged and highly respected across the House. The last in the 2010 parliament as election delayed following death of UKIP candidate. Elected Chair, select cttee: Environment, Food & Rural Affairs 2010-. Shad Min: EFRA 2007-10; Children, Young People & Families 2006-07; Work & Pensions 2005-06; Foreign 2005; Environment & Transport 2003-05; Transport 2002-03. Opposition spokesperson 2001-02. MP Vale of York 1997-2010. MEP 1989-99. Advocate, adviser. Married. Education: Harrogate Ladies' College; Edinburgh (LLB); Rhus University, Denmark (European law).

Howard Keal (LD) Freelance PR. Cllr, Ryedale DC.
Jonathan Roberts (Lab) b. Feb 7, 1982. Chamber of Shipping. Cllr, Thirsk TC, 2005-07.
Toby Horton (UKIP) Contested Sedgefield 2007; Rother Valley (as Con) 1992.

Constituency
This new seat encompasses most of the old Ryedale seat, excluding fringes of York but including the eastern half of the defunct Vale of York seat. It stretches from Filey on the coast to Thirsk in the west; Malton lies roughly in the centre. There is a significant agricultural sector and Thirsk was the market town at the heart of the James Herriot veterinary tales. Food and drink industries, engineering and tourism are big employers. This area has long been staunchly Conservative.

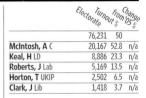

	Electorate	Turnout %	from '05 % Change
	76,231	50	
McIntosh, A C	20,167	52.8	n/a
Keal, H LD	8,886	23.3	n/a
Roberts, J Lab	5,169	13.5	n/a
Horton, T UKIP	2,502	6.5	n/a
Clark, J Lib	1,418	3.7	n/a

50%
Majority 11,281

| C | LD | Lab | UKIP |

Thornbury & Yate — Liberal Democrat hold

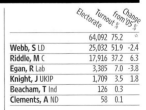

Steve Webb
b. Jul 18, 1965
MP 1997-

Softly spoken, left-leaning economist with detailed knowledge of the benefits system which earned him a ministerial role in first coalition Government (Min: Work & Pensions 2010-). Ran Simon Hughes' leadership campaign in 2006. Lost influence under Nick Clegg's leadership because of personal clashes. LD Shad Sec: Work & Pensions 2009-10; Energy & Climate Change 2008-09. LD Shad Min: Countryside 2008. LD Shad Sec: EFRA 2007-08. Chair, LD Manifesto team 2006-07. LD Shad Sec: Health 2005-; Work & Pensions 2001-05. LD spokes: soc sec/welfare 1997-2001. Commission on Social Justice. Institute for Fiscal Studies. Social policy professor, Bath Univ. Committed Christian. Married, one daughter, one son. Ed: Oxford Uni.

Matthew Riddle (C) Lecturer, Bridgwater College, associate lecturer at University of Plymouth, 2002. Cllr.
Roxanne Egan (Lab) b. Jul 28, 1989. Architecture student, Greenwich Uni.

Constituency
This new constituency covers most of the old Northavon seat but loses a stretch of coast around Severn Beach. Retains Severn Bridge, which takes the M48 to Wales. Main population centres are Thornbury, a fairly affluent market town with new estates on the outskirts; Chipping Sodbury, similar in character; and Yate, a 1950-60s dormitory town for commuters to Bristol. Rural area has dairy and sheep farming. High economic growth, low unemployment. Lib Dems gained from the Tories in 1997.

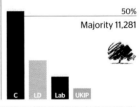

	Electorate	Turnout %	from '05 % Change
	64,092	75.2	
Webb, S LD	25,032	51.9	-2.4
Riddle, M C	17,916	37.2	6.3
Egan, R Lab	3,385	7.0	-3.8
Knight, J UKIP	1,709	3.5	1.8
Beacham, T Ind	126	0.3	
Clements, A ND	58	0.1	

50%
Majority 7,116

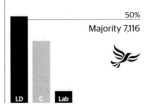

| LD | C | Lab |

Thurrock — Conservative gain

Jackie Doyle-Price
b. Aug 5, 1969
MP 2010-

Interested in financial services and the economy – worked as an associate for the Financial Services Authority. Contested Sheffield Hillsborough 2005. Long-term activist. Assistant private secretary. Lord Mayor of the City of London 2000-05. Parliamentary officer, City of London. Roman Catholic. Enjoys theatre, reading and soaps. Education: Notre Dame RC School, Sheffield; Durham (economics and politics).

Carl Morris (Lab) b. Jun 6, 1956. Mayor of Thurrock, 1999-2000. Cllr, Thurrock (deputy leader 2000-04). Education: Culverhouse Secondary School.

Carys Davis (LD) b. Jun 18, 1981. Parliamentary relations officer for UK charity. Researcher for: Danny Alexander MP; Julia Goldsworthy MP.
Emma Colgate (BNP) Cllr.
Clive Broad (UKIP)

Constituency
This seat covers the urban half of the Thurrock unitary authority, at the gateway to London. The M25 runs through the seat, including the northern end of the Dartford bridge and tunnel crossings. The Lakeside Shopping Centre, with more than 300 stores, is a major employer. It also has Procter & Gamble's main UK base nearby. Purfleet, South Ockendon, Grays and Tilbury are some of the town centres within the Thurrock conurbation. The seat has been Labour since the Second World War with the exception of one term from 1987 when it went Tory.

	Electorate	Turnout %	Change from '05 %
	92,390	49.6	☆
Doyle-Price, J C	16,869	36.8	3.6
Morris, C Lab	16,777	36.6	-9.6
Davis, C LD	4,901	10.7	-0.4
Colgate, E BNP	3,618	7.9	
Broad, C UKIP	3,390	7.4	4.0
Araba, A Ch	266	0.6	

Majority 92

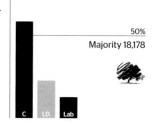

C | Lab | LD | BNP | UKIP

Tiverton & Honiton — Conservative hold

Neil Parish
b. May 26, 1956
MP 2010-

Very pugnacious attack-dog. Jovial and mischevious. Helped set up inquiry into foot-and-mouth outbreak as MEP South West 1999-2009 (agriculture spokes, deputy Con chief whip, member cttee Agriculture and Rural Development, chair 2007-09). Contested Pontypool 1997. Cllr, Sedgemoor District 1983-96, Somerset County 1989-93. Parish/District/County, Somerset. Election monitor Zimbabwe 2000 – criticism resulted in ban from the country. Animal welfare campaigner, managed family farm. Married, one daughter, one son. Education: Brymore Agricultural School; Taunton College.

Jon Underwood (LD) Financial trader, previously worked for NatWest. Ed: Oxford; Imperial College London.
Vernon Whitlock (Lab) b. Aug 28, 1947. Former police officer. Workforce development officer.
Daryl Stanbury (UKIP)

Constituency
Substantially redrawn, the constituency is now a strip of Devonshire heartland along the border with Somerset and Dorset. From Tiverton at the north its main towns are Cullompton, Honiton – a popular cream-tea stop for holidaymakers heading west – Axminster at Devon's eastern tip and Seaton on the coast. Much of the rolling countryside between is agricultural, employing nearly 7 per cent of the population. The seat is less affluent but less ageing than most of the county. It has returned Tory MPs for decades.

	Electorate	Turnout %	Change from '05 %
	76,810	71.5	☆
Parish, N C	27,614	50.3	3.6
Underwood, J LD	18,294	33.3	4.2
Whitlock, V Lab	4,907	8.9	-4.4
Stanbury, D UKIP	3,277	6.0	1.2
Connor, C Green	802	1.5	-1.3

Majority 9,320

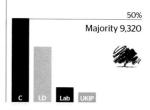

C | LD | Lab | UKIP

Tonbridge and Malling — Conservative hold

Sir John Stanley
b. Jan 19, 1942
MP 1974-

Old-school, knight of the shire, mildly bombastic. Right-wing with an interest in foreign affairs. A figure from the past who has never had much influence. Minister: NI 1987-88; Armed Forces 1983-87; Housing/Construction 1979-83. PPS to Margaret Thatcher 1976-79. Con research dept 1967-68. Research associate, Strategic Studies Institute. Rio Tinto-Zinc Corp. Married, one daughter, one son. Ed: Repton Sch; Lincoln College, Oxford (modern history); Syracuse, USA.

Elizabeth Simpson (LD) b. 1955. Business manager in probation service. Cllr, Tonbridge & Malling 1991-. Chair of Housing.

Daniel Griffiths (Lab) b. Nov 3, 1972. Journalist, BBC. Born in Germany, brought up in Grampion. Ed: Durham.

Constituency
From Edenbridge in the southwestern corner of Kent, by the border with Surrey and Sussex, the seat curves east to Tonbridge and Hildenborough, and then north to the M20 and beyond. West and East Malling give their name to the predominantly rural northern area, which includes Mereworth Woods. GlaxoSmithKline, near Leigh in the south, is an important employer. It is generally an affluent seat and popular with commuters, although 15 per cent of residents live in social housing. The constituency has been safely Tory for generations.

	Electorate	Turnout %	Change from '05 %
	71,790	71.5	
Stanley, J C	29,723	57.9	5.1
Simpson, E LD	11,545	22.5	3.0
Griffiths, D Lab	6,476	12.6	-11.2
Waller, D UKIP	1,911	3.7	0.0
Dawe, S Green	764	1.5	
Easter, M NF	505	1.0	
Rogers, L Eng	390	0.8	

Majority 18,178

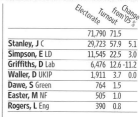

C | LD | Lab

Tooting — Labour hold

Sadiq Khan
b. Aug 18, 1970
MP 2005-

Bright, personable, fast-talking with slightly intense manner. Exiled under Blair for opposing 90-day detention power for terror suspects. Bugged by police when visiting constituent in prison over terrorism enquiry. Was first Muslim to attend Cabinet. Min: Transport (attending cabinet) 2009-10. Parly Under-Sec: DCLG 2008-09. Asst govt whip 2007-08. PPS to Jack Straw 2007. Cllr, Wandsworth 1994- (dep leader Lab Group 1996-2001). GMB, Unison, CWU. Chair, legal affairs cttee. Muslim Council of Britain. Vice-Chair Legal Action Group. Solicitor. Founder, Human Rights Lawyers Assoc. Married, two daughters. Ed: Uni of North London (LLB); Coll of Law, Guildford (Law Soc finals).

Mark Clarke (C) b. 1977. Runs own consultancy business. Ed: Dulwich College, Durham University.
Nasser Butt (LD) Accountant. Cllr, Sutton, 2002-2006.

Constituency
Sandwiched between Wimbledon and Streatham, this South London seat boasts green spaces at Wandsworth and Tooting Bec commons. Earlsfield and Tooting are the main centres and the rest of the seat has residential streets built in the 1930s. Fairly well off, it is less affluent and more ethnically diverse than the other Wandsworth seats. More than 30 per cent live in social housing and there are notable Indian and black Caribbean communities. It has returned Labour since its creation in 1974.

	Electorate	Turnout %	Change from '05 %
	73,836	68.6	☆
Khan, S Lab	22,038	43.5	0.8
Clarke, M C	19,514	38.5	8.0
Butt, N LD	7,509	14.8	-4.8
McDonald, S UKIP	624	1.2	0.2
Vickery, R Green	609	1.2	-2.9
John-Richards, S Ind	190	0.4	
Paul, S Ch	171	0.3	

Majority 2,524

Torbay — Liberal Democrat hold

Adrian Sanders
b. Apr 25, 1959
MP 1997-

Constituency-focused local champion. Diabetes campaigner – he has Type 1 diabetes. LD dep chief whip 2006-10; whip 2006-10, 1997-2001. LD spokes: Tourism 2002-05; Transport/ Local Govt/Regions/Social Justice 1999-2002; Housing 1997-2001. Cllr, Torbay 1984-86. NVCO policy officer. Assistant to Paddy Ashdown. Parly officer, LD whips office. Liberal Cllrs Assoc info officer. Member CPA, IPU. Grants adviser to charities. Married. Ed: Torquay Boys' GS.

Marcus Wood (C) b. 1959. Runs Fleming Banfu International. Contested Torbay, 2005. Education: Maidenhead GS; Slough College.

David Pedrick-Friend (Lab) b. Jan 17, 1943. Lecturer. Involved in British Legion. Ed: Exeter University.
Julien Parrott (UKIP)

Constituency
The densely populated constituency takes in much of the "English Riviera" borough of Torbay. It includes the sandy beaches of Paignton and palm-lined promenades of Torquay, which is still trying to shrug off the Basil Fawlty image that has dogged hoteliers since John Cleese's television comedy series *Fawlty Towers* was filmed there in the 1970s. These resorts, and villages such as Cockington, attract hordes of tourists and retired people. It was staunchly Conservative until 1997, when the Lib Dems took it by 12 votes.

	Electorate	Turnout %	Change from '05 %
	76,151	64.6	☆
Sanders, A LD	23,126	47.0	5.2
Wood, M C	19,048	38.7	3.0
Pedrick-Friend, D Lab	3,231	6.6	-7.9
Parrott, J UKIP	2,628	5.3	-2.7
Conway, A BNP	709	1.4	
Moss, S Green	468	1.0	

Majority 4,078

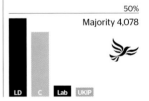

Torfaen — Labour hold

Paul Murphy
b. Nov 25, 1948
MP 1987-

Traditional Labour mollifier, played key role in Northern Ireland peace talks. Catholic. Sec: Wales 2008-09, 1999-2005. Min: NI Office 1997-99. Opp spokes 1988-97. Cllr, Torfaen BC 1973-87. Royal Inst of Internat Affairs. Lecturer in govt. Management trainee CWS. Knight of St Gregory. TGWU. Ed: St Francis Sch, Abersychan; West Monmouth Sch, Pontypool; Oriel Coll, Oxford (MA mod hist).

Jonathan Burns (C) b. 1981. Consultant in Public Relations. Cllr, Cardiff County Council 2004-. Contested Blaenau Gwent by-election 2006.

David Morgan (LD) IT officer. Cllr, Bridgend. Ed: Brynglas Primary; Bettws Comprehensive.
Rhys ab Elis (PC)

Constituency
This southeast Wales seat has a number of towns along the River Lwyd. These include Cwmbran in the south, Pontypool, Abertillery and Blaenavon – which grew around the iron works and subsequent steel and coal industries and is preserved as a Unesco World Heritage Site. Still a working-class, manufacturing-orientated seat, about 25 per cent of its residents live in social housing. Roy Jenkins, who was Home Secretary, hailed from Abersychan but never represented the seat, which has been Labour for decades.

	Electorate	Turnout %	Change from '05 %
	61,178	61.5	☆
Murphy, P Lab	16,847	44.8	-12.1
Burns, J C	7,541	20.0	4.3
Morgan, D LD	6,264	16.6	0.9
ab Elis, R PC	2,005	5.3	
Noble, J BNP	1,657	4.4	
Wildgust, F Ind	1,419	3.8	1.7
Dunn, G UKIP	862	2.3	-0.9
Turner-Thomas, R Ind	607	1.6	-0.5
Clarke, O Green	438	1.2	

Majority 9,306

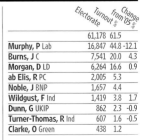

Dr Sarah Wollaston
b. Feb 17, 1962
MP 2010-

Down-to-earth, political outsider – joined Tories in 2006 and won open primary. South Devon GP for 16 years. Part-time educationalist and examiner. Former police surgeon. Cites political heroes as Emmeline Pankhurst and 'more Darwin than Disraeli'. Member: BMA; RCGP. Enjoys tandeming, cross-country running. Daughter of RAF catering officer, varied upbringing. Married, two daughters, one son. Ed: Tal-Handaq Service Children's Sch, Malta; Watford GS; Guy's Hospital Medical Sch.

Julian Brazil (LD) Teacher. Cllr, Devon CC. Special adviser to Charles Kennedy on the environment.

Carole Whitty (Lab) b. May 18, 1948. Deputy Gen Sec NAHT, former head teacher. RSA Fellow and involved in the National Education Trust. Ed: Birmingham.
Jeff Beer (UKIP)

Constituency
Totnes hosts a colony of ecofriendly New Agers who are more likely to offer visitors a cup of chai than PG Tips. The constituency extends northwest to the fringes of Dartmoor and south to the coastal town of Salcombe, taking in a chunk of South Hams with its sheltered countryside and pretty beaches. Other towns include Dartmouth and the Torbay fishing port of Brixham. Tourism drives the economy though farming and fishing remain. The seat has returned Tory MPs for decades but Lib Dems have recently reduced the majorities.

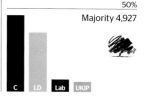

	Electorate	Turnout %	Change from '05 %
	67,937	70.4	*
Wollaston, S C	21,940	45.9	3.1
Brazil, J LD	17,013	35.6	-1.5
Whitty, C Lab	3,538	7.4	-4.7
Beer, J UKIP	2,890	6.0	-1.5
Somerville, L Green	1,181	2.5	
Turner, M BNP	624	1.3	
Drew, S Ind	390	0.8	
Hopwood, S Ind	267	0.6	

50%
Majority 4,927

C   LD   Lab   UKIP

David Lammy
b. Jul 19, 1972
MP 2000-

Articulate, never quite fulfilled potential. Made much of Harvard links with Barack Obama. Min: DIUS/BIS 2008-. Parly Under-Sec: DIUS 2007-08; CMS 2005-07; Constitutional Affairs 2003-05; Health 2002-03. PPS to Estelle Morris 2001-02. Member, GLA 2000, Archbishop's Council 1999-2002. Member, Fabian Soc, Christian Socialist Movement. Barrister. Former trustee, ActionAid. Married, two sons. Ed: The King's Sch, Peterborough (scholarship); SOAS (LLB); Harvard (LLM).

David Schmitz (LD) Barrister. Former welfare caseworker in the Bronx. Ed: Syracuse University, USA.

Sean Sullivan (C) .b 1981. Criminal barrister. Cllr, Epsom & Ewell. Ed: Oxford University.

Constituency
This North London seat, stretching from Finsbury Park to White Hart Lane, encompasses the poorer and more deprived eastern half of Haringey. It is a densely populated Labour stronghold with high unemployment and large areas of deprivation, especially in the north east. Manufacturing remains an important sector but is in decline. There is a large black population and other ethnic minority groups including Turkish and Cypriot. This has been safely Labour for decades.

	Electorate	Turnout %	Change from '05 %
	69,933	58.2	
Lammy, D Lab	24,128	59.3	1.4
Schmitz, D LD	7,197	17.7	1.0
Sullivan, S C	6,064	14.9	1.4
Sutton, J TUSC	1,057	2.6	
Gray, A Green	980	2.4	-2.2
McKenzie, W UKIP	466	1.2	
Watson, N Ind	265	0.7	
Kadara, A Ch	262	0.6	
Thompson, S Ind	143	0.4	
Carr, E Ind	125	0.3	

50%
Majority 16,931

Lab   LD   C

Sarah Newton
b. Jul, 1961
MP 2010-

Campaigned on healthcare issues. Cllr, Merton BC. Director, International Longevity Centre thinktank. Dir, Age Concern England. Marketing career: IBIS, Citibank, American Express. FRSA. Member, Falmouth Tall Ships Assoc, Falmouth Rotary Club, several charities. Enjoys sailing, skiing and bee-keeping. Married, two daughters, one son. Ed: Falmouth School.

Terrye Teverson (LD) b. 1952. Founded stationery manufacturing company KCS. Contested Falmouth & Camborne, 1997, 1992; European elections (south west) 1999. Ed: Helston GS; Cornwall College.

Charlotte Mackenzie (Lab) b. Jun 7, 1957. Researcher and consultant. Former associate director of HEFCE and QAA. Cllr, Truro 2007-. Contested Truro & St Austell 2005. Ed: Cambridge Uni; UCL.

Constituency
The cathedral city of Truro is the centre of Cornwall's trade and commerce, and geographic heart of this constituency, which has lost St Austell but gained Falmouth. On the eastern side is St Mawes peninsula, whose secluded beaches draw tourists. There are relatively high numbers of working-class and self-employed. Despite the recession, Truro remained one of Britain's most desirable places to live, with house prices several per cent higher than elsewhere in Cornwall. The predecessor seat had been Liberal or Lib Dem since 1974.

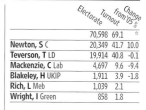

	Electorate	Turnout %	Change from '05 %
	70,598	69.1	*
Newton, S C	20,349	41.7	10.0
Teverson, T LD	19,914	40.8	-0.1
Mackenzie, C Lab	4,697	9.6	-9.4
Blakeley, H UKIP	1,911	3.9	-1.8
Rich, L Meb	1,039	2.1	
Wright, I Green	858	1.8	

50%
Majority 435

C   LD   Lab

Tunbridge Wells
Conservative hold

Greg Clark
b. Aug 28, 1967
MP 2005-

Mild-mannered, erudite, thoughtful moderniser from party's soft left. Behind-the-scenes, the new David Willetts. Bright and ambitious, performed well as Shadow SoS: Energy and Climate Change (2008-10) against Ed Miliband. Min: Communities & Local Govt 2010-. Shadow Minister: Cabinet Office 2007-08; Charities 2006-07. Director of policy, Con Party 2001-05; Special adviser to Ian Lang MP 1996-97. BBC controller of Commercial Policy. Boston Consulting Group. Married, two daughters, one son. Ed: St Peter's Comprehensive, Middlesbrough; Magdalene College, Cambridge (BA economics, MA); LSE (PhD).

David Hallas (LD) b. Oct 27, 1980. Primary school teacher. Ed: Kent Uni; Christ Church Uni, Canterbury.
Gary Heather (Lab) b. Dec 30, 1953. BT telephone engineer, Trade Unionist. Board member, Well-being and Health Institute at the University of Westminster. Ed: Southampton Uni.

Constituency
The spa town of Royal Tunbridge Wells lies at Kent's border with East Sussex, from where the seat stretches southeast along the county boundary as far as the villages of Hawkhurst and Sandhurst, newly included after boundary changes. It includes Paddock Wood. Tourism is a notable sector in this affluent seat and the pretty villages amid High Weald countryside are popular with commuters. The constituency has long been a Tory stronghold.

	Electorate	Turnout %	Change from '05 %
	72,042	69.9	*
Clark, G C	28,302	56.2	5.6
Hallas, D LD	12,726	25.3	0.0
Heather, G Lab	5,448	10.8	-9.6
Webb, V UKIP	2,054	4.1	0.5
Dawe, H Green	914	1.8	
McBride, A BNP	704	1.4	
Bradbury, F Ind	172	0.3	

Majority 15,576

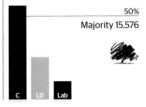

50%

C   LD   Lab

Twickenham
Liberal Democrat hold

Vince Cable
b. May 9, 1943
MP 1997-

Became the Liberal Democrats' best known politician in 2008-09 for his tell-it-as-it-is approach to the economy. SoS: Business 2010-. LD Shad Chancellor of Exchequer 2003-10. LD spokes 1997-2003. Member, cttee: Treasury 1998-99. Cllr (Lab), Glasgow CC 1971-74. Special adviser to: World Environ & Devt Commission; Commonwealth Gen Sec; John Smith. Chief economist, Shell. Finance officer, economics lecturer, diplomatic service. Dep dir, Overseas Devt Inst. Accomplished ballroom/latin dancer. Widowed, one daughter, two sons. Remarried. Ed: Fitzwilliam Coll, Cambridge (BA natsci/econ; pres Union); Glasgow (PhD internat econ).

Deborah Thomas (C) b. Nov 9, 1977. Owns consulting business. PPC for Birmingham Hodge Hill, 2005. Member, Economic Competitiveness Policy Group 2006-2007.
Brian Tomlinson (Lab) b. Jun 15, 1979. Lawyer. Worked for National Assembly for Wales.

Constituency
Known for its rugby stadium, Twickenham lies in the north east of the seat. Other population centres are Hampton in the west and Teddington in the east, with its canal and locks. Hampton Court Palace and park, and Bushy Park, cover the south of the seat. Although there is an Indian population in the north west, the seat is predominantly white. The seat is generally affluent and was Tory from the Second World War until 1997, when the Lib Dems took it.

	Electorate	Turnout %	Change from '05 %
	79,861	74.8	
Cable, V LD	32,483	54.4	2.8
Thomas, D C	20,343	34.1	1.8
Tomlinson, B Lab	4,583	7.7	-3.6
Gilbert, B UKIP	868	1.5	0.0
Roest, S Green	674	1.1	-1.7
Hurst, C BNP	654	1.1	
Cole, H R&E	76.0	0.13	
Armstrong, P Magna	40	0.1	

Majority 12,140

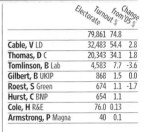

50%

LD   C   Lab

Tynemouth
Labour hold

Alan Campbell
b. Jul 8, 1957
MP 1997-

Parly Under-Sec: Home 2008-10. Whip: govt 2006-08; asst govt 2005-06. PPS to: Adam Ingram 2003-05; Lord Macdonald of Tradeston 2001-03. Member, select cttee: Public Accounts 1997-2001. Campaign coordinator, Tynemouth Labour. School teacher. Married, one daughter, one son. Ed: Blackfyne Sec, Consett; Lancaster (BA politics); Leeds (PGCE); Newcastle Poly (MA hist).

Wendy Morton (C) b. 1967. Runs small manufacturing and electronics business. Diplomatic Service. Contested Newcastle Central 2005. Ed: Wensleydale Comprehensive School; Open University.

John Appleby (LD) b. Nov, 1956. Head of School of Mechanical & Systems Engineering, Newcastle University. Cllr, Newcastle City 2004-2007. Ed: Cambridge University.

Constituency
The north of the Tyne is generally the better-off side, with numbers of professionals and owner-occupiers high for the region. There are still some severely deprived areas in the very south, around North Shields, and north west, around Backworth, which is newly included after boundary changes. The coast toward the tourist resort of Whitley Bay in the north is far more affluent. The Tories held this seat for 47 years until 1997, when it formed part of Labour's seaside success story.

	Electorate	Turnout %	Change from '05 %
	75,680	69.6	*
Campbell, A Lab	23,860	45.3	-3.0
Morton, W C	18,121	34.4	-2.2
Appleby, J LD	7,845	14.9	-0.2
Brooke, D BNP	1,404	2.7	
Payne, N UKIP	900	1.7	
Erskine, J Green	538	1.0	

Majority 5,739

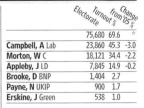

50%

Lab   C   LD

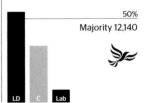

Tyneside North

Mary Glindon
b. Jan 13, 1957
MP 2010-

Vivacious, down-to-earth Geordie who never planned on becoming an MP until an all-woman shortlist was imposed on the seat shortly before the election. Long-serving cllr from working class background, dedicated to her constituency. Interested in renewable energies, health and older people. Cllr, North Tyneside 1995-2010 (Civic Mayor 1999-2000). Worked in call centres, hospital, and as a dept store sales assistant. Administrator for Child Support Agency. Voluntary sector work - ran North Shields People's Centre. GMB. Married, one stepson, one stepdaughter, one daughter. Ed: Sacred Heart; Newcastle; Newcastle Poly (BSc Hons sociology).

David Ord (LD) b. 1961. Computer programmer, NHS. Cllr, North Tyneside 1998-. Contested Wallsend & Newcastle East, 2005, 2001.
Gagan Mohindra (C) Businessman. Cllr, Epping Forest DC. Ed: King's College London.

Constituency
This slightly redrawn seat forms a corridor between Newcastle and Tynemouth. There are some severely deprived areas in the industrial Riverside ward, which reaches from Wallsend East to North Shields and includes power plants, docks and shipyards. Longbenton and Killingworth are dense urban areas in the middle of the seat, while the north is more rural and no single economic sector dominates. About a third of residents live in social housing in this solid Labour constituency.

		Electorate	Turnout %	Change from '05 %
		77,690	59.7	☆
Glindon, M	Lab	23,505	50.7	-8.7
Ord, D	LD	10,621	22.9	0.9
Mohindra, G	C	8,514	18.4	-0.3
Burrows, J	BNP	1,860	4.0	
Blake, C	UKIP	1,306	2.8	
Batten, B	NF	599	1.3	

50%
Majority 12,884

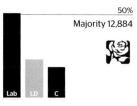

Lab LD C

Tyrone West

Pat Doherty
b. Jul 18, 1945
MP 2001-

Named by the UUP MP David Burnside under Parliamentary privilege in 2002 as a member of Provisional IRA's ruling army council, his brother was a member of the notorious Balcombe Street Gang. SF spokes: Enterprise, Trade & Investment 2000-. Member NI Assembly 1998 (member/chair, Enterprise Trade & Investment cttee 1999-). Sinn Fein VP/nat organiser/dir of elections/activist. Ldr delegation to Dublin Forum for Peace & Reconciliation. Member talks team 1997-98. Former member Local Credit Union. Site Engineer. Likes building stone walls. Married, three daughters, two sons. Ed: St Joseph's Coll, Lochwinnoch.

Thomas Buchanan (DUP) b. Jul 30, 1963. Cllr, Omagh DC 1993-. Member Omagh 2010 Task Force.
Ross Hussey (UCUNF) b. Feb 25, 1959. Cllr, Omagh DC 2005-.
Joe Byrne (SDLP) Cllr, Omagh, 2003-2005. Former teacher and economist. SDLP Chairman.

Constituency
This large, sparsely populated seat is Northern Ireland's newest and 18th, created by the Boundary Commissioners for the 1997 general election. It has the highest levels of rural poverty and is the third most Catholic constituency, with its population concentrated in the poorer highlands and the Protestants in the valleys. It is overwhelmingly nationalist, but had an Ulster Unionist MP for one term on its inception until the nationalists united behind Sinn Féin, who have held it since 2001.

		Electorate	Turnout %	Change from '05 %
		61,148	61.0	
Doherty, P	SF	18,050	48.4	9.6
Buchanan, T	DUP	7,365	19.8	2.0
Hussey, R	UCUNF	5,281	14.2	
Byrne, J	SDLP	5,212	14.0	4.9
Bower, M	Alliance	859	2.3	
McClean, C	Ind	508	1.4	-25.9

50%
Majority 10,685

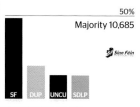

SF DUP UNCU SDLP

Ulster Mid

Martin McGuinness
b. May 23, 1950
MP 1997-

A remarkable personal journey from guns to government, McGuinness for decades embodied the Provisional IRA but in 2009 called the IRA murderers of two soldiers and a policeman "traitors". Member, NI Assembly 1999-; Deputy First Minister 2007-. Min for Education 1999-. Member NI Assembly 1982. SF chief negotiator mid-1980s. Rep to Dublin Forum for Peace and Reconciliation 1994-95. Married, two daughters, two sons. Ed: Christian Brothers Tech Coll.

Ian McCrea (DUP) b. Jun 12, 1976. Cllr, Cookstown DC 2001-. Member, NI Assembly, 2007-. Ed: Rainey Endowed Grammar School.

Tony Quinn (SDLP) Credit controller. Cllr, Cookstown.
Sandra Overend (UCUNF) Office manager for Billy Armstrong MLA. Ed: Cookstorn High School; University of Ulster (accountancy).
Walter Millar (TUV)

Constituency
The boundary changes of 1997 created a Republican Catholic constituency for the sitting MP Martin McGuinness. Previously the seat had been held by the DUP by virtue of a silent pact with the UUP, which did not stand. The mainly rural farmland is on the front line of the struggle between the two communities. Its heartland rests in the strongly segregated villages.

		Electorate	Turnout %	Change from '05 %
		64,594	63.2	
McGuinness, M	SF	21,239	52.0	4.4
McCrea, I	DUP	5,876	14.4	-9.0
Quinn, T	SDLP	5,826	14.3	-3.1
Overend, S	UCUNF	4,509	11.0	
Millar, W	TUV	2,995	7.3	
Butler, I	Alliance	397	1.0	

50%
Majority 15,363

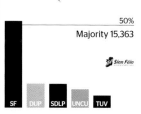

SF DUP SDLP UNCU TUV

Upper Bann — DUP hold

David Simpson
b. Feb 16, 1959
MP 2005-

On the DUP's fundamentalist wing, he supports the teaching of "intelligent design' alongside evolution. DUP spokes: Transport, Int Devt, Young People 2007-; Trade & Industry 2005-07. Member, NI Assembly 2003-. VP DUP. Vice-Chair, DUP Victims Cttee, DUP Council Assoc. Cllr, Craigavon BC. Food manufacturing industry. Senior Partner, Universal Meat Co. Married, two daughters, one son. Ed: Killicomaine HS, Portadown; Coll of Bus Studies, Belfast.

Harry Hamilton (UCUNF) Business development manager. Musician.
John O'Dowd (SF) Member, NI Assembly. Cllr, Craigavon BC.

Dolores Kelly (SDLP) b. Sep 3, 1959. Member, NI Assembly 2003. Cllr, Loughside DC 2005. Mayor of Craigavon, 1999. Ed: St Michael's Grammar School, Lurgan; University of Ulster (occupational therapy).

Constituency
This is a constituency of divisions in an area of Ulster that has been central to sectarian conflict. Although it reflects the Northern Ireland balance of 43 per cent Catholic, 55 per cent Protestant, many of its towns are segregated. The violent protests of Drumcree in the Nineties, pitting Protestant Orangemen against the Catholic residents of Garvaghy Road in Portadown, remain a defining feature. The DUP gained the seat in 2005.

	Electorate	Turnout %	Change from '05 %
	74,732	55.4	
Simpson, T DUP	14,000	33.8	-3.7
Hamilton, H UCUNF	10,639	25.7	
O'Dowd, J SF	10,237	24.7	3.8
Kelly, D SDLP	5,276	12.8	-0.2
Heading, B Alliance	1,231	3.0	0.8

50%

Majority 3,361

Uxbridge & Ruislip South — Conservative hold

John Randall
b. Aug 5, 1955
MP Jul 1997-

Reliable backroom party man who was MD of family department store, Randall's of Uxbridge, and is a small-businessman populist. Dep Chief Whip (Treasurer of HM Household) 2010-. Opposition: Asst chief whip 2005-10. Previously opposition whip, 2000-05, interrupted in 2003 when he resigned in opposition to the Iraq war. Chaired Uxbridge Con Assoc 1994-97. Chaired Uxbridge Retailers Association. Ornithologist tour leader 1986-97. Married, one daughter, two sons. Ed: Slavonic and E European Studies Sch (BA Serbo-Croat).

Sidharath Garg (Lab) b. Feb 5, 1976. Lawyer/conveyancer. Cllr, Hillingdon.

Michael Cox (LD) Chartered accountant and auditor. Cllr, Hillingdon 2002-. Contested Ruislip-Northwood 2005, 2001.

Constituency
On the western edge of London, the old Uxbridge seat has been redrawn with Ickenham lost from the north west and West Drayton from the south. However, it has gained a large chunk of Manor, South Ruislip and Cavendish in the north east, divided from the main Uxbridge town and Hillingdon by RAF Northolt. Brunel University is a major presence and employer in the area. Bordering with Buckinghamshire, the seat is well connected and part of the affluent commuter belt. The old Uxbridge constituency had been Tory since 1970.

	Electorate	Turnout %	Change from '05 %
	71,168	63.3	☆
Randall, J C	21,758	48.3	3.8
Garg, S Lab	10,542	23.4	-3.0
Cox, M LD	8,995	20.0	-2.7
Neal, D BNP	1,396	3.1	
Wadsworth, M UKIP	1,234	2.7	1.1
Harling, M Green	477	1.1	-1.1
Cooper, R Eng	403	0.9	
Mcallister, F NF	271	0.6	

50%

Majority 11,216

Vale of Clwyd — Labour hold

Chris Ruane
b. Jul 18, 1958
MP 1997-

Noisy heckler of opponents from backbenches in Commons chamber. Champion of seaside towns (Member, Lab group of seaside MPs). PPS to: David Miliband 2009-10; Caroline Flint 2007-08; Peter Hain 2002-07. Member, select cttee: Welsh Affairs 1999-2002. Cllr, Rhyl Town 1988-99. Founder member Rhyl anti-apartheid, environmental assoc. Amnesty Int Pres. NUT Vale of Clwyd/West Clwyd. Primary sch dep head/teacher. Married, two daughters. Ed: Blessed Edward Jones Comp; Uni of Wales, Aberystwyth (BSc econ, hist, politics); Liverpool (PGCE).

Matt Wright (C) Freelance consultant. Cllr, Flintshire CC. Contested Vale of Clwyd 2007; Alyn & Deeside 2003.
Paul Penlington (LD) b. Apr 17, 1964. College lecturer.
Caryl Wyn Jones (PC)

Constituency
This seat spans from the coast, at Rhyl and Prestatyn, inland to Denbigh and beyond. Rhyl includes some of the most deprived areas in Wales, with a high claimant rate and social problems, but the town is undergoing regeneration. It was also where John Prescott punched a countryside protester who had thrown an egg at him in 2001. A varied seat, it has a slight working-class demographic skew but the middle classes are also well represented. Health is the biggest economic sector. Labour won this seat on its creation in 1997 but the Tories had previously been strong in predecessor constituencies.

	Electorate	Turnout %	Change from '05 %
	55,781	63.7	☆
Ruane, C Lab	15,017	42.3	-3.6
Wright, M C	12,508	35.2	3.5
Penlington, P LD	4,472	12.6	0.8
Wyn, C Jones PC	2,068	5.8	
Si'Ree, I BNP	827	2.3	
Turner, T UKIP	515	1.5	0.3
Butler, M Green	127	0.4	

50%

Majority 2,509

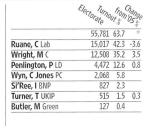

Alun Cairns
b. Jul 20, 1970
MP 2010-

Tweed-wearing Tory, interested in special educational needs and the economy. Contested Vale of Glamorgan 2005, Gower 1997. Member, Welsh Assembly 1999-, when Welsh Tories adopted mild nationalist tinge. Career: Lloyds TSB. Enjoys shooting and skiing. Married, one son. Education: Ysgol Gyfun Ysalyfera; University of Wales (MBA).

Alana Davies (Lab) b. Mar 9, 1948. Retired lecturer. Cllr, Bridgend 1999-. Cabinet member, Children and Young People. Twice Mayor of Porthcawl. Education: Bridgend Girls' Grammar School; Open University; University of Wales.

Eluned Parrott (LD) b. 1974. Community engagement manager for Cardiff Uni. Ed: St Peter's Collegiate School; Cardiff University; Chartered Institute of Marketing.
Ian Johnson (PC) Head of research in Westminster for Plaid Cymru.

Constituency
This South Wales seat spans from Ogmore-by-Sea to Barry, which has come to prominence as the setting for the television show *Gavin and Stacey*. Other coastal towns include St Athan and Llantwit Major, while inland lies Cowbridge. The coast is home to the "Crachach" – the elite of Welsh life. This predominantly middle-class seat was once regarded as safe for the Tories. However, Labour won it in a 1989 by-election, lost it in 1992, but regained in 1997 and held on with reduced majorities in 2001 and 2005.

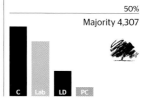

	Electorate	Turnout %	from '05 % Change
	70,262	69.3	☆
Cairns, A C	20,341	41.8	4.4
Davies, A Lab	16,034	33.0	-7.8
Parrott, E LD	7,403	15.2	2.0
Johnson, I PC	2,667	5.5	0.3
Mahoney, K UKIP	1,529	3.1	1.4
Thomas, R Green	457	0.9	
Harrold, J Ch	236	0.5	

50%
Majority 4,307

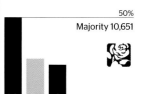

C | Lab | LD | PC

Kate Hoey
b. Jun 21, 1946
MP Jun 1989-

Maverick rebel, Unionist, pro-fox hunting (Chair, Countryside Alliance). Parly Under-Sec: CMS 1999-2001; Home 1998-99. PPS to Frank Field 1997-98. Member, select cttees: NI Affairs 2007-; Science & Technology 2004-05; Social Security 1994-97; Broadcasting 1991-97. Cllr, Hackney BC 1978-92; Southwark BC 1988-89. Senior lecturer. Educational adviser, Arsenal FC. Ed: Belfast Royal Academy; Ulster Coll of Phys Ed (teaching dip); City of London Coll (BSC economics).

Caroline Pidgeon (LD) b. 1972. Cllr, Southwark 1998-2010. Memb, GLA; Met Police Authority. Contested Dulwich & West Norwood 2001.

Glyn Chambers (C) Economist. Contested Belfast East 2007.

Constituency
From the north side of Clapham Common, the seat tracks the A3 north through Stockwell and Vauxhall as far as the Oval, then follows the riverside from Vauxhall Bridge to the Southbank. It is a seat of contrasts with affluent areas in Clapham Old Town and Thames-side residences backing on to housing estates with severe deprivation. About half the residents lived in social housing at the last census, but it has lost the deprived Coldharbour ward. There are large black African and Caribbean communities and more than 30 per cent of residents were born outside Britain. The seat has been Labour since 1983.

	Electorate	Turnout %	from '05 % Change
	74,811	57.7	☆
Hoey, K Lab	21,498	49.8	-2.0
Pidgeon, C LD	10,847	25.1	-2.1
Chambers, G C	9,301	21.5	7.0
Healy, J Green	708	1.6	-2.8
Navarro, J Eng	289	0.7	
Martin, L Ch	200	0.5	
Lambert, D Soc	143	0.3	
Drinkall, J WP	109	0.3	
Kapetanos, J APP	96	0.2	

50%
Majority 10,651

Lab | LD | C

Mary Creagh
b. Dec 2, 1967
MP 2005-

Elfin, Peter-Pan looks. Sharp but approachable. Introduced Bill for values to regulate bath water temperature and prevent scalding. Asst govt whip 2009-10. PPS to: Andy Burnham 2006-09; Lord Warner 2006. Member, cttees: Joint cttee on Human Rights 2005-07; Finance & Services 2007-10. Cllr, Islington BC 1998-2005 (leader Lab group 2000-04). Lecturer in entrepreneurship Cranfield Sch of Management 1997-. Catholic. Married, one daughter, one son. Ed: Bishop Ullathorne RC Comp, Coventry; Pembroke Coll, Oxford (BA modern langs); LSE (MSC European studies).

Alex Story (C) b. 1974. Film and documentary producer. Former Olympic rower. 2012 Olympics spokesman for Taxpayers' Alliance.
David Smith (LD) b. 1957. Director, Leeds Voice.
Ian Senior (BNP)

Constituency
At the heart of West Yorkshire's former mining area, Wakefield is yet to recover fully from the industry's decline and has patches of severe deprivation. The city's economy is increasingly diverse and, though the seat has always returned Labour MPs since the Second World War, margins of victory under old boundaries were sometimes narrow. Substantial boundary changes mean the seat loses a large, sparsely populated rural area to its south west and gains the market town of Ossett in the north. Under old boundaries, the constituency was reliably Labour.

	Electorate	Turnout %	from '05 % Change
	70,834	62.7	☆
Creagh, M Lab	17,454	39.3	-4.8
Story, A C	15,841	35.6	9.1
Smith, D LD	7,256	16.3	-2.5
Senior, I BNP	2,581	5.8	
Hawkins, M Green	873	2.0	0.0
Harrop, M Ind	439	1.0	

50%
Majority 1,613

Lab | C | LD | BNP

Wallasey | Labour hold

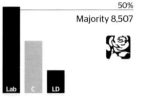

Angela Eagle
b. Feb 17, 1961
MP 1992-

Determined campaigner on equality issues; one of few publicly acknowledged lesbians in the Commons. Minister: DWP 2009. Exchequer Sec, Treasury 2007-09. Parly Under-Sec: Home 2001-02; Social Security 1998-2001; Green issues 1997-98. Opp whip 1996-97. Twin sister of Maria Eagle MP. Member select cttees: Treasury 2003-07; Public Accounts 2007-09, 2002-03, 1995-97. COHSE parly liaison officer/press officer/researcher. Civil partnership. Ed: Formby HS; St John's Coll, Oxford (BA PPE).

Leah Fraser (C) b. 1959. Cllr, Wirral BC, 2003. Contested Wallasey 2005. Ed: Weatherhead School for Girls.

Steve Pitt (LD) b. Dec 1, 1956. Former soldier. Worked in electrical installation, warehouse management and supervisor for adults with autism. Ed: Wallasey Tech GS; Liverpool John Moores Uni; Liverpool Uni.

Constituency
On the western bank at the head of the Mersey Estuary, this seat looks across to Bootle and the north end of Liverpool and is well connected to them through road and rail tunnels. A mixed seat, there is severe deprivation in Seacombe, by the docks, and Moreton, to the west, while regeneration is under way in the seaside town of New Brighton. There are, however, some better-off areas in Wallasey and it only switched to Labour in 1992.

	Electorate	Turnout %	Change from 05 %
	65,915	63.2	*
Eagle, A Lab	21,578	51.8	-2.7
Fraser, L C	13,071	31.4	0.8
Pitt, S LD	5,693	13.7	0.9
Snowden, D UKIP	1,205	2.9	0.6
Mwaba, E Ind	107	0.3	

50%
Majority 8,507

Walsall North | Labour hold

David Winnick
b. Jun 26, 1933
MP 1979-, 1966-70

Long-serving centrist with instinct for popular mood. Member, select cttee: Home 1997-; Procedure 1989-97. MP Croydon S 1966-70. Cllr, Willesden BC 1959-64, Brent BC 1964-66. Chair UK Immigrants advisory service. VP, Assocn of Professional, Executive, Clerical & Computer Staff (APEX). Divorced. One son. Education: London School of Economics (Dip social admin).

Helyn Clack (C) Managing director. Cllr, Surrey CC 2001-.
Nadia Fazal (LD) Contested Walsall South 2005 as Respect candidate.
Christopher Woodall (BNP) Local BNP organiser.

Constituency
Once the "leather capital of the world" Walsall has long been dependent on traditional manufacturing industries, which have been in decline for decades. The seat has areas of severe deprivation, especially to the east, and its residents are working class, along with high numbers who have never worked. About a third live in council housing. This is a predominantly white seat with a small Asian community. The exception in Labour's post-1950 dominance was a three-year Conservative stint after the John Stonehouse scandal triggered a by-election in 1976.

	Electorate	Turnout %	Change from 05 %
	65,183	55.5	*
Winnick, D Lab	13,385	37.0	-11.2
Clack, H C	12,395	34.3	6.8
Fazal, N LD	4,754	13.1	0.8
Woodall, C BNP	2,930	8.1	
Hazell, E UKIP	1,737	4.8	1.1
Smith, P Dem	842	2.3	
Shakir, B Ch	144	0.4	

50%
Majority 990

Walsall South | Labour hold

Valerie Vaz
b. 1955
MP 2010-

Sister of Keith Vaz MP. Contested Twickenham 1987. Cllr, Ealing 1986-90. TV presenter on Network East in 1980s. Deputy District Judge. Government legal service. Solicitor. Set up community law firm Townsend Vaz. Member of the Lay Advisory Panel of the College of Optometrists, the National Trust, the Law Society and a Friend of Kew Gardens. Married, one daughter. Education: Twickenham County Grammar School, London (BSc Biochemistry).

Richard Hunt (C) b. Jun 29, 1958. Company secretary, International Management. Cllr, Hart. Contested Barrow & Furness 1997. Education: St Aidan's CofE High School; University of Huddersfield (accountancy).
Dr Murli Sinha (LD) NHS GP for over 30 years. Focus on obesity in the community.
Derek Bennett (UKIP) Contested Walsall South, 2005, 2001.

Constituency
Walsall town centre lies in this seat. There is severe deprivation here and in Darlaston, bisected by the M6, in the west. Both are the scene of major regeneration projects aimed at reversing decades of economic decline. This part of the seat is strongly working-class with high numbers of those who have never worked and tend to vote Labour. Moving east through semi-rural areas towards Aldridge, it becomes much more affluent and Tory-leaning. Around a fifth of residents are Asian.

	Electorate	Turnout %	Change from 05 %
	64,830	63.1	*
Vaz, V Lab	16,211	39.7	-9.6
Hunt, R C	14,456	35.4	6.9
Sinha, M LD	5,880	14.4	4.6
Bennett, D UKIP	3,449	8.4	3.6
Khan, G Ch	482	1.2	
Mulia, M ND	404	1.0	

50%
Majority 1,755

Walthamstow

Stella Creasy
b. Apr 5, 1977
MP 2010-

Highly ambitious, well-spoken New Labourite with a fondness for unfashionably coloured lipsticks. Known for her intellectual rigour. Cllr, Waltham Forest 2002-06 (Mayor, Dep Mayor, Chief Whip). Speechwriter/researcher to Douglas Alexander MP, Charles Clarke MP, Ross Cranston MP. Head of campaigns/PR at The Scout Association. Dep dir, Involve (citizenship organisation). Trustee for voluntary action group. Member, Unite, Fabians, Socialist Environment & Research Association, Labour Women's Network. Education: Colchester HS; Magdalene Coll, Cambridge (Psychology); LSE (PhD psychology, won Richard Titmuss prize).

Farid Ahmed (LD) b. Aug 23, 1961, Pakistan. Business consultant. Former investment banker. PPC, 2005. Education: Sir George Monoux School, King's College London, University of Hull.
Andy Hemsted (C), finance consultant. Councillor, Waltham Forest 2002-.

Constituency
This East London seat was made famous by the band East 17, while its dog track was one of the last in London. Its reputation as the traditional working-class southern half of Waltham Forest is not undeserved, with patches of severe deprivation. It is a diverse area with about half of residents white British, and large Pakistani, Caribbean and African populations. Clement Attlee once held a seat under old boundaries, and Labour have traditionally been strong.

			Electorate	Turnout %	Change from 05 %
			64,625	63.4	
Creasy, S	Lab		21,252	51.8	1.6
Ahmed, F	LD		11,774	28.7	1.7
Hemsted, A	C		5,734	14.0	-4.1
Chisholm-Benli, J	UKIP		823	2.0	-0.3
Perrett, D	Green		767	1.9	
Taaffe, N	TUSC		279	0.7	
Mall, A	Ch		248	0.6	
Warburton, P	Ind		117	0.3	

50%
Majority 9,478

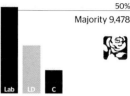

Lab LD C

Wansbeck

Ian Lavery
b. Jan 6, 1963
MP 2010-

Firebrand socialist class warrior, successor to Arthur Scargill as NUM leader (2002-), on the front line of the 1984-85 miners' strike. Branded New Labour an "abject failure". Declared he had no respect for the police following conviction for public order offence after a football match in 1985. Cllr, Wansbeck DC 1995-2003. Sec, NUM Northumberland branch. NCB miner, Ellington/Lynemouth collieries. Construction worker. Chair: Ashington FC; Hirst Welfare Centre. Married, two sons. Ed: Ashington Community HS; New Coll, Durham (HNC mining).

Simon Reed (LD) b. Jan 14, 1969. Teacher. Former soldier and Gulf War veteran. Cllr, Northumberland CC, 1999-. Ed: Newcastle University.
Campbell Storey (C) Computing manager, policy researcher. Ed: Hirst High, Oxford (BA History), Newcastle (PhD).

Constituency
This coastal Northumberland seat is densely populated and predominantly working class because of its coalmining heritage. The last deep mine in the North East was at Ellington, just beyond the northern boundary; its 2005 closure had a much greater impact on Wansbeck than the Berwick-upon-Tweed seat to which it belongs. The main settlements are Bedlington, Newbiggin-by-the-Sea, the more affluent commuter town of Morpeth and Ashington, famous for its sporting greats, including the footballers Jack and Sir Bobby Charlton and the cricketer Stephen Harmison. The seat has been Labour since 1945.

			Electorate	Turnout %	Change from 05 %
			63,045	60.7	
Lavery, I	Lab		17,548	45.9	-9.3
Reed, S	LD		10,517	27.5	1.1
Storey, C	C		6,714	17.5	2.6
Finlay, S	BNP		1,418	3.7	
Lee-Stokoe, L	UKIP		974	2.5	
Best, N	Green		601	1.6	-1.8
Reid, M	Ind		359	0.9	
Flynn, M	Ch		142	0.4	

50%
Majority 7,031

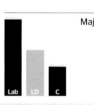

Lab LD C

Wantage

Ed Vaizey
b. Jun 5, 1968
MP 2005-

Tory moderniser, close to Cameron. Bouncy, bumptious and never taken seriously. Parly Under-Sec: Business/CMS (Culture Minister) 2010-. Shadow Min: Arts 2006-10. Speechwriter for Michael Howard as leader, election aide to Iain Duncan Smith, 2001GE. Contested Bristol East 1997. Barrister, family law/childcare. Editor, Blue Books. Freelance journalist. Dir, Consolidated Comms (PR). Trustee, the Trident Trust. Married, one daughter, one son. Education: St Paul's Sch; Merton Coll, Oxford (BA modern history); City (Dip Law).

Alan Armitage (LD) Specialist in computer security. Cllr, Oxfordshire CC, Oxford CC. Part-time member of the Asylum & Immigration Tribunal. Born in Africa. Ed: University of York.
Steven Mitchell (Lab) b. Jun 28, 1966. Business consultant. Former English teacher and project engineer. Ed: Manchester Uni.

Constituency
Much of the rolling countryside in the Vale of the White Horse – including the prehistoric chalk equine itself – lies within Wantage constituency, named after the small town at its centre. The seat takes in Faringdon and two south Oxfordshire towns: Wallingford, a pretty market town, and Didcot, which like Wantage has been earmarked for significant development. The seat has been safely Tory since the Second World War.

			Electorate	Turnout %	Change from 05 %
			80,456	70.0	☆
Vaizey, E	C		29,284	52.0	8.9
Armitage, A	LD		15,737	27.9	0.3
Mitchell, S	Lab		7,855	13.9	-10.0
Jones, J	UKIP		2,421	4.3	2.8
Twine, A	Green		1,044	1.9	-0.7

50%
Majority 13,547

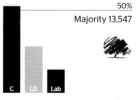

C LD Lab

Warley — Labour hold

John Spellar
b. Aug 5, 1947
MP 1992-, 1982-83

Leading figure on Labour Right and opponent of elected Lords. Hopes of Cabinet post never realised. Govt whip 2008-10. Min: NI 2003-05; Transport 2001-03; Armed Forces 1999-2001. Parly Under-Sec: Defence 1997-99. Opp spokes: Defence 1995-97; NI 1994-95. Opp whip 1992-94. MP Warley West 1992-97, Birmingham Northfield 1982-83. Nat Officer Electrical, Telecommunication & Plumbing Union. Widowed. One daughter. Education: Dulwich College; St Edmund's Hall, Oxford (BA PPE).

Jasbir Parmar (C) Cllr, Bedford BC. Runs commercial post office. Education: Ludhiana, Punjab (agriculture).

Edward Keating (LD) Freelance media and marketing consultant. Education: Cornwall College; Brunel University.
Nigel Harvey (UKIP)

Constituency
This seat lies about three miles from Birmingham, in the southeast corner of the Black Country. Very deprived areas around the Victorian terraces of Smethwick in the east give way to the slightly better-off, semi-detached 1930s housing of Warley in the west. About a fifth of residents are ethnic minority, the biggest community being of Indian origin. This remains an overwhelmingly working-class seat with high unemployment, large numbers of residents who have never worked and council housing. It has been Labour since 1966.

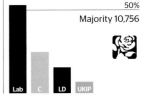

	Electorate	Turnout %	Change from '05 %
	63,106	60.6	☆
Spellar, J Lab	20,240	52.9	-2.0
Parmar, J C	9,484	24.8	1.9
Keating, E LD	5,929	15.5	2.3
Harvey, N UKIP	2,617	6.8	4.7

50%
Majority 10,756

Lab C LD UKIP

Warrington North — Labour hold

Helen Jones
b. Dec 24, 1954
MP 1997-

Chatty. Whip: govt 2009-10; asst 2008-09. PPS to: Dawn Primarolo 2007-08. Member, select cttees: Selection 2009-; Administration 2005-07; Education and Skills 2003-07; Standing Orders 2001, Unopposed Bills (Panel) 1999-, Education and Employment 1999-2001, Standing Orders 1999-2000, Public Administration 1998-2000, Catering 1997-98. Cllr, Chester CC 1984-91. MSF Lab Party liaison officer. Solicitor. Eng teacher. Justice/peace officer. MIND devt officer. Education: UCL (BA); Chester Coll; Liverpool (Med); Manchester Metropolitan Uni.

Paul Campbell (C) Cllr, Warrington BC. Retired police officer.

David Eccles (LD) Education consultant. Cllr. Teacher. Ed: Chorley GS; Chester Coll of Higher Education: Manchester Uni.

Constituency
Containing the densely packed inner-urban residential areas of Warrington – although not the actual town centre – this corner of the former industrial town, north of the Mersey and Manchester Ship Canal, has traditionally been working-class. Areas of deprivation remain in the centre but the east is increasingly affluent, with professionals enjoying semi-rural Cheshire and good transport links, with the M6 and M62 meeting in the middle of this seat. Business parks have a strategic location for distribution. This has been a Labour stronghold for decades.

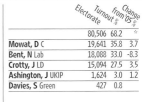

	Electorate	Turnout %	Change from '05 %
	71,601	61.8	☆
Jones, H Lab	20,135	45.5	-7.4
Campbell, P C	13,364	30.2	5.9
Eccles, D LD	9,196	20.8	2.1
Scott, A Ind	1,516	3.4	

50%
Majority 6,771

Lab C LD

Warrington South — Conservative gain

David Mowat
b. Feb 20, 1957
MP 2010-

Experienced businessman. Cllr, Macclesfield 2007-09. Arthur Andersen and Accenture, Global Industry Managing Partner (Energy). Chairman, Fairbridge. Member, ACA, Institute of Petroleum. Cites Frank Field among political heroes. Director, Warrington FC. Cadet pilot, RAFVR. Keen chess and golf player. Church of Scotland. Married, three daughters, one son. Ed: Lawrence Sheriff GS; Imperial Coll (civil engineering).

Nick Bent (Lab) b. 1972. Business consultant on corporate ethics and corporate responsibility. Ed: Oxford (law); Harvard (politics and public policy at JFK sch of govt).

Jo Crotty (LD) b. 1975. University lecturer. Cllr, Warrington BC. Ed: Nottingham University (PhD economics).

Constituency
Warrington's retail and commercial town centre lies in the north of the seat, with some deprived urban areas around it. Much industry was traditionally based here, by the Mersey and Manchester Ship Canal, which bisects the seat. However, the centre is undergoing regeneration and the surrounding areas have long been more affluent. Penketh in the west, Stockton Heath and Appleton Thorn in the south and Lymm in the east are home to high numbers of professionals. The seat was held by the Conservatives before switching to Labour in 1992.

	Electorate	Turnout %	Change from '05 %
	80,506	68.2	☆
Mowat, D C	19,641	35.8	3.7
Bent, N Lab	18,088	33.0	-8.3
Crotty, J LD	15,094	27.5	3.5
Ashington, J UKIP	1,624	3.0	1.2
Davies, S Green	427	0.8	

50%
Majority 1,553

C Lab LD

Warwick & Leamington — Conservative gain

Chris White
b. Apr 28, 1967
MP 2010-

Amiable former engineer. Cllr, Warwick DC 2008-10. Contested Warwick & Leamington 2005 (missed out by 266 votes), Birmingham Hall Green 2001. Freelance PR consultant, formerly of Century Public Relations. Worked in supply and development engineering at MG Rover in Longbridge. Divorced. Education: St Gregory's Comp, Tunbridge Wells; Manchester (BEng); Bath (MBA).

James Plaskitt (Lab) b. Jun 23, 1954. MP 1997-2010. MP Warwick and Leamington 1997-2010, Parly Under-Sec DWP 2005-, Member, Treasury cttee 1999-2005. Cllr, Oxfordshire CC. Former lecturer, director of consultancy. Ed: Pilgrim Sch, Bedford; Oxford University (MA and MPhil).
Alan Beddow (LD) IT project manager.

Constituency

Historic Warwick, with its medieval castle, sits on the west bank of the River Avon, with Royal Leamington Spa on the east bank. Leamington was once a centre for car manufacture and is the less well off of the two towns, although its economy has increasingly diversified, including into the computer game industry. The seat is generally affluent, with good transport links as the M40 cuts through the rural area to the south of the towns. The seat has been significantly cut back, losing about 16,000 electors. Labour overturned decades of Tory dominance when they won here in 1992.

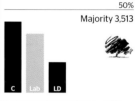

	Electorate	Turnout %	Change from '05 %
	58,030	84.5	☆
White, C C	20,876	42.6	8.2
Plaskitt, J Lab	17,363	35.4	-9.3
Beddow, A LD	8,977	18.3	2.4
Lenton, C UKIP	926	1.9	0.2
Davison, I Green	693	1.4	-2.0
Cullinane, J Ind	197	0.4	

Majority 3,513

Warwickshire North — Conservative gain

Dan Byles
b. Jun 24, 1974
MP 2010-

Action man, former soldier and adventurer who campaigned on political outsider ticket; independent minded. Holds two Guinness world records for expeditions with his mother: across Atlantic Ocean in wooden rowing boat; and trekking to Magnetic N Pole. Motivational/after-dinner speaker. Headhunter helping former soldiers. Army career: operational tours in Kosovo and Bosnia. Served in MoD during Iraq invasion. Royal Army Medical Corps. Light Infantry. Fellow, Royal Geographical Soc. Cites Boris Johnson among political heroes. Brought up by single mother, first in family to go to uni. Married. Ed: Warwick Sch; Leeds Uni (econ); RMA Sandhurst.

Mike O'Brien (Lab) b. Jun 19, 1954. MP 1992-2010. Min: Health 2009-10; DECC 2008-09; Pensions 2007-08; Solicitor Gen 2005-07; Energy 2004-05; FCO 2002-04; Home 1992-01 (left govt). Solicitor and lecturer.
Stephen Martin (LD) Sustainable development consultant. Former cllr.

Constituency

On the eastern border of Birmingham, this C-shaped seat curves around Nuneaton constituency, under boundary changes that lost a rural chunk from its centre. The main towns are Bedworth, Polesworth, Atherstone and Coleshill – which lies by the junction of the M42 and M6 toll roads at the west and is more affluent. There are patches of deprivation in the urban areas at the east and this seat, once dominated by mining, retains a strong working class. Labour won it from the Conservatives in 1992.

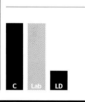

	Electorate	Turnout %	Change from '05 %
	70,143	67.4	☆
Byles, D C	18,993	40.2	8.1
O'Brien, M Lab	18,939	40.1	-7.3
Martin, S LD	5,481	11.6	-1.9
Holmes, J BNP	2,106	4.5	
Fowler, S UKIP	1,335	2.8	0.2
Lane, D Eng	411	0.9	

Majority 54

Washington & Sunderland West — Labour hold

Sharon Hodgson
b. Apr 1, 1966
MP 2005-

Asst govt whip 2009-. Parliamentary private secretary to: Dawn Primarolo 2008-09; Bob Ainsworth 2007-08; Liam Byrne 2006-07. Member, cttees: North East 2009-; Children Schools & Families 2007-; Court of Referees 2007-; European Scrutiny 2006; Regulatory Reform 2005-. Lab party constituency worker/regional organiser/women's officer. Payroll and accounting clerk. Married, one daughter, one son. Ed: Heathfield Senior HS, Gateshead. Newcastle Coll (HEFC English); National Education Centre (TUC dip in Lab party organising).

Ian Cuthbert (C) b. 1967. Trained as an accountant, now a marketing manager for Orange. Cllr, Sunderland CC.
Peter Andras (LD) b. May 26, 1971. University reader at School of Computing Science, Newcastle Uni. Founding director of the Civitas Foundation.
Ian McDonald (BNP)

Constituency

Washington New Town was built postwar around an old village, once home to the ancestors of George Washington. It forms the bulk of the seat, which extends east to the fringes of Sunderland, including the Nissan motor plant, one of the biggest employers. New business parks are being built amid regeneration works but deprivation – legacy of the coal industry's decline – remains, especially in the east; Washington is better off than most of Sunderland. The area has long been Labour-supporting.

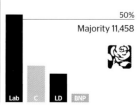

	Electorate	Turnout %	Change from '05 %
	68,910	54.2	☆
Hodgson, S Lab	19,615	52.5	-16.3
Cuthbert, I C	8,157	21.9	6.9
Andras, P LD	6,382	17.1	0.9
McDonald, I BNP	1,913	5.1	
Hudson, L UKIP	1,267	3.4	

Majority 11,458

Watford — Conservative gain

Richard Harrington
b. Nov 4, 1957
MP 2010-

Larger than life; a less fogey Nick Soames. Wealthy businessman. Member, Tory Reform Group, Conservative Friends of Israel. Conservative party treasurer 2008-. Shareholder and non-exec dir, Eden Financial. Founded Harvington Properties. Was responsible for re-development of One Devonshire Gardens hotel in Glasgow. Began career at John Lewis. Jewish. Married, two sons. Ed: Leeds GS; Keble Coll, Oxford (Law).

Sal Brinton (LD) b. 1955. Company director and businesswoman, consultant with IDeA. Former vice-chair, Federal Policy Committee; former member, Federal Conference Committee.

Claire Ward (Lab) b. May 9, 1972. MP 1997-2010. Govt whip 2006-08. Chair, select cttee for Culture, Media and Sport 2002.

Constituency

In the south west of Hertfordshire, Watford lies within the M25 and is mainly urban with pockets of green space. About 50 per cent of residents commute out to work, and nearly three fifths of the jobs are taken by non-residents. More than a fifth of residents are ethnic minorities. Watford is relatively prosperous although there are pockets of deprivation and crime. There is a strong service sector but the proportion of managerial and professional workers is below the national average. The Tories held the seat from 1979 until Labour's 1997 landslide.

	Electorate	Turnout %	Change from '05 %
	80,798	68.3	☆
Harrington, R C	19,291	34.9	5.3
Brinton, S LD	17,866	32.4	1.1
Ward, C Lab	14,750	26.7	-6.8
Emerson, A BNP	1,217	2.2	
Eardley, G UKIP	1,199	2.2	-0.5
Brandon, I Green	885	1.6	-1.4

50%
Majority 1,425

Waveney — Conservative gain

Peter Aldous
b. Aug 26, 1961
MP 2010-

Local man from farming background – involved in family pig and arable farm. Member, Countryside Alliance. Contested Waveney 2005. Cllr: Waveney DC; Suffolk CC (dep leader Con group 2002-05). Chartered Surveyor. CofE. Sports enthusiast, season ticket holder Ipswich Town FC. Ed: Harrow; Reading (BSc land management).

Bob Blizzard (Lab) b. May 31, 1950. MP 1997-2010. Whip: Govt 2008-10; asst 2007-08. PPS to: Douglas Alexander 2005-07; Nicholas Brown 2001-03; Baroness Hayman 1999-2001. Cllr Waveney DC 1987-97 (ldr 1991-97). Head of English: Crayford Sch Bexley;

Lynn Grove HS, Gorleston Norfolk. Ed: Culford Sch, Bury St Edmunds; Birmingham Uni (BA).
Alan Dean (LD) b. May 23, 1946. Cllr.
Jack Tyler (UKIP)

Constituency

Lowestoft, Britain's most easterly point, is Suffolk's second-largest town and the coastal focus of this seat. Stretching inland it includes the towns of Beccles and Bungay and, beyond them, villages and small hamlets. Notable economic sectors include tourism, manufacturing and services related to offshore energy. The seat is well connected to Europe through nearby Felixstowe. Parts of Lowestoft are within the 10 per cent most deprived nationwide, with Kirkley in the worst 1 per cent. However, regeneration is under way. This seat switched from Tory to Labour in 1997.

	Electorate	Turnout %	Change from '05 %
	78,532	65.1	
Aldous, P C	20,571	40.2	6.9
Blizzard, B Lab	19,802	38.7	-6.6
Dean, A LD	6,811	13.3	-1.8
Tyler, J UKIP	2,684	5.3	1.5
Elliott, G Green	1,167	2.3	-0.1
Barfe, L Ind	106	0.2	

50%
Majority 769

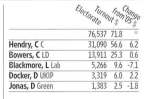

Wealden — Conservative hold

Charles Hendry
b. May 6, 1959
MP 2001-; 1992-7

Earnest, slightly bumbling. Min: Energy & Climate Change 2010-. Shadow Minister: Energy 2008-10 Trade & Industry 2005; Higher Ed 2005; Young People 2002-05. Opposition whip 2001-02. Deputy Chairman Con Party 2003-05. PPS to: Gillian Shepherd 1995, William Hague, Lord Mackay of Ardbrecknish 1994-95. MP High Peak 1992-97. Public relations career, Ogilvy & Mather, Burson Marsteller. Special adviser to John Moore and Tony Newton. Married, two sons, one stepson, one stepdaughter. Ed: Rugby; Edinburgh (business studies).

Chris Bowers (LD) b. 1961. Journalist (Eurosport, BBC Radio). Consultant

editor, European Federation for Transport & Environment. Cllr, Wealden DC and Lewes DC.
Lorna Blackmore (Lab) b. 1953. Financial crime manager for bank. Former cllr, Tunbridge Wells BC.
Dan Docker (UKIP)

Constituency

A large and generally affluent seat, Wealden encompasses the heart of East Sussex. From the border with Kent in the north it stretches down through High Weald, taking in Crowborough, Uckfield and, at its south, Hailsham. Under boundary changes it has lost the town of Heathfield. There are above-average numbers of professionals and large numbers of self-employed – much of the land is given over to agriculture, although the sector no longer dominates employment. There is a long history of Tory representation.

	Electorate	Turnout %	Change from '05 %
	76,537	71.8	☆
Hendry, C C	31,090	56.6	6.2
Bowers, C LD	13,911	25.3	0.6
Blackmore, L Lab	5,266	9.6	-7.1
Docker, D UKIP	3,319	6.0	2.2
Jonas, D Green	1,383	2.5	-1.8

50%
Majority 17,179

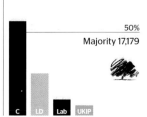

Weaver Vale — Conservative gain

Graham Evans
b. Nov 10, 1963
MP 2010-

Campaigned on Northwich Vision regeneration, and against the closure of Northwich Victoria infirmary. Cllr, Macclesfield 2000-. Contested Worsley 2005. Sales and marketing management, roles in Hewlett Packard and BAE Systems. Christian. Married, three children. Ed: Poynton County HS; Manchester Met Uni Business School (evenings).

John Stockton (Lab) Cllr, Halton Brook BC. Labour constituency secretary.
Peter Hampson (LD) Works for the Co-operative Bank. Previously worked with Mark Williams MP in Ceredigion and Westminster. Ed: Weaverham HS; Sir John Deane's Sixth Form Coll; Aberystwyth (law with econ; legal practice).

Constituency
Reaching from the banks of the Mersey down into Cheshire countryside, Weaver Vale is a varied seat. The main town of Northwich lies in the east and, along with Frodsham and Norton in the north, has areas of severe deprivation. About 25 per cent of residents in these white, working-class towns live in council housing. Regeneration projects are, however, slowly improving the urban areas, while smaller towns in the rural areas are more affluent and home to large numbers of professionals commuting to Liverpool. The seat was won by Labour on its creation in 1997.

	Electorate	Turnout %	Change from '05 %
	66,538	66.1	☆
Evans, G C	16,953	38.5	6.9
Stockton, J Lab	15,962	36.3	-9.4
Hampson, P LD	8,196	18.6	-1.1
Marsh, C BNP	1,063	2.4	
Remfry, P UKIP	1,018	2.3	-0.5
Thorp, H Green	338	0.8	
Cooksley, M Ind	270	0.6	
Reynolds, T Ind	133	0.3	
Charlton, W Ind	57	0.1	

50%
Majority 991

Wellingborough — Conservative hold

Peter Bone
b. Oct 19, 1952
MP 2005-

One of a crop of hyperactive back-benchers elected in 2005. Self-proclaimed founding member of member of HOTS – Harriet [Harman]'s Official Tory Supporters. Speeches were greeted with calls of "Sven" owing to resemblance to Sven-Göran Eriksson. 1922 executive committee, 2010-. Right-winger, member of Cornerstone Group. Chartered accountant, ran PLC and family business, electronics and travel companies; dubbed Britain's meanest boss in 1995 for paying trainee 87p an hour. Southend-on-Sea cllr 1977-86. Contested three seats before 2005 success. Married, one daughter, two sons. Ed: Stewards Comp, Harlow; Westcliff-on-Sea GS, Essex.

Jayne Buckland (Lab) b. Dec 13, 1956. Teacher. Cllr, Enfield BC 2002-10. Ed: Gloucestershire Coll of art & design.
Kevin Barron (LD) IT security consultant. Contested Northampton South 2005.

Constituency
This Northamptonshire seat covers not only the eponymous town but also Rushden and Higham Ferrers to its east, towards the border with Bedfordshire. Boundary changes have cut it back, losing the Earls Barton area from its west. This is a seat of contrasts between relatively affluent rural areas and significantly poorer urban ones, with large numbers of working classes and a strong manufacturing sector. Accordingly it has a history of marginality. It was won by Labour with just 187 votes in 1997, and by the Tories by 687 votes in 2005.

	Electorate	Turnout %	Change from '05 %
	76,857	67.2	☆
Bone, P C	24,918	48.2	5.5
Buckland, J Lab	13,131	25.4	-16.0
Barron, K LD	8,848	17.1	5.6
Haynes, A UKIP	1,636	3.2	0.9
Walker, R BNP	1,596	3.1	
Spencer, T Eng	530	1.0	
Hornett, J Green	480	0.9	
Crofts, P TUSC	249	0.5	
Donaldson, G Ind	240	0.5	
Lavin, M Ind	33	0.1	

50%
Majority 11,787

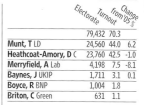

Wells — Liberal Democrat gain

Tessa Munt
b. Oct 16, 1959
MP 2010-

Inspired by her grandfather Ernest Vasey, who served in the Kenyan Government. Contested Wells 2005, Ipswich 2001 by-election, Suffolk South 2001. Trainer, marketing, and sales roles in hotel and leisure industry. FE lecturer. Teacher. Social services manager. PA to co dir. Fee earner for lawyers' firms. Cllr for Childline. Campaigner (domestic violence, environment). Separated, two children. Ed: St Joseph's Priory, Dorking; Reigate County Sch; Sutton HS for Girls.

David Heathcoat-Amory (C) b. 1949. MP for Wells 1983-2010. Shad SoS: DTI 2000-01. Shad Chief Treasury Sec 1997-2000. Paymaster Gen 1994-96 (resigned). Min: FCO 1993-94. Dep Chief whip 1992-93. Ed: Eton Coll; Oxford Uni (MA PPE).
Andy Merryfield (Lab) b. Jul 18, 1954. Asst Dir for Community and Mental Health. Ed: Uni of Plymouth (MPhil).

Constituency
England's smallest city gives its name to this North Somerset seat. Wells Cathedral's magnificent 14th-century clock shows the Sun and Moon revolving round Earth and it sometimes feels as if time has stood still here since the days of that dogma. The Mendip Hills and Cheddar Gorge to the north, wetlands and Somerset Levels to the west and Glastonbury at the south are big tourist draws. To the east is Shepton Mallet and to the west the resort of Burnham-on-Sea. Conservatives have held the seat since 1945, but in 1997 margin was only 528 votes.

	Electorate	Turnout %	Change from '05 %
	79,432	70.3	
Munt, T LD	24,560	44.0	6.2
Heathcoat-Amory, D C	23,760	42.5	-1.0
Merryfield, A Lab	4,198	7.5	-8.1
Baynes, J UKIP	1,711	3.1	0.1
Boyce, R BNP	1,004	1.8	
Briton, C Green	631	1.1	

50%
Majority 800

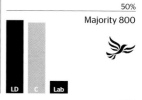

Welwyn Hatfield Conservative hold

Grant Shapps
b. Sep 14, 1968
MP 2005-

Populist attack dog – any depths well hidden. Self-made, undogmatic moderniser and early Cameron supporter. Min: CLG 2010-. Shadow Minister: Housing 2007-10. Vice-Chair (Campaigning) Con Party 2005-09. Contested Welwyn Hatfield 2001 and N Southwark & Bermondsey 1997. Founded PrintHouse Corporation, design print & web dev't co, remains chairman. Married, one girl, two boys. Education: Watford Boys Grammar School; Cassio College, Watford (OND business & finance); Manchester Polytechnic (HND business and finance).

Mike Hobday (Lab) b. Feb 18, 1964. Senior manager for campaigning at MacMillan Cancer support, prev worked for League Against Cruel Sports. Cllr 1997-2005. Ed: Cambridge Uni (BA social and political sciences). **Paul Zukowskyj** (LD) b. Feb 18, 1967. Geography lecturer at University of Hertfordshire. Ed: Uni of Greenwich.

Constituency
In central Hertfordshire, this seat is named after Welwyn and Hatfield, both designated New Towns after the Second World War to rehouse those displaced from London. Nearly 90 per cent of jobs are service sector including education with the University of Hertfordshire. Companies such as GlaxoSmithKline contribute to a notable pharmaceuticals presence. About 20 per cent of working residents commute elsewhere in Hertfordshire and a similar proportion to London. Labour took this from the Tories in 1997 but lost it in 2005.

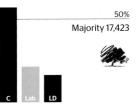

	Electorate	Turnout %	Change from '05 %
	72,058	68.0	
Shapps, G C	27,894	57.0	7.5
Hobday, M Lab	10,471	21.4	-14.8
Zukowskyj, P LD	8,010	16.4	2.3
Platt, D UKIP	1,643	3.4	
Weston, J Green	796	1.6	
Parker, N Ind	158	0.3	

50%
Majority 17,423

C / Lab / LD

Wentworth & Dearne Labour hold

John Healey
b. Feb 13, 1960
MP 1997-

Longstanding ally of Gordon Brown, well versed in local government policy. Minister: Housing 2009-10; Communities & Local Government 2007-09. Treasury: Financial Secretary of State 2005-07; Economic Secretary of State 2002-05. Parly Under-Sec: Education & Skills 2001-02. Parliamentary private secretary to Gordon Brown 1999-2001. MP, Wentworth 1997-2010. Member, GMB. Head of communications: TUC/MSF. Tutor, campaigns manager. Disability charity campaigner. Journalist and editor, *The House Magazine*. Married, one son. Education: Lady Lumley's Comp, Pickering; St Peter's Sch, York; Christ's College, Cambridge (Scholar, BA).

Michelle Donelan (C) Marketing, AETN UK. Ed: Uni of York (hist/pol). Nat Exec for Con Future (media). **Nick Love** (LD) Business dev't manager, software. Ed: York (Engl/music). **John Wilkinson** (UKIP) Semi-retired accountant. Publican, civil servant.

Constituency
To the north east of Rotherham, the seat has lost some areas from the south, now extending only as far as Bramley. It gains the lowlands area of Dearne Valley in the north, mainly deprived former mining communities. Wath-upon-Dearne and Swinton are the chief towns and the industrial area near the former Manvers Main Colliery provides employment for many. The west is more rural while, farther south, the Corus steelworks at Aldwarke have been hard hit by job cuts. Labour majorities have historically been large.

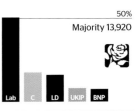

	Electorate	Turnout %	Change from '05 %
	72,586	58.0	☆
Healey, J Lab	21,316	50.6	-11.2
Donelan, M C	7,396	17.6	3.8
Love, N LD	6,787	16.1	-0.1
Wilkinson, J UKIP	3,418	8.1	4.6
Baldwin, G BNP	3,189	7.6	

50%
Majority 13,920

Lab / C / LD / UKIP / BNP

West Bromwich East Labour hold

Tom Watson
b. Jan 8, 1967
MP 2001-

Political enforcer for Gordon Brown, led failed coup against Tony Blair in 2006 prompting resignation as junior defence minister. Web-savvy blogger. Parly Sec, Cab Office 2008-09. Asst govt whip 2007-08. Parly-Under Sec, Defence 2006. Whip: govt 2005-06; asst govt 2004-05. PPS to Dawn Primarolo 2003-04. Member, select cttees: CMS 2009-; Home 2001-03. Nat coordinator Lab FPTP campaign. Lab party nat devt officer. Dir: Tribune; Policy Network. AEEU nat political officer. Advertising account exec. Marketing officer Save the City of Wells. Married, one daughter, one son. Education: King Charles I Sch, Kidderminster.

Alistair Thompson (C) b. 1978. Former journalist, works for Media Intelligence Partners, a communications company. Cllr, Portsmouth, CC 2000-2010. **Ian Garrett** (LD) History teacher. Cllr, Sandwell Met BC 1994-2002. Ed: St Catherine's Coll, Oxford (BA history); University of Birmingham (PGCE). **Terry Lewin** (BNP)

Constituency
The affluent north east of this seat, around the junction of the M5 and M6, contrasts with the deprived south west around West Bromwich town centre. In the east of the seat is a large recreational area at Sandwell Valley Country Park. The majority of residents are working-class, with many living in council housing. There is a significant population of Indian origin. This seat has been Labour for decades.

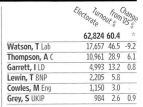

	Electorate	Turnout %	Change from '05 %
	62,824	60.4	
Watson, T Lab	17,657	46.5	-9.2
Thompson, A C	10,961	28.9	6.1
Garrett, I LD	4,993	13.2	0.8
Lewin, T BNP	2,205	5.8	
Cowles, M Eng	1,150	3.0	·
Grey, S UKIP	984	2.6	0.9

50%
Majority 6,696

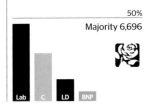

Lab / C / LD / BNP

West Bromwich West
Labour hold

Adrian Bailey
b. Dec 11, 1945
MP Nov 2000- (by-election)

Unimpressive back-bencher. Dull, even by the standards of librarians. Elected Chair, select committee: Business, Innovation & Skills 2010-. Parliamentary private secretary to: Bob Ainsworth 2007; Adam Ingram 2006-07; Hilary Armstrong 2006; John Hutton 2005-06. Co-operative Party political organiser 1982-2000. Councillor Sandwell BC 1991-2000 (deputy leader 1997-2000). Librarian Cheshire CC. GMBATU member. Married, one stepson. Education: Cheltenham Grammar School; Exeter University (BA economic history); Loughborough Coll of Librarianship (postgrad dip).

Andrew Hardie (C) b. 1955. Doctor. Ed: Bromsgrove School, Birmingham University (medicine).
Sadie Smith (LD) Previously worked in the health service for a national charity. Cllr, Sandwell.
Russ Green (BNP) Former cllr.

Constituency
Good transport connections make the Sandwell area popular for industry and it is home to multinationals such as Rhodia. Bordering on Walsall in the north lies Wednesbury, once a prosperous coalmining centre but now a large residential area. The seat includes some deprived areas with large housing estates such as Tibbington and Friar Park. Traditionally Labour, the seat found itself with the Speaker for eight years when Betty Boothroyd was MP here.

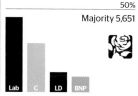

	Electorate	Turnout %	Change from 05 %
	65,013	55.6	☆
Bailey, A Lab	16,263	45.0	-8.7
Hardie, A C	10,612	29.3	6.6
Smith, S LD	4,336	12.0	1.8
Green, R BNP	3,394	9.4	
Ford, M UKIP	1,566	4.3	1.8

50%

Majority 5,651

West Ham
Labour hold

Lyn Brown
b. Apr 13, 1960
MP 2005-

Popular organiser of social events among Labour MPs from 2005 intake. Assistant government whip 2009-10. PPS to: John Denham 2007-09; Phil Woolas 2006-07. Member, select cttee: ODPM/CLG 2005-07. Unison. Member, Co-op Party, Fabian Society. Contested Wanstead & Woodford 1992. Founder, London Library Dev't Board. Member: London Region Sports Board; London Arts Board; Museums, Libraries and Archives Council, London. Married. Ed: Plashet Comp; Whitelands Coll, Roehampton (BA English & religious studies).

Virginia Morris (C) b. 1969. Author and engineer. Former partner and dir

Max Fordham engineering consultants, Ed: PhD in engineering.
Martin Pierce (LD) b. Jun 29, 1964. Freelance project manager. Cllr.

Constituency
This diverse seat in inner London has been enlarged to include Canning Town and Custom House, a large area in the south west with parts that are within the most deprived 10 per cent nationwide. The rest of the seat is slightly more affluent although Stratford is undergoing regeneration with most of the Olympic Village based there. The largest Asian populations are concentrated around Green Street at the east of the seat. It also includes Plaistow, while West Ham United's stadium is just over the boundary in the neighbouring East Ham seat. The seat has been safely Labour for decades.

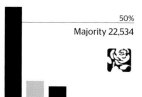

	Electorate	Turnout %	Change from 05 %
	85,313	55.0	☆
Brown, L Lab	29,422	62.7	10.9
Morris, V C	6,888	14.7	2.6
Pierce, M LD	5,392	11.5	1.3
Gain, S CPA	1,327	2.8	
Malik, K Ind	1,245	2.7	
Davidson, M NF	1,089	2.3	
Gandy, K UKIP	766	1.6	0.6
Lithgow, J Green	645	1.4	-1.6
Agbogun-Toko, G Ind	177	0.4	

50%

Majority 22,534

Westminster North
Labour hold

Karen Buck
b. Aug 30, 1958
MP 1997-

Combative, important figure in London Labour party who saw off concerted Conservative challenge. Parly assistant to Tony McNulty 2008-10. Parly Under-Sec: Transport 2005-06. Chair, committee: London 2009-10. Member, committees: Children, Schools & Families 2009-10; Home 2006-09; Work & Pensions 2001-05; Selection 1999-2001; Soc Security 1997-2001. Councillor, Westminster 1990-97. Disabled people services. Employment charity worker. Hackney Borough specialist officer. Public health officer. Married, one son. Education: Chelmsford High School; LSE (BSc Economics, MSc Economics, MA social policy & administration).

Joanne Cash (C) b. Dec 28, 1969. Barrister (libel and privacy law). Adviser to Policy Exchange think-tank. On the Tory A-list.
Mark Blackburn (LD) b. 1958. Retail, sold his chain of shoe shops in 2007.

Constituency
This new London seat is based on the Westminster borough parts of the old Regent's Park & Kensington North seat. Its western boundary spans from Queen's Park to Lancaster Gate while the eastern edge is Regent's Park. There is a variety of affluence in this residential seat. Most of the south and west is in the most deprived 5 per cent nationwide, while the St John's Wood area in the north is home to celebrities. The old seat had been held by Labour from 1997.

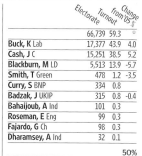

	Electorate	Turnout %	Change from 05 %
	66,739	59.3	☆
Buck, K Lab	17,377	43.9	4.0
Cash, J C	15,251	38.5	5.2
Blackburn, M LD	5,513	13.9	-5.7
Smith, T Green	478	1.2	-3.5
Curry, S BNP	334	0.8	
Badzak, J UKIP	315	0.8	-0.4
Bahaijoub, A Ind	101	0.3	
Roseman, E Eng	99	0.3	
Fajardo, G Ch	98	0.3	
Dharamsey, A Ind	32	0.1	

50%

Majority 2,126

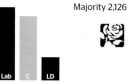

Westmoreland & Lonsdale

Liberal Democrat hold

Tim Farron
b. May 27, 1970
MP 2005-

From the Lib Dems' cen-tre-left, active in Simon Hughes' leadership campaign in 2006. Candidate for LD Dep Leader 2010. Active Christian. Quit LD front bench to vote for EU referendum in 2008. LD Shad Sec: EFRA 2008-10. LD Shad Min: Countryside 2007-08; Home 2007. PPS to Sir Menzies Campbell 2006-07. LD spokes: Youth Affairs 2005-06. Member, cttees: Environ Audit 2006-07; Education & Skills 2005-06. Contested Westmorland & Lonsdale 2001. Cllr, South Lakeland DC 2004-, Lancashire CC (group dep leader 1993-2000). Head of faculty admin St Martin's Coll. Ed: Lostock Hall HS, Preston; Runshaw Tertiary Coll; Newcastle (BA politics).

Gareth McKeever (C) Former senior executive and equity adviser to Japanese markets, quit on his selection. Education: Coleraine Academical Institution; Oxford University (philosophy, politics and economics).

Constituency
From Morecambe Bay this seat reaches up through some of the Lake District's most popular tourist destinations, including Coniston, Grasmere and Ambleside, at the head of Windermere. Beyond the park lie Kendal and smaller towns such as Milnthorpe. To the east the seat stretches to the Yorkshire Dales National Park. About 5 per cent of the population is engaged in agriculture. The most middle-class of the Cumbria seats, the area had returned Tory MPs for decades but the Lib Dems took it in 2005.

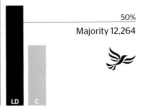

	Electorate	Turnout %	Change from '05 %
	67,881	75.9	☆
Farron, T LD	30,896	60.0	14.1
McKeever, G C	18,632	36.2	-8.1
Todd, J Lab	1,158	2.3	-5.6
Mander, J UKIP	801	1.6	0.2

50%

Majority 12,264

Weston-super-Mare

Conservative hold

John Penrose
b. Jun 22, 1964
MP 2005-

Bringing a management consultant's rigour to government. Dapper and hard-working though, in the last Parliament, often out of the limelight. Parly Under-Sec: CMS 2010-. Shadow Min: Business 2009-10. PPS to Oliver Letwin as Chair, Con Policy Review 2006-09. Member cttees: Work & Pens 2005-09; Regulatory Reform 2009- Contested Ealing Southall 1997, Weston-super-Mare 2001. Publishing career: chair Logotron (educational software); MD, Longman, Thomson. Management consultant, McKinsey. Banking, JP Morgan. Head of research, Bow Group. Married, two daughters. Ed: Ipswich Sch; Downing Coll, Cambridge (BA Law); Columbia (MBA).

Mike Bell (LD) b. 1974. Production manager, runs publishing company. Former cllr and Adviser/aide to Brian Cotter MP, Graham Watson MEP.
David Bradley (Lab) b. 1981. Insurance adviser.

Constituency
Weston-super-Mare was once the queen of bucket-and-spade resorts, catering to workers from the Midlands. The tide of tourism has turned, leaving behind retired people and social security claimants, and the town has pockets of severe deprivation. However, the wider North Somerset constituency is generally prosperous, stretching east beyond the M5 to rural areas toward the Mendip Hills, and has a growing commuter population. The seat was Tory for 74 years, the Lib Dems took it in 1997 and Conservatives regained it in 2005.

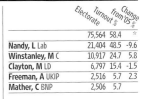

	Electorate	Turnout %	Change from '05 %
	78,487	67.2	☆
Penrose, J C	23,356	44.3	4.0
Bell, M LD	20,665	39.2	3.1
Bradley, D Lab	5,772	11.0	-7.7
Spencer, P UKIP	1,406	2.7	0.2
Parsons, P BNP	1,098	2.1	
Peverelle, J Eng	275	0.5	
Satch, S Ind	144	0.3	

50%

Majority 2,691

Wigan

Labour hold

Lisa Nandy
b. Mon 0 09-Aug-79
MP 2010-

Respected campaigner on children and housing, unafraid to take on party establishment. From Labour's pragmatic "soft left". Cites JS Mill among political heroes. Cllr, Shad Cab Member for Housing and Regeneration, Hammersmith & Fulham BC 2006-10. Senior policy adviser, The Children's Society. Prev. policy researcher, Centrepoint (youth homelessness charity). Parly researcher to Neil Gerrard MP. Member: Unite, Compass, the Co-operative Party, Amnesty International. Local theatre director. Rugby league and football fan Ed: Parrs Wood Comp, Manchester; Newcastle Upon Tyne (BA politics); Birkbeck Coll, London (MSc politics & government).

Michael Winstanley (C) b. 1971. Senior data analyst for St Helens and Knowsley Hospitals NHS Trust. Ed: St Edmund Arrowsmith RC HS; St Helens Tech Coll.
Mark Clayton (LD) Systems consultant, former MD of IT company. Cllr, Manchester CC. Ed: Manchester Uni.
Alan Freeman (UKIP)
Charles Mather (BNP)

Constituency
Wigan lies at the western end of Greater Manchester, around halfway between Liverpool and Manchester. Despite an industrial reputation, the town has a pretty centre and the constituency, which extends to its north, has countryside and lakes, with former mining communities such as Standish in-between. After boundary changes the seat includes Ince-in-Makerfield. It has been solidly Labour since 1918.

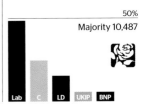

	Electorate	Turnout %	Change from '05 %
	75,564	58.4	☆
Nandy, L Lab	21,404	48.5	-9.6
Winstanley, M C	10,917	24.7	5.8
Clayton, M LD	6,797	15.4	-1.5
Freeman, A UKIP	2,516	5.7	2.3
Mather, C BNP	2,506	5.7	

50%

Majority 10,487

Wiltshire North Conservative hold

James Gray
b. Nov 7, 1954
MP 1997-

Controversial, horse-riding, shire Tory of excitable nature. Survived two de-selection attempts after revelations he had an affair while wife was battling cancer. Shadow Sec: Scotland (briefly, 2005). Shadow Min: Countryside 2002-05; Defence 2001; Opposition whip 2000-01. Special adviser to John Gummer, Michael Howard 1991-95. Management trainee/broker/managing director/director. Director, Baltic Futures Exchange. Territorial Army. Divorced, remarried. One daughter, two sons from previous marriage. Education: Glasgow High School; Glasgow University (MA history), Christ Church, Oxford (history thesis).

Mike Evemy (LD) Senior marketing manager for Nationwide. Cllr. Ed: University of York (economics and statistics).
Jason Hughes (Lab) b. 1970. Barrister (pupil). Ed: College of Law.

Constituency
The old Wiltshire North seat has been cut by nearly 18,000 electors and loses Chippenham (which gets its own seat) to gain the smaller town of Calne. It is a predominantly rural area, dotted with limestone villages. Wootton Bassett has become the focus of national mourning for soldiers killed in Afghanistan, whose bodies are repatriated via RAF Lyneham – due to close in 2012. To the north of the M4, which bisects the constituency, lie Malmesbury and Cricklade, small market towns. The seat has been Tory since 1924.

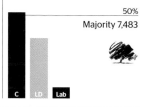

	Electorate	Turnout %	Change from '05 %
	66,313	73.4	☆
Gray, J C	25,114	51.6	1.9
Evemy, M LD	17,631	36.2	1.8
Hughes, J Lab	3,239	6.7	-5.3
Bennett, C UKIP	1,908	3.9	1.3
Chamberlain, P Green	599	1.2	
Allnatt, P Ind	208	0.4	

50%
Majority 7,483

Wiltshire South West Conservative hold

Andrew Murrison
b. Apr 24, 1961
MP 2001-

Former medical officer in Royal Navy, recalled in 2003 for Iraq war. Shadow Minister: Defence 2007-10; Health 2004-07; Public Services/Health/Education 2003-04. MP Westbury 2001-10. Research assistant to Lord Freeman. PH7 magazine editorial advisory board. Surgeon Commander Royal Navy 1981-2000. Locum consultant occupational physician and GP. Married, five daughters. Education: The Harwich School; Bristol (medicine MD CHB MD); Cambridge (DPH).

Trevor Carbin (LD) b. Jun 8, 1951. Self-employed driving instructor, former archaeologist. Cllr, West Wiltshire DC, 1995-2009. Cllr, Wiltshire UA, and leader of the opposition. Ed: Durham Uni (BSc), Leeds Uni (MSc).
Rebecca Rennison (Lab) b. Nov 10, 1981. Lobbyist for a disability charity. Treasurer Young Fabians
Mike Cuthbert-Murray (UKIP)

Constituency
This large rural seat was renamed from Westbury and shifted south to make way for the Chippenham seat. In the old county town of Trowbridge, technology enterprises have replaced old wool industries. Twinned with Oujda in Morocco, it has one of the largest Moroccan populations outside North Africa. Warminster, home of the Army's Land Warfare Centre and Headquarters Infantry, borders Salisbury Plain. In the south, small towns, villages and farms are dotted about in an Area of Outstanding Natural Beauty. The seat has been Tory since the 1920s.

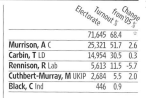

	Electorate	Turnout %	Change from '05 %
	71,645	68.4	☆
Murrison, A C	25,321	51.7	2.6
Carbin, T LD	14,954	30.5	0.3
Rennison, R Lab	5,613	11.5	-5.7
Cuthbert-Murray, M UKIP	2,684	5.5	2.0
Black, C Ind	446	0.9	

50%
Majority 10,367

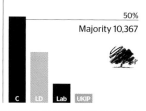

Wimbledon Conservative hold

Stephen Hammond
b. Feb 4, 1962
MP 2005-

Rotund, worthy – an obvious Minister of State. Shadow Minister: Transport 2005-10. Former Merton Cllr and long-term Tory activist. Stockbroker, UBS Philips and Drew. Directorial roles, Dresdner Kleinwort Benson Securities and Commerzbank Securities. Married, one daughter. Education: King Edward VI School, Southampton; Richard Hale School, Hertford; Queen Mary College, London (BSc econ).

Shas Sheehan (LD) Office manager for Susan Kramer MP. Cllr, Richmond BC 2006-. Ed: Franciscan sch; Graveney sch; University College London (BSc); Imperial College London (MSc).

Andrew Judge (Lab) b. Sep 11, 1962. Barrister, environmental lawyer and activist. Cllr, Merton BC (Leader 2001-06)

Constituency
Famous for the All England Lawn Tennis Club, Wimbledon has two main areas, with the most affluent Wimbledon Village and the main town area, with the Centre Court Shopping Centre. Well connected with several mainline rail stations and two Underground lines, Wimbledon is popular with commuters and primarily residential. The centres of Morden, Raynes Park and West Barnes are also in this seat. Labour overturned decades of Tory representation with their win here in 1997 but lost it in 2005.

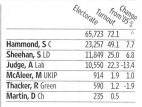

	Electorate	Turnout %	Change from '05 %
	65,723	72.1	☆
Hammond, S C	23,257	49.1	7.7
Sheehan, S LD	11,849	25.0	6.8
Judge, A Lab	10,550	22.3	-13.4
McAleer, M UKIP	914	1.9	1.0
Thacker, R Green	590	1.2	-1.9
Martin, D Ch	235	0.5	

50%
Majority 11,408

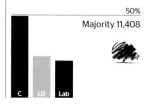

Winchester — Conservative gain

Steve Brine
b. Jan 28, 1974
MP 2010-

Former journalist, interested in health and the media. Member, Conservative Way Forward. Works with specialist golf marketing agency, The Azalea Group. Reporter and producer, BBC Radio Surrey / Southern Counties Radio. Consultant Conservative Research Department. Christian. Keen golfer and skier. Married, one daughter. Education: Bohunt Comprehensive, Liphook; Liverpool Uni (history).

Martin Tod (LD) Independent marketing consultant. Former member, Liberal Democrats' Federal Executive. Ed: Lancing College; Cambridge.
Patrick Davies (Lab) b. 1943. Solicitor. Cllr, Winchester CC 1980-2006; 1973-

1976. Contested Winchester 2005, 1997, 1997 by-election. Ed: Perse School; Oxford University.

Constituency
The small city of Winchester, with its cathedral and prestigious school, sits in the heart of Hampshire amid countryside dotted with picturesque villages. Dramatic boundary changes to make way for the new Meon Valley constituency have almost halved this seat's area, losing a large rural district. The electorate has been cut by only 12,000 because Chandler's Ford and Hiltingbury, in the southern tip, are added. An overwhelmingly white, middle-class seat, traditionally Tory, it was won by the Lib Dems in 1997. Mark Oaten announced that he was standing down after a sex scandal in 2006.

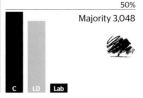

	Electorate	Turnout %	Change from '05 %
	73,806	75.8	☆
Brine, S C	27,155	48.5	11.2
Tod, M LD	24,107	43.1	-7.0
Davies, P Lab	3,051	5.5	-3.9
Penn-Bull, J UKIP	1,139	2.0	-0.2
Lancaster, M Eng	503	0.9	

50%
Majority 3,048

C | LD | Lab

Windsor — Conservative hold

Adam Afriyie
b. Aug 4, 1965
MP 2005-

Wealthy, dapper entrepreneur, the first black Tory MP. Struggled to adjust to cut-and-thrust of politics. Smooth, but has made little impact. Shadow Minister: Innovation and Science 2007-10. Founder of Connect Support Services, successful IT company. Chairman Adfero. London Chairman of Business for Sterling, campaigned against Euro. Born in Wimbledon to Ghanaian father. Divorced, remarried, one daughter, two sons, one stepson. Education: Imperial College (BSc agricultural economics).

Julian Tisi (LD) Finance manager. Chair, Lib Dems for Electoral Reform.

Amanjit Jhund (Lab) b. Feb 3, 1981. Entrepreneur and doctor.

Constituency
Stretching from the M25 to Bracknell Forest, this constituency encompasses areas synonymous with upper-class wealth: Windsor, with its medieval royal castle, Eton, with Britain's most famous school, and Ascot, of racecourse fame. It contains the Household Cavalry's Combermere barracks and Windsor Great Park. Residents are overwhelmingly affluent and work in the service sector – some campaigned for a new postcode to disassociate themselves from Slough, across the M4. House prices are sky-high as ex-Londoners snap up its Victorian housing stock, despite its position beneath Heathrow flight paths. There is a long Tory tradition, although the Lib Dems have enjoyed some success locally.

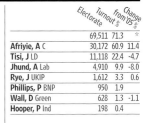

	Electorate	Turnout %	Change from '05 %
	69,511	71.3	☆
Afriyie, A C	30,172	60.9	11.4
Tisi, J LD	11,118	22.4	-4.7
Jhund, A Lab	4,910	9.9	-8.0
Rye, J UKIP	1,612	3.3	0.6
Phillips, P BNP	950	1.9	
Wall, D Green	628	1.3	-1.1
Hooper, P Ind	198	0.4	

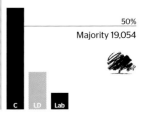

50%
Majority 19,054

C | LD | Lab

Wirral South — Labour hold

Alison McGovern
b. Dec 30, 1980
MP 2010-

Mainstream Labour, locally-raised candidate. Cllr, Southwark Borough Council 2006-10 (deputy leader Labour group). Public Affairs Manager for Network Rail, The Art Fund and Creativity Culture & Education. Grew up in Bromborough. Liverpool FC fan. Married. Ed: Wirral GS for Girls; UCL (philosophy); Birkbeck College (economics).

Jeff Clarke (C) Barrister, specialising in criminal law. Cllr, Chester CC. Contested Wirral West in 2005; Preseli Pembrokeshire in 1997, both for the Liberal Democrats, before joining the Conservative party. Ed: Keele University (BA law and economics).

Jamie Saddler (LD) b. Apr 28, 1986. Researcher to Andrew Stunell MP. Ed: Lingham Lane Primary, Moreton; Calday Grange Grammar School; University of Leeds.

Constituency
Spanning the width of the Wirral peninsula, the seat's main settlements lie at either side and are home to relatively affluent middle classes, although the docks and industry lining the east coast support an above-average manufacturing sector. Bebington looks across the Mersey to the south side of Liverpool, the M53 runs through the centre of the seat, while Heswall and Gayton, popular with retired people, are in the west, on the Dee Estuary. The seat was held by the Tories from its creation in 1982 until Labour took it with a dramatic win in a 1997 by-election.

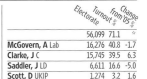

	Electorate	Turnout %	Change from '05 %
	56,099	71.1	☆
McGovern, A Lab	16,276	40.8	-1.7
Clarke, J C	15,745	39.5	6.3
Saddler, J LD	6,611	16.6	-5.0
Scott, D UKIP	1,274	3.2	1.6

50%
Majority 531

Lab | C | LD

Wirral West — Conservative hold

Esther McVey
b. Oct 24, 1967
MP 2010-

Former GMTV presenter/producer turned successful businesswoman. Plays on Liverpudlian accent and everywoman appeal. Contested Wirral West (old boundaries), 2005. MD, Making It (UK) Ltd (helping small companies set up business, PR agency). School friend of Kate McCann; former trustee, Madeleine fund. Founder 'Winning Women'. Dir, JG McVey and Co (family construction company). Patron, Wirral Holistic Therapeutic Cancer Care. Former girlfriend of Ed Vaizey MP. Ed: Belvedere Sch; Queen Mary and Westfield Uni (law); City (radio journalism); Liverpool John Moores (MSc corporate governance; studying for PhD in leadership & entrepreneurship.

Phillip Davies (Lab) Cllr, Wirral. Dep leader Lab Group. Chair, Wirral Learning Partnership.
Peter Reisdorf (LD) b. Jun 26, 1962. Mature student. Contested Wallasey 2001, 1997. Cllr, Wirral 2000-.

Constituency
The affluent northwestern corner of the Wirral peninsula is home to many middle-class professionals, often working in the public sector, health and education, and commuting to Liverpool. The coastal towns of Hoylake and West Kirby are popular with retired people. The seat, which was Conservative until 1997, reaches down to the northern part of Heswall and is bounded to the east by the M53. Its boundary has been cut back with the loss of Prenton.

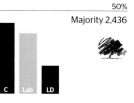

	Electorate	Turnout %	Change from 05 %
	55,050	71.5	☆
McVey, E C	16,726	42.5	0.7
Davies, P Lab	14,290	36.3	-4.0
Reisdorf, P LD	6,630	16.8	0.5
Griffiths, P UKIP	899	2.3	1.1
Kirwan, D Ind	506	1.3	
James, D CSP	321	0.8	

50%
Majority 2,436

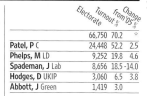

C | Lab | LD

Witham — Conservative hold

Priti Patel
b. Mar 29, 1972
MP 2010-

The first female Asian Tory MP. Has robust right-wing views and is staunchly Eurosceptic; left the Tory party to work on the Referendum Party's 1997 election campaign before rejoining under William Hague. 1922 executive committee, 2010-. Interested in small businesses. Contested Nottingham North 2005. Dir, Weber Shandwick Corporate Communications. Diageo plc. Shandwick PR. Deputy Press Sec to William Hague as Leader of Opposition. Enjoys racing, cricket and rock music. Hindu. Married, one son. Ed: Westfield Girls Sch; Watford; Keele (BA economics); Essex (British government).

Margaret Phelps (LD) b. Feb 2, 1945. Teacher. Contested Cynon Valley 2005. Ed: St Hugh's Coll, Oxford.
John Spademan (Lab) b. Jun 1, 1960. Railway safety engineer.
David Hodges (UKIP)

Constituency
This new seat incorporates parts of Maldon and Braintree districts and Colchester borough, reaching to the outskirts of the three eponymous towns. It has a stretch of coastline along the Blackwater Estuary. Witham is a small town, with a pleasant Georgian centre but some areas of deprivation, and lies in the centre of the seat by the A12. The rest of the seat is mostly rural with attractive villages such as Coggeshall and Kelvedon. The predecessor seats here tended to return Conservative MPs.

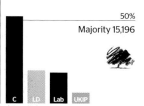

	Electorate	Turnout %	Change from 05 %
	66,750	70.2	☆
Patel, P C	24,448	52.2	2.5
Phelps, M LD	9,252	19.8	4.6
Spademan, J Lab	8,656	18.5	-14.0
Hodges, D UKIP	3,060	6.5	3.8
Abbott, J Green	1,419	3.0	

50%
Majority 15,196

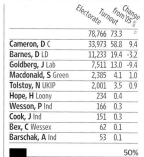

C | LD | Lab | UKIP

Witney — Conservative hold

David Cameron
b. Oct 9, 1966
MP 2001-

Prime Minister 2010-. Leader of the Opposition 2005-10. Leader of the Conservative Party 2005-. Shadow Secretary of State: Education 2005. Shadow Minister: Local Government 2004; Privy Council Office 2003. Head political section, Conservative research department 1988-92, member John Major's Prime Minister's Question Time briefing team. Special adviser to: Norman Lamont; Michael Howard. Carlton Communications. Married, one daughter, two sons – one deceased; Ivan, who had cerebral palsy and severe epilepsy, died Feb 25, 2009. Education: Eton College; Brasenose College, Oxford (BA PPE).

Dawn Barnes (LD) b. Nov 1, 1976. Media and communications manager. Ed: Chartered Institute of Marketing.
Joe Goldberg (Lab) b. Aug 7, 1976. Strategy consultant. School governor. Ed: Bristol University.

Constituency
The seat had turned Labour against its will in 1999 when Shaun Woodward, the incumbent Tory, defected to Labour. When he moved to represent another constituency in 2001, Witney elected Mr Cameron and re-elected him in 2005, with 49 per cent of the votes. Witney town is largely residential and industrial but the wider constituency boasts beautiful scenery, Cotswold stone cottages and Blenheim Palace. The RAF base at Brize Norton is a notable feature and other towns include Woodstock and Chipping Norton.

	Electorate	Turnout %	Change from 05 %
	78,766	73.3	☆
Cameron, D C	33,973	58.8	9.4
Barnes, D LD	11,233	19.4	-3.2
Goldberg, J Lab	7,511	13.0	-9.4
Macdonald, S Green	2,385	4.1	1.0
Tolstoy, N UKIP	2,001	3.5	0.9
Hope, H Loony	234	0.4	
Wesson, P Ind	166	0.3	
Cook, J Ind	151	0.3	
Bex, C Wessex	62	0.1	
Barschak, A Ind	53	0.1	

50%
Majority 22,740

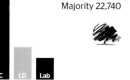

C | LD | Lab

Woking — Conservative hold

Jonathan Lord
b. Sep 17, 1972
MP 2010-

Marketing consultant who won open primary selection. Chairman of Guildford Conservative Association and campaign manager to Anne Milton in successful 2005 campaign. Cllr, Surrey 2009-; Westminster (1994-2002; Deputy Leader). Oldham-born, cut his teeth contesting Oldham West & Royton 1997. Former dir, Saatchi & Saatchi. Keen cricketer. Married, one daughter, one son. Education: Shrewsbury School; Kent Sch, Conneticut (scholarship); Merton College, Oxford (OUCA president).

Rosie Sharpley (LD) Former NHS worker. Cllr, Woking BC for 20 years.

Tom Miller (Lab) b. Nov 5, 1985. PR and advertising officer. Ed: Manchester University. Representative on the Young Labour National Committee and former editorial assistant at LabourList.org.

Constituency

The largest town in Surrey has been heavily developed in recent decades and gives its name to this constituency, which includes Byfleet and Pirbright, where there are military barracks. The constituency is mainly affluent commuter territory, although the Sheerwater estate, which houses more than 1,300 families and an unusually high ethnic minority population for Surrey, is deprived even by national standards. The Lib Dems have made progress but it remains a safe Tory seat.

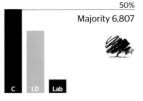

	Electorate	Turnout %	Change from '05 %
	73,838	71.5	
Lord, J C	26,551	50.3	2.9
Sharpley, R LD	19,744	37.4	4.4
Miller, T Lab	4,246	8.0	-8.3
Burberry, R UKIP	1,997	3.8	0.9
Roxburgh, J PPN-V	204	0.4	
Temple, R Magna	44	0.1	

50%
Majority 6,807

C LD Lab

Wokingham — Conservative hold

John Redwood
b. Jun 15, 1951
MP 1987-

Right-wing intellectual with maverick streak, challenged John Major's leadership in 1995 and contested again in 1997. A populist lacking the popular touch; though clever and original he cannot escape the 'Vulcan' tag. Chair, Con Econ competitiveness policy group 2005-. Shadow SoS: Deregulation 2004-05; Environment, Transport & Regions 1999-2000; T&I 1997-99. SoS: Wales 1993-95. Minister: Environment 1992-93; 1990-2. Parly Under-Sec; DT&I 1989-90. Cllr, Oxon. Chief policy adviser to Thatcher, 1990s. Fellow, All Souls. Tutor, lecturer, investment analyst, NM Rothschild, Chair Concentric plc. Divorced, one daughter, one son. Ed: Kent Coll; Magdalen Coll, Oxford

(MA mod hist); St Antony's College (DPhil mod hist).

Prue Bray (LD) b. May 14, 1957. Former IT consultant. Cllr, Wokingham. Contested seat in 2005.
George Davidson (Lab) b. Jan 4, 1971. Market researcher. Cllr, Slough BC 2000-2004.

Constituency

This Berkshire constituency spans the rural area south of Reading but the population is concentrated in the east, in an area criss-crossed by motorways. It encompasses the eastern tip of the Reading conurbation, with Earley, Sindlesham, Winnersh, part of the University of Reading and Wokingham itself. With high numbers of professionals and few manual labourers, this affluent seat has a long history of returning Tory MPs.

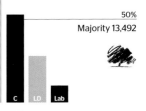

	Electorate	Turnout %	Change from '05 %
	76,219	71.5	☆
Redwood, J C	28,754	52.7	4.6
Bray, P LD	15,262	28.0	-4.7
Davidson, G Lab	5,516	10.1	-4.9
Ashwell, M Ind	2,340	4.3	
Zebedee, A UKIP	1,664	3.1	0.9
Bisset, M Green	567	1.0	
Cat, T Owen	329	0.6	
Smith, R Ind	96	0.2	

50%
Majority 13,492

C LD Lab

Wolverhampton North East — Labour hold

Emma Reynolds
b. Nov 2, 1977
MP 2010-

Centrist, lobbyist (Cogitamus) and special adviser to Geoff Hoon MP as minister for Europe/chief whip. Political adviser to Robin Cook as President, Party of European Socialists in Brussels. Small Business Europe. Multi-lingual. GMB. Locally-raised, Wolverhampton Wanderers fan. Ed: Perton Middle Sch; Codsall HS; Wulfren Coll; Wadham Coll, Oxford (PPE).

Julie Rook (C) b. Sep 23, 1965. Local businesswoman. Cllr: Dover DC 2003-; Kent CC 2009-.
Colin Ross (LD) b. Oct 29, 1975. Works for West Midland Local Authority; campaigns officer, RSPB.

Simon Patten (BNP)

Constituency

Reaching from Wolverhampton city centre ring road out to the border with Staffordshire, this Black Country seat includes a large and severely deprived industrial area built around the convergence of rail, road and canals. Beyond this are residential suburbs typified by the early 20th-century housing in the Fallings Park estate. Traditionally a Labour seat, the Conservatives held it briefly in 1987-92.

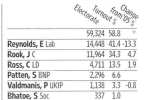

	Electorate	Turnout %	Change from '05 %
	59,324	58.8	☆
Reynolds, E Lab	14,448	41.4	-13.3
Rook, J C	11,964	34.3	4.7
Ross, C LD	4,711	13.5	1.9
Patten, S BNP	2,296	6.6	
Valdmanis, P UKIP	1,138	3.3	-0.8
Bhatoe, S Soc	337	1.0	

50%
Majority 2,484

Lab C LD BNP

Wolverhampton South East — Labour hold

Pat McFadden
b. Mar 26, 1965
MP 2005-

Long-standing back room boy, party fixer turned politician. Shrewd, good union links. Disciple of Donald Dewar. Exudes caution and pessimism about life and politics. Political secretary, PM's Office 2002-05. Min: Employment Relations & Postal Affairs (Dep BERR / BIS) 2007-, attending Cabinet 2009-. Parly Sec, Cabinet Office 2006-07. TGWU. Passionate Celtic fan. Ed: Holyrood Sch; Edinburgh (MA politics).

Ken Wood (C) Recruitment consultancy director. Cllr, Birmingham CC (chairman of the Housing and Urban Renewal Overview & Scrutiny Committee).

Richard Whitehouse (LD) Former teacher. Cllr, Wolverhampton CC for 26 years (chair, Scrutiny board). Former Mayor of Wolverhampton. Ed: Hull.
Gordon Fanthom (UKIP) Owns a car repair garage.

Constituency
From just south of Wolverhampton centre, this seat stretches to Bilston, with its large industrial developments. Sitting at the core of the Black Country, this is former colliery land, some of which remains disused, while much has been replaced with housing. Areas of severe deprivation remain and job losses from manufacturing have worsened the situation. Unlike the other Wolverhampton seats, its predecessor remained Labour throughout the 1980s. The seat also includes the Coseley East ward from Dudley Borough.

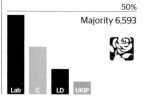

	Electorate	Turnout %	Change from '05 %
	60,450	57.4	☆
McFadden, P Lab	16,505	47.6	-12.0
Wood, K C	9,912	28.6	5.6
Whitehouse, R LD	5,277	15.2	2.9
Fanthom, G UKIP	2,675	7.7	2.5
Handa, S Ind	338	1.0	

50%
Majority 6,593

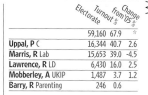

Lab · C · LD · UKIP

Wolverhampton South West — Conservative gain

Paul Uppal
b. Jun 14, 1967
MP 2010-

Eloquent and softly-spoken, avid devotee of David Cameron. Interested in business and foreign affairs, building business relations with Indian sub-continent. Contested Birmingham Yardley 2005. Self-employed businessman - commercial property manager. Cites Gorbachev, Reagan and Lincoln as political heroes. Sikh of East African descent, trustee of a Sikh temple. Wolverhampton Wanderers season ticket holder. Married, three children. Ed: Harborne Hill School, Birmingham; Warwick Uni (BA Hons politics & sociology).

Rob Marris (Lab) b. Apr 8, 1955. MP 2001-10. PPS to Shaun Woodward

2007, member of the Trade & Industry Committee 2005-07.
Robin Lawrence (LD) Drama teacher. Cllr, Wolverhampton CC 2007-.

Constituency
Wolverhampton city centre, with its university, museums and commercial heart, lies on higher ground looking out over the rest of this seat to its west, which stretches to Tettenhall. Hospitals, the Wanderers football stadium, a racecourse and golf courses lie amid middle-class residential suburban neighbourhoods typified by semi-detached properties. Enoch Powell was MP in 1950-74 and the seat was Conservative until 1997.

	Electorate	Turnout %	Change from '05 %
	59,160	67.9	☆
Uppal, P C	16,344	40.7	2.6
Marris, R Lab	15,653	39.0	-4.5
Lawrence, R LD	6,430	16.0	2.5
Mobberley, A UKIP	1,487	3.7	1.2
Barry, R Parenting	246	0.6	

50%
Majority 691

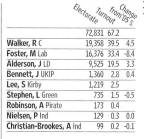

C · Lab · LD

Worcester — Conservative gain

Robin Walker
b. Apr 12, 1978
MP 2010-

Son of long-serving former Worcester MP Lord Walker. Press officer to Oliver Letwin, 2005. Assistant to Richard Adams PPC for Worcester 2001. PA/driver to Stephen Dorrell 1997. Partner of Finsbury Ltd, advising industry on press/financial communications. Formerly worked in recruitment. Anglican. Member, TRG. Ed: St Paul's Sch; Balliol College, Oxford (ancient & modern history).

Michael Foster (Lab) b. Mar 14, 1963. MP 1997-2010. Parly Under-Sec, International Development 2008-10. Asst whip 2006-08. PPS to Peter Hain 2005-06. Ed: Great Wyrley HS, Cannock, Wolverhampton.

Jackie Alderson (LD) Director of a marketing company. Ed: Liverpool Institute of Higher Education.

Constituency
The cathedral city and county town of Worcestershire is built around the River Severn and flanked by the M5 to its east, taking commuters up to Birmingham. Worcester is very active economically, predominantly in the service sector, but with car and aerospace engineering industries surviving from its traditional manufacturing base. There are patches of severe deprivation in the centre of the seat but farther out is affluent. Although historically a safe Tory seat, albeit under different boundaries, Labour won here in 1997.

	Electorate	Turnout %	Change from '05 %
	72,831	67.2	
Walker, R C	19,358	39.5	4.5
Foster, M Lab	16,376	33.4	-8.4
Alderson, J LD	9,525	19.5	3.3
Bennett, J UKIP	1,360	2.8	0.4
Lee, S Kirby	1,219	2.5	
Stephen, L Green	735	1.5	-0.5
Robinson, A Pirate	173	0.4	
Nielsen, P Ind	129	0.3	0.0
Christian-Brookes, A Ind	99	0.2	-0.1

50%
Majority 2,982

C · Lab · LD

Worcestershire Mid Conservative hold

Peter Luff
b. Feb 18, 1955
MP 1992-

Affable, popular and well-regarded. Campaigned for MPs to retain right to employ their spouses. Led Middle Way Group on hunting. Parly Under-Sec: Defence 2010-. Chairman of Business and Skills Committee 2005-10. Opposition whip 2000-05. PPS to: Ann Widdecombe/Lord Mackay of Clashfern 1996-97; Tim Eggar 1993-96. Chaired Agriculture committee 1997-2000. MP research assistant, head of Edward Heath's private office. Company sec, family retail stationery firm. PR consultant, special adviser DTI. Married, one daughter, one son. Ed: Windsor Grammar; Corpus Christi College, Cambridge (BA economics).

Margaret Rowley (LD) Works for Worcestershire Health ICT Services. Cllr, Wychavon DC 1995-. Contested Mid-Worcs 2005; Bromsgrove 2001. **Robin Lunn** (Lab) b. Jun 13, 1968. Business development manager. **John White** (UKIP)

Constituency
This lengthy rural seat borders Kidderminster in the north and skirts round the east of Worcester, stretching south to the border with Gloucestershire. The two main towns are Droitwich Spa and Evesham. Well connected to the West Midlands conurbation, it is economically active and popular with affluent professionals. Working classes are also well represented, with some light industry in the towns and agricultural work. The area has been a Tory stronghold for decades.

	Electorate	Turnout %	Change from 05 %
	72,171	70.6	☆
Luff, P C	27,770	54.5	3.2
Rowley, M LD	11,906	23.4	3.1
Lunn, R Lab	7,613	15.0	-9.1
White, J UKIP	3,049	6.0	1.6
Matthews, G Green	593	1.2	

50%
Majority 15,864

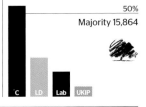

Worcestershire West Conservative hold

Harriett Baldwin
b. May 2, 1960
MP 2010-

One of CCHQ's favourite of the new intake, not least for solid media performances. Smart, enthusiastic and straightforward. Contested Stockton North 2005. Twenty-year career at JP Morgan - investment manager. Campaigned, anti-Euro group Business for Sterling. Involvement with Centre for Policy Studies - published a study - and Centre for Social Justice supporter/fundraiser, helped write social enterprise policy. Married, one son, two step-daughters. Ed: Quaker Friends' School; Marlborough College; Lady Margaret Hall, Oxford (French & Russian); McGill University, Canada (MBA).

Richard Burt (LD) Journalist. Ed: Birmingham University; Open University. **Penelope Barber** (Lab) Accountant and auditor.

Constituency
This large, rural seat encompasses the Malvern Hills district, as well as an area from Wychavon at its southwest. The spa town of Great Malvern and the smaller towns of Tenbury Wells and Upton-upon-Severn are the main population centres but several villages are strewn across the district. Agriculture influences the seat but its population is overwhelmingly affluent professionals. Both this and its predecessor seats have traditionally been Conservative.

	Electorate	Turnout %	Change from 05 %
	73,270	73.8	☆
Baldwin, H C	27,213	50.3	5.4
Burt, R LD	20,459	37.8	-1.1
Barber, P Lab	3,661	6.8	-3.7
Bovey, C UKIP	2,119	3.9	0.7
Victory, M Green	641	1.2	-1.2

50%
Majority 6,754

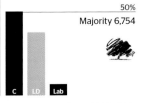

Workington Labour hold

Tony Cunningham
b. Sep 16, 1952
MP 2001-

Earnest and quietly effective. Once said he didn't need a whips' 'black book' of MPs' secrets as it was all in his head. Govt whip 2008-10; Asst whip 2005-08. PPS to Elliot Morley 2003-05. Member, select cttees: Catering 2001-; European Scrutiny 2001-04. MEP Cumbria and North Lancashire 1994-99 (Member, European standing cttee C). Cllr, Allerdale BC: leader 1992-94. NUT local sec 1985-94. Chief exec Human Rights NGO. Teacher. Patron, Mines Advisory Group, VSO. Married, one daughter, one son, one stepdaughter, one stepson. Education: Workington Grammar School; Liverpool (BA history/politics); Didsbury College (PGCE).

Judith Pattinson (C) Retired partner in insurance brokers. Chair, Brampton PC. Former cllr and Mayor of Carlisle. Contested Workington 2005. **Stan Collins** (LD) Retired, environmental insurance. Cllr, Cumbria CC; South Lakeland DC 1979-.

Constituency
This northwestern Cumbrian seat divides roughly into three parts. At the north is the Solway Firth, an Area of Outstanding Natural Beauty on the border with Scotland. A fork south along the coast leads to Maryport and Workington, which have struggled since the decline of the coal, iron and steel industries. They are working class, with more than a fifth living in social housing. The seat's other fork, to the south east, runs down to Bassenthwaite Lake, in the Lake District National Park. This seat has been Labour since 1931.

	Electorate	Turnout %	Change from 05 %
	59,607	65.9	☆
Cunningham, T Lab	17,865	45.5	-6.5
Pattinson, J C	13,290	33.9	4.8
Collins, S LD	5,318	13.6	-0.9
Wingfield, M BNP	1,496	3.8	
Lee, S UKIP	876	2.2	-1.3
Logan, R Eng	414	1.1	

50%
Majority 4,575

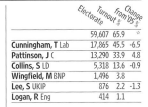

Worsley & Eccles South
Labour hold

Barbara Keeley
b. Mar 26, 1952
MP 2005-

Close interest in improving support services for support carers. Dep Leader House of Commons 2009-10. Asst govt whip 2007-08. PPS to: Harriet Harman 2006-07; Jim Murphy 2006-07. MP for Worsley 2005-10. Cllr, Trafford Borough Council 1995-2004. Voluntary sector consultant. Married. Ed: Mount St Mary's RC Coll, Leeds; Salford (politics & contemporary history).

Iain Lindley (C) Member of the Greater Manchester Fire Rescue Authority. Election agent for Nigel Adams, 2005. Cllr, Salford CC 2004-. School governor. Ed: Walkden High School; Eccles College; University of York.

Richard Gadsden (LD) b. Apr 5, 1973. Computer programmer.

Constituency
This city of Salford seat is loosely based on the old Worsley seat but with the loss of the Wigan wards and the gain of a sizeable chunk from the southwest of the old Eccles seat. It contains the deprived, formerly industrial areas of south Eccles, Little Hulton and other built-up areas that lie between the M62 and the ship canal. To the west of the motorway is Worsley, an historic town astride the Bridgewater Canal that is home to some affluent residents, including the footballer Ryan Giggs. The predecessor seats here were both Labour.

		Electorate	Turnout %	Change from '05 %
		72,473	57.5	☆
Keeley, B	Lab	17,892	42.9	-10.4
Lindley, I	C	13,555	32.5	4.8
Gadsden, R	LD	6,883	16.5	3.6
Townsend, A	UKIP	2,037	4.9	-1.2
Whitelegg, P	Eng	1,334	3.2	

50%
Majority 4,337

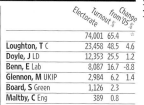

Worthing East & Shoreham
Conservative hold

Tim Loughton
b. May 30, 1962
MP 1997-

Smooth and plausible but slightly pompous. Often seen wearing jeans around Westminster. Has a laconic sense of humour and performed an excruciating rap dance on TV reality show. Parly Under-Sec: Education 2010-. Shadow Minister: Children 2003-10; Health and Education 2003. Opposition spokes, various 2000-03. General election PA to Tim Eggar 1987. Fund manager, Flemings. Non-exec director, internet start-up Netlink. Married, two daughters, one son. Ed: The Priory School; Warwick (BA classical civilisation); Clare College, Cambridge (research Mesopotamian archaeology).

James Doyle (LD) b. Oct 3, 1964. IT consultant and website designer.
Emily Benn (Lab) b. Oct 4, 1989. Student, granddaughter of Tony Benn.
Mike Glennon (UKIP) b. Oct 1, 1957. Teacher. Contested W Sussex 2009.

Constituency
Just west of Brighton, this coastal seat encompasses only the eastern fringe of Worthing, with its trading estates, and stretches along the coast through Sompting and Lancing to Shoreham-by-Sea and Southwick. Typically for resorts with seasonal tourism employment, much of the seafront area is relatively poor, though there is little serious deprivation. Farther inland there are more affluent patches. The constituency has above-average numbers of retired people and health is a prominent economic sector. It has returned Tory MPs since its inception in 1997.

		Electorate	Turnout %	Change from '05 %
		74,001	65.4	☆
Loughton, T	C	23,458	48.5	4.6
Doyle, J	LD	12,353	25.5	1.2
Benn, E	Lab	8,087	16.7	-8.8
Glennon, M	UKIP	2,984	6.2	1.4
Board, S	Green	1,126	2.3	
Maltby, C	Eng	389	0.8	

50%
Majority 11,105

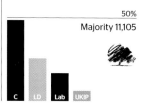

Worthing West
Conservative hold

Peter Bottomley
b. Jul 20, 1944
MP 1975-

Old-style Tory wet and independent-minded trade unionist. A loner who, despite his long experience, has always been seen as a slightly cranky outsider, and whose career has been in decline for more than a decade. Husband of Baroness Bottomley, Health SoS in Major's Cabinet. Parly Under-Sec: NI (1989-90); Transport (1986-89); Employment (1984-86). MP: Eltham 1983-97; Greenwich, Woolwich West 1975-83. President, Con Trade Unionists (1978-80), former TWGU member. Lorry driver, industrial relations, industrial economist. Married, two daughters, one son. Ed: Westminster Sch; Trinity Coll, Cambridge (BA economics, MA).

Hazel Thorpe (LD) Teacher. Cllr, Worthing BC 2000- (dep leader LD group). Contested Brighton Pavilion 2005.
Ian Ross (Lab) Policy officer, national disability charity. Former civil servant.
John Wallace (UKIP)

Constituency
As well as encompassing most of the large seaside town of Worthing, complete with pier, this West Sussex seat stretches along the coast through Goring-by-Sea, Ferring and East Preston to Rustington at its western extremity. It is the more affluent of the Worthing seats, with only a few patches of deprivation. The working population is chiefly in the service sector – notably health, because of its hospital – but the seat is most notable for the large number of retired people, who have helped to ensure that it returned Tory MPs in recent years.

		Electorate	Turnout %	Change from '05 %
		75,945	64.7	☆
Bottomley, P	C	25,416	51.7	4.1
Thorpe, H	LD	13,687	27.9	1.1
Ross, I	Lab	5,800	11.8	-7.4
Wallace, J	UKIP	2,924	6.0	0.7
Aherne, D	Green	996	2.0	
Dearsley, S	Christian	300	0.6	

50%
Majority 11,729

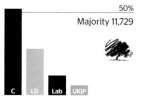

Wrekin, The Conservative hold

Mark Pritchard
b. Nov 22, 1966
MP 2005-

Animal welfare campaigner. Sec, 1922 committee, 2010-. Member, select committees: Environmental Audit 2005-07; Work & Pensions 2006-09; Welsh Affairs 2007-; Transport 2009-. Contested Warley 2001. Cllr, Harrow, Woking. CCO press officer 1997. Career in marketing - company director. Married. Education: Afan Comprehensive, Cymmer; Aylestone School, Hereford; London Guildhall University.

Paul Kalinauckas (Lab Co-op) b. Sep 19, 1954. Chief Exec of a community finance initiative. Ran for Staffordshire South 2005, 2001.

Ali Cameron-Daw (LD) Manager of business training company. Former music teacher; founded the Lavant Churches Youth Music Group. Former membership sec of Chichester LDs.

Constituency
Surrounding Telford on three sides, this West Midlands seat includes the towns of Wellington, Hadley, Shifnal and Newport, which is an historic market town on the border with Staffordshire, popular with pensioners and the middle classes. The sparsely populated countryside is the site of some farming and the Harper Adams University College is a renowned provider of agricultural training. The Wrekin is a hill visible from miles around, giving rise to the regional phrase "all around the Wrekin", meaning to take the long way round. This seat was Labour from 1997 to 2005.

	Electorate	Turnout %	Change from '05 %
	65,544	70.1	*
Pritchard, M C	21,922	47.7	5.6
Kalinauckas, P Lab	12,472	27.1	-12.1
Cameron-Daw, A LD	8,019	17.4	2.4
Hurst, M UKIP	2,050	4.5	0.9
Harwood, S BNP	1,505	3.3	

50%
Majority 9,450

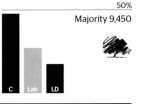

Wrexham Labour hold

Ian Lucas
b. Sep 18, 1960
MP 2001-

Claim to fame as solicitor to Trevor Rees-Jones, the sole survivor of the crash that killed Princess Diana. Parly Under-Sec: BIS 2009-10. Asst govt whip 2008-09. PPS to: Liam Byrne 2007-08; Bill Rammell 2005-06. Member, select cttees: Public Accounts 2007; Transport 2003-05; Environmental Audit 2001-03; Procedure 2001-02. Member, Gresford Community Council, Wrexham 1987-91. Fabian Society. Amicus/MSF. Keen cricketer. Married, one daughter, one son. Ed: Greenwell Comprehensive School, Gateshead; RGS, Newcastle; New College, Oxford (BA jurisprudence); Coll of Law, Christleton law.

Tom Rippeth (LD) b. 1966. Scientist and lecturer. Contested Wrexham 2005, 2003 (Welsh Assembly).
Gareth Hughes (C) Barrister. Chair and director of the British Comedy Society.
Arfon Jones (PC) Former police officer. Cllr, Wrexham 2008-.

Constituency
The eponymous town lies southwest of this seat, which fans out north including the town of Gresford, and east to the River Dee, which forms the border with England. Once a market town in a coalmining area, Wrexham's economy has diversified successfully and it is home to a huge industrial estate. About 25 per cent of residents live in social housing. However, the seat also has a sizeable middle-class and although it has been Labour for decades, its MPs have not always enjoyed great majorities.

	Electorate	Turnout %	Change from '05 %
	50,872	64.8	
Lucas, I Lab	12,161	36.9	-9.1
Rippeth, T LD	8,503	25.8	2.2
Hughes, G C	8,375	25.4	5.4
Jones, A PC	2,029	6.2	0.4
Roberts, M BNP	1,134	3.4	0.4
Humberstone, J UKIP	774	2.4	

50%
Majority 3,658

Wycombe Conservative hold

Steven Baker
b. Jun 6, 1971
MP 2010-

Little political experience; won the first seat he was interviewed for. Cornwall-born, Christian, RAF engineer officer, chartered engineer. Technology consultant for various companies including Lehman Brothers. Director, The Cobden Centre; banking reform think-tank. Associate consultant, Centre for Social Justice. Claims to offset his carbon footprint from sky-diving and other high-octane hobbies. Married. Education: Poltair Comprehensive School, Cornwall; St Austell Sixth Form College; Southampton (BEng aerospace systems engineering); St Cross College, Oxford (MSc computer science).

Steve Guy (LD) b. Mar 6, 1963. Project manager in telecommunications. Cllr, Wycombe DC (LD group leader).
Andrew Lomas (Lab) b. Sep 17, 1983. Studying for PhD in cancer research.

Constituency
The M40 neatly slices this Buckinghamshire constituency in two, with High Wycombe to the north and largely rural areas dotted with villages to the south. RAF High Wycombe is the headquarters of Air Command. There is a sizeable amount of light industry and manufacturing in High Wycombe but it is an affluent constituency, enjoying the natural beauty of the Chiltern Hills, and has little council housing. The ethnic minority population is more than twice the national average and there is a large Muslim community. A safe Tory seat, it withstood even Labour's 1997 onslaught – albeit with reduced majorities.

	Electorate	Turnout %	Change from '05 %
	74,502	64.6	*
Baker, S C	23,423	48.6	1.2
Guy, S LD	13,863	28.8	10.9
Lomas, A Lab	8,326	17.3	-12.8
Wiseman, J UKIP	2,123	4.4	0.5
Khokar, M Ind	228	0.5	
Fitton, D Ind	188	0.4	

50%
Majority 9,560

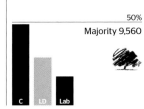

Wyre & Preston North — Conservative hold

Ben Wallace
b. May 15, 1970
MP 2005-

Personable but aggressive. Overlooked in first coalition government. Shadow Min: Scotland 2007-10. MP Lancaster & Wyre 2005-10. MSP (North-East Scotland) 1999-2003. EU/overseas dir, Qinetiq. Army officer, Scots Guard. Ski instructor, Austrian National Ski school. Married, one daughter, two sons. Ed: Millfield Sch, Somerset; RMA Sandhurst.

Danny Gallagher (LD) b. May 14, 1959. Business consultant and cllr, Preston CC. Leader of Preston LDs.
Cat Smith (Lab) Parliamentary researcher and disability officer for London Young Labour. Christian Socialist Movement.

Constituency
The M6 runs up the spine of this new Lancashire seat with Fulwood, a suburb of Preston with sought-after residential streets of terraced and detached houses, just inside the seat's southern boundary. Garstang in the north is similarly well connected and the good road links make the rural area popular with affluent commuters. The seat extends northwest across the River Wyre to Thornton and Poulton-le-Fylde, just inland from Blackpool. This seat has tended to vote Tory in the past.

	Electorate	Turnout %	Change from '05 %
	71,201	72.1	*
Wallace, B C	26,877	52.4	-2.3
Gallagher, D LD	11,033	21.5	5.4
Smith, C Lab	10,932	21.3	-5.9
Cecil, N UKIP	2,466	4.8	2.7

50%
Majority 15,844

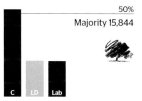

Wyre Forest — Conservative gain

Mark Garnier
b. Feb 26, 1963
MP 2010-

Investment banker and hedge fund adviser, cousin of Edward Garnier MP. Enjoys shooting and fishing. Contested Wyre Forest 2005. Cllr, Forest of Dean DC 2003-07. Partner, AugMentor. Management consultant, Strategic Planning Solutions. Var roles: Severn Capital LLP; CGR Capital; Bear Sterns; Edmond DeRothschild Securities; Daiwa Securities Europe; South China Securities; Swiss Bank Corp Int; WI Carr. History buff. Married, one daughter, two sons. Ed: Charterhouse.

Dr Richard Taylor (Ind CHC) b. Jul 7, 1934. MP 2001-2010. Doctor. Member, select cttee: Health 2001-10.

Nigel Knowles (Lab) b. Dec 5, 1946. Politician and writer. Former Mayor of Kidderminster and chairman, Worcestershire CC.
Neville Farmer (LD) Television producer, author and journalist.

Constituency
Bisected by the River Severn, this northern seat has a triangle of three main towns: Kidderminster, by far the biggest, Stourport-on-Severn and Bewdley. A mixed seat, there are pockets of severe deprivation in Kidderminster but also some extremely affluent areas. The seat is generally averagely well off. Labour overturned decades of Tory rule in 1997, only to be defeated in 2001 by Richard Taylor fighting as an Independent to maintain services at Kidderminster Hospital.

	Electorate	Turnout %	Change from '05 %
	76,711	66.4	
Garnier, M C	18,793	36.9	7.8
Taylor, R Ind CHC	16,150	31.7	
Knowles, N Lab	7,298	14.3	-8.2
Farmer, N LD	6,040	11.9	10.6
Wrench, M UKIP	1,498	2.9	0.6
Howells, G BNP	1,120	2.2	

50%
Majority 2,643

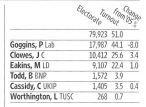

Wythenshaw & Sale East — Labour hold

Paul Goggins
b. Jun 16, 1953
MP 1997-

Reliable, undemonstrative minister. Quietly effective but low-key. Active Christian. Minister: Northern Ireland 2007-10. Parly Under-Sec: NIO 2006-07; Home 2003-06. PPS to: David Blunkett 2000-03, John Denham 1998-2000. Councillor, Salford City Council 1990-98. Youth worker. National Director, Church Action on Poverty. Member CAFOD board. TGWU. Married, one daughter, two sons. Education: St Bede's, Manchester; Ushaw College, Durham; Birmingham Polytechnic (certificate, residential care of children & young people); Manchester Polytechnic (cert of qual social work).

Janet Clowes (C) Works for an educational charity. Co-ordinated the party campaign offices during the 2008 Crewe & Nantwich by-election.
Martin Eakins (LD) b. 1977. Former IT consultant. Cllr, Manchester CC 2008-.

Constituency
The M60 runs along the north of this constituency, which lies to the southwest of Manchester. Five wards of the seat are Wythenshawe, created in the 1920s as a "garden city" but better known as one of Europe's largest council house estates, with its social problems caricatured in the television drama Shameless. The main employers are industrial estates such as Roundthorn and Sharston. The other three wards, Sale East, are taken from Trafford borough. They are dramatically different and have a population of more affluent commuters. Labour has represented here for years.

	Electorate	Turnout %	Change from '05 %
	79,923	51.0	
Goggins, P Lab	17,987	44.1	-8.0
Clowes, J C	10,412	25.6	3.4
Eakins, M LD	9,107	22.4	1.0
Todd, B BNP	1,572	3.9	
Cassidy, C UKIP	1,405	3.5	0.4
Worthington, L TUSC	268	0.7	

50%
Majority 7,575

Yeovil

Liberal Democrat hold

David Laws
b. Nov 30, 1965
MP 2001-

Serious-minded, policy-focused with sharp political skills, key member of LD coalition negotiating team. Chief Sec to Treasury May 2010, resigned pending inquiry into Commons allowances for second home rent to male lover. Joint editor in 2004 of *The Orange Book* urging his party to reclaim its economic liberal roots. LD Shad Sec: Children, Schools & Families 2007-10; Work & Pensions 2005-07; Chief Sec to Treasury 2002-05. LD spokes: defence 2001-02. LD party economics/policy and research dir. Investment banker: MD Barclays de Zoete Wedd Ltd; VP JP Morgan & Co. Ed: St George Coll, Surrey; King's Coll, Cambridge (BA economics).

Kevin Davis (C) Chief executive of a national disability charity. Former leader of Kingston CC. Contested Kingston & Surbiton 2005.
Lee Skevington (Lab) b. Aug 4, 1987. Student and freelance web designer.

Constituency
Yeovil, at the extreme east, is by far the biggest town and is famous for its aerospace industries: AgustaWestland, the helicopter manufacturer, employs 4,000 people. After boundary changes the seat includes the Royal Naval Air Station at Yeovilton, at the northern tip, also a notable employer. Chard, the second-biggest town, lies to the west, surrounded by a particularly sparsely populated rural area of hamlets and isolated houses. The seat's Liberal tradition began with the election of Paddy Ashdown in 1983.

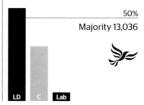

	Electorate	Turnout %	Change from '05 %
	82,314	69.4	☆
Laws, D LD	31,843	55.7	4.2
Davis, K C	18,807	32.9	-1.2
Skevington, L Lab	2,991	5.2	-5.3
Pearson, N UKIP	2,357	4.1	0.3
Baehr, R BNP	1,162	2.0	

50%
Majority 13,036

Ynys Môn

Labour hold

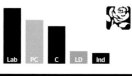

Albert Owen
b. Aug 10, 1959
MP 2001-

Member, select cttees: Welsh Affairs 2006-10, 2001-05; Accomm & Works 2001-05. Pres officer, const Lab Party 1996-2000. Cllr, 1997-99. RMT/NUS official. Merchant seafarer. Welfare rights & Employment adviser. Isle of Anglesey CC centre manager. Member, WEA N Wales management cttee. Chair, Anglesey regeneration partnership. Married, two daughters. Ed: Holyhead County Comp, Anglesey; Coleg Harlech (dip ind relations); York (BA politics).

Dylan Rees (PC) b. Jul 8, 1955. Former police inspector. Senior homelessness officer for Ynys Môn Council 2003-.
Anthony Ridge-Newman (C) Journal-ist, social scientist. Cllr, Runnymede DC.
Matt Wood (LD) Independent financial adviser. Volunteer with the Samaritans.
Peter Rogers (Ind)

Constituency
In the northwest corner of Wales, Anglesey lies across the Menai Strait from the mainland and is known by its Welsh name, Ynys Môn. Towns include Menai Bridge, Llangefni, Amlwch and Holyhead. The seat includes a nuclear power plant, RAF bases and Llanfair PG. It is home to one of the largest concentrations of Welsh-speakers in the country. The Tories overturned decades of Labour representation in 1979 and held on for two terms, before Plaid Cymru won in 1987. Labour took it in 2001 and held on in 2005 but their majorities over PC were narrow.

	Electorate	Turnout %	Change from '05 %
	50,075	68.8	
Owen, A Lab	11,490	33.4	-1.2
Rees, D PC	9,029	26.2	-4.9
Ridge-Newman, A C	7,744	22.5	11.5
Wood, M LD	2,592	7.5	0.7
Rogers, P Ind	2,225	6.5	-8.2
Gill, E UKIP	1,201	3.5	2.5
Owen, D Ch P	163	0.47	

50%
Majority 2,461

York Central

Labour hold

Hugh Bayley
b. Jan 9, 1952
MP 1992-

Mild-mannered, failed to make impact as minister. Parly Under-Sec, Soc Security 1999-2001. PPS to Frank Dobson 1997-99. Member select cttees: Int Devt 2001-; Health 1992-7. Cllr, Camden BC 1980-86. (MP York 1992-2010, City of York 1997-2010) York Health Authority. Research/lecturer, York Uni. General Sec, International Broadcasting Trust. NALGO dist/nat officer. Married, one daughter, one son. Education: Haileybury Sch; Bristol (BSc pol); York (BPhil Southern African studies).

Susan Wade Weeks (C) b. 1957. Creative director of advertising company. Former cllr, Chichester CC.

Christian Vassie (LD) b. Jan 17, 1958. Composer for film & TV and writer. Cllr, York CC 2003-. York's "Energy Champion" and the Chair of City Strategy.

Constituency
The renamed City of York seat has lost one populous ward from the south west and a couple of part wards but the heart remains the same. Its Roman, Viking and medieval heritage make it a popular tourist destination. Dominating the city is York Minster, Northern Europe's largest Gothic cathedral. The mixed economy includes manufacturing, notably confectionery with Nestlé, and financial services, with Aviva. The inner city has a young professional feel. The constituency changed hands several times, most recently to Labour in 1992.

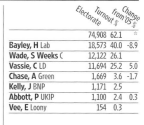

	Electorate	Turnout %	Change from '05 %
	74,908	62.1	☆
Bayley, H Lab	18,573	40.0	-8.9
Wade, S Weeks C	12,122	26.1	
Vassie, C LD	11,694	25.2	5.0
Chase, A Green	1,669	3.6	-1.7
Kelly, J BNP	1,171	2.5	
Abbott, P UKIP	1,100	2.4	0.3
Vee, E Loony	154	0.3	

50%
Majority 6,451

Julian Sturdy
b. Jun 3, 1971
MP 2010-

Plain-speaking Yorkshire farmer, supplies McCain with potatoes. Cllr, Harrogate BC 2002-07. Contested Scunthorpe 2005. Son of Robert Sturdy MEP. Runs farming and property business. Keen cricketer and Leeds Utd FC fan. Married, one daughter, one son, Ed: Ashville College, Harrogate; Harper Adams (agriculture).

Madeleine Kirk (LD) b. Feb 13, 1953. Accountant, Joseph Rowntree Foundation. Dir, York Theatre Royal Board; vice-chair, Connexions York & N Yorkshire; governor, York Hospitals NHS Foundation Trust. Cllr, York CC 1991-. Contested Elmet 2005, 2001.

James Alexander (Lab) b. Feb 27, 1982. Project and outreach worker for York St John University. Cllr, York CC 2007- (leader of the Labour group)

Constituency
Forming a ring around York, this seat is created out of territory from four others. The inner boundary includes the University of York at Heslington, which contributes a significant student vote and shapes the economy through science and technology sectors. The constituency includes the suburbs of Woodthorpe, Dringhouses, Huntingdon and Rawcliffe. Beyond the ring road are commuter villages including Wheldrake, Haxby and the Poppletons. This affluent seat has higher numbers of retired people than the city centre. Predecessor seats had a mixed political history.

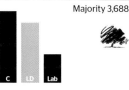

	Electorate	Turnout %	Change from '05 %
	74,965	71.1	
Sturdy, J C	22,912	43.0	6.7
Kirk, M LD	19,224	36.1	-0.6
Alexander, J Lab	9,108	17.1	-9.9
Morris, J UKIP	1,100	2.1	
Smurthwaite, C BNP	956	1.8	

50%

Majority 3,688

Greg Knight
b. Apr 4, 1949
MP 2001-; 1983-97

A classic Whips' Office insider. Plays drums in MP rock band, MP4. Elected unopposed as Chair, select cttee: Procedure 2010-. Shadow Minister: Transport 2005; Environment and Transport 2003-05; CMS 2003. Dep Shadow Leader of the House 2002-03. Minister: DTI 1996-7. Whip, 1989-96. PPS to David Mellor, 1987-89. Chair, committee ODPM 1993-2002. Vice-Chair Con Parly candidates assoc 1997-2001. MP Derby North 1983-97. Cllr, Leicester/Leics. Solicitor, ran own practice. Education: Alderman Newton's Grammar; London and Guildford Law Colleges.

Robert Adamson (LD) b. Aug 8, 1949. Retired. Contested Darlington 2005, 2001. Ed: University of Lancaster.
Paul Rounding (Lab) b. Nov 18, 1955. Major of Driffield. Former Cllr, Driffield TC for 22 years.

Constituency
Stretching from the coast at Bridlington almost to York, with Driffield at the centre, this is a large and predominantly rural seat. A notable sector of the population works in agriculture and there are above-average numbers of self-employed. Too distant for convenient commuting to Hull, it is less affluent than other rural seats in the East Riding. The resort of Bridlington is very much the poor relation of Scarborough and Whitby. The constituency has been Tory since its creation in 1997 but not always with great majorities.

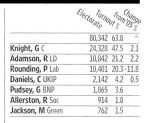

	Electorate	Turnout %	Change from '05 %
	80,342	63.8	☆
Knight, G C	24,328	47.5	2.1
Adamson, R LD	10,842	21.2	2.2
Rounding, P Lab	10,401	20.3	-11.8
Daniels, C UKIP	2,142	4.2	0.5
Pudsey, G BNP	1,865	3.6	
Allerston, R Soc	914	1.8	
Jackson, M Green	762	1.5	

50%

Majority 13,486

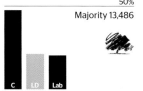

MPs with majorities of less than 10 per cent

Conservative

	Majority Votes	%
Byles, D	54	0.11
Eustice, G	66	0.16
Doyle-Price, J	92	0.2
Offord, M	106	0.23
Blackwood, N	176	0.32
Evans, J	194	0.41
Spencer, M	214	0.43
Wharton, J	332	0.66
Soubry, A	389	0.74
Ollerenshaw, E	333	0.78
Newton, S	435	0.9
Morris, A	523	1.09
Mills, N	536	1.16
Aldous, P	769	1.5
Uppal, P	691	1.72
Jones, A	1,039	1.95
Morris, D	866	1.99
Stevenson, J	853	2.02
Carmichael, N	1,299	2.24
Evans, G	991	2.25
McCartney, K	1,058	2.32
Colville, O	1,149	2.62
Reevell, S	1,526	2.82
Mowat, D	1,553	2.83
Fuller, R	1,353	3
Kirby, S	1,328	3.11
Andrew, S	1,659	3.38
Davies, G	1,184	3.5
Bagshawe, L	1,895	3.5
Macleod, M	1,958	3.64
Weatherley, M	1,868	3.75
de Bois, N	1,692	3.81
Rudd, A	1,993	4
Main, A	2,305	4.37
Gummer, B	2,079	4.43
Morris, J	2,023	4.6
Jones, M	2,069	4.64
Graham, R	2,420	4.76
Ellis, M	1,936	4.81
Nuttall, D	2,243	4.99
Skidmore, C	2,445	5.11
Penrose, J	2,691	5.11
Norman, J	2,481	5.13
Garnier, M	2,643	5.19
Lee, J	2,501	5.25
Maynard, P	2,150	5.29
Brine, S	3,048	5.45
Mosley, S	2,583	5.52
Barwell, G	2,969	5.97
Walker, R	2,982	6.09
Hopkins, K	2,940	6.16
McVey, E	2,436	6.19
Murray, S	3,220	6.49
Leslie, C	3,274	6.5
Letwin, O	3,923	6.84
Goldsmith, Z	4,091	6.9
Sturdy, J	3,688	6.92
Burley, A	3,195	7.01
Morgan, N	3,744	7.08
Blackman, B	3,403	7.09
Redwood, J	3,482	7.48
Buckland, R	3,544	7.52
Bray, A	3,716	7.88
Stephenson, A	3,585	7.96
McPartland, S	3,578	8.01
Shelbrooke, A	4,521	8.1

	Majority Votes	%
Hart, S	3,423	8.45
Nokes, C	4,156	8.5
McCartney, J	4,837	8.74
Cairns, A	4,307	8.85
Mundell, D	4,194	9.14
Smith, C	3,901	9.16
Tredinnick, D	5,032	9.27
Bingham, A	4,677	9.29
Burns, S	5,110	9.36
Stewart, I	5,201	9.4
Berry, J	4,493	9.53
Vickers, M	4,298	9.56
Rees-Mogg, J	4,914	9.6
Lewis, B	4,276	9.93

Labour

	Majority Votes	%
Jackson, G	42	0.08
Hilling, J	92	0.19
Woolas, P	103	0.23
de Piero, G	192	0.39
Blomfield, P	165	0.4
Denham, J	192	0.43
Murray, I	316	0.72
Perkins, T	549	1.2
McGovern, A	531	1.33
Williamson, C	613	1.36
Davies, G	504	1.42
Austin, I	649	1.68
Johnson, D	641	1.92
Danczuk, S	889	1.94
Mitchell, A	714	2.16
Balls, E	1,101	2.25
Wright, D	978	2.37
Winnick, D	990	2.74
Stuart, G	1,274	3.07
Riordan, L	1,472	3.38
Farrelly, P	1,552	3.59
Creagh, M	1,613	3.63
Blenkinsop, T	1,677	3.63
Lazarowicz, M	1,724	3.64
Seabeck, A	1,588	3.82
Coaker, V	1,859	3.86
Efford, C	1,663	3.96
Vaz, V	1,755	4.29
Greenwood, L	1,772	4.35
Watson, T	1,533	4.45
Morden, J	1,650	4.78
Khan, S	2,524	4.99
Engel, N	2,445	5.2
Hoyle, L	2,593	5.21
Bradshaw, B	2,721	5.21
Marsden, G	1,851	5.26
Buck, K	2,126	5.37
Whitehead, A	2,413	5.47
Shuker, G	2,329	5.52
Moon, M	2,263	5.9
Cruddas, J	2,630	5.94
Hanson, D	2,272	6.14
Caton, M	2,683	6.43
Smith, A	3,049	6.55
Blackman-Woods, R	3,067	6.63
Burden, R	2,782	6.66
Reynolds, J	2,744	6.71
Thomas, G	3,143	6.82
Lewis, I	3,292	6.82
Dakin, N	2,549	6.88
Umunna, C	3,259	6.96
Ruane, C	2,509	7.06

	Majority Votes	%
Reynolds, E	2,484	7.12
Tami, M	2,919	7.32
Slaughter, A	3,549	7.47
McCabe, S	3,482	7.48
Smith, O	2,791	7.61
McKinnell, C	3,414	7.77
Godsiff, R	3,799	7.8
Chapman, J	3,388	7.9
Esterson, B	3,862	7.97
Begg, A	3,506	8.14
Elan Jones, S	2,834	8.17
Thornberry, E	3,569	8.19
McCarthy, K	3,722	8.27
Flint, C	3,595	8.28
Cunningham, J	3,845	8.37
Wood, M	4,406	8.62
Smith, A	4,581	8.87
Flynn, P	3,544	8.92
Cooper, R	4,343	8.95
Reed, J	3,833	8.96
Dromey, J	3,277	9.22
Crausby, D	4,084	9.43
Hamilton, F	4,545	9.56
Keen, A	4,658	9.59
Primarolo, D	4,734	9.79
Miller, A	4,331	9.79

Liberal Democrat

	Majority Votes	%
Burt, L	175	0.32
Brooke, A	269	0.58
Wright, S	310	0.65
Ward, D	365	0.9
Munt, T	800	1.43
Gilbert, S	1312	2.78
Teather, S	1345	2.96
Heath, D	1817	2.99
Burstow, P	1608	3.31
George, A	1719	3.74
Leech, J	1894	4.21
Birtwistle, G	1818	4.34
Swinson, J	2184	4.56
Hames, D	2470	4.72
Hunter, M	3272	6.23
Rogerson, D	2981	6.37
Lloyd, S	3435	6.59
Browne, J	3993	6.86
Beith, A	2690	7
Hemming, J	3002	7.34
Reid, A	3431	7.58
Smith, R	3684	8.16
Crockart, M	3803	8.19
Sanders, A	4078	8.28
Horwood, M	4920	9.32
Williams, R	3747	9.65

Others

	Majority Votes	%
Gildernew, M (SF)	4	0.01
McCrea, W (DUP)	1,183	3.48
Long, N (Alliance)	1,533	4.45
Hosie, S (SNP)	1,821	4.49
Williams, H (PC)	1,455	5.58
Dodds, N (DUP)	2,224	6.01
Simpson, T (DUP)	3,361	8.12
Weir, M (SNP)	3,282	8.65
Wishart, P (SNP)	4,379	9.07
Edwards, J (PC)	3,481	9.16

How the nation voted
2010

	C*	Lab	LD	Others	Total
Votes	10,806,105	8,606,518	6,836,198	3,432,843	29,681,664
% (change '05)	36.4 (+3.6)	29.0 (-6.2)	23.0 (+1)	11.6 (+1.6)	100
Seats (change '05)	306 (+96)	258 (-90)	57 (-5)	29 (-1)	650
Candidates	648	631	631	2,245	4,138

Great Britain

	C	Lab	LD	Others	Total
Votes	10,703,744	8,606,518	6,836,198	2,758,943	28,905,403
% ('05)	37 (+3.8)	29.8 (-6.3)	23.7 (+1)	9.5 (+1.5)	100
Seats ('05)	306 (+96)	258 (-90)	57 (-5)	11 (-1)	632
Candidates	631	631	631	2,137	4,030

England

	C	Lab	LD	Others	Total
Votes	9,908,100	7,039,400	6,075,600	2,052,200	25,075,300
% ('05)	39.5 (+3.8)	28.1 (-7.4)	24.2 (+1.3)	8.2 (+2.3)	100
Seats ('05)	297 (+91)	191 (-87)	43 (-4)	2 (-)	533
Candidates	531	531	531	1,817	3,410

Scotland

	C	Lab	LD	SDP	Others	Total
Votes	412,900	1,035,500	465,500	491,400	60,400	2,465,700
% ('05)	16.7 (+0.9)	42.0 (+3.1)	18.9 (-3.7)	19.9 (+2.3)	2.4 (-2.6)	
Seats ('05)	1 (-)	41 (+)	11 (-)	6 (-)	0 (-1)	59
Candidates	59	59	59	59	172	349

Wales

	C	Lab	LD	PC	Others	Total
Votes	382,700	531,600	295,200	165,400	91,300	1,466,200
% ('05)	26.1 (+4.7)	36.3 (-6.5)	20.1 (+1.7)	11.3 (-1.3)	6.2 (+1.3)	
Seats ('05)	8 (+5)	26 (-4)	3 (-1)	3 (+1)	0 (-1)	40
Candidates	40	40	40	40	146	266

Northern Ireland

	DUP	SINN FEIN	SDLP	UCU	All	Others	Total
Votes	168,200	171,900	111,000	102,400	47,800	72,600	673,900
% ('05)	25.0% (-8.7)	25.5% (+1.2)	16.5% (-1)	15.2% (-2.6)	7.1% (+3.1)	10.8% (+8)	
Seats ('05)	8 (-1)	5 (-)	3 (-)	0 (-1)	1 (+1)	2 (+)	18
Candidates	16	17	18	17	18	39	108

* includes Ulster Conservatives and Unionists in Northern Ireland. **NB** England, Scotland, Wales and Northern Ireland votes to nearest hundred.

Tories rediscovered the art of by-election victory

Greg Hurst
Editor of the guide

By-elections returned to a level approaching historical norms during the 2005-10 Parliament. There were 14 such contests, compared with six during Tony Blair's second term from 2001-05, as Labour and the Conservatives placed enormous pressure on its sitting MPs not to stand down prematurely for fear of defeat by the Liberal Democrats. By comparison, there were 17 by-elections in Mr Blair's first Parliament from 1997-2001, 18 in John Major's full term of 1992-97 and 24 in the Parliament before that.

The higher frequency of parliamentary by-elections from 2005 ushered in several trends of interest, most notably the rediscovery by the Conservatives of the art of winning these peculiar campaigns just as the Liberal Democrats ran out of steam after a succession of triumphs. Labour veered from being ruthlessly effective campaigners to whipping boys, as a severe mid-term slump in popularity allowed voters to use by-elections to punish the party of government, a long-established tradition. The party also experimented with extremes of over-long and very short campaigns.

Labour held four seats, reclaimed a fifth represented by the Speaker, lost two to the Conservatives and one apiece to the Lib Dems and Scottish Nationalists. The Tories held three, the Lib Dems one and, a rarity, another seat remained in independent hands. Only one by-election, in Norwich North, returned a woman MP.

The first such contest after the 2005 election was a harbinger of things to come. The Liberal Democrats, more familiar with chasing by-election gains from other parties, were forced by the death of Patsy Carlton to defend her seat of Cheadle during a difficult period for their leader, Charles Kennedy. It was the first time the Lib Dems had defended a seat in a by-election: the nearest parallel was a by-election at Truro in 1987, held by the Liberals. The Tories mounted a ferocious, but clumsy, attempt to retake the seat, which they had held until 2001, flooding the constituency with locally focused literature and demonising the Lib Dem candidate. The Lib Dems held on with an increased vote but the Conservatives' serious intent was clear.

Robin Cook, the former Foreign Secretary, died after collapsing while hill-walking in the Scottish Highlands in August 2005, aged 59. Labour selected as its candidate Jim Devine, his agent in Livingston, who was later deselected over his parliamentary expenses. Labour held the by-election in late September, during its annual party conference, and won reasonably comfortably.

The first upset came in Dunfermline & West Fife, af-

ter the death of the Labour MP Rachel Squire. To widespread astonishment her seat, bordering Gordon Brown's, was captured by the Liberal Democrats, then without a leader after the resignation of Mr Kennedy. It proved, however, to be the party's last hurrah, the final flourish of 12 upsets since the Eastbourne by-election in 1990.

Labour failed to win back Blaenau Gwent, the South Wales valleys seat once held by Aneurin Bevan and Michael Foot but won in 2005 by an independent, disaffected Labour politician, Peter Law, in a protest over women-only shortlists. His death in April 2006 produced a constitutional oddity: he had no party to move the by-election writ. The Labour Chief Whip did so but the election was won by Mr Law's agent, Dai Davies, standing for the Blaenau Gwent People's Voice Group.

The Lib Dems ran the Conservatives a very close second in Bromley & Chislehurst after the death of Eric Forth, cutting the Tory majority from 13,342 to 633 after branding the Conservative candidate Bob Neill – a barrister, politician in the London Assembly and health authority board member – "three jobs Bob".

When Tony Blair quit Parliament on the day he left Downing Street, Labour returned to a strategy it had used successfully in 2004, when it held difficult by-elections at Leicester South and Birmingham Hodge Hill on the same day in order to overstretch the Lib Dems. The writ for Sedgefield, Mr Blair's seat, was moved immediately for the day of another by-election in Ealing Southall, following the death of the Labour MP Piara Khabra. This proved much the more lively contest. Again the Conservatives attempted a spirited if flawed campaign but the credibility of their candidate, Tony Lit, the son of a local Sikh businessman, was shot to pieces when Labour, with ruthless brilliance, produced recent photographs of him smiling with Mr Blair at an event where his company donated £5,000 to Labour. Both seats were held, with reduced majorities, giving an early boost to Gordon Brown's premiership and destabilising David Cameron, whose candidates came a humiliating third in Ealing Southall and fourth in Sedgefield, behind UKIP.

Thereafter the tide turned. A by-election in Crewe & Nantwich a year later, caused by the death of Gwyneth Dunwoody, coincided with controversy over Mr Brown's abolition of a 10p income tax threshold, the effect of which was to penalise millions of the lower paid. This time fortune smiled on Mr Cameron, whose party was in second place with the Lib Dems a distant third. He made the issue central to the by-election, while Labour floundered with misjudged attempts to portray the wealthy Tory candidate, Edward Timpson, as a "toff". Mr Timpson triumphed in the Tories' first by-election gain since 1982, itself an oddity, when the MP Bruce Douglas Mann, honourably but misguidedly resigned to contest his seat of Mitcham & Morden under his new colours on leaving Labour to join the SDP. The last time the Tories had gained a seat from Labour in a by-election was in March 1978 at Ilford North.

Within months the Conservatives comfortably held

two seats in short by-election campaigns. One was for Henley, after Boris Johnson's election as Mayor of London, in which Labour came a humiliating fifth. The second was more bizarre. David Davis, the Tory Home Affairs spokesman, resigned his seat of Haltemprice & Howden after MPs voted to extend police powers to hold terrorist suspects for up to 42 days without charge, saying that he wished to fight a by-election in protest. The Lib Dems, and then Labour, decided not to field candidates, leaving Mr Davis to debate with a crop of cranks and self-publicists. He won a hollow victory.

Following the resignation that month of David Marshall, the Labour MP for Glasgow East, citing ill-health, Labour again moved the writ within a day. With Mr Brown by now plumbing new depths of un-popularity, the Scottish Nationalists added to his woes, winning with a huge swing of 22.54 per cent.

The death within a month of another of its MPs in Scotland, John MacDougall, prompted Labour to try a different approach in Glenrothes, delaying the process for three months to give maximum opportunity to overhaul the SNP. It worked, with Labour's successful defence boosted by several campaign visits from Sarah Brown, the Prime Minister's wife.

The Conservatives secured a second triumph in another unusual by-election in Norwich North, where Ian Gibson was barred by Labour from standing again as a candidate over his Commons expenses claims. He responded by resigning his seat immediately. It was too good a chance to miss for the Tories, who again started in second place. Their victorious candidate, Chloe Smith, became, at 27, Britain's youngest MP.

The Parliament's final by-election was also triggered by the controversy over MPs' expenses, and fury at its handling by the Commons authorities. MPs blamed the Speaker, Michael Martin, who was forced to stand down, the first holder of his office to do so for 300 years. Labour, his party before his election as Speaker, strung out the by-election in his seat of Glasgow North East for 142 days, well beyond the convention of three months, defeating the SNP's attempt to move the writ earlier. The interval, the longest in records held by the Commons since 1974, earned a rebuke from the Electoral Commission but worked: Labour held on comfortably, albeit with the lowest turnout in a Scottish Westminster by-election, 33 per cent.

Three seats were left vacant before the election, two after the deaths of Labour MPs: Leicestershire North West, which went unrepresented for four months, and Middlesbrough South & East Cleveland. The third was Strangford, where Iris Robinson, wife of the Democratic Unionist Party leader, Peter Robinson, resigned over financial assistance for her teenage lover's business. The DUP decided against contesting a by-election.

At the general election, Labour regained the seats it had lost in Scotland and Blaenau Gwent in Wales but not Crewe & Nantwich or Norwich North, both of which stayed Conservative.

By-elections 2005-10

2005

Cheadle July 15
Caused by the death of Patsy Calton

Mark Hunter LD	19,593
Stephen Day C	15,936
Martin Miller Lab	1,739
Leslie Leggett Veritas	218
John Allman Alliance for Change	81

LD majority 3,657 LD hold
Electorate 68,051; total vote 37,567; turnout 55.2%

Livingston September 29
Caused by the death of death of Robin Cook

Jim Devine Lab	12,319
Angela Constance SNP	9,639
Charles Dundas LD	4,362
Gordon Lindhurst C	1,993
David Robertson Green	529
Steve Nimmo SNP	407
Peter Adams UKIP	108
Melville Brown Ind	55
John Allman All for Change	33
Brian Gardner Soc Party of GB	32

Lab majority 2,680 Lab hold
Electorate 76,365; total vote 19,447; turnout 38.6%

2006

Dunfermline & W Fife February 9
Caused by the death of Rachel Squire

Willie Rennie LD	12,391
Catherine Stihler Lab	10,591
Douglas Chapman SNP	7,261
Carrie Ruxton C	2,702
John McAllion SNP	537
James Hargreaves Scot Christian Party	411
Thomas Minogue Abolish Forth Bridge Tolls	374
Ian Borland UKIP Scotland	208
Dick Rodgers Common Good	103

LD majority 1,800 LD gain
Electorate 71,017; total vote 34,578; turnout 48.7%

Blaenau Gwent June 29
Caused by the death of Peter Law

Dai Davies Ind	12,543
Owen Smith Lab	10,059
Steffan Lewis PC	1,755
Amy Kitcher LD	1,477
Margrit Williams C	1,013
Alan Hope Raving Loony	318

Ind majority 2,484 Ind hold
Electorate 52,512; total vote 27,165; turnout 51.7%

Bromley & Chislehurst June 29

Caused by the death of Eric Forth

Robert Neill C	11,621
Benjamin Abbotts LD	10,988
Nigel Farage UKIP	2,347
Rachel Reeves Lab	1,925
Ann Garrett Green	811
Paul Winnett NF Britain	476
John Hemming-Clarke Ind	442
Steven Uncles Eng Democrats	212
John Cartwright Raving Loony	132
Nick Hadziannis Ind	65
Anne Besley Money Reform	33

C majority 633 C hold
Electorate 71,818; total vote 29,052; turnout 40.5%

2007

Ealing, Southall July 19

Caused by the death of Piara Khabra

Virendra Kumar Sharma Lab	15,188
Nigel Bakhai LD	10,118
Tony Lit C	8,230
Sarah Janet Edwards Green	1,135
Salvindern Singh Dhillon Respect	588
K.T. Rajan UKIP	285
Yaqub Masih Christian	280
Kuldeep Singh Grewal Ind	275
John Sydney Cartwright Raving Loony	188
Sati Chaggar Eng Democrats	152
Jasdev Singh Rai Ind	92
Gulbash Singh Ind	87

Lab majority 5,070 Lab hold
Electorate 85,262; total vote 36,618; turnout 42.9%

Sedgefield July 19

Caused by the resignation of Tony Blair

Philip Wilson Lab	12,528
Greg Stone LD	5,572
Graham Michael Robb C	4,082
Andrew Spence BNP	2,494
Paul Gittins Ind	1,885
Toby Horton UKIP	536
Christopher Michael Haine Green	348
Stepen Paul Gash Eng Democrats	177
Tim Grainger Christian	177
Alan "Howling Laud" Hope Raving Loony	129
Norman Scarth Anti-Crime	34

Lab majority 6,956 Lab hold
Electorate 67,314; total vote 27,962; turnout 41.5%

2008

Crewe & Nantwich May 22

Caused by the death of Gwyneth Dunwoody

Edward Timpson C	20,539
Tamsin Dunwoody Lab	12,679
Elizabeth Shenton LD	6,040
Mike Nattrass UKIP	922
Robert Andrew Smith Green	359
David Alan Roberts Eng Democrats	275
The Flying Brick Raving Loony	236
Mark Walklate Ind	217
Paul Richard Thorogood Cut Tax on Petrol	118
Gemma Dawn Garrett Ind	113

C majority 7,860 C gain
Electorate 71,963; total vote 41,498; turnout 57.7%

Henley June 26

Caused by the resignation of Boris Johnson

John Howell C	19,796
Stephen Kearney LD	9,680
Mark Stevenson Greens	1,321
Timothy Rait BNP	1,243
Richard McKenzie Lab	1,066
Chris Adams UKIP	843
Bananaman Owen Raving Loony	242
Derek Allpass Eng Democrats	157
Amanda Harrington Ind (Miss GB Party)	128
Dick Rodgers Common Good	121
Louise Cole Ind (Miss GB Party)	91
Harry Bear The Fur Play Party	73

C majority 10.116 C hold
Electorate 69,086; total vote 34,761; turnout 50.3%

Haltemprice & Howden July 10

Caused by the resignation of David Davis

David Michael Davis C	17,113
Shan Oakes Green	1,758
Joanne Robinson Eng Democrats	1,714
Tess Culnane NF Britain for British	544
Gemma Dawn Garrett Miss GB Party	521
Jill Saward Ind	492
Mad Cow Girl Raving Loony	412
Walter Edward Sweeney Ind	238
John Nicholson Ind	162
David Craig Ind	135
David Pinder New Party	135
David Icke No party listed	110
Hamish Howitt Freedom 4 Choice	91
Christopher John Talbot Soc Equality	84
Grace Christine Astley Ind	77
George Hargreaves Christian	76
David Laurence Bishop Church of Militant Elvis	44
John Randle Upex Ind	38
Greg Wood Ind	32
Eamonn Fitzpatrick Ind	31
Ronnie Carroll Make Politicians History	29
Thomas Faithful Darwood Ind	25

Christopher Mark Foren Ind	23
Herbert Winford Crossman Ind	11
Tony Farnon Ind	8
Norman Scarth Ind	8

C majority 15,355 C hold
Electorate 70,100; total vote 23,911; turnout 34.1%

Glasgow East July 24
Caused by the resignation of David Marshall

John Mason SNP	11,277
Margaret Curran Lab	10,912
Davena Rankin C	1,639
Ian Robertson LD	915
Frances Curran Scot Socialist	555
Tricia McLeish Solidarity	512
Dr Eileen Duke Scot Greens	232
Chris Creighton Ind	67
Hamish Howitt Freedom 4 Choice	65

SNP majority 365 SNP gain
Electorate 62,051; total vote 26,174; turnout 42.2%

Glenrothes November 26
Caused by the death of John MacDougall

Lindsay Roy Lab	19,946
Peter Grant SNP	13,209
Maurice Golden C	1,381
Harry Wills LD	947
Jim Parker Scot Senior Citizens Unity	296
Morag Balfour Scottish Socialists	212
Kris Seunarine UKIP	117
Louise McLeary Solidarity	87

Lab majority 6,737 Lab hold
Electorate 69,155; total vote 36,195; turnout 52.3%

2009

Norwich North July 23
Caused by the resignation of Dr Ian Gibson

Chloe Smith C	13,591
Chris Ostrowski Lab	6,243
April Pond LD	4,803
Glenn Tingle UKIP	4,068
Rupert Read Green	3,350
Peter Baggs Ind	23
Thomas Burridge Libertarian	36
Anne Fryatt None of The Above Party	59
Bill Holden Ind	166
Laud Howling Raving Loony	144
Craig Murray Put Honest Man into Parliament	953
Robert West BNP	941

C majority 7,348 C gain
Electorate 75,124; total vote 34,337; turnout 45.8%

Glasgow North East November 12
Caused by the resignation of Michael Martin

Willie Bain Lab	12,231
David Kerr SNP	4,120
Ruth Davidson C	1,075
Charlie Baillie BNP	1,013
Tommy Sheridan Solidarity	794
Eileen Baxendale LD	474
David Doherty Scot Green Party	332
John Smeaton The Jury Team	258
Kevin McVey Scottish Socialist	152
Mikey Hughes Ind	54
Louise McDaid Socialist Labour	47
Mev Brown Ind	32
Colin Campbell Ind Labour and Tory (Tilt)	3

Lab majority 8,111 Lab win
Electorate 62,475; total vote 20,595; turnout 33%

Manifestos

*"Halving the deficit by 2014 –
is that a target, a pledge, an
aspiration, or a bedtime story?"*

Coalition programme for government

FOREWORD

By David Cameron and Nick Clegg

This is an historic document in British politics: the first time in over half a century two parties have come together to put forward a programme for partnership government.

As our parties have worked together it has become increasingly clear to us that, although there are differences, there is also common ground. We share a conviction that the days of big government are over; that centralisation and top-down control have proved a failure. We believe that the time has come to disperse power more widely in Britain today; to recognise that we will only make progress if we help people to come together to make life better. In short, it is our ambition to distribute power and opportunity to people rather than hoarding authority within government. That way, we can build the free, fair and responsible society we want to see.

We are agreed that the first duty of government is to safeguard our national security and support our troops in Afghanistan and elsewhere – and we will fulfil that duty. We are also agreed that the most urgent task facing this coalition is to tackle our record debts, because without sound finances, none of our ambitions will be deliverable. Difficult decisions will have to be taken in the months and years ahead, but we will ensure that fairness is at the heart of those decisions so that all those most in need are protected. Working together, we are confident that we can take the country through difficult times to better days ahead.

Tackling the deficit is essential, but it is not what we came into politics to achieve. We stood for Parliament – and for the leadership of our parties – with visions of a Britain better in every way. And we have found in this coalition that our visions are not compromised by working together; they are strengthened and enhanced. That is why this coalition has the potential for era-changing, convention-challenging, radical reform.

For example, we both want to build a new economy from the rubble of the old. We will support sustainable growth and enterprise, balanced across all regions and all industries, and promote the green industries that are so essential for our future. This document shows how, with radical plans to reform our broken banking system and new incentives for green growth.

We both want a Britain where social mobility is unlocked; where everyone, regardless of background, has the chance to rise as high as their talents and ambition allow them. To pave the way, we have both agreed to sweeping reform of welfare, taxes and, most of all, our schools – with a breaking open of the state monopoly and extra money following the poorest pupils so that they, at last, get to go to the best schools, not the worst.

We both want a Britain where our political system is looked at with admiration, not anger. We have a shared ambition to clean up Westminster and a determination to oversee a radical redistribution of power away from Westminster and Whitehall to councils, communities and homes across the nation. Wherever possible, we want people to call the shots over the decisions that affect their lives.

And we are both committed to turning old thinking on its head and developing new approaches to government. For years, politicians could argue that because they held all the information, they needed more power. But today, technological innovation has – with astonishing speed – developed the opportunity to spread information and decentralise power in a way we have never seen before. So we will extend transparency to every area of public life. Similarly, there has been the assumption that central government can only change people's behaviour through rules and regulations. Our government will be a much smarter one, shunning the bureaucratic levers of the past and finding intelligent ways to encourage, support and enable people to make better choices for themselves.

In every part of this agreement, we have gone further than simply adopting those policies where we previously overlapped. We have found that a combination of our parties' best ideas and attitudes has produced a programme for government that is more radical and comprehensive than our individual manifestos.

For example, when you take Conservative plans to strengthen families and encourage social responsibility, and add to them the Liberal Democrat passion for protecting our civil liberties and stopping the relentless incursion of the state into the lives of individuals, you create a Big Society matched by big citizens.

This offers the potential to completely recast the relationship between people and the state: citizens empowered; individual opportunity extended; communities coming together to make lives better. We believe that the combination of our ideas will help us to create a much stronger society: one where those who can, do; and those who cannot, we always help.

In the crucial area of public service reform, we have found that Liberal Democrat and Conservative ideas are stronger combined. For example, in the NHS, take Conservative thinking on markets, choice and competition and add to it the Liberal Democrat belief in advancing democracy at a much more local level, and you have a united vision for the NHS that is truly radical: GPs with authority over commissioning; patients with much more control; elections for your local NHS health board. Together, our ideas will bring an emphatic end to the bureaucracy, top-down control and centralisation that has so diminished our NHS.

Three weeks ago we could never have predicted the publication of this document. After the election, of course, there was the option of minority government – but we were uninspired by it. Instead, there was the option of a coalition in the national interest – and we seized it. When we set off on this journey we were two parties with some policies in common and a shared desire to work in the national interest.

We arrive at this programme for government a strong, progressive coalition inspired by the values of freedom, fairness and responsibility. This programme is for five years of partnership government driven by those values. We believe that it can deliver radical, reforming government, a stronger society, a smaller state, and power and responsibility in the hands of every citizen. Great change and real progress lie ahead.

David Cameron, Prime Minister
Nick Clegg, Deputy Prime Minister

1. BANKING

In recent years, we have seen a massive financial meltdown due to over-lending, over-borrowing and poor regulation. The Government believes that the current system of financial regulation is fundamentally flawed and needs to be replaced with a framework that promotes responsible and sustainable banking, where regulators have greater powers to curb unsustainable lending practices and we take action to promote more competition in the banking sector. In addition, we recognise that much more needs to be done to protect taxpayers from financial malpractice and to help the public manage their own debts.

• We will reform the banking system to avoid a repeat of the financial crisis, to promote a competitive economy, to sustain the recovery and to protect and sustain jobs.

• We will introduce a banking levy and seek a detailed agreement on implementation.

• We will bring forward detailed proposals for robust action to tackle unacceptable bonuses in the financial services sector; in developing these proposals, we will ensure they are effective in reducing risk.

• We want the banking system to serve business, not the other way round. We will bring forward detailed proposals to foster diversity in financial services, promote mutuals and create a more competitive banking industry.

• We will develop effective proposals to ensure the flow of credit to viable SMEs. This will include consideration of both a major loan guarantee scheme and the use of net lending targets for the nationalised banks.

• We will take steps to reduce systemic risk in the banking system and will establish an independent commission to investigate the complex issue of separating retail and investment banking in a sustainable way; while recognising that this will take time to get right, the commission will be given an initial time frame of one year to report.

• We will reform the regulatory system to avoid a repeat of the financial crisis. We will bring forward proposals to give the Bank of England control of macro-prudential regulation and oversight of micro-prudential regulation.

• We rule out joining or preparing to join the European Single Currency for the duration of this agreement.

• We will work with the Bank of England to investigate how the process of including housing costs in the CPI measure of inflation can be accelerated.

• We will create Britain's first free national financial advice service, which will be funded in full from a new social responsibility levy on the financial services sector.

• We take white collar crime as seriously as other crime, so we will create a single agency to take on the work of tackling serious economic crime that is currently done by, among others, the Serious Fraud Office, Financial Services Authority and Office of Fair Trading.

2. BUSINESS

The Government believes that business is the driver of economic growth and innovation, and that we need to take urgent action to boost enterprise, support green growth and build a new and more responsible economic model. We want to create a fairer and more balanced economy, where we are not so dependent on a narrow range of economic sectors, and where new businesses and economic opportunities are more evenly shared between regions and industries.

• We will cut red tape by introducing a 'one-in, one-out' rule whereby no new regulation is brought in without other regulation being cut by a greater amount.

• We will end the culture of 'tick-box' regulation, and instead target inspections on high-risk organisations through co-regulation and improving professional standards.

• We will impose 'sunset clauses' on regulations and regulators to ensure that the need for each regulation is regularly reviewed.

• We will review IR 35, as part of a wholesale review of all small business taxation, and seek to replace it with simpler measures that prevent tax avoidance but do not place undue administrative burdens or uncertainty on the self-employed, or restrict labour market flexibility.

• We will find a practical way to make small business rate relief automatic.

• We will reform the corporate tax system by simplifying reliefs and allowances, and tackling avoidance, in order to reduce headline rates. Our aim is to create the most competitive corporate tax regime in the G20, while protecting manufacturing industries.

• We will seek to ensure an injection of private capital into Royal Mail, including opportunities for employee ownership. We will retain Post Office Ltd in public ownership.

• We will seek to ensure a level playing field between small and large retailers by enabling councils to take competition issues into account when drawing up their local plans to shape the direction and type of new retail development.

• We will give the public the opportunity to challenge the worst regulations.

• We will review employment and workplace laws, for employers and employees, to ensure they maximise flexibility for both parties while protecting fairness and providing the competitive environment required for enterprise to thrive.

• We will make it easier for people to set up new enterprises by cutting the time it takes to start a new business. Our ambition is to make the UK one of the fastest countries in the world to start up a new business. We will reduce the number of forms needed to register a new business, and move towards a 'one-click' registration model.

• We will end the ban on social tenants starting businesses in their own homes.

• We will promote small business procurement, in particular by introducing an aspiration that 25% of government contracts should be awarded to small and medium-sized businesses and by publishing government tenders in full online and free of charge.

• We will consider the implementation of the Dyson Review to make the UK the leading hi-tech exporter in Europe, and refocus the research and development tax credit on hi-tech companies, small firms and start-ups.

• We will review the range of factors that can be considered by regulators when takeovers are proposed.

• We will reinstate an Operating and Financial Review to ensure that directors' social and environmental duties have to be covered in company reporting, and investigate further ways of improving corporate accountability and transparency.

• We will ensure that Post Offices are allowed to offer a wide range of services in order to sustain the network, and we will look at the case for developing new sources of revenue, such as the creation of a Post Office Bank.

• We will end the so-called 'gold-plating' of EU rules, so that British businesses are not disadvantaged relative to their European competitors.

• We will support the creation of Local Enterprise Partnerships – joint local authority-business bodies brought forward by local authorities themselves to promote local economic development – to replace Regional Development Agencies (RDAs). These may take the form of the existing RDAs in areas where they are popular.

• We will take steps to improve the competitiveness of the UK tourism industry, recognising the important part it plays in our national economy.

3. CIVIL LIBERTIES

We will be strong in defence of freedom. The Government believes that the British state has become too authoritarian, and that over the past decade it has abused and eroded fundamental human freedoms and historic civil liberties. We need to restore the rights of individuals in the face of encroaching state power, in keeping with Britain's tradition of freedom and fairness.

• We will implement a full programme of measures to reverse the substantial erosion of civil liberties and roll back state intrusion.

• We will introduce a Freedom Bill.

• We will scrap the ID card scheme, the National Identity register and the ContactPoint database, and halt the next generation of biometric passports.

• We will outlaw the finger-printing of children at school without parental permission.

• We will extend the scope of the Freedom of Information Act to provide greater transparency.

• We will adopt the protections of the Scottish model for the DNA database.

- We will protect historic freedoms through the defence of trial by jury.
- We will restore rights to non-violent protest.
- We will review libel laws to protect freedom of speech.
- We will introduce safeguards against the misuse of anti-terrorism legislation.
- We will further regulate CCTV.
- We will end the storage of internet and email records without good reason.
- We will introduce a new mechanism to prevent the proliferation of unnecessary new criminal offences.
- We will establish a Commission to investigate the creation of a British Bill of Rights that incorporates and builds on all our obligations under the European Convention on Human Rights, ensures that these rights continue to be enshrined in British law, and protects and extends British liberties. We will seek to promote a better understanding of the true scope of these obligations and liberties.

4. COMMUNITIES AND LOCAL GOVERNMENT

The Government believes that it is time for a fundamental shift of power from Westminster to people. We will promote decentralisation and democratic engagement, and we will end the era of top-down government by giving new powers to local councils, communities, neighbourhoods and individuals.

- We will promote the radical devolution of power and greater financial autonomy to local government and community groups. This will include a review of local government finance.
- We will rapidly abolish Regional Spatial Strategies and return decision-making powers on housing and planning to local councils, including giving councils new powers to stop 'garden grabbing'.
- In the longer term, we will radically reform the planning system to give neighbourhoods far more ability to determine the shape of the places in which their inhabitants live, based on the principles set out in the Conservative Party publication Open Source Planning.
- We will abolish the unelected Infrastructure Planning Commission and replace it with an efficient and democratically accountable system that provides a fast-track process for major infrastructure projects.
- We will publish and present to Parliament a simple and consolidated national planning framework covering all forms of development and setting out national economic, environmental and social priorities.
- We will maintain the Green Belt, Sites of Special Scientific Interest (SSSIs) and other environmental protections, and create a new designation – similar to SSSIs – to protect green areas of particular importance to local communities.
- We will abolish the Government Office for London and consider the case for abolishing the remaining Government Offices.
- We will provide more protection against aggressive bailiffs and unreasonable charging orders, ensure that courts have the power to insist that repossession is always a last resort, and ban orders for sale on unsecured debts of less than £25,000.
- We will explore a range of measures to bring empty homes into use.
- We will promote shared ownership schemes and help social tenants and others to own or part-own their home.
- We will promote 'Home on the Farm' schemes that encourage farmers to convert existing buildings into affordable housing.
- We will create new trusts that will make it simpler for communities to provide homes for local people.
- We will phase out the ring-fencing of grants to local government and review the unfair Housing Revenue Account.
- We will freeze Council Tax in England for at least one year, and seek to freeze it for a further year, in partnership with local authorities.

- We will create directly elected mayors in the 12 largest English cities, subject to confirmatory referendums and full scrutiny by elected councillors.
- We will give councils a general power of competence.
- We will ban the use of powers in the Regulation of Investigatory Powers Act (RIPA) by councils, unless they are signed off by a magistrate and required for stopping serious crime.
- We will allow councils to return to the committee system, should they wish to.
- We will abolish the Standards Board regime.
- We will stop the restructuring of councils in Norfolk, Suffolk and Devon, and stop plans to force the regionalisation of the fire service.
- We will impose tougher rules to stop unfair competition by local authority newspapers.
- We will introduce new powers to help communities save local facilities and services threatened with closure, and give communities the right to bid to take over local state-run services.
- We will implement the Sustainable Communities Act, so that citizens know how taxpayers' money is spent in their area and have a greater say over how it is spent.
- We will cut local government inspection and abolish the Comprehensive Area Assessment.
- We will require continuous improvements to the energy efficiency of new housing.
- We will provide incentives for local authorities to deliver sustainable development, including for new homes and businesses.
- We will review the effectiveness of the raising of the stamp duty threshold for first-time buyers.
- We will give councillors the power to vote on large salary packages for unelected council officials.

5. CONSUMER PROTECTION

The Government believes that action is needed to protect consumers, particularly the most vulnerable, and to promote greater competition across the economy. We need to promote more responsible corporate and consumer behaviour through greater transparency and by harnessing the insights from behavioural economics and social psychology.

- We will give regulators new powers to define and ban excessive interest rates on credit and store cards; and we will introduce a seven-day cooling-off period for store cards.
- We will oblige credit card companies to provide better information to their customers in a uniform electronic format that will allow consumers to find out whether they are receiving the best deal.
- We will introduce stronger consumer protections, including measures to end unfair bank and financial transaction charges.
- We will take forward measures to enhance customer service in the private and public sectors.
- We will introduce, as a first step, an Ombudsman in the Office of Fair Trading who can proactively enforce the Grocery Supply Code of Practice and curb abuses of power, which undermine our farmers and act against the long-term interest of consumers.
- We will introduce honesty in food labelling so that consumers can be confident about where their food comes from and its environmental impact.
- We will increase households' control over their energy costs by ensuring that energy bills provide information on how to move to the cheapest tariff offered by their supplier, and how each household's energy usage compares to similar households.
- We will give Post Office Card account holders the chance to benefit from direct debit discounts and ensure that social tariffs offer access to the best prices available.
- We will seek to extend protection and support to 'off-grid' energy consumers.

6. CRIME AND POLICING

The Government believes that we need radical action to reform our criminal justice system. We need police forces that have greater freedom from Ministerial control and are better able to deal with the crime and anti-social behaviour that blights people's lives, but which are much more accountable to the public they serve.

• We will reduce time-wasting bureaucracy that hampers police operations, and introduce better technology to make policing more effective while saving taxpayers' money.

• We will amend the health and safety laws that stand in the way of common sense policing.

• We will seek to spread information on which policing techniques and sentences are most effective at cutting crime across the Criminal Justice System.

• We will have a full review of the terms and conditions for police officer employment.

• We will introduce measures to make the police more accountable through oversight by a directly elected individual, who will be subject to strict checks and balances by locally elected representatives.

• We will oblige the police to publish detailed local crime data statistics every month, so the public can get proper information about crime in their neighbourhoods and hold the police to account for their performance.

• We will require police forces to hold regular 'beat meetings' so that residents can hold them to account.

• We will make hospitals share non-confidential information with the police so they know where gun and knife crime is happening and can target stop-and-search in gun and knife crime hot spots.

• We will give people greater legal protection to prevent crime and apprehend criminals.

• We will ensure that people have the protection that they need when they defend themselves against intruders.

• We will ban the sale of alcohol below cost price.

• We will review alcohol taxation and pricing to ensure it tackles binge drinking without unfairly penalising responsible drinkers, pubs and important local industries.

• We will overhaul the Licensing Act to give local authorities and the police much stronger powers to remove licences from, or refuse to grant licences to, any premises that are causing problems.

• We will allow councils and the police to shut down permanently any shop or bar found to be persistently selling alcohol to children.

• We will double the maximum fine for under-age alcohol sales to £20,000.

• We will permit local councils to charge more for late-night licences to pay for additional policing.

• We will promote better recording of hate crimes against disabled, homosexual and transgender people, which are frequently not centrally recorded.

• We will introduce a system of temporary bans on new 'legal highs' while health issues are considered by independent experts. We will not permanently ban a substance without receiving full advice from the Advisory Council on the Misuse of Drugs.

• We will review the operation of the Extradition Act – and the US/UK extradition treaty – to make sure it is even-handed.

7. CULTURE, OLYMPICS, MEDIA AND SPORT

The Government believes that a vibrant cultural, media and sporting sector is crucial for our well-being and quality of life. We need to promote excellence in these fields, with government funding used where appropriate to encourage philanthropic and corporate investment.

• We will maintain the independence of the BBC, and give the National Audit Office full access to the BBC's accounts to ensure transparency.

• We will enable partnerships between local newspapers, radio and television stations to promote a strong and diverse local media industry.

• We will maintain free entry to national museums and galleries, and give national museums greater freedoms.

• We will work with the Scottish Government to deliver a successful Commonwealth Games in Glasgow in 2014, and ensure that the 2013 Rugby League and the 2015 Rugby Union World Cups are successful. We will strongly support the England 2018 World Cup bid.

• We will work with the Mayor of London to ensure a safe and successful Olympic and Paralympic Games in London in 2012, and urgently form plans to deliver a genuine and lasting legacy.

• We will examine the case for moving to a 'gross profits tax' system for the National Lottery, and reform the National Lottery so that more money goes into sport, the arts and heritage.

• We will stop wasteful spending by National Lottery distributors by banning lobbying activities and restricting administration costs to 5% of total income.

• We will use cash in dormant betting accounts to improve local sports facilities and support sports clubs.

• We will encourage the reform of football governance rules to support the co-operative ownership of football clubs by supporters.

• We will support the creation of an annual Olympic-style schools sport event to encourage competitive sport in schools, and we will seek to protect school playing fields.

• We will cut red tape to encourage the performance of more live music.

• We will introduce measures to ensure the rapid roll-out of superfast broadband across the country. We will ensure that BT and other infrastructure providers allow the use of their assets to deliver such broadband, and we will seek to introduce superfast broadband in remote areas at the same time as in more populated areas. If necessary, we will consider using the part of the TV licence fee that is supporting the digital switchover to fund broadband in areas that the market alone will not reach.

8. DEFENCE

The Government believes that we need to take action to safeguard our national security at home and abroad. We also recognise that we need to do much more to ensure that our Armed Forces have the support they need, and that veterans and their families are treated with the dignity that they deserve.

• We will maintain Britain's nuclear deterrent, and have agreed that the renewal of Trident should be scrutinised to ensure value for money. Liberal Democrats will continue to make the case for alternatives. We will immediately play a strong role in the Nuclear Non-Proliferation Treaty Review Conference, and press for continued progress on multilateral disarmament.

• We will aim to reduce Ministry of Defence running costs by at least 25%.

• We will work to rebuild the Military Covenant by:

– ensuring that Service personnel's rest and recuperation leave can be maximised;

– changing the rules so that Service personnel only have to register once on the Service register;

– exploring the potential for including Service children as part of our proposals for a pupil premium;

– providing university and further education scholarships for the children of Servicemen and women who have been killed on active duty since 1990;

– providing support for ex-Service personnel to study at university;

– creating a new programme, 'Troops for Teachers', to recruit ex-Service personnel into the teaching profession;

– providing extra support for veteran mental health needs; and

– reviewing the rules governing the awarding of medals.

• We will double the operational allowance for Armed

Forces personnel serving in Afghanistan, and include Armed Forces pay in our plans for a fair pay review.

• We will ensure that injured personnel are treated in dedicated military wards.

• We will look at whether there is scope to refurbish Armed Forces' accommodation from efficiencies within the Ministry of Defence.

• We will support defence jobs through exports that are used for legitimate purposes, not internal repression, and will work for a full international ban on cluster munitions.

9. DEFICIT REDUCTION

The Government believes that it is the most vulnerable who are most at risk from the debt crisis, and that it is deeply unfair that the Government could have to spend more on debt interest payments than on schools. So we need immediate action to tackle the deficit in a fair and responsible way, ensure that taxpayers' money is spent responsibly, and get the public finances back on track.

• We recognise that deficit reduction, and continuing to ensure economic recovery, is the most urgent issue facing Britain.

• We will significantly accelerate the reduction of the structural deficit over the course of a Parliament, with the main burden of deficit reduction borne by reduced spending rather than increased taxes.

• We will introduce arrangements that will protect those on low incomes from the effect of public sector pay constraint and other spending constraints.

• We will protect jobs by stopping the proposed jobs tax.

• We will set out a plan for deficit reduction in an emergency budget. We have created an independent Office for Budget Responsibility to make new forecasts of growth and borrowing for this emergency budget.

• We will make modest cuts of £6 billion to non-front-line services within the financial year 2010/11, subject to advice from the Treasury and the Bank of England on their feasibility and advisability. A proportion of these savings can be used to support jobs.

• We will hold a full Spending Review reporting this autumn, following a fully consultative process involving all tiers of government and the private sector.

• We will reduce spending on the Child Trust Fund and tax credits for higher earners.

• We will create strong financial discipline at all levels of government and place an obligation on public servants to manage taxpayers' money wisely.

• We will reduce the number and cost of quangos.

10. ENERGY AND CLIMATE CHANGE

The Government believes that climate change is one of the gravest threats we face, and that urgent action at home and abroad is required. We need to use a wide range of levers to cut carbon emissions, decarbonise the economy and support the creation of new green jobs and technologies. We will implement a full programme of measures to fulfil our joint ambitions for a low carbon and eco-friendly economy.

• We will push for the EU to demonstrate leadership in tackling international climate change, including by supporting an increase in the EU emission reduction target to 30% by 2020.

• We will seek to increase the target for energy from renewable sources, subject to the advice of the Climate Change Committee.

• We will continue public sector investment in carbon capture and storage (CCS) technology for four coal-fired power stations.

• We will establish a smart grid and roll out smart meters.

• We will establish a full system of feed-in tariffs in electricity – as well as the maintenance of banded Renewables Obligation Certificates.

• We will introduce measures to promote a huge increase in energy from waste through anaerobic digestion.

• We will create a green investment bank.

• We will retain energy performance certificates while scrapping HIPs.

• We will introduce measures to encourage marine energy.

• We will establish an emissions performance standard that will prevent coal-fired power stations being built unless they are equipped with sufficient carbon capture and storage to meet the emissions performance standard.

• We will cancel the third runway at Heathrow.

• We will refuse permission for additional runways at Gatwick and Stansted.

• We will replace Air Passenger Duty with a per-flight duty.

• We will introduce a floor price for carbon, and make efforts to persuade the EU to move towards full auctioning of ETS permits.

• Through our 'Green Deal', we will encourage home energy efficiency improvements paid for by savings from energy bills. We will also take measures to improve energy efficiency in businesses and public sector buildings. We will reduce central government carbon emissions by 10% within 12 months.

• We will reform energy markets to deliver security of supply and investment in low carbon energy, and ensure fair competition including a review of the role of Ofgem.

• We will instruct Ofgem to establish a security guarantee of energy supplies.

• We will give an Annual Energy Statement to Parliament to set strategic energy policy and guide investment.

• We will deliver an offshore electricity grid in order to support the development of a new generation of offshore wind power.

• We will encourage community-owned renewable energy schemes where local people benefit from the power produced. We will also allow communities that host renewable energy projects to keep the additional business rates they generate.

• As part of the creation of a green investment bank, we will create green financial products to provide individuals with opportunities to invest in the infrastructure needed to support the new green economy.

• We will work towards an ambitious global climate deal that will limit emissions and explore the creation of new international sources of funding for the purpose of climate change adaptation and mitigation.

• Liberal Democrats have long opposed any new nuclear construction. Conservatives, by contrast, are committed to allowing the replacement of existing nuclear power stations provided that they are subject to the normal planning process for major projects (under a new National Planning Statement), and also provided that they receive no public subsidy.

• We will implement a process allowing the Liberal Democrats to maintain their opposition to nuclear power while permitting the Government to bring forward the National Planning Statement for ratification by Parliament so that new nuclear construction becomes possible. This process will involve:

– the Government completing the drafting of a national planning statement and putting it before Parliament;

– specific agreement that a Liberal Democrat spokesperson will speak against the Planning Statement, but that Liberal Democrat MPs will abstain; and

– clarity that this will not be regarded as an issue of confidence.

11. ENVIRONMENT, FOOD AND RURAL AFFAIRS

The Government believes that we need to protect the environment for future generations, make our economy more environmentally sustainable, and improve our quality of life and well-being. We also believe that much more needs to be done to support the farming industry, protect biodiversity and encourage sustainable food production.

- We will introduce measures to make the import or possession of illegal timber a criminal offence.
- We will introduce measures to protect wildlife and promote green spaces and wildlife corridors in order to halt the loss of habitats and restore biodiversity.
- We will launch a national tree planting campaign.
- We will review the governance arrangements of National Parks in order to increase local accountability.
- We will work towards full compliance with European Air Quality standards.
- We will take forward the findings of the Pitt Review to improve our flood defences, and prevent unnecessary building in areas of high flood risk.
- We will examine the conclusions of the Cave and Walker Reviews, and reform the water industry to ensure more efficient use of water and the protection of poorer households.
- We will work towards a 'zero waste' economy, encourage councils to pay people to recycle, and reduce littering.
- We will reduce the regulatory burden on farmers by moving to a risk-based system of regulation, and will develop a system of extra support for hill farmers.
- We will investigate ways to share with livestock keepers the responsibility for preparing for and dealing with outbreaks of disease.
- We will take forward the Marine and Coastal Access Act and ensure that its conservation measures are implemented.
- As part of a package of measures, we will introduce a carefully managed and science-led policy of badger control in areas with high and persistent levels of bovine tuberculosis.
- We will promote high standards of farm animal welfare. We will end the testing of household products on animals and work to reduce the use of animals in scientific research. We will promote responsible pet ownership by introducing effective codes of practice under the Animal Welfare Act, and will ensure that enforcement agencies target irresponsible owners of dangerous dogs.
- We will ensure that food procured by government departments, and eventually the whole public sector, meets British standards of production wherever this can be achieved without increasing overall cost.
- We will investigate measures to help with fuel costs in remote rural areas, starting with pilot schemes.
- We will create a presumption in favour of sustainable development in the planning system.
- We oppose the resumption of commercial whaling, will press for a ban on ivory sales, and will tackle the smuggling and illegal trade on wildlife through a Border Police Force.
- We will bring forward a motion on a free vote enabling the House of Commons to express its view on the repeal of the Hunting Act.

12. EQUALITIES

The Government believes that there are many barriers to social mobility and equal opportunities in Britain today, with too many children held back because of their social background, and too many people of all ages held back because of their gender, race, religion or sexuality. We need concerted government action to tear down these barriers and help to build a fairer society.

- We will promote equal pay and take a range of measures to end discrimination in the workplace.
- We will extend the right to request flexible working to all employees, consulting with business on how best to do so.
- We will undertake a fair pay review in the public sector to implement our proposed '20 times' pay multiple.
- We will look to promote gender equality on the boards of listed companies.
- We will promote improved community relations and opportunities for Black, Asian and Minority Ethnic (BAME) communities, including by providing internships for underrepresented minorities in every Whitehall department and funding a targeted national enterprise mentoring scheme for BAME people who want to start a business.
- We will stop the deportation of asylum seekers who have

had to leave particular countries because their sexual orientation or gender identification puts them at proven risk of imprisonment, torture or execution.
- We will use our relationships with other countries to push for unequivocal support for gay rights and for UK civil partnerships to be recognised internationally.

13. EUROPE

The Government believes that Britain should play a leading role in an enlarged European Union, but that no further powers should be transferred to Brussels without a referendum. This approach strikes the right balance between constructive engagement with the EU to deal with the issues that affect us all, and protecting our national sovereignty.

- We will ensure that the British Government is a positive participant in the European Union, playing a strong and positive role with our partners, with the goal of ensuring that all the nations of Europe are equipped to face the challenges of the 21st century: global competitiveness, global warming and global poverty.
- We will ensure that there is no further transfer of sovereignty or powers over the course of the next Parliament. We will examine the balance of the EU's existing competences and will, in particular, work to limit the application of the Working Time Directive in the United Kingdom.
- We will amend the 1972 European Communities Act so that any proposed future treaty that transferred areas of power, or competences, would be subject to a referendum on that treaty – a 'referendum lock'. We will amend the 1972 European Communities Act so that the use of any passerelle would require primary legislation.
- We will examine the case for a United Kingdom Sovereignty Bill to make it clear that ultimate authority remains with Parliament.
- We will ensure that Britain does not join or prepare to join the Euro in this Parliament.
- We will strongly defend the UK's national interests in the forthcoming EU budget negotiations and agree that the EU budget should only focus on those areas where the EU can add value.
- We will press for the European Parliament to have only one seat, in Brussels.
- We will approach forthcoming legislation in the area of criminal justice on a case-by-case basis, with a view to maximising our country's security, protecting Britain's civil liberties and preserving the integrity of our criminal justice system. Britain will not participate in the establishment of any European Public Prosecutor.
- We support the further enlargement of the EU.

14. FAMILIES AND CHILDREN

The Government believes that strong and stable families of all kinds are the bedrock of a strong and stable society. That is why we need to make our society more family friendly, and to take action to protect children from excessive commercialisation and premature sexualisation.

- We will maintain the goal of ending child poverty in the UK by 2020.
- We will reform the administration of tax credits to reduce fraud and overpayments.
- We will bring forward plans to reduce the couple penalty in the tax credit system as we make savings from our welfare reform plans.
- We support the provision of free nursery care for preschool children, and we want that support to be provided by a diverse range of providers, with a greater gender balance in the early years workforce.
- We will take Sure Start back to its original purpose of early intervention, increase its focus on the neediest families, and better involve organisations with a track record of supporting families. We will investigate ways of ensuring that providers are paid in part by the results they achieve.
- We will refocus funding from Sure Start peripatetic out-

reach services, and from the Department of Health budget, to pay for 4,200 extra Sure Start health visitors.
• We will investigate a new approach to helping families with multiple problems.
• We will publish serious case reviews, with identifying details removed.
• We will review the criminal records and vetting and barring regime and scale it back to common sense levels.
• We will crack down on irresponsible advertising and marketing, especially to children. We will also take steps to tackle the commercialisation and sexualisation of childhood.
• We will encourage shared parenting from the earliest stages of pregnancy – including the promotion of a system of flexible parental leave.
• We will put funding for relationship support on a stable, long-term footing, and make sure that couples are given greater encouragement to use existing relationship support.
• We will conduct a comprehensive review of family law in order to increase the use of mediation when couples do break up, and to look at how best to provide greater access rights to non-resident parents and grandparents.

15. FOREIGN AFFAIRS

The Government believes that Britain must always be an active member of the global community, promoting our national interests while standing up for the values of freedom, fairness and responsibility. This means working as a constructive member of the United Nations, NATO and other multilateral organisations including the Commonwealth; working to promote stability and security; and pushing for reform of global institutions to ensure that they reflect the modern world.
• We will take forward our shared resolve to safeguard the UK's national security and support our Armed Forces in Afghanistan and elsewhere.
• We will push for peace in the Middle East, with a secure and universally recognised Israel living alongside a sovereign and viable Palestinian state.
• We will work to establish a new 'special relationship' with India and seek closer engagement with China, while standing firm on human rights in all our bilateral relationships.
• We will maintain a strong, close and frank relationship with the United States.
• We want to strengthen the Commonwealth as a focus for promoting democratic values and development.
• We will work to promote stability in the Western Balkans.
• We will support concerted international efforts to prevent Iran from obtaining a nuclear weapon.
• We support reform of the UN Security Council, including permanent seats for Japan, India, Germany, Brazil and African representation.
• We will work to intensify our cultural, educational, commercial and diplomatic links with many nations beyond Europe and North America to strengthen the UK's relations with the fastest-growing areas of the world economy.
• We will never condone the use of torture.

16. GOVERNMENT TRANSPARENCY

The Government believes that we need to throw open the doors of public bodies, to enable the public to hold politicians and public bodies to account. We also recognise that this will help to deliver better value for money in public spending, and help us achieve our aim of cutting the record deficit. Setting government data free will bring significant economic benefits by enabling businesses and non-profit organisations to build innovative applications and websites.
• We will require public bodies to publish online the job titles of every member of staff and the salaries and expenses of senior officials paid more than the lowest salary permissible in Pay Band 1 of the Senior Civil Service pay scale, and organograms that include all positions in those bodies.

• We will require anyone paid more than the Prime Minister in the centrally funded public sector to have their salary signed off by the Treasury.
• We will regulate lobbying through introducing a statutory register of lobbyists and ensuring greater transparency.
• We will also pursue a detailed agreement on limiting donations and reforming party funding in order to remove big money from politics.
• We will strengthen the powers of Select Committees to scrutinise major public appointments.
• We will introduce new protections for whistleblowers in the public sector.
• We will take steps to open up government procurement and reduce costs; and we will publish government ICT contracts online.
• We will create a level playing field for opensource software and will enable large ICT projects to be split into smaller components.
• We will require full, online disclosure of all central government spending and contracts over £25,000.
• We will create a new 'right to data' so that government-held datasets can be requested and used by the public, and then published on a regular basis.
• We will require all councils to publish meeting minutes and local service and performance data.
• We will require all councils to publish items of spending above £500, and to publish contracts and tender documents in full.
• We will ensure that all data published by public bodies is published in an open and standardised format, so that it can be used easily and with minimal cost by third parties.

17. IMMIGRATION

The Government believes that immigration has enriched our culture and strengthened our economy, but that it must be controlled so that people have confidence in the system. We also recognise that to ensure cohesion and protect our public services, we need to introduce a cap on immigration and reduce the number of non-EU immigrants.
• We will introduce an annual limit on the number of non-EU economic migrants admitted into the UK to live and work. We will consider jointly the mechanism for implementing the limit.
• We will end the detention of children for immigration purposes.
• We will create a dedicated Border Police Force, as part of a refocused Serious Organised Crime Agency, to enhance national security, improve immigration controls and crack down on the trafficking of people, weapons and drugs. We will work with police forces to strengthen arrangements to deal with serious crime and other cross-boundary policing challenges, and extend collaboration between forces to deliver better value for money.
• We support E-borders and will reintroduce exit checks.
• We will apply transitional controls as a matter of course in the future for all new EU Member States.
• We will introduce new measures to minimise abuse of the immigration system, for example via student routes, and will tackle human trafficking as a priority.
• We will explore new ways to improve the current asylum system to speed up the processing of applications.

18. INTERNATIONAL DEVELOPMENT

The Government believes that even in these difficult economic times, the UK has a moral responsibility to help the poorest people in the world. We will honour our aid commitments, but at the same time will ensure much greater transparency and scrutiny of aid spending to deliver value for money for British taxpayers and to maximise the impact of our aid budget.
• We will honour our commitment to spend 0.7% of GNI on overseas aid from 2013, and to enshrine this commitment in law.

- We will encourage other countries to fulfil their aid commitments.
- We will support actions to achieve the Millennium Development Goals. In particular, we will prioritise aid spending on programmes to ensure that everyone has access to clean water, sanitation, healthcare and education; to reduce maternal and infant mortality; and to restrict the spread of major diseases like HIV/ AIDS, TB and malaria. We will recognise the vital role of women in development, promote gender equality and focus on the rights of women, children and disabled people to access services.
- We will use the aid budget to support the development of local democratic institutions, civil society groups, the media and enterprise; and support efforts to tackle corruption.
- We will introduce full transparency in aid and publish details of all UK aid spending online. We will push for similarly high levels of transparency internationally.
- We will create new mechanisms to give British people a direct say in how an element of the aid budget is spent.
- We will keep aid untied from commercial interests, and will maintain DfID as an independent department focused on poverty reduction.
- We will stick to the rules laid down by the OECD about what spending counts as aid.
- We will push hard in 2010 to make greater progress in tackling maternal and infant mortality.
- We will work to accelerate the process of relieving Heavily Indebted Poor Countries of their debt.
- We will support efforts to establish an International Arms Trade Treaty to limit the sale of arms to dangerous regimes.
- We will support pro-development trade deals, including the proposed Pan-African Free Trade Area.
- We will support innovative and effective smaller British non-governmental organisations that are committed to tackling poverty.
- We will explore ways of helping the very poorest developing countries to take part in international climate change negotiations.
- We will ensure that UK Trade and Investment and the Export Credits Guarantee Department become champions for British companies that develop and export innovative green technologies around the world, instead of supporting investment in dirty fossil-fuel energy production.
- We will provide a more integrated approach to post-conflict reconstruction where the British military is involved – building on the Stabilisation Unit in Whitehall and creating a new Stabilisation and Reconstruction Force to bridge the gap between the military and the reconstruction effort.
- We will review what action can be taken against 'vulture funds'.
- We will support reform of global financial institutions such as the World Bank and the International Monetary Fund to increase the involvement of developing nations.

19. JOBS AND WELFARE

The Government believes that we need to encourage responsibility and fairness in the welfare system. That means providing help for those who cannot work, training and targeted support for those looking for work, but sanctions for those who turn down reasonable offers of work or training.

- We will end all existing welfare to work programmes and create a single welfare to work programme to help all unemployed people get back into work.
- We will ensure that Jobseeker's Allowance claimants facing the most significant barriers to work are referred to the new welfare to work programme immediately, not after 12 months as is currently the case. We will ensure that Jobseeker's Allowance claimants aged under 25 are referred to the programme after a maximum of six months.
- We will realign contracts with welfare to work service providers to reflect more closely the results they achieve in getting people back into work.

- We will reform the funding mechanism used by government to finance welfare to work programmes to reflect the fact that initial investment delivers later savings through lower benefit expenditure, including creating an integrated work programme with outcome funding based upon the DEL/AME switch.
- We will ensure that receipt of benefits for those able to work is conditional on their willingness to work.
- We support the National Minimum Wage because of the protection it gives lowincome workers and the incentives to work it provides.
- We will re-assess all current claimants of Incapacity Benefit for their readiness to work. Those assessed as fully capable for work will be moved onto Jobseeker's Allowance.
- We will support would-be entrepreneurs through a new programme – Work for Yourself – which will give the unemployed access to business mentors and start-up loans.
- We will draw on a range of Service Academies to offer pre-employment training and work placements for unemployed people.
- We will develop local Work Clubs – places where unemployed people can gather to exchange skills, find opportunities, make contacts and provide mutual support.
- We will investigate how to simplify the benefit system in order to improve incentives to work.

20. JUSTICE

The Government believes that more needs to be done to ensure fairness in the justice system. This means introducing more effective sentencing policies, as well as overhauling the system of rehabilitation to reduce reoffending and provide greater support and protection for the victims of crime.

- We will introduce a 'rehabilitation revolution' that will pay independent providers to reduce reoffending, paid for by the savings this will generate in the criminal justice system.
- We will conduct a full review of sentencing policy to ensure that it is effective in deterring crime, protecting the public, punishing offenders and cutting reoffending. In particular, we will ensure that sentencing for drug use helps offenders come off drugs.
- We will explore alternative forms of secure, treatment-based accommodation for mentally ill and drugs offenders.
- We will implement the Prisoners' Earnings Act 1996 to allow deductions from the earnings of prisoners in properly paid work to be paid into the Victims' Fund.
- We will consider how to use proceeds from the Victim Surcharge to deliver up to 15 new rape crisis centres, and give existing rape crisis centres stable, long-term funding.
- We will carry out a fundamental review of Legal Aid to make it work more efficiently.
- We will change the law so that historical convictions for consensual gay sex with over-16s will be treated as spent and will not show up on criminal records checks.
- We will extend anonymity in rape cases to defendants.
- We will introduce effective measures to tackle anti-social behaviour and low-level crime, including forms of restorative justice such as Neighbourhood Justice Panels.

21. NATIONAL SECURITY

The Government believes that its primary responsibility is to ensure national security. We need a coherent approach to national security across government, and we will take action to tackle terrorism and its causes at home and abroad.

- We have established a National Security Council and appointed a National Security Adviser.
- We have commenced a Strategic Defence and Security Review, commissioned and overseen by the National Security Council, with strong Treasury involvement. We will also develop and publish a new National Security Strategy.
- We will urgently review Control Orders, as part of a wider review of counter-terrorist legislation, measures and programmes. We will seek to find a practical way to allow the use of intercept evidence in court.

• We will deny public funds to any group that has recently espoused or incited violence or hatred. We will proscribe such organisations, subject to the advice of the police and security and intelligence agencies.

• We believe that Britain should be able to deport foreign nationals who threaten our security to countries where there are verifiable guarantees that they will not be tortured. We will seek to extend these guarantees to more countries.

22. NHS

The Government believes that the NHS is an important expression of our national values. We are committed to an NHS that is free at the point of use and available to everyone based on need, not the ability to pay. We want to free NHS staff from political micromanagement, increase democratic participation in the NHS and make the NHS more accountable to the patients that it serves. That way we will drive up standards, support professional responsibility, deliver better value for money and create a healthier nation.

• We will guarantee that health spending increases in real terms in each year of the Parliament, while recognising the impact this decision will have on other departments.

• We will stop the top-down reorganisations of the NHS that have got in the way of patient care. We are committed to reducing duplication and the resources spent on administration, and diverting these resources back to front-line care.

• We will significantly cut the number of health quangos.

• We will cut the cost of NHS administration by a third and transfer resources to support doctors and nurses on the front line.

• We will stop the centrally dictated closure of A&E and maternity wards, so that people have better access to services.

• We will strengthen the power of GPs as patients' expert guides through the health system by enabling them to commission care on their behalf.

• We will ensure that there is a stronger voice for patients locally through directly elected individuals on the boards of their local primary care trust (PCT). The remainder of the PCT's board will be appointed by the relevant local authority or authorities, and the Chief Executive and principal officers will be appointed by the Secretary of State on the advice of the new independent NHS board. This will ensure the right balance between locally accountable individuals and technical expertise.

• The local PCT will act as a champion for patients and commission those residual services that are best undertaken at a wider level, rather than directly by GPs. It will also take responsibility for improving public health for people in their area, working closely with the local authority and other local organisations.

• If a local authority has concerns about a significant proposed closure of local services, for example an A&E department, it will have the right to challenge health organisations, and refer the case to the Independent Reconfiguration Panel. The Panel would then provide advice to the Secretary of State for Health.

• We will give patients the right to choose to register with the GP they want, without being restricted by where they live.

• We will develop a 24/7 urgent care service in every area of England, including GP out-of-hours services, and ensure every patient can access a local GP. We will make care more accessible by introducing a single number for every kind of urgent care and by using technology to help people communicate with their doctors.

• We will renegotiate the GP contract and incentivise ways of improving access to primary care in disadvantaged areas.

• We will make the NHS work better by extending best practice on improving discharge from hospital, maximising the number of day care operations, reducing delays prior to operations, and where possible enabling community access to care and treatments.

• We will help elderly people live at home for longer through solutions such as home adaptations and community support programmes.

• We will prioritise dementia research within the health research and development budget.

• We will seek to stop foreign healthcare professionals working in the NHS unless they have passed robust language and competence tests.

• Doctors and nurses need to be able to use their professional judgement about what is right for patients and we will support this by giving front-line staff more control of their working environment.

• We will strengthen the role of the Care Quality Commission so it becomes an effective quality inspectorate. We will develop Monitor into an economic regulator that will oversee access, competition and price-setting in the NHS.

• We will establish an independent NHS board to allocate resources and provide commissioning guidelines.

• We will enable patients to rate hospitals and doctors according to the quality of care they received, and we will require hospitals to be open about mistakes and always tell patients if something has gone wrong.

• We will measure our success on the health results that really matter – such as improving cancer and stroke survival rates or reducing hospital infections.

• We will publish detailed data about the performance of healthcare providers online, so everyone will know who is providing a good service and who is falling behind.

• We will put patients in charge of making decisions about their care, including control of their health records.

• We will create a Cancer Drugs Fund to enable patients to access the cancer drugs their doctors think will help them, paid for using money saved by the NHS through our pledge to stop the rise in Employer National Insurance contributions from April 2011.

• We will reform NICE and move to a system of value-based pricing, so that all patients can access the drugs and treatments their doctors think they need.

• We will introduce a new dentistry contract that will focus on achieving good dental health and increasing access to NHS dentistry, with an additional focus on the oral health of schoolchildren.

• We will provide £10 million a year beyond 2011 from the budget of the Department of Health to support children's hospices in their vital work. And so that proper support for the most sick children and adults can continue in the setting of their choice, we will introduce a new per-patient funding system for all hospices and providers of palliative care.

• We will encourage NHS organisations to work better with their local police forces to clamp down on anyone who is aggressive and abusive to staff.

• We are committed to the continuous improvement of the quality of services to patients, and to achieving this through much greater involvement of independent and voluntary providers.

• We will give every patient the power to choose any healthcare provider that meets NHS standards, within NHS prices. This includes independent, voluntary and community sector providers.

23. PENSIONS AND OLDER PEOPLE

The Government believes that people deserve dignity and respect in old age, and that they should be provided with the support they need. That means safeguarding key benefits and pensions, and taking action to make it easier for older people to work or volunteer.

• We will restore the earnings link for the basic state pension from April 2011, with a 'triple guarantee' that pensions are raised by the higher of earnings, prices or 2.5%.

• We will commit to establishing an independent commission to review the long-term affordability of public sector pensions, while protecting accrued rights.

• We will phase out the default retirement age and hold a review to set the date at which the state pension age starts to rise to 66, although it will not be sooner than 2016 for men and 2020 for women. We will end the rules requiring compulsory annuitisation at 75.

- We will implement the Parliamentary and Health Ombudsman's recommendation to make fair and transparent payments to Equitable Life policy holders, through an independent payment scheme, for their relative loss as a consequence of regulatory failure.
- We will explore the potential to give people greater flexibility in accessing part of their personal pension fund early.
- We will protect key benefits for older people such as the winter fuel allowance, free TV licences, free bus travel, and free eye tests and prescriptions.
- We will simplify the rules and regulations relating to pensions to help reinvigorate occupational pensions, encouraging companies to offer high-quality pensions to all employees, and we will work with business and the industry to support auto enrolment.

24. POLITICAL REFORM

The Government believes that our political system is broken. We urgently need fundamental political reform, including a referendum on electoral reform, much greater co-operation across party lines, and changes to our political system to make it far more transparent and accountable.
- We will establish five-year fixed-term Parliaments. We will put a binding motion before the House of Commons stating that the next general election will be held on the first Thursday of May 2015. Following this motion, we will legislate to make provision for fixed-term Parliaments of five years. This legislation will also provide for dissolution if 55% or more of the House votes in favour.
- We will bring forward a Referendum Bill on electoral reform, which includes provision for the introduction of the Alternative Vote in the event of a positive result in the referendum, as well as for the creation of fewer and more equal sized constituencies. We will whip both Parliamentary parties in both Houses to support a simple majority referendum on the Alternative Vote, without prejudice to the positions parties will take during such a referendum.
- We will bring forward early legislation to introduce a power of recall, allowing voters to force a by-election where an MP is found to have engaged in serious wrongdoing and having had a petition calling for a by-election signed by 10% of his or her constituents.
- We will establish a committee to bring forward proposals for a wholly or mainly elected upper chamber on the basis of proportional representation. The committee will come forward with a draft motion by December 2010. It is likely that this will advocate single long terms of office. It is also likely that there will be a grandfathering system for current Peers. In the interim, Lords appointments will be made with the objective of creating a second chamber that is reflective of the share of the vote secured by the political parties in the last general election.
- We will bring forward the proposals of the Wright Committee for reform to the House of Commons in full – starting with the proposed committee for management of backbench business. A House Business Committee, to consider government business, will be established by the third year of the Parliament.
- We will reduce electoral fraud by speeding up the implementation of individual voter registration.
- We will establish a commission to consider the 'West Lothian question'.
- We will prevent the possible misuse of Parliamentary privilege by MPs accused of serious wrongdoing.
- We will cut the perks and bureaucracy associated with Parliament.
- We will consult with the Independent Parliamentary Standards Authority on how to move away from the generous final-salary pension system for MPs.
- We will fund 200 all-postal primaries over this Parliament, targeted at seats which have not changed hands for many years. These funds will be allocated to all political parties with seats in Parliament that they take up, in proportion to their share of the total vote in the last general election.

- We will ensure that any petition that secures 100,000 signatures will be eligible for debate in Parliament. The petition with the most signatures will enable members of the public to table a bill eligible to be voted on in Parliament.
- We will introduce a new 'public reading stage' for bills to give the public an opportunity to comment on proposed legislation online, and a dedicated 'public reading day' within a bill's committee stage where those comments will be debated by the committee scrutinising the bill.
- We will improve the civil service, and make it easier to reward the best civil servants and remove the least effective.
- We will reform the Civil Service Compensation Scheme to bring it into line with practice in the private sector.
- We will put a limit on the number on Special Advisers.
- We will introduce extra support for people with disabilities who want to become MPs, councillors or elected officials.
- We will open up Whitehall recruitment by publishing central government job vacancies online.
- We will publish details of every UK project that receives over £25,000 of EU funds.
- We will give residents the power to instigate local referendums on any local issue.
- We will stop plans to impose supplementary business rates on firms if a majority of the firms affected do not give their consent.
- We will give residents the power to veto excessive council tax increases.
- We will continue to promote peace, stability and economic prosperity in Northern Ireland, standing firmly behind the agreements negotiated and institutions they establish. We will work to bring Northern Ireland back into the mainstream of UK politics, including producing a government paper examining potential mechanisms for changing the corporation tax rate in Northern Ireland.
- We will implement the proposals of the Calman Commission and hold a referendum on further Welsh devolution.
- We will review the control and use of accumulated and future revenues from the Fossil Fuel Levy in Scotland.
- We recognise the concerns expressed by the Holtham Commission on the system of devolution funding. However, at this time, the priority must be to reduce the deficit and therefore any change to the system must await the stabilisation of the public finances. Depending on the outcome of the forthcoming referendum, we will establish a process similar to the Calman Commission for the Welsh Assembly. We will take forward the Sustainable Homes Legislative Competence Order.
- We will make government more efficient by introducing enhanced Departmental Boards which will form collective operational leadership of government departments.

25. PUBLIC HEALTH

The Government believes that we need action to promote public health, and encourage behaviour change to help people live healthier lives. We need an ambitious strategy to prevent ill-health which harnesses innovative techniques to help people take responsibility for their own health.
- We will give local communities greater control over public health budgets with payment by the outcomes they achieve in improving the health of local residents.
- We will give GPs greater incentives to tackle public health problems.
- We will investigate ways of improving access to preventative healthcare for those in disadvantaged areas to help tackle health inequalities.
- We will ensure greater access to talking therapies to reduce long-term costs for the NHS.

26. SCHOOLS

The Government believes that we need to reform our school system to tackle educational inequality, which has widened in recent years, and to give greater powers to parents and pupils to choose a good school. We want to ensure high standards of discipline in the classroom, robust standards and the highest quality teaching. We also believe that the state should help parents, community groups and others come together to improve the education system by starting new schools.

• We will promote the reform of schools in order to ensure that new providers can enter the state school system in response to parental demand; that all schools have greater freedom over the curriculum; and that all schools are held properly to account.

• We will fund a significant premium for disadvantaged pupils from outside the schools budget by reductions in spending elsewhere.

• We will give parents, teachers, charities and local communities the chance to set up new schools, as part of our plans to allow new providers to enter the state school system in response to parental demand.

• We will support Teach First, create Teach Now to build on the Graduate Teacher Programme, and seek other ways to improve the quality of the teaching profession.

• We will reform the existing rigid national pay and conditions rules to give schools greater freedoms to pay good teachers more and deal with poor performance.

• We will help schools tackle bullying in schools, especially homophobic bullying.

• We will simplify the regulation of standards in education and target inspection on areas of failure.

• We will give anonymity to teachers accused by pupils and take other measures to protect against false accusations.

• We will seek to attract more top science and maths graduates to be teachers.

• We will publish performance data on educational providers, as well as past exam papers.

• We will create more flexibility in the exams systems so that state schools can offer qualifications like the IGCSE.

• We will reform league tables so that schools can focus on, and demonstrate, the progress of children of all abilities.

• We will give heads and teachers the powers they need to ensure discipline and promote good behaviour.

• We believe the most vulnerable children deserve the highest quality of care. We will improve diagnostic assessment for schoolchildren, prevent the unnecessary closure of special schools, and remove the bias towards inclusion.

• We will improve the quality of vocational education, including increasing flexibility for 14–19 year olds and creating new Technical Academies as part of our plans to diversify skills provision.

• We will keep external assessment, but will review how Key Stage 2 tests operate in future.

• We will ensure that all new Academies follow an inclusive admissions policy. We will work with faith groups to enable more faith schools and facilitate inclusive admissions policies in as many of these schools as possible.

27. SOCIAL ACTION

The Government believes that the innovation and enthusiasm of civil society is essential in tackling the social, economic and political challenges that the UK faces today. We will take action to support and encourage social responsibility, volunteering and philanthropy, and make it easier for people to come together to improve their communities and help one another.

• We will support the creation and expansion of mutuals, co-operatives, charities and social enterprises, and enable these groups to have much greater involvement in the running of public services.

• We will give public sector workers a new right to form employee-owned co-operatives and bid to take over the services they deliver. This will empower millions of public sector workers to become their own boss and help them to deliver better services.

• We will train a new generation of community organisers and support the creation of neighbourhood groups across the UK, especially in the most deprived areas.

• We will take a range of measures to encourage charitable giving and philanthropy.

• We will introduce National Citizen Service. The initial project will provide a programme for 16-year-olds to give them a chance to develop the skills needed to be active and responsible citizens, mix with people from different backgrounds, and start getting involved in their communities.

• We will use funds from dormant bank accounts to establish a 'Big Society Bank', which will provide new finance for neighbourhood groups, charities, social enterprises and other non-governmental bodies.

• We will take a range of measures to encourage volunteering and involvement in social action, including launching a national day to celebrate and encourage social action, and make regular community service an element of civil service staff appraisals.

28. SOCIAL CARE AND DISABILITY

The Government believes that people needing care deserve to be treated with dignity and respect. We understand the urgency of reforming the system of social care to provide much more control to individuals and their carers, and to ease the cost burden that they and their families face.

• We will establish a commission on long-term care, to report within a year. The commission will consider a range of ideas, including both a voluntary insurance scheme to protect the assets of those who go into residential care, and a partnership scheme as proposed by Derek Wanless.

• We will break down barriers between health and social care funding to incentivise preventative action.

• We will extend the greater roll-out of personal budgets to give people and their carers more control and purchasing power.

• We will use direct payments to carers and better community-based provision to improve access to respite care.

• We will reform Access to Work, so disabled people can apply for jobs with funding already secured for any adaptations and equipment they will need.

29. TAXATION

The Government believes that the tax system needs to be reformed to make it more competitive, simpler, greener and fairer. We need to take action to ensure that the tax framework better reflects the values of this Government.

• We will increase the personal allowance for income tax to help lower and middle-income earners. We will announce in the first Budget a substantial increase in the personal allowance from April 2011, with the benefits focused on those with lower and middle incomes. This will be funded with the money that would have been used to pay for the increase in employee National Insurance thresholds proposed by the Conservative Party, as well as revenues from increases in Capital Gains Tax rates for non-business assets as described below. The increase in employer National Insurance thresholds proposed by the Conservatives will go ahead to stop the planned jobs tax.

• We will further increase the personal allowance to £10,000, making real terms steps each year towards meeting this as a longterm policy objective. We will prioritise this over other tax cuts, including cuts to Inheritance Tax.

• We will also ensure that provision is made for Liberal Democrat MPs to abstain on budget resolutions to introduce transferable tax allowances for married couples without prejudice to the coalition agreement.

• We will reform the taxation of air travel by switching from a per-passenger to a per-plane duty, and will ensure that a proportion of any increased revenues over time will be used to help fund increases in the personal allowance.

• We will seek ways of taxing non-business capital gains at rates similar or close to those applied to income, with generous exemptions for entrepreneurial business activities.

• We will make every effort to tackle tax avoidance, including detailed development of Liberal Democrat proposals.

- We will increase the proportion of tax revenue accounted for by environmental taxes.
- We will take measures to fulfil our EU treaty obligations in regard to the taxation of holiday letting that do not penalise UK-based businesses.
- We will review the taxation of non-domiciled individuals.

30. TRANSPORT

The Government believes that a modern transport infrastructure is essential for a dynamic and entrepreneurial economy, as well as to improve well-being and quality of life. We need to make the transport sector greener and more sustainable, with tougher emission standards and support for new transport technologies.

- We will mandate a national recharging network for electric and plug-in hybrid vehicles.
- We will grant longer rail franchises in order to give operators the incentive to invest in the improvements passengers want – like better services, better stations, longer trains and better rolling stock.
- We will reform the way decisions are made on which transport projects to prioritise, so that the benefits of low carbon proposals (including light rail schemes) are fully recognised.
- We will make Network Rail more accountable to its customers.
- We will establish a high speed rail network as part of our programme of measures to fulfil our ambitions to create a low-carbon economy. Our vision is of a truly national high speed rail network for the whole of Britain. Given financial constraints, we will have to achieve this in phases.
- We support Crossrail and further electrification of the rail network.
- We will turn the rail regulator into a powerful passenger champion.
- We will support sustainable travel initiatives, including the promotion of cycling and walking, and will encourage joint working between bus operators and local authorities.
- We are committed to fair pricing for rail travel.
- We will work towards the introduction of a new system of HGV road user charging to ensure a fairer arrangement for UK hauliers.
- We will stop central government funding for new fixed speed cameras and switch to more effective ways of making our roads safer, including 'drugalyser' technology.
- We will tackle rogue private sector wheel clampers.

31. UNIVERSITIES AND FURTHER EDUCATION

The Government believes that our universities are essential for building a strong and innovative economy. We will take action to create more college and university places, as well as help to foster stronger links between universities, colleges and industries.

- We will seek ways to support the creation of apprenticeships, internships, work pairings, and college and workplace training places as part of our wider programme to get Britain working.
- We will set colleges free from direct state control and abolish many of the further education quangos. Public funding should be fair and follow the choices of students.
- We will await Lord Browne's report into higher education funding, and will judge its proposals against the need to:
  – increase social mobility;
  – take into account the impact on student debt;
  – ensure a properly funded university sector;
  – improve the quality of teaching;
  – advance scholarship; and
  – attract a higher proportion of students from disadvantaged backgrounds.
- If the response of the Government to Lord Browne's report is one that Liberal Democrats cannot accept, then arrangements will be made to enable Liberal Democrat MPs to abstain in any vote.
- We will review support for part-time students in terms of loans and fees.
- We will publish more information about the costs, graduate earnings and student satisfaction of different university courses.
- We will ensure that public funding mechanisms for university research safeguard its academic integrity.

The deficit reduction programme takes precedence over any of the other measures in this agreement, and the speed of implementation of any measures that have a cost to the public finances will depend on decisions to be made in the Comprehensive Spending Review.

The Government fully supports the devolution of powers to Northern Ireland, Scotland and Wales. As a result of devolution, many decisions made by UK Ministers or in the Westminster Parliament now apply to England only. The Northern Ireland Executive, the Scottish Executive and the Welsh Assembly Government make their own policy on their devolved issues. This document therefore sets out the agreed priorities for the Coalition Government in Westminster.

Conservative manifesto

CHANGE THE ECONOMY

Urgent action is needed if we are to avoid the higher borrowing costs that would inevitably follow from a credit rating downgrade. So we will cut wasteful government spending to bring the deficit down and restore stability. We will increase spending on health in real terms every year and honour our commitments on international aid, but our plan to get a grip on the deficit will include cuts to wasteful spending in many other departmental budgets. That will enable the independent Bank of England to keep interest rates as low as possible for as long as possible.

To ensure that no Labour government can ever attempt to bankrupt our public finances again, we will set up an independent Office for Budget Responsibility to restore trust in the government's ability to manage the public finances. We will provide an emergency Budget within 50 days of taking office to set out a credible plan for eliminating the bulk of the structural current budget deficit over a Parliament. The case for starting early to re-establish our economic credibility is overwhelming, and is backed by economists and business leaders. We will start by cutting a net £6 billion of wasteful departmental spending in the financial year 2010/11. In addition, we will make the following savings:

• freeze public sector pay for one year in 2011, excluding the one million lowest paid workers;
• hold a review to bring forward the date at which the state pension age starts to rise to 66, although it will not be sooner than 2016 for men and 2020 for women;
• stop paying tax credits to better-off families with incomes over £50,000;
• cut government contributions to Child Trust Funds for all but the poorest third of families and families with disabled children;
• cap public sector pensions above £50,000;
• cut Ministers' pay by 5 per cent, followed by a five year freeze; and,
• reduce the number of MPs by 10 per cent. Over the course of a Parliament, we will cut Whitehall policy, funding and regulation costs by a third, saving £2 billion a year, and save a further £1 billion a year from quango bureaucracy.

Cut government waste to stop Labour's jobs tax

Labour are planning to increase national insurance in 2011. Anyone earning over £20,000 will pay more tax, and employers will pay more tax on all jobs paid over £5,700. This jobs tax, which will hit small businesses especially hard, will kill off the recovery. Experts predict it will cost 57,000 jobs in small and medium-sized businesses alone. At the same time, Labour will not take action to cut waste in government. They have identified £11 billion of waste, but they do not plan to start dealing with it until April 2011. So Labour will continue wasting money while putting up taxes on working people. We will act immediately to cut government waste so we can stop the most damaging part of the national insurance rise for employers and for anyone earning under £35,000. We will make the following changes in April 2011, relative to Labour's plans:

• raise the primary threshold for national insurance by £24 a week and raise the Upper Earnings Limit by £29 a week; and,
• raise the secondary threshold at which employers start paying National Insurance by £21 a week.

Seven out of ten working people – those earning between £7,100 and £45,400 – and almost every employer will save up to £150 a year per person compared to under Labour. Lower earners will get the greatest benefit as a percentage of their earnings. Nobody will be worse off as a result of these changes. Our plans are backed by many of Britain's top business leaders, who between them employ more than half a million people, as well as by Britain's leading business organisations. To pay for this we will take immediate action to cut a net £6 billion of wasteful departmental spending in the financial year 2010/11, with further savings in future years. This is in addition to the savings made by cutting tax credits and Child Trust Funds for better off families.

These actions will allow us to reduce the deficit more quickly than Labour year-on-year while avoiding the most damaging part of their jobs tax. It will also lower the proportion of the reduction of the structural deficit that is accounted for by tax increases, from about one third towards one fifth. This is in line with international best practice, as well as the Treasury's own internal analysis. Former government advisers Sir Peter Gershon and Dr Martin Read have advised us that savings of £12 billion across all departmental spending are possible in-year without affecting the quality of frontline services. These are over and above any savings already planned by Labour. We will achieve this through:

• a freeze on major new Information and Communications Technologies (ICT) spending;
• immediate negotiations to achieve cost reductions from major suppliers;
• tighter control of public sector recruitment;
• reductions in discretionary spending, including travel, expenses, advertising, consultancy and office supplies; and,
• reductions in public sector property costs. We will match Labour's spending plans for 2010-11 in health and overseas aid. Given our commitment to carry out a Strategic Defence and Security Review, it would also not be appropriate to make in-year reductions to the existing defence budget in 2010/11. Savings in these protected areas will be channelled back into frontline services. The net £6 billion savings will be made from the remaining departmental budgets.

Make Britain the leading hi-tech exporter in Europe

We will implement key recommendations from Sir James Dyson's Review into how to achieve our goal of making Britain Europe's leading hi-tech exporter, including:

• encouraging the establishment of joint university-business research and development institutes;
• initiating a multi-year Science and Research Budget to provide a stable investment climate for Research Councils;
• creating a better focus on Science, Technology, Engineering and Maths (STEM) subjects in schools; and,
• establishing a new prize for engineering. Research and development tax credits will be improved and refocused on hi-tech companies, small businesses and new start-ups. At the same time, we will give strong backing to the growth industries that generate high-quality jobs around the country.

We will improve the performance of UK Trade and Investment with a renewed focus on high priority sectors and markets where the return on taxpayers' money is highest. We will regularly compare government support for exporters and inward investment against the services provided by our competitors. We will work for the successful conclusion of the Doha trade round and support bilateral free trade negotiations between the European Union (EU) and other countries.

Encourage saving and investment

Only by saving more can we finance investment for the future without being dependent on unsustainable inflows of capital from abroad. We will help stop the spread of means-testing by restoring the link between the basic state pension and average earnings, making it worthwhile for people to save. Other measures we will take to encourage saving include:

• reinvigorating occupational pensions and working with and industry to support auto-enrolment into pensions;

• working with the trade unions, businesses and others to address the growing disparity between public sector pensions and private sector pensions, while protecting accrued rights; and,

• when resources allow, starting to reverse the effects of the abolition of the dividend tax credit for pension funds.

We will reward those who have saved for their retirement by ending the effective obligation to buy an annuity at age 75. And we will raise the inheritance tax threshold to £1 million to help millions of people who aspire to pass something on to their children, paid for by a simple flat-rate levy on all non-domiciled individuals. We must not let the mis-selling of financial products put people off saving. We will implement the Ombudsman's recommendation to make fair and transparent payments to Equitable Life policy holders, through an independent payment scheme, for their relative loss as a consequence of regulatory failure.

Help households manage their debts

Going into the recession, Britain's consumer debt was the highest in the G7. A Conservative government will promote responsible consumer finance by creating a powerful Consumer Protection Agency (CPA) to take over the Financial Services Authority's consumer protection role. In addition, we will:

• give the CPA new powers to define and ban excessive borrowing rates on store cards;

• launch Britain's first free national financial advice service, funded in full through a new social responsibility levy on the financial services sector;

• introduce a seven-day cooling off period for store cards;

• require credit card companies to provide clear information; and,

• ensure that no-one is forced to sell their home to pay unsecured debts of less than £25,000.

Reduce welfare dependency

We will scrap Labour's failing employment schemes and create a single Work Programme for everyone who is unemployed, including the 2.6 million people claiming Incapacity Benefit who do not get enough help from existing programmes. We will reassess all current claimants of Incapacity Benefit. Those found fit for work will be transferred onto Jobseeker's Allowance. Recipients of Incapacity Benefit who are genuinely disabled will continue to receive the financial support to which they are entitled. Our Work Programme will:

• offer people targeted, personalised help sooner – straight away for those with serious barriers to work and at six months for those aged under 25;

• be delivered through private and voluntary sector providers, which will be rewarded on a payment by results basis for getting people into sustainable work;

• draw on a range of Service Academies to offer pre-employment training for unemployed people – our first Service Academy, for hospitality and leisure, will provide up to 50,000 training places and work placements; and,

• involve the development of local Work Clubs – places where people looking for work can gather together to exchange skills, find opportunities, make useful contacts and provide mutual support.

Unemployed people must be prepared to take up job offers. So, with the Conservatives, long-term benefit claimants who fail to find work will be required to 'work for the dole' on community work programmes. Anyone on Jobseeker's Allowance who refuses to join the Work Programme will lose the right to claim out-of-work benefits until they do, while people who refuse to accept reasonable job offers could forfeit their benefits for up to three years.

Boost small business

As well as stopping Labour's jobs tax, for the first two years of a Conservative government any new business will pay no Employers National Insurance on the first ten employees it hires during its first year. To support small businesses further, we will:

• make small business rate relief automatic; and,

• aim to deliver 25 per cent of government research and procurement contracts through SME s by cutting the administrative costs of bidding.

We will support would-be entrepreneurs through a new programme – Work for Yourself – which will give unemployed people direct access to business mentors and substantial loans. We need to make work pay, so we will keep the minimum wage and work to reduce the very high marginal tax rates faced by many people on low incomes who want to return to work or increase their earnings. We will look at how to abolish the default retirement age, as many older people want to carry on working. And we will force equal pay audits on any company found to be discriminating on the basis of gender.

Improve skills and strengthen higher education

We will promote fair access to universities, the professions, and good jobs for young people from all backgrounds. We will use funding that currently supports Labour's ineffective employment and training schemes, such as Train-2Gain, to provide our own help for people looking to improve their skills. This will allow us to:

• create 400,000 work pairing, apprenticeship, college and training places over two years;

• give SMEs a £2,000 bonus for every apprentice they hire;

• establish a Community Learning Fund to help people restart their careers; and,

• create a new all-age careers service so that everyone can access the advice they need.

To meet the skills challenge we face, the training sector needs to be given the freedom to innovate. We will set colleges free from direct state control and abolish many of the further education quangos Labour have put in place. Public funding will follow the choices of students and be delivered by a single agency, the Further Education Funding Council. Universities contribute enormously to the economy. But not all of this contribution comes directly – it can come from fundamental research with no immediate application – and universities also have a crucial cultural role. We will ensure that Britain's universities enjoy the freedom to pursue academic excellence and focus on raising the quality of the student experience. To enable this to happen, we will:

• delay the implementation of the Research Excellence Framework so that it can be reviewed – because of doubts about whether there is a robust and acceptable way of measuring the impact of all research;

• consider carefully the results of Lord Browne's review into the future of higher education funding, so that we can unlock the potential of universities to transform our economy, to enrich students' lives through teaching of the highest quality, and to advance scholarship; and,

• provide 10,000 extra university places this year, paid for by giving graduates incentives to pay back their student loans early on an entirely voluntary basis.

Cut and simplify business taxes

The Conservative Party believes in lower and simpler taxation. That is why we will ensure that by far the largest part of the burden of dealing with the deficit falls on lower spending rather than higher taxes. Cutting the deficit is the most urgent task we need to undertake if we are to get the economy moving, but it is not enough. So, initially, we will cut the headline rate of corporation tax to 25p and the small companies' rate to 20p, funded by reducing complex reliefs and allowances. Over time, we hope to reduce these rates further. Our ambition is to create the most competitive tax system in the G20 within five years.

We will restore the tax system's reputation for simplicity, stability and predictability. In our first Budget, we will set out a five year road map for the direction of corporate tax reform, providing greater certainty and stability to businesses. We will create an independent Office of Tax Simplification to suggest reforms to the tax system. We will take a series of measures to encourage Foreign Direct Investment into the UK, including:

• making the UK a more attractive location for multinationals by simplifying the complex Controlled Foreign Companies rules;

• consulting on moving towards a territorial corporate tax system that only taxes profits generated in the UK; and,

• creating an attractive tax environment for intellectual property.

Reduce regulation

A Conservative government will introduce regulatory budgets: forcing any government body wanting to introduce a new regulation to reduce regulation elsewhere by a greater amount. And we will give the public the opportunity to force the worst regulations to be repealed.

To encourage new businesses to start up, we will reduce the number of forms needed to register a new business – moving towards a 'one-click' registration model – to make Britain the fastest place in the world to start a business, and end the restrictions on social tenants starting a business from their homes. We are proud of the last Conservative government's industrial relations reforms, which helped bring about our economic revival in the 1980s, and we will always be prepared to build on them if necessary.

Support innovation and sustainable development

Government procurement is a £200 billion a year market that can be used much better to stimulate enterprise and innovation. We will take steps to open up government procurement to small and innovative businesses by:

• publishing online all government tender documents for contracts worth over £10,000 via the Supply2Gov website;

• creating a level playing field for open source ICT in government procurement; and,

• opening up contracts to SMEs by breaking up large ICT projects into smaller components.

Britain's complex and unwieldy planning system has long been cited as a significant barrier to growth and wealth creation. We will create a presumption in favour of sustainable development in the planning system. We will abolish the unelected Infrastructure Planning Commission (IPC) and replace it with an efficient and democratically-accountable system that provides a fast-track process for major infrastructure projects. We will:

• use private or hybrid Bills to promote major projects, such as our plans for a national high speed rail network;

• ensure that all other major infrastructure projects are considered at planning inquiries which have binding timetables and which focus on planning issues – with final permission given by a Minister; and,

• provide transitional arrangements for projects already before the IPC to ensure that these projects are not disrupted or delayed.

Attract the brightest and best to our country

Immigration has enriched our nation over the years and we want to attract the brightest and the best people who can make a real difference to our economic growth. But immigration today is too high and needs to be reduced. We do not need to attract people to do jobs that could be carried out by British citizens, given the right training and support. So we will take steps to take net migration back to the levels of the 1990s – tens of thousands a year, not hundreds of thousands. To help achieve this goal, we will introduce a number of measures, such as:

• setting an annual limit on the number of non-EU economic migrants admitted into the UK to live and work;

• limiting access only to those who will bring the most value to the British economy; and,

• applying transitional controls as a matter of course in the future for all new EU Member States.

In addition, we will promote integration into British society, as we believe that everyone coming to this country must be ready to embrace our core values and become a part of their local community. So there will be an English language test for anyone coming here to get married.

We want to encourage students to come to our universities and colleges, but our student visa system has become the biggest weakness in our border controls. A Conservative government will strengthen the system of granting student visas so that it is less open to abuse. We want to make it easier for reputable universities and colleges to accept applications, while putting extra scrutiny on new institutions looking to accept foreign students or existing institutions not registered with Companies House. In addition, we will:

• insist foreign students at new or unregistered institutions pay a bond in order to study in this country, to be repaid after the student has left at the end of their studies;

• ensure foreign students can prove that they have the financial means to support themselves in the UK; and,

• require that students must usually leave the country and reapply if they want to switch to another course or apply for a work permit.

Too many areas of the UK lack a vibrant private sector and are too dependent on public spending. These regional imbalances have got worse over the last decade, despite billions of pounds spent by the Regional Development Agencies (RDAs). Our aim is to increase the private sector's share of the economy in every part of the country by boosting enterprise and creating a better business environment. We will work closely with local government, and with the Scottish Parliament, Welsh Assembly and Northern Ireland Assembly, to achieve this goal.

Create a modern transport network

A Conservative government will begin work immediately to create a high speed rail line connecting London and Heathrow with Birmingham, Manchester and Leeds. This is the first step towards achieving our vision of creating a national high speed rail network to join up major cities across England, Scotland and Wales. Stage two will deliver two new lines bringing the North East, Scotland and Wales into the high speed rail network. Because travel abroad is so important for our economy and for family holidays, we need to improve our airports and reduce the environmental impact of flying. Our goal is to make Heathrow airport better, not bigger. We will stop the third runway and instead link Heathrow directly to our high speed rail network, providing an alternative to thousands of flights. In addition, we will:

• block plans for second runways at Stansted and Gatwick;

• reform Air Passenger Duty to encourage a switch to fuller and cleaner planes.

To improve life for commuters and encourage people to switch to lower carbon public transport, we will reform our railways to provide a better focus on tackling problems that matter most to passengers, such as overcrowding. We will grant longer, more flexible rail franchises to incentivise private sector investment in improvements like longer trains and better stations.

We support Crossrail and the electrification of the Great Western line to South Wales. We will turn the rail regulator into a powerful passenger champion and reform Network Rail to make it more accountable to its customers. And we will introduce a moratorium on building on disused rail lines still in public ownership, so they are available to be re-opened. Britain has the chance to lead the world in making our transport system greener. So we will introduce incentives for electricity network operators to establish a new national car recharging network, making it much easier for drivers to move to electric and plug-in hybrid vehicles. We will support sustainable travel initiatives that work best for local communities by:

• giving the concerns of cyclists much greater priority;
• encouraging partnerships between bus operators and local authorities; and,
• helping people cut down on work-related travel.

We will stop central government funding for new fixed speed cameras, and switch to more effective ways to make our roads safer, including authorising 'drugalyser' technology for use in testing for drug-driving. We will make companies that dig up our roads accountable for the congestion they cause and crack down on rogue clampers. Councils will get more powers to keep traffic flowing.

We will consult on the introduction of a 'Fair Fuel Stabiliser'. This would cut fuel duty when oil prices rise, and vice versa. It would ensure families, businesses and the whole British economy are less exposed to volatile oil markets, and that there is a more stable environment for low carbon investment.

Spread prosperity

We want Britain to become a European hub for hi-tech, digital and creative industries – but this can only happen if we have the right infrastructure in place. Establishing a superfast broadband network throughout the UK could generate 600,000 additional jobs and add £18 billion to Britain's GDP. We will scrap Labour's phone tax and instead require BT and other infrastructure providers to allow the use of their assets to deliver superfast broadband across the country. If necessary, we will consider using the part of the licence fee that is supporting the digital switchover to fund broadband in areas that the market alone will not reach.

We will give councils and businesses the power to form their own business-led local enterprise partnerships instead of RDAs. Where local councils and businesses want to maintain regionally-based enterprise partnerships, they will be able to. Local government should be at the heart of our economic recovery, so we will:

• allow councils to keep above-average increases in business rate revenue so that communities which go for growth can reap the benefits;
• give councils new powers to introduce further discounts on business rates; and,
• introduce an immediate freeze of, and inquiry into, the Government's punitive programme of back-dating business rates on ports.

Decentralisation, accountability and transparency

We will raise public sector productivity by increasing diversity of provision, extending payment by results and giving more power to consumers. Giving public sector workers ownership of the services they deliver is a powerful way to drive efficiency, so we will support co-operatives and mutualisation as a way of transferring public assets and revenue streams to public sector workers. We will encourage them to come together to form employee-led co-operatives and bid to take over the services they run. This will empower millions of public sector workers to become their own boss and help them to deliver better services – the most significant shift in power from the state to working people since the sale of council houses in the 1980s.

Transparency is crucial to creating a value-for-money culture. We will publish all items of spending over £25,000 online, and the salaries of senior civil servants in central government will also be published. We will create strong financial discipline at all levels of government and place an obligation to manage taxpayers' money wisely at the heart of Civil Service employment contracts. In addition, we will:

• introduce and publish a standard set of cost measures that capture the key drivers of departmental spending;
• help departmental Finance Directors to manage resources more efficiently;

• implement clear financial performance targets for senior civil servants; and,
• create a focus on delivering strong financial management across government.

Reform financial services

The financial services sector is one of our most globally successful industries, and we want the City to be the leading location for global finance. But the financial sector must not put the stability of the whole economy at risk. We will put in place a levy on banks. We are prepared to act unilaterally if necessary, but there is emerging international agreement on this approach and the US and German governments have both announced similar plans.

We need fundamental reform of our failed regulatory system, avoiding badly designed regulations that will damage our competitiveness and ensuring that the financial sector can supply the affordable credit that businesses need. We will abolish Gordon Brown's failed tripartite system of regulation and put the Bank of England in charge of prudential supervision. We will restore the Bank's historic role in monitoring the overall growth of credit and debt in the economy. In addition, we will:

• pursue international agreement to prevent retail banks from engaging in activities, such as large-scale proprietary trading, that put the stability of the system at risk;
• empower the Bank of England to crack down on risky bonus arrangements;
• increase competition in the banking industry, starting with a study of competition in the sector to inform our strategy for selling the government's stakes in the banks; and,
• as the government comes to sell off its holdings in the banks, offer a 'people's bank bonus', so that everybody in the country has the chance to buy a stake in the state-owned banks.

We will create more diverse sources of affordable credit for small businesses, building on our proposals for a National Loan Guarantee Scheme.

Create a low carbon future

The wave of low carbon innovation we want to unleash requires investment, so we will create Britain's first Green Investment Bank – which will draw together money currently divided across existing government initiatives, leveraging private sector capital to finance new green technology start-ups. We will create green Individual Savings Accounts to help provide the financial backing we need to create a low carbon economy.

A credible and sustainable price for carbon is vital if we are to see adequate and timely investment in new electricity generation. Whatever the carbon content of electricity generated, operators considering new investments in projects with a life of several decades need to know where they stand. We will reform the Climate Change Levy to provide a floor price for carbon, delivering the right climate for investment in low carbon energy production. We will increase the proportion of tax revenues accounted for by environmental taxes, ensuring that any additional revenues from new green taxes that are principally designed as an environmental measure to change behaviour are used to reduce the burden of taxation elsewhere.

CHANGE SOCIETY

Our public service reform programme will enable social enterprises, charities and voluntary groups to play a leading role in delivering public services and tackling deep-rooted social problems. We will strengthen and support social enterprises to help deliver our public service reforms by creating a Big Society Bank, funded from unclaimed bank assets, to provide new finance for neighbourhood groups, charities, social enterprises and other nongovernmental bodies. This will provide social enterprises with the start-up funding and support they need to bid for government contracts or work towards delivering services under a payment by results model. Britain has a proud and longstanding charitable tradition, and we are convinced that the voluntary sector should play a major part in our civic renewal. We will introduce a fair deal on grants to give voluntary sector organisations more stability and allow them to earn a competitive return for providing public services. We will work with local authorities to promote the delivery of public services by social enterprises, charities and the voluntary sector.

Our ambition is for every adult in the country to be a member of an active neighbourhood group. We will stimulate the creation and development of neighbourhood groups, which can take action to improve their local area. We will use Cabinet Office budgets to fund the training of independent community organisers to help people establish and run neighbourhood groups, and provide neighbourhood grants to the UK's poorest areas to ensure they play a leading role in the rebuilding of civic society. To stimulate social action further, we will:

- transform the civil service into a 'civic service' by making sure that participation in social action is recognised in civil servants' appraisals;
- launch an annual Big Society Day to celebrate the work of neighbourhood groups and encourage more people to take part in social action;
- provide funding from the Big Society Bank to intermediary bodies with a track record of supporting and growing social enterprises; and,
- develop a measure of well-being that encapsulates the social value of state action.

We will introduce National Citizen Service. The initial project will provide a programme for 16-year-olds to give them a chance to develop the skills needed to be active, responsible citizens, mix with people from different backgrounds and start getting involved in their communities. Even in these difficult times, the British people have demonstrated their desire to give money and time to good causes. We will introduce new ways to increase philanthropy, and use the latest insights from behavioural economics to encourage people to make volunteering and community participation something they do on a regular basis.

We will restore the National Lottery to its original purpose and, by cutting down on administration costs, make sure more money goes to good causes. The Big Lottery Fund will focus purely on supporting social action through the voluntary and community sector, instead of Ministers' pet projects as at present. Sports, heritage and the arts will each see their original allocations of 20 per cent of good cause money restored.

We will deliver a successful Olympics that brings lasting benefits for the country as a whole. Part of the community sports budget of the National Lottery will be responsible for delivering an Olympic legacy, including the vigorous promotion of competitive sports through a national Olympic-style school competition. To support high-level sport further, we will:

- work with the Scottish government to deliver a top-quality Commonwealth Games in Glasgow in 2014;
- ensure that the 2013 Rugby League and the 2015 Rugby Union World Cups are successful; and,
- strongly support England's bid to host the 2018 Football World Cup.

Make Britain the most family friendly country in Europe

Today, Labour's tax and benefits system rewards couples who split up. A Conservative government will end the couple penalty for all couples in the tax credit system as we make savings from our welfare reform plans. We will recognise marriage and civil partnerships in the tax system in the next Parliament. This will send an important signal that we value couples and the commitment that people make when they get married.

To help Britain's families further, a Conservative government will freeze council tax for two years, in partnership with local councils. This will be paid for by reducing spending on government consultants and advertising, and

could save families and pensioners up to £219 over two years on a Band D bill. We will also scrap Labour's plans for an expensive and intrusive council tax revaluation.

We support tax credits and will continue to provide the range of tax credits to families, although we can no longer justify paying tax credits to households earning more than £50,000. We will reform the administration of tax credits to reduce fraud and overpayments, which hit the poorest families hardest. We strongly value the role older people play in families and in society, and will not let them suffer because of the economic mistakes of others. That is why we have made a pledge to pensioners to re-link the basic state pension to earnings, and protect: the winter fuel payment, free bus passes, free TV licences, disability living allowance and attendance allowance and the pension credit.

Give families more control over their lives

Making Britain more family-friendly means helping families spend more time together. That is why we will initially extend the right to request flexible working to every parent with a child under the age of eighteen. We want our government to lead from the front, so we will extend the right to request flexible working to all those in the public sector, recognising that this may need to be done in stages. In addition, we will:

- in the longer term, extend the right to request flexible working to all, but only in the light of experience and after full consultation with business on how to do this in a way which is administratively simple and without burdening them with extra costs; and,
- oblige JobCentre Plus to ask employers if their vacancies could be advertised on a part-time or flexible basis.

We will introduce a new system of flexible parental leave which lets parents share maternity leave between them, while ensuring that parents on leave can stay in touch with their employer. We support the provision of free nursery care for pre-school children, and we want that support to be provided by a diverse range of providers. A Conservative government will review the way the childcare industry is regulated and funded to ensure that no providers, including childminders, are put at a disadvantage. To give families more control over their lives, we will put funding for relationship support on a stable, long-term footing and make sure couples are given greater encouragement to use existing relationship support. We will review family law in order to increase the use of mediation when couples do break up, and look at how best to provide greater access rights to non-resident parents and grandparents.

Protect childhood

Children should be allowed to grow up at their own pace, without excessive pressure placed on them by businesses. We will take a series of measures to help reverse the commercialisation of childhood. We prefer to gain voluntary consent to these actions but we are prepared to legislate if necessary. We will:

- prevent any marketing or advertising company found to be in serious breach of rules governing marketing to children from bidding for government advertising contracts for three years;
- ban companies from using new peer-to-peer marketing techniques targeted at children, and tackle marketing on corporate websites targeted at children;
- establish a new online system that gives parents greater powers to take action against irresponsible commercial activities targeted at children; and,
- empower head teachers and governors to ban advertising and vending machines in schools.

A new approach to early intervention

We will take Sure Start back to its original purpose of early intervention, increase its focus on the neediest families, and better involve organisations with a track record in supporting families. Families need the best possible advice and support while their children are young. We will provide 4,200 more Sure Start health visitors – giving all parents a guaranteed level of support before and after birth until their child starts school. This will be paid for out of the Department of Health budget and by refocusing Sure Start's peripatetic outreach services. To improve the early interventions we make to help families, we will:

• ensure that new Sure Start providers are paid in part by the results they achieve;

• bring all funding for early intervention and parenting support into one budget, to be overseen by a single, newly-created Early Years Support Team; and,

• set out a new approach to help families with multiple problems.

Back the NHS
We understand the pressures the NHS faces, so we will increase health spending in real terms every year. But on its own this will not be enough to deliver the rising standards of care that people expect. We need to allow patients to choose the best care available, giving healthcare providers the incentives they need to drive up quality. So we will give every patient the power to choose any healthcare provider that meets NHS standards, within NHS prices. This includes independent, voluntary and community sector providers. We will make patients' choices meaningful by:

• putting patients in charge of making decisions about their care, including control of their health records;

• spreading the use of the NHS tariff, so funding follows patients' choices; and,

• making sure good performance is rewarded by implementing a payment by results system, improving quality.

We will publish detailed data about the performance of healthcare providers online, so everyone will know who is providing a good service and who is falling behind, and we will measure our success on the health results that really matter – such as improving cancer and stroke survival rates or reducing hospital infections. Patients will be able to rate hospitals and doctors according to the quality of care they received. We will give the public a strong and independent voice through HealthWatch, a statutory body with the power to investigate and support complaints. We will strengthen the power of GPs as patients' expert guides through the health system by:

• giving them the power to hold patients' budgets and commission care on their behalf;

• linking their pay to the quality of their results; and,

• putting them in charge of commissioning local health services.

Trust healthcare professionals
Doctors and nurses need to be able to use their professional judgement about what is right for patients, instead of being forced to follow bureaucratic processes that often put lives at risk. That is why we will scrap the politically-motivated targets that have no clinical justification. We will set NHS providers free to innovate by ensuring that they become autonomous Foundation Trusts. We will make sure that funding decisions are made on the basis of need, and commissioning decisions according to evidence-based quality standards, by creating an independent NHS board to allocate resources and provide commissioning guidelines. We will ensure that NHS staff are protected if they raise concerns about patient safety.

NHS staff will be properly accountable to patients for their performance, removing the need for expensive layers of bureaucracy to oversee the NHS. As a result, we will be able to cut the cost of NHS administration by a third and transfer resources to support doctors and nurses.

Increase access to vital drugs and services
People want an NHS that is easy to access at any time of day or night. We will commission a 24/7 urgent care service in every area of England, including GP out of hours services, and ensure that every patient can access a GP in their area between 8am and 8pm, seven days a week. We will introduce a single number for every kind of urgent care – to run in parallel with the emergency number 999.

We will stop the forced closure of A&E and maternity wards, so that people have better access to services, and give mothers a real choice over where to have their baby, with NHS funding following their decisions. We will create 'maternity networks' to ensure that mothers can safely access the right care, in the right place, at the right time.

When patients are forced to go to hospital, they expect the highest standards of cleanliness. But infections like MRSA now kill more than three times as many people as are killed on the roads each year. We will increase the number of single rooms in hospitals, as resources allow, helping the battle against infection and providing safety and privacy. As a result, we will end the scandal of mixed-sex accommodation – which Labour have failed to do. And we will not pay hospitals in full when a patient is left with an avoidable infection. NHS patients rightly expect to be among the first in the world to access effective treatments, but under Labour they are among the last. We want more people to access the drugs and treatments that would prolong or improve their lives by reforming the way drug companies are paid for NHS medicines. Using money saved by the NHS through our pledge to stop Labour's jobs tax, we will create a Cancer Drug Fund to enable patients to access the cancer drugs that doctors think will help them. To help the fight against cancer further, we will:

• give thousands more people – especially young people – access to effective drugs to treat rare cancers by changing the way these drugs are commissioned;

• encourage clinical trials of innovative techniques to diagnose and treat cancer; and,

• support the roll out of screening programmes for common cancers.

We will introduce a dentistry contract that will focus on achieving good dental health, not simply the number of treatments achieved. This will tie newly qualified dentists into the NHS for five years and allow dentists to fine people who consistently miss appointments. These changes will allow us to give one million more people access to an NHS dentist and give every five-year-old a dental check-up.

Take control of your care
The UK's six million carers play an indispensable role in looking after friends or family members who need support. Not only do they provide help to some of the most vulnerable people in society, the unpaid work they do contributes £87 billion worth of value a year – sometimes at the cost of carers' finances and even their health. We will support carers, and those they look after, by providing direct payments to help with care needs and by improving access to respite care. We will provide £10 million a year beyond 2011 to support children's hospices in their vital work. And so that proper support for the most sick children and adults can continue in the setting of their choice, we will introduce a new per-patient funding system for all hospices and other providers of palliative care.

We reject Labour's plans for a compulsory 'death tax' on everyone to pay for social care, regardless of their needs. We want to create a system which is based on choice and which rewards the hundreds of thousands of people who care for an elderly relative full-time. So we will allow anyone to protect their home from being sold to fund residential care costs by paying a one-off insurance premium that is entirely voluntary. Independent experts suggest this should cost around £8,000. We will support older people to live independently at home and have access to the personal care they need. We will work to design a system where people can top up their premium – also voluntarily – to cover the costs of receiving care in their own home.

A healthier nation
We will turn the Department of Health into a Department for Public Health so that the promotion of good health and prevention of illness get the attention they need. We

will provide separate public health funding to local communities, which will be accountable for – and paid according to – how successful they are in improving their residents' health. In addition, we will:
• introduce a health premium, weighting public health funding towards the poorest areas with the worst outcomes;
• enable welfare-to-work providers and employers to purchase services from Mental Health Trusts; and,
• increase access to effective 'talking' therapies.

Raise standards in schools
The single most important thing for a good education is for every child to have access to a good teacher. We will take steps to enhance the status of the teaching profession and ensure it attracts the best people. Schools – especially struggling ones – must be able to attract the best teachers and subject specialists, so we will give all head teachers the power to pay good teachers more.

We will expand Teach First and introduce two new programmes – Teach Now, for people looking to change career, and Troops to Teachers, for ex-service personnel – to get experienced, high-quality people into the profession.

We will make it easier for teachers to deal with violent incidents and remove disruptive pupils or items from the classroom. We believe heads are best placed to improve behaviour, which is why we will stop them being overruled by bureaucrats on exclusions. To raise the status of teaching and toughen school discipline further, we will:
• raise the entry requirement for taxpayer-funded primary school teacher training;
• expect new graduates to have at least a 2:2 in their degree in order to qualify for state-funded training;
• pay the student loan repayments for top Maths and Science graduates for as long as they remain teachers, by redirecting some of the current teacher training budget;
• give teachers the strongest possible protection from false accusations; and,
• reinforce powers of discipline by strengthening home-school behaviour contracts.

A rigorous curriculum and exam system
Every child who is capable of reading should be doing so after two years in primary school. To make this happen, we will promote the teaching of systematic synthetic phonics and ensure that teachers are properly trained to teach using this method. To provide parents with the reassurance they need that their child is making progress, we will establish a simple reading test at the age of six. We will reform the National Curriculum so that it is more challenging and based on evidence about what knowledge can be mastered by children at different ages. We will ensure that the primary curriculum is organised around subjects like Maths, Science and History. We will encourage setting so those who are struggling get extra help and the most able are stretched.

We will ensure that our exam system is measured against the most rigorous systems in the world. We will keep Key Stage 2 tests and league tables. We will reform them to make them more rigorous. We will make other exams more robust by giving universities and academics more say over their form and content. We want to develop proper vocational and technical education that engages young people and meets the needs of modern business. So we will establish Technical Academies across England, starting in at least twelve cities. People expect to be able to make choices about the services they use, based on robust information about the quality on offer. So a Conservative government will reform school league tables so that schools can demonstrate they are stretching the most able and raising the attainment of the less able.

To improve school standards further, we will:
• allow all state schools the freedom to offer the same high quality international exams that private schools offer – including giving every pupil the chance to study separate sciences at GCSE;
• create 20,000 additional young apprenticeships;
• allow schools and colleges to offer workplace training;
• publish all performance data currently kept secret by the Department for Children, Schools and Families; and,
• establish a free online database of exam papers and marking schemes.

Give every parent access to a good school
Drawing on the experience of the Swedish school reforms and the charter school movement in the US, we will break down barriers to entry so that any good education provider can set up a new Academy school. Our schools revolution will create a new generation of good small schools with smaller class sizes and high standards of discipline. Our school reform programme is a major part of our anti-poverty strategy, which is why our first task will be to establish new Academy schools in the most deprived areas of the country. They will be beacons of excellence in areas where school standards are unacceptably low.

We want every child to benefit from our reforms. So all existing schools will have the chance to achieve Academy status, with 'outstanding' schools pre-approved, and we will extend the Academy programme to primary schools. Education's real power lies in its ability to transform life chances, but we can't go on giving the poorest children the worst education. That is why we will introduce a pupil premium – extra funding for children from disadvantaged backgrounds. The most vulnerable children deserve the very highest quality of care, so we will call a moratorium on the ideologically-driven closure of special schools. We will end the bias towards the inclusion of children with special needs in mainstream schools. We will ensure that the schools inspectorate Ofsted adopts a more rigorous and targeted inspection regime, reporting on performance only in the core areas related to teaching and learning. And any school that is in special measures for more than a year will be taken over immediately by a successful Academy provider. To give parents better access to a good school, we will:
• give parents the power to save local schools threatened by closure, allowing communities the chance to take over and run good small schools;
• make sure Academies have the freedoms that helped to make them so successful in the first place; and,
• ensure failing schools are inspected more often – with the best schools visited less frequently.

Fight back against crime
Under Labour's lax licensing regime, drink-fuelled violence and disorder are a blight on many communities. We will overhaul the Licensing Act to give local authorities and the police much stronger powers to remove licences from, or refuse to grant licences to, any premises that are causing problems. In addition, we will:
• allow councils and the police to shut permanently any shop or bar found persistently selling alcohol to children;
• double the maximum fine for under-age alcohol sales to £20,000;
• raise taxes on drinks linked to antisocial drinking, while abolishing Labour's new 'cider tax' on ordinary drinkers;
• ban off-licences and supermarkets from selling alcohol below cost price; and,
• permit local councils to charge more for late night licences to pay for additional policing.

We recognise the need for criminal sanctions like ASBOs and fixed penalty notices, but they are blunt instruments that often fail their purpose of deterring people from committing crime. We will introduce early intervention measures, including grounding orders, to allow the police to use instant sanctions to deal with anti-social behaviour without criminalising young people unnecessarily.

Put the criminal justice system on the side of the public
We will make it clear that anyone convicted of a knife crime can expect to face a prison sentence. We will

introduce mobile knife scanners on streets and public transport, and extend the length of custodial sentences that can be awarded in a Magistrates' Court from six to twelve months. So that the public can be confident their views are accounted for in deciding sentences, we will examine the case for greater Parliamentary scrutiny of sentencing guidelines. We will carry out a fundamental review of legal aid to make it work more efficiently, and examine ways of bringing in alternative sources of funding.

We will change the law so that anyone acting reasonably to stop a crime or apprehend a criminal is not arrested or prosecuted, and we will give householders greater legal protection if they have to defend themselves against intruders in their homes.

We will implement the Prisoners' Earnings Act 1996 to allow deductions from the earnings of prisoners in properly paid work to be paid into the Victims' Fund. We will use this Fund to deliver up to fifteen new rape crisis centres and give existing rape crisis centres stable, long-term funding. To help stop sexual violence before it occurs, we will ensure that the school curriculum includes teaching young people about sexual consent.

Reform the police

A Conservative government will reduce the amount of paperwork that the police have to deal with, starting by scrapping the stop form entirely and reducing the burden of stop-and-search procedures. To allow the police to focus on fighting crime, we will:

• amend the health and safety laws that stand in the way of common sense policing;

• give police the power to identify offenders in order to protect the public and prevent crime;

• return charging discretion to the police for minor offences; and,

• process criminals more quickly by videolinking custody cells and courts.

We will replace the existing, invisible and unaccountable police authorities and make the police accountable to a directly-elected individual who will set policing priorities for local communities. They will be responsible for setting the budget and the strategy for local police forces, with the police retaining their operational independence.

We will oblige the police to publish detailed local crime data statistics every month, in an open and standardised format. Extremists, serious criminals and others find our borders far too easy to penetrate. That is why we will create a dedicated Border Police Force, as part of a refocused Serious Organised Crime Agency, to enhance national security, improve immigration controls, and crack down on the trafficking of people, weapons and drugs. We will work with police forces to strengthen arrangements to deal with serious crime and other cross-boundary policing challenges, and extend collaboration between forces to deliver better value for money.

Prisons with a purpose

In the last three years, 80,000 criminals have been released early from prison because the Government failed to build enough places. We are determined that early release will not be introduced again, so we will redevelop the prison estate and increase capacity as necessary to stop it. Under Labour, the number of foreign criminals in our prisons has more than doubled. We will extend early deportation of foreign national prisoners to reduce further the pressure on our prison population. Many people feel that sentencing in Britain is dishonest and misleading. So we will introduce a system where the courts can specify minimum and maximum sentences for certain offenders. These prisoners will only be able to leave jail after their minimum sentence is served by having earned their release, not simply by right.

We will never bring our crime rate down or start to reduce the costs of crime until we properly rehabilitate ex-prisoners. So, with a Conservative government, when offenders leave prison, they will be trained and rehabilitated by private and voluntary sector providers, under supervision. We will use the same approach that lies behind our welfare reform plans, payment by results, to cut re-offending, with organisations paid using savings in the criminal justice system from the resulting lower levels of crime.

Drug and alcohol addiction are behind many of the crimes that are committed on our streets, but the treatment that too many addicts receive just maintains their habits. We will give courts the power to use abstinence-based Drug Rehabilitation Orders to help offenders kick drugs once and for all. We will introduce a system of temporary bans on new 'legal highs' while health issues are considered by independent experts.

To reform our system of rehabilitation further, we will:

• apply our payment by results reforms to the youth justice system;

• engage with specialist organisations to provide education, mentoring and drug rehabilitation programmes to help young offenders go straight; and,

• pilot a scheme to create Prison and Rehabilitation Trusts so that just one organisation is responsible for helping to stop a criminal re-offending.

CHANGE POLITICS

A Conservative government will introduce a power of 're-call' to allow electors to kick out MPs, a power that will be triggered by proven serious wrongdoing. And we will introduce a Parliamentary Privilege Act to make clear that privilege cannot be abused by MPs to evade justice. We will cut the perks and bureaucracy associated with Parliament to save over £100 million a year. We will consult with the Independent Parliamentary Standards Authority on how to move away from the generous final-salary pension system for MPs. The public are concerned about the influence of money on politics, whether it is from trade unions, individuals, or the lobbying industry. We will seek an agreement on a comprehensive package of reform that will encourage individual donations and include an across-the-board cap on donations. This will mark the end of the big donor era and the problems it has sometimes entailed.

A Conservative government will introduce new measures to ensure that the contacts and knowledge Ministers gain while being paid by the public to serve the public are not unfairly used for private gain. We will:

• ensure that ex-Ministers are banned from lobbying government for two years after leaving office;

• ensure that ex-Ministers have to seek advice on the business posts they take up for ten years after leaving office;

• rewrite the Ministerial Code to make clear that any former Minister who breaks the rules on appointments will be forced to give up some or all of their Ministerial pension; and,

• introduce new rules to stop central government bodies using public money to hire lobbyists to lobby other government bodies. The lobbying industry must regulate itself to ensure its practices are transparent – if it does not, then we will legislate to do so.

Give citizens more power

Having a single vote every four or five years is not good enough – we need to give people real control over how they are governed. So, with a Conservative government, any petition that secures 100,000 signatures will be eligible for formal debate in Parliament. The petition with the most signatures will enable members of the public to table a Bill eligible to be voted on in Parliament. And we will introduce a new Public Reading Stage for Bills to give the public an opportunity to comment on proposed legislation online. Labour have meddled shamelessly with the electoral system to try to gain political advantage. A Conservative government will ensure every vote will have equal value by introducing 'fair vote' reforms to equalise the size of constituency electorates, and conduct a boundary review to implement these changes within five years.

We will swiftly implement individual voter registration, giving everyone the right to cast their vote in person and making it easier for UK citizens living overseas to vote. We support the first-past-the-post system for Westminster elections because it gives voters the chance to kick out a government they are fed up with. We will work to build a consensus for a mainly-elected second chamber to replace the current House of Lords, recognising that an efficient and effective second chamber should play an important role in our democracy and requires both legitimacy and public confidence.

Make government more accountable and representative
We will restore the balance between government and Parliament, by:
• establishing a Backbench Business Committee to give the House of Commons more control over its timetable;
• allowing MPs the time to scrutinise law effectively;
• providing more free votes, and protecting the principle that issues of conscience – like abortion – remain subject to a free vote; and,
• making the use of the Royal Prerogative subject to greater democratic control so that Parliament is properly involved in all big national decisions.

We will scrap Labour's failed target regime and instead require every department to publish a business plan, with senior management accountable to more rigorous departmental boards for their performance. We will make it easier to reward the best civil servants and remove the least effective. We will reform the Civil Service Compensation Scheme to bring it more into line with practice in the private sector. We will put a limit on the number of special advisers and protect the impartiality of the civil service.

We will introduce a £1 million fund to help people with disabilities who want to become MPs, councillors or other elected officials with the extra costs they face in running for office. This will be funded from the existing budget of the Government Equalities Office.

Publish data so the public can hold government to account
A Conservative government will bring in new measures to enable the public to scrutinise the government's accounts to see whether it is providing value for money. All data will be published in an open and standardised format. We will:
• require public bodies to publish online the job titles of every member of staff and the salaries and expenses of senior officials paid more than the lowest salary permissible in Pay Band 1 of the Senior Civil Service pay scale, and organograms that include all positions in those bodies;
• require anyone paid more than the Prime Minister in the public sector to have their salary agreed by the Treasury;
• require senior civil servants to publish online details of expense claims and meetings with lobbyists;
• apply these transparency principles to local government, with the threshold for publication of spending items and contracts set at £500, and for the publication of salaries the same as at the national level; and,
• give councillors the power to vote on large salary packages for unelected council officials.

Curtail the quango state
Any quangos that do not perform a technical function or a function that requires political impartiality, or act independently to establish facts, will be abolished. To increase the scrutiny of quangos, we will:
• give Select Committees the right to hold confirmation hearings for major public appointments;
• examine the case for giving Select Committees the power to prevent increases in quango budgets; and,
• ensure that the National Audit Office has full access to the BBC's accounts.

Reduce the cost of procurement
We will tackle wasteful government procurement by:
• strengthening the role of the Chief Information Officer

to get a grip on government ICT projects;
• introducing a series of changes to ICT procurement to deliver better value for money;
• appointing senior private sector nonexecutives to departmental boards to deliver better value for money;
• publishing in full government contracts for goods and services worth over £25,000; and,
• increasing the accountability of EU spending by publishing details of every UK project that receives over £25,000 of EU funds.

Make politics more local
The planning system is vital for a strong economy, for an attractive and sustainable environment, and for a successful democracy. A Conservative government will introduce a new 'open source' planning system. This will mean that people in each neighbourhood will be able to specify what kind of development they want to see in their area. These neighbourhood plans will be consolidated into a local plan.

We will abolish the entire bureaucratic and undemocratic tier of regional planning, including the Regional Spatial Strategies and building targets.

Developers will have to pay a tariff to the local authority to compensate the community for loss of amenity and costs of additional infrastructure. The tariff will replace the payments and levies on development that have grown up under Labour. A portion of this tariff will be kept by the neighbourhoods in which a given development takes place, providing clear incentives for communities which go for growth. Significant local projects, like new housing estates, will have to be designed through a collaborative process that has involved the neighbourhood. Immediate neighbours will have a new role – with a faster approvals process for planning applications where neighbours raise no objections. At the national level, for all forms of development, we will publish and present to Parliament for debate a simple and consolidated national planning framework, which will set out national economic and environmental priorities. To give communities greater control over planning, we will:
• abolish the power of planning inspectors to rewrite local plans;
• amend the 'Use Classes Order' so that people can use buildings for any purpose allowed in the local plan;
• limit appeals against planning decisions to cases that involve abuse of process or failure to apply the local plan;
• encourage county councils and unitary authorities to compile infrastructure plans;
• give local planning authorities and other public authorities a duty to co-operate with one another; and,
• allow neighbourhoods to stop 'garden grabbing'.

Deliver more affordable homes
We want to create a property-owning democracy where everyone has the chance to own their own home. That is why we will permanently raise the stamp duty threshold to £250,000 for first-time buyers, meaning nine out of ten of them will pay no tax on their first home purchase.

Communities should benefit when they choose to develop sustainably, so we will match pound-for-pound the council tax receipts that local authorities receive from new homes to encourage sensitive local development. We will create new local housing trusts to allow communities to grant planning permission for new housing within villages and towns so that the benefits of development remain within the local area. We will also abolish Home Information Packs, which have made a significant contribution to problems in our housing market.

A Conservative government will make it easier for social tenants to own or part-own their home. We will:
• introduce a 'foot on the ladder' programme to offer an equity stake to good social tenants, which can be cashed in when they move out of social rented accommodation;
• pilot a 'right to move' scheme and introduce a nationwide social home swap programme, so social tenants can

transfer their tenancy to another home; and,
• respect the tenures and rents of social housing tenants.

We will implement a range of measures to address the problems of the homeless, including introducing more accurate street counts and ensuring a Minister in each relevant department has homelessness in their brief.

Give people more power and control over their lives

Mirroring our reforms at the national level, we will give residents the power to instigate local referendums on any local issue if 5 per cent of the local population sign up, and they will also be able to veto any proposed high council tax increases. We will stop Labour's plans to impose supplementary business rates on firms if a majority do not give their consent.

Nothing underlines the powerlessness that many communities feel more than the loss of essential services, like post offices and pubs, because of decisions made by distant bureaucrats. Our 'community right to buy' scheme will give local people the power to protect any community assets that are threatened with closure. In addition, we will:
• give people a 'right to bid' to run any community service instead of the state; and,
• reform the governance arrangements in football to enable co-operative ownership models to be established by supporters.

We will give democratically accountable local government greater power to improve their citizens' lives by:
• giving local councils a 'general power of competence', so that they have explicit authority to do what is necessary to improve their communities;
• ending ring-fencing so that funding can be spent on local priorities;
• scrapping the hundreds of process targets Labour have imposed on councils;
• ending the bureaucratic inspection regime that stops councils focusing on residents' main concerns;
• scrapping Labour's uncompleted plans to impose unwieldy and expensive unitary councils and to force the regionalisation of the fire service;
• ending the 'predetermination rules' that prevent councillors speaking up about issues that they have campaigned on; and,
• encouraging greater use of ward budgets for councillors.

We have seen that a single municipal leader can inject dynamism and ambition into their communities. So, initially, we will give the citizens in each of England's twelve largest cities the chance of having an elected mayor. We will abolish the Government Office for London as part of our plan to devolve more power downwards to the London Boroughs and the Mayor of London. Decentralising control must go hand in hand with creating much greater transparency in local government. Power without information is not enough. We will implement fully the Sustainable Communities Act, and reintroduce the Sustainable Communities Act (Amendment) Bill as government legislation, to give people greater information on, and control over, what is being spent by each government agency in their area.

We will sweep away the rules that stop local newspapers owning other local media platforms and create a new network of local television stations. And we will tighten the rules on taxpayer-funded publicity spending by town halls.

Restore our civil liberties

Labour's approach to our personal privacy is the worst of all worlds – intrusive, ineffective and enormously expensive. We will scrap ID cards, the National Identity Register and the Contactpoint database. To protect our freedoms from state encroachment and encourage greater social responsibility, we will replace the Human Rights Act with a UK Bill of Rights. We will review and reform libel laws to protect freedom of speech, reduce costs and discourage libel tourism. We will strengthen the powers of the Information Commissioner to penalise any public body found guilty of mismanaging data. We will take further steps to protect people from unwarranted intrusion by the state, including:
• cutting back intrusive powers of entry into homes, which have been massively extended under Labour;
• curtailing the surveillance powers that allow some councils to use anti-terrorism laws to spy on people making trivial mistakes or minor breaches of the rules;
• requiring Privacy Impact Assessments of any proposal that involves data collection or sharing; and,
• ensuring proper Parliamentary scrutiny of any new powers of data-sharing.

We will legislate to make sure that our DNA database is used primarily to store information about those who are guilty of committing crimes rather than those who are innocent. We will collect the DNA of all existing prisoners, those under state supervision who have been convicted of an offence, and anyone convicted of a serious recordable offence. We pushed the Government to end the permanent retention of innocent people's DNA, and we will change the guidance to give people on the database who have been wrongly accused of a minor crime an automatic right to have their DNA withdrawn. We believe that people working in positions of trust with children should go through a proper criminal record check. We will review the criminal records and 'vetting and barring' regime and scale it back to common sense levels.

The Hunting Act has proved unworkable. A Conservative government will give Parliament the opportunity to repeal the Hunting Act on a free vote, with a government bill in government time.

Support devolution

We support the changes proposed by the Calman Commission for clarifying the devolution settlement and creating a relationship of mutual respect between Westminster and Holyrood:
• The Prime Minister and other Ministers will go to Holyrood for questioning on a regular basis.
• The Scottish Parliament should have more responsibility for raising the money it spends.

We will produce our own White Paper by May 2011 to set out how we will deal with the issues raised by Calman, and we will legislate to implement those proposals within the next Parliament.

We will not stand in the way of the referendum on further legislative powers requested by the Welsh Assembly. The people of Wales will decide the outcome and Conservatives will have a free vote. But our priority remains getting people back into work and strengthening the Welsh economy. So we will seek ways to work with the Welsh Assembly Government to increase economic growth and improve people's quality of life.

In Northern Ireland, we support the political institutions established in the past decade and we are committed to making devolution work. We will continue to promote peace, stability and economic prosperity and work to bring Northern Ireland back into the mainstream of UK politics. We will produce a government paper examining the mechanism for changing the corporation tax rate in Northern Ireland, in order to attract significant new investment. And we will stop the practice of 'double-jobbing', whereby elected representatives sit in both Westminster and Stormont.

Labour have refused to address the so-called 'West Lothian Question': the unfair situation of Scottish MPs voting on matters which are devolved. A Conservative government will introduce new rules so that legislation referring specifically to England, or to England and Wales, cannot be enacted without the consent of MPs representing constituencies of those countries.

PROTECT THE ENVIRONMENT

Climate change is a global phenomenon, and that means the world must work together to reduce harmful emissions. A Conservative government will work towards an ambitious global deal that will limit emissions and make available substantial financial resources for adaptation and mitigation. As part of our commitment to move towards a low carbon future, we can confirm our aim of reducing carbon emissions by 80 per cent by 2050. In government, we will lead from the front by delivering a 10 per cent cut in central government emissions within twelve months and by working with local authorities and others to deliver emissions reductions.

Promote low carbon energy production

The way our energy is produced and transmitted is stuck in the last century. A Conservative government will transform this 'dumb', unresponsive network and create an 'electricity internet' – a highly interactive network, based on a new smart grid that will interact with smart meters in people's homes, to manage supply and demand. This will allow a huge increase in renewable power, and far greater choice for consumers. To limit harmful emissions from UK power stations, we will take steps to encourage new low carbon energy production, including:
• introducing an Emissions Performance Standard to limit the levels of greenhouse gases our power stations produce;
• clearing the way for new nuclear power stations – provided they receive no public subsidy;
• creating four carbon capture and storage equipped plants, taking coal – one of the most polluting fuels of all – and transforming it into a low carbon fuel of the future;
• delivering an offshore electricity grid in order to support the development of a new generation of offshore wind power, and establishing at least two Marine Energy Parks;
• giving local authorities the power to establish new district heating networks which use biogas and other low carbon fuels;
• allowing communities that host renewable energy projects like wind farms to keep the additional business rates they generate for six years; and,
• giving incentives for smaller-scale energy generation, including capturing heat that is currently wasted.

Safeguard the UK's energy security

Britain needs an energy policy that is clear, consistent and stable. That means that Ministers will be unambiguously responsible for determining energy policy and delivering an Annual Energy Statement to Parliament to set a clear direction for energy policy. To safeguard our energy security, we will reform the energy regulator Ofgem so that:
• it focuses on executing energy policy;
• it is tasked with monitoring the spare capacity in the energy market and making provisions for additional capacity where required; and,
• its competition policy and consumer protection powers pass to the Office of Fair Trading.

As a result, we will cut the number of quangos intervening in the energy market.

We will work to diversify the sources of the gas we need, secure long term contracts and increase storage capacity to guarantee supplies throughout the year.

Help people go green

We will improve the energy efficiency of everyday appliances by drawing on the experience of the 'top runner' scheme from Japan. To help further, we will:
• ensure that 10 per cent of the staff directly employed by 'Green Deal' providers are apprentices, helping to build a green collar workforce for the future;
• keep Energy Performance Certificates to help people improve the environmental rating of their property; and,
• give Post Office Card Account holders the chance to benefit from direct debit discounts, worth up to £150 a year.

Conserve wildlife

We will support the strongest protection for endangered species and work to protect vital habitats from destruction. We will tackle the smuggling and illegal trade in wild-

life through our new Border Police Force. We will fight for wholesale reform of the Common Fisheries Policy to encourage sustainable practices, give communities a greater say over the future of their fishing industries, and end the scandal of fish discards. We will take forward the Marine and Coastal Access Act and ensure that its conservation measures are implemented effectively, including the creation of Marine Conservation Zones.

We will work to reduce the use of animals in scientific research. We will promote responsible pet ownership by introducing codes of practice under the Animal Welfare Act, and target irresponsible owners of dangerous dogs.

To give wildlife greater protection, we will:
• firmly oppose any resumption of commercial whaling and do all we can to ensure that the international moratorium stays in place;
• press for a total ban on ivory sales and the destruction of existing stockpiles; and,
• promote new green spaces and wildlife corridors to help animals adapt and thrive in the face of climate change.

Protect habitats

The natural world faces great pressure from development and climate change. We will produce a White Paper on protecting the natural environment, including a focus on restoring habitat. We will pioneer a new system of conservation credits to protect habitats. We will maintain national Green Belt protection, Areas of Outstanding Natural Beauty (AONBs), National Parks, Sites of Special Scientific Interest and other environmental designations which protect the character of our country's landscape. In addition, we will:
• review the governance arrangements for National Parks and AONBs to ensure that they are more accountable to local communities; and,
• work to reduce litter, which spoils too much of our countryside and urban environment.

Since 1997, the area of new woodland created in England each year has more than halved. In addition to ongoing woodland creation, we will launch a national tree planting campaign, planting up to one million new trees in the next Parliament. We will tackle illegal logging by:
• pressing for financial support from within a reformed EU budget to be given to developing countries to halt deforestation;
• pressing for only legally-harvested timber and timber products to be made available on the market; and,
• introducing a new criminal offence under UK law for the import and possession of illegal timber.

Promote sustainable and productive farming practices

Our farmland is a national resource for future generations and the foundation of our food security. We will prevent development on the most fertile farmland, in all but exceptional circumstances. To promote sustainable farming practices further, we will:
• support the Campaign for the Farmed Environment and seek to create a more effective system of environmental stewardship;
• ensure that consumers have the right to choose non-GM foods through clear labelling;
• not permit any commercial planting of GM crops until and unless it has been assessed as safe for people and the environment; and,
• develop a legally-binding protocol covering the separation of GM and non-GM material, including industry liability.

We will negotiate for further reform of the Common Agricultural Policy (CAP) to deliver greater value for money while supporting the sustainability of British farming. The new CAP should reflect the importance we attach to the environment, to ensuring food security and to tackling global poverty. We advocate the dismantling of market-distorting subsidies at a pace that allows time for British farmers and producers in developing countries to adapt. We will minimise and reform on-farm inspections, and abolish the Agricultural Wages Board. The most pressing animal health problem in the UK today is bovine tuberculosis (bTB), which has led to the slaughter of over 250,000 cattle since 1997. As part of a package of measures, we will introduce a carefully-managed and science-led policy of badger control in areas with high and persistent levels of bTB . Government should take the lead by procuring more sustainably. We will ensure that food procured by government departments, and eventually the whole public sector, meets British standards of production, wherever this can be achieved without increasing overall costs. We will introduce honesty in food labelling, if necessary through legislation, so consumers can be confident about where their food comes from. This will ensure that meat labelled as 'British' is born and bred in Britain, and raised to our high welfare standards. And we will promote local food networks so that homes and businesses can obtain supplies of locally produced food.

We will ensure a fair market for food suppliers, especially farmers, by reducing the burden of regulation. To ensure the grocery supply code of practice is applied fairly, we will introduce an independent supermarket ombudsman.

Use natural resources responsibly

We will introduce a Responsibility Deal on waste – a voluntary arrangement among producers to cut back on the production of waste and improve its disposal – as we move towards our goal of a zero-waste society. Households need new incentives to go green, so we will reward people who do the right thing by encouraging councils to pay people to recycle, while scrapping Labour's plans for new bin taxes on families. To help this happen, we will put a floor under the standard rate of landfill tax until 2020 to encourage alternative forms of waste disposal.

We will reform the water industry, and bring in new measures to encourage businesses and households to value this precious resource more highly, and protect poorer households from excessive rises in water bills. To cope with the increased risk of flooding associated with climate change, we will take forward the findings of the Pitt Review to improve our flood defences, prevent unnecessary building in areas of high flood risk, and ensure the country is better equipped when flooding does take place.

PROMOTE OUR NATIONAL INTEREST

We will establish a National Security Council to coordinate responses to the dangers we face, which will be chaired by the Prime Minister. In addition, we will:
- create a National Security Adviser and a new National Resilience Team for Homeland Security;
- develop a National Security Strategy and oversee a Strategic Defence and Security Review that implements that strategy; and,
- establish a new Permanent Military Command for Homeland Defence and Security to provide a more structured military contribution to homeland security.

A Conservative government will ban any organisations which advocate hate or the violent overthrow of our society, such as Hizb-ut-Tahrir, and close down organisations which attempt to fund terrorism from the UK. In Northern Ireland, we will continue to give our fullest support to the police and other agencies in their efforts to combat the threat from dissident republican and other terrorist organisations.

Support our brave Armed Forces

Our mission in Afghanistan is vital to our national security. Success in Afghanistan will be achieved when it is a more stable state, able to manage its own security, resist outside interference, and prevent terrorists from using its territory as a safe haven. We will always ensure our Forces have the resources they need to carry out their mission properly, and we will press other members of NATO to take their fair share of the military burden. The training of Afghanistan's own security forces is key to the success of the mission, and we will continue to make it a priority.

Our Strategic Defence and Security Review will ensure that resources for our Armed Forces are matched to our foreign policy requirements. We support the decision to renew Britain's submarine-based nuclear deterrent, based on the Trident missile system. We will review the structure of the Ministry of Defence to reduce running costs by 25 per cent. We will reform the procurement process to ensure the delivery of equipment on time and on budget. We will release spending on unnecessary and bureaucratic EU defence initiatives and spend the money on our Armed Forces. As part of that process, we will re-evaluate our position with the European Defence Agency.

Our commitment to look after the Armed Forces and their families – the Military Covenant – has been allowed to fall into disrepair. This is one of the most damning failures of Gordon Brown's government. We will restore the Military Covenant and ensure that our Armed Forces, their families and veterans are properly taken care of. To make that happen, we will:
- double the operational allowance;
- maximise rest and recuperation leave;
- ensure our servicemen and women are treated in dedicated military wards in hospital;
- change the rules so that service personnel are not locked out of the voting system by rules that Labour introduced;
- use 'pupil level annual school census' data to include service children within our plans for a pupil premium in schools, ensuring they attract extra funding;
- provide university and further education scholarships for the children of servicemen and women killed while on active duty, backdated to 1990;
- pilot a mental health follow-up service for those who have left the services; and,
- review the rules governing the awarding of medals.

A liberal Conservative foreign policy

A Conservative government will champion a distinctive British foreign policy. We will renew and reinforce our engagement with the rest of the world and build up British influence by deepening our alliances beyond Europe and the United States, not only diplomatically but in culture, education, commerce and security. A Conservative government will always speak up for freedom and human rights. Torture is unacceptable and abhorrent, and we will never condone it.

We will support humanitarian intervention when it is practical and necessary, while working with other countries to prevent conflict arising.

Promoting Britain's interests and values means developing and strengthening our alliances and reforming international institutions. To achieve these goals, we will:
- work to establish a new special relationship with India, the world's largest democracy;
- seek closer engagement with China while standing firm on human rights;
- elevate our relationships with many friendly nations, including in the Middle East, as well as North Africa, South Asia and Latin America;
- press to keep the EU's doors open to those countries, including Turkey, that wish to join, conditional on the rigorous application of the accession criteria;
- support permanent seats on the United Nations Security Council for Japan, India, Germany, Brazil and African representation; and,
- strengthen the Commonwealth as a focus for promoting democratic values and development.

We will work with our allies across the world to prevent conflict and secure peace. We will maintain a strong, close and frank relationship with the United States. We will work closely with other European countries to establish a common approach to common problems, such as climate change. We will be committed to NATO as the ultimate guarantor of Europe's security. To ensure our global security further, we will:

• work towards stability in Afghanistan and Pakistan;
• support concerted international efforts to prevent Iran from obtaining a nuclear weapon;
• support a two-state solution in the Middle East;
• promote stability in the Western Balkans;
• be ready to assist Cypriots in their efforts to agree a just, balanced and lasting settlement to reunite their island; and,
• play our part in efforts to make the world safer from the dangers of nuclear weapons and nuclear proliferation.

European countries need to work together to boost global economic growth, fight global poverty, and combat global climate change. The European Union has a crucial part to play in enabling the countries of Europe to meet these great challenges of the 21st century. A Conservative government will play an active and energetic role in the European Union to advance these causes. We will stand for open markets, and a strong transatlantic relationship; for an EU that looks out to the world, and that builds strong and open relations with rising powers like China and India. And, like every other Member State, we will fight our corner to promote our national interests.

We believe Britain's interests are best served by membership of a European Union that is an association of its Member States. We will never allow Britain to slide into a federal Europe. Labour's ratification of the Lisbon Treaty without the consent of the British people has been a betrayal of this country's democratic traditions. In government, we will put in place a number of measures to make sure this shameful episode can never happen again.

Restore democratic control

In future, the British people must have their say on any transfer of powers to the European Union. We will amend the 1972 European Communities Act so that any proposed future Treaty that transferred areas of power, or competences, would be subject to a referendum – a 'referendum lock'. A Conservative government would never take the UK into the Euro. Our amendment to the 1972 Act will prevent any future government from doing so without a referendum.

Unlike other European countries, the UK does not have a written constitution. We will introduce a United Kingdom Sovereignty Bill to make it clear that ultimate authority stays in this country, in our Parliament. The Lisbon Treaty contains a number of so called 'ratchet clauses', which allow the powers of the EU to expand in the future without a new Treaty. We do not believe that any of these 'ratchet clauses' should be used to hand over more powers from Britain to the EU. So a Conservative government will not agree to the UK's participation in the establishment of a European Public Prosecutor's Office or permit its jurisdiction over the UK. We will change the 1972 Act so that an Act of Parliament would be required before any 'ratchet clause' could be used. Additionally, the use of a major 'ratchet clause' which amounted to the transfer of an area of power to the EU would be subject to a referendum.

The steady and unaccountable intrusion of the European Union into almost every aspect of our lives has gone too far. A Conservative government will negotiate for three specific guarantees – on the Charter of Fundamental Rights, on criminal justice, and on social and employment legislation – with our European partners to return powers that we believe should reside with the UK, not the EU. We seek a mandate to negotiate the return of these powers from the EU to the UK

One world Conservatism

A new Conservative government will be fully committed to achieving, by 2013, the UN target of spending 0.7 per cent of national income as aid. We will stick to the rules laid down by the OE CD about what spending counts as aid. We will legislate in the first session of a new Parliament to lock in this level of spending for every year from 2013. We support the Millennium Development Goals and will continue to work towards them. We will maintain an independent Department for International Development (DFID) and keep aid untied from commercial interests. We will be completely transparent about the cost and performance of DFID programmes by independently evaluating programmes and by introducing, where appropriate, payment by results.

We will ensure British aid money is properly spent by publishing full details of British aid on the DFID website. This will include spending data on a project-by-project basis, published in an open and standardised format so that it can be used by third party websites. In addition, we will work to bring about improved transparency of aid spending by other development organisations.

We will create a new MyAid Fund to allow British people a direct say on aid spending, as well as giving people in developing countries more say over how aid is spent in their communities. We will stop giving aid to China and Russia and review which other countries should get British aid. We will focus more on the poorest, paying particular attention to development within the Commonwealth. A key aim of our aid is to make sure everyone gets access to the basics: clean water, sanitation, healthcare and education. We will focus particularly on the rights of women, children and disabled people to access these services. Malaria continues to kill nearly a million people per year, despite the fact that it is easily preventable and treatable. So, as part of our commitment to increase aid funding, a Conservative government will spend at least £500 million per year tackling malaria and will strongly support efforts to develop a malaria vaccine.

Trade and economic growth are the only sustainable way for developing countries to escape poverty, which is why we will put maximum effort into achieving an ambitious, pro-development global trade deal. Our aid programme will help poor countries put in place the building blocks of wealth creation: property rights, effective public services, stability and the rule of law.

We will provide a more integrated approach to post-conflict reconstruction where the British military is involved – building on the Stabilisation Unit in Whitehall and creating a new Stabilisation and Reconstruction Force to bridge the gap between the military and the reconstruction effort. To help deliver on our commitment to developing countries, we will:
• establish a Poverty Impact Fund to support innovative and effective British poverty fighting groups which do not currently qualify for government funding;
• explore ways to help the very poorest developing countries take part in international climate change negotiations, and work to make our aid 'climate-smart';
• end Labour's use of the Export Credit Guarantee Department to support investment in dirty fossil fuel power stations, and instead use it to help spread new green energy technology to developing countries; and,
• encourage the establishment of a Pan-African Free Trade Area, which has the potential to transform that continent's economies.

This is an edited version of the Conservative Party manifesto.

Liberal Democrat manifesto

Fair taxes and fair benefits to help every family get by

Liberal Democrats want to make the tax and benefits system fair, so that everyone, be they young or old, can afford to get by. We have plans for the most radical, far-reaching tax reforms in a generation. These changes are desperately needed. Conservative and Labour governments have changed Britain into one of the most unequal societies in the developed world, where ordinary people struggle to make ends meet while the richest benefit from tax breaks. The poorest fifth of the population pay a higher proportion of their income in tax than the richest fifth. We set out in this manifesto a clear plan to bring the budget back under control, being honest about the tough choices we need to take. We will cut taxes for millions of working people and pensioners, paid for by making sure that the very wealthy pay their fair share and that polluting air travel is properly taxed. We will boost the state pension by immediately restoring the link with earnings growth.

Tax fairness for everyone

Under a Liberal Democrat government, you will not have to pay any income tax on the first £10,000 you earn. This will put £700 back into the pockets of millions of people on low and middle incomes and free 3.6 million more people on low incomes from having to pay any income tax at all. In this way, we will help people who are struggling to make ends meet and provide an incentive to work and save. This change will be paid for by:

• Giving tax relief on pensions only at the basic rate, so that everyone gets the same tax relief on their pension contributions.
• Taxing capital gains at the same rates as income, so that all the money you make is taxed in the same way.
• Tackling tax avoidance and evasion, with new powers for HM Revenue & Customs.
• Ensuring pollution is properly taxed by replacing the per-passenger Air Passenger Duty with a per-plane duty (PPD), ensuring that air freight is taxed for the first time. We will also introduce an additional, higher rate of PPD on domestic flights if realistic alternative and less polluting travel is available.
• Introducing a Mansion Tax at a rate of 1 per cent on properties worth over £2 million, paid on the value of the property above that level. In addition we will reform the system of 'non-domiciled' status, allowing people to hold such status for up to seven years.

Dealing with the deficit

A Liberal Democrat government will be straight with people about the tough choices ahead. Not only must waste be eliminated, but we must also be bold about finding big areas of spending that can be cut completely. That way we can control borrowing, protect the services people rely on most and still find some money to invest in building a fair future. We have already identified over £15 billion of savings in government spending per year, vastly in excess of the £5 billion per year that we have set aside for additional spending commitments. All our spending commitments will be funded from this pool of identified savings, with all remaining savings used to reduce the deficit. We must ensure the timing is right. If spending is cut too soon, it would undermine the much-needed recovery and cost jobs. We will base the timing of cuts on an objective assessment of economic conditions, not political dogma. Our working assumption is that the economy will be in a stable enough condition to bear cuts from the beginning of 2011–12. Through making tough choices, as well as increasing efficiency, our savings will include:

• Setting a £400 pay rise cap for all public sector workers, initially for two years, ensuring that the lowest paid are eligible for the biggest percentage rise.
• Restricting tax credits.
• Ending government payments into Child Trust Funds.
• Introducing a Banking Levy so that banks pay for the financial support they have received, until such time as they can be split up in order to insulate retail banking from investment risks.
• Scrapping ID cards and the next generation of biometric passports.
• Cancelling Eurofighter Tranche 3b.
• Scaling back HomeBuy schemes.
• Reforming prisons, including through reducing the number of short sentences.
• Cutting back burdensome regulation of local authorities.

Further details of our savings, including a number of smaller savings items, can be found in the tables annexed to the chapter on Credible and Responsible Finances on page 96. In the longer term, as part of a Comprehensive Spending Review (CSR) involving wide consultation, we will seek to identify additional savings which can be used to pay down the deficit further. These will include:

• Saying no to the like-for-like replacement of the Trident nuclear weapons system, which could cost £100 billion. We will hold a full defence review to establish the best alternative for Britain's future security.
• Reforming public sector pensions to ensure that they are sustainable and affordable for the long term, with an independent review to agree a settlement that is fair for all taxpayers as well as for public servants.
• Better government IT procurement, investigating the potential of different approaches such as cloud computing and open-source software.
• A wholesale review of value for money in the public sector based on the findings of the National Audit Office and the House of Commons Public Accounts Committee. We will establish a Council on Financial Stability, involving representatives of all parties, the Governor of the Bank of England and the Chair of the Financial Services Authority. This group would agree the timeframe and scale of a deficit reduction plan to set the framework (not the detail) for the CSR and seek to promote it externally and domestically. Any agreement would be without prejudice to parties retaining and advocating distinctive views on a wide range of issues (such as fair taxes and spending priorities).

Fairness in pensions, savings and benefits

We will make pensions and benefits fair and reward savers by:

• Immediately restoring the link between the basic state pension and earnings. We will uprate the state pension annually by whichever is the higher of growth in earnings, growth in prices or 2.5 per cent.
• Increasing the income tax threshold to £10,000.
• Giving people greater flexibility in accessing part of their personal pension fund early, for example to help in times of financial hardship.
• Giving people control over their pension by scrapping the rule that compels you to buy an annuity when you reach age 75.
• Allowing individuals to save through our UK Infrastructure Bank, offering stable long-term returns.
• Meeting the government's obligations towards Equitable Life policyholders who have suffered loss. We will set up a swift, simple, transparent and fair payment scheme.
• Ending the rollercoaster of tax credit overpayments by fixing payments for six months at a time. We will

also target payments towards those who need them most.
• Reforming Winter Fuel Payments to extend them to all severely disabled people, paid for by delaying age-related Winter Fuel Payments until people reach 65. We will continue to pay Winter Fuel Payments to all current recipients of Pension Credit.

Opportunities for all in a fair, green economy
Banks must be made to behave responsibly. And we need to support and develop new ways of financing growing businesses, with equity rather than debt, and without relying too heavily on the financial centre of the City of London. More diverse sources of finance will provide the funding needed to develop innovative new products and reverse the decline in the UK's manufacturing base.

In order to put the economy on a new footing, we will:
• Break up the banks, to ensure taxpayers are never again expected to underwrite high-risk banking. We would establish a clear separation between low-risk retail banking and high-risk investment banking, and encourage the development of local and regional banks. We will introduce a Banking Levy, so that banks pay for their tax-payer guarantee, until the break-up is complete.
• Get the banks lending responsibly again. The taxpayers' representatives on the boards of the banks the public own or part-own should insist banks lend to viable businesses on fair terms again.
• Ensure that the bonus system can never again encourage banks to behave in a way that puts the financial system at risk or offers rewards for failure.
• Support the establishment of Local Enterprise Funds and Regional Stock Exchanges. Local Enterprise Funds will help local investors put money into growing businesses in their own part of the country and support the development of new products from research to production. Regional Stock Exchanges will be a route for businesses to access equity without the heavy regulatory requirements of a London listing.

Creating jobs that last
We have identified £3.1 billion of public spending that can be used to create 100,000 jobs. This will be a first step towards our target for a zero-carbon Britain by 2050. Our green stimulus plan will create 100,000 jobs. It comprises:
• Investing up to £400 million in refurbishing shipyards in the North of England and Scotland so that they can manufacture offshore wind turbines and other marine renewable energy equipment. As part of this scheme we will write off backdated business rates demands from before April 2008 for businesses in ports.
• Launching an 'Eco Cash-Back' scheme, for one year only, which will give you £400 if you install double glazing, replace an old boiler, or install micro-generation. If you choose micro-generation, you will be able to sell the energy back to the National Grid at a profit, with a more attractive feed-in tariff than under current government plans.
• Setting aside extra money for schools who want to improve the energy efficiency of their buildings. They will pay back the loan over time from energy savings, creating a rolling fund to help insulate every public building.
• Bringing 250,000 empty homes back into use. People who own these homes will get a grant or a cheap loan to renovate them so that they can be used: grants if the home is for social housing, loans for private use.
• Investing £140 million in a bus scrappage scheme that helps bus companies to replace old polluting buses with new, accessible low-carbon ones and creates jobs.

We will also create hundreds of thousands of opportunities for young people affected by the recession. A work placement scheme with up to 800,000 places will ensure that young people have the opportunity to gain skills, qualifications and work experience even if they can't find a job. Young people on the scheme would be paid £55 a week for up to three months. We will also fund 15,000 extra Foundation Degree places, fully meet the up-front costs of adult apprenticeships, and increase the Adult Learning Grant to £45 a week for 18 to 24-year-olds in Further Education.

To help the transition to a green economy over the longer-term, we will set up a United Kingdom Infrastructure Bank (UKIB) to attract private finance – essential to delivering the much-needed expansion of Britain's transport and energy infrastructure when public finances are tight. The UKIB will:
• Create a new route to provide capital, guarantees and equity to infrastructure projects, using public money to attract upfront private investment.
• Increase the funding available from the private sector by tapping into the funds of institutional investors, namely annuity funds looking for a home in the UK.
• Reduce the cost of long-term funding as compared with the Private Finance Initiative.
• Provide the opportunity for retail investors to save in safe long-term assets.
• Be a stand-alone public entity, independent from government but with a long-term strategic remit. It would have the ability to reject or accept proposals based on whether they are financially viable or within its remit.
• Start with government seed funding which it can use as a capital base to borrow against. This seed funding could be raised from the sell-off of the student loan book or the Tote as the government has already proposed. In addition borrowing could be secured against or raised from government-owned assets such as the Dartford Crossing. We will investigate other ways of raising seed capital such as auctioning airport landing slots and parts of the radio spectrum.

Enabling enterprise that benefits Britain
Liberal Democrats will:
• Reduce the burden of unnecessary red tape by properly assessing the cost and effectiveness of regulations before and after they are introduced, using 'sunset clauses' to ensure that the need for a regulation is regularly reviewed, and working towards the principle of 'one in, one out' for new rules.
• Put an end to the so-called 'gold-plating' of EU rules, so that British businesses are not disadvantaged relative to their European competitors.
• Reform business rates, creating a fairer system where rates are based on site values rather than rental values and are the responsibility of local authorities. We will make small company relief automatic and also seek to ensure that the burden is spread more equitably between small and large businesses.
• Reform Regional Development Agencies (RDAs) to focus solely on economic development, removing duplication with other parts of government and allowing substantial budget reductions. We will give responsibility for economic development to local authorities. Where existing RDAs have strong local support, they may continue with refocused economic development objectives. Where they do not, they will be scrapped and their functions taken over by local authorities.
• Ensure that takeover rules serve the UK economy. We will restore a public interest test so that a broader range of factors than just competition can be considered by regulators when takeovers are proposed and we will ensure that the outcome of takeover bids is determined by the long-term shareholder base. We will reintroduce the Operating and Financial Review, dropped in November 2005, to ensure that directors' social and environmental duties will have to be covered in company reporting.
• Support public investment in the roll-out of superfast broadband, targeted first at those areas which are least likely to be provided for by the market.
• Keep the tax regime and allowances that apply to the oil and gas industry under review to secure the maximum long-term benefit to the UK economy of the remaining North Sea reserves.
• Use the substantial purchasing power of government to expand the markets for green products and technologies.

Manifestos

Supporting mutuals, co-ops and social enterprises
We believe that mutuals, co-operatives and social enterprises have an important role to play in the creation of a more balanced and mixed economy. Mutuals give people a proper stake in the places they work, spreading wealth through society, and bringing innovative and imaginative business ideas to bear on meeting local needs. We will:
- Give financial regulators a clear objective of maintaining a diversity of providers in the financial services industry.
- Seek to turn Northern Rock into a building society.
- Give both Royal Mail and post offices a long-term future, by separating Post Office Ltd from the Royal Mail and retaining Post Office Ltd in full public ownership. 49 per cent of Royal Mail will be sold to create funds for investment. The ownership of the other 51 per cent will be divided between an employee trust and the government.
- Encourage community-owned renewable energy schemes where local people benefit from the power produced.
- Pass a new Mutuals, Co-operatives and Social Enterprises Bill to bring the law up to date and give responsibility for mutuals to a specific minister.

Creating a dynamic environment for science and innovation
In the current economic climate it is not possible to commit to growth in spending, but Liberal Democrats recognise the importance of science investment to the recovery and to the reshaping of the economy, making it less reliant on the City of London and creating new green industries instead. We will:
- Respect the convention that the science budget, once allocated through the Comprehensive Spending Review process, is not used for other purposes.
- Ensure that the decisions on the funding of research projects are made on the basis of peer review not Whitehall interference, while recognising the need for government to identify broad strategic priorities in a transparent manner.
- Ensure that all state-funded research, including clinical trials, is publicly accessible and that the results are published and subject to peer review.
- Reform science funding to ensure that genuinely innovative scientific research is identified and supported, instead of basing funding decisions on narrow impact factors. We need to safeguard the future of the science and engineering workforce and break the vicious cycle linking fewer University science, engineering and maths applicants to fewer teachers with specialist qualifications. We will:
- Tackle the gender gap at all levels of scientific study and research to help increase the supply of scientists. It is vital that policy, especially that relating to public health, criminal justice and environmental protection, benefits from being based on the best available evidence. We will:
- Safeguard academic freedom and the independence of scientific advisers by amending the Ministerial Code to prevent government from bullying or mistreating advisers and distorting evidence or statistics.

Fair treatment at work for everyone
We want to give employees fair opportunities to make the best use of their talents, and greater control over their working lives and conditions. Women are still paid less than men. People from Black, Asian and Minority Ethnic communities are still more likely to suffer discrimination. And there are far too many barriers to work for people with disabilities. We will change this by:
- Extending the right to request flexible working to all employees.
- Requiring name-blind job application forms to reduce sex and race discrimination in employment, initially for every company with over 100 employees.
- Introducing fair pay audits for every company with over 100 employees to combat discrimination. We will also require all public companies to declare in full all remunerations of £200,000 per year or more.

- Giving disabled job seekers better practical help to get to work, using voluntary and private sector providers, as well as JobCentre Plus services. We will also reform Access to Work, so disabled people can apply for jobs with funding already in place for equipment and adaptation that they need.

The best chance for every child
Liberal Democrats want every child to receive an excellent education, to unlock children's potential and to ensure that they can succeed in life. Too many children are still leaving school without the knowledge and skills to be successful. And your family background still has a huge effect: a typical child from a poor family will fall behind a richer classmate by the age of seven and never catch up. We will seek to ensure that all pupils leaving primary and secondary education have the skills they need.

We will free schools from the present stranglehold of central government control and encourage them to be genuinely innovative. We will invest additional money in the schools system to allow schools to cut class sizes, pay for one-to-one tuition, introduce catch-up classes, or take other steps to ensure that every child has the best possible education. We will therefore ensure that every neighbourhood is served by an excellent local school or college. We will:
- Increase the funding of the most disadvantaged pupils, around one million children. We will invest £2.5 billion in this 'Pupil Premium' to boost education opportunities for every child. This is additional money going into the schools budget, and headteachers will be free to spend it in the best interests of children.
- The extra money could be used to cut class sizes, attract the best teachers, offer extra one-to-one tuition and provide for after-school and holiday support. This will allow an average primary school to cut classes to 20 and an average secondary school to introduce catch-up classes for 160 pupils.
- Improve discipline by early intervention to tackle the poor basic education of those children who are otherwise most likely to misbehave and become demotivated.
- Guarantee Special Educational Needs (SEN) diagnostic assessments for all 5-year-olds, improve SEN provision and improve SEN training for teachers.
- Improve teacher training by increasing the size of the school-based Graduate Teacher Programme and support the expansion of Teach First to attract more top graduates into teaching. We will improve training for existing teachers over the course of their careers to keep them up to date with best practice. We will seek to ensure that science at Key Stage 4 and above is taught by appropriately qualified teachers.
- Confront bullying, including homophobic bullying, and include bullying prevention in teacher training.
- Set aside extra money for schools to improve the energy efficiency of their buildings. They will pay back the loan over time from energy savings, creating a rolling fund to help insulate other public buildings.

A better education: standards and the curriculum
To make the most of their years at school, every child needs an education tailored to suit their abilities and interests. The National Curriculum and the arbitrary split between academic and vocational qualifications isn't working. We will:
- Establish a fully independent Educational Standards Authority (ESA) with real powers to stand up to ministers and restore confidence in standards. The ESA would oversee the examinations system, the systems of school inspection and accountability, and the detail of the curriculum. It would replace the Qualifications and Curriculum Development Agency and the Office of the Qualifications and Examinations Regulator (OFQUAL), and include OFSTED, the schools inspectorate.
- Replace the Early Years Foundation Stage with a slimmed-down framework which includes a range of educational approaches and enough flexibility for every child.

- Axe the rigid National Curriculum, and replace it with a slimmed down 'Minimum Curriculum Entitlement' to be delivered by every state-funded school.
- Scale back Key Stage 2 tests at age 11, and use teacher assessment, with external checking, to improve marking.
- Create a General Diploma to bring GCSEs, A-Levels and high quality vocational qualifications together, enabling pupils to mix vocational and academic learning.
- Give 14 to 19-year-olds the right to take up a course at college, rather than at school, if it suits them better. This will enable all children to choose to study, for example, separate sciences or modern languages at GCSE, or a vocational subject.
- Seek to close the unfair funding gap between pupils in school sixth forms and Further Education colleges, as resources allow.
- Scrap the Government's plan to criminalise those who leave education between ages 16 and 18.
- Reform league tables to give parents more meaningful information which truly reflects the performance of a school. Schools should be working to get the best from all their pupils but government league tables are forcing them to focus on those who are just above or below the key C-grade borderline.

Freeing schools for excellence

Liberal Democrats want an education system where all schools will have the freedom to innovate, not be dictated to by central government. We will:
- Introduce an Education Freedom Act banning politicians from getting involved in the day-to-day running of schools. Teachers are held back by constant government interference which distracts from teaching. We would cut the size of the central department of Children, Schools and Families, and focus its activities on a few strategic priorities. Local authorities will not run schools, but will have a central strategic role, including responsibility for oversight of school performance and fair admissions. They will be expected to intervene where school leadership or performance is weak.
- Give all schools the freedom to innovate. We will ensure a level playing field for admissions and funding and replace Academies with our own model of 'Sponsor-Managed Schools'. These schools will be commissioned by and accountable to local authorities and not Whitehall, and would allow other appropriate providers, such as educational charities and parent groups, to be involved in delivering state-funded education.
- Allow parents to continue to choose faith-based schools within the state-funded sector and allow the establishment of new faith schools. We will ensure that all faith schools develop an inclusive admissions policy and end unfair discrimination on grounds of faith when recruiting staff, except for those principally responsible for optional religious instruction.
- Reform the existing rigid national pay and conditions rules to give schools and colleges more freedom, including in offering financial and other incentives to attract and retain excellent teachers, while ensuring that all staff receive the minimum national pay award.

Opportunities at college and university

There should be a wide range of opportunities for everyone at the age of 16. Liberal Democrats believe that education is important for all young people, and will create, finally, a level playing field between academic and vocational courses. And we will ensure that adults who wish to study, including those wanting to return to education later on in life, are able to do so without being put off by the burden of debt. We will:
- Scrap unfair university tuition fees for all students taking their first degree, including those studying part-time, saving them over £10,000 each. We have a financially responsible plan to phase fees out over six years, so that the change is affordable even in these difficult economic times, and without cutting university income. We will immediately scrap fees for final year students.
- Reform bursary schemes to create a National Bursary Scheme for students, so that each university gets a bursary budget suited to its students' needs. These bursaries would be awarded on the basis of studying strategic subjects (such as sciences and mathematics) and on financial hardship.
- Replace wasteful quangos (the Skills Funding Agency and the Higher Education Funding Council for England) with a single Council for Adult Skills and Higher Education.
- Scrap the arbitrary target of 50 per cent of young people attending university, focusing effort instead on a balance of college education, vocational training and apprenticeships.
- Start discussions with universities and schools about the design of a trial scheme whereby the best students from the lowest achieving schools are guaranteed a place in Higher Education.
- As part of our immediate job creation package, fund 15,000 new places on Foundation Degree courses and fully fund the off-the-job costs of adult apprenticeships, which currently have to be met by employers, for one year.
- Better target spending on adult skills. We will end Train to Gain funding for large companies, restricting the funds to the small and medium-sized firms that need the support. The money saved will be used to cover the course fees for adults taking a first Level 3 qualification (such as A-levels or an adult apprenticeship), allowing a significant reduction in the overall budget.

Protecting and improving our NHS

We are proud of the NHS – it's built on the basic British principle of fairness. Liberal Democrats believe that we can improve the NHS; in fact, we believe it's our duty to do so at a time like this when budgets are tight. We all know that too much precious NHS money is wasted on bureaucracy, and doctors and nurses spend too much time trying to meet government targets.

So our first priority is to increase spending in some parts of the NHS by cutting waste in others. We have identified specific savings that can be made in management costs, bureaucracy and quangos, and we will reinvest that money back into the health care you need. Because of the rising costs of treatments and an ageing population, there will be particular pressure on services like cancer treatment, mental health care, maternity services, and dementia care; only by going through this process of finding savings elsewhere can we protect these services in the coming years. The NHS is a huge system, and we will make changes to ensure it works as effectively as possible. We will:
- Give priority to preventing people getting ill by linking payments to health boards and GPs more directly to prevention measures.
- Cut the size of the Department of Health by half, abolish unnecessary quangos such as Connecting for Health and cut the budgets of the rest, scrap Strategic Health Authorities and seek to limit the pay and bonuses of top NHS managers so that none are paid more than the Prime Minister.
- Make the NHS work better by extending best practice on improving hospital discharge, maximising the number of day case operations, reducing delays prior to operations, and where possible moving consultations into the community.
- Integrate health and social care to create a seamless service, ending bureaucratic barriers and saving money to allow people to stay in their homes for longer rather than going into hospital or long term residential care.
- Use the money for Labour's flawed Personal Care At Home Bill to provide guaranteed respite care for the one million carers who work the longest hours. We will establish an independent commission, with cross-party support, to develop proposals for long-term care of the elderly.
- Prioritise dementia research within the health research and development budget.
- Improve access to counselling for people with mental health problems, by continuing the roll-out of cognitive and behavioural therapies.

• Reduce the ill health and crime caused by excessive drinking. We support a ban on below-cost selling, and are in favour of the principle of minimum pricing, subject to detailed work to establish how it could be used in tackling problems of irresponsible drinking. We will also review the complex, ill-thought-through system of taxation for alcohol to ensure it tackles binge drinking without unfairly penalising responsible drinkers, pubs and important local industries.

• Save lives and reduce pressure on NHS budgets by cutting air pollution. We will cancel plans for a third runway at Heathrow and other airport expansion in the South East, and reduce pollution from vehicle exhausts through tighter regulation. We will aim to fully meet European air quality targets by 2012.

More control over the health care you need

Liberal Democrats believe that one important way to improve the NHS is to make care flexible, designed to suit what patients need, not what managers want. And we believe that care would improve if local people had more control over how their health services were run.

The NHS often feels too remote and complex. Local services – especially maternity wards and accident and emergency departments – keep being closed, even though local people desperately want them to stay open. People often struggle to get convenient access to GP services, and poorer areas are less well served by the NHS, contributing to widening health inequalities. We will change this by:

• Sharply reducing centralised targets and bureaucracy, replacing them with entitlements guaranteeing that patients get diagnosis and treatment on time. If they do not, the NHS will pay for the treatment to be provided privately.

• Putting front-line staff in charge of their ward or unit budgets, and allowing staff to establish employee trusts giving them a say over how their service is run.

• Empowering local communities to improve health services through elected Local Health Boards, which will take over the role of Primary Care Trust boards in commissioning care for local people, working in co-operation with local councils. Over time, Local Health Boards should be able to take on greater responsibility for revenue and resources to allow people to fund local services that need extra money.

• Giving every patient the right to choose to register with the GP they want, without being restricted by where they live, and the right to access their GP by email.

• Ensuring that local GPs are directly involved in providing out-of-hours care.

• Reforming payments to GPs so that those who accept patients from areas with the worst health and deprivation scores receive an extra payment for each one they take.

• Giving Local Health Boards the freedom to commission services for local people from a range of different types of provider, including for example staff co-operatives, on the basis of a level playing field in any competitive tendering – ending any current bias in favour of private providers.

Quality care for all patients

We all need to be assured that, if we become unwell, the care we get will be of good quality. Most of all, we need to be confident that our safety comes first, and that the treatment we get doesn't put us in more danger. We will introduce a series of reforms to improve patient safety. We will:

• Require hospitals to be open about mistakes, and always tell patients if something has gone wrong.

• Make it illegal for a doctor to work in the UK without passing language and competence tests.

• Clamp down on anyone who is aggressive or abusive to staff in accident and emergency departments. We would encourage better working relationships between hospitals and the local police to provide an increased police presence at times of high risk, and increase prosecutions. At the same time, we will ensure that problem drinkers or substance abusers are referred for appropriate treatment. It is deeply disappointing that the Government has failed to provide adequate support for those affected by the contamination of

blood products with HIV. A Liberal Democrat government will establish a working group involving patient groups to determine appropriate levels of financial assistance.

Access to culture and sport

Liberal Democrats believe that the arts are a central part of civic and community life. They contribute to innovation, education, diversity, and social inclusion, and the creative industries are one of the fastest growing sectors of the economy. Britain's culture and heritage play a vital role in attracting visitors to the UK and boosting the very important tourism industry. We will foster an environment in which all forms of creativity are able to flourish.

We are proud that Britain is hosting the Olympic and Paralympic Games in 2012, and we support bids for other high-profile events such as the 2018 World Cup – but we believe that grassroots sport is just as important. We will give people from all backgrounds and generations the opportunity to participate in sports. Liberal Democrats will:

• Maintain free entry to national museums and galleries and open the Government Art Collection for greater public use.

• Set up a 'Creative Enterprise Fund' offering training, mentoring and small grants or loans to help creative businesses get off the ground.

• Cut red tape for putting on live music. We will reintroduce the rule allowing two performers of unamplified music in any licensed premises without the need for an entertainment licence, allow licensed venues for up to 200 people to host live music without the need for an entertainment licence, and remove the requirement for schools and hospitals to apply for a licence.

• Reform the National Lottery. We will change the way the National Lottery is taxed from a ticket tax to a gross profits tax, which is forecast to deliver more for good causes and the Exchequer.

• Use cash in dormant betting accounts to set up a capital fund for improving local sports facilities.

• Close loopholes that allow playing fields to be sold or built upon without going through the normal planning procedures. A strong and diverse media, free from government interference and pressure is essential to a free and democratic society. We will:

• Ensure that the BBC remains strong, free from interference and securely funded, not least to provide impartial news, independent of political and commercial pressures. We will also ensure that the BBC does not undermine the viability of other media providers through unfair competition based on its public funding and dominant position.

• Support a diverse regional and local media. We will help to maintain independent local sources of news and information by enabling partnerships between TV, radio and newspaper companies to reduce costs, and by limiting publicly-subsidised competition for paid advertising from local council free-sheets.

A fair deal for families of every shape and size

In Britain today, families come in all shapes and sizes. Liberal Democrats believe every family should get the support it needs to thrive, from help with childcare through to better support for carers and elderly parents.

Liberal Democrats will improve life for your family. On top of our tax cuts to put £700 in the pockets of millions of low and middle-income earners, we will allow mums and dads to share parental leave between them so they can arrange family life in the way that suits them best. We will provide better support for children at risk and young adults to help them thrive. We will restore the earnings link for pensions, and offer respite breaks for carers. And we will protect families from unfair bills.

Help for families – right from the start

The first weeks, months and years after a child is born are enormously important, but the support arrangements are simply too inflexible at the moment. When a baby is born, the mother gets a year's leave and the father gets just two

weeks, meaning the mother has to take the lion's share of the responsibility, even if their partner would rather share things more equally. Liberal Democrats will:
• Give fathers time off for ante-natal appointments.
• Allow parents to share the allocation of maternity and paternity leave between them in whatever way suits them.
• Protect existing childcare support arrangements until the nation's finances can support a longer term solution: a move to 20 hours free childcare for every child, from the age of 18 months.
• Seek to extend the period of shared parental leave up to 18 months when resources and economic circumstances allow.
• Support efforts by childcare providers to encourage more men to work in this profession.
• Extend the right to request flexible working to all employees, making it easier for grandparents, for example, to take a caring role.

Helping families stay strong

Every child deserves a happy life free from poverty and free from fear. Children face too many difficulties in today's Britain; the Government is going to fall far short of its target to cut child poverty, and young people have been demonised by a generation of politicians more interested in sounding tough than in offering help. Children are also the main victims of family breakdown. Liberal Democrats will:
• Maintain the commitment to end child poverty in the UK by 2020.
• Incorporate the UN Convention on the Rights of the Child into UK law, ending the detention of children for immigration purposes.
• Enhance child protection. We will enforce the publication of an anonymised version of Serious Case Reviews to ensure that lessons are learned.
• Support the objective of at least a 70 per cent reduction in child maltreatment by 2030, promoted by the WAVE trust.
• Help protect children and young people from developing negative body images by regulating airbrushing in adverts.
• Tackle online bullying by backing quick-report buttons on social networking sites, enabling offensive postings to be speedily removed.
• Strengthen the Youth Service by making it a statutory service, and by encouraging local authorities to provide youth services in partnership with young people and the voluntary sector.
• Set the minimum wage at the same level for all workers over 16 (except for those on apprenticeships).
• Introduce a Default Contact Arrangement which would divide the child's time between their two parents in the event of family breakdown, if there is no threat to the safety of the child.

Dignity and security in later life

Liberal Democrats will:
• Immediately restore the link between the basic state pension and earnings. We will uprate the state pension annually by whichever is the higher of growth in earnings, growth in prices or 2.5 per cent.
• Increase the income tax threshold to £10,000, saving most pensioners around £100 a year.
• Offer a week's respite for the one million carers who spend 50 hours every week looking after a sick relative.
• Scrap compulsory retirement ages, allowing those who wish to continue in work to do so.
• Give you control over your pension by scrapping the rules that compel you to buy an annuity when you reach 75.
• In the long term, aim to bring in a Citizen's Pension that will be paid to all UK citizens who are long-term residents, set at the level of the Pension Credit, though this can only be done when resources allow.
• Begin a national programme to insulate many more homes paid for by the savings from lower energy bills.

There is a further, serious, long-term crisis facing older people: the sustainability of the systems for providing long-term care. It is unacceptable that this challenge has been treated as a political football. A Liberal Democrat Government would immediately establish an independent commission to develop future proposals for long-term care that will attract all-party support and so be sustainable. We believe that the eventual solution must be based on the principles of fairness, affordability and sustainability.

A fair deal for consumers

We will:
• Change the tariffs used by energy supply companies so that the first, essential, energy you use is the cheapest. We'll ensure that effective energy efficiency measures are introduced to keep bills low and that 'social tariffs' are available to guarantee the best price for all those in most need. We will seek to extend protection and support to 'off-gasgrid' consumers.
• Address unfairness in water charges by consulting on the implementation of the Walker Review.
• Legislate to end unfair bank and financial transaction charges, so you cannot be charged more than the costs incurred.
• Improve access to banking with a PostBank, revenues from which will also help to secure the future of the Post Office.
• Impose maximum interest rates for credit cards and store cards, following consultation with the financial industry and consumer groups.
• Introduce a Universal Service Code to secure high-quality customer service in the private and public sectors, for example by requiring that the customer service phone number is free from mobiles and landlines.
• Require a local competition test for all planning applications for new retail developments and establish a local competition office within the Office of Fair Trading to investigate anti-competitive practices at a local and regional level.
• Require airlines to be honest and upfront about pricing, ending the practice of adding hidden charges.
• Cut rail fares, changing the rules in contracts with Train Operating Companies so that regulated fares fall behind inflation by 1 per cent each year, meaning a real-terms cut.
• Make Network Rail refund a third of your ticket price if you have to take a rail replacement bus service.
• Regulate the parking system to remove unfairness and stop private sector wheel-clamping.

Enhanced protection for animals

Liberal Democrats believe that ownership and use of animals is a responsibility that should not be abused. We will:
• Merge existing quangos to establish an Animal Protection Commission to investigate abuses, educate the public and enforce the law; it will also be able to publish reports on its own initiative.
• End testing of household products on animals.
• Work for the proper enforcement of regulations for the transportation of live animals across all EU member states.

Securing Britain's future with global action

Liberal Democrats believe that Britain must work together with its partners abroad if we are to have the best hope of meeting the challenges the world faces. We believe in freedom, justice, prosperity and human rights for all and will do all we can to work towards a world where these hopes become reality.

Never has there been such a need for global action. There are only a few years to take action to stop runaway climate change. The global recession proved the need for better international regulation of the financial markets. New security threats are emerging, for which Britain's armed forces are not yet fully equipped, whilst terrorists and organised criminals exploit international networks. The challenge of tackling global poverty remains, with the Millennium Development Goals still far from being achieved. And the battle for human rights remains to be fought in many countries.

Liberal Democrats will work through the European Union to deliver a global deal on climate change. We will transform the armed forces, meeting the nation's obligations under the military covenant, and conducting a defence review to ensure they are equipped for modern threats. We will push for better global financial regulation. We will strive for global nuclear disarmament, showing leadership by committing not to replace the Trident nuclear weapons system on a like-for-like basis.

We will meet the UK's obligations to the developing world by committing to spending 0.7 per cent of GNI on aid. And we will put Britain at the heart of Europe, to ensure we use our influence to achieve prosperity, security and opportunity for Britain.

Tackling climate change

Climate change is the greatest challenge facing this generation. Liberal Democrats are unwavering in our commitment: runaway climate change must be stopped, and politicians must follow the science in order to make that happen.

We will set a target for a zero-carbon Britain that doesn't contribute at all to global warming – making the British economy carbon-neutral overall by 2050, reducing carbon emissions in the UK by over 40 per cent of 1990 levels by 2020 as a step on the way.

Our response to climate change will give the British people more secure energy supplies, reduce air pollution and related health costs – and create thousands of new jobs.

Liberal Democrats will:

• Begin a ten-year programme of home insulation, offering a home energy improvement package of up to £10,000 per home, paid for by the savings from lower energy bills, and make sure every new home is fully energy-efficient by improving building regulations.

• Set a target for 40 per cent of UK electricity to come from clean, non-carbon-emitting sources by 2020, rising to 100 per cent by 2050, underpinned by guaranteed price support; and ensure that at least three-quarters of this new renewable energy comes from marine and offshore sources.

• Set out a clear renewables route map to 2050, covering grid access and investment in electricity networks, and develop new incentives to promote renewable heat.

• Transform the electricity networks into a dynamic electricity grid that can better connect and integrate new, clean energy technologies particularly through the better use of sub-sea connections, leading to a European Supergrid.

• Invest up to £400 million in refurbishing shipyards in the North of England and Scotland so that they can manufacture offshore wind turbines and other marine renewable energy equipment.

• Launch an 'Eco Cash-Back' scheme, for one year only, which will give you £400 if you install double glazing, replace an old boiler, or install micro-generation. If you choose micro-generation, you will be able to sell the energy back to the National Grid at a profit, with a more attractive feed-in tariff than under current government plans.

• Set aside extra money for schools to improve the energy efficiency of their buildings. They will pay back the loan over time from energy savings, creating a rolling fund to help insulate all public buildings.

• Invest £140 million in a bus scrappage scheme that helps bus companies to replace old polluting buses with new low-carbon ones and creates jobs.

• Block any new coal-fired power stations – the most polluting form of power generation – unless they are accompanied by the highest level of carbon capture and storage facilities.

• Reject a new generation of nuclear power stations; based on the evidence nuclear is a far more expensive way of reducing carbon emissions than promoting energy conservation and renewable energy.

• Improve energy efficiency in the commercial and public sectors, by strengthening the Carbon Reduction Commitment Energy Efficiency Scheme and requiring companies and government departments to report on their energy use and set targets for reducing it. We will set a 30 per cent energy efficiency improvement target for 2020, and will commit to the goals of the 10:10 campaign as a first step.

Leading the fight against climate change

Liberal Democrats are committed to securing a legally binding global agreement on limiting the increase in global temperatures to below 1.7 degrees Celsius. We believe that such an agreement must be based on reducing emissions overall, while equalising emissions between the developed and developing worlds – the principle of contraction and convergence. Strong and credible EU ambition, with effective UK leadership, are essential for achieving a global agreement, so that total greenhouse gas emissions peak no later than 2015. Liberal Democrats will work within Europe and internationally to give renewed urgency to global efforts to combat climate change. We will press the EU to:

• Promote the transition to a low-carbon economy in Europe, by moving unilaterally and immediately to an EU emissions reduction target of 30 per cent by 2020, adopting new long-term targets and policies for clean energy and energy efficiency; and expand investment in energy technology innovation, within Europe and internationally.

• Boost investment in clean energy by reforming the EU emissions trading scheme – bringing in a tighter cap on emissions, auctioning as many allowances as possible, and encouraging other European countries to increase the use of reserve prices in allowance auctions.

• Engage with major emitters and deepen diplomatic co-operation between the EU and emerging economies and developing countries, provide enhanced financial support for low-carbon solutions and lead international efforts to promote the transfer of technologies that will help to tackle climate change.

• Work for the adoption of 'quick win' measures that could be initiated within the next few years such as reducing the use of hydrofluorocarbons (HFCs). At the UN level, we will support the provision of UN Adaptation Funds for developing countries, financed from international emissions markets, such as a cap-and-trade system for international emissions from aviation and shipping.

Protecting the global environment

Humans are living beyond the ability of the planet to support life; more than 60 per cent of the basic ecosystems that support life on Earth are being degraded or used unsustainably. Co-ordinated international action and effective global institutions are necessary to help to create a sustainable future and improve quality of life.

Liberal Democrats will:

• Work through the EU to make sure that the environment is fully integrated into the objectives of international institutions such as the World Bank, International Monetary Fund and World Trade Organisation.

• Work to increase the resourcing of the UN Environment Programme and improve the enforcement of international environmental treaties.

• Protect the world's forests, not only to reduce carbon emissions but also to preserve this crucial reservoir of biodiversity. We will argue for an international target of zero net deforestation by 2020; support a new system of payments to developing countries to enable them to reduce deforestation; and adopt at EU – or, if necessary, at UK – level a new law making it illegal to import or possess timber produced illegally in foreign countries.

• Work with other countries to develop an international labelling system for the environmental impact of products, helping consumers choose those with the least impact on resource use and pollution.

Meeting Britain's obligations to the developing world

Liberal Democrats will:

• Increase the UK's aid budget to reach the UN target of 0.7 per cent of GNI by 2013 and enshrine that target in law. We will hold the G8 to its Gleneagles pledges on aid, including on the 0.7 per cent target.

• Work with other countries to establish new sources of development financing, including bringing forward urgent proposals for a financial transaction tax and a cap-and-trade

system for carbon emissions from aviation and shipping.
• Support reform of the global financial institutions such as the World Bank and IMF.
• Ban banks from facilitating the transfer of funds obtained by corruption. We will crack down on tax havens which allow individuals and corporations to avoid paying taxes to developing countries.
• Ensure that the developing world is prepared to deal with the consequences of a changing climate. We will ensure that adaptation and mitigation measures are financed by industrialised nations on top of existing aid commitments.
• Prioritise health and education programmes which aim to promote gender equality, reduce maternal and infant mortality, and restrict the spread of major diseases like HIV/AIDS, TB and malaria. We will focus effort on supplying basic needs like clean water.
• Support a global fund for social protection to help developing countries build viable welfare systems.
• Push for a renewed international effort on debt and support 100 per cent cancellation of the unpayable debts of the world's poorest countries. We will also take measures against 'vulture funds' and lobby for similar action at international level.

Equipping Britain's armed forces for the 21st century
The world has changed enormously since the end of the Cold War. New threats are emerging and yet Britain's armed forces remain largely equipped to fight the old ones. The Iraq War, and allegations over British complicity in torture and in secret 'rendition' flights of terrorist suspects, highlight the dangers of a subservient relationship with the United States that neglects Britain's core values and interests.

The threats of tomorrow are likely to be driven by failed states, mass migration, climate change and regional instability. So we will ensure that taxpayers' money is spent more effectively on equipping the forces for the tasks of the future, not old Cold War threats. We will:
• Hold an immediate Strategic Security and Defence Review (SSDR) to ensure that Britain can face the most serious threats to its citizens' security and well-being, including non-military challenges such as climate change.
• With strong Treasury involvement, review all major defence procurement projects through the SSDR to ensure money is being spent effectively. We will not purchase tranche 3B of the Eurofighter.
• Rule out the like-for-like replacement of the Trident nuclear weapons system. At a cost of £100 billion over a lifetime it is unaffordable, and Britain's security would be better served by alternatives. We support multilateral nuclear disarmament and will ensure that the UK plays a proactive role in the arms reduction talks starting later this year.
• Reinvigorate Franco-British and wider European defence co-operation to ensure procurement costs are kept low.

A fair deal for our service personnel
The brave men and women of Britain's armed forces are the most precious military asset we have. They must be treated fairly, with pay and conditions that reflect their outstanding commitment to this country, and properly valued and supported after they leave the services. Liberal Democrats will put the forces' welfare first. We will:
• Give a pay rise to the lower ranks so that their pay is brought into line with the starting salary of their emergency services counterparts.
• Double the rate of modernisation of forces' family homes to ensure they are fit for heroes. While it is necessary to find resources to support the troops properly, at the same time fairness requires that we make savings where possible within the defence budget as a whole. We will reduce the number of civilian staff in the Ministry of Defence and reduce numbers of top brass officers.

Putting Britain at the heart of Europe
Liberal Democrats believe that European co-operation is the best way for Britain to be strong, safe and influential in the future. We will ensure that Britain maximises its influence through a strong and positive commitment. But just because Europe is essential, that doesn't mean the European Union is perfect. We will continue to campaign for improved accountability, efficiency and effectiveness. Working together, the member states of the EU have a better chance of managing the impacts of globalisation, such as cross-border crime and environmental pollution.
Liberal Democrats will:
• Work with Britain's European neighbours to create thousands of new jobs by breaking down trade barriers and boosting support for green jobs.
• Work through the European Union for stricter international regulation of financial services and banking.
• Keep Britain part of international crime-fighting measures such as the European Arrest Warrant, European Police Office, Eurojust, and the European Criminal Records Information System, while ensuring high standards of justice.
• Keep the pressure on for reform of agricultural subsidies so that farmers, consumers and taxpayers get a fair deal, and the environment is protected.
• Fight to stop MEPs having to travel to the Strasbourg Parliament every month, wasting €200 million a year.
• Campaign for continuing reform of the EU budget so that money is spent only on the things the EU really needs to do. The European Union has evolved significantly since the last public vote on membership over thirty years ago. Liberal Democrats therefore remain committed to an in/out referendum the next time a British government signs up for fundamental change in the relationship between the UK and the EU. We believe that it is in Britain's long-term interest to be part of the euro. But Britain should only join when the economic conditions are right, and in the present economic situation, they are not. Britain should join the euro only if that decision were supported by the people of Britain in a referendum.

Standing up for liberal values around the world
We will:
• Make the EU use its collective weight effectively in other areas of foreign policy. Britain can have a far stronger voice on relations with Russia, China, Iran and the Middle East peace process when it joins with the rest of Europe.
• Be critical supporters of the Afghanistan mission. The military surge must be accompanied by a strategy to ensure a more legitimate government, tackle corruption and win over moderate elements in the insurgency. We will continue to demand a strategy that involves other players in the region. We believe that a successful strategy will stabilise Afghanistan enough to allow British troops to come home during the next Parliament.
• Support the establishment of an International Arms Trade Treaty to limit the sale of arms to dangerous regimes and work for a full international ban on cluster munitions. We will ensure that British arms are not sold to states that would use them for internal repression. We will require arms brokers to register under a code of conduct and revoke the licences of those who break the code.
• Support action by the international community to stop Iran obtaining nuclear weapons. We would follow a diplomatic route of active engagement, and are ready to back targeted sanctions, but we oppose military action against Iran and believe those calling for such action undermine the growing reform movement in Iran.
• Hold a full judicial inquiry into allegations of British complicity in torture and state kidnapping as part of a process to restore Britain's reputation for decency and fairness.
• Remain committed to the search for a peaceful resolution of the Israeli-Palestinian conflict. A sustainable solution can be reached in the context of two separate Israeli and Palestinian states, mutually recognised and internationally accepted within borders which are secure and based on the situation before the 1967 conflict. We condemn disproportionate force used by all sides. We believe

Britain and the EU must put pressure on Israel and Egypt to end the blockade of Gaza.

Rebuilding security, opportunity, homes and hope

Liberal Democrats believe in strong communities, where local people can come together to meet local needs, enjoy a pleasant local environment, and feel free from the threat of crime. We want every community to be safe and fair, and offer opportunities to people of every background. Under Labour and Conservative rule, communities have been let down. Governments have talked tough on crime but failed to take effective action. Lack of affordable housing has driven many young people out of the communities where they were born. Public transport is expensive when it is there at all. Key local services like the Post Office have declined dramatically. Liberal Democrats will put thousands more police on the beat and make them work more effectively to cut crime. We value Britain's open, welcoming character, and will protect it by changing the immigration system to make it firm and fair so that people can once again put their faith in it. We will invest in public transport and cut rail fares, as well as providing more affordable homes and protecting people from unfair repossessions. We will keep post offices open, and will protect and restore the natural environment.

Cutting crime with more and better police

We will focus on what works to cut crime. We will support more positive activities for young people to stop them getting involved in a life of crime. Labour and the Conservatives posture on penalties, which do not deter criminals. What does deter them is increasing the chances of being caught. That is why more police are needed on the streets – to provide a longer arm for the law. And we need to help the police to be more effective at catching criminals, spend less time on bureaucracy and more time preventing crime, reassuring the public and helping keep everyone safe.

Liberal Democrats will:

• Pay for 3,000 more police on the beat, affordable because we are cutting other spending, such as scrapping pointless ID cards.

• Reduce time-wasting bureaucracy at police stations with better technology that can be deployed on the streets.

• Give local people a real say over their police force through the direct election of police authorities. Authorities would still be able to co-opt extra members to ensure diversity, experience and expertise.

• Give far more power to elected police authorities, including the right to sack and appoint the Chief Constable, set local policing priorities, and agree and determine budgets.

• Strengthen the Youth Service by making it a statutory service, and encourage local authorities to provide youth services in partnership with young people and the voluntary sector.

• Reform the police, with a full review of the very restrictive terms and conditions for police officer employment.

• Turn the National Policing Improvement Agency into a National Crime Reduction Agency with a wider remit to test what policing techniques and sentences work and spread best practice across police services and the criminal justice system.

Practical steps to make you safer

We will do all we can to prevent crime with practical measures that we know will make a difference and keep people safe. We will:

• Make hospitals share non-confidential information with the police so they know where gun and knife crime is happening and can target stop-and-search in gun and knife crime hot spots.

• Bring in stop-on-request for night buses. You should be able to ask the driver to let you off between stops, so you're as close to home as possible.

• Require better recording of hate crimes against disabled, homosexual and transgender people, which are frequently not centrally recorded.

• Ensure that financial resources, and police and court time, are not wasted on the unnecessary prosecution and imprisonment of drug users and addicts; the focus instead should be on getting addicts the treatment they need. Police should concentrate their efforts on organised drug pushers and gangs.

• Always base drugs policy on independent scientific advice, including making the Advisory Council on the Misuse of Drugs completely independent of government.

Making the justice system work to rehabilitate criminals and reduce crime

Too many politicians have talked tough, meting out ever-longer prison sentences, but doing far too little to tackle reoffending and to stop crime happening in the first place. As a result, the government is spending more and more on prisons, but those released from them are as likely as ever to commit more crimes. We will:

• Make prisoners work and contribute from their prison wages to a compensation fund for victims. As resources allow, we will increase the number of hours prisoners spend in education and training.

• Introduce a presumption against short-term sentences of less than six months – replaced by rigorously enforced community sentences which evidence shows are better at cutting reoffending.

• Move offenders who are drug addicts or mentally ill into more appropriate secure accommodation.

• As a consequence of these changes, be able to cancel the Government's billion-pound prison building programme.

• Give people a direct say in how petty criminals and those who engage in anti-social behaviour are punished by setting up Neighbourhood Justice Panels (NJPs), like the one run by Liberal Democrats in Somerset where 95 per cent of offenders have been turned away from further crimes.

• Champion restorative justice programmes, like NJPs, which make offenders confront their behaviour and are more successful at reducing crime than traditional punishments.

Firm but fair immigration system

The immigration system is in chaos after decades of incompetent management. The Government has failed to plan properly for new migrants, making it harder for people to integrate. No-one has any idea how many people are here illegally, and there aren't even exit checks at all ports and airports to ensure that people here on temporary visas go home on time. We will create a fair system that works and promotes integration. We will:

• Immediately reintroduce exit checks at ports and airports.

• Secure Britain's borders by giving a National Border Force police powers.

• Introduce a regional points-based system to ensure that migrants can work only where they are needed. We need to enforce any immigration system through rigorous checks on businesses and a crackdown on rogue employers who profit from illegal labour.

• Prioritise deportation efforts on criminals, people-traffickers and other high-priority cases. We will let law-abiding families earn citizenship. We will allow people who have been in Britain without the correct papers for ten years, but speak English, have a clean record and want to live here long-term to earn their citizenship. This route to citizenship will not apply to people arriving after 2010.

A safe haven for those fleeing persecution

Britain has a responsibility to welcome refugees fleeing wars and persecution around the world. Liberal Democrats will abide by Britain's international obligations and restore confidence in the asylum system by making it firm and fair. We will:

• Take responsibility for asylum away from the Home Office and give it to a wholly independent agency, as has been successful in Canada.

• Push for an EU-wide asylum system to ensure that the responsibility is fairly shared between member states.

• Allow asylum seekers to work, saving taxpayers' money and allowing them the dignity of earning their living instead of having to depend on handouts.

• End the detention of children in immigration detention centres. Alternative systems such as electronic tagging, stringent reporting requirements and residence restrictions can be used for adults in families considered high flight risks.

• End deportations of refugees to countries where they face persecution, imprisonment, torture or execution and end the detention of individuals for whom removal is not possible or imminent, except where there is a significant risk of absconding.

Better and more affordable homes

Liberal Democrats will:

• Make sure that repossession is always the last resort by changing the powers of the courts.

• Bring 250,000 empty homes back into use with cheap loans and grants as part of our job creation plan.

• Begin a national programme to insulate more homes paid for by the savings from lower energy bills.

• Make sure every new home is fully energy efficient by improving building regulations.

• Investigate reforming public sector borrowing requirements to free councils to borrow money against their assets in order to build a new generation of council homes, and allow them to keep all the revenue from these new homes. Over time, we will seek to provide a greater degree of subsidy as resources allow to increase the number of new sustainable homes being built.

• Scrap Home Information Packs, retaining the requirement for homes to have an energy performance certificate.

Public transport you can rely on

Public transport is an important part of a fair society and the best way to cut carbon emissions from transport without trying to limit people's opportunities to travel. We want to improve the experience for the traveller and cut carbon emissions. We will:

• Switch traffic from road to rail by investing in rail improvements, such as opening closed rail lines and adding extra tracks, paid for by cutting the major roads budget.

• Cut rail fares, changing the contracts with Train Operating Companies so that regulated fares fall behind inflation by 1 per cent each year, meaning a real-terms cut.

• Make Network Rail refund a third of your ticket price if you have to take a rail replacement bus service.

• Overhaul Network Rail to put the interests of passengers first and bring it under the Freedom of Information Act.

• Set up a UK Infrastructure Bank to invest in public transport like high speed rail.

• Give councils greater powers to regulate bus services according to community needs so that local people get a real say over routes and fares.

• Include the promotion of safer cycling and pedestrian routes in all local transport plans.

Restricting aviation growth

The emissions from rising aviation are a serious problem in the fight against climate change. But in some more remote parts of the country, flights are a vital lifeline, and aviation is important for the economy as a whole. Liberal Democrats believe that we should do all we can to ensure people use alternatives where that makes sense. We will:

• Replace the per-passenger Air Passenger Duty with a per-plane duty (PPD), so capturing freight movements by air for the first time.

• Introduce a higher rate of PPD on domestic flights for which alternative and less polluting travel is available.

• Cancel plans for the third runway at Heathrow and any expansion of other airports in the South East.

A fair deal for motorists

Our planned expansion of public transport will provide much-needed alternatives to private cars, and cut carbon emissions. However, in many places there will always be a need for car travel, so we need to ensure that it is as environmentally friendly as possible. We will:

• Work through the EU for a zero emissions target for all new cars by 2040 and extend targets to other vehicles.

• Undertake preparations for the introduction of a system of road pricing in a second parliament. Any such system would be revenue-neutral for motorists, with revenue from cars used to abolish Vehicle Excise Duty and reduce fuel duty, helping those in rural areas who have no alternatives to road travel. Some of the revenue from lorries would be used to fund further extensions of high speed rail through the UK Infrastructure Bank.

• Introduce a rural fuel discount scheme which would allow a reduced rate of fuel duty to be paid in remote rural areas, as is allowed under EU law.

A green and pleasant land

Liberal Democrats will:

• Increase the general right of access to the countryside, along the lines of the model introduced by the Liberal Democrats in Scotland.

• Abolish the Infrastructure Planning Commission and return decision-making, including housing targets, to local people. We will create a third-party right of appeal in cases where planning decisions go against locally agreed plans.

• Set targets for 'zero waste', aiming to end the use of landfill. That means less packaging, more recycling, and a huge increase in anaerobic digestion to generate energy from food and farm waste. We will also improve resource efficiency and reduce waste by requiring better design and durability product standards and reducing excess packaging.

• Introduce a new strategy to bring the UK back on target to halt the loss of habitats and species and as far as possible restore biodiversity by 2020.

• Protect greenfield land and our built heritage by reducing the cost of repairs. We will equalise VAT on new build and repair on an overall revenue-neutral basis. This will also help to reduce the costs of repairs to historic buildings.

• Make National Parks more democratically accountable, allowing a proportion of the Park boards to be elected.

• Create a new designation – similar to Site of Special Scientific Interest status – to protect green areas of particular importance or value to the community. We will aim to double the UK's woodland cover by 2050. We will stop 'garden grabbing' by defining gardens as greenfield sites in planning law so that they cannot so easily be built over.

Manage water for everyone

Britain has real problems in managing its scarce water resources. Some people face devastating floods, while others have drought conditions most summers. We will:

• Stop major new housing developments in flood risk areas.

• Crack down on waste from the water companies and introduce compulsory smart meters in areas of shortage.

• Introduce landscape-scale planning policies with a specific remit to restore water channels, rivers and wetlands and reduce flood risk by properly utilising the natural capacity of the landscape to retain water.

A fair deal for the countryside

Liberal Democrats are proud that we represent a large part of rural Britain. We believe a fair society is one where people can afford to work and live in the countryside with accessible public services. Liberal Democrats will:

• Give local authorities the power to set higher Council Tax rates for second homes and the option to require specific planning permission for new second homes, in areas where the number of such homes is threatening the viability of a community.

• Through our policy on Capital Gains Tax, ensure that those who use second homes as speculative investments will pay tax on enhanced capital value at the same rate as on earned income, not at 18 per cent as at present.

• End the post office closure programme to keep post offices open in rural areas where they're the linchpin of community life, improve access to banking and help to secure the future of the Post Office through a PostBank.

- Promote schemes for affordable homes like equity mortgages and 'Home on the Farm' which encourage farmers to convert existing buildings into affordable housing.
- Refund VAT to mountain rescue services.

Fair trade for British farmers
Liberal Democrats will:
- Create a legal Supermarket Code and a powerful independent regulator of Britain's food market.
- Introduce a minimum level for the Single Farm Payment and concentrate future reductions on the highest claims so that big landowners get less, and the money goes to working farmers who need it, not people who farm one field as a hobby.
- Use the money freed by our reform to Single Farm Payments to provide extra support for hill farmers, cheap loans to help farmers invest in environmentally friendly biogas digesters and a Farming Apprenticeship scheme.
- Work within Europe for further reform of the Common Agricultural Policy, while continuing direct support for farmers, especially in upland and less favoured areas. We believe that a greater proportion of that support should be targeted at conservation, the environment and tackling climate change, as well as at providing food security for a rapidly growing world population. Organic and reduced-input foodstuffs should be encouraged.
- Help consumers to choose foods with the least environmental impact, through clearer labelling, and work with the EU to make sure country-of-origin labels identify the source of the products, not where they are packaged. We will use government procurement policy to expand the market for sustainable and fair-traded products.

Supporting the voluntary sector
Liberal Democrats will support the voluntary sector by:
- Introducing 'easy giving accounts' at publicly-owned banks to allow people to operate charitable giving accounts alongside their current accounts.
- Reforming Gift Aid to operate at a single rate of 23 per cent – giving more money to charity while closing down a loophole for higher rate tax payers.
- Reforming the process of criminal record checking so that volunteers need only one record that is portable, rather than multiple checks for each activity.

Fair and local politics, protecting your freedom
As the expenses scandal showed, the political system is rotten. Hundreds of MPs have safe seats where they can ignore their constituents. Party funding rules mean big donors have huge influence. Power has been concentrated in Westminster and Whitehall by a succession of governments. And Britain's hard-won civil liberties have been eaten away. Liberal Democrats will do things differently, because we believe that power should be in the hands of people, not politicians. We will give people a real say in who governs the country by introducing fair votes. We will stop big donations and give people the power to sack corrupt MPs. We will increase the powers of the Welsh Assembly and Scottish Parliament. We will cut back central government and all the stifling targets that it sets and make sure local taxes are spent locally. And we will introduce a Freedom Bill to restore the civil liberties that are so precious to the British character.

Fairer politics
Liberal Democrats will:
- Change politics and abolish safe seats by introducing a fair, more proportional voting system for MPs. Our preferred Single Transferable Vote system gives people the choice between candidates as well as parties. We would be able to reduce the number of MPs by 150.
- Give the right to vote from age 16.

- Introduce fixed-term parliaments to ensure that the Prime Minister of the day cannot change the date of an election to suit themselves.
- Strengthen the House of Commons to increase accountability. We will increase Parliamentary scrutiny of the budget and of government appointments and give Parliament control over its own agenda so that all bills leaving the Commons have been fully debated.
- Replace the House of Lords with a fully-elected second chamber with fewer members than the current House.
- Get better politics for less. Liberal Democrats would save this country nearly £2 billion by reforms that cut waste in central government and the Houses of Parliament.
- Introduce a written constitution. We would give people the power to determine this constitution in a citizens' convention, subject to final approval in a referendum.
- Strengthen the Data Protection Act and the Office of the Information Commissioner, extending Freedom of Information legislation to private companies delivering monopoly public services such as Network Rail.

Cleaner politics
We will:
- Give you the right to sack MPs who have broken the rules. We would introduce a recall system so that constituents could force a by-election for any MP found responsible for serious wrongdoing. We are campaigning for this right of recall to be introduced to the European Parliament too.
- Get big money out of politics by capping donations at £10,000 and limiting spending throughout the electoral cycle.
- Require all MPs, Lords and parliamentary candidates to be resident, ordinarily resident and domiciled in Britain for tax.
- Curb the improper influence of lobbyists by introducing a statutory register of lobbyists, changing the Ministerial Code so that ministers and officials are forbidden from meeting MPs on issues where the MP is paid to lobby, requiring companies to declare how much they spend on lobbying in their annual reports, and introducing a statutory register of interests for parliamentary candidates based on the current Register of Members' Interests.

More power for local people
Liberal Democrats will:
- Make local government more accountable to local people by introducing fair votes for local elections in England.
- Reform local taxation. The Council Tax is an unfair tax. Liberal Democrats believe that it should be scrapped and replaced with a fair local tax, based on people's ability to pay. It is necessary to pilot Local Income Tax to resolve any practical issues of implementation before it can be rolled out nationally, so we would invite councils to put themselves forward to be involved in the piloting phase in the second year of a Parliament.
- Return business rates to councils and base them on site values, as a first step towards the radical decentralisation of taxation and spending powers to local people.
- Review local government finance as part of these tax changes, including reviewing the unfair Housing Revenue Account system and the mainstreaming of central grants.
- Give people a say in policing and the NHS with elected police authorities and health boards.
- Scrap nearly £1 billion of central government inspection regimes on local councils.
- Scrap the Government Offices for the Regions and regional ministers.
- Implement the Sustainable Communities Act Amendment Bill, which gives local communities the right to propose actions in their area to improve sustainability.

A federal Britain
Liberal Democrats will:
- Implement the recommendations of the Calman Com-

mission to give significant new powers and responsibilities to the Scottish Parliament.

• Give the National Assembly primary legislative powers so that it becomes a true Welsh Parliament. We also support passing on a greater number of responsibilities to the National Assembly.

• Replace the current Barnett formula for allocating funding to the Scottish, Welsh and Northern Irish governments with a new needs-based formula, to be agreed by a Finance Commission of the Nations.

• Address the status of England within a federal Britain, through the Constitutional Convention set up to draft a written constitution for the UK as a whole.

Tensions between Labour and the SNP have undermined the devolved settlement in Scotland. This has led to unjustified and unnecessary financial disputes which have locked up money due to Scotland. We will restore revenue to Scotland from the reserves of Registers of Scotland and from Scottish money paid to OFGEM under the Fossil Fuel Levy as one-off payments in the 2011 budget and give control of future revenues to the Scottish Government. This will likely lead to an increase in revenue for Scotland of around £250 million in 2011-12.

Restoring your freedoms

Liberal Democrats will protect and restore your freedoms. We will:

• Introduce a Freedom Bill. We will regulate CCTV, stop councils from spying on people, stop unfair extradition to the US, defend trial by jury, and stop children being fingerprinted at school without their parents' permission.

• Restore the right to protest by reforming the Public Order Act to safeguard non-violent protest even if it offends; and restrict the scope of injunctions issued by vested interests.

• Protect free speech, investigative journalism and academic peer-reviewed publishing through reform of the English and Welsh libel laws – including by requiring corporations to show damage and prove malice or recklessness, and by providing a robust responsible journalism defence.

• Scrap intrusive Identity Cards and have more police instead, and also scrap plans for expensive, unnecessary new passports with additional biometric data.

• Halt the increase in unnecessary new offences with the creation of a 'stop unit' in the Cabinet Office. Every department in Whitehall would have to convince this unit of the need for a new offence.

• End plans to store your email and internet records without good cause.

• Remove innocent people from the police DNA database and stop storing DNA from innocent people in the future.

• Ensure that everyone has the same protections under the law by protecting the Human Rights Act.

• Scrap the intrusive ContactPoint database which is intended to hold the details of every child in England.

We believe that the best way to combat terrorism is to prosecute terrorists, not give away hard-won British freedoms. That is why we will:

• Reach out to the communities most at risk of radicalisation to improve the relationships between them and the police and increase the flow of intelligence.

• Scrap control orders, which can use secret evidence to place people under house arrest.

• Cut the maximum pre-charge detention to 14 days.

• Make it easier to prosecute and convict terrorists by allowing intercept evidence in court and by making greater use of post-charge questioning.

Credible and responsible finances

The savings we have identified far outweigh the amount of spending we are proposing, and it is these savings which will be used to start to reduce the deficit. All the savings we have identified are either instead of or additional to proposals the Government has already made. It is our working assumption that we will start to reduce the deficit from 2011-12 onwards. The savings identified below are only the start of a programme to tackle the deficit and in government we will go further, holding a comprehensive review of all government spending, on which we will consult fully with the public. This will identify the remaining savings which will need to be made to balance the government's books. This comprehensive review will not reverse or undermine any of the spending commitments we make in this manifesto. Over and above our planned new levy on the profits of banks, we will seek to eliminate the deficit through spending cuts. If, in order to protect fairness, sufficient cuts could not be found, tax rises would be a last resort. While it will be impossible to remove the Government's tax rises while the deficit is so huge, the increase in National Insurance Contributions is a damaging tax on jobs and an unfair tax on employees, so when resources allow we would seek to reverse it.

Following the election of a Liberal Democrat Government, an emergency budget and interim spending review would be held by no later than the end of June 2010. This budget and spending review would have four purposes:

• To put in place the necessary tax changes in order to raise the personal allowance to £10,000 for the start of the financial year 2011-12.

• To put in place cuts which could be realised within the financial year, such as scrapping the Child Trust Fund or restricting tax credits, to release money for our jobs and infrastructure package.

• Subject to our five economic tests being met, to put into place cuts for 2011-12 identified in our manifesto.

• To confirm the departmental spending shifts necessary to deliver our core manifesto commitments.

We will establish a Council on Financial Stability, involving representatives of all parties, the Governor of the Bank of England, and the Chair of the Financial Services Authority. This group would agree the timeframe and scale of a deficit reduction plan to set the framework (though not the detail) for the Comprehensive Spending Review and seek to promote it externally and domestically. Any such agreement would be without prejudice to parties retaining and advocating distinctive views on a wide range of issues, such as fair taxes and spending priorities.

Throughout the summer and early autumn a Comprehensive Spending Review of all departments would be conducted with the objective of identifying the remaining cuts needed to, at a minimum, halve the deficit by 2013-14. A Strategic Security and Defence Review would form part of this spending review, working within the same financial and time constraints. This review will focus particularly on savings that can be made across government – such as on pay, public sector pensions, and IT provision – and on low-priority spending. It will not reverse or undermine any of the spending commitments that we make in this manifesto.

In education, that means that additional funding for schools through the Pupil Premium will continue to be delivered throughout the next Parliament. Instead of ring-fencing education, we are doing better than that by bringing in new money to fund the Pupil Premium.

In health, our first priority will continue to be to increase spending in some parts of the NHS by cutting waste in others. We do not plan to make net cuts in spending on frontline health services.

The cross-government economies needed to reduce the deficit such as on pay, pensions, and IT procurement will affect all departments, so it would simply be dishonest to say that entire departmental budget can be ringfenced from cuts. For example, it is only because we refuse to ring-fence departments from the search for savings that we have been able to identify the funds for the Pupil Premium and to protect frontline health services. The results of this spending review would be widely consulted on with the public sector and general public throughout the end of 2010 and beginning of 2011. Based on this consultation a full spending review up to 2013-14 would be published alongside the 2011 Budget.

This is an edited version of the Liberal Democrat manifesto.

Labour manifesto

SECURING BRITAIN'S FUTURE

The plans set out in this Manifesto take full account of the fiscal position we face. We will protect frontline public services while meeting our commitment to halve the deficit over the next four years. We are now emerging from the global financial crisis. It has had a lasting effect on tax receipts, here and across the world. We are sticking to our spending plans this year so that support for families and businesses remains as we secure the recovery. But from 2011-12, as growth takes hold, spending will be tighter.

As the economy steadily recovers, there will be no return to business as usual: financial institutions cannot continue the practices of the past. Radical change is needed. Without long-term investment in wealth-creating infrastructure and enterprise, accompanied by the diversification of our industrial base, Britain will not emerge from the recession ready for a stronger, fairer future. The engine of growth is private enterprise: we will give business our full support in creating wealth and jobs. Strong and sustained growth is fundamental to a credible strategy for keeping the public finances on a stable long-term footing. To be successful, business needs stability, but to achieve stability after the seismic shock of the global banking crisis, the governance of our economic and financial institutions must be radically reformed.

And to support business in securing prosperity for future generations, an activist industrial strategy is needed: learning the lessons from those nations that have succeeded in developing advanced manufacturing and leading-edge service industries. In these countries the role of government is not to stand aside, but to nurture private-sector dynamism, properly supporting infrastructure and the sectors of the future.

GROWTH

Deficit reduction and fiscal sustainability

Once the recovery is secure, we will rapidly reduce the budget deficit. We have set out a clear, balanced and fair plan to more than halve the deficit over the next four years and we will stick to it. We will achieve this through a combination of: fair tax increases; a firm grip on public spending including cuts in lower-priority areas; and strategies for growth that increase tax revenues and reduce spending on benefits. Over the next Parliament the structural deficit will be cut by more than two thirds.

As part of our plan to ensure we protect frontline services while halving the deficit over four years, we have announced that National Insurance will rise by one penny. This will not happen until next year, once growth is firmly established. This is the fairest way to protect key frontline services. Our National Insurance changes will mean that no one earning under £20,000, or any pensioners, will pay more. It is fairer than alternative options like VAT, which we have not increased since 1997.

We will not raise the basic, higher and new top rates of tax in the next Parliament and we renew our pledge not to extend VAT to food, children's clothes, books, newspapers and public transport fares. We will maintain tax credits, not cut them. And we have made our choice to protect frontline investment in childcare and schools, the NHS and policing.

Tough choices

We will overhaul how government works: cutting back-office and property running costs; abolishing unnecessary arms-length bodies; sharply reducing spending on consultancy and marketing; and cutting lower-priority spend. We have already shown in Budget 2010 how these steps will help us to achieve savings of £20 billion a year by 2012-13, on top of the £15 billion savings that are being delivered this year. We will take a tough stance on public-sector pay, saving over £3 billion by capping public-sector pay rises at 1 per cent in 2011-12 and 2012-13. We have agreed tough reforms to public-sector pensions, which will make significant savings and ensure that pensions for the public sector workforce are secure and sustainable in the long term. Any government-controlled appointment involving a salary over £150,000 will require ministerial sign-off. Savings from our tougher approach will help to realise a fair rate of pay for all those working for central government.

We have made the new fiscal responsibility framework legally binding, and we will maintain our inflation target of 2 per cent so that mortgage rates can be kept as low as possible.

Rebuilding our banking system

We are determined to support our financial sector and for it to be a major employer and wealth creator, but there will be no return to the excesses of the past – banks will face tighter regulation. The banking system must support domestic businesses, including start-ups and entrepreneurs, as well as mortgages. We have agreed lending targets with those banks in which we have a stake, and there will be consequences for executive remuneration if targets are not met. We will compel banks to keep more capital and create 'living wills' so that should they fail there will be no danger of that failure spreading. We will continue to work with our international partners to require all banks to hold more and better-quality capital, to ensure counter-cyclical protection, and to introduce a global levy on financial services so that banks across the world contribute fairly to the society in which they are based.

The new Council for Financial Stability will monitor and help to address asset bubbles and financial imbalances. We will give the FSA additional powers if necessary to constrain and quash executive remuneration where it is a source of risk and instability. If there is evidence of bonus rules being evaded, we will act. We will ensure greater competition in the banking sector, breaking up those banks in which the Government currently has a controlling stake. The proposed Office of Fair Trading review into how City markets operate is welcome.

We value the role of building societies owned by their customers and the strength and diversity that a healthy mutual sector brings to our financial services, and we will consult on measures to help to strengthen the sector. As one option for the disposal of Northern Rock, we will encourage a mutual solution, while ensuring that the sale generates maximum value for money for the taxpayer.

Rebuilding our industrial base:
new industries, new jobs, new knowledge

After the financial crisis, we will ensure that growing companies can access the investment they need to expand. Finance must be at the service of industry, as new public channels are built to deliver private funds to innovative and fast-growing companies. The new UK Finance for Growth Fund will bring together a total of £4 billion of public funds and combine it with private money to channel equity to businesses looking to develop and grow. Within this, the Growth CapitalFund will focus on SMEs which need capital injections of between £2 and £10 million, while the Innovation Investment Fund will focus on the needs of high-tech firms.

The Strategic Investment Fund is supporting important new investment in the nuclear and renewables industries. We will provide incentives for companies to invest through R&D tax credits, and protect and increase the size of capital allowances that help to grow key sectors such as manufacturing. We will ensure a competitive regime through the development of the patent-box, a lower rate of corporation tax to encourage UK-based innovation.

Investing in science and research
We are committed to a ring-fenced science budget in the next spending review. To help us to do better in turning research outputs into innovation, we will provide focused investment for Technology and Innovation Centres, developing technologies where the UK has world-leading expertise. We will also support university research through the Higher Education Innovation Fund, and through the development of a new University Enterprise Capital Fund.

As we create a more diverse economy, we will strengthen support for exporters to help us to increase our market share with our traditional markets in Europe and the United States, while breaking further into the emerging markets of China, India and Brazil.

Universities will be encouraged to develop international links and research partnerships, and we want the Open University and learndirect to reach the global market in distance learning. We will develop a new gateway for the export of NHS intellectual property and cutting-edge services.

Restoring full employment
We expect our growing economic and sectoral strengths to create at least one million skilled jobs by 2015. These jobs of the future will increasingly come from the new growth sectors in which we are investing – low-carbon, digital and creative industries, life sciences – and professional services in business, healthcare and education. A regional growth fund will be established by the Regional Development Agencies with regional ministers given an enhanced role, and we will help our core cities and city regions to become powerhouses of innovation and growth, with a major devolution of power to shape transport and skills.

Championing an enterprise economy
We will keep business taxation competitive at the same time as we increase capital allowances to encourage investment. We will support small businesses and help with their cash flow by continuing our Time to Pay scheme, which has already, through tax and NICs deferral, helped thousands of firms; offering a one-year holiday on business rates for small businesses; widening support for training and apprenticeships; and in recognising the special contribution of entrepreneurs we are doubling the Entrepreneurs Relief lifetime limit to £2 million. We will also create a new Small Business Credit Adjudicator with statutory powers ensuring that SMEs are not turned down unfairly when applying to banks for finance.

We will help to create a new generation of entrepreneurs, ensuring that those studying for vocational skills are offered the opportunity to learn how to start and run a business, while the Flying Start programme will do the same for final-year university students. We will continue to simplify regulation and avoid unnecessary red tape. We will seek to reduce the costs of regulation by more than £6 billion by 2015.

21st-century infrastructure
To ensure that Britain's infrastructure needs are properly resourced, we will work with the private sector, reforming the regulation of energy to improve incentives for the private sector to invest. We will establish a Green Investment Bank to invest in low-carbon infrastructure, with the Government's stake funded by the sale of infrastructure assets. The Government will seek to match its contribution with at least £1 billion of private-sector investment.

The newly formed Infrastructure Planning Commission will, within a democratically determined framework, help to streamline and speed up decision-making on major projects. We now propose to extend the public interest test so that it is applied to potential takeovers of infrastructure and utility companies.

Broadband Britain
We will reach the long-term vision of superfast broadband for all through a public-private partnership in three stages: first, giving virtually every household in the country a broadband service of at least two megabits per second by 2012; second, making possible superfast broadband for the vast majority of Britain in partnership with private operators, with Government investing over £1 billion in the next seven years; and lastly reaching the final 10 per cent using satellites and mobile broadband. We will raise revenue to pay for this from a modest levy on fixed telephone lines. And we will continue to work with business, the BBC and other broadcasters to increase take-up of broadband and to ensure Britain becomes a leading digital economy.

Rebuilding our transport infrastructure
At the heart of our growth plan is the commitment to a new high-speed rail line, linking North and South. Built in stages, the initial line will link London to Birmingham, Manchester, the East Midlands, Sheffield and Leeds, and then to the North and Scotland. By running through-trains from day one, cities including Glasgow, Edinburgh, Newcastle and Liverpool will also be part of the initial network. Journey times will be slashed – those from the West Midlands to London will be as little as 31 minutes. We will consult fully on legislation to take forward our high-speed rail plans within the next Parliament.

We will press ahead with a major investment programme in existing rail services, hugely improving commuter services into and through London, and electrifying new rail-lines including the Great Western Main Line from London to South Wales. We will complete the new east-west Crossrail line in London adding ten per cent to London transport capacity. We will encourage more people to switch to rail with an enforceable right to the cheapest fare, while trebling the number of secure cycle-storage spaces at rail stations. We will welcome rail franchise bids from not-for-profit, mutual or co-operative franchise enterprises and will look to remove unfair barriers that prevent such bids benefiting passengers and taxpayers.

We will extend hard-shoulder running on motorways, alongside targeted motorway widening including on the M25. We will increase tenfold the penalties on utilities who allow work to overrun. We rule out the introduction of national road pricing in the next Parliament.

We support a third runway at Heathrow, subject to strict conditions on environmental impact and flight numbers, but we will not allow additional runways to proceed at any other airport in the next Parliament.

To promote the rapid take-up of electric and low-carbon cars, we will ensure there are 100,000 electric vehicle charging points by the end of the next Parliament.

Corporate governance reform
We will strengthen the 2006 Companies Act, where necessary. The UK's Stewardship Code for institutional shareholders should be strengthened and we will require institutional shareholders to declare how they vote and for banks to put their remuneration policies to shareholders for explicit approval.

Companies should be more transparent about their long-term plans for the business they want to acquire. There needs to be more disclosure of who owns shares, a requirement for bidders to set out how they will finance their bids and greater transparency on advisers' fees. There should be a higher threshold of support – two thirds of shareholders – for securing a change of ownership and the case for limiting votes to those on the register before the bid should be examined.

Creating a shareholding society

We want Britain's workers to have a stake in their company by widening share ownership and creating more employee-owned and trust-owned businesses. We want to see a step change in the role of employee-owned companies in the economy, recognising that many entrepreneurs would like to see their companies in the hands of their employees when they retire. We will review any outstanding barriers to the formation of more employee companies like the John Lewis Partnership.

Our job guarantees will put an end to long-term unemployment and a life on benefits. No one fit for work should be abandoned to a life on benefit, so all those who can work will be required to do so. At the same time, we believe that people should be able to earn enough to live and be better off than on welfare. We will enable more people to get on the housing ladder; offer a helping hand to build up savings; and secure a fair deal with the banks to strengthen people's personal finances.

LIVING STANDARDS

A modern welfare state for all

No young person in Britain should be long-term unemployed: those out of work for six months or more will be guaranteed employment or training through the £1 billion Future Jobs Fund, with mandatory participation after ten months. The fund will support 200,000 jobs. All those who are long-term unemployed for two years will be guaranteed a job placement, which they will be required to take up or have their benefits cut.

More people with disabilities and health conditions will be helped to move into work from Incapacity Benefit and Employment Support Allowance, as we extend the use of our tough-but-fair work capability test. This will help to reduce the benefit bill by £1.5 billion over the next four years. We will reassess the Incapacity Benefit claims of 1.5 million people by 2014, as we move those able to work back into jobs. For those with the most serious conditions or disabilities who want to work there will be a new guarantee of supported employment after two years on benefit.

We are radically reforming how Job Centre Plus helps lone parents: providing extra help with childcare, training and support to find family-friendly work, while requiring those with children aged three to take steps to prepare for work and actively to seek employment once their youngest child is seven years old.

Housing Benefit will be reformed to ensure that we do not subsidise people to live in the private sector on rents that other working families could not afford. And we will continue to crack down on those who try to cheat the benefit system.

Making work pay

The Low Pay Commission's remit will have the goal of the National Minimum Wage rising at least in line with average earnings over the period to 2015. We will ask all Whitehall Departments, within their budgets, to follow the lead of those who already pay the Living Wage. This will be supported by measures to address high pay in the public sector – reducing pay-bill pressure in the years ahead.

We will guarantee that when someone who has found it difficult to get into work comes off benefits, their family will be at least £40 a week better off. This is our Better Off in Work guarantee: together the National Minimum Wage and tax credits should always make work pay. And we will consult on further reforms to simplify the benefits system and make sure it gives people the right incentives and personal support to get into work and progress in their jobs. We will give the Low Pay Commission additional responsibilities to report on productivity and career progression in low-skilled, low-paid sectors, bringing together representatives from the business community and social partners.

Getting ahead: investing in you

We have rescued the apprenticeship system supporting more than 250,000 places a year, and we will now expand technician-level apprenticeships to ensure Britain has the skills it needs for the future.

We have legislated for a right to request time for training and will continue to invest in workplace training through Train to Gain. New Skills Accounts will enable every worker to make choices that drive improvement and quality in the skills system. Accounts will help learners know what training they are entitled to, the level of funding available and the benefits of training for their careers. We will continue to promote more effective employee engagement in the workplace.

Improving your living standards

We have done all we can to keep mortgage rates low – at 0.5 per cent during this recession compared to 15 per cent in the 1990s – and will continue to do so in the future. Tax credits will be increased not cut. Council Tax increases have fallen to their lowest ever rate and we expect them to stay low. There will be more help with energy bills through the Social Tariff and Winter Fuel Payments, and we will work with the regulator to promote greater competition and diversity in the supply of energy to ensure falling wholesale prices get passed on to households in lower bills.

Fairness at work

We will strive to ensure fairness at work for all employees, continuing our crackdown on exploitative gang-masters and rogue employers. We will extend the licensing approach to labour providers in the construction industry if the evidence shows that is the best way to enforce employment rights. We have strengthened HMRC's enforcement of the minimum wage. In future it will cooperate more closely with local authorities to enforce minimum wage legislation. We are enacting the Agency Workers Directive to offer additional protection to agency workers in relation to pay and conditions. New legislation and the Equality and Human Rights Commission will ensure that people are not held back at work because of their gender, age, disability, race and religious or sexual orientation. The new Equality Act will be enforced, promoting fairness across our society. The public duty to promote equality of opportunity is being extended. We will encourage employers to make greater use of pay reviews and equality checks to eliminate unfair pay gaps, including inequalities in pay between men and women.

More home ownership

We will widen home ownership: over 160,000 households have been supported into ownership through government action since 1997. We will exempt purchases below £250,000 from stamp duty for the next two years, benefiting more than nine out of ten first-time buyers. This will be paid for by increasing stamp duty to five per cent for homes worth more than £1 million. Our highly popular Home Buy Direct scheme will continue. We will work with Housing Associations to develop a new form of affordable housing targeted at working families on modest incomes who struggle in the private sector and rarely qualify for social housing. This will focus on enabling working people to rent an affordable home at below market rates while they build up an equity stake.

We will strengthen regulation to ensure consistent standards of consumer protection from repossession, making the FSA responsible for the regulation of all mortgages. This means transferring second charge loans such as debt consolidation loans, which are often issued by sub-prime lenders, into the FSA's tougher regime – guaranteeing equal protection for homeowners.

We are investing £7.5 billion over two years to 2011 to build new houses, delivering 110,000 additional energy-efficient, affordable homes to rent or buy. We will reform the council house financing system to enable local authorities to maintain properties at the Decent Home standard and to build up to 10,000 council houses a year by the end of the next Parliament. Tenant involvement in the management of social housing properties will be encouraged.

Better housing

We will guarantee the three million households who rent from a private landlord the right to a written tenancy agreement and access to free and impartial advice; and we will establish a new National Landlord Register. We are committed to ending rough sleeping by 2012, and we will tackle the problems faced by homeless people with multiple needs. We will provide homeless 16 and 17-year-olds with Foyer-based supported accommodation and training including help with parenting skills. Once there is enough provision to provide universal coverage we will legislate to change the law so that for 16 and 17-year-olds the right to housing is met solely through supported housing.

Support with saving

The annual limits for Individual Savings Accounts have been raised to £10,200 and will be index linked. The Pension Credit capital disregard will increase from £6,000 to £10,000. The pioneering Savings Gateway account for people on lower incomes will be available to over eight million families from July 2010, providing a match of 50p for each £1 saved up to a limit of £300. We will extend this approach even further, giving a boost to savings for more people on middle incomes. To help to encourage the savings habit among young adults, we will develop a matched savings account for all 18-30 basic-rate taxpayers, as set out in the Budget. For the next generation we will protect – not cut – the Child Trust Fund. We will contribute an additional £100 a year to the Child Trust Funds of all disabled children.

A new deal on personal finances

We will transform the Post Office into a People's Bank offering a full range of competitive, affordable products. We are firmly committed to the 28 million homes and businesses across the country receiving mail six days a week, with the promise that one price goes everywhere. Continuing modernisation and investment will be needed by the Royal Mail in the public sector.

We will introduce a universal service obligation on retail banks, so that all consumers with a valid address have a legal right to a basic bank account, and a right to redress if this is refused. Banks will have to publicly report on the extent to which they are under-serving communities and we will introduce a new levy on the banks to help to fund a step-change in the scale of affordable lending by third sector organisations, including a new partnership with the Post Office, offering an alternative to loan sharks and high-cost doorstep lending.

Over the lifetime of the next Parliament, we will clamp down on the interest rates and other fees charged by instant loan companies and payday or doorstep lenders, tackling the very high-cost lending that hits low-income communities hardest. We will introduce a single regulator for consumer finance to restore confidence and trust with responsibility for the supervision of all unsecured lending being passed to the Financial Services Authority. And new rules governing how financial products are sold will be introduced with a crackdown on unfair terms in contracts.

Finally, we will seek to promote competition in high-street banking by introducing portable bank account and cash ISA numbers that stimulate switching where consumers are dissatisfied, along with consistent, easily understood labelling of financial products.

EDUCATION

Frontline spending on Sure Start, childcare, schools and 16-19 learning will be increased, safeguarding our priorities such as an additional 41,000 teachers and 120,000 teaching assistants. But funding will not rise as fast as in recent years, making tough choices necessary to focus resources

on the front line, with £950m saved through collaboration and efficiency in back office functions and procurement and £500m from quangos and central budgets.

The early years

Children's Centres will become the bedrock of a new national under-fives service: 'one-stop shops', open to all families, offering excellent affordable childcare, healthcare and parenting advice. The number of free early learning places for disadvantaged two-year-olds will be expanded, on the way to our long-term goal of universal free childcare for this age group.

Flexible childcare

Busy working parents will have more flexibility over the hours their children have access to nursery education, such as taking them over two full working days, as well as greater choice over when children start school. We will also explore allowing parents to carry over their free hours of nursery education from year to year. Childcare vouchers will be retained, with all families receiving income tax relief at the basic rate, and childcare standards will be raised by a more qualified workforce. We want to strengthen parental engagement with Sure Start Children's Centres. Some voluntary and third-sector organisations already run networks of Centres, and we will now pioneer mutual federations running groups of local Children's Centres in the community interest.

Excellence for all: every school a good school

For pupils and parents we will set out in law guarantees of the excellent education and personal support they can expect. Teach First will be extended to attract more of the best graduates into teaching, including teaching in primary schools. We have invested heavily in the professionalism and expertise of the workforce, and will build on this success with a new right for every teacher to continuous professional development; in return they will have to demonstrate high standards of teaching to maintain their licence to practise. We will promote new Teacher Training Academies and £10,000 'golden handcuffs' to attract the best teachers into the most challenging schools.

Our task now is to devolve more power and responsibility to strong school leaders and to spread excellence, with up to 1,000 schools, through mergers and take-overs, part of an accredited school group by 2015 – a new generation of not-for-profit chains of schools with a proven track record. These will include excellent school leaders from the maintained sector, universities, colleges, faith schools, academy chains and independent schools. We are pioneering new cooperative trust schools where parents, teachers and the local community come together to help to govern their local school.

More power for parents

Where parents are dissatisfied with the choice of secondary schools in an area, local authorities will be required to act, securing take-overs of poor schools, the expansion of good schools, or in some cases, entirely new provision. Where parents at an individual school want change, they will be able to trigger a ballot on whether to bring in a new leadership team from a proven and trusted accredited provider. School Report Cards will give every parent clear information on standards, levels of parental satisfaction and behaviour and bullying. They will provide information on the progress being made by all pupils, not just by some. We will consult on giving every school an overall grade for its performance.

Ensuring all pupils make progress also requires a fair funding system, so we will introduce a local pupil premium to guarantee that extra funding to take account of deprivation follows the pupil. Barriers to social mobility will be tackled by giving disadvantaged families free access to broadband to support their child's learning. All parents will be guaranteed online information about their child's progress and behaviour. We have high expectations for children with special educational needs and schools will be held to account for how well they meet the needs of these pupils. We are expanding the number of specialist dyslexia teachers and improving teacher training for children with autism. The statementing process will be improved to give more support to parents, and the supply of teachers with specialist skills to teach pupils with severe learning disabilities in special schools will be increased.

Primary schools: no child left behind

Our primary curriculum reforms will create more flexibility for teachers to offer a broad, challenging and engaging education, with opportunities to play sport, and to take part in arts, culture and music, including the chance to learn a musical instrument. As part of these reforms, all primary schools will teach a modern foreign language. We will create a specialist Mandarin teacher training qualification, so that many more primary schools have access to a qualified primary teacher able to teach Mandarin.

Parents will be given a '3Rs Guarantee' that every pupil who falls behind at primary school and early in secondary school will receive one-to-one or small-group catch-up provision. This will include up to 40,000 six and seven-year-olds benefiting from extra tuition in English and Maths through 'Every Child a Reader' and 'Every Child Counts', and 300,000 receiving ten hours of one-to-one tuition in both English and Maths when they are older.

For primary-age children, we are guaranteeing childcare and constructive activities from 8am until 6pm in termtime at their own or a neighbouring school; this entitlement will particularly help busy working parents to juggle work and family life. We are extending the provision of free school meals so that an additional half a million primary school children in families on low incomes will benefit from healthy and nutritious food, and we are trialling free school meals for all primary school children in pilot areas across the country.

Secondary schools: excellence for all, personal to each

All secondary school pupils will have a Personal Tutor of Studies, and we will work with schools to extend one-to-one or small-group tuition to pupils in the run-up to their GCSEs. More young people will be able to study single science subjects and modern foreign languages. Diplomas will strengthen the status and quality of vocational study and bring together academic and vocational programmes. And the Gifted and Talented programme will be reformed and improved, guaranteeing additional personalised support. We will review the qualifications system in 2013, with any changes taking place in the Parliament after next. Meanwhile, the new independent exam regulator will ensure that standards are being maintained. We will take forward our Building Schools for the Future programme to rebuild or refurbish secondary schools.

Zero tolerance of poor behaviour

Home School Agreements will be strengthened, making clear the responsibilities of families and pupils. Every parent will agree to adhere to the school's behaviour rules, signing contracts each year facing real consequences if they fail to live up to them, including the option of a court-imposed parenting order. Safer School Partnerships will be extended to every school where the head or parents demand it. Alternative education for excluded pupils will be transformed. New providers will be encouraged to take over existing Pupil Referral Units, pioneering approaches that bring order and discipline back to young people's lives. More will be invested in anti-bullying interventions including tackling homophobic bullying.

Cadet forces will move increasingly into state schools and we will expand spare time activities for young people, doubling those available, including sport, on Friday and Saturday nights, with neighbourhood police teams involved in areas where youth crime is highest. Teacher training institutions will be asked to provide courses for teachers in promoting pupils' resilience and responsibility.

All children safe and thriving

We will expand specialised foster care for the most vulnerable children and the Care2Work programme for all care leavers. Through Children's Trusts, children and youth services will work closely with schools and colleges, increasingly co-locating wider children's services with schools. Early intervention programmes with a proven impact will be promoted. We will continue to reduce teenage pregnancy rates, with compulsory, high-quality sex and relationship education.

The new vetting and barring system will protect children without being unduly burdensome or interfering in private family arrangements. Social work training will be radically overhauled, raising the status and standards of the profession, and we will establish a National College of Social Work. We will publish detailed Serious Case Review summaries that explain the facts, but keep full reports out of the public domain in order to protect children's identities.

Staying on to get ahead

We are committed to an historic change: raising the education and training leaving age to 18. All young people will stay on in learning until 18, Education Maintenance Allowances will be retained and there will be an entitlement to an apprenticeship place in 2013 for all suitably qualified 16-18 year olds. We will introduce greater freedom for all colleges to respond to local community needs and free them from red tape. Students will be given clearer information on the quality of courses on offer, with a 'traffic-light' grading system for all courses and colleges. To complement vocational learning for 14-19 year olds in schools and colleges, we will pioneer University Technical Colleges and new Studio Schools that offer innovative curricula involving practical learning and paid work.

Advanced apprenticeships will be radically expanded, creating up to 70,000 places a year. These provide well-respected routes into high-skilled careers and further study at university and will support our ambition that three-quarters of young people enter higher education or complete an advanced apprenticeship or equivalent technician-level qualification by the time they are 30. New apprenticeship scholarships will enable the best apprentices to go on to higher education.

We will open up opportunity for people from families on low incomes to enter professions like the media and law, expanding paid internships for students. Careers advice for young people, including for younger children, will be overhauled, ensuring much better information and guidance.

World-class higher education

We will guarantee mentoring and support for higher education applications to all low-income pupils with the potential for university study, with extra summer schools and help with UCAS applications; and expand programmes to encourage highly able students from low-income backgrounds to attend Russell Group universities. We support universities that already widen access by taking into account the context of applicants' achievement at school. In the coming years, priority in the expansion of student places will be given to Foundation Degrees and part-time study, and to science, technology, engineering and mathematics degrees, as well as applied study in key economic growth sectors.

HEALTH

Protecting the NHS and investing in the front line

As we complete our once-in-a-generation programme of hospital building, we will refocus capital investment on primary and community services so that we rival the best healthcare systems in the world with our ability to identify disease early. The reforms of recent years will allow us to do more than ever to release savings by cutting red tape and directing resources to where they matter most. We will scale down the NHS IT programme, saving hundreds of millions of pounds, and over the next four years, we will deliver up to £20 billion of efficiencies in the frontline NHS, ensuring that every pound is reinvested in frontline care.

Getting the most from NHS resources: sustained investment and reform

All hospitals will become Foundation Trusts, with successful FTs given the support and incentives to take over those that are underperforming. Failing hospitals will have their management replaced. Foundation Trusts will be given the freedom to expand their provision into primary and community care, and to increase their private services – where these are consistent with NHS values, and provided they generate surpluses that are invested directly into the NHS. We will support an active role for the independent sector working alongside the NHS in the provision of care, particularly where they bring innovation – such as in end-of-life care and cancer services, and increase capacity. We will be uncompromising in expecting high standards from all NHS services – and in the coming period we will expect PCTs to challenge all services to achieve the highest quality. Where changes are needed, we will be fair to NHS services and staff and give them a chance to improve, but where they fail to do so we will look to alternative provision.

Patients requiring elective care will have the right, in law, to choose from any provider who meets NHS standards at NHS costs. And we will also increase year-on-year the payments made to hospitals linked to patient satisfaction and quality outcomes – up to ten per cent of payment.

Prevention and early intervention

GPs will be encouraged to keep their patients healthy through exercise and healthy eating advice. The ambitious Change 4 Life programme will support a more active, health-conscious country. We will pioneer better mental healthcare and tackle the scourge of mental illness. Over the next Parliament more than 8,000 new therapists will ensure access to psychological therapy for all who need it as we seek to change our society's attitudes to mental illness.

Empowering NHS staff and enabling Mutuals

We will continue the process of empowering staff – freeing them from bureaucracy and ensuring they get proper support. We will expand the role of NHS nurses, particularly in primary care, in line with the best clinical evidence. And across the NHS we will extend the right for staff, particularly nurses, to request to run their own services in the not-for-profit sector. We will increase the membership of Foundation Trusts to over three million by the end of the next Parliament. The NHS will benefit from a period of organisational stability: we will make no top-down changes to the structure of Primary Care Trusts or Strategic Health Authorities during the next Parliament, and we will ensure stability in the hospital payment system.

Real guarantees and real choices for patients

We will expand patient choice, empowering patients with information, and giving individuals the right to determine the time and place of treatment. At the heart of this will be legally binding guarantees enshrined in the NHS constitution:
• The waiting-time guarantee will ensure that treatment begins within 18 weeks of seeing your GP, or the NHS will fund you to go private.
• The cancer guarantee will ensure that all patients see a cancer specialist within two weeks of GP referral and that all cancer tests will be completed and the results received within just one week.
• The health-check guarantee will ensure that everyone between 40 and 74 will be guaranteed routine health checks on the NHS.
• The GP access guarantee will ensure everyone has the right to choose a GP in their area offering evening and weekend opening.

A personal NHS

We will ensure the NHS suits the lives of busy families expanding further the availability of GP-led health centres open seven days a week '8 til 8' in towns and cities. NHS organisations will offer telephone and online booking via the NHS Choices website. Online patient comments about the quality of any NHS service will inform people's choices. A new national Ill telephone number will make non-emergency services far easier for people to access and book. We will bring the NHS closer to people through a major expansion in care available at home, including chemotherapy and dialysis. More services will be available from GPs and through local pharmacists. Patients will have the right to register with a GP anywhere they choose, including near their place of work. Choice of when and where you are treated will be extended whenever patients are booking routine appointments.

All cancer patients will be offered one-to-one dedicated nursing for the duration of their care and we will work with Marie Curie Cancer Care and other providers to guarantee everyone who wants it the opportunity for palliative care in their own home at the end of their lives. Everyone with a long-term condition, such as those with diabetes, will have the right to a care plan and an individual budget.

All women will have the right, wherever it is safe, to a homebirth, and every expectant mother will have a named midwife providing continuity of care. More mums and dads will be offered single rooms if they need to stay overnight, and post-natal care will be further expanded so that every area of the country has a Family Nurse Partnership. Patients who fail to turn up for pre-booked appointments will not be guaranteed fast-track treatment. The NHS Constitution will guarantee the legal rights of patients, wherever they live, to all treatments and drugs approved by NICE for use in the NHS. We will continue to improve the process of approving new drugs and treatments so that these can be made available to NHS patients more quickly. We will ensure all leading drugs available internationally are assessed by NICE and those which are deemed effective will be available within six months of referral.

We will establish a new National Care Service working in partnership with the NHS to transform the way care is provided to the elderly and disabled people.

Safety and cleanliness

More than 3,000 matrons across the NHS will have the power to manage wards, order deep cleaning, and report problems directly to hospital boards. Every patient who comes into an NHS hospital will be screened for MRSA. We will establish national standards of infection control that get tougher every year and which every hospital and ward must meet. The safety regulator will have the power to close wards, impose fines or order cleaning wherever necessary.

CRIME AND IMMIGRATION

Protecting frontline policing

We are committed to giving the police the resources to maintain their numbers, with funding assured for the next three years. To protect the front line we are making tough choices elsewhere: continuing to cut bureaucracy and inefficiency in procurement, IT and overtime.

To ensure that communities can determine local policing priorities, neighbourhood police teams will hold monthly beat meetings at which local people will have a right to hold senior commanders to account. We will protect the police from politicisation, but take swift action where they are not performing. Where a police force or local Basic Command Unit consistently fails local people, we will ensure either that the senior management team including the borough commander or chief constable is replaced, or it is taken over by a neighbouring force or BCU.

Early intervention and preventing crime

We will expand Family Nurse Partnerships to vulnerable

young mothers, reducing future crime and behavioural problems. For the 50,000 most dysfunctional families who cause misery to their neighbours, we will provide Family Intervention Projects – proven to tackle antisocial behaviour – a no-nonsense regime of one-to-one support with tough sanctions for non-compliance.

We will expand US-style street teams, which use youth pastors and vetted ex-offenders to reach out to disaffected young people; Youth Conditional Cautions, which focus on rehabilitation and reparation; and we will introduce a preventative element for all Anti-Social Behaviour Orders for under 16s. We will double the availability of organised youth activities on Friday and Saturday nights. We will expand joint working between police and the probation service to supervise prolific young offenders after they get out of prison, and the use of mentors including vetted ex-prisoners to meet offenders 'at the gate' so they don't slip back into crime. And alcohol treatment places will be trebled to cover all persistent criminals where alcohol is identified as a cause of their crimes.

We will pioneer Social Impact Bonds, encouraging private investors to support social entrepreneurs and the third sector – and harnessing additional investment for crime prevention at minimal cost to the taxpayer.

We will bring in a Restorative Justice Act to ensure it is available wherever victims approve it. We have reclassified cannabis to Class B and banned 'legal highs'. We will switch investment towards those programmes that are shown to sustain drug-free lives and reduce crime.

Tough action on crime and antisocial behaviour

We are committed to zero tolerance of violence against women, so we will continue to drive up prosecution rates, tackle causes, and raise awareness – as well as maintaining women-only services including a Sexual Assault Referral Centre in every area. Labour is proud to be the party that legislated first to criminalise incitement to racial hatred, religious hatred, and homophobic hatred – and we will reverse the Tory attempt to undermine this legislation, invoking the Parliament Act if necessary to force it through.

We will guarantee an initial response to any complaint about antisocial behaviour within 24 hours. Local authorities and other agencies will be required to give people a named case worker who will report back on progress, and escalate action if the problem persists. All relevant agencies – not just neighbourhood police teams – will hold monthly public meetings to hear people's concerns; all PCSOs will have stronger powers to tackle ASB; a 'Respect' standard for the private rented sector will be introduced; and local ASB champions will make agencies work together to tackle cases.

Enforcement will also be strengthened: we will ensure that the great majority of applications for ASBOs take under a month and that whenever an ASBO is breached there is an expectation of prosecution. And when someone suffers repeated ASB and the police, council, courts or other agencies fail to act, there must be a stronger form of redress. So we will legislate to give people financial support to pursue legal injunctions, with the costs met by the agency that let them down.

Using technology to cut crime

Labour will ensure that the most serious offenders are added to the DNA database no matter where or when they were convicted – and retain for six years the DNA profiles of those arrested but not convicted.

The new biometric ID scheme, which already covers foreign nationals, will be offered to an increasing number of British citizens, but will not be compulsory for them. It will help to fight the growing threat of identity theft and fraud, as well as crime, illegal immigration and terrorism. In the next Parliament ID cards and the ID scheme will be self-financing. The price of the passport and ID cards together with savings from reduced fraud across the public services will fully cover the costs of the scheme.

Punishment and reform

We will provide a total of 96,000 prison places by 2014. More EU and other foreign prisoners will be transferred abroad, and we will work to reduce the number of women, young and mentally ill people in prison. Any spare capacity generated will reduce costs while protecting the public.

For offenders not sentenced to prison we have brought in tough new 'Community Payback': hard work in public, wearing orange jackets. We will extend nationwide the right for local people to vote on what work offenders do to pay back to the communities they have harmed. We are creating a National Victims Service to guarantee all victims of crime and antisocial behaviour seven-day- a-week cover and a named, dedicated worker offering one-to-one support through the trial and beyond. The compensation offenders have to pay to victims has been increased, and we will now ensure victims get this payment up front.

To help to protect frontline services, we will find greater savings in legal aid and the courts system – increasing the use of successful 'virtual courts' which move from arrest, to trial, to sentencing in hours rather than weeks or months. We will use the tax system to claw back from higher-earning offenders a proportion of the costs of prison. Asset confiscation will be a standard principle in sentencing, extended from cash to houses and cars. Every community will have the right to vote on how these assets are used to pay back to the community.

Terrorism and organised crime

We condemn torture, and our police and security services will not co-operate with those who use torture. We will develop our Prevent strategy to combat extremism.

We will continue to make Britain a hostile place for organised criminals, harassing them with asset seizures, tax investigations and other powers; strengthening the Serious Organised Crime Agency and encouraging police forces to cooperate across force boundaries and international borders; and responding quickly to new threats including cybercrime.

Strong borders and immigration controls

Genuine refugees will continue to receive protection. Our new Australian-style points-based system is ensuring we get the migrants our economy needs, but no more. We will gradually tighten the criteria in line with the needs of the British economy and the values of British citizenship, and step up our action against illegal immigration. The points-based system will be used to control migration with limits for high-skilled workers and university students. We will expand the Migration Impact Fund, paid for by contributions from migrants, to help local areas.

We know that migrants who are fluent in English are more likely to work and find it easier to integrate. So as well as making our English test harder, we will ensure it is taken by all applicants before they arrive. Local councils and other public services should keep funding for translation services to a minimum. Many public-sector workers are already required to meet minimum standards of English; we will build on this to ensure that all employees who have contact with the public possess an appropriate level of English language competence.

We will break the link between staying here for a set period and being able to settle or gain citizenship. In future, staying will be dependent on the points-based system, and access to benefits and social housing will increasingly be reserved for British citizens and permanent residents.

FAMILIES AND OLDER PEOPLE

Strengthening family life

We will continue to promote internet safety for children, building on the recommendations of Dr Tanya Byron's review. We will support parents who challenge aggressive or sexualised commercial marketing. We will ask Consumer Focus to develop a website for parents to register their concerns about sexualised products aimed at their children.

No child left behind in poverty

We will continue to make progress towards our historic goal of ending child poverty by 2020, building on the 2010 Child Poverty Act. In the next Parliament, we will focus on helping families into jobs and out of poverty. Where parents, especially mothers, want to stay at home or work part time we will do more to help families with younger children, reducing poverty in those vital early years of a child's life. We will ensure that work always pays for hard-working lone parents.

The child element of the Child Tax Credit will be increased by £4 a week for families with children aged one and two from 2012, paid regardless of the marital status of the parents – a Toddler Tax Credit.

A better work-life balance

We will extend real choice to parents over how they organise their parental leave. We have already increased paid maternity leave to nine months. We continue to believe that one year's paid leave in the baby's first year would be of great benefit to parents and their children. However, in the current economic circumstances, progress will inevitably be tougher. So we will introduce more flexibility to the nine months' paid leave that mothers currently enjoy – allowing them to share this entitlement with fathers after a minimum of six months. We will introduce a new Fathers' Month, four weeks of paid leave rather than the current two. We will also work with employers on how this can be taken flexibly – for instance, two weeks around the birth, and the remaining two weeks taken flexibly over the first year of the baby's life, including the option of sharing these extra weeks between parents. This will be paid for as savings accrue from housing benefit through our reforms.

We will promote the creation of more highly skilled, quality jobs for parents who choose to work more flexibly.

By the end of the next Parliament we will ensure that the right to flexible working is extended for older people, recognising that many, including grandparents, want to vary their hours to the benefit of their families and to accommodate changing lifestyles. We will consult on the age at which this right should apply.

Helping older people who want to work

We will proceed to end default retirement at 65, with a review to establish the right way in which to support more people to work longer should they choose to do so. To expand the choices available for those wishing to work after retirement, we will enable people aged 60 and over to claim Working Tax Credit if they work at least 16 hours a week, rather than 30 hours as at present.

A good quality of life in older age

We will continue to support older people in getting involved in their community by providing matched funding for community projects.

Grandparents who give up work to help to care for their grandchildren must not lose out, so they will receive National Insurance Credits towards their state pension. We will remove the requirement on grandparents to apply for the court's permission before making an application for contact with their grandchildren and we will ensure that grandparents and other family members are always given first consideration for adoption or fostering.

Better pensions for all, tackling pensioner poverty

We will restore the link between the basic state pension and earnings from 2012 – a link broken by the Tories in 1980. Pension credit, which ensures that no pensioner need live on less than £132.60 per week or £202.40 for couples, and supports the income of 2.7 million pensioner households, will also rise in line with earnings.

We will continue to provide help to pensioners, with the Winter Fuel Payments (maintained this winter at £250 for those over state retirement age and £400 for those aged 80 or over); concessionary public-transport fares; free TV licences for the over-75s; and free eye tests and prescriptions.

Saving for pensions

We will support ten million low and middle-income people to build up savings through automatic enrolment in occupational pensions and new Personal Pension Accounts, ensuring that everyone in work is entitled to matched contributions from employers and government. We will continue to make pension saving more attractive for individuals through favourable tax treatment. And we will promote stakeholder pensions offering simple, low-cost and flexible products, obliging employers to provide access to a pension for all employees.

We will continue to protect pension schemes when a firm's company scheme goes bust. We are also introducing more flexibility to make it easier for companies to run good schemes. Between now and 2020 the State Pension Age for woman will rise to 65; and between 2024 and 2046, it will rise to 68 for both men and women, helping to keep state pensions affordable in the long term. The reforms we are making to public-sector pensions will keep them sustainable and affordable over the long term.

The National Care Service and an age-friendly NHS

We will establish a new National Care Service and forge a new settlement for our country as enduring as that that the Labour Government built after 1945. The care of both older people and disabled adults will be transformed; unfair postcode lotteries removed; more people will be looked after at home; and family homes and savings will be protected from catastrophic care costs. To provide independence and control for everyone with a care need we will continue to expand the use of individual budgets.

The first stage of reform will be to create a step-change in the provision of services in the home and in our communities. From 2011 we will protect more than 400,000 of those with the greatest needs from all charges for care in the home, and we will create a national physio support service helping people in every area of the country to regain their independence and confidence after a crisis or the first time they need care. These services will be funded through savings and efficiencies in the health budget and in local government.

During the next Parliament, the second stage of reform will centre on the development of national standards and entitlements to ensure high-quality care for all, and an end to the unfair postcode lotteries that affect too many families. We also want to remove the fear that families will lose the family home in order to pay for care bills. So, from 2014, the National Care Service will cap the costs of residential care so that everyone's homes and savings are protected from care charges after two years. We will pay for this through our decision to freeze Inheritance Tax Thresholds until 2014-15, by supporting more people over the State Pension Age to stay in work if they so wish, and through efficiencies across the NHS and the care system.

The final stage of reform, after 2015, will be a comprehensive National Care Service, free at the point of use not just for older people, but all adults with an eligible care need. At the start of the next Parliament we will establish a Commission to reach a consensus on the right way of financing this system.

Across the NHS we will improve and personalise care for the elderly and their families. This will mean more NHS services available in the home, with greater use of tele-care and personal nursing; reform of the GP contract to help ensure those with late-life depression and anxiety are diagnosed and supported; and better services for those with dementia and Alzheimer's so that every area of the country has access to psychological therapy, counselling and memory clinics.

There will be an end to the age discrimination that has

too often seen older people disadvantaged in the provision of health services.

COMMUNITIES AND CREATIVE BRITAIN

2012: creating an Olympic generation
We will ensure that the Olympics are delivered on time and on budget, to the highest standards.

Sport for All
We are providi ng more resources to give every child the opportunity to do at least five hours' sport per week. This will be provided through extended schools, community sports clubs and 3,000 new Olympic-inspired sports clubs. We will invest in a new national network of school sports coaches to increase the quality and quantity of coaching in some of the most deprived areas.

This will be backed by a Pupil Guarantee ensuring that every pupil should have access to regular competitive sport along with coaching, a choice of different sports, and pathways to elite and club development. We will continue our investment in free swimming for children and the over-60s. People of all ages and abilities can apply to join one of the tens of thousands of sports clubs receiving public funding.

We will toughen measures to combat cheating and the use of illegal substances in sport. We will work with governing authorities to ensure that professional clubs are accountable to their stakeholders, and run transparently on sound financial principles, with greater involvement of local communities and supporter representation. Sports governing bodies will be empowered to scrutinise takeovers of clubs, ensuring they are in the long-term interests of the club and the sport. We will develop proposals to enable registered Supporters Trusts to buy stakes in their club. We aim to bring more major international sporting competitions to Britain, beginning with our current partnership with the English FA to bring the 2018 World Cup to England.

Arts, culture and museums
Every child and young person should be entitled to five hours of art, music and culture per week, through learning to play a musical instrument, visiting local museums and joining film clubs, or taking part in local theatre. Through Creative Partnerships we are ensuring that young people in the most deprived areas are able to fulfil their artistic talents by working with local arts and cultural organisations. Creative Bursaries will support the most artistically gifted young people in their early professional careers. We will review how incentives for philanthropic support can be strengthened. Our major museums and galleries should be operationally independent of government, so we will legislate to ensure their managerial and financial autonomy. We will maintain our commitment to free admissions. Every child will have lifetime library membership from birth.

We will review the structures that oversee English Heritage, putting mutual principles at the heart of its governance so that people can have a direct say over the protection and maintenance of Britain's built historical legacy. We will give public institutions new rights to borrow works of art from the national collection, so that more people can benefit from access to our national artistic heritage.

We will promote greater public involvement in the way that National Lottery proceeds are spent on good causes. A proportion of Lottery funding is going to the Olympics. After 2012, this proportion will return to culture, heritage and sport.

Protecting community life
We are investing £235 million to create new or refurbished play spaces and adventure playgrounds. We will protect the Post Office network, so that it can fulfil its historic role as a trusted institution serving the community.

We will support pubs that have a viable future with a new fund for community ownership in 2010-11. Councils must take full account of the importance of pubs to the local community when assessing proposals that change their use, and we will make it more difficult to demolish pubs. Restrictive covenants applied by pub companies to property sales will be curbed and flexibility for pubs to provide related services promoted, making it easier to have live entertainment without a licence. A non-tie option should be available for pub tenants; we will act if the industry fails to make progress on this. We will give councils new powers to oppose gambling licences if there are too many betting shops operating in a high street.

The 'cleaner neighbourhoods' legislation will be used to clamp down on litter, fly-tipping and vandalism. We will extend the use of participatory budgeting to give local people a stronger say. Community Land Trusts enable people to purchase and run local amenities and assets in their area such as youth facilities, parks and open spaces. We will promote the transfer of buildings and land to the ownership or control of voluntary and community groups.

Supporting social enterprise
The Social Investment Bank will make additional capital available to social enterprises with an initial endowment of £75 million funded by dormant accounts alongside existing funding streams. We will promote the creation of more social enterprise hubs in every community – helping more to get off the ground. We will extend the right of public-sector workers to request that they deliver frontline services through a social enterprise. Public-sector workers in the NHS currently enjoy this right. We will extend this to more public services, including social care, with greater community involvement in their governance.

The new mutualism
We want to see more local organisations run on cooperative principles with an expansion of Community Interest Companies and third-sector mutual organisations that reinvest profits for the public good. We will promote this through the Co-operative Party, Business Link, enterprise education and the Regional Development Agencies. To give more people a stake in a highly valued national asset, British Waterways will be turned into a mutually owned co-operative. We will promote the use of community shares that support investment in football clubs, pubs, renewable energy and shops.

A vibrant voluntary sector
There will be greater support for third-sector organisations in competing for public-sector contracts, ensuring there is a level playing field with the public and private sectors. We will consult on putting the Compact Commission – which sets guidelines for effective partnership working between government and the third sector in Britain – on a statutory footing, and ensure greater support for the Compact at local level.

We are taking forward plans for a National Youth Community Service, with the goal that all young people contribute at least 50 hours to their communities by the age of 19, building on citizenship education and community engagement in schools.

We will actively combat extremist groups who promote fear, hatred and violence on the basis of faith or race.

Britain's creative industries
We will maintain the film tax credit and create a merged British Film Institute and UK Film Council to establish a single body to promote film production and film heritage.

Subject to state aid clearance, we will introduce a tax relief for the UK video games industry. We will support film festivals around the country, and establish a new biennial Festival of Britain, beginning in 2013, showcasing our major cultural achievements and young British talent across all of our creative industries.

We support an independent and world-class BBC at the heart of a vibrant public broadcasting system. Our strong support for its editorial independence and the licence fee that finances the BBC's programmes and activities will continue. The BBC Trust should fully involve the public in decision-making. The licence-fee is guaranteed for the ten-year Royal Charter that took effect on 1 January 2007.

Channel 4 will continue as a public-service broadcaster providing distinctive competition to the BBC, alongside ITV and Channel 5. We are committed to maintaining plurality in regional news provision. We will fund three regional news programme pilots from the digital switchover under-spend in the current licence-fee period.

We are working with the BBC and Digital UK to ensure that TV's digital switch-over takes place smoothly by 2012, providing financial support and helping elderly people and the most vulnerable households in the UK. To ensure we preserve competition and protect children and consumers on the Internet, we will safeguard the independence of Ofcom. We are extending broadband access to every business and home, ensuring universal access within a decade to high-speed broadband across the country.

We will update the intellectual property framework that is crucial to the creative industries – and take further action to tackle online piracy.

A GREEN RECOVERY

Towards a green economy
Internationally, we will continue to work for an ambitious, fair and legally binding climate change agreement, building on the Copenhagen Accord to limit global temperature rises to two degrees Celsius. In the next Parliament, we will use our leadership in the EU to push for a strengthening of Europe's 2020 emission reductions from 20 to 30 per cent by 2020 as part of an ambitious global deal. This would mean the UK increasing its current target of a 34 per cent reduction. As part of the negotiations, we believe Europe should agree a second Kyoto commitment period, provided all countries are brought within a clear legal framework.

Developing countries need help to adapt, reduce deforestation and emissions. From 2013 we will provide climate assistance additional to our commitment to provide 0.7 per cent of national income in overseas aid. No more than 10 per cent of our aid will be counted towards climate finance.

Clean energy
We are planning for around 40 per cent of our electricity to come from low-carbon sources by 2020 – renewables, nuclear and clean fossil fuels. A major drive for energy efficiency will be enhanced by a 'smart grid' using new information technologies.

We are committed to meeting 15 per cent of our energy demand from renewables by 2020. We already have more offshore wind-power than any other country in the world, and our plans could see this increase up to 40 times, alongside other renewable technologies such as tidal and marine, solar and sustainable bio-energy. We will make a decision early in the next Parliament on the feasibility of alternative options for a tidal energy project on the Severn, taking full account of the environmental impacts.

We have reformed the planning system to reduce delays for major infrastructure. We will now reform the regulatory system to provide the certainty that investors need, and create a Green Investment Bank to help to finance this transformation.

In stimulating the sustainable use of resources, we will move towards a 'zero waste' Britain, banning recyclable and biodegradable materials from landfill and continuing the move towards universal water metering in areas of water stress. Our industrial strategy will ensure that the drive to green our economy will create jobs and businesses in Britain in the manufacture and installation of low-carbon and environmental technologies.

Making green living easier and fairer
Through our requirement that energy companies provide subsidies for insulation, we will ensure that all household lofts and cavity walls are insulated, where practical, by 2015. By 2020 every home will have a smart meter to help to control energy use and enable cheaper tariffs; and we will enable seven million homes to have a fuller 'eco-upgrade'.

We will legislate to introduce 'Pay As You Save' financing schemes under which home energy improvements can be paid for from the savings they generate on energy bills.

We will introduce a new Warm Home Standard for social housing and regulate landlords so that privately rented accommodation is properly insulated. We have legislated for compulsory contributions from energy companies to protect the vulnerable.

We will ensure greater competition in the energy supply market and we will review the role of the water regulator, Ofwat, to ensure customers get the best deal and their voice is heard in price-setting.

We will devolve power to local councils to hold energy companies to account for community energy efficiency programmes, and give them powers to develop local energy systems such as renewables and district heating. We will support community organisations, co-ops and social enterprises to provide energy services, meaning lower prices through bulk purchasing, and the development of small-scale renewables. We will drive the introduction of 'recycling on the go', with separated public bins on the street and in shopping centres. We will work with community organisations to make it easier to find and use sites for 'grow your own' schemes.

Valuing nature for everyone
We will maintain the target that 60 per cent of new development should be on brownfield land. We will extend the Right to Roam to the whole English coastline.

We will introduce a new framework for managing our land that can more effectively reconcile competing pressures. We will put forward new areas for protected landscape and habitat status, focusing on green corridors and wildlife networks to link up existing sites. And we will commit to increasing the area covered by forest and woodland. Having doubled spending on flood defence over the last decade we will bring forward legislation to improve floods and water management.

We will campaign internationally to end illegal trading in ivory and to protect species such as polar bears, seals and blue-fin tuna, as well as for an EU-wide ban on illegally logged timber, banning it domestically if this does not succeed.

Sustainable farming, healthy food
In order to protect farmers and food suppliers from unfair and uncompetitive practices by major retailers, we will create a Supermarket Ombudsman.

Consumers have the right to know where food comes from. We are working with the food industry and retailers to ensure proper food labelling, including tougher and clearer 'country of origin' information.

An economically viable and environmentally sustainable fishing industry is vital for our coastal communities. We will push for fundamental reform of the EU Common Fisheries Policy.

Thriving rural communities
Already £3.9 billion is being spent on support for the rural economy and we will continue to provide specific support to rural businesses. We are building 10,000 homes in rural areas up to 2011. We are protecting rural bus services and making it more difficult for rural schools to be closed.

Rural businesses and communities must have the broadband connections they need. We are committed to universal broadband access, irrespective of location. The levy on fixed phone lines will pay for expansion of fast broadband connections to rural areas.

DEMOCRATIC REFORM

Cleaning up politics

We acted swiftly to clean up politics by creating an Independent Parliamentary Standards Authority (IPSA) to set pay and pensions for MPs, as well as their allowances. And we will take further measures to restore trust in our politics. MPs who are found responsible for financial misconduct will be subject to a right of recall if Parliament itself has failed to act against them. The House of Lords and the new Second Chamber will be brought under the aegis of IPSA. We will create a Statutory Register of Lobbyists to ensure complete transparency in their activities. We will ban MPs from working for generic lobbying companies and require those who want to take up paid outside appointments to seek approval from an independent body to avoid jobs that conflict with their responsibilities to the public.

A new politics

We will let the British people decide on whether to make Parliament more democratic and accountable in referenda on reform of the House of Commons and House of Lords, to be held on the same day, by October 2011.

We will hold a referendum on introducing the Alternative Vote for elections to the House of Commons. We will ensure that the hereditary principle is removed from the House of Lords.

Further democratic reform to create a fully elected Second Chamber will then be achieved in stages. At the end of the next Parliament one third of the House of Lords will be elected; a further one third of members will be elected at the general election after that. Until the final stage, the representation of all groups should be maintained in equal proportions to now. We will consult widely on these proposals, and on an open-list proportional representation electoral system for the Second Chamber, before putting them to the people in a referendum. We will legislate for Fixed Term Parliaments and set up an All Party Commission to chart a course to a Written Constitution.

The success of elections for local Youth Mayors and the UK Youth Parliament strengthens the case for reducing the voting age to 16, a change to which Labour is committed. However, we believe that prior to this happening, we need further to improve citizenship education in schools so that young people are better prepared for their democratic responsibilities; a report will be commissioned on how best to achieve this so that we can raise standards in citizenship education, before providing a free vote in Parliament on reducing the voting age to 16, for which we will make government time available.

Stronger accountability

The public will be given a new right to petition the House of Commons to trigger debates on issues of significant public concern. Parliament must better reflect the diversity of modern Britain. We will take forward the proposals of the recent Speaker's Conference so that the House of Commons properly reflects the diversity of modern Britain. To encourage freedom of speech and access to information, we will bring forward new legislation on libel to protect the right of defendants to speak freely.

We will establish a non-partisan Parliamentary Boundaries Review to examine the rules for constructing parliamentary constituencies. We have already legislated to enable the individual registration of voters. We will now act, legislating further if necessary, to end the unacceptable situation where three million eligible voters cannot vote because they are not registered to do so.

We believe that the funding of political parties must be reformed if the public is to regain trust in politics. Our starting point should be the Hayden Phillips proposals of 2008. We will seek to reopen discussions on party funding reform, with a clear understanding that any changes should only be made on the basis of cross-party agreement and widespread public support.

Devolving power

Local government and its partners in public services are already pooling budgets across localities. Our radical Total Place agenda will take this further, giving local areas additional freedom to achieve better services and more savings, cutting bureaucracy and management costs, while placing a greater on early intervention. Ring-fenced budgets, central targets and indicators will be cut back.

We will give local government new powers to lead in the provision and financing of social and affordable housing, tackle climate change and work with the NHS in our new National Care Service. Alongside enhanced scrutiny powers for councillors, we are introducing petitioning powers for local residents to demand action, and extending neighbourhood agreements where citizens set out the standards of services they expect locally.

We will also extend the powers available to our major city-regions, building upon the pioneering arrangements in Greater Manchester, Leeds and Birmingham. City-regions will be able to gain additional powers to improve transport, skills and economic development and acquire greater borrowing flexibility. Where new city-region authorities are created, we will give residents the opportunity to trigger a referendum for directly electing a Mayor, with London-style powers.

We will support tram schemes into the major cities, including upgrades to the Manchester, Nottingham, Birmingham and Tyne & Wear light-rail systems, a modern trolley bus in Leeds, and more Oyster-style electronic ticketing promoting cheap and easy interchange between public transport in cities. We will provide punctuality data on all bus routes so passengers can hold services to account. We want greater use of London-style powers to regulate bus routes where local bus services are not serving communities well, and we will work with the Competition Commission to ensure that the bus companies do not make excess profits at the expense of passengers.

Excessive Council Tax rises will be capped. We will not hold a Council Tax revaluation in the next Parliament and we will establish a cross-party commission to review local government finance to ensure it is meeting our goals of accountability, equity and efficiency across the country.

Public services in the digital age

Citizens should be able to compare local services, demand improvements, choose between providers, and hold government to account. We have led the world with the creation of data.gov.uk, putting over 3,000 government datasets online. Entrepreneurs and developers have used these datasets to unleash social innovation, creating applications and websites for citizens from local crime maps to new guides to help find good care homes or GPs. We will now publish a Domesday Book of all non-personal datasets held by government and its agencies, with a default assumption that these will be made public. We will explore how to give citizens direct access to the data held on them by public agencies.

We can use new technologies to give people a say on policymaking; enable citizens to carry out more of their dealings with government online; and save money for taxpayers as we switch services over to digital-only delivery. We will build on our network of UK Online centres and public libraries to spread free internet access points within the community, and develop new incentives for users to switch to online services.

Protecting the UK and supporting the Union

We will implement the recommendations of the Calman Commission, including giving the Scottish Parliament additional tax-raising powers, and seek ways to build consensus behind these changes. We will work with the Welsh Assembly Government on a referendum to enhance the powers to make laws affecting Wales in Wales; and to ensure that Wales is not disproportionately disadvantaged by the application of the central government funding formula. Supported by unprecedented public funding, we will continue to invest in the institutions of devolution in Northern Ireland, so that the Unionist and Republican traditions can work together for all the people of Northern Ireland.

We believe that there is a case for reform of the laws concerning marriage to Roman Catholics and the primacy of male members of the Royal family. However, any reform would need the agreement of all the Commonwealth countries of which the Queen is the Sovereign.

A GLOBAL FUTURE

Afghanistan: our commitment
Afghanistan is not a war without end. Together the military and civilian effort is designed to create the conditions for a political settlement that keeps Al Qaeda out, reconciles tribal interests, and involves Afghanistan's neighbours. It will lock in the long-term gains delivered by our aid programme since 2002 – with millions more children, especially girls, going to school, big reductions in child mortality, and better access to basic healthcare. It requires stronger local administration and less corruption, combined with a way back for former fighters who are prepared to renounce links to Al Qaeda and abide by the Afghan constitution.

Strengthening our Armed Forces and national security
Defence spending has increased by ten per cent in real terms since 1997. Funding for Iraq and Afghanistan is additional to that, with the Treasury Reserve providing £18 billion in total so far and an estimated £5 billion in the next year. A Strategic Defence Review will look at all areas of defence, but we will maintain our independent nuclear deterrent. We will fight for multilateral disarmament, working for a world free of nuclear weapons, in the Non Proliferation Treaty Review conference and beyond – combining support for civilian nuclear energy with concerted action against proliferation.

We are committed to a strong Navy based on the new aircraft carriers, an Air Force with two state-of-the-art fast-jet fleets as well as additional helicopters, transport planes and unmanned drones, and a strong, high-tech Army, vastly better equipped than it was in 1997.

The growth in the core defence budget has also enabled us to guarantee fair pay for all our forces, including the first ever tax-free bonus for those on operations abroad, while strengthening our support for their welfare. Service families can now retain their place on NHS waiting lists when they are deployed to another part of the country. Further education is free for those leaving the forces with six years' service or more. We have invested hundreds of millions of pounds to reverse a legacy of decades of neglect of forces' accommodation, and we are helping service personnel to get on to the housing ladder. Homelessness among service leavers has been sharply reduced, and the law changed to give them better access to social housing.

The new Queen Elizabeth Hospital in Birmingham will have a military-run ward and the largest single-floor critical care unit in the world. Headley Court and the new Army Recovery Capability will continue to offer world-leading support to those rehabilitating after serious injury. We have doubled the lump-sum payments for the most seriously injured to £570,000, and increased the lifetime-income payments by up to a third. We will introduce a Forces Charter to enshrine in law the rights of forces, their families, and veterans. A Veterans ID card will help Veterans to access their improved benefits and will be free to service leavers. We will continue to strengthen mental health provision in partnership with the Combat Stress charity, and roll out our Welfare Pathway to give personnel and their families better support and advice.

A strong Britain in a reformed Europe
Fundamental reform of the EU budget remains necessary, with further changes to the Common Agricultural Policy on the way to ending export subsidies. Transfers within the EU must target those areas that are least well off. On the Euro, we hold to our promise that there will be no membership of the single currency without the consent of the British people in a referendum.

We support the enlargement of EU membership to include Croatia, and believe that all Western Balkan states should open negotiations on EU accession by 2014 – one hundred years after the start of the First World War. Turkey's future membership is a key test of Europe's potential to become a bridge between religions and regions; there must be continued progress on its application to join the EU. In its foreign policy, Europe should play a key role in conflict resolution and the promotion of security, and work bilaterally to achieve its goals with the leading global powers in each region of the world.

On climate change, the EU has a critical leadership role to play in securing a legally binding UN agreement, reducing its emissions by 30 per cent on 1990 levels in the context of an ambitious global deal. It must also offer stronger leadership on global poverty reduction. We will strengthen co-operation with our EU partners in fighting crime and international terrorism, and support practical European co-operation on defence, in partnership with NATO. To symbolise its commitment to global peace and justice, and energise its young people, we propose a European Peace Corps.

Strengthening global security and preventing conflict
We will continue to press for stronger international action against terrorism and learn the lessons of recent experience to prevent and defuse conflict and build stability and the rule of law in places that would otherwise shelter terrorist networks. We will spend at least half of our new bilateral aid in fragile and conflict-affected states.

We are leading the campaign for a legally binding global arms trade treaty in 2012. We will continue to drive reform of the humanitarian agencies at the UN and work to build an international consensus on 'responsibility to protect', while supporting the International Criminal Court in bringing previously untouchable criminals to justice. We will advocate a new international convention to enable the prosecution of perpetrators of genocide and crimes against humanity.

We support the creation of a viable Palestinian state that can live alongside a secure Israel. We support engagement and pressure on the Iranian regime; it is threatening its own people as well as the security of the region and the world. We will support the final stages of the Comprehensive Peace Agreement in Sudan, and maintain the pressure for Zimbabwe to transition back to democracy as quickly as possible.

We will work with Greece and Turkey for long-term stability in Cyprus; and continue to support bilateral efforts by India and Pakistan to improve relations. We will keep up the pressure for the release of Aung Sang Suu Kyi and a return to democracy in Burma. We strongly support reconstruction and reconciliation in Sri Lanka.

The global poverty emergency: our moral duty, our common interest
We will lead an international campaign to get the Millennium Development Goals back on track. We remain committed to spending 0.7 per cent of national income on aid from 2013, and we will enshrine this commitment in law early in the next Parliament. Our aid will target the poorest and most excluded – spent transparently and evaluated independently. We will fight corruption, investing more to track, freeze, and recover assets stolen from developing countries.

Further action will be taken to strengthen developing countries' tax systems, reduce tax evasion, improve reporting, and crack down on tax havens. To increase accountability, we will allocate at least five per cent of all funding developing country budgets for the purpose of strengthening the role of Parliaments and civil society.

Our leadership on debt cancellation has freed 28 countries from the shackles of debt. We will continue to drive this agenda, building on legislation to clamp down on vulture funds. We will spend £8.5 billion over eight years to help more children go to school; maintain our pledge to spend £6 billion on health between 2008 and 2015 and £1 billion through the Global Fund to support the fight against HIV/AIDS, TB and malaria; fight for universal access to prevention, treatment and care for HIV/AIDS by 2010; and deliver at least 30 million additional anti-malarial bed-nets over the next three years.

We will provide £1 billion for water and sanitation by 2013, driving this issue up the international agenda, and over £1 billion on food security and agriculture. We will push for the establishment of a Global Council on Child Hunger. We will help to save the lives of six million mothers and babies by 2015 and, because international focus on the needs of women and girls is vital, we will double core funding to the new UN Women's agency. We will work closely with NGOs and developing countries to eliminate user fees and promote healthcare and education free at the point of access. We will encourage other countries to ratify the ILO conventions on labour standards, as we have done. We will work with the private sector, trade unions and co-operatives to promote sustainable development, quadruple our funding for fair and ethical trade, and press for a fair World Trade Organisation deal, with no enforced liberalisation for poor countries, and increased duty-free and quota-free access.

Reforming global institutions

To secure global change, we will make the case for:
- The extension of the G8.
- A clearer mandate for the World Bank to focus on the poorest countries and promote low-carbon development; and for the IMF to focus on financial stability, with both becoming more inclusive.
- Radical UN reform, including new membership of the Security Council, budgetary reform, and an overhaul of UN agencies.
- Continuing reform of NATO and stronger international co-operation to tackle security challenges, while building the capacity of regional security organisations including the African Union.
- The enduring role of the Commonwealth – a unique organisation for fostering understanding and trust, spanning a quarter of the world's population.

This is an edited version of the Labour Party manifesto.

Smaller parties' manifestos

GREEN PARTY

The principal themes of the Greens' election message were the environment, fairness and the economy. The party proposed to invest £44 billion in renewable energy sources, free insulation for homes, transport and recycling. It proposed a large increase in spending on pubic transport, paid for by reallocating £30 billion earmarked for road building. Nuclear power would be phased out.

On the economy, the party argued for measures to promote equality, specifically a "living wage" of £8.10 an hour, a 50 per cent marginal tax rate on incomes above £100,000, a non-means-tested "citizen's pension", opposition to public sector job cuts, permanent taxes on bankers' bonuses and the creation of a million new jobs in favoured occupations. The party also proposed a 35-hour week to provide a better balance between work and life, and to enable jobs to be shared. The Greens proposed also the abolition of charges in healthcare, the reversal of all cuts and the maintenance of local treatment. The party placed much store on its anti-nuclear credentials, opposing the acquisition of a new generation of Trident nuclear submarines and thereby saving, so the Greens maintained, £80 billion.

UK INDEPENDENCE PARTY

UKIP's key policy was to withdraw from the EU, which the party claimed would save £120 billion a year. The party aimed, however, to broaden its electoral message. It voiced a strongly anti-immigration theme, proposing a medium-term freeze on immigration for permanent residency and a future limit of 50,000 immigrants a year. It argued for the deportation of illegal immigrants.

On the economy, the party argued for a rise in the threshold for income tax to £11,500 and a flat tax of 31 per cent to encompass income tax and national insurance contributions. It proposed to cut the size of the public sector, which it saw as unproductive, and thereby divert employment to manufacturing. The party's protectionist message was clear in proposals to bar foreign interests from taking controlling stakes in "strategic British companies".

BRITISH NATIONAL PARTY

The core proposal of the BNP was to stop immigration. The party was particularly hostile to immigration from Muslim countries. It said it would allow legally settled ethnic minorities to remain but would review citizenship grants. It further proposed to deport illegal immigrants and exhort British citizens of various unspecified national origins to "return" to their supposed lands of ethnic origin.

The party's other main electoral message was on crime. It proposed allowing householders to defend themselves and their property "using whatever means they deem necessary", reintroducing capital punishment and establishing a penal colony on South Georgia for dangerous offenders.

The party proposed withdrawing British troops from Afghanistan and renegotiating the UK's role within Nato.

The BNP's proposals on constitutional issues included the creation of an English parliament, withdrawal from the European Convention on Human Rights and the creation of a Bill of Rights. On the economy, the party proposed to save what it claimed would be at least £40 billion on spending on international aid, contributions to the EU and immigration and asylum.

SCOTTISH NATIONAL PARTY

The SNP's priority was Scottish independence after a referendum but its broader electoral message put it distinctively on the left in its plans for public spending and taxation. It urged a continued fiscal stimulus to protect the emerging but fitful economic recovery and preserve jobs. The savings that it proposed were a claimed £5 billion by scrapping ID cards and £100 billion by not renewing Trident, a figure vigorously disputed by defence experts but also appearing in the Liberal Democrat manifesto. Minor savings would come from abolition of the House of Lords and the Scottish Office and a reduction in the number of quangos.

The SNP proposed restoration of the link between earnings and state pensions and protection of concessionary travel schemes and free personal care from Westminster cuts. It supported an international levy on banks, taxing bank bonuses, and regulation to return to prudent banking.

On constitutional issues, the SNP proposed to work case-by-case in Westminster with Plaid Cymru and sought fiscal autonomy and borrowing powers for Scotland.

PLAID CYMRU

The party called for a referendum on law-making powers. The people of Wales wanted stronger legislative powers for the National Assembly of Wales, replacing the expensive, complicated and bureaucratic system of Legislative Competence Orders, its manifesto said. In time, further powers might be transferred to the National Assembly, beginning with the police and criminal justice.

Plaid said that UK spending departments faced a reduction of 3.2% a year, based on calculations using Treasury forecasts. On these figures, the Assembly's budget faced a reduction of about £2.8 billion. Plaid called for reform of the funding formula, demanding the adoption of interim recommendations from the Holtham Commission, which calls for a new formula based on relative need, saying that this would add £300 million per annum to the Assembly budget.

The manifesto proposed increasing a single person's pension to at least £130 a week and a couple's pension to £202 a week, paid for by limiting income tax relief on pension contributions to the standard rate.

DEMOCRATIC UNIONIST PARTY

The DUP promised to "build stability and prosperity in Northern Ireland through improved and more efficient local political institutions". It proposed this through more public spending pledges and tax cuts. It promised to create a wealth-generating export-oriented economy; reduce corporation tax; introduce a 5 per cent VAT rate for construction; and claim special economic zone status for Northern Ireland. It would reduce the regulatory burden on business; improve basic skills; overhaul public sector procurement; have a single government department for the economy; create jobs and more small business start-ups.

It wanted extra funding in primary schools and more classroom assistants; enhanced extended schools programmes; an increased youth services budget; pupils matched to post-primary school on basis of ability; an end to special privileges for integrated and Irish medium sectors; and a single body to own and promote controlled schools.

The manifesto called for more visible neighbourhood police officers; a new sentencing framework; reduced legal aid bill; fewer prisoners on remand; and support for extended pre-charge detention. It also wanted a rise in the winter fuel payment said it would scrap plans for a national ID cards system and cut the BBC licence fee from £142.50 to £50.

SINN FEIN

Sinn Fein launched its paperless manifesto on a memory stick, but the message was reassuringly familiar. The pro-Irish unity party wants an increase in Northern Ireland's block grant with devolution of fiscal powers from Westminster. It also called for the currency of Northern Ireland to become the euro and, in a nod to next year's Northern Ireland Assembly elections, it also vowed to continue resisting the introduction of water charges.

Sinn Fein also pledged "harmonisation" of the education systems in Ireland North and South as well as continuing the "radical restructuring" of schools and colleges. It promised 20 new trains, a £400 million investment in fishing and rural communities over three years and the doubling of forest cover across the province over the next 50 years. The party also insisted that MI5 and the Serious and Organised Crime Agency "must go". It called for an inquiry into the extent of historical institutional and clerical abuse in Ireland and an inquiry into the murder of Pat Finucane, a Belfast solicitor.

It called for an all-Ireland referendum with the British Government becoming "persuaders" for a united Ireland.

ULSTER CONSERVATIVES AND UNIONISTS NEW FORCE

This party's big idea is to turn all of Northern Ireland into an economic enterprise zone. It promised to produce a government paper to examine the mechanism for changing the corporation tax rate in Northern Ireland, in order to attract significant new investment.

It proposed a long-term programme to "rebalance" the Northern Irish economy and boost the private sector, adding: "We can't go on with a situation where two thirds of economic activity in Northern Ireland is directly or indirectly dependent on government spending."

The manifesto says that the party will look at enabling Stormont to bring in a regional aviation strategy. They also support academic selection. The party would also ban double jobbing for elected representatives and it rejects a separate Bill of Rights for Northern Ireland, as envisaged in the 1998 Good Friday Agreement.

SOCIAL AND DEMOCRATIC LABOUR PARTY

The SDLP promised to create 42,000 new jobs for Northern Ireland over the lifetime of the next Parliament, 12,000 from the harmonisation of corporation tax north and south of the Irish border but others from "green" environmental policies, particularly renewable energy, and an additional promise to invest in construction and tourism.

It proposed scrapping Labour government "catastrophes" including ID cards, the National Health IT system and the Trident nuclear submarines replacement and it wanted a 50p 'Robin Hood' levy on every £1,000 of speculative transactions between banks, a policy the party says "has the ability to raise hundreds of billions of pounds every year and transform public finances".

It said that broadcasting, telecommunications and fisheries should become devolved issues for the NI Assembly, while simultaneously deepening cross-border ties to integrate an all-island economy.

ALLIANCE PARTY

The Alliance Party prioritised breaking down Northern Ireland's sectarian divide, which the party said costs the average household £1,000 a year. The bill for duplicating the public services required to provide separately for Protestant and Catholic communities is in excess of a £1 billion per annum, it said. It proposed the creation of tens of thousands of jobs with the implementation of a Green New Deal based on sustainable and renewable energy. Tax-varying powers should be given to Stormont in order to cut the rate of business/corporation tax, it said.

It promised to safeguard and reform frontline public services and resist "reckless" cuts; restore earnings link to pensions and increase winter fuel grants for older people; extend the national minimum wage to 16-year-olds; push for the introduction of an independent Environment Protection Agency in Northern Ireland; crack down on double jobbing politicians at Westminster and Stormont and toughen up regulations on MPs' expenses.

TRADITIONAL UNIONIST VOICE

Traditional Unionist Voice placed stopping Martin McGuinness becoming Northern Ireland's First Minister as its first priority. It called for a system of voluntary coalition to replace the mandatory partnership between unionists and nationalists.

RESPECT

The Respect campaign was concentrated on three constituencies, with a principal message of opposition to the British commitment of troops to the war in Afghanistan. The party declared that it would demand an early date for ending the British commitment there and in Iraq, and would cancel the Trident nuclear programme. The money saved would be devoted instead to public services. The Respect manifesto opposed what it called the "cuts consensus" of the main parties, and argued for the protection of jobs and services. The party also called for fairer taxation and stood for the benefits of a multicultural society.

CHRISTIAN PARTY

The Christian Party declared its aim of "integrity, truth, justice for all", and of reconciliation. It criticised a "hostile, non-Christian liberal elite" at work in the main parties. It espoused a programme of opposition to sex education for young children, protection of the sanctity of life from conception to death, prevention of immigrants from jumping the housing queue, lifting the low-paid out of the tax system, and requiring employers rather than taxpayers to finance the healthcare of new immigrants. The party supported the maintenance of an independent nuclear deterrent, but opposed "military adventurism".

ENGLISH DEMOCRATS

The English Democrats called for a defence of Englishness and proposed the creation of a post of English First Minister, equivalent to the Scottish First Minister. It likewise sought the creation of an English assembly. It opposed politcal correctness and multiculturalism and sought the closure of Quangos that promote these ends. It maintained that immigration was out of control and proposed to end mass immigration. It advocated withdrawal from the EU and defence of the family. It opposed treating members of the same sex as equivalent to married couples.

TRADE UNION AND SOCIALIST COALITION

A collection of small left-wing groups and independent activists that campaigned on a platform of "no to cuts and privatisation – make the bosses pay". It proposed a steeply progressive income tax, large increases in pensions and public ownership of the banks. It sought the abandonment of the Private Finance Initiative and the British military commitment in Afghanistan.

SCOTTISH SOCIALIST PARTY

The party's key message was for an independent socialist Scotland. It opposed cuts in public spending and demanded instead emergency funding to protect youth employment in Scotland. The party opposed the British military commitment in Afghanistan.

INDEPENDENT COMMUNITY AND HEALTH CONCERN

ICHC centred its campaign on the Independent candidature of Richard Taylor in Wyre Forest, who had been successful in the 2001 and 2005 elections. Its principal message is the "provision and protection of free, quality, healthcare on demand and at the point of need for local residents". The party promised to consult and listen in the community, and offer an independent voice free of dogma for local benefit. While primarily a party of concern about health issues, it argued more broadly that social provision should be from the bottom up rather then driven by national politics.

Summarised by Oliver Kamm and David Sharrock

Index to candidates

"Ever the bad loser"

Index

Index

Index

Index

376

Index

Index